LECTIONARY FOR MASS

THE ROMAN MISSAL
RESTORED BY DECREE OF THE SECOND ECUMENICAL
COUNCIL OF THE VATICAN AND PROMULGATED BY
AUTHORITY OF POPE PAUL VI

LECTIONARY FOR MASS

FOR USE IN THE DIOCESES
OF THE UNITED STATES OF AMERICA

SECOND TYPICAL EDITION

Volume III:
Proper of Seasons for Weekdays, Year II
Proper of Saints
Common of Saints

UNITED STATES CONFERENCE OF CATHOLIC BISHOPS

A Liturgical Press Book

THE LITURGICAL PRESS COLLEGEVILLE, MINNESOTA

Concordat cum originali:

Reverend James P. Moroney
Executive Director, Secretariat for the Liturgy
United States Conference of Catholic Bishops

Published by the authority of the Bishops' Committee on the Liturgy, United States Conference of Catholic Bishops.

ACKNOWLEDGMENTS

Design by Frank Kacmarcik, Obl.S.B.

Copyright © 2001, 1998, 1992, 1986, 1970 Confraternity of Christian Doctrine, Washington, D.C. All rights reserved.

The English translation of the Introduction to the *Lectionary for Mass* © 1981, International Committee on English in the Liturgy, Inc. All rights reserved. Altered by the National Conference of Catholic Bishops.

The English translation of the Psalm Responses, the Alleluia and Gospel Verses, and the Lenten Gospel Acclamations, and the Titles, Summaries, and Conclusion of the Readings, from the *Lectionary for Mass* © 1997, 1981, 1968, International Committee on English in the Liturgy, Inc. All rights reserved.

The poetic English translations of the sequences of the Roman Missal are taken from the *Roman Missal* approved by the National Conference of Catholic Bishops of the United States © 1964 by the National Catholic Welfare Conference, Inc. All rights reserved.

© 2002 by The Order of St. Benedict, Inc., Collegeville, Minnesota. All rights reserved.

ISBN 0-8146-2879-6

CONTENTS

Decree of the Sacred Congregation for Divine Worship, 1st Edition   vii
Decree of the Sacred Congregation for the Sacraments and Divine Worship, 2nd Edition   viii
Decree of the Congregation for Divine Worship and the Discipline of the Sacraments   x
Decree of the National Conference of Catholic Bishops   xi

INTRODUCTION
Preamble
Chapter One: General Principles for the Liturgical Celebration of the Word of God   xiii

First Part: The Word of God in the Celebration of Mass
Chapter Two: The Celebration of the Liturgy of the Word at Mass   xvi
Chapter Three: Offices and Ministries in the Celebration of the Liturgy of the Word Within Mass   xx

Second Part: The Structure of the Order of Readings for Mass
Chapter Four: The General Arrangement of Readings for Mass   xxiii
Chapter Five: Description of the Order of Readings   xxx
Chapter Six: Adaptations, Translations, and Format of the Order of Readings   xxxvi

TABLES
Table I: Principal Celebrations of the Liturgical Year   xlvi
Table II: Order of the First Reading for Weekdays in Ordinary Time   xlviii
Table III: Abbreviations of the Books of the Bible   xlix

PROPER OF SEASONS
WEEKDAY READINGS
Season of Advent   5
Season of Christmas   93

Season of Lent   143
Holy Week and Season of Easter   281
Ordinary Time   443
Alleluia Verses for Weekdays in Ordinary Time   1099
Common Texts for Sung Responsorial Psalms   1109

PROPER OF SAINTS
January   1131
February   1171
March   1208
April   1236
May   1275
June   1319
July   1375
August   1429
September   1513
October   1559
November   1606
December   1682

COMMONS
The Common of the Anniversary of the Dedication of a Church   1733
The Common of the Blessed Virgin Mary   1751
The Common of Martyrs   1782
The Common of Pastors   1805
The Common of Doctors of the Church   1838
The Common of Virgins   1857
The Common of Holy Men and Women   1868

APPENDICES
Appendix I: Sequence   1931
Appendix II: Table of Readings   1935
Appendix III: Table of Responsorial Psalms and Canticles   1955

SACRED CONGREGATION FOR DIVINE WORSHIP

Prot. n. 106/69

DECREE

The Order of Readings from the Sacred Scriptures to be used at Mass was prepared by the Consilium for the Implementation of the Constitution on the Sacred Liturgy in accordance with the requirement of the Constitution that a more lavish table of the word of God be spread before the faithful, that the treasures of the Bible be opened up more widely, and that the more important part of the Holy Scriptures be read to the people over a prescribed number of years (art. 51). The Supreme Pontiff Paul VI approved it by the Apostolic Constitution *Missale Romanum*, on 3 April 1969.

Accordingly, this Sacred Congregation for Divine Worship, by special mandate of the Supreme Pontiff, promulgates this same Order of Readings for Mass, establishing that it enter into force on 30 November, the First Sunday of Advent, in the year 1969. However, in the coming liturgical year series B will be used for the Sunday readings and series II for the first reading on weekdays of Ordinary Time.

Since in the present Order of Readings only the references are given for the individual readings, the Episcopal Conferences will have complete texts prepared in the vernacular languages, observing the norms laid down in the Instruction on vernacular translations issued by the Consilium for the Implementation of the Constitution on the Sacred Liturgy on 25 January 1969. The vernacular texts may either be taken from translations of the Sacred Scriptures already lawfully approved for particular regions, and confirmed by the Apostolic See, or, newly translated, in which case they should be submitted for confirmation to this Sacred Congregation.

All things to the contrary notwithstanding.

From the offices of the Sacred Congregation for Divine Worship, 25 May 1969, Pentecost Sunday.

✠ Benno Cardinal Gut
Prefect

✠ A. Bugnini
Secretary

SACRED CONGREGATION FOR THE SACRAMENTS AND DIVINE WORSHIP

Prot. CD 240/81

DECREE

REGARDING THE SECOND TYPICAL EDITION

The Order of Readings for Mass, first published in *editio typica* in 1969, was promulgated on 25 May of that year by special mandate of the Supreme Pontiff Paul VI, in accordance with the requirement of the Constitution on the Sacred Liturgy, in order to provide Bishops' Conferences with the references for the individual biblical readings at Mass with a view to the preparation of lectionaries in the vernacular languages in the different regions.

In that edition were lacking the biblical references of readings for celebration of the sacraments and other rites that have been published since May 1969. Moreover, following the issuing of the Neo-Vulgate edition of the Sacred Scriptures, it was laid down by the Apostolic Constitution *Scripturarum thesaurus* of 25 April 1979 that thereafter the text of the Neo-Vulgate must be adopted as the typical edition for liturgical use. Since the first *editio typica* is no longer available, it seemed opportune to prepare a second edition, having the following features with regard to the previous one:

1. The text of the Introduction has been expanded.

2. In compliance with the Apostolic Constitution *Scripturarum thesaurus*, the Neo-Vulgate edition of the Sacred Scriptures has been used in indicating the biblical references.

3. There have been incorporated all the biblical references to be found in the lectionaries for the celebration of sacraments and sacramentals that have been published since the first edition of the Order of Readings for Mass.

4. The biblical references have also been added for readings for certain Masses "for various needs" and for readings in other Masses which were inserted into the Roman Missal for the first time in its second edition of 1975.

5. As regards the celebrations of the Holy Family, the Baptism of the Lord, the Ascension, and Pentecost, references have been added for optional read-

ings in such a way that biblical texts arranged for cycles A, B, and C in the Lectionary for Sundays and feasts are completed.

The Supreme Pontiff John Paul II has by his authority approved this second edition of the Order of Readings for Mass and the Sacred Congregation for the Sacraments and Divine Worship now promulgates it and declares it to be the *editio typica*.

The Episcopal Conferences will introduce the changes found in this second edition into the editions to be prepared in the vernacular.

All things to the contrary notwithstanding.

From the offices of the Sacred Congregation for the Sacraments and Divine Worship, 21 January 1981.

☩ James R. Cardinal Knox
Prefect

☩ Virgilio Noè
Associate Secretary

CONGREGATION FOR DIVINE WORSHIP
AND THE DISCIPLINE OF THE SACRAMENTS

Prot. 492/00/L

THE UNITED STATES OF AMERICA

At the request of His Excellency, Joseph A. Fiorenza, Bishop of Galveston–Houston, President of the Conference of Bishops of the United States of America, made in a letter dated February 25, 2001, and in virtue of the faculties granted to this Congregation by the Supreme Pontiff JOHN PAUL II, we gladly confirm and approve also according to the norms of the Instruction, *Liturgiam authenticam*, dated March 28, 2001, Volume II of the *Lectionarium Missae*, drawn up in English, as in the attached copy, with the title of *Lectionary for Mass for use in the Dioceses of the United States of America*.

In printed editions of the text there should be inserted in its entirety this Decree by which the Apostolic See accords the requested confirmation of the sole translation to be used in the celebration of holy Mass in all the dioceses of the United States of America. Moreover, two copies of the printed text should be forwarded to this Congregation.

All things to the contrary notwithstanding.

From the offices of the Congregation for Divine Worship and the Discipline of the Sacraments, June 6, 2001.

✠ Jorge A. Cardinal Medina Estévez
Prefect

✠ Franciscus Pius Tamburrino
Archbishop-Secretary

NATIONAL CONFERENCE OF CATHOLIC BISHOPS
UNITED STATES OF AMERICA

DECREE

In accord with the norms established by decree of the Sacred Congregation of Rites in *Cum, nostra ætate* (January 27, 1966), this edition of the *Lectionary for Mass, Volume II: Proper of Seasons for Weekdays, Proper of Saints, Ritual Masses, Masses for Various Needs, Votive Masses and Masses for the Dead,* is declared to be the vernacular typical edition of the *Ordo Lectionum Missæ, editio typica altera* in the dioceses of the United States of America, and is published by authority of the National Conference of Catholic Bishops.

The second volume of the *Lectionary for Mass* was canonically approved for use by the National Conference of Catholic Bishops on June 20, 1992, and was subsequently confirmed by the Apostolic See by decree of the Congregation for Divine Worship and the Discipline of the Sacraments on June 6, 2001 (Prot. 492/00/L).

On Ash Wednesday, February 13, 2002, the second volume of the *Lectionary for Mass* may be used in the liturgy. On Pentecost Sunday, May 19, 2002, the use of the entire *Lectionary for Mass* is mandatory. After that date no other edition of the *Lectionary for Mass* may be used in the dioceses of the United States of America.

Given at the General Secretariat of the National Conference of Catholic Bishops, Washington, D.C. on June 29, 2001, the Solemnity of Saints Peter and Paul.

✠ Most Reverend Joseph A. Fiorenza
Bishop of Galveston-Houston

President
National Conference of Catholic Bishops

Reverend Monsignor William P. Fay
General Secretary

INTRODUCTION

PREAMBLE

CHAPTER ONE

**GENERAL PRINCIPLES
FOR THE LITURGICAL CELEBRATION OF THE WORD OF GOD**

1. CERTAIN PRELIMINARIES

a) The Importance of the Word of God in Liturgical Celebration

1. The Second Vatican Council,[1] the magisterium of the Popes,[2] and various documents promulgated after the Council by the organisms of the Holy See[3] have already had many excellent things to say about the importance of the word of God and about reestablishing the use of Sacred Scripture in every celebration of the Liturgy. The Introduction to the 1969 edition of the Order of Readings for Mass has clearly stated and briefly explained some of the more important principles.[4]

On the occasion of this new edition of the Order of Readings for Mass, requests have come from many quarters for a more detailed exposition of the same principles. Hence, this expanded and more suitable arrangement of the Introduction first gives a general statement on the essential bond between the word of God and the liturgical celebration,[5] then deals in greater detail with the word of God in the celebration of Mass, and, finally, explains the precise structure of the Order of Readings for Mass.

b) Terms Used to Refer to the Word of God

2. For the sake of clear and precise language on this topic, a definition of terms might well be expected as a prerequisite. Nevertheless this Introduction will simply use the same terms employed in conciliar and postconciliar documents. Furthermore it will use "Sacred Scripture" and "word of God" interchangeably throughout when referring to the books written under the inspiration of the Holy Spirit, thus avoiding any confusion of language or meaning.[6]

c) The Significance of the Word of God in the Liturgy

3. The many riches contained in the one word of God are admirably brought out in the different kinds of liturgical celebration and in the different gatherings of the faithful who take part in those celebrations. This takes place as the unfolding mystery of Christ is recalled during the course of the liturgical year, as the Church's sacraments and sacramentals are celebrated, or as the faithful respond individually to the Holy Spirit working within them.[7] For then the liturgical celebration, founded primarily on the word of God and sustained by it, becomes a new event and enriches the word itself with new meaning and power. Thus in the Liturgy the Church faithfully adheres to the way Christ himself read and explained the Sacred Scriptures, beginning with the "today" of his coming forward in the synagogue and urging all to search the Scriptures.[8]

2. LITURGICAL CELEBRATION OF THE WORD OF GOD

a) The Proper Character of the Word of God in the Liturgical Celebration

4. In the celebration of the Liturgy the word of God is not announced in only one way[9] nor does it always stir the hearts of the hearers with the same efficacy. Always, however, Christ is present in his word,[10] as he carries out the mystery of salvation, he sanctifies humanity and offers the Father perfect worship.[11]

Moreover, the word of God unceasingly calls to mind and extends the economy of salvation, which achieves its fullest expression in the Liturgy. The liturgical celebration becomes therefore the continuing, complete, and effective presentation of God's word.

The word of God constantly proclaimed in the Liturgy is always, then, a living and effective word[12] through the power of the Holy Spirit. It expresses the Father's love that never fails in its effectiveness toward us.

b) The Word of God in the Economy of Salvation

5. When in celebrating the Liturgy the Church proclaims both the Old and New Testament, it is proclaiming one and the same mystery of Christ.

The New Testament lies hidden in the Old; the Old Testament comes fully to light in the New.[13] Christ himself is the center and fullness of the whole of Scripture, just as he is of all liturgical celebration.[14] Thus the Scriptures are the living waters from which all who seek life and salvation must drink.

The more profound our understanding of the celebration of the Liturgy, the higher our appreciation of the importance of God's word. Whatever we say of the one, we can in turn say of the other, because each recalls the mystery of Christ and each in its own way causes the mystery to be carried forward.

c) The Word of God in the Liturgical Participation of the Faithful

6. In celebrating the Liturgy the Church faithfully echoes the "Amen" that Christ, the mediator between God and men and women, uttered once for all as he shed his blood to seal God's new covenant in the Holy Spirit.[15]

When God communicates his word, he expects a response, one, that is, of listening and adoring "in Spirit and in truth" (Jn 4:23). The Holy Spirit makes that response effective, so that what is heard in the celebration of the Liturgy may be carried out in a way of life: "Be doers of the word and not hearers only" (Jas 1:22).

The liturgical celebration and the participation of the faithful receive outward expression in actions, gestures, and words. These derive their full meaning not simply from their origin in human experience but from the word of God and the economy of salvation, to which they refer. Accordingly, the participation of the faithful in the Liturgy increases to the degree that, as they listen to the word of God proclaimed in the Liturgy, they strive harder to commit themselves to the Word of God incarnate in Christ. Thus, they endeavor to conform their way of life to what they celebrate in the Liturgy, and then in turn to bring to the celebration of the Liturgy all that they do in life.[16]

3. THE WORD OF GOD IN THE LIFE OF THE PEOPLE OF THE COVENANT

a) The Word of God in the Life of the Church

7. In the hearing of God's word the Church is built up and grows, and in the signs of the liturgical celebration God's wonderful, past works in the history of salvation are presented anew

as mysterious realities. God in turn makes use of the congregation of the faithful that celebrates the Liturgy in order that his word may speed on and be glorified and that his name be exalted among the nations.[17]

Whenever, therefore, the Church, gathered by the Holy Spirit for liturgical celebration,[18] announces and proclaims the word of God, she is aware of being a new people in whom the covenant made in the past is perfected and fulfilled. Baptism and confirmation in the Spirit have made all Christ's faithful into messengers of God's word because of the grace of hearing they have received. They must therefore be the bearers of the same word in the Church and in the world, at least by the witness of their lives.

The word of God proclaimed in the celebration of God's mysteries does not only address present conditions but looks back to past events and forward to what is yet to come. Thus God's word shows us what we should hope for with such a longing that in this changing world our hearts will be set on the place where our true joys lie.[19]

b) The Church's Explanation of the Word of God

8. By Christ's own will there is a marvelous diversity of members in the new people of God and each has different duties and responsibilities with respect to the word of God. Accordingly, the faithful listen to God's word and meditate on it, but only those who have the office of teaching by virtue of sacred ordination or who have been entrusted with exercising that ministry expound the word of God.

This is how in doctrine, life, and worship the Church keeps alive and passes on to every generation all that she is, all that she believes. Thus with the passage of the centuries, the Church is ever to advance toward the fullness of divine truth until God's word is wholly accomplished in her.[20]

c) The Connection between the Word of God Proclaimed and the Working of the Holy Spirit

9. The working of the Holy Spirit is needed if the word of God is to make what we hear outwardly have its effect inwardly. Because of the Holy Spirit's inspiration and support, the word of God becomes the foundation of the liturgical celebration and the rule and support of all our life.

The working of the Holy Spirit precedes, accompanies, and brings to completion the whole celebration of the Liturgy. But the Spirit also brings home[21] to each person individually everything that in the proclamation of the word of God is spoken for the good of the whole gathering of the faithful. In strengthening the unity of all, the Holy Spirit at the same time fosters a diversity of gifts and furthers their multiform operation.

d) The Essential Bond between the Word of God and the Mystery of the Eucharist

10. The Church has honored the word of God and the Eucharistic mystery with the same reverence, although not with the same worship, and has always and everywhere insisted upon and sanctioned such honor. Moved by the example of its Founder, the Church has never ceased to celebrate his paschal mystery by coming together to read "what referred to him in all the Scriptures" (Lk 24:27) and to carry out the work of salvation through the celebration of the memorial of the Lord and through the sacraments. "The preaching of the word is necessary for the ministry of the sacraments, for these are sacraments of faith, which is born and nourished from the word."[22]

The Church is nourished spiritually at the twofold table of God's word and of the Eucharist:[23] from the one it grows in wisdom and from the other in holiness. In the word of God the divine covenant is announced; in the Eucharist the new and everlasting covenant is renewed. On the one hand the history of salvation is brought to mind by means of human sounds; on the other it is made manifest in the sacramental signs of the Liturgy.

It can never be forgotten, therefore, that the divine word read and proclaimed by the Church in the Liturgy has as its one purpose the sacrifice of the New Covenant and the banquet of grace, that is, the Eucharist. The celebration of Mass in which the word is heard and the Eucharist is offered and received forms but one single act of divine worship.[24] That act offers the sacrifice of praise to God and makes available to God's creatures the fullness of redemption.

FIRST PART

THE WORD OF GOD IN THE CELEBRATION OF MASS

CHAPTER TWO

THE CELEBRATION OF THE LITURGY OF THE WORD AT MASS

1. THE ELEMENTS OF THE LITURGY OF THE WORD AND THEIR RITES

11. "Readings from Sacred Scripture and the chants between the readings form the main part of the Liturgy of the Word. The homily, the profession of faith, and the universal prayer or prayer of the faithful carry it forward and conclude it."[25]

a) The Biblical Readings

12. In the celebration of Mass the biblical readings with their accompanying chants from the Sacred Scriptures may not be omitted, shortened, or, worse still, replaced by nonbiblical readings.[26] For it is out of the word of God handed down in writing that even now "God speaks to his people"[27] and it is from the continued use of Sacred Scripture that the people of God, docile to the Holy Spirit under the light of faith, is enabled to bear witness to Christ before the world by its manner of life.

13. The reading of the Gospel is the high point of the Liturgy of the Word. For this the other readings, in their established sequence from the Old to the New Testament, prepare the assembly.

14. A speaking style on the part of the readers that is audible, clear, and intelligent is the first means of transmitting the word of God properly to the congregation. The readings, taken from the approved editions,[28] may be sung in a way suited to different languages. This singing, however, must serve to bring out the sense of the words, not obscure them. On occasions when the readings are in Latin, the manner given in the *Ordo cantus Missae* is to be maintained.[29]

15. There may be concise introductions before the readings, especially the first. The style proper to such comments must be respected, that is, they must be simple, faithful to the text, brief, well prepared, and properly varied to suit the text they introduce.[30]

16. In a Mass with the people the readings are always to be proclaimed at the ambo.[31]

17. Of all the rites connected with the Liturgy of the Word, the reverence due to the Gospel reading must receive special attention.[32] Where there is an Evangeliary or Book of Gospels that has been carried in by the deacon or reader during the entry procession,[33] it is most fitting that the deacon or a priest, when there is no deacon, take the book from the altar[34] and carry it to the ambo. He is preceded by servers with candles and incense or other symbols of reverence that may be customary. As the faithful stand and acclaim the Lord, they show honor to the Book of Gospels. The deacon who is to read the Gospel, bowing in front of the one presiding, asks and receives the blessing. When no deacon is present, the priest, bowing before the altar, prays inaudibly, *Almighty God, cleanse my heart* . . . .[35]

At the ambo the one who proclaims the Gospel greets the people, who are standing, and announces the reading as he makes the sign of the cross on forehead, mouth, and breast. If incense is used, he next incenses the book, then reads the Gospel. When finished, he kisses the book, saying the appointed words inaudibly.

Even if the Gospel itself is not sung, it is appropriate for the greeting *The Lord be with you*, and *A reading from the holy Gospel according to* . . ., and at the end *The Gospel of the Lord* to be sung, in order that the congregation may also sing its acclamations. This is a way both of bringing out the importance of the Gospel reading and of stirring up the faith of those who hear it.

18. At the conclusion of the other readings, *The word of the Lord* may be sung, even by someone other than the reader; all respond with the acclamation. In this way the assembled congregation pays reverence to the word of God it has listened to in faith and gratitude.

b) The Responsorial Psalm

19. The responsorial psalm, also called the gradual, has great liturgical and pastoral significance because it is an "integral part of the liturgy of the word."[36] Accordingly, the faithful must be continually instructed on the way to perceive the word of God speaking in the psalms and to turn these psalms into the prayer of the Church. This, of course, "will be achieved more readily if a deeper understanding of the psalms, according to the meaning with which they are sung in the sacred Liturgy, is more diligently promoted among the clergy and communicated to all the faithful by means of appropriate catechesis."[37]

Brief remarks about the choice of the psalm and response as well as their correspondence to the readings may be helpful.

20. As a rule the responsorial psalm should be sung. There are two established ways of singing the psalm after the first reading: responsorially and directly. In responsorial singing, which, as far as possible, is to be given preference, the psalmist, or cantor of the psalm, sings the psalm verse and the whole congregation joins in by singing the response. In direct singing of the psalm there is no intervening response by the community; either the psalmist, or cantor of the psalm, sings the psalm alone as the community listens or else all sing it together.

21. The singing of the psalm, or even of the response alone, is a great help toward understanding and meditating on the psalm's spiritual meaning.

To foster the congregation's singing, every means available in each individual culture is to be employed. In particular, use is to be made of all the relevant options provided in the Order of Readings for Mass[38] regarding responses corresponding to the different liturgical seasons.

22. When not sung, the psalm after the reading is to be recited in a manner conducive to meditation on the word of God.[39]

The responsorial psalm is sung or recited by the psalmist or cantor at the ambo.[40]

c) The Acclamation before the Reading of the Gospel

23. The *Alleluia* or, as the liturgical season requires, the verse before the Gospel, is also a "rite or act standing by itself."[41] It serves as the greeting of welcome of the assembled faithful to the Lord who is about to speak to them and as an expression of their faith through song.

The *Alleluia* or the verse before the Gospel must be sung and during it all stand. It is not to be sung only by the cantor who intones it or by the choir, but by the whole of the people together.[42]

d) The Homily

24. Through the course of the liturgical year the homily sets forth the mysteries of faith and the standards of the Christian life on the basis of the sacred text. Beginning with the Constitution on the Liturgy, the homily as part of the Liturgy of the Word[43] has been repeatedly and strongly recommended and in some cases it is obligatory. As a rule it is to be given by the one presiding.[44] The purpose of the homily at Mass is that the spoken word of God and the Liturgy of the Eucharist may together become "a proclamation of God's wonderful works in the history of salvation, the mystery of Christ."[45] Through the readings and homily Christ's paschal mystery is proclaimed; through the sacrifice of the Mass it becomes present.[46] Moreover Christ himself is always present and active in the preaching of his Church.[47]

Whether the homily explains the text of the Sacred Scriptures proclaimed in the readings or some other text of the Liturgy,[48] it must always lead the community of the faithful to celebrate the Eucharist actively, "so that they may hold fast in their lives to what they have grasped by faith."[49] From this living explanation, the word of God proclaimed in the readings and the Church's celebration of the day's Liturgy will have greater impact. But this demands that the homily be truly the fruit of meditation, carefully prepared, neither too long nor too short, and suited to all those present, even children and the uneducated.[50]

At a concelebration, the celebrant or one of the concelebrants as a rule gives the homily.[51]

25. On the prescribed days, that is, Sundays and holydays of obligation, there must be a homily in all Masses celebrated with a congregation, even Masses on the preceding evening; the homily may not be omitted without a serious reason.[52] There is also to be a homily in Masses with children and with special groups.[53]

A homily is strongly recommended on the weekdays of Advent, Lent, and the Easter season for the sake of the faithful who regularly take part in the celebration of Mass; also on other feasts and occasions when a large congregation is present.[54]

26. The priest celebrant gives the homily, standing either at the chair or at the ambo.[55]

27. Any necessary announcements are to be kept completely separate from the homily; they must take place following the prayer after Communion.[56]

e) Silence

28. The Liturgy of the Word must be celebrated in a way that fosters meditation; clearly, any sort of haste that hinders recollection must be avoided. The dialogue between God and his people taking place through the Holy Spirit demands short intervals of silence, suited to the assembled congregation, as an opportunity to take the word of God to heart and to prepare a response to it in prayer.

Proper times for silence during the Liturgy of the Word are, for example, before this Liturgy begins, after the first and the second reading, after the homily.[57]

f) The Profession of Faith

29. The symbol, creed, or profession of faith, said when the rubrics require, has as its purpose in the celebration of Mass that the assembled congregation may respond and give assent to the word of God heard in the readings and through the homily, and that before beginning to celebrate in the Eucharist the mystery of faith it may call to mind the rule of faith in a formulary approved by the Church.[58]

g) The Universal Prayer or Prayer of the Faithful

30. In the light of God's word and in a sense in response to it, the congregation of the faithful prays in the universal prayer as a rule for the needs of the universal Church and the local community, for the salvation of the world and those oppressed by any burden, and for special categories of people.

The celebrant introduces the prayer; a deacon, another minister, or some of the faithful may propose intentions that are short and phrased with a measure of freedom. In these petitions "the people, exercising its priestly function, makes intercession for all men and women,"[59] with the result that, as the Liturgy of the Word has its full effects in the faithful, they are better prepared to proceed to the Liturgy of the Eucharist.

31. For the prayer of the faithful the celebrant presides at the chair and the intentions are announced at the ambo.[60]

The assembled congregation takes part in the prayer of the faithful while standing and by saying or singing a common response after each intention or by silent prayer.[61]

2. AIDS TO THE PROPER CELEBRATION OF THE LITURGY OF THE WORD

a) The Place for the Proclamation of the Word of God

32. There must be a place in the church that is somewhat elevated, fixed, and of a suitable design and nobility. It should reflect the dignity of God's word and be a clear reminder to the people that in the Mass the table of God's word and of Christ's body is placed before them.[62] The place for the readings must also truly help the people's listening and attention during the Liturgy of the Word. Great pains must therefore be taken, in keeping with the design of each church, over the harmonious and close relationship of the ambo with the altar.

33. Either permanently or at least on occasions of greater solemnity, the ambo should be decorated simply and in keeping with its design.

Since the ambo is the place from which the word of God is proclaimed by the ministers, it must of its nature be reserved for the readings, the responsorial psalm, and the Easter Proclamation (the *Exsultet*). The ambo may rightly be used for the homily and the prayer of the faithful, however, because of their close connection with the entire Liturgy of the Word. It is better for the commentator, cantor, or director of singing, for example, not to use the ambo.[63]

34. In order that the ambo may properly serve its liturgical purpose, it is to be rather large, since on occasion several ministers must use it at the same time. Provision must also be made for the readers to have enough light to read the text and, as required, to have modern sound equipment enabling the faithful to hear them without difficulty.

b) The Books for Proclamation of the Word of God in the Liturgy

35. Along with the ministers, the actions, the allocated places, and other elements, the books containing the readings of the word of God remind the hearers of the presence of God speaking to his people. Since in liturgical celebrations the books too serve as signs and symbols of the higher realities, care must be taken to ensure that they truly are worthy, dignified, and beautiful.[64]

36. The proclamation of the Gospel always stands as the high point of the Liturgy of the Word. Thus the liturgical tradition of both West and East has consistently made a certain distinction between the books for the readings. The Book of Gospels was always fabricated and decorated with the utmost care and shown greater respect than any of the other books of readings. In our times also, then, it is very desirable that cathedrals and at least the larger, more populous parishes and the churches with a larger attendance possess a beautifully designed Book of Gospels, separate from any other book of readings. For good reason it is the Book of Gospels that is presented to a deacon at his ordination and that at an ordination to the episcopate is laid upon the head of the bishop-elect and held there.[65]

37. Because of the dignity of the word of God, the books of readings used in the celebration are not to be replaced by other pastoral aids, for example, by leaflets printed for the preparation of the readings by the faithful or for their personal meditation.

CHAPTER THREE

OFFICES AND MINISTRIES IN THE CELEBRATION OF THE LITURGY OF THE WORD WITHIN MASS

1. THE FUNCTION OF THE PRESIDENT AT THE LITURGY OF THE WORD

38. The one presiding at the Liturgy of the Word communicates the spiritual nourishment it contains to those present, especially in the homily. Even if he too is a listener to the word of God proclaimed by others, the duty of proclaiming it has been entrusted above all to him. Personally or through others he sees to it that the word of God is properly proclaimed. He then as a rule reserves to himself the tasks of composing comments to help the people listen more attentively and of preaching a homily that fosters in them a richer understanding of the word of God.

39. The first requirement for one who is to preside over the celebration is a thorough knowledge of the structure of the Order of Readings, so that he will know how to work a fruitful effect in the hearts of the faithful. Through study and prayer he must also develop a full understanding of the coordination and connection of the various texts in the Liturgy of the Word, so that the Order of Readings will become the source of a sound understanding of the mystery of Christ and his saving work.

40. The one presiding is to make ready use of the various options provided in the Lectionary regarding readings, responses, responsorial psalms, and Gospel acclamations;[66] but he is to do so in harmony[67] with all concerned and after listening to the opinions of the faithful in what concerns them.[68]

41. The one presiding exercises his proper office and the ministry of word of God also as he preaches the homily.[69] In this way he leads his brothers and sisters to an affective knowledge of Scripture. He opens their minds to thanksgiving for the wonderful works of God. He strengthens the faith of those present in the word that in the celebration becomes sacrament through the Holy Spirit. Finally, he prepares them for a fruitful reception of Communion and invites them to take upon themselves the demands of the Christian life.

42. The president is responsible for preparing the faithful for the Liturgy of the Word on occasion by means of introductions before the readings.[70] These comments can help the assembled congregation toward a better hearing of the word of God, because they stir up an attitude of faith and good will. He may also carry out this responsibility through others, a deacon, for example, or a commentator.[71]

43. As he directs the prayer of the faithful and through their introduction and conclusion connects them, if possible, with the day's readings and the homily, the president leads the faithful toward the Liturgy of the Eucharist.[72]

2. THE ROLE OF THE FAITHFUL IN THE LITURGY OF THE WORD

44. Christ's word gathers the people of God as one and increases and sustains them. "This applies above all to the Liturgy of the Word in the celebration of Mass, where there are inseparably united the proclamation of the death of the Lord, the response of the people listening, and the very offering through which Christ has confirmed the New Covenant in his Blood, and in which the people share by their intentions and by reception of the sacrament."[73] For "not only when things are read 'that were written for our instruction' (Rom 15:4), but also when the Church prays or sings or acts, the faith of those taking part is nourished and their minds are raised to God, so that they may offer him rightful worship and receive his grace more abundantly."[74]

45. In the Liturgy of the Word, the congregation of Christ's faithful even today receives from God the word of his covenant through the faith that comes by hearing, and must respond to that word in faith, so that they may become more and more truly the people of the New Covenant.

The people of God have a spiritual right to receive abundantly from the treasury of God's word. Its riches are presented to them through use of the Order of Readings, the homily, and pastoral efforts.

For their part, the faithful at the celebration of Mass are to listen to the word of God with an inward and outward reverence that will bring them continuous growth in the spiritual life and draw them more deeply into the mystery which is celebrated.[75]

46. As a help toward celebrating the memorial of the Lord with eager devotion, the faithful should be keenly aware of the one presence of Christ in both the word of God—it is himself "who speaks when the Sacred Scriptures are read in the Church"—and "above all under the Eucharistic species."[76]

47. To be received and integrated into the life of Christ's faithful, the word of God demands a living faith.[77] Hearing the word of God unceasingly proclaimed arouses that faith.

xxii Introduction

The Sacred Scriptures, above all in their liturgical proclamation, are the source of life and strength. As the Apostle Paul attests, the Gospel is the saving power of God for everyone who believes.[78] Love of the Scriptures is therefore a force reinvigorating and renewing the entire people of God.[79] All the faithful without exception must therefore always be ready to listen gladly to God's word.[80] When this word is proclaimed in the Church and put into living practice, it enlightens the faithful through the working of the Holy Spirit and draws them into the entire mystery of the Lord as a reality to be lived.[81] The word of God reverently received moves the heart and its desires toward conversion and toward a life resplendent with both individual and community faith,[82] since God's word is the food of Christian life and the source of the prayer of the whole Church.[83]

48. The intimate connection between the Liturgy of the Word and the Liturgy of the Eucharist in the Mass should prompt the faithful to be present right from the beginning of the celebration,[84] to take part attentively, and to prepare themselves in so far as possible to hear the word, especially by learning beforehand more about Sacred Scripture. That same connection should also awaken in them a desire for a liturgical understanding of the texts read and a readiness to respond through singing.[85]

When they hear the word of God and reflect deeply on it, Christ's faithful are enabled to respond to it actively with full faith, hope, and charity through prayer and self-giving, and not only during Mass but in their entire Christian life.

3. MINISTRIES IN THE LITURGY OF THE WORD

49. Liturgical tradition assigns responsibility for the biblical readings in the celebration of Mass to ministers: to readers and the deacon. But when there is no deacon or no other priest present, the priest celebrant is to read the Gospel[86] and when there is no reader present, all the readings.[87]

50. It pertains to the deacon in the Liturgy of the Word at Mass to proclaim the Gospel, sometimes to give the homily, as occasion suggests, and to propose to the people the intentions of the prayer of the faithful.[88]

51. "The reader has his own proper function in the Eucharistic celebration and should exercise this even though ministers of a higher rank may be present."[89] The ministry of reader, conferred through a liturgical rite, must be held in respect. When there are instituted readers available, they are to carry out their office at least on Sundays and festive days, especially at the principal Mass of the day. These readers may also be given responsibility for assisting in the arrangement of the Liturgy of the Word, and, to the extent necessary, of seeing to the preparation of others of the faithful who may be appointed on a given occasion to read at Mass.[90]

52. The liturgical assembly truly requires readers, even those not instituted. Proper measures must therefore be taken to ensure that there are certain suitable laypeople who have been trained to carry out this ministry.[91] Whenever there is more than one reading, it is better to assign the readings to different readers, if available.

53. In Masses without a deacon, the function of announcing the intentions for the prayer of the faithful is to be assigned to the cantor, particularly when they are to be sung, to a reader, or to someone else.[92]

54. During the celebration of Mass with a congregation a second priest, a deacon, and an instituted reader must wear the distinctive vestment of their office when they go up to the ambo

to read the word of God. Those who carry out the ministry of reader just for the occasion or even regularly but without institution may go to the ambo in ordinary attire, but this should be in keeping with the customs of the different regions.

55. "It is necessary that those who exercise the ministry of reader, even if they have not received institution, be truly suited and carefully prepared, so that the faithful may develop a warm and living love for Sacred Scripture from listening to the sacred readings."[93]

Their preparation must above all be spiritual, but what may be called a technical preparation is also needed. The spiritual preparation presupposes at least a biblical and liturgical formation. The purpose of their biblical formation is to give readers the ability to understand the readings in context and to perceive by the light of faith the central point of the revealed message. The liturgical formation ought to equip the readers to have some grasp of the meaning and structure of the Liturgy of the Word and of the significance of its connection with the Liturgy of the Eucharist. The technical preparation should make the readers more skilled in the art of reading publicly, either with the power of their own voice or with the help of sound equipment.

56. The psalmist, or cantor of the psalm, is responsible for singing, responsorially or directly, the chants between the readings—the psalm or other biblical canticle, the gradual and *Alleluia*, or other chant. The psalmist may, as occasion requires, intone the *Alleluia* and verse.[94]

For carrying out the function of psalmist it is advantageous to have in each ecclesial community laypeople with the ability to sing and read with correct diction. The points made about the formation of readers apply to cantors as well.

57. The commentator also fulfills a genuine liturgical ministry, which consists in presenting to the congregation of the faithful, from a suitable place, relevant explanations and comments that are clear, of marked sobriety, meticulously prepared, and as a rule written out and approved beforehand by the celebrant.[95]

SECOND PART

THE STRUCTURE OF THE ORDER OF READINGS FOR MASS

CHAPTER FOUR

THE GENERAL ARRANGEMENT OF READINGS FOR MASS

1. THE PASTORAL PURPOSE OF THE ORDER OF READINGS FOR MASS

58. On the basis of the intention of the Second Vatican Council, the Order of Readings provided by the Lectionary of the Roman Missal has been composed above all for a pastoral purpose.

To achieve this aim, not only the principles underlying this new Order of Readings but also the lists of texts that it provides have been discussed and revised over and over again, with the cooperation of a great many experts in exegetical, liturgical, catechetical, and pastoral studies from all parts of the world. The Order of Readings is the fruit of this combined effort.

The prolonged use of this Order of Readings to proclaim and explain Sacred Scripture in the Eucharistic celebration will, it is hoped, prove to be an effective step toward achieving the objective stated repeatedly by the Second Vatican Council.[96]

59. The decision on revising the Lectionary for Mass was to draw up and edit a single, rich, and full Order of Readings that would be in complete accord with the intent and prescriptions of the Second Vatican Council.[97] At the same time, however, the Order was meant to be of a kind that would meet the requirements and usages of particular Churches and celebrating congregations. For this reason, those responsible for the revision took pains to safeguard the liturgical tradition of the Roman Rite, but valued highly the merits of all the systems of selecting, arranging, and using the biblical readings in other liturgical families and in certain particular Churches. The revisers made use of those elements that experience has confirmed, but with an effort to avoid certain shortcomings found in the preceding form of the tradition.

60. The present Order of Readings for Mass, then, is an arrangement of biblical readings that provides the faithful with a knowledge of the whole of God's word, in a pattern suited to the purpose. Throughout the liturgical year, but above all during the seasons of Easter, Lent, and Advent, the choice and sequence of readings are aimed at giving Christ's faithful an ever-deepening perception of the faith they profess and of the history of salvation.[98] Accordingly, the Order of Readings corresponds to the requirements and interests of the Christian people.

61. The celebration of the Liturgy is not in itself simply a form of catechesis, but it does contain an element of teaching. The Lectionary of the Roman Missal brings this out[99] and therefore deserves to be regarded as a pedagogical resource aiding catechesis.

This is so because the Order of Readings for Mass aptly presents from Sacred Scripture the principal deeds and words belonging to the history of salvation. As its many phases and events are recalled in the Liturgy of the Word, it will become clear to the faithful that the history of salvation is continued here and now in the representation of Christ's paschal mystery celebrated through the Eucharist.

62. The pastoral advantage of having in the Roman Rite a single Order of Readings for the Lectionary is obvious on other grounds. All the faithful, particularly those who for various reasons do not always take part in Mass with the same assembly, will everywhere be able to hear the same readings on any given day or in any liturgical season and to meditate on the application of these readings to their own concrete circumstances. This is the case even in places that have no priest and where a deacon or someone else deputed by the bishop conducts a celebration of the word of God.[100]

63. Pastors may wish to respond specifically from the word of God to the concerns of their own congregations. Although they must be mindful that they are above all to be heralds of the entire mystery of Christ and of the Gospel, they may rightfully use the options provided in the Order of Readings for Mass. This applies particularly to the celebration of a ritual or votive Mass, a Mass in honor of the Saints, or one of the Masses for various needs and occasions. With due regard for the general norms, special faculties are granted concerning the readings in Masses celebrated for particular groups.[101]

2. THE PRINCIPLES OF COMPOSITION OF THE ORDER OF READINGS FOR MASS

64. To achieve the purpose of the Order of Readings for Mass, the parts have been selected and arranged in such a way as to take into account the sequence of the liturgical seasons and the hermeneutical principles whose understanding and definition has been facilitated by modern biblical research.

It was judged helpful to state here the principles guiding the composition of the Order of Readings for Mass.

a) The Choice of Texts

65. The course of readings in the Proper of Seasons is arranged as follows. Sundays and festive days present the more important biblical passages. In this way the more significant parts of God's revealed word can be read to the assembled faithful within an appropriate period of time. Weekdays present a second series of texts from Sacred Scripture and in a sense these complement the message of salvation explained on festive days. But neither series in these main parts of the Order of Readings—the series for Sundays and festive days and that for weekdays—is dependent on the other. The Order of Readings for Sundays and festive days extends over three years; for weekdays, over two. Thus each runs its course independently of the other.

The sequence of readings in other parts of the Order of Readings is governed by its own rules. This applies to the series of readings for celebrations of the Saints, ritual Masses, Masses for various needs and occasions, votive Masses, or Masses for the dead.

b) The Arrangement of the Readings for Sundays and Festive Days

66. The following are features proper to the readings for Sundays and festive days:

1. Each Mass has three readings: the first from the Old Testament, the second from an Apostle (that is, either from a Letter or from the Book of Revelation, depending on the season), and the third from the Gospels. This arrangement brings out the unity of the Old and New Testaments and of the history of salvation, in which Christ is the central figure, commemorated in his paschal mystery.

2. A more varied and richer reading of Sacred Scripture on Sundays and festive days results from the three-year cycle provided for these days, in that the same texts are read only every fourth year.[102]

3. The principles governing the Order of Reading for Sundays and festive days are called the principles of "harmony" and of "semicontinuous reading." One or the other applies according to the different seasons of the year and the distinctive character of the particular liturgical season.

67. The best instance of harmony between the Old and New Testament readings occurs when it is one that Scripture itself suggests. This is the case when the doctrine and events recounted in texts of the New Testament bear a more or less explicit relationship to the doctrine and events of the Old Testament. The present Order of Readings selects Old Testament texts mainly because of their correlation with New Testament texts read in the same Mass, and particularly with the Gospel text.

Harmony of another kind exists between texts of the readings for each Mass during Advent, Lent, and Easter, the seasons that have a distinctive importance or character.

In contrast, the Sundays in Ordinary Time do not have a distinctive character. Thus the text of both the apostolic and Gospel readings are arranged in order of semicontinuous reading, whereas the Old Testament reading is harmonized with the Gospel.

68. The decision was made not to extend to Sundays the arrangement suited to the liturgical seasons mentioned, that is, not to have an organic harmony of themes devised with a view to facilitating homiletic instruction. Such an arrangement would be in conflict with the genuine conception of liturgical celebration, which is always the celebration of the mystery of Christ and which by its own tradition makes use of the word of God not only at the prompting of logical or extrinsic concerns but spurred by the desire to proclaim the Gospel and to lead those who believe to the fullness of truth.

c) The Arrangement of the Readings for Weekdays

69. The weekday readings have been arranged in the following way:

1. Each Mass has two readings: the first is from the Old Testament or from an Apostle (that is, either from a Letter or from the Book of Revelation), and during the Easter season from the Acts of the Apostles; the second, from the Gospels.

2. The yearly cycle for Lent has its own principles of arrangement, which take into account the baptismal and penitential character of this season.

3. The cycle for the weekdays of Advent, the Christmas season, and the Easter season is also yearly and the readings thus remain the same each year.

4. For the thirty-four weeks of Ordinary Time, the weekday Gospel readings are arranged in a single cycle, repeated each year. But the first reading is arranged in a two-year cycle and is thus read every other year. Year I is used during odd-numbered years; Year II, during even-numbered years.

Like the Order for Sundays and festive days, then, the weekday Order of Readings is governed by similar application of the principles of harmony and of semicontinuous reading, especially in the case of seasons with their own distinctive character.

d) The Readings for Celebrations of the Saints

70. Two series of readings are provided for celebrations of the Saints.

1. The Proper of Saints provides the first series, for solemnities, feasts, or memorials and particularly when there are proper texts for one or other such celebration. Sometimes in the Proper, however, there is a reference to the most appropriate among the texts in the Commons as the one to be given preference.

2. The Commons of Saints provide the second, more extensive group of readings. There are, first, appropriate texts for the different classes of Saints (martyrs, pastors, virgins, etc.), then numerous texts that deal with holiness in general. These may be freely chosen whenever the Commons are indicated as the source for the choice of readings.

71. As to their sequence, all the texts in this part of the Order of Readings appear in the order in which they are to be read at Mass. Thus the Old Testament texts are first, then the texts from the Apostles, followed by the psalms and verses between the readings, and finally the texts from the Gospels. The rationale of this arrangement is that, unless otherwise noted, the celebrant may choose at will from such texts, in view of the pastoral needs of the congregation taking part in the celebration.

e) Readings for Ritual Masses, Masses for Various Needs and Occasions, Votive Masses, and Masses for the Dead

72. For ritual Masses, Masses for various needs and occasions, votive Masses, and Masses for the dead, the texts for the readings are arranged as just described, that is, numerous texts are grouped together in the order of their use, as in the Commons of Saints.

f) The Main Criteria Applied in Choosing and Arranging the Readings

73. In addition to the guiding principles already given for the arrangement of readings in the individual parts of the Order of Readings, others of a more general nature follow.

1) THE RESERVATION OF SOME BOOKS TO PARTICULAR LITURGICAL SEASONS

74. In this Order of Readings, some biblical books are set aside for particular liturgical seasons on the basis both of the intrinsic importance of subject matter and of liturgical tradition. For example, the Western (Ambrosian and Hispanic) and Eastern tradition of reading the Acts of the Apostles during the Easter season is maintained. This usage results in a clear presentation of how the Church's entire life derives its beginning from the paschal mystery. The tradition of both West and East is also retained, namely the reading of the Gospel of John in the latter weeks of Lent and in the Easter season.

Tradition assigns the reading of Isaiah, especially the first part, to Advent. Some texts of this book, however, are read during the Christmas season, to which the First Letter of John is also assigned.

2) THE LENGTH OF THE TEXTS

75. A *middle way* is followed in regard to the length of texts. A distinction has been made between narratives, which require reading a fairly long passage but which usually hold the attention of the faithful, and texts that should not be lengthy because of the profundity of their doctrine.

In the case of certain rather lengthy texts, longer and shorter versions are provided to suit different situations. The editing of the shorter version has been carried out with great caution.

3) DIFFICULT TEXTS

76. In readings for Sundays and solemnities, texts that present real difficulties are avoided for pastoral reasons. The difficulties may be objective, in that the texts themselves raise profound literary, critical, or exegetical problems; or the difficulties may lie, at least to a certain extent, in the ability of the faithful to understand the texts. But there could be no justification for concealing from the faithful the spiritual riches of certain texts on the grounds of difficulty if the problem arises from the inadequacy either of the religious education that every Christian should have or of the biblical formation that every pastor of souls should have. Often a difficult reading is clarified by its correlation with another in the same Mass.

4) THE OMISSION OF CERTAIN VERSES

77. The omission of verses in readings from Scripture has at times been the tradition of many liturgies, including the Roman liturgy. Admittedly such omissions may not be made lightly, for fear of distorting the meaning of the text or the intent and style of Scripture. Yet on pastoral grounds it was decided to continue the traditional practice in the present Order of Readings, but at the same time to ensure that the essential meaning of the text remained intact. One

reason for the decision is that otherwise some texts would have been unduly long. It would also have been necessary to omit completely certain readings of high spiritual value for the faithful because those readings include some verse that is pastorally less useful or that involves truly difficult questions.

3. PRINCIPLES TO BE FOLLOWED IN THE USE OF THE ORDER OF READINGS

a) The Freedom of Choice Regarding Some Texts

78. The Order of Readings sometimes leaves it to the celebrant to choose between alternative texts or to choose one from the several listed together for the same reading. The option seldom exists on Sundays, solemnities, or feasts, in order not to obscure the character proper to the particular liturgical season or needlessly interrupt the semicontinuous reading of some biblical book. On the other hand, the option is given readily in celebrations of the Saints, in ritual Masses, Masses for various needs and occasions, votive Masses, and Masses for the dead.

These options, together with those indicated in the General Instruction of the Roman Missal and the *Ordo cantus Missae*,[103] have a pastoral purpose. In arranging the Liturgy of the Word, then, the priest should "consider the general spiritual good of the congregation rather than his personal outlook. He should be mindful that the choice of texts is to be made in harmony with the ministers and others who have a role in the celebration and should listen to the opinions of the faithful in what concerns them more directly."[104]

1) THE TWO READINGS BEFORE THE GOSPEL

79. In Masses to which three readings are assigned, all three are to be used. If, however, for pastoral reasons the Conference of Bishops has given permission for two readings only to be used,[105] the choice between the two first readings is to be made in such a way as to safeguard the Church's intent to instruct the faithful more completely in the mystery of salvation. Thus, unless the contrary is indicated in the text of the Lectionary, the reading to be chosen as the first reading is the one that is more closely in harmony with the Gospel, or, in accord with the intent just mentioned, the one that is more helpful toward a coherent catechesis over an extended period, or that preserves the semicontinuous reading of some biblical book.[106]

2) THE LONGER AND SHORTER FORMS OF TEXTS

80. A pastoral criterion must also guide the choice between the longer and shorter forms of the same text. The main consideration must be the capacity of the hearers to listen profitably either to the longer or to the shorter reading; or to listen to a more complete text that will be explained through the homily.

3) WHEN TWO TEXTS ARE PROVIDED

81. When a choice is allowed between alternative texts, whether they are fixed or optional, the first consideration must be the best interest of those taking part. It may be a matter of using the easier texts or the one more relevant to the assembled congregation or, as pastoral advantage may suggest, of repeating or replacing a text that is assigned as proper to one celebration and optional to another.

The issue may arise when it is feared that some text will create difficulties for a particular congregation or when the same text would have to be repeated within a few days, as on a Sunday and on a day during the week following.

4) THE WEEKDAY READINGS

82. The arrangement of weekday readings provides texts for every day of the week throughout the year. In most cases, therefore, these readings are to be used on their assigned days, unless a solemnity, a feast, or else a memorial with proper readings occurs.[107]

In using the Order of Readings for weekdays attention must be paid to whether one reading or another from the same biblical book will have to be omitted because of some celebration occurring during the week. With the arrangement of readings for the entire week in mind, the priest in that case arranges to omit the less significant passages or combines them in the most appropriate manner with other readings, if they contribute to an integral view of a particular theme.

5) THE CELEBRATIONS OF THE SAINTS

83. When they exist, proper readings are given for celebrations of the Saints, that is, biblical passages about the Saint or the mystery that the Mass is celebrating. Even in the case of a memorial these readings must take the place of the weekday readings for the same day. This Order of Readings makes explicit note of every case of proper readings on a memorial.

In some cases there are accommodated readings, those, namely, that bring out some particular aspect of a Saint's spiritual life or work. Use of such readings does not seem binding, except for compelling pastoral reasons. For the most part references are given to readings in the Commons in order to facilitate choice. But these are merely suggestions: in place of an accommodated reading or the particular reading proposed from a Common, any other reading from the Commons referred to may be selected.

The first concern of a priest celebrating with a congregation is the spiritual benefit of the faithful and he will be careful not to impose his personal preference on them. Above all he will make sure not to omit too often or without sufficient cause the readings assigned for each day in the weekday Lectionary: the Church's desire is that a more lavish table of the word of God be spread before the faithful.[108]

There are also common readings, that is, those placed in the Commons either for some determined class of Saints (martyrs, virgins, pastors) or for the Saints in general. Because in these cases several texts are listed for the same reading, it will be up to the priest to choose the one best suited to those listening.

In all celebrations of Saints the readings may be taken not only from the Commons to which the references are given in each case, but also from the Common of Holy Men and Women, whenever there is special reason for doing so.

84. For celebrations of the Saints the following should be observed:

1. On solemnities and feasts the readings must be those that are given in the Proper or in the Commons. For solemnities and feasts of the General Roman Calendar proper readings are always assigned.

2. On solemnities inscribed in particular calendars, three readings are to be assigned, unless the Conference of Bishops has decreed that there are to be only two readings.[109] The first reading is from the Old Testament (but during the Easter season, from the Acts of the Apostles or the Book of Revelation); the second, from an Apostle; the third, from the Gospels.

3. On feasts and memorials, which have only two readings, the first reading can be chosen from either the Old Testament or from an Apostle; the second is from the Gospels. Following the Church's traditional practice, however, the first reading during the Easter season is to be taken from an Apostle; the second, as far as possible, from the Gospel of John.

6) OTHER PARTS OF THE ORDER OF READINGS

85. In the Order of Readings for ritual Masses the references given are to the texts already published for the individual rites. This obviously does not include the texts belonging to celebrations that must not be integrated with Mass.[110]

86. The Order of Readings for Masses for various needs and occasions, votive Masses, and Masses for the dead provides many texts that can be of assistance in adapting such celebrations to the situation, circumstances, and concerns of the particular groups taking part.[111]

87. In ritual Masses, Masses for various needs and occasions, votive Masses, and Masses for the dead, since many texts are given for the same reading, the choice of readings follows the criteria already indicated for the choice of readings from the Common of Saints.

88. On a day when some ritual Mass is not permitted and when the norms in the individual rite allow the choice of one reading from those provided for ritual Masses, the general spiritual welfare of the participants must be considered.[112]

b) The Responsorial Psalm and the Acclamation before the Gospel Reading

89. Among the chants between the readings, the psalm which follows the first reading is of great importance. As a rule the psalm to be used is the one assigned to the reading. But in the case of readings for the Common of Saints, ritual Masses, Masses for various needs and occasions, votive Masses, and Masses for the dead the choice is left up to the priest celebrating. He will base his choice on the principle of the pastoral benefit of those present.

But to make it easier for the people to join in the response to the psalm, the Order of Readings lists certain other texts of psalms and responses that have been chosen according to the various seasons or classes of Saints. Whenever the psalm is sung, these texts may replace the text corresponding to the reading.[113]

90. The chant between the second reading and the Gospel is either specified in each Mass and correlated with the Gospel or else it is left as a choice to be made from those in the series given for a liturgical season or one of the Commons.

91. During Lent one of the acclamations from those given in the Order of Readings may be used, depending on the occasion.[114] This acclamation precedes and follows the verse before the Gospel.

CHAPTER FIVE

DESCRIPTION OF THE ORDER OF READINGS

92. It seems useful to provide here a brief description of the Order of Readings, at least for the principal celebrations and the different seasons of the liturgical year. With these in mind, readings were selected on the basis of the rules already stated. This description is meant to assist

pastors of souls to understand the structure of the Order of Readings, so that their use of it will become more perceptive and the Order of Readings a source of good for Christ's faithful.

1. ADVENT

a) The Sundays

93. Each Gospel reading has a distinctive theme: the Lord's coming at the end of time (First Sunday of Advent), John the Baptist (Second and Third Sunday), and the events that prepared immediately for the Lord's birth (Fourth Sunday).

The Old Testament readings are prophecies about the Messiah and the Messianic age, especially from the Book of Isaiah.

The readings from an Apostle contain exhortations and proclamations, in keeping with the different themes of Advent.

b) The Weekdays

94. There are two series of readings: one to be used from the beginning of Advent until 16 December; the other from 17 to 24 December.

In the first part of Advent there are readings from the Book of Isaiah, distributed in accord with the sequence of the book itself and including the more important texts that are also read on the Sundays. For the choice of the weekday Gospel the first reading has been taken into consideration.

On Thursday of the second week the readings from the Gospel concerning John the Baptist begin. The first reading is either a continuation of Isaiah or a text chosen in view of the Gospel.

In the last week before Christmas the events that immediately prepared for the Lord's birth are presented from the Gospels of Matthew (chapter 1) and Luke (chapter 1). The texts in the first reading, chosen in view of the Gospel reading, are from different Old Testament books and include important Messianic prophecies.

2. THE CHRISTMAS SEASON

a) The Solemnities, Feasts, and Sundays

95. For the vigil and the three Masses of Christmas both the prophetic readings and the others have been chosen from the Roman tradition.

The Gospel on the Sunday within the Octave of Christmas, Feast of the Holy Family, is about Jesus' childhood and the other readings are about the virtues of family life.

On the Octave Day of Christmas, Solemnity of the Blessed Virgin Mary, the Mother of God, the readings are about the Virgin Mother of God and the giving of the holy Name of Jesus.

On the second Sunday after Christmas, the readings are about the mystery of the Incarnation.

On the Epiphany of the Lord, the Old Testament reading and the Gospel continue the Roman tradition; the text for the reading from the Letters of the Apostles is about the calling of the nations to salvation.

On the Feast of the Baptism of the Lord, the texts chosen are about this mystery.

b) The Weekdays

96. From 29 December on, there is a continuous reading of the whole of the First Letter of John, which actually begins earlier, on 27 December, the Feast of St. John the Evangelist, and on 28 December, the Feast of the Holy Innocents. The Gospels relate manifestations of the

Lord: events of Jesus' childhood from the Gospel of Luke (29–30 December); passages from the first chapter of the Gospel of John (31 December–5 January); other manifestations of the Lord from the four Gospels (7–12 January).

3. LENT

a) The Sundays

97. The Gospel readings are arranged as follows:

> The first and second Sundays maintain the accounts of the Temptation and Transfiguration of the Lord, with readings, however, from all three Synoptics.
>
> On the next three Sundays, the Gospels about the Samaritan woman, the man born blind, and the raising of Lazarus have been restored in Year A. Because these Gospels are of major importance in regard to Christian initiation, they may also be read in Year B and Year C, especially in places where there are catechumens.
>
> Other texts, however, are provided for Year B and Year C: for Year B, a text from John about Christ's coming glorification through his Cross and Resurrection and for Year C, a text from Luke about conversion.
>
> On Palm Sunday of the Lord's Passion the texts for the procession are selections from the Synoptic Gospels concerning the Lord's solemn entry into Jerusalem. For the Mass the reading is the account of the Lord's Passion.
>
> The Old Testament readings are about the history of salvation, which is one of the themes proper to the catechesis of Lent. The series of texts for each Year presents the main elements of salvation history from its beginning until the promise of the New Covenant.
>
> The readings from the Letters of the Apostles have been selected to fit the Gospel and the Old Testament readings and, to the extent possible, to provide a connection between them.

b) The Weekdays

98. The readings from the Gospels and the Old Testament were selected because they are related to each other. They treat various themes of the Lenten catechesis that are suited to the spiritual significance of this season. Beginning with Monday of the Fourth Week of Lent, there is a semicontinuous reading of the Gospel of John, made up of texts that correspond more closely to the themes proper to Lent.

> Because the readings about the Samaritan woman, the man born blind, and the raising of Lazarus are now assigned to Sundays, but only for Year A (in Year B and Year C they are optional), provision has been made for their use on weekdays. Thus at the beginning of the Third, Fourth, and Fifth Weeks of Lent optional Masses with these texts for the Gospel have been inserted and may be used in place of the readings of the day on any weekday of the respective week.
>
> In the first days of Holy Week the readings are about the mystery of Christ's passion. For the Chrism Mass the readings bring out both Christ's Messianic mission and its continuation in the Church by means of the sacraments.

4. THE SACRED TRIDUUM AND THE EASTER SEASON

a) The Sacred Easter Triduum

99. On Holy Thursday at the evening Mass the remembrance of the meal preceding the Exodus casts its own special light because of Christ's example in washing the feet of his disciples and Paul's account of the institution of the Christian Passover in the Eucharist.

On Good Friday the liturgical service has as its center John's narrative of the Passion of him who was proclaimed in Isaiah as the Servant of the Lord and who became the one High Priest by offering himself to the Father.

At the Vigil on the holy night of Easter there are seven Old Testament readings which recall the wonderful works of God in the history of salvation. There are two New Testament readings, the announcement of the Resurrection according to one of the Synoptic Gospels and a reading from St. Paul on Christian baptism as the sacrament of Christ's Resurrection.

The Gospel reading for the Mass on Easter day is from John on the finding of the empty tomb. There is also, however, the option to use the Gospel texts from the Easter Vigil or, when there is an evening Mass on Easter Sunday, to use the account in Luke of the Lord's appearance to the disciples on the road to Emmaus. The first reading is from the Acts of the Apostles, which throughout the Easter season replaces the Old Testament reading. The reading from the Apostle Paul concerns the living out of the paschal mystery in the Church.

b) The Sundays

100. The Gospel readings for the first three Sundays recount the appearances of the risen Christ. The readings about the Good Shepherd are assigned to the Fourth Sunday. On the Fifth, Sixth, and Seventh Sundays, there are excerpts from the Lord's discourse and prayer at the end of the Last Supper.

The first reading is from the Acts of the Apostles, in a three-year cycle of parallel and progressive selections: material is presented on the life of the early Church, its witness, and its growth.

For the reading from the Apostles, the First Letter of Peter is in Year A, the First Letter of John in Year B, the Book of Revelation in Year C. These are the texts that seem to fit in especially well with the spirit of joyous faith and sure hope proper to this season.

c) The Weekdays

101. As on the Sundays, the first reading is a semicontinuous reading from the Acts of the Apostles. The Gospel readings during the Easter octave are accounts of the Lord's appearances. After that there is a semicontinuous reading of the Gospel of John, but with texts that have a paschal character, in order to complete the reading from John during Lent. This paschal reading is made up in large part of the Lord's discourse and prayer at the end of the Last Supper.

d) The Solemnities of the Ascension and of Pentecost

102. For the first reading the Solemnity of the Ascension retains the account of the Ascension according to the Acts of the Apostles. This text is complemented by the second reading from the Apostle on Christ in exaltation at the right hand of the Father. For the Gospel reading, each of the three Years has its own text in accord with the differences in the Synoptic Gospels.

In the evening Mass celebrated on the Vigil of Pentecost four Old Testament texts are provided; any one of them may be used, in order to bring out the many aspects of Pentecost. The reading from the Apostles shows the actual working of the Holy Spirit in the Church. The Gospel reading recalls the promise of the Spirit made by Christ before his own glorification.

For the Mass on Pentecost day itself, in accord with received usage, the account in the Acts of the Apostles of the great occurrence on Pentecost day is taken as the first reading. The texts from the Apostle Paul bring out the effect of the action of the Spirit in the life of the Church. The Gospel reading is a remembrance of Jesus bestowing his Spirit on the disciples on the evening of Easter day; other optional texts describe the action of the Spirit on the disciples and on the Church.

5. ORDINARY TIME

a) The Arrangement and Choice of Texts

103. Ordinary Time begins on the Monday after the Sunday following 6 January; it lasts until the Tuesday before Lent inclusive. It begins again on the Monday after Pentecost Sunday and finishes before evening prayer I of the First Sunday of Advent.

The Order of Readings provides readings for thirty-four Sundays and the weeks following them. In some years, however, there are only thirty-three weeks of Ordinary Time. Further, some Sundays either belong to another season (the Sunday on which the Feast of the Baptism of the Lord falls and Pentecost Sunday) or else are impeded by a solemnity that coincides with Sunday (e.g., The Most Holy Trinity or Christ the King).

104. For the correct arrangement in the use of the readings for Ordinary Time, the following are to be respected:

1. The Sunday on which the Feast of the Baptism of the Lord falls replaces the First Sunday in Ordinary Time. Therefore the readings of the First Week of Ordinary Time begin on the Monday after the Sunday following 6 January. When the Feast of the Baptism of the Lord is celebrated on Monday because the Epiphany has been celebrated on the Sunday, the readings of the First Week begin on Tuesday.

2. The Sunday following the Feast of the Baptism of the Lord is the Second Sunday of Ordinary Time. The remaining Sundays are numbered consecutively up to the Sunday preceding the beginning of Lent. The readings for the week in which Ash Wednesday falls are interrupted after the Tuesday readings.

3. For the resumption of the readings of Ordinary Time after Pentecost Sunday:

—when there are thirty-four Sundays in Ordinary Time, the week to be used is the one that immediately follows the last week used before Lent;[115]

—when there are thirty-three Sundays in Ordinary Time, the first week that would have been used after Pentecost is omitted, in order to reserve for the end of the year the eschatological texts that are assigned to the last two weeks.[116]

b) The Sunday Readings

1) THE GOSPEL READINGS

105. On the Second Sunday of Ordinary Time the Gospel continues to center on the manifestation of the Lord, which is celebrated on the Solemnity of the Epiphany, through the traditional passage about the wedding feast at Cana and two other passages from the Gospel of John.

Beginning with the Third Sunday, there is a semicontinuous reading of the Synoptic Gospels. This reading is arranged in such a way that as the Lord's life and preaching unfold the doctrine proper to each of these Gospels is presented.

This distribution also provides a certain coordination between the meaning of each Gospel and the progress of the liturgical year. Thus after Epiphany the readings are on the beginning of the Lord's preaching and they fit in well with Christ's baptism and the first events in which he manifests himself. The liturgical year leads quite naturally to a conclusion in the eschatological theme proper to the last Sundays, since the chapters of the Synoptics that precede the account of the Passion treat this eschatological theme rather extensively.

After the Sixteenth Sunday in Year B, five readings are incorporated from John chapter 6 (the discourse on the bread of life). This is the natural place for these readings because the multiplication of the loaves from the Gospel of John takes the place of the same account in Mark. In the semicontinuous reading of Luke for Year C, the introduction of this Gospel has been prefixed to the first text (that is, on the Third Sunday). This passage expresses the author's intention very beautifully and there seemed to be no better place for it.

2) THE OLD TESTAMENT READINGS

106. These readings have been chosen to correspond to the Gospel passages in order to avoid an excessive diversity between the readings of different Masses and above all to bring out the unity between the Old and the New Testament. The connection between the readings of the same Mass is shown by a precise choice of the readings prefixed to the individual readings.

To the degree possible, the readings were chosen in such a way that they would be short and easy to grasp. But care has been taken to ensure that many Old Testament texts of major significance would be read on Sundays. Such readings are distributed not according to a logical order but on the basis of what the Gospel reading requires. Still, the treasury of the word of God will be opened up in such a way that nearly all the principal pages of the Old Testament will become familiar to those taking part in the Mass on Sundays.

3) THE READINGS FROM THE APOSTLES

107. There is a semicontinuous reading of the Letters of Paul and James (the Letters of Peter and John being read during the Easter and Christmas seasons).

Because it is quite long and deals with such diverse issues, the First Letter to the Corinthians has been spread over the three years of the cycle at the beginning of Ordinary Time. It also was thought best to divide the Letter to the Hebrews into two parts; the first part is read in Year B and the second in Year C.

Only readings that are short and readily grasped by the people have been chosen.

Table II at the end of this Introduction[117] indicates the distribution of Letters of the Apostles over the three-year cycle of the Sundays of Ordinary Time.

c) The Readings for Solemnities of the Lord during Ordinary Time

108. On the solemnities of Holy Trinity, Corpus Christi, and the Sacred Heart, the texts chosen correspond to the principal themes of these celebrations.

The readings of the Thirty-Fourth and last Sunday of Ordinary Time celebrate Christ the universal King. He was prefigured by David and proclaimed as King amid the humiliations of his Passion and Cross; he reigns in the Church and will come again at the end of time.

d) The Weekday Readings

109. The *Gospels* are so arranged that Mark is read first (First to Ninth Week), then Matthew (Tenth to Twenty-First Week), then Luke (Twenty-Second to Thirty-Fourth Week). Mark chapters 1–12 are read in their entirety, with the exception only of the two passages of Mark chapter 6 that are read on weekdays in other seasons. From Matthew and Luke the readings comprise all the material not contained in Mark. All the passages that either are distinctively presented in each Gospel or are needed for a proper understanding of its progression are read

two or three times. Jesus' eschatological discourse as contained in its entirety in Luke is read at the end of the liturgical year.

110. The *First Reading* is taken in periods of several weeks at a time first from one then from the other Testament; the number of weeks depends on the length of the biblical books read.

Rather large sections are read from the New Testament books in order to give the substance, as it were, of each of the Letters.

From the Old Testament there is room only for select passages that, as far as possible, bring out the character of the individual books. The historical texts have been chosen in such a way as to provide an overall view of the history of salvation before the Incarnation of the Lord. But lengthy narratives could hardly be presented; sometimes verses have been selected that make for a reading of moderate length. In addition, the religious significance of the historical events is sometimes brought out by means of certain texts from the wisdom books that are placed as prologues or conclusions to a series of historical readings.

Nearly all the Old Testament books have found a place in the Order of Readings for weekdays in the Proper of Seasons. The only omissions are the shortest of the prophetic books (Obadiah and Zephaniah) and a poetic book (the Song of Songs). Of those narratives of edification requiring a lengthy reading if they are to be understood, Tobit and Ruth are included, but the others (Esther and Judith) are omitted. Texts from these latter two books are assigned, however, to Sundays and weekdays at other times of the year.

Table III at the end of this Introduction[118] lists the way the books of the Old and the New Testaments are distributed over the weekdays in Ordinary Time in the course of two years.

At the end of the liturgical year the readings are from the books that correspond to the eschatological character of this period, Daniel and the Book of Revelation.

CHAPTER SIX

ADAPTATIONS, TRANSLATIONS, AND FORMAT OF THE ORDER OF READINGS

1. ADAPTATIONS AND TRANSLATIONS

111. In the liturgical assembly the word of God must always be read either from the Latin texts prepared by the Holy See or from vernacular translations approved for liturgical use by the Conferences of Bishops, according to existing norms.[119]

112. The Lectionary for Mass must be translated integrally in all its parts, including the Introduction. If the Conference of Bishops has judged it necessary and useful to add certain adaptations, these are to be incorporated after their confirmation by the Holy See.[120]

113. The size of the Lectionary will necessitate editions in more than one volume; no particular division of the volumes is prescribed. But each volume is to contain the explanatory texts on the structure and purpose of the section it contains.

The ancient custom is recommended of having separate books, one for the Gospels and the other for the other readings for the Old and New Testaments.

It may also be useful to publish separately a Sunday lectionary (which could also contain selected excerpts from the sanctoral cycle), and a weekday lectionary. A practical basis for

Introduction xxxvii

dividing the Sunday lectionary is the three-year cycle, so that all the readings for each year are presented in sequence.

But there is freedom to adopt other arrangements that may be devised and seem to have pastoral advantages.

114. The texts for the chants are always to be adjoined to the readings, but separate books containing the chants alone are permitted. It is recommended that the texts be printed with divisions into stanzas.

115. Whenever a text consists of different parts, the typography must make this structure of the text clear. It is likewise recommended that even non-poetic texts be printed with division into sense lines to assist the proclamation of the readings.

116. Where there are longer and shorter forms of a text, they are to be printed separately, so that each can be read with ease. But if such a separation does not seem feasible, a way is to be found to ensure that each text can be proclaimed without mistakes.

117. In vernacular editions the texts are not to be printed without headings prefixed. If it seems advisable, an introductory note on the general meaning of the passage may be added to the heading. This note is to carry some distinctive symbol or is to be set in different type to show clearly that it is an optional text.[121]

118. It would be useful for every volume to have an index of the passages of the Bible, modeled on the biblical index of the present volume.[122] This will provide ready access to texts of the lectionaries for Mass that may be needed or helpful for specific occasions.

2. THE FORMAT OF INDIVIDUAL READINGS

For each reading the present volume carries the textual reference, the headings, and the *incipit*.

a) The Biblical References

119. The text reference (that is, to chapter and verses) is always given according to the Neo-Vulgate edition for the psalms.[123] But a second reference according to the original text (Hebrew, Aramaic, or Greek) has been added wherever there is a discrepancy. Depending on the decrees of the competent Authorities for the individual languages, vernacular versions may retain the enumeration corresponding to the version of the Bible approved for liturgical use by the same Authorities. Exact references to chapter and verses, however, must always appear and may be given in the text or in the margin.

120. These references provide liturgical books with the basis of the "announcement" of the text that must be read in the celebration, but which is not printed in this volume. This "announcement" of the text will observe the following norms, but they may be altered by decree of the competent Authorities on the basis of what is customary and useful for different places and languages.

121. The formula to be used is always: "A *reading* from the Book of . . .," "A *reading* from the Letter of . . .," or "A *reading* from the holy Gospel according to . . .," and not: "The *beginning* of . . . ," (unless this seems advisable in particular instances), nor: "The *continuation* of . . . ."

122. The traditionally accepted titles for books are to be retained with the following exceptions:

1. Where there are two books with the same name, the title is to be: The first Book, The second Book (for example, of Kings, of Maccabees) or The first Letter, The second Letter.

2. The title more common in current usage is to be accepted for the following books:

—I and II Samuel instead of I and II Kings;

—I and II Kings instead of III and IV Kings;

—I and II Chronicles instead of I and II Paralipomenon;

—The Books of Ezra and Nehemiah instead of I and II Ezra.

3. The distinguishing titles for the wisdom books are: The Book of Job, the Book of Proverbs, the Book of Ecclesiastes, the Song of Songs, the Book of Wisdom, and the Book of Sirach.

4. For all the books that are included among the prophets in the Neo-Vulgate, the formula is to be: "A reading from the Book of the Prophet Isaiah, or of the Prophet Jeremiah or of the Prophet Baruch" and: "A reading from the Book of the Prophet Ezekiel, of the Prophet Daniel, of the Prophet Hosea, of the Prophet Malachi," even in the case of books not regarded by some as being in actual fact prophetic.

5. The title is to be Book of Lamentations and Letter to the Hebrews, with no mention of Jeremiah or Paul.

b) The Heading

123. There is a *heading* prefixed to each text, chosen carefully (usually from the words of the text itself) in order to point out the main theme of the reading and, when necessary, to make the connection between the readings of the same Mass clear.

c) The "Incipit"

124. In this Order of Readings the first element of the *incipit* is the customary introductory phrase: "At that time," "In those days," "Brothers and sisters," "Beloved," "Dearly beloved," "Dearest brothers and sisters," or "Thus says the Lord," "Thus says the Lord God." These words are not given when the text itself provides sufficient indication of the time or the persons involved or where such phrases would not fit in with the very nature of the text. For the individual languages, such phrases may be changed or omitted by decree of the competent Authorities.

After the first words of the *incipit* the Order of Readings gives the proper beginning of the reading, with some words deleted or supplied for intelligibility, inasmuch as the text is separated from its context. When the text for a reading is made up of non-consecutive verses and this has required changes in wording, these are appropriately indicated.

d) The Final Acclamation

125. In order to facilitate the congregation's acclamation, the words for the reader *The word of the Lord*, or similar words suited to local custom, are to be printed at the end of the reading for use by the reader.

NOTES

[1] Cf. especially Second Vatican Council, Constitution on the Sacred Liturgy, *Sacrosanctum Concilium*, nn. 7, 24, 33, 35, 48, 51, 52, 56; Dogmatic Constitution on Divine Revelation, *Dei Verbum*, nn. 1, 21, 25, 26; Decree on the Missionary Activity of the Church, *Ad gentes*, n. 6; Decree on the Ministry and Life of Priests, *Presbyterorum Ordinis*, n. 18.

[2] Among the spoken or written statements of the Supreme Pontiffs, see especially: Paul VI, Motu Proprio, *Ministeria quaedam*, 15 August 1972, n. V: *Acta Apostolicae Sedis* [*AAS*] 64 (1972) 532; Apostolic Exhortation, *Marialis cultus*, 2 February 1974, n. 12: *AAS* 66 (1974) 125–126; Apostolic Exhortation, *Evangelii nuntiandi*, 8 December 1975, n. 28: *AAS* 68 (1976) 24–25, n. 43: *ibid.*, pp. 33–34, n. 47: *ibid.*, pp. 36–37; John Paul II, Apostolic Constitution, *Scripturarum thesaurus*, 25 April 1979 in *Nova Vulgata Bibliorum Sacrorum editione*, Typis Polyglottis Vaticanis 1979, pp. V–VIII; Apostolic Exhortation, *Catechesi tradendae*, 16 October 1979, nn. 23, 27, 48: *AAS* 71 (1979) 1296–1297, 1298–1299, 1316; Letter, *Dominicae Cenae*, 24 February 1980, n. 10: *AAS* 72 (1980) 134–137.

[3] Cf. V. gr. Sacred Congregation of Rites, Instruction, *Eucharisticum Mysterium*, 25 May 1967, n. 10: *AAS* 59 (1967) 547–548; Sacred Congregation for Divine Worship, Instruction, *Liturgicae instaurationes*, 5 September 1970, n. 2: *AAS* 62 (1970) 695–696; Sacred Congregation for the Clergy, *Directorum catecheticum generale,* 11 April 1971: *AAS* 64 (1972) 106–107; n. 25: *ibid.*, p. 114; Sacred Congregation for Divine Worship, *Institutio Generalis Missalis Romani*, nn. 9, 11, 24, 33, 60, 62, 316, 320; Sacred Congregation for Catholic Education, Instruction on liturgical formation in seminaries, *In ecclesiasticam futurorum sacerdotum*, 3 June 1979, nn. 11, 52; *ibid.*, Appendix, n. 15; Sacred Congregation for the Sacraments and Divine Worship, Instruction, *Inaestimabile Donum*, 3 April 1980, nn. 1, 2, 3; *AAS* 72 (1980) 333–334.

[4] Cf. Missale Romanum ex Decreto Sacrosancti Oecumenici Concilii Vaticani II instauratum auctoritate Pauli VI promulgatum, *Ordo lectionum Missae* (Typis Polyglottis Vaticanis, 1969) pp. IX–XII (Praenotanda); Decree of promulgation: *AAS* 61 (1969) 548–549.

[5] Cf. Second Vatican Council, Constitution on the Sacred Liturgy, *Sacrosanctum Concilium*, nn. 35, 56; Paul VI, Apostolic Exhortation, *Evangelii nuntiandi*, 8 December 1975, nn. 28, 47: *AAS* 68 (1976) 24–25, 36–37; John Paul II, Letter, *Dominicae Cenae*, 24 February 1980, nn. 10, 11, 12: *AAS* 72 (1980) 134–146.

[6] For example, the terms "word of God," "Sacred Scripture," "Old" and "New Testament," "Reading (readings) of the word of God," "Reading (readings) from Sacred Scripture," "Celebration (celebrations) of the word of God," etc.

[7] Thus one and the same text may be read or used for various reasons on various occasions and celebrations of the Church's liturgical year. This is to be recalled in the homily, in pastoral exegesis, and in catechesis. The indexes of this volume will show, for example, that Romans chapter 6 or Romans chapter 8 is used in various seasons of the liturgical year and in various celebrations of the sacraments and sacramentals.

[8] Cf. Lk 4:16-21; 24:25-35, 44-49.

[9] Thus, for example, in the celebration of Mass, there is proclamation, reading, etc. (cf. *Institutio Generalis Missalis Romani*, nn. 21, 23, 95, 131, 146, 234, 235). There are also other celebrations of the word of God in the *Pontificale Romanum*, the *Rituale Romanum*, and the *Liturgia Horarum*, as restored by decree of Second Vatican Council.

[10] Cf. Second Vatican Council, Constitution on the Sacred Liturgy, *Sacrosanctum Concilium*, nn. 7, 33; Mk 16:19-20; Mt 28:20; St. Augustine, *Sermo 85*, 1: "The Gospel is the mouth of Christ. He is seated in heaven yet does not cease to speak on earth": *PL* 38, 520; cf. also *In Io. Ev. tract.* XXX, 1: *PL* 35, 1632; *CCL* 36, 289; *Pontificale Romano–Germanicum*: "The Gospel is read, in which Christ speaks by his own mouth to the people . . . the Gospel resounds in the church as though Christ himself were speaking to the

people" (see C. Vogel & R. Elze, edd., *Le Pontifical romano–germanique du dixième siècle. Le Texte I*, Città del Vaticano, 1963, XCIV, 18, p. 334); or "At the approach of Christ, that is the Gospel, we put aside our staffs, because we have no need of human assistance" (*ibid.* XCIV, 23, p. 335).

[11] Cf. Second Vatican Council, Constitution on the Sacred Liturgy, *Sacrosanctum Concilium*, n. 7.

[12] Cf. Heb 4:12.

[13] Cf. St. Augustine, *Quaestionum in Heptateuchum liber* 2, 73: *PL* 34, 623; *CCL* 33, 106; Second Vatican Council, Dogmatic Constitution on Divine Revelation, *Dei Verbum*, n. 16.

[14] Cf. St. Jerome: "If, as St. Paul says (1 Cor 1:24), Christ is the power of God and the wisdom of God, anyone who is ignorant of the Scriptures is ignorant of the power of God and his wisdom. For ignorance of the Scriptures is ignorance of Christ" (*Commentarii in Isaiam prophetam, Prologus*: *PL* 24, 17A; *CCL* 73, 1); Second Vatican Council, Dogmatic Constitution on Divine Revelation, *Dei Verbum*, n. 25.

[15] Cf. 2 Cor 1:20-22.

[16] Cf. Second Vatican Council, Constitution on the Sacred Liturgy, *Sacrosanctum Concilium*, n. 10.

[17] Cf. 2 Thes 3:1.

[18] Cf. *Collectae, Pro Sancta Ecclesia,* in *Missale Romanum ex Decreto Sacrosancti Oecumenici Concilii Vaticani II instauratum auctoritate Pauli VI promulgatum* (Typis Polyglottis Vaticanis, 1975) pp. 786, 787, 790: St. Cyprian, *De oratione dominica* 23: *PL* 4, 553; *CSEL* 3/2, 285; *CCL* 3A, 105; St. Augustine, *Sermo* 71, 20, 33: *PL* 38, 463f.

[19] Cf. *Collecta, Dominica XXI "per annum,"* in *Missale Romanum*, p. 360.

[20] Cf. Second Vatican Council, Dogmatic Constitution on Divine Revelation, *Dei Verbum*, n. 8.

[21] Cf. Jn 14:15-17, 25-26–16:15.

[22] Second Vatican Council, Decree on the Ministry and Life of Priests, *Presbyterorum Ordinis*, n. 4.

[23] Cf. Second Vatican Council, Constitution on the Sacred Liturgy, *Sacrosanctum Concilium*, n. 51; Decree on the Ministry and Life of Priests, *Presbyterorum Ordinis*, n. 18; also Dogmatic Constitution on Divine Revelation, *Dei Verbum*, n. 21; Decree on the Missionary Activity of the Church, *Ad gentes*, n. 6. Cf. *Institutio Generalis Missalis Romani*, n. 8.

[24] Second Vatican Council, Constitution on the Sacred Liturgy, *Sacrosanctum Concilium*, n. 56.

[25] *Institutio Generalis Missalis Romani*, n. 33.

[26] Cf. Sacred Congregation for Divine Worship, Instruction, *Liturgicae instaurationes*, 5 September 1970, n. 2: *AAS* 62 (1970) 695–696; John Paul II, Letter, *Dominicae Cenae*, 24 February 1980, n. 10: *AAS* 72 (1980) 134–137; Sacred Congregation for the Sacraments and Divine Worship, Instruction, *Inaestimabile Donum*, 3 April 1980, n. 1: *AAS* 72 (1980) 333.

[27] Second Vatican Council, Constitution on the Sacred Liturgy, *Sacrosanctum Concilium*, n. 33.

[28] Cf. below, n. 111 of this Introduction.

[29] Cf. *Missale Romanum ex Decreto Sacrosancti Oecumenici Concilii Vaticani II instauratum auctoritate Pauli VI promulgatum, Ordo cantus Missae, editio typica* 1972, *Praenotanda*, nn. 4, 6, 10.

[30] Cf. *Institutio Generalis Missalis Romani*, n. 11.

[31] Cf. *ibid.*, n. 272; and nn. 32–34 of this Introduction.

[32] Cf. *ibid.*, nn. 35, 95.

[33] Cf. *ibid.*, nn. 82–84.

[34] Cf. *ibid.*, nn. 94, 131.

[35] Cf. *Ordo Missae cum populo*, 11, in: *Missale Romanum ex Decreto Sacrosancti Oecumenici Concilii Vaticani II instauratum auctoritate Pauli VI promulgatum* (Typis Polyglottis Vaticanis, 1975) p. 388.

[36] *Institutio Generalis Missalis Romani*, n. 36.

[37] Paul VI, Apostolic Constitution, *Laudis canticum,* in *Liturgia Horarum ex Decreto Sacrosancti Oecumenici Concilii Vaticani II instaurata, auctoritate Pauli VI promulgata* (Typis Polyglottis Vaticanis, 1971); cf. also Second Vatican Council, Constitution on the Sacred Liturgy, *Sacrosanctum Concilium*, nn. 24, 90; Sacred Congregation of Rites, Instruction, *Musicam sacram*, 5 March 1967, n. 39: *AAS* 59 (1967) 311; *Liturgia Horarum, Institutio Generalis*, nn. 23, 109; Sacred Congregation for Catholic Education, *Ratio fundamentalis,* n. 53.

[38] Cf. below, nn. 89–90 of this Introduction.

[39] Cf. *Institutio Generalis Missalis Romani*, nn. 18, 39.

[40] Cf. *ibid.*, n. 272; and below, nn. 32ff. of this Introduction.

[41] Cf. *ibid.*, n. 39.

[42] Cf. *ibid.*, nn. 37–39; *Missale Romanum ex Decreto Sacrosancti Oecumenici Concilii Vaticani II instauratum auctoritate Pauli VI promulgatum, Ordo cantus Missae, Praenotanda*, nn. 7–9; *Graduale Romanum*, 1974, *Praenotanda,* n. 7; *Graduale simplex, editio typica altera* 1975, *Praenotanda,* n. 16.

[43] Second Vatican Council, Constitution on the Sacred Liturgy, *Sacrosanctum Concilium*, n. 52; Sacred Congregation of Rites, Instruction, *Inter Oecumenici*, 26 September 1964, n. 54: *AAS* 56 (1964) 890.

[44] Cf. *Institutio Generalis Missalis Romani*, n. 42.

[45] Second Vatican Council, Constitution on the Sacred Liturgy, *Sacrosanctum Concilium*, n. 35, 2.

[46] Cf. Second Vatican Council, Constitution on the Sacred Liturgy, *Sacrosanctum Concilium*, nn. 6 and 47.

[47] Cf. Paul VI, Encyclical, *Mysterium Fidei*, 3 September 1965, n. 36: *AAS* 57 (1965) 753; Second Vatican Council, Decree on the Missionary Activity of the Church, *Ad gentes*, n. 9; Paul VI, Apostolic Exhortation, *Evangelii nuntiandi*, 8 December 1975, n. 43: *AAS* 69 (1976) 33–34.

[48] Cf. Second Vatican Council, Constitution on the Sacred Liturgy, *Sacrosanctum Concilium*, n. 35, 2; *Institutio Generalis Missalis Romani*, n. 41.

[49] Second Vatican Council, Constitution on the Sacred Liturgy, *Sacrosanctum Concilium*, n. 10.

[50] Cf. John Paul II, Apostolic Exhortation, *Catechesi tradendae*, 16 October 1979, n. 48: *AAS* 71 (1979) 1316.

[51] Cf. *Institutio Generalis Missalis Romani*, n. 165.

[52] Cf. *ibid.*, n. 42; and also Sacred Congregation of Rites, Instruction, *Eucharisticum Mysterium*, 25 May 1967, n. 28: *AAS* 59 (1967) 556–557.

[53] Cf. Sacred Congregation for Divine Worship, Instruction, *Actio pastoralis*, 15 May 1969, n. 6g: *AAS* 61 (1969) 809; *Directorium de Missis cum pueris*, 1 November 1973, n. 48: *AAS* 66 (1974) 44.

[54] Cf. *Institutio Generalis Missalis Romani*, nn. 42, 338; *Rituale Romanum ex Decreto Sacrosancti Oecumenici Concilii Vaticani II instauratum, auctoritate Pauli VI promulgatum, Ordo celebrandi Matrimonium*

xlii Notes to the Introduction

(Typis Polyglottis Vaticanis, 1969) nn. 22, 42, 57; *Ordo Exsequiarum* (Typis Polyglottis Vaticanis, 1969) nn. 41, 64.

[55] Cf. *Institutio Generalis Missalis Romani*, n. 97.

[56] Cf. *ibid.*, n. 139.

[57] Cf. *ibid.*, n. 23.

[58] Cf. *ibid.*, n. 43.

[59] Cf. *ibid.*, n. 45.

[60] Cf. *ibid.*, n. 99.

[61] Cf. *ibid.*, n 47.

[62] Cf. above, note 23 of this Introduction.

[63] Cf. *Institutio Generalis Missalis Romani*, n. 272.

[64] Cf. Second Vatican Council, Constitution on the Sacred Liturgy, *Sacrosanctum Concilium*, n. 122.

[65] Cf. *Pontificale Romanum ex Decreto Sacrosancti Oecumenici Concilii Vaticani II instauratum auctoritate Pauli VI promulgatum, De Ordinatione Diaconi, Presbyteri et Episcopi* (Typis Polyglottis Vaticanis, 1968) p. 28, n. 24; p. 58, n. 21; p. 85, n. 24; p. 70, n. 25; p. 110, n. 25.

[66] Cf. below, nn. 78–91 of this Introduction.

[67] Cf. *Institutio Generalis Missalis Romani*, nn. 318–320, 324–325.

[68] Cf. *ibid.*, n. 313.

[69] Cf. *ibid.*, n. 42; Sacred Congregation for the Sacraments and Divine Worship, Instruction, *Inaestimabile Donum*, 3 April 1980, n. 3: *AAS* 72 (1980) 334.

[70] Cf. *Institutio Generalis Missalis Romani*, n. 11.

[71] Cf. *ibid.*, n. 68.

[72] Cf. *ibid.*, nn. 33, 47.

[73] Second Vatican Council, Decree on the Ministry and Life of Priests, *Presbyterorum Ordinis*, n. 4.

[74] Second Vatican Council, Constitution on the Sacred Liturgy, *Sacrosanctum Concilium*, n. 33.

[75] Cf. *Institutio Generalis Missalis Romani*, n. 9.

[76] Second Vatican Council, Constitution on the Sacred Liturgy, *Sacrosanctum Concilium*, n. 7.

[77] Cf. *ibid.*, n. 9.

[78] Cf. Rom 1:16.

[79] Cf. Second Vatican Council, Dogmatic Constitution on Divine Revelation, *Dei Verbum*, n. 21.

[80] Quoted *ibid.*

[81] Cf. Jn 14:15-26; 15:26–16:4, 5-15.

[82] Cf. Second Vatican Council, Decree on the Missionary Activity of the Church, *Ad gentes*, nn. 6 and 15; and also Dogmatic Constitution on Divine Revelation, *Dei Verbum*, n. 26.

[83] Cf. Second Vatican Council, Constitution on the Sacred Liturgy, *Sacrosanctum Concilium*, n. 24; and also Sacred Congregation for the Clergy, *Directorium Catechisticum Generale*, 11 April 1971, n. 25: *AAS* 64 (1972) 114.

[84] Cf. Second Vatican Council, Constitution on the Sacred Liturgy, *Sacrosanctum Concilium*, n. 56; see also Sacred Congregation for the Sacraments and Divine Worship, Instruction, *Inaestimabile Donum*, 3 April 1980, n. 1: *AAS* 72 (1980) 333–334.

[85] Cf. Second Vatican Council, Constitution on the Sacred Liturgy, *Sacrosanctum Concilium*, nn. 24 and 35.

[86] Cf. *Institutio Generalis Missalis Romani*, n. 34.

[87] Cf. *ibid.*, n. 96.

[88] Cf. *ibid.*, nn. 47, 61, 132; Sacred Congregation for the Sacraments and Divine Worship, Instruction, *Inaestimabile Donum*, 3 April 1980, n. 3: *AAS* 72 (1980) 334.

[89] Cf. *Institutio Generalis Missalis Romani*, n. 66.

[90] Cf. Paul VI, Motu Proprio, *Ministeria quaedam*, 15 August 1972, n. V: *AAS* 64 (1972) 532.

[91] Cf. Sacred Congregation for the Sacraments and Divine Worship, Instruction, *Inaestimabile Donum*, 3 April 1980, nn. 2 and 18: *AAS* 72 (1980) 334; cf. also Sacred Congregation for Divine Worship, *Directorium de Missis cum pueris*, 1 November 1973, nn. 22, 24, 27: *AAS* 66 (1974) 43.

[92] Cf. *Institutio Generalis Missalis Romani*, nn. 47, 66, 151; cf. also Consilium ad exsequendam Constitutionem de Sacra Liturgia, *De oratione communi fidelium* (Città del Vaticano, 1966) n. 8.

[93] Cf. *Institutio Generalis Missalis Romani*, n. 66.

[94] Cf. *ibid.*, nn. 37a and 67.

[95] Cf. *ibid.*, n. 68.

[96] Cf., for example, Pope Paul VI, Apostolic Constitution, *Missale Romanum*, 3 April 1969, in *Missale Romanum ex Decreto Sacrosancti Oecumenici Concilii Vaticani II instauratum auctoritate Pauli VI promulgatum* (Typis Polyglottis Vaticanis, 1975) p. 15, quoted in *Missale Romanum ex Decreto Sacrosancti Oecumenici Concilii Vaticani II instauratum auctoritate Pauli VI promulgatum, Ordo lectionum Missae, editio typica altera* (Typis Polyglottis Vaticanis, 1981) p. XXX.

[97] Cf. Second Vatican Council, Constitution on the Sacred Liturgy, *Sacrosanctum Concilium*, nn. 35 and 51.

[98] Cf. Pope Paul VI, Apostolic Constitution, *Missale Romanum*: in *Missale Romanum ex Decreto Sacrosancti Oecumenici Concilii Vaticani II instauratum auctoritate Pauli VI promulgatum* (Typis Polyglottis Vaticanis, 1975) p. 15, quoted in *Missale Romanum ex Decreto Sacrosancti Oecumenici Concilii Vaticani II instauratum auctoritate Pauli VI promulgatum, Ordo lectionum Missae, editio typica altera* (Typis Polyglottis Vaticanis, 1981) p. XXXI.

[99] Cf. Second Vatican Council, Constitution on the Sacred Liturgy, *Sacrosanctum Concilium*, nn. 9 and 33; Sacred Congregation of Rites, Instruction, *Inter Oecumenici*, 26 September 1964, n. 7: *AAS* 56 (1964) 878; John Paul II, Apostolic Exhortation, *Catechesi tradendae*, 16 October 1979, n. 23: *AAS* 71 (1979) 1296–1297.

[100] Cf. Second Vatican Council, Constitution on the Sacred Liturgy, *Sacrosanctum Concilium*, n. 35, 4; Sacred Congregation of Rites, Instruction, *Inter Oecumenici*, 26 September 1964, nn. 37–38: *AAS* 56 (1964) 884.

[101] Cf. Sacred Congregation for Divine Worship, Instruction, *Actio pastoralis*, 15 May 1969, n. 6: *AAS* 61 (1969) 809; Sacred Congregation for Divine Worship, *Directorium de Missis cum pueris*, 1 November 1973,

xliv Notes to the Introduction

nn. 41–47: *AAS* 66 (1974) 43; Paul VI, Apostolic Exhortation *Marialis cultus*, 2 February 1974, n. 12: *AAS* 66 (1974) 125–126.

[102] Each of the years is designated by the letter A, B, or C. The following is the procedure to determine which year is A, B, or C. The letter C designates a year whose number is divisible into three equal parts, as though the cycle had taken its beginning from the first year of the Christian era. Thus the year 1 would have been Year A; year 2, Year B; year 3, Year C (as would years 6, 9, and 12). Thus, for example, year 1980 is Year C; 1981, Year A; 1982, Year B; and 1983, Year C again. And so forth. Obviously each cycle runs in accord with the plan of the liturgical year, that is, it begins with the First Week of Advent, which falls in the preceding year of the civil calendar.

The years in each cycle are marked in a sense by the principal characteristic of the Synoptic Gospel used for the semicontinuous reading of Ordinary Time. Thus the first Year of the cycle is the Year for the reading of the Gospel of Matthew and is so named; the second and third Years are the Year of Mark and the Year of Luke.

[103] Cf. *Institutio Generalis Missalis Romani*, nn. 36–40; *Missale Romanum ex Decreto Sacrosancti Oecumenici Concilii Vaticani II instauratum auctoritate Pauli VI promulgatum, Ordo cantus Missae* (Typis Polyglottis Vaticanis) nn. 5–9.

[104] Cf. *Institutio Generalis Missalis Romani*, n. 313.

[105] Cf. *ibid.*, n. 318; Sacred Congregation for the Sacraments and Divine Worship, Instruction, *Inaestimabile donum*, n. 1: *AAS* 72 (1980) 333–334.

[106] For example: in Lent the continuity of the Old Testament readings corresponds to the unfolding of the history of salvation; the Sundays in Ordinary Time provide the semicontinuous reading of one of the Letters of the Apostles. In these cases it is right that the pastor of souls choose one or other of the readings in a systematic way over a series of Sundays, so that he may establish a coherent plan for catechesis. It is not right to read indiscriminately on one day from the Old Testament, on another from the Letter of an Apostle, without any orderly plan for the texts that follow.

[107] Cf. *Institutio Generalis Missalis Romani*, n. 319.

[108] Cf. *ibid.*, n. 316c; see Second Vatican Council, Constitution on the Sacred Liturgy, *Sacrosanctum Concilium*, n. 51.

[109] Cf. *Institutio Generalis Missalis Romani*, n. 318.

[110] Cf. *Rituale Romanum ex Decreto Sacrosancti Oecumenici Concilii Vaticani II instauratum, auctoritate Pauli VI promulgatum, Ordo Paenitentiae* (Typis Polyglottis Vaticanis, 1974) *Praenotanda*, n. 13.

[111] Cf. *Institutio Generalis Missalis Romani*, n. 320.

[112] Cf. *ibid.*, n. 313.

[113] Cf. nn. 173–174, of this Order of Readings.

[114] Cf. n. 233, of this Order of Readings.

[115] So, for example, when there are six weeks before Lent, the seventh week begins on the Monday after Pentecost. The Solemnity of the Most Holy Trinity replaces the Sunday of Ordinary Time.

[116] When there are, for example, five weeks before Lent, the Monday after Pentecost begins with the Seventh Week of Ordinary Time and the Sixth Week is omitted.

[117] Cf. Table II at the end of this Introduction [found in volume I].

[118] Cf. Table III at the end of this Introduction [Table II in this volume].

[119] Cf. Consilium ad exsequendam Constitutionem de Sacra Liturgia, Instruction, *De popularibus interpretationibus conficiendis*, 25 January 1969: Notitiae 5 (1969), pp. 3–12; *Declaratio circa interpretationes textuum liturgicorum "ad interim" paratas*: Notitiae 5 (1969), p. 69; Sacred Congregation for Divine Worship, *Declaratio de interpretatione textuum liturgicorum*: Notitiae 5 (1969), pp. 333–334 (cf. also *Responsiones ad dubia*, in Notitiae 9 (1973) pp. 153–154); *De unica interpretatione textuum liturgicorum*: Notitiae 6 (1970), pp. 84–85; Sacred Congregation for the Sacraments and Divine Worship, *Epistula ad Praesides Conferentiarum Episcopalium de linguis vulgaribus in S. Liturgiam inducendis*: Notitiae 12 (1976), pp. 300–302.

[120] Cf. Sacred Congregation for Divine Worship, Instruction, *Liturgicae instaurationes*, 5 September 1970, n. 11: *AAS* 62 (1970) 702–703; *Institutio Generalis Missalis Romani*, n. 325.

[121] Cf. *ibid., Institutio Generalis Missalis Romani*, nn. 11, 29, 68a, 139.

[122] Cf. Index of Readings, p. 1935 of this Order of Readings.

[123] The references for the psalms follow the order of the *Liber Psalmorum*, published by the Pontifical Commission for the Neo-Vulgate (Typis Polyglottis Vaticanis, 1969).

TABLE IA
PRINCIPAL CELEBRATIONS OF THE LITURGICAL YEAR

Year	Lectionary Cycle Sunday	Lectionary Cycle Weekday	Ash Wednesday	Easter	Ascension Thursday	Pentecost
1998	C	II	25 Feb	12 Apr	21 May	31 May
1999	A	I	17 Feb	4 Apr	13 May	23 May
2000	B	II	8 Mar	23 Apr	1 June	11 June
2001	C	I	28 Feb	15 Apr	24 May	3 June
2002	A	II	13 Feb	31 Mar	9 May	19 May
2003	B	I	5 Mar	20 Apr	29 May	8 June
2004	C	II	25 Feb	11 Apr	20 May	30 May
2005	A	I	9 Feb	27 Mar	5 May	15 May
2006	B	II	1 Mar	16 Apr	25 May	4 June
2007	C	I	21 Feb	8 Apr	17 May	27 May
2008	A	II	6 Feb	23 Mar	1 May	11 May
2009	B	I	25 Feb	12 Apr	21 May	31 May
2010	C	II	17 Feb	4 Apr	13 May	23 May
2011	A	I	9 Mar	24 Apr	2 June	12 June
2012	B	II	22 Feb	8 Apr	17 May	27 May
2013	C	I	13 Feb	31 Mar	9 May	19 May
2014	A	II	5 Mar	20 Apr	29 May	8 June
2015	B	I	18 Feb	5 Apr	14 May	24 May
2016	C	II	10 Feb	27 Mar	5 May	15 May
2017	A	I	1 Mar	16 Apr	25 May	4 June
2018	B	II	14 Feb	1 Apr	10 May	20 May
2019	C	I	6 Mar	21 Apr	30 May	9 June
2020	A	II	26 Feb	12 Apr	21 May	31 May
2021	B	I	17 Feb	4 Apr	13 May	23 May
2022	C	II	2 Mar	17 Apr	26 May	5 June
2023	A	I	22 Feb	9 Apr	18 May	28 May
2024	B	II	14 Feb	31 Mar	9 May	19 May
2025	C	I	5 Mar	20 Apr	29 May	8 June

TABLE IB
PRINCIPAL CELEBRATIONS OF THE LITURGICAL YEAR

| | | | *Weeks in Ordinary Time* | | | | |
| | | | *before Lent* | | *after Easter Season* | | |
Year	*Lectionary Cycle Sunday*	*Lectionary Cycle Weekday*	*Number of Weeks*	*Ending*	*Beginning*	*Week Number*	*First Sunday of Advent*
1998	C	II	7	24 Feb	1 June	9	29 Nov
1999	A	I	6	16 Feb	24 May	8	28 Nov
2000	B	II	9	7 Mar	12 June	10	3 Dec
2001	C	I	7	27 Feb	4 June	9	2 Dec
2002	A	II	5	12 Feb	20 May	7	1 Dec
2003	B	I	8	4 Mar	9 June	10	30 Nov
2004	C	II	7	24 Feb	31 May	9	28 Nov
2005	A	I	5	8 Feb	16 May	7	27 Nov
2006	B	II	8	28 Feb	5 June	9	3 Dec
2007	C	I	7	20 Feb	28 May	8	2 Dec
2008	A	II	4	5 Feb	12 May	6	30 Nov
2009	B	I	7	24 Feb	1 June	9	29 Nov
2010	C	II	6	16 Feb	24 May	8	28 Nov
2011	A	I	9	8 Mar	13 June	11	27 Nov
2012	B	II	7	21 Feb	28 May	8	2 Dec
2013	C	I	5	12 Feb	20 May	7	1 Dec
2014	A	II	8	4 Mar	9 June	10	30 Nov
2015	B	I	6	17 Feb	25 May	8	29 Nov
2016	C	II	5	9 Feb	16 May	7	27 Nov
2017	A	I	8	28 Feb	5 June	9	3 Dec
2018	B	II	6	13 Feb	21 May	7	2 Dec
2019	C	I	8	5 Mar	10 June	10	1 Dec
2020	A	II	7	25 Feb	1 June	9	29 Nov
2021	B	I	6	16 Feb	24 May	8	28 Nov
2022	C	II	8	1 Mar	6 June	10	27 Nov
2023	A	I	7	21 Feb	29 May	8	3 Dec
2024	B	II	6	13 Feb	20 May	7	1 Dec
2025	C	I	8	4 Mar	9 June	10	30 Nov

TABLE II

ORDER OF THE FIRST READING FOR WEEKDAYS IN ORDINARY TIME

Week	Year I	Year II
1	Hebrews	1 Samuel
2	Hebrews	1 Samuel
3	Hebrews	2 Samuel
4	Hebrews	2 Samuel; 1 Kings, 1–16
5	Genesis, 1–11	1 Kings, 1–16
6	Genesis, 1–11	James
7	Sirach	James
8	Sirach	1 Peter; Jude
9	Tobit	2 Peter; 2 Timothy
10	2 Corinthians	1 Kings, 17–22
11	2 Corinthians	1 Kings, 17–22; 2 Kings
12	Genesis, 12–50	2 Kings; Lamentations
13	Genesis, 12–50	Amos
14	Genesis, 12–50	Hosea; Isaiah
15	Exodus	Isaiah; Micah
16	Exodus	Micah; Jeremiah
17	Exodus; Leviticus	Jeremiah
18	Numbers; Deuteronomy	Jeremiah; Nahum; Habakkuk
19	Deuteronomy; Joshua	Ezekiel
20	Judges; Ruth	Ezekiel
21	1 Thessalonians	2 Thessalonians; 1 Corinthians
22	1 Thessalonians; Colossians	1 Corinthians
23	Colossians; 1 Timothy	1 Corinthians
24	1 Timothy	1 Corinthians
25	Ezra; Haggai; Zechariah	Proverbs; Ecclesiastes
26	Zechariah; Nehemiah; Baruch	Job
27	Jonah; Malachi; Joel	Galatians
28	Romans	Galatians; Ephesians
29	Romans	Ephesians
30	Romans	Ephesians
31	Romans	Ephesians; Philippians
32	Wisdom	Titus; Philemon; 2 and 3 John
33	1 and 2 Maccabees	Revelation
34	Daniel	Revelation

TABLE III
ABBREVIATIONS OF THE BOOKS OF THE BIBLE

Acts	Acts of the Apostles	2 Kgs	2 Kings
Am	Amos	Lam	Lamentations
Bar	Baruch	Lk	Luke
1 Chr	1 Chronicles	Lv	Leviticus
2 Chr	2 Chronicles	Mal	Malachi
1 Cor	1 Corinthians	1 Mc	1 Maccabees
2 Cor	2 Corinthians	2 Mc	2 Maccabees
Col	Colossians	Mi	Micah
Dn	Daniel	Mk	Mark
Dt	Deuteronomy	Mt	Matthew
Eccl	Ecclesiastes	Na	Nahum
Eph	Ephesians	Neh	Nehemiah
Est	Esther	Nm	Numbers
Ex	Exodus	Ob	Obadiah
Ez	Ezekiel	Phil	Philippians
Ezr	Ezra	Phlm	Philemon
Gal	Galatians	Prv	Proverbs
Gen	Genesis	Ps(s)	Psalm(s)
Hab	Habakkuk	1 Pt	1 Peter
Heb	Hebrews	2 Pt	2 Peter
Hg	Haggai	Rom	Romans
Hos	Hosea	Ru	Ruth
Is	Isaiah	Rv	Revelation
Jas	James	Sg	Song of Songs
Jb	Job	Sir	Sirach
Jdt	Judith	1 Sm	1 Samuel
Jer	Jeremiah	2 Sm	2 Samuel
Jgs	Judges	1 Thes	1 Thessalonians
Jl	Joel	2 Thes	2 Thessalonians
Jn	John	Ti	Titus
1 Jn	1 John	1 Tm	1 Timothy
2 Jn	2 John	2 Tm	2 Timothy
3 Jn	3 John	Tb	Tobit
Jon	Jonah	Wis	Wisdom
Jos	Joshua	Zec	Zechariah
Jud	Jude	Zep	Zephaniah
1 Kgs	1 Kings		

PROPER OF SEASONS

WEEKDAY READINGS

SEASON OF ADVENT

175 MONDAY OF THE FIRST WEEK OF ADVENT

FIRST READING

Isaiah 2:1-5   The Lord will gather all nations into the eternal peace of the Kingdom of God.

A reading from the Book of the Prophet Isaiah

**This is what Isaiah, son of Amoz,
    saw concerning Judah and Jerusalem.**

**In days to come,
The mountain of the Lord's house
    shall be established as the highest mountain
    and raised above the hills.
All nations shall stream toward it;
    many peoples shall come and say:
"Come, let us climb the Lord's mountain,
    to the house of the God of Jacob,
That he may instruct us in his ways,
    and we may walk in his paths."
For from Zion shall go forth instruction,
    and the word of the Lord from Jerusalem.
He shall judge between the nations,
    and impose terms on many peoples.
They shall beat their swords into plowshares
    and their spears into pruning hooks;
One nation shall not raise the sword against another,
    nor shall they train for war again.**

**O house of Jacob, come,
    let us walk in the light of the Lord!**

The word of the Lord.

In Year A, when this reading is used on the First Sunday of Advent, the following reading replaces it.

Monday of the First Week of Advent II

FIRST READING

Isaiah 4:2-6   There will be splendor for the survivors.

A reading from the Book of the Prophet Isaiah

**On that day,
The branch of the L**ORD **will be luster and glory,**
   and the fruit of the earth will be honor and splendor
   for the survivors of Israel.
He who remains in Zion
   and he who is left in Jerusalem
Will be called holy:
   every one marked down for life in Jerusalem.
When the LORD **washes away**
   the filth of the daughters of Zion,
And purges Jerusalem's blood from her midst
   with a blast of searing judgment,
Then will the LORD **create,**
   over the whole site of Mount Zion
   and over her place of assembly,
A smoking cloud by day
   and a light of flaming fire by night.
For over all, the LORD**'s glory will be shelter and protection:**
   shade from the parching heat of day,
   refuge and cover from storm and rain.

The word of the Lord.

RESPONSORIAL PSALM

Psalm 122:1-2, 3-4b, 4cd-5, 6-7, 8-9

℟. **Let us go rejoicing to the house of the Lord.**

I rejoiced because they said to me,
 "We will go up to the house of the Lord."
And now we have set foot
 within your gates, O Jerusalem.

℟. **Let us go rejoicing to the house of the Lord.**

Jerusalem, built as a city
 with compact unity.
To it the tribes go up,
 the tribes of the Lord.

℟. **Let us go rejoicing to the house of the Lord.**

According to the decree for Israel,
 to give thanks to the name of the Lord.
In it are set up judgment seats,
 seats for the house of David.

℟. **Let us go rejoicing to the house of the Lord.**

Pray for the peace of Jerusalem!
 May those who love you prosper!
May peace be within your walls,
 prosperity in your buildings.

℟. **Let us go rejoicing to the house of the Lord.**

Because of my relatives and friends
 I will say, "Peace be within you!"
Because of the house of the Lord, our God,
 I will pray for your good.

℟. **Let us go rejoicing to the house of the Lord.**

ALLELUIA

See Psalm 80:4

℟. Alleluia, alleluia.

Come and save us, Lord our God;
let your face shine upon us, that we may be saved.

℟. Alleluia, alleluia.

GOSPEL

Matthew 8:5-11   Many will come from the east and the west into the Kingdom of heaven.

✠ A reading from the holy Gospel according to Matthew

When Jesus entered Capernaum,
   a centurion approached him and appealed to him, saying,
   "Lord, my servant is lying at home paralyzed, suffering dreadfully."
He said to him, "I will come and cure him."
The centurion said in reply,
   "Lord, I am not worthy to have you enter under my roof;
   only say the word and my servant will be healed.
For I too am a man subject to authority,
   with soldiers subject to me.
And I say to one, 'Go,' and he goes;
   and to another, 'Come here,' and he comes;
   and to my slave, 'Do this,' and he does it."
When Jesus heard this, he was amazed and said to those following him,
   "Amen, I say to you, in no one in Israel have I found such faith.
I say to you, many will come from the east and the west,
   and will recline with Abraham, Isaac, and Jacob
   at the banquet in the Kingdom of heaven."

The Gospel of the Lord.

176 TUESDAY OF THE FIRST WEEK OF ADVENT

FIRST READING

Isaiah 11:1-10   The Spirit of the Lord God shall rest upon him.

A reading from the Book of the Prophet Isaiah

On that day,
A shoot shall sprout from the stump of Jesse,
and from his roots a bud shall blossom.
The Spirit of the Lord shall rest upon him:
a Spirit of wisdom and of understanding,
A Spirit of counsel and of strength,
a Spirit of knowledge and of fear of the Lord,
and his delight shall be the fear of the Lord.
Not by appearance shall he judge,
nor by hearsay shall he decide,
But he shall judge the poor with justice,
and decide aright for the land's afflicted.
He shall strike the ruthless with the rod of his mouth,
and with the breath of his lips he shall slay the wicked.
Justice shall be the band around his waist,
and faithfulness a belt upon his hips.

Then the wolf shall be a guest of the lamb,
and the leopard shall lie down with the kid;
The calf and the young lion shall browse together,
with a little child to guide them.
The cow and the bear shall be neighbors,
together their young shall rest;
the lion shall eat hay like the ox.
The baby shall play by the cobra's den,
and the child lay his hand on the adder's lair.
There shall be no harm or ruin on all my holy mountain;
for the earth shall be filled with knowledge of the Lord,
as water covers the sea.

On that day,
The root of Jesse,
set up as a signal for the nations,
The Gentiles shall seek out,
for his dwelling shall be glorious.

The word of the Lord.

RESPONSORIAL PSALM

Psalm 72:1-2, 7-8, 12-13, 17

℟. (see 7) **Justice shall flourish in his time, and fullness of peace for ever.**

O God, with your judgment endow the king,
   and with your justice, the king's son;
He shall govern your people with justice
   and your afflicted ones with judgment.

℟. **Justice shall flourish in his time, and fullness of peace for ever.**

Justice shall flower in his days,
   and profound peace, till the moon be no more.
May he rule from sea to sea,
   and from the River to the ends of the earth.

℟. **Justice shall flourish in his time, and fullness of peace for ever.**

He shall rescue the poor when he cries out,
   and the afflicted when he has no one to help him.
He shall have pity for the lowly and the poor;
   the lives of the poor he shall save.

℟. **Justice shall flourish in his time, and fullness of peace for ever.**

May his name be blessed forever;
   as long as the sun his name shall remain.
In him shall all the tribes of the earth be blessed;
   all the nations shall proclaim his happiness.

℟. **Justice shall flourish in his time, and fullness of peace for ever.**

ALLELUIA

℟. Alleluia, alleluia.

Behold, our Lord shall come with power;
he will enlighten the eyes of his servants.

℟. Alleluia, alleluia.

GOSPEL

Luke 10:21-24   Jesus rejoices in the Holy Spirit.

✛ A reading from the holy Gospel according to Luke

Jesus rejoiced in the Holy Spirit and said,
  "I give you praise, Father, Lord of heaven and earth,
  for although you have hidden these things
  from the wise and the learned
  you have revealed them to the childlike.
Yes, Father, such has been your gracious will.
All things have been handed over to me by my Father.
No one knows who the Son is except the Father,
  and who the Father is except the Son
  and anyone to whom the Son wishes to reveal him."

Turning to the disciples in private he said,
  "Blessed are the eyes that see what you see.
For I say to you,
  many prophets and kings desired to see what you see,
  but did not see it,
  and to hear what you hear, but did not hear it."

The Gospel of the Lord.

177 WEDNESDAY OF THE FIRST WEEK OF ADVENT

FIRST READING

Isaiah 25:6-10a   The Lord invites us to his feast and will wipe away the tears from all faces.

A reading from the Book of the Prophet Isaiah

**On this mountain the Lord of hosts
  will provide for all peoples
A feast of rich food and choice wines,
  juicy, rich food and pure, choice wines.
On this mountain he will destroy
  the veil that veils all peoples,
The web that is woven over all nations;
  he will destroy death forever.
The Lord God will wipe away
  the tears from all faces;
The reproach of his people he will remove
  from the whole earth; for the Lord has spoken.**

  **On that day it will be said:
"Behold our God, to whom we looked to save us!
  This is the Lord for whom we looked;
  let us rejoice and be glad that he has saved us!"
For the hand of the Lord will rest on this mountain.**

The word of the Lord.

RESPONSORIAL PSALM

Psalm 23:1-3a, 3b-4, 5, 6

℟. (6cd) **I shall live in the house of the Lord all the days of my life.**

The Lord **is my shepherd; I shall not want.**
  In verdant pastures he gives me repose;
Beside restful waters he leads me;
  he refreshes my soul.

℟. **I shall live in the house of the Lord all the days of my life.**

He guides me in right paths
  for his name's sake.
Even though I walk in the dark valley
  I fear no evil; for you are at my side
With your rod and your staff
  that give me courage.

℟. **I shall live in the house of the Lord all the days of my life.**

You spread the table before me
  in the sight of my foes;
You anoint my head with oil;
  my cup overflows.

℟. **I shall live in the house of the Lord all the days of my life.**

Only goodness and kindness follow me
  all the days of my life;
And I shall dwell in the house of the Lord
  for years to come.

℟. **I shall live in the house of the Lord all the days of my life.**

ALLELUIA

℟. **Alleluia, alleluia.**

Behold, the Lord comes to save his people;
blessed are those prepared to meet him.

℟. **Alleluia, alleluia.**

GOSPEL

Matthew 15:29-37   Jesus heals many and multiplies the bread.

✠ A reading from the holy Gospel according to Matthew

At that time:
Jesus walked by the Sea of Galilee,
 went up on the mountain, and sat down there.
Great crowds came to him,
 having with them the lame, the blind, the deformed, the mute,
 and many others.
They placed them at his feet, and he cured them.
The crowds were amazed when they saw the mute speaking,
 the deformed made whole,
 the lame walking,
 and the blind able to see,
 and they glorified the God of Israel.

Jesus summoned his disciples and said,
 "My heart is moved with pity for the crowd,
 for they have been with me now for three days
 and have nothing to eat.
I do not want to send them away hungry,
 for fear they may collapse on the way."
The disciples said to him,
 "Where could we ever get enough bread in this deserted place
 to satisfy such a crowd?"
Jesus said to them, "How many loaves do you have?"
"Seven," they replied, "and a few fish."
He ordered the crowd to sit down on the ground.
Then he took the seven loaves and the fish,
 gave thanks, broke the loaves,
 and gave them to the disciples, who in turn gave them to the crowds.
They all ate and were satisfied.
They picked up the fragments left over—seven baskets full.

The Gospel of the Lord.

178 THURSDAY OF THE FIRST WEEK OF ADVENT

FIRST READING

Isaiah 26:1-6   Let in a nation that is just, one that keeps faith.

A reading from the Book of the Prophet Isaiah

On that day they will sing this song in the land of Judah:

> "A strong city have we;
>   he sets up walls and ramparts to protect us.
> Open up the gates
>   to let in a nation that is just,
>   one that keeps faith.
> A nation of firm purpose you keep in peace;
>   in peace, for its trust in you."
>
> Trust in the Lord forever!
>   For the Lord is an eternal Rock.
> He humbles those in high places,
>   and the lofty city he brings down;
> He tumbles it to the ground,
>   levels it with the dust.
> It is trampled underfoot by the needy,
>   by the footsteps of the poor.

The word of the Lord.

RESPONSORIAL PSALM

Psalm 118:1 and 8-9, 19-21, 25-27a

℟. (26a) **Blessed is he who comes in the name of the Lord.**
   or:
℟. **Alleluia.**

**Give thanks to the Lord, for he is good,
   for his mercy endures forever.
It is better to take refuge in the Lord
   than to trust in man.
It is better to take refuge in the Lord
   than to trust in princes.**

℟. **Blessed is he who comes in the name of the Lord.**
   or:
℟. **Alleluia.**

**Open to me the gates of justice;
   I will enter them and give thanks to the Lord.
This gate is the Lord's;
   the just shall enter it.
I will give thanks to you, for you have answered me
   and have been my savior.**

℟. **Blessed is he who comes in the name of the Lord.**
   or:
℟. **Alleluia.**

**O Lord, grant salvation!
   O Lord, grant prosperity!
Blessed is he who comes in the name of the Lord;
   we bless you from the house of the Lord.
   The Lord is God, and he has given us light.**

℟. **Blessed is he who comes in the name of the Lord.**
   or:
℟. **Alleluia.**

ALLELUIA

Isaiah 55:6

℟. Alleluia, alleluia.

**Seek the Lord while he may be found;
call him while he is near.**

℟. Alleluia, alleluia.

GOSPEL

Matthew 7:21, 24-27   Whoever does the will of my Father will enter the Kingdom of heaven.

✠ **A reading from the holy Gospel according to Matthew**

Jesus said to his disciples:
"Not everyone who says to me, 'Lord, Lord,'
    will enter the Kingdom of heaven,
    but only the one who does the will of my Father in heaven.

"Everyone who listens to these words of mine and acts on them
    will be like a wise man who built his house on rock.
The rain fell, the floods came,
    and the winds blew and buffeted the house.
But it did not collapse; it had been set solidly on rock.
And everyone who listens to these words of mine
    but does not act on them
    will be like a fool who built his house on sand.
The rain fell, the floods came,
    and the winds blew and buffeted the house.
And it collapsed and was completely ruined."

The Gospel of the Lord.

179 FRIDAY OF THE FIRST WEEK OF ADVENT

FIRST READING

Isaiah 29:17-24   On that day, the eyes of the blind shall see.

A reading from the Book of the Prophet Isaiah

Thus says the Lord God:
But a very little while,
  and Lebanon shall be changed into an orchard,
  and the orchard be regarded as a forest!
On that day the deaf shall hear
  the words of a book;
And out of gloom and darkness,
  the eyes of the blind shall see.
The lowly will ever find joy in the Lord,
  and the poor rejoice in the Holy One of Israel.
For the tyrant will be no more
  and the arrogant will have gone;
All who are alert to do evil will be cut off,
  those whose mere word condemns a man,
Who ensnare his defender at the gate,
  and leave the just man with an empty claim.
Therefore thus says the Lord,
  the God of the house of Jacob,
  who redeemed Abraham:
Now Jacob shall have nothing to be ashamed of,
  nor shall his face grow pale.
When his children see
  the work of my hands in his midst,
They shall keep my name holy;
  they shall reverence the Holy One of Jacob,
  and be in awe of the God of Israel.
Those who err in spirit shall acquire understanding,
  and those who find fault shall receive instruction.

The word of the Lord.

RESPONSORIAL PSALM

Psalm 27:1, 4, 13-14

℟. (1a) The Lord is my light and my salvation.

The LORD is my light and my salvation;
    whom should I fear?
The LORD is my life's refuge;
    of whom should I be afraid?

℟. The Lord is my light and my salvation.

One thing I ask of the LORD;
    this I seek:
To dwell in the house of the LORD
    all the days of my life,
That I may gaze on the loveliness of the LORD
    and contemplate his temple.

℟. The Lord is my light and my salvation.

I believe that I shall see the bounty of the LORD
    in the land of the living.
Wait for the LORD with courage;
    be stouthearted, and wait for the LORD.

℟. The Lord is my light and my salvation.

ALLELUIA

℟. Alleluia, alleluia.

Behold, our Lord shall come with power;
he will enlighten the eyes of his servants.

℟. Alleluia, alleluia.

GOSPEL

Matthew 9:27-31   Believing in Jesus, two who were blind are cured.

✛ A reading from the holy Gospel according to Matthew

As Jesus passed by, two blind men followed him, crying out,
   "Son of David, have pity on us!"
When he entered the house,
   the blind men approached him and Jesus said to them,
   "Do you believe that I can do this?"
"Yes, Lord," they said to him.
Then he touched their eyes and said,
   "Let it be done for you according to your faith."
And their eyes were opened.
Jesus warned them sternly,
   "See that no one knows about this."
But they went out and spread word of him through all that land.

The Gospel of the Lord.

180 SATURDAY OF THE FIRST WEEK OF ADVENT

FIRST READING

Isaiah 30:19-21, 23-26   The Merciful One will show you mercy when you cry out.

A reading from the Book of the Prophet Isaiah

Thus says the Lord God,
  the Holy One of Israel:
O people of Zion, who dwell in Jerusalem,
  no more will you weep;
He will be gracious to you when you cry out,
  as soon as he hears he will answer you.
The Lord will give you the bread you need
  and the water for which you thirst.
No longer will your Teacher hide himself,
  but with your own eyes you shall see your Teacher,
While from behind, a voice shall sound in your ears:
  "This is the way; walk in it,"
  when you would turn to the right or to the left.

He will give rain for the seed
  that you sow in the ground,
And the wheat that the soil produces
  will be rich and abundant.
On that day your flock will be given pasture
  and the lamb will graze in spacious meadows;
The oxen and the asses that till the ground
  will eat silage tossed to them
  with shovel and pitchfork.
Upon every high mountain and lofty hill
  there will be streams of running water.
On the day of the great slaughter,
  when the towers fall,
The light of the moon will be like that of the sun
  and the light of the sun will be seven times greater
  like the light of seven days.
On the day the Lord binds up the wounds of his people,
  he will heal the bruises left by his blows.

The word of the Lord.

RESPONSORIAL PSALM

Psalm 147:1-2, 3-4, 5-6

℟. (see Isaiah 30:18d) **Blessed are all who wait for the Lord.**

Praise the Lord, for he is good;
  sing praise to our God, for he is gracious;
  it is fitting to praise him.
The Lord rebuilds Jerusalem;
  the dispersed of Israel he gathers.

℟. **Blessed are all who wait for the Lord.**

He heals the brokenhearted
  and binds up their wounds.
He tells the number of the stars;
  he calls each by name.

℟. **Blessed are all who wait for the Lord.**

Great is our Lord and mighty in power:
  to his wisdom there is no limit.
The Lord sustains the lowly;
  the wicked he casts to the ground.

℟. **Blessed are all who wait for the Lord.**

ALLELUIA

Isaiah 33:22

℟. **Alleluia, alleluia.**

The Lord is our Judge, our Lawgiver, our King;
he it is who will save us.

℟. **Alleluia, alleluia.**

GOSPEL

Matthew 9:35–10:1, 5a, 6-8   At the sight of the crowds, Jesus' heart was moved with pity for them.

✠ **A reading from the holy Gospel according to Matthew**

**Jesus went around to all the towns and villages,
   teaching in their synagogues,
   proclaiming the Gospel of the Kingdom,
   and curing every disease and illness.
At the sight of the crowds, his heart was moved with pity for them
   because they were troubled and abandoned,
   like sheep without a shepherd.
Then he said to his disciples,
   "The harvest is abundant but the laborers are few;
   so ask the master of the harvest
   to send out laborers for his harvest."**

**Then he summoned his Twelve disciples
   and gave them authority over unclean spirits to drive them out
   and to cure every disease and every illness.**

**Jesus sent out these twelve after instructing them thus,
   "Go to the lost sheep of the house of Israel.
As you go, make this proclamation: 'The Kingdom of heaven is at hand.'
Cure the sick, raise the dead,
   cleanse lepers, drive out demons.
Without cost you have received; without cost you are to give."**

The Gospel of the Lord.

181 MONDAY OF THE SECOND WEEK OF ADVENT

FIRST READING

Isaiah 35:1-10   *God himself will come and save you.*

A reading from the Book of the Prophet Isaiah

> The desert and the parched land will exult;
>   the steppe will rejoice and bloom.
> They will bloom with abundant flowers,
>   and rejoice with joyful song.
> The glory of Lebanon will be given to them,
>   the splendor of Carmel and Sharon;
> They will see the glory of the LORD,
>   the splendor of our God.
> Strengthen the hands that are feeble,
>   make firm the knees that are weak,
> Say to those whose hearts are frightened:
>   Be strong, fear not!
> Here is your God,
>   he comes with vindication;
> With divine recompense
>   he comes to save you.
> Then will the eyes of the blind be opened,
>   the ears of the deaf be cleared;
> Then will the lame leap like a stag,
>   then the tongue of the mute will sing.
>
> Streams will burst forth in the desert,
>   and rivers in the steppe.
> The burning sands will become pools,
>   and the thirsty ground, springs of water;
> The abode where jackals lurk
>   will be a marsh for the reed and papyrus.
> A highway will be there,
>   called the holy way;
> No one unclean may pass over it,
>   nor fools go astray on it.
> No lion will be there,
>   nor beast of prey go up to be met upon it.

It is for those with a journey to make,
   and on it the redeemed will walk.
Those whom the LORD **has ransomed will return**
   and enter Zion singing,
   crowned with everlasting joy;
They will meet with joy and gladness,
   sorrow and mourning will flee.

The word of the Lord.

RESPONSORIAL PSALM

Psalm 85:9ab and 10, 11-12, 13-14

℟. (Isaiah 35:4f) **Our God will come to save us!**

I will hear what God proclaims;
   the LORD**—for he proclaims peace to his people.**
Near indeed is his salvation to those who fear him,
   glory dwelling in our land.

℟. **Our God will come to save us!**

Kindness and truth shall meet;
   justice and peace shall kiss.
Truth shall spring out of the earth,
   and justice shall look down from heaven.

℟. **Our God will come to save us!**

The LORD **himself will give his benefits;**
   our land shall yield its increase.
Justice shall walk before him,
   and salvation, along the way of his steps.

℟. **Our God will come to save us!**

ALLELUIA

℟. Alleluia, alleluia.

Behold the king will come, the Lord of the earth,
and he himself will lift the yoke of our captivity.

℟. Alleluia, alleluia.

GOSPEL

Luke 5:17-26   We have seen incredible things today.

✢ A reading from the holy Gospel according to Luke

One day as Jesus was teaching,
   Pharisees and teachers of the law,
   who had come from every village of Galilee and Judea and Jerusalem,
   were sitting there,
   and the power of the Lord was with him for healing.
And some men brought on a stretcher a man who was paralyzed;
   they were trying to bring him in and set him in his presence.
But not finding a way to bring him in because of the crowd,
   they went up on the roof
   and lowered him on the stretcher through the tiles
   into the middle in front of Jesus.
When Jesus saw their faith, he said,
   "As for you, your sins are forgiven."

Then the scribes and Pharisees began to ask themselves,
   "Who is this who speaks blasphemies?
Who but God alone can forgive sins?"
Jesus knew their thoughts and said to them in reply,
   "What are you thinking in your hearts?
Which is easier, to say, 'Your sins are forgiven,'
   or to say, 'Rise and walk'?
But that you may know
   that the Son of Man has authority on earth to forgive sins"—
   he said to the one who was paralyzed,
   "I say to you, rise, pick up your stretcher, and go home."

He stood up immediately before them,
   picked up what he had been lying on,
   and went home, glorifying God.
Then astonishment seized them all and they glorified God,
   and, struck with awe, they said,
   "We have seen incredible things today."

The Gospel of the Lord.

182 TUESDAY OF THE SECOND WEEK OF ADVENT

FIRST READING

Isaiah 40:1-11   God consoles his people.

A reading from the Book of the Prophet Isaiah

Comfort, give comfort to my people,
   says your God.
Speak tenderly to Jerusalem, and proclaim to her
   that her service is at an end,
   her guilt is expiated;
Indeed, she has received from the hand of the Lord
   double for all her sins.

   A voice cries out:
In the desert prepare the way of the Lord!
   Make straight in the wasteland a highway for our God!
Every valley shall be filled in,
   every mountain and hill shall be made low;
The rugged land shall be made a plain,
   the rough country, a broad valley.
Then the glory of the Lord shall be revealed,
   and all people shall see it together;
   for the mouth of the Lord has spoken.

A voice says, "Cry out!"
   I answer, "What shall I cry out?"
"All flesh is grass,
   and all their glory like the flower of the field.
The grass withers, the flower wilts,
   when the breath of the Lord blows upon it.
   So then, the people is the grass.
Though the grass withers and the flower wilts,
   the word of our God stands forever."

Go up onto a high mountain,
   Zion, herald of glad tidings;
Cry out at the top of your voice,
   Jerusalem, herald of good news!

Fear not to cry out
  and say to the cities of Judah:
  Here is your God!
Here comes with power
  the Lord GOD,
  who rules by his strong arm;
Here is his reward with him,
  his recompense before him,
Like a shepherd he feeds his flock;
  in his arms he gathers the lambs,
Carrying them in his bosom,
  and leading the ewes with care.

The word of the Lord.

RESPONSORIAL PSALM

Psalm 96:1-2, 3 and 10ac, 11-12, 13

℟. (see Isaiah 40:10ab) **The Lord our God comes with power.**

Sing to the LORD a new song;
  sing to the LORD, all you lands.
Sing to the LORD; bless his name;
  announce his salvation, day after day.

℟. **The Lord our God comes with power.**

Tell his glory among the nations;
  among all peoples, his wondrous deeds.
Say among the nations: The LORD is king;
  he governs the peoples with equity.

℟. **The Lord our God comes with power.**

Let the heavens be glad and the earth rejoice;
  let the sea and what fills it resound;
  let the plains be joyful and all that is in them!
Then let all the trees of the forest rejoice.

℟. **The Lord our God comes with power.**

They shall exult before the Lord, for he comes;
   for he comes to rule the earth.
He shall rule the world with justice
   and the peoples with his constancy.

℟. **The Lord our God comes with power.**

ALLELUIA

℟. **Alleluia, alleluia.**

The day of the Lord is near:
Behold, he comes to save us.

℟. **Alleluia, alleluia.**

GOSPEL

Matthew 18:12-14   God does not will that the little ones be lost.

✟ **A reading from the holy Gospel according to Matthew**

Jesus said to his disciples:
"What is your opinion?
If a man has a hundred sheep and one of them goes astray,
   will he not leave the ninety-nine in the hills
   and go in search of the stray?
And if he finds it, amen, I say to you, he rejoices more over it
   than over the ninety-nine that did not stray.
In just the same way, it is not the will of your heavenly Father
   that one of these little ones be lost."

The Gospel of the Lord.

183 WEDNESDAY OF THE SECOND WEEK OF ADVENT

FIRST READING

Isaiah 40:25-31   The Lord God is almighty and gives strength to the fainting.

A reading from the Book of the Prophet Isaiah

To whom can you liken me as an equal?
  says the Holy One.
Lift up your eyes on high
  and see who has created these things:
He leads out their army and numbers them,
  calling them all by name.
By his great might and the strength of his power
  not one of them is missing!
Why, O Jacob, do you say,
  and declare, O Israel,
"My way is hidden from the Lord,
  and my right is disregarded by my God"?

Do you not know
  or have you not heard?
The Lord is the eternal God,
  creator of the ends of the earth.
He does not faint nor grow weary,
  and his knowledge is beyond scrutiny.
He gives strength to the fainting;
  for the weak he makes vigor abound.
Though young men faint and grow weary,
  and youths stagger and fall,
They that hope in the Lord will renew their strength,
  they will soar as with eagles' wings;
They will run and not grow weary,
  walk and not grow faint.

The word of the Lord.

RESPONSORIAL PSALM

Psalm 103:1-2, 3-4, 8 and 10

℟. (1) O bless the Lord, my soul!

Bless the LORD, O my soul;
   and all my being, bless his holy name.
Bless the LORD, O my soul,
   and forget not all his benefits.

℟. O bless the Lord, my soul!

He pardons all your iniquities,
   he heals all your ills.
He redeems your life from destruction,
   he crowns you with kindness and compassion.

℟. O bless the Lord, my soul!

Merciful and gracious is the LORD,
   slow to anger and abounding in kindness.
Not according to our sins does he deal with us,
   nor does he requite us according to our crimes.

℟. O bless the Lord, my soul!

ALLELUIA

℟. **Alleluia, alleluia.**

**Behold, the Lord comes to save his people;
blessed are those prepared to meet him.**

℟. **Alleluia, alleluia.**

GOSPEL

Matthew 11:28-30   Come to me, all you who labor.

✠ **A reading from the holy Gospel according to Matthew**

**Jesus said to the crowds:
"Come to me, all you who labor and are burdened,
  and I will give you rest.
Take my yoke upon you and learn from me,
  for I am meek and humble of heart;
  and you will find rest for yourselves.
For my yoke is easy, and my burden light."**

The Gospel of the Lord.

184 THURSDAY OF THE SECOND WEEK OF ADVENT

FIRST READING

Isaiah 41:13-20   I am your redeemer, the Holy One of Israel.

A reading from the Book of the Prophet Isaiah

I am the LORD, your God,
 who grasp your right hand;
It is I who say to you, "Fear not,
 I will help you."
Fear not, O worm Jacob,
 O maggot Israel;
I will help you, says the LORD;
 your redeemer is the Holy One of Israel.
I will make of you a threshing sledge,
 sharp, new, and double-edged,
To thresh the mountains and crush them,
 to make the hills like chaff.
When you winnow them, the wind shall carry them off
 and the storm shall scatter them.
But you shall rejoice in the LORD,
 and glory in the Holy One of Israel.

The afflicted and the needy seek water in vain,
 their tongues are parched with thirst.
I, the LORD, will answer them;
 I, the God of Israel, will not forsake them.
I will open up rivers on the bare heights,
 and fountains in the broad valleys;
I will turn the desert into a marshland,
 and the dry ground into springs of water.
I will plant in the desert the cedar,
 acacia, myrtle, and olive;
I will set in the wasteland the cypress,
 together with the plane tree and the pine,
That all may see and know,
 observe and understand,
That the hand of the LORD has done this,
 the Holy One of Israel has created it.

The word of the Lord.

RESPONSORIAL PSALM

Psalm 145:1 and 9, 10-11, 12-13ab

℟. (8) **The Lord is gracious and merciful; slow to anger, and of great kindness.**

I will extol you, O my God and King,
   and I will bless your name forever and ever.
The Lord is good to all
   and compassionate toward all his works.

℟. The Lord is gracious and merciful; slow to anger, and of great kindness.

Let all your works give you thanks, O Lord,
   and let your faithful ones bless you.
Let them discourse of the glory of your Kingdom
   and speak of your might.

℟. The Lord is gracious and merciful; slow to anger, and of great kindness.

Let them make known to men your might
   and the glorious splendor of your Kingdom.
Your Kingdom is a Kingdom for all ages,
   and your dominion endures through all generations.

℟. The Lord is gracious and merciful; slow to anger, and of great kindness.

ALLELUIA

See Isaiah 45:8

℟. Alleluia, alleluia.

**Let the clouds rain down the Just One,
and the earth bring forth a Savior.**

℟. Alleluia, alleluia.

GOSPEL

Matthew 11:11-15   None greater than John the Baptist has been born.

✠ **A reading from the holy Gospel according to Matthew**

**Jesus said to the crowds:
   "Amen, I say to you,
   among those born of women
   there has been none greater than John the Baptist;
   yet the least in the Kingdom of heaven is greater than he.
From the days of John the Baptist until now,
   the Kingdom of heaven suffers violence,
   and the violent are taking it by force.
All the prophets and the law prophesied up to the time of John.
And if you are willing to accept it,
   he is Elijah, the one who is to come.
Whoever has ears ought to hear."**

The Gospel of the Lord.

185 FRIDAY OF THE SECOND WEEK OF ADVENT

FIRST READING

Isaiah 48:17-19   If only you would hearken to my commandments.

A reading from the Book of the Prophet Isaiah

Thus says the Lord, your redeemer,
  the Holy One of Israel:
I, the Lord, your God,
  teach you what is for your good,
  and lead you on the way you should go.
If you would hearken to my commandments,
  your prosperity would be like a river,
  and your vindication like the waves of the sea;
Your descendants would be like the sand,
  and those born of your stock like its grains,
Their name never cut off
  or blotted out from my presence.

The word of the Lord.

RESPONSORIAL PSALM

Psalm 1:1-2, 3, 4 and 6

℟. (see John 8:12) **Those who follow you, Lord, will have the light of life.**

**Blessed the man who follows not
  the counsel of the wicked
Nor walks in the way of sinners,
  nor sits in the company of the insolent,
But delights in the law of the Lord
  and meditates on his law day and night.**

℟. **Those who follow you, Lord, will have the light of life.**

**He is like a tree
  planted near running water,
That yields its fruit in due season,
  and whose leaves never fade.
  Whatever he does, prospers.**

℟. **Those who follow you, Lord, will have the light of life.**

**Not so the wicked, not so;
  they are like chaff which the wind drives away.
For the Lord watches over the way of the just,
  but the way of the wicked vanishes.**

℟. **Those who follow you, Lord, will have the light of life.**

ALLELUIA

℟. Alleluia, alleluia.

The Lord will come; go out to meet him!
He is the prince of peace.

℟. Alleluia, alleluia.

GOSPEL

Matthew 11:16-19   They listened to neither John nor to the Son of Man.

✠ **A reading from the holy Gospel according to Matthew**

Jesus said to the crowds:
"To what shall I compare this generation?
It is like children who sit in marketplaces and call to one another,
    'We played the flute for you, but you did not dance,
    we sang a dirge but you did not mourn.'
For John came neither eating nor drinking, and they said,
    'He is possessed by a demon.'
The Son of Man came eating and drinking and they said,
    'Look, he is a glutton and a drunkard,
    a friend of tax collectors and sinners.'
But wisdom is vindicated by her works."

The Gospel of the Lord.

186 SATURDAY OF THE SECOND WEEK OF ADVENT

FIRST READING

Sirach 48:1-4, 9-11   Elijah was enveloped in a whirlwind.

A reading from the Book of Sirach

> In those days,
> like a fire there appeared the prophet Elijah
>   whose words were as a flaming furnace.
> Their staff of bread he shattered,
>   in his zeal he reduced them to straits;
> By the Lord's word he shut up the heavens
>   and three times brought down fire.
> How awesome are you, Elijah, in your wondrous deeds!
>   Whose glory is equal to yours?
> You were taken aloft in a whirlwind of fire,
>   in a chariot with fiery horses.
> You were destined, it is written, in time to come
>   to put an end to wrath before the day of the LORD,
> To turn back the hearts of fathers toward their sons,
>   and to re-establish the tribes of Jacob.
> Blessed is he who shall have seen you
>   and who falls asleep in your friendship.

The word of the Lord.

RESPONSORIAL PSALM

Psalm 80:2ac and 3b, 15-16, 18-19

℟. (4) **Lord, make us turn to you; let us see your face and we shall be saved.**

O shepherd of Israel, hearken,
From your throne upon the cherubim, shine forth.
Rouse your power.

℟. **Lord, make us turn to you; let us see your face and we shall be saved.**

Once again, O Lord of hosts,
   look down from heaven, and see;
Take care of this vine,
   and protect what your right hand has planted
   the son of man whom you yourself made strong.

℟. Lord, make us turn to you; let us see your face and we shall be saved.

May your help be with the man of your right hand,
   with the son of man whom you yourself made strong.
Then we will no more withdraw from you;
   give us new life, and we will call upon your name.

℟. Lord, make us turn to you; let us see your face and we shall be saved.

ALLELUIA

Luke 3:4, 6

℟. Alleluia, alleluia.

Prepare the way of the Lord, make straight his paths:
All flesh shall see the salvation of God.

℟. Alleluia, alleluia.

GOSPEL

Matthew 17:9a, 10-13   Elijah has already come, and they did not recognize him.

✠ A reading from the holy Gospel according to Matthew

As they were coming down from the mountain,
   the disciples asked Jesus,
     "Why do the scribes say that Elijah must come first?"
He said in reply, "Elijah will indeed come and restore all things;
   but I tell you that Elijah has already come,
   and they did not recognize him but did to him whatever they pleased.
So also will the Son of Man suffer at their hands."
Then the disciples understood
   that he was speaking to them of John the Baptist.

The Gospel of the Lord.

187 MONDAY OF THE THIRD WEEK OF ADVENT

If today is December 17 or 18, omit these readings (no. 187) and use those given for the weekdays of Advent, nos. 193 or 194.

FIRST READING

Numbers 24:2-7, 15-17a A star shall advance from Jacob.

A reading from the Book of Numbers

When Balaam raised his eyes and saw Israel encamped, tribe by tribe,
   the spirit of God came upon him,
   and he gave voice to his oracle:

The utterance of Balaam, son of Beor,
   the utterance of a man whose eye is true,
The utterance of one who hears what God says,
   and knows what the Most High knows,
Of one who sees what the Almighty sees,
   enraptured, and with eyes unveiled:
How goodly are your tents, O Jacob;
   your encampments, O Israel!
They are like gardens beside a stream,
   like the cedars planted by the Lord.
His wells shall yield free-flowing waters,
   he shall have the sea within reach;
His king shall rise higher,
   and his royalty shall be exalted.

Then Balaam gave voice to his oracle:

The utterance of Balaam, son of Beor,
   the utterance of the man whose eye is true,
The utterance of one who hears what God says,
   and knows what the Most High knows,
Of one who sees what the Almighty sees,
   enraptured, and with eyes unveiled.
I see him, though not now;
   I behold him, though not near:
A star shall advance from Jacob,
   and a staff shall rise from Israel.

The word of the Lord.

RESPONSORIAL PSALM

Psalm 25:4-5ab, 6 and 7bc, 8-9

℟. (4) **Teach me your ways, O Lord.**

**Your ways, O Lord, make known to me;
    teach me your paths,
Guide me in your truth and teach me,
    for you are God my savior.**

℟. **Teach me your ways, O Lord.**

**Remember that your compassion, O Lord,
    and your kindness are from of old.
In your kindness remember me,
    because of your goodness, O Lord.**

℟. **Teach me your ways, O Lord.**

**Good and upright is the Lord;
    thus he shows sinners the way.
He guides the humble to justice,
    he teaches the humble his way.**

℟. **Teach me your ways, O Lord.**

ALLELUIA

Psalm 85:8

℟. **Alleluia, alleluia.**

**Show us, Lord, your love,
and grant us your salvation.**

℟. **Alleluia, alleluia.**

GOSPEL

Matthew 21:23-27   John's baptism: where did it come from?

✛ **A reading from the holy Gospel according to Matthew**

When Jesus had come into the temple area,
   the chief priests and the elders of the people approached him
   as he was teaching and said,
   "By what authority are you doing these things?
And who gave you this authority?"
Jesus said to them in reply,
   "I shall ask you one question, and if you answer it for me,
   then I shall tell you by what authority I do these things.
Where was John's baptism from?
Was it of heavenly or of human origin?"
They discussed this among themselves and said,
   "If we say 'Of heavenly origin,' he will say to us,
   'Then why did you not believe him?'
But if we say, 'Of human origin,' we fear the crowd,
   for they all regard John as a prophet."
So they said to Jesus in reply, "We do not know."
He himself said to them,
   "Neither shall I tell you by what authority I do these things."

The Gospel of the Lord.

188 TUESDAY OF THE THIRD WEEK OF ADVENT

If today is December 17 or 18, omit these readings (no. 188) and use those given for the weekdays of Advent, nos. 193 or 194.

FIRST READING

Zephaniah 3:1-2, 9-13   Messianic salvation is promised to all of the poor.

A reading from the Book of the Prophet Zephaniah

Thus says the Lord:
Woe to the city, rebellious and polluted,
   to the tyrannical city!
She hears no voice,
   accepts no correction;
In the Lord she has not trusted,
   to her God she has not drawn near.

For then I will change and purify
   the lips of the peoples,
That they all may call upon the name of the Lord,
   to serve him with one accord;
From beyond the rivers of Ethiopia
   and as far as the recesses of the North,
   they shall bring me offerings.

   On that day
You need not be ashamed
   of all your deeds,
   your rebellious actions against me;
For then will I remove from your midst
   the proud braggarts,
And you shall no longer exalt yourself
   on my holy mountain.
But I will leave as a remnant in your midst
   a people humble and lowly,
Who shall take refuge in the name of the Lord:
   the remnant of Israel.
They shall do no wrong
   and speak no lies;

Nor shall there be found in their mouths
  a deceitful tongue;
They shall pasture and couch their flocks
  with none to disturb them.

The word of the Lord.

RESPONSORIAL PSALM

Psalm 34:2-3, 6-7, 17-18, 19 and 23

℟. (7a) **The Lord hears the cry of the poor.**

I will bless the Lord at all times;
  his praise shall be ever in my mouth.
Let my soul glory in the Lord;
  the lowly will hear me and be glad.

℟. **The Lord hears the cry of the poor.**

Look to him that you may be radiant with joy,
  and your faces may not blush with shame.
When the poor one called out, the Lord heard,
  and from all his distress he saved him.

℟. **The Lord hears the cry of the poor.**

The Lord confronts the evildoers,
  to destroy remembrance of them from the earth.
When the just cry out, the Lord hears them,
  and from all their distress he rescues them.

℟. **The Lord hears the cry of the poor.**

The Lord is close to the brokenhearted;
  and those who are crushed in spirit he saves.
The Lord redeems the lives of his servants;
  no one incurs guilt who takes refuge in him.

℟. **The Lord hears the cry of the poor.**

ALLELUIA

℟. **Alleluia, alleluia.**

**Come, O Lord, do not delay;
forgive the sins of your people.**

℟. **Alleluia, alleluia.**

GOSPEL

Matthew 21:28-32   John came and sinners believed in him.

✚ **A reading from the holy Gospel according to Matthew**

**Jesus said to the chief priests and the elders of the people:
"What is your opinion?
A man had two sons.
He came to the first and said,
    'Son, go out and work in the vineyard today.'
The son said in reply, 'I will not,'
    but afterwards he changed his mind and went.
The man came to the other son and gave the same order.
He said in reply, 'Yes, sir,' but did not go.
Which of the two did his father's will?"
They answered, "The first."
Jesus said to them, "Amen, I say to you,
    tax collectors and prostitutes
    are entering the Kingdom of God before you.
When John came to you in the way of righteousness,
    you did not believe him;
    but tax collectors and prostitutes did.
Yet even when you saw that,
    you did not later change your minds and believe him."**

The Gospel of the Lord.

189 WEDNESDAY OF THE THIRD WEEK OF ADVENT

If today is December 17 or 18, omit these readings (no. 189) and use those given for the weekdays of Advent, nos. 193 or 194.

FIRST READING

Isaiah 45:6c-8, 18, 21c-25   Let the clouds rain down.

A reading from the Book of the Prophet Isaiah

I am the LORD, there is no other;
   I form the light, and create the darkness,
I make well-being and create woe;
   I, the LORD, do all these things.
Let justice descend, O heavens, like dew from above,
   like gentle rain let the skies drop it down.
Let the earth open and salvation bud forth;
   let justice also spring up!
   I, the LORD, have created this.

   For thus says the LORD,
The creator of the heavens,
   who is God,
The designer and maker of the earth
   who established it,
Not creating it to be a waste,
   but designing it to be lived in:
I am the LORD, and there is no other.

Who announced this from the beginning
   and foretold it from of old?
Was it not I, the LORD,
   besides whom there is no other God?
   There is no just and saving God but me.

Turn to me and be safe,
   all you ends of the earth,
   for I am God; there is no other!
By myself I swear,
   uttering my just decree
   and my unalterable word:

**To me every knee shall bend;
   by me every tongue shall swear,
Saying, "Only in the L**ORD
   **are just deeds and power.
Before him in shame shall come
   all who vent their anger against him.
In the L**ORD **shall be the vindication and the glory
   of all the descendants of Israel."**

The word of the Lord.

RESPONSORIAL PSALM

Psalm 85:9ab and 10, 11-12, 13-14

℟. (Isaiah 45:8) **Let the clouds rain down the Just One, and the earth bring forth a Savior.**

I will hear what God proclaims;
   the Lord—for he proclaims peace to his people.
Near indeed is his salvation to those who fear him,
   glory dwelling in our land.

℟. **Let the clouds rain down the Just One, and the earth bring forth a Savior.**

Kindness and truth shall meet;
   justice and peace shall kiss.
Truth shall spring out of the earth,
   and justice shall look down from heaven.

℟. **Let the clouds rain down the Just One, and the earth bring forth a Savior.**

The Lord himself will give his benefits;
   our land shall yield its increase.
Justice shall walk before him,
   and salvation, along the way of his steps.

℟. **Let the clouds rain down the Just One, and the earth bring forth a Savior.**

ALLELUIA

See Isaiah 40:9-10

℟. **Alleluia, alleluia.**

Raise your voice and tell the Good News:
Behold, the Lord God comes with power.

℟. **Alleluia, alleluia.**

GOSPEL

Luke 7:18b-23   Go back and tell John what you have seen and heard.

✝ **A reading from the holy Gospel according to Luke**

**At that time,
John summoned two of his disciples and sent them to the Lord to ask,
   "Are you the one who is to come, or should we look for another?"
When the men came to the Lord, they said,
   "John the Baptist has sent us to you to ask,
   'Are you the one who is to come, or should we look for another?'"
At that time Jesus cured many of their diseases, sufferings, and evil spirits;
   he also granted sight to many who were blind.
And Jesus said to them in reply,
   "Go and tell John what you have seen and heard:
   the blind regain their sight,
   the lame walk,
   lepers are cleansed,
   the deaf hear, the dead are raised,
   the poor have the good news proclaimed to them.
And blessed is the one who takes no offense at me."**

The Gospel of the Lord.

190 THURSDAY OF THE THIRD WEEK OF ADVENT

If today is December 17 or 18, omit these readings (no. 190) and use those given for the weekdays of Advent, nos. 193 or 194.

FIRST READING

Isaiah 54:1-10   Like a forsaken wife, the LORD has called you back.

A reading from the Book of the Prophet Isaiah

> Raise a glad cry, you barren one who did not bear,
>   Break forth in jubilant song, you who were not in labor,
> For more numerous are the children of the deserted wife
>   than the children of her who has a husband,
>   says the LORD.
> Enlarge the space for your tent,
>   spread out your tent cloths unsparingly;
>   lengthen your ropes and make firm your stakes.
> For you shall spread abroad to the right and to the left;
>   Your descendants shall dispossess the nations
>   and shall people the desolate cities.
>
> Fear not, you shall not be put to shame;
>   you need not blush, for you shall not be disgraced.
> The shame of your youth you shall forget,
>   the reproach of your widowhood no longer remember.
> For he who has become your husband is your Maker;
>   his name is the LORD of hosts;
> Your redeemer is the Holy One of Israel,
>   called God of all the earth.
> The LORD calls you back,
>   like a wife forsaken and grieved in spirit,
> A wife married in youth and then cast off,
>   says your God.
> For a brief moment I abandoned you,
>   but with great tenderness I will take you back.
> In an outburst of wrath, for a moment
>   I hid my face from you;
> but with enduring love I take pity on you,
>   says the LORD, your redeemer.

This is for me like the days of Noah,
   when I swore that the waters of Noah
   should never again deluge the earth;
So I have sworn not to be angry with you,
   or to rebuke you.
Though the mountains leave their place
   and the hills be shaken,
My love shall never leave you
   nor my covenant of peace be shaken,
   says the Lord, who has mercy on you.

The word of the Lord.

RESPONSORIAL PSALM

Psalm 30:2 and 4, 5-6, 11-12a and 13b

℟. (2a) I will praise you, Lord, for you have rescued me.

I will extol you, O Lord, for you drew me clear
   and did not let my enemies rejoice over me.
O Lord, you brought me up from the nether world;
   you preserved me from among those going down into the pit.

℟. I will praise you, Lord, for you have rescued me.

Sing praise to the Lord, you his faithful ones,
   and give thanks to his holy name.
For his anger lasts but a moment;
   a lifetime, his good will.
At nightfall, weeping enters in,
   but with the dawn, rejoicing.

℟. I will praise you, Lord, for you have rescued me.

"Hear, O Lord, and have pity on me;
   O Lord, be my helper."
You changed my mourning into dancing;
   O Lord, my God, forever will I give you thanks.

℟. I will praise you, Lord, for you have rescued me.

ALLELUIA

Luke 3:4, 6

℟. Alleluia, alleluia.

Prepare the way of the Lord, make straight his paths:
All flesh shall see the salvation of God.

℟. Alleluia, alleluia.

GOSPEL

Luke 7:24-30   John is the messenger who prepares the way of the Lord.

☩ A reading from the holy Gospel according to Luke

When the messengers of John the Baptist had left,
   Jesus began to speak to the crowds about John.
"What did you go out to the desert to see—a reed swayed by the wind?
Then what did you go out to see?
Someone dressed in fine garments?
Those who dress luxuriously and live sumptuously
   are found in royal palaces.
Then what did you go out to see?
A prophet? Yes, I tell you, and more than a prophet.
This is the one about whom Scripture says:

   Behold, I am sending my messenger ahead of you,
   he will prepare your way before you.

I tell you,
   among those born of women, no one is greater than John;
   yet the least in the Kingdom of God is greater than he."
(All the people who listened, including the tax collectors,
   who were baptized with the baptism of John,
   acknowledged the righteousness of God;
   but the Pharisees and scholars of the law,
   who were not baptized by him,
   rejected the plan of God for themselves.)

The Gospel of the Lord.

191 FRIDAY OF THE THIRD WEEK OF ADVENT

If today is December 17 or 18, omit these readings (no. 191) and use those given for the weekdays of Advent, nos. 193 or 194.

FIRST READING

Isaiah 56:1-3a, 6-8   My house shall be called a house of prayer for all peoples.

A reading from the Book of the Prophet Isaiah

Thus says the Lord:
Observe what is right, do what is just;
   for my salvation is about to come,
   my justice, about to be revealed.
Blessed is the man who does this,
   the son of man who holds to it;
Who keeps the sabbath free from profanation,
   and his hand from any evildoing.
Let not the foreigner say,
   when he would join himself to the Lord,
   "The Lord will surely exclude me from his people."

The foreigners who join themselves to the Lord,
   ministering to him,
Loving the name of the Lord,
   and becoming his servants—
All who keep the sabbath free from profanation
   and hold to my covenant,
Them I will bring to my holy mountain
   and make joyful in my house of prayer;
Their burnt offerings and sacrifices
   will be acceptable on my altar,
For my house shall be called
   a house of prayer for all peoples.
Thus says the Lord God,
   who gathers the dispersed of Israel:
Others will I gather to him
   besides those already gathered.

The word of the Lord.

RESPONSORIAL PSALM

Psalm 67:2-3, 5, 7-8

℟. (4) O God, let all the nations praise you!

May God have pity on us and bless us;
   may he let his face shine upon us.
So may your way be known upon earth;
   among all nations, your salvation.

℟. O God, let all the nations praise you!

May the nations be glad and exult
   because you rule the peoples in equity;
   the nations on the earth you guide.

℟. O God, let all the nations praise you!

The earth has yielded its fruits;
   God, our God, has blessed us.
May God bless us,
   and may all the ends of the earth fear him!

℟. O God, let all the nations praise you!

ALLELUIA

℟. Alleluia, alleluia.

Come, Lord, bring us your peace
that we may rejoice before you with a perfect heart.

℟. Alleluia, alleluia.

GOSPEL

John 5:33-36   John was a burning and shining lamp.

✠ A reading from the holy Gospel according to John

Jesus said to the Jews:
"You sent emissaries to John, and he testified to the truth.
I do not accept testimony from a human being,
　but I say this so that you may be saved.
John was a burning and shining lamp,
　and for a while you were content to rejoice in his light.
But I have testimony greater than John's.
The works that the Father gave me to accomplish,
　these works that I perform testify on my behalf
　that the Father has sent me."

The Gospel of the Lord.

192 ALLELUIA VERSES FOR WEEKDAYS OF ADVENT UP TO DECEMBER 16

These texts may be used in place of the texts proposed for each day.

1.

See Psalm 80:4

**Come and save us, Lord our God;
let your face shine upon us that we may be saved.**

2.

Psalm 85:8

**Show us, Lord, your love,
and grant us your salvation.**

3.

Isaiah 33:22

**The Lord is our Judge, our Lawgiver, our King;
he it is who will save us.**

4.

See Isaiah 40:9-10

**Raise your voice and tell the Good News:
Behold, the Lord God comes with power.**

5.

See Isaiah 45:8

**Let the clouds rain down the Just One,
and the earth bring forth a Savior.**

6.

Isaiah 55:6

**Seek the Lord while he may be found;
call him while he is near.**

7.

Luke 3:4, 6

**Prepare the way of the Lord, make straight his paths:
All flesh shall see the salvation of God.**

8.

**The Lord will come; go out to meet him!
He is the prince of peace.**

9.

**Behold, our Lord shall come with power;
he will enlighten the eyes of his servants.**

10.

**Behold, the Lord comes to save his people;
blessed are those prepared to meet him.**

11.

**Behold, the King will come, the Lord of earth:
and he will take away the yoke of our captivity.**

12.

**The day of the Lord is near:
Behold, he comes to save us.**

13.

**Come, O Lord, do not delay:
forgive the sins of your people.**

14.

**Come, Lord, bring us your peace;
that we may rejoice before you with a perfect heart.**

WEEKDAYS OF ADVENT
DECEMBER 17 TO DECEMBER 24

The following readings are used from December 17 to 24. If a Sunday occurs during this time, the weekday readings for that day are omitted, but they may be anticipated or used later on another day during the week, especially to avoid duplicating the Sunday readings.

193 DECEMBER 17

FIRST READING

Genesis 49:2, 8-10   The scepter shall not depart from Judah.

A reading from the Book of Genesis

Jacob called his sons and said to them:
  "Assemble and listen, sons of Jacob,
    listen to Israel, your father.

"You, Judah, shall your brothers praise
    —your hand on the neck of your enemies;
    the sons of your father shall bow down to you.
Judah, like a lion's whelp,
    you have grown up on prey, my son.
He crouches like a lion recumbent,
    the king of beasts—who would dare rouse him?
The scepter shall never depart from Judah,
    or the mace from between his legs,
While tribute is brought to him,
    and he receives the people's homage."

The word of the Lord.

RESPONSORIAL PSALM

Psalm 72:1-2, 3-4ab, 7-8, 17

℟. (see 7) **Justice shall flourish in his time, and fullness of peace for ever.**

**O God, with your judgment endow the king,
 and with your justice, the king's son;
He shall govern your people with justice
 and your afflicted ones with judgment.**

℟. **Justice shall flourish in his time, and fullness of peace for ever.**

**The mountains shall yield peace for the people,
 and the hills justice.
He shall defend the afflicted among the people,
 save the children of the poor.**

℟. **Justice shall flourish in his time, and fullness of peace for ever.**

**Justice shall flower in his days,
 and profound peace, till the moon be no more.
May he rule from sea to sea,
 and from the River to the ends of the earth.**

℟. **Justice shall flourish in his time, and fullness of peace for ever.**

**May his name be blessed forever;
 as long as the sun his name shall remain.
In him shall all the tribes of the earth be blessed;
 all the nations shall proclaim his happiness.**

℟. **Justice shall flourish in his time, and fullness of peace for ever.**

ALLELUIA

℟. Alleluia, alleluia.

O Wisdom of our God Most High,
guiding creation with power and love:
come to teach us the path of knowledge!

℟. Alleluia, alleluia.

GOSPEL

Matthew 1:1-17   The genealogy of Jesus Christ, the son of David.

☩ A reading from the beginning of the holy Gospel according to Matthew

The book of the genealogy of Jesus Christ,
   the son of David, the son of Abraham.

Abraham became the father of Isaac,
   Isaac the father of Jacob,
   Jacob the father of Judah and his brothers.
Judah became the father of Perez and Zerah,
   whose mother was Tamar.
Perez became the father of Hezron,
   Hezron the father of Ram,
   Ram the father of Amminadab.
Amminadab became the father of Nahshon,
   Nahshon the father of Salmon,
   Salmon the father of Boaz,
   whose mother was Rahab.
Boaz became the father of Obed,
   whose mother was Ruth.
Obed became the father of Jesse,
   Jesse the father of David the king.

David became the father of Solomon,
   whose mother had been the wife of Uriah.
Solomon became the father of Rehoboam,
   Rehoboam the father of Abijah,
   Abijah the father of Asaph.
Asaph became the father of Jehoshaphat,
   Jehoshaphat the father of Joram,
   Joram the father of Uzziah.

Uzziah became the father of Jotham,
    Jotham the father of Ahaz,
    Ahaz the father of Hezekiah.
Hezekiah became the father of Manasseh,
    Manasseh the father of Amos,
    Amos the father of Josiah.
Josiah became the father of Jechoniah and his brothers
    at the time of the Babylonian exile.

After the Babylonian exile,
    Jechoniah became the father of Shealtiel,
    Shealtiel the father of Zerubbabel,
    Zerubbabel the father of Abiud.
Abiud became the father of Eliakim,
    Eliakim the father of Azor,
    Azor the father of Zadok.
Zadok became the father of Achim,
    Achim the father of Eliud,
    Eliud the father of Eleazar.
Eleazar became the father of Matthan,
    Matthan the father of Jacob,
    Jacob the father of Joseph, the husband of Mary.
Of her was born Jesus who is called the Christ.

Thus the total number of generations
    from Abraham to David
    is fourteen generations;
    from David to the Babylonian exile, fourteen generations;
    from the Babylonian exile to the Christ,
    fourteen generations.

The Gospel of the Lord.

194 DECEMBER 18

FIRST READING

Jeremiah 23:5-8   I will raise up a righteous shoot to David.

A reading from the Book of the Prophet Jeremiah

> **Behold, the days are coming, says the Lord,
>   when I will raise up a righteous shoot to David;
> As king he shall reign and govern wisely,
>   he shall do what is just and right in the land.
> In his days Judah shall be saved,
>   Israel shall dwell in security.
> This is the name they give him:
>   "The Lord our justice."**

**Therefore, the days will come, says the Lord,
   when they shall no longer say, "As the Lord lives,
   who brought the children of Israel out of the land of Egypt";
   but rather, "As the Lord lives,
   who brought the descendants of the house of Israel
   up from the land of the north"—
   and from all the lands to which I banished them;
   they shall again live on their own land.**

The word of the Lord.

RESPONSORIAL PSALM

Psalm 72:1-2, 12-13, 18-19

℟. (see 7) **Justice shall flourish in his time, and fullness of peace for ever.**

**O God, with your judgment endow the king,
and with your justice, the king's son;
He shall govern your people with justice
and your afflicted ones with judgment.**

℟. **Justice shall flourish in his time, and fullness of peace for ever.**

**For he shall rescue the poor when he cries out,
and the afflicted when he has no one to help him.
He shall have pity for the lowly and the poor;
the lives of the poor he shall save.**

℟. **Justice shall flourish in his time, and fullness of peace for ever.**

**Blessed be the Lord, the God of Israel,
who alone does wondrous deeds.
And blessed forever be his glorious name;
may the whole earth be filled with his glory.**

℟. **Justice shall flourish in his time, and fullness of peace for ever.**

ALLELUIA

℟. **Alleluia, alleluia.**

**O Leader of the House of Israel,
giver of the Law to Moses on Sinai:
come to rescue us with your mighty power!**

℟. **Alleluia, alleluia.**

GOSPEL

Matthew 1:18-25   Jesus was born of Mary, the betrothed of Joseph, a son of David.

✠ **A reading from the holy Gospel according to Matthew**

**This is how the birth of Jesus Christ came about.
When his mother Mary was betrothed to Joseph,
   but before they lived together,
   she was found with child through the Holy Spirit.
Joseph her husband, since he was a righteous man,
   yet unwilling to expose her to shame,
   decided to divorce her quietly.
Such was his intention when, behold,
   the angel of the Lord appeared to him in a dream and said,
   "Joseph, son of David,
   do not be afraid to take Mary your wife into your home.
For it is through the Holy Spirit
   that this child has been conceived in her.
She will bear a son and you are to name him Jesus,
   because he will save his people from their sins."
All this took place to fulfill
   what the Lord had said through the prophet:**

   *Behold, the virgin shall be with child and bear a son,
      and they shall name him Emmanuel,*

which means "God is with us."
When Joseph awoke,
   he did as the angel of the Lord had commanded him
   and took his wife into his home.
He had no relations with her until she bore a son,
   and he named him Jesus.

The Gospel of the Lord.

195 DECEMBER 19

FIRST READING

Judges 13:2-7, 24-25a   The birth of Samson is announced by an angel.

A reading from the Book of Judges

**There was a certain man from Zorah, of the clan of the Danites,
   whose name was Manoah.
His wife was barren and had borne no children.
An angel of the Lord appeared to the woman and said to her,
   "Though you are barren and have had no children,
   yet you will conceive and bear a son.
Now, then, be careful to take no wine or strong drink
   and to eat nothing unclean.
As for the son you will conceive and bear,
   no razor shall touch his head,
   for this boy is to be consecrated to God from the womb.
It is he who will begin the deliverance of Israel
   from the power of the Philistines."

The woman went and told her husband,
   "A man of God came to me;
   he had the appearance of an angel of God, terrible indeed.
I did not ask him where he came from, nor did he tell me his name.
But he said to me,
   'You will be with child and will bear a son.
So take neither wine nor strong drink, and eat nothing unclean.
For the boy shall be consecrated to God from the womb,
   until the day of his death.'"

The woman bore a son and named him Samson.
The boy grew up and the Lord blessed him;
   the Spirit of the Lord stirred him.**

The word of the Lord.

RESPONSORIAL PSALM

Psalm 71:3-4a, 5-6ab, 16-17

℟. (see 8) **My mouth shall be filled with your praise, and I will sing your glory!**

Be my rock of refuge,
 a stronghold to give me safety,
  for you are my rock and my fortress.
O my God, rescue me from the hand of the wicked.

℟. **My mouth shall be filled with your praise, and I will sing your glory!**

For you are my hope, O Lord;
 my trust, O God, from my youth.
On you I depend from birth;
 from my mother's womb you are my strength.

℟. **My mouth shall be filled with your praise, and I will sing your glory!**

I will treat of the mighty works of the Lord;
 O God, I will tell of your singular justice.
O God, you have taught me from my youth,
 and till the present I proclaim your wondrous deeds.

℟. **My mouth shall be filled with your praise, and I will sing your glory!**

ALLELUIA

℟. Alleluia, alleluia.

O Root of Jesse's stem,
sign of God's love for all his people:
come to save us without delay!

℟. Alleluia, alleluia.

GOSPEL

Luke 1:5-25   The birth of John the Baptist is announced by Gabriel.

✠ A reading from the holy Gospel according to Luke

In the days of Herod, King of Judea,
   there was a priest named Zechariah
   of the priestly division of Abijah;
   his wife was from the daughters of Aaron,
   and her name was Elizabeth.
Both were righteous in the eyes of God,
   observing all the commandments
   and ordinances of the Lord blamelessly.
But they had no child, because Elizabeth was barren
   and both were advanced in years.

Once when he was serving as priest
   in his division's turn before God,
   according to the practice of the priestly service,
   he was chosen by lot
   to enter the sanctuary of the Lord to burn incense.
Then, when the whole assembly of the people was praying outside
   at the hour of the incense offering,
   the angel of the Lord appeared to him,
   standing at the right of the altar of incense.
Zechariah was troubled by what he saw, and fear came upon him.

But the angel said to him, "Do not be afraid, Zechariah,
   because your prayer has been heard.
Your wife Elizabeth will bear you a son,
   and you shall name him John.
And you will have joy and gladness,
   and many will rejoice at his birth,
   for he will be great in the sight of the Lord.
He will drink neither wine nor strong drink.
He will be filled with the Holy Spirit even from his mother's womb,
   and he will turn many of the children of Israel
   to the Lord their God.
He will go before him in the spirit and power of Elijah
   to turn the hearts of fathers toward children
   and the disobedient to the understanding of the righteous,
   to prepare a people fit for the Lord."

Then Zechariah said to the angel,
   "How shall I know this?
For I am an old man, and my wife is advanced in years."
And the angel said to him in reply,
   "I am Gabriel, who stand before God.
I was sent to speak to you and to announce to you this good news.
But now you will be speechless and unable to talk
   until the day these things take place,
   because you did not believe my words,
   which will be fulfilled at their proper time."
Meanwhile the people were waiting for Zechariah
   and were amazed that he stayed so long in the sanctuary.
But when he came out, he was unable to speak to them,
   and they realized that he had seen a vision in the sanctuary.
He was gesturing to them but remained mute.

Then, when his days of ministry were completed, he went home.

After this time his wife Elizabeth conceived,
   and she went into seclusion for five months, saying,
   "So has the Lord done for me at a time when he has seen fit
   to take away my disgrace before others."

The Gospel of the Lord.

196 DECEMBER 20

FIRST READING

Isaiah 7:10-14 Behold, the virgin shall be with child.

A reading from the Book of the Prophet Isaiah

The Lord spoke to Ahaz:
Ask for a sign from the Lord, your God;
> let it be deep as the nether world, or high as the sky!

But Ahaz answered,
> "I will not ask! I will not tempt the Lord!"

Then Isaiah said:
> Listen, O house of David!

Is it not enough for you to weary men,
> must you also weary my God?

Therefore the Lord himself will give you this sign:
> the virgin shall conceive and bear a son,
> and shall name him Emmanuel.

The word of the Lord.

RESPONSORIAL PSALM

Psalm 24:1-2, 3-4ab, 5-6

℟. (see 7c and 10b) **Let the Lord enter; he is the king of glory.**

**The Lord's are the earth and its fullness;
the world and those who dwell in it.
For he founded it upon the seas
and established it upon the rivers.**

℟. **Let the Lord enter; he is the king of glory.**

**Who can ascend the mountain of the Lord?
or who may stand in his holy place?
He whose hands are sinless, whose heart is clean,
who desires not what is vain.**

℟. **Let the Lord enter; he is the king of glory.**

**He shall receive a blessing from the Lord,
a reward from God his savior.
Such is the race that seeks for him,
that seeks the face of the God of Jacob.**

℟. **Let the Lord enter; he is the king of glory.**

ALLELUIA

℟. **Alleluia, alleluia.**

**O Key of David,
opening the gates of God's eternal Kingdom:
come and free the prisoners of darkness!**

℟. **Alleluia, alleluia.**

GOSPEL

Luke 1:26-38   You will conceive in your womb and bear a son.

☩ A reading from the holy Gospel according to Luke

In the sixth month,
>the angel Gabriel was sent from God
>to a town of Galilee called Nazareth,
>to a virgin betrothed to a man named Joseph,
>of the house of David,
>and the virgin's name was Mary.

And coming to her, he said,
>"Hail, full of grace! The Lord is with you."

But she was greatly troubled at what was said
>and pondered what sort of greeting this might be.

Then the angel said to her,
>"Do not be afraid, Mary,
>for you have found favor with God.

Behold, you will conceive in your womb and bear a son,
>and you shall name him Jesus.

He will be great and will be called Son of the Most High,
>and the Lord God will give him the throne of David his father,
>and he will rule over the house of Jacob forever,
>and of his Kingdom there will be no end."

But Mary said to the angel,
>"How can this be,
>since I have no relations with a man?"

And the angel said to her in reply,
>"The Holy Spirit will come upon you,
>and the power of the Most High will overshadow you.

Therefore the child to be born
>will be called holy, the Son of God.

And behold, Elizabeth, your relative,
>has also conceived a son in her old age,
>and this is the sixth month for her who was called barren;
>for nothing will be impossible for God."

Mary said, "Behold, I am the handmaid of the Lord.
May it be done to me according to your word."
Then the angel departed from her.

The Gospel of the Lord.

197 DECEMBER 21

FIRST READING

First Option

Song of Songs 2:8-14   Hark! my lover comes, springing across the mountains.

A reading from the Song of Songs

**Hark! my lover—here he comes
   springing across the mountains,
   leaping across the hills.
My lover is like a gazelle
   or a young stag.
Here he stands behind our wall,
   gazing through the windows,
   peering through the lattices.
My lover speaks; he says to me,
   "Arise, my beloved, my dove, my beautiful one,
   and come!
"For see, the winter is past,
   the rains are over and gone.
The flowers appear on the earth,
   the time of pruning the vines has come,
   and the song of the dove is heard in our land.
The fig tree puts forth its figs,
   and the vines, in bloom, give forth fragrance.
Arise, my beloved, my beautiful one,
   and come!**

**"O my dove in the clefts of the rock,
   in the secret recesses of the cliff,
Let me see you,
   let me hear your voice,
For your voice is sweet,
   and you are lovely."**

The word of the Lord.

   OR

Second Option

Zephaniah 3:14-18a   The King of Israel, the Lord, is in your midst.

A reading from the Book of the Prophet Zephaniah

**Shout for joy, O daughter Zion!
  Sing joyfully, O Israel!
Be glad and exult with all your heart,
  O daughter Jerusalem!
The Lord has removed the judgment against you,
  he has turned away your enemies;
The King of Israel, the Lord, is in your midst,
  you have no further misfortune to fear.
On that day, it shall be said to Jerusalem:
  Fear not, O Zion, be not discouraged!
The Lord, your God, is in your midst,
  a mighty savior;
He will rejoice over you with gladness,
  and renew you in his love,
He will sing joyfully because of you,
  as one sings at festivals.**

The word of the Lord.

RESPONSORIAL PSALM

Psalm 33:2-3, 11-12, 20-21

℟. (1a; 3a) **Exult, you just, in the Lord! Sing to him a new song.**

**Give thanks to the Lord on the harp;
  with the ten-stringed lyre chant his praises.
Sing to him a new song;
  pluck the strings skillfully, with shouts of gladness.**

℟. **Exult, you just, in the Lord! Sing to him a new song.**

**But the plan of the Lord stands forever;
  the design of his heart, through all generations.
Blessed the nation whose God is the Lord,
  the people he has chosen for his own inheritance.**

℟. **Exult, you just, in the Lord! Sing to him a new song.**

Our soul waits for the LORD,
>who is our help and our shield,
For in him our hearts rejoice;
>in his holy name we trust.

℟. **Exult, you just, in the Lord! Sing to him a new song.**

ALLELUIA

℟. **Alleluia, alleluia.**

O Emmanuel, our King and Giver of Law:
come to save us, Lord our God!

℟. **Alleluia, alleluia.**

GOSPEL

Luke 1:39-45   And how does this happen to me, that the mother of my Lord should come to me?

✠ A reading from the holy Gospel according to Luke

**Mary set out in those days
>and traveled to the hill country in haste
>to a town of Judah,
>where she entered the house of Zechariah
>and greeted Elizabeth.
When Elizabeth heard Mary's greeting,
>the infant leaped in her womb,
>and Elizabeth, filled with the Holy Spirit,
>cried out in a loud voice and said,
>"Most blessed are you among women,
>and blessed is the fruit of your womb.
And how does this happen to me,
>that the mother of my Lord should come to me?
For at the moment the sound of your greeting reached my ears,
>the infant in my womb leaped for joy.
Blessed are you who believed
>that what was spoken to you by the Lord
>would be fulfilled."**

The Gospel of the Lord.

198 DECEMBER 22

FIRST READING

1 Samuel 1:24-28   Hannah gives thanks for the birth of Samuel.

A reading from the first Book of Samuel

In those days,
Hannah brought Samuel with her,
  along with a three-year-old bull,
  an ephah of flour, and a skin of wine,
  and presented him at the temple of the Lord in Shiloh.
After the boy's father had sacrificed the young bull,
  Hannah, his mother, approached Eli and said:
  "Pardon, my lord!
As you live, my lord,
  I am the woman who stood near you here, praying to the Lord.
I prayed for this child, and the Lord granted my request.
Now I, in turn, give him to the Lord;
  as long as he lives, he shall be dedicated to the Lord."
She left Samuel there.

The word of the Lord.

RESPONSORIAL PSALM

1 Samuel 2:1, 4-5, 6-7, 8abcd

℟. (see 1a) **My heart exults in the Lord, my Savior.**

"My heart exults in the LORD,
 my horn is exalted in my God.
I have swallowed up my enemies;
 I rejoice in my victory."

℟. **My heart exults in the Lord, my Savior.**

"The bows of the mighty are broken,
 while the tottering gird on strength.
The well-fed hire themselves out for bread,
 while the hungry batten on spoil.
The barren wife bears seven sons,
 while the mother of many languishes."

℟. **My heart exults in the Lord, my Savior.**

"The LORD puts to death and gives life;
 he casts down to the nether world;
 he raises up again.
The Lord makes poor and makes rich,
 he humbles, he also exalts."

℟. **My heart exults in the Lord, my Savior.**

"He raises the needy from the dust;
 from the dung heap he lifts up the poor,
To seat them with nobles
 and make a glorious throne their heritage."

℟. **My heart exults in the Lord, my Savior.**

ALLELUIA

℟. Alleluia, alleluia.

O King of all nations and keystone of the Church;
come and save man, whom you formed from the dust!

℟. Alleluia, alleluia.

GOSPEL

Luke 1:46-56   The Mighty One has done great things for me.

✠ A reading from the holy Gospel according to Luke

Mary said:

> "My soul proclaims the greatness of the Lord;
>   my spirit rejoices in God my savior,
>   for he has looked upon his lowly servant.
> From this day all generations will call me blessed;
>   the Almighty has done great things for me,
>   and holy is his Name.
> He has mercy on those who fear him
>   in every generation.
> He has shown the strength of his arm,
>   and has scattered the proud in their conceit.
> He has cast down the mighty from their thrones
>   and has lifted up the lowly.
> He has filled the hungry with good things,
>   and the rich he has sent away empty.
> He has come to the help of his servant Israel
>   for he remembered his promise of mercy,
>   the promise he made to our fathers,
>   to Abraham and his children for ever."

Mary remained with Elizabeth about three months
  and then returned to her home.

The Gospel of the Lord.

199 DECEMBER 23

FIRST READING

Malachi 3:1-4, 23-24   I will send you Elijah, the prophet, before the day of the Lord comes.

A reading from the Book of the Prophet Malachi

Thus says the Lord God:
Lo, I am sending my messenger
 to prepare the way before me;
And suddenly there will come to the temple
 the Lord whom you seek,
And the messenger of the covenant whom you desire.
 Yes, he is coming, says the Lord of hosts.
But who will endure the day of his coming?
 And who can stand when he appears?
For he is like the refiner's fire,
 or like the fuller's lye.
He will sit refining and purifying silver,
 and he will purify the sons of Levi,
Refining them like gold or like silver
 that they may offer due sacrifice to the Lord.
Then the sacrifice of Judah and Jerusalem
 will please the Lord,
 as in the days of old, as in years gone by.

Lo, I will send you
 Elijah, the prophet,
Before the day of the Lord comes,
 the great and terrible day,
To turn the hearts of the fathers to their children,
 and the hearts of the children to their fathers,
Lest I come and strike
 the land with doom.

The word of the Lord.

RESPONSORIAL PSALM

Psalm 25:4-5ab, 8-9, 10 and 14

℟. (see Luke 21:28) **Lift up your heads and see; your redemption is near at hand.**

Your ways, O LORD, make known to me;
    teach me your paths,
Guide me in your truth and teach me,
    for you are God my savior.

℟. **Lift up your heads and see; your redemption is near at hand.**

Good and upright is the LORD;
    thus he shows sinners the way.
He guides the humble to justice,
    he teaches the humble his way.

℟. **Lift up your heads and see; your redemption is near at hand.**

All the paths of the LORD are kindness and constancy
    toward those who keep his covenant and his decrees.
The friendship of the LORD is with those who fear him,
    and his covenant, for their instruction.

℟. **Lift up your heads and see; your redemption is near at hand.**

ALLELUIA

℟. **Alleluia, alleluia.**

O King of all nations and keystone of the Church;
come and save man, whom you formed from the dust!

℟. **Alleluia, alleluia.**

GOSPEL

Luke 1:57-66   The birth of John the Baptist.

✠ A reading from the holy Gospel according to Luke

When the time arrived for Elizabeth to have her child
   she gave birth to a son.
Her neighbors and relatives heard
   that the Lord had shown his great mercy toward her,
   and they rejoiced with her.
When they came on the eighth day to circumcise the child,
   they were going to call him Zechariah after his father,
   but his mother said in reply,
   "No. He will be called John."
But they answered her,
   "There is no one among your relatives who has this name."
So they made signs, asking his father what he wished him to be called.
He asked for a tablet and wrote, "John is his name,"
   and all were amazed.
Immediately his mouth was opened, his tongue freed,
   and he spoke blessing God.
Then fear came upon all their neighbors,
   and all these matters were discussed
   throughout the hill country of Judea.
All who heard these things took them to heart, saying,
   "What, then, will this child be?
For surely the hand of the Lord was with him."

The Gospel of the Lord.

200 DECEMBER 24

MASS IN THE MORNING

FIRST READING

2 Samuel 7:1-5, 8b-12, 14a, 16   The Kingdom of David shall endure forever in the sight of the Lord.

A reading from the second Book of Samuel

When King David was settled in his palace,
>   and the Lord had given him rest from his enemies on every side,
>   he said to Nathan the prophet,
>   "Here I am living in a house of cedar,
>   while the ark of God dwells in a tent!"

Nathan answered the king,
>   "Go, do whatever you have in mind,
>   for the Lord is with you."

But that night the Lord spoke to Nathan and said:
>   "Go, tell my servant David, 'Thus says the Lord:
>   Should you build me a house to dwell in?

"'It was I who took you from the pasture
>   and from the care of the flock
>   to be commander of my people Israel.

I have been with you wherever you went,
>   and I have destroyed all your enemies before you.

And I will make you famous like the great ones of the earth.

I will fix a place for my people Israel;
>   I will plant them so that they may dwell in their place
>   without further disturbance.

Neither shall the wicked continue to afflict them as they did of old,
>   since the time I first appointed judges over my people Israel.

I will give you rest from all your enemies.

The Lord also reveals to you
>   that he will establish a house for you.

And when your time comes and you rest with your ancestors,
>   I will raise up your heir after you, sprung from your loins,
>   and I will make his Kingdom firm.

I will be a father to him,
>   and he shall be a son to me.

Your house and your Kingdom shall endure forever before me;
> your throne shall stand firm forever.'"

The word of the Lord.

RESPONSORIAL PSALM

Psalm 89:2-3, 4-5, 27 and 29

℟. (2) **For ever I will sing the goodness of the Lord.**

The favors of the LORD **I will sing forever;**
> **through all generations my mouth shall proclaim your faithfulness.**
For you have said, "My kindness is established forever";
> **in heaven you have confirmed your faithfulness.**

℟. **For ever I will sing the goodness of the Lord.**

"I have made a covenant with my chosen one,
> **I have sworn to David my servant:**
Forever will I confirm your posterity
> **and establish your throne for all generations."**

℟. **For ever I will sing the goodness of the Lord.**

"He shall say of me, 'You are my father,
> **my God, the rock, my savior.'**
Forever I will maintain my kindness toward him,
> **and my covenant with him stands firm."**

℟. **For ever I will sing the goodness of the Lord.**

ALLELUIA

℟. **Alleluia, alleluia.**

O Radiant Dawn,
splendor of eternal light, sun of justice:
come and shine on those who dwell in darkness and in the shadow of death.

℟. **Alleluia, alleluia.**

GOSPEL

Luke 1:67-79   The daybreak from on high has visited us.

✠ A reading from the holy Gospel according to Luke

Zechariah his father, filled with the Holy Spirit, prophesied, saying:

> "Blessed be the Lord, the God of Israel;
>   for he has come to his people and set them free.
> He has raised up for us a mighty Savior,
>   born of the house of his servant David.
> Through his prophets he promised of old
>   that he would save us from our enemies,
>   from the hands of all who hate us.
> He promised to show mercy to our fathers
>   and to remember his holy covenant.
> This was the oath he swore to our father Abraham:
>   to set us free from the hand of our enemies,
>   free to worship him without fear,
>   holy and righteous in his sight
>   all the days of our life.
> You, my child, shall be called the prophet of the Most High,
>   for you will go before the Lord to prepare his way,
>   to give his people knowledge of salvation
>   by the forgiveness of their sins.
> In the tender compassion of our God
>   the dawn from on high shall break upon us,
>   to shine on those who dwell in darkness and the shadow of death,
>   and to guide our feet into the way of peace."

The Gospel of the Lord.

201 ALLELUIA VERSES FOR WEEKDAYS OF ADVENT FROM DECEMBER 17 TO DECEMBER 24

These texts may be used in place of the texts proposed for each day.

1.

O Wisdom of our God Most High,
guiding creation with power and love:
come to teach us the path of knowledge!

2.

O Leader of the House of Israel,
giver of the Law to Moses on Sinai:
come to rescue us with your mighty power!

3.

O Root of Jesse's stem,
sign of God's love for all his people:
come to save us without delay!

4.

O Key of David,
opening the gates of God's eternal Kingdom:
come and free the prisoners of darkness!

5.

O Radiant Dawn,
splendor of eternal light, sun of justice:
come and shine on those who dwell in darkness and in the shadow of death!

6.

O King of all nations and keystone of the Church;
come and save man, whom you formed from the dust!

7.

O Emmanuel, our King, and Giver of Law:
come to save us, Lord our God!

SEASON OF CHRISTMAS

202 DECEMBER 29

THE FIFTH DAY IN THE OCTAVE OF CHRISTMAS

FIRST READING

1 John 2:3-11   Those who love their brother remain in the light.

A reading from the first Letter of Saint John

Beloved:
The way we may be sure that we know Jesus
  is to keep his commandments.
Whoever says, "I know him," but does not keep his commandments
  is a liar, and the truth is not in him.
But whoever keeps his word,
  the love of God is truly perfected in him.
This is the way we may know that we are in union with him:
  whoever claims to abide in him ought to walk just as he walked.

Beloved, I am writing no new commandment to you
  but an old commandment that you had from the beginning.
The old commandment is the word that you have heard.
And yet I do write a new commandment to you,
  which holds true in him and among you,
  for the darkness is passing away,
  and the true light is already shining.
Whoever says he is in the light,
  yet hates his brother, is still in the darkness.
Whoever loves his brother remains in the light,
  and there is nothing in him to cause a fall.
Whoever hates his brother is in darkness;
  he walks in darkness
  and does not know where he is going
  because the darkness has blinded his eyes.

The word of the Lord.

RESPONSORIAL PSALM

Psalm 96:1-2a, 2b-3, 5b-6

℟. (11a) **Let the heavens be glad and the earth rejoice!**

**Sing to the Lord a new song;
   sing to the Lord, all you lands.
Sing to the Lord; bless his name.**

℟. **Let the heavens be glad and the earth rejoice!**

**Announce his salvation, day after day.
Tell his glory among the nations;
   among all peoples, his wondrous deeds.**

℟. **Let the heavens be glad and the earth rejoice!**

**The Lord made the heavens.
Splendor and majesty go before him;
   praise and grandeur are in his sanctuary.**

℟. **Let the heavens be glad and the earth rejoice!**

ALLELUIA

Luke 2:32

℟. **Alleluia, alleluia.**

**A light of revelation to the Gentiles
and glory for your people Israel.**

℟. **Alleluia, alleluia.**

GOSPEL

Luke 2:22-35   This is the light of revelation to the Gentiles.

✝ A reading from the holy Gospel according to Luke

When the days were completed for their purification
   according to the law of Moses,
   the parents of Jesus took him up to Jerusalem
   to present him to the Lord,
   just as it is written in the law of the Lord,
   Every male that opens the womb shall be consecrated to the Lord,
   and to offer the sacrifice of
   a pair of turtledoves or two young pigeons,
   in accordance with the dictate in the law of the Lord.

Now there was a man in Jerusalem whose name was Simeon.
This man was righteous and devout,
   awaiting the consolation of Israel,
   and the Holy Spirit was upon him.
It had been revealed to him by the Holy Spirit
   that he should not see death
   before he had seen the Christ of the Lord.
He came in the Spirit into the temple;
   and when the parents brought in the child Jesus
   to perform the custom of the law in regard to him,
   he took him into his arms and blessed God, saying:

"Lord, now let your servant go in peace;
   your word has been fulfilled:
my own eyes have seen the salvation
   which you prepared in the sight of every people,
a light to reveal you to the nations
   and the glory of your people Israel."

The child's father and mother were amazed at what was said about him;
   and Simeon blessed them and said to Mary his mother,
   "Behold, this child is destined
   for the fall and rise of many in Israel,
   and to be a sign that will be contradicted
   (and you yourself a sword will pierce)
   so that the thoughts of many hearts may be revealed."

The Gospel of the Lord.

203 DECEMBER 30

THE SIXTH DAY IN THE OCTAVE OF CHRISTMAS

FIRST READING

1 John 2:12-17   Those who do the will of God remain forever.

A reading from the first Letter of Saint John

I am writing to you, children,
> because your sins have been forgiven for his name's sake.

I am writing to you, fathers,
> because you know him who is from the beginning.

I am writing to you, young men,
> because you have conquered the Evil One.

I write to you, children,
> because you know the Father.

I write to you, fathers,
> because you know him who is from the beginning.

I write to you, young men,
> because you are strong and the word of God remains in you,
> and you have conquered the Evil One.

Do not love the world or the things of the world.
If anyone loves the world, the love of the Father is not in him.
For all that is in the world,
> sensual lust, enticement for the eyes, and a pretentious life,
> is not from the Father but is from the world.

Yet the world and its enticement are passing away.
But whoever does the will of God remains forever.

The word of the Lord.

RESPONSORIAL PSALM

Psalm 96:7-8a, 8b-9, 10

℟. (11a) **Let the heavens be glad and the earth rejoice!**

Give to the Lord, you families of nations,
 give to the Lord glory and praise;
 give to the Lord the glory due his name!

℟. **Let the heavens be glad and the earth rejoice!**

Bring gifts, and enter his courts;
 worship the Lord in holy attire.
Tremble before him, all the earth.

℟. **Let the heavens be glad and the earth rejoice!**

Say among the nations: The Lord is king.
He has made the world firm, not to be moved;
 he governs the peoples with equity.

℟. **Let the heavens be glad and the earth rejoice!**

ALLELUIA

℟. Alleluia, alleluia.

A holy day has dawned upon us.
Come, you nations, and adore the Lord.
Today a great light has come upon the earth.

℟. Alleluia, alleluia.

GOSPEL

Luke 2:36-40   She spoke about the child to all who were awaiting the redemption of Jerusalem.

✠ A reading from the holy Gospel according to Luke

There was a prophetess, Anna,
   the daughter of Phanuel, of the tribe of Asher.
She was advanced in years,
   having lived seven years with her husband after her marriage,
   and then as a widow until she was eighty-four.
She never left the temple,
   but worshiped night and day with fasting and prayer.
And coming forward at that very time,
   she gave thanks to God and spoke about the child
   to all who were awaiting the redemption of Jerusalem.

When they had fulfilled all the prescriptions
   of the law of the Lord,
   they returned to Galilee,
   to their own town of Nazareth.
The child grew and became strong, filled with wisdom;
   and the favor of God was upon him.

The Gospel of the Lord.

204 DECEMBER 31

THE SEVENTH DAY IN THE OCTAVE OF CHRISTMAS

FIRST READING

1 John 2:18-21   You have the anointing that comes from the Holy One, and you have all knowledge.

A reading from the first Letter of Saint John

Children, it is the last hour;
  and just as you heard that the antichrist was coming,
  so now many antichrists have appeared.
Thus we know this is the last hour.
They went out from us, but they were not really of our number;
  if they had been, they would have remained with us.
Their desertion shows that none of them was of our number.
But you have the anointing that comes from the Holy One,
  and you all have knowledge.
I write to you not because you do not know the truth
  but because you do, and because every lie is alien to the truth.

The word of the Lord.

RESPONSORIAL PSALM

Psalm 96:1-2, 11-12, 13

℟. (11a) **Let the heavens be glad and the earth rejoice!**

Sing to the Lord a new song;
  sing to the Lord, all you lands.
Sing to the Lord; bless his name;
  announce his salvation, day after day.

℟. **Let the heavens be glad and the earth rejoice!**

Let the heavens be glad and the earth rejoice;
  let the sea and what fills it resound;
  let the plains be joyful and all that is in them!
Then shall all the trees of the forest exult before the Lord.

℟. **Let the heavens be glad and the earth rejoice!**

The Lord comes,
> he comes to rule the earth.
He shall rule the world with justice
> and the peoples with his constancy.

℟. Let the heavens be glad and the earth rejoice!

ALLELUIA

John 1:14a, 12a

℟. Alleluia, alleluia.

The Word of God became flesh and dwelt among us.
To those who accepted him
he gave power to become the children of God.

℟. Alleluia, alleluia.

GOSPEL

John 1:1-18   The Word became flesh.

☩ A reading from the beginning of the holy Gospel according to John

In the beginning was the Word,
> and the Word was with God,
> and the Word was God.
He was in the beginning with God.
All things came to be through him,
> and without him nothing came to be.
What came to be through him was life,
> and this life was the light of the human race;
> the light shines in the darkness,
> and the darkness has not overcome it.

A man named John was sent from God.
He came for testimony, to testify to the light,
> so that all might believe through him.
He was not the light,
> but came to testify to the light.
The true light, which enlightens everyone, was coming into the world.

He was in the world,
> and the world came to be through him,
> but the world did not know him.

He came to what was his own,
> but his own people did not accept him.

But to those who did accept him
> he gave power to become children of God,
> to those who believe in his name,
> who were born not by natural generation
> nor by human choice nor by a man's decision
> but of God.

And the Word became flesh
> and made his dwelling among us,
> and we saw his glory,
> the glory as of the Father's only-begotten Son,
> full of grace and truth.

John testified to him and cried out, saying,
> "This was he of whom I said,
> 'The one who is coming after me ranks ahead of me
> because he existed before me.'"

From his fullness we have all received,
> grace in place of grace,
> because while the law was given through Moses,
> grace and truth came through Jesus Christ.

No one has ever seen God.

The only-begotten Son, God, who is at the Father's side,
> has revealed him.

The Gospel of the Lord.

205 JANUARY 2

FIRST READING

1 John 2:22-28 Let what you heard from the beginning remain in you.

A reading from the first Letter of Saint John

Beloved:
Who is the liar?
Whoever denies that Jesus is the Christ.
Whoever denies the Father and the Son, this is the antichrist.
Anyone who denies the Son does not have the Father,
   but whoever confesses the Son has the Father as well.

Let what you heard from the beginning remain in you.
If what you heard from the beginning remains in you,
   then you will remain in the Son and in the Father.
And this is the promise that he made us: eternal life.
I write you these things about those who would deceive you.
As for you,
   the anointing that you received from him remains in you,
   so that you do not need anyone to teach you.
But his anointing teaches you about everything and is true and not false;
   just as it taught you, remain in him.

And now, children, remain in him,
   so that when he appears we may have confidence
   and not be put to shame by him at his coming.

The word of the Lord.

RESPONSORIAL PSALM

Psalm 98:1, 2-3ab, 3cd-4

℟. (3cd) **All the ends of the earth have seen the saving power of God.**

Sing to the Lord **a new song,
for he has done wondrous deeds;
His right hand has won victory for him,
his holy arm.**

℟. **All the ends of the earth have seen the saving power of God.**

The Lord **has made his salvation known:
in the sight of the nations he has revealed his justice.
He has remembered his kindness and his faithfulness
toward the house of Israel.**

℟. **All the ends of the earth have seen the saving power of God.**

**All the ends of the earth have seen
the salvation by our God.
Sing joyfully to the L**ord**, all you lands;
break into song; sing praise.**

℟. **All the ends of the earth have seen the saving power of God.**

ALLELUIA

Hebrews 1:1-2

℟. **Alleluia, alleluia.**

**In times past, God spoke to our ancestors through the prophets:
in these last days, he has spoken to us through his Son.**

℟. **Alleluia, alleluia.**

GOSPEL

John 1:19-28   There is one who is coming after me.

✠ A reading from the holy Gospel according to John

This is the testimony of John.
When the Jews from Jerusalem sent priests and Levites to him
   to ask him, "Who are you?"
He admitted and did not deny it, but admitted,
   "I am not the Christ."
So they asked him,
   "What are you then? Are you Elijah?"
And he said, "I am not."
"Are you the Prophet?"
He answered, "No."
So they said to him,
   "Who are you, so we can give an answer to those who sent us?
What do you have to say for yourself?"
He said:
     "I am *the voice of one crying out in the desert,*
     'Make straight the way of the Lord,'
   as Isaiah the prophet said."
Some Pharisees were also sent.
They asked him,
   "Why then do you baptize
   if you are not the Christ or Elijah or the Prophet?"
John answered them,
   "I baptize with water;
   but there is one among you whom you do not recognize,
   the one who is coming after me,
   whose sandal strap I am not worthy to untie."
This happened in Bethany across the Jordan,
   where John was baptizing.

The Gospel of the Lord.

206 JANUARY 3

FIRST READING

1 John 2:29–3:6   No one who remains in him sins.

A reading from the first Letter of Saint John

**If you consider that God is righteous,
   you also know that everyone who acts in righteousness
   is begotten by him.**

**See what love the Father has bestowed on us
   that we may be called the children of God.
Yet so we are.
The reason the world does not know us is that it did not know him.
Beloved, we are God's children now;
   what we shall be has not yet been revealed.
We do know that when it is revealed we shall be like him,
   for we shall see him as he is.
Everyone who has this hope based on him makes himself pure,
   as he is pure.**

**Everyone who commits sin commits lawlessness,
   for sin is lawlessness.
You know that he was revealed to take away sins,
   and in him there is no sin.
No one who remains in him sins;
   no one who sins has seen him or known him.**

The word of the Lord.

RESPONSORIAL PSALM

Psalm 98:1, 3cd-4, 5-6

℟. (3cd) **All the ends of the earth have seen the saving power of God.**

Sing to the LORD **a new song,**
   for he has done wondrous deeds;
His right hand has won victory for him,
   his holy arm.

℟. **All the ends of the earth have seen the saving power of God.**

All the ends of the earth have seen
   the salvation by our God.
Sing joyfully to the LORD**, all you lands;**
   break into song; sing praise.

℟. **All the ends of the earth have seen the saving power of God.**

Sing praise to the LORD **with the harp,**
   with the harp and melodious song.
With trumpets and the sound of the horn
   sing joyfully before the King, the LORD**.**

℟. **All the ends of the earth have seen the saving power of God.**

ALLELUIA

John 1:14a, 12a

℟. **Alleluia, alleluia.**

The Word of God became flesh and dwelt among us.
To those who accepted him
he gave power to become the children of God.

℟. **Alleluia, alleluia.**

GOSPEL

John 1:29-34   Behold the Lamb of God.

☩ A reading from the holy Gospel according to John

John the Baptist saw Jesus coming toward him and said,
  "Behold, the Lamb of God, who takes away the sin of the world.
He is the one of whom I said,
  'A man is coming after me who ranks ahead of me
  because he existed before me.'
I did not know him,
  but the reason why I came baptizing with water
  was that he might be made known to Israel."
John testified further, saying,
  "I saw the Spirit come down like a dove from the sky
  and remain upon him.
I did not know him,
  but the one who sent me to baptize with water told me,
  'On whomever you see the Spirit come down and remain,
  he is the one who will baptize with the Holy Spirit.'
Now I have seen and testified that he is the Son of God."

The Gospel of the Lord.

207 JANUARY 4

FIRST READING

1 John 3:7-10   Those who are begotten by God commit no sin.

A reading from the first Letter of Saint John

Children, let no one deceive you.
The person who acts in righteousness is righteous,
 just as he is righteous.
Whoever sins belongs to the Devil,
 because the Devil has sinned from the beginning.
Indeed, the Son of God was revealed to destroy the works of the Devil.
No one who is begotten by God commits sin,
 because God's seed remains in him;
 he cannot sin because he is begotten by God.
In this way,
 the children of God and the children of the Devil are made plain;
 no one who fails to act in righteousness belongs to God,
 nor anyone who does not love his brother.

The word of the Lord.

RESPONSORIAL PSALM

Psalm 98:1, 7-8, 9

℟. (3cd) **All the ends of the earth have seen the saving power of God.**

**Sing to the Lord a new song,
  for he has done wondrous deeds;
His right hand has won victory for him,
  his holy arm.**

℟. **All the ends of the earth have seen the saving power of God.**

**Let the sea and what fills it resound,
  the world and those who dwell in it;
Let the rivers clap their hands,
  the mountains shout with them for joy before the Lord.**

℟. **All the ends of the earth have seen the saving power of God.**

**The Lord comes;
  he comes to rule the earth;
He will rule the world with justice
  and the peoples with equity.**

℟. **All the ends of the earth have seen the saving power of God.**

ALLELUIA

Hebrews 1:1-2

℟. **Alleluia, alleluia.**

**In the past God spoke to our ancestors through the prophets:
in these last days, he has spoken to us through the Son.**

℟. **Alleluia, alleluia.**

GOSPEL

John 1:35-42   We have found the Messiah.

☩ **A reading from the holy Gospel according to John**

**John was standing with two of his disciples,
and as he watched Jesus walk by, he said,
"Behold, the Lamb of God."
The two disciples heard what he said and followed Jesus.
Jesus turned and saw them following him and said to them,
"What are you looking for?"
They said to him, "Rabbi" (which translated means Teacher),
"where are you staying?"
He said to them, "Come, and you will see."
So they went and saw where he was staying,
and they stayed with him that day.
It was about four in the afternoon.
Andrew, the brother of Simon Peter,
was one of the two who heard John and followed Jesus.
He first found his own brother Simon and told him,
"We have found the Messiah," which is translated Christ.
Then he brought him to Jesus.
Jesus looked at him and said,
"You are Simon the son of John;
you will be called Cephas," which is translated Peter.**

The Gospel of the Lord.

208 JANUARY 5

FIRST READING

1 John 3:11-21   We have passed from death to life because we love our brothers.

A reading from the first Letter of Saint John

Beloved:
This is the message you have heard from the beginning:
   we should love one another,
   unlike Cain who belonged to the Evil One
   and slaughtered his brother.
Why did he slaughter him?
Because his own works were evil,
   and those of his brother righteous.
Do not be amazed, then, brothers and sisters, if the world hates you.
We know that we have passed from death to life
   because we love our brothers.
Whoever does not love remains in death.
Everyone who hates his brother is a murderer,
   and you know that no murderer has eternal life remaining in him.
The way we came to know love
   was that he laid down his life for us;
   so we ought to lay down our lives for our brothers.
If someone who has worldly means
   sees a brother in need and refuses him compassion,
   how can the love of God remain in him?
Children, let us love not in word or speech
   but in deed and truth.

Now this is how we shall know that we belong to the truth
   and reassure our hearts before him
   in whatever our hearts condemn,
   for God is greater than our hearts and knows everything.
Beloved, if our hearts do not condemn us,
   we have confidence in God.

The word of the Lord.

RESPONSORIAL PSALM

Psalm 100:1b-2, 3, 4, 5

℟. (2a) **Let all the earth cry out to God with joy.**

**Sing joyfully to the Lord, all you lands;
serve the Lord with gladness;
come before him with joyful song.**

℟. **Let all the earth cry out to God with joy.**

**Know that the Lord is God;
he made us, his we are;
his people, the flock he tends.**

℟. **Let all the earth cry out to God with joy.**

**Enter his gates with thanksgiving,
his courts with praise;
Give thanks to him; bless his name.**

℟. **Let all the earth cry out to God with joy.**

**The Lord is good:
the Lord, whose kindness endures forever,
and his faithfulness, to all generations.**

℟. **Let all the earth cry out to God with joy.**

ALLELUIA

℟. **Alleluia, alleluia.**

**A holy day has dawned upon us.
Come, you nations, and adore the Lord.
Today a great light has come upon the earth.**

℟. **Alleluia, alleluia.**

GOSPEL

John 1:43-51   You are the Son of God; you are the King of Israel.

✠ A reading from the holy Gospel according to John

**Jesus decided to go to Galilee, and he found Philip.
And Jesus said to him, "Follow me."
Now Philip was from Bethsaida, the town of Andrew and Peter.
Philip found Nathanael and told him,
   "We have found the one about whom Moses wrote in the law,
   and also the prophets, Jesus, son of Joseph, from Nazareth."
But Nathanael said to him,
   "Can anything good come from Nazareth?"
Philip said to him, "Come and see."
Jesus saw Nathanael coming toward him and said of him,
   "Here is a true child of Israel.
There is no duplicity in him."
Nathanael said to him, "How do you know me?"
Jesus answered and said to him,
   "Before Philip called you, I saw you under the fig tree."
Nathanael answered him,
   "Rabbi, you are the Son of God; you are the King of Israel."
Jesus answered and said to him,
   "Do you believe
   because I told you that I saw you under the fig tree?
You will see greater things than this."
And he said to him, "Amen, amen, I say to you,
   you will see the sky opened and the angels of God
   ascending and descending on the Son of Man."**

The Gospel of the Lord.

209 JANUARY 6

If the Epiphany is celebrated on Sunday, January 7 or 8, the following readings are used for the Mass on January 6.

FIRST READING

1 John 5:5-13   The Spirit, the water, and the Blood.

A reading from the first Letter of Saint John

Beloved:
Who indeed is the victor over the world
    but the one who believes that Jesus is the Son of God?

This is the one who came through water and Blood, Jesus Christ,
    not by water alone, but by water and Blood.
The Spirit is the one who testifies,
    and the Spirit is truth.
So there are three that testify,
    the Spirit, the water, and the Blood,
    and the three are of one accord.
If we accept human testimony,
    the testimony of God is surely greater.
Now the testimony of God is this,
    that he has testified on behalf of his Son.
Whoever believes in the Son of God
    has this testimony within himself.
Whoever does not believe God has made him a liar
    by not believing the testimony God has given about his Son.
And this is the testimony:
    God gave us eternal life,
    and this life is in his Son.
Whoever possesses the Son has life;
    whoever does not possess the Son of God does not have life.

I write these things to you so that you may know
    that you have eternal life,
    you who believe in the name of the Son of God.

The word of the Lord.

RESPONSORIAL PSALM

Psalm 147:12-13, 14-15, 19-20

℟. (12a) **Praise the Lord, Jerusalem.**
   or:
℟. **Alleluia.**

**Glorify the Lord, O Jerusalem;
   praise your God, O Zion.
For he has strengthened the bars of your gates;
   he has blessed your children within you.**

℟. **Praise the Lord, Jerusalem.**
   or:
℟. **Alleluia.**

**He has granted peace in your borders;
   with the best of wheat he fills you.
He sends forth his command to the earth;
   swiftly runs his word!**

℟. **Praise the Lord, Jerusalem.**
   or:
℟. **Alleluia.**

**He has proclaimed his word to Jacob,
   his statutes and his ordinances to Israel.
He has not done thus for any other nation;
   his ordinances he has not made known to them. Alleluia.**

℟. **Praise the Lord, Jerusalem.**
   or:
℟. **Alleluia.**

ALLELUIA

See Mark 9:6

℟. **Alleluia, alleluia.**

**The heavens were opened and the voice of the Father thundered:
This is my beloved Son. Listen to him.**

℟. **Alleluia, alleluia.**

GOSPEL

First Option

Mark 1:7-11   You are my beloved Son; with you I am well pleased.

✠   **A reading from the holy Gospel according to Mark**

This is what John the Baptist proclaimed:
   "One mightier than I is coming after me.
I am not worthy to stoop and loosen the thongs of his sandals.
I have baptized you with water;
   he will baptize you with the Holy Spirit."

It happened in those days that Jesus came from Nazareth of Galilee
   and was baptized in the Jordan by John.
On coming up out of the water he saw the heavens being torn open
   and the Spirit, like a dove, descending upon him.
And a voice came from the heavens,
   "You are my beloved Son; with you I am well pleased."

The Gospel of the Lord.

OR Second Option

Long Form

Luke 3:23-38   The genealogy of Jesus Christ, the son of Adam, the son of God.

✠   **A reading from the holy Gospel according to Luke**

When Jesus began his ministry he was about thirty years of age.
He was the son, as was thought, of Joseph, the son of Heli,
   the son of Matthat, the son of Levi, the son of Melchi,
   the son of Jannai, the son of Joseph, the son of Mattathias,
   the son of Amos, the son of Nahum, the son of Esli,
   the son of Naggai, the son of Maath, the son of Mattathias,
   the son of Semein, the son of Josech, the son of Joda,
   the son of Joanan, the son of Rhesa, the son of Zerubbabel,
   the son of Shealtiel, the son of Neri, the son of Melchi,
   the son of Addi, the son of Cosam, the son of Elmadam,
   the son of Er, the son of Joshua, the son of Eliezer,
   the son of Jorim, the son of Matthat, the son of Levi,
   the son of Simeon, the son of Judah, the son of Joseph,
   the son of Jonam, the son of Eliakim, the son of Melea,

the son of Menna, the son of Mattatha, the son of Nathan,
the son of David, the son of Jesse, the son of Obed,
the son of Boaz, the son of Sala, the son of Nahshon,
the son of Amminadab, the son of Admin, the son of Arni,
the son of Hezron, the son of Perez, the son of Judah,
the son of Jacob, the son of Isaac, the son of Abraham,
the son of Terah, the son of Nahor, the son of Serug,
the son of Reu, the son of Peleg, the son of Eber,
the son of Shelah, the son of Cainan, the son of Arphaxad,
the son of Shem, the son of Noah, the son of Lamech,
the son of Methuselah, the son of Enoch, the son of Jared,
the son of Mahalaleel, the son of Cainan, the son of Enos,
the son of Seth, the son of Adam, the son of God.

The Gospel of the Lord.

OR

Short Form

Luke 3:23, 31-34, 36, 38   The genealogy of Jesus Christ, the son of Adam, the son of God.

☩ **A reading from the holy Gospel according to Luke**

**When Jesus began his ministry he was about thirty years of age.
He was the son, as was thought, of Joseph, the son of Heli,**
the son of Melea, the son of Menna, the son of Mattatha,
the son of Nathan, the son of David, the son of Jesse,
the son of Obed, the son of Boaz, the son of Sala,
the son of Nahshon, the son of Amminadab, the son of Admin,
the son of Arni, the son of Hezron, the son of Perez,
the son of Judah, the son of Jacob, the son of Isaac,
the son of Abraham, the son of Terah, the son of Nahor,
the son of Cainan, the son of Arphaxad, the son of Shem,
the son of Noah, the son of Lamech, the son of Enos,
the son of Seth, the son of Adam, the son of God.

The Gospel of the Lord.

210 JANUARY 7

If the Epiphany is celebrated on Sunday, January 8, the following readings are used for the Mass on January 7.

FIRST READING

1 John 5:14-21 God hears us in regard to whatever we ask.

A reading from the first Letter of Saint John

Beloved:
We have this confidence in God,
  that if we ask anything according to his will, he hears us.
And if we know that he hears us in regard to whatever we ask,
  we know that what we have asked him for is ours.
If anyone sees his brother sinning, if the sin is not deadly,
  he should pray to God and he will give him life.
This is only for those whose sin is not deadly.
There is such a thing as deadly sin,
  about which I do not say that you should pray.
All wrongdoing is sin, but there is sin that is not deadly.

We know that no one begotten by God sins;
  but the one begotten by God he protects,
  and the Evil One cannot touch him.
We know that we belong to God,
  and the whole world is under the power of the Evil One.
We also know that the Son of God has come
  and has given us discernment to know the one who is true.
And we are in the one who is true, in his Son Jesus Christ.
He is the true God and eternal life.
Children, be on your guard against idols.

The word of the Lord.

RESPONSORIAL PSALM

Psalm 149:1-2, 3-4, 5 and 6a and 9b

℟. (see 4a) **The Lord takes delight in his people.**
   or:
℟. **Alleluia.**

Sing to the Lord a new song
   of praise in the assembly of the faithful.
Let Israel be glad in their maker,
   let the children of Zion rejoice in their king.

℟. **The Lord takes delight in his people.**
   or:
℟. **Alleluia.**

Let them praise his name in the festive dance,
   let them sing praise to him with timbrel and harp.
For the Lord loves his people,
   and he adorns the lowly with victory.

℟. **The Lord takes delight in his people.**
   or:
℟. **Alleluia.**

Let the faithful exult in glory;
   let them sing for joy upon their couches;
let the high praises of God be in their throats.
   This is the glory of all his faithful. Alleluia.

℟. **The Lord takes delight in his people.**
   or:
℟. **Alleluia.**

ALLELUIA

Luke 7:16

℟. **Alleluia, alleluia.**

**A great prophet has arisen in our midst
and God has visited his people.**

℟. **Alleluia, alleluia.**

GOSPEL

John 2:1-11   Jesus did this as the beginning of his signs at Cana in Galilee.

✟ A reading from the holy Gospel according to John

There was a wedding at Cana in Galilee,
   and the mother of Jesus was there.
Jesus and his disciples were also invited to the wedding.
When the wine ran short,
   the mother of Jesus said to him,
   "They have no wine."
And Jesus said to her,
   "Woman, how does your concern affect me?
My hour has not yet come."
His mother said to the servers,
   "Do whatever he tells you."
Now there were six stone water jars there for Jewish ceremonial washings,
   each holding twenty to thirty gallons.
Jesus told them,
   "Fill the jars with water."
So they filled them to the brim.
Then he told them,
   "Draw some out now and take it to the headwaiter."
So they took it.
And when the headwaiter tasted the water that had become wine,
   without knowing where it came from
   (although the servers who had drawn the water knew),
   the headwaiter called the bridegroom and said to him,
   "Everyone serves good wine first,
   and then when people have drunk freely, an inferior one;
   but you have kept the good wine until now."
Jesus did this as the beginning of his signs at Cana in Galilee
   and so revealed his glory,
   and his disciples began to believe in him.

The Gospel of the Lord.

211 ALLELUIA VERSES FOR WEEKDAYS BEFORE EPIPHANY

These texts may be used in place of the texts proposed for each day.

1.

John 1:14a, 12a

**The Word of God became flesh and dwelt among us.
To those who accepted him
he gave power to become the children of God.**

2.

Hebrews 1:1-2

**In the past God spoke to our ancestors through the prophets:
in these last days, he has spoken to us through the Son.**

3.

**A holy day has dawned upon us.
Come, you nations, and adore the Lord.
Today a great light has come upon the earth.**

Monday after Epiphany or January 7 II

In the dioceses of the United States of America, where Epiphany is celebrated on the Sunday between January 2 and January 8, the following readings are used on the days that follow Epiphany up to the following Saturday. Nevertheless, on Monday after the Sunday on which the Baptism of the Lord is celebrated (that is, the Sunday after January 6), the readings of Ordinary Time begin, and any readings left over from those assigned for January 7 to January 12 are omitted.

212 MONDAY AFTER EPIPHANY OR JANUARY 7

FIRST READING

1 John 3:22—4:6   Test the spirits to see whether they belong to God.

A reading from the first Letter of Saint John

Beloved:
We receive from him whatever we ask,
  because we keep his commandments and do what pleases him.
And his commandment is this:
  we should believe in the name of his Son, Jesus Christ,
  and love one another just as he commanded us.
Those who keep his commandments remain in him, and he in them,
  and the way we know that he remains in us
  is from the Spirit whom he gave us.

Beloved, do not trust every spirit
  but test the spirits to see whether they belong to God,
  because many false prophets have gone out into the world.
This is how you can know the Spirit of God:
  every spirit that acknowledges Jesus Christ come in the flesh
  belongs to God,
  and every spirit that does not acknowledge Jesus
  does not belong to God.
This is the spirit of the antichrist
  who, as you heard, is to come,
  but in fact is already in the world.
You belong to God, children, and you have conquered them,
  for the one who is in you
  is greater than the one who is in the world.

They belong to the world;
    accordingly, their teaching belongs to the world,
    and the world listens to them.
We belong to God, and anyone who knows God listens to us,
    while anyone who does not belong to God refuses to hear us.
This is how we know the spirit of truth and the spirit of deceit.

The word of the Lord.

RESPONSORIAL PSALM

Psalm 2:7bc-8, 10-12a

℟. (8ab) **I will give you all the nations for an inheritance.**

The Lord said to me, "You are my Son;
    this day I have begotten you.
Ask of me and I will give you
    the nations for an inheritance
    and the ends of the earth for your possession."

℟. **I will give you all the nations for an inheritance.**

And now, O kings, give heed;
    take warning, you rulers of the earth.
Serve the Lord with fear, and rejoice before him;
    with trembling rejoice.

℟. **I will give you all the nations for an inheritance.**

ALLELUIA

See Matthew 4:23

℟. **Alleluia, alleluia.**

Jesus proclaimed the Gospel of the Kingdom
and cured every disease among the people.

℟. **Alleluia, alleluia.**

GOSPEL

Matthew 4:12-17, 23-25   The Kingdom of heaven is at hand.

✠ A reading from the holy Gospel according to Matthew

When Jesus heard that John had been arrested,
  he withdrew to Galilee.
He left Nazareth and went to live in Capernaum by the sea,
    in the region of Zebulun and Naphtali,
    that what had been said through Isaiah the prophet
    might be fulfilled:

Land of Zebulun and land of Naphtali,
  the way to the sea, beyond the Jordan,
  Galilee of the Gentiles,
the people who sit in darkness
  have seen a great light,
on those dwelling in a land overshadowed by death
  light has arisen.

From that time on, Jesus began to preach and say,
  "Repent, for the Kingdom of heaven is at hand."

He went around all of Galilee,
    teaching in their synagogues, proclaiming the Gospel of the Kingdom,
    and curing every disease and illness among the people.
His fame spread to all of Syria,
    and they brought to him all who were sick with various diseases
    and racked with pain,
    those who were possessed, lunatics, and paralytics,
    and he cured them.
And great crowds from Galilee, the Decapolis, Jerusalem, and Judea,
    and from beyond the Jordan followed him.

The Gospel of the Lord.

213 TUESDAY AFTER EPIPHANY OR JANUARY 8

FIRST READING

1 John 4:7-10   God is love.

A reading from the first Letter of Saint John

**Beloved, let us love one another,
 because love is of God;
 everyone who loves is begotten by God and knows God.
Whoever is without love does not know God, for God is love.
In this way the love of God was revealed to us:
 God sent his only-begotten Son into the world
 so that we might have life through him.
In this is love:
 not that we have loved God, but that he loved us
 and sent his Son as expiation for our sins.**

The word of the Lord.

RESPONSORIAL PSALM

Psalm 72:1-2, 3-4, 7-8

℟. (see 11) **Lord, every nation on earth will adore you.**

**O God, with your judgment endow the king,
 and with your justice, the king's son;
He shall govern your people with justice
 and your afflicted ones with judgment.**

℟. **Lord, every nation on earth will adore you.**

**The mountains shall yield peace for the people,
 and the hills justice.
He shall defend the afflicted among the people,
 save the children of the poor.**

℟. **Lord, every nation on earth will adore you.**

**Justice shall flower in his days,
 and profound peace, till the moon be no more.
May he rule from sea to sea,
 and from the River to the ends of the earth.**

℟. **Lord, every nation on earth will adore you.**

ALLELUIA

Luke 4:18

℟. **Alleluia, alleluia.**

The Lord has sent me to bring glad tidings to the poor and to proclaim liberty to captives.

℟. **Alleluia, alleluia.**

GOSPEL

Mark 6:34-44   Multiplying the loaves, Jesus shows himself as a prophet.

☩ A reading from the holy Gospel according to Mark

When Jesus saw the vast crowd, his heart was moved with pity for them,
   for they were like sheep without a shepherd;
   and he began to teach them many things.
By now it was already late and his disciples approached him and said,
   "This is a deserted place and it is already very late.
Dismiss them so that they can go
   to the surrounding farms and villages
   and buy themselves something to eat."
He said to them in reply,
   "Give them some food yourselves."
But they said to him,
   "Are we to buy two hundred days' wages worth of food
   and give it to them to eat?"
He asked them, "How many loaves do you have? Go and see."
And when they had found out they said,
   "Five loaves and two fish."
So he gave orders to have them sit down in groups on the green grass.
The people took their places in rows by hundreds and by fifties.
Then, taking the five loaves and the two fish and looking up to heaven,
he said the blessing, broke the loaves, and gave them to his disciples
   to set before the people;
   he also divided the two fish among them all.
They all ate and were satisfied.
And they picked up twelve wicker baskets full of fragments
   and what was left of the fish.
Those who ate of the loaves were five thousand men.

The Gospel of the Lord.

214 WEDNESDAY AFTER EPIPHANY OR JANUARY 9

FIRST READING

1 John 4:11-18   If we love one another, God remains in us.

A reading from the first Letter of John

Beloved, if God so loved us,
  we also must love one another.
No one has ever seen God.
Yet, if we love one another, God remains in us,
  and his love is brought to perfection in us.

This is how we know that we remain in him and he in us,
  that he has given us of his Spirit.
Moreover, we have seen and testify
  that the Father sent his Son as savior of the world.
Whoever acknowledges that Jesus is the Son of God,
  God remains in him and he in God.
We have come to know and to believe in the love God has for us.

God is love, and whoever remains in love remains in God and God in him.
In this is love brought to perfection among us,
  that we have confidence on the day of judgment
  because as he is, so are we in this world.
There is no fear in love,
  but perfect love drives out fear
  because fear has to do with punishment,
  and so one who fears is not yet perfect in love.

The word of the Lord.

RESPONSORIAL PSALM

Psalm 72:1-2, 10, 12-13

℟. (see 11) **Lord, every nation on earth will adore you.**

**O God, with your judgment endow the king,
  and with your justice, the king's son;
He shall govern your people with justice
  and your afflicted ones with judgment.**

℟. **Lord, every nation on earth will adore you.**

**The kings of Tarshish and the Isles shall offer gifts;
  the kings of Arabia and Seba shall bring tribute.**

℟. **Lord, every nation on earth will adore you.**

**For he shall rescue the poor when he cries out,
  and the afflicted when he has no one to help him.
He shall have pity for the lowly and the poor;
  the lives of the poor he shall save.**

℟. **Lord, every nation on earth will adore you.**

ALLELUIA

See 1 Timothy 3:16

℟. **Alleluia, alleluia.**

**Glory to you, O Christ, proclaimed to the Gentiles.
Glory to you, O Christ, believed in throughout the world.**

℟. **Alleluia, alleluia.**

GOSPEL

Mark 6:45-52   They saw Jesus walking on the sea.

✛ A reading from the holy Gospel according to Mark

After the five thousand had eaten and were satisfied,
    Jesus made his disciples get into the boat
    and precede him to the other side toward Bethsaida,
    while he dismissed the crowd.
And when he had taken leave of them,
    he went off to the mountain to pray.
When it was evening,
    the boat was far out on the sea and he was alone on shore.
Then he saw that they were tossed about while rowing,
    for the wind was against them.
About the fourth watch of the night,
    he came toward them walking on the sea.
He meant to pass by them.
But when they saw him walking on the sea,
    they thought it was a ghost and cried out.
They had all seen him and were terrified.
But at once he spoke with them,
    "Take courage, it is I, do not be afraid!"
He got into the boat with them and the wind died down.
They were completely astounded.
They had not understood the incident of the loaves.
On the contrary, their hearts were hardened.

The Gospel of the Lord.

215 THURSDAY AFTER EPIPHANY OR JANUARY 10

FIRST READING

1 John 4:19–5:4   Those who love God must also love their brother and sister.

A reading from the first Letter of Saint John

Beloved, we love God because
  he first loved us.
If anyone says, "I love God,"
  but hates his brother, he is a liar;
  for whoever does not love a brother whom he has seen
  cannot love God whom he has not seen.
This is the commandment we have from him:
Whoever loves God must also love his brother.

Everyone who believes that Jesus is the Christ is begotten by God,
  and everyone who loves the father
  loves also the one begotten by him.
In this way we know that we love the children of God
  when we love God and obey his commandments.
For the love of God is this,
  that we keep his commandments.
And his commandments are not burdensome,
  for whoever is begotten by God conquers the world.
And the victory that conquers the world is our faith.

The word of the Lord.

RESPONSORIAL PSALM

Psalm 72:1-2, 14 and 15bc, 17

℟. (see 11) **Lord, every nation on earth will adore you.**

**O God, with your judgment endow the king,
  and with your justice, the king's son;
He shall govern your people with justice
  and your afflicted ones with judgment.**

℟. **Lord, every nation on earth will adore you.**

**From fraud and violence he shall redeem them,
  and precious shall their blood be in his sight.
May they be prayed for continually;
  day by day shall they bless him.**

℟. **Lord, every nation on earth will adore you.**

**May his name be blessed forever;
  as long as the sun his name shall remain.
In him shall all the tribes of the earth be blessed;
  all the nations shall proclaim his happiness.**

℟. **Lord, every nation on earth will adore you.**

ALLELUIA

Luke 4:18

℟. **Alleluia, alleluia.**

**The Lord has sent me to bring glad tidings to the poor
and to proclaim liberty to captives.**

℟. **Alleluia, alleluia.**

GOSPEL

Luke 4:14-22   Today this Scripture passage is fulfilled.

✠ **A reading from the holy Gospel according to Luke**

Jesus returned to Galilee in the power of the Spirit,
  and news of him spread throughout the whole region.
He taught in their synagogues and was praised by all.

He came to Nazareth, where he had grown up,
  and went according to his custom
    into the synagogue on the sabbath day.
He stood up to read and was handed a scroll of the prophet Isaiah.
He unrolled the scroll and found the passage where it was written:

The Spirit of the Lord is upon me,
  because he has anointed me
    to bring glad tidings to the poor.
He has sent me to proclaim liberty to captives
  and recovery of sight to the blind,
    to let the oppressed go free,
and to proclaim a year acceptable to the Lord.

Rolling up the scroll, he handed it back to the attendant and sat down,
  and the eyes of all in the synagogue looked intently at him.
He said to them,
  "Today this Scripture passage is fulfilled in your hearing."
And all spoke highly of him
  and were amazed at the gracious words that came from his mouth.

The Gospel of the Lord.

216 FRIDAY AFTER EPIPHANY OR JANUARY 11

FIRST READING

1 John 5:5-13   The Spirit, the water, and the Blood.

A reading from the first Letter of Saint John

Beloved:
Who indeed is the victor over the world
 but the one who believes that Jesus is the Son of God?

This is the one who came through water and Blood, Jesus Christ,
 not by water alone, but by water and Blood.
The Spirit is the one who testifies,
 and the Spirit is truth.
So there are three who testify,
 the Spirit, the water, and the Blood,
 and the three are of one accord.
If we accept human testimony,
 the testimony of God is surely greater.
Now the testimony of God is this,
 that he has testified on behalf of his Son.
Whoever believes in the Son of God
 has this testimony within himself.
Whoever does not believe God has made him a liar
 by not believing the testimony God has given about his Son.
And this is the testimony:
 God gave us eternal life,
 and this life is in his Son.
Whoever possesses the Son has life;
 whoever does not possess the Son of God does not have life.

I write these things to you so that you may know
 that you have eternal life,
 you who believe in the name of the Son of God.

The word of the Lord.

RESPONSORIAL PSALM

Psalm 147:12-13, 14-15, 19-20

℟. (12a) **Praise the Lord, Jerusalem.**
   or:
℟. **Alleluia.**

Glorify the Lord, O Jerusalem;
   praise your God, O Zion.
For he has strengthened the bars of your gates;
   he has blessed your children within you.

℟. **Praise the Lord, Jerusalem.**
   or:
℟. **Alleluia.**

He has granted peace in your borders;
   with the best of wheat he fills you.
He sends forth his command to the earth;
   swiftly runs his word!

℟. **Praise the Lord, Jerusalem.**
   or:
℟. **Alleluia.**

He has proclaimed his word to Jacob,
   his statutes and his ordinances to Israel.
He has not done thus for any other nation;
   his ordinances he has not made known to them. Alleluia.

℟. **Praise the Lord, Jerusalem.**
   or:
℟. **Alleluia.**

ALLELUIA

See Matthew 4:23

℟. Alleluia, alleluia.

**Jesus proclaimed the Gospel of the Kingdom
and cured every disease among the people.**

℟. Alleluia, alleluia.

GOSPEL

Luke 5:12-16   The leprosy left him immediately.

✢ A reading from the holy Gospel according to Luke

**It happened that there was a man full of leprosy in one of the towns
    where Jesus was;
  and when he saw Jesus,
  he fell prostrate, pleaded with him, and said,
  "Lord, if you wish, you can make me clean."
Jesus stretched out his hand, touched him, and said,
  "I do will it. Be made clean."
And the leprosy left him immediately.
Then he ordered him not to tell anyone, but
  "Go, show yourself to the priest and offer for your cleansing
  what Moses prescribed; that will be proof for them."
The report about him spread all the more,
  and great crowds assembled to listen to him
  and to be cured of their ailments,
  but he would withdraw to deserted places to pray.**

The Gospel of the Lord.

217 SATURDAY AFTER EPIPHANY OR JANUARY 12

FIRST READING

1 John 5:14-21   God hears us in regard to whatever we ask.

A reading from the first Letter of Saint John

Beloved:
We have this confidence in him
   that if we ask anything according to his will, he hears us.
And if we know that he hears us in regard to whatever we ask,
   we know that what we have asked him for is ours.
If anyone sees his brother sinning, if the sin is not deadly,
   he should pray to God and he will give him life.
This is only for those whose sin is not deadly.
There is such a thing as deadly sin,
   about which I do not say that you should pray.
All wrongdoing is sin, but there is sin that is not deadly.

We know that anyone begotten by God does not sin;
   but the one begotten by God he protects,
   and the Evil One cannot touch him.
We know that we belong to God,
   and the whole world is under the power of the Evil One.
We also know that the Son of God has come
   and has given us discernment to know the one who is true.
And we are in the one who is true,
   in his Son Jesus Christ.
He is the true God and eternal life.
Children, be on your guard against idols.

The word of the Lord.

RESPONSORIAL PSALM

Psalm 149:1-2, 3-4, 5-6a and 9b

℟. (see 4a) **The Lord takes delight in his people.**
   or:
℟. **Alleluia.**

Sing to the LORD **a new song**
   of praise in the assembly of the faithful.
Let Israel be glad in their maker,
   let the children of Zion rejoice in their king.

℟. **The Lord takes delight in his people.**
   or:
℟. **Alleluia.**

Let them praise his name in the festive dance,
   let them sing praise to him with timbrel and harp.
For the LORD **loves his people,**
   and he adorns the lowly with victory.

℟. **The Lord takes delight in his people.**
   or:
℟. **Alleluia.**

Let the faithful exult in glory;
   let them sing for joy upon their couches;
Let the high praises of God be in their throats.
   This is the glory of all his faithful. Alleluia.

℟. **The Lord takes delight in his people.**
   or:
℟. **Alleluia.**

ALLELUIA

Matthew 4:16

℟. **Alleluia, alleluia.**

The people who sit in darkness have seen a great light,
on those dwelling in a land overshadowed by death
light has arisen.

℟. **Alleluia, alleluia.**

GOSPEL

John 3:22-30   The friend of the bridegroom rejoices at the bridegroom's voice.

✢ A reading from the holy Gospel according to John

**Jesus and his disciples went into the region of Judea,
 where he spent some time with them baptizing.
John was also baptizing in Aenon near Salim,
 because there was an abundance of water there,
 and people came to be baptized,
 for John had not yet been imprisoned.
Now a dispute arose between the disciples of John and a Jew
 about ceremonial washings.
So they came to John and said to him,
 "Rabbi, the one who was with you across the Jordan,
 to whom you testified,
 here he is baptizing and everyone is coming to him."
John answered and said,
 "No one can receive anything except what has been given from heaven.
You yourselves can testify that I said that I am not the Christ,
 but that I was sent before him.
The one who has the bride is the bridegroom;
 the best man, who stands and listens for him,
 rejoices greatly at the bridegroom's voice.
So this joy of mine has been made complete.
He must increase; I must decrease."**

The Gospel of the Lord.

218 ALLELUIA VERSES FOR WEEKDAYS AFTER EPIPHANY

These texts may be used in place of the texts proposed for each day.

1.

Matthew 4:16

**The people who sit in darkness have seen a great light;
on those dwelling in a land overshadowed by death,
light has arisen.**

2.

See Matthew 4:23

**Jesus proclaimed the Gospel of the Kingdom
and cured every disease among the people.**

3.

Luke 4:18

**The Lord sent me to bring glad tidings to the poor,
and to proclaim liberty to captives.**

4.

Luke 7:16

**A great prophet has arisen in our midst
and God has visited his people.**

5.

See 1 Timothy 3:16

**Glory to you, O Christ, proclaimed to the Gentiles.
Glory to you, O Christ, believed in throughout the world.**

SEASON OF LENT

219 ASH WEDNESDAY

If the blessing and distribution of ashes take place outside Mass, it is appropriate that the Liturgy of the Word precede it, using texts assigned to the Mass of Ash Wednesday.

FIRST READING

Joel 2:12-18   Rend your hearts, not your garments.

A reading from the Book of the Prophet Joel

Even now, says the Lord,
   return to me with your whole heart,
   with fasting, and weeping, and mourning;
Rend your hearts, not your garments,
   and return to the Lord, your God.
For gracious and merciful is he,
   slow to anger, rich in kindness,
   and relenting in punishment.
Perhaps he will again relent
   and leave behind him a blessing,
Offerings and libations
   for the Lord, your God.

Blow the trumpet in Zion!
   proclaim a fast,
   call an assembly;
Gather the people,
   notify the congregation;
Assemble the elders,
   gather the children
   and the infants at the breast;
Let the bridegroom quit his room
   and the bride her chamber.
Between the porch and the altar
   let the priests, the ministers of the Lord, weep,
And say, "Spare, O Lord, your people,
   and make not your heritage a reproach,
   with the nations ruling over them!
Why should they say among the peoples,
   'Where is their God?'"

Then the Lord was stirred to concern for his land
   and took pity on his people.

The word of the Lord.

RESPONSORIAL PSALM

Psalm 51:3-4, 5-6ab, 12-13, 14 and 17

℟. (see 3a) **Be merciful, O Lord, for we have sinned.**

Have mercy on me, O God, in your goodness;
   in the greatness of your compassion wipe out my offense.
Thoroughly wash me from my guilt
   and of my sin cleanse me.

℟. **Be merciful, O Lord, for we have sinned.**

For I acknowledge my offense,
   and my sin is before me always:
"Against you only have I sinned,
   and done what is evil in your sight."

℟. **Be merciful, O Lord, for we have sinned.**

A clean heart create for me, O God,
   and a steadfast spirit renew within me.
Cast me not out from your presence,
   and your Holy Spirit take not from me.

℟. **Be merciful, O Lord, for we have sinned.**

Give me back the joy of your salvation,
   and a willing spirit sustain in me.
O Lord, open my lips,
   and my mouth shall proclaim your praise.

℟. **Be merciful, O Lord, for we have sinned.**

SECOND READING

2 Corinthians 5:20—6:2   Be reconciled to God. Behold, now is the acceptable time.

A reading from the second Letter of Saint Paul to the Corinthians

**Brothers and sisters:
We are ambassadors for Christ,
   as if God were appealing through us.
We implore you on behalf of Christ,
   be reconciled to God.
For our sake he made him to be sin who did not know sin,
   so that we might become the righteousness of God in him.**

**Working together, then,
   we appeal to you not to receive the grace of God in vain.
For he says:**

   *In an acceptable time I heard you,
      and on the day of salvation I helped you.*

**Behold, now is a very acceptable time;
   behold, now is the day of salvation.**

The word of the Lord.

VERSE BEFORE THE GOSPEL

See Psalm 95:8

**If today you hear his voice,
harden not your hearts.**

GOSPEL

Matthew 6:1-6, 16-18   Your Father who sees in secret will repay you.

☩ A reading from the holy Gospel according to Matthew

Jesus said to his disciples:
   "Take care not to perform righteous deeds
   in order that people may see them;
   otherwise, you will have no recompense from your heavenly Father.
When you give alms,
   do not blow a trumpet before you,
   as the hypocrites do in the synagogues and in the streets
   to win the praise of others.
Amen, I say to you,
   they have received their reward.
But when you give alms,
   do not let your left hand know what your right is doing,
   so that your almsgiving may be secret.
And your Father who sees in secret will repay you.

"When you pray,
   do not be like the hypocrites,
   who love to stand and pray in the synagogues and on street corners
   so that others may see them.
Amen, I say to you,
   they have received their reward.
But when you pray, go to your inner room,
   close the door, and pray to your Father in secret.
And your Father who sees in secret will repay you.

"When you fast,
   do not look gloomy like the hypocrites.
They neglect their appearance,
   so that they may appear to others to be fasting.
Amen, I say to you, they have received their reward.
But when you fast,
   anoint your head and wash your face,
   so that you may not appear to be fasting,
   except to your Father who is hidden.
And your Father who sees what is hidden will repay you."

The Gospel of the Lord.

220 THURSDAY AFTER ASH WEDNESDAY

FIRST READING

Deuteronomy 30:15-20   Behold, I set before you the blessing and the curse (Deuteronomy 11:26).

A reading from the Book of Deuteronomy

Moses said to the people:
"Today I have set before you
life and prosperity, death and doom.
If you obey the commandments of the LORD, **your God,**
which I enjoin on you today,
loving him, and walking in his ways,
and keeping his commandments, statutes and decrees,
you will live and grow numerous,
and the LORD, your God,
will bless you in the land you are entering to occupy.
If, however, you turn away your hearts and will not listen,
but are led astray and adore and serve other gods,
I tell you now that you will certainly perish;
you will not have a long life
on the land that you are crossing the Jordan to enter and occupy.
I call heaven and earth today to witness against you:
I have set before you life and death,
the blessing and the curse.
Choose life, then,
that you and your descendants may live, by loving the LORD, your God,
heeding his voice, and holding fast to him.
For that will mean life for you,
a long life for you to live on the land that the LORD swore
he would give to your fathers Abraham, Isaac and Jacob."

The word of the Lord.

RESPONSORIAL PSALM

Psalm 1:1-2, 3, 4 and 6

℟. (40:5a) **Blessed are they who hope in the Lord.**

**Blessed the man who follows not
   the counsel of the wicked
Nor walks in the way of sinners,
   nor sits in the company of the insolent,
But delights in the law of the Lord
   and meditates on his law day and night.**

℟. **Blessed are they who hope in the Lord.**

**He is like a tree
   planted near running water,
That yields its fruit in due season,
   and whose leaves never fade.
   Whatever he does, prospers.**

℟. **Blessed are they who hope in the Lord.**

**Not so the wicked, not so;
   they are like chaff which the wind drives away.
For the Lord watches over the way of the just,
   but the way of the wicked vanishes.**

℟. **Blessed are they who hope in the Lord.**

VERSE BEFORE THE GOSPEL

Matthew 4:17

**Repent, says the Lord;
the Kingdom of heaven is at hand.**

GOSPEL

Luke 9:22-25   Whoever loses his life for my sake will save it.

✠ **A reading from the holy Gospel according to Luke**

Jesus said to his disciples:
   "The Son of Man must suffer greatly and be rejected
   by the elders, the chief priests, and the scribes,
   and be killed and on the third day be raised."

Then he said to all,
   "If anyone wishes to come after me, he must deny himself
   and take up his cross daily and follow me.
For whoever wishes to save his life will lose it,
   but whoever loses his life for my sake will save it.
What profit is there for one to gain the whole world
   yet lose or forfeit himself?"

The Gospel of the Lord.

221 FRIDAY AFTER ASH WEDNESDAY

FIRST READING

Isaiah 58:1-9a   Is this the manner of fasting I wish?

A reading from the Book of the Prophet Isaiah

**Thus says the Lord God:
Cry out full-throated and unsparingly,
  lift up your voice like a trumpet blast;
Tell my people their wickedness,
  and the house of Jacob their sins.
They seek me day after day,
  and desire to know my ways,
Like a nation that has done what is just
  and not abandoned the law of their God;
They ask me to declare what is due them,
  pleased to gain access to God.
"Why do we fast, and you do not see it?
  afflict ourselves, and you take no note of it?"**

**Lo, on your fast day you carry out your own pursuits,
  and drive all your laborers.
Yes, your fast ends in quarreling and fighting,
  striking with wicked claw.
Would that today you might fast
  so as to make your voice heard on high!
Is this the manner of fasting I wish,
  of keeping a day of penance:
That a man bow his head like a reed
  and lie in sackcloth and ashes?
Do you call this a fast,
  a day acceptable to the Lord?
This, rather, is the fasting that I wish:
  releasing those bound unjustly,
  untying the thongs of the yoke;
Setting free the oppressed,
  breaking every yoke;
Sharing your bread with the hungry,
  sheltering the oppressed and the homeless;**

Clothing the naked when you see them,
   and not turning your back on your own.
Then your light shall break forth like the dawn,
   and your wound shall quickly be healed;
Your vindication shall go before you,
   and the glory of the LORD shall be your rear guard.
Then you shall call, and the LORD will answer,
   you shall cry for help, and he will say: Here I am!

The word of the Lord.

RESPONSORIAL PSALM

Psalm 51:3-4, 5-6ab, 18-19

R/. (19b) **A heart contrite and humbled, O God, you will not spurn.**

Have mercy on me, O God, in your goodness;
   in the greatness of your compassion wipe out my offense.
Thoroughly wash me from my guilt
   and of my sin cleanse me.

R/. **A heart contrite and humbled, O God, you will not spurn.**

For I acknowledge my offense,
   and my sin is before me always:
"Against you only have I sinned,
   and done what is evil in your sight."

R/. **A heart contrite and humbled, O God, you will not spurn.**

For you are not pleased with sacrifices;
   should I offer a burnt offering, you would not accept it.
My sacrifice, O God, is a contrite spirit;
   a heart contrite and humbled, O God, you will not spurn.

R/. **A heart contrite and humbled, O God, you will not spurn.**

VERSE BEFORE THE GOSPEL

See Amos 5:14

**Seek good and not evil so that you may live,
and the Lord will be with you.**

GOSPEL

Matthew 9:14-15   When the bridegroom is taken from them, then they will fast.

☩ **A reading from the holy Gospel according to Matthew**

**The disciples of John approached Jesus and said,
   "Why do we and the Pharisees fast much,
   but your disciples do not fast?"
Jesus answered them, "Can the wedding guests mourn
   as long as the bridegroom is with them?
The days will come when the bridegroom is taken away from them,
   and then they will fast."**

The Gospel of the Lord.

222 SATURDAY AFTER ASH WEDNESDAY

FIRST READING

Isaiah 58:9b-14   If you bestow your bread on the hungry, then light shall rise for you in the darkness.

A reading from the Book of the Prophet Isaiah

Thus says the Lord:
If you remove from your midst oppression,
    false accusation and malicious speech;
If you bestow your bread on the hungry
    and satisfy the afflicted;
Then light shall rise for you in the darkness,
    and the gloom shall become for you like midday;
Then the Lord will guide you always
    and give you plenty even on the parched land.
He will renew your strength,
    and you shall be like a watered garden,
    like a spring whose water never fails.
The ancient ruins shall be rebuilt for your sake,
    and the foundations from ages past you shall raise up;
"Repairer of the breach," they shall call you,
    "Restorer of ruined homesteads."

If you hold back your foot on the sabbath
    from following your own pursuits on my holy day;
If you call the sabbath a delight,
    and the Lord's holy day honorable;
If you honor it by not following your ways,
    seeking your own interests, or speaking with malice–
Then you shall delight in the Lord,
    and I will make you ride on the heights of the earth;
I will nourish you with the heritage of Jacob, your father,
    for the mouth of the Lord has spoken.

The word of the Lord.

RESPONSORIAL PSALM

Psalm 86:1-2, 3-4, 5-6

℟. (11ab) **Teach me your way, O Lord, that I may walk in your truth.**

**Incline your ear, O Lord; answer me,
    for I am afflicted and poor.
Keep my life, for I am devoted to you;
    save your servant who trusts in you.
    You are my God.**

℟. **Teach me your way, O Lord, that I may walk in your truth.**

**Have mercy on me, O Lord,
    for to you I call all the day.
Gladden the soul of your servant,
    for to you, O Lord, I lift up my soul.**

℟. **Teach me your way, O Lord, that I may walk in your truth.**

**For you, O Lord, are good and forgiving,
    abounding in kindness to all who call upon you.
Hearken, O Lord, to my prayer
    and attend to the sound of my pleading.**

℟. **Teach me your way, O Lord, that I may walk in your truth.**

VERSE BEFORE THE GOSPEL

Ezekiel 33:11

I take no pleasure in the death of the wicked man, says the Lord, but rather in his conversion, that he may live.

GOSPEL

Luke 5:27-32   I have not come to call righteous to repentance but sinners.

☩ A reading from the holy Gospel according to Luke

**Jesus saw a tax collector named Levi sitting at the customs post.
He said to him, "Follow me."
And leaving everything behind, he got up and followed him.
Then Levi gave a great banquet for him in his house,
and a large crowd of tax collectors
and others were at table with them.
The Pharisees and their scribes complained to his disciples, saying,
"Why do you eat and drink with tax collectors and sinners?"
Jesus said to them in reply,
"Those who are healthy do not need a physician, but the sick do.
I have not come to call the righteous to repentance but sinners."**

The Gospel of the Lord.

223 VERSES BEFORE THE GOSPEL FOR WEEKDAYS OF LENT

1.

Psalm 51:12a, 14a

**A clean heart create for me, O God;
give me back the joy of your salvation.**

2.

See Psalm 95:8

**If today you hear his voice,
harden not your hearts.**

3.

Psalm 130:5, 7bc

**I hope in the LORD, I trust in his word;
with him there is kindness and plenteous redemption.**

4.

Ezekiel 18:31

**Cast away from you all the crimes you have committed, says the Lord,
and make for yourselves a new heart and a new spirit.**

5.

Ezekiel 33:11

**I take no pleasure in the death of the wicked man, says the Lord,
but rather in his conversion, that he may live.**

6.

Joel 2:12-13

**Even now, says the LORD,
return to me with your whole heart;
for I am gracious and merciful.**

7.

See Amos 5:14

**Seek good and not evil so that you may live,
and the LORD will be with you.**

8.

Matthew 4:4b

**One does not live on bread alone,
but on every word that comes forth from the mouth of God.**

9.

Matthew 4:17

**Repent, says the Lord;
the Kingdom of heaven is at hand.**

10.

See Luke 8:15

**Blessed are they who have kept the word with a generous heart
and yield a harvest through perseverance.**

11.

Luke 15:18

**I will get up and go to my father and shall say to him:
Father, I have sinned against heaven and against you.**

12.

John 3:16

**God so loved the world that he gave his only-begotten Son,
so that everyone who believes in him might have eternal life.**

13.

See John 6:63c, 68c

**Your words, Lord, are Spirit and life;
you have the words of everlasting life.**

14.

John 8:12

**I am the light of the world, says the Lord;
whoever follows me will have the light of life.**

15.

John 11:25a, 26

**I am the resurrection and the life, says the Lord;
whoever believes in me will never die.**

16.

2 Corinthians 6:2b

**Behold, now is a very acceptable time;
behold, now is the day of salvation.**

17.

**The seed is the word of God, Christ is the sower;
all who come to him will live for ever.**

GOSPEL ACCLAMATIONS FOR LENT

1.

**Glory and praise to you,
Lord Jesus Christ!**

2.

**Glory to you, Lord Jesus Christ,
Wisdom of God the Father!**

3.

Glory to you, Word of God, Lord Jesus Christ!

4.

**Glory to you, Lord Jesus Christ,
Son of the living God!**

5.

Praise and honor to you, Lord Jesus Christ!

6.

**Praise to you, Lord Jesus Christ,
King of endless glory!**

7.

Marvelous and great are your works, O Lord!

8.

Salvation, glory, and power to the Lord Jesus Christ!

224 MONDAY OF THE FIRST WEEK OF LENT

FIRST READING

Leviticus 19:1-2, 11-18   *Judge your fellow man justly.*

A reading from the Book of Leviticus

The Lord said to Moses,
 "Speak to the whole assembly of the children of Israel and tell them:
 Be holy, for I, the Lord, your God, am holy.

"You shall not steal.
You shall not lie or speak falsely to one another.
You shall not swear falsely by my name,
 thus profaning the name of your God.
I am the Lord.

"You shall not defraud or rob your neighbor.
You shall not withhold overnight the wages of your day laborer.
You shall not curse the deaf,
 or put a stumbling block in front of the blind,
 but you shall fear your God.
I am the Lord.

"You shall not act dishonestly in rendering judgment.
Show neither partiality to the weak nor deference to the mighty,
 but judge your fellow men justly.
You shall not go about spreading slander among your kin;
 nor shall you stand by idly when your neighbor's life is at stake.
I am the Lord.

"You shall not bear hatred for your brother in your heart.
Though you may have to reprove him,
 do not incur sin because of him.
Take no revenge and cherish no grudge against your fellow countrymen.
You shall love your neighbor as yourself.
I am the Lord."

The word of the Lord.

RESPONSORIAL PSALM

Psalm 19:8, 9, 10, 15

℟. (John 6:63b) **Your words, Lord, are Spirit and life.**

The law of the LORD **is perfect,
 refreshing the soul.
The decree of the L**ORD **is trustworthy,
 giving wisdom to the simple.**

℟. **Your words, Lord, are Spirit and life.**

The precepts of the LORD **are right,
 rejoicing the heart.
The command of the L**ORD **is clear,
 enlightening the eye.**

℟. **Your words, Lord, are Spirit and life.**

The fear of the LORD **is pure,
 enduring forever;
The ordinances of the L**ORD **are true,
 all of them just.**

℟. **Your words, Lord, are Spirit and life.**

**Let the words of my mouth and the thought of my heart
 find favor before you,
 O L**ORD**, my rock and my redeemer.**

℟. **Your words, Lord, are Spirit and life.**

VERSE BEFORE THE GOSPEL

2 Corinthians 6:2b

**Behold, now is a very acceptable time;
behold, now is the day of salvation.**

GOSPEL

Matthew 25:31-46   Whatever you have done to the very least of my brothers, you have done to me.

✠ A reading from the holy Gospel according to Matthew

Jesus said to his disciples:
   "When the Son of Man comes in his glory,
   and all the angels with him,
   he will sit upon his glorious throne,
   and all the nations will be assembled before him.
And he will separate them one from another,
   as a shepherd separates the sheep from the goats.
He will place the sheep on his right and the goats on his left.
Then the king will say to those on his right,
   'Come, you who are blessed by my Father.
Inherit the kingdom prepared for you from the foundation of the world.
For I was hungry and you gave me food,
   I was thirsty and you gave me drink,
   a stranger and you welcomed me,
   naked and you clothed me,
   ill and you cared for me,
   in prison and you visited me.'
Then the righteous will answer him and say,
   'Lord, when did we see you hungry and feed you,
   or thirsty and give you drink?
When did we see you a stranger and welcome you,
   or naked and clothe you?
When did we see you ill or in prison, and visit you?'
And the king will say to them in reply,
   'Amen, I say to you, whatever you did
   for one of these least brothers of mine, you did for me.'
Then he will say to those on his left,
   'Depart from me, you accursed,
   into the eternal fire prepared for the Devil and his angels.
For I was hungry and you gave me no food,
   I was thirsty and you gave me no drink,
   a stranger and you gave me no welcome,
   naked and you gave me no clothing,
   ill and in prison, and you did not care for me.'

Then they will answer and say,
   'Lord, when did we see you hungry or thirsty
   or a stranger or naked or ill or in prison,
   and not minister to your needs?'
He will answer them, 'Amen, I say to you,
   what you did not do for one of these least ones,
   you did not do for me.'
And these will go off to eternal punishment,
   but the righteous to eternal life."

The Gospel of the Lord.

225 TUESDAY OF THE FIRST WEEK OF LENT

FIRST READING

Isaiah 55:10-11   *My word will do whatever I will.*

A reading from the Book of the Prophet Isaiah

Thus says the Lord:
Just as from the heavens
   the rain and snow come down
And do not return there
   till they have watered the earth,
   making it fertile and fruitful,
Giving seed to the one who sows
   and bread to the one who eats,
So shall my word be
   that goes forth from my mouth;
It shall not return to me void,
   but shall do my will,
   achieving the end for which I sent it.

The word of the Lord.

RESPONSORIAL PSALM

Psalm 34:4-5, 6-7, 16-17, 18-19

℟. (18b) **From all their distress God rescues the just.**

Glorify the LORD **with me,**
   let us together extol his name.
I sought the LORD**, and he answered me**
   and delivered me from all my fears.

℟. **From all their distress God rescues the just.**

Look to him that you may be radiant with joy,
   and your faces may not blush with shame.
When the poor one called out, the LORD **heard,**
   and from all his distress he saved him.

℟. **From all their distress God rescues the just.**

The LORD **has eyes for the just,**
   and ears for their cry.
The LORD **confronts the evildoers,**
   to destroy remembrance of them from the earth.

℟. **From all their distress God rescues the just.**

When the just cry out, the LORD **hears them,**
   and from all their distress he rescues them.
The LORD **is close to the brokenhearted;**
   and those who are crushed in spirit he saves.

℟. **From all their distress God rescues the just.**

VERSE BEFORE THE GOSPEL

Matthew 4:4b

One does not live on bread alone,
but on every word that comes forth from the mouth of God.

GOSPEL

Matthew 6:7-15   This is how you are to pray.

✠ A reading from the holy Gospel according to Matthew

Jesus said to his disciples:
   "In praying, do not babble like the pagans,
   who think that they will be heard because of their many words.
Do not be like them.
Your Father knows what you need before you ask him.

"This is how you are to pray:

   Our Father who art in heaven,
      hallowed be thy name,
      thy Kingdom come,
   thy will be done,
      on earth as it is in heaven.
   Give us this day our daily bread;
   and forgive us our trespasses,
      as we forgive those who trespass against us;
   and lead us not into temptation,
      but deliver us from evil.

"If you forgive men their transgressions,
   your heavenly Father will forgive you.
But if you do not forgive men,
   neither will your Father forgive your transgressions."

The Gospel of the Lord.

226 WEDNESDAY OF THE FIRST WEEK OF LENT

FIRST READING

Jonah 3:1-10   The Ninevites turned from their evil way.

A reading from the Book of the Prophet Jonah

The word of the Lord came to Jonah a second time:
   "Set out for the great city of Nineveh,
   and announce to it the message that I will tell you."
So Jonah made ready and went to Nineveh,
   according to the Lord's bidding.
Now Nineveh was an enormously large city;
   it took three days to go through it.
Jonah began his journey through the city,
   and had gone but a single day's walk announcing,
   "Forty days more and Nineveh shall be destroyed,"
   when the people of Nineveh believed God;
   they proclaimed a fast
   and all of them, great and small, put on sackcloth.

When the news reached the king of Nineveh,
   he rose from his throne, laid aside his robe,
   covered himself with sackcloth, and sat in the ashes.
Then he had this proclaimed throughout Nineveh,
   by decree of the king and his nobles:
   "Neither man nor beast, neither cattle nor sheep,
   shall taste anything;
   they shall not eat, nor shall they drink water.
Man and beast shall be covered with sackcloth and call loudly to God;
   every man shall turn from his evil way
   and from the violence he has in hand.
Who knows, God may relent and forgive, and withhold his blazing wrath,
   so that we shall not perish."
When God saw by their actions how they turned from their evil way,
   he repented of the evil that he had threatened to do to them;
   he did not carry it out.

The word of the Lord.

RESPONSORIAL PSALM

Psalm 51:3-4, 12-13, 18-19

℟. (19b) **A heart contrite and humbled, O God, you will not spurn.**

Have mercy on me, O God, in your goodness;
  in the greatness of your compassion wipe out my offense.
Thoroughly wash me from my guilt
  and of my sin cleanse me.

℟. **A heart contrite and humbled, O God, you will not spurn.**

A clean heart create for me, O God,
  and a steadfast spirit renew within me.
Cast me not out from your presence,
  and your Holy Spirit take not from me.

℟. **A heart contrite and humbled, O God, you will not spurn.**

For you are not pleased with sacrifices;
  should I offer a burnt offering, you would not accept it.
My sacrifice, O God, is a contrite spirit;
  a heart contrite and humbled, O God, you will not spurn.

℟. **A heart contrite and humbled, O God, you will not spurn.**

VERSE BEFORE THE GOSPEL

Joel 2:12-13

Even now, says the LORD**,
return to me with your whole heart
for I am gracious and merciful.**

GOSPEL

Luke 11:29-32   No sign will be given to this generation except the sign of Jonah.

✠ A reading from the holy Gospel according to Luke

While still more people gathered in the crowd, Jesus said to them,
   "This generation is an evil generation;
   it seeks a sign, but no sign will be given it,
   except the sign of Jonah.
Just as Jonah became a sign to the Ninevites,
   so will the Son of Man be to this generation.
At the judgment
   the queen of the south will rise with the men of this generation
   and she will condemn them,
   because she came from the ends of the earth
   to hear the wisdom of Solomon,
   and there is something greater than Solomon here.
At the judgment the men of Nineveh will arise with this generation
   and condemn it,
   because at the preaching of Jonah they repented,
   and there is something greater than Jonah here."

The Gospel of the Lord.

227 THURSDAY OF THE FIRST WEEK OF LENT

FIRST READING

Esther C:12, 14-16, 23-25   I have no protector other than you, Lord.

A reading from the Book of Esther

Queen Esther, seized with mortal anguish,
  had recourse to the LORD.
She lay prostrate upon the ground, together with her handmaids,
  from morning until evening, and said:
    "God of Abraham, God of Isaac, and God of Jacob, blessed are you.
Help me, who am alone and have no help but you,
  for I am taking my life in my hand.
As a child I used to hear from the books of my forefathers
  that you, O LORD, always free those who are pleasing to you.
Now help me, who am alone and have no one but you,
  O LORD, my God.

"And now, come to help me, an orphan.
Put in my mouth persuasive words in the presence of the lion
    and turn his heart to hatred for our enemy,
    so that he and those who are in league with him may perish.
Save us from the hand of our enemies;
  turn our mourning into gladness
  and our sorrows into wholeness."

The word of the Lord.

RESPONSORIAL PSALM

Psalm 138:1-2ab, 2cde-3, 7c-8

℟. (3a) Lord, on the day I called for help, you answered me.

I will give thanks to you, O LORD, with all my heart,
  for you have heard the words of my mouth;
  in the presence of the angels I will sing your praise;
I will worship at your holy temple
  and give thanks to your name.

℟. Lord, on the day I called for help, you answered me.

Because of your kindness and your truth;
   for you have made great above all things
   your name and your promise.
When I called, you answered me;
   you built up strength within me.

℟. Lord, on the day I called for help, you answered me.

Your right hand saves me.
The Lord will complete what he has done for me;
   your kindness, O Lord, endures forever;
   forsake not the work of your hands.

℟. Lord, on the day I called for help, you answered me.

VERSE BEFORE THE GOSPEL

Psalm 51:12a, 14a

A clean heart create for me, O God;
give me back the joy of your salvation.

GOSPEL

Matthew 7:7-12   Everyone who asks, receives.

☩ A reading from the holy Gospel according to Matthew

Jesus said to his disciples:
   "Ask and it will be given to you;
   seek and you will find;
   knock and the door will be opened to you.
For everyone who asks, receives; and the one who seeks, finds;
   and to the one who knocks, the door will be opened.
Which one of you would hand his son a stone
   when he asked for a loaf of bread,
   or a snake when he asked for a fish?
If you then, who are wicked,
   know how to give good gifts to your children,
   how much more will your heavenly Father give good things
   to those who ask him.

"Do to others whatever you would have them do to you.
This is the law and the prophets."

The Gospel of the Lord.

228 FRIDAY OF THE FIRST WEEK OF LENT

FIRST READING

Ezekiel 18:21-28 Do I derive any pleasure from the death of the wicked and not rejoice when he turns from his evil way that he may live?

A reading from the Book of the Prophet Ezekiel

Thus says the Lord God:
If the wicked man turns away from all the sins he committed,
   if he keeps all my statutes and does what is right and just,
   he shall surely live, he shall not die.
None of the crimes he committed shall be remembered against him;
   he shall live because of the virtue he has practiced.
Do I indeed derive any pleasure from the death of the wicked?
   says the Lord God.
Do I not rather rejoice when he turns from his evil way
   that he may live?

And if the virtuous man turns from the path of virtue to do evil,
   the same kind of abominable things that the wicked man does,
   can he do this and still live?
None of his virtuous deeds shall be remembered,
   because he has broken faith and committed sin;
   because of this, he shall die.
You say, "The Lord's way is not fair!"
Hear now, house of Israel:
   Is it my way that is unfair, or rather, are not your ways unfair?
When someone virtuous turns away from virtue to commit iniquity, and dies,
   it is because of the iniquity he committed that he must die.
But if the wicked, turning from the wickedness he has committed,
   does what is right and just,
   he shall preserve his life;
   since he has turned away from all the sins that he committed,
   he shall surely live, he shall not die.

The word of the Lord.

RESPONSORIAL PSALM

Psalm 130:1-2, 3-4, 5-7a, 7bc-8

℟. (3) **If you, O Lord, mark iniquities, who can stand?**

Out of the depths I cry to you, O Lord;
  Lord, hear my voice!
Let your ears be attentive
  to my voice in supplication.

℟. **If you, O Lord, mark iniquities, who can stand?**

If you, O Lord, mark iniquities,
  Lord, who can stand?
But with you is forgiveness,
  that you may be revered.

℟. **If you, O Lord, mark iniquities, who can stand?**

I trust in the Lord;
  my soul trusts in his word.
My soul waits for the Lord
  more than sentinels wait for the dawn.
  Let Israel wait for the Lord.

℟. **If you, O Lord, mark iniquities, who can stand?**

For with the Lord is kindness
  and with him is plenteous redemption;
And he will redeem Israel
  from all their iniquities.

℟. **If you, O Lord, mark iniquities, who can stand?**

VERSE BEFORE THE GOSPEL

Ezekiel 18:31

Cast away from you all the crimes you have committed, says the Lord, and make for yourselves a new heart and a new spirit.

Friday of the First Week of Lent II

GOSPEL

Matthew 5:20-26   Go first and be reconciled with your brother.

✞ **A reading from the holy Gospel according to Matthew**

**Jesus said to his disciples:
"I tell you,
   unless your righteousness surpasses that
   of the scribes and Pharisees,
   you will not enter into the Kingdom of heaven.**

"You have heard that it was said to your ancestors,
   You shall not kill; and whoever kills will be liable to judgment.
**But I say to you, whoever is angry with his brother
   will be liable to judgment,
   and whoever says to his brother,** *Raqa,*
   **will be answerable to the Sanhedrin,
   and whoever says, 'You fool,' will be liable to fiery Gehenna.
Therefore, if you bring your gift to the altar,
   and there recall that your brother
   has anything against you,
   leave your gift there at the altar,
   go first and be reconciled with your brother,
   and then come and offer your gift.
Settle with your opponent quickly while on the way to court.
Otherwise your opponent will hand you over to the judge,
   and the judge will hand you over to the guard,
   and you will be thrown into prison.
Amen, I say to you,
   you will not be released until you have paid the last penny."**

The Gospel of the Lord.

229 SATURDAY OF THE FIRST WEEK OF LENT

FIRST READING

Deuteronomy 26:16-19   You will be a people sacred to the Lord God.

A reading from the Book of Deuteronomy

Moses spoke to the people, saying:
"This day the Lord, your God,
commands you to observe these statutes and decrees.
Be careful, then,
to observe them with all your heart and with all your soul.
Today you are making this agreement with the Lord:
he is to be your God and you are to walk in his ways
and observe his statutes, commandments and decrees,
and to hearken to his voice.
And today the Lord is making this agreement with you:
you are to be a people peculiarly his own, as he promised you;
and provided you keep all his commandments,
he will then raise you high in praise and renown and glory
above all other nations he has made,
and you will be a people sacred to the Lord, your God,
as he promised."

The word of the Lord.

RESPONSORIAL PSALM

Psalm 119:1-2, 4-5, 7-8

℟. (1b) Blessed are they who follow the law of the Lord!

Blessed are they whose way is blameless,
 who walk in the law of the Lord.
Blessed are they who observe his decrees,
 who seek him with all their heart.

℟. Blessed are they who follow the law of the Lord!

You have commanded that your precepts
 be diligently kept.
Oh, that I might be firm in the ways
 of keeping your statutes!

℟. Blessed are they who follow the law of the Lord!

I will give you thanks with an upright heart,
 when I have learned your just ordinances.
I will keep your statutes;
 do not utterly forsake me.

℟. Blessed are they who follow the law of the Lord!

VERSE BEFORE THE GOSPEL

2 Corinthians 6:2b

Behold, now is a very acceptable time;
behold, now is the day of salvation.

GOSPEL

Matthew 5:43-48 Be perfect, just as your heavenly Father is perfect.

✢ **A reading from the holy Gospel according to Matthew**

**Jesus said to his disciples:
  "You have heard that it was said,
    You shall love your neighbor and hate your enemy.
But I say to you, love your enemies,
  and pray for those who persecute you,
  that you may be children of your heavenly Father,
  for he makes his sun rise on the bad and the good,
  and causes rain to fall on the just and the unjust.
For if you love those who love you, what recompense will you have?
Do not the tax collectors do the same?
And if you greet your brothers and sisters only,
  what is unusual about that?
Do not the pagans do the same?
So be perfect, just as your heavenly Father is perfect."**

The Gospel of the Lord.

230 MONDAY OF THE SECOND WEEK OF LENT

FIRST READING

Daniel 9:4b-10   We have sinned, been wicked and done evil.

A reading from the Book of the Prophet Daniel

"Lord, great and awesome God,
   you who keep your merciful covenant toward those who love you
   and observe your commandments!
We have sinned, been wicked and done evil;
   we have rebelled and departed from your commandments and your laws.
We have not obeyed your servants the prophets,
   who spoke in your name to our kings, our princes,
   our fathers, and all the people of the land.
Justice, O Lord, is on your side;
   we are shamefaced even to this day:
   we, the men of Judah, the residents of Jerusalem,
   and all Israel, near and far,
   in all the countries to which you have scattered them
   because of their treachery toward you.
O Lord, we are shamefaced, like our kings, our princes, and our fathers,
   for having sinned against you.
But yours, O Lord, our God, are compassion and forgiveness!
Yet we rebelled against you
   and paid no heed to your command, O Lord, our God,
   to live by the law you gave us through your servants the prophets."

The word of the Lord.

RESPONSORIAL PSALM

Psalm 79:8, 9, 11 and 13

℟. (see 103:10a) **Lord, do not deal with us according to our sins.**

Remember not against us the iniquities of the past;
   may your compassion quickly come to us,
   for we are brought very low.

℟. **Lord, do not deal with us according to our sins.**

Help us, O God our savior,
   because of the glory of your name;
Deliver us and pardon our sins
   for your name's sake.

℟. **Lord, do not deal with us according to our sins.**

Let the prisoners' sighing come before you;
   with your great power free those doomed to death.
Then we, your people and the sheep of your pasture,
   will give thanks to you forever;
      through all generations we will declare your praise.

℟. **Lord, do not deal with us according to our sins.**

VERSE BEFORE THE GOSPEL

See John 6:63c, 68c

Your words, Lord, are Spirit and life;
you have the words of everlasting life.

GOSPEL

Luke 6:36-38   Forgive and you will be forgiven.

✠ A reading from the holy Gospel according to Luke

Jesus said to his disciples:
   "Be merciful, just as your Father is merciful.

"Stop judging and you will not be judged.
Stop condemning and you will not be condemned.
Forgive and you will be forgiven.
Give and gifts will be given to you;
   a good measure, packed together, shaken down, and overflowing,
   will be poured into your lap.
For the measure with which you measure
   will in return be measured out to you."

The Gospel of the Lord.

231 TUESDAY OF THE SECOND WEEK OF LENT

FIRST READING

Isaiah 1:10, 16-20   Learn to do good; make justice your aim.

A reading from the Book of the Prophet Isaiah

**Hear the word of the Lord,
 princes of Sodom!
Listen to the instruction of our God,
 people of Gomorrah!**

**Wash yourselves clean!
Put away your misdeeds from before my eyes;
 cease doing evil; learn to do good.
Make justice your aim: redress the wronged,
 hear the orphan's plea, defend the widow.**

**Come now, let us set things right,
 says the Lord:
Though your sins be like scarlet,
 they may become white as snow;
Though they be crimson red,
 they may become white as wool.
If you are willing, and obey,
 you shall eat the good things of the land;
But if you refuse and resist,
 the sword shall consume you:
 for the mouth of the Lord has spoken!**

The word of the Lord.

RESPONSORIAL PSALM

Psalm 50:8-9, 16bc-17, 21 and 23

℟. (23b) **To the upright I will show the saving power of God.**

"Not for your sacrifices do I rebuke you,
   for your burnt offerings are before me always.
I take from your house no bullock,
   no goats out of your fold."

℟. **To the upright I will show the saving power of God.**

"Why do you recite my statutes,
   and profess my covenant with your mouth,
Though you hate discipline
   and cast my words behind you?"

℟. **To the upright I will show the saving power of God.**

"When you do these things, shall I be deaf to it?
   Or do you think that I am like yourself?
   I will correct you by drawing them up before your eyes.
He that offers praise as a sacrifice glorifies me;
   and to him that goes the right way I will show the salvation of God."

℟. **To the upright I will show the saving power of God.**

VERSE BEFORE THE GOSPEL

Ezekiel 18:31

Cast away from you all the crimes you have committed, says the Lord, and make for yourselves a new heart and a new spirit.

GOSPEL

Matthew 23:1-12   They preach but they do not practice.

✠ A reading from the holy Gospel according to Matthew

Jesus spoke to the crowds and to his disciples, saying,
   "The scribes and the Pharisees
   have taken their seat on the chair of Moses.
Therefore, do and observe all things whatsoever they tell you,
   but do not follow their example.
For they preach but they do not practice.
They tie up heavy burdens hard to carry
   and lay them on people's shoulders,
   but they will not lift a finger to move them.
All their works are performed to be seen.
They widen their phylacteries and lengthen their tassels.
They love places of honor at banquets, seats of honor in synagogues,
   greetings in marketplaces, and the salutation 'Rabbi.'
As for you, do not be called 'Rabbi.'
You have but one teacher, and you are all brothers.
Call no one on earth your father;
   you have but one Father in heaven.
Do not be called 'Master';
   you have but one master, the Christ.
The greatest among you must be your servant.
Whoever exalts himself will be humbled;
   but whoever humbles himself will be exalted."

The Gospel of the Lord.

232 WEDNESDAY OF THE SECOND WEEK OF LENT

FIRST READING

Jeremiah 18:18-20   Come, let us persecute him.

A reading from the Book of the Prophet Jeremiah

The people of Judah and the citizens of Jerusalem said,
 "Come, let us contrive a plot against Jeremiah.
It will not mean the loss of instruction from the priests,
 nor of counsel from the wise, nor of messages from the prophets.
And so, let us destroy him by his own tongue;
 let us carefully note his every word."

Heed me, O Lord,
 and listen to what my adversaries say.
Must good be repaid with evil
 that they should dig a pit to take my life?
Remember that I stood before you
 to speak in their behalf,
 to turn away your wrath from them.

The word of the Lord.

RESPONSORIAL PSALM

Psalm 31:5-6, 14, 15-16

℟. (17b) **Save me, O Lord, in your kindness.**

**You will free me from the snare they set for me,
 for you are my refuge.
Into your hands I commend my spirit;
 you will redeem me, O Lord, O faithful God.**

℟. **Save me, O Lord, in your kindness.**

**I hear the whispers of the crowd,
 that frighten me from every side,
as they consult together against me,
 plotting to take my life.**

℟. **Save me, O Lord, in your kindness.**

**But my trust is in you, O Lord;
 I say, "You are my God."
In your hands is my destiny; rescue me
 from the clutches of my enemies and my persecutors.**

℟. **Save me, O Lord, in your kindness.**

VERSE BEFORE THE GOSPEL

John 8:12

**I am the light of the world, says the Lord;
whoever follows me will have the light of life.**

GOSPEL

Matthew 20:17-28   They will condemn the Son of Man to death.

✝ **A reading from the holy Gospel according to Matthew**

As Jesus was going up to Jerusalem,
  he took the Twelve disciples aside by themselves,
  and said to them on the way,
  "Behold, we are going up to Jerusalem,
  and the Son of Man will be handed over to the chief priests
  and the scribes,
  and they will condemn him to death,
  and hand him over to the Gentiles
  to be mocked and scourged and crucified,
  and he will be raised on the third day."

Then the mother of the sons of Zebedee approached Jesus with her sons
  and did him homage, wishing to ask him for something.
He said to her, "What do you wish?"
She answered him,
  "Command that these two sons of mine sit,
  one at your right and the other at your left, in your kingdom."
Jesus said in reply,
  "You do not know what you are asking.
Can you drink the chalice that I am going to drink?"
They said to him, "We can."
He replied,
  "My chalice you will indeed drink,
  but to sit at my right and at my left,
  this is not mine to give
  but is for those for whom it has been prepared by my Father."
When the ten heard this,
  they became indignant at the two brothers.
But Jesus summoned them and said,
  "You know that the rulers of the Gentiles lord it over them,
  and the great ones make their authority over them felt.
But it shall not be so among you.
Rather, whoever wishes to be great among you shall be your servant;
  whoever wishes to be first among you shall be your slave.
Just so, the Son of Man did not come to be served but to serve
  and to give his life as a ransom for many."

The Gospel of the Lord.

233 THURSDAY OF THE SECOND WEEK OF LENT

FIRST READING

Jeremiah 17:5-10   A curse on those who trust in mortals; a blessing on those who trust in the Lord God.

A reading from the Book of the Prophet Jeremiah

Thus says the Lord:
Cursed is the man who trusts in human beings,
  who seeks his strength in flesh,
  whose heart turns away from the Lord.
He is like a barren bush in the desert
  that enjoys no change of season,
But stands in a lava waste,
  a salt and empty earth.
Blessed is the man who trusts in the Lord,
  whose hope is the Lord.
He is like a tree planted beside the waters
  that stretches out its roots to the stream:
It fears not the heat when it comes,
  its leaves stay green;
In the year of drought it shows no distress,
  but still bears fruit.
More tortuous than all else is the human heart,
  beyond remedy; who can understand it?
I, the Lord, alone probe the mind
  and test the heart,
To reward everyone according to his ways,
  according to the merit of his deeds.

The word of the Lord.

RESPONSORIAL PSALM

Psalm 1:1-2, 3, 4 and 6

℟. (40:5a) **Blessed are they who hope in the Lord.**

**Blessed the man who follows not
   the counsel of the wicked
Nor walks in the way of sinners,
   nor sits in the company of the insolent,
But delights in the law of the Lord
   and meditates on his law day and night.**

℟. **Blessed are they who hope in the Lord.**

**He is like a tree
   planted near running water,
That yields its fruit in due season,
   and whose leaves never fade.
   Whatever he does, prospers.**

℟. **Blessed are they who hope in the Lord.**

**Not so, the wicked, not so;
   they are like chaff which the wind drives away.
For the Lord watches over the way of the just,
   but the way of the wicked vanishes.**

℟. **Blessed are they who hope in the Lord.**

VERSE BEFORE THE GOSPEL

See Luke 8:15

Blessed are they who have kept the word with a generous heart
and yield a harvest through perseverance.

GOSPEL

Luke 16:19-31   Good things came to you and bad things to Lazarus; now he is comforted while you are in agony.

✠   A reading from the holy Gospel according to Luke

Jesus said to the Pharisees:
"There was a rich man who dressed in purple garments and fine linen
    and dined sumptuously each day.
And lying at his door was a poor man named Lazarus, covered with sores,
    who would gladly have eaten his fill of the scraps
    that fell from the rich man's table.
Dogs even used to come and lick his sores.
When the poor man died,
    he was carried away by angels to the bosom of Abraham.
The rich man also died and was buried,
    and from the netherworld, where he was in torment,
    he raised his eyes and saw Abraham far off
    and Lazarus at his side.
And he cried out, 'Father Abraham, have pity on me.
Send Lazarus to dip the tip of his finger in water and cool my tongue,
    for I am suffering torment in these flames.'
Abraham replied, 'My child,
    remember that you received what was good during your lifetime
    while Lazarus likewise received what was bad;
    but now he is comforted here, whereas you are tormented.
Moreover, between us and you a great chasm is established
    to prevent anyone from crossing
    who might wish to go from our side to yours
    or from your side to ours.'
He said, 'Then I beg you, father, send him
    to my father's house,
    for I have five brothers, so that he may warn them,
    lest they too come to this place of torment.'

But Abraham replied, 'They have Moses and the prophets.
Let them listen to them.'
He said, 'Oh no, father Abraham,
   but if someone from the dead goes to them, they will repent.'
Then Abraham said,
   'If they will not listen to Moses and the prophets,
   neither will they be persuaded
   if someone should rise from the dead.'"

The Gospel of the Lord.

234 FRIDAY OF THE SECOND WEEK OF LENT

FIRST READING

Genesis 37:3-4, 12-13a, 17b-28a Here comes the man of dreams; let us kill him.

A reading from the Book of Genesis

Israel loved Joseph best of all his sons,
   for he was the child of his old age;
   and he had made him a long tunic.
When his brothers saw that their father loved him best of all his sons,
   they hated him so much that they would not even greet him.

One day, when his brothers had gone
   to pasture their father's flocks at Shechem,
   Israel said to Joseph,
   "Your brothers, you know, are tending our flocks at Shechem.
Get ready; I will send you to them."

So Joseph went after his brothers and caught up with them in Dothan.
They noticed him from a distance,
   and before he came up to them, they plotted to kill him.
They said to one another: "Here comes that master dreamer!
Come on, let us kill him and throw him into one of the cisterns here;
   we could say that a wild beast devoured him.
We shall then see what comes of his dreams."

When Reuben heard this,
   he tried to save him from their hands, saying,
   "We must not take his life.
Instead of shedding blood," he continued,
   "just throw him into that cistern there in the desert;
   but do not kill him outright."
His purpose was to rescue him from their hands
   and return him to his father.
So when Joseph came up to them,
   they stripped him of the long tunic he had on;
   then they took him and threw him into the cistern,
   which was empty and dry.

They then sat down to their meal.
Looking up, they saw a caravan of Ishmaelites coming from Gilead,
   their camels laden with gum, balm and resin
   to be taken down to Egypt.
Judah said to his brothers:
   "What is to be gained by killing our brother and concealing his blood?
Rather, let us sell him to these Ishmaelites,
   instead of doing away with him ourselves.
After all, he is our brother, our own flesh."
His brothers agreed.
They sold Joseph to the Ishmaelites for twenty pieces of silver.

The word of the Lord.

RESPONSORIAL PSALM

Psalm 105:16-17, 18-19, 20-21

℟. (5a) **Remember the marvels the Lord has done.**

When the LORD called down a famine on the land
   and ruined the crop that sustained them,
He sent a man before them,
   Joseph, sold as a slave.

℟. **Remember the marvels the Lord has done.**

They had weighed him down with fetters,
   and he was bound with chains,
Till his prediction came to pass
   and the word of the LORD proved him true.

℟. **Remember the marvels the Lord has done.**

The king sent and released him,
   the ruler of the peoples set him free.
He made him lord of his house
   and ruler of all his possessions.

℟. **Remember the marvels the Lord has done.**

VERSE BEFORE THE GOSPEL

John 3:16

**God so loved the world that he gave his only-begotten Son;
so that everyone who believes in him might have eternal life.**

GOSPEL

Matthew 21:33-43, 45-46   This is the heir; let us kill him.

✠   A reading from the holy Gospel according to Matthew

**Jesus said to the chief priests and the elders of the people:
"Hear another parable.
There was a landowner who planted a vineyard,
   put a hedge around it,
   dug a wine press in it, and built a tower.
Then he leased it to tenants and went on a journey.
When vintage time drew near,
   he sent his servants to the tenants to obtain his produce.
But the tenants seized the servants and one they beat,
   another they killed, and a third they stoned.
Again he sent other servants, more numerous than the first ones,
   but they treated them in the same way.
Finally, he sent his son to them,
   thinking, 'They will respect my son.'
But when the tenants saw the son, they said to one another,
   'This is the heir.
Come, let us kill him and acquire his inheritance.'
They seized him, threw him out of the vineyard, and killed him.
What will the owner of the vineyard do to those tenants when he comes?"
They answered him,
   "He will put those wretched men to a wretched death
   and lease his vineyard to other tenants
   who will give him the produce at the proper times."
Jesus said to them, "Did you never read in the Scriptures:**

   *The stone that the builders rejected
      has become the cornerstone;
   by the Lord has this been done,
      and it is wonderful in our eyes?*

Therefore, I say to you,
> **the Kingdom of God will be taken away from you**
> **and given to a people that will produce its fruit."**

When the chief priests and the Pharisees heard his parables,
> **they knew that he was speaking about them.**

And although they were attempting to arrest him,
> **they feared the crowds, for they regarded him as a prophet.**

The Gospel of the Lord.

235 SATURDAY OF THE SECOND WEEK OF LENT

FIRST READING

Micah 7:14-15, 18-20   God will cast our sins into the depths of the sea.

A reading from the Book of the Prophet Micah

Shepherd your people with your staff,
   the flock of your inheritance,
That dwells apart in a woodland,
   in the midst of Carmel.
Let them feed in Bashan and Gilead,
   as in the days of old;
As in the days when you came from the land of Egypt,
   show us wonderful signs.

Who is there like you, the God who removes guilt
   and pardons sin for the remnant of his inheritance;
Who does not persist in anger forever,
   but delights rather in clemency,
And will again have compassion on us,
   treading underfoot our guilt?
You will cast into the depths of the sea all our sins;
You will show faithfulness to Jacob,
   and grace to Abraham,
As you have sworn to our fathers
   from days of old.

The word of the Lord.

RESPONSORIAL PSALM

Psalm 103:1-2, 3-4, 9-10, 11-12

℟. (8a) **The Lord is kind and merciful.**

Bless the LORD**, O my soul;**
 and all my being, bless his holy name.
Bless the LORD**, O my soul,**
 and forget not all his benefits.

℟. **The Lord is kind and merciful.**

He pardons all your iniquities,
 he heals all your ills.
He redeems your life from destruction,
 he crowns you with kindness and compassion.

℟. **The Lord is kind and merciful.**

He will not always chide,
 nor does he keep his wrath forever.
Not according to our sins does he deal with us,
 nor does he requite us according to our crimes.

℟. **The Lord is kind and merciful.**

For as the heavens are high above the earth,
 so surpassing is his kindness toward those who fear him.
As far as the east is from the west,
 so far has he put our transgressions from us.

℟. **The Lord is kind and merciful.**

VERSE BEFORE THE GOSPEL

Luke 15:18

I will get up and go to my father and shall say to him,
Father, I have sinned against heaven and against you.

Saturday of the Second Week of Lent II

GOSPEL

Luke 15:1-3, 11-32   Your brother was dead and has come to life.

✠ A reading from the holy Gospel according to Luke

Tax collectors and sinners were all drawing near to listen to Jesus,
  but the Pharisees and scribes began to complain, saying,
  "This man welcomes sinners and eats with them."
So to them Jesus addressed this parable.
"A man had two sons, and the younger son said to his father,
  'Father, give me the share of your estate that should come to me.'
So the father divided the property between them.
After a few days, the younger son collected all his belongings
  and set off to a distant country
  where he squandered his inheritance on a life of **dissipation.**
When he had freely spent everything,
  a severe famine struck that country,
  and he found himself in dire need.
So he hired himself out to one of the local citizens
  who sent him to his farm to tend the swine.
And he longed to eat his fill of the pods on which the **swine fed,**
  but nobody gave him any.
Coming to his senses he thought,
  'How many of my father's hired workers
  have more than enough food to eat,
  but here am I, dying from hunger.
I shall get up and go to my father and I shall say to him,
  "Father, I have sinned against heaven and **against you.**
I no longer deserve to be called your son;
  treat me as you would treat one of your hired workers."'
So he got up and went back to his father.
While he was still a long way off,
  his father caught sight of him, and was filled with **compassion.**
He ran to his son, embraced him and kissed him.
His son said to him,
  'Father, I have sinned against heaven and against you;
  I no longer deserve to be called your son.'
But his father ordered his servants,
  'Quickly, bring the finest robe and put it on him;
  put a ring on his finger and sandals on his feet.
Take the fattened calf and slaughter it.

Then let us celebrate with a feast,
> because this son of mine was dead, and has come to life again;
> he was lost, and has been found.'

Then the celebration began.
Now the older son had been out in the field
> and, on his way back, as he neared the house,
> he heard the sound of music and dancing.

He called one of the servants and asked what this might mean.
The servant said to him,
> 'Your brother has returned
> and your father has slaughtered the fattened calf
> because he has him back safe and sound.'

He became angry,
> and when he refused to enter the house,
> his father came out and pleaded with him.

He said to his father in reply,
> 'Look, all these years I served you
> and not once did I disobey your orders;
> yet you never gave me even a young goat to feast on with my friends.

But when your son returns
> who swallowed up your property with prostitutes,
> for him you slaughter the fattened calf.'

He said to him,
> 'My son, you are here with me always;
> everything I have is yours.

But now we must celebrate and rejoice,
> because your brother was dead and has come to life again;
> he was lost and has been found.'"

The Gospel of the Lord.

236 OPTIONAL MASS OF THE THIRD WEEK OF LENT

This Mass may be used on any day of this week, especially in Years B and C when the Gospel of the Samaritan woman is not read on the Third Sunday of Lent.

FIRST READING

Exodus 17:1-7   The Lord showed Moses water, that the people might drink.

A reading from the Book of Exodus

**From the desert of Sin the whole congregation of the children of Israel
 journeyed by stages, as the Lord directed,
 and encamped at Rephidim.**

**There was no water for the people to drink.
They quarreled, therefore, with Moses and said,
 "Give us water to drink."
Moses replied, "Why do you quarrel with me?
Why do you put the Lord to a test?"
Then, in their thirst for water,
 the people grumbled against Moses,
  saying, "Why did you ever make us leave Egypt?
Was it just to have us die here of thirst
 with our children and our livestock?"
So Moses cried out to the Lord,
 "What shall I do with this people?
A little more and they will stone me!"
The Lord answered Moses,
 "Go over there in front of the people,
 along with some of the elders of Israel,
 holding in your hand, as you go,
 the staff with which you struck the river.
I will be standing there in front of you on the rock in Horeb.
Strike the rock, and the water will flow from it
 for the people to drink."
This Moses did, in the presence of the elders of Israel.**

The place was called Massah and Meribah,
   because the children of Israel quarreled there
   and tested the LORD, saying,
   "Is the LORD in our midst or not?"

The word of the Lord.

RESPONSORIAL PSALM

Psalm 95:1-2, 6-7ab, 7c-9

℟. (8) **If today you hear his voice, harden not your hearts.**

Come, let us sing joyfully to the LORD;
   let us acclaim the Rock of our salvation.
Let us come into his presence with thanksgiving;
   let us joyfully sing psalms to him.

℟. **If today you hear his voice, harden not your hearts.**

Come, let us bow down in worship;
   let us kneel before the LORD who made us.
For he is our God,
   and we are the people he shepherds, the flock he guides.

℟. **If today you hear his voice, harden not your hearts.**

Oh, that today you would hear his voice:
   "Harden not your hearts as at Meribah,
   as in the day of Massah in the desert,
Where your fathers tempted me;
   they tested me though they had seen my works."

℟. **If today you hear his voice, harden not your hearts.**

VERSE BEFORE THE GOSPEL

See John 4:42, 15

**Lord, you are truly the Savior of the world;
give me living water, that I may never thirst again.**

GOSPEL

John 4:5-42   The water that I shall give will become a spring of eternal life.

✢   A reading from the holy Gospel according to John

At that time,
Jesus came to a town of Samaria called Sychar,
  near the plot of land that Jacob had given to his son Joseph.
Jacob's well was there.
Jesus, tired from his journey, sat down there at the well.
It was about noon.

A woman of Samaria came to draw water.
Jesus said to her,
  "Give me a drink."
His disciples had gone into the town to buy food.
The Samaritan woman said to him,
  "How can you, a Jew, ask me, a Samaritan woman, for a drink?"
—For Jews use nothing in common with Samaritans.—
Jesus answered and said to her,
  "If you knew the gift of God
  and who is saying to you, 'Give me a drink,'
  you would have asked him
  and he would have given you living water."
The woman said to him,
  "Sir, you do not even have a bucket and the cistern is deep;
  where then can you get this living water?
Are you greater than our father Jacob,
  who gave us this cistern and drank from it himself
  with his children and his flocks?"
Jesus answered and said to her,
  "Everyone who drinks this water will be thirsty again;
  but whoever drinks the water I shall give will never thirst;
  the water I shall give will become in him
  a spring of water welling up to eternal life."
The woman said to him,
  "Sir, give me this water, so that I may not be thirsty
  or have to keep coming here to draw water."

Jesus said to her,
  "Go call your husband and come back."

The woman answered and said to him,
  "I do not have a husband."
Jesus answered her,
  "You are right in saying, 'I do not have a husband.'
For you have had five husbands,
  and the one you have now is not your husband.
What you have said is true."
The woman said to him,
  "Sir, I can see that you are a prophet.
Our ancestors worshiped on this mountain;
  but you people say that the place to worship is in Jerusalem."
Jesus said to her,
  "Believe me, woman, the hour is coming
  when you will worship the Father
  neither on this mountain nor in Jerusalem.
You people worship what you do not understand;
  we worship what we understand,
  because salvation is from the Jews.
But the hour is coming, and is now here,
  when true worshipers will worship the Father in Spirit and truth;
  and indeed the Father seeks such people to worship him.
God is Spirit, and those who worship him
  must worship in Spirit and truth."
The woman said to him,
  "I know that the Christ is coming, the one called the Anointed;
  when he comes, he will tell us everything."
Jesus said to her,
  "I am he, the one speaking with you."

At that moment his disciples returned,
  and were amazed that he was talking with a woman,
  but still no one said, "What are you looking for?"
  or "Why are you talking with her?"
The woman left her water jar
  and went into the town and said to the people,
  "Come see a man who told me everything I have done.
Could he possibly be the Christ?"
They went out of the town and came to him.
Meanwhile, the disciples urged him, "Rabbi, eat."
But he said to them,
  "I have food to eat of which you do not know."

So the disciples said to one another,
   "Could someone have brought him something to eat?"
Jesus said to them,
   "My food is to do the will of the one who sent me
   and to finish his work.
Do you not say, 'In four months the harvest will be here'?
I tell you, look up and see the fields ripe for the harvest.
The reaper is already receiving payment
   and gathering crops for eternal life,
   so that the sower and reaper can rejoice together.
For here the saying is verified that 'One sows and another reaps.'
I sent you to reap what you have not worked for;
   others have done the work,
   and you are sharing the fruits of their work."

Many of the Samaritans of that town began to believe in him
   because of the word of the woman who testified,
   "He told me everything I have done."
When the Samaritans came to him,
   they invited him to stay with them;
   and he stayed there two days.
Many more began to believe in him because of his word,
   and they said to the woman,
   "We no longer believe because of your word;
   for we have heard for ourselves,
   and we know that this is truly the savior of the world."

The Gospel of the Lord.

237 MONDAY OF THE THIRD WEEK OF LENT

FIRST READING

2 Kings 5:1-15ab   There were many people with leprosy in Israel, but none were made clean, except Naaman the Syrian (Luke 4:27).

A reading from the second Book of Kings

Naaman, the army commander of the king of Aram,
   was highly esteemed and respected by his master,
   for through him the Lord had brought victory to Aram.
But valiant as he was, the man was a leper.
Now the Arameans had captured in a raid on the land of Israel
   a little girl, who became the servant of Naaman's wife.
"If only my master would present himself to the prophet in Samaria,"
   she said to her mistress, "he would cure him of his leprosy."
Naaman went and told his lord
   just what the slave girl from the land of Israel had said.
"Go," said the king of Aram.
"I will send along a letter to the king of Israel."
So Naaman set out, taking along ten silver talents,
   six thousand gold pieces, and ten festal garments.
To the king of Israel he brought the letter, which read:
   "With this letter I am sending my servant Naaman to you,
   that you may cure him of his leprosy."

When he read the letter,
   the king of Israel tore his garments and exclaimed:
   "Am I a god with power over life and death,
   that this man should send someone to me to be cured of leprosy?
Take note! You can see he is only looking for a quarrel with me!"
When Elisha, the man of God,
   heard that the king of Israel had torn his garments,
   he sent word to the king:
   "Why have you torn your garments?
Let him come to me and find out
   that there is a prophet in Israel."

Naaman came with his horses and chariots
   and stopped at the door of Elisha's house.

The prophet sent him the message:
   "Go and wash seven times in the Jordan,
   and your flesh will heal, and you will be clean."
But Naaman went away angry, saying,
   "I thought that he would surely come out and stand there
   to invoke the LORD his God,
   and would move his hand over the spot,
   and thus cure the leprosy.
Are not the rivers of Damascus, the Abana and the Pharpar,
   better than all the waters of Israel?
Could I not wash in them and be cleansed?"
With this, he turned about in anger and left.

But his servants came up and reasoned with him.
"My father," they said,
   "if the prophet had told you to do something extraordinary,
   would you not have done it?
All the more now, since he said to you,
   'Wash and be clean,' should you do as he said."
So Naaman went down and plunged into the Jordan seven times
   at the word of the man of God.
His flesh became again like the flesh of a little child, and he was clean.

He returned with his whole retinue to the man of God.
On his arrival he stood before him and said,
   "Now I know that there is no God in all the earth,
   except in Israel."

The word of the Lord.

RESPONSORIAL PSALM

Psalm 42:2, 3; 43:3, 4

℟. (see 42:3) **Athirst is my soul for the living God.
When shall I go and behold the face of God?**

**As the hind longs for the running waters,
 so my soul longs for you, O God.**

℟. **Athirst is my soul for the living God.
When shall I go and behold the face of God?**

**Athirst is my soul for God, the living God.
 When shall I go and behold the face of God?**

℟. **Athirst is my soul for the living God.
When shall I go and behold the face of God?**

**Send forth your light and your fidelity;
 they shall lead me on
And bring me to your holy mountain,
 to your dwelling-place.**

℟. **Athirst is my soul for the living God.
When shall I go and behold the face of God?**

**Then will I go in to the altar of God,
 the God of my gladness and joy;
Then will I give you thanks upon the harp,
 O God, my God!**

℟. **Athirst is my soul for the living God.
When shall I go and behold the face of God?**

VERSE BEFORE THE GOSPEL

See Psalm 130:5, 7

I hope in the L*ord***, I trust in his word;
with him there is kindness and plenteous redemption.**

GOSPEL

Luke 4:24-30   Like Elijah and Elisha, Jesus was sent not only to the Jews.

✠ **A reading from the holy Gospel according to Luke**

**Jesus said to the people in the synagogue at Nazareth:
"Amen, I say to you,
   no prophet is accepted in his own native place.
Indeed, I tell you, there were many widows in Israel
   in the days of Elijah
   when the sky was closed for three and a half years
   and a severe famine spread over the entire land.
It was to none of these that Elijah was sent,
   but only to a widow in Zarephath in the land of Sidon.
Again, there were many lepers in Israel
   during the time of Elisha the prophet;
   yet not one of them was cleansed, but only Naaman the Syrian."
When the people in the synagogue heard this,
   they were all filled with fury.
They rose up, drove him out of the town,
   and led him to the brow of the hill
   on which their town had been built,
   to hurl him down headlong.
But he passed through the midst of them and went away.**

The Gospel of the Lord.

238 TUESDAY OF THE THIRD WEEK OF LENT

FIRST READING

Daniel 3:25, 34-43   We ask you to receive us with humble and contrite hearts.

A reading from the Book of the Prophet Daniel

Azariah stood up in the fire and prayed aloud:

"For your name's sake, O Lord, do not deliver us up forever,
>   or make void your covenant.
Do not take away your mercy from us,
>   for the sake of Abraham, your beloved,
>   Isaac your servant, and Israel your holy one,
To whom you promised to multiply their offspring
>   like the stars of heaven,
>   or the sand on the shore of the sea.
For we are reduced, O Lord, beyond any other nation,
>   brought low everywhere in the world this day
>   because of our sins.
We have in our day no prince, prophet, or leader,
>   no burnt offering, sacrifice, oblation, or incense,
>   no place to offer first fruits, to find favor with you.
But with contrite heart and humble spirit
>   let us be received;
As though it were burnt offerings of rams and bullocks,
>   or thousands of fat lambs,
So let our sacrifice be in your presence today
>   as we follow you unreservedly;
>   for those who trust in you cannot be put to shame.
And now we follow you with our whole heart,
>   we fear you and we pray to you.
Do not let us be put to shame,
>   but deal with us in your kindness and great mercy.
Deliver us by your wonders,
>   and bring glory to your name, O Lord."

The word of the Lord.

RESPONSORIAL PSALM

Psalm 25:4-5ab, 6 and 7bc, 8-9

℟. (6a) **Remember your mercies, O Lord.**

**Your ways, O Lord, make known to me;
 teach me your paths,
Guide me in your truth and teach me,
 for you are God my savior.**

℟. **Remember your mercies, O Lord.**

**Remember that your compassion, O Lord,
 and your kindness are from of old.
In your kindness remember me,
 because of your goodness, O Lord.**

℟. **Remember your mercies, O Lord.**

**Good and upright is the Lord;
 thus he shows sinners the way.
He guides the humble to justice,
 he teaches the humble his way.**

℟. **Remember your mercies, O Lord.**

VERSE BEFORE THE GOSPEL

Joel 2:12-13

Even now, says the Lord,
return to me with your whole heart;
for I am gracious and merciful.

GOSPEL

Matthew 18:21-35   Unless each of you forgives your brother and sister, the Father will not forgive you.

✠ A reading from the holy Gospel according to Matthew

Peter approached Jesus and asked him,
    "Lord, if my brother sins against me,
    how often must I forgive him?
As many as seven times?"
Jesus answered, "I say to you, not seven times but seventy-seven times.
That is why the Kingdom of heaven may be likened to a king
    who decided to settle accounts with his servants.
When he began the accounting,
    a debtor was brought before him who owed him a huge amount.
Since he had no way of paying it back,
    his master ordered him to be sold,
    along with his wife, his children, and all his property,
    in payment of the debt.
At that, the servant fell down, did him homage, and said,
    'Be patient with me, and I will pay you back in full.'
Moved with compassion the master of that servant
    let him go and forgave him the loan.
When that servant had left, he found one of his fellow servants
    who owed him a much smaller amount.
He seized him and started to choke him, demanding,
    'Pay back what you owe.'
Falling to his knees, his fellow servant begged him,
    'Be patient with me, and I will pay you back.'
But he refused.
Instead, he had him put in prison
    until he paid back the debt.

Now when his fellow servants saw what had happened,
> they were deeply disturbed, and went to their master
> and reported the whole affair.
His master summoned him and said to him, 'You wicked servant!
I forgave you your entire debt because you begged me to.
Should you not have had pity on your fellow servant,
> as I had pity on you?'
Then in anger his master handed him over to the torturers
> until he should pay back the whole debt.
So will my heavenly Father do to you,
> unless each of you forgives your brother from your heart."

The Gospel of the Lord.

239 WEDNESDAY OF THE THIRD WEEK OF LENT

FIRST READING

Deuteronomy 4:1, 5-9   Keep the commandments and your work will be complete.

A reading from the Book of Deuteronomy

Moses spoke to the people and said:
"Now, Israel, hear the statutes and decrees
   which I am teaching you to observe,
     that you may live, and may enter in and take possession of the land
   which the LORD, the God of your fathers, is giving you.
Therefore, I teach you the statutes and decrees
   as the LORD, my God, has commanded me,
     that you may observe them in the land you are entering to occupy.
Observe them carefully,
   for thus will you give evidence
     of your wisdom and intelligence to the nations,
   who will hear of all these statutes and say,
     'This great nation is truly a wise and intelligent people.'
For what great nation is there
   that has gods so close to it as the LORD, our God, is to us
     whenever we call upon him?
Or what great nation has statutes and decrees
   that are as just as this whole law
     which I am setting before you today?

"However, take care and be earnestly on your guard
   not to forget the things which your own eyes have seen,
     nor let them slip from your memory as long as you live,
     but teach them to your children and to your children's children."

The word of the Lord.

RESPONSORIAL PSALM

Psalm 147:12-13, 15-16, 19-20

℟. (12a) **Praise the Lord, Jerusalem.**

**Glorify the LORD, O Jerusalem;
    praise your God, O Zion.
For he has strengthened the bars of your gates;
    he has blessed your children within you.**

℟. **Praise the Lord, Jerusalem.**

**He sends forth his command to the earth;
    swiftly runs his word!
He spreads snow like wool;
    frost he strews like ashes.**

℟. **Praise the Lord, Jerusalem.**

**He has proclaimed his word to Jacob,
    his statutes and his ordinances to Israel.
He has not done thus for any other nation;
    his ordinances he has not made known to them.**

℟. **Praise the Lord, Jerusalem.**

VERSE BEFORE THE GOSPEL

See John 6:63c, 68c

**Your words, Lord, are Spirit and life;
you have the words of everlasting life.**

GOSPEL

Matthew 5:17-19   Whoever keeps and teaches the law will be called great.

✝ **A reading from the holy Gospel according to Matthew**

Jesus said to his disciples:
"Do not think that I have come to abolish the law or the prophets.
I have come not to abolish but to fulfill.
Amen, I say to you, until heaven and earth pass away,
  not the smallest letter or the smallest part of a letter
  will pass from the law,
  until all things have taken place.
Therefore, whoever breaks one of the least of these commandments
  and teaches others to do so
  will be called least in the Kingdom of heaven.
But whoever obeys and teaches these commandments
  will be called greatest in the Kingdom of heaven."

The Gospel of the Lord.

240 THURSDAY OF THE THIRD WEEK OF LENT

FIRST READING

Jeremiah 7:23-28   This is the nation that will not listen to the voice of the Lord God.

A reading from the Book of the Prophet Jeremiah

Thus says the Lord:
>This is what I commanded my people:
>>Listen to my voice;
>>then I will be your God and you shall be my people.
>
>Walk in all the ways that I command you,
>>so that you may prosper.

But they obeyed not, nor did they pay heed.
They walked in the hardness of their evil hearts
>and turned their backs, not their faces, to me.

From the day that your fathers left the land of Egypt even to this day,
>I have sent you untiringly all my servants the prophets.

Yet they have not obeyed me nor paid heed;
>they have stiffened their necks and done worse than their fathers.

When you speak all these words to them,
>they will not listen to you either;
>when you call to them, they will not answer you.

Say to them:
>This is the nation that does not listen
>to the voice of the Lord, its God,
>or take correction.

Faithfulness has disappeared;
>the word itself is banished from their speech.

The word of the Lord.

RESPONSORIAL PSALM

Psalm 95:1-2, 6-7, 8-9

℟. (8) **If today you hear his voice, harden not your hearts.**

Come, let us sing joyfully to the LORD**;**
   let us acclaim the Rock of our salvation.
Let us come into his presence with thanksgiving;
   let us joyfully sing psalms to him.

℟. **If today you hear his voice, harden not your hearts.**

Come, let us bow down in worship;
   let us kneel before the LORD **who made us.**
For he is our God,
   and we are the people he shepherds, the flock he guides.

℟. **If today you hear his voice, harden not your hearts.**

Oh, that today you would hear his voice:
   "Harden not your hearts as at Meribah,
   as in the day of Massah in the desert,
Where your fathers tempted me;
   they tested me though they had seen my works."

℟. **If today you hear his voice, harden not your hearts.**

VERSE BEFORE THE GOSPEL

Joel 2:12-13

Even now, says the LORD**,**
return to me with your whole heart,
for I am gracious and merciful.

GOSPEL

Luke 11:14-23   Whoever is not with me is against me.

✝ A reading from the holy Gospel according to Luke

Jesus was driving out a demon that was mute,
  and when the demon had gone out,
  the mute man spoke and the crowds were amazed.
Some of them said, "By the power of Beelzebul, the prince of demons,
  he drives out demons."
Others, to test him, asked him for a sign from heaven.
But he knew their thoughts and said to them,
  "Every kingdom divided against itself will be laid waste
  and house will fall against house.
And if Satan is divided against himself,
  how will his kingdom stand?
For you say that it is by Beelzebul that I drive out demons.
If I, then, drive out demons by Beelzebul,
  by whom do your own people drive them out?
Therefore they will be your judges.
But if it is by the finger of God that I drive out demons,
  then the Kingdom of God has come upon you.
When a strong man fully armed guards his palace,
  his possessions are safe.
But when one stronger than he attacks and overcomes him,
  he takes away the armor on which he relied
  and distributes the spoils.
Whoever is not with me is against me,
  and whoever does not gather with me scatters."

The Gospel of the Lord.

241 FRIDAY OF THE THIRD WEEK OF LENT

FIRST READING

Hosea 14:2-10   We will not say to the work of our hands: our god.

A reading from the Book of the Prophet Hosea

>Thus says the Lord:
Return, O Israel, to the Lord, your God;
>   you have collapsed through your guilt.
Take with you words,
>   and return to the Lord;
Say to him, "Forgive all iniquity,
>   and receive what is good, that we may render
>   as offerings the bullocks from our stalls.
Assyria will not save us,
>   nor shall we have horses to mount;
We shall say no more, 'Our god,'
>   to the work of our hands;
>   for in you the orphan finds compassion."

I will heal their defection, says the Lord,
>   I will love them freely;
>   for my wrath is turned away from them.
I will be like the dew for Israel:
>   he shall blossom like the lily;
He shall strike root like the Lebanon cedar,
>   and put forth his shoots.
His splendor shall be like the olive tree
>   and his fragrance like the Lebanon cedar.
Again they shall dwell in his shade
>   and raise grain;
They shall blossom like the vine,
>   and his fame shall be like the wine of Lebanon.

Ephraim! What more has he to do with idols?
>   I have humbled him, but I will prosper him.
"I am like a verdant cypress tree"—
>   Because of me you bear fruit!

Let him who is wise understand these things;
>   let him who is prudent know them.

Straight are the paths of the LORD**,**
   in them the just walk,
      but sinners stumble in them.

The word of the Lord.

RESPONSORIAL PSALM

Psalm 81:6c-8a, 8bc-9, 10-11ab, 14 and 17

℟. (see 11 and 9a) **I am the Lord your God: hear my voice.**

An unfamiliar speech I hear:
   "I relieved his shoulder of the burden;
   his hands were freed from the basket.
In distress you called, and I rescued you."

℟. **I am the Lord your God: hear my voice.**

"Unseen, I answered you in thunder;
   I tested you at the waters of Meribah.
Hear, my people, and I will admonish you;
   O Israel, will you not hear me?"

℟. **I am the Lord your God: hear my voice.**

"There shall be no strange god among you
   nor shall you worship any alien god.
I, the LORD**, am your God**
   who led you forth from the land of Egypt."

℟. **I am the Lord your God: hear my voice.**

"If only my people would hear me,
   and Israel walk in my ways,
I would feed them with the best of wheat,
   and with honey from the rock I would fill them."

℟. **I am the Lord your God: hear my voice.**

VERSE BEFORE THE GOSPEL

Matthew 4:17

**Repent, says the Lord;
the Kingdom of heaven is at hand.**

GOSPEL

Mark 12:28-34   The Lord our God is one Lord, and you shall love the Lord your God.

✠ **A reading from the holy Gospel according to Mark**

**One of the scribes came to Jesus and asked him,
   "Which is the first of all the commandments?"
Jesus replied, "The first is this:**
   Hear, O Israel!
   The Lord our God is Lord alone!
You shall love the Lord your God with all your heart,
   with all your soul,
   with all your mind,
   and with all your strength.
The second is this:
   You shall love your neighbor as yourself.
**There is no other commandment greater than these."
The scribe said to him, "Well said, teacher.
You are right in saying,**
   He is One and there is no other than he.
And *to love him with all your heart,*
   with all your understanding,
   with all your strength,
   and to love your neighbor as yourself
   **is worth more than all burnt offerings and sacrifices."
And when Jesus saw that he answered with understanding,
   he said to him,
   "You are not far from the Kingdom of God."
And no one dared to ask him any more questions.**

The Gospel of the Lord.

242 SATURDAY OF THE THIRD WEEK OF LENT

FIRST READING

Hosea 6:1-6   What I want is love, not sacrifice.

A reading from the Book of the Prophet Hosea

"Come, let us return to the Lord,
   it is he who has rent, but he will heal us;
   he has struck us, but he will bind our wounds.
He will revive us after two days;
   on the third day he will raise us up,
   to live in his presence.
Let us know, let us strive to know the Lord;
   as certain as the dawn is his coming,
   and his judgment shines forth like the light of day!
He will come to us like the rain,
   like spring rain that waters the earth."

What can I do with you, Ephraim?
What can I do with you, Judah?
Your piety is like a morning cloud,
   like the dew that early passes away.
For this reason I smote them through the prophets,
   I slew them by the words of my mouth;
For it is love that I desire, not sacrifice,
   and knowledge of God rather than burnt offerings.

The word of the Lord.

RESPONSORIAL PSALM

Psalm 51:3-4, 18-19, 20-21ab

℟. (see Hosea 6:6) **It is mercy I desire, and not sacrifice.**

**Have mercy on me, O God, in your goodness;
   in the greatness of your compassion wipe out my offense.
Thoroughly wash me from my guilt
   and of my sin cleanse me.**

℟. **It is mercy I desire, and not sacrifice.**

**For you are not pleased with sacrifices;
   should I offer a burnt offering, you would not accept it.
My sacrifice, O God, is a contrite spirit;
   a heart contrite and humbled, O God, you will not spurn.**

℟. **It is mercy I desire, and not sacrifice.**

**Be bountiful, O Lord, to Zion in your kindness
   by rebuilding the walls of Jerusalem;
Then shall you be pleased with due sacrifices,
   burnt offerings and holocausts.**

℟. **It is mercy I desire, and not sacrifice.**

VERSE BEFORE THE GOSPEL

Psalm 95:8

**If today you hear his voice,
harden not your hearts.**

GOSPEL

Luke 18:9-14   The tax collector went home justified, not the Pharisee.

✠ **A reading from the holy Gospel according to Luke**

Jesus addressed this parable
   to those who were convinced of their own righteousness
   and despised everyone else.
"Two people went up to the temple area to pray;
   one was a Pharisee and the other was a tax collector.
The Pharisee took up his position and spoke this prayer to himself,
   'O God, I thank you that I am not like the rest of humanity—
   greedy, dishonest, adulterous—or even like this tax collector.
I fast twice a week,
   and I pay tithes on my whole income.'
But the tax collector stood off at a distance
   and would not even raise his eyes to heaven
   but beat his breast and prayed,
   'O God, be merciful to me a sinner.'
I tell you, the latter went home justified, not the former;
   for everyone who exalts himself will be humbled,
   and the one who humbles himself will be exalted."

The Gospel of the Lord.

243 OPTIONAL MASS OF THE FOURTH WEEK OF LENT

This Mass may be used on any day of this week, especially in years B and C when the Gospel of the man born blind is not read on the Fourth Sunday of Lent.

FIRST READING

Micah 7:7-9   I will arise; though I sit in darkness, the LORD is my light.

A reading from the Book of the Prophet Micah

I will look to the LORD,
   I will put my trust in God my savior;
   my God will hear me!

Rejoice not over me, O my enemy!
   though I have fallen, I will arise;
   though I sit in darkness, the LORD is my light.
The wrath of the LORD I will endure
   because I have sinned against him,
Until he takes up my cause,
   and establishes my right.
He will bring me forth to the light;
   I will see his justice.

The word of the Lord.

RESPONSORIAL PSALM

Psalm 27:1, 7-8a, 8b-9abc, 13-14

℟. (1a) **The Lord is my light and my salvation.**

The LORD is my light and my salvation;
   whom should I fear?
The LORD is my life's refuge;
   of whom should I be afraid?

℟. **The Lord is my light and my salvation.**

Hear, O LORD, the sound of my call;
   have pity on me and answer me.
Of you my heart speaks; you my glance seeks.

℟. **The Lord is my light and my salvation.**

Your presence, O LORD, I seek!
Hide not your face from me;
   do not in anger repel your servant.
You are my helper; cast me not off.

℟. **The Lord is my light and my salvation.**

I believe that I shall see the bounty of the LORD
   in the land of the living.
Wait for the LORD with courage;
   be stouthearted, and wait for the LORD!

℟. **The Lord is my light and my salvation.**

VERSE BEFORE THE GOSPEL

John 8:12

I am the light of the world, says the Lord;
whoever follows me will have the light of life.

GOSPEL

John 9:1-41   He went, washed and came back able to see.

✠ A reading from the holy Gospel according to John

**As Jesus passed by he saw a man blind from birth.
His disciples asked him,
    "Rabbi, who sinned, this man or his parents,
    that he was born blind?"
Jesus answered,
    "Neither he nor his parents sinned;
    it is so that the works of God might be made visible through him.
We have to do the works of the one who sent me while it is day.
Night is coming when no one can work.
While I am in the world, I am the light of the world."
When he had said this, he spat on the ground
    and made clay with the saliva,
    and smeared the clay on his eyes, and said to him,
    "Go, wash in the Pool of Siloam"—which means Sent—.
So he went and washed, and came back able to see.**

**His neighbors and those who had seen him earlier as a beggar said,
    "Isn't this the one who used to sit and beg?"
Some said, "It is,"
    but others said, "No, he just looks like him."
He said, "I am."
So they said to him, "How were your eyes opened?"
He replied,
    "The man called Jesus made clay and anointed my eyes
    and told me, 'Go to Siloam and wash.'
So I went there and washed and was able to see."
And they said to him, "Where is he?"
He said, "I don't know."**

They brought the one who was once blind to the Pharisees.
Now Jesus had made clay and opened his eyes on a sabbath.
So then the Pharisees also asked him how he was able to see.
He said to them,
    "He put clay on my eyes, and I washed, and now I can see."
So some of the Pharisees said,
    "This man is not from God,
    because he does not keep the sabbath."

But others said,
> "How can a sinful man do such signs?"

And there was a division among them.
So they said to the blind man again,
> "What do you have to say about him,
> since he opened your eyes?"

He said, "He is a prophet."

Now the Jews did not believe
> that he had been blind and gained his sight
> until they summoned the parents of the one who had gained his sight.

They asked them,
> "Is this your son, who you say was born blind?

How does he now see?"
His parents answered and said,
> "We know that this is our son and that he was born blind.

We do not know how he sees now,
> nor do we know who opened his eyes.

Ask him, he is of age;
> he can speak for himself."

His parents said this because they were afraid
> of the Jews, for the Jews had already agreed
> that if anyone acknowledged him as the Christ,
> he would be expelled from the synagogue.

For this reason his parents said,
> "He is of age; question him."

So a second time they called the man who had been blind
> and said to him, "Give God the praise!

We know that this man is a sinner."
He replied,
> "If he is a sinner, I do not know.

One thing I do know is that I was blind and now I see."
So they said to him,
> "What did he do to you?
> How did he open your eyes?"

He answered them,
> "I told you already and you did not listen.

Why do you want to hear it again?
Do you want to become his disciples, too?"

They ridiculed him and said,
> "You are that man's disciple;
> we are disciples of Moses!

We know that God spoke to Moses,
> but we do not know where this one is from."

The man answered and said to them,
> "This is what is so amazing,
> that you do not know where he is from, yet he opened my eyes.

We know that God does not listen to sinners,
> but if one is devout and does his will, he listens to him.

It is unheard of that anyone ever opened the eyes of a person born blind.
If this man were not from God,
> he would not be able to do anything."

They answered and said to him,
> "You were born totally in sin,
> and are you trying to teach us?"

Then they threw him out.

When Jesus heard that they had thrown him out,
> he found him and said, "Do you believe in the Son of Man?"

He answered and said,
> "Who is he, sir, that I may believe in him?"

Jesus said to him,
> "You have seen him, and
> the one speaking with you is he."

He said,
> "I do believe, Lord," and he worshiped him.

Then Jesus said,
> "I came into this world for judgment,
> so that those who do not see might see,
> and those who do see might become blind."

Some of the Pharisees who were with him heard this
> and said to him, "Surely we are not also blind, are we?"

Jesus said to them,
> "If you were blind, you would have no sin;
> but now you are saying, 'We see,' so your sin remains."

The Gospel of the Lord.

244 MONDAY OF THE FOURTH WEEK OF LENT

FIRST READING

Isaiah 65:17-21   No longer shall the sound of weeping or the sound of crying be heard.

A reading from the Book of the Prophet Isaiah

**Thus says the Lord:
Lo, I am about to create new heavens
 and a new earth;
The things of the past shall not be remembered
 or come to mind.
Instead, there shall always be rejoicing and happiness
 in what I create;
For I create Jerusalem to be a joy
 and its people to be a delight;
I will rejoice in Jerusalem
 and exult in my people.
No longer shall the sound of weeping be heard there,
 or the sound of crying;
no longer shall there be in it
 an infant who lives but a few days,
 or an old man who does not round out his full lifetime;
He dies a mere youth who reaches but a hundred years,
 and he who fails of a hundred shall be thought accursed.
They shall live in the houses they build,
 and eat the fruit of the vineyards they plant.**

The word of the Lord.

RESPONSORIAL PSALM

Psalm 30:2 and 4, 5-6, 11-12a and 13b

℟. (2a) **I will praise you, Lord, for you have rescued me.**

**I will extol you, O LORD, for you drew me clear
    and did not let my enemies rejoice over me.
O LORD, you brought me up from the nether world;
    you preserved me from among those going down into the pit.**

℟. **I will praise you, Lord, for you have rescued me.**

**Sing praise to the LORD, you his faithful ones,
    and give thanks to his holy name.
For his anger lasts but a moment;
    a lifetime, his good will.
At nightfall, weeping enters in,
    but with the dawn, rejoicing.**

℟. **I will praise you, Lord, for you have rescued me.**

**"Hear, O LORD, and have pity on me;
    O LORD, be my helper."
You changed my mourning into dancing;
    O LORD, my God, forever will I give you thanks.**

℟. **I will praise you, Lord, for you have rescued me.**

VERSE BEFORE THE GOSPEL

Amos 5:14

**Seek good and not evil so that you may live,
and the LORD will be with you.**

GOSPEL

John 4:43-54   Go, your son will live.

✠ A reading from the holy Gospel according to John

At that time Jesus left [Samaria] for Galilee.
For Jesus himself testified
  that a prophet has no honor in his native place.
When he came into Galilee, the Galileans welcomed him,
  since they had seen all he had done in Jerusalem at the feast;
  for they themselves had gone to the feast.

Then he returned to Cana in Galilee,
  where he had made the water wine.
Now there was a royal official whose son was ill in Capernaum.
When he heard that Jesus had arrived in Galilee from Judea,
  he went to him and asked him to come down
  and heal his son, who was near death.
Jesus said to him,
  "Unless you people see signs and wonders, you will not believe."
The royal official said to him,
  "Sir, come down before my child dies."
Jesus said to him, "You may go; your son will live."
The man believed what Jesus said to him and left.
While the man was on his way back,
  his slaves met him and told him that his boy would live.
He asked them when he began to recover.
They told him,
  "The fever left him yesterday, about one in the afternoon."
The father realized that just at that time Jesus had said to him,
  "Your son will live,"
  and he and his whole household came to believe.
Now this was the second sign Jesus did
  when he came to Galilee from Judea.

The Gospel of the Lord.

245 TUESDAY OF THE FOURTH WEEK OF LENT

FIRST READING

Ezekiel 47:1-9, 12   I saw water flowing from the temple, and all who were touched by it were saved (see Roman Missal).

A reading from the Book of the Prophet Ezekiel

The angel brought me, Ezekiel,
   back to the entrance of the temple of the Lord,
   and I saw water flowing out
   from beneath the threshold of the temple toward the east,
   for the façade of the temple was toward the east;
   the water flowed down from the right side of the temple,
   south of the altar.
He led me outside by the north gate,
   and around to the outer gate facing the east,
   where I saw water trickling from the right side.
Then when he had walked off to the east
   with a measuring cord in his hand,
   he measured off a thousand cubits
   and had me wade through the water,
   which was ankle-deep.
He measured off another thousand
   and once more had me wade through the water,
   which was now knee-deep.
Again he measured off a thousand and had me wade;
   the water was up to my waist.
Once more he measured off a thousand,
   but there was now a river through which I could not wade;
   for the water had risen so high it had become a river
   that could not be crossed except by swimming.
He asked me, "Have you seen this, son of man?"
Then he brought me to the bank of the river, where he had me sit.
Along the bank of the river I saw very many trees on both sides.
He said to me,
   "This water flows into the eastern district down upon the Arabah,
   and empties into the sea, the salt waters, which it makes fresh.
Wherever the river flows,
   every sort of living creature that can multiply shall live,

and there shall be abundant fish,
    for wherever this water comes the sea shall be made fresh.
Along both banks of the river, fruit trees of every kind shall grow;
    their leaves shall not fade, nor their fruit fail.
Every month they shall bear fresh fruit,
    for they shall be watered by the flow from the sanctuary.
Their fruit shall serve for food, and their leaves for medicine."

The word of the Lord.

RESPONSORIAL PSALM

Psalm 46:2-3, 5-6, 8-9

℟. (8) **The Lord of hosts is with us; our stronghold is the God of Jacob.**

God is our refuge and our strength,
    an ever-present help in distress.
Therefore we fear not, though the earth be shaken
    and mountains plunge into the depths of the sea.

℟. **The Lord of hosts is with us; our stronghold is the God of Jacob.**

There is a stream whose runlets gladden the city of God,
    the holy dwelling of the Most High.
God is in its midst; it shall not be disturbed;
    God will help it at the break of dawn.

℟. **The Lord of hosts is with us; our stronghold is the God of Jacob.**

The LORD of hosts is with us;
    our stronghold is the God of Jacob.
Come! behold the deeds of the LORD,
    the astounding things he has wrought on earth.

℟. **The Lord of hosts is with us; our stronghold is the God of Jacob.**

VERSE BEFORE THE GOSPEL

Psalm 51:12a, 14a

A clean heart create for me, O God;
give me back the joy of your salvation.

GOSPEL

John 5:1-16   Immediately the man became well.

✢   A reading from the holy Gospel according to John

There was a feast of the Jews, and Jesus went up to Jerusalem.
Now there is in Jerusalem at the Sheep Gate
   a pool called in Hebrew Bethesda, with five porticoes.
In these lay a large number of ill, blind, lame, and crippled.
One man was there who had been ill for thirty-eight years.
When Jesus saw him lying there
   and knew that he had been ill for a long time, he said to him,
   "Do you want to be well?"
The sick man answered him,
   "Sir, I have no one to put me into the pool
   when the water is stirred up;
   while I am on my way, someone else gets down there before me."
Jesus said to him, "Rise, take up your mat, and walk."
Immediately the man became well, took up his mat, and walked.

Now that day was a sabbath.
So the Jews said to the man who was cured,
   "It is the sabbath, and it is not lawful for you to carry your mat."
He answered them, "The man who made me well told me,
   'Take up your mat and walk.'"
They asked him,
   "Who is the man who told you, 'Take it up and walk'?"
The man who was healed did not know who it was,
   for Jesus had slipped away, since there was a crowd there.
After this Jesus found him in the temple area and said to him,
   "Look, you are well; do not sin any more,
   so that nothing worse may happen to you."
The man went and told the Jews
   that Jesus was the one who had made him well.
Therefore, the Jews began to persecute Jesus
   because he did this on a sabbath.

The Gospel of the Lord.

246 WEDNESDAY OF THE FOURTH WEEK OF LENT

FIRST READING

Isaiah 49:8-15 I have given you as a covenant to the people, to restore the land.

A reading from the Book of the Prophet Isaiah

>Thus says the LORD:
In a time of favor I answer you,
>>on the day of salvation I help you;
>>and I have kept you and given you as a covenant to the people,
>To restore the land
>>and allot the desolate heritages,
>Saying to the prisoners: Come out!
>To those in darkness: Show yourselves!
>Along the ways they shall find pasture,
>>on every bare height shall their pastures be.
>They shall not hunger or thirst,
>>nor shall the scorching wind or the sun strike them;
>For he who pities them leads them
>>and guides them beside springs of water.
>I will cut a road through all my mountains,
>>and make my highways level.
>See, some shall come from afar,
>>others from the north and the west,
>>and some from the land of Syene.
>Sing out, O heavens, and rejoice, O earth,
>>break forth into song, you mountains.
>For the LORD comforts his people
>>and shows mercy to his afflicted.

>But Zion said, "The LORD has forsaken me;
>>my Lord has forgotten me."
>Can a mother forget her infant,
>>be without tenderness for the child of her womb?
>Even should she forget,
>>I will never forget you.

The word of the Lord.

RESPONSORIAL PSALM

Psalm 145:8-9, 13cd-14, 17-18

℟. (8a) **The Lord is gracious and merciful.**

**The Lord is gracious and merciful,
 slow to anger and of great kindness.
The Lord is good to all
 and compassionate toward all his works.**

℟. **The Lord is gracious and merciful.**

**The Lord is faithful in all his words
 and holy in all his works.
The Lord lifts up all who are falling
 and raises up all who are bowed down.**

℟. **The Lord is gracious and merciful.**

**The Lord is just in all his ways
 and holy in all his works.
The Lord is near to all who call upon him,
 to all who call upon him in truth.**

℟. **The Lord is gracious and merciful.**

VERSE BEFORE THE GOSPEL

John 11:25a, 26

**I am the resurrection and the life, says the Lord;
whoever believes in me will never die.**

GOSPEL

John 5:17-30   As the Father raises the dead and gives them life, so also does the Son give life to those whom he chooses.

✜ **A reading from the holy Gospel according to John**

**Jesus answered the Jews:
"My Father is at work until now, so I am at work."
For this reason they tried all the more to kill him,
 because he not only broke the sabbath
 but he also called God his own father, making himself equal to God.**

Jesus answered and said to them,
> "Amen, amen, I say to you, the Son cannot do anything on his own,
> but only what he sees the Father doing;
> for what he does, the Son will do also.

For the Father loves the Son
> and shows him everything that he himself does,
> and he will show him greater works than these,
> so that you may be amazed.

For just as the Father raises the dead and gives life,
> so also does the Son give life to whomever he wishes.

Nor does the Father judge anyone,
> but he has given all judgment to the Son,
> so that all may honor the Son just as they honor the Father.

Whoever does not honor the Son
> does not honor the Father who sent him.

Amen, amen, I say to you, whoever hears my word
> and believes in the one who sent me
> has eternal life and will not come to condemnation,
> but has passed from death to life.

Amen, amen, I say to you, the hour is coming and is now here
> when the dead will hear the voice of the Son of God,
> and those who hear will live.

For just as the Father has life in himself,
> so also he gave to the Son the possession of life in himself.

And he gave him power to exercise judgment,
> because he is the Son of Man.

Do not be amazed at this,
> because the hour is coming in which all who are in the tombs
> will hear his voice and will come out,
> those who have done good deeds
> to the resurrection of life,
> but those who have done wicked deeds
> to the resurrection of condemnation.

"I cannot do anything on my own;
> I judge as I hear, and my judgment is just,
> because I do not seek my own will
> but the will of the one who sent me."

The Gospel of the Lord.

247 THURSDAY OF THE FOURTH WEEK OF LENT

FIRST READING

Exodus 32:7-14   Relent in punishing your people.

A reading from the Book of Exodus

The Lord said to Moses,
   "Go down at once to your people
   whom you brought out of the land of Egypt,
   for they have become depraved.
They have soon turned aside from the way I pointed out to them,
   making for themselves a molten calf and worshiping it,
   sacrificing to it and crying out,
   'This is your God, O Israel,
   who brought you out of the land of Egypt!'
The Lord said to Moses,
   "I see how stiff-necked this people is.
Let me alone, then,
   that my wrath may blaze up against them to consume them.
Then I will make of you a great nation."

But Moses implored the Lord, his God, saying,
   "Why, O Lord, should your wrath blaze up against your own people,
   whom you brought out of the land of Egypt
   with such great power and with so strong a hand?
Why should the Egyptians say,
   'With evil intent he brought them out,
   that he might kill them in the mountains
   and exterminate them from the face of the earth'?
Let your blazing wrath die down;
   relent in punishing your people.
Remember your servants Abraham, Isaac and Israel,
   and how you swore to them by your own self, saying,
   'I will make your descendants as numerous as the stars in the sky;
   and all this land that I promised,
   I will give your descendants as their perpetual heritage.'"
So the Lord relented in the punishment
   he had threatened to inflict on his people.

The word of the Lord.

RESPONSORIAL PSALM

Psalm 106:19-20, 21-22, 23

℟. (4a) **Remember us, O Lord, as you favor your people.**

**Our fathers made a calf in Horeb
 and adored a molten image;
They exchanged their glory
 for the image of a grass-eating bullock.**

℟. **Remember us, O Lord, as you favor your people.**

**They forgot the God who had saved them,
 who had done great deeds in Egypt,
Wondrous deeds in the land of Ham,
 terrible things at the Red Sea.**

℟. **Remember us, O Lord, as you favor your people.**

**Then he spoke of exterminating them,
 but Moses, his chosen one,
Withstood him in the breach
 to turn back his destructive wrath.**

℟. **Remember us, O Lord, as you favor your people.**

VERSE BEFORE THE GOSPEL

John 3:16

**God so loved the world that he gave his only-begotten Son,
so that everyone who believes in him might have eternal life.**

GOSPEL

John 5:31-47   The one who will accuse you is Moses, in whom you have placed your hope.

✠ A reading from the holy Gospel according to John

**Jesus said to the Jews:
"If I testify on my own behalf, my testimony is not true.
But there is another who testifies on my behalf,
and I know that the testimony he gives on my behalf is true.
You sent emissaries to John, and he testified to the truth.
I do not accept human testimony,
but I say this so that you may be saved.
He was a burning and shining lamp,
and for a while you were content to rejoice in his light.
But I have testimony greater than John's.
The works that the Father gave me to accomplish,
these works that I perform testify on my behalf
that the Father has sent me.
Moreover, the Father who sent me has testified on my behalf.
But you have never heard his voice nor seen his form,
and you do not have his word remaining in you,
because you do not believe in the one whom he has sent.
You search the Scriptures,
because you think you have eternal life through them;
even they testify on my behalf.
But you do not want to come to me to have life.**

**"I do not accept human praise;
moreover, I know that you do not have the love of God in you.
I came in the name of my Father,
but you do not accept me;
yet if another comes in his own name,
you will accept him.**

How can you believe, when you accept praise from one another
   and do not seek the praise that comes from the only God?
Do not think that I will accuse you before the Father:
   the one who will accuse you is Moses,
   in whom you have placed your hope.
For if you had believed Moses,
   you would have believed me,
   because he wrote about me.
But if you do not believe his writings,
   how will you believe my words?"

The Gospel of the Lord.

248 FRIDAY OF THE FOURTH WEEK OF LENT

FIRST READING

Wisdom 2:1a, 12-22   Let us condemn him to a shameful death.

A reading from the Book of Wisdom

**The wicked said among themselves,
 thinking not aright:
"Let us beset the just one, because he is obnoxious to us;
 he sets himself against our doings,
Reproaches us for transgressions of the law
 and charges us with violations of our training.
He professes to have knowledge of God
 and styles himself a child of the Lord.
To us he is the censure of our thoughts;
 merely to see him is a hardship for us,
Because his life is not like that of others,
 and different are his ways.
He judges us debased;
 he holds aloof from our paths as from things impure.
He calls blest the destiny of the just
 and boasts that God is his Father.
Let us see whether his words be true;
 let us find out what will happen to him.
For if the just one be the son of God, he will defend him
 and deliver him from the hand of his foes.
With revilement and torture let us put him to the test
 that we may have proof of his gentleness
 and try his patience.
Let us condemn him to a shameful death;
 for according to his own words, God will take care of him."
These were their thoughts, but they erred;
 for their wickedness blinded them,
and they knew not the hidden counsels of God;
 neither did they count on a recompense of holiness
 nor discern the innocent souls' reward.**

The word of the Lord.

RESPONSORIAL PSALM

Psalm 34:17-18, 19-20, 21 and 23

℟. (19a) **The Lord is close to the brokenhearted.**

**The LORD confronts the evildoers,
 to destroy remembrance of them from the earth.
When the just cry out, the LORD hears them,
 and from all their distress he rescues them.**

℟. **The Lord is close to the brokenhearted.**

**The LORD is close to the brokenhearted;
 and those who are crushed in spirit he saves.
Many are the troubles of the just man,
 but out of them all the LORD delivers him.**

℟. **The Lord is close to the brokenhearted.**

**He watches over all his bones;
 not one of them shall be broken.
The LORD redeems the lives of his servants;
 no one incurs guilt who takes refuge in him.**

℟. **The Lord is close to the brokenhearted.**

VERSE BEFORE THE GOSPEL

Matthew 4:4b

**One does not live on bread alone,
but on every word that comes forth from the mouth of God.**

GOSPEL

John 7:1-2, 10, 25-30   They tried to arrest him, but his hour had not yet come.

☩ A reading from the holy Gospel according to John

Jesus moved about within Galilee;
> he did not wish to travel in Judea,
> because the Jews were trying to kill him.

But the Jewish feast of Tabernacles was near.

But when his brothers had gone up to the feast,
> he himself also went up, not openly but as it were in secret.

Some of the inhabitants of Jerusalem said,
> "Is he not the one they are trying to kill?

And look, he is speaking openly and they say nothing to him.
Could the authorities have realized that he is the Christ?
But we know where he is from.
When the Christ comes, no one will know where he is from."
So Jesus cried out in the temple area as he was teaching and said,
> "You know me and also know where I am from.

Yet I did not come on my own,
> but the one who sent me, whom you do not know, is true.

I know him, because I am from him, and he sent me."
So they tried to arrest him,
> but no one laid a hand upon him,
> because his hour had not yet come.

The Gospel of the Lord.

249 SATURDAY OF THE FOURTH WEEK OF LENT

FIRST READING

Jeremiah 11:18-20   I am like a trusting lamb led to slaughter.

A reading from the Book of the Prophet Jeremiah

I knew their plot because the Lord informed me;
   at that time you, O Lord, showed me their doings.

Yet I, like a trusting lamb led to slaughter,
   had not realized that they were hatching plots against me:
   "Let us destroy the tree in its vigor;
   let us cut him off from the land of the living,
   so that his name will be spoken no more."

But, you, O Lord of hosts, O just Judge,
    searcher of mind and heart,
Let me witness the vengeance you take on them,
    for to you I have entrusted my cause!

The word of the Lord.

RESPONSORIAL PSALM

Psalm 7:2-3, 9bc-10, 11-12

℟. (2a) O Lord, my God, in you I take refuge.

O LORD, my God, in you I take refuge;
   save me from all my pursuers and rescue me,
Lest I become like the lion's prey,
   to be torn to pieces, with no one to rescue me.

℟. O Lord, my God, in you I take refuge.

Do me justice, O LORD, because I am just,
   and because of the innocence that is mine.
Let the malice of the wicked come to an end,
   but sustain the just,
   O searcher of heart and soul, O just God.

℟. O Lord, my God, in you I take refuge.

A shield before me is God,
   who saves the upright of heart;
A just judge is God,
   a God who punishes day by day.

℟. O Lord, my God, in you I take refuge.

VERSE BEFORE THE GOSPEL

See Luke 8:15

Blessed are they who have kept the word with a generous heart and yield a harvest through perseverance.

GOSPEL

John 7:40-53   The Christ will not come from Galilee, will he?

✜ A reading from the holy Gospel according to John

Some in the crowd who heard these words of Jesus said,
  "This is truly the Prophet."
Others said, "This is the Christ."
But others said, "The Christ will not come from Galilee, will he?
Does not Scripture say that the Christ will be of David's family
  and come from Bethlehem, the village where David lived?"
So a division occurred in the crowd because of him.
Some of them even wanted to arrest him,
  but no one laid hands on him.

So the guards went to the chief priests and Pharisees,
  who asked them, "Why did you not bring him?"
The guards answered, "Never before has anyone spoken like this man."
So the Pharisees answered them, "Have you also been deceived?
Have any of the authorities or the Pharisees believed in him?
But this crowd, which does not know the law, is accursed."
Nicodemus, one of their members who had come to him earlier, said to them,
  "Does our law condemn a man before it first hears him
  and finds out what he is doing?"
They answered and said to him,
  "You are not from Galilee also, are you?
Look and see that no prophet arises from Galilee."

Then each went to his own house.

The Gospel of the Lord.

250 OPTIONAL MASS OF THE FIFTH WEEK OF LENT

This Mass may be used on any day of this week, especially in Years B and C when the Gospel of Lazarus is not read on the Fifth Sunday of Lent.

FIRST READING

2 Kings 4:18b-21, 32-37   The man of God stretched himself over the boy, and the child's flesh grew warm.

A reading from the second Book of Kings

**The day came when the child of the Shunammite woman
   was old enough to go out to his father among the reapers.
"My head hurts!" he complained to his father.
"Carry him to his mother," the father said to a servant.
The servant picked him up and carried him to his mother;
   he stayed with her until noon, when he died in her lap.
The mother took him upstairs and laid him on the bed of the man of God.
Closing the door on him, she went out.**

**When Elisha reached the house,
   he found the boy lying dead.
He went in, closed the door on them both,
   and prayed to the Lord.
Then he lay upon the child on the bed,
   placing his mouth upon the child's mouth,
   his eyes upon the eyes, and his hands upon the hands.
As Elisha stretched himself over the child, the body became warm.
He arose, paced up and down the room,
   and then once more lay down upon the boy,
   who now sneezed seven times and opened his eyes.
Elisha summoned Gehazi and said,
   "Call the Shunammite."
She came at his call, and Elisha said to her, "Take your son."
She came in and fell at his feet in gratitude;
   then she took her son and left the room.**

The word of the Lord.

RESPONSORIAL PSALM

Psalm 17:1, 6-7, 8b and 15

℟. (15b) **Lord, when your glory appears, my joy will be full.**

Hear, O LORD, a just suit;
  attend to my outcry;
  hearken to my prayer from lips without deceit.

℟. **Lord, when your glory appears, my joy will be full.**

I call upon you, for you will answer me, O God;
  incline your ear to me; hear my word.
Show your wondrous mercies,
  O savior of those who flee
    from their foes to refuge at your right hand.

℟. **Lord, when your glory appears, my joy will be full.**

Hide me in the shadow of your wings.
But I in justice shall behold your face;
  on waking, I shall be content in your presence.

℟. **Lord, when your glory appears, my joy will be full.**

VERSE BEFORE THE GOSPEL

John 11:25a, 26

I am the resurrection and the life, says the Lord;
whoever believes in me will never die.

GOSPEL

John 11:1-45   I am the resurrection and the life.

✢ A reading from the holy Gospel according to John

There was a man who was ill, Lazarus from Bethany,
  the village of Mary and her sister Martha.
Mary was the one who had anointed the Lord with perfumed oil
  and dried his feet with her hair;
  it was her brother Lazarus who was ill.
So the sisters sent word to Jesus saying,
  "Master, the one you love is ill."
When Jesus heard this he said,
  "This illness is not to end in death,
  but is for the glory of God,
  that the Son of God may be glorified through it."
Now Jesus loved Martha and her sister and Lazarus.
So when he heard that he was ill,
  he remained for two days in the place where he was.
Then after this he said to his disciples,
  "Let us go back to Judea."
The disciples said to him,
  "Rabbi, the Jews were just trying to stone you,
  and you want to go back there?"
Jesus answered,
  "Are there not twelve hours in a day?
If one walks during the day, he does not stumble,
  because he sees the light of this world.
But if one walks at night, he stumbles,
  because the light is not in him."
He said this, and then told them,
  "Our friend Lazarus is asleep,
  but I am going to awaken him."
So the disciples said to him,
  "Master, if he is asleep, he will be saved."
But Jesus was talking about his death,
  while they thought that he meant ordinary sleep.
So then Jesus said to them clearly,
  "Lazarus has died.
And I am glad for you that I was not there,
  that you may believe.

Let us go to him."
So Thomas, called Didymus, said to his fellow disciples,
   "Let us also go to die with him."

When Jesus arrived, he found that Lazarus
   had already been in the tomb for four days.
Now Bethany was near Jerusalem, only about two miles away.
And many of the Jews had come to Martha and Mary
   to comfort them about their brother.
When Martha heard that Jesus was coming,
   she went to meet him;
   but Mary sat at home.
Martha said to Jesus,
   "Lord, if you had been here,
   my brother would not have died.
But even now I know that whatever you ask of God,
   God will give you."
Jesus said to her,
   "Your brother will rise."
Martha said to him,
   "I know he will rise,
   in the resurrection on the last day."
Jesus told her,
   "I am the resurrection and the life;
   whoever believes in me, even if he dies, will live,
   and everyone who lives and believes in me will never die.
Do you believe this?"
She said to him, "Yes, Lord.
I have come to believe that you are the Christ, the Son of God,
   the one who is coming into the world."

When she had said this,
   she went and called her sister Mary secretly, saying,
   "The teacher is here and is asking for you."
As soon as she heard this,
   she rose quickly and went to him.
For Jesus had not yet come into the village,
   but was still where Martha had met him.
So when the Jews who were with her in the house comforting her
   saw Mary get up quickly and go out,
     they followed her,
     presuming that she was going to the tomb to weep there.

When Mary came to where Jesus was and saw him,
> she fell at his feet and said to him,
> "Lord, if you had been here,
> my brother would not have died."

When Jesus saw her weeping and the Jews who had come with her weeping,
> he became perturbed and deeply troubled, and said,
> "Where have you laid him?"

They said to him, "Sir, come and see."
And Jesus wept.
So the Jews said, "See how he loved him."
But some of them said,
> "Could not the one who opened the eyes of the blind man
> have done something so that this man would not have died?"

So Jesus, perturbed again, came to the tomb.
It was a cave, and a stone lay across it.
Jesus said, "Take away the stone."
Martha, the dead man's sister, said to him,
> "Lord, by now there will be a stench;
> he has been dead for four days."

Jesus said to her,
> "Did I not tell you that if you believe
> you will see the glory of God?"

So they took away the stone.
And Jesus raised his eyes and said,
> "Father, I thank you for hearing me.

I know that you always hear me;
> but because of the crowd here I have said this,
> that they may believe that you sent me."

And when he had said this,
> he cried out in a loud voice,
> "Lazarus, come out!"

The dead man came out,
> tied hand and foot with burial bands,
> and his face was wrapped in a cloth.

So Jesus said to them,
> "Untie him and let him go."

Now many of the Jews who had come to Mary
> and seen what he had done began to believe in him.

The Gospel of the Lord.

251 MONDAY OF THE FIFTH WEEK OF LENT

FIRST READING

Long Form

Daniel 13:1-9, 15-17, 19-30, 33-62   Here I am about to die, though I have done none of the things charged against me.

A reading from the Book of the Prophet Daniel

In Babylon there lived a man named Joakim,
> who married a very beautiful and God-fearing woman, Susanna,
> the daughter of Hilkiah;
> her pious parents had trained their daughter
> according to the law of Moses.

Joakim was very rich;
> he had a garden near his house,
> and the Jews had recourse to him often
> because he was the most respected of them all.

That year, two elders of the people were appointed judges,
> of whom the Lord said, "Wickedness has come out of Babylon:
> from the elders who were to govern the people as judges."

These men, to whom all brought their cases,
> frequented the house of Joakim.

When the people left at noon,
> Susanna used to enter her husband's garden for a walk.

When the old men saw her enter every day for her walk,
> they began to lust for her.

They suppressed their consciences;
> they would not allow their eyes to look to heaven,
> and did not keep in mind just judgments.

One day, while they were waiting for the right moment,
> she entered the garden as usual, with two maids only.

She decided to bathe, for the weather was warm.

Nobody else was there except the two elders,
> who had hidden themselves and were watching her.

"Bring me oil and soap," she said to the maids,
> "and shut the garden doors while I bathe."

As soon as the maids had left,
> the two old men got up and hurried to her.

"Look," they said, "the garden doors are shut, and no one can see us;
   give in to our desire, and lie with us.
If you refuse, we will testify against you
   that you dismissed your maids because a young man was here with you."

"I am completely trapped," Susanna groaned.
"If I yield, it will be my death;
   if I refuse, I cannot escape your power.
Yet it is better for me to fall into your power without guilt
   than to sin before the Lord."
Then Susanna shrieked, and the old men also shouted at her,
   as one of them ran to open the garden doors.
When the people in the house heard the cries from the garden,
   they rushed in by the side gate to see what had happened to her.
At the accusations by the old men,
   the servants felt very much ashamed,
   for never had any such thing been said about Susanna.

When the people came to her husband Joakim the next day,
   the two wicked elders also came,
   fully determined to put Susanna to death.
Before all the people they ordered:
   "Send for Susanna, the daughter of Hilkiah,
   the wife of Joakim."
When she was sent for,
   she came with her parents, children and all her relatives.
All her relatives and the onlookers were weeping.

In the midst of the people the two elders rose up
   and laid their hands on her head.
Through tears she looked up to heaven,
   for she trusted in the Lord wholeheartedly.
The elders made this accusation:
   "As we were walking in the garden alone,
   this woman entered with two girls
   and shut the doors of the garden, dismissing the girls.
A young man, who was hidden there, came and lay with her.
When we, in a corner of the garden, saw this crime,
   we ran toward them.
We saw them lying together,
   but the man we could not hold, because he was stronger than we;
   he opened the doors and ran off.

Then we seized her and asked who the young man was,
>   but she refused to tell us.

We testify to this."
The assembly believed them,
>   since they were elders and judges of the people,
>   and they condemned her to death.

But Susanna cried aloud:
>   "O eternal God, you know what is hidden
>   and are aware of all things before they come to be:
>   you know that they have testified falsely against me.

Here I am about to die,
>   though I have done none of the things
>   with which these wicked men have charged me."

The Lord heard her prayer.
As she was being led to execution,
>   God stirred up the holy spirit of a young boy named Daniel,
>   and he cried aloud:
>   "I will have no part in the death of this woman."

All the people turned and asked him, "What is this you are saying?"
He stood in their midst and continued,
>   "Are you such fools, O children of Israel!

To condemn a woman of Israel without examination
>   and without clear evidence?

Return to court, for they have testified falsely against her."

Then all the people returned in haste.
To Daniel the elders said,
>   "Come, sit with us and inform us,
>   since God has given you the prestige of old age."

But he replied,
>   "Separate these two far from each other that I may examine them."

After they were separated one from the other,
>   he called one of them and said:
>   "How you have grown evil with age!

Now have your past sins come to term:
>   passing unjust sentences, condemning the innocent,
>   and freeing the guilty, although the Lord says,
>   'The innocent and the just you shall not put to death.'

Now, then, if you were a witness,
>   tell me under what tree you saw them together."

"Under a mastic tree," he answered.
Daniel replied, "Your fine lie has cost you your head,
   for the angel of God shall receive the sentence from him
   and split you in two."
Putting him to one side, he ordered the other one to be brought.
Daniel said to him,
   "Offspring of Canaan, not of Judah, beauty has seduced you,
   lust has subverted your conscience.
This is how you acted with the daughters of Israel,
   and in their fear they yielded to you;
   but a daughter of Judah did not tolerate your wickedness.
Now, then, tell me under what tree you surprised them together."
"Under an oak," he said.
Daniel replied, "Your fine lie has cost you also your head,
   for the angel of God waits with a sword to cut you in two
   so as to make an end of you both."

The whole assembly cried aloud,
   blessing God who saves those who hope in him.
They rose up against the two elders,
   for by their own words Daniel had convicted them of perjury.
According to the law of Moses,
   they inflicted on them
      the penalty they had plotted to impose on their neighbor:
   they put them to death.
Thus was innocent blood spared that day.

The word of the Lord.

OR

Short Form

Daniel 13:41c-62   Here I am about to die, though I have done none of the things charged against me.

A reading from the Book of the Prophet Daniel

The assembly condemned Susanna to death.

But Susanna cried aloud:
  "O eternal God, you know what is hidden
  and are aware of all things before they come to be:
  you know that they have testified falsely against me.
Here I am about to die,
  though I have done none of the things
  with which these wicked men have charged me."

The Lord heard her prayer.
As she was being led to execution,
  God stirred up the holy spirit of a young boy named Daniel,
  and he cried aloud:
  "I will have no part in the death of this woman."
All the people turned and asked him,
  "What is this you are saying?"
He stood in their midst and continued,
  "Are you such fools, O children of Israel!
To condemn a woman of Israel without examination
  and without clear evidence?
Return to court, for they have testified falsely against her."

Then all the people returned in haste.
To Daniel the elders said,
  "Come, sit with us and inform us,
  since God has given you the prestige of old age."
But he replied,
  "Separate these two far from each other that I may examine them."

After they were separated one from the other,
  he called one of them and said:
  "How you have grown evil with age!
Now have your past sins come to term:
  passing unjust sentences, condemning the innocent,
  and freeing the guilty, although the Lord says,
  'The innocent and the just you shall not put to death.'

Now, then, if you were a witness,
> tell me under what tree you saw them together."

"Under a mastic tree," he answered.

Daniel replied, "Your fine lie has cost you your head,
> for the angel of God shall receive the sentence from him
> and split you in two."

Putting him to one side, he ordered the other one to be brought.

Daniel said to him, "Offspring of Canaan, not of Judah,
> beauty has seduced you, lust has subverted your conscience.

This is how you acted with the daughters of Israel,
> and in their fear they yielded to you;
> but a daughter of Judah did not tolerate your wickedness.

Now, then, tell me under what tree you surprised them together."

"Under an oak," he said.

Daniel replied, "Your fine lie has cost you also your head,
> for the angel of God waits with a sword to cut you in two
> so as to make an end of you both."

The whole assembly cried aloud,
> blessing God who saves those who hope in him.

They rose up against the two elders,
> for by their own words Daniel had convicted them of perjury.

According to the law of Moses,
> they inflicted on them
>> the penalty they had plotted to impose on their neighbor:
> they put them to death.

Thus was innocent blood spared that day.

The word of the Lord.

RESPONSORIAL PSALM

Psalm 23:1-3a, 3b-4, 5, 6

℟. (4ab) **Even though I walk in the dark valley I fear no evil; for you are at my side.**

The Lord is my shepherd; I shall not want.
   In verdant pastures he gives me repose;
Beside restful waters he leads me;
   he refreshes my soul.

℟. **Even though I walk in the dark valley I fear no evil; for you are at my side.**

He guides me in right paths
   for his name's sake.
Even though I walk in the dark valley
   I fear no evil; for you are at my side
With your rod and your staff
   that give me courage.

℟. **Even though I walk in the dark valley I fear no evil; for you are at my side.**

You spread the table before me
   in the sight of my foes;
You anoint my head with oil;
   my cup overflows.

℟. **Even though I walk in the dark valley I fear no evil; for you are at my side.**

Only goodness and kindness follow me
   all the days of my life;
And I shall dwell in the house of the Lord
   for years to come.

℟. **Even though I walk in the dark valley I fear no evil; for you are at my side.**

VERSE BEFORE THE GOSPEL

Ezekiel 33:11

I take no pleasure in the death of the wicked man, says the Lord,
but rather in his conversion, that he may live.

Monday of the Fifth Week of Lent II

GOSPEL

John 8:1-11   Let the person without sin be the first to throw a stone.

✠ A reading from the holy Gospel according to John

**Jesus went to the Mount of Olives.
But early in the morning he arrived again in the temple area,
   and all the people started coming to him,
   and he sat down and taught them.
Then the scribes and the Pharisees brought a woman
   who had been caught in adultery
   and made her stand in the middle.
They said to him,
   "Teacher, this woman was caught
   in the very act of committing adultery.
Now in the law, Moses commanded us to stone such women.
So what do you say?"
They said this to test him,
   so that they could have some charge to bring against him.
Jesus bent down and began to write on the ground with his finger.
But when they continued asking him,
   he straightened up and said to them,
   "Let the one among you who is without sin
   be the first to throw a stone at her."
Again he bent down and wrote on the ground.
And in response, they went away one by one,
   beginning with the elders.
So he was left alone with the woman before him.
Then Jesus straightened up and said to her,
   "Woman, where are they?
Has no one condemned you?"
She replied, "No one, sir."
Then Jesus said, "Neither do I condemn you.
Go, and from now on do not sin any more."**

The Gospel of the Lord.

In Year C, when this Gospel is read on the preceding Sunday, the following text is used.

GOSPEL

John 8:12-20   I am the light of the world.

☩ A reading from the holy Gospel according to John

Jesus spoke to them again, saying,
  "I am the light of the world.
Whoever follows me will not walk in darkness,
  but will have the light of life."
So the Pharisees said to him,
  "You testify on your own behalf,
  so your testimony cannot be verified."
Jesus answered and said to them,
  "Even if I do testify on my own behalf, my testimony can be verified,
  because I know where I came from and where I am going.
But you do not know where I come from or where I am going.
You judge by appearances, but I do not judge anyone.
And even if I should judge, my judgment is valid,
  because I am not alone,
  but it is I and the Father who sent me.
Even in your law it is written
  that the testimony of two men can be verified.
I testify on my behalf and so does the Father who sent me."
So they said to him, "Where is your father?"
Jesus answered, "You know neither me nor my Father.
If you knew me, you would know my Father also."
He spoke these words
  while teaching in the treasury in the temple area.
But no one arrested him, because his hour had not yet come.

The Gospel of the Lord.

252 TUESDAY OF THE FIFTH WEEK OF LENT

FIRST READING

Numbers 21:4-9   Whoever looks at the bronze serpent, shall live.

A reading from the Book of Numbers

From Mount Hor the children of Israel set out on the Red Sea road,
 to bypass the land of Edom.
But with their patience worn out by the journey,
 the people complained against God and Moses,
 "Why have you brought us up from Egypt to die in this desert,
 where there is no food or water?
We are disgusted with this wretched food!"

In punishment the LORD sent among the people saraph serpents,
 which bit the people so that many of them died.
Then the people came to Moses and said,
 "We have sinned in complaining against the LORD and you.
Pray the LORD to take the serpents away from us."
So Moses prayed for the people, and the LORD said to Moses,
 "Make a saraph and mount it on a pole,
 and whoever looks at it after being bitten will live."
Moses accordingly made a bronze serpent and mounted it on a pole,
 and whenever anyone who had been bitten by a serpent
 looked at the bronze serpent, he lived.

The word of the Lord.

RESPONSORIAL PSALM

Psalm 102:2-3, 16-18, 19-21

℟. (2) O Lord, hear my prayer, and let my cry come to you.

O LORD, hear my prayer,
   and let my cry come to you.
Hide not your face from me
   in the day of my distress.
Incline your ear to me;
   in the day when I call, answer me speedily.

℟. O Lord, hear my prayer, and let my cry come to you.

The nations shall revere your name, O LORD,
   and all the kings of the earth your glory,
When the LORD has rebuilt Zion
   and appeared in his glory;
When he has regarded the prayer of the destitute,
   and not despised their prayer.

℟. O Lord, hear my prayer, and let my cry come to you.

Let this be written for the generation to come,
   and let his future creatures praise the LORD:
"The LORD looked down from his holy height,
   from heaven he beheld the earth,
To hear the groaning of the prisoners,
   to release those doomed to die."

℟. O Lord, hear my prayer, and let my cry come to you.

VERSE BEFORE THE GOSPEL

**The seed is the word of God, Christ is the sower;
all who come to him will live for ever.**

GOSPEL

John 8:21-30   When you have lifted up the Son of Man, then you will know that I am he.

✠ A reading from the holy Gospel according to John

Jesus said to the Pharisees:
"I am going away and you will look for me,
  but you will die in your sin.
Where I am going you cannot come."
So the Jews said,
  "He is not going to kill himself, is he,
  because he said, 'Where I am going you cannot come'?"
He said to them, "You belong to what is below,
  I belong to what is above.
You belong to this world,
  but I do not belong to this world.
That is why I told you that you will die in your sins.
For if you do not believe that I AM,
  you will die in your sins."
So they said to him, "Who are you?"
Jesus said to them, "What I told you from the beginning.
I have much to say about you in condemnation.
But the one who sent me is true,
  and what I heard from him I tell the world."
They did not realize that he was speaking to them of the Father.
So Jesus said to them,
  "When you lift up the Son of Man,
  then you will realize that I AM,
  and that I do nothing on my own,
  but I say only what the Father taught me.
The one who sent me is with me.
He has not left me alone,
  because I always do what is pleasing to him."
Because he spoke this way, many came to believe in him.

The Gospel of the Lord.

253 WEDNESDAY OF THE FIFTH WEEK OF LENT

FIRST READING

Daniel 3:14-20, 91-92, 95 *The Lord has sent his angel to deliver his servants.*

A reading from the Book of the Prophet Daniel

King Nebuchadnezzar said:
"Is it true, Shadrach, Meshach, and Abednego,
  that you will not serve my god,
  or worship the golden statue that I set up?
Be ready now to fall down and worship the statue I had made,
  whenever you hear the sound of the trumpet,
  flute, lyre, harp, psaltery, bagpipe,
  and all the other musical instruments;
  otherwise, you shall be instantly cast into the white-hot furnace;
  and who is the God who can deliver you out of my hands?"
Shadrach, Meshach, and Abednego answered King Nebuchadnezzar,
  "There is no need for us to defend ourselves before you
  in this matter.
If our God, whom we serve,
  can save us from the white-hot furnace
  and from your hands, O king, may he save us!
But even if he will not, know, O king,
  that we will not serve your god
  or worship the golden statue that you set up."

King Nebuchadnezzar's face became livid with utter rage
  against Shadrach, Meshach, and Abednego.
He ordered the furnace to be heated seven times more than usual
  and had some of the strongest men in his army
    bind Shadrach, Meshach, and Abednego
  and cast them into the white-hot furnace.

Nebuchadnezzar rose in haste and asked his nobles,
  "Did we not cast three men bound into the fire?"
"Assuredly, O king," they answered.
"But," he replied, "I see four men unfettered and unhurt,
  walking in the fire, and the fourth looks like a son of God."

Nebuchadnezzar exclaimed,
"Blessed be the God of Shadrach, Meshach, and Abednego,
who sent his angel to deliver the servants who trusted in him;
they disobeyed the royal command and yielded their bodies
rather than serve or worship any god
except their own God."

The word of the Lord.

RESPONSORIAL PSALM

Daniel 3:52, 53, 54, 55, 56

℟. (52b) **Glory and praise for ever!**

"Blessed are you, O Lord, the God of our fathers,
   praiseworthy and exalted above all forever;
And blessed is your holy and glorious name,
   praiseworthy and exalted above all for all ages."

℟. **Glory and praise for ever!**

"Blessed are you in the temple of your holy glory,
   praiseworthy and exalted above all forever."

℟. **Glory and praise for ever!**

"Blessed are you on the throne of your kingdom,
   praiseworthy and exalted above all forever."

℟. **Glory and praise for ever!**

"Blessed are you who look into the depths
   from your throne upon the cherubim;
   praiseworthy and exalted above all forever."

℟. **Glory and praise for ever!**

"Blessed are you in the firmament of heaven,
   praiseworthy and glorious forever."

℟. **Glory and praise for ever!**

VERSE BEFORE THE GOSPEL

See Luke 8:15

Blessed are they who have kept the word with a generous heart and yield a harvest through perseverance.

GOSPEL

John 8:31-42   If the Son makes you free, you will be free indeed.

✠ **A reading from the holy Gospel according to John**

**Jesus said to those Jews who believed in him,
  "If you remain in my word, you will truly be my disciples,
  and you will know the truth, and the truth will set you free."
They answered him, "We are descendants of Abraham
  and have never been enslaved to anyone.
How can you say, 'You will become free'?"
Jesus answered them, "Amen, amen, I say to you,
  everyone who commits sin is a slave of sin.
A slave does not remain in a household forever,
  but a son always remains.
So if the Son frees you, then you will truly be free.
I know that you are descendants of Abraham.
But you are trying to kill me,
  because my word has no room among you.
I tell you what I have seen in the Father's presence;
  then do what you have heard from the Father."

They answered and said to him, "Our father is Abraham."
Jesus said to them, "If you were Abraham's children,
  you would be doing the works of Abraham.
But now you are trying to kill me,
  a man who has told you the truth that I heard from God;
  Abraham did not do this.
You are doing the works of your father!"
So they said to him, "We were not born of fornication.
We have one Father, God."
Jesus said to them, "If God were your Father, you would love me,
  for I came from God and am here;
  I did not come on my own, but he sent me."

The Gospel of the Lord.**

254 THURSDAY OF THE FIFTH WEEK OF LENT

FIRST READING

Genesis 17:3-9　You will be the father of a multitude of nations.

A reading from the Book of Genesis

When Abram prostrated himself, God spoke to him:
"My covenant with you is this:
 you are to become the father of a host of nations.
No longer shall you be called Abram;
 your name shall be Abraham,
 for I am making you the father of a host of nations.
I will render you exceedingly fertile;
 I will make nations of you;
 kings shall stem from you.
I will maintain my covenant with you
 and your descendants after you
 throughout the ages as an everlasting pact,
 to be your God and the God of your descendants after you.
I will give to you
 and to your descendants after you
 the land in which you are now staying,
 the whole land of Canaan, as a permanent possession;
 and I will be their God."

God also said to Abraham:
 "On your part, you and your descendants after you
 must keep my covenant throughout the ages."

The word of the Lord.

RESPONSORIAL PSALM

Psalm 105:4-5, 6-7, 8-9

℟. (8a) **The Lord remembers his covenant for ever.**

Look to the LORD **in his strength;**
  seek to serve him constantly.
Recall the wondrous deeds that he has wrought,
  his portents, and the judgments he has uttered.

℟. **The Lord remembers his covenant for ever.**

You descendants of Abraham, his servants,
  sons of Jacob, his chosen ones!
He, the LORD**, is our God;**
  throughout the earth his judgments prevail.

℟. **The Lord remembers his covenant for ever.**

He remembers forever his covenant
  which he made binding for a thousand generations—
Which he entered into with Abraham
  and by his oath to Isaac.

℟. **The Lord remembers his covenant for ever.**

VERSE BEFORE THE GOSPEL

Psalm 95:8

If today you hear his voice,
harden not your hearts.

GOSPEL

John 8:51-59   Your father, Abraham, rejoiced because he saw my day.

✠ **A reading from the holy Gospel according to John**

Jesus said to the Jews:
"Amen, amen, I say to you,
  whoever keeps my word will never see death."
So the Jews said to him,
  "Now we are sure that you are possessed.
Abraham died, as did the prophets, yet you say,
  'Whoever keeps my word will never taste death.'
Are you greater than our father Abraham, who died?
Or the prophets, who died?
Who do you make yourself out to be?"
Jesus answered, "If I glorify myself, my glory is worth nothing;
  but it is my Father who glorifies me,
  of whom you say, 'He is our God.'
You do not know him, but I know him.
And if I should say that I do not know him,
  I would be like you a liar.
But I do know him and I keep his word.
Abraham your father rejoiced to see my day;
  he saw it and was glad."
So the Jews said to him,
  "You are not yet fifty years old and you have seen **Abraham?**"
Jesus said to them, "Amen, amen, I say to you,
  before Abraham came to be, I AM."
So they picked up stones to throw at him;
  but Jesus hid and went out of the temple area.

The Gospel of the Lord.

255 FRIDAY OF THE FIFTH WEEK OF LENT

FIRST READING

Jeremiah 20:10-13   The Lord God is with me, a mighty hero.

A reading from the Book of the Prophet Jeremiah

I hear the whisperings of many:
   "Terror on every side!
   Denounce! let us denounce him!"
All those who were my friends
   are on the watch for any misstep of mine.
"Perhaps he will be trapped; then we can prevail,
   and take our vengeance on him."
But the Lord is with me, like a mighty champion:
   my persecutors will stumble, they will not triumph.
In their failure they will be put to utter shame,
   to lasting, unforgettable confusion.
O Lord of hosts, you who test the just,
   who probe mind and heart,
Let me witness the vengeance you take on them,
   for to you I have entrusted my cause.
Sing to the Lord,
   praise the Lord,
For he has rescued the life of the poor
   from the power of the wicked!"

The word of the Lord.

RESPONSORIAL PSALM

Psalm 18:2-3a, 3bc-4, 5-6, 7

℟. (see 7) **In my distress I called upon the Lord, and he heard my voice.**

I love you, O LORD**, my strength,**
  O LORD**, my rock, my fortress, my deliverer.**

℟. **In my distress I called upon the Lord, and he heard my voice.**

My God, my rock of refuge,
  my shield, the horn of my salvation, my stronghold!
Praised be the LORD**, I exclaim,**
  and I am safe from my enemies.

℟. **In my distress I called upon the Lord, and he heard my voice.**

The breakers of death surged round about me,
  the destroying floods overwhelmed me;
The cords of the nether world enmeshed me,
  the snares of death overtook me.

℟. **In my distress I called upon the Lord, and he heard my voice.**

In my distress I called upon the LORD
  and cried out to my God;
From his temple he heard my voice,
  and my cry to him reached his ears.

℟. **In my distress I called upon the Lord, and he heard my voice.**

VERSE BEFORE THE GOSPEL

See John 6:63c, 68c

Your words, Lord, are Spirit and life;
you have the words of everlasting life.

GOSPEL

John 10:31-42   They wanted to arrest Jesus, but he eluded them.

✚ A reading from the holy Gospel according to John

The Jews picked up rocks to stone Jesus.
Jesus answered them, "I have shown you many good works from my Father.
For which of these are you trying to stone me?"
The Jews answered him,
"We are not stoning you for a good work but for blasphemy.
You, a man, are making yourself God."
Jesus answered them,
"Is it not written in your law, 'I said, "You are gods"'?
If it calls them gods to whom the word of God came,
and Scripture cannot be set aside,
can you say that the one
whom the Father has consecrated and sent into the world
blasphemes because I said, 'I am the Son of God'?
If I do not perform my Father's works, do not believe me;
but if I perform them, even if you do not believe me,
believe the works, so that you may realize and understand
that the Father is in me and I am in the Father."
Then they tried again to arrest him;
but he escaped from their power.

He went back across the Jordan
to the place where John first baptized, and there he remained.
Many came to him and said,
"John performed no sign,
but everything John said about this man was true."
And many there began to believe in him.

The Gospel of the Lord.

256 SATURDAY OF THE FIFTH WEEK OF LENT

FIRST READING

Ezekiel 37:21-28   I will make them into one nation.

A reading from the Book of the Prophet Ezekiel

Thus says the Lord God:
I will take the children of Israel from among the nations
   to which they have come,
   and gather them from all sides to bring them back to their land.
I will make them one nation upon the land,
   in the mountains of Israel,
   and there shall be one prince for them all.
Never again shall they be two nations,
   and never again shall they be divided into two kingdoms.

No longer shall they defile themselves with their idols,
   their abominations, and all their transgressions.
I will deliver them from all their sins of apostasy,
   and cleanse them so that they may be my people
   and I may be their God.
My servant David shall be prince over them,
   and there shall be one shepherd for them all;
   they shall live by my statutes and carefully observe my decrees.
They shall live on the land that I gave to my servant Jacob,
   the land where their fathers lived;
   they shall live on it forever,
   they, and their children, and their children's children,
   with my servant David their prince forever.
I will make with them a covenant of peace;
   it shall be an everlasting covenant with them,
   and I will multiply them, and put my sanctuary among them forever.
My dwelling shall be with them;
   I will be their God, and they shall be my people.
Thus the nations shall know that it is I, the Lord,
   who make Israel holy,
   when my sanctuary shall be set up among them forever.

The word of the Lord.

RESPONSORIAL PSALM

Jeremiah 31:10, 11-12abcd, 13

℟. (see 10d) **The Lord will guard us, as a shepherd guards his flock.**

Hear the word of the LORD**, O nations,
   proclaim it on distant isles, and say:
He who scattered Israel, now gathers them together,
   he guards them as a shepherd his flock.**

℟. **The Lord will guard us, as a shepherd guards his flock.**

The LORD **shall ransom Jacob,
   he shall redeem him from the hand of his conqueror.
Shouting, they shall mount the heights of Zion,
   they shall come streaming to the L**ORD**'s blessings:
The grain, the wine, and the oil,
   the sheep and the oxen.**

℟. **The Lord will guard us, as a shepherd guards his flock.**

**Then the virgins shall make merry and dance,
   and young men and old as well.
I will turn their mourning into joy,
   I will console and gladden them after their sorrows.**

℟. **The Lord will guard us, as a shepherd guards his flock.**

VERSE BEFORE THE GOSPEL

Ezekiel 18:31

Cast away from you all the crimes you have committed, says the Lord, and make for yourselves a new heart and a new spirit.

GOSPEL

John 11:45-56   To gather together in unity the scattered children of God.

✟ A reading from the holy Gospel according to John

Many of the Jews who had come to Mary
  and seen what Jesus had done began to believe in him.
But some of them went to the Pharisees
  and told them what Jesus had done.
So the chief priests and the Pharisees
  convened the Sanhedrin and said,
  "What are we going to do?
This man is performing many signs.
If we leave him alone, all will believe in him,
  and the Romans will come
  and take away both our land and our nation."
But one of them, Caiaphas,
  who was high priest that year, said to them,
  "You know nothing,
  nor do you consider that it is better for you
  that one man should die instead of the people,
  so that the whole nation may not perish."
He did not say this on his own,
  but since he was high priest for that year,
  he prophesied that Jesus was going to die for the nation,
  and not only for the nation,
  but also to gather into one the dispersed children of God.
So from that day on they planned to kill him.

So Jesus no longer walked about in public among the Jews,
  but he left for the region near the desert,
  to a town called Ephraim,
  and there he remained with his disciples.

Now the Passover of the Jews was near,
  and many went up from the country to Jerusalem
  before Passover to purify themselves.
They looked for Jesus and said to one another
  as they were in the temple area, "What do you think?
That he will not come to the feast?"

The Gospel of the Lord.

HOLY WEEK

257 MONDAY OF HOLY WEEK

FIRST READING

Isaiah 42:1-7   He will not cry out, nor make his voice heard in the street.
(First oracle of the Servant of the Lord)

A reading from the Book of the Prophet Isaiah

Here is my servant whom I uphold,
   my chosen one with whom I am pleased,
Upon whom I have put my Spirit;
   he shall bring forth justice to the nations,
Not crying out, not shouting,
   not making his voice heard in the street.
A bruised reed he shall not break,
   and a smoldering wick he shall not quench,
Until he establishes justice on the earth;
   the coastlands will wait for his teaching.

Thus says God, the LORD,
   who created the heavens and stretched them out,
   who spreads out the earth with its crops,
Who gives breath to its people
   and spirit to those who walk on it:
I, the LORD, have called you for the victory of justice,
   I have grasped you by the hand;
I formed you, and set you
   as a covenant of the people,
   a light for the nations,
To open the eyes of the blind,
   to bring out prisoners from confinement,
   and from the dungeon, those who live in darkness.

The word of the Lord.

RESPONSORIAL PSALM

Psalm 27:1, 2, 3, 13-14

℟. (1a) **The Lord is my light and my salvation.**

The Lord is my light and my salvation;
   whom should I fear?
The Lord is my life's refuge;
   of whom should I be afraid?

℟. The Lord is my light and my salvation.

When evildoers come at me
   to devour my flesh,
My foes and my enemies
   themselves stumble and fall.

℟. The Lord is my light and my salvation.

Though an army encamp against me,
   my heart will not fear;
Though war be waged upon me,
   even then will I trust.

℟. The Lord is my light and my salvation.

I believe that I shall see the bounty of the Lord
   in the land of the living.
Wait for the Lord with courage;
   be stouthearted, and wait for the Lord.

℟. The Lord is my light and my salvation.

VERSE BEFORE THE GOSPEL

Hail to you, our King;
you alone are compassionate with our faults.

GOSPEL

John 12:1-11   Let her keep this for the day of my burial.

✠ **A reading from the holy Gospel according to John**

Six days before Passover Jesus came to Bethany,
   where Lazarus was, whom Jesus had raised from the dead.
They gave a dinner for him there, and Martha served,
   while Lazarus was one of those reclining at table with him.
Mary took a liter of costly perfumed oil
   made from genuine aromatic nard
   and anointed the feet of Jesus and dried them with her hair;
   the house was filled with the fragrance of the oil.
Then Judas the Iscariot, one of his disciples,
   and the one who would betray him, said,
   "Why was this oil not sold for three hundred days' wages
   and given to the poor?"
He said this not because he cared about the poor
   but because he was a thief and held the money bag
   and used to steal the contributions.
So Jesus said, "Leave her alone.
Let her keep this for the day of my burial.
You always have the poor with you, but you do not always have me."

The large crowd of the Jews found out that he was there and came,
   not only because of him, but also to see Lazarus,
   whom he had raised from the dead.
And the chief priests plotted to kill Lazarus too,
   because many of the Jews were turning away
   and believing in Jesus because of him.

The Gospel of the Lord.

258 TUESDAY OF HOLY WEEK

FIRST READING

Isaiah 49:1-6   I will make you a light to the nations, that my salvation may reach to the ends of the earth.
(Second oracle of the Servant of the Lord)

A reading from the Book of the Prophet Isaiah

Hear me, O islands,
   listen, O distant peoples.
The Lord called me from birth,
   from my mother's womb he gave me my name.
He made of me a sharp-edged sword
   and concealed me in the shadow of his arm.
He made me a polished arrow,
   in his quiver he hid me.
You are my servant, he said to me,
   Israel, through whom I show my glory.

Though I thought I had toiled in vain,
   and for nothing, uselessly, spent my strength,
Yet my reward is with the Lord,
   my recompense is with my God.
For now the Lord has spoken
   who formed me as his servant from the womb,
That Jacob may be brought back to him
   and Israel gathered to him;
And I am made glorious in the sight of the Lord,
   and my God is now my strength!
It is too little, he says, for you to be my servant,
   to raise up the tribes of Jacob,
   and restore the survivors of Israel;
I will make you a light to the nations,
   that my salvation may reach to the ends of the earth.

The word of the Lord.

RESPONSORIAL PSALM

Psalm 71:1-2, 3-4a, 5ab-6ab, 15 and 17

℟. (see 15ab) **I will sing of your salvation.**

In you, O LORD**, I take refuge;**
  let me never be put to shame.
In your justice rescue me, and deliver me;
  incline your ear to me, and save me.

℟. **I will sing of your salvation.**

Be my rock of refuge,
  a stronghold to give me safety,
  for you are my rock and my fortress.
O my God, rescue me from the hand of the wicked.

℟. **I will sing of your salvation.**

For you are my hope, O Lord;
  my trust, O God, from my youth.
On you I depend from birth;
  from my mother's womb you are my strength.

℟. **I will sing of your salvation.**

My mouth shall declare your justice,
  day by day your salvation.
O God, you have taught me from my youth,
  and till the present I proclaim your wondrous deeds.

℟. **I will sing of your salvation.**

VERSE BEFORE THE GOSPEL

Hail to you, our King, obedient to the Father;
you were led to your crucifixion like a gentle lamb to the slaughter.

GOSPEL

John 13:21-33, 36-38   One of you will betray me; the cock will not crow before you deny me three times.

✠ A reading from the holy Gospel according to John

Reclining at table with his disciples, Jesus was deeply troubled and testified,
  "Amen, amen, I say to you, one of you will betray me."
The disciples looked at one another, at a loss as to whom he meant.
One of his disciples, the one whom Jesus loved,
  was reclining at Jesus' side.
So Simon Peter nodded to him to find out whom he meant.
He leaned back against Jesus' chest and said to him,
  "Master, who is it?"
Jesus answered,
  "It is the one to whom I hand the morsel after I have dipped it."
So he dipped the morsel and took it and handed it to Judas,
  son of Simon the Iscariot.
After Judas took the morsel, Satan entered him.
So Jesus said to him, "What you are going to do, do quickly."
Now none of those reclining at table realized why he said this to him.
Some thought that since Judas kept the money bag, Jesus had told him,
  "Buy what we need for the feast,"
  or to give something to the poor.
So Judas took the morsel and left at once. And it was night.

When he had left, Jesus said,
  "Now is the Son of Man glorified, and God is glorified in him.
If God is glorified in him, God will also glorify him in himself,
  and he will glorify him at once.
My children, I will be with you only a little while longer.
You will look for me, and as I told the Jews,
  'Where I go you cannot come,' so now I say it to you."

Simon Peter said to him, "Master, where are you going?"
Jesus answered him,

"Where I am going, you cannot follow me now,
though you will follow later."
Peter said to him,
"Master, why can I not follow you now?
I will lay down my life for you."
Jesus answered, "Will you lay down your life for me?
Amen, amen, I say to you, the cock will not crow
before you deny me three times."

The Gospel of the Lord.

259 WEDNESDAY OF HOLY WEEK

FIRST READING

Isaiah 50:4-9a   My face I did not shield from buffets and spitting.
(Third oracle of the Servant of the Lord)

A reading from the Book of the Prophet Isaiah

The Lord God has given me
  a well-trained tongue,
That I might know how to speak to the weary
  a word that will rouse them.
Morning after morning
  he opens my ear that I may hear;
And I have not rebelled,
  have not turned back.
I gave my back to those who beat me,
  my cheeks to those who plucked my beard;
My face I did not shield
  from buffets and spitting.

The Lord God is my help,
  therefore I am not disgraced;
I have set my face like flint,
  knowing that I shall not be put to shame.
He is near who upholds my right;
  if anyone wishes to oppose me,
  let us appear together.
Who disputes my right?
  Let him confront me.
See, the Lord God is my help;
  who will prove me wrong?

The word of the Lord.

RESPONSORIAL PSALM

Psalm 69:8-10, 21-22, 31 and 33-34

℟. (14c) **Lord, in your great love, answer me.**

**For your sake I bear insult,
 and shame covers my face.
I have become an outcast to my brothers,
 a stranger to my mother's sons,
because zeal for your house consumes me,
 and the insults of those who blaspheme you fall upon me.**

℟. **Lord, in your great love, answer me.**

**Insult has broken my heart, and I am weak,
 I looked for sympathy, but there was none;
 for consolers, not one could I find.
Rather they put gall in my food,
 and in my thirst they gave me vinegar to drink.**

℟. **Lord, in your great love, answer me.**

**I will praise the name of God in song,
 and I will glorify him with thanksgiving:
"See, you lowly ones, and be glad;
 you who seek God, may your hearts revive!
For the L<small>ORD</small> hears the poor,
 and his own who are in bonds he spurns not."**

℟. **Lord, in your great love, answer me.**

VERSE BEFORE THE GOSPEL

A

**Hail to you, our King;
you alone are compassionate with our errors.**

OR

B

**Hail to you, our King, obedient to the Father;
you were led to your crucifixion like a gentle lamb to the slaughter.**

GOSPEL

Matthew 26:14-25   The Son of Man indeed goes, as it is written of him, but woe to that man by whom the Son of Man is betrayed.

☩ **A reading from the holy Gospel according to Matthew**

One of the Twelve, who was called Judas Iscariot,
   went to the chief priests and said,
   "What are you willing to give me
   if I hand him over to you?"
They paid him thirty pieces of silver,
   and from that time on he looked for an opportunity to hand him over.

On the first day of the Feast of Unleavened Bread,
   the disciples approached Jesus and said,
   "Where do you want us to prepare
   for you to eat the Passover?"
He said,
   "Go into the city to a certain man and tell him,
   'The teacher says, "My appointed time draws near;
   in your house I shall celebrate the Passover with my disciples."'"
The disciples then did as Jesus had ordered,
   and prepared the Passover.

When it was evening,
   he reclined at table with the Twelve.
And while they were eating, he said,
   "Amen, I say to you, one of you will betray me."
Deeply distressed at this,
   they began to say to him one after another,
   "Surely it is not I, Lord?"
He said in reply,
   "He who has dipped his hand into the dish with me
   is the one who will betray me.
The Son of Man indeed goes, as it is written of him,
   but woe to that man by whom the Son of Man is betrayed.
It would be better for that man if he had never been born."
Then Judas, his betrayer, said in reply,
   "Surely it is not I, Rabbi?"
He answered, "You have said so."

The Gospel of the Lord.

260 THURSDAY OF HOLY WEEK
CHRISM MASS

FIRST READING

Isaiah 61:1-3a, 6a, 8b-9   The Lord anointed me and sent me to bring glad tidings to the lowly, and to give them oil of gladness.

A reading from the Book of the Prophet Isaiah

> **The Spirit of the Lord God is upon me,**
> **because the Lord has anointed me;**
> **He has sent me to bring glad tidings to the lowly,**
> **to heal the brokenhearted,**
> **To proclaim liberty to the captives**
> **and release to the prisoners,**
> **To announce a year of favor from the Lord**
> **and a day of vindication by our God,**
> **to comfort all who mourn;**
> **To place on those who mourn in Zion**
> **a diadem instead of ashes,**
> **To give them oil of gladness in place of mourning,**
> **a glorious mantle instead of a listless spirit.**
>
> **You yourselves shall be named priests of the Lord,**
> **ministers of our God shall you be called.**
>
> **I will give them their recompense faithfully,**
> **a lasting covenant I will make with them.**
> **Their descendants shall be renowned among the nations,**
> **and their offspring among the peoples;**
> **All who see them shall acknowledge them**
> **as a race the Lord has blessed.**

The word of the Lord.

RESPONSORIAL PSALM

Psalm 89:21-22, 25 and 27

℟. (2) **For ever I will sing the goodness of the Lord.**

"I have found David, my servant;
  with my holy oil I have anointed him.
That my hand may always be with him;
  and that my arm may make him strong."

℟. **For ever I will sing the goodness of the Lord.**

"My faithfulness and my mercy shall be with him;
  and through my name shall his horn be exalted.
He shall say of me, 'You are my father,
  my God, the Rock, my savior!'"

℟. **For ever I will sing the goodness of the Lord.**

SECOND READING

Revelation 1:5-8   Christ has made us into a Kingdom, priests for his God and Father.

A reading from the Book of Revelation

[Grace to you and peace] **from Jesus Christ, who is the faithful witness,**
  the firstborn of the dead and ruler of the kings of the earth.
To him who loves us and has freed us from our sins by his Blood,
  who has made us into a Kingdom, priests for his God and Father,
  to him be glory and power forever and ever. Amen.

  Behold, he is coming amid the clouds,
    and every eye will see him,
    even those who pierced him.
  All the peoples of the earth will lament him.
    Yes. Amen.

"I am the Alpha and the Omega," says the Lord God,
  "the one who is and who was and who is to come, the Almighty."

The word of the Lord.

VERSE BEFORE THE GOSPEL

Isaiah 61:1 (cited in Luke 4:18)

The Spirit of the LORD **is upon me;
for he has sent me to bring glad tidings to the poor.**

GOSPEL

Luke 4:16-21   The Spirit of the Lord is upon me, because of which he has anointed me.

✛ **A reading from the holy Gospel according to Luke**

**Jesus came to Nazareth, where he had grown up,
   and went according to his custom
   into the synagogue on the sabbath day.
He stood up to read and was handed a scroll of the prophet Isaiah.
He unrolled the scroll and found the passage where it was written:**

> *The Spirit of the Lord is upon me,
> because he has anointed me
>   to bring glad tidings to the poor.
> He has sent me to proclaim liberty to captives
>   and recovery of sight to the blind,
>   to let the oppressed go free,
> and to proclaim a year acceptable to the Lord.*

**Rolling up the scroll, he handed it back to the attendant and sat down,
   and the eyes of all in the synagogue looked intently at him.
He said to them,
   "Today this Scripture passage is fulfilled in your hearing."**

The Gospel of the Lord.

SEASON OF EASTER

261 MONDAY OF THE OCTAVE OF EASTER

FIRST READING

Acts 2:14, 22-33 God raised this Jesus; of this we are all witnesses.

A reading from the Acts of the Apostles

On the day of Pentecost, Peter stood up with the Eleven,
  raised his voice, and proclaimed:
    "You who are Jews, indeed all of you staying in Jerusalem.
Let this be known to you, and listen to my words.

"You who are children of Israel, hear these words.
Jesus the Nazorean was a man commended to you by God
  with mighty deeds, wonders, and signs,
    which God worked through him in your midst, as you yourselves know.
This man, delivered up by the set plan and foreknowledge of God,
  you killed, using lawless men to crucify him.
But God raised him up, releasing him from the throes of death,
  because it was impossible for him to be held by it.
For David says of him:

> *I saw the Lord ever before me,*
>   *with him at my right hand I shall not be disturbed.*
> *Therefore my heart has been glad and my tongue has exulted;*
>   *my flesh, too, will dwell in hope,*
> *because you will not abandon my soul to the nether world,*
>   *nor will you suffer your holy one to see corruption.*
> *You have made known to me the paths of life;*
>   *you will fill me with joy in your presence.*

My brothers, one can confidently say to you
  about the patriarch David that he died and was buried,
    and his tomb is in our midst to this day.
But since he was a prophet and knew that God had sworn an oath to him
  that he would set one of his descendants upon his throne,
    he foresaw and spoke of the resurrection of the Christ,
    that neither was he abandoned to the netherworld
    nor did his flesh see corruption.
God raised this Jesus;
  of this we are all witnesses.
Exalted at the right hand of God,
  he poured forth the promise of the Holy Spirit
  that he received from the Father, as you both see and hear."

The word of the Lord.

RESPONSORIAL PSALM

Psalm 16:1-2a and 5, 7-8, 9-10, 11

℟. (1) **Keep me safe, O God; you are my hope.**
   or:
℟. **Alleluia.**

Keep me, O God, for in you I take refuge;
   I say to the Lord, "My Lord are you."
O Lord, my allotted portion and my cup,
   you it is who hold fast my lot.

℟. **Keep me safe, O God; you are my hope.**
   or:
℟. **Alleluia.**

I bless the Lord who counsels me;
   even in the night my heart exhorts me.
I set the Lord ever before me;
   with him at my right hand I shall not be disturbed.

℟. **Keep me safe, O God; you are my hope.**
   or:
℟. **Alleluia.**

Therefore my heart is glad and my soul rejoices,
   my body, too, abides in confidence;
Because you will not abandon my soul to the nether world,
   nor will you suffer your faithful one to undergo corruption.

℟. **Keep me safe, O God; you are my hope.**
   or:
℟. **Alleluia.**

You will show me the path to life,
   fullness of joys in your presence,
   the delights at your right hand forever.

℟. **Keep me safe, O God; you are my hope.**
   or:
℟. **Alleluia.**

ALLELUIA

Psalm 118:24

℟. Alleluia, alleluia.

**This is the day the Lord has made;
let us be glad and rejoice in it.**

℟. Alleluia, alleluia.

GOSPEL

Matthew 28:8-15   Go tell my brothers to go to Galilee, and there they will see me.

✛ **A reading from the holy Gospel according to Matthew**

**Mary Magdalene and the other Mary went away quickly from the tomb,
   fearful yet overjoyed,
   and ran to announce the news to his disciples.
And behold, Jesus met them on their way and greeted them.
They approached, embraced his feet, and did him homage.
Then Jesus said to them, "Do not be afraid.
Go tell my brothers to go to Galilee,
   and there they will see me."**

**While they were going, some of the guard went into the city
   and told the chief priests all that had happened.
The chief priests assembled with the elders and took counsel;
   then they gave a large sum of money to the soldiers,
   telling them, "You are to say,
   'His disciples came by night and stole him while we were asleep.'
And if this gets to the ears of the governor,
   we will satisfy him and keep you out of trouble."
The soldiers took the money and did as they were instructed.
And this story has circulated among the Jews to the present day.**

The Gospel of the Lord.

262 TUESDAY OF THE OCTAVE OF EASTER

FIRST READING

Acts 2:36-41   Repent and be baptized, every one of you, in the name of Jesus Christ.

A reading from the Acts of the Apostles

**On the day of Pentecost, Peter said to the Jewish people,
 "Let the whole house of Israel know for certain
 that God has made him both Lord and Christ,
 this Jesus whom you crucified."**

**Now when they heard this, they were cut to the heart,
 and they asked Peter and the other Apostles,
 "What are we to do, my brothers?"
Peter said to them,
 "Repent and be baptized, every one of you,
 in the name of Jesus Christ, for the forgiveness of your sins;
 and you will receive the gift of the Holy Spirit.
For the promise is made to you and to your children
 and to all those far off,
 whomever the Lord our God will call."
He testified with many other arguments, and was exhorting them,
 "Save yourselves from this corrupt generation."
Those who accepted his message were baptized,
 and about three thousand persons were added that day.**

The word of the Lord.

RESPONSORIAL PSALM

Psalm 33:4-5, 18-19, 20 and 22

℟. (5b) **The earth is full of the goodness of the Lord.**
   or:
℟. **Alleluia.**

Upright is the word of the LORD**,
   and all his works are trustworthy.
He loves justice and right;
   of the kindness of the L**ORD **the earth is full.**

℟. **The earth is full of the goodness of the Lord.**
   or:
℟. **Alleluia.**

See, the eyes of the LORD **are upon those who fear him,
   upon those who hope for his kindness,
To deliver them from death
   and preserve them in spite of famine.**

℟. **The earth is full of the goodness of the Lord.**
   or:
℟. **Alleluia.**

Our soul waits for the LORD**,
   who is our help and our shield.
May your kindness, O L**ORD**, be upon us
   who have put our hope in you.**

℟. **The earth is full of the goodness of the Lord.**
   or:
℟. **Alleluia.**

ALLELUIA

Psalm 118:24

℟. **Alleluia, alleluia.**

**This is the day the Lord has made;
let us be glad and rejoice in it.**

℟. **Alleluia, alleluia.**

GOSPEL

John 20:11-18   I have seen the Lord, and he said these things to me.

☩ A reading from the holy Gospel according to John

Mary Magdalene stayed outside the tomb weeping.
And as she wept, she bent over into the tomb
   and saw two angels in white sitting there,
   one at the head and one at the feet
   where the Body of Jesus had been.
And they said to her, "Woman, why are you weeping?"
She said to them, "They have taken my Lord,
   and I don't know where they laid him."
When she had said this, she turned around and saw Jesus there,
   but did not know it was Jesus.
Jesus said to her, "Woman, why are you weeping?
Whom are you looking for?"
She thought it was the gardener and said to him,
   "Sir, if you carried him away,
   tell me where you laid him,
   and I will take him."
Jesus said to her, "Mary!"
She turned and said to him in Hebrew, "Rabbouni,"
   which means Teacher.
Jesus said to her, "Stop holding on to me,
   for I have not yet ascended to the Father.
But go to my brothers and tell them,
   'I am going to my Father and your Father,
   to my God and your God.'"
Mary went and announced to the disciples,
   "I have seen the Lord,"
   and then reported what he had told her.

The Gospel of the Lord.

263 WEDNESDAY OF THE OCTAVE OF EASTER

FIRST READING

Acts 3:1-10   What I do have I give you: in the name of the Lord Jesus, rise and walk.

A reading from the Acts of the Apostles

**Peter and John were going up to the temple area
 for the three o'clock hour of prayer.
And a man crippled from birth was carried
 and placed at the gate of the temple called "the Beautiful Gate" every day
 to beg for alms from the people who entered the temple.
When he saw Peter and John about to go into the temple,
 he asked for alms.
But Peter looked intently at him, as did John,
 and said, "Look at us."
He paid attention to them, expecting to receive something from them.
Peter said, "I have neither silver nor gold,
 but what I do have I give you:
 in the name of Jesus Christ the Nazorean, rise and walk."
Then Peter took him by the right hand and raised him up,
 and immediately his feet and ankles grew strong.
He leaped up, stood, and walked around,
 and went into the temple with them,
 walking and jumping and praising God.
When all the people saw him walking and praising God,
 they recognized him as the one
 who used to sit begging at the Beautiful Gate of the temple,
 and they were filled with amazement and astonishment
 at what had happened to him.**

The word of the Lord.

RESPONSORIAL PSALM

Psalm 105:1-2, 3-4, 6-7, 8-9

℟. (3b) **Rejoice, O hearts that seek the Lord.**
   or:
℟. **Alleluia.**

Give thanks to the LORD**, invoke his name;**
   make known among the nations his deeds.
Sing to him, sing his praise,
   proclaim all his wondrous deeds.

℟. **Rejoice, O hearts that seek the Lord.**
   or:
℟. **Alleluia.**

Glory in his holy name;
   rejoice, O hearts that seek the LORD**!**
Look to the LORD **in his strength;**
   seek to serve him constantly.

℟. **Rejoice, O hearts that seek the Lord.**
   or:
℟. **Alleluia.**

You descendants of Abraham, his servants,
   sons of Jacob, his chosen ones!
He, the LORD**, is our God;**
   throughout the earth his judgments prevail.

℟. **Rejoice, O hearts that seek the Lord.**
   or:
℟. **Alleluia.**

He remembers forever his covenant
   which he made binding for a thousand generations–
Which he entered into with Abraham
   and by his oath to Isaac.

℟. **Rejoice, O hearts that seek the Lord.**
   or:
℟. **Alleluia.**

ALLELUIA

Psalm 118:24

℟. Alleluia, alleluia.

**This is the day the Lord has made;
let us be glad and rejoice in it.**

℟. Alleluia, alleluia.

GOSPEL

Luke 24:13-35   They recognized Jesus in the breaking of the bread.

✠ A reading from the holy Gospel according to Luke

That very day, the first day of the week,
   two of Jesus' disciples were going
   to a village seven miles from Jerusalem called Emmaus,
   and they were conversing about all the things that had occurred.
And it happened that while they were conversing and debating,
   Jesus himself drew near and walked with them,
   but their eyes were prevented from recognizing him.
He asked them,
   "What are you discussing as you walk along?"
They stopped, looking downcast.
One of them, named Cleopas, said to him in reply,
   "Are you the only visitor to Jerusalem
   who does not know of the things
   that have taken place there in these days?"
And he replied to them, "What sort of things?"
They said to him,
   "The things that happened to Jesus the Nazarene,
   who was a prophet mighty in deed and word
   before God and all the people,
   how our chief priests and rulers both handed him over
   to a sentence of death and crucified him.
But we were hoping that he would be the one to redeem Israel;
   and besides all this,
   it is now the third day since this took place.
Some women from our group, however, have astounded us:
   they were at the tomb early in the morning
   and did not find his Body;
   they came back and reported
   that they had indeed seen a vision of angels
   who announced that he was alive.
Then some of those with us went to the tomb
   and found things just as the women had described,
   but him they did not see."

And he said to them, "Oh, how foolish you are!
How slow of heart to believe all that the prophets spoke!
Was it not necessary that the Christ should suffer these things
   and enter into his glory?"
Then beginning with Moses and all the prophets,
   he interpreted to them what referred to him
   in all the Scriptures.
As they approached the village to which they were going,
   he gave the impression that he was going on farther.
But they urged him, "Stay with us,
   for it is nearly evening and the day is almost over."
So he went in to stay with them.
And it happened that, while he was with them at table,
   he took bread, said the blessing,
   broke it, and gave it to them.
With that their eyes were opened and they recognized him,
   but he vanished from their sight.
Then they said to each other,
   "Were not our hearts burning within us
   while he spoke to us on the way and opened the Scriptures to us?"
So they set out at once and returned to Jerusalem
   where they found gathered together
   the Eleven and those with them who were saying,
   "The Lord has truly been raised and has appeared to Simon!"
Then the two recounted what had taken place on the way
   and how he was made known to them in the breaking of the bread.

The Gospel of the Lord.

264 THURSDAY OF THE OCTAVE OF EASTER

FIRST READING

Acts 3:11-26 The author of life you put to death, but God raised him from the dead.

A reading from the Acts of the Apostles

As the crippled man who had been cured clung to Peter and John,
> all the people hurried in amazement toward them
> in the portico called "Solomon's Portico."

When Peter saw this, he addressed the people,
> "You children of Israel, why are you amazed at this,
> and why do you look so intently at us
> as if we had made him walk by our own power or piety?

The God of Abraham, the God of Isaac, and the God of Jacob,
> the God of our fathers, has glorified his servant Jesus
> whom you handed over and denied in Pilate's presence,
> when he had decided to release him.

You denied the Holy and Righteous One
> and asked that a murderer be released to you.

The author of life you put to death,
> but God raised him from the dead; of this we are witnesses.

And by faith in his name,
> this man, whom you see and know, his name has made strong,
> and the faith that comes through it
> has given him this perfect health,
> in the presence of all of you.

Now I know, brothers and sisters,
> that you acted out of ignorance, just as your leaders did;
> but God has thus brought to fulfillment
> what he had announced beforehand
> through the mouth of all the prophets,
> that his Christ would suffer.

Repent, therefore, and be converted, that your sins may be wiped away,
> and that the Lord may grant you times of refreshment
> and send you the Christ already appointed for you, Jesus,
> whom heaven must receive until the times of universal restoration
> of which God spoke through the mouth
> of his holy prophets from of old.

For Moses said:

> *A prophet like me will the Lord, your God, raise up for you*
>   *from among your own kin;*
> *to him you shall listen in all that he may say to you.*
> *Everyone who does not listen to that prophet*
>   *will be cut off from the people.*

"Moreover, all the prophets who spoke,
   from Samuel and those afterwards, also announced these days.
You are the children of the prophets
   and of the covenant that God made with your ancestors
   when he said to Abraham,
In your offspring all the families of the earth shall be blessed.
For you first, God raised up his servant and sent him to bless you
   by turning each of you from your evil ways."

The word of the Lord.

RESPONSORIAL PSALM

Psalm 8:2ab and 5, 6-7, 8-9

℟. (2ab) **O Lord, our God, how wonderful your name in all the earth!**
 or:
℟. **Alleluia.**

**O LORD, our Lord,
 how glorious is your name over all the earth!
What is man that you should be mindful of him,
 or the son of man that you should care for him?**

℟. **O Lord, our God, how wonderful your name in all the earth!**
 or:
℟. **Alleluia.**

**You have made him little less than the angels,
 and crowned him with glory and honor.
You have given him rule over the works of your hands,
 putting all things under his feet.**

℟. **O Lord, our God, how wonderful your name in all the earth!**
 or:
℟. **Alleluia.**

**All sheep and oxen,
 yes, and the beasts of the field,
The birds of the air, the fishes of the sea,
 and whatever swims the paths of the seas.**

℟. **O Lord, our God, how wonderful your name in all the earth!**
 or:
℟. **Alleluia.**

ALLELUIA

Psalm 118:24

℟. **Alleluia, alleluia.**

**This is the day the Lord has made;
let us be glad and rejoice in it.**

℟. **Alleluia, alleluia.**

GOSPEL

Luke 24:35-48   Thus it was written that the Christ would suffer and rise from the dead on the third day.

✠ A reading from the holy Gospel according to Luke

The disciples of Jesus recounted what had taken place along the way,
  and how they had come to recognize him in the breaking of bread.

While they were still speaking about this,
  he stood in their midst and said to them,
  "Peace be with you."
But they were startled and terrified
  and thought that they were seeing a ghost.
Then he said to them, "Why are you troubled?
And why do questions arise in your hearts?
Look at my hands and my feet, that it is I myself.
Touch me and see, because a ghost does not have flesh and bones
  as you can see I have."
And as he said this,
  he showed them his hands and his feet.
While they were still incredulous for joy and were amazed,
  he asked them, "Have you anything here to eat?"
They gave him a piece of baked fish;
  he took it and ate it in front of them.

He said to them,
  "These are my words that I spoke to you while I was still with you,
  that everything written about me in the law of Moses
  and in the prophets and psalms must be fulfilled."
Then he opened their minds to understand the Scriptures.
And he said to them,
  "Thus it is written that the Christ would suffer
  and rise from the dead on the third day
  and that repentance, for the forgiveness of sins,
  would be preached in his name
  to all the nations, beginning from Jerusalem.
You are witnesses of these things."

The Gospel of the Lord.

265 FRIDAY OF THE OCTAVE OF EASTER

FIRST READING

Acts 4:1-12   There is no salvation through anyone else.

A reading from the Acts of the Apostles

After the crippled man had been cured,
   while Peter and John were still speaking to the people,
   the priests, the captain of the temple guard,
   and the Sadducees confronted them,
      disturbed that they were teaching the people
      and proclaiming in Jesus the resurrection of the dead.
They laid hands on Peter and John
   and put them in custody until the next day,
   since it was already evening.
But many of those who heard the word came to believe
   and the number of men grew to about five thousand.

On the next day, their leaders, elders, and scribes
   were assembled in Jerusalem, with Annas the high priest,
   Caiaphas, John, Alexander,
   and all who were of the high-priestly class.
They brought them into their presence and questioned them,
   "By what power or by what name have you done this?"
Then Peter, filled with the Holy Spirit, answered them,
   "Leaders of the people and elders:
   If we are being examined today
   about a good deed done to a cripple,
   namely, by what means he was saved,
   then all of you and all the people of Israel should know
   that it was in the name of Jesus Christ the Nazorean
   whom you crucified, whom God raised from the dead;
   in his name this man stands before you healed.
He is *the stone rejected by you, the builders,*
   which has become the cornerstone.
There is no salvation through anyone else,
   nor is there any other name under heaven
   given to the human race by which we are to be saved."

The word of the Lord.

RESPONSORIAL PSALM

Psalm 118:1-2 and 4, 22-24, 25-27a

℟. (22) **The stone rejected by the builders has become the cornerstone.**
   or:
℟. **Alleluia.**

Give thanks to the Lord, for he is good,
   for his mercy endures forever.
Let the house of Israel say,
   "His mercy endures forever."
Let those who fear the Lord say,
   "His mercy endures forever."

℟. **The stone rejected by the builders has become the cornerstone.**
   or:
℟. **Alleluia.**

The stone which the builders rejected
   has become the cornerstone.
By the Lord has this been done;
   it is wonderful in our eyes.
This is the day the Lord has made;
   let us be glad and rejoice in it.

℟. **The stone rejected by the builders has become the cornerstone.**
   or:
℟. **Alleluia.**

O Lord, grant salvation!
   O Lord, grant prosperity!
Blessed is he who comes in the name of the Lord;
   we bless you from the house of the Lord.
   The Lord is God, and he has given us light.

℟. **The stone rejected by the builders has become the cornerstone.**
   or:
℟. **Alleluia.**

ALLELUIA

Psalm 118:24

℟. Alleluia, alleluia.

This is the day the Lord has made;
let us be glad and rejoice in it.

℟. Alleluia, alleluia.

GOSPEL

John 21:1-14   Jesus came over and took the bread and gave it to them, and in like manner the fish.

✛ A reading from the holy Gospel according to John

Jesus revealed himself again to his disciples at the Sea of Tiberias.
He revealed himself in this way.
Together were Simon Peter, Thomas called Didymus,
   Nathanael from Cana in Galilee,
   Zebedee's sons, and two others of his disciples.
Simon Peter said to them, "I am going fishing."
They said to him, "We also will come with you."
So they went out and got into the boat,
   but that night they caught nothing.
When it was already dawn, Jesus was standing on the shore;
   but the disciples did not realize that it was Jesus.
Jesus said to them, "Children, have you caught anything to eat?"
They answered him, "No."
So he said to them, "Cast the net over the right side of the boat
   and you will find something."
So they cast it, and were not able to pull it in
   because of the number of fish.
So the disciple whom Jesus loved said to Peter, "It is the Lord."
When Simon Peter heard that it was the Lord,
   he tucked in his garment, for he was lightly clad,
   and jumped into the sea.
The other disciples came in the boat,
   for they were not far from shore, only about a hundred yards,
   dragging the net with the fish.

When they climbed out on shore,
> they saw a charcoal fire with fish on it and bread.

Jesus said to them, "Bring some of the fish you just caught."

So Simon Peter went over and dragged the net ashore
> full of one hundred fifty-three large fish.

Even though there were so many, the net was not torn.

Jesus said to them, "Come, have breakfast."

And none of the disciples dared to ask him, "Who are you?"
> because they realized it was the Lord.

Jesus came over and took the bread and gave it to them,
> and in like manner the fish.

This was now the third time Jesus was revealed to his disciples
> after being raised from the dead.

The Gospel of the Lord.

266 SATURDAY OF THE OCTAVE OF EASTER

FIRST READING

Acts 4:13-21 It is impossible for us not to speak about what we have seen and heard.

A reading from the Acts of the Apostles

Observing the boldness of Peter and John
　and perceiving them to be uneducated, ordinary men,
　the leaders, elders, and scribes were amazed,
　and they recognized them as the companions of Jesus.
Then when they saw the man who had been cured standing there with them,
　they could say nothing in reply.
So they ordered them to leave the Sanhedrin,
　and conferred with one another, saying,
　"What are we to do with these men?
Everyone living in Jerusalem knows that a remarkable sign
　was done through them, and we cannot deny it.
But so that it may not be spread any further among the people,
　let us give them a stern warning
　never again to speak to anyone in this name."

So they called them back
　and ordered them not to speak or teach at all in the name of Jesus.
Peter and John, however, said to them in reply,
　"Whether it is right in the sight of God
　for us to obey you rather than God, you be the judges.
It is impossible for us not to speak about what we have seen and heard."
After threatening them further,
　they released them,
　finding no way to punish them,
　on account of the people who were all praising God
　for what had happened.

The word of the Lord.

RESPONSORIAL PSALM

Psalm 118:1 and 14-15ab, 16-18, 19-21

℟. (21a) **I will give thanks to you, for you have answered me.**
    or:
℟. **Alleluia.**

Give thanks to the LORD, for he is good,
    for his mercy endures forever.
My strength and my courage is the LORD,
    and he has been my savior.
The joyful shout of victory
    in the tents of the just.

℟. **I will give thanks to you, for you have answered me.**
    or:
℟. **Alleluia.**

"The right hand of the LORD is exalted;
    the right hand of the LORD has struck with power."
I shall not die, but live,
    and declare the works of the LORD.
Though the LORD has indeed chastised me,
    yet he has not delivered me to death.

℟. **I will give thanks to you, for you have answered me.**
    or:
℟. **Alleluia.**

Open to me the gates of justice;
    I will enter them and give thanks to the LORD.
This is the gate of the LORD;
    the just shall enter it.
I will give thanks to you, for you have answered me
    and have been my savior.

℟. **I will give thanks to you, for you have answered me.**
    or:
℟. **Alleluia.**

ALLELUIA

Psalm 118:24

℟. Alleluia, alleluia.

This is the day the Lord has made;
let us be glad and rejoice in it.

℟. Alleluia, alleluia.

GOSPEL

Mark 16:9-15   Go into the whole world and proclaim the Gospel to every creature.

✠ A reading from the holy Gospel according to Mark

When Jesus had risen, early on the first day of the week,
   he appeared first to Mary Magdalene,
   out of whom he had driven seven demons.
She went and told his companions who were mourning and weeping.
When they heard that he was alive
   and had been seen by her, they did not believe.

After this he appeared in another form
   to two of them walking along on their way to the country.
They returned and told the others;
   but they did not believe them either.

But later, as the Eleven were at table, he appeared to them
   and rebuked them for their unbelief and hardness of heart
   because they had not believed those
   who saw him after he had been raised.
He said to them, "Go into the whole world
   and proclaim the Gospel to every creature."

The Gospel of the Lord.

267 MONDAY OF THE SECOND WEEK OF EASTER

FIRST READING

Acts 4:23-31   As they prayed, they were all filled with the Holy Spirit and continued to speak the word of God with boldness.

A reading from the Acts of the Apostles

**After their release Peter and John went back to their own people
   and reported what the chief priests and elders had told them.
And when they heard it,
   they raised their voices to God with one accord
   and said, "Sovereign Lord, maker of heaven and earth
   and the sea and all that is in them,
   you said by the Holy Spirit
   through the mouth of our father David, your servant:**

*Why did the Gentiles rage
   and the peoples entertain folly?
The kings of the earth took their stand
   and the princes gathered together
   against the Lord and against his anointed.*

**"Indeed they gathered in this city
   against your holy servant Jesus whom you anointed,
   Herod and Pontius Pilate,
   together with the Gentiles and the peoples of Israel,
   to do what your hand and your will
   had long ago planned to take place.
And now, Lord, take note of their threats,
   and enable your servants to speak your word
   with all boldness, as you stretch forth your hand to heal,
   and signs and wonders are done
   through the name of your holy servant Jesus."
As they prayed, the place where they were gathered shook,
   and they were all filled with the Holy Spirit
   and continued to speak the word of God with boldness.**

The word of the Lord.

RESPONSORIAL PSALM

Psalm 2:1-3, 4-7a, 7b-9

℟. (see 11d) **Blessed are all who take refuge in the Lord.**
   or:
℟. **Alleluia.**

Why do the nations rage
   and the peoples utter folly?
The kings of the earth rise up,
   and the princes conspire together
   against the Lord and against his anointed:
"Let us break their fetters
   and cast their bonds from us!"

℟. **Blessed are all who take refuge in the Lord.**
   or:
℟. **Alleluia.**

He who is throned in heaven laughs;
   the Lord derides them.
Then in anger he speaks to them;
   he terrifies them in his wrath:
"I myself have set up my king
   on Zion, my holy mountain."
I will proclaim the decree of the Lord.

℟. **Blessed are all who take refuge in the Lord.**
   or:
℟. **Alleluia.**

The Lord said to me, "You are my Son;
   this day I have begotten you.
Ask of me and I will give you
   the nations for an inheritance
   and the ends of the earth for your possession.
You shall rule them with an iron rod;
   you shall shatter them like an earthen dish."

℟. **Blessed are all who take refuge in the Lord.**
   or:
℟. **Alleluia.**

ALLELUIA

Colossians 3:1

℟. Alleluia, alleluia.

**If then you were raised with Christ,
seek what is above,
where Christ is seated at the right hand of God.**

℟. Alleluia, alleluia.

GOSPEL

John 3:1-8   No one can enter the Kingdom of God without being born of water and Spirit.

✠ **A reading from the holy Gospel according to John**

**There was a Pharisee named Nicodemus, a ruler of the Jews.
He came to Jesus at night and said to him,
"Rabbi, we know that you are a teacher who has come from God,
for no one can do these signs that you are doing
unless God is with him."
Jesus answered and said to him,
"Amen, amen, I say to you,
unless one is born from above, he cannot see the Kingdom of God."
Nicodemus said to him,
"How can a man once grown old be born again?
Surely he cannot reenter his mother's womb and be born again, can he?"
Jesus answered,
"Amen, amen, I say to you,
unless one is born of water and Spirit
he cannot enter the Kingdom of God.
What is born of flesh is flesh
and what is born of spirit is spirit.
Do not be amazed that I told you,
'You must be born from above.'
The wind blows where it wills,
and you can hear the sound it makes,
but you do not know where it comes from or where it goes;
so it is with everyone who is born of the Spirit."**

The Gospel of the Lord.

268 TUESDAY OF THE SECOND WEEK OF EASTER

FIRST READING

Acts 4:32-37   The community of believers was of one heart and mind.

A reading from the Acts of the Apostles

**The community of believers was of one heart and mind,
 and no one claimed that any of his possessions was his own,
 but they had everything in common.
With great power the Apostles bore witness
 to the resurrection of the Lord Jesus,
 and great favor was accorded them all.
There was no needy person among them,
 for those who owned property or houses would sell them,
 bring the proceeds of the sale,
 and put them at the feet of the Apostles,
 and they were distributed to each according to need.**

**Thus Joseph, also named by the Apostles Barnabas
 (which is translated "son of encouragement"),
 a Levite, a Cypriot by birth,
 sold a piece of property that he owned,
 then brought the money and put it at the feet of the Apostles.**

The word of the Lord.

RESPONSORIAL PSALM

Psalm 93:1ab, 1cd-2, 5

℟. (1a) **The Lord is king; he is robed in majesty.**
   or:
℟. **Alleluia.**

The Lord is king, in splendor robed;
   robed is the Lord and girt about with strength.

℟. **The Lord is king; he is robed in majesty.**
   or:
℟. **Alleluia.**

And he has made the world firm,
   not to be moved.
Your throne stands firm from of old;
   from everlasting you are, O Lord.

℟. **The Lord is king; he is robed in majesty.**
   or:
℟. **Alleluia.**

Your decrees are worthy of trust indeed:
   holiness befits your house,
   O Lord, for length of days.

℟. **The Lord is king; he is robed in majesty.**
   or:
℟. **Alleluia.**

ALLELUIA

John 3:14-15

℟. Alleluia, alleluia.

**The Son of Man must be lifted up,
so that everyone who believes in him
may have eternal life.**

℟. Alleluia, alleluia.

GOSPEL

John 3:7b-15   No one has gone up to heaven except the one who has come down from heaven, the Son of Man.

✠ **A reading from the holy Gospel according to John**

Jesus said to Nicodemus:
   "'You must be born from above.'
The wind blows where it wills, and you can hear the sound it makes,
   but you do not know where it comes from or where it goes;
   so it is with everyone who is born of the Spirit."
Nicodemus answered and said to him,
   "How can this happen?"
Jesus answered and said to him,
   "You are the teacher of Israel and you do not understand this?
Amen, amen, I say to you,
   we speak of what we know and we testify to what we have seen,
   but you people do not accept our testimony.
If I tell you about earthly things and you do not believe,
   how will you believe if I tell you about heavenly things?
No one has gone up to heaven
   except the one who has come down from heaven, the Son of Man.
And just as Moses lifted up the serpent in the desert,
   so must the Son of Man be lifted up,
   so that everyone who believes in him may have eternal life."

The Gospel of the Lord.

269 WEDNESDAY OF THE SECOND WEEK OF EASTER

FIRST READING

Acts 5:17-26   *The men whom you put in prison are in the temple area and are teaching the people.*

A reading from the Acts of the Apostles

The high priest rose up and all his companions,
   that is, the party of the Sadducees,
   and, filled with jealousy,
   laid hands upon the Apostles and put them in the public jail.
But during the night, the angel of the Lord opened the doors of the prison,
   led them out, and said,
   "Go and take your place in the temple area,
   and tell the people everything about this life."
When they heard this,
   they went to the temple early in the morning and taught.
When the high priest and his companions arrived,
   they convened the Sanhedrin,
   the full senate of the children of Israel,
   and sent to the jail to have them brought in.
But the court officers who went did not find them in the prison,
   so they came back and reported,
   "We found the jail securely locked
   and the guards stationed outside the doors,
   but when we opened them, we found no one inside."
When the captain of the temple guard and the chief priests heard this report,
   they were at a loss about them,
   as to what this would come to.
Then someone came in and reported to them,
   "The men whom you put in prison are in the temple area
   and are teaching the people."
Then the captain and the court officers went and brought them,
   but without force,
   because they were afraid of being stoned by the people.

The word of the Lord.

RESPONSORIAL PSALM

Psalm 34:2-3, 4-5, 6-7, 8-9

℟. (7a) **The Lord hears the cry of the poor.**
   or:
℟. **Alleluia.**

I will bless the Lord at all times;
   his praise shall be ever in my mouth.
Let my soul glory in the Lord;
   the lowly will hear me and be glad.

℟. **The Lord hears the cry of the poor.**
   or:
℟. **Alleluia.**

Glorify the Lord with me,
   let us together extol his name.
I sought the Lord, and he answered me
   and delivered me from all my fears.

℟. **The Lord hears the cry of the poor.**
   or:
℟. **Alleluia.**

Look to him that you may be radiant with joy,
   and your faces may not blush with shame.
When the poor one called out, the Lord heard,
   and from all his distress he saved him.

℟. **The Lord hears the cry of the poor.**
   or:
℟. **Alleluia.**

The angel of the Lord encamps
   around those who fear him, and delivers them.
Taste and see how good the Lord is;
   blessed the man who takes refuge in him.

℟. **The Lord hears the cry of the poor.**
   or:
℟. **Alleluia.**

ALLELUIA

John 3:16

℟. Alleluia, alleluia.

**God so loved the world that he gave his only-begotten Son,
so that everyone who believes in him might have eternal life.**

℟. Alleluia, alleluia.

GOSPEL

John 3:16-21   God sent his Son that the world might be saved through him.

✠ A reading from the holy Gospel according to John

**God so loved the world that he gave his only-begotten Son,
   so that everyone who believes in him might not perish
   but might have eternal life.
For God did not send his Son into the world to condemn the world,
   but that the world might be saved through him.
Whoever believes in him will not be condemned,
   but whoever does not believe has already been condemned,
   because he has not believed in the name of the only-begotten Son of God.
And this is the verdict,
   that the light came into the world,
   but people preferred darkness to light,
   because their works were evil.
For everyone who does wicked things hates the light
   and does not come toward the light,
   so that his works might not be exposed.
But whoever lives the truth comes to the light,
   so that his works may be clearly seen as done in God.**

The Gospel of the Lord.

270 THURSDAY OF THE SECOND WEEK OF EASTER

FIRST READING

Acts 5:27-33   We are witnesses of these words, as is the Holy Spirit.

A reading from the Acts of the Apostles

**When the court officers had brought the Apostles in
 and made them stand before the Sanhedrin,
 the high priest questioned them,
 "We gave you strict orders did we not,
 to stop teaching in that name.
Yet you have filled Jerusalem with your teaching
 and want to bring this man's blood upon us."
But Peter and the Apostles said in reply,
 "We must obey God rather than men.
The God of our ancestors raised Jesus,
 though you had him killed by hanging him on a tree.
God exalted him at his right hand as leader and savior
 to grant Israel repentance and forgiveness of sins.
We are witnesses of these things,
 as is the Holy Spirit whom God has given to those who obey him."**

**When they heard this,
 they became infuriated and wanted to put them to death.**

The word of the Lord.

RESPONSORIAL PSALM

Psalm 34:2 and 9, 17-18, 19-20

℟. (7a) **The Lord hears the cry of the poor.**
or:
℟. **Alleluia.**

I will bless the LORD **at all times;**
   his praise shall be ever in my mouth.
Taste and see how good the LORD **is;**
   blessed the man who takes refuge in him.

℟. **The Lord hears the cry of the poor.**
or:
℟. **Alleluia.**

The LORD **confronts the evildoers,**
   to destroy remembrance of them from the earth.
When the just cry out, the LORD **hears them,**
   and from all their distress he rescues them.

℟. **The Lord hears the cry of the poor.**
or:
℟. **Alleluia.**

The LORD **is close to the brokenhearted;**
   and those who are crushed in spirit he saves.
Many are the troubles of the just man,
   but out of them all the LORD **delivers him.**

℟. **The Lord hears the cry of the poor.**
or:
℟. **Alleluia.**

ALLELUIA

John 20:29

℟. Alleluia, alleluia.

You believe in me, Thomas, because you have seen me, says the Lord; blessed are those who have not seen, but still believe!

℟. Alleluia, alleluia.

GOSPEL

John 3:31-36   The Father loves the Son and has given everything over to him.

✠ **A reading from the holy Gospel according to John**

**The one who comes from above is above all.
The one who is of the earth is earthly and speaks of earthly things.
But the one who comes from heaven is above all.
He testifies to what he has seen and heard,
   but no one accepts his testimony.
Whoever does accept his testimony certifies that God is trustworthy.
For the one whom God sent speaks the words of God.
He does not ration his gift of the Spirit.
The Father loves the Son and has given everything over to him.
Whoever believes in the Son has eternal life,
   but whoever disobeys the Son will not see life,
   but the wrath of God remains upon him.**

The Gospel of the Lord.

271 FRIDAY OF THE SECOND WEEK OF EASTER

FIRST READING

Acts 5:34-42   The Apostles went out rejoicing that they had been found worthy to suffer dishonor for the sake of the name.

A reading from the Acts of the Apostles

A Pharisee in the Sanhedrin named Gamaliel,
 a teacher of the law, respected by all the people,
 stood up, ordered the Apostles to be put outside for a short time,
 and said to the Sanhedrin, "Fellow children of Israel,
 be careful what you are about to do to these men.
Some time ago, Theudas appeared, claiming to be someone important,
 and about four hundred men joined him, but he was killed,
 and all those who were loyal to him
 were disbanded and came to nothing.
After him came Judas the Galilean at the time of the census.
He also drew people after him,
 but he too perished and all who were loyal to him were scattered.
So now I tell you,
 have nothing to do with these men, and let them go.
For if this endeavor or this activity is of human origin,
 it will destroy itself.
But if it comes from God, you will not be able to destroy them;
 you may even find yourselves fighting against God."
They were persuaded by him.
After recalling the Apostles, they had them flogged,
 ordered them to stop speaking in the name of Jesus,
 and dismissed them.
So they left the presence of the Sanhedrin,
 rejoicing that they had been found worthy
 to suffer dishonor for the sake of the name.
And all day long, both at the temple and in their homes,
 they did not stop teaching and proclaiming the Christ, Jesus.

The word of the Lord.

RESPONSORIAL PSALM

Psalm 27:1, 4, 13-14

℟. (see 4abc) **One thing I seek: to dwell in the house of the Lord.**
   or:
℟. **Alleluia.**

The Lord is my light and my salvation;
   whom should I fear?
The Lord is my life's refuge;
   of whom should I be afraid?

℟. **One thing I seek: to dwell in the house of the Lord.**
   or:
℟. **Alleluia.**

One thing I ask of the Lord;
   this I seek:
To dwell in the house of the Lord
   all the days of my life,
That I may gaze on the loveliness of the Lord
   and contemplate his temple.

℟. **One thing I seek: to dwell in the house of the Lord.**
   or:
℟. **Alleluia.**

I believe that I shall see the bounty of the Lord
   in the land of the living.
Wait for the Lord with courage;
   be stouthearted, and wait for the Lord.

℟. **One thing I seek: to dwell in the house of the Lord.**
   or:
℟. **Alleluia.**

ALLELUIA

Matthew 4:4b

℟. **Alleluia, alleluia.**

One does not live on bread alone,
but on every word that comes forth from the mouth of God.

℟. **Alleluia, alleluia.**

GOSPEL

John 6:1-15   Jesus distributed to those who were reclining as much as they wanted.

✠   A reading from the holy Gospel according to John

Jesus went across the Sea of Galilee.
A large crowd followed him,
　because they saw the signs he was performing on the sick.
Jesus went up on the mountain,
　and there he sat down with his disciples.
The Jewish feast of Passover was near.
When Jesus raised his eyes and saw that a large crowd was coming to him,
　he said to Philip, "Where can we buy enough food for them to eat?"
He said this to test him,
　because he himself knew what he was going to do.
Philip answered him,
　"Two hundred days' wages worth of food would not be enough
　for each of them to have a little."
One of his disciples,
　Andrew, the brother of Simon Peter, said to him,
　"There is a boy here who has five barley loaves and two fish;
　but what good are these for so many?"
Jesus said, "Have the people recline."
Now there was a great deal of grass in that place.
So the men reclined, about five thousand in number.
Then Jesus took the loaves, gave thanks,
　and distributed them to those who were reclining,
　and also as much of the fish as they wanted.
When they had had their fill, he said to his disciples,
　"Gather the fragments left over,
　so that nothing will be wasted."
So they collected them,
　and filled twelve wicker baskets with fragments
　from the five barley loaves that had been more than they could eat.
When the people saw the sign he had done, they said,
　"This is truly the Prophet, the one who is to come into the world."
Since Jesus knew that they were going to come and carry him off
　to make him king,
　he withdrew again to the mountain alone.

The Gospel of the Lord.

272 SATURDAY OF THE SECOND WEEK OF EASTER

FIRST READING

Acts 6:1-7 They chose seven men filled with the Holy Spirit.

A reading from the Acts of the Apostles

**As the number of disciples continued to grow,
   the Hellenists complained against the Hebrews
   because their widows
   were being neglected in the daily distribution.
So the Twelve called together the community of the disciples and said,
   "It is not right for us to neglect the word of God to serve at table.
Brothers, select from among you seven reputable men,
   filled with the Spirit and wisdom,
   whom we shall appoint to this task,
   whereas we shall devote ourselves to prayer
   and to the ministry of the word."
The proposal was acceptable to the whole community,
   so they chose Stephen, a man filled with faith and the Holy Spirit,
   also Philip, Prochorus, Nicanor, Timon, Parmenas,
   and Nicholas of Antioch, a convert to Judaism.
They presented these men to the Apostles
   who prayed and laid hands on them.
The word of God continued to spread,
   and the number of the disciples in Jerusalem increased greatly;
   even a large group of priests were becoming obedient to the faith.**

The word of the Lord.

RESPONSORIAL PSALM

Psalm 33:1-2, 4-5, 18-19

℟. (22) **Lord, let your mercy be on us, as we place our trust in you.**
   or:
℟. **Alleluia.**

**Exult, you just, in the LORD;
   praise from the upright is fitting.
Give thanks to the LORD on the harp;
   with the ten-stringed lyre chant his praises.**

℟. **Lord, let your mercy be on us, as we place our trust in you.**
   or:
℟. **Alleluia.**

**Upright is the word of the LORD,
   and all his works are trustworthy.
He loves justice and right;
   of the kindness of the LORD the earth is full.**

℟. **Lord, let your mercy be on us, as we place our trust in you.**
   or:
℟. **Alleluia.**

**See, the eyes of the LORD are upon those who fear him,
   upon those who hope for his kindness,
To deliver them from death
   and preserve them in spite of famine.**

℟. **Lord, let your mercy be on us, as we place our trust in you.**
   or:
℟. **Alleluia.**

ALLELUIA

℟. **Alleluia, alleluia.**

**Christ is risen, who made all things;
he has shown mercy on all people.**

℟. **Alleluia, alleluia.**

GOSPEL

John 6:16-21   They saw Jesus, walking on the sea.

✠ **A reading from the holy Gospel according to John**

**When it was evening, the disciples of Jesus went down to the sea,
    embarked in a boat, and went across the sea to Capernaum.
It had already grown dark, and Jesus had not yet come to them.
The sea was stirred up because a strong wind was blowing.
When they had rowed about three or four miles,
    they saw Jesus walking on the sea and coming near the boat,
    and they began to be afraid.
But he said to them, "It is I. Do not be afraid."
They wanted to take him into the boat,
    but the boat immediately arrived at the shore
    to which they were heading.**

The Gospel of the Lord.

273 MONDAY OF THE THIRD WEEK OF EASTER

FIRST READING

Acts 6:8-15 They could not withstand the wisdom and the Spirit with which he spoke.

A reading from the Acts of the Apostles

**Stephen, filled with grace and power,
was working great wonders and signs among the people.
Certain members of the so-called Synagogue of Freedmen,
Cyreneans, and Alexandrians,
and people from Cilicia and Asia,
came forward and debated with Stephen,
but they could not withstand the wisdom and the Spirit with which he spoke.
Then they instigated some men to say,
"We have heard him speaking blasphemous words
against Moses and God."
They stirred up the people, the elders, and the scribes,
accosted him, seized him,
and brought him before the Sanhedrin.
They presented false witnesses who testified,
"This man never stops saying things against this holy place and the law.
For we have heard him claim
that this Jesus the Nazorean will destroy this place
and change the customs that Moses handed down to us."
All those who sat in the Sanhedrin looked intently at him
and saw that his face was like the face of an angel.**

The word of the Lord.

RESPONSORIAL PSALM

Psalm 119:23-24, 26-27, 29-30

℟. (1ab) **Blessed are they who follow the law of the Lord!**
   or:
℟. **Alleluia.**

**Though princes meet and talk against me,
   your servant meditates on your statutes.
Yes, your decrees are my delight;
   they are my counselors.**

℟. **Blessed are they who follow the law of the Lord!**
   or:
℟. **Alleluia.**

**I declared my ways, and you answered me;
   teach me your statutes.
Make me understand the way of your precepts,
   and I will meditate on your wondrous deeds.**

℟. **Blessed are they who follow the law of the Lord!**
   or:
℟. **Alleluia.**

**Remove from me the way of falsehood,
   and favor me with your law.
The way of truth I have chosen;
   I have set your ordinances before me.**

℟. **Blessed are they who follow the law of the Lord!**
   or:
℟. **Alleluia.**

ALLELUIA

Matthew 4:4b

℟. **Alleluia, alleluia.**

**One does not live on bread alone
but on every word that comes forth from the mouth of God.**

℟. **Alleluia, alleluia.**

GOSPEL

John 6:22-29   Do not work for food that perishes but for food that endures for eternal life.

☩ A reading from the holy Gospel according to John

[After Jesus had fed the five thousand men, his disciples saw him walking
    on the sea.]
The next day, the crowd that remained across the sea
   saw that there had been only one boat there,
   and that Jesus had not gone along with his disciples in the boat,
   but only his disciples had left.
Other boats came from Tiberias
   near the place where they had eaten the bread
   when the Lord gave thanks.
When the crowd saw that neither Jesus nor his disciples were there,
   they themselves got into boats
   and came to Capernaum looking for Jesus.
And when they found him across the sea they said to him,
   "Rabbi, when did you get here?"
Jesus answered them and said,
   "Amen, amen, I say to you, you are looking for me
   not because you saw signs
   but because you ate the loaves and were filled.
Do not work for food that perishes
   but for the food that endures for eternal life,
   which the Son of Man will give you.
For on him the Father, God, has set his seal."
So they said to him,
   "What can we do to accomplish the works of God?"
Jesus answered and said to them,
   "This is the work of God, that you believe in the one he sent."

The Gospel of the Lord.

274 TUESDAY OF THE THIRD WEEK OF EASTER

FIRST READING

Acts 7:51—8:1a   Lord Jesus, receive my spirit.

A reading from the Acts of the Apostles

Stephen said to the people, the elders, and the scribes:
"You stiff-necked people, uncircumcised in heart and ears,
   you always oppose the Holy Spirit;
   you are just like your ancestors.
Which of the prophets did your ancestors not persecute?
They put to death those who foretold the coming of the righteous one,
   whose betrayers and murderers you have now become.
You received the law as transmitted by angels,
   but you did not observe it."

When they heard this, they were infuriated,
   and they ground their teeth at him.
But Stephen, filled with the Holy Spirit,
   looked up intently to heaven and saw the glory of God
   and Jesus standing at the right hand of God,
   and Stephen said, "Behold, I see the heavens opened
   and the Son of Man standing at the right hand of God."
But they cried out in a loud voice,
   covered their ears, and rushed upon him together.
They threw him out of the city, and began to stone him.
The witnesses laid down their cloaks
   at the feet of a young man named Saul.
As they were stoning Stephen, he called out,
   "Lord Jesus, receive my spirit."
Then he fell to his knees and cried out in a loud voice,
   "Lord, do not hold this sin against them";
   and when he said this, he fell asleep.

Now Saul was consenting to his execution.

The word of the Lord.

RESPONSORIAL PSALM

Psalm 31:3cd-4, 6 and 7b and 8a, 17 and 21ab

℟. (6a) **Into your hands, O Lord, I commend my spirit.**
   or:
℟. **Alleluia.**

**Be my rock of refuge,
   a stronghold to give me safety.
You are my rock and my fortress;
   for your name's sake you will lead and guide me.**

℟. **Into your hands, O Lord, I commend my spirit.**
   or:
℟. **Alleluia.**

**Into your hands I commend my spirit;
   you will redeem me, O Lord, O faithful God.
My trust is in the Lord;
   I will rejoice and be glad of your mercy.**

℟. **Into your hands, O Lord, I commend my spirit.**
   or:
℟. **Alleluia.**

**Let your face shine upon your servant;
   save me in your kindness.
You hide them in the shelter of your presence
   from the plottings of men.**

℟. **Into your hands, O Lord, I commend my spirit.**
   or:
℟. **Alleluia.**

ALLELUIA

John 6:35ab

℟. Alleluia, alleluia.

I am the bread of life, says the Lord;
whoever comes to me will never hunger.

℟. Alleluia, alleluia.

GOSPEL

John 6:30-35   It was not Moses, but my Father who gives you the true bread from heaven.

✠ A reading from the holy Gospel according to John

The crowd said to Jesus:
"What sign can you do, that we may see and believe in you?
What can you do?
Our ancestors ate manna in the desert, as it is written:

He gave them bread from heaven to eat."

So Jesus said to them,
    "Amen, amen, I say to you,
    it was not Moses who gave the bread from heaven;
    my Father gives you the true bread from heaven.
For the bread of God is that which comes down from heaven
    and gives life to the world."

So they said to Jesus,
    "Sir, give us this bread always."
Jesus said to them, "I am the bread of life;
    whoever comes to me will never hunger,
    and whoever believes in me will never thirst."

The Gospel of the Lord.

275 WEDNESDAY OF THE THIRD WEEK OF EASTER

FIRST READING

Acts 8:1b-8 They went about preaching the word.

A reading from Acts of the Apostles

**There broke out a severe persecution of the Church in Jerusalem,
 and all were scattered
  throughout the countryside of Judea and Samaria,
  except the Apostles.
Devout men buried Stephen and made a loud lament over him.
Saul, meanwhile, was trying to destroy the Church;
  entering house after house and dragging out men and women,
  he handed them over for imprisonment.**

**Now those who had been scattered went about preaching the word.
Thus Philip went down to the city of Samaria
  and proclaimed the Christ to them.
With one accord, the crowds paid attention to what was said by Philip
  when they heard it and saw the signs he was doing.
For unclean spirits, crying out in a loud voice,
  came out of many possessed people,
  and many paralyzed and crippled people were cured.
There was great joy in that city.**

The word of the Lord.

RESPONSORIAL PSALM

Psalm 66:1-3a, 4-5, 6-7a

℟. (1) **Let all the earth cry out to God with joy.**
or:
℟. **Alleluia.**

**Shout joyfully to God, all the earth,
sing praise to the glory of his name;
proclaim his glorious praise.
Say to God, "How tremendous are your deeds!"**

℟. **Let all the earth cry out to God with joy.**
or:
℟. **Alleluia.**

**"Let all on earth worship and sing praise to you,
sing praise to your name!"
Come and see the works of God,
his tremendous deeds among the children of Adam.**

℟. **Let all the earth cry out to God with joy.**
or:
℟. **Alleluia.**

**He has changed the sea into dry land;
through the river they passed on foot;
therefore let us rejoice in him.
He rules by his might forever.**

℟. **Let all the earth cry out to God with joy.**
or:
℟. **Alleluia.**

ALLELUIA

See John 6:40

℟. Alleluia, alleluia.

**Everyone who believes in the Son has eternal life,
and I shall raise him on the last day, says the Lord.**

℟. Alleluia, alleluia.

GOSPEL

John 6:35-40   This is the will of my Father, that all who see the Son may have eternal life.

✢ **A reading from the holy Gospel according to John**

**Jesus said to the crowds,
   "I am the bread of life;
   whoever comes to me will never hunger,
   and whoever believes in me will never thirst.
But I told you that although you have seen me,
   you do not believe.
Everything that the Father gives me will come to me,
   and I will not reject anyone who comes to me,
      because I came down from heaven not to do my own will
      but the will of the one who sent me.
And this is the will of the one who sent me,
   that I should not lose anything of what he gave me,
   but that I should raise it on the last day.
For this is the will of my Father,
   that everyone who sees the Son and believes in him
   may have eternal life,
   and I shall raise him on the last day."**

The Gospel of the Lord.

276 THURSDAY OF THE THIRD WEEK OF EASTER

FIRST READING

Acts 8:26-40   Look, there is water. What is to prevent my being baptized?

A reading from the Acts of the Apostles

The angel of the Lord spoke to Philip,
  "Get up and head south on the road
  that goes down from Jerusalem to Gaza, the desert route."
So he got up and set out.
Now there was an Ethiopian eunuch,
  a court official of the Candace,
  that is, the queen of the Ethiopians,
  in charge of her entire treasury,
  who had come to Jerusalem to worship, and was returning home.
Seated in his chariot, he was reading the prophet Isaiah.
The Spirit said to Philip,
  "Go and join up with that chariot."
Philip ran up and heard him reading Isaiah the prophet and said,
  "Do you understand what you are reading?"
He replied,
  "How can I, unless someone instructs me?"
So he invited Philip to get in and sit with him.
This was the Scripture passage he was reading:

  Like a sheep he was led to the slaughter,
    and as a lamb before its shearer is silent,
      so he opened not his mouth.
  In his humiliation justice was denied him.
    Who will tell of his posterity?
      For his life is taken from the earth.

Then the eunuch said to Philip in reply,
  "I beg you, about whom is the prophet saying this?
About himself, or about someone else?"
Then Philip opened his mouth and, beginning with this Scripture passage,
  he proclaimed Jesus to him.

As they traveled along the road
    they came to some water,
    and the eunuch said, "Look, there is water.
What is to prevent my being baptized?"
Then he ordered the chariot to stop,
    and Philip and the eunuch both went down into the water,
    and he baptized him.
When they came out of the water,
    the Spirit of the Lord snatched Philip away,
    and the eunuch saw him no more,
    but continued on his way rejoicing.
Philip came to Azotus, and went about proclaiming the good news
    to all the towns until he reached Caesarea.

The word of the Lord.

RESPONSORIAL PSALM

Psalm 66:8-9, 16-17, 20

℟. (1) **Let all the earth cry out to God with joy.**
   or:
℟. **Alleluia.**

**Bless our God, you peoples,
   loudly sound his praise;
He has given life to our souls,
   and has not let our feet slip.**

℟. **Let all the earth cry out to God with joy.**
   or:
℟. **Alleluia.**

**Hear now, all you who fear God, while I declare
   what he has done for me.
When I appealed to him in words,
   praise was on the tip of my tongue.**

℟. **Let all the earth cry out to God with joy.**
   or:
℟. **Alleluia.**

**Blessed be God who refused me not
   my prayer or his kindness!**

℟. **Let all the earth cry out to God with joy.**
   or:
℟. **Alleluia.**

ALLELUIA

John 6:51

℟. **Alleluia, alleluia.**

**I am the living bread that came down from heaven, says the Lord;
whoever eats this bread will live forever.**

℟. **Alleluia, alleluia.**

GOSPEL

John 6:44-51   I am the living bread that came down from heaven.

✠ **A reading from the holy Gospel according to John**

**Jesus said to the crowds:
"No one can come to me unless the Father who sent me draw him,
    and I will raise him on the last day.
It is written in the prophets:**

> *They shall all be taught by God.*

**Everyone who listens to my Father and learns from him comes to me.
Not that anyone has seen the Father
    except the one who is from God;
    he has seen the Father.
Amen, amen, I say to you,
    whoever believes has eternal life.
I am the bread of life.
Your ancestors ate the manna in the desert, but they died;
    this is the bread that comes down from heaven
    so that one may eat it and not die.
I am the living bread that came down from heaven;
    whoever eats this bread will live forever;
    and the bread that I will give
    is my Flesh for the life of the world."**

The Gospel of the Lord.

277 FRIDAY OF THE THIRD WEEK OF EASTER

FIRST READING

Acts 9:1-20   This man is a chosen instrument of mine to carry my name before the Gentiles.

A reading from the Acts of the Apostles

Saul, still breathing murderous threats against the disciples of the Lord,
 went to the high priest and asked him
 for letters to the synagogues in Damascus, that,
 if he should find any men or women who belonged to the Way,
 he might bring them back to Jerusalem in chains.
On his journey, as he was nearing Damascus,
 a light from the sky suddenly flashed around him.
He fell to the ground and heard a voice saying to him,
 "Saul, Saul, why are you persecuting me?"
He said, "Who are you, sir?"
The reply came, "I am Jesus, whom you are persecuting.
Now get up and go into the city and you will be told what you must do."
The men who were traveling with him stood speechless,
 for they heard the voice but could see no one.
Saul got up from the ground,
 but when he opened his eyes he could see nothing;
 so they led him by the hand and brought him to Damascus.
For three days he was unable to see, and he neither ate nor drank.

There was a disciple in Damascus named Ananias,
 and the Lord said to him in a vision, "Ananias."
He answered, "Here I am, Lord."
The Lord said to him, "Get up and go to the street called Straight
 and ask at the house of Judas for a man from Tarsus named Saul.
He is there praying,
 and in a vision he has seen a man named Ananias
 come in and lay his hands on him,
 that he may regain his sight."
But Ananias replied,
 "Lord, I have heard from many sources about this man,
 what evil things he has done to your holy ones in Jerusalem.
And here he has authority from the chief priests
 to imprison all who call upon your name."

But the Lord said to him,
> "Go, for this man is a chosen instrument of mine
> to carry my name before Gentiles, kings, and children of Israel,
> and I will show him what he will have to suffer for my name."

So Ananias went and entered the house;
> laying his hands on him, he said,
> "Saul, my brother, the Lord has sent me,
> Jesus who appeared to you on the way by which you came,
> that you may regain your sight and be filled with the Holy Spirit."

Immediately things like scales fell from his eyes
> and he regained his sight.

He got up and was baptized,
> and when he had eaten, he recovered his strength.

He stayed some days with the disciples in Damascus,
> and he began at once to proclaim Jesus in the synagogues,
> that he is the Son of God.

The word of the Lord.

RESPONSORIAL PSALM

Psalm 117:1bc, 2

℟. (Mark 16:15) **Go out to all the world and tell the Good News.**
   or:
℟. **Alleluia.**

Praise the Lord, all you nations;
   glorify him, all you peoples!

℟. **Go out to all the world and tell the Good News.**
   or:
℟. **Alleluia.**

For steadfast is his kindness toward us,
   and the fidelity of the Lord endures forever.

℟. **Go out to all the world and tell the Good News.**
   or:
℟. **Alleluia.**

ALLELUIA

John 6:56

℟. **Alleluia, alleluia.**

Whoever eats my Flesh and drinks my Blood,
remains in me and I in him, says the Lord.

℟. **Alleluia, alleluia.**

Friday of the Third Week of Easter II 355

GOSPEL

John 6:52-59   My Flesh is true food, and my Blood is true drink.

✞ **A reading from the holy Gospel according to John**

The Jews quarreled among themselves, saying,
 "How can this man give us his Flesh to eat?"
Jesus said to them,
 "Amen, amen, I say to you,
 unless you eat the Flesh of the Son of Man and drink his Blood,
 you do not have life within you.
Whoever eats my Flesh and drinks my Blood
 has eternal life,
 and I will raise him on the last day.
For my Flesh is true food,
 and my Blood is true drink.
Whoever eats my Flesh and drinks my Blood
 remains in me and I in him.
Just as the living Father sent me
 and I have life because of the Father,
 so also the one who feeds on me will have life because of me.
This is the bread that came down from heaven.
Unlike your ancestors who ate and still died,
 whoever eats this bread will live forever."
These things he said while teaching in the synagogue in Capernaum.

The Gospel of the Lord.

278 SATURDAY OF THE THIRD WEEK OF EASTER

FIRST READING

Acts 9:31-42   The Church was being built up, and with the consolation of the Holy Spirit she grew in numbers.

A reading from the Acts of the Apostles

The Church throughout all Judea, Galilee, and Samaria
 was at peace.
She was being built up and walked in the fear of the Lord,
 and with the consolation of the Holy Spirit she grew in numbers.

As Peter was passing through every region,
 he went down to the holy ones living in Lydda.
There he found a man named Aeneas,
 who had been confined to bed for eight years, for he was paralyzed.
Peter said to him,
 "Aeneas, Jesus Christ heals you. Get up and make your bed."
He got up at once.
And all the inhabitants of Lydda and Sharon saw him,
 and they turned to the Lord.

Now in Joppa there was a disciple named Tabitha
 (which translated is Dorcas).
She was completely occupied with good deeds and almsgiving.
Now during those days she fell sick and died,
 so after washing her, they laid her out in a room upstairs.
Since Lydda was near Joppa,
 the disciples, hearing that Peter was there,
 sent two men to him with the request,
 "Please come to us without delay."
So Peter got up and went with them.
When he arrived, they took him to the room upstairs
 where all the widows came to him weeping
 and showing him the tunics and cloaks
 that Dorcas had made while she was with them.

Peter sent them all out and knelt down and prayed.
Then he turned to her body and said, "Tabitha, rise up."
She opened her eyes, saw Peter, and sat up.
He gave her his hand and raised her up,
    and when he had called the holy ones and the widows,
    he presented her alive.
This became known all over Joppa,
    and many came to believe in the Lord.

The word of the Lord.

RESPONSORIAL PSALM

Psalm 116:12-13, 14-15, 16-17

℟. (12) **How shall I make a return to the Lord for all the good he has done for me?**
 or:
℟. **Alleluia.**

How shall I make a return to the Lord
  for all the good he has done for me?
The cup of salvation I will take up,
  and I will call upon the name of the Lord.

℟. **How shall I make a return to the Lord for all the good he has done for me?**
 or:
℟. **Alleluia.**

My vows to the Lord I will pay
  in the presence of all his people.
Precious in the eyes of the Lord
  is the death of his faithful ones.

℟. **How shall I make a return to the Lord for all the good he has done for me?**
 or:
℟. **Alleluia.**

O Lord, I am your servant;
  I am your servant, the son of your handmaid;
  you have loosed my bonds.
To you will I offer sacrifice of thanksgiving,
  and I will call upon the name of the Lord.

℟. **How shall I make a return to the Lord for all the good he has done for me?**
 or:
℟. **Alleluia.**

ALLELUIA

See John 6:63c, 68c

℟. Alleluia, alleluia.

Your words, Lord, are Spirit and life;
you have the words of everlasting life.

℟. Alleluia, alleluia.

GOSPEL

John 6:60-69   To whom shall we go? You have the words of eternal life.

✠ A reading from the holy Gospel according to John

Many of the disciples of Jesus who were listening said,
   "This saying is hard; who can accept it?"
Since Jesus knew that his disciples were murmuring about this,
   he said to them, "Does this shock you?
What if you were to see the Son of Man ascending to where he was before?
It is the Spirit that gives life, while the flesh is of no avail.
The words I have spoken to you are Spirit and life.
But there are some of you who do not believe."
Jesus knew from the beginning the ones who would not believe
   and the one who would betray him.
And he said, "For this reason I have told you that no one can come to me
   unless it is granted him by my Father."

As a result of this,
   many of his disciples returned to their former way of life
   and no longer walked with him.
Jesus then said to the Twelve, "Do you also want to leave?"
Simon Peter answered him, "Master, to whom shall we go?
You have the words of eternal life.
We have come to believe
   and are convinced that you are the Holy One of God."

The Gospel of the Lord.

279 MONDAY OF THE FOURTH WEEK OF EASTER

FIRST READING

Acts 11:1-18   God has then granted life-giving repentance to the Gentiles too.

A reading from the Acts of the Apostles

The Apostles and the brothers who were in Judea
   heard that the Gentiles too had accepted the word of God.
So when Peter went up to Jerusalem
   the circumcised believers confronted him, saying,
   "You entered the house of uncircumcised people and ate with them."
Peter began and explained it to them step by step, saying,
   "I was at prayer in the city of Joppa
   when in a trance I had a vision,
   something resembling a large sheet coming down,
   lowered from the sky by its four corners, and it came to me.
Looking intently into it,
   I observed and saw the four-legged animals of the earth,
   the wild beasts, the reptiles, and the birds of the sky.
I also heard a voice say to me, 'Get up, Peter. Slaughter and eat.'
But I said, 'Certainly not, sir,
   because nothing profane or unclean has ever entered my mouth.'
But a second time a voice from heaven answered,
   'What God has made clean, you are not to call profane.'
This happened three times,
   and then everything was drawn up again into the sky.
Just then three men appeared at the house where we were,
   who had been sent to me from Caesarea.
The Spirit told me to accompany them without discriminating.
These six brothers also went with me,
   and we entered the man's house.
He related to us how he had seen the angel standing in his house, saying,
   'Send someone to Joppa and summon Simon, who is called Peter,
   who will speak words to you
   by which you and all your household will be saved.'
As I began to speak, the Holy Spirit fell upon them
   as it had upon us at the beginning,
   and I remembered the word of the Lord, how he had said,

'John baptized with water
   but you will be baptized with the Holy Spirit.'
If then God gave them the same gift he gave to us
   when we came to believe in the Lord Jesus Christ,
   who was I to be able to hinder God?"
When they heard this,
   they stopped objecting and glorified God, saying,
      "God has then granted life-giving repentance to the Gentiles too."

The word of the Lord.

RESPONSORIAL PSALM

Psalm 42:2-3; 43:3, 4

℟. (see 3a) **Athirst is my soul for the living God.**
   or:

℟. **Alleluia.**

As the hind longs for the running waters,
   so my soul longs for you, O God.
Athirst is my soul for God, the living God.
   When shall I go and behold the face of God?

℟. **Athirst is my soul for the living God.**
   or:

℟. **Alleluia.**

Send forth your light and your fidelity;
   they shall lead me on
And bring me to your holy mountain,
   to your dwelling-place.

℟. **Athirst is my soul for the living God.**
   or:

℟. **Alleluia.**

Then will I go in to the altar of God,
   the God of my gladness and joy;
Then will I give you thanks upon the harp,
   O God, my God!

℟. **Athirst is my soul for the living God.**
   or:

℟. **Alleluia.**

ALLELUIA

John 10:14

℟. Alleluia, alleluia.

I am the good shepherd, says the Lord;
I know my sheep, and mine know me.

℟. Alleluia, alleluia.

GOSPEL

John 10:1-10   I am the gate for the sheep.

✠ A reading from the holy Gospel according to John

Jesus said:
"Amen, amen, I say to you,
   whoever does not enter a sheepfold through the gate
   but climbs over elsewhere is a thief and a robber.
But whoever enters through the gate is the shepherd of the sheep.
The gatekeeper opens it for him, and the sheep hear his voice,
   as he calls his own sheep by name and leads them out.
When he has driven out all his own,
   he walks ahead of them, and the sheep follow him,
   because they recognize his voice.
But they will not follow a stranger;
   they will run away from him,
   because they do not recognize the voice of strangers."
Although Jesus used this figure of speech,
   they did not realize what he was trying to tell them.

So Jesus said again, "Amen, amen, I say to you,
   I am the gate for the sheep.
All who came before me are thieves and robbers,
   but the sheep did not listen to them.
I am the gate.
Whoever enters through me will be saved,
   and will come in and go out and find pasture.
A thief comes only to steal and slaughter and destroy;
   I came so that they might have life and have it more abundantly."

The Gospel of the Lord.

OR

In Year A, when this Gospel is read on the preceding Sunday, the following text is used.

GOSPEL

John 10:11-18   A good shepherd lays down his life for the sheep.

☩ A reading from the holy Gospel according to John

Jesus said:
"I am the good shepherd.
A good shepherd lays down his life for the sheep.
A hired man, who is not a shepherd
  and whose sheep are not his own,
  sees a wolf coming and leaves the sheep and runs away,
  and the wolf catches and scatters them.
This is because he works for pay and has no concern for the sheep.
I am the good shepherd,
  and I know mine and mine know me,
    just as the Father knows me and I know the Father;
  and I will lay down my life for the sheep.
I have other sheep that do not belong to this fold.
These also I must lead, and they will hear my voice,
  and there will be one flock, one shepherd.
This is why the Father loves me,
  because I lay down my life in order to take it up again.
No one takes it from me, but I lay it down on my own.
I have power to lay it down, and power to take it up again.
This command I have received from my Father."

The Gospel of the Lord.

280 TUESDAY OF THE FOURTH WEEK OF EASTER

FIRST READING

Acts 11:19-26   They began speaking to the Greeks as well, proclaiming the Good News of Jesus Christ.

A reading from the Acts of the Apostles

**Those who had been scattered by the persecution
   that arose because of Stephen
   went as far as Phoenicia, Cyprus, and Antioch,
   preaching the word to no one but Jews.
There were some Cypriots and Cyrenians among them, however,
   who came to Antioch and began to speak to the Greeks as well,
   proclaiming the Lord Jesus.
The hand of the Lord was with them
   and a great number who believed turned to the Lord.
The news about them reached the ears of the Church in Jerusalem,
   and they sent Barnabas to go to Antioch.
When he arrived and saw the grace of God,
   he rejoiced and encouraged them all
   to remain faithful to the Lord in firmness of heart,
   for he was a good man, filled with the Holy Spirit and faith.
And a large number of people was added to the Lord.
Then he went to Tarsus to look for Saul,
   and when he had found him he brought him to Antioch.
For a whole year they met with the Church
   and taught a large number of people,
   and it was in Antioch that the disciples
   were first called Christians.**

The word of the Lord.

RESPONSORIAL PSALM

Psalm 87:1b-3, 4-5, 6-7

℟. (117:1a) **All you nations, praise the Lord.**
   or:
℟. **Alleluia.**

**His foundation upon the holy mountains
   the LORD loves:
The gates of Zion,
   more than any dwelling of Jacob.
Glorious things are said of you,
   O city of God!**

℟. **All you nations, praise the Lord.**
   or:
℟. **Alleluia.**

**I tell of Egypt and Babylon
   among those who know the LORD;
Of Philistia, Tyre, Ethiopia:
   "This man was born there."
And of Zion they shall say:
   "One and all were born in her;
And he who has established her
   is the Most High LORD."**

℟. **All you nations, praise the Lord.**
   or:
℟. **Alleluia.**

**They shall note, when the peoples are enrolled:
   "This man was born there."
And all shall sing, in their festive dance:
   "My home is within you."**

℟. **All you nations, praise the Lord.**
   or:
℟. **Alleluia.**

ALLELUIA

John 10:27

℟. Alleluia, alleluia.

My sheep hear my voice, says the Lord;
I know them, and they follow me.

℟. Alleluia, alleluia.

GOSPEL

John 10:22-30   The Father and I are one.

✛ A reading from the holy Gospel according to John

The feast of the Dedication was taking place in Jerusalem.
It was winter.
And Jesus walked about in the temple area on the Portico of Solomon.
So the Jews gathered around him and said to him,
   "How long are you going to keep us in suspense?
If you are the Christ, tell us plainly."
Jesus answered them, "I told you and you do not believe.
The works I do in my Father's name testify to me.
But you do not believe, because you are not among my sheep.
My sheep hear my voice;
   I know them, and they follow me.
I give them eternal life, and they shall never perish.
No one can take them out of my hand.
My Father, who has given them to me, is greater than all,
   and no one can take them out of the Father's hand.
The Father and I are one."

The Gospel of the Lord.

281 WEDNESDAY OF THE FOURTH WEEK OF EASTER

FIRST READING

Acts 12:24—13:5a   Set apart for me Barnabas and Saul.

A reading from the Acts of the Apostles

The word of God continued to spread and grow.

After Barnabas and Saul completed their relief mission,
 they returned to Jerusalem,
 taking with them John, who is called Mark.

Now there were in the Church at Antioch prophets and teachers:
 Barnabas, Symeon who was called Niger, Lucius of Cyrene,
 Manaen who was a close friend of Herod the tetrarch, and Saul.
While they were worshiping the Lord and fasting, the Holy Spirit said,
 "Set apart for me Barnabas and Saul
 for the work to which I have called them."
Then, completing their fasting and prayer,
 they laid hands on them and sent them off.

So they, sent forth by the Holy Spirit,
 went down to Seleucia
 and from there sailed to Cyprus.
When they arrived in Salamis,
 they proclaimed the word of God in the Jewish synagogues.

The word of the Lord.

RESPONSORIAL PSALM

Psalm 67:2-3, 5, 6 and 8

℟. (4) **O God, let all the nations praise you!**
   or:
℟. **Alleluia.**

**May God have pity on us and bless us;
   may he let his face shine upon us.
So may your way be known upon earth;
   among all nations, your salvation.**

℟. **O God, let all the nations praise you!**
   or:
℟. **Alleluia.**

**May the nations be glad and exult
   because you rule the peoples in equity;
   the nations on the earth you guide.**

℟. **O God, let all the nations praise you!**
   or:
℟. **Alleluia.**

**May the peoples praise you, O God;
   may all the peoples praise you!
May God bless us,
   and may all the ends of the earth fear him!**

℟. **O God, let all the nations praise you!**
   or:
℟. **Alleluia.**

ALLELUIA

John 8:12

℟. Alleluia, alleluia.

I am the light of the world, says the Lord;
whoever follows me will have the light of life.

℟. Alleluia, alleluia.

GOSPEL

John 12:44-50   I came into the world as light.

✠ A reading from the holy Gospel according to John

Jesus cried out and said,
   "Whoever believes in me believes not only in me
   but also in the one who sent me,
   and whoever sees me sees the one who sent me.
I came into the world as light,
   so that everyone who believes in me might not remain in darkness.
And if anyone hears my words and does not observe them,
   I do not condemn him,
   for I did not come to condemn the world but to save the world.
Whoever rejects me and does not accept my words
   has something to judge him: the word that I spoke,
   it will condemn him on the last day,
   because I did not speak on my own,
   but the Father who sent me commanded me what to say and speak.
And I know that his commandment is eternal life.
So what I say, I say as the Father told me."

The Gospel of the Lord.

282 THURSDAY OF THE FOURTH WEEK OF EASTER

FIRST READING

Acts 13:13-25   From this man's descendants God, according to his promise, has brought to Israel a savior, Jesus.

A reading from the Acts of Apostles

From Paphos, Paul and his companions
   set sail and arrived at Perga in Pamphylia.
But John left them and returned to Jerusalem.
They continued on from Perga and reached Antioch in Pisidia.
On the sabbath they entered into the synagogue and took their seats.
After the reading of the law and the prophets,
   the synagogue officials sent word to them,
   "My brothers, if one of you has a word of exhortation
   for the people, please speak."
So Paul got up, motioned with his hand, and said,
   "Fellow children of Israel and you others who are God-fearing, listen.
The God of this people Israel chose our ancestors
   and exalted the people during their sojourn in the land of Egypt.
With uplifted arm he led them out,
   and for about forty years he put up with them in the desert.
When he had destroyed seven nations in the land of Canaan,
   he gave them their land as an inheritance
   at the end of about four hundred and fifty years.
After these things he provided judges up to Samuel the prophet.
Then they asked for a king.
God gave them Saul, son of Kish,
   a man from the tribe of Benjamin, for forty years.
Then he removed him and raised up David as their king;
   of him he testified,
   I have found David, son of Jesse, a man after my own heart;
   he will carry out my every wish.
From this man's descendants God, according to his promise,
   has brought to Israel a savior, Jesus.

John heralded his coming by proclaiming a baptism of repentance
   to all the people of Israel;
   and as John was completing his course, he would say,
   'What do you suppose that I am? I am not he.
Behold, one is coming after me;
   I am not worthy to unfasten the sandals of his feet.'"

The word of the Lord.

RESPONSORIAL PSALM

Psalm 89:2-3, 21-22, 25 and 27

℟. (2) **For ever I will sing the goodness of the Lord.**
   or:
℟. **Alleluia.**

The favors of the LORD I will sing forever;
   through all generations my mouth shall proclaim your faithfulness.
For you have said, "My kindness is established forever";
   in heaven you have confirmed your faithfulness.

℟. **For ever I will sing the goodness of the Lord.**
   or:
℟. **Alleluia.**

"I have found David, my servant;
   with my holy oil I have anointed him,
That my hand may be always with him,
   and that my arm may make him strong."

℟. **For ever I will sing the goodness of the Lord.**
   or:
℟. **Alleluia.**

"My faithfulness and my mercy shall be with him,
   and through my name shall his horn be exalted.
He shall say of me, 'You are my father,
   my God, the Rock, my savior.'"

℟. **For ever I will sing the goodness of the Lord.**
   or:
℟. **Alleluia.**

ALLELUIA

See Revelation 1:5ab

℟. **Alleluia, alleluia.**

**Jesus Christ, you are the faithful witness,
the firstborn of the dead,
you have loved us and freed us from our sins by your Blood.**

℟. **Alleluia, alleluia.**

GOSPEL

John 13:16-20   Whoever receives the one I send receives me.

✛ **A reading from the holy Gospel according to John**

**When Jesus had washed the disciples' feet, he said to them:
"Amen, amen, I say to you, no slave is greater than his master
   nor any messenger greater than the one who sent him.
If you understand this, blessed are you if you do it.
I am not speaking of all of you.
I know those whom I have chosen.
But so that the Scripture might be fulfilled,
   The one who ate my food has raised his heel against me.
From now on I am telling you before it happens,
   so that when it happens you may believe that I AM.
Amen, amen, I say to you, whoever receives the one I send
   receives me, and whoever receives me receives the one who sent me."**

The Gospel of the Lord.

283 FRIDAY OF THE FOURTH WEEK OF EASTER

FIRST READING

Acts 13:26-33   God has fulfilled his promise by raising Jesus from the dead.

A reading from the Acts of the Apostles

When Paul came to Antioch in Pisidia, he said in the synagogue:
"My brothers, children of the family of Abraham,
and those others among you who are God-fearing,
to us this word of salvation has been sent.
The inhabitants of Jerusalem and their leaders failed to recognize him,
and by condemning him they fulfilled the oracles of the prophets
that are read sabbath after sabbath.
For even though they found no grounds for a death sentence,
they asked Pilate to have him put to death,
and when they had accomplished all that was written about him,
they took him down from the tree and placed him in a tomb.
But God raised him from the dead,
and for many days he appeared to those
who had come up with him from Galilee to Jerusalem.
These are now his witnesses before the people.
We ourselves are proclaiming this good news to you
that what God promised our fathers
he has brought to fulfillment for us, their children, by raising up Jesus,
as it is written in the second psalm,
You are my Son; this day I have begotten you."

The word of the Lord.

RESPONSORIAL PSALM

Psalm 2:6-7, 8-9, 10-11ab

℟. (7bc) **You are my Son; this day I have begotten you.**
  or:
℟. **Alleluia.**

"I myself have set up my king
  on Zion, my holy mountain."
I will proclaim the decree of the Lord:
  The Lord said to me, "You are my Son;
  this day I have begotten you."

℟. You are my Son; this day I have begotten you.
  or:
℟. Alleluia.

"Ask of me and I will give you
  the nations for an inheritance
  and the ends of the earth for your possession.
You shall rule them with an iron rod;
  you shall shatter them like an earthen dish."

℟. You are my Son; this day I have begotten you.
  or:
℟. Alleluia.

And now, O kings, give heed;
  take warning, you rulers of the earth.
Serve the Lord with fear, and rejoice before him;
  with trembling rejoice.

℟. You are my Son; this day I have begotten you.
  or:
℟. Alleluia.

ALLELUIA

John 14:6

℟. Alleluia, alleluia.

**I am the way and the truth and the life, says the Lord;
no one comes to the Father except through me.**

℟. Alleluia, alleluia.

GOSPEL

John 14:1-6   I am the way and the truth and the life.

✠ A reading from the holy Gospel according to John

**Jesus said to his disciples:
"Do not let your hearts be troubled.
You have faith in God; have faith also in me.
In my Father's house there are many dwelling places.
If there were not,
   would I have told you that I am going to prepare a place for you?
And if I go and prepare a place for you,
   I will come back again and take you to myself,
   so that where I am you also may be.
Where I am going you know the way."
Thomas said to him,
   "Master, we do not know where you are going;
   how can we know the way?"
Jesus said to him, "I am the way and the truth and the life.
No one comes to the Father except through me."**

The Gospel of the Lord.

284 SATURDAY OF THE FOURTH WEEK OF EASTER

FIRST READING

Acts 13:44-52   We now turn to the Gentiles.

A reading from the Acts of the Apostles

On the following sabbath
	almost the whole city
	gathered to hear the word of the Lord.
When the Jews saw the crowds, they were filled with jealousy
	and with violent abuse contradicted what Paul said.
Both Paul and Barnabas spoke out boldly and said,
	"It was necessary that the word of God be spoken to you first,
	but since you reject it
	and condemn yourselves as unworthy of eternal life,
	we now turn to the Gentiles.
For so the Lord has commanded us,
	I have made you a light to the Gentiles,
	that you may be an instrument of salvation
	to the ends of the earth."

The Gentiles were delighted when they heard this
	and glorified the word of the Lord.
All who were destined for eternal life came to believe,
	and the word of the Lord continued to spread
	through the whole region.
The Jews, however, incited the women of prominence who were worshipers
		and the leading men of the city,
	stirred up a persecution against Paul and Barnabas,
	and expelled them from their territory.
So they shook the dust from their feet in protest against them
	and went to Iconium.
The disciples were filled with joy and the Holy Spirit.

The word of the Lord.

RESPONSORIAL PSALM

Psalm 98:1, 2-3ab, 3cd-4

℟. (3cd) **All the ends of the earth have seen the saving power of God.**
   or:
℟. **Alleluia.**

**Sing to the Lord a new song,
   for he has done wondrous deeds;
His right hand has won victory for him,
   his holy arm.**

℟. **All the ends of the earth have seen the saving power of God.**
   or:
℟. **Alleluia.**

**The Lord has made his salvation known:
   in the sight of the nations he has revealed his justice.
He has remembered his kindness and his faithfulness
   toward the house of Israel.**

℟. **All the ends of the earth have seen the saving power of God.**
   or:
℟. **Alleluia.**

**All the ends of the earth have seen
   the salvation by our God.
Sing joyfully to the Lord, all you lands;
   break into song; sing praise.**

℟. **All the ends of the earth have seen the saving power of God.**
   or:
℟. **Alleluia.**

ALLELUIA

John 8:31b-32

℟. Alleluia, alleluia.

If you remain in my word, you will truly be my disciples, and you will know the truth, says the Lord.

℟. Alleluia, alleluia.

GOSPEL

John 14:7-14   Whoever has seen me has seen the Father.

✝ **A reading from the holy Gospel according to John**

Jesus said to his disciples:
"If you know me, then you will also know my Father.
From now on you do know him and have seen him."
Philip said to Jesus,
  "Master, show us the Father, and that will be enough for us."
Jesus said to him, "Have I been with you for so long a time
  and you still do not know me, Philip?
Whoever has seen me has seen the Father.
How can you say, 'Show us the Father'?
Do you not believe that I am in the Father and the Father is in me?
The words that I speak to you I do not speak on my own.
The Father who dwells in me is doing his works.
Believe me that I am in the Father and the Father is in me,
  or else, believe because of the works themselves.
Amen, amen, I say to you,
  whoever believes in me will do the works that I do,
  and will do greater ones than these,
  because I am going to the Father.
And whatever you ask in my name, I will do,
  so that the Father may be glorified in the Son.
If you ask anything of me in my name, I will do it."

The Gospel of the Lord.

285 MONDAY OF THE FIFTH WEEK OF EASTER

FIRST READING

Acts 14:5-18   We proclaim to you Good News that you should turn from these idols to the living God.

A reading from the Acts of the Apostles

There was an attempt in Iconium
>   by both the Gentiles and the Jews,
>   together with their leaders,
>   to attack and stone Paul and Barnabas.

They realized it,
>   and fled to the Lycaonian cities of Lystra and Derbe
>   and to the surrounding countryside,
>   where they continued to proclaim the Good News.

At Lystra there was a crippled man, lame from birth,
>   who had never walked.

He listened to Paul speaking, who looked intently at him,
>   saw that he had the faith to be healed,
>   and called out in a loud voice, "Stand up straight on your feet."

He jumped up and began to walk about.

When the crowds saw what Paul had done,
>   they cried out in Lycaonian,
>   "The gods have come down to us in human form."

They called Barnabas "Zeus" and Paul "Hermes,"
>   because he was the chief speaker.

And the priest of Zeus, whose temple was at the entrance to the city,
>   brought oxen and garlands to the gates,
>   for he together with the people intended to offer sacrifice.

The Apostles Barnabas and Paul tore their garments
>   when they heard this and rushed out into the crowd, shouting,
>   "Men, why are you doing this?

We are of the same nature as you, human beings.

We proclaim to you good news
>   that you should turn from these idols to the living God,
>   *who made heaven and earth and sea and all that is in them.*

In past generations he allowed all Gentiles to go their own ways;
   yet, in bestowing his goodness,
   he did not leave himself without witness,
   for he gave you rains from heaven and fruitful seasons,
   and filled you with nourishment and gladness for your hearts."
Even with these words, they scarcely restrained the crowds
   from offering sacrifice to them.

The word of the Lord.

RESPONSORIAL PSALM

Psalm 115:1-2, 3-4, 15-16

℟. (1ab) Not to us, O Lord, but to your name give the glory.
   or:
℟. Alleluia.

Not to us, O LORD**, not to us**
   but to your name give glory
   because of your mercy, because of your truth.
Why should the pagans say,
   "Where is their God?"

℟. Not to us, O Lord, but to your name give the glory.
   or:
℟. Alleluia.

Our God is in heaven;
   whatever he wills, he does.
Their idols are silver and gold,
   the handiwork of men.

℟. Not to us, O Lord, but to your name give the glory.
   or:
℟. Alleluia.

May you be blessed by the LORD**,**
   who made heaven and earth.
Heaven is the heaven of the LORD**,**
   but the earth he has given to the children of men.

℟. Not to us, O Lord, but to your name give the glory.
   or:
℟. Alleluia.

ALLELUIA

John 14:26

℟. Alleluia, alleluia.

The Holy Spirit will teach you everything
and remind you of all I told you.

℟. Alleluia, alleluia.

GOSPEL

John 14:21-26   The Advocate whom the Father will send will teach you everything.

✝ A reading from the holy Gospel according to John

Jesus said to his disciples:
"Whoever has my commandments and observes them
 is the one who loves me.
Whoever loves me will be loved by my Father,
 and I will love him and reveal myself to him."
Judas, not the Iscariot, said to him,
 "Master, then what happened that you will reveal yourself to us
 and not to the world?"
Jesus answered and said to him,
 "Whoever loves me will keep my word,
 and my Father will love him,
 and we will come to him and make our dwelling with him.
Whoever does not love me does not keep my words;
 yet the word you hear is not mine
 but that of the Father who sent me.

"I have told you this while I am with you.
The Advocate, the Holy Spirit
 whom the Father will send in my name–
 he will teach you everything
 and remind you of all that I told you."

The Gospel of the Lord.

286 TUESDAY OF THE FIFTH WEEK OF EASTER

FIRST READING

Acts 14:19-28   They called the Church together and reported what God had done with them.

A reading from the Acts of the Apostles

In those days, some Jews from Antioch and Iconium
   arrived and won over the crowds.
They stoned Paul and dragged him out of the city,
   supposing that he was dead.
But when the disciples gathered around him,
   he got up and entered the city.
On the following day he left with Barnabas for Derbe.

After they had proclaimed the good news to that city
   and made a considerable number of disciples,
   they returned to Lystra and to Iconium and to Antioch.
They strengthened the spirits of the disciples
   and exhorted them to persevere in the faith, saying,
   "It is necessary for us to undergo many hardships
   to enter the Kingdom of God."
They appointed presbyters for them in each Church and,
   with prayer and fasting, commended them to the Lord
   in whom they had put their faith.
Then they traveled through Pisidia and reached Pamphylia.
After proclaiming the word at Perga they went down to Attalia.
From there they sailed to Antioch,
   where they had been commended to the grace of God
   for the work they had now accomplished.
And when they arrived, they called the Church together
   and reported what God had done with them
   and how he had opened the door of faith to the Gentiles.
Then they spent no little time with the disciples.

The word of the Lord.

RESPONSORIAL PSALM

Psalm 145:10-11, 12-13ab, 21

℟. (see 12) **Your friends make known, O Lord, the glorious splendor of your kingdom.**
   or:
℟. **Alleluia.**

Let all your works give you thanks, O Lord,
   and let your faithful ones bless you.
Let them discourse of the glory of your kingdom
   and speak of your might.

℟. **Your friends make known, O Lord, the glorious splendor of your kingdom.**
   or:
℟. **Alleluia.**

Making known to men your might
   and the glorious splendor of your kingdom.
Your kingdom is a kingdom for all ages,
   and your dominion endures through all generations.

℟. **Your friends make known, O Lord, the glorious splendor of your kingdom.**
   or:
℟. **Alleluia.**

May my mouth speak the praise of the Lord,
   and may all flesh bless his holy name forever and ever.

℟. **Your friends make known, O Lord, the glorious splendor of your kingdom.**
   or:
℟. **Alleluia.**

ALLELUIA

See Luke 24:46, 26

℟. Alleluia, alleluia.

**Christ had to suffer and to rise from the dead,
and so enter into his glory.**

℟. Alleluia, alleluia.

GOSPEL

John 14:27-31a   My peace I give to you.

✠ A reading from the holy Gospel according to John

**Jesus said to his disciples:
"Peace I leave with you; my peace I give to you.
Not as the world gives do I give it to you.
Do not let your hearts be troubled or afraid.
You heard me tell you,
    'I am going away and I will come back to you.'
If you loved me,
    you would rejoice that I am going to the Father;
    for the Father is greater than I.
And now I have told you this before it happens,
    so that when it happens you may believe.
I will no longer speak much with you,
    for the ruler of the world is coming.
He has no power over me,
    but the world must know that I love the Father
    and that I do just as the Father has commanded me."**

The Gospel of the Lord.

287 WEDNESDAY OF THE FIFTH WEEK OF EASTER

FIRST READING

Acts 15:1-6   They decided to go up to Jerusalem to the Apostles and presbyters about this question.

A reading from the Acts of the Apostles

Some who had come down from Judea were instructing the brothers,
"Unless you are circumcised according to the Mosaic practice,
you cannot be saved."
Because there arose no little dissension and debate
by Paul and Barnabas with them,
it was decided that Paul, Barnabas, and some of the others
should go up to Jerusalem to the Apostles and presbyters
about this question.
They were sent on their journey by the Church,
and passed through Phoenicia and Samaria
telling of the conversion of the Gentiles,
and brought great joy to all the brethren.
When they arrived in Jerusalem,
they were welcomed by the Church,
as well as by the Apostles and the presbyters,
and they reported what God had done with them.
But some from the party of the Pharisees who had become believers
stood up and said, "It is necessary to circumcise them
and direct them to observe the Mosaic law."

The Apostles and the presbyters met together to see about this matter.

The word of the Lord.

RESPONSORIAL PSALM

Psalm 122:1-2, 3-4ab, 4cd-5

℟. (see 1) **Let us go rejoicing to the house of the Lord.**
   or:
℟. **Alleluia.**

**I rejoiced because they said to me,
   "We will go up to the house of the Lord."
And now we have set foot
   within your gates, O Jerusalem.**

℟. **Let us go rejoicing to the house of the Lord.**
   or:
℟. **Alleluia.**

**Jerusalem, built as a city
   with compact unity.
To it the tribes go up,
   the tribes of the Lord.**

℟. **Let us go rejoicing to the house of the Lord.**
   or:
℟. **Alleluia.**

**According to the decree for Israel,
   to give thanks to the name of the Lord.
In it are set up judgment seats,
   seats for the house of David.**

℟. **Let us go rejoicing to the house of the Lord.**
   or:
℟. **Alleluia.**

ALLELUIA

John 15:4a, 5b

℟. Alleluia, alleluia.

Remain in me, as I remain in you, says the Lord; whoever remains in me will bear much fruit.

℟. Alleluia, alleluia.

GOSPEL

John 15:1-8   Whoever remains in me and I in him will bear much fruit.

✣ A reading from the holy Gospel according to John

Jesus said to his disciples:
"I am the true vine, and my Father is the vine grower.
He takes away every branch in me that does not bear fruit,
   and everyone that does he prunes so that it bears more fruit.
You are already pruned because of the word that I spoke to you.
Remain in me, as I remain in you.
Just as a branch cannot bear fruit on its own
   unless it remains on the vine,
   so neither can you unless you remain in me.
I am the vine, you are the branches.
Whoever remains in me and I in him will bear much fruit,
   because without me you can do nothing.
Anyone who does not remain in me
   will be thrown out like a branch and wither;
   people will gather them and throw them into a fire
   and they will be burned.
If you remain in me and my words remain in you,
   ask for whatever you want and it will be done for you.
By this is my Father glorified,
   that you bear much fruit and become my disciples."

The Gospel of the Lord.

288 THURSDAY OF THE FIFTH WEEK OF EASTER

FIRST READING

Acts 15:7-21　It is my judgment, therefore, that we ought to stop troubling the Gentiles who turn to God.

A reading from the Acts of the Apostles

After much debate had taken place,
　　Peter got up and said to the Apostles and the presbyters,
　　"My brothers, you are well aware that from early days
　　God made his choice among you that through my mouth
　　the Gentiles would hear the word of the Gospel and believe.
And God, who knows the heart,
　　bore witness by granting them the Holy Spirit
　　just as he did us.
He made no distinction between us and them,
　　for by faith he purified their hearts.
Why, then, are you now putting God to the test
　　by placing on the shoulders of the disciples
　　a yoke that neither our ancestors nor we have been able to bear?
On the contrary, we believe that we are saved
　　through the grace of the Lord Jesus, in the same way as they."
The whole assembly fell silent,
　　and they listened
　　while Paul and Barnabas described the signs and wonders
　　God had worked among the Gentiles through them.

After they had fallen silent, James responded,
　　"My brothers, listen to me.
Symeon has described how God first concerned himself
　　with acquiring from among the Gentiles a people for his name.
The words of the prophets agree with this, as is written:

*　　After this I shall return*
*　　　　and rebuild the fallen hut of David;*
*　　from its ruins I shall rebuild it*
*　　　　and raise it up again,*
*　　so that the rest of humanity may seek out the Lord,*
*　　　　even all the Gentiles on whom my name is invoked.*

***Thus says the Lord who accomplishes these things,
   known from of old.***

**It is my judgment, therefore,
   that we ought to stop troubling the Gentiles who turn to God,
   but tell them by letter to avoid pollution from idols,
   unlawful marriage, the meat of strangled animals, and blood.
For Moses, for generations now,
   has had those who proclaim him in every town,
   as he has been read in the synagogues every sabbath."**

The word of the Lord.

RESPONSORIAL PSALM

Psalm 96:1-2a, 2b-3, 10

℟. (3) **Proclaim God's marvelous deeds to all the nations.**
   or:
℟. **Alleluia.**

Sing to the L**ORD** **a new song;
   sing to the** L**ORD,** **all you lands.
Sing to the** L**ORD;** **bless his name.**

℟. **Proclaim God's marvelous deeds to all the nations.**
   or:
℟. **Alleluia.**

**Announce his salvation, day after day.
Tell his glory among the nations;
   among all peoples, his wondrous deeds.**

℟. **Proclaim God's marvelous deeds to all the nations.**
   or:
℟. **Alleluia.**

Say among the nations: The L**ORD** **is king.
He has made the world firm, not to be moved;
   he governs the peoples with equity.**

℟. **Proclaim God's marvelous deeds to all the nations.**
   or:
℟. **Alleluia.**

ALLELUIA

John 10:27

℟. Alleluia, alleluia.

**My sheep hear my voice, says the Lord;
I know them, and they follow me.**

℟. Alleluia, alleluia.

GOSPEL

John 15:9-11   Remain in my love, that your joy might be complete.

✛ **A reading from the holy Gospel according to John**

**Jesus said to his disciples:
"As the Father loves me, so I also love you.
Remain in my love.
If you keep my commandments, you will remain in my love,
just as I have kept my Father's commandments
and remain in his love.**

**"I have told you this so that
my joy might be in you and
your joy might be complete."**

The Gospel of the Lord.

289 FRIDAY OF THE FIFTH WEEK OF EASTER

FIRST READING

Acts 15:22-31 It is the decision of the Holy Spirit and of us not to place on you any burden beyond these necessities.

A reading from the Acts of the Apostles

The Apostles and presbyters, in agreement with the whole Church,
   decided to choose representatives
   and to send them to Antioch with Paul and Barnabas.
The ones chosen were Judas, who was called Barsabbas,
   and Silas, leaders among the brothers.
This is the letter delivered by them:
"The Apostles and the presbyters, your brothers,
   to the brothers in Antioch, Syria, and Cilicia
   of Gentile origin: greetings.
Since we have heard that some of our number
   who went out without any mandate from us
   have upset you with their teachings
   and disturbed your peace of mind,
   we have with one accord decided to choose representatives
   and to send them to you along with our beloved Barnabas and Paul,
   who have dedicated their lives to the name of our Lord Jesus Christ.
So we are sending Judas and Silas
   who will also convey this same message by word of mouth:
   'It is the decision of the Holy Spirit and of us
   not to place on you any burden beyond these necessities,
   namely, to abstain from meat sacrificed to idols,
   from blood, from meats of strangled animals,
   and from unlawful marriage.
If you keep free of these,
   you will be doing what is right. Farewell.'"

And so they were sent on their journey.
Upon their arrival in Antioch
   they called the assembly together and delivered the letter.
When the people read it, they were delighted with the exhortation.

The word of the Lord.

RESPONSORIAL PSALM

Psalm 57:8-9, 10 and 12

℟. (10a) **I will give you thanks among the peoples, O Lord.**
   or:
℟. **Alleluia.**

My heart is steadfast, O God; my heart is steadfast;
   I will sing and chant praise.
Awake, O my soul; awake, lyre and harp!
   I will wake the dawn.

℟. **I will give you thanks among the peoples, O Lord.**
   or:
℟. **Alleluia.**

I will give thanks to you among the peoples, O LORD,
   I will chant your praise among the nations.
For your mercy towers to the heavens,
   and your faithfulness to the skies.
Be exalted above the heavens, O God;
   above all the earth be your glory!

℟. **I will give you thanks among the peoples, O Lord.**
   or:
℟. **Alleluia.**

ALLELUIA

John 15:15b

℟. Alleluia, alleluia.

**I call you my friends, says the Lord,
for I have made known to you all that the Father has told me.**

℟. Alleluia, alleluia.

GOSPEL

John 15:12-17   This is my commandment: love one another.

✛ **A reading from the holy Gospel according to John**

**Jesus said to his disciples:
"This is my commandment: love one another as I love you.
No one has greater love than this,
   to lay down one's life for one's friends.
You are my friends if you do what I command you.
I no longer call you slaves,
   because a slave does not know what his master is doing.
I have called you friends,
   because I have told you everything I have heard from my Father.
It was not you who chose me, but I who chose you
   and appointed you to go and bear fruit that will remain,
   so that whatever you ask the Father in my name he may give you.
This I command you: love one another."**

The Gospel of the Lord.

290 SATURDAY OF THE FIFTH WEEK OF EASTER

FIRST READING

Acts 16:1-10   Come over to Macedonia and help us.

A reading from the Acts of the Apostles

Paul reached also Derbe and Lystra
   where there was a disciple named Timothy,
   the son of a Jewish woman who was a believer,
   but his father was a Greek.
The brothers in Lystra and Iconium spoke highly of him,
   and Paul wanted him to come along with him.
On account of the Jews of that region, Paul had him circumcised,
   for they all knew that his father was a Greek.
As they traveled from city to city,
   they handed on to the people for observance the decisions
   reached by the Apostles and presbyters in Jerusalem.
Day after day the churches grew stronger in faith
   and increased in number.

They traveled through the Phrygian and Galatian territory
   because they had been prevented by the Holy Spirit
   from preaching the message in the province of Asia.
When they came to Mysia, they tried to go on into Bithynia,
   but the Spirit of Jesus did not allow them,
   so they crossed through Mysia and came down to Troas.
During the night Paul had a vision.
A Macedonian stood before him and implored him with these words,
   "Come over to Macedonia and help us."
When he had seen the vision,
   we sought passage to Macedonia at once,
   concluding that God had called us to proclaim the Good News to them.

The word of the Lord.

RESPONSORIAL PSALM

Psalm 100:1b-2, 3, 5

℟. (2a) **Let all the earth cry out to God with joy.**
   or:
℟. **Alleluia.**

Sing joyfully to the LORD**, all you lands;**
   serve the LORD **with gladness;**
   come before him with joyful song.

℟. **Let all the earth cry out to God with joy.**
   or:
℟. **Alleluia.**

Know that the LORD **is God;**
   he made us, his we are;
   his people, the flock he tends.

℟. **Let all the earth cry out to God with joy.**
   or:
℟. **Alleluia.**

The LORD **is good:**
   his kindness endures forever,
   and his faithfulness, to all generations.

℟. **Let all the earth cry out to God with joy.**
   or:
℟. **Alleluia.**

ALLELUIA

Colossians 3:1

℟. Alleluia, alleluia.

If then you were raised with Christ,
seek what is above,
where Christ is seated at the right hand of God.

℟. Alleluia, alleluia.

GOSPEL

John 15:18-21   You do not belong to the world, and I have chosen you out of the world.

✠ A reading from the holy Gospel according to John

Jesus said to his disciples:
"If the world hates you, realize that it hated me first.
If you belonged to the world, the world would love its own;
　but because you do not belong to the world,
　and I have chosen you out of the world,
　the world hates you.
Remember the word I spoke to you,
　'No slave is greater than his master.'
If they persecuted me, they will also persecute you.
If they kept my word, they will also keep yours.
And they will do all these things to you on account of my name,
　because they do not know the one who sent me."

The Gospel of the Lord.

291 MONDAY OF THE SIXTH WEEK OF EASTER

FIRST READING

Acts 16:11-15   The Lord opened her heart to pay attention to what Paul taught.

A reading from the Acts of the Apostles

**We set sail from Troas, making a straight run for Samothrace,
   and on the next day to Neapolis, and from there to Philippi,
   a leading city in that district of Macedonia and a Roman colony.
We spent some time in that city.
On the sabbath we went outside the city gate along the river
   where we thought there would be a place of prayer.
We sat and spoke with the women who had gathered there.
One of them, a woman named Lydia, a dealer in purple cloth,
   from the city of Thyatira, a worshiper of God, listened,
   and the Lord opened her heart to pay attention
   to what Paul was saying.
After she and her household had been baptized,
   she offered us an invitation,
   "If you consider me a believer in the Lord,
   come and stay at my home," and she prevailed on us.**

The word of the Lord.

RESPONSORIAL PSALM

Psalm 149:1b-2, 3-4, 5-6a and 9b

℟. (see 4a) **The Lord takes delight in his people.**
   or:
℟. **Alleluia.**

**Sing to the LORD a new song
   of praise in the assembly of the faithful.
Let Israel be glad in their maker,
   let the children of Zion rejoice in their king.**

℟. **The Lord takes delight in his people.**
   or:
℟. **Alleluia.**

**Let them praise his name in the festive dance,
   let them sing praise to him with timbrel and harp.
For the LORD loves his people,
   and he adorns the lowly with victory.**

℟. **The Lord takes delight in his people.**
   or:
℟. **Alleluia.**

**Let the faithful exult in glory;
   let them sing for joy upon their couches.
Let the high praises of God be in their throats.
   This is the glory of all his faithful. Alleluia.**

℟. **The Lord takes delight in his people.**
   or:
℟. **Alleluia.**

ALLELUIA

John 15:26b, 27a

℞. Alleluia, alleluia.

The Spirit of truth will testify to me, says the Lord,
and you also will testify.

℞. Alleluia, alleluia.

GOSPEL

John 15:26—16:4a   The Spirit of truth will testify to me.

✠ A reading from the holy Gospel according to John

Jesus said to his disciples:
"When the Advocate comes whom I will send you from the Father,
   the Spirit of truth who proceeds from the Father,
   he will testify to me.
And you also testify,
   because you have been with me from the beginning.

"I have told you this so that you may not fall away.
They will expel you from the synagogues;
   in fact, the hour is coming when everyone who kills you
   will think he is offering worship to God.
They will do this because they have not known either the Father or me.
I have told you this so that when their hour comes
   you may remember that I told you."

The Gospel of the Lord.

292 TUESDAY OF THE SIXTH WEEK OF EASTER

FIRST READING

Acts 16:22-34   Believe in the Lord Jesus and you and your household will be saved.

A reading from the Acts of the Apostles

The crowd in Philippi joined in the attack on Paul and Silas,
   and the magistrates had them stripped
   and ordered them to be beaten with rods.
After inflicting many blows on them,
   they threw them into prison
   and instructed the jailer to guard them securely.
When he received these instructions, he put them in the innermost cell
   and secured their feet to a stake.

About midnight, while Paul and Silas were praying
   and singing hymns to God as the prisoners listened,
   there was suddenly such a severe earthquake
   that the foundations of the jail shook;
   all the doors flew open, and the chains of all were pulled loose.
When the jailer woke up and saw the prison doors wide open,
   he drew his sword and was about to kill himself,
   thinking that the prisoners had escaped.
But Paul shouted out in a loud voice,
   "Do no harm to yourself; we are all here."
He asked for a light and rushed in and,
   trembling with fear, he fell down before Paul and Silas.
Then he brought them out and said,
   "Sirs, what must I do to be saved?"
And they said, "Believe in the Lord Jesus
   and you and your household will be saved."
So they spoke the word of the Lord to him and to everyone in his house.
He took them in at that hour of the night and bathed their wounds;
   then he and all his family were baptized at once.
He brought them up into his house and provided a meal
   and with his household rejoiced at having come to faith in God.

The word of the Lord.

RESPONSORIAL PSALM

Psalm 138:1-2ab, 2cde-3, 7c-8

℟. (7c) **Your right hand saves me, O Lord.**
   or:
℟. **Alleluia.**

**I will give thanks to you, O Lord, with all my heart,
   for you have heard the words of my mouth;
   in the presence of the angels I will sing your praise;
I will worship at your holy temple,
   and give thanks to your name.**

℟. **Your right hand saves me, O Lord.**
   or:
℟. **Alleluia.**

**Because of your kindness and your truth,
   you have made great above all things
   your name and your promise.
When I called, you answered me;
   you built up strength within me.**

℟. **Your right hand saves me, O Lord.**
   or:
℟. **Alleluia.**

**Your right hand saves me.
The Lord will complete what he has done for me;
   your kindness, O Lord, endures forever;
   forsake not the work of your hands.**

℟. **Your right hand saves me, O Lord.**
   or:
℟. **Alleluia.**

ALLELUIA

See John 16:7, 13

℟. Alleluia, alleluia.

I will send to you the Spirit of truth, says the Lord; he will guide you to all truth.

℟. Alleluia, alleluia.

GOSPEL

John 16:5-11   For if I do not go, the Advocate will not come to you.

✝ **A reading from the holy Gospel according to John**

Jesus said to his disciples:
"Now I am going to the one who sent me,
   and not one of you asks me, 'Where are you going?'
But because I told you this, grief has filled your hearts.
But I tell you the truth, it is better for you that I go.
For if I do not go, the Advocate will not come to you.
But if I go, I will send him to you.
And when he comes he will convict the world
   in regard to sin and righteousness and condemnation:
   sin, because they do not believe in me;
   righteousness, because I am going to the Father
   and you will no longer see me;
   condemnation, because the ruler of this world has been condemned."

The Gospel of the Lord.

293 WEDNESDAY OF THE SIXTH WEEK OF EASTER

FIRST READING

Acts 17:15, 22–18:1   What therefore you unknowingly worship, I proclaim to you.

A reading from the Acts of the Apostles

After Paul's escorts had taken him to Athens,
- they came away with instructions for Silas and Timothy
- to join him as soon as possible.

Then Paul stood up at the Areopagus and said:
- "You Athenians, I see that in every respect
- you are very religious.

For as I walked around looking carefully at your shrines,
- I even discovered an altar inscribed, 'To an Unknown God.'

What therefore you unknowingly worship, I proclaim to you.
The God who made the world and all that is in it,
- the Lord of heaven and earth,
- does not dwell in sanctuaries made by human hands,
- nor is he served by human hands because he needs anything.

Rather it is he who gives to everyone life and breath and everything.
He made from one the whole human race
- to dwell on the entire surface of the earth,
- and he fixed the ordered seasons and the boundaries of their regions,
- so that people might seek God,
- even perhaps grope for him and find him,
- though indeed he is not far from any one of us.

For 'In him we live and move and have our being,'
- as even some of your poets have said,
- 'For we too are his offspring.'

Since therefore we are the offspring of God,
- we ought not to think that the divinity is like an image
- fashioned from gold, silver, or stone by human art and imagination.

God has overlooked the times of ignorance,
> **but now he demands that all people everywhere repent**
> **because he has established a day on which he will 'judge the world**
> **with justice' through a man he has appointed,**
> **and he has provided confirmation for all**
> **by raising him from the dead."**

When they heard about resurrection of the dead,
> **some began to scoff, but others said,**
> **"We should like to hear you on this some other time."**

And so Paul left them.

But some did join him, and became believers.

Among them were Dionysius,
> **a member of the Court of the Areopagus,**
> **a woman named Damaris, and others with them.**

After this he left Athens and went to Corinth.

The word of the Lord.

RESPONSORIAL PSALM

Psalm 148:1-2, 11-12, 13, 14

℟. Heaven and earth are full of your glory.
 or:
℟. Alleluia.

Praise the Lord from the heavens;
 praise him in the heights.
Praise him, all you his angels;
 praise him, all you his hosts.

℟. Heaven and earth are full of your glory.
 or:
℟. Alleluia.

Let the kings of the earth and all peoples,
 the princes and all the judges of the earth,
Young men too, and maidens,
 old men and boys.

℟. Heaven and earth are full of your glory.
 or:
℟. Alleluia.

Praise the name of the Lord,
 for his name alone is exalted;
His majesty is above earth and heaven.

℟. Heaven and earth are full of your glory.
 or:
℟. Alleluia.

He has lifted up the horn of his people;
Be this his praise from all his faithful ones,
 from the children of Israel, the people close to him.
 Alleluia.

℟. Heaven and earth are full of your glory.
 or:
℟. Alleluia.

ALLELUIA

John 14:16

℟. Alleluia, alleluia.

**I will ask the Father
and he will give you another Advocate
to be with you always.**

℟. Alleluia, alleluia.

GOSPEL

John 16:12-15   When the Spirit of truth comes, he will guide you to all truth.

✠ **A reading from the holy Gospel according to John**

**Jesus said to his disciples:
"I have much more to tell you, but you cannot bear it now.
But when he comes, the Spirit of truth,
   he will guide you to all truth.
He will not speak on his own,
   but he will speak what he hears,
   and will declare to you the things that are coming.
He will glorify me,
   because he will take from what is mine and declare it to you.
Everything that the Father has is mine;
   for this reason I told you that he will take from what is mine
   and declare it to you."**

The Gospel of the Lord.

294 THURSDAY OF THE SIXTH WEEK OF EASTER

In Provinces where the celebration of Ascension is transferred to the Seventh Sunday of Easter, the following readings are used on this Thursday.

FIRST READING

Acts 18:1-8   Paul stayed with them and worked and entered into discussions in the synagogue.

A reading from the Acts of the Apostles

**Paul left Athens and went to Corinth.
There he met a Jew named Aquila, a native of Pontus,
   who had recently come from Italy with his wife Priscilla
   because Claudius had ordered all the Jews to leave Rome.
He went to visit them and, because he practiced the same trade,
   stayed with them and worked, for they were tentmakers by trade.
Every sabbath, he entered into discussions in the synagogue,
   attempting to convince both Jews and Greeks.**

**When Silas and Timothy came down from Macedonia,
   Paul began to occupy himself totally with preaching the word,
   testifying to the Jews that the Christ was Jesus.
When they opposed him and reviled him,
   he shook out his garments and said to them,
   "Your blood be on your heads!
I am clear of responsibility.
From now on I will go to the Gentiles."
So he left there and went to a house
   belonging to a man named Titus Justus, a worshiper of God;
   his house was next to a synagogue.
Crispus, the synagogue official, came to believe in the Lord
   along with his entire household, and many of the Corinthians
   who heard believed and were baptized.**

The word of the Lord.

RESPONSORIAL PSALM

Psalm 98:1, 2-3ab, 3cd-4

℟. (see 2b) **The Lord has revealed to the nations his saving power.**
  or:
℟. **Alleluia.**

Sing to the Lord **a new song,**
  for he has done wondrous deeds;
His right hand has won victory for him,
  his holy arm.

℟. **The Lord has revealed to the nations his saving power.**
  or:
℟. **Alleluia.**

The Lord **has made his salvation known:**
  in the sight of the nations he has revealed his justice.
He has remembered his kindness and his faithfulness
  toward the house of Israel.

℟. **The Lord has revealed to the nations his saving power.**
  or:
℟. **Alleluia.**

All the ends of the earth have seen
  the salvation by our God.
Sing joyfully to the Lord**, all you lands;**
  break into song; sing praise.

℟. **The Lord has revealed to the nations his saving power.**
  or:
℟. **Alleluia.**

ALLELUIA

See John 14:18

℟. Alleluia, alleluia.

I will not leave you orphans, says the Lord;
I will come back to you, and your hearts will rejoice.

℟. Alleluia, alleluia.

GOSPEL

John 16:16-20 You will grieve, but your grief will become joy.

✢ A reading from the holy Gospel according to John

Jesus said to his disciples:
"A little while and you will no longer see me,
 and again a little while later and you will see me."
So some of his disciples said to one another,
  "What does this mean that he is saying to us,
  'A little while and you will not see me,
  and again a little while and you will see me,'
  and 'Because I am going to the Father'?"
So they said, "What is this 'little while' of which he speaks?
We do not know what he means."
Jesus knew that they wanted to ask him, so he said to them,
  "Are you discussing with one another what I said,
  'A little while and you will not see me,
  and again a little while and you will see me'?
Amen, amen, I say to you,
  you will weep and mourn, while the world rejoices;
  you will grieve, but your grief will become joy."

The Gospel of the Lord.

295 FRIDAY OF THE SIXTH WEEK OF EASTER

FIRST READING

Acts 18:9-18   I have many people in this city.

A reading from the Acts of the Apostles

**One night while Paul was in Corinth, the Lord said to him in a vision,
   "Do not be afraid.
Go on speaking, and do not be silent, for I am with you.
No one will attack and harm you,
   for I have many people in this city."
He settled there for a year and a half
   and taught the word of God among them.**

**But when Gallio was proconsul of Achaia,
   the Jews rose up together against Paul
   and brought him to the tribunal, saying,
   "This man is inducing people to worship God contrary to the law."
When Paul was about to reply, Gallio spoke to the Jews,
   "If it were a matter of some crime or malicious fraud,
   I should with reason hear the complaint of you Jews;
   but since it is a question of arguments over doctrine and titles
   and your own law, see to it yourselves.
I do not wish to be a judge of such matters."
And he drove them away from the tribunal.
They all seized Sosthenes, the synagogue official,
   and beat him in full view of the tribunal.
But none of this was of concern to Gallio.**

**Paul remained for quite some time,
   and after saying farewell to the brothers he sailed for Syria,
   together with Priscilla and Aquila.
At Cenchreae he had shaved his head because he had taken a vow.**

The word of the Lord.

RESPONSORIAL PSALM

Psalm 47:2-3, 4-5, 6-7

℟. (8a) **God is king of all the earth.**
   or:
℟. **Alleluia.**

**All you peoples, clap your hands,
   shout to God with cries of gladness,
For the L**ORD**, the Most High, the awesome,
   is the great king over all the earth.**

℟. **God is king of all the earth.**
   or:
℟. **Alleluia.**

**He brings people under us;
   nations under our feet.
He chooses for us our inheritance,
   the glory of Jacob, whom he loves.**

℟. **God is king of all the earth.**
   or:
℟. **Alleluia.**

**God mounts his throne amid shouts of joy;
   the L**ORD**, amid trumpet blasts.
Sing praise to God, sing praise;
   sing praise to our king, sing praise.**

℟. **God is king of all the earth.**
   or:
℟. **Alleluia.**

ALLELUIA

See Luke 24:46, 26

℟. Alleluia, alleluia.

**Christ had to suffer and to rise from the dead,
and so enter into his glory.**

℟. Alleluia, alleluia.

GOSPEL

John 16:20-23   No one will take your joy away from you.

✠ **A reading from the holy Gospel according to John**

**Jesus said to his disciples:
"Amen, amen, I say to you, you will weep and mourn,
  while the world rejoices;
  you will grieve, but your grief will become joy.
When a woman is in labor, she is in anguish because her hour has arrived;
  but when she has given birth to a child,
  she no longer remembers the pain because of her joy
  that a child has been born into the world.
So you also are now in anguish.
But I will see you again, and your hearts will rejoice,
  and no one will take your joy away from you.
On that day you will not question me about anything.
Amen, amen, I say to you,
  whatever you ask the Father in my name he will give you."**

The Gospel of the Lord.

296 SATURDAY OF THE SIXTH WEEK OF EASTER

FIRST READING

Acts 18:23-28   Apollos established from the Scriptures that the Christ is Jesus.

A reading from the Acts of the Apostles

**After staying in Antioch some time,
Paul left and traveled in orderly sequence
through the Galatian country and Phrygia,
bringing strength to all the disciples.**

**A Jew named Apollos, a native of Alexandria,
an eloquent speaker, arrived in Ephesus.
He was an authority on the Scriptures.
He had been instructed in the Way of the Lord and,
with ardent spirit, spoke and taught accurately about Jesus,
although he knew only the baptism of John.
He began to speak boldly in the synagogue;
but when Priscilla and Aquila heard him,
they took him aside
and explained to him the Way of God more accurately.
And when he wanted to cross to Achaia,
the brothers encouraged him
and wrote to the disciples there to welcome him.
After his arrival he gave great assistance
to those who had come to believe through grace.
He vigorously refuted the Jews in public,
establishing from the Scriptures that the Christ is Jesus.**

The word of the Lord.

RESPONSORIAL PSALM

Psalm 47:2-3, 8-9, 10

℟. (8a) **God is king of all the earth.**
   or:
℟. **Alleluia.**

All you peoples, clap your hands;
   shout to God with cries of gladness.
For the LORD**, the Most High, the awesome,**
   is the great king over all the earth.

℟. **God is king of all the earth.**
   or:
℟. **Alleluia.**

For king of all the earth is God;
   sing hymns of praise.
God reigns over the nations,
   God sits upon his holy throne.

℟. **God is king of all the earth.**
   or:
℟. **Alleluia.**

The princes of the peoples are gathered together
   with the people of the God of Abraham.
For God's are the guardians of the earth;
   he is supreme.

℟. **God is king of all the earth.**
   or:
℟. **Alleluia.**

ALLELUIA

John 16:28

℟. Alleluia, alleluia.

I came from the Father and have come into the world;
now I am leaving the world and going back to the Father.

℟. Alleluia, alleluia.

GOSPEL

John 16:23b-28   My Father loves you because you have loved me and believed in me.

✠ A reading from the holy Gospel according to John

Jesus said to his disciples:
"Amen, amen, I say to you,
   whatever you ask the Father in my name he will give you.
Until now you have not asked anything in my name;
   ask and you will receive, so that your joy may be complete.

"I have told you this in figures of speech.
The hour is coming when I will no longer speak to you in figures
   but I will tell you clearly about the Father.
On that day you will ask in my name,
   and I do not tell you that I will ask the Father for you.
For the Father himself loves you, because you have loved me
   and have come to believe that I came from God.
I came from the Father and have come into the world.
Now I am leaving the world and going back to the Father."

The Gospel of the Lord.

297 MONDAY OF THE SEVENTH WEEK OF EASTER

FIRST READING

Acts 19:1-8 Did you receive the Holy Spirit when you became believers?

A reading from the Acts of the Apostles

While Apollos was in Corinth,
   Paul traveled through the interior of the country
   and down to Ephesus where he found some disciples.
He said to them,
   "Did you receive the Holy Spirit when you became believers?"
They answered him,
   "We have never even heard that there is a Holy Spirit."
He said, "How were you baptized?"
They replied, "With the baptism of John."
Paul then said, "John baptized with a baptism of repentance,
   telling the people to believe in the one who was to come after him,
   that is, in Jesus."
When they heard this,
   they were baptized in the name of the Lord Jesus.
And when Paul laid his hands on them,
   the Holy Spirit came upon them,
   and they spoke in tongues and prophesied.
Altogether there were about twelve men.

He entered the synagogue, and for three months debated boldly
   with persuasive arguments about the Kingdom of God.

The word of the Lord.

RESPONSORIAL PSALM

Psalm 68:2-3ab, 4-5acd, 6-7ab

℟. (33a) **Sing to God, O kingdoms of the earth.**
   or:
℟. **Alleluia.**

**God arises; his enemies are scattered,
   and those who hate him flee before him.
As smoke is driven away, so are they driven;
   as wax melts before the fire.**

℟. **Sing to God, O kingdoms of the earth.**
   or:
℟. **Alleluia.**

**But the just rejoice and exult before God;
   they are glad and rejoice.
Sing to God, chant praise to his name;
   whose name is the Lord.**

℟. **Sing to God, O kingdoms of the earth.**
   or:
℟. **Alleluia.**

**The father of orphans and the defender of widows
   is God in his holy dwelling.
God gives a home to the forsaken;
   he leads forth prisoners to prosperity.**

℟. **Sing to God, O kingdoms of the earth.**
   or:
℟. **Alleluia.**

ALLELUIA

Colossians 3:1

℟. Alleluia, alleluia.

**If then you were raised with Christ,
seek what is above,
where Christ is seated at the right hand of God.**

℟. Alleluia, alleluia.

GOSPEL

John 16:29-33   Take courage, I have conquered the world.

✠ **A reading from the holy Gospel according to John**

**The disciples said to Jesus,
 "Now you are talking plainly, and not in any figure of speech.
Now we realize that you know everything
 and that you do not need to have anyone question you.
Because of this we believe that you came from God."
Jesus answered them, "Do you believe now?
Behold, the hour is coming and has arrived
   when each of you will be scattered to his own home
   and you will leave me alone.
But I am not alone, because the Father is with me.
I have told you this so that you might have peace in me.
In the world you will have trouble,
   but take courage, I have conquered the world."**

The Gospel of the Lord.

298 TUESDAY OF THE SEVENTH WEEK OF EASTER

FIRST READING

Acts 20:17-27 I am finishing my course and the ministry that I received from the Lord Jesus.

A reading from the Acts of the Apostles

From Miletus Paul had the presbyters
  of the Church at Ephesus summoned.
When they came to him, he addressed them,
  "You know how I lived among you
  the whole time from the day I first came to the province of Asia.
I served the Lord with all humility
  and with the tears and trials that came to me
  because of the plots of the Jews,
  and I did not at all shrink from telling you
  what was for your benefit,
  or from teaching you in public or in your homes.
I earnestly bore witness for both Jews and Greeks
  to repentance before God and to faith in our Lord Jesus.
But now, compelled by the Spirit, I am going to Jerusalem.
What will happen to me there I do not know,
  except that in one city after another
  the Holy Spirit has been warning me
  that imprisonment and hardships await me.
Yet I consider life of no importance to me,
  if only I may finish my course
  and the ministry that I received from the Lord Jesus,
  to bear witness to the Gospel of God's grace.

"But now I know that none of you
  to whom I preached the kingdom during my travels
  will ever see my face again.
And so I solemnly declare to you this day
  that I am not responsible for the blood of any of you,
  for I did not shrink from proclaiming to you the entire plan of God."

The word of the Lord.

RESPONSORIAL PSALM

Psalm 68:10-11, 20-21

℟. (33a) **Sing to God, O kingdoms of the earth.**
   or:
℟. **Alleluia.**

A bountiful rain you showered down, O God, upon your inheritance;
   you restored the land when it languished;
Your flock settled in it;
   in your goodness, O God, you provided it for the needy.

℟. **Sing to God, O kingdoms of the earth.**
   or:
℟. **Alleluia.**

Blessed day by day be the Lord,
   who bears our burdens; God, who is our salvation.
God is a saving God for us;
   the LORD, my Lord, controls the passageways of death.

℟. **Sing to God, O kingdoms of the earth.**
   or:
℟. **Alleluia.**

ALLELUIA

John 14:16

℟. **Alleluia, alleluia.**

I will ask the Father
and he will give you another Advocate
to be with you always.

℟. **Alleluia, alleluia.**

GOSPEL

John 17:1-11a   Father, glorify your Son.

✠ A reading from the holy Gospel according to John

Jesus raised his eyes to heaven and said,
  "Father, the hour has come.
Give glory to your son, so that your son may glorify you,
  just as you gave him authority over all people,
  so that your son may give eternal life to all you gave him.
Now this is eternal life,
  that they should know you, the only true God,
  and the one whom you sent, Jesus Christ.
I glorified you on earth
  by accomplishing the work that you gave me to do.
Now glorify me, Father, with you,
  with the glory that I had with you before the world began.

"I revealed your name to those whom you gave me out of the world.
They belonged to you, and you gave them to me,
  and they have kept your word.
Now they know that everything you gave me is from you,
  because the words you gave to me I have given to them,
  and they accepted them and truly understood that I came from you,
  and they have believed that you sent me.
I pray for them.
I do not pray for the world but for the ones you have given me,
  because they are yours, and everything of mine is yours
  and everything of yours is mine,
  and I have been glorified in them.
And now I will no longer be in the world,
  but they are in the world, while I am coming to you."

The Gospel of the Lord.

299 WEDNESDAY OF THE SEVENTH WEEK OF EASTER

FIRST READING

Acts 20:28-38 I commend you to God who has the power to build you up and to give you an inheritance.

A reading from the Acts of the Apostles

At Miletus, Paul spoke to the presbyters of the Church of Ephesus:
"Keep watch over yourselves and over the whole flock
   of which the Holy Spirit has appointed you overseers,
   in which you tend the Church of God
   that he acquired with his own Blood.
I know that after my departure savage wolves will come among you,
   and they will not spare the flock.
And from your own group, men will come forward perverting the truth
   to draw the disciples away after them.
So be vigilant and remember that for three years, night and day,
   I unceasingly admonished each of you with tears.
And now I commend you to God
   and to that gracious word of his that can build you up
   and give you the inheritance among all who are consecrated.
I have never wanted anyone's silver or gold or clothing.
You know well that these very hands
   have served my needs and my companions.
In every way I have shown you that by hard work of that sort
   we must help the weak,
   and keep in mind the words of the Lord Jesus who himself said,
   'It is more blessed to give than to receive.'"

When he had finished speaking
   he knelt down and prayed with them all.
They were all weeping loudly
   as they threw their arms around Paul and kissed him,
   for they were deeply distressed that he had said
   that they would never see his face again.
Then they escorted him to the ship.

The word of the Lord.

RESPONSORIAL PSALM

Psalm 68:29-30, 33-35a, 35bc-36ab

℟. (33a) **Sing to God, O kingdoms of the earth.**
   or:
℟. **Alleluia.**

**Show forth, O God, your power,
   the power, O God, with which you took our part;
For your temple in Jerusalem
   let the kings bring you gifts.**

℟. **Sing to God, O kingdoms of the earth.**
   or:
℟. **Alleluia.**

**You kingdoms of the earth, sing to God,
   chant praise to the Lord
   who rides on the heights of the ancient heavens.
Behold, his voice resounds, the voice of power:
   "Confess the power of God!"**

℟. **Sing to God, O kingdoms of the earth.**
   or:
℟. **Alleluia.**

**Over Israel is his majesty;
   his power is in the skies.
Awesome in his sanctuary is God, the God of Israel;
   he gives power and strength to his people.**

℟. **Sing to God, O kingdoms of the earth.**
   or:
℟. **Alleluia.**

ALLELUIA

See John 17:17b, 17a

℟. **Alleluia, alleluia.**

**Your word, O Lord, is truth;
consecrate us in the truth.**

℟. **Alleluia, alleluia.**

GOSPEL

John 17:11b-19   May they be one just as we are one.

✠ A reading from the holy Gospel according to John

Lifting up his eyes to heaven, Jesus prayed, saying:
"Holy Father, keep them in your name
    that you have given me,
    so that they may be one just as we are one.
When I was with them I protected them in your name that you gave me,
    and I guarded them, and none of them was lost
    except the son of destruction,
    in order that the Scripture might be fulfilled.
But now I am coming to you.
I speak this in the world
    so that they may share my joy completely.
I gave them your word, and the world hated them,
    because they do not belong to the world
    any more than I belong to the world.
I do not ask that you take them out of the world
    but that you keep them from the Evil One.
They do not belong to the world
    any more than I belong to the world.
Consecrate them in the truth.
Your word is truth.
As you sent me into the world,
    so I sent them into the world.
And I consecrate myself for them,
    so that they also may be consecrated in truth."

The Gospel of the Lord.

300 THURSDAY OF THE SEVENTH WEEK OF EASTER

FIRST READING

Acts 22:30; 23:6-11   You must bear witness in Rome.

A reading from the Acts of the Apostles

Wishing to determine the truth
   about why Paul was being accused by the Jews,
   the commander freed him
   and ordered the chief priests and the whole Sanhedrin to convene.
Then he brought Paul down and made him stand before them.

Paul was aware that some were Sadducees and some Pharisees,
   so he called out before the Sanhedrin,
   "My brothers, I am a Pharisee, the son of Pharisees;
   I am on trial for hope in the resurrection of the dead."
When he said this,
   a dispute broke out between the Pharisees and Sadducees,
   and the group became divided.
For the Sadducees say that there is no resurrection
   or angels or spirits,
   while the Pharisees acknowledge all three.
A great uproar occurred,
   and some scribes belonging to the Pharisee party
   stood up and sharply argued,
   "We find nothing wrong with this man.
Suppose a spirit or an angel has spoken to him?"
The dispute was so serious that the commander,
   afraid that Paul would be torn to pieces by them,
   ordered his troops to go down and rescue Paul from their midst
   and take him into the compound.
The following night the Lord stood by him and said, "Take courage.
For just as you have borne witness to my cause in Jerusalem,
   so you must also bear witness in Rome."

The word of the Lord.

RESPONSORIAL PSALM

Psalm 16:1-2a and 5, 7-8, 9-10, 11

℟. (1) **Keep me safe, O God; you are my hope.**
   or:
℟. **Alleluia.**

Keep me, O God, for in you I take refuge;
   I say to the LORD, **"My Lord are you."**
O LORD, **my allotted portion and my cup,**
   you it is who hold fast my lot.

℟. **Keep me safe, O God; you are my hope.**
   or:
℟. **Alleluia.**

I bless the LORD **who counsels me;**
   even in the night my heart exhorts me.
I set the LORD **ever before me;**
   with him at my right hand I shall not be disturbed.

℟. **Keep me safe, O God; you are my hope.**
   or:
℟. **Alleluia.**

Therefore my heart is glad and my soul rejoices,
   my body, too, abides in confidence;
Because you will not abandon my soul to the nether world,
   nor will you suffer your faithful one to undergo corruption.

℟. **Keep me safe, O God; you are my hope.**
   or:
℟. **Alleluia.**

You will show me the path to life,
   fullness of joys in your presence,
   the delights at your right hand forever.

℟. **Keep me safe, O God; you are my hope.**
   or:
℟. **Alleluia.**

ALLELUIA

John 17:21

℟. Alleluia, alleluia.

May they all be one as you, Father, are in me and I in you,
that the world may believe that you sent me, says the Lord.

℟. Alleluia, alleluia.

GOSPEL

John 17:20-26   May they all be one.

✠ A reading from the holy Gospel according to John

Lifting up his eyes to heaven, Jesus prayed saying:
"I pray not only for these,
   but also for those who will believe in me through their word,
   so that they may all be one,
   as you, Father, are in me and I in you,
   that they also may be in us,
   that the world may believe that you sent me.
And I have given them the glory you gave me,
   so that they may be one, as we are one,
   I in them and you in me,
   that they may be brought to perfection as one,
   that the world may know that you sent me,
   and that you loved them even as you loved me.
Father, they are your gift to me.
I wish that where I am they also may be with me,
   that they may see my glory that you gave me,
   because you loved me before the foundation of the world.
Righteous Father, the world also does not know you,
   but I know you, and they know that you sent me.
I made known to them your name and I will make it known,
   that the love with which you loved me
   may be in them and I in them."

The Gospel of the Lord.

301 FRIDAY OF THE SEVENTH WEEK OF EASTER

FIRST READING

Acts 25:13b-21 *Jesus was dead, whom Paul claimed to be alive.*

A reading from the Acts of the Apostles

King Agrippa and Bernice arrived in Caesarea
   on a visit to Festus.
Since they spent several days there,
   Festus referred Paul's case to the king, saying,
   "There is a man here left in custody by Felix.
When I was in Jerusalem the chief priests and the elders of the Jews
   brought charges against him and demanded his condemnation.
I answered them that it was not Roman practice
   to hand over an accused person before he has faced his accusers
   and had the opportunity to defend himself against their charge.
So when they came together here, I made no delay;
   the next day I took my seat on the tribunal
   and ordered the man to be brought in.
His accusers stood around him,
   but did not charge him with any of the crimes I suspected.
Instead they had some issues with him about their own religion
   and about a certain Jesus who had died
   but who Paul claimed was alive.
Since I was at a loss how to investigate this controversy,
   I asked if he were willing to go to Jerusalem
   and there stand trial on these charges.
And when Paul appealed that he be held in custody
   for the Emperor's decision,
   I ordered him held until I could send him to Caesar."

The word of the Lord.

RESPONSORIAL PSALM

Psalm 103:1-2, 11-12, 19-20ab

℟. (19a) **The Lord has established his throne in heaven.**
   or:
℟. **Alleluia.**

Bless the Lord, O my soul;
   and all my being, bless his holy name.
Bless the Lord, O my soul,
   and forget not all his benefits.

℟. **The Lord has established his throne in heaven.**
   or:
℟. **Alleluia.**

For as the heavens are high above the earth,
   so surpassing is his kindness toward those who fear him.
As far as the east is from the west,
   so far has he put our transgressions from us.

℟. **The Lord has established his throne in heaven.**
   or:
℟. **Alleluia.**

The Lord has established his throne in heaven,
   and his kingdom rules over all.
Bless the Lord, all you his angels,
   you mighty in strength, who do his bidding.

℟. **The Lord has established his throne in heaven.**
   or:
℟. **Alleluia.**

ALLELUIA

John 14:26

℟. **Alleluia, alleluia.**

The Holy Spirit will teach you everything
and remind you of all I told you.

℟. **Alleluia, alleluia.**

GOSPEL

John 21:15-19 Feed my lambs, feed my sheep.

✣ A reading from the holy Gospel according to John

After Jesus had revealed himself to his disciples and eaten breakfast with them,
  he said to Simon Peter,
    "Simon, son of John, do you love me more than these?"
Simon Peter answered him, "Yes, Lord, you know that I love you."
Jesus said to him, "Feed my lambs."
He then said to Simon Peter a second time,
  "Simon, son of John, do you love me?"
Simon Peter answered him, "Yes, Lord, you know that I love you."
He said to him, "Tend my sheep."
He said to him the third time,
  "Simon, son of John, do you love me?"
Peter was distressed that he had said to him a third time,
  "Do you love me?" and he said to him,
  "Lord, you know everything; you know that I love you."
Jesus said to him, "Feed my sheep.
Amen, amen, I say to you, when you were younger,
  you used to dress yourself and go where you wanted;
  but when you grow old, you will stretch out your hands,
  and someone else will dress you
  and lead you where you do not want to go."
He said this signifying by what kind of death he would glorify God.
And when he had said this, he said to him, "Follow me."

The Gospel of the Lord.

302 SATURDAY OF THE SEVENTH WEEK OF EASTER

MASS IN THE MORNING

FIRST READING

Acts 28:16-20, 30-31   Paul remained at Rome, proclaiming the Kingdom of God.

A reading from the Acts of the Apostles

When he entered Rome, Paul was allowed to live by himself,
  with the soldier who was guarding him.

Three days later he called together the leaders of the Jews.
When they had gathered he said to them, "My brothers,
  although I had done nothing against our people
  or our ancestral customs,
  I was handed over to the Romans as a prisoner from Jerusalem.
After trying my case the Romans wanted to release me,
  because they found nothing against me deserving the death penalty.
But when the Jews objected, I was obliged to appeal to Caesar,
  even though I had no accusation to make against my own nation.
This is the reason, then, I have requested to see you
  and to speak with you, for it is on account of the hope of Israel
  that I wear these chains."

He remained for two full years in his lodgings.
He received all who came to him, and with complete assurance
  and without hindrance he proclaimed the Kingdom of God
  and taught about the Lord Jesus Christ.

The word of the Lord.

RESPONSORIAL PSALM

Psalm 11:4, 5 and 7

℟. (see 7b) **The just will gaze on your face, O Lord.**
   or:
℟. **Alleluia.**

The L<small>ORD</small> is in his holy temple;
   the L<small>ORD</small>'s throne is in heaven.
His eyes behold,
   his searching glance is on mankind.

℟. **The just will gaze on your face, O Lord.**
   or:
℟. **Alleluia.**

The L<small>ORD</small> searches the just and the wicked;
   the lover of violence he hates.
For the L<small>ORD</small> is just, he loves just deeds;
   the upright shall see his face.

℟. **The just will gaze on your face, O Lord.**
   or:
℟. **Alleluia.**

ALLELUIA

John 16:7, 13

℟. Alleluia, alleluia.

I will send to you the Spirit of truth, says the Lord;
he will guide you to all truth.

℟. Alleluia, alleluia.

GOSPEL

John 21:20-25   This is the disciple who has written these things and his testimony is true.

✠ A reading from the conclusion of the holy Gospel according to John

Peter turned and saw the disciple following whom Jesus loved,
 the one who had also reclined upon his chest during the supper
 and had said, "Master, who is the one who will betray you?"
When Peter saw him, he said to Jesus, "Lord, what about him?"
Jesus said to him, "What if I want him to remain until I come?
What concern is it of yours?
You follow me."
So the word spread among the brothers that that disciple would not die.
But Jesus had not told him that he would not die,
 just "What if I want him to remain until I come?
What concern is it of yours?"

It is this disciple who testifies to these things
 and has written them, and we know that his testimony is true.
There are also many other things that Jesus did,
 but if these were to be described individually,
 I do not think the whole world would contain the books
 that would be written.

The Gospel of the Lord.

303 ALLELUIA VERSES FOR WEEKDAYS OF THE SEASON OF EASTER UP TO THE ASCENSION

These texts may be used in place of the texts proposed for each day.

1.

Matthew 4:4b

**One does not live on bread alone,
but on every word that comes forth from the mouth of God.**

2.

See Luke 24:46, 26

**Christ had to suffer and to rise from the dead,
and so enter into his glory.**

3.

John 3:14-15

**The Son of Man must be lifted up,
so that everyone who believes in him
may have eternal life.**

4.

John 3:16

**God so loved the world that he gave his only-begotten Son,
so that everyone who believes in him might have eternal life.**

5.

John 6:35ab

**I am the bread of life, says the Lord;
whoever comes to me will never hunger.**

6.

See John 6:40

**Everyone who believes in the Son has eternal life,
and I shall raise him on the last day, says the Lord.**

7.

John 6:51

**I am the living bread that came down from heaven,
says the Lord;
whoever eats this bread will live forever.**

8.

John 6:56

**Whoever eats my Flesh and drinks my Blood
remains in me and I in him, says the Lord.**

9.

See John 6:63c, 68c

**Your words, Lord, are Spirit and life;
you have the words of everlasting life.**

10.

John 8:12

**I am the light of the world, says the Lord;
whoever follows me will have the light of life.**

11.

John 8:31b-32

**If you remain in my word, you will truly be my disciples,
and you will know the truth, says the Lord.**

12.

John 10:14

**I am the good shepherd, says the Lord;
I know my sheep, and mine know me.**

13.

John 10:27

**My sheep hear my voice, says the Lord;
I know them, and they follow me.**

14.

John 14:6

**I am the way and the truth and the life, says the Lord;
no one comes to the Father except through me.**

15.

John 15:4a, 5b

**Remain in me, as I remain in you, says the Lord;
whoever remains in me will bear much fruit.**

16.

John 15:15b

I call you my friends, says the Lord,
for I have made known to you all that the Father has told me.

17.

John 20:29

You believe in me, Thomas, because you have seen me, says the Lord;
Blessed are those who have not seen, but still believe!

18.

Romans 6:9

Christ now raised from the dead, dies no more;
death no longer has power over him.

19.

Colossians 3:1

If then you were raised with Christ,
seek what is above,
where Christ is seated at the right hand of God.

20.

See Revelation 1:5ab

Jesus Christ, you are the faithful witness,
the firstborn of the dead;
you have loved us and freed us from our sins by your Blood.

21.

We know that Christ is truly risen from the dead;
victorious king, have mercy on us.

22.

Nailed to the cross for our sake,
the Lord is now risen from the grave.

23.

Christ is risen and shines upon us,
whom he has redeemed by his Blood.

24.

Christ is risen, who made all things;
he has shown mercy on all people.

304 ALLELUIA VERSES FOR WEEKDAYS OF THE SEASON OF EASTER AFTER THE ASCENSION

These texts may be used in place of the texts proposed for each day.

1.

Matthew 28:19a, 20b

**Go and teach all nations, says the Lord;
I am with you always, until the end of the world.**

2.

John 14:16

**I will ask the Father,
and he will give you another Advocate,
to be with you always.**

3.

See John 14:18

**I will not leave you orphans, says the Lord;
I will come back to you, and your hearts will rejoice.**

4.

John 14:26

**The Holy Spirit will teach you everything
and remind you of all I told you.**

5.

John 15:26b, 27a

**The Spirit of truth will testify to me, says the Lord,
and you also will testify.**

6.

See John 16:7, 13

**I will send to you the Spirit of truth, says the Lord;
he will guide you to all truth.**

7.

John 16:28

**I came from the Father and have come into the world;
now I am leaving the world and going back to the Father.**

8.

See John 17:17b, 17a

**Your word, O Lord, is truth;
consecrate us in the truth.**

9.

John 17:21

**May they all be one as you, Father, are in me, and I in you,
that the world may believe that you sent me, says the Lord.**

10.

Colossians 3:1

**If then you were raised with Christ,
seek what is above,
where Christ is seated at the right hand of God.**

ORDINARY TIME

305 MONDAY OF THE FIRST WEEK IN ORDINARY TIME

When the Baptism of the Lord occurs on Monday of the First Week in Ordinary Time, the readings assigned to Monday may be joined to those of Tuesday so that the opening of each book will be read.

FIRST READING   Year II

1 Samuel 1:1-8   Hannah's rival turned it into a constant reproach to her that the Lord had left her barren.

A reading from the beginning of the first Book of Samuel

**There was a certain man from Ramathaim, Elkanah by name,
   a Zuphite from the hill country of Ephraim.
He was the son of Jeroham, son of Elihu,
   son of Tohu, son of Zuph, an Ephraimite.
He had two wives, one named Hannah, the other Peninnah;
   Peninnah had children, but Hannah was childless.
This man regularly went on pilgrimage from his city
   to worship the Lord of hosts and to sacrifice to him at Shiloh,
   where the two sons of Eli, Hophni and Phinehas,
   were ministering as priests of the Lord.
When the day came for Elkanah to offer sacrifice,
   he used to give a portion each to his wife Peninnah
   and to all her sons and daughters,
   but a double portion to Hannah because he loved her,
   though the Lord had made her barren.
Her rival, to upset her, turned it into a constant reproach to her
   that the Lord had left her barren.
This went on year after year;
   each time they made their pilgrimage to the sanctuary of the Lord,
   Peninnah would approach her,
   and Hannah would weep and refuse to eat.
Her husband Elkanah used to ask her:
   "Hannah, why do you weep, and why do you refuse to eat?
Why do you grieve?
Am I not more to you than ten sons?"

The word of the Lord.**

RESPONSORIAL PSALM

Psalm 116:12-13, 14-17, 18-19

℟. (17a) **To you, Lord, I will offer a sacrifice of praise.**
  or:
℟. **Alleluia.**

How shall I make a return to the Lord
  for all the good he has done for me?
The cup of salvation I will take up,
  and I will call upon the name of the Lord.

℟. **To you, Lord, I will offer a sacrifice of praise.**
  or:
℟. **Alleluia.**

My vows to the Lord I will pay
  in the presence of all his people.
Precious in the eyes of the Lord
  is the death of his faithful ones.
O Lord, I am your servant;
  I am your servant, the son of your handmaid;
  you have loosed my bonds.

℟. **To you, Lord, I will offer a sacrifice of praise.**
  or:
℟. **Alleluia.**

My vows to the Lord I will pay
  in the presence of all his people,
In the courts of the house of the Lord,
  in your midst, O Jerusalem.

℟. **To you, Lord, I will offer a sacrifice of praise.**
  or:
℟. **Alleluia.**

ALLELUIA

Mark 1:15

℟. Alleluia, alleluia.

**The Kingdom of God is at hand;
repent and believe in the Gospel.**

℟. Alleluia, alleluia.

GOSPEL   Years I and II

Mark 1:14-20   Repent, and believe in the Gospel.

✠ **A reading from the holy Gospel according to Mark**

**After John had been arrested,
Jesus came to Galilee proclaiming the Gospel of God:
"This is the time of fulfillment.
The Kingdom of God is at hand.
Repent, and believe in the Gospel."**

**As he passed by the Sea of Galilee,
he saw Simon and his brother Andrew casting their nets into the sea;
they were fishermen.
Jesus said to them,
"Come after me, and I will make you fishers of men."
Then they left their nets and followed him.
He walked along a little farther
and saw James, the son of Zebedee, and his brother John.
They too were in a boat mending their nets.
Then he called them.
So they left their father Zebedee in the boat
along with the hired men and followed him.**

The Gospel of the Lord.

306 TUESDAY OF THE FIRST WEEK IN ORDINARY TIME

FIRST READING   Year II

1 Samuel 1:9-20   The Lord God remembered Hannah, and she gave birth to Samuel.

A reading from the first Book of Samuel

Hannah rose after a meal at Shiloh,
   and presented herself before the Lord;
   at the time, Eli the priest was sitting on a chair
   near the doorpost of the Lord's temple.
In her bitterness she prayed to the Lord, weeping copiously,
   and she made a vow, promising: "O Lord of hosts,
   if you look with pity on the misery of your handmaid,
   if you remember me and do not forget me,
   if you give your handmaid a male child,
   I will give him to the Lord for as long as he lives;
   neither wine nor liquor shall he drink,
   and no razor shall ever touch his head."
As she remained long at prayer before the Lord,
   Eli watched her mouth, for Hannah was praying silently;
   though her lips were moving, her voice could not be heard.
Eli, thinking her drunk, said to her,
   "How long will you make a drunken show of yourself?
Sober up from your wine!"
"It isn't that, my lord," Hannah answered.
"I am an unhappy woman.
I have had neither wine nor liquor;
   I was only pouring out my troubles to the Lord.
Do not think your handmaid a ne'er-do-well;
   my prayer has been prompted by my deep sorrow and misery."
Eli said, "Go in peace,
   and may the God of Israel grant you what you have asked of him."
She replied, "Think kindly of your maidservant," and left.
She went to her quarters, ate and drank with her husband,
   and no longer appeared downcast.
Early the next morning they worshiped before the Lord,
   and then returned to their home in Ramah.

When Elkanah had relations with his wife Hannah,
  the Lord remembered her.
She conceived, and at the end of her term bore a son
  whom she called Samuel, since she had asked the Lord for him.

The word of the Lord.

RESPONSORIAL PSALM

1 Samuel 2:1, 4-5, 6-7, 8abcd

R/. (see 1) **My heart exults in the Lord, my Savior.**

"My heart exults in the Lord,
  my horn is exalted in my God.
I have swallowed up my enemies;
  I rejoice in my victory."

R/. **My heart exults in the Lord, my Savior.**

"The bows of the mighty are broken,
  while the tottering gird on strength.
The well-fed hire themselves out for bread,
  while the hungry batten on spoil.
The barren wife bears seven sons,
  while the mother of many languishes."

R/. **My heart exults in the Lord, my Savior.**

"The Lord puts to death and gives life;
  he casts down to the nether world;
  he raises up again.
The Lord makes poor and makes rich;
  he humbles, he also exalts."

R/. **My heart exults in the Lord, my Savior.**

"He raises the needy from the dust;
  from the dung heap he lifts up the poor,
To seat them with nobles
  and make a glorious throne their heritage."

R/. **My heart exults in the Lord, my Savior.**

ALLELUIA

See 1 Thessalonians 2:13

℟. Alleluia, alleluia.

Receive the word of God, not as the word of men,
but as it truly is, the word of God.

℟. Alleluia, alleluia.

GOSPEL Years I and II

Mark 1:21-28   Jesus taught them as one having authority.

✠ A reading from the holy Gospel according to Mark

Jesus came to Capernaum with his followers,
  and on the sabbath he entered the synagogue and taught.
The people were astonished at his teaching,
  for he taught them as one having authority and not as the scribes.
In their synagogue was a man with an unclean spirit;
  he cried out, "What have you to do with us, Jesus of Nazareth?
Have you come to destroy us?
I know who you are—the Holy One of God!"
Jesus rebuked him and said, "Quiet! Come out of him!"
The unclean spirit convulsed him and with a loud cry came out of him.
All were amazed and asked one another,
"What is this?
A new teaching with authority.
He commands even the unclean spirits and they obey him."
His fame spread everywhere throughout the whole region of Galilee.

The Gospel of the Lord.

307 WEDNESDAY OF THE FIRST WEEK IN ORDINARY TIME

FIRST READING   Year II

1 Samuel 3:1-10, 19-20   Speak, O Lord, for your servant is listening.

A reading from the first Book of Samuel

During the time young Samuel was minister to the Lord under Eli,
   a revelation of the Lord was uncommon and vision infrequent.
One day Eli was asleep in his usual place.
His eyes had lately grown so weak that he could not see.
The lamp of God was not yet extinguished,
   and Samuel was sleeping in the temple of the Lord
   where the ark of God was.
The Lord called to Samuel, who answered, "Here I am."

Samuel ran to Eli and said, "Here I am. You called me."
"I did not call you," Eli said. "Go back to sleep."
So he went back to sleep.
Again the Lord called Samuel, who rose and went to Eli.
"Here I am," he said. "You called me."
But Eli answered, "I did not call you, my son. Go back to sleep."
At that time Samuel was not familiar with the Lord,
   because the Lord had not revealed anything to him as yet.
The Lord called Samuel again, for the third time.
Getting up and going to Eli, he said, "Here I am.
You called me."
Then Eli understood that the Lord was calling the youth.
So Eli said to Samuel, "Go to sleep, and if you are called, reply,
   'Speak, Lord, for your servant is listening.'"
When Samuel went to sleep in his place,
   the Lord came and revealed his presence,
   calling out as before, "Samuel, Samuel!"
Samuel answered, "Speak, for your servant is listening."

Samuel grew up, and the Lord was with him,
   not permitting any word of his to be without effect.
Thus all Israel from Dan to Beersheba
   came to know that Samuel was an accredited prophet of the Lord.

The word of the Lord.

RESPONSORIAL PSALM

Psalm 40:2 and 5, 7-8a, 8b-9, 10

℟. (8a and 9a) **Here am I, Lord; I come to do your will.**

I have waited, waited for the Lord,
 and he stooped toward me and heard my cry.
Blessed the man who makes the Lord **his trust;**
 who turns not to idolatry
 or to those who stray after falsehood.

℟. **Here am I, Lord; I come to do your will.**

Sacrifice or oblation you wished not,
 but ears open to obedience you gave me.
Burnt offerings or sin-offerings you sought not;
 then said I, "Behold I come."

℟. **Here am I, Lord; I come to do your will.**

"In the written scroll it is prescribed for me.
To do your will, O my God, is my delight,
 and your law is within my heart!"

℟. **Here am I, Lord; I come to do your will.**

I announced your justice in the vast assembly;
 I did not restrain my lips, as you, O Lord, know.

℟. **Here am I, Lord; I come to do your will.**

ALLELUIA

John 10:27

℟. **Alleluia, alleluia.**

My sheep hear my voice, says the Lord.
I know them, and they follow me.

℟. **Alleluia, alleluia.**

GOSPEL   Years I and II

Mark 1:29-39   Jesus cured many who were sick with various diseases.

✠ **A reading from the holy Gospel according to Mark**

**On leaving the synagogue
Jesus entered the house of Simon and Andrew with James and John.
Simon's mother-in-law lay sick with a fever.
They immediately told him about her.
He approached, grasped her hand, and helped her up.
Then the fever left her and she waited on them.**

**When it was evening, after sunset,
they brought to him all who were ill or possessed by demons.
The whole town was gathered at the door.
He cured many who were sick with various diseases,
and he drove out many demons,
not permitting them to speak because they knew him.**

**Rising very early before dawn,
he left and went off to a deserted place, where he prayed.
Simon and those who were with him pursued him
and on finding him said, "Everyone is looking for you."
He told them, "Let us go on to the nearby villages
that I may preach there also.
For this purpose have I come."
So he went into their synagogues, preaching and driving out demons
throughout the whole of Galilee.**

The Gospel of the Lord.

308 THURSDAY OF THE FIRST WEEK IN ORDINARY TIME

FIRST READING   Year II

1 Samuel 4:1-11   Israel was defeated and the ark of God was captured.

A reading from the first Book of Samuel

The Philistines gathered for an attack on Israel.
Israel went out to engage them in battle and camped at Ebenezer,
 while the Philistines camped at Aphek.
The Philistines then drew up in battle formation against Israel.
After a fierce struggle Israel was defeated by the Philistines,
 who slew about four thousand men on the battlefield.
When the troops retired to the camp, the elders of Israel said,
 "Why has the Lord permitted us to be defeated today
  by the Philistines?
Let us fetch the ark of the Lord from Shiloh
 that it may go into battle among us
 and save us from the grasp of our enemies."

So the people sent to Shiloh and brought from there
 the ark of the Lord of hosts, who is enthroned upon the cherubim.
The two sons of Eli, Hophni and Phinehas, were with the ark of God.
When the ark of the Lord arrived in the camp,
 all Israel shouted so loudly that the earth resounded.
The Philistines, hearing the noise of shouting, asked,
 "What can this loud shouting in the camp of the Hebrews mean?"
On learning that the ark of the Lord had come into the camp,
 the Philistines were frightened.
They said, "Gods have come to their camp."
They said also, "Woe to us! This has never happened before. Woe to us!
Who can deliver us from the power of these mighty gods?
These are the gods that struck the Egyptians
 with various plagues and with pestilence.
Take courage and be manly, Philistines;
 otherwise you will become slaves to the Hebrews,
 as they were your slaves.
So fight manfully!"

The Philistines fought and Israel was defeated;
   every man fled to his own tent.
It was a disastrous defeat,
   in which Israel lost thirty thousand foot soldiers.
The ark of God was captured,
   and Eli's two sons, Hophni and Phinehas, were among the dead.

The word of the Lord.

RESPONSORIAL PSALM

Psalm 44:10-11, 14-15, 24-25

℟. (27b) **Redeem us, Lord, because of your mercy.**

Yet now you have cast us off and put us in disgrace,
   and you go not forth with our armies.
You have let us be driven back by our foes;
   those who hated us plundered us at will.

℟. **Redeem us, Lord, because of your mercy.**

You made us the reproach of our neighbors,
   the mockery and the scorn of those around us.
You made us a byword among the nations,
   a laughingstock among the peoples.

℟. **Redeem us, Lord, because of your mercy.**

Why do you hide your face,
   forgetting our woe and our oppression?
For our souls are bowed down to the dust,
   our bodies are pressed to the earth.

℟. **Redeem us, Lord, because of your mercy.**

ALLELUIA

See Matthew 4:23

℟. Alleluia, alleluia.

**Jesus preached the Gospel of the Kingdom
and cured every disease among the people.**

℟. Alleluia, alleluia.

GOSPEL   Years I and II

Mark 1:40-45   The leprosy left him, and he was made clean.

✟ A reading from the holy Gospel according to Mark

A leper came to him and kneeling down begged him and said,
   "If you wish, you can make me clean."
Moved with pity, he stretched out his hand,
   touched the leper, and said to him,
   "I do will it. Be made clean."
The leprosy left him immediately, and he was made clean.
Then, warning him sternly, he dismissed him at once.
Then he said to him, "See that you tell no one anything,
   but go, show yourself to the priest
   and offer for your cleansing what Moses prescribed;
   that will be proof for them."
The man went away and began to publicize the whole matter.
He spread the report abroad
   so that it was impossible for Jesus to enter a town openly.
He remained outside in deserted places,
   and people kept coming to him from everywhere.

The Gospel of the Lord.

309 FRIDAY OF THE FIRST WEEK IN ORDINARY TIME

FIRST READING   Year II

1 Samuel 8:4-7, 10-22a   *You will complain against the king whom you have chosen, but on that day the L*ORD *will not answer you.*

A reading from the first Book of Samuel

All the elders of Israel came in a body to Samuel at Ramah
   and said to him, "Now that you are old,
   and your sons do not follow your example,
   appoint a king over us, as other nations have, to judge us."

Samuel was displeased when they asked for a king to judge them.
He prayed to the LORD, however, who said in answer:
   "Grant the people's every request.
It is not you they reject, they are rejecting me as their king."

Samuel delivered the message of the LORD in full
   to those who were asking him for a king.
He told them:
   "The rights of the king who will rule you will be as follows:
   He will take your sons and assign them to his chariots and horses,
   and they will run before his chariot.
He will also appoint from among them his commanders of groups
   of a thousand and of a hundred soldiers.
He will set them to do his plowing and his harvesting,
   and to make his implements of war and the equipment of his chariots.
He will use your daughters as ointment makers, as cooks, and as bakers.
He will take the best of your fields, vineyards, and olive groves,
   and give them to his officials.
He will tithe your crops and your vineyards,
   and give the revenue to his eunuchs and his slaves.
He will take your male and female servants,
   as well as your best oxen and your asses,
   and use them to do his work.
He will tithe your flocks and you yourselves will become his slaves.
When this takes place,
   you will complain against the king whom you have chosen,
   but on that day the LORD will not answer you."

The people, however, refused to listen to Samuel's warning and said,
   "Not so! There must be a king over us.
We too must be like other nations,
   with a king to rule us and to lead us in warfare
   and fight our battles."
When Samuel had listened to all the people had to say,
   he repeated it to the Lord, who then said to him,
   "Grant their request and appoint a king to rule them."

The word of the Lord.

RESPONSORIAL PSALM

Psalm 89:16-17, 18-19

℟. (2) **For ever I will sing the goodness of the Lord.**

Blessed the people who know the joyful shout;
   in the light of your countenance, O Lord, they walk.
At your name they rejoice all the day,
   and through your justice they are exalted.

℟. **For ever I will sing the goodness of the Lord.**

For you are the splendor of their strength,
   and by your favor our horn is exalted.
For to the Lord belongs our shield,
   and to the Holy One of Israel, our King.

℟. **For ever I will sing the goodness of the Lord.**

ALLELUIA

Luke 7:16

℟. **Alleluia, alleluia.**

A great prophet has arisen in our midst
and God has visited his people.

℟. **Alleluia, alleluia.**

GOSPEL — Years I and II

Mark 2:1-12   The Son of Man has authority to forgive sins on earth.

☩ A reading from the holy Gospel according to Mark

When Jesus returned to Capernaum after some days,
  it became known that he was at home.
Many gathered together so that there was no longer room for them,
  not even around the door,
  and he preached the word to them.
They came bringing to him a paralytic carried by four men.
Unable to get near Jesus because of the crowd,
  they opened up the roof above him.
After they had broken through,
  they let down the mat on which the paralytic was lying.
When Jesus saw their faith, he said to him,
  "Child, your sins are forgiven."
Now some of the scribes were sitting there asking themselves,
  "Why does this man speak that way? He is blaspheming.
Who but God alone can forgive sins?"
Jesus immediately knew in his mind what
  they were thinking to themselves,
  so he said, "Why are you thinking such things in your hearts?
Which is easier, to say to the paralytic,
  'Your sins are forgiven,'
  or to say, 'Rise, pick up your mat and walk'?
But that you may know
  that the Son of Man has authority to forgive sins on earth"
  —he said to the paralytic,
  "I say to you, rise, pick up your mat, and go home."
He rose, picked up his mat at once,
  and went away in the sight of everyone.
They were all astounded
  and glorified God, saying, "We have never seen anything like this."

The Gospel of the Lord.

310 SATURDAY OF THE FIRST WEEK IN ORDINARY TIME

FIRST READING   Year II

1 Samuel 9:1-4, 17-19; 10:1   This is the man of whom the Lord God spoke, Saul who will rule his people.

A reading from the first Book of Samuel

There was a stalwart man from Benjamin named Kish,
   who was the son of Abiel, son of Zeror,
   son of Becorath, son of Aphiah, a Benjaminite.
He had a son named Saul, who was a handsome young man.
There was no other child of Israel more handsome than Saul;
   he stood head and shoulders above the people.

Now the asses of Saul's father, Kish, had wandered off.
Kish said to his son Saul, "Take one of the servants with you
   and go out and hunt for the asses."
Accordingly they went through the hill country of Ephraim,
   and through the land of Shalishah.
Not finding them there,
   they continued through the land of Shaalim without success.
They also went through the land of Benjamin,
   but they failed to find the animals.

When Samuel caught sight of Saul, the Lord assured him,
   "This is the man of whom I told you; he is to govern my people."

Saul met Samuel in the gateway and said,
   "Please tell me where the seer lives."
Samuel answered Saul: "I am the seer.
Go up ahead of me to the high place and eat with me today.
In the morning, before dismissing you,
   I will tell you whatever you wish."

Then, from a flask he had with him, Samuel poured oil on Saul's head;
   he also kissed him, saying:
   "The Lord anoints you commander over his heritage.
You are to govern the Lord's people Israel,
   and to save them from the grasp of their enemies roundabout.
"This will be the sign for you
   that the Lord has anointed you commander over his heritage."

The word of the Lord.

RESPONSORIAL PSALM

Psalm 21:2-3, 4-5, 6-7

℟. (2a) **Lord, in your strength the king is glad.**

O LORD, in your strength the king is glad;
  in your victory how greatly he rejoices!
You have granted him his heart's desire;
  you refused not the wish of his lips.

℟. **Lord, in your strength the king is glad.**

For you welcomed him with goodly blessings,
  you placed on his head a crown of pure gold.
He asked life of you: you gave him
  length of days forever and ever.

℟. **Lord, in your strength the king is glad.**

Great is his glory in your victory;
  majesty and splendor you conferred upon him.
For you made him a blessing forever;
  you gladdened him with the joy of your face.

℟. **Lord, in your strength the king is glad.**

ALLELUIA

Luke 4:18

℟. **Alleluia, alleluia.**

The Lord sent me to bring glad tidings to the poor and to proclaim liberty to captives.

℟. **Alleluia, alleluia.**

GOSPEL Years I and II

Mark 2:13-17   I did not come to call the righteous but sinners.

✠ **A reading from the holy Gospel according to Mark**

**Jesus went out along the sea.
All the crowd came to him and he taught them.
As he passed by, he saw Levi, son of Alphaeus,
   sitting at the customs post.
Jesus said to him, "Follow me."
And he got up and followed Jesus.
While he was at table in his house,
   many tax collectors and sinners sat with Jesus and his disciples;
   for there were many who followed him.
Some scribes who were Pharisees saw that Jesus was eating with sinners
   and tax collectors and said to his disciples,
   "Why does he eat with tax collectors and sinners?"
Jesus heard this and said to them,
   "Those who are well do not need a physician, but the sick do.
I did not come to call the righteous but sinners."**

The Gospel of the Lord.

311 MONDAY OF THE SECOND WEEK IN ORDINARY TIME

FIRST READING   Year II

1 Samuel 15:16-23   Obedience is better than sacrifice. Because you have rejected the command of the Lord, he, too, has rejected you as ruler.

A reading from the first Book of Samuel

**Samuel said to Saul:
"Stop! Let me tell you what the Lord said to me last night."
Saul replied, "Speak!"
Samuel then said: "Though little in your own esteem,
   are you not leader of the tribes of Israel?
The Lord anointed you king of Israel and sent me on a mission, saying,
   'Go and put the sinful Amalekites under a ban of destruction.
Fight against them until you have exterminated them.'
Why then have you disobeyed the Lord?
You have pounced on the spoil, thus displeasing the Lord."
Saul answered Samuel: "I did indeed obey the Lord
   and fulfill the mission on which the Lord sent me.
I have brought back Agag, and I have destroyed Amalek under the ban.
But from the spoil the men took sheep and oxen,
   the best of what had been banned,
   to sacrifice to the Lord their God in Gilgal."
But Samuel said:
   "Does the Lord so delight in burnt offerings and sacrifices
   as in obedience to the command of the Lord?
   Obedience is better than sacrifice,
      and submission than the fat of rams.
   For a sin like divination is rebellion,
      and presumption is the crime of idolatry.
   Because you have rejected the command of the Lord,
      he, too, has rejected you as ruler."**

The word of the Lord.

RESPONSORIAL PSALM

Psalm 50:8-9, 16bc-17, 21 and 23

℟. (23b) **To the upright I will show the saving power of God.**

"Not for your sacrifices do I rebuke you,
  for your burnt offerings are before me always.
I take from your house no bullock,
  no goats out of your fold."

℟. **To the upright I will show the saving power of God.**

"Why do you recite my statutes,
  and profess my covenant with your mouth,
Though you hate discipline
  and cast my words behind you?"

℟. **To the upright I will show the saving power of God.**

"When you do these things, shall I be deaf to it?
  Or do you think that I am like yourself?
  I will correct you by drawing them up before your eyes.
He that offers praise as a sacrifice glorifies me;
  and to him that goes the right way I will show the salvation of God."

℟. **To the upright I will show the saving power of God.**

ALLELUIA

Hebrews 4:12

℟. Alleluia, alleluia.

**The word of God is living and effective,
able to discern reflections and thoughts of the heart.**

℟. Alleluia, alleluia.

GOSPEL Years I and II

Mark 2:18-22 *The bridegroom is with them.*

✠ **A reading from the holy Gospel according to Mark**

The disciples of John and of the Pharisees were accustomed to fast.
People came to Jesus and objected,
   "Why do the disciples of John and the disciples of the Pharisees fast,
   but your disciples do not fast?"
Jesus answered them,
   "Can the wedding guests fast while the bridegroom is with them?
As long as they have the bridegroom with them they cannot fast.
But the days will come when the bridegroom is taken away from them,
   and then they will fast on that day.
No one sews a piece of unshrunken cloth on an old cloak.
   If he does, its fullness pulls away,
   the new from the old, and the tear gets worse.
Likewise, no one pours new wine into old wineskins.
Otherwise, the wine will burst the skins,
   and both the wine and the skins are ruined.
Rather, new wine is poured into fresh wineskins."

The Gospel of the Lord.

312 TUESDAY OF THE SECOND WEEK IN ORDINARY TIME

FIRST READING   Year II

1 Samuel 16:1-13   Samuel anointed David in the presence of his brothers, and the Spirit of the Lord God rushed upon him.

A reading from the first Book of Samuel

The Lord said to Samuel:
"How long will you grieve for Saul,
　whom I have rejected as king of Israel?
Fill your horn with oil, and be on your way.
I am sending you to Jesse of Bethlehem,
　for I have chosen my king from among his sons."
But Samuel replied:
　"How can I go?
　Saul will hear of it and kill me."
To this the Lord answered:
　"Take a heifer along and say,
　'I have come to sacrifice to the Lord.'
Invite Jesse to the sacrifice, and I myself will tell you what to do;
　you are to anoint for me the one I point out to you."

Samuel did as the Lord had commanded him.
When he entered Bethlehem,
　the elders of the city came trembling to meet him and inquired,
　"Is your visit peaceful, O seer?"
He replied:
　"Yes! I have come to sacrifice to the Lord.
So cleanse yourselves and join me today for the banquet."
He also had Jesse and his sons cleanse themselves
　and invited them to the sacrifice.
As they came, he looked at Eliab and thought,
　"Surely the Lord's anointed is here before him."
But the Lord said to Samuel:
　"Do not judge from his appearance or from his lofty stature,
　because I have rejected him.
Not as man sees does God see,
　because he sees the appearance
　but the Lord looks into the heart."

Then Jesse called Abinadab and presented him before Samuel,
who said, "The Lord **has not chosen him."**
Next Jesse presented Shammah, but Samuel said,
"The Lord **has not chosen this one either."**
In the same way Jesse presented seven sons before Samuel,
but Samuel said to Jesse,
"The Lord **has not chosen any one of these."**
Then Samuel asked Jesse,
"Are these all the sons you have?"
Jesse replied,
"There is still the youngest, who is tending the sheep."
Samuel said to Jesse,
"Send for him;
we will not begin the sacrificial banquet until he arrives here."
Jesse sent and had the young man brought to them.
He was ruddy, a youth handsome to behold
and making a splendid appearance.
The Lord **said,**
"There—anoint him, for this is he!"
Then Samuel, with the horn of oil in hand,
anointed him in the midst of his brothers;
and from that day on, the Spirit of the Lord **rushed upon David.**
When Samuel took his leave, he went to Ramah.

The word of the Lord.

RESPONSORIAL PSALM

Psalm 89:20, 21-22, 27-28

℟. (21a) **I have found David, my servant.**

**Once you spoke in a vision,
 and to your faithful ones you said:
"On a champion I have placed a crown;
 over the people I have set a youth."**

℟. **I have found David, my servant.**

**"I have found David, my servant;
 with my holy oil I have anointed him,
That my hand may be always with him,
 and that my arm may make him strong."**

℟. **I have found David, my servant.**

**"He shall say of me, 'You are my father,
 my God, the Rock, my savior.'
And I will make him the first-born,
 highest of the kings of the earth."**

℟. **I have found David, my servant.**

ALLELUIA

See Ephesians 1:17-18

℟. **Alleluia, alleluia.**

**May the Father of our Lord Jesus Christ
enlighten the eyes of our hearts,
that we may know what is the hope
that belongs to our call.**

℟. **Alleluia, alleluia.**

GOSPEL   Years I and II

Mark 2:23-28   The sabbath was made for people, not people for the sabbath.

✙ **A reading from the holy Gospel according to Mark**

As Jesus was passing through a field of grain on the sabbath,
   his disciples began to make a path while picking the heads of grain.
At this the Pharisees said to him,
   "Look, why are they doing what is unlawful on the sabbath?"
He said to them,
   "Have you never read what David did
   when he was in need and he and his companions were hungry?
How he went into the house of God when Abiathar was high priest
   and ate the bread of offering that only the priests could lawfully eat,
   and shared it with his companions?"
Then he said to them,
   "The sabbath was made for man, not man for the sabbath.
That is why the Son of Man is lord even of the sabbath."

The Gospel of the Lord.

313 WEDNESDAY OF THE SECOND WEEK IN ORDINARY TIME

FIRST READING   Year II

1 Samuel 17:32-33, 37, 40-51   David overcame the Philistine with sling and stone.

A reading from the first Book of Samuel

David spoke to Saul:
"Let your majesty not lose courage.
I am at your service to go and fight this Philistine."
But Saul answered David,
　"You cannot go up against this Philistine and fight with him,
　for you are only a youth, while he has been a warrior from his youth."

David continued:
　"The Lord, who delivered me from the claws of the lion and the bear,
　will also keep me safe from the clutches of this Philistine."
Saul answered David, "Go! the Lord will be with you."

Then, staff in hand, David selected five smooth stones from the wadi
　and put them in the pocket of his shepherd's bag.
With his sling also ready to hand, he approached the Philistine.

With his shield bearer marching before him,
　the Philistine also advanced closer and closer to David.
When he had sized David up,
　and seen that he was youthful, and ruddy, and handsome in appearance,
　the Philistine held David in contempt.
The Philistine said to David,
　"Am I a dog that you come against me with a staff?"
Then the Philistine cursed David by his gods
　and said to him, "Come here to me,
　and I will leave your flesh for the birds of the air
　and the beasts of the field."
David answered him:
　"You come against me with sword and spear and scimitar,
　but I come against you in the name of the Lord of hosts,
　the God of the armies of Israel that you have insulted.

Today the LORD shall deliver you into my hand;
> I will strike you down and cut off your head.

This very day I will leave your corpse
> and the corpses of the Philistine army for the birds of the air
> and the beasts of the field;
> thus the whole land shall learn that Israel has a God.

All this multitude, too,
> shall learn that it is not by sword or spear that the LORD saves.

For the battle is the LORD's and he shall deliver you into our hands."

The Philistine then moved to meet David at close quarters,
> while David ran quickly toward the battle line
> in the direction of the Philistine.

David put his hand into the bag and took out a stone,
> hurled it with the sling,
> and struck the Philistine on the forehead.

The stone embedded itself in his brow,
> and he fell prostrate on the ground.

Thus David overcame the Philistine with sling and stone;
> he struck the Philistine mortally, and did it without a sword.

Then David ran and stood over him;
> with the Philistine's own sword which he drew from its sheath
> he dispatched him and cut off his head.

The word of the Lord.

RESPONSORIAL PSALM

Psalm 144:1b, 2, 9-10

℟. (1) **Blessed be the Lord, my Rock!**

Blessed be the LORD**, my rock,
   who trains my hands for battle, my fingers for war.**

℟. **Blessed be the Lord, my Rock!**

**My refuge and my fortress,
   my stronghold, my deliverer,
My shield, in whom I trust,
   who subdues my people under me.**

℟. **Blessed be the Lord, my Rock!**

**O God, I will sing a new song to you;
   with a ten-stringed lyre I will chant your praise,
You who give victory to kings,
   and deliver David, your servant from the evil sword.**

℟. **Blessed be the Lord, my Rock!**

ALLELUIA

See Matthew 4:23

℟. **Alleluia, alleluia.**

**Jesus preached the Gospel of the Kingdom
and cured every disease among the people.**

℟. **Alleluia, alleluia.**

GOSPEL Years I and II

Mark 3:1-6   Is it lawful on the sabbath to save life rather than to destroy it?

✢ **A reading from the holy Gospel according to Mark**

Jesus entered the synagogue.
There was a man there who had a withered hand.
They watched Jesus closely
   to see if he would cure him on the sabbath
   so that they might accuse him.
He said to the man with the withered hand,
   "Come up here before us."
Then he said to the Pharisees,
   "Is it lawful to do good on the sabbath rather than to do evil,
   to save life rather than to destroy it?"
But they remained silent.
Looking around at them with anger
   and grieved at their hardness of heart,
   Jesus said to the man, "Stretch out your hand."
He stretched it out and his hand was restored.
The Pharisees went out and immediately took counsel
   with the Herodians against him to put him to death.

The Gospel of the Lord.

314 THURSDAY OF THE SECOND WEEK IN ORDINARY TIME

FIRST READING Year II

1 Samuel 18:6-9; 19:1-7   My father Saul is trying to kill you.

A reading from the first Book of Samuel

When David and Saul approached
    (on David's return after slaying the Philistine),
    women came out from each of the cities of Israel to meet King Saul,
    singing and dancing, with tambourines, joyful songs, and sistrums.
The women played and sang:

    "Saul has slain his thousands,
    and David his ten thousands."

Saul was very angry and resentful of the song, for he thought:
    "They give David ten thousands, but only thousands to me.
All that remains for him is the kingship."
And from that day on, Saul was jealous of David.

Saul discussed his intention of killing David
    with his son Jonathan and with all his servants.
But Saul's son Jonathan, who was very fond of David, told him:
    "My father Saul is trying to kill you.
Therefore, please be on your guard tomorrow morning;
    get out of sight and remain in hiding.
I, however, will go out and stand beside my father
    in the countryside where you are, and will speak to him about you.
If I learn anything, I will let you know."

Jonathan then spoke well of David to his father Saul, saying to him:
    "Let not your majesty sin against his servant David,
    for he has committed no offense against you,
    but has helped you very much by his deeds.
When he took his life in his hands and slew the Philistine,
    and the Lord brought about a great victory
    for all Israel through him,
    you were glad to see it.

Why, then, should you become guilty of shedding innocent blood
  by killing David without cause?"
Saul heeded Jonathan's plea and swore,
  "As the Lord lives, he shall not be killed."
So Jonathan summoned David and repeated the whole conversation to him.
Jonathan then brought David to Saul, and David served him as before.

The word of the Lord.

RESPONSORIAL PSALM

Psalm 56:2-3, 9-10a, 10b-11, 12-13

℟. (5b) **In God I trust; I shall not fear.**

**Have mercy on me, O God, for men trample upon me;
    all the day they press their attack against me.
My adversaries trample upon me all the day;
    yes, many fight against me.**

℟. **In God I trust; I shall not fear.**

**My wanderings you have counted;
    my tears are stored in your flask;
    are they not recorded in your book?
Then do my enemies turn back,
    when I call upon you.**

℟. **In God I trust; I shall not fear.**

**Now I know that God is with me.
    In God, in whose promise I glory,
    in God I trust without fear;
    what can flesh do against me?**

℟. **In God I trust; I shall not fear.**

**I am bound, O God, by vows to you;
    your thank offerings I will fulfill.
For you have rescued me from death,
    my feet, too, from stumbling;
    that I may walk before God in the light of the living.**

℟. **In God I trust; I shall not fear.**

ALLELUIA

See 2 Timothy 1:10

℟. Alleluia, alleluia.

**Our Savior Jesus Christ has destroyed death
and brought life to light through the Gospel.**

℟. Alleluia, alleluia.

GOSPEL   Years I and II

Mark 3:7-12   The unclean spirits shouted, "You are the Son of God," but Jesus warned them sternly not to make him known.

☩ **A reading from the holy Gospel according to Mark**

**Jesus withdrew toward the sea with his disciples.
A large number of people followed from Galilee and from Judea.
Hearing what he was doing,
   a large number of people came to him also from Jerusalem,
   from Idumea, from beyond the Jordan,
   and from the neighborhood of Tyre and Sidon.
He told his disciples to have a boat ready for him because of the crowd,
   so that they would not crush him.
He had cured many and, as a result, those who had diseases
   were pressing upon him to touch him.
And whenever unclean spirits saw him they would fall down before him
   and shout, "You are the Son of God."
He warned them sternly not to make him known.**

The Gospel of the Lord.

315 FRIDAY OF THE SECOND WEEK IN ORDINARY TIME

FIRST READING   Year II

1 Samuel 24:3-21   I will not raise a hand against my lord, for he is the Lord's anointed.

A reading from the first Book of Samuel

Saul took three thousand picked men from all Israel
  and went in search of David and his men
  in the direction of the wild goat crags.
When he came to the sheepfolds along the way, he found a cave,
  which he entered to relieve himself.
David and his men were occupying the inmost recesses of the cave.

David's servants said to him,
  "This is the day of which the Lord said to you,
  'I will deliver your enemy into your grasp;
  do with him as you see fit.'"
So David moved up and stealthily cut off an end of Saul's mantle.
Afterward, however, David regretted that he had cut off
  an end of Saul's mantle.
He said to his men,
  "The Lord forbid that I should do such a thing to my master,
  the Lord's anointed, as to lay a hand on him,
  for he is the Lord's anointed."
With these words David restrained his men
  and would not permit them to attack Saul.
Saul then left the cave and went on his way.
David also stepped out of the cave, calling to Saul,
  "My lord the king!"
When Saul looked back, David bowed to the ground in homage and asked Saul:
  "Why do you listen to those who say,
  'David is trying to harm you'?
You see for yourself today that the Lord just now delivered you
  into my grasp in the cave.
I had some thought of killing you, but I took pity on you instead.

I decided, 'I will not raise a hand against my lord,
   for he is the Lord's anointed and a father to me.'
Look here at this end of your mantle which I hold.
Since I cut off an end of your mantle and did not kill you,
   see and be convinced that I plan no harm and no rebellion.
I have done you no wrong,
   though you are hunting me down to take my life.
The Lord will judge between me and you,
   and the Lord will exact justice from you in my case.
I shall not touch you.
The old proverb says, 'From the wicked comes forth wickedness.'
So I will take no action against you.
Against whom are you on campaign, O king of Israel?
Whom are you pursuing? A dead dog, or a single flea!
The Lord will be the judge; he will decide between me and you.
May he see this, and take my part,
   and grant me justice beyond your reach!"

When David finished saying these things to Saul, Saul answered,
   "Is that your voice, my son David?"
And Saul wept aloud.
Saul then said to David: "You are in the right rather than I;
   you have treated me generously, while I have done you harm.
Great is the generosity you showed me today,
   when the Lord delivered me into your grasp
   and you did not kill me.
For if a man meets his enemy, does he send him away unharmed?
May the Lord reward you generously for what you have done this day.
And now, I know that you shall surely be king
   and that sovereignty over Israel shall come into your possession."

The word of the Lord.

RESPONSORIAL PSALM

Psalm 57:2, 3-4, 6 and 11

℟. (2a) Have mercy on me, God, have mercy.

Have mercy on me, O God; have mercy on me,
   for in you I take refuge.
In the shadow of your wings I take refuge,
   till harm pass by.

℟. Have mercy on me, God, have mercy.

I call to God the Most High,
   to God, my benefactor.
May he send from heaven and save me;
   may he make those a reproach who trample upon me;
   may God send his mercy and his faithfulness.

℟. Have mercy on me, God, have mercy.

Be exalted above the heavens, O God;
   above all the earth be your glory!
For your mercy towers to the heavens,
   and your faithfulness to the skies.

℟. Have mercy on me, God, have mercy.

ALLELUIA

2 Corinthians 5:19

℟. Alleluia, alleluia.

God was reconciling the world to himself in Christ,
and entrusting to us the message of reconciliation.

℟. Alleluia, alleluia.

GOSPEL — Years I and II

Mark 3:13-19   Jesus summoned those whom he wanted and they came to him.

✟ **A reading from the holy Gospel according to Mark**

**Jesus went up the mountain and summoned those whom he wanted
and they came to him.
He appointed Twelve, whom he also named Apostles,
that they might be with him
and he might send them forth to preach
and to have authority to drive out demons:
He appointed the Twelve:
Simon, whom he named Peter;
James, son of Zebedee,
and John the brother of James, whom he named Boanerges,
that is, sons of thunder;
Andrew, Philip, Bartholomew,
Matthew, Thomas, James the son of Alphaeus;
Thaddeus, Simon the Cananean,
and Judas Iscariot who betrayed him.**

The Gospel of the Lord.

316 SATURDAY OF THE SECOND WEEK IN ORDINARY TIME

FIRST READING   Year II

2 Samuel 1:1-4, 11-12, 19, 23-27   How can the warriors have fallen in battle!

A reading from the second Book of Samuel

David returned from his defeat of the Amalekites
  and spent two days in Ziklag.
On the third day a man came from Saul's camp,
  with his clothes torn and dirt on his head.
Going to David, he fell to the ground in homage.
David asked him, "Where do you come from?"
He replied, "I have escaped from the camp of the children of Israel."
"Tell me what happened," David bade him.
He answered that many of the soldiers had fled the battle
  and that many of them had fallen and were dead,
  among them Saul and his son Jonathan.

David seized his garments and rent them,
  and all the men who were with him did likewise.
They mourned and wept and fasted until evening
  for Saul and his son Jonathan,
  and for the soldiers of the Lord of the clans of Israel,
  because they had fallen by the sword.

  "Alas! the glory of Israel, Saul,
    slain upon your heights;
  how can the warriors have fallen!

  "Saul and Jonathan, beloved and cherished,
    separated neither in life nor in death,
    swifter than eagles, stronger than lions!
  Women of Israel, weep over Saul,
    who clothed you in scarlet and in finery,
    who decked your attire with ornaments of gold.

  "How can the warriors have fallen—
    in the thick of the battle,
    slain upon your heights!

"I grieve for you, Jonathan my brother!
  most dear have you been to me;
  more precious have I held love for you than love for women.

"How can the warriors have fallen,
  the weapons of war have perished!"

The word of the Lord.

RESPONSORIAL PSALM

Psalm 80:2-3, 5-7

℟. (4b) **Let us see your face, Lord, and we shall be saved.**

O shepherd of Israel, hearken,
  O guide of the flock of Joseph!
From your throne upon the cherubim, shine forth
  before Ephraim, Benjamin and Manasseh.
Rouse your power,
  and come to save us.

℟. **Let us see your face, Lord, and we shall be saved.**

O Lord of hosts, how long will you burn with anger
  while your people pray?
You have fed them with the bread of tears
  and given them tears to drink in ample measure.
You have left us to be fought over by our neighbors,
  and our enemies mock us.

℟. **Let us see your face, Lord, and we shall be saved.**

ALLELUIA

See Acts 16:14b

℟. Alleluia, alleluia.

**Open our hearts, O Lord,
to listen to the words of your Son.**

℟. Alleluia, alleluia.

GOSPEL — Years I and II

Mark 3:20-21   They said, "He is out of his mind."

✠ **A reading from the holy Gospel according to Mark**

**Jesus came with his disciples into the house.
Again the crowd gathered,
   making it impossible for them even to eat.
When his relatives heard of this they set out to seize him,
   for they said, "He is out of his mind."**

The Gospel of the Lord.

317 MONDAY OF THE THIRD WEEK IN ORDINARY TIME

FIRST READING   Year II

2 Samuel 5:1-7, 10   You shall shepherd my people Israel.

A reading from the second Book of Samuel

All the tribes of Israel came to David in Hebron and said:
"Here we are, your bone and your flesh.
In days past, when Saul was our king,
 it was you who led the children of Israel out and brought them back.
And the Lord said to you, 'You shall shepherd my people Israel
 and shall be commander of Israel.'"
When all the elders of Israel came to David in Hebron,
 King David made an agreement with them there before the Lord,
 and they anointed him king of Israel.
David was thirty years old when he became king,
 and he reigned for forty years:
 seven years and six months in Hebron over Judah,
 and thirty-three years in Jerusalem
 over all Israel and Judah.

Then the king and his men set out for Jerusalem
 against the Jebusites who inhabited the region.
David was told, "You cannot enter here:
 the blind and the lame will drive you away!"
 which was their way of saying, "David cannot enter here."
But David did take the stronghold of Zion, which is the City of David.

David grew steadily more powerful,
 for the Lord of hosts was with him.

The word of the Lord.

RESPONSORIAL PSALM

Psalm 89:20, 21-22, 25-26

℟. (25a) **My faithfulness and my mercy shall be with him.**

**Once you spoke in a vision,
 and to your faithful ones you said:
"On a champion I have placed a crown;
 over the people I have set a youth."**

℟. **My faithfulness and my mercy shall be with him.**

**"I have found David, my servant;
 with my holy oil I have anointed him,
That my hand may be always with him,
 and that my arm may make him strong."**

℟. **My faithfulness and my mercy shall be with him.**

**"My faithfulness and my mercy shall be with him,
 and through my name shall his horn be exalted.
I will set his hand upon the sea,
 his right hand upon the rivers."**

℟. **My faithfulness and my mercy shall be with him.**

ALLELUIA

See 2 Timothy 1:10

℟. **Alleluia, alleluia.**

**Our Savior Jesus Christ has destroyed death
and brought life to light through the Gospel.**

℟. **Alleluia, alleluia.**

GOSPEL — Years I and II

Mark 3:22-30   It is the end of Satan.

✢ **A reading from the holy Gospel according to Mark**

**The scribes who had come from Jerusalem said of Jesus,
"He is possessed by Beelzebul," and
"By the prince of demons he drives out demons."**

**Summoning them, he began to speak to them in parables,
"How can Satan drive out Satan?
If a kingdom is divided against itself, that kingdom cannot stand.
And if a house is divided against itself,
that house will not be able to stand.
And if Satan has risen up against himself and is divided,
he cannot stand;
that is the end of him.
But no one can enter a strong man's house to plunder his property
unless he first ties up the strong man.
Then he can plunder his house.
Amen, I say to you, all sins and all blasphemies
that people utter will be forgiven them.
But whoever blasphemes against the Holy Spirit
will never have forgiveness,
but is guilty of an everlasting sin."
For they had said, "He has an unclean spirit."**

The Gospel of the Lord.

318 TUESDAY OF THE THIRD WEEK IN ORDINARY TIME

FIRST READING   Year II

2 Samuel 6:12b-15, 17-19   *David and all the children of Israel were bringing up the ark of the Lord with shouts of joy.*

A reading from the second Book of Samuel

**David went to bring up the ark of God from the house of Obed-edom
  into the City of David amid festivities.
As soon as the bearers of the ark of the Lord had advanced six steps,
  he sacrificed an ox and a fatling.
Then David, girt with a linen apron,
  came dancing before the Lord with abandon,
  as he and all the house of Israel were bringing up the ark of the Lord
  with shouts of joy and to the sound of the horn.
The ark of the Lord was brought in and set in its place
  within the tent David had pitched for it.
Then David offered burnt offerings and peace offerings before the Lord.
When he finished making these offerings,
  he blessed the people in the name of the Lord of hosts.
He then distributed among all the people,
  to each man and each woman in the entire multitude of Israel,
  a loaf of bread, a cut of roast meat, and a raisin cake.
With this, all the people left for their homes.**

The word of the Lord.

RESPONSORIAL PSALM

Psalm 24:7, 8, 9, 10

℟. (8) **Who is this king of glory? It is the Lord!**

**Lift up, O gates, your lintels;
  reach up, you ancient portals,
  that the king of glory may come in!**

℟. **Who is this king of glory? It is the Lord!**

Who is this king of glory?
  The Lord**, strong and mighty,**
  the Lord**, mighty in battle.**

℟. **Who is this king of glory? It is the Lord!**

Lift up, O gates, your lintels;
  reach up, you ancient portals,
  that the king of glory may come in!

℟. **Who is this king of glory? It is the Lord!**

Who is this king of glory?
  The Lord **of hosts; he is the king of glory.**

℟. **Who is this king of glory? It is the Lord!**

ALLELUIA

See Matthew 11:25

℟. **Alleluia, alleluia.**

Blessed are you, Father, Lord of heaven and earth;
you have revealed to little ones the mysteries of the Kingdom.

℟. **Alleluia, alleluia.**

GOSPEL Years I and II

Mark 3:31-35   Whoever does the will of God is my brother and sister and mother.

✠ **A reading from the holy Gospel according to Mark**

The mother of Jesus and his brothers arrived at the house.
Standing outside, they sent word to Jesus and called him.
A crowd seated around him told him,
  "Your mother and your brothers and your sisters
  are outside asking for you."
But he said to them in reply,
  "Who are my mother and my brothers?"
And looking around at those seated in the circle he said,
  "Here are my mother and my brothers.
For whoever does the will of God
  is my brother and sister and mother."

The Gospel of the Lord.

319 WEDNESDAY OF THE THIRD WEEK IN ORDINARY TIME

FIRST READING   Year II

2 Samuel 7:4-17   *I will raise up your heir after you and I will make his Kingdom firm.*

A reading from the second Book of Samuel

That night the Lord spoke to Nathan and said:
"Go, tell my servant David, 'Thus says the Lord:
   Should you build me a house to dwell in?
I have not dwelt in a house
   from the day on which I led the children of Israel
   out of Egypt to the present,
   but I have been going about in a tent under cloth.
In all my wanderings everywhere among the children of Israel,
   did I ever utter a word to any one of the judges
   whom I charged to tend my people Israel, to ask:
   Why have you not built me a house of cedar?'

"Now then, speak thus to my servant David,
   'The Lord of hosts has this to say:
   It was I who took you from the pasture
   and from the care of the flock
   to be commander of my people Israel.
I have been with you wherever you went,
   and I have destroyed all your enemies before you.
And I will make you famous like the great ones of the earth.
I will fix a place for my people Israel;
   I will plant them so that they may dwell in their place
   without further disturbance.
Neither shall the wicked continue to afflict them as they did of old,
   since the time I first appointed judges over my people Israel.
I will give you rest from all your enemies.
The Lord also reveals to you that he will establish a house for you.
And when your time comes and you rest with your ancestors,
   I will raise up your heir after you, sprung from your loins,
   and I will make his Kingdom firm.
It is he who shall build a house for my name.
And I will make his royal throne firm forever.

I will be a father to him,
   and he shall be a son to me.
And if he does wrong,
   I will correct him with the rod of men
   and with human chastisements;
   but I will not withdraw my favor from him
   as I withdrew it from your predecessor Saul,
   whom I removed from my presence.
Your house and your kingdom shall endure forever before me;
   your throne shall stand firm forever.'"

Nathan reported all these words and this entire vision to David.

The word of the Lord.

RESPONSORIAL PSALM

Psalm 89:4-5, 27-28, 29-30

℟. (29a) **For ever I will maintain my love for my servant.**

"I have made a covenant with my chosen one;
   I have sworn to David my servant:
I will make your dynasty stand forever
   and establish your throne through all ages."

℟. **For ever I will maintain my love for my servant.**

"He shall cry to me, 'You are my father,
   my God, the Rock that brings me victory!'
I myself make him firstborn,
   Most High over the kings of the earth."

℟. **For ever I will maintain my love for my servant.**

"Forever I will maintain my love for him;
   my covenant with him stands firm.
I will establish his dynasty forever,
   his throne as the days of the heavens."

℟. **For ever I will maintain my love for my servant.**

ALLELUIA

℟. Alleluia, alleluia.

The seed is the word of God, Christ is the sower;
all who come to him will live for ever.

℟. Alleluia, alleluia.

GOSPEL   Years I and II

Mark 4:1-20   A sower went out to sow.

☩ A reading from the holy Gospel according to Mark

On another occasion, Jesus began to teach by the sea.
A very large crowd gathered around him
　so that he got into a boat on the sea and sat down.
And the whole crowd was beside the sea on land.
And he taught them at length in parables,
　and in the course of his instruction he said to them,
　"Hear this! A sower went out to sow.
And as he sowed, some seed fell on the path,
　and the birds came and ate it up.
Other seed fell on rocky ground where it had little soil.
It sprang up at once because the soil was not deep.
And when the sun rose, it was scorched and it withered for lack of roots.
Some seed fell among thorns, and the thorns grew up and choked it
　and it produced no grain.
And some seed fell on rich soil and produced fruit.
It came up and grew and yielded thirty, sixty, and a hundredfold."
He added, "Whoever has ears to hear ought to hear."

And when he was alone,
　those present along with the Twelve
　questioned him about the parables.
He answered them,
　"The mystery of the Kingdom of God has been granted to you.
But to those outside everything comes in parables, so that
　they may look and see but not perceive,
　　and hear and listen but not understand,
　　in order that they may not be converted and be forgiven."

**Jesus said to them, "Do you not understand this parable?
Then how will you understand any of the parables?
The sower sows the word.
These are the ones on the path where the word is sown.
As soon as they hear, Satan comes at once
   and takes away the word sown in them.
And these are the ones sown on rocky ground who,
   when they hear the word, receive it at once with joy.
But they have no roots; they last only for a time.
Then when tribulation or persecution comes because of the word,
   they quickly fall away.
Those sown among thorns are another sort.
They are the people who hear the word,
   but worldly anxiety, the lure of riches,
   and the craving for other things intrude and choke the word,
   and it bears no fruit.
But those sown on rich soil are the ones who hear the word and accept it
   and bear fruit thirty and sixty and a hundredfold."**

The Gospel of the Lord.

320 THURSDAY OF THE THIRD WEEK IN ORDINARY TIME

FIRST READING   Year II

2 Samuel 7:18-19, 24-29   *Who am I, Lord God, and who are the members of my house?*

A reading from the second Book of Samuel

**After Nathan had spoken to King David,
 the king went in and sat before the Lord and said,
 "Who am I, Lord God, and who are the members of my house,
 that you have brought me to this point?
Yet even this you see as too little, Lord God;
 you have also spoken of the house of your servant
 for a long time to come:
 this too you have shown to man, Lord God!**

**"You have established for yourself your people Israel as yours forever,
 and you, Lord, have become their God.
And now, Lord God, confirm for all time the prophecy you have made
 concerning your servant and his house,
 and do as you have promised.
Your name will be forever great, when men say,
 'The Lord of hosts is God of Israel,'
 and the house of your servant David stands firm before you.
It is you, Lord of hosts, God of Israel,
 who said in a revelation to your servant,
 'I will build a house for you.'
Therefore your servant now finds the courage to make this prayer to you.
And now, Lord God, you are God and your words are truth;
 you have made this generous promise to your servant.
Do, then, bless the house of your servant
 that it may be before you forever;
 for you, Lord God, have promised,
 and by your blessing the house of your servant
 shall be blessed forever."**

The word of the Lord.

RESPONSORIAL PSALM

Psalm 132:1-2, 3-5, 11, 12, 13-14

℟. (Luke 1:32b) **The Lord God will give him the throne of David, his father.**

Lord, remember David
   and all his anxious care;
How he swore an oath to the Lord,
   vowed to the Mighty One of Jacob.

℟. **The Lord God will give him the throne of David, his father.**

"I will not enter the house where I live,
   nor lie on the couch where I sleep;
I will give my eyes no sleep,
   my eyelids no rest,
Till I find a home for the Lord,
   a dwelling for the Mighty One of Jacob."

℟. **The Lord God will give him the throne of David, his father.**

The Lord swore an oath to David
   a firm promise from which he will not withdraw:
"Your own offspring
   I will set upon your throne."

℟. **The Lord God will give him the throne of David, his father.**

"If your sons keep my covenant,
   and the decrees which I shall teach them,
Their sons, too, forever
   shall sit upon your throne."

℟. **The Lord God will give him the throne of David, his father.**

For the Lord has chosen Zion,
   he prefers her for his dwelling:
"Zion is my resting place forever;
   in her I will dwell, for I prefer her."

℟. **The Lord God will give him the throne of David, his father.**

ALLELUIA

Psalm 119:105

℟. **Alleluia, alleluia.**

**A lamp to my feet is your word,
a light to my path.**

℟. **Alleluia, alleluia.**

GOSPEL — Years I and II

Mark 4:21-25   A lamp is to be placed on a lampstand. The measure with which you measure will be measured out to you.

✢ A reading from the holy Gospel according to Mark

Jesus said to his disciples,
    "Is a lamp brought in to be placed under a bushel basket
    or under a bed,
    and not to be placed on a lampstand?
For there is nothing hidden except to be made visible;
    nothing is secret except to come to light.
Anyone who has ears to hear ought to hear."
He also told them, "Take care what you hear.
The measure with which you measure will be measured out to you,
    and still more will be given to you.
To the one who has, more will be given;
    from the one who has not, even what he has will be taken away."

The Gospel of the Lord.

321 FRIDAY OF THE THIRD WEEK IN ORDINARY TIME

FIRST READING Year II

2 Samuel 11:1-4a, 5-10a, 13-17 *You have despised me and have taken the wife of Uriah to be your wife (see 2 Samuel 12:10).*

A reading from the second Book of Samuel

At the turn of the year, when kings go out on campaign,
  David sent out Joab along with his officers
  and the army of Israel,
  and they ravaged the Ammonites and besieged Rabbah.
David, however, remained in Jerusalem.
One evening David rose from his siesta
  and strolled about on the roof of the palace.
From the roof he saw a woman bathing, who was very beautiful.
David had inquiries made about the woman and was told,
  "She is Bathsheba, daughter of Eliam,
  and wife of Joab's armor bearer Uriah the Hittite."
Then David sent messengers and took her.
When she came to him, he had relations with her.
She then returned to her house.
But the woman had conceived,
  and sent the information to David, "I am with child."

David therefore sent a message to Joab,
  "Send me Uriah the Hittite."
So Joab sent Uriah to David.
When he came, David questioned him about Joab, the soldiers,
  and how the war was going, and Uriah answered that all was well.
David then said to Uriah, "Go down to your house and bathe your feet."
Uriah left the palace,
  and a portion was sent out after him from the king's table.
But Uriah slept at the entrance of the royal palace
  with the other officers of his lord, and did not go down
  to his own house.
David was told that Uriah had not gone home.

On the day following, David summoned him,
    and he ate and drank with David, who made him drunk.
But in the evening Uriah went out to sleep on his bed
    among his lord's servants, and did not go down to his home.
The next morning David wrote a letter to Joab
    which he sent by Uriah.
In it he directed:
    "Place Uriah up front, where the fighting is fierce.
Then pull back and leave him to be struck down dead."
So while Joab was besieging the city, he assigned Uriah
    to a place where he knew the defenders were strong.
When the men of the city made a sortie against Joab,
    some officers of David's army fell,
    and among them Uriah the Hittite died.

The word of the Lord.

RESPONSORIAL PSALM

Psalm 51:3-4, 5-6a, 6bcd-7, 10-11

℟. (see 3a) **Be merciful, O Lord, for we have sinned.**

Have mercy on me, O God, in your goodness;
  in the greatness of your compassion wipe out my offense.
Thoroughly wash me from my guilt
  and of my sin cleanse me.

℟. **Be merciful, O Lord, for we have sinned.**

For I acknowledge my offense,
  and my sin is before me always:
"Against you only have I sinned,
  and done what is evil in your sight."

℟. **Be merciful, O Lord, for we have sinned.**

I have done such evil in your sight
  that you are just in your sentence,
  blameless when you condemn.
True, I was born guilty,
  a sinner, even as my mother conceived me.

℟. **Be merciful, O Lord, for we have sinned.**

Let me hear the sounds of joy and gladness;
  the bones you have crushed shall rejoice.
Turn away your face from my sins,
  and blot out all my guilt.

℟. **Be merciful, O Lord, for we have sinned.**

ALLELUIA

See Matthew 11:25

℟. **Alleluia, alleluia.**

Blessed are you, Father, Lord of heaven and earth;
you have revealed to little ones the mysteries of the Kingdom.

℟. **Alleluia, alleluia.**

GOSPEL   Years I and II

Mark 4:26-34   *A man scatters seed on the land and would sleep and the seed would sprout and grow, he knows not how.*

✠   **A reading from the holy Gospel according to Mark**

Jesus said to the crowds:
"This is how it is with the Kingdom of God;
  it is as if a man were to scatter seed on the land
  and would sleep and rise night and day
  and the seed would sprout and grow,
  he knows not how.
Of its own accord the land yields fruit,
  first the blade, then the ear, then the full grain in the ear.
And when the grain is ripe, he wields the sickle at once,
  for the harvest has come."

He said,
  "To what shall we compare the Kingdom of God,
  or what parable can we use for it?
It is like a mustard seed that, when it is sown in the ground,
  is the smallest of all the seeds on the earth.
But once it is sown, it springs up and becomes the largest of plants
  and puts forth large branches,
  so that the birds of the sky can dwell in its shade."
With many such parables
  he spoke the word to them as they were able to understand it.
Without parables he did not speak to them,
  but to his own disciples he explained everything in private.

The Gospel of the Lord.

322 SATURDAY OF THE THIRD WEEK IN ORDINARY TIME

FIRST READING   Year II

2 Samuel 12:1-7a, 10-17   I have sinned against the Lord.

A reading from the second Book of Samuel

The Lord sent Nathan to David, and when he came to him,
   Nathan said: "Judge this case for me!
In a certain town there were two men, one rich, the other poor.
The rich man had flocks and herds in great numbers.
But the poor man had nothing at all
   except one little ewe lamb that he had bought.
He nourished her, and she grew up with him and his children.
She shared the little food he had
   and drank from his cup and slept in his bosom.
She was like a daughter to him.
Now, the rich man received a visitor,
   but he would not take from his own flocks and herds
   to prepare a meal for the wayfarer who had come to him.
Instead he took the poor man's ewe lamb
   and made a meal of it for his visitor."
David grew very angry with that man and said to him:
   "As the Lord lives, the man who has done this merits death!
He shall restore the ewe lamb fourfold
   because he has done this and has had no pity."

Then Nathan said to David: "You are the man!
Thus says the Lord God of Israel:
   'The sword shall never depart from your house,
   because you have despised me
   and have taken the wife of Uriah to be your wife.'
Thus says the Lord:
   'I will bring evil upon you out of your own house.
I will take your wives while you live to see it,
   and will give them to your neighbor.
He shall lie with your wives in broad daylight.
You have done this deed in secret,
   but I will bring it about in the presence of all Israel,
   and with the sun looking down.'"

Then David said to Nathan, "I have sinned against the Lord."
Nathan answered David: "The Lord on his part has forgiven your sin:
   you shall not die.
But since you have utterly spurned the Lord by this deed,
   the child born to you must surely die."
Then Nathan returned to his house.

The Lord struck the child that the wife of Uriah had borne to David,
   and it became desperately ill.
David besought God for the child.
He kept a fast, retiring for the night
   to lie on the ground clothed in sackcloth.
The elders of his house stood beside him
   urging him to rise from the ground; but he would not,
   nor would he take food with them.

The word of the Lord.

RESPONSORIAL PSALM

Psalm 51:12-13, 14-15, 16-17

℟. (12a) **Create a clean heart in me, O God.**

**A clean heart create for me, O God,
 and a steadfast spirit renew within me.
Cast me not out from your presence,
 and your Holy Spirit take not from me.**

℟. **Create a clean heart in me, O God.**

**Give me back the joy of your salvation,
 and a willing spirit sustain in me.
I will teach transgressors your ways,
 and sinners shall return to you.**

℟. **Create a clean heart in me, O God.**

**Free me from blood guilt, O God, my saving God;
 then my tongue shall revel in your justice.
O Lord, open my lips,
 and my mouth shall proclaim your praise.**

℟. **Create a clean heart in me, O God.**

ALLELUIA

John 3:16

℟. **Alleluia, alleluia.**

**God so loved the world that he gave his only-begotten Son,
so that everyone who believes in him might have eternal life.**

℟. **Alleluia, alleluia.**

GOSPEL — Years I and II

Mark 4:35-41   Who then is this whom even wind and sea obey?

✛ **A reading from the holy Gospel according to Mark**

**On that day, as evening drew on, Jesus said to his disciples:
"Let us cross to the other side."
Leaving the crowd, they took Jesus with them in the boat just as he was.
And other boats were with him.
A violent squall came up and waves were breaking over the boat,
   so that it was already filling up.
Jesus was in the stern, asleep on a cushion.
They woke him and said to him,
   "Teacher, do you not care that we are perishing?"
He woke up,
   rebuked the wind,
   and said to the sea, "Quiet! Be still!"
The wind ceased and there was great calm.
Then he asked them, "Why are you terrified?
Do you not yet have faith?"
They were filled with great awe and said to one another,
   "Who then is this whom even wind and sea obey?"**

The Gospel of the Lord.

323 MONDAY OF THE FOURTH WEEK IN ORDINARY TIME

FIRST READING   Year II

2 Samuel 15:13-14, 30; 16:5-13   Let us take flight, or none of us will escape from Absalom. Let Shimei alone and let him curse, for the LORD has told him to.

A reading from the second Book of Samuel

An informant came to David with the report,
  "The children of Israel have transferred their loyalty to Absalom."
At this, David said to all his servants
  who were with him in Jerusalem:
  "Up! Let us take flight, or none of us will escape from Absalom.
Leave quickly, lest he hurry and overtake us,
  then visit disaster upon us and put the city to the sword."

As David went up the Mount of Olives, he wept without ceasing.
His head was covered, and he was walking barefoot.
All those who were with him also had their heads covered
  and were weeping as they went.

As David was approaching Bahurim,
  a man named Shimei, the son of Gera
  of the same clan as Saul's family,
  was coming out of the place, cursing as he came.
He threw stones at David and at all the king's officers,
  even though all the soldiers, including the royal guard,
  were on David's right and on his left.
Shimei was saying as he cursed:
  "Away, away, you murderous and wicked man!
The LORD has requited you for all the bloodshed in the family of Saul,
  in whose stead you became king,
  and the LORD has given over the kingdom to your son Absalom.
And now you suffer ruin because you are a murderer."
Abishai, son of Zeruiah, said to the king:
  "Why should this dead dog curse my lord the king?
Let me go over, please, and lop off his head."
But the king replied: "What business is it of mine or of yours,
  sons of Zeruiah, that he curses?

Suppose the L<small>ORD</small> has told him to curse David;
> who then will dare to say, 'Why are you doing this?'"

Then the king said to Abishai and to all his servants:
> "If my own son, who came forth from my loins, is seeking my life,
> how much more might this Benjaminite do so?

Let him alone and let him curse, for the L<small>ORD</small> has told him to.
Perhaps the L<small>ORD</small> will look upon my affliction
> and make it up to me with benefits
> for the curses he is uttering this day."

David and his men continued on the road,
> while Shimei kept abreast of them on the hillside,
> all the while cursing and throwing stones and dirt as he went.

The word of the Lord.

RESPONSORIAL PSALM

Psalm 3:2-3, 4-5, 6-7

℟. (8a) **Lord, rise up and save me.**

O L<small>ORD</small>, how many are my adversaries!
> Many rise up against me!

Many are saying of me,
> "There is no salvation for him in God."

℟. **Lord, rise up and save me.**

But you, O L<small>ORD</small>, are my shield;
> my glory, you lift up my head!

When I call out to the L<small>ORD</small>,
> he answers me from his holy mountain.

℟. **Lord, rise up and save me.**

When I lie down in sleep,
> I wake again, for the L<small>ORD</small> sustains me.

I fear not the myriads of people
> arrayed against me on every side.

℟. **Lord, rise up and save me.**

ALLELUIA

Luke 7:16

℟. Alleluia, alleluia.

A great prophet has arisen in our midst
and God has visited his people.

℟. Alleluia, alleluia.

GOSPEL   Years I and II

Mark 5:1-20   Unclean spirit, come out of the man!

✠ A reading from the holy Gospel according to Mark

Jesus and his disciples came to the other side of the sea,
   to the territory of the Gerasenes.
When he got out of the boat,
   at once a man from the tombs who had an unclean spirit met him.
The man had been dwelling among the tombs,
   and no one could restrain him any longer, even with a chain.
In fact, he had frequently been bound with shackles and chains,
   but the chains had been pulled apart by him and the shackles smashed,
   and no one was strong enough to subdue him.
Night and day among the tombs and on the hillsides
   he was always crying out and bruising himself with stones.
Catching sight of Jesus from a distance,
   he ran up and prostrated himself before him,
   crying out in a loud voice,
   "What have you to do with me, Jesus, Son of the Most High God?
I adjure you by God, do not torment me!"
(He had been saying to him, "Unclean spirit, come out of the man!")
He asked him, "What is your name?"
He replied, "Legion is my name. There are many of us."
And he pleaded earnestly with him
   not to drive them away from that territory.

Now a large herd of swine was feeding there on the hillside.
And they pleaded with him,
 "Send us into the swine. Let us enter them."
And he let them, and the unclean spirits came out and entered the swine.
The herd of about two thousand rushed down a steep bank into the sea,
 where they were drowned.
The swineherds ran away and reported the incident in the town
 and throughout the countryside.
And people came out to see what had happened.
As they approached Jesus,
 they caught sight of the man who had been possessed by Legion,
 sitting there clothed and in his right mind.
And they were seized with fear.
Those who witnessed the incident explained to them what had happened
 to the possessed man and to the swine.
Then they began to beg him to leave their district.
As he was getting into the boat,
 the man who had been possessed pleaded to remain with him.
But Jesus would not permit him but told him instead,
 "Go home to your family and announce to them
 all that the Lord in his pity has done for you."
Then the man went off and began to proclaim in the Decapolis
 what Jesus had done for him; and all were amazed.

The Gospel of the Lord.

324 TUESDAY OF THE FOURTH WEEK IN ORDINARY TIME

FIRST READING   Year II

2 Samuel 18:9-10, 14b, 24-25a, 30–19:3   My son Absalom, if only I had died instead of you.

A reading from the second Book of Samuel

Absalom unexpectedly came up against David's servants.
He was mounted on a mule,
   and, as the mule passed under the branches of a large terebinth,
   his hair caught fast in the tree.
He hung between heaven and earth
   while the mule he had been riding ran off.
Someone saw this and reported to Joab
   that he had seen Absalom hanging from a terebinth.
And taking three pikes in hand,
   he thrust for the heart of Absalom,
   still hanging from the tree alive.

Now David was sitting between the two gates,
   and a lookout went up to the roof of the gate above the city wall,
   where he looked about and saw a man running all alone.
The lookout shouted to inform the king, who said,
   "If he is alone, he has good news to report."
The king said, "Step aside and remain in attendance here."
So he stepped aside and remained there.
When the Cushite messenger came in, he said,
   "Let my lord the king receive the good news
   that this day the Lord has taken your part,
   freeing you from the grasp of all who rebelled against you."
But the king asked the Cushite, "Is young Absalom safe?"
The Cushite replied, "May the enemies of my lord the king
   and all who rebel against you with evil intent
   be as that young man!"

The king was shaken,
> and went up to the room over the city gate to weep.
He said as he wept,
> "My son Absalom! My son, my son Absalom!
If only I had died instead of you,
> Absalom, my son, my son!"

Joab was told that the king was weeping and mourning for Absalom;
> and that day's victory was turned into mourning for the whole army
> when they heard that the king was grieving for his son.

The word of the Lord.

RESPONSORIAL PSALM

Psalm 86:1-2, 3-4, 5-6

℟. (1a) **Listen, Lord, and answer me.**

Incline your ear, O Lord; answer me,
> for I am afflicted and poor.
Keep my life, for I am devoted to you;
> save your servant who trusts in you.
> You are my God.

℟. **Listen, Lord, and answer me.**

Have mercy on me, O Lord,
> for to you I call all the day.
Gladden the soul of your servant,
> for to you, O Lord, I lift up my soul.

℟. **Listen, Lord, and answer me.**

For you, O Lord, are good and forgiving,
> abounding in kindness to all who call upon you.
Hearken, O Lord, to my prayer
> and attend to the sound of my pleading.

℟. **Listen, Lord, and answer me.**

ALLELUIA

Matthew 8:17

℟. Alleluia, alleluia.

**Christ took away our infirmities
and bore our diseases.**

℟. Alleluia, alleluia.

GOSPEL Years I and II

Mark 5:21-43   Little girl, I say to you, arise!

✠ A reading from the holy Gospel according to Mark

**When Jesus had crossed again in the boat
   to the other side,
   a large crowd gathered around him, and he stayed close to the sea.
One of the synagogue officials, named Jairus, came forward.
Seeing him he fell at his feet and pleaded earnestly with him, saying,
   "My daughter is at the point of death.
Please, come lay your hands on her
   that she may get well and live."
He went off with him
   and a large crowd followed him.**

**There was a woman afflicted with hemorrhages for twelve years.
She had suffered greatly at the hands of many doctors
   and had spent all that she had.
Yet she was not helped but only grew worse.
She had heard about Jesus and came up behind him in the crowd
   and touched his cloak.
She said, "If I but touch his clothes, I shall be cured."
Immediately her flow of blood dried up.
She felt in her body that she was healed of her affliction.
Jesus, aware at once that power had gone out from him,
   turned around in the crowd and asked, "Who has touched my clothes?"
But his disciples said to him,
   "You see how the crowd is pressing upon you,
   and yet you ask, Who touched me?"
And he looked around to see who had done it.**

The woman, realizing what had happened to her,
    approached in fear and trembling.
She fell down before Jesus and told him the whole truth.
He said to her, "Daughter, your faith has saved you.
Go in peace and be cured of your affliction."

While he was still speaking,
    people from the synagogue official's house arrived and said,
    "Your daughter has died; why trouble the teacher any longer?"
Disregarding the message that was reported,
    Jesus said to the synagogue official,
    "Do not be afraid; just have faith."
He did not allow anyone to accompany him inside
    except Peter, James, and John, the brother of James.
When they arrived at the house of the synagogue official,
    he caught sight of a commotion,
    people weeping and wailing loudly.
So he went in and said to them,
    "Why this commotion and weeping?
The child is not dead but asleep."
And they ridiculed him.
Then he put them all out.
He took along the child's father and mother
    and those who were with him
    and entered the room where the child was.
He took the child by the hand and said to her, *"Talitha koum,"*
    which means, "Little girl, I say to you, arise!"
The girl, a child of twelve, arose immediately and walked around.
At that they were utterly astounded.
He gave strict orders that no one should know this
    and said that she should be given something to eat.

The Gospel of the Lord.

325 WEDNESDAY OF THE FOURTH WEEK IN ORDINARY TIME

FIRST READING Year II

2 Samuel 24:2, 9-17   It is I who have sinned; but these are sheep; what have they done?

A reading from the second Book of Samuel

King David said to Joab and the leaders of the army who were with him,
   "Tour all the tribes in Israel from Dan to Beer-sheba
   and register the people, that I may know their number."
Joab then reported to the king the number of people registered:
   in Israel, eight hundred thousand men fit for military service;
   in Judah, five hundred thousand.

Afterward, however, David regretted having numbered the people,
   and said to the Lord:
   "I have sinned grievously in what I have done.
But now, Lord, forgive the guilt of your servant,
   for I have been very foolish."
When David rose in the morning,
   the Lord had spoken to the prophet Gad, David's seer, saying:
   "Go and say to David, 'This is what the Lord says:
   I offer you three alternatives;
   choose one of them, and I will inflict it on you.'"
Gad then went to David to inform him.
He asked: "Do you want a three years' famine to come upon your land,
   or to flee from your enemy three months while he pursues you,
   or to have a three days' pestilence in your land?
Now consider and decide what I must reply to him who sent me."
David answered Gad: "I am in very serious difficulty.
Let us fall by the hand of God, for he is most merciful;
   but let me not fall by the hand of man."
Thus David chose the pestilence.
Now it was the time of the wheat harvest
   when the plague broke out among the people.
The Lord then sent a pestilence over Israel
   from morning until the time appointed,
   and seventy thousand of the people from Dan to Beer-sheba died.

But when the angel stretched forth his hand toward Jerusalem to destroy it,
>	the Lord regretted the calamity
>		and said to the angel causing the destruction among the people,
>	"Enough now! Stay your hand."

The angel of the Lord was then standing
>	at the threshing floor of Araunah the Jebusite.

When David saw the angel who was striking the people,
>	he said to the Lord: "It is I who have sinned;
>		it is I, the shepherd, who have done wrong.

But these are sheep; what have they done?
Punish me and my kindred."

The word of the Lord.

RESPONSORIAL PSALM

Psalm 32:1-2, 5, 6, 7

℟. (see 5c) **Lord, forgive the wrong I have done.**

Blessed is he whose fault is taken away,
>	whose sin is covered.

Blessed the man to whom the Lord imputes not guilt,
>	in whose spirit there is no guile.

℟. Lord, forgive the wrong I have done.

Then I acknowledged my sin to you,
>	my guilt I covered not.

I said, "I confess my faults to the Lord,"
>	and you took away the guilt of my sin.

℟. Lord, forgive the wrong I have done.

For this shall every faithful man pray to you
>	in time of stress.

Though deep waters overflow,
>	they shall not reach him.

℟. Lord, forgive the wrong I have done.

You are my shelter; from distress you will preserve me;
>	with glad cries of freedom you will ring me round.

℟. Lord, forgive the wrong I have done.

ALLELUIA

John 10:27

℟. Alleluia, alleluia.

My sheep hear my voice, says the Lord;
I know them, and they follow me.

℟. Alleluia, alleluia.

GOSPEL Years I and II

Mark 6:1-6 A prophet is not without honor except in his native place.

✠ A reading from the holy Gospel according to Mark

Jesus departed from there and came to his native place,
   accompanied by his disciples.
When the sabbath came he began to teach in the synagogue,
   and many who heard him were astonished.
They said, "Where did this man get all this?
What kind of wisdom has been given him?
What mighty deeds are wrought by his hands!
Is he not the carpenter, the son of Mary,
   and the brother of James and Joseph and Judas and Simon?
And are not his sisters here with us?"
And they took offense at him.
Jesus said to them,
   "A prophet is not without honor except in his native place
   and among his own kin and in his own house."
So he was not able to perform any mighty deed there,
   apart from curing a few sick people by laying his hands on them.
He was amazed at their lack of faith.

The Gospel of the Lord.

326 THURSDAY OF THE FOURTH WEEK IN ORDINARY TIME

FIRST READING   Year II

1 Kings 2:1-4, 10-12   I am going the way of all flesh. Take courage and be a man.

A reading from the first Book of Kings

When the time of David's death drew near,
   he gave these instructions to his son Solomon:
   "I am going the way of all flesh.
Take courage and be a man.
Keep the mandate of the Lord, your God, following his ways
   and observing his statutes, commands, ordinances, and decrees
   as they are written in the law of Moses,
   that you may succeed in whatever you do,
   wherever you turn, and the Lord may fulfill
   the promise he made on my behalf when he said,
   'If your sons so conduct themselves
   that they remain faithful to me with their whole heart
   and with their whole soul,
   you shall always have someone of your line
   on the throne of Israel.'"

David rested with his ancestors and was buried in the City of David.
The length of David's reign over Israel was forty years:
   he reigned seven years in Hebron
   and thirty-three years in Jerusalem.

Solomon was seated on the throne of his father David,
   with his sovereignty firmly established.

The word of the Lord.

RESPONSORIAL PSALM

1 Chronicles 29:10, 11ab, 11d-12a, 12bcd

℟. (12b) **Lord, you are exalted over all.**

"Blessed may you be, O L<small>ORD</small>,
 God of Israel our father,
 from eternity to eternity."

℟. **Lord, you are exalted over all.**

"Yours, O L<small>ORD</small>, are grandeur and power,
 majesty, splendor, and glory."

℟. **Lord, you are exalted over all.**

"L<small>ORD</small>, you are exalted over all.
 Yours, O L<small>ORD</small>, is the sovereignty;
 you are exalted as head over all.
Riches and honor are from you."

℟. **Lord, you are exalted over all.**

"In your hand are power and might;
 it is yours to give grandeur and strength to all."

℟. **Lord, you are exalted over all.**

ALLELUIA

Mark 1:15

℟. **Alleluia, alleluia.**

**The Kingdom of God is at hand;
repent and believe in the Gospel.**

℟. **Alleluia, alleluia.**

GOSPEL   Years I and II

Mark 6:7-13   Jesus summoned the Twelve and began to send them out.

✚ **A reading from the holy Gospel according to Mark**

**Jesus summoned the Twelve and began to send them out two by two
   and gave them authority over unclean spirits.
He instructed them to take nothing for the journey but a walking stick
   —no food, no sack, no money in their belts.
They were, however, to wear sandals but not a second tunic.
He said to them,
   "Wherever you enter a house, stay there until you leave from there.
Whatever place does not welcome you or listen to you,
   leave there and shake the dust off your feet
in testimony against them."
So they went off and preached repentance.
The Twelve drove out many demons,
   and they anointed with oil many who were sick and cured them.**

The Gospel of the Lord.

327 FRIDAY OF THE FOURTH WEEK IN ORDINARY TIME

FIRST READING   Year II

Sirach 47:2-11   With his every deed David offered thanks to God Most High; in words of praise he loved his Maker.

A reading from the Book of Sirach

Like the choice fat of the sacred offerings,
  so was David in Israel.
He made sport of lions as though they were kids,
  and of bears, like lambs of the flock.
As a youth he slew the giant
  and wiped out the people's disgrace,
When his hand let fly the slingstone
  that crushed the pride of Goliath.
Since he called upon the Most High God,
  who gave strength to his right arm
To defeat the skilled warrior
  and raise up the might of his people,
Therefore the women sang his praises,
  and ascribed to him tens of thousands
  and praised him when they blessed the Lord.
When he assumed the royal crown, he battled
  and subdued the enemy on every side.
He destroyed the hostile Philistines
  and shattered their power till our own day.
With his every deed he offered thanks
  to God Most High, in words of praise.
With his whole being he loved his Maker
  and daily had his praises sung;
  He set singers before the altar and by their voices
    he made sweet melodies,
He added beauty to the feasts
  and solemnized the seasons of each year
So that when the Holy Name was praised,
  before daybreak the sanctuary would resound.

The LORD forgave him his sins
   and exalted his strength forever;
He conferred on him the rights of royalty
   and established his throne in Israel.

The word of the Lord.

RESPONSORIAL PSALM

Psalm 18:31, 47 and 50, 51

℟. (see 47b) **Blessed be God my salvation!**

God's way is unerring,
   the promise of the LORD is fire-tried;
   he is a shield to all who take refuge in him.

℟. **Blessed be God my salvation!**

The LORD live! And blessed be my Rock!
   Extolled be God my savior.
Therefore will I proclaim you, O LORD, among the nations,
   and I will sing praise to your name.

℟. **Blessed be God my salvation!**

You who gave great victories to your king
   and showed kindness to your anointed,
   to David and his posterity forever.

℟. **Blessed be God my salvation!**

ALLELUIA

See Luke 8:15

℟. Alleluia, alleluia.

Blessed are they who have kept the word with a generous heart,
and yield a harvest through perseverance.

℟. Alleluia, alleluia.

GOSPEL   Years I and II

Mark 6:14-29   It is John whom I beheaded. He has been raised up.

✠ A reading from the holy Gospel according to Mark

King Herod heard about Jesus, for his fame had become widespread,
  and people were saying,
    "John the Baptist has been raised from the dead;
    that is why mighty powers are at work in him."
Others were saying, "He is Elijah";
  still others, "He is a prophet like any of the prophets."
But when Herod learned of it, he said,
  "It is John whom I beheaded. He has been raised up."

Herod was the one who had John arrested and bound in prison
  on account of Herodias,
  the wife of his brother Philip, whom he had married.
John had said to Herod,
  "It is not lawful for you to have your brother's wife."
Herodias harbored a grudge against him
  and wanted to kill him but was unable to do so.
Herod feared John, knowing him to be a righteous and holy man,
  and kept him in custody.
When he heard him speak he was very much perplexed,
  yet he liked to listen to him.
Herodias had an opportunity one day when Herod, on his birthday,
  gave a banquet for his courtiers, his military officers,
  and the leading men of Galilee.
His own daughter came in and performed a dance
  that delighted Herod and his guests.
The king said to the girl,
  "Ask of me whatever you wish and I will grant it to you."

He even swore many things to her,
   "I will grant you whatever you ask of me,
   even to half of my kingdom."
She went out and said to her mother,
   "What shall I ask for?"
Her mother replied, "The head of John the Baptist."
The girl hurried back to the king's presence and made her request,
   "I want you to give me at once on a platter
   the head of John the Baptist."
The king was deeply distressed,
   but because of his oaths and the guests
   he did not wish to break his word to her.
So he promptly dispatched an executioner
   with orders to bring back his head.
He went off and beheaded him in the prison.
He brought in the head on a platter
   and gave it to the girl.
The girl in turn gave it to her mother.
When his disciples heard about it,
   they came and took his body and laid it in a tomb.

The Gospel of the Lord.

328 SATURDAY OF THE FOURTH WEEK IN ORDINARY TIME

FIRST READING   Year II

1 Kings 3:4-13   Give your servant an understanding heart to judge your people.

A reading from the first Book of Kings

Solomon went to Gibeon to sacrifice there,
    because that was the most renowned high place.
Upon its altar Solomon offered a thousand burnt offerings.
In Gibeon the Lord appeared to Solomon in a dream at night.
God said, "Ask something of me and I will give it to you."
Solomon answered:
    "You have shown great favor to your servant, my father David,
    because he behaved faithfully toward you,
    with justice and an upright heart;
    and you have continued this great favor toward him, even today,
    seating a son of his on his throne.
O Lord, my God, you have made me, your servant,
    king to succeed my father David;
    but I am a mere youth, not knowing at all how to act.
I serve you in the midst of the people whom you have chosen,
    a people so vast that it cannot be numbered or counted.
Give your servant, therefore, an understanding heart
    to judge your people and to distinguish right from wrong.
For who is able to govern this vast people of yours?"

The Lord was pleased that Solomon made this request.
So God said to him: "Because you have asked for this—
    not for a long life for yourself,
    nor for riches, nor for the life of your enemies,
    but for understanding so that you may know what is right—
    I do as you requested.

I give you a heart so wise and understanding
 that there has never been anyone like you up to now,
 and after you there will come no one to equal you.
In addition, I give you what you have not asked for,
 such riches and glory that among kings there is not your like."

The word of the Lord.

RESPONSORIAL PSALM

Psalm 119:9, 10, 11, 12, 13, 14

℟. (12b) **Lord, teach me your statutes.**

How shall a young man be faultless in his way?
    By keeping to your words.

℟. **Lord, teach me your statutes.**

With all my heart I seek you;
    let me not stray from your commands.

℟. **Lord, teach me your statutes.**

Within my heart I treasure your promise,
    that I may not sin against you.

℟. **Lord, teach me your statutes.**

Blessed are you, O Lord;
    teach me your statutes.

℟. **Lord, teach me your statutes.**

With my lips I declare
    all the ordinances of your mouth.

℟. **Lord, teach me your statutes.**

In the way of your decrees I rejoice,
    as much as in all riches.

℟. **Lord, teach me your statutes.**

ALLELUIA

John 10:27

℟. Alleluia, alleluia.

My sheep hear my voice, says the Lord;
I know them, and they follow me.

℟. Alleluia, alleluia.

GOSPEL   Years I and II

Mark 6:30-34   They were like sheep without a shepherd.

✠ A reading from the holy Gospel according to Mark

The Apostles gathered together with Jesus
 and reported all they had done and taught.
He said to them,
 "Come away by yourselves to a deserted place and rest a while."
People were coming and going in great numbers,
 and they had no opportunity even to eat.
So they went off in the boat by themselves to a deserted place.
People saw them leaving and many came to know about it.
They hastened there on foot from all the towns
 and arrived at the place before them.

When Jesus disembarked and saw the vast crowd,
 his heart was moved with pity for them,
 for they were like sheep without a shepherd;
 and he began to teach them many things.

The Gospel of the Lord.

329 MONDAY OF THE FIFTH WEEK IN ORDINARY TIME

FIRST READING   Year II

1 Kings 8:1-7, 9-13   *They brought the ark of the covenant into the holy of holies, and a cloud filled the temple of the Lord.*

A reading from the first Book of Kings

The elders of Israel and all the leaders of the tribes,
   the princes in the ancestral houses of the children of Israel,
   came to King Solomon in Jerusalem,
   to bring up the ark of the Lord's covenant
   from the City of David, which is Zion.
All the people of Israel assembled before King Solomon
   during the festival in the month of Ethanim (the seventh month).
When all the elders of Israel had arrived,
   the priests took up the ark;
   they carried the ark of the Lord
   and the meeting tent with all the sacred vessels
   that were in the tent.
(The priests and Levites carried them.)

King Solomon and the entire community of Israel
   present for the occasion
   sacrificed before the ark sheep and oxen
   too many to number or count.
The priests brought the ark of the covenant of the Lord
   to its place beneath the wings of the cherubim in the sanctuary,
   the holy of holies of the temple.
The cherubim had their wings spread out over the place of the ark,
   sheltering the ark and its poles from above.
There was nothing in the ark but the two stone tablets
   which Moses had put there at Horeb,
   when the Lord made a covenant with the children of Israel
   at their departure from the land of Egypt.

When the priests left the holy place,
   the cloud filled the temple of the LORD
   so that the priests could no longer minister because of the cloud,
   since the LORD's glory had filled the temple of the LORD.
Then Solomon said, "The LORD intends to dwell in the dark cloud;
   I have truly built you a princely house,
   a dwelling where you may abide forever."

The word of the Lord.

RESPONSORIAL PSALM

Psalm 132:6-7, 8-10

℟. (8a) **Lord, go up to the place of your rest!**

Behold, we heard of it in Ephrathah;
   we found it in the fields of Jaar.
Let us enter into his dwelling,
   let us worship at his footstool.

℟. **Lord, go up to the place of your rest!**

Advance, O LORD, to your resting place,
   you and the ark of your majesty.
May your priests be clothed with justice;
   let your faithful ones shout merrily for joy.
For the sake of David your servant,
   reject not the plea of your anointed.

℟. **Lord, go up to the place of your rest!**

ALLELUIA

See Matthew 4:23

℟. Alleluia, alleluia.

**Jesus preached the Gospel of the Kingdom
and cured every disease among the people.**

℟. Alleluia, alleluia.

GOSPEL   Years I and II

Mark 6:53-56   As many as touched it were healed.

✛ **A reading from the holy Gospel according to Mark**

**After making the crossing to the other side of the sea,
    Jesus and his disciples came to land at Gennesaret
    and tied up there.
As they were leaving the boat, people immediately recognized him.
They scurried about the surrounding country
    and began to bring in the sick on mats
    to wherever they heard he was.
Whatever villages or towns or countryside he entered,
    they laid the sick in the marketplaces
    and begged him that they might touch only the tassel on his cloak;
    and as many as touched it were healed.**

The Gospel of the Lord.

330 TUESDAY OF THE FIFTH WEEK IN ORDINARY TIME

FIRST READING Year II

1 Kings 8:22-23, 27-30   You have said: My name shall be there, to hear the prayers of your people Israel.

A reading from the first Book of Kings

Solomon stood before the altar of the Lord
   in the presence of the whole community of Israel,
   and stretching forth his hands toward heaven,
   he said, "Lord, God of Israel,
   there is no God like you in heaven above or on earth below;
   you keep your covenant of mercy with your servants
   who are faithful to you with their whole heart.

"Can it indeed be that God dwells on earth?
If the heavens and the highest heavens cannot contain you,
   how much less this temple which I have built!
Look kindly on the prayer and petition of your servant, O Lord, my God,
   and listen to the cry of supplication which I, your servant,
   utter before you this day.
May your eyes watch night and day over this temple,
   the place where you have decreed you shall be honored;
   may you heed the prayer which I, your servant, offer in this place.
Listen to the petitions of your servant and of your people Israel
   which they offer in this place.
Listen from your heavenly dwelling and grant pardon."

The word of the Lord.

RESPONSORIAL PSALM

Psalm 84:3, 4, 5 and 10, 11

℟. (2) **How lovely is your dwelling place, Lord, mighty God!**

My soul yearns and pines
   for the courts of the Lord.
My heart and my flesh
   cry out for the living God.

℟. **How lovely is your dwelling place, Lord, mighty God!**

Even the sparrow finds a home,
  and the swallow a nest
  in which she puts her young—
Your altars, O Lord of hosts,
  my king and my God!

℞. How lovely is your dwelling place, Lord, mighty God!

Blessed they who dwell in your house!
  continually they praise you.
O God, behold our shield,
  and look upon the face of your anointed.

℞. How lovely is your dwelling place, Lord, mighty God!

I had rather one day in your courts
  than a thousand elsewhere;
I had rather lie at the threshold of the house of my God
  than dwell in the tents of the wicked.

℞. How lovely is your dwelling place, Lord, mighty God!

ALLELUIA

Psalm 119:36, 29b

℞. Alleluia, alleluia.

Incline my heart, O God, to your decrees;
and favor me with your law.

℞. Alleluia, alleluia.

GOSPEL   Years I and II

Mark 7:1-13   You disregard God's commandment but cling to human tradition.

✢ A reading from the holy Gospel according to Mark

When the Pharisees with some scribes who had come from Jerusalem
  gathered around Jesus,
    they observed that some of his disciples ate their meals
    with unclean, that is, unwashed, hands.

(For the Pharisees and, in fact, all Jews,
> do not eat without carefully washing their hands,
> keeping the tradition of the elders.

And on coming from the marketplace
> they do not eat without purifying themselves.

And there are many other things that they have traditionally observed,
> the purification of cups and jugs and kettles and beds.)

So the Pharisees and scribes questioned him,
> "Why do your disciples not follow the tradition of the elders
> but instead eat a meal with unclean hands?"

He responded,
> "Well did Isaiah prophesy about you hypocrites,
> as it is written:

> *This people honors me with their lips,*
>> *but their hearts are far from me;*
> *In vain do they worship me,*
>> *teaching as doctrines human precepts.*

You disregard God's commandment but cling to human tradition."
He went on to say,
> "How well you have set aside the commandment of God
> in order to uphold your tradition!

For Moses said,
> *Honor your father and your mother,*
> and *Whoever curses father or mother shall die.*

Yet you say,
> 'If someone says to father or mother,
> "Any support you might have had from me is *qorban*"'
> (meaning, dedicated to God),
> you allow him to do nothing more for his father or mother.

You nullify the word of God
> in favor of your tradition that you have handed on.

And you do many such things."

The Gospel of the Lord.

331 WEDNESDAY OF THE FIFTH WEEK IN ORDINARY TIME

FIRST READING   Year II

1 Kings 10:1-10   The Queen of Sheba saw all the wisdom of Solomon.

A reading from the first Book of Kings

The queen of Sheba, having heard of Solomon's fame,
　came to test him with subtle questions.
She arrived in Jerusalem with a very numerous retinue,
　and with camels bearing spices,
　a large amount of gold, and precious stones.
She came to Solomon and questioned him on every subject
　in which she was interested.
King Solomon explained everything she asked about,
　and there remained nothing hidden from him
　that he could not explain to her.

When the queen of Sheba witnessed Solomon's great wisdom,
　the palace he had built, the food at his table,
　the seating of his ministers, the attendance and garb of his waiters,
　his banquet service,
　and the burnt offerings he offered in the temple of the Lord,
　she was breathless.
"The report I heard in my country
　about your deeds and your wisdom is true," she told the king.
"Though I did not believe the report until I came and saw with my own eyes,
　I have discovered that they were not telling me the half.
Your wisdom and prosperity surpass the report I heard.
Blessed are your men, blessed these servants of yours,
　who stand before you always and listen to your wisdom.
Blessed be the Lord, your God,
　whom it has pleased to place you on the throne of Israel.
In his enduring love for Israel,
　the Lord has made you king to carry out judgment and justice."
Then she gave the king one hundred and twenty gold talents,
　a very large quantity of spices, and precious stones.
Never again did anyone bring such an abundance of spices
　as the queen of Sheba gave to King Solomon.

The word of the Lord.

RESPONSORIAL PSALM

Psalm 37:5-6, 30-31, 39-40

℟. (30a) **The mouth of the just murmurs wisdom.**

Commit to the LORD your way;
   trust in him, and he will act.
He will make justice dawn for you like the light;
   bright as the noonday shall be your vindication.

℟. **The mouth of the just murmurs wisdom.**

The mouth of the just man tells of wisdom
   and his tongue utters what is right.
The law of his God is in his heart,
   and his steps do not falter.

℟. **The mouth of the just murmurs wisdom.**

The salvation of the just is from the LORD;
   he is their refuge in time of distress.
And the LORD helps them and delivers them;
   he delivers them from the wicked and saves them,
   because they take refuge in him.

℟. **The mouth of the just murmurs wisdom.**

ALLELUIA

See John 17:17b, 17a

℟. Alleluia, alleluia.

Your word, O Lord, is truth:
consecrate us in the truth.

℟. Alleluia, alleluia.

GOSPEL   Years I and II

Mark 7:14-23   What comes out of the man, that is what defiles him.

✠ A reading from the holy Gospel according to Mark

Jesus summoned the crowd again and said to them,
   "Hear me, all of you, and understand.
Nothing that enters one from outside can defile that person;
   but the things that come out from within are what defile."

When he got home away from the crowd
   his disciples questioned him about the parable.
He said to them,
   "Are even you likewise without understanding?
Do you not realize that everything
   that goes into a person from outside cannot defile,
   since it enters not the heart but the stomach
   and passes out into the latrine?"
(Thus he declared all foods clean.)
"But what comes out of the man, that is what defiles him.
From within the man, from his heart,
   come evil thoughts, unchastity, theft, murder,
   adultery, greed, malice, deceit,
   licentiousness, envy, blasphemy, arrogance, folly.
All these evils come from within and they defile."

The Gospel of the Lord.

332 THURSDAY OF THE FIFTH WEEK IN ORDINARY TIME

FIRST READING   Year II

1 Kings 11:4-13   Since you have not kept my covenant, I will deprive you of the kingdom, but I will leave your son one tribe for the sake of my servant David.

A reading from the first Book of Kings

**When Solomon was old his wives had turned his heart to strange gods,
    and his heart was not entirely with the Lord, his God,
    as the heart of his father David had been.
By adoring Astarte, the goddess of the Sidonians,
    and Milcom, the idol of the Ammonites,
    Solomon did evil in the sight of the Lord;
    he did not follow him unreservedly as his father David had done.
Solomon then built a high place to Chemosh, the idol of Moab,
    and to Molech, the idol of the Ammonites,
    on the hill opposite Jerusalem.
He did the same for all his foreign wives
    who burned incense and sacrificed to their gods.
The Lord, therefore, became angry with Solomon,
    because his heart was turned away from the Lord, the God of Israel,
    who had appeared to him twice
    (for though the Lord had forbidden him
    this very act of following strange gods,
    Solomon had not obeyed him).**

**So the Lord said to Solomon: "Since this is what you want,
    and you have not kept my covenant and my statutes
    which I enjoined on you,
    I will deprive you of the kingdom and give it to your servant.
I will not do this during your lifetime, however,
    for the sake of your father David;
    it is your son whom I will deprive.
Nor will I take away the whole kingdom.
I will leave your son one tribe for the sake of my servant David
    and of Jerusalem, which I have chosen."**

The word of the Lord.

RESPONSORIAL PSALM

Psalm 106:3-4, 35-36, 37 and 40

℟. (4a) **Remember us, O Lord, as you favor your people.**

**Blessed are they who observe what is right,
 who do always what is just.
Remember us, O Lord, as you favor your people;
 visit us with your saving help.**

℟. **Remember us, O Lord, as you favor your people.**

**But they mingled with the nations
 and learned their works.
They served their idols,
 which became a snare for them.**

℟. **Remember us, O Lord, as you favor your people.**

**They sacrificed their sons
 and their daughters to demons.
And the Lord grew angry with his people,
 and abhorred his inheritance.**

℟. **Remember us, O Lord, as you favor your people.**

ALLELUIA

James 1:21bc

℟. **Alleluia, alleluia.**

Humbly welcome the word that has been planted in you and is able to save your souls.

℟. **Alleluia, alleluia.**

GOSPEL Years I and II

Mark 7:24-30   The dogs under the table eat the children's scraps.

☩ A reading from the holy Gospel according to Mark

Jesus went to the district of Tyre.
He entered a house and wanted no one to know about it,
   but he could not escape notice.
Soon a woman whose daughter had an unclean spirit heard about him.
She came and fell at his feet.
The woman was a Greek, a Syrophoenician by birth,
   and she begged him to drive the demon out of her daughter.
He said to her, "Let the children be fed first.
For it is not right to take the food of the children
   and throw it to the dogs."
She replied and said to him,
   "Lord, even the dogs under the table eat the children's scraps."
Then he said to her, "For saying this, you may go.
The demon has gone out of your daughter."
When the woman went home, she found the child lying in bed
   and the demon gone.

The Gospel of the Lord.

333 FRIDAY OF THE FIFTH WEEK IN ORDINARY TIME

FIRST READING   Year II

1 Kings 11:29-32; 12:19   Israel went into rebellion against David's house to this day.

A reading from the first Book of Kings

Jeroboam left Jerusalem,
   and the prophet Ahijah the Shilonite met him on the road.
The two were alone in the area,
   and the prophet was wearing a new cloak.
Ahijah took off his new cloak,
   tore it into twelve pieces, and said to Jeroboam:

"Take ten pieces for yourself;
   the Lord, the God of Israel, says:
   'I will tear away the kingdom from Solomon's grasp
   and will give you ten of the tribes.
One tribe shall remain to him for the sake of David my servant,
   and of Jerusalem,
   the city I have chosen out of all the tribes of Israel.'"

Israel went into rebellion against David's house to this day.

The word of the Lord.

RESPONSORIAL PSALM

Psalm 81:10-11ab, 12-13, 14-15

℟. (11a and 9a) **I am the Lord, your God: hear my voice.**

"There shall be no strange god among you
   nor shall you worship any alien god.
I, the L<small>ORD</small>, am your God
   who led you forth from the land of Egypt."

℟. **I am the Lord, your God: hear my voice.**

"My people heard not my voice,
   and Israel obeyed me not;
So I gave them up to the hardness of their hearts;
   they walked according to their own counsels."

℟. **I am the Lord, your God: hear my voice.**

"If only my people would hear me,
   and Israel walk in my ways,
Quickly would I humble their enemies;
   against their foes I would turn my hand."

℟. **I am the Lord, your God: hear my voice.**

ALLELUIA

See Acts 16:14b

℟. Alleluia, alleluia.

**Open our hearts, O Lord,
to listen to the words of your Son.**

℟. Alleluia, alleluia.

GOSPEL   Years I and II

Mark 7:31-37   He makes the deaf hear and the mute speak.

✠ **A reading from the holy Gospel according to Mark**

**Jesus left the district of Tyre
   and went by way of Sidon to the Sea of Galilee,
      into the district of the Decapolis.
And people brought to him a deaf man who had a speech impediment
   and begged him to lay his hand on him.
He took him off by himself away from the crowd.
He put his finger into the man's ears
   and, spitting, touched his tongue;
      then he looked up to heaven and groaned, and said to him,
         "Ephphatha!" (that is, "Be opened!")
And immediately the man's ears were opened,
   his speech impediment was removed,
   and he spoke plainly.
He ordered them not to tell anyone.
But the more he ordered them not to,
   the more they proclaimed it.
They were exceedingly astonished and they said,
   "He has done all things well.
He makes the deaf hear and the mute speak."**

The Gospel of the Lord.

334 SATURDAY OF THE FIFTH WEEK IN ORDINARY TIME

FIRST READING   Year II

1 Kings 12:26-32; 13:33-34   Jeroboam made two golden calves.

A reading from the first Book of Kings

Jeroboam thought to himself:
"The kingdom will return to David's house.
If now this people go up to offer sacrifices
   in the temple of the LORD in Jerusalem,
   the hearts of this people will return to their master,
   Rehoboam, king of Judah,
   and they will kill me."
After taking counsel, the king made two calves of gold
   and said to the people:
   "You have been going up to Jerusalem long enough.
Here is your God, O Israel, who brought you up from the land of Egypt."
And he put one in Bethel, the other in Dan.
This led to sin, because the people frequented those calves
   in Bethel and in Dan.
He also built temples on the high places
   and made priests from among the people who were not Levites.
Jeroboam established a feast in the eighth month
   on the fifteenth day of the month
   to duplicate in Bethel the pilgrimage feast of Judah,
   with sacrifices to the calves he had made;
   and he stationed in Bethel priests of the high places he had built.

Jeroboam did not give up his evil ways after this,
   but again made priests for the high places
   from among the common people.
Whoever desired it was consecrated
   and became a priest of the high places.
This was a sin on the part of the house of Jeroboam
   for which it was to be cut off and destroyed from the earth.

The word of the Lord.

RESPONSORIAL PSALM

Psalm 106:6-7ab, 19-20, 21-22

℟. (4a) **Remember us, O Lord, as you favor your people.**

We have sinned, we and our fathers;
   we have committed crimes; we have done wrong.
Our fathers in Egypt
   considered not your wonders.

℟. **Remember us, O Lord, as you favor your people.**

They made a calf in Horeb
   and adored a molten image;
They exchanged their glory
   for the image of a grass-eating bullock.

℟. **Remember us, O Lord, as you favor your people.**

They forgot the God who had saved them,
   who had done great deeds in Egypt,
Wondrous deeds in the land of Ham,
   terrible things at the Red Sea.

℟. **Remember us, O Lord, as you favor your people.**

ALLELUIA

Matthew 4:4b

℟. **Alleluia, alleluia.**

One does not live on bread alone,
but on every word that comes forth from the mouth of God.

℟. **Alleluia, alleluia.**

GOSPEL Years I and II

Mark 8:1-10   They ate and were satisfied.

✢ **A reading from the holy Gospel according to Mark**

**In those days when there again was a great crowd without anything to eat,
    Jesus summoned the disciples and said,
    "My heart is moved with pity for the crowd,
    because they have been with me now for three days
    and have nothing to eat.
If I send them away hungry to their homes,
    they will collapse on the way,
    and some of them have come a great distance."
His disciples answered him, "Where can anyone get enough bread
    to satisfy them here in this deserted place?"
Still he asked them, "How many loaves do you have?"
They replied, "Seven."
He ordered the crowd to sit down on the ground.
Then, taking the seven loaves he gave thanks, broke them,
    and gave them to his disciples to distribute,
    and they distributed them to the crowd.
They also had a few fish.
He said the blessing over them
    and ordered them distributed also.
They ate and were satisfied.
They picked up the fragments left over—seven baskets.
There were about four thousand people.**

**He dismissed the crowd and got into the boat with his disciples
    and came to the region of Dalmanutha.**

The Gospel of the Lord.

335 MONDAY OF THE SIXTH WEEK IN ORDINARY TIME

FIRST READING Year II

James 1:1-11   The testing of your faith produces perseverance so that you may be perfect and complete.

A reading from the beginning of the Letter of Saint James

**James, a servant of God and of the Lord Jesus Christ,
to the twelve tribes in the dispersion, greetings.**

**Consider it all joy, my brothers and sisters,
when you encounter various trials,
for you know that the testing of your faith produces perseverance.
And let perseverance be perfect,
so that you may be perfect and complete, lacking in nothing.
But if any of you lacks wisdom,
he should ask God who gives to all generously and ungrudgingly,
and he will be given it.
But he should ask in faith, not doubting,
for the one who doubts is like a wave of the sea
that is driven and tossed about by the wind.
For that person must not suppose that he will receive anything from the Lord,
since he is a man of two minds, unstable in all his ways.**

**The brother in lowly circumstances
should take pride in high standing,
and the rich one in his lowliness,
for he will pass away "like the flower of the field."
For the sun comes up with its scorching heat and dries up the grass,
its flower droops, and the beauty of its appearance vanishes.
So will the rich person fade away in the midst of his pursuits.**

The word of the Lord.

RESPONSORIAL PSALM

Psalm 119:67, 68, 71, 72, 75, 76

℟. (77a) **Be kind to me, Lord, and I shall live.**

**Before I was afflicted I went astray,
 but now I hold to your promise.**

℟. **Be kind to me, Lord, and I shall live.**

**You are good and bountiful;
 teach me your statutes.**

℟. **Be kind to me, Lord, and I shall live.**

**It is good for me that I have been afflicted,
 that I may learn your statutes.**

℟. **Be kind to me, Lord, and I shall live.**

**The law of your mouth is to me more precious
 than thousands of gold and silver pieces.**

℟. **Be kind to me, Lord, and I shall live.**

I know, O Lord**, that your ordinances are just,
 and in your faithfulness you have afflicted me.**

℟. **Be kind to me, Lord, and I shall live.**

**Let your kindness comfort me
 according to your promise to your servants.**

℟. **Be kind to me, Lord, and I shall live.**

ALLELUIA

John 14:6

℟. Alleluia, alleluia.

I am the way and the truth and the life, says the Lord;
no one comes to the Father except through me.

℟. Alleluia, alleluia.

GOSPEL   Years I and II

Mark 8:11-13   Why does this generation seek a sign?

✠ A reading from the holy Gospel according to Mark

The Pharisees came forward and began to argue with Jesus,
  seeking from him a sign from heaven to test him.
He sighed from the depth of his spirit and said,
  "Why does this generation seek a sign?
Amen, I say to you, no sign will be given to this generation."
Then he left them, got into the boat again,
  and went off to the other shore.

The Gospel of the Lord.

336 TUESDAY OF THE SIXTH WEEK IN ORDINARY TIME

FIRST READING   Year II

James 1:12-18   God himself tempts no one.

A reading from the Letter of Saint James

**Blessed is he who perseveres in temptation,
   for when he has been proven he will receive the crown of life
   that he promised to those who love him.
No one experiencing temptation should say,
   "I am being tempted by God";
   for God is not subject to temptation to evil,
   and he himself tempts no one.
Rather, each person is tempted when lured and enticed by his desire.
Then desire conceives and brings forth sin,
   and when sin reaches maturity it gives birth to death.**

**Do not be deceived, my beloved brothers and sisters:
   all good giving and every perfect gift is from above,
   coming down from the Father of lights,
   with whom there is no alteration or shadow caused by change.
He willed to give us birth by the word of truth
   that we may be a kind of firstfruits of his creatures.**

The word of the Lord.

RESPONSORIAL PSALM

Psalm 94:12-13a, 14-15, 18-19

℟. (12a) **Blessed the man you instruct, O Lord.**

**Blessed the man whom you instruct, O Lord,
  whom by your law you teach,
Giving him rest from evil days.**

℟. **Blessed the man you instruct, O Lord.**

**For the Lord will not cast off his people,
  nor abandon his inheritance;
But judgment shall again be with justice,
  and all the upright of heart shall follow it.**

℟. **Blessed the man you instruct, O Lord.**

**When I say, "My foot is slipping,"
  your mercy, O Lord, sustains me;
When cares abound within me,
  your comfort gladdens my soul.**

℟. **Blessed the man you instruct, O Lord.**

ALLELUIA

John 14:23

℟. **Alleluia, alleluia.**

**Whoever loves me will keep my word, says the Lord;
and my Father will love him
and we will come to him.**

℟. **Alleluia, alleluia.**

GOSPEL Years I and II

Mark 8:14-21 Watch out, guard against the leaven of the Pharisees and the leaven of Herod.

✠ **A reading from the holy Gospel according to Mark**

**The disciples had forgotten to bring bread,
   and they had only one loaf with them in the boat.
Jesus enjoined them, "Watch out,
   guard against the leaven of the Pharisees
   and the leaven of Herod."
They concluded among themselves that
   it was because they had no bread.
When he became aware of this he said to them,
   "Why do you conclude that it is because you have no bread?
Do you not yet understand or comprehend?
Are your hearts hardened?
Do you have eyes and not see, ears and not hear?
And do you not remember,
   when I broke the five loaves for the five thousand,
   how many wicker baskets full of fragments you picked up?"
They answered him, "Twelve."
"When I broke the seven loaves for the four thousand,
   how many full baskets of fragments did you pick up?"
They answered him, "Seven."
He said to them, "Do you still not understand?"**

The Gospel of the Lord.

337 WEDNESDAY OF THE SIXTH WEEK IN ORDINARY TIME

FIRST READING   Year II

James 1:19-27   Be doers of the word and not hearers only.

A reading from the Letter of Saint James

Know this, my dear brothers and sisters:
   everyone should be quick to hear, slow to speak, slow to anger
   for anger does not accomplish
   the righteousness of God.
Therefore, put away all filth and evil excess
   and humbly welcome the word that has been planted in you
   and is able to save your souls.

Be doers of the word and not hearers only, deluding yourselves.
For if anyone is a hearer of the word and not a doer,
   he is like a man who looks at his own face in a mirror.
He sees himself, then goes off and promptly forgets
   what he looked like.
But the one who peers into the perfect law of freedom and perseveres,
   and is not a hearer who forgets but a doer who acts;
   such a one shall be blessed in what he does.

If anyone thinks he is religious and does not bridle his tongue
   but deceives his heart, his religion is vain.
Religion that is pure and undefiled before God and the Father is this:
   to care for orphans and widows in their affliction
   and to keep oneself unstained by the world.

The word of the Lord.

RESPONSORIAL PSALM

Psalm 15:2-3a, 3bc-4ab, 5

℟. (1b) Who shall live on your holy mountain, O Lord?

He who walks blamelessly and does justice;
   who thinks the truth in his heart
   and slanders not with his tongue.

℟. Who shall live on your holy mountain, O Lord?

Who harms not his fellow man,
   nor takes up a reproach against his neighbor;
By whom the reprobate is despised,
   while he honors those who fear the Lord.

℟. **Who shall live on your holy mountain, O Lord?**

Who lends not his money at usury
   and accepts no bribe against the innocent.
He who does these things
   shall never be disturbed.

℟. **Who shall live on your holy mountain, O Lord?**

ALLELUIA

See Ephesians 1:17-18

℟. **Alleluia, alleluia.**

May the Father of our Lord Jesus Christ
enlighten the eyes of our hearts,
that we may know what is the hope
that belongs to his call.

℟. **Alleluia, alleluia.**

GOSPEL   Years I and II

Mark 8:22-26   His sight was restored and he could see everything distinctly.

✠ **A reading from the holy Gospel according to Mark**

When Jesus and his disciples arrived at Bethsaida,
   people brought to him a blind man and begged Jesus to touch him.
He took the blind man by the hand and led him outside the village.
Putting spittle on his eyes he laid his hands on the man and asked,
   "Do you see anything?"
Looking up the man replied, "I see people looking like trees and walking."
Then he laid hands on the man's eyes a second time and he saw clearly;
   his sight was restored and he could see everything distinctly.
Then he sent him home and said, "Do not even go into the village."

The Gospel of the Lord.

338 THURSDAY OF THE SIXTH WEEK IN ORDINARY TIME

FIRST READING   Year II

James 2:1-9   Did not God choose those who are poor in the world? You, however, dishonored the person who is poor.

A reading from the Letter of Saint James

My brothers and sisters, show no partiality
   as you adhere to the faith in our glorious Lord Jesus Christ.
For if a man with gold rings and fine clothes
   comes into your assembly,
   and a poor person with shabby clothes also comes in,
   and you pay attention to the one wearing the fine clothes
   and say, "Sit here, please,"
   while you say to the poor one, "Stand there," or "Sit at my feet,"
   have you not made distinctions among yourselves
   and become judges with evil designs?

Listen, my beloved brothers and sisters.
Did not God choose those who are poor in the world
   to be rich in faith and heirs of the Kingdom
   that he promised to those who love him?
But you dishonored the poor.
Are not the rich oppressing you?
And do they themselves not haul you off to court?
Is it not they who blaspheme the noble name that was invoked over you?
However, if you fulfill the royal law according to the Scripture,
   You shall love your neighbor as yourself, you are doing well.
But if you show partiality, you commit sin,
   and are convicted by the law as transgressors.

The word of the Lord.

RESPONSORIAL PSALM

Psalm 34:2-3, 4-5, 6-7

℟. (7a) **The Lord hears the cry of the poor.**

I will bless the LORD **at all times;
his praise shall be ever in my mouth.
Let my soul glory in the L**ORD**;
the lowly will hear me and be glad.**

℟. **The Lord hears the cry of the poor.**

Glorify the LORD **with me,
let us together extol his name.
I sought the L**ORD**, and he answered me
and delivered me from all my fears.**

℟. **The Lord hears the cry of the poor.**

**Look to him that you may be radiant with joy,
and your faces may not blush with shame.
When the poor one called out, the L**ORD **heard,
and from all his distress he saved him.**

℟. **The Lord hears the cry of the poor.**

ALLELUIA

See John 6:63c, 68c

℟. **Alleluia, alleluia.**

**Your words, Lord, are Spirit and life;
you have the words of everlasting life.**

℟. **Alleluia, alleluia.**

GOSPEL Years I and II

Mark 8:27-33   You are the Christ. The Son of Man must suffer much.

✠ A reading from the holy Gospel according to Mark

Jesus and his disciples set out
   for the villages of Caesarea Philippi.
Along the way he asked his disciples,
   "Who do people say that I am?"
They said in reply,
   "John the Baptist, others Elijah,
   still others one of the prophets."
And he asked them,
   "But who do you say that I am?"
Peter said to him in reply,
   "You are the Christ."
Then he warned them not to tell anyone about him.

He began to teach them
   that the Son of Man must suffer greatly
   and be rejected by the elders, the chief priests, and the scribes,
   and be killed, and rise after three days.
He spoke this openly.
Then Peter took him aside and began to rebuke him.
At this he turned around and, looking at his disciples,
   rebuked Peter and said, "Get behind me, Satan.
You are thinking not as God does, but as human beings do."

The Gospel of the Lord.

339 FRIDAY OF THE SIXTH WEEK IN ORDINARY TIME

FIRST READING   Year II

James 2:14-24, 26   For just as a body without a spirit is dead, so also faith without works is dead.

A reading from the Letter of Saint James

What good is it, my brothers and sisters,
  if someone says he has faith but does not have works?
Can that faith save him?
If a brother or sister has nothing to wear
  and has no food for the day,
  and one of you says to them,
  "Go in peace, keep warm, and eat well,"
  but you do not give them the necessities of the body,
  what good is it?
So also faith of itself,
  if it does not have works, is dead.

Indeed someone might say,
  "You have faith and I have works."
Demonstrate your faith to me without works,
  and I will demonstrate my faith to you from my works.
You believe that God is one.
You do well.
Even the demons believe that and tremble.
Do you want proof, you ignoramus,
  that faith without works is useless?
Was not Abraham our father justified by works
  when he offered his son Isaac upon the altar?
You see that faith was active along with his works,
  and faith was completed by the works.
Thus the Scripture was fulfilled that says,
  __Abraham believed God,__
  __and it was credited to him as righteousness,__
  and he was called *__the friend of God.__*
See how a person is justified by works and not by faith alone.
For just as a body without a spirit is dead,
  so also faith without works is dead.

The word of the Lord.

RESPONSORIAL PSALM

Psalm 112:1-2, 3-4, 5-6

℟. (see 1b) **Blessed the man who greatly delights in the Lord's commands.**

**Blessed the man who fears the Lord,
 who greatly delights in his commands.
His posterity shall be mighty upon the earth;
 the upright generation shall be blessed.**

℟. **Blessed the man who greatly delights in the Lord's commands.**

**Wealth and riches shall be in his house;
 his generosity shall endure forever.
Light shines through the darkness for the upright;
 he is gracious and merciful and just.**

℟. **Blessed the man who greatly delights in the Lord's commands.**

**Well for the man who is gracious and lends,
 who conducts his affairs with justice;
He shall never be moved;
 the just man shall be in everlasting remembrance.**

℟. **Blessed the man who greatly delights in the Lord's commands.**

ALLELUIA

John 15:15b

℟. **Alleluia, alleluia.**

**I call you my friends, says the Lord,
for I have made known to you all that the Father has told me.**

℟. **Alleluia, alleluia.**

GOSPEL Years I and II

Mark 8:34–9:1   Those who lose their lives for my sake and that of the Gospel, will save them.

✠ **A reading from the holy Gospel according to Mark**

Jesus summoned the crowd with his disciples and said to them,
   "Whoever wishes to come after me must deny himself,
   take up his cross, and follow me.
For whoever wishes to save his life will lose it,
   but whoever loses his life for my sake
   and that of the Gospel will save it.
What profit is there for one to gain the whole world
   and forfeit his life?
What could one give in exchange for his life?
Whoever is ashamed of me and of my words
   in this faithless and sinful generation,
   the Son of Man will be ashamed of
   when he comes in his Father's glory with the holy angels."

He also said to them,
   "Amen, I say to you,
   there are some standing here who will not taste death
   until they see that the Kingdom of God has come in power."

The Gospel of the Lord.

340 SATURDAY OF THE SIXTH WEEK IN ORDINARY TIME

FIRST READING   Year II

James 3:1-10   No human being can tame the tongue.

A reading from the Letter of Saint James

**Not many of you should become teachers, my brothers and sisters,
    for you realize that we will be judged more strictly,
    for we all fall short in many respects.
If anyone does not fall short in speech, he is a perfect man,
    able to bridle the whole body also.
If we put bits into the mouths of horses to make them obey us,
    we also guide their whole bodies.
It is the same with ships:
    even though they are so large and driven by fierce winds,
    they are steered by a very small rudder
    wherever the pilot's inclination wishes.
In the same way the tongue is a small member
    and yet has great pretensions.**

**Consider how small a fire can set a huge forest ablaze.
The tongue is also a fire.
It exists among our members as a world of malice,
    defiling the whole body
    and setting the entire course of our lives on fire,
    itself set on fire by Gehenna.
For every kind of beast and bird, of reptile and sea creature,
    can be tamed and has been tamed by the human species,
    but no man can tame the tongue.
It is a restless evil, full of deadly poison.
With it we bless the Lord and Father,
    and with it we curse men
    who are made in the likeness of God.
From the same mouth come blessing and cursing.
My brothers and sisters, this need not be so.**

The word of the Lord.

RESPONSORIAL PSALM

Psalm 12:2-3, 4-5, 7-8

℟. (8a) **You will protect us, Lord.**

**Help, O LORD! for no one now is dutiful;
 faithfulness has vanished from among the children of men.
Everyone speaks falsehood to his neighbor;
 with smooth lips they speak, and double heart.**

℟. **You will protect us, Lord.**

**May the LORD destroy all smooth lips,
 every boastful tongue,
Those who say, "We are heroes with our tongues;
 our lips are our own; who is lord over us?"**

℟. **You will protect us, Lord.**

**The promises of the LORD are sure,
 like tried silver, freed from dross, sevenfold refined.
You, O LORD, will keep us
 and preserve us always from this generation.**

℟. **You will protect us, Lord.**

ALLELUIA

See Mark 9:6

℟. **Alleluia, alleluia.**

**The heavens were opened and the voice of the Father thundered:
This is my beloved Son. Listen to him.**

℟. **Alleluia, alleluia.**

GOSPEL   Years I and II

Mark 9:2-13   Jesus was transfigured before them.

✠ A reading from the holy Gospel according to Mark

Jesus took Peter, James, and John
  and led them up a high mountain apart by themselves.
And he was transfigured before them,
  and his clothes became dazzling white,
  such as no fuller on earth could bleach them.
Then Elijah appeared to them along with Moses,
  and they were conversing with Jesus.
Then Peter said to Jesus in reply,
  "Rabbi, it is good that we are here!
Let us make three tents:
  one for you, one for Moses, and one for Elijah."
He hardly knew what to say, they were so terrified.
Then a cloud came, casting a shadow over them;
  then from the cloud came a voice,
  "This is my beloved Son. Listen to him."
Suddenly, looking around, the disciples no longer saw anyone
  but Jesus alone with them.

As they were coming down from the mountain,
  he charged them not to relate what they had seen to anyone,
  except when the Son of Man had risen from the dead.
So they kept the matter to themselves,
  questioning what rising from the dead meant.
Then they asked him,
  "Why do the scribes say that Elijah must come first?"
He told them, "Elijah will indeed come first and restore all things,
  yet how is it written regarding the Son of Man
  that he must suffer greatly and be treated with contempt?
But I tell you that Elijah has come
  and they did to him whatever they pleased,
  as it is written of him."

The Gospel of the Lord.

341 MONDAY OF THE SEVENTH WEEK IN ORDINARY TIME

FIRST READING   Year II

James 3:13-18   If you have bitter jealousy and selfish ambition in your hearts, do not boast.

A reading from the Letter of Saint James

Beloved:
Who among you is wise and understanding?
Let him show his works by a good life
   in the humility that comes from wisdom.
But if you have bitter jealousy and selfish ambition in your hearts,
   do not boast and be false to the truth.
Wisdom of this kind does not come down from above
   but is earthly, unspiritual, demonic.
For where jealousy and selfish ambition exist,
   there is disorder and every foul practice.
But the wisdom from above is first of all pure,
   then peaceable, gentle, compliant,
   full of mercy and good fruits,
   without inconstancy or insincerity.
And the fruit of righteousness is sown in peace
   for those who cultivate peace.

The word of the Lord.

RESPONSORIAL PSALM

Psalm 19:8, 9, 10, 15

℟. (9a) **The precepts of the Lord give joy to the heart.**

The law of the Lord is perfect,
   refreshing the soul;
The decree of the Lord is trustworthy,
   giving wisdom to the simple.

℟. **The precepts of the Lord give joy to the heart.**

The precepts of the LORD are right,
   rejoicing the heart;
The command of the LORD is clear,
   enlightening the eye.

℟. The precepts of the Lord give joy to the heart.

The fear of the LORD is pure,
   enduring forever;
The ordinances of the LORD are true,
   all of them just.

℟. The precepts of the Lord give joy to the heart.

Let the words of my mouth and the thought of my heart
   find favor before you,
     O LORD, my rock and my redeemer.

℟. The precepts of the Lord give joy to the heart.

ALLELUIA

See 2 Timothy 1:10

℟. Alleluia, alleluia.

Our Savior Jesus Christ has destroyed death
and brought life to light through the Gospel.

℟. Alleluia, alleluia.

GOSPEL   Years I and II

Mark 9:14-29   I do believe, help my unbelief!

✝ A reading from the holy Gospel according to Mark

As Jesus came down from the mountain with Peter, James, and John
   and approached the other disciples,
     they saw a large crowd around them and scribes arguing with them.
Immediately on seeing him,
   the whole crowd was utterly amazed.
They ran up to him and greeted him.
He asked them, "What are you arguing about with them?"
Someone from the crowd answered him,
   "Teacher, I have brought to you my son possessed by a mute spirit.

Wherever it seizes him, it throws him down;
>   he foams at the mouth, grinds his teeth, and becomes rigid.
I asked your disciples to drive it out, but they were unable to do so."
He said to them in reply,
>   "O faithless generation, how long will I be with you?
How long will I endure you? Bring him to me."
They brought the boy to him.
And when he saw him,
>   the spirit immediately threw the boy into convulsions.
As he fell to the ground, he began to roll around
>   and foam at the mouth.
Then he questioned his father,
>   "How long has this been happening to him?"
He replied, "Since childhood.
It has often thrown him into fire and into water to kill him.
But if you can do anything, have compassion on us and help us."
Jesus said to him,
>   "'If you can!' Everything is possible to one who has faith."
Then the boy's father cried out, "I do believe, help my unbelief!"
Jesus, on seeing a crowd rapidly gathering,
>   rebuked the unclean spirit and said to it,
>   "Mute and deaf spirit, I command you:
>   come out of him and never enter him again!"
Shouting and throwing the boy into convulsions, it came out.
He became like a corpse, which caused many to say, "He is dead!"
But Jesus took him by the hand, raised him, and he stood up.
When he entered the house, his disciples asked him in private,
>   "Why could we not drive the spirit out?"
He said to them, "This kind can only come out through prayer."

The Gospel of the Lord.

342 TUESDAY OF THE SEVENTH WEEK IN ORDINARY TIME

FIRST READING   Year II

James 4:1-10   You ask but you do not receive, because you ask wrongly.

A reading from the Letter of Saint James

Beloved:
Where do the wars and where do the conflicts among you come from?
Is it not from your passions that make war within your members?
You covet but do not possess.
You kill and envy but you cannot obtain;
   you fight and wage war.
You do not possess because you do not ask.
You ask but do not receive, because you ask wrongly,
   to spend it on your passions.
Adulterers!
Do you not know that to be a lover of the world means enmity with God?
Therefore, whoever wants to be a lover of the world
   makes himself an enemy of God.
Or do you suppose that the Scripture speaks without meaning when it says,
   The spirit that he has made to dwell in us tends toward jealousy?
But he bestows a greater grace; therefore, it says:
   God resists the proud,
      but gives grace to the humble.

So submit yourselves to God.
Resist the Devil, and he will flee from you.
Draw near to God, and he will draw near to you.
Cleanse your hands, you sinners,
   and purify your hearts, you of two minds.
Begin to lament, to mourn, to weep.
Let your laughter be turned into mourning
   and your joy into dejection.
Humble yourselves before the Lord
   and he will exalt you.

The word of the Lord.

RESPONSORIAL PSALM

Psalm 55:7-8, 9-10a, 10b-11a, 23

℟. (23a) **Throw your cares on the Lord, and he will support you.**

And I say, "Had I but wings like a dove,
   I would fly away and be at rest.
Far away I would flee;
   I would lodge in the wilderness."

℟. **Throw your cares on the Lord, and he will support you.**

"I would wait for him who saves me
   from the violent storm and the tempest."
Engulf them, O Lord; divide their counsels.

℟. **Throw your cares on the Lord, and he will support you.**

In the city I see violence and strife,
   day and night they prowl about upon its walls.

℟. **Throw your cares on the Lord, and he will support you.**

Cast your care upon the Lord,
   and he will support you;
   never will he permit the just man to be disturbed.

℟. **Throw your cares on the Lord, and he will support you.**

ALLELUIA

Galatians 6:14

℟. **Alleluia, alleluia.**

**May I never boast except in the Cross of our Lord Jesus Christ,
through which the world has been crucified to me and I to the world.**

℟. **Alleluia, alleluia.**

GOSPEL   Years I and II

Mark 9:30-37   The Son of Man is to be handed over. Whoever wishes to be first, shall be last of all.

✠ **A reading from the holy Gospel according to Mark**

**Jesus and his disciples left from there and began a journey through Galilee,
   but he did not wish anyone to know about it.
He was teaching his disciples and telling them,
   "The Son of Man is to be handed over to men
   and they will kill him,
   and three days after his death the Son of Man will rise."
But they did not understand the saying,
   and they were afraid to question him.**

**They came to Capernaum and, once inside the house,
   he began to ask them,
   "What were you arguing about on the way?"
But they remained silent.
For they had been discussing among themselves on the way
   who was the greatest.
Then he sat down, called the Twelve, and said to them,
   "If anyone wishes to be first,
   he shall be the last of all and the servant of all."
Taking a child, he placed it in their midst,
   and putting his arms around it, he said to them,
   "Whoever receives one child such as this in my name, receives me;
   and whoever receives me,
   receives not me but the One who sent me."**

The Gospel of the Lord.

343 WEDNESDAY OF THE SEVENTH WEEK IN ORDINARY TIME

FIRST READING   Year II

James 4:13-17   You have no idea what your life will be like. Instead you should say: If the Lord wills it.

A reading from the Letter of Saint James

Beloved:
Come now, you who say,
  "Today or tomorrow we shall go into such and such a town,
  spend a year there doing business, and make a profit"—
  you have no idea what your life will be like tomorrow.
You are a puff of smoke that appears briefly and then disappears.
Instead you should say,
  "If the Lord wills it, we shall live to do this or that."
But now you are boasting in your arrogance.
All such boasting is evil.
So for one who knows the right thing to do
  and does not do it, it is a sin.

The word of the Lord.

RESPONSORIAL PSALM

Psalm 49:2-3, 6-7, 8-10, 11

℟. (Matthew 5:3) **Blessed are the poor in spirit; the Kingdom of heaven is theirs!**

Hear this, all you peoples;
  hearken, all who dwell in the world,
Of lowly birth or high degree,
  rich and poor alike.

℟. **Blessed are the poor in spirit; the Kingdom of heaven is theirs!**

Why should I fear in evil days
  when my wicked ensnarers ring me round?
They trust in their wealth;
  the abundance of their riches is their boast.

℟. **Blessed are the poor in spirit; the Kingdom of heaven is theirs!**

Yet in no way can a man redeem himself,
   or pay his own ransom to God;
Too high is the price to redeem one's life; he would never have enough
   to remain alive always and not see destruction.

℟. Blessed are the poor in spirit; the Kingdom of heaven is theirs!

For he can see that wise men die,
   and likewise the senseless and the stupid pass away,
   leaving to others their wealth.

℟. Blessed are the poor in spirit; the Kingdom of heaven is theirs!

ALLELUIA

John 14:6

℟. Alleluia, alleluia.

I am the way and the truth and the life, says the Lord;
no one comes to the Father except through me.

℟. Alleluia, alleluia.

GOSPEL   Years I and II

Mark 9:38-40   Whoever is not against us is for us.

✝ A reading from the holy Gospel according to Mark

John said to Jesus,
   "Teacher, we saw someone driving out demons in your name,
   and we tried to prevent him because he does not follow us."
Jesus replied, "Do not prevent him.
There is no one who performs a mighty deed in my name
   who can at the same time speak ill of me.
For whoever is not against us is for us."

The Gospel of the Lord.

344 THURSDAY OF THE SEVENTH WEEK IN ORDINARY TIME

FIRST READING   Year II

James 5:1-6   The workers from whom you withheld the wages, are crying aloud; their cries have reached the ears of the Lord of hosts.

A reading from the Letter of Saint James

Come now, you rich, weep and wail over your impending miseries.
Your wealth has rotted away, your clothes have become moth-eaten,
   your gold and silver have corroded,
   and that corrosion will be a testimony against you;
   it will devour your flesh like a fire.
You have stored up treasure for the last days.
Behold, the wages you withheld from the workers
   who harvested your fields are crying aloud;
   and the cries of the harvesters
   have reached the ears of the Lord of hosts.
You have lived on earth in luxury and pleasure;
   you have fattened your hearts for the day of slaughter.
You have condemned;
   you have murdered the righteous one;
   he offers you no resistance.

The word of the Lord.

RESPONSORIAL PSALM

Psalm 49:14-15ab, 15cd-16, 17-18, 19-20

℟. (Matthew 5:3) **Blessed are the poor in spirit; the Kingdom of heaven is theirs!**

**This is the way of those whose trust is folly,
 the end of those contented with their lot:
Like sheep they are herded into the nether world;
 death is their shepherd and the upright rule over them.**

℟. **Blessed are the poor in spirit; the Kingdom of heaven is theirs!**

**Quickly their form is consumed;
 the nether world is their palace.
But God will redeem me
 from the power of the nether world by receiving me.**

℟. **Blessed are the poor in spirit; the Kingdom of heaven is theirs!**

**Fear not when a man grows rich,
 when the wealth of his house becomes great,
For when he dies, he shall take none of it;
 his wealth shall not follow him down.**

℟. **Blessed are the poor in spirit; the Kingdom of heaven is theirs!**

**Though in his lifetime he counted himself blessed,
 "They will praise you for doing well for yourself,"
He shall join the circle of his forebears
 who shall never more see light.**

℟. **Blessed are the poor in spirit; the Kingdom of heaven is theirs!**

ALLELUIA

See 1 Thessalonians 2:13

℟. **Alleluia, alleluia.**

Receive the word of God, not as the word of men,
but as it truly is, the word of God.

℟. **Alleluia, alleluia.**

GOSPEL Years I and II

Mark 9:41-50 It is better for you to enter into life with one hand, than with two hands to go into Gehenna.

☩ **A reading from the holy Gospel according to Mark**

Jesus said to his disciples:
"Anyone who gives you a cup of water to drink
   because you belong to Christ,
   amen, I say to you, will surely not lose his reward.

"Whoever causes one of these little ones who believe in me to sin,
   it would be better for him if a great millstone
   were put around his neck
   and he were thrown into the sea.
If your hand causes you to sin, cut it off.
It is better for you to enter into life maimed
   than with two hands to go into Gehenna,
   into the unquenchable fire.
And if your foot causes you to sin, cut if off.
It is better for you to enter into life crippled
   than with two feet to be thrown into Gehenna.
And if your eye causes you to sin, pluck it out.
Better for you to enter into the Kingdom of God with one eye
   than with two eyes to be thrown into Gehenna,
   where *their worm does not die, and the fire is not quenched.*

"Everyone will be salted with fire.
Salt is good, but if salt becomes insipid,
   with what will you restore its flavor?
Keep salt in yourselves and you will have peace with one another."

The Gospel of the Lord.

345 FRIDAY OF THE SEVENTH WEEK IN ORDINARY TIME

FIRST READING   Year II

James 5:9-12   The Judge is standing before the gates.

A reading from the Letter of Saint James

Do not complain, brothers and sisters, about one another,
   that you may not be judged.
Behold, the Judge is standing before the gates.
Take as an example of hardship and patience, brothers and sisters,
   the prophets who spoke in the name of the Lord.
Indeed we call blessed those who have persevered.
You have heard of the perseverance of Job,
   and you have seen the purpose of the Lord,
   because *the Lord is compassionate and merciful.*

But above all, my brothers and sisters, do not swear,
   either by heaven or by earth or with any other oath,
   but let your "Yes" mean "Yes" and your "No" mean "No,"
   that you may not incur condemnation.

The word of the Lord.

RESPONSORIAL PSALM

Psalm 103:1-2, 3-4, 8-9, 11-12

℟. (8a) **The Lord is kind and merciful.**

Bless the Lord, O my soul;
   and all my being, bless his holy name.
Bless the Lord, O my soul,
   and forget not all his benefits.

℟. **The Lord is kind and merciful.**

He pardons all your iniquities,
   he heals all your ills.
He redeems your life from destruction,
   he crowns you with kindness and compassion.

℟. **The Lord is kind and merciful.**

Merciful and gracious is the Lord,
   slow to anger and abounding in kindness.
He will not always chide,
   nor does he keep his wrath forever.

℟. **The Lord is kind and merciful.**

For as the heavens are high above the earth,
   so surpassing is his kindness toward those who fear him.
As far as the east is from the west,
   so far has he put our transgressions from us.

℟. **The Lord is kind and merciful.**

ALLELUIA

See John 17:17b, 17a

℟. **Alleluia, alleluia.**

Your word, O Lord, is truth;
consecrate us in the truth.

℟. **Alleluia, alleluia.**

GOSPEL Years I and II

Mark 10:1-12 What God has joined together, no human being must separate.

✝ A reading from the holy Gospel according to Mark

Jesus came into the district of Judea and across the Jordan.
Again crowds gathered around him and, as was his custom,
   he again taught them.
The Pharisees approached him and asked,
   "Is it lawful for a husband to divorce his wife?"
They were testing him.
He said to them in reply, "What did Moses command you?"
They replied,
   "Moses permitted a husband to write a bill of divorce
   and dismiss her."
But Jesus told them,
   "Because of the hardness of your hearts
   he wrote you this commandment.
But from the beginning of creation, *God made them male and female.*
For this reason a man shall leave his father and mother
   and be joined to his wife,
   and the two shall become one flesh.
So they are no longer two but one flesh.
Therefore what God has joined together,
   no human being must separate."
In the house the disciples again questioned Jesus about this.
He said to them,
   "Whoever divorces his wife and marries another
   commits adultery against her;
   and if she divorces her husband and marries another,
   she commits adultery."

The Gospel of the Lord.

346 SATURDAY OF THE SEVENTH WEEK IN ORDINARY TIME

FIRST READING   Year II

James 5:13-20   The fervent prayer of a righteous person is very powerful.

A reading from the Letter of Saint James

Beloved:
Is anyone among you suffering?
He should pray.
Is anyone in good spirits?
He should sing a song of praise.
Is anyone among you sick?
He should summon the presbyters of the Church,
   and they should pray over him
   and anoint him with oil in the name of the Lord.
The prayer of faith will save the sick person,
   and the Lord will raise him up.
If he has committed any sins, he will be forgiven.

Therefore, confess your sins to one another
   and pray for one another, that you may be healed.
The fervent prayer of a righteous person is very powerful.
Elijah was a man like us;
   yet he prayed earnestly that it might not rain,
   and for three years and six months it did not rain upon the land.
Then Elijah prayed again, and the sky gave rain
   and the earth produced its fruit.

My brothers and sisters,
   if anyone among you should stray from the truth
   and someone bring him back,
   he should know that whoever brings back a sinner
   from the error of his way will save his soul from death
   and will cover a multitude of sins.

The word of the Lord.

RESPONSORIAL PSALM

Psalm 141:1-2, 3 and 8

℟. (2a) **Let my prayer come like incense before you.**

O Lord, to you I call; hasten to me;
  hearken to my voice when I call upon you.
Let my prayer come like incense before you;
  the lifting up of my hands, like the evening sacrifice.

℟. **Let my prayer come like incense before you.**

O Lord, set a watch before my mouth,
  a guard at the door of my lips.
For toward you, O God, my Lord, my eyes are turned;
  in you I take refuge; strip me not of life.

℟. **Let my prayer come like incense before you.**

ALLELUIA

See Matthew 11:25

℟. **Alleluia, alleluia.**

Blessed are you, Father, Lord of heaven and earth;
you have revealed to little ones the mysteries of the Kingdom.

℟. **Alleluia, alleluia.**

GOSPEL Years I and II

Mark 10:13-16   Whoever does not accept the Kingdom of God like a child will not enter it.

✠ **A reading from the holy Gospel according to Mark**

**People were bringing children to Jesus that he might touch them,
 but the disciples rebuked them.
When Jesus saw this he became indignant and said to them,
 "Let the children come to me; do not prevent them,
 for the Kingdom of God belongs to such as these.
Amen, I say to you,
 whoever does not accept the Kingdom of God like a child
 will not enter it."
Then he embraced the children and blessed them,
 placing his hands on them.**

The Gospel of the Lord.

347 MONDAY OF THE EIGHTH WEEK IN ORDINARY TIME

FIRST READING   Year II

1 Peter 1:3-9   Although you have not seen him, you love him; you rejoice with an indescribable and glorious joy.

A reading from the first Letter of Saint Peter

Blessed be the God and Father of our Lord Jesus Christ,
>   who in his great mercy gave us a new birth to a living hope
>   through the resurrection of Jesus Christ from the dead,
>   to an inheritance that is imperishable, undefiled, and unfading,
>   kept in heaven for you
>   who by the power of God are safeguarded through faith,
>   to a salvation that is ready to be revealed in the final time.

In this you rejoice, although now for a little while
>   you may have to suffer through various trials,
>   so that the genuineness of your faith,
>   more precious than gold that is perishable even though tested by fire,
>   may prove to be for praise, glory, and honor
>   at the revelation of Jesus Christ.

Although you have not seen him you love him;
>   even though you do not see him now yet you believe in him,
>   you rejoice with an indescribable and glorious joy,
>   as you attain the goal of faith, the salvation of your souls.

The word of the Lord.

RESPONSORIAL PSALM

Psalm 111:1-2, 5-6, 9 and 10c

℟. (5) **The Lord will remember his covenant for ever.**
  or:
℟. **Alleluia.**

I will give thanks to the LORD **with all my heart**
  in the company and assembly of the just.
Great are the works of the LORD**,**
  exquisite in all their delights.

℟. **The Lord will remember his covenant for ever.**
  or:
℟. **Alleluia.**

He has given food to those who fear him;
  he will forever be mindful of his covenant.
He has made known to his people the power of his works,
  giving them the inheritance of the nations.

℟. **The Lord will remember his covenant for ever.**
  or:
℟. **Alleluia.**

He has sent deliverance to his people;
  he has ratified his covenant forever;
  holy and awesome is his name.
  His praise endures forever.

℟. **The Lord will remember his covenant for ever.**
  or:
℟. **Alleluia.**

ALLELUIA

2 Corinthians 8:9

℟. **Alleluia, alleluia.**

Jesus Christ became poor although he was rich,
so that by his poverty you might become rich.

℟. **Alleluia, alleluia.**

GOSPEL   Years I and II

Mark 10:17-27   Go, sell what you have, and give to the poor.

☩ A reading from the holy Gospel according to Mark

As Jesus was setting out on a journey, a man ran up,
 knelt down before him, and asked him,
 "Good teacher, what must I do to inherit eternal life?"
Jesus answered him, "Why do you call me good?
No one is good but God alone.
You know the commandments: *You shall not kill;*
 you shall not commit adultery;
 you shall not steal;
 you shall not bear false witness;
 you shall not defraud;
 honor your father and your mother."
He replied and said to him,
 "Teacher, all of these I have observed from my youth."
Jesus, looking at him, loved him and said to him,
 "You are lacking in one thing.
Go, sell what you have, and give to the poor
 and you will have treasure in heaven; then come, follow me."
At that statement, his face fell,
 and he went away sad, for he had many possessions.

Jesus looked around and said to his disciples,
 "How hard it is for those who have wealth
 to enter the Kingdom of God!"
The disciples were amazed at his words.
So Jesus again said to them in reply,
 "Children, how hard it is to enter the Kingdom of God!
It is easier for a camel to pass through the eye of a needle
 than for one who is rich to enter the Kingdom of God."
They were exceedingly astonished and said among themselves,
 "Then who can be saved?"
Jesus looked at them and said,
 "For men it is impossible, but not for God.
All things are possible for God."

The Gospel of the Lord.

348 TUESDAY OF THE EIGHTH WEEK IN ORDINARY TIME

FIRST READING   Year II

1 Peter 1:10-16   They prophesied about the grace that was to be yours; therefore, live soberly and set your hopes completely on the grace to be brought to you.

A reading from the first Letter of Saint Peter

Beloved:
Concerning the salvation of your souls
> the prophets who prophesied about the grace that was to be yours
> searched and investigated it
> investigating the time and circumstances
> that the Spirit of Christ within them indicated
> when it testified in advance
> to the sufferings destined for Christ
> and the glories to follow them.

It was revealed to them that they were serving not themselves but you
> with regard to the things that have now been announced to you
> by those who preached the Good News to you
> through the Holy Spirit sent from heaven,
> things into which angels longed to look.

Therefore, gird up the loins of your mind, live soberly,
> and set your hopes completely on the grace to be brought to you
> at the revelation of Jesus Christ.

Like obedient children,
> do not act in compliance with the desires of your former ignorance
> but, as he who called you is holy,
> be holy yourselves in every aspect of your conduct,
> for it is written, *Be holy because I am holy.*

The word of the Lord.

RESPONSORIAL PSALM

Psalm 98:1, 2-3ab, 3cd-4

℟. (2a) **The Lord has made known his salvation.**

Sing to the LORD **a new song,
 for he has done wondrous deeds;
His right hand has won victory for him,
 his holy arm.**

℟. **The Lord has made known his salvation.**

The LORD **has made his salvation known:
 in the sight of the nations he has revealed his justice.
He has remembered his kindness and his faithfulness
 toward the house of Israel.**

℟. **The Lord has made known his salvation.**

**All the ends of the earth have seen
 the salvation by our God.
Sing joyfully to the L**ORD**, all you lands;
 break into song; sing praise.**

℟. **The Lord has made known his salvation.**

ALLELUIA

See Matthew 11:25

℟. **Alleluia, alleluia.**

**Blessed are you, Father, Lord of heaven and earth;
you have revealed to little ones the mysteries of the Kingdom.**

℟. **Alleluia, alleluia.**

GOSPEL Years I and II

Mark 10:28-31   You will receive a hundred times as much persecution in this present age, and eternal life in the age to come.

✟ **A reading from the holy Gospel according to Mark**

Peter began to say to Jesus,
  "We have given up everything and followed you."
Jesus said, "Amen, I say to you,
   there is no one who has given up house or brothers or sisters
   or mother or father or children or lands
   for my sake and for the sake of the Gospel
   who will not receive a hundred times more now in this present age:
   houses and brothers and sisters
   and mothers and children and lands,
   with persecutions, and eternal life in the age to come.
But many that are first will be last, and the last will be first."

The Gospel of the Lord.

349 WEDNESDAY OF THE EIGHTH WEEK IN ORDINARY TIME

FIRST READING   Year II

1 Peter 1:18-25   *You were ransomed with the precious Blood of Christ, as of a spotless unblemished Lamb.*

A reading from the first Letter of Saint Peter

Beloved:
Realize that you were ransomed from your futile conduct,
   handed on by your ancestors,
   not with perishable things like silver or gold
   but with the precious Blood of Christ
   as of a spotless unblemished Lamb.
He was known before the foundation of the world
   but revealed in the final time for you,
   who through him believe in God
   who raised him from the dead and gave him glory,
   so that your faith and hope are in God.

Since you have purified yourselves
   by obedience to the truth for sincere brotherly love,
   love one another intensely from a pure heart.
You have been born anew,
   not from perishable but from imperishable seed,
   through the living and abiding word of God, for:

   "All flesh is like grass,
      and all its glory like the flower of the field;
   the grass withers,
      and the flower wilts;
   but the word of the Lord remains forever."
This is the word that has been proclaimed to you.

The word of the Lord.

RESPONSORIAL PSALM

Psalm 147:12-13, 14-15, 19-20

℟. (12a) **Praise the Lord, Jerusalem.**
  or:
℟. **Alleluia.**

**Glorify the Lord, O Jerusalem;
  praise your God, O Zion.
For he has strengthened the bars of your gates;
  he has blessed your children within you.**

℟. **Praise the Lord, Jerusalem.**
  or:
℟. **Alleluia.**

**He has granted peace in your borders;
  with the best of wheat he fills you.
He sends forth his command to the earth;
  swiftly runs his word!**

℟. **Praise the Lord, Jerusalem.**
  or:
℟. **Alleluia.**

**He has proclaimed his word to Jacob,
  his statutes and his ordinances to Israel.
He has not done thus for any other nation;
  his ordinances he has not made known to them. Alleluia.**

℟. **Praise the Lord, Jerusalem.**
  or:
℟. **Alleluia.**

ALLELUIA

Mark 10:45

℟. Alleluia, alleluia.

The Son of Man came to serve,
and to give his life as a ransom for many.

℟. Alleluia, alleluia.

GOSPEL   Years I and II

Mark 10:32-45   Behold, we are going up to Jerusalem and the Son of Man will be handed over.

✠ A reading from the holy Gospel according to Mark

The disciples were on the way, going up to Jerusalem,
   and Jesus went ahead of them.
They were amazed, and those who followed were afraid.
Taking the Twelve aside again, he began to tell them
   what was going to happen to him.
"Behold, we are going up to Jerusalem, and the Son of Man
   will be handed over to the chief priests and the scribes,
   and they will condemn him to death
   and hand him over to the Gentiles who will mock him,
   spit upon him, scourge him, and put him to death,
   but after three days he will rise."

Then James and John, the sons of Zebedee,
   came to Jesus and said to him,
   "Teacher, we want you to do for us whatever we ask of you."
He replied, "What do you wish me to do for you?"
They answered him,
   "Grant that in your glory
   we may sit one at your right and the other at your left."
Jesus said to them, "You do not know what you are asking.
Can you drink the chalice that I drink
   or be baptized with the baptism with which I am baptized?"
They said to him, "We can."

**Jesus said to them, "The chalice that I drink, you will drink,
   and with the baptism with which I am baptized, you will be baptized;
   but to sit at my right or at my left is not mine to give
   but is for those for whom it has been prepared."
When the ten heard this, they became indignant at James and John.
Jesus summoned them and said to them,
   "You know that those who are recognized as rulers over the Gentiles
   lord it over them,
   and their great ones make their authority over them felt.
But it shall not be so among you.
Rather, whoever wishes to be great among you will be your servant;
   whoever wishes to be first among you will be the slave of all.
For the Son of Man did not come to be served but to serve
   and to give his life as a ransom for many."**

The Gospel of the Lord.

350 THURSDAY OF THE EIGHTH WEEK IN ORDINARY TIME

FIRST READING   Year II

1 Peter 2:2-5, 9-12   *You are a chosen race, a royal priesthood, so that you may announce the praises of him who called you.*

A reading from the first Letter of Saint Peter

Beloved:
Like newborn infants, long for pure spiritual milk
   so that through it you may grow into salvation,
   for you have tasted that the Lord is good.
Come to him, a living stone, rejected by human beings
   but chosen and precious in the sight of God,
   and, like living stones,
   let yourselves be built into a spiritual house
   to be a holy priesthood to offer spiritual sacrifices
   acceptable to God through Jesus Christ.

You are *a chosen race, a royal priesthood,*
   a holy nation, a people of his own,
   so that you may announce the praises of him
   who called you out of darkness into his wonderful light.

Once you were *no people*
   but now you are God's people;
   you *had not received mercy*
   but now you have received mercy.

Beloved, I urge you as aliens and sojourners
   to keep away from worldly desires that wage war against the soul.
Maintain good conduct among the Gentiles,
   so that if they speak of you as evildoers,
   they may observe your good works
   and glorify God on the day of visitation.

The word of the Lord.

RESPONSORIAL PSALM

Psalm 100:2, 3, 4, 5

℟. (2c) **Come with joy into the presence of the Lord.**

Sing joyfully to the LORD**, all you lands;**
  serve the LORD **with gladness;**
  come before him with joyful song.

℟. **Come with joy into the presence of the Lord.**

Know that the LORD **is God;**
  he made us, his we are;
  his people, the flock he tends.

℟. **Come with joy into the presence of the Lord.**

Enter his gates with thanksgiving,
  his courts with praise;
Give thanks to him;
  bless his name.

℟. **Come with joy into the presence of the Lord.**

The LORD **is good:**
  his kindness endures forever,
  and his faithfulness, to all generations.

℟. **Come with joy into the presence of the Lord.**

ALLELUIA

John 8:12

℟. Alleluia, alleluia.

I am the light of the world, says the Lord;
whoever follows me will have the light of life.

℟. Alleluia, alleluia.

GOSPEL   Years I and II

Mark 10:46-52   Master, I want to see.

✠ A reading from the holy Gospel according to Mark

As Jesus was leaving Jericho with his disciples and a sizable crowd,
    Bartimaeus, a blind man, the son of Timaeus,
    sat by the roadside begging.
On hearing that it was Jesus of Nazareth,
    he began to cry out and say,
    "Jesus, son of David, have pity on me."
And many rebuked him, telling him to be silent.
But he kept calling out all the more, "Son of David, have pity on me."
Jesus stopped and said, "Call him."
So they called the blind man, saying to him,
    "Take courage; get up, Jesus is calling you."
He threw aside his cloak, sprang up, and came to Jesus.
Jesus said to him in reply, "What do you want me to do for you?"
The blind man replied to him, "Master, I want to see."
Jesus told him, "Go your way; your faith has saved you."
Immediately he received his sight
    and followed him on the way.

The Gospel of the Lord.

351 FRIDAY OF THE EIGHTH WEEK IN ORDINARY TIME

FIRST READING   Year II

1 Peter 4:7-13   Be good stewards of God's varied grace.

A reading from the first Letter of Saint Peter

Beloved:
The end of all things is at hand.
Therefore be serious and sober-minded
 so that you will be able to pray.
Above all, let your love for one another be intense,
 because love covers a multitude of sins.
Be hospitable to one another without complaining.
As each one has received a gift, use it to serve one another
 as good stewards of God's varied grace.
Whoever preaches, let it be with the words of God;
 whoever serves, let it be with the strength that God supplies,
 so that in all things God may be glorified through Jesus Christ,
 to whom belong glory and dominion forever and ever. Amen.

Beloved, do not be surprised that a trial by fire is occurring among you,
 as if something strange were happening to you.
But rejoice to the extent that you share in the sufferings of Christ,
 so that when his glory is revealed
 you may also rejoice exultantly.

The word of the Lord.

RESPONSORIAL PSALM

Psalm 96:10, 11-12, 13

℟. (13b) **The Lord comes to judge the earth.**

Say among the nations: The Lord is king.
He has made the world firm, not to be moved;
 he governs the peoples with equity.

℟. **The Lord comes to judge the earth.**

Let the heavens be glad and the earth rejoice;
>   let the sea and what fills it resound;
>   let the plains be joyful and all that is in them!
Then shall all the trees of the forest exult.

℟. The Lord comes to judge the earth.

Before the Lord, for he comes;
>   for he comes to rule the earth.
He shall rule the world with justice
>   and the peoples with his constancy.

℟. The Lord comes to judge the earth.

ALLELUIA

See John 15:16

℟. Alleluia, alleluia.

I chose you from the world,
to go and bear fruit that will last, says the Lord.

℟. Alleluia, alleluia.

GOSPEL   Years I and II

Mark 11:11-26   My house will be called a house of prayer for all peoples. Have faith in God.

✠ A reading from the holy Gospel according to Mark

Jesus entered Jerusalem and went into the temple area.
He looked around at everything and, since it was already late,
>   went out to Bethany with the Twelve.

The next day as they were leaving Bethany he was hungry.
Seeing from a distance a fig tree in leaf,
>   he went over to see if he could find anything on it.
When he reached it he found nothing but leaves;
>   it was not the time for figs.
And he said to it in reply, "May no one ever eat of your fruit again!"
And his disciples heard it.

They came to Jerusalem,
   and on entering the temple area
   he began to drive out those selling and buying there.
He overturned the tables of the money changers
   and the seats of those who were selling doves.
He did not permit anyone to carry anything through the temple area.
Then he taught them saying, "Is it not written:

> *My house shall be called a house of prayer for all peoples?*
>   *But you have made it a den of thieves."*

The chief priests and the scribes came to hear of it
   and were seeking a way to put him to death,
     yet they feared him
   because the whole crowd was astonished at his teaching.
When evening came, they went out of the city.

Early in the morning, as they were walking along,
   they saw the fig tree withered to its roots.
Peter remembered and said to him, "Rabbi, look!
The fig tree that you cursed has withered."
Jesus said to them in reply, "Have faith in God.
Amen, I say to you, whoever says to this mountain,
   'Be lifted up and thrown into the sea,'
     and does not doubt in his heart
     but believes that what he says will happen,
     it shall be done for him.
Therefore I tell you, all that you ask for in prayer,
   believe that you will receive it and it shall be yours.
When you stand to pray,
   forgive anyone against whom you have a grievance,
   so that your heavenly Father may in turn
   forgive you your transgressions."

The Gospel of the Lord.

352 SATURDAY OF THE EIGHTH WEEK IN ORDINARY TIME

FIRST READING   Year II

Jude 17, 20b-25   To the one who is able to keep you from stumbling and to present you unblemished and exultant in the presence of his glory.

A reading from the Letter of Saint Jude

**Beloved, remember the words spoken beforehand
   by the Apostles of our Lord Jesus Christ.
Build yourselves up in your most holy faith; pray in the Holy Spirit.
Keep yourselves in the love of God
   and wait for the mercy of our Lord Jesus Christ
   that leads to eternal life.
On those who waver, have mercy;
   save others by snatching them out of the fire;
   on others have mercy with fear,
   abhorring even the outer garment stained by the flesh.**

**To the one who is able to keep you from stumbling
   and to present you unblemished and exultant,
   in the presence of his glory,
   to the only God, our savior,
   through Jesus Christ our Lord
   be glory, majesty, power, and authority
   from ages past, now, and for ages to come. Amen.**

The word of the Lord.

RESPONSORIAL PSALM

Psalm 63:2, 3-4, 5-6

℟. (2b) **My soul is thirsting for you, O Lord my God.**

**O God, you are my God whom I seek;
 for you my flesh pines and my soul thirsts
  like the earth, parched, lifeless and without water.**

℟. **My soul is thirsting for you, O Lord my God.**

**Thus have I gazed toward you in the sanctuary
 to see your power and your glory,
For your kindness is a greater good than life;
 my lips shall glorify you.**

℟. **My soul is thirsting for you, O Lord my God.**

**Thus will I bless you while I live;
 lifting up my hands, I will call upon your name.
As with the riches of a banquet shall my soul be satisfied,
 and with exultant lips my mouth shall praise you.**

℟. **My soul is thirsting for you, O Lord my God.**

ALLELUIA

See Colossians 3:16a, 17c

℟. Alleluia, alleluia.

Let the word of Christ dwell in you richly;
giving thanks to God the Father through him.

℟. Alleluia, alleluia.

GOSPEL   Years I and II

Mark 11:27-33   By what authority are you doing these things?

☩ A reading from the holy Gospel according to Mark

Jesus and his disciples returned once more to Jerusalem.
As he was walking in the temple area,
   the chief priests, the scribes, and the elders
   approached him and said to him,
     "By what authority are you doing these things?
Or who gave you this authority to do them?"
Jesus said to them, "I shall ask you one question.
Answer me, and I will tell you by what authority I do these things.
Was John's baptism of heavenly or of human origin? Answer me."
They discussed this among themselves and said,
   "If we say, 'Of heavenly origin,' he will say,
   'Then why did you not believe him?'
But shall we say, 'Of human origin'?"–
   they feared the crowd,
   for they all thought John really was a prophet.
So they said to Jesus in reply, "We do not know."
Then Jesus said to them,
   "Neither shall I tell you by what authority I do these things."

The Gospel of the Lord.

353 MONDAY OF THE NINTH WEEK IN ORDINARY TIME

FIRST READING   Year II

2 Peter 1:2-7   God has bestowed on us the precious and very great promises, so that through them you may come to share in the divine nature.

A reading from the second Letter of Saint Peter

Beloved:
May grace and peace be yours in abundance
through knowledge of God and of Jesus our Lord.

His divine power has bestowed on us
   everything that makes for life and devotion,
   through the knowledge of him
   who called us by his own glory and power.
Through these, he has bestowed on us
   the precious and very great promises,
   so that through them you may come to share in the divine nature,
   after escaping from the corruption that is in the world
   because of evil desire.
For this very reason,
   make every effort to supplement your faith with virtue,
   virtue with knowledge, knowledge with self-control,
   self-control with endurance, endurance with devotion,
   devotion with mutual affection, mutual affection with love.

The word of the Lord.

RESPONSIAL PSALM

Psalm 91:1-2, 14-15b, 15c-16

℟. (see 2b) **In you, my God, I place my trust.**

**You who dwell in the shelter of the Most High,
 who abide in the shadow of the Almighty,
Say to the L**ORD**, "My refuge and my fortress,
 my God, in whom I trust."**

℟. **In you, my God, I place my trust.**

**Because he clings to me, I will deliver him;
 I will set him on high because he acknowledges my name.
He shall call upon me, and I will answer him;
 I will be with him in distress.**

℟. **In you, my God, I place my trust.**

**I will deliver him and glorify him;
 with length of days I will gratify him
 and will show him my salvation.**

℟. **In you, my God, I place my trust.**

ALLELUIA

See Revelation 1:5ab

℟. **Alleluia, alleluia.**

**Jesus Christ, you are the faithful witness,
the firstborn of the dead;
you have loved us and freed us from our sins by your Blood.**

℟. **Alleluia, alleluia.**

GOSPEL Years I and II

Mark 12:1-12   They seized the beloved son, killed him, and threw him out of the vineyard.

✠ A reading from the holy Gospel according to Mark

Jesus began to speak to the chief priests, the scribes,
   and the elders in parables.
"A man planted a vineyard, put a hedge around it,
   dug a wine press, and built a tower.
Then he leased it to tenant farmers and left on a journey.
At the proper time he sent a servant to the tenants
   to obtain from them some of the produce of the vineyard.
But they seized him, beat him,
   and sent him away empty-handed.
Again he sent them another servant.
And that one they beat over the head and treated shamefully.
He sent yet another whom they killed.
So, too, many others; some they beat, others they killed.
He had one other to send, a beloved son.
He sent him to them last of all, thinking, 'They will respect my son.'
But those tenants said to one another, 'This is the heir.
Come, let us kill him, and the inheritance will be ours.'
So they seized him and killed him,
   and threw him out of the vineyard.
What then will the owner of the vineyard do?
He will come, put the tenants to death,
   and give the vineyard to others.
Have you not read this Scripture passage:**

   The stone that the builders rejected
      has become the cornerstone;
   by the Lord has this been done,
      and it is wonderful in our eyes?"

**They were seeking to arrest him, but they feared the crowd,
   for they realized that he had addressed the parable to them.
So they left him and went away.**

The Gospel of the Lord.

354 TUESDAY OF THE NINTH WEEK IN ORDINARY TIME

FIRST READING   Year II

2 Peter 3:12-15a, 17-18   We await new heavens and a new earth.

A reading from the second Letter of Saint Peter

Beloved:
Wait for and hasten the coming of the day of God,
 because of which the heavens will be dissolved in flames
 and the elements melted by fire.
But according to his promise
 we await new heavens and a new earth
 in which righteousness dwells.

Therefore, beloved, since you await these things,
 be eager to be found without spot or blemish before him, at peace.
And consider the patience of our Lord as salvation.

Therefore, beloved, since you are forewarned,
 be on your guard not to be led into the error of the unprincipled
 and to fall from your own stability.
But grow in grace
 and in the knowledge of our Lord and savior Jesus Christ.
To him be glory now and to the day of eternity. Amen.

The word of the Lord.

RESPONSORIAL PSALM

Psalm 90:2, 3-4, 10, 14 and 16

℟. (1) **In every age, O Lord, you have been our refuge.**

**Before the mountains were begotten
and the earth and the world were brought forth,
from everlasting to everlasting you are God.**

℟. **In every age, O Lord, you have been our refuge.**

**You turn man back to dust,
saying, "Return, O children of men."
For a thousand years in your sight
are as yesterday, now that it is past,
or as a watch of the night.**

℟. **In every age, O Lord, you have been our refuge.**

**Seventy is the sum of our years,
or eighty, if we are strong,
And most of them are fruitless toil,
for they pass quickly and we drift away.**

℟. **In every age, O Lord, you have been our refuge.**

**Fill us at daybreak with your kindness,
that we may shout for joy and gladness all our days.
Let your work be seen by your servants
and your glory by their children.**

℟. **In every age, O Lord, you have been our refuge.**

ALLELUIA

See Ephesians 1:17-18

℟. **Alleluia, alleluia.**

**May the Father of our Lord Jesus Christ
enlighten the eyes of our hearts,
that we may know what is the hope
that belongs to his call.**

℟. **Alleluia, alleluia.**

GOSPEL   Years I and II

Mark 12:13-17   Repay to Caesar what belongs to Caesar and to God what belongs to God.

☩ A reading from the holy Gospel according to Mark

Some Pharisees and Herodians were sent
  to Jesus to ensnare him in his speech.
They came and said to him,
  "Teacher, we know that you are a truthful man
  and that you are not concerned with anyone's opinion.
You do not regard a person's status
  but teach the way of God in accordance with the truth.
Is it lawful to pay the census tax to Caesar or not?
Should we pay or should we not pay?"
Knowing their hypocrisy he said to them,
  "Why are you testing me?
Bring me a denarius to look at."
They brought one to him and he said to them,
  "Whose image and inscription is this?"
They replied to him, "Caesar's."
So Jesus said to them,
  "Repay to Caesar what belongs to Caesar
  and to God what belongs to God."
They were utterly amazed at him.

The Gospel of the Lord.

355 WEDNESDAY OF THE NINTH WEEK IN ORDINARY TIME

FIRST READING   Year II

2 Timothy 1:1-3, 6-12   Stir into flame the gift of God that you have through the laying on of my hands.

A reading from the beginning of the second Letter of Saint Paul to Timothy

Paul, an Apostle of Christ Jesus by the will of God
   for the promise of life in Christ Jesus,
   to Timothy, my dear child:
   grace, mercy, and peace from God the Father
   and Christ Jesus our Lord.

I am grateful to God,
   whom I worship with a clear conscience as my ancestors did,
   as I remember you constantly in my prayers, night and day.

For this reason, I remind you to stir into flame
   the gift of God that you have through the imposition of my hands.
For God did not give us a spirit of cowardice
   but rather of power and love and self-control.
So do not be ashamed of your testimony to our Lord,
   nor of me, a prisoner for his sake;
   but bear your share of hardship for the Gospel
with the strength that comes from God.

He saved us and called us to a holy life,
   not according to our works
   but according to his own design
   and the grace bestowed on us in Christ Jesus before time began,
   but now made manifest
   through the appearance of our savior Christ Jesus,
   who destroyed death and brought life and immortality
   to light through the Gospel,
   for which I was appointed preacher and Apostle and teacher.
On this account I am suffering these things;
   but I am not ashamed,
   for I know him in whom I have believed
   and am confident that he is able to guard
   what has been entrusted to me until that day.

The word of the Lord.

RESPONSORIAL PSALM

Psalm 123:1b-2ab, 2cdef

℟. (1b) **To you, O Lord, I lift up my eyes.**

**To you I lift up my eyes
who are enthroned in heaven.
Behold, as the eyes of servants
are on the hands of their masters.**

℟. **To you, O Lord, I lift up my eyes.**

**As the eyes of a maid
are on the hands of her mistress,
So are our eyes on the L**ORD**, our God,
till he have pity on us.**

℟. **To you, O Lord, I lift up my eyes.**

ALLELUIA

John 11:25a, 26

℟. **Alleluia, alleluia.**

**I am the resurrection and the life, says the Lord;
whoever believes in me will never die.**

℟. **Alleluia, alleluia.**

GOSPEL Years I and II

Mark 12:18-27 He is not God of the dead but of the living.

✢ **A reading from the holy Gospel according to Mark**

Some Sadducees, who say there is no resurrection,
   came to Jesus and put this question to him, saying,
   "Teacher, Moses wrote for us,
   If someone's brother dies, leaving a wife but no child,
   his brother must take the wife
   and raise up descendants for his brother.
Now there were seven brothers.
The first married a woman and died, leaving no descendants.
So the second brother married her and died, leaving no descendants,
   and the third likewise.
And the seven left no descendants.
Last of all the woman also died.
At the resurrection when they arise whose wife will she be?
For all seven had been married to her."
Jesus said to them, "Are you not misled
   because you do not know the Scriptures or the power of God?
When they rise from the dead,
   they neither marry nor are given in marriage,
   but they are like the angels in heaven.
As for the dead being raised,
   have you not read in the Book of Moses,
in the passage about the bush, how God told him,
   I am the God of Abraham, the God of Isaac,
   and the God of Jacob?
He is not God of the dead but of the living.
You are greatly misled."

The Gospel of the Lord.

356 THURSDAY OF THE NINTH WEEK IN ORDINARY TIME

FIRST READING   Year II

2 Timothy 2:8-15   The word of God is not chained. If we have died with Christ, we shall also live with him.

A reading from the second Letter of Saint Paul to Timothy

Beloved:
Remember Jesus Christ, raised from the dead, a descendant of David:
   such is my Gospel, for which I am suffering,
   even to the point of chains, like a criminal.
But the word of God is not chained.
Therefore, I bear with everything for the sake of those who are chosen,
   so that they too may obtain the salvation that is in Christ Jesus,
   together with eternal glory.
This saying is trustworthy:

>If we have died with him
>   we shall also live with him;
>if we persevere
>   we shall also reign with him.
>But if we deny him
>   he will deny us.
>If we are unfaithful
>   he remains faithful,
>   for he cannot deny himself.

Remind people of these things
   and charge them before God to stop disputing about words.
This serves no useful purpose since it harms those who listen.
Be eager to present yourself as acceptable to God,
   a workman who causes no disgrace,
imparting the word of truth without deviation.

The word of the Lord.

RESPONSORIAL PSALM

Psalm 25:4-5ab, 8-9, 10 and 14

℟. (4) **Teach me your ways, O Lord.**

**Your ways, O Lord, make known to me;
  teach me your paths,
Guide me in your truth and teach me,
  for you are God my savior.**

℟. **Teach me your ways, O Lord.**

**Good and upright is the Lord;
  thus he shows sinners the way.
He guides the humble to justice,
  he teaches the humble his way.**

℟. **Teach me your ways, O Lord.**

**All the paths of the Lord are kindness and constancy
  toward those who keep his covenant and his decrees.
The friendship of the Lord is with those who fear him,
  and his covenant, for their instruction.**

℟. **Teach me your ways, O Lord.**

ALLELUIA

See 2 Timothy 1:10

℟. **Alleluia, alleluia.**

**Our Savior Jesus Christ has destroyed death
and brought life to light through the Gospel.**

℟. **Alleluia, alleluia.**

GOSPEL Years I and II

Mark 12:28-34   There is no commandment greater than these.

☩ **A reading from the holy Gospel according to Mark**

One of the scribes came to Jesus and asked him,
  "Which is the first of all the commandments?"
Jesus replied, "The first is this:
  Hear, O Israel!
  The Lord our God is Lord alone!
  You shall love the Lord your God with all your heart,
  with all your soul, with all your mind,
  and with all your strength.
  The second is this:
  You shall love your neighbor as yourself.
There is no other commandment greater than these."
The scribe said to him, "Well said, teacher.
You are right in saying,
  He is One and there is no other than he.
And *to love him with all your heart,*
  with all your understanding,
  with all your strength,
  and to love your neighbor as yourself
  is worth more than all burnt offerings and sacrifices."
And when Jesus saw that he answered with understanding,
  he said to him, "You are not far from the Kingdom of God."
And no one dared to ask him any more questions.

The Gospel of the Lord.

357 FRIDAY OF THE NINTH WEEK IN ORDINARY TIME

FIRST READING   Year II

2 Timothy 3:10-17   All who want to live religiously in Christ Jesus will be persecuted.

A reading from the second Letter of Saint Paul to Timothy

**You have followed my teaching, way of life,
 purpose, faith, patience, love, endurance, persecutions,
 and sufferings, such as happened to me
 in Antioch, Iconium, and Lystra,
 persecutions that I endured.
Yet from all these things the Lord delivered me.
In fact, all who want to live religiously in Christ Jesus
 will be persecuted.
But wicked people and charlatans will go from bad to worse,
 deceivers and deceived.
But you, remain faithful to what you have learned and believed,
 because you know from whom you learned it,
 and that from infancy you have known the sacred Scriptures,
 which are capable of giving you wisdom for salvation
 through faith in Christ Jesus.
All Scripture is inspired by God and is useful for teaching,
 for refutation, for correction,
 and for training in righteousness,
 so that one who belongs to God may be competent,
 equipped for every good work.**

The word of the Lord.

RESPONSORIAL PSALM

Psalm 119:157, 160, 161, 165, 166, 168

℟. (165a) **O Lord, great peace have they who love your law.**

**Though my persecutors and my foes are many,
   I turn not away from your decrees.**

℟. **O Lord, great peace have they who love your law.**

**Permanence is your word's chief trait;
   each of your just ordinances is everlasting.**

℟. **O Lord, great peace have they who love your law.**

**Princes persecute me without cause
   but my heart stands in awe of your word.**

℟. **O Lord, great peace have they who love your law.**

**Those who love your law have great peace,
   and for them there is no stumbling block.**

℟. **O Lord, great peace have they who love your law.**

**I wait for your salvation, O Lord,
   and your commands I fulfill.**

℟. **O Lord, great peace have they who love your law.**

**I keep your precepts and your decrees,
   for all my ways are before you.**

℟. **O Lord, great peace have they who love your law.**

ALLELUIA

John 14:23

℟. Alleluia, alleluia.

Whoever loves me will keep my word,
and my Father will love him
and we will come to him.

℟. Alleluia, alleluia.

GOSPEL   Years I and II

Mark 12:35-37   How do the scribes claim that the Christ is the son of David?

✠ A reading from the holy Gospel according to Mark

As Jesus was teaching in the temple area he said,
    "How do the scribes claim that the Christ is the son of David?
David himself, inspired by the Holy Spirit, said:
    The Lord said to my lord,
    'Sit at my right hand
    until I place your enemies under your feet.'
David himself calls him 'lord';
    so how is he his son?"
The great crowd heard this with delight.

The Gospel of the Lord.

358 SATURDAY OF THE NINTH WEEK IN ORDINARY TIME

FIRST READING   Year II

2 Timothy 4:1-8   *I am already being poured out and the crown of righteousness awaits me which the Lord will award to me.*

A reading from the second Letter of Saint Paul to Timothy

Beloved:
I charge you in the presence of God and of Christ Jesus,
 who will judge the living and the dead,
 and by his appearing and his kingly power:
 proclaim the word;
 be persistent whether it is convenient or inconvenient;
 convince, reprimand, encourage through all patience and teaching.
For the time will come when people will not tolerate sound doctrine
 but, following their own desires and insatiable curiosity,
 will accumulate teachers and will stop listening to the truth
 and will be diverted to myths.
But you, be self-possessed in all circumstances;
 put up with hardship;
 perform the work of an evangelist;
 fulfill your ministry.

For I am already being poured out like a libation,
 and the time of my departure is at hand.
I have competed well;
 I have finished the race; I have kept the faith.
From now on the crown of righteousness awaits me,
 which the Lord, the just judge,
 will award to me on that day, and not only to me,
 but to all who have longed for his appearance.

The word of the Lord.

RESPONSORIAL PSALM

Psalm 71:8-9, 14-15ab, 16-17, 22

℟. (see 15ab) **I will sing of your salvation.**

**My mouth shall be filled with your praise,
   with your glory day by day.
Cast me not off in my old age;
   as my strength fails, forsake me not.**

℟. **I will sing of your salvation.**

**But I will always hope
   and praise you ever more and more.
My mouth shall declare your justice,
   day by day your salvation.**

℟. **I will sing of your salvation.**

**I will treat of the mighty works of the Lord;
   O God, I will tell of your singular justice.
O God, you have taught me from my youth,
   and till the present I proclaim your wondrous deeds.**

℟. **I will sing of your salvation.**

**So will I give you thanks with music on the lyre,
   for your faithfulness, O my God!
I will sing your praises with the harp,
   O Holy One of Israel!**

℟. **I will sing of your salvation.**

ALLELUIA

Matthew 5:3

℟. Alleluia, alleluia.

Blessed are the poor in spirit;
for theirs is the Kingdom of heaven.

℟. Alleluia, alleluia.

GOSPEL Years I and II

Mark 12:38-44   This poor widow has given more than all others.

✝ A reading from the holy Gospel according to Mark

In the course of his teaching Jesus said,
 "Beware of the scribes, who like to go around in long robes
   and accept greetings in the marketplaces,
   seats of honor in synagogues,
   and places of honor at banquets.
They devour the houses of widows and, as a pretext,
   recite lengthy prayers.
They will receive a very severe condemnation."

He sat down opposite the treasury
   and observed how the crowd put money into the treasury.
Many rich people put in large sums.
A poor widow also came and put in two small coins worth a few cents.
Calling his disciples to himself, he said to them,
 "Amen, I say to you, this poor widow put in more
   than all the other contributors to the treasury.
For they have all contributed from their surplus wealth,
   but she, from her poverty, has contributed all she had,
   her whole livelihood."

The Gospel of the Lord.

359 MONDAY OF THE TENTH WEEK IN ORDINARY TIME

FIRST READING Year II

1 Kings 17:1-6   Elijah stands before the LORD God of Israel.

A reading from the first Book of Kings

Elijah the Tishbite, from Tishbe in Gilead, said to Ahab:
    "As the LORD, the God of Israel, lives, whom I serve,
    during these years there shall be no dew or rain except at my word."
The LORD then said to Elijah:
    "Leave here, go east
    and hide in the Wadi Cherith, east of the Jordan.
You shall drink of the stream,
    and I have commanded ravens to feed you there."
So he left and did as the LORD had commanded.
He went and remained by the Wadi Cherith, east of the Jordan.
Ravens brought him bread and meat in the morning,
    and bread and meat in the evening,
    and he drank from the stream.

The word of the Lord.

RESPONSORIAL PSALM

Psalm 121:1bc-2, 3-4, 5-6, 7-8

℟. (see 2) **Our help is from the Lord, who made heaven and earth.**

**I lift up my eyes toward the mountains;
 whence shall help come to me?
My help is from the Lord,
 who made heaven and earth.**

℟. **Our help is from the Lord, who made heaven and earth.**

**May he not suffer your foot to slip;
 may he slumber not who guards you:
Indeed he neither slumbers nor sleeps,
 the guardian of Israel.**

℟. **Our help is from the Lord, who made heaven and earth.**

**The Lord is your guardian; the Lord is your shade;
 he is beside you at your right hand.
The sun shall not harm you by day,
 nor the moon by night.**

℟. **Our help is from the Lord, who made heaven and earth.**

**The Lord will guard you from all evil;
 he will guard your life.
The Lord will guard your coming and your going,
 both now and forever.**

℟. **Our help is from the Lord, who made heaven and earth.**

ALLELUIA

Matthew 5:12a

℟. **Alleluia, alleluia.**

**Rejoice and be glad;
for your reward will be great in heaven.**

℟. **Alleluia, alleluia.**

GOSPEL — Years I and II

Matthew 5:1-12   Blessed are the poor in spirit.

✠ **A reading from the holy Gospel according to Matthew**

**When Jesus saw the crowds, he went up the mountain,
 and after he had sat down, his disciples came to him.
He began to teach them, saying:**

> "Blessed are the poor in spirit,
>   for theirs is the Kingdom of heaven.
> Blessed are they who mourn,
>   for they will be comforted.
> Blessed are the meek,
>   for they will inherit the land.
> Blessed are they who hunger and thirst for righteousness,
>   for they will be satisfied.
> Blessed are the merciful,
>   for they will be shown mercy.
> Blessed are the clean of heart,
>   for they will see God.
> Blessed are the peacemakers,
>   for they will be called children of God.
> Blessed are they who are persecuted for the sake of righteousness,
>   for theirs is the Kingdom of heaven.

**Blessed are you when they insult you and persecute you
  and utter every kind of evil against you falsely because of me.
Rejoice and be glad,
  for your reward will be great in heaven.
Thus they persecuted the prophets who were before you."**

The Gospel of the Lord.

360 TUESDAY OF THE TENTH WEEK IN ORDINARY TIME

FIRST READING   Year II

1 Kings 17:7-16   The jar of flour shall not go empty, as the Lord had foretold through Elijah.

A reading from the first Book of Kings

**The brook near where Elijah was hiding ran dry,
 because no rain had fallen in the land.
So the Lord said to Elijah:
 "Move on to Zarephath of Sidon and stay there.
I have designated a widow there to provide for you."
He left and went to Zarephath.
As he arrived at the entrance of the city,
 a widow was gathering sticks there; he called out to her,
 "Please bring me a small cupful of water to drink."
She left to get it, and he called out after her,
 "Please bring along a bit of bread."
She answered, "As the Lord, your God, lives,
 I have nothing baked;
 there is only a handful of flour in my jar
 and a little oil in my jug.
Just now I was collecting a couple of sticks,
 to go in and prepare something for myself and my son;
 when we have eaten it, we shall die."
Elijah said to her, "Do not be afraid.
Go and do as you propose.
But first make me a little cake and bring it to me.
Then you can prepare something for yourself and your son.
For the Lord, the God of Israel, says,
 'The jar of flour shall not go empty,
 nor the jug of oil run dry,
 until the day when the Lord sends rain upon the earth.'"
She left and did as Elijah had said.
She was able to eat for a year, and Elijah and her son as well;
 the jar of flour did not go empty,
 nor the jug of oil run dry,
 as the Lord had foretold through Elijah.**

The word of the Lord.

RESPONSORIAL PSALM

Psalm 4:2-3, 4-5, 7b-8

℟. (7a) **Lord, let your face shine on us.**

**When I call, answer me, O my just God,
    you who relieve me when I am in distress;
    Have pity on me, and hear my prayer!
Men of rank, how long will you be dull of heart?
    Why do you love what is vain and seek after falsehood?**

℟. **Lord, let your face shine on us.**

Know that the LORD **does wonders for his faithful one;
    the L**ORD **will hear me when I call upon him.
Tremble, and sin not;
    reflect, upon your beds, in silence.**

℟. **Lord, let your face shine on us.**

O LORD**, let the light of your countenance shine upon us!
You put gladness into my heart,
    more than when grain and wine abound.**

℟. **Lord, let your face shine on us.**

ALLELUIA

Matthew 5:16

℟. Alleluia, alleluia.

**Let your light shine before others
that they may see your good deeds and glorify your heavenly Father.**

℟. Alleluia, alleluia.

GOSPEL   Years I and II

Matthew 5:13-16   You are the light of the world.

✝ **A reading from the holy Gospel according to Matthew**

**Jesus said to his disciples:
"You are the salt of the earth.
But if salt loses its taste, with what can it be seasoned?
It is no longer good for anything
   but to be thrown out and trampled underfoot.
You are the light of the world.
A city set on a mountain cannot be hidden.
Nor do they light a lamp and then put it under a bushel basket;
   it is set on a lampstand,
      where it gives light to all in the house.
Just so, your light must shine before others,
   that they may see your good deeds
   and glorify your heavenly Father."**

The Gospel of the Lord.

361 WEDNESDAY OF THE TENTH WEEK IN ORDINARY TIME

FIRST READING   Year II

1 Kings 18:20-39   Let it be known this day that you, Lord, are God.

A reading from the first Book of Kings

**Ahab sent to all the children of Israel
   and had the prophets assemble on Mount Carmel.**

**Elijah appealed to all the people and said,
   "How long will you straddle the issue?
If the Lord is God, follow him; if Baal, follow him."
The people, however, did not answer him.
So Elijah said to the people,
   "I am the only surviving prophet of the Lord,
   and there are four hundred and fifty prophets of Baal.
Give us two young bulls.
Let them choose one, cut it into pieces, and place it on the wood,
   but start no fire.
I shall prepare the other and place it on the wood,
   but shall start no fire.
You shall call on your gods, and I will call on the Lord.
The God who answers with fire is God."
All the people answered, "Agreed!"**

**Elijah then said to the prophets of Baal,
   "Choose one young bull and prepare it first,
   for there are more of you.
Call upon your gods, but do not start the fire."
Taking the young bull that was turned over to them, they prepared it
   and called on Baal from morning to noon, saying,
   "Answer us, Baal!"
But there was no sound, and no one answering.
And they hopped around the altar they had prepared.
When it was noon, Elijah taunted them:
   "Call louder, for he is a god and may be meditating,
   or may have retired, or may be on a journey.
Perhaps he is asleep and must be awakened."**

They called out louder and slashed themselves with swords and spears,
  as was their custom, until blood gushed over them.
Noon passed and they remained in a prophetic state
  until the time for offering sacrifice.
But there was not a sound;
  no one answered, and no one was listening.

Then Elijah said to all the people, "Come here to me."
When the people had done so, he repaired the altar of the LORD
  that had been destroyed.
He took twelve stones, for the number of tribes of the sons of Jacob,
  to whom the LORD had said, "Your name shall be Israel."
He built an altar in honor of the LORD with the stones,
  and made a trench around the altar
  large enough for two measures of grain.
When he had arranged the wood,
  he cut up the young bull and laid it on the wood.
"Fill four jars with water," he said,
  "and pour it over the burnt offering and over the wood."
"Do it again," he said, and they did it again.
"Do it a third time," he said,
  and they did it a third time.
The water flowed around the altar,
  and the trench was filled with the water.

At the time for offering sacrifice,
  the prophet Elijah came forward and said,
"LORD, God of Abraham, Isaac, and Israel,
  let it be known this day that you are God in Israel
  and that I am your servant
  and have done all these things by your command.
Answer me, LORD!
Answer me, that this people may know that you, LORD, are God
  and that you have brought them back to their senses."
The LORD's fire came down
  and consumed the burnt offering, wood, stones, and dust,
  and it lapped up the water in the trench.
Seeing this, all the people fell prostrate and said,
  "The LORD is God! The LORD is God!"

The word of the Lord.

RESPONSORIAL PSALM

Psalm 16:1b-2ab, 4, 5ab and 8, 11

℟. (1b) **Keep me safe, O God; you are my hope.**

**Keep me, O God, for in you I take refuge;
   I say to the Lord, "My Lord are you."**

℟. **Keep me safe, O God; you are my hope.**

**They multiply their sorrows
   who court other gods.
Blood libations to them I will not pour out,
   nor will I take their names upon my lips.**

℟. **Keep me safe, O God; you are my hope.**

**O Lord, my allotted portion and cup,
   you it is who hold fast my lot.
I set the Lord ever before me;
   with him at my right hand I shall not be disturbed.**

℟. **Keep me safe, O God; you are my hope.**

**You will show me the path to life,
   fullness of joys in your presence,
   the delights at your right hand forever.**

℟. **Keep me safe, O God; you are my hope.**

ALLELUIA

Psalm 25:4b, 5a

℟. Alleluia, alleluia.

Teach me your paths, my God,
and guide me in your truth.

℟. Alleluia, alleluia.

GOSPEL Years I and II

Matthew 5:17-19   I have come not to abolish the law, but to fulfill it.

✠ A reading from the holy Gospel according to Matthew

**Jesus said to his disciples:
"Do not think that I have come to abolish the law or the prophets.
I have come not to abolish but to fulfill.
Amen, I say to you, until heaven and earth pass away,
   not the smallest letter or the smallest part of a letter
   will pass from the law,
   until all things have taken place.
Therefore, whoever breaks one of the least of these commandments
   and teaches others to do so
   will be called least in the Kingdom of heaven.
But whoever obeys and teaches these commandments
   will be called greatest in the Kingdom of heaven."**

The Gospel of the Lord.

362 THURSDAY OF THE TENTH WEEK IN ORDINARY TIME

FIRST READING   Year II

1 Kings 18:41-46   Elijah prayed and the sky gave rain (James 5:18).

A reading from the first Book of Kings

Elijah said to Ahab, "Go up, eat and drink,
  for there is the sound of a heavy rain."
So Ahab went up to eat and drink,
  while Elijah climbed to the top of Carmel,
  crouched down to the earth,
  and put his head between his knees.
"Climb up and look out to sea," he directed his servant,
  who went up and looked, but reported, "There is nothing."
Seven times he said, "Go, look again!"
And the seventh time the youth reported,
  "There is a cloud as small as a man's hand rising from the sea."
Elijah said, "Go and say to Ahab,
  'Harness up and leave the mountain before the rain stops you.'"
In a trice the sky grew dark with clouds and wind,
  and a heavy rain fell.
Ahab mounted his chariot and made for Jezreel.
But the hand of the Lord was on Elijah,
  who girded up his clothing and ran before Ahab
  as far as the approaches to Jezreel.

The word of the Lord.

RESPONSORIAL PSALM

Psalm 65:10, 11, 12-13

℟. (2a) **It is right to praise you in Zion, O God.**

You have visited the land and watered it;
   greatly have you enriched it.
God's watercourses are filled;
   you have prepared the grain.

℟. **It is right to praise you in Zion, O God.**

Thus have you prepared the land:
   drenching its furrows, breaking up its clods,
Softening it with showers,
   blessing its yield.

℟. **It is right to praise you in Zion, O God.**

You have crowned the year with your bounty,
   and your paths overflow with a rich harvest;
The untilled meadows overflow with it,
   and rejoicing clothes the hills.

℟. **It is right to praise you in Zion, O God.**

ALLELUIA

John 13:34

℟. Alleluia, alleluia.

I give you a new commandment:
love one another as I have loved you.

℟. Alleluia, alleluia.

GOSPEL   Years I and II

Matthew 5:20-26   Whoever is angry with his brother will be liable to judgment.

✠ A reading from the holy Gospel according to Matthew

Jesus said to his disciples:
 "I tell you, unless your righteousness surpasses that
 of the scribes and Pharisees,
 you will not enter into the Kingdom of heaven.

"You have heard that it was said to your ancestors,
 You shall not kill; and whoever kills will be liable to judgment.
But I say to you, whoever is angry with his brother
 will be liable to judgment,
 and whoever says to his brother,
 'Raqa,' will be answerable to the Sanhedrin,
 and whoever says, 'You fool,' will be liable to fiery Gehenna.
Therefore, if you bring your gift to the altar,
 and there recall that your brother
 has anything against you,
 leave your gift there at the altar,
 go first and be reconciled with your brother,
 and then come and offer your gift.
Settle with your opponent quickly while on the way to court with him.
Otherwise your opponent will hand you over to the judge,
 and the judge will hand you over to the guard,
 and you will be thrown into prison.
Amen, I say to you,
 you will not be released until you have paid the last penny."

The Gospel of the Lord.

363 FRIDAY OF THE TENTH WEEK IN ORDINARY TIME

FIRST READING   Year II

1 Kings 19:9a, 11-16   Stand on the mountain before the Lord.

A reading from the first Book of Kings

At the mountain of God, Horeb,
  Elijah came to a cave, where he took shelter.
But the word of the Lord came to him,
  "Go outside and stand on the mountain before the Lord;
  the Lord will be passing by."
A strong and heavy wind was rending the mountains
  and crushing rocks before the Lord—
  but the Lord was not in the wind.
After the wind there was an earthquake—
  but the Lord was not in the earthquake.
After the earthquake there was fire—
  but the Lord was not in the fire.
After the fire there was a tiny whispering sound.
When he heard this,
  Elijah hid his face in his cloak
  and went and stood at the entrance of the cave.
A voice said to him, "Elijah, why are you here?"
He replied, "I have been most zealous for the Lord,
  the God of hosts.
But the children of Israel have forsaken your covenant,
  torn down your altars,
  and put your prophets to the sword.
I alone am left, and they seek to take my life."
The Lord said to him,
  "Go, take the road back to the desert near Damascus.
When you arrive, you shall anoint Hazael as king of Aram.
Then you shall anoint Jehu, son of Nimshi, as king of Israel,
  and Elisha, son of Shaphat of Abel-meholah,
  as prophet to succeed you."

The word of the Lord.

RESPONSORIAL PSALM

Psalm 27:7-8a, 8b-9abc, 13-14

℟. (8b) **I long to see your face, O Lord.**

**Hear, O LORD, the sound of my call;
    have pity on me, and answer me.
Of you my heart speaks; you my glance seeks.**

℟. **I long to see your face, O Lord.**

**Your presence, O LORD, I seek.
Hide not your face from me;
    do not in anger repel your servant.
You are my helper: cast me not off.**

℟. **I long to see your face, O Lord.**

**I believe that I shall see the bounty of the LORD
    in the land of the living.
Wait for the LORD with courage;
    be stouthearted, and wait for the LORD.**

℟. **I long to see your face, O Lord.**

ALLELUIA

Philippians 2:15d, 16a

℟. **Alleluia, alleluia.**

**Shine like lights on the world,
as you hold on to the word of life.**

℟. **Alleluia, alleluia.**

GOSPEL Years I and II

Matthew 5:27-32 Everyone who looks at a woman with lust has already committed adultery with her in his heart.

✠ **A reading from the holy Gospel according to Matthew**

Jesus said to his disciples:
"You have heard that it was said, *You shall not commit adultery.*
But I say to you,
   everyone who looks at a woman with lust
   has already committed adultery with her in his heart.
If your right eye causes you to sin,
   tear it out and throw it away.
It is better for you to lose one of your members
   than to have your whole body thrown into Gehenna.
And if your right hand causes you to sin,
   cut it off and throw it away.
It is better for you to lose one of your members
   than to have your whole body go into Gehenna.

"It was also said,
   Whoever divorces his wife must give her a bill of divorce.
But I say to you,
   whoever divorces his wife (unless the marriage is unlawful)
   causes her to commit adultery,
   and whoever marries a divorced woman commits adultery."

The Gospel of the Lord.

364 SATURDAY OF THE TENTH WEEK IN ORDINARY TIME

FIRST READING   Year II

1 Kings 19:19-21   Then Elisha left and followed Elijah.

A reading from the first Book of Kings

Elijah set out, and came upon Elisha, son of Shaphat,
    as he was plowing with twelve yoke of oxen;
    he was following the twelfth.
Elijah went over to him and threw his cloak over him.
Elisha left the oxen, ran after Elijah, and said,
    "Please, let me kiss my father and mother goodbye,
    and I will follow you."
Elijah answered, "Go back!
Have I done anything to you?"
Elisha left him and, taking the yoke of oxen, slaughtered them;
    he used the plowing equipment for fuel to boil their flesh,
    and gave it to his people to eat.
Then he left and followed Elijah as his attendant.

The word of the Lord.

RESPONSORIAL PSALM

Psalm 16:1b-2a and 5, 7-8, 9-10

℟. (see 5a) You are my inheritance, O Lord.

Keep me, O God, for in you I take refuge;
    I say to the Lord, "My Lord are you."
O Lord, my allotted portion and my cup,
    you it is who hold fast my lot.

℟. You are my inheritance, O Lord.

I bless the Lord who counsels me;
    even in the night my heart exhorts me.
I set the Lord ever before me;
    with him at my right hand I shall not be disturbed.

℟. You are my inheritance, O Lord.

Therefore my heart is glad and my soul rejoices,
  my body, too, abides in confidence;
Because you will not abandon my soul to the nether world,
  nor will you suffer your faithful one to undergo corruption.

℟. You are my inheritance, O Lord.

ALLELUIA

Psalm 119:36a, 29b

℟. Alleluia, alleluia.

Incline my heart, O God, to your decrees;
and favor me with your law.

℟. Alleluia, alleluia.

GOSPEL   Years I and II

Matthew 5:33-37   I say to you, do not swear at all.

☩ A reading from the holy Gospel according to Matthew

Jesus said to his disciples:
"You have heard that it was said to your ancestors,
  Do not take a false oath,
  but make good to the Lord all that you vow.
But I say to you, do not swear at all;
  not by heaven, for it is God's throne;
  nor by the earth, for it is his footstool;
  nor by Jerusalem, for it is the city of the great King.
Do not swear by your head,
  for you cannot make a single hair white or black.
Let your 'Yes' mean 'Yes,' and your 'No' mean 'No.'
Anything more is from the Evil One."

The Gospel of the Lord.

365 MONDAY OF THE ELEVENTH WEEK IN ORDINARY TIME

FIRST READING   Year II

1 Kings 21:1-16   Naboth has been stoned to death.

A reading from the first Book of Kings

Naboth the Jezreelite had a vineyard in Jezreel
  next to the palace of Ahab, king of Samaria.
Ahab said to Naboth, "Give me your vineyard to be my vegetable garden,
  since it is close by, next to my house.
I will give you a better vineyard in exchange, or,
  if you prefer, I will give you its value in money."
Naboth answered him, "The Lord forbid
  that I should give you my ancestral heritage."
Ahab went home disturbed and angry at the answer
  Naboth the Jezreelite had made to him:
  "I will not give you my ancestral heritage."
Lying down on his bed, he turned away from food and would not eat.

His wife Jezebel came to him and said to him,
  "Why are you so angry that you will not eat?"
He answered her, "Because I spoke to Naboth the Jezreelite
  and said to him, 'Sell me your vineyard, or,
  if you prefer, I will give you a vineyard in exchange.'
But he refused to let me have his vineyard."
His wife Jezebel said to him,
  "A fine ruler over Israel you are indeed!
Get up.
Eat and be cheerful.
I will obtain the vineyard of Naboth the Jezreelite for you."

So she wrote letters in Ahab's name and,
  having sealed them with his seal,
  sent them to the elders and to the nobles
  who lived in the same city with Naboth.
This is what she wrote in the letters:
  "Proclaim a fast and set Naboth at the head of the people.
Next, get two scoundrels to face him
  and accuse him of having cursed God and king.
Then take him out and stone him to death."

His fellow citizens—the elders and nobles who dwelt in his city—
   did as Jezebel had ordered them in writing,
   through the letters she had sent them.
They proclaimed a fast and placed Naboth at the head of the people.
Two scoundrels came in and confronted him with the accusation,
   "Naboth has cursed God and king."
And they led him out of the city and stoned him to death.
Then they sent the information to Jezebel
   that Naboth had been stoned to death.

When Jezebel learned that Naboth had been stoned to death,
   she said to Ahab,
   "Go on, take possession of the vineyard
   of Naboth the Jezreelite that he refused to sell you,
   because Naboth is not alive, but dead."
On hearing that Naboth was dead, Ahab started off on his way
   down to the vineyard of Naboth the Jezreelite,
   to take possession of it.

The word of the Lord.

RESPONSORIAL PSALM

Psalm 5:2-3ab, 4b-6a, 6b-7

℟. (2b) **Lord, listen to my groaning.**

**Hearken to my words, O LORD,
  attend to my sighing.
Heed my call for help,
  my king and my God!**

℟. **Lord, listen to my groaning.**

**At dawn I bring my plea expectantly before you.
For you, O God, delight not in wickedness;
  no evil man remains with you;
  the arrogant may not stand in your sight.**

℟. **Lord, listen to my groaning.**

**You hate all evildoers.
  You destroy all who speak falsehood;
The bloodthirsty and the deceitful
  the LORD abhors.**

℟. **Lord, listen to my groaning.**

ALLELUIA

Psalm 119:105

℟. Alleluia, alleluia.

A lamp to my feet is your word,
a light to my path.

℟. Alleluia, alleluia.

GOSPEL   Years I and II

Matthew 5:38-42   But I say to you, offer no resistance to one who is evil.

☩ A reading from the holy Gospel according to Matthew

Jesus said to his disciples:
"You have heard that it was said,
An eye for an eye and a tooth for a tooth.
But I say to you, offer no resistance to one who is evil.
When someone strikes you on your right cheek,
turn the other one to him as well.
If anyone wants to go to law with you over your tunic,
hand him your cloak as well.
Should anyone press you into service for one mile,
go with him for two miles.
Give to the one who asks of you,
and do not turn your back on one who wants to borrow."

The Gospel of the Lord.

366 TUESDAY OF THE ELEVENTH WEEK IN ORDINARY TIME

FIRST READING   Year II

1 Kings 21:17-29   You have provoked me by leading Israel into sin.

A reading from the first Book of Kings

After the death of Naboth the Lord said to Elijah the Tishbite:
   "Start down to meet Ahab, king of Israel,
   who rules in Samaria.
He will be in the vineyard of Naboth,
   of which he has come to take possession.
This is what you shall tell him,
   'The Lord says: After murdering, do you also take possession?
For this, the Lord says:
   In the place where the dogs licked up the blood of Naboth,
   the dogs shall lick up your blood, too.'"
Ahab said to Elijah, "Have you found me out, my enemy?"
"Yes," he answered.
"Because you have given yourself up to doing evil in the Lord's sight,
   I am bringing evil upon you: I will destroy you
   and will cut off every male in Ahab's line,
   whether slave or freeman, in Israel.
I will make your house like that of Jeroboam, son of Nebat,
   and like that of Baasha, son of Ahijah,
   because of how you have provoked me by leading Israel into sin."
(Against Jezebel, too, the Lord declared,
   "The dogs shall devour Jezebel in the district of Jezreel.")
"When one of Ahab's line dies in the city,
   dogs will devour him;
   when one of them dies in the field,
   the birds of the sky will devour him."
Indeed, no one gave himself up to the doing of evil
   in the sight of the Lord as did Ahab,
   urged on by his wife Jezebel.
He became completely abominable by following idols,
   just as the Amorites had done,
   whom the Lord drove out before the children of Israel.

When Ahab heard these words, he tore his garments
    and put on sackcloth over his bare flesh.
He fasted, slept in the sackcloth, and went about subdued.
Then the Lord said to Elijah the Tishbite,
    "Have you seen that Ahab has humbled himself before me?
Since he has humbled himself before me,
    I will not bring the evil in his time.
I will bring the evil upon his house during the reign of his son."

The word of the Lord.

RESPONSORIAL PSALM

Psalm 51:3-4, 5-6ab, 11 and 16

℟. (see 3a) **Be merciful, O Lord, for we have sinned.**

**Have mercy on me, O God, in your goodness;
   in the greatness of your compassion wipe out my offense.
Thoroughly wash me from my guilt
   and of my sin cleanse me.**

℟. **Be merciful, O Lord, for we have sinned.**

**For I acknowledge my offense,
   and my sin is before me always:
"Against you only have I sinned,
   and done what is evil in your sight."**

℟. **Be merciful, O Lord, for we have sinned.**

**Turn away your face from my sins,
   and blot out all my guilt.
Free me from blood guilt, O God, my saving God;
   then my tongue shall revel in your justice.**

℟. **Be merciful, O Lord, for we have sinned.**

ALLELUIA

John 13:34

℟. Alleluia, alleluia.

I give you a new commandment:
love one another as I have loved you.

℟. Alleluia, alleluia.

GOSPEL Years I and II

Matthew 5:43-48 Love your enemies.

✢ A reading from the holy Gospel according to Matthew

Jesus said to his disciples:
"You have heard that it was said,
 You shall love your neighbor and hate your enemy.
But I say to you, love your enemies
  and pray for those who persecute you,
  that you may be children of your heavenly Father,
  for he makes his sun rise on the bad and the good,
  and causes rain to fall on the just and the unjust.
For if you love those who love you, what recompense will you have?
Do not the tax collectors do the same?
And if you greet your brothers only,
  what is unusual about that?
Do not the pagans do the same?
So be perfect, just as your heavenly Father is perfect."

The Gospel of the Lord.

367 WEDNESDAY OF THE ELEVENTH WEEK IN ORDINARY TIME

FIRST READING   Year II

2 Kings 2:1, 6-14   A flaming chariot came between them, and Elijah went up to heaven.

A reading from the second Book of Kings

**When the LORD was about to take Elijah up to heaven in a whirlwind,
   he and Elisha were on their way from Gilgal.
Elijah said to Elisha, "Please stay here;
   the LORD has sent me on to the Jordan."
"As the LORD lives, and as you yourself live,
   I will not leave you," Elisha replied.
And so the two went on together.
Fifty of the guild prophets followed and
   when the two stopped at the Jordan,
   they stood facing them at a distance.
Elijah took his mantle, rolled it up
   and struck the water, which divided,
   and both crossed over on dry ground.**

**When they had crossed over, Elijah said to Elisha,
   "Ask for whatever I may do for you, before I am taken from you."
Elisha answered, "May I receive a double portion of your spirit."
"You have asked something that is not easy," Elijah replied.
"Still, if you see me taken up from you,
   your wish will be granted; otherwise not."
As they walked on conversing,
   a flaming chariot and flaming horses came between them,
   and Elijah went up to heaven in a whirlwind.
When Elisha saw it happen he cried out,
   "My father! my father! Israel's chariots and drivers!"
But when he could no longer see him,
   Elisha gripped his own garment and tore it in two.**

**Then he picked up Elijah's mantle that had fallen from him,
    and went back and stood at the bank of the Jordan.
Wielding the mantle that had fallen from Elijah,
    Elisha struck the water in his turn and said,
    "Where is the LORD, the God of Elijah?"
When Elisha struck the water it divided and he crossed over.**

The word of the Lord.

RESPONSORIAL PSALM

Psalm 31:20, 21, 24

℟. (25) **Let your hearts take comfort, all who hope in the Lord.**

**How great is the goodness, O Lord,
  which you have in store for those who fear you,
And which, toward those who take refuge in you,
  you show in the sight of the children of men.**

℟. **Let your hearts take comfort, all who hope in the Lord.**

**You hide them in the shelter of your presence
  from the plottings of men;
You screen them within your abode
  from the strife of tongues.**

℟. **Let your hearts take comfort, all who hope in the Lord.**

**Love the Lord, all you his faithful ones!
  The Lord keeps those who are constant,
  but more than requites those who act proudly.**

℟. **Let your hearts take comfort, all who hope in the Lord.**

ALLELUIA

John 14:23

℟. **Alleluia, alleluia.**

**Whoever loves me will keep my word,
and my Father will love him
and we will come to him.**

℟. **Alleluia, alleluia.**

GOSPEL Years I and II

Matthew 6:1-6, 16-18   And your Father who sees what is hidden will repay you.

✠ **A reading from the holy Gospel according to Matthew**

**Jesus said to his disciples:
"Take care not to perform righteous deeds
   in order that people may see them;
   otherwise, you will have no recompense from your heavenly Father.
When you give alms, do not blow a trumpet before you,
   as the hypocrites do in the synagogues and in the streets
   to win the praise of others.
Amen, I say to you, they have received their reward.
But when you give alms,
   do not let your left hand know what your right is doing,
   so that your almsgiving may be secret.
And your Father who sees in secret will repay you.**

**"When you pray, do not be like the hypocrites,
   who love to stand and pray in the synagogues and on street corners
   so that others may see them.
Amen, I say to you, they have received their reward.
But when you pray, go to your inner room, close the door,
   and pray to your Father in secret.
And your Father who sees in secret will repay you.**

**"When you fast, do not look gloomy like the hypocrites.
They neglect their appearance,
   so that they may appear to others to be fasting.
Amen, I say to you, they have received their reward.
But when you fast, anoint your head and wash your face,
   so that you may not appear to others to be fasting,
   except to your Father who is hidden.
And your Father who sees what is hidden will repay you."**

The Gospel of the Lord.

368 THURSDAY OF THE ELEVENTH WEEK IN ORDINARY TIME

FIRST READING   Year II

Sirach 48:1-14   Elijah was enveloped in a whirlwind, and Elisha was filled with the twofold portion of his spirit.

A reading from the Book of Sirach

Like a fire there appeared the prophet Elijah
  whose words were as a flaming furnace.
Their staff of bread he shattered,
  in his zeal he reduced them to straits;
By the Lord's word he shut up the heavens
  and three times brought down fire.
How awesome are you, Elijah, in your wondrous deeds!
  Whose glory is equal to yours?
You brought a dead man back to life
  from the nether world, by the will of the Lord.
You sent kings down to destruction,
  and easily broke their power into pieces.
You brought down nobles, from their beds of sickness.
You heard threats at Sinai,
  at Horeb avenging judgments.
You anointed kings who should inflict vengeance,
  and a prophet as your successor.
You were taken aloft in a whirlwind of fire,
  in a chariot with fiery horses.
You were destined, it is written, in time to come
  to put an end to wrath before the day of the Lord,
To turn back the hearts of fathers toward their sons,
  and to re-establish the tribes of Jacob.
Blessed is he who shall have seen you
And who falls asleep in your friendship.
For we live only in our life,
  but after death our name will not be such.
  O Elijah, enveloped in the whirlwind!

Then Elisha, filled with the twofold portion of his spirit,
   wrought many marvels by his mere word.
During his lifetime he feared no one,
   nor was any man able to intimidate his will.
Nothing was beyond his power;
   beneath him flesh was brought back into life.
In life he performed wonders,
   and after death, marvelous deeds.

The word of the Lord.

RESPONSORIAL PSALM

Psalm 97:1-2, 3-4, 5-6, 7

℟. (12a) **Rejoice in the Lord, you just!**

**The Lord is king; let the earth rejoice;
   let the many isles be glad.
Clouds and darkness are round about him,
   justice and judgment are the foundation of his throne.**

℟. **Rejoice in the Lord, you just!**

**Fire goes before him
   and consumes his foes round about.
His lightnings illumine the world;
   the earth sees and trembles.**

℟. **Rejoice in the Lord, you just!**

**The mountains melt like wax before the Lord,
   before the Lord of all the earth.
The heavens proclaim his justice,
   and all peoples see his glory.**

℟. **Rejoice in the Lord, you just!**

**All who worship graven things are put to shame,
   who glory in the things of nought;
   all gods are prostrate before him.**

℟. **Rejoice in the Lord, you just!**

ALLELUIA

Romans 8:15bc

℟. **Alleluia, alleluia.**

**You have received a spirit of adoption as sons
through which we cry: Abba! Father!**

℟. **Alleluia, alleluia.**

GOSPEL   Years I and II

Matthew 6:7-15   This is how you are to pray.

✠ **A reading from the holy Gospel according to Matthew**

**Jesus said to his disciples:
"In praying, do not babble like the pagans,
    who think that they will be heard because of their many words.
Do not be like them.
Your Father knows what you need before you ask him.**

"This is how you are to pray:

   **'Our Father who art in heaven,
      hallowed be thy name,
      thy Kingdom come,
      thy will be done,
         on earth as it is in heaven.
      Give us this day our daily bread;
      and forgive us our trespasses,
         as we forgive those who trespass against us;
      and lead us not into temptation,
         but deliver us from evil.'**

**"If you forgive others their transgressions,
   your heavenly Father will forgive you.
But if you do not forgive others,
   neither will your Father forgive your transgressions."**

The Gospel of the Lord.

369 FRIDAY OF THE ELEVENTH WEEK IN ORDINARY TIME

FIRST READING   Year II

2 Kings 11:1-4, 9-18, 20   They anointed him and shouted: "Long live the king!"

A reading from the second Book of Kings

When Athaliah, the mother of Ahaziah,
  saw that her son was dead,
  she began to kill off the whole royal family.
But Jehosheba, daughter of King Jehoram and sister of Ahaziah,
  took Joash, his son, and spirited him away, along with his nurse,
  from the bedroom where the princes were about to be slain.
She concealed him from Athaliah, and so he did not die.
For six years he remained hidden in the temple of the Lord,
  while Athaliah ruled the land.

But in the seventh year,
  Jehoiada summoned the captains of the Carians
  and of the guards.
He had them come to him in the temple of the Lord,
  exacted from them a sworn commitment,
  and then showed them the king's son.

The captains did just as Jehoiada the priest commanded.
Each one with his men, both those going on duty for the sabbath
  and those going off duty that week,
  came to Jehoiada the priest.
He gave the captains King David's spears and shields,
  which were in the temple of the Lord.
And the guards, with drawn weapons,
  lined up from the southern to the northern limit of the enclosure,
  surrounding the altar and the temple on the king's behalf.
Then Jehoiada led out the king's son
  and put the crown and the insignia upon him.
They proclaimed him king and anointed him,
  clapping their hands and shouting, "Long live the king!"

Athaliah heard the noise made by the people,
    and appeared before them in the temple of the Lord.
When she saw the king standing by the pillar, as was the custom,
    and the captains and trumpeters near him,
        with all the people of the land rejoicing and blowing trumpets,
    she tore her garments and cried out, "Treason, treason!"
Then Jehoiada the priest instructed the captains
    in command of the force:
    "Bring her outside through the ranks.
If anyone follows her," he added, "let him die by the sword."
He had given orders that she
    should not be slain in the temple of the Lord.
She was led out forcibly to the horse gate of the royal palace,
    where she was put to death.

Then Jehoiada made a covenant between the Lord as one party
    and the king and the people as the other,
        by which they would be the Lord's people;
        and another covenant, between the king and the people.
Thereupon all the people of the land went to the temple of Baal
    and demolished it.
They shattered its altars and images completely,
    and slew Mattan, the priest of Baal, before the altars.
Jehoiada appointed a detachment for the temple of the Lord.
All the people of the land rejoiced and the city was quiet,
    now that Athaliah had been slain with the sword
    at the royal palace.

The word of the Lord.

RESPONSORIAL PSALM

Psalm 132:11, 12, 13-14, 17-18

℟. (13) **The Lord has chosen Zion for his dwelling.**

**The LORD swore to David
 a firm promise from which he will not withdraw:
"Your own offspring
 I will set upon your throne."**

℟. The Lord has chosen Zion for his dwelling.

**"If your sons keep my covenant
 and the decrees which I shall teach them,
Their sons, too, forever
 shall sit upon your throne."**

℟. The Lord has chosen Zion for his dwelling.

**For the LORD has chosen Zion;
 he prefers her for his dwelling.
"Zion is my resting place forever;
 in her will I dwell, for I prefer her."**

℟. The Lord has chosen Zion for his dwelling.

**"In her will I make a horn to sprout forth for David;
 I will place a lamp for my anointed.
His enemies I will clothe with shame,
 but upon him my crown shall shine."**

℟. The Lord has chosen Zion for his dwelling.

ALLELUIA

Matthew 5:3

℟. **Alleluia, alleluia.**

**Blessed are the poor in spirit;
for theirs is the Kingdom of heaven.**

℟. **Alleluia, alleluia.**

GOSPEL   Years I and II

Matthew 6:19-23   For where your treasure is, there also will your heart be.

✠ **A reading from the holy Gospel according to Matthew**

**Jesus said to his disciples:
"Do not store up for yourselves treasures on earth,
   where moth and decay destroy, and thieves break in and steal.
But store up treasures in heaven,
   where neither moth nor decay destroys, nor thieves break in and steal.
For where your treasure is, there also will your heart be.**

**"The lamp of the body is the eye.
If your eye is sound, your whole body will be filled with light;
   but if your eye is bad, your whole body will be in darkness.
And if the light in you is darkness, how great will the darkness be."**

The Gospel of the Lord.

370 SATURDAY OF THE ELEVENTH WEEK IN ORDINARY TIME

FIRST READING   Year II

2 Chronicles 24:17-25   They murdered Zechariah between the sanctuary and the altar (Matthew 23:35).

A reading from the second Book of Chronicles

After the death of Jehoiada,
   the princes of Judah came and paid homage to King Joash,
   and the king then listened to them.
They forsook the temple of the LORD, the God of their fathers,
   and began to serve the sacred poles and the idols;
   and because of this crime of theirs,
   wrath came upon Judah and Jerusalem.
Although prophets were sent to them to convert them to the LORD,
   the people would not listen to their warnings.
Then the Spirit of God possessed Zechariah,
   son of Jehoiada the priest.
He took his stand above the people and said to them:
   "God says, 'Why are you transgressing the LORD's commands,
   so that you cannot prosper?
Because you have abandoned the LORD, he has abandoned you.'"
But they conspired against him,
   and at the king's order they stoned him to death
   in the court of the LORD's temple.
Thus King Joash was unmindful of the devotion shown him
   by Jehoiada, Zechariah's father, and slew his son.
And as Zechariah was dying, he said, "May the LORD see and avenge."

At the turn of the year a force of Arameans came up against Joash.
They invaded Judah and Jerusalem,
   did away with all the princes of the people,
   and sent all their spoil to the king of Damascus.
Though the Aramean force came with few men,
   the LORD surrendered a very large force into their power,
   because Judah had abandoned the LORD, the God of their fathers.
So punishment was meted out to Joash.

After the Arameans had departed from him,
   leaving him in grievous suffering,
   his servants conspired against him
   because of the murder of the son of Jehoiada the priest.
He was buried in the City of David,
   but not in the tombs of the kings.

The word of the Lord.

RESPONSORIAL PSALM

Psalm 89:4-5, 29-30, 31-32, 33-34

℟. (29a) **For ever I will maintain my love for my servant.**

**"I have made a covenant with my chosen one,
   I have sworn to David my servant:
Forever will I confirm your posterity
   and establish your throne for all generations."**

℟. **For ever I will maintain my love for my servant.**

**"Forever I will maintain my kindness toward him,
   and my covenant with him stands firm.
I will make his posterity endure forever
   and his throne as the days of heaven."**

℟. **For ever I will maintain my love for my servant.**

**"If his sons forsake my law
   and walk not according to my ordinances,
If they violate my statutes
   and keep not my commands."**

℟. **For ever I will maintain my love for my servant.**

**"I will punish their crime with a rod
   and their guilt with stripes.
Yet my mercy I will not take from him,
   nor will I belie my faithfulness."**

℟. **For ever I will maintain my love for my servant.**

ALLELUIA

2 Corinthians 8:9

℟. **Alleluia, alleluia.**

**Jesus Christ became poor although he was rich,
so that by his poverty you might become rich.**

℟. **Alleluia, alleluia.**

GOSPEL   Years I and II

Matthew 6:24-34   Do not worry about tomorrow.

✢ A reading from the holy Gospel according to Matthew

Jesus said to his disciples:
"No one can serve two masters.
He will either hate one and love the other,
   or be devoted to one and despise the other.
You cannot serve God and mammon.

"Therefore I tell you, do not worry about your life,
   what you will eat or drink,
   or about your body, what you will wear.
Is not life more than food and the body more than clothing?
Look at the birds in the sky;
   they do not sow or reap, they gather nothing into barns,
   yet your heavenly Father feeds them.
Are not you more important than they?
Can any of you by worrying add a single moment to your life-span?
Why are you anxious about clothes?
Learn from the way the wild flowers grow.
They do not work or spin.
But I tell you that not even Solomon in all his splendor
   was clothed like one of them.
If God so clothes the grass of the field,
   which grows today and is thrown into the oven tomorrow,
   will he not much more provide for you, O you of little faith?
So do not worry and say, 'What are we to eat?'
   or 'What are we to drink?' or 'What are we to wear?'
All these things the pagans seek.
Your heavenly Father knows that you need them all.
But seek first the Kingdom of God and his righteousness,
   and all these things will be given you besides.
Do not worry about tomorrow; tomorrow will take care of itself.
Sufficient for a day is its own evil."

The Gospel of the Lord.

371 MONDAY OF THE TWELFTH WEEK IN ORDINARY TIME

FIRST READING   Year II

2 Kings 17:5-8, 13-15a, 18   In his great anger against Israel, the LORD put them away out of his sight. Only the tribe of Judah was left.

A reading from the second Book of Kings

Shalmaneser, king of Assyria, occupied the whole land
   and attacked Samaria, which he besieged for three years.
In the ninth year of Hoshea, king of Israel
   the king of Assyria took Samaria,
   and deported the children of Israel to Assyria,
     setting them in Halah, at the Habor, a river of Gozan,
     and the cities of the Medes.

This came about because the children of Israel sinned against the LORD,
   their God, who had brought them up from the land of Egypt,
     from under the domination of Pharaoh, king of Egypt,
     and because they venerated other gods.
They followed the rites of the nations
   whom the LORD had cleared out of the way of the children of Israel
   and the kings of Israel whom they set up.

And though the LORD warned Israel and Judah
   by every prophet and seer,
   "Give up your evil ways and keep my commandments and statutes,
   in accordance with the entire law which I enjoined on your fathers
   and which I sent you by my servants the prophets,"
   they did not listen, but were as stiff-necked as their fathers,
   who had not believed in the LORD, their God.
They rejected his statutes,
   the covenant which he had made with their fathers,
   and the warnings which he had given them, till,
   in his great anger against Israel,
   the LORD put them away out of his sight.
Only the tribe of Judah was left.

The word of the Lord.

RESPONSORIAL PSALM

Psalm 60:3, 4-5, 12-13

℟. (7b) **Help us with your right hand, O Lord, and answer us.**

**O God, you have rejected us and broken our defenses;
   you have been angry; rally us!**

℟. **Help us with your right hand, O Lord, and answer us.**

**You have rocked the country and split it open;
   repair the cracks in it, for it is tottering.
You have made your people feel hardships;
   you have given us stupefying wine.**

℟. **Help us with your right hand, O Lord, and answer us.**

**Have not you, O God, rejected us,
   so that you go not forth, O God, with our armies?
Give us aid against the foe,
   for worthless is the help of men.**

℟. **Help us with your right hand, O Lord, and answer us.**

ALLELUIA

Hebrews 4:12

℟. Alleluia, alleluia.

**The word of God is living and effective,
able to discern reflections and thoughts of the heart.**

℟. Alleluia, alleluia.

GOSPEL   Years I and II

Matthew 7:1-5   Remove the wooden beam from your eye first.

☩ **A reading from the holy Gospel according to Matthew**

**Jesus said to his disciples:
"Stop judging, that you may not be judged.
For as you judge, so will you be judged,
   and the measure with which you measure will be measured out to you.
Why do you notice the splinter in your brother's eye,
   but do not perceive the wooden beam in your own eye?
How can you say to your brother,
   'Let me remove that splinter from your eye,'
   while the wooden beam is in your eye?
You hypocrite, remove the wooden beam from your eye first;
   then you will see clearly
   to remove the splinter from your brother's eye."**

The Gospel of the Lord.

372 TUESDAY OF THE TWELFTH WEEK IN ORDINARY TIME

FIRST READING   Year II

2 Kings 19:9b-11, 14-21, 31-35a, 36   I will shield and save this city for my own sake and for the sake of my servant David.

A reading from the second Book of Kings

Sennacherib, king of Assyria, sent envoys to Hezekiah
  with this message:
  "Thus shall you say to Hezekiah, king of Judah:
  'Do not let your God on whom you rely deceive you
  by saying that Jerusalem will not be handed over
  to the king of Assyria.
You have heard what the kings of Assyria have done
  to all other countries: they doomed them!
Will you, then, be saved?'"

Hezekiah took the letter from the hand of the messengers and read it;
  then he went up to the temple of the Lord,
  and spreading it out before him,
  he prayed in the Lord's presence:
  "O Lord, God of Israel, enthroned upon the cherubim!
You alone are God over all the kingdoms of the earth.
You have made the heavens and the earth.
Incline your ear, O Lord, and listen!
Open your eyes, O Lord, and see!
Hear the words of Sennacherib which he sent to taunt the living God.
Truly, O Lord, the kings of Assyria have laid waste the nations
  and their lands, and cast their gods into the fire;
  they destroyed them because they were not gods,
  but the work of human hands, wood and stone.
Therefore, O Lord, our God, save us from the power of this man,
  that all the kingdoms of the earth may know
  that you alone, O Lord, are God."

Then Isaiah, son of Amoz, sent this message to Hezekiah:
  "Thus says the Lord, the God of Israel,
  in answer to your prayer for help against Sennacherib, king of Assyria:
  I have listened!

This is the word the LORD has spoken concerning him:

"'She despises you, laughs you to scorn,
   the virgin daughter Zion!
Behind you she wags her head,
   daughter Jerusalem.

"'For out of Jerusalem shall come a remnant,
   and from Mount Zion, survivors.
   The zeal of the LORD of hosts shall do this.'

"Therefore, thus says the LORD concerning the king of Assyria:
   'He shall not reach this city, nor shoot an arrow at it,
   nor come before it with a shield,
   nor cast up siege-works against it.
He shall return by the same way he came,
   without entering the city, says the LORD.
I will shield and save this city for my own sake,
   and for the sake of my servant David.'"

That night the angel of the LORD went forth and struck down
   one hundred and eighty-five thousand men in the Assyrian camp.
So Sennacherib, the king of Assyria, broke camp,
   and went back home to Nineveh.

The word of the Lord.

RESPONSORIAL PSALM

Psalm 48:2-3ab, 3cd-4, 10-11

℟. (see 9d) **God upholds his city for ever.**

Great is the LORD **and wholly to be praised
   in the city of our God.
His holy mountain, fairest of heights,
   is the joy of all the earth.**

℟. **God upholds his city for ever.**

**Mount Zion, "the recesses of the North,"
   is the city of the great King.
God is with her castles;
   renowned is he as a stronghold.**

℟. **God upholds his city for ever.**

**O God, we ponder your mercy
   within your temple.
As your name, O God, so also your praise
   reaches to the ends of the earth.
Of justice your right hand is full.**

℟. **God upholds his city for ever.**

ALLELUIA

John 8:12

℟. **Alleluia, alleluia.**

**I am the light of the world, says the Lord;
whoever follows me will have the light of life.**

℟. **Alleluia, alleluia.**

GOSPEL   Years I and II

Matthew 7:6, 12-14   Do to others whatever you would have them do to you.

✠ **A reading from the holy Gospel according to Matthew**

Jesus said to his disciples:
"**Do not give what is holy to dogs, or throw your pearls before swine,
    lest they trample them underfoot, and turn and tear you to pieces.**

"**Do to others whatever you would have them do to you.
This is the Law and the Prophets.**

"**Enter through the narrow gate;
    for the gate is wide and the road broad that leads to destruction,
    and those who enter through it are many.
How narrow the gate and constricted the road that leads to life.
And those who find it are few.**"

The Gospel of the Lord.

373 WEDNESDAY OF THE TWELFTH WEEK IN ORDINARY TIME

FIRST READING   Year II

2 Kings 22:8-13; 23:1-3   The king had the book that had been found in the temple read out to them, and he made a covenant before the Lord.

A reading from the second Book of Kings

The high priest Hilkiah informed the scribe Shaphan,
  "I have found the book of the law in the temple of the Lord."
Hilkiah gave the book to Shaphan, who read it.
Then the scribe Shaphan went to the king and reported,
  "Your servants have smelted down the metals available in the temple
  and have consigned them to the master workmen
  in the temple of the Lord."
The scribe Shaphan also informed the king
  that the priest Hilkiah had given him a book,
  and then read it aloud to the king.
When the king heard the contents of the book of the law,
  he tore his garments and issued this command to Hilkiah the priest,
  Ahikam, son of Shaphan,
  Achbor, son of Micaiah, the scribe Shaphan,
  and the king's servant Asaiah:
  "Go, consult the Lord for me, for the people, for all Judah,
  about the stipulations of this book that has been found,
  for the anger of the Lord has been set furiously ablaze against us,
  because our fathers did not obey the stipulations of this book,
  nor fulfill our written obligations."

The king then had all the elders of Judah
  and of Jerusalem summoned together before him.
The king went up to the temple of the Lord with all the men of Judah
  and all the inhabitants of Jerusalem:
  priests, prophets, and all the people, small and great.
He had the entire contents of the book of the covenant
  that had been found in the temple of the Lord, read out to them.

Standing by the column, the king made a covenant before the Lord
that they would follow him
and observe his ordinances, statutes and decrees
with their whole hearts and souls,
thus reviving the terms of the covenant
which were written in this book.
And all the people stood as participants in the covenant.

The word of the Lord.

RESPONSORIAL PSALM

Psalm 119:33, 34, 35, 36, 37, 40

℟. (33a) **Teach me the way of your decrees, O Lord.**

**Instruct me, O LORD, in the way of your statutes,
    that I may exactly observe them.**

℟. **Teach me the way of your decrees, O Lord.**

**Give me discernment, that I may observe your law
    and keep it with all my heart.**

℟. **Teach me the way of your decrees, O Lord.**

**Lead me in the path of your commands,
    for in it I delight.**

℟. **Teach me the way of your decrees, O Lord.**

**Incline my heart to your decrees
    and not to gain.**

℟. **Teach me the way of your decrees, O Lord.**

**Turn away my eyes from seeing what is vain:
    by your way give me life.**

℟. **Teach me the way of your decrees, O Lord.**

**Behold, I long for your precepts;
    in your justice give me life.**

℟. **Teach me the way of your decrees, O Lord.**

ALLELUIA

John 15:4a, 5b

℟. Alleluia, alleluia.

Remain in me, as I remain in you, says the Lord;
whoever remains in me will bear much fruit.

℟. Alleluia, alleluia.

GOSPEL   Years I and II

Matthew 7:15-20   By their fruits you will know them.

✢ A reading from the holy Gospel according to Matthew

Jesus said to his disciples:
"Beware of false prophets, who come to you in sheep's clothing,
  but underneath are ravenous wolves.
By their fruits you will know them.
Do people pick grapes from thornbushes, or figs from thistles?
Just so, every good tree bears good fruit,
  and a rotten tree bears bad fruit.
A good tree cannot bear bad fruit,
  nor can a rotten tree bear good fruit.
Every tree that does not bear good fruit will be cut down
  and thrown into the fire.
So by their fruits you will know them."

The Gospel of the Lord.

374 THURSDAY OF THE TWELFTH WEEK IN ORDINARY TIME

FIRST READING   Year II

2 Kings 24:8-17   The king of Babylon also led captive to Babylon Jehoiachin and the chief men of the land.

A reading from the second Book of Kings

Jehoiachin was eighteen years old when he began to reign,
 and he reigned three months in Jerusalem.
His mother's name was Nehushta,
 daughter of Elnathan of Jerusalem.
He did evil in the sight of the Lord,
 just as his forebears had done.

At that time the officials of Nebuchadnezzar, king of Babylon,
 attacked Jerusalem, and the city came under siege.
Nebuchadnezzar, king of Babylon,
 himself arrived at the city
 while his servants were besieging it.
Then Jehoiachin, king of Judah, together with his mother,
 his ministers, officers, and functionaries,
 surrendered to the king of Babylon, who,
 in the eighth year of his reign, took him captive.
And he carried off all the treasures
 of the temple of the Lord and those of the palace,
 and broke up all the gold utensils that Solomon, king of Israel,
 had provided in the temple of the Lord, as the Lord had foretold.
He deported all Jerusalem:
 all the officers and men of the army, ten thousand in number,
 and all the craftsmen and smiths.
None were left among the people of the land except the poor.
He deported Jehoiachin to Babylon,
 and also led captive from Jerusalem to Babylon
 the king's mother and wives,
 his functionaries, and the chief men of the land.
The king of Babylon also led captive to Babylon
 all seven thousand men of the army,
 and a thousand craftsmen and smiths,
 all of them trained soldiers.

In place of Jehoiachin,
> the king of Babylon appointed his uncle Mattaniah king,
> and changed his name to Zedekiah.

The word of the Lord.

RESPONSORIAL PSALM

Psalm 79:1b-2, 3-5, 8, 9

℟. (9) **For the glory of your name, O Lord, deliver us.**

O God, the nations have come into your inheritance;
> they have defiled your holy temple,
> they have laid Jerusalem in ruins.
They have given the corpses of your servants
> as food to the birds of heaven,
> the flesh of your faithful ones to the beasts of the earth.

℟. **For the glory of your name, O Lord, deliver us.**

They have poured out their blood like water
> round about Jerusalem,
> and there is no one to bury them.
We have become the reproach of our neighbors,
> the scorn and derision of those around us.
O Lord, how long? Will you be angry forever?
> Will your jealousy burn like fire?

℟. **For the glory of your name, O Lord, deliver us.**

Remember not against us the iniquities of the past;
> may your compassion quickly come to us,
> for we are brought very low.

℟. **For the glory of your name, O Lord, deliver us.**

Help us, O God our savior,
> because of the glory of your name;
Deliver us and pardon our sins
> for your name's sake.

℟. **For the glory of your name, O Lord, deliver us.**

ALLELUIA

John 14:23

℟. Alleluia, alleluia.

**Whoever loves me will keep my word,
and my Father will love him
and we will come to him.**

℟. Alleluia, alleluia.

GOSPEL Years I and II

Matthew 7:21-29   The house built on rock and the house built on sand.

✠ A reading from the holy Gospel according to Matthew

**Jesus said to his disciples:
"Not everyone who says to me, 'Lord, Lord,'
will enter the Kingdom of heaven,
but only the one who does the will of my Father in heaven.
Many will say to me on that day,
'Lord, Lord, did we not prophesy in your name?
Did we not drive out demons in your name?
Did we not do mighty deeds in your name?'
Then I will declare to them solemnly,
'I never knew you. Depart from me, you evildoers.'**

**"Everyone who listens to these words of mine and acts on them
will be like a wise man who built his house on rock.
The rain fell, the floods came,
and the winds blew and buffeted the house.
But it did not collapse; it had been set solidly on rock.
And everyone who listens to these words of mine
but does not act on them
will be like a fool who built his house on sand.
The rain fell, the floods came,
and the winds blew and buffeted the house.
And it collapsed and was completely ruined."**

**When Jesus finished these words,
the crowds were astonished at his teaching,
for he taught them as one having authority,
and not as their scribes.**

The Gospel of the Lord.

375 FRIDAY OF THE TWELFTH WEEK IN ORDINARY TIME

FIRST READING   Year II

2 Kings 25:1-12   Thus was Judah exiled from her land (2 Kings 25:21).

A reading from the second Book of Kings

In the tenth month of the ninth year of Zedekiah's reign,
   on the tenth day of the month,
   Nebuchadnezzar, king of Babylon, and his whole army
   advanced against Jerusalem, encamped around it,
   and built siege walls on every side.
The siege of the city continued until the eleventh year of Zedekiah.
On the ninth day of the fourth month,
   when famine had gripped the city,
   and the people had no more bread,
   the city walls were breached.
Then the king and all the soldiers left the city by night
   through the gate between the two walls
   that was near the king's garden.
Since the Chaldeans had the city surrounded,
   they went in the direction of the Arabah.
But the Chaldean army pursued the king
   and overtook him in the desert near Jericho,
   abandoned by his whole army.

The king was therefore arrested and brought to Riblah
   to the king of Babylon, who pronounced sentence on him.
He had Zedekiah's sons slain before his eyes.
Then he blinded Zedekiah, bound him with fetters,
   and had him brought to Babylon.

On the seventh day of the fifth month
   (this was in the nineteenth year of Nebuchadnezzar,
   king of Babylon),
   Nebuzaradan, captain of the bodyguard,
   came to Jerusalem as the representative
   of the king of Babylon.
He burned the house of the Lord,
   the palace of the king, and all the houses of Jerusalem;
   every large building was destroyed by fire.

**Then the Chaldean troops who were with the captain of the guard
   tore down the walls that surrounded Jerusalem.**

**Then Nebuzaradan, captain of the guard,
   led into exile the last of the people remaining in the city,
   and those who had deserted to the king of Babylon,
   and the last of the artisans.
But some of the country's poor, Nebuzaradan, captain of the guard,
   left behind as vinedressers and farmers.**

The word of the Lord.

RESPONSORIAL PSALM

Psalm 137:1-2, 3, 4-5, 6

℟. (6ab) **Let my tongue be silenced, if I ever forget you!**

**By the streams of Babylon
  we sat and wept
  when we remembered Zion.
On the aspens of that land
  we hung up our harps.**

℟. **Let my tongue be silenced, if I ever forget you!**

**Though there our captors asked of us
  the lyrics of our songs,
And our despoilers urged us to be joyous:
  "Sing for us the songs of Zion!"**

℟. **Let my tongue be silenced, if I ever forget you!**

How could we sing a song of the LORD
  **in a foreign land?
If I forget you, Jerusalem,
  may my right hand be forgotten!**

℟. **Let my tongue be silenced, if I ever forget you!**

**May my tongue cleave to my palate
  if I remember you not,
If I place not Jerusalem
  ahead of my joy.**

℟. **Let my tongue be silenced, if I ever forget you!**

ALLELUIA

Matthew 8:17

℟. Alleluia, alleluia.

**Christ took away our infirmities
and bore our diseases.**

℟. Alleluia, alleluia.

GOSPEL   Years I and II

Matthew 8:1-4   If you wish, you can make me clean.

✠ **A reading from the holy Gospel according to Matthew**

**When Jesus came down from the mountain, great crowds followed him.
And then a leper approached, did him homage, and said,
   "Lord, if you wish, you can make me clean."
He stretched out his hand, touched him, and said,
   "I will do it. Be made clean."
His leprosy was cleansed immediately.
Then Jesus said to him, "See that you tell no one,
   but go show yourself to the priest,
   and offer the gift that Moses prescribed;
   that will be proof for them."**

The Gospel of the Lord.

376 SATURDAY OF THE TWELFTH WEEK IN ORDINARY TIME

FIRST READING   Year II

Lamentations 2:2, 10-14, 18-19   Cry out to the Lord over the fortresses of daughter Zion.

A reading from the Book of Lamentations

The Lord has consumed without pity
 all the dwellings of Jacob;
He has torn down in his anger
 the fortresses of daughter Judah;
He has brought to the ground in dishonor
 her king and her princes.

On the ground in silence sit
 the old men of daughter Zion;
They strew dust on their heads
 and gird themselves with sackcloth;
The maidens of Jerusalem
 bow their heads to the ground.

Worn out from weeping are my eyes,
 within me all is in ferment;
My gall is poured out on the ground
 because of the downfall of the daughter of my people,
As child and infant faint away
 in the open spaces of the town.

In vain they ask their mothers,
 "Where is the grain?"
As they faint away like the wounded
 in the streets of the city,
And breathe their last
 in their mothers' arms.

To what can I liken or compare you,
 O daughter Jerusalem?
What example can I show you for your comfort,
 virgin daughter Zion?
For great as the sea is your downfall;
 who can heal you?

**Your prophets had for you
   false and specious visions;
They did not lay bare your guilt,
   to avert your fate;
They beheld for you in vision
   false and misleading portents.**

**Cry out to the Lord;
   moan, O daughter Zion!
Let your tears flow like a torrent
   day and night;
Let there be no respite for you,
   no repose for your eyes.**

**Rise up, shrill in the night,
   at the beginning of every watch;
Pour out your heart like water
   in the presence of the Lord;
Lift up your hands to him
   for the lives of your little ones
Who faint from hunger
   at the corner of every street.**

The word of the Lord.

RESPONSORIAL PSALM

Psalm 74:1b-2, 3-5, 6-7, 20-21

℟. (19b) Lord, forget not the souls of your poor ones.

Why, O God, have you cast us off forever?
　　Why does your anger smolder against the sheep of your pasture?
Remember your flock which you built up of old,
　　the tribe you redeemed as your inheritance,
　　Mount Zion, where you took up your abode.

℟. Lord, forget not the souls of your poor ones.

Turn your steps toward the utter ruins;
　　toward all the damage the enemy has done in the sanctuary.
Your foes roar triumphantly in your shrine;
　　they have set up their tokens of victory.
They are like men coming up with axes to a clump of trees.

℟. Lord, forget not the souls of your poor ones.

With chisel and hammer they hack at all the paneling of the sanctuary.
They set your sanctuary on fire;
　　the place where your name abides they have razed and profaned.

℟. Lord, forget not the souls of your poor ones.

Look to your covenant,
　　for the hiding places in the land and the plains are full of violence.
May the humble not retire in confusion;
　　may the afflicted and the poor praise your name.

℟. Lord, forget not the souls of your poor ones.

ALLELUIA

Matthew 8:17

℟. Alleluia, alleluia.

Christ took away our infirmities
and bore our diseases.

℟. Alleluia, alleluia.

GOSPEL   Years I and II

Matthew 8:5-17   Many will come from east and west and will recline with Abraham, Isaac, and Jacob.

☩ A reading from the holy Gospel according to Matthew

When Jesus entered Capernaum,
    a centurion approached him and appealed to him, saying,
    "Lord, my servant is lying at home paralyzed, suffering dreadfully."
He said to him, "I will come and cure him."
The centurion said in reply,
    "Lord, I am not worthy to have you enter under my roof;
    only say the word and my servant will be healed.
For I too am a man subject to authority,
    with soldiers subject to me.
And I say to one, 'Go,' and he goes;
    and to another, 'Come here,' and he comes;
    and to my slave, 'Do this,' and he does it."
When Jesus heard this, he was amazed and said to those following him,
    "Amen, I say to you, in no one in Israel have I found such faith.
I say to you, many will come from the east and the west,
    and will recline with Abraham, Isaac, and Jacob
    at the banquet in the Kingdom of heaven,
    but the children of the Kingdom
    will be driven out into the outer darkness,
    where there will be wailing and grinding of teeth."
And Jesus said to the centurion,
    "You may go; as you have believed, let it be done for you."
And at that very hour his servant was healed.

Jesus entered the house of Peter,
    and saw his mother-in-law lying in bed with a fever.
He touched her hand, the fever left her,
    and she rose and waited on him.

When it was evening, they brought him many
    who were possessed by demons,
    and he drove out the spirits by a word and cured all the sick,
    to fulfill what had been said by Isaiah the prophet:

He took away our infirmities and bore our diseases.

The Gospel of the Lord.

377 MONDAY OF THE THIRTEENTH WEEK IN ORDINARY TIME

FIRST READING   Year II

Amos 2:6-10, 13-16   They trample the heads of the weak into the dust of the earth.

A reading from the Book of the Prophet Amos

Thus says the Lord:
For three crimes of Israel, and for four,
   I will not revoke my word;
Because they sell the just man for silver,
   and the poor man for a pair of sandals.
They trample the heads of the weak
   into the dust of the earth,
   and force the lowly out of the way.
Son and father go to the same prostitute,
   profaning my holy name.
Upon garments taken in pledge
   they recline beside any altar;
And the wine of those who have been fined
   they drink in the house of their god.

Yet it was I who destroyed the Amorites before them,
   who were as tall as the cedars,
   and as strong as the oak trees.
I destroyed their fruit above,
   and their roots beneath.
It was I who brought you up from the land of Egypt,
   and who led you through the desert for forty years,
   to occupy the land of the Amorites.

Beware, I will crush you into the ground
    as a wagon crushes when laden with sheaves.
Flight shall perish from the swift,
    and the strong man shall not retain his strength;
The warrior shall not save his life,
    nor the bowman stand his ground;
The swift of foot shall not escape,
    nor the horseman save his life.
And the most stouthearted of warriors
    shall flee naked on that day, says the Lord.

The word of the Lord.

RESPONSORIAL PSALM

Psalm 50:16bc-17, 18-19, 20-21, 22-23

℟. (22a) **Remember this, you who never think of God.**

"Why do you recite my statutes,
 and profess my covenant with your mouth,
Though you hate discipline
 and cast my words behind you?"

℟. **Remember this, you who never think of God.**

"When you see a thief, you keep pace with him,
 and with adulterers you throw in your lot.
To your mouth you give free rein for evil,
 you harness your tongue to deceit."

℟. **Remember this, you who never think of God.**

"You sit speaking against your brother;
 against your mother's son you spread rumors.
When you do these things, shall I be deaf to it?
 Or do you think that I am like yourself?
 I will correct you by drawing them up before your eyes."

℟. **Remember this, you who never think of God.**

"Consider this, you who forget God,
 lest I rend you and there be no one to rescue you.
He that offers praise as a sacrifice glorifies me;
 and to him that goes the right way I will show the salvation of God."

℟. **Remember this, you who never think of God.**

ALLELUIA

Psalm 95:8

℟. Alleluia, alleluia.

If today you hear his voice,
harden not your hearts.

℟. Alleluia, alleluia.

GOSPEL   Years I and II

Matthew 8:18-22   Follow me.

☩ A reading from the holy Gospel according to Matthew

When Jesus saw a crowd around him,
   he gave orders to cross to the other shore.
A scribe approached and said to him,
   "Teacher, I will follow you wherever you go."
Jesus answered him, "Foxes have dens and birds of the sky have nests,
   but the Son of Man has nowhere to rest his head."
Another of his disciples said to him,
   "Lord, let me go first and bury my father."
But Jesus answered him, "Follow me,
   and let the dead bury their dead."

The Gospel of the Lord.

378 TUESDAY OF THE THIRTEENTH WEEK IN ORDINARY TIME

FIRST READING   Year II

Amos 3:1-8; 4:11-12   The Lord GOD speaks—who will not prophesy!

A reading from the Book of the Prophet Amos

Hear this word, O children of Israel, that the LORD **pronounces over you,**
   over the whole family that I brought up from the land of Egypt:

You alone have I favored,
   more than all the families of the earth;
Therefore I will punish you
   for all your crimes.

Do two walk together
   unless they have agreed?
Does a lion roar in the forest
   when it has no prey?
Does a young lion cry out from its den
   unless it has seized something?
Is a bird brought to earth by a snare
   when there is no lure for it?
Does a snare spring up from the ground
   without catching anything?
If the trumpet sounds in a city,
   will the people not be frightened?
If evil befalls a city,
   has not the LORD caused it?
Indeed, the Lord GOD does nothing
   without revealing his plan
   to his servants, the prophets.

The lion roars–
   who will not be afraid!
The Lord GOD speaks–
   who will not prophesy!

I brought upon you such upheaval
   as when God overthrew Sodom and Gomorrah:
   you were like a brand plucked from the fire;
Yet you returned not to me,
   says the Lord.

So now I will deal with you in my own way, O Israel!
   and since I will deal thus with you,
   prepare to meet your God, O Israel.

The word of the Lord.

RESPONSORIAL PSALM

Psalm 5:4b-6a, 6b-7, 8

℟. (9a) Lead me in your justice, Lord.

At dawn I bring my plea expectantly before you.
For you, O God, delight not in wickedness;
   no evil man remains with you;
   the arrogant may not stand in your sight.

℟. Lead me in your justice, Lord.

You hate all evildoers;
   you destroy all who speak falsehood;
The bloodthirsty and the deceitful
   the Lord abhors.

℟. Lead me in your justice, Lord.

But I, because of your abundant mercy,
   will enter your house;
I will worship at your holy temple
   in fear of you, O Lord.

℟. Lead me in your justice, Lord.

ALLELUIA

Psalm 130:5

℟. Alleluia, alleluia.

I trust in the Lord;
my soul trusts in his word.

℟. Alleluia, alleluia.

GOSPEL Years I and II

Matthew 8:23-27   Jesus rebuked the winds and the sea, and there was great calm.

✠ A reading from the holy Gospel according to Matthew

As Jesus got into a boat, his disciples followed him.
Suddenly a violent storm came up on the sea,
   so that the boat was being swamped by waves;
   but he was asleep.
They came and woke him, saying,
   "Lord, save us! We are perishing!"
He said to them, "Why are you terrified, O you of little faith?"
Then he got up, rebuked the winds and the sea,
   and there was great calm.
The men were amazed and said, "What sort of man is this,
   whom even the winds and the sea obey?"

The Gospel of the Lord.

379 WEDNESDAY OF THE THIRTEENTH WEEK IN ORDINARY TIME

FIRST READING   Year II

Amos 5:14-15, 21-24   Away with your noisy songs! Let justice surge like an unfailing stream.

A reading from the Book of the Prophet Amos

**Seek good and not evil,
   that you may live;
Then truly will the Lord, the God of hosts,
   be with you as you claim!
Hate evil and love good,
   and let justice prevail at the gate;
Then it may be that the Lord, the God of hosts,
   will have pity on the remnant of Joseph.**

**I hate, I spurn your feasts, says the Lord,
   I take no pleasure in your solemnities;
Your cereal offerings I will not accept,
   nor consider your stall-fed peace offerings.
Away with your noisy songs!
   I will not listen to the melodies of your harps.
But if you would offer me burnt offerings,
   then let justice surge like water,
   and goodness like an unfailing stream.**

The word of the Lord.

RESPONSORIAL PSALM

Psalm 50:7, 8-9, 10-11, 12-13, 16bc-17

℟. (23b) **To the upright I will show the saving power of God.**

"Hear, my people, and I will speak;
 Israel, I will testify against you;
 God, your God, am I."

℟. To the upright I will show the saving power of God.

"Not for your sacrifices do I rebuke you,
 for your burnt offerings are before me always.
I take from your house no bullock,
 no goats out of your fold."

℟. To the upright I will show the saving power of God.

"For mine are all the animals of the forests,
 beasts by the thousand on my mountains.
I know all the birds of the air,
 and whatever stirs in the plains, belongs to me."

℟. To the upright I will show the saving power of God.

"If I were hungry, I should not tell you,
 for mine are the world and its fullness.
Do I eat the flesh of strong bulls,
 or is the blood of goats my drink?"

℟. To the upright I will show the saving power of God.

"Why do you recite my statutes,
 and profess my covenant with your mouth,
Though you hate discipline
 and cast my words behind you?"

℟. To the upright I will show the saving power of God.

ALLELUIA

James 1:18

℟. Alleluia, alleluia.

The Father willed to give us birth by the word of truth
that we may be a kind of firstfruits of his creatures.

℟. Alleluia, alleluia.

GOSPEL   Years I and II

Matthew 8:28-34   Have you come here to torment us before the appointed time?

✠ A reading from the holy Gospel according to Matthew

When Jesus came to the territory of the Gadarenes,
  two demoniacs who were coming from the tombs met him.
They were so savage that no one could travel by that road.
They cried out, "What have you to do with us, Son of God?
Have you come here to torment us before the appointed time?"
Some distance away a herd of many swine was feeding.
The demons pleaded with him,
  "If you drive us out, send us into the herd of swine."
And he said to them, "Go then!"
They came out and entered the swine,
  and the whole herd rushed down the steep bank into the sea
  where they drowned.
The swineherds ran away,
  and when they came to the town they reported everything,
  including what had happened to the demoniacs.
Thereupon the whole town came out to meet Jesus,
  and when they saw him they begged him to leave their district.

The Gospel of the Lord.

380 THURSDAY OF THE THIRTEENTH WEEK IN ORDINARY TIME

FIRST READING   Year II

Amos 7:10-17   Go, prophesy to my people Israel.

A reading from the Book of the Prophet Amos

Amaziah, the priest of Bethel, sent word to Jeroboam,
    king of Israel:
    "Amos has conspired against you here within Israel;
    the country cannot endure all his words.
For this is what Amos says:
    Jeroboam shall die by the sword,
        and Israel shall surely be exiled from its land."

To Amos, Amaziah said:
    "Off with you, visionary, flee to the land of Judah!
There earn your bread by prophesying,
    but never again prophesy in Bethel;
    for it is the king's sanctuary and a royal temple."
Amos answered Amaziah, "I was no prophet,
    nor have I belonged to a company of prophets;
    I was a shepherd and a dresser of sycamores.
The Lord took me from following the flock, and said to me,
    'Go, prophesy to my people Israel.'
Now hear the word of the Lord!"

    You say: prophesy not against Israel,
        preach not against the house of Isaac.
            Now thus says the Lord:
        Your wife shall be made a harlot in the city,
            and your sons and daughters shall fall by the sword;
        Your land shall be divided by measuring line,
            and you yourself shall die in an unclean land;
                Israel shall be exiled far from its land.

The word of the Lord.

RESPONSORIAL PSALM

Psalm 19:8, 9, 10, 11

℟. (10cd) **The judgments of the Lord are true, and all of them are just.**

**The law of the Lord is perfect,
refreshing the soul;
The decree of the Lord is trustworthy,
giving wisdom to the simple.**

℟. **The judgments of the Lord are true, and all of them are just.**

**The precepts of the Lord are right,
rejoicing the heart;
The command of the Lord is clear,
enlightening the eye.**

℟. **The judgments of the Lord are true, and all of them are just.**

**The fear of the Lord is pure,
enduring forever;
The ordinances of the Lord are true,
all of them just.**

℟. **The judgments of the Lord are true, and all of them are just.**

**They are more precious than gold,
than a heap of purest gold;
Sweeter also than syrup
or honey from the comb.**

℟. **The judgments of the Lord are true, and all of them are just.**

ALLELUIA

2 Corinthians 5:19

℟. Alleluia, alleluia.

**God was reconciling the world to himself in Christ
and entrusting to us the message of reconciliation.**

℟. Alleluia, alleluia.

GOSPEL   Years I and II

Matthew 9:1-8   They glorified God who had given such authority to men.

✠ A reading from the holy Gospel according to Matthew

**After entering a boat, Jesus made the crossing, and came into his own town.
And there people brought to him a paralytic lying on a stretcher.
When Jesus saw their faith, he said to the paralytic,
    "Courage, child, your sins are forgiven."
At that, some of the scribes said to themselves,
    "This man is blaspheming."
Jesus knew what they were thinking, and said,
    "Why do you harbor evil thoughts?
Which is easier, to say, 'Your sins are forgiven,'
    or to say, 'Rise and walk'?
But that you may know that the Son of Man
    has authority on earth to forgive sins"–
    he then said to the paralytic,
    "Rise, pick up your stretcher, and go home."
He rose and went home.
When the crowds saw this they were struck with awe
    and glorified God who had given such authority to men.**

The Gospel of the Lord.

381 FRIDAY OF THE THIRTEENTH WEEK IN ORDINARY TIME

FIRST READING   Year II

Amos 8:4-6, 9-12   I will send famine upon the land: not a famine of bread or thirst for water, but for hearing the word of the Lord.

A reading from the Book of the Prophet Amos

Hear this, you who trample upon the needy
   and destroy the poor of the land!
"When will the new moon be over," you ask,
   "that we may sell our grain,
   and the sabbath, that we may display the wheat?"
We will diminish the containers for measuring,
   add to the weights,
   and fix our scales for cheating!
We will buy the lowly man for silver,
   and the poor man for a pair of sandals;
   even the refuse of the wheat we will sell!"

On that day, says the Lord God,
   I will make the sun set at midday
   and cover the earth with darkness in broad daylight.
I will turn your feasts into mourning
   and all your songs into lamentations.
I will cover the loins of all with sackcloth
   and make every head bald.
I will make them mourn as for an only son,
   and bring their day to a bitter end.

Yes, days are coming, says the Lord God,
   when I will send famine upon the land:
Not a famine of bread, or thirst for water,
   but for hearing the word of the Lord.
Then shall they wander from sea to sea
   and rove from the north to the east
In search of the word of the Lord,
   but they shall not find it.

The word of the Lord.

RESPONSORIAL PSALM

Psalm 119:2, 10, 20, 30, 40, 131

℟. (Matthew 4:4) **One does not live by bread alone, but by every word that comes from the mouth of God.**

Blessed are they who observe his decrees,
who seek him with all their heart.

℟. **One does not live by bread alone, but by every word that comes from the mouth of God.**

With all my heart I seek you;
let me not stray from your commands.

℟. **One does not live by bread alone, but by every word that comes from the mouth of God.**

My soul is consumed with longing
for your ordinances at all times.

℟. **One does not live by bread alone, but by every word that comes from the mouth of God.**

The way of truth I have chosen;
I have set your ordinances before me.

℟. **One does not live by bread alone, but by every word that comes from the mouth of God.**

Behold, I long for your precepts;
in your justice give me life.

℟. **One does not live by bread alone, but by every word that comes from the mouth of God.**

I gasp with open mouth
in my yearning for your commands.

℟. **One does not live by bread alone, but by every word that comes from the mouth of God.**

ALLELUIA

Matthew 11:28

℟. Alleluia, alleluia.

Come to me, all you who labor and are burdened,
and I will give you rest, says the Lord.

℟. Alleluia, alleluia.

GOSPEL   Years I and II

Matthew 9:9-13   Those who are well do not need a physician; I desire mercy, not sacrifice.

☩ A reading from the holy Gospel according to Matthew

As Jesus passed by,
  he saw a man named Matthew sitting at the customs post.
He said to him, "Follow me."
And he got up and followed him.
While he was at table in his house,
  many tax collectors and sinners came
  and sat with Jesus and his disciples.
The Pharisees saw this and said to his disciples,
  "Why does your teacher eat with tax collectors and sinners?"
He heard this and said,
  "Those who are well do not need a physician, but the sick do.
Go and learn the meaning of the words,
  I desire mercy, not sacrifice.
I did not come to call the righteous but sinners."

The Gospel of the Lord.

382 SATURDAY OF THE THIRTEENTH WEEK IN ORDINARY TIME

FIRST READING   Year II

Amos 9:11-15   *I will bring about the restoration of my people Israel; I will plant them upon their own ground.*

A reading from the Book of the Prophet Amos

Thus says the Lord:
On that day I will raise up
   the fallen hut of David;
I will wall up its breaches,
   raise up its ruins,
   and rebuild it as in the days of old,
That they may conquer what is left of Edom
   and all the nations that shall bear my name,
   say I, the Lord, who will do this.
Yes, days are coming,
   says the Lord,
When the plowman shall overtake the reaper,
   and the vintager, him who sows the seed;
The juice of grapes shall drip down the mountains,
   and all the hills shall run with it.
I will bring about the restoration of my people Israel;
   they shall rebuild and inhabit their ruined cities,
Plant vineyards and drink the wine,
   set out gardens and eat the fruits.
I will plant them upon their own ground;
   never again shall they be plucked
From the land I have given them,
   say I, the Lord, your God.

The word of the Lord.

RESPONSORIAL PSALM

Psalm 85:9ab and 10, 11-12, 13-14

℟. (see 9b) **The Lord speaks of peace to his people.**

**I will hear what God proclaims;
   the Lord–for he proclaims peace to his people.
Near indeed is his salvation to those who fear him,
   glory dwelling in our land.**

℟. **The Lord speaks of peace to his people.**

**Kindness and truth shall meet;
   justice and peace shall kiss.
Truth shall spring out of the earth,
   and justice shall look down from heaven.**

℟. **The Lord speaks of peace to his people.**

**The Lord himself will give his benefits;
   our land shall yield its increase.
Justice shall walk before him,
   and salvation, along the way of his steps.**

℟. **The Lord speaks of peace to his people.**

ALLELUIA

John 10:27

℟. Alleluia, alleluia.

My sheep hear my voice, says the Lord;
I know them, and they follow me.

℟. Alleluia, alleluia.

GOSPEL Years I and II

Matthew 9:14-17 Can the wedding guests mourn as long as the bridegroom is with them?

✟ A reading from the holy Gospel according to Matthew

The disciples of John approached Jesus and said,
  "Why do we and the Pharisees fast much,
  but your disciples do not fast?"
Jesus answered them, "Can the wedding guests mourn
  as long as the bridegroom is with them?
The days will come when the bridegroom is taken away from them,
  and then they will fast.
No one patches an old cloak with a piece of unshrunken cloth,
  for its fullness pulls away from the cloak and the tear gets worse.
People do not put new wine into old wineskins.
Otherwise the skins burst, the wine spills out, and the skins are ruined.
Rather, they pour new wine into fresh wineskins, and both are preserved."

The Gospel of the Lord.

383 MONDAY OF THE FOURTEENTH WEEK IN ORDINARY TIME

FIRST READING   Year II

Hosea 2:16, 17c-18, 21-22   I will espouse you to me forever.

A reading from the Book of the Prophet Hosea

**Thus says the Lord:
I will allure her;
   I will lead her into the desert
   and speak to her heart.
She shall respond there as in the days of her youth,
   when she came up from the land of Egypt.**

   **On that day, says the Lord,
She shall call me "My husband,"
   and never again "My baal."**

**I will espouse you to me forever:
   I will espouse you in right and in justice,
   in love and in mercy;
I will espouse you in fidelity,
   and you shall know the Lord.**

The word of the Lord.

RESPONSORIAL PSALM

Psalm 145:2-3, 4-5, 6-7, 8-9

℟. (8a) The Lord is gracious and merciful.

Every day will I bless you,
 and I will praise your name forever and ever.
Great is the LORD and highly to be praised;
 his greatness is unsearchable.

℟. The Lord is gracious and merciful.

Generation after generation praises your works
 and proclaims your might.
They speak of the splendor of your glorious majesty
 and tell of your wondrous works.

℟. The Lord is gracious and merciful.

They discourse of the power of your terrible deeds
 and declare your greatness.
They publish the fame of your abundant goodness
 and joyfully sing of your justice.

℟. The Lord is gracious and merciful.

The LORD is gracious and merciful,
 slow to anger and of great kindness.
The LORD is good to all
 and compassionate toward all his works.

℟. The Lord is gracious and merciful.

ALLELUIA

See 2 Timothy 1:10

℟. Alleluia, alleluia.

**Our Savior Jesus Christ has destroyed death
and brought life to light through the Gospel.**

℟. Alleluia, alleluia.

GOSPEL Years I and II

Matthew 9:18-26   My daughter has just died, but come and she will live.

✠ A reading from the holy Gospel according to Matthew

**While Jesus was speaking, an official came forward,
   knelt down before him, and said,
   "My daughter has just died.
But come, lay your hand on her, and she will live."
Jesus rose and followed him, and so did his disciples.
A woman suffering hemorrhages for twelve years came up behind him
   and touched the tassel on his cloak.
She said to herself, "If only I can touch his cloak, I shall be cured."
Jesus turned around and saw her, and said,
   "Courage, daughter! Your faith has saved you."
And from that hour the woman was cured.**

**When Jesus arrived at the official's house
   and saw the flute players and the crowd who were making a commotion,
   he said, "Go away! The girl is not dead but sleeping."
And they ridiculed him.
When the crowd was put out, he came and took her by the hand,
   and the little girl arose.
And news of this spread throughout all that land.**

The Gospel of the Lord.

384 TUESDAY OF THE FOURTEENTH WEEK IN ORDINARY TIME

FIRST READING   Year II

Hosea 8:4-7, 11-13   When they sow the wind, they shall reap the whirlwind.

A reading from the Book of the Prophet Hosea

Thus says the LORD:
They made kings in Israel, but not by my authority;
 they established princes, but without my approval.
With their silver and gold they made
 idols for themselves, to their own destruction.
Cast away your calf, O Samaria!
 my wrath is kindled against them;
How long will they be unable to attain
 innocence in Israel?
The work of an artisan,
 no god at all,
Destined for the flames—
 such is the calf of Samaria!

When they sow the wind,
 they shall reap the whirlwind;
The stalk of grain that forms no ear
 can yield no flour;
Even if it could,
 strangers would swallow it.

When Ephraim made many altars to expiate sin,
 his altars became occasions of sin.
Though I write for him my many ordinances,
 they are considered as a stranger's.
Though they offer sacrifice,
 immolate flesh and eat it,
 the LORD is not pleased with them.
He shall still remember their guilt
 and punish their sins;
 they shall return to Egypt.

The word of the Lord.

RESPONSORIAL PSALM

Psalm 115:3-4, 5-6, 7ab-8, 9-10

℟. (9a) **The house of Israel trusts in the Lord.**
   or:
℟. **Alleluia.**

**Our God is in heaven;
   whatever he wills, he does.
Their idols are silver and gold,
   the handiwork of men.**

℟. **The house of Israel trusts in the Lord.**
   or:
℟. **Alleluia.**

**They have mouths but speak not;
   they have eyes but see not;
They have ears but hear not;
   they have noses but smell not.**

℟. **The house of Israel trusts in the Lord.**
   or:
℟. **Alleluia.**

**They have hands but feel not;
   they have feet but walk not.
Their makers shall be like them,
   everyone that trusts in them.**

℟. **The house of Israel trusts in the Lord.**
   or:
℟. **Alleluia.**

ALLELUIA

John 10:14

℟. Alleluia, alleluia.

I am the good shepherd, says the Lord;
I know my sheep, and mine know me.

℟. Alleluia, alleluia.

GOSPEL   Years I and II

Matthew 9:32-38   The harvest is abundant but the laborers are few.

✠ A reading from the holy Gospel according to Matthew

A demoniac who could not speak was brought to Jesus,
    and when the demon was driven out the mute man spoke.
The crowds were amazed and said,
    "Nothing like this has ever been seen in Israel."
But the Pharisees said,
    "He drives out demons by the prince of demons."

Jesus went around to all the towns and villages,
    teaching in their synagogues,
    proclaiming the Gospel of the Kingdom,
    and curing every disease and illness.
At the sight of the crowds, his heart was moved with pity for them
    because they were troubled and abandoned,
    like sheep without a shepherd.
Then he said to his disciples,
    "The harvest is abundant but the laborers are few;
    so ask the master of the harvest
    to send out laborers for his harvest."

The Gospel of the Lord.

385 WEDNESDAY OF THE FOURTEENTH WEEK IN ORDINARY TIME

FIRST READING   Year II

Hosea 10:1-3, 7-8, 12   It is time to seek the Lord.

A reading from the Book of the Prophet Hosea

Israel is a luxuriant vine
  whose fruit matches its growth.
The more abundant his fruit,
  the more altars he built;
The more productive his land,
  the more sacred pillars he set up.
Their heart is false,
  now they pay for their guilt;
God shall break down their altars
  and destroy their sacred pillars.
If they would say,
  "We have no king"—
Since they do not fear the Lord,
  what can the king do for them?

The king of Samaria shall disappear,
  like foam upon the waters.
The high places of Aven shall be destroyed,
  the sin of Israel;
  thorns and thistles shall overgrow their altars.
Then they shall cry out to the mountains, "Cover us!"
  and to the hills, "Fall upon us!"

"Sow for yourselves justice,
  reap the fruit of piety;
break up for yourselves a new field,
  for it is time to seek the Lord,
  till he come and rain down justice upon you."

The word of the Lord.

RESPONSORIAL PSALM

Psalm 105:2-3, 4-5, 6-7

℟. (4b) Seek always the face of the Lord.
or:
℟. Alleluia.

Sing to him, sing his praise,
   proclaim all his wondrous deeds.
Glory in his holy name;
   rejoice, O hearts that seek the Lord!

℟. Seek always the face of the Lord.
or:
℟. Alleluia.

Look to the Lord in his strength;
   seek to serve him constantly.
Recall the wondrous deeds that he has wrought,
   his portents, and the judgments he has uttered.

℟. Seek always the face of the Lord.
or:
℟. Alleluia.

You descendants of Abraham, his servants,
   sons of Jacob, his chosen ones!
He, the Lord, is our God;
   throughout the earth his judgments prevail.

℟. Seek always the face of the Lord.
or:
℟. Alleluia.

ALLELUIA

Mark 1:15

℞. Alleluia, alleluia.

The Kingdom of God is at hand:
repent and believe in the Gospel.

℞. Alleluia, alleluia.

GOSPEL   Years I and II

Matthew 10:1-7   Go rather to the lost sheep of the house of Israel.

✢ A reading from the holy Gospel according to Matthew

**Jesus summoned his Twelve disciples
and gave them authority over unclean spirits to drive them out
and to cure every disease and every illness.
The names of the Twelve Apostles are these:
first, Simon called Peter, and his brother Andrew;
James, the son of Zebedee, and his brother John;
Philip and Bartholomew,
Thomas and Matthew the tax collector;
James, the son of Alphaeus, and Thaddeus;
Simon the Cananean, and Judas Iscariot
who betrayed Jesus.**

**Jesus sent out these Twelve after instructing them thus,
"Do not go into pagan territory or enter a Samaritan town.
Go rather to the lost sheep of the house of Israel.
As you go, make this proclamation: 'The Kingdom of heaven is at hand.'"**

The Gospel of the Lord.

386 THURSDAY OF THE FOURTEENTH WEEK IN ORDINARY TIME

FIRST READING   Year II

Hosea 11:1-4, 8e-9   My heart is overwhelmed.

A reading from the Book of the Prophet Hosea

Thus says the Lord:
When Israel was a child I loved him,
  out of Egypt I called my son.
The more I called them,
  the farther they went from me,
Sacrificing to the Baals
  and burning incense to idols.
Yet it was I who taught Ephraim to walk,
  who took them in my arms;
I drew them with human cords,
  with bands of love;
I fostered them like one
  who raises an infant to his cheeks;
Yet, though I stooped to feed my child,
  they did not know that I was their healer.

My heart is overwhelmed,
  my pity is stirred.
I will not give vent to my blazing anger,
  I will not destroy Ephraim again;
For I am God and not man,
  the Holy One present among you;
I will not let the flames consume you.

The word of the Lord.

RESPONSORIAL PSALM

Psalm 80:2ac and 3b, 15-16

℟. (4b) **Let us see your face, Lord, and we shall be saved.**

**O shepherd of Israel, hearken.
From your throne upon the cherubim, shine forth.
Rouse your power.**

℟. **Let us see your face, Lord, and we shall be saved.**

Once again, O LORD **of hosts,
   look down from heaven, and see:
Take care of this vine,
   and protect what your right hand has planted,
   the son of man whom you yourself made strong.**

℟. **Let us see your face, Lord, and we shall be saved.**

ALLELUIA

Mark 1:15

℟. Alleluia, alleluia.

**The Kingdom of God is at hand:
repent and believe in the Gospel.**

℟. Alleluia, alleluia.

GOSPEL Years I and II

Matthew 10:7-15   Without cost you have received; without cost you are to give.

✠ A reading from the holy Gospel according to Matthew

**Jesus said to his Apostles:
"As you go, make this proclamation:
   'The Kingdom of heaven is at hand.'
Cure the sick, raise the dead,
   cleanse the lepers, drive out demons.
Without cost you have received; without cost you are to give.
Do not take gold or silver or copper for your belts;
   no sack for the journey, or a second tunic,
   or sandals, or walking stick.
The laborer deserves his keep.
Whatever town or village you enter, look for a worthy person in it,
   and stay there until you leave.
As you enter a house, wish it peace.
If the house is worthy,
   let your peace come upon it;
   if not, let your peace return to you.
Whoever will not receive you or listen to your words—
   go outside that house or town and shake the dust from your feet.
Amen, I say to you, it will be more tolerable
   for the land of Sodom and Gomorrah on the day of judgment
   than for that town."**

The Gospel of the Lord.

387 FRIDAY OF THE FOURTEENTH WEEK IN ORDINARY TIME

FIRST READING   Year II

Hosea 14:2-10   We shall say no more "Our god" to the work of our hands.

A reading from the Book of the Prophet Hosea

    Thus says the LORD:
Return, O Israel, to the LORD, your God;
    you have collapsed through your guilt.
Take with you words,
    and return to the LORD;
Say to him, "Forgive all iniquity,
    and receive what is good, that we may render
    as offerings the bullocks from our stalls.
Assyria will not save us,
    nor shall we have horses to mount;
We shall say no more, 'Our god,'
    to the work of our hands;
    for in you the orphan finds compassion."
I will heal their defection, says the LORD,
    I will love them freely;
    for my wrath is turned away from them.
I will be like the dew for Israel:
    he shall blossom like the lily;
He shall strike root like the Lebanon cedar,
    and put forth his shoots.
His splendor shall be like the olive tree
    and his fragrance like the Lebanon cedar.
Again they shall dwell in his shade
    and raise grain;
They shall blossom like the vine,
    and his fame shall be like the wine of Lebanon.

Ephraim! What more has he to do with idols?
    I have humbled him, but I will prosper him.
"I am like a verdant cypress tree"—
    because of me you bear fruit!

Let him who is wise understand these things;
   let him who is prudent know them.
Straight are the paths of the LORD,
   in them the just walk,
   but sinners stumble in them.

The word of the Lord.

RESPONSORIAL PSALM

Psalm 51:3-4, 8-9, 12-13, 14 and 17

℟. (17b) **My mouth will declare your praise.**

Have mercy on me, O God, in your goodness;
   in the greatness of your compassion wipe out my offense.
Thoroughly wash me from my guilt
   and of my sin cleanse me.

℟. **My mouth will declare your praise.**

Behold, you are pleased with sincerity of heart,
   and in my inmost being you teach me wisdom.
Cleanse me of sin with hyssop, that I may be purified;
   wash me, and I shall be whiter than snow.

℟. **My mouth will declare your praise.**

A clean heart create for me, O God,
   and a steadfast spirit renew within me.
Cast me not out from your presence,
   and your Holy Spirit take not from me.

℟. **My mouth will declare your praise.**

Give me back the joy of your salvation,
   and a willing spirit sustain in me.
O Lord, open my lips,
   and my mouth shall proclaim your praise.

℟. **My mouth will declare your praise.**

ALLELUIA

John 16:13a; 14:26d

℟. Alleluia, alleluia.

When the Spirit of truth comes,
he will guide you to all truth
and remind you of all I told you.

℟. Alleluia, alleluia.

GOSPEL   Years I and II

Matthew 10:16-23   For it will not be you who speak, but the Spirit of your Father speaking through you.

✠ A reading from the holy Gospel according to Matthew

Jesus said to his Apostles:
"Behold, I am sending you like sheep in the midst of wolves;
   so be shrewd as serpents and simple as doves.
But beware of men,
   for they will hand you over to courts
   and scourge you in their synagogues,
   and you will be led before governors and kings for my sake
   as a witness before them and the pagans.
When they hand you over,
   do not worry about how you are to speak
   or what you are to say.
You will be given at that moment what you are to say.
For it will not be you who speak
   but the Spirit of your Father speaking through you.
Brother will hand over brother to death,
   and the father his child;
   children will rise up against parents and have them put to death.
You will be hated by all because of my name,
   but whoever endures to the end will be saved.
When they persecute you in one town, flee to another.
Amen, I say to you, you will not finish the towns of Israel
   before the Son of Man comes."

The Gospel of the Lord.

388 SATURDAY OF THE FOURTEENTH WEEK IN ORDINARY TIME

FIRST READING   Year II

Isaiah 6:1-8   I am a man of unclean lips; yet my eyes have seen the King, the Lord of hosts!

A reading from the Book of the Prophet Isaiah

In the year King Uzziah died,
   I saw the Lord seated on a high and lofty throne,
   with the train of his garment filling the temple.
Seraphim were stationed above; each of them had six wings:
   with two they veiled their faces,
   with two they veiled their feet,
   and with two they hovered aloft.

They cried one to the other,
   "Holy, holy, holy is the Lord of hosts!
All the earth is filled with his glory!"
At the sound of that cry, the frame of the door shook
   and the house was filled with smoke.

Then I said, "Woe is me, I am doomed!
For I am a man of unclean lips,
   living among a people of unclean lips;
   yet my eyes have seen the King, the Lord of hosts!"
Then one of the seraphim flew to me,
   holding an ember that he had taken with tongs from the altar.

He touched my mouth with it and said,
   "See, now that this has touched your lips,
   your wickedness is removed, your sin purged."

Then I heard the voice of the Lord saying,
   "Whom shall I send? Who will go for us?"
"Here I am," I said; "send me!"

The word of the Lord.

RESPONSORIAL PSALM

Psalm 93:1ab, 1cd-2, 5

℟. (1a) **The Lord is king; he is robed in majesty.**

The Lord is king, in splendor robed;
  robed is the Lord and girt about with strength.

℟. **The Lord is king; he is robed in majesty.**

And he has made the world firm,
  not to be moved.
Your throne stands firm from of old;
  from everlasting you are, O Lord.

℟. **The Lord is king; he is robed in majesty.**

Your decrees are worthy of trust indeed:
  holiness befits your house,
  O Lord, for length of days.

℟. **The Lord is king; he is robed in majesty.**

ALLELUIA

1 Peter 4:14

℟. **Alleluia, alleluia.**

If you are insulted for the name of Christ, blessed are you, for the Spirit of God rests upon you.

℟. **Alleluia, alleluia.**

GOSPEL Years I and II

Matthew 10:24-33　　Do not be afraid of those who kill the body.

✠ A reading from the holy Gospel according to Matthew

Jesus said to his Apostles:
"No disciple is above his teacher,
　no slave above his master.
It is enough for the disciple that he become like his teacher,
　for the slave that he become like his master.
If they have called the master of the house Beelzebul,
　how much more those of his household!

"Therefore do not be afraid of them.
Nothing is concealed that will not be revealed,
　nor secret that will not be known.
What I say to you in the darkness, speak in the light;
　what you hear whispered, proclaim on the housetops.
And do not be afraid of those who kill the body but cannot kill the soul;
　rather, be afraid of the one who can destroy
　both soul and body in Gehenna.
Are not two sparrows sold for a small coin?
Yet not one of them falls to the ground without your Father's knowledge.
Even all the hairs of your head are counted.
So do not be afraid; you are worth more than many sparrows.
Everyone who acknowledges me before others
　I will acknowledge before my heavenly Father.
But whoever denies me before others,
　I will deny before my heavenly Father."

The Gospel of the Lord.

389 MONDAY OF THE FIFTEENTH WEEK IN ORDINARY TIME

FIRST READING   Year II

Isaiah 1:10-17   Wash yourselves clean! Put away your misdeeds from before my eyes.

A reading from the Book of the Prophet Isaiah

**Hear the word of the Lord,
  princes of Sodom!
Listen to the instruction of our God,
  people of Gomorrah!
What care I for the number of your sacrifices?
  says the Lord.
I have had enough of whole-burnt rams
  and fat of fatlings;
In the blood of calves, lambs and goats
  I find no pleasure.**

**When you come in to visit me,
  who asks these things of you?
Trample my courts no more!
  Bring no more worthless offerings;
  your incense is loathsome to me.
New moon and sabbath, calling of assemblies,
  octaves with wickedness: these I cannot bear.
Your new moons and festivals I detest;
  they weigh me down, I tire of the load.
When you spread out your hands,
  I close my eyes to you;
Though you pray the more,
  I will not listen.
Your hands are full of blood!
  Wash yourselves clean!
Put away your misdeeds from before my eyes;
  cease doing evil; learn to do good.
Make justice your aim: redress the wronged,
  hear the orphan's plea, defend the widow.**

The word of the Lord.

RESPONSORIAL PSALM

Psalm 50:8-9, 16bc-17, 21 and 23

℟. (23b) **To the upright I will show the saving power of God.**

"Not for your sacrifices do I rebuke you,
  for your burnt offerings are before me always.
I take from your house no bullock,
  no goats out of your fold."

℟. **To the upright I will show the saving power of God.**

"Why do you recite my statutes,
  and profess my covenant with your mouth,
Though you hate discipline
  and cast my words behind you?"

℟. **To the upright I will show the saving power of God.**

"When you do these things, shall I be deaf to it?
  Or do you think that I am like yourself?
  I will correct you by drawing them up before your eyes.
He that offers praise as a sacrifice glorifies me;
  and to him that goes the right way I will show the salvation of God."

℟. **To the upright I will show the saving power of God.**

ALLELUIA

Matthew 5:10

℟. **Alleluia, alleluia.**

Blessed are they who are persecuted for the sake of righteousness, for theirs is the Kingdom of heaven.

℟. **Alleluia, alleluia.**

GOSPEL Years I and II

Matthew 10:34—11:1 I have come to bring not peace, but the sword.

☩ A reading from the holy Gospel according to Matthew

Jesus said to his Apostles:
"Do not think that I have come to bring peace upon the earth.
I have come to bring not peace but the sword.
For I have come to set
    a man against his father,
        a daughter against her mother,
    and a daughter-in-law against her mother-in-law;
        and one's enemies will be those of his household.

"Whoever loves father or mother more than me is not worthy of me,
    and whoever loves son or daughter more than me is not worthy of me;
    and whoever does not take up his cross
    and follow after me is not worthy of me.
Whoever finds his life will lose it,
    and whoever loses his life for my sake will find it.

"Whoever receives you receives me,
    and whoever receives me receives the one who sent me.
Whoever receives a prophet because he is a prophet
    will receive a prophet's reward,
    and whoever receives a righteous man
    because he is righteous
    will receive a righteous man's reward.
And whoever gives only a cup of cold water
    to one of these little ones to drink
    because he is a disciple—
    amen, I say to you, he will surely not lose his reward."

When Jesus finished giving these commands to his Twelve disciples,
    he went away from that place to teach and to preach in their towns.

The Gospel of the Lord.

390 TUESDAY OF THE FIFTEENTH WEEK IN ORDINARY TIME

FIRST READING   Year II

Isaiah 7:1-9   Unless your faith is firm, you shall not be firm!

A reading from the Book of the Prophet Isaiah

In the days of Ahaz, king of Judah, son of Jotham, son of Uzziah,
  Rezin, king of Aram,
  and Pekah, king of Israel, son of Remaliah,
  went up to attack Jerusalem,
  but they were not able to conquer it.
When word came to the house of David that Aram
  was encamped in Ephraim,
  the heart of the king and the heart of the people trembled,
  as the trees of the forest tremble in the wind.

Then the LORD said to Isaiah: Go out to meet Ahaz,
  you and your son Shear-jashub,
  at the end of the conduit of the upper pool,
  on the highway of the fuller's field, and say to him:
  Take care you remain tranquil and do not fear;
  let not your courage fail
  before these two stumps of smoldering brands
  the blazing anger of Rezin and the Arameans,
  and of the son Remaliah,
  because of the mischief that
  Aram, Ephraim and the son of Remaliah,
  plots against you, saying,
  "Let us go up and tear Judah asunder, make it our own by force,
  and appoint the son of Tabeel king there."

Thus says the LORD:
   This shall not stand, it shall not be!
  Damascus is the capital of Aram,
     and Rezin is the head of Damascus;
  Samaria is the capital of Ephraim,
     and Remaliah's son the head of Samaria.

But within sixty years and five,
>   Ephraim shall be crushed, no longer a nation.
> Unless your faith is firm
>   you shall not be firm!

The word of the Lord.

RESPONSORIAL PSALM

Psalm 48:2-3a, 3b-4, 5-6, 7-8

℟. (see 9d) **God upholds his city for ever.**

Great is the Lord and wholly to be praised
   in the city of our God.
His holy mountain, fairest of heights,
   is the joy of all the earth.

℟. **God upholds his city for ever.**

Mount Zion, "the recesses of the North,"
   is the city of the great King.
God is with her castles;
   renowned is he as a stronghold.

℟. **God upholds his city for ever.**

For lo! the kings assemble,
   they come on together;
They also see, and at once are stunned,
   terrified, routed.

℟. **God upholds his city for ever.**

Quaking seizes them there;
   anguish, like a woman's in labor,
As though a wind from the east
   were shattering ships of Tarshish.

℟. **God upholds his city for ever.**

ALLELUIA

Psalm 95:8

℟. Alleluia, alleluia.

If today you hear his voice,
harden not your hearts.

℟. Alleluia, alleluia.

GOSPEL   Years I and II

Matthew 11:20-24   It will be more tolerable for Tyre and Sidon and for the land of Sodom on the day of judgment than for you.

✞ A reading from the holy Gospel according to Matthew

Jesus began to reproach the towns
 where most of his mighty deeds had been done,
 since they had not repented.
"Woe to you, Chorazin! Woe to you, Bethsaida!
For if the mighty deeds done in your midst
 had been done in Tyre and Sidon,
 they would long ago have repented in sackcloth and ashes.
But I tell you, it will be more tolerable
 for Tyre and Sidon on the day of judgment than for you.
And as for you, Capernaum:

*Will you be exalted to heaven?
 You will go down to the nether world.*

For if the mighty deeds done in your midst had been done in Sodom,
 it would have remained until this day.
But I tell you, it will be more tolerable
 for the land of Sodom on the day of judgment than for you."

The Gospel of the Lord.

391 WEDNESDAY OF THE FIFTEENTH WEEK IN ORDINARY TIME

FIRST READING — Year II

Isaiah 10:5-7, 13b-16 — Will the axe boast against the one who hews with it?

A reading from the Book of the Prophet Isaiah

> Thus says the Lord:
> Woe to Assyria! My rod in anger,
>   my staff in wrath.
> Against an impious nation I send him,
>   and against a people under my wrath I order him
> To seize plunder, carry off loot,
>   and tread them down like the mud of the streets.
> But this is not what he intends,
>   nor does he have this in mind;
> Rather, it is in his heart to destroy,
>   to make an end of nations not a few.
>
> For he says:
> "By my own power I have done it,
>   and by my wisdom, for I am shrewd.
> I have moved the boundaries of peoples,
>   their treasures I have pillaged,
>   and, like a giant, I have put down the enthroned.
> My hand has seized like a nest
>   the riches of nations;
> As one takes eggs left alone,
>   so I took in all the earth;
> No one fluttered a wing,
>   or opened a mouth, or chirped!"
>
> Will the axe boast against him who hews with it?
>   Will the saw exalt itself above him who wields it?
> As if a rod could sway him who lifts it,
>   or a staff him who is not wood!
> Therefore the Lord, the Lord of hosts,
>   will send among his fat ones leanness,
> And instead of his glory there will be kindling
>   like the kindling of fire.

The word of the Lord.

RESPONSORIAL PSALM

Psalm 94:5-6, 7-8, 9-10, 14-15

℟. (14a) **The Lord will not abandon his people.**

Your people, O Lord, they trample down,
   your inheritance they afflict.
Widow and stranger they slay,
   the fatherless they murder.

℟. **The Lord will not abandon his people.**

And they say, "The Lord sees not;
   the God of Jacob perceives not."
Understand, you senseless ones among the people;
   and, you fools, when will you be wise?

℟. **The Lord will not abandon his people.**

Shall he who shaped the ear not hear?
   or he who formed the eye not see?
Shall he who instructs nations not chastise,
   he who teaches men knowledge?

℟. **The Lord will not abandon his people.**

For the Lord will not cast off his people,
   nor abandon his inheritance;
But judgment shall again be with justice,
   and all the upright of heart shall follow it.

℟. **The Lord will not abandon his people.**

ALLELUIA

See Matthew 11:25

℟. Alleluia, alleluia.

Blessed are you, Father, Lord of heaven and earth;
you have revealed to little ones the mysteries of the Kingdom.

℟. Alleluia, alleluia.

GOSPEL   Years I and II

Matthew 11:25-27   Although you have hidden these things from the wise and the learned you have revealed them to the childlike.

✢ A reading from the holy Gospel according to Matthew

At that time Jesus exclaimed:
"I give praise to you, Father, Lord of heaven and earth,
   for although you have hidden these things
   from the wise and the learned
   you have revealed them to the childlike.
Yes, Father, such has been your gracious will.
All things have been handed over to me by my Father.
No one knows the Son except the Father,
   and no one knows the Father except the Son
   and anyone to whom the Son wishes to reveal him."

The Gospel of the Lord.

392 THURSDAY OF THE FIFTEENTH WEEK IN ORDINARY TIME

FIRST READING   Year II

Isaiah 26:7-9, 12, 16-19   Awake and sing, you who lie in the dust.

A reading from the Book of the Prophet Isaiah

The way of the just is smooth;
 the path of the just you make level.
Yes, for your way and your judgments, O Lord,
 we look to you;
Your name and your title
 are the desire of our souls.
My soul yearns for you in the night,
 yes, my spirit within me keeps vigil for you;
When your judgment dawns upon the earth,
 the world's inhabitants learn justice.
O Lord, you mete out peace to us,
 for it is you who have accomplished all we have done.

O Lord, oppressed by your punishment,
 we cried out in anguish under your chastising.
As a woman about to give birth
 writhes and cries out in her pains,
 so were we in your presence, O Lord.
We conceived and writhed in pain,
 giving birth to wind;
Salvation we have not achieved for the earth,
 the inhabitants of the world cannot bring it forth.
But your dead shall live, their corpses shall rise;
 awake and sing, you who lie in the dust.
For your dew is a dew of light,
 and the land of shades gives birth.

The word of the Lord.

RESPONSORIAL PSALM

Psalm 102:13-14ab and 15, 16-18, 19-21

℟. (20b) **From heaven the Lord looks down on the earth.**

**You, O Lord, abide forever,
    and your name through all generations.
You will arise and have mercy on Zion,
    for it is time to pity her.
For her stones are dear to your servants,
    and her dust moves them to pity.**

℟. **From heaven the Lord looks down on the earth.**

**The nations shall revere your name, O Lord,
    and all the kings of the earth your glory,
When the Lord has rebuilt Zion
    and appeared in his glory;
When he has regarded the prayer of the destitute,
    and not despised their prayer.**

℟. **From heaven the Lord looks down on the earth.**

**Let this be written for the generation to come,
    and let his future creatures praise the Lord:
"The Lord looked down from his holy height,
    from heaven he beheld the earth,
To hear the groaning of the prisoners,
    to release those doomed to die."**

℟. **From heaven the Lord looks down on the earth.**

ALLELUIA

Matthew 11:28

℟. Alleluia, alleluia.

Come to me, all you who labor and are burdened,
and I will give you rest, says the Lord.

℟. Alleluia, alleluia.

GOSPEL   Years I and II

Matthew 11:28-30   I am meek and humble of heart.

☩ A reading from the holy Gospel according to Matthew

Jesus said:
"Come to me, all you who labor and are burdened,
　　and I will give you rest.
Take my yoke upon you and learn from me,
　　for I am meek and humble of heart;
　　and you will find rest for yourselves.
For my yoke is easy, and my burden light."

The Gospel of the Lord.

393 FRIDAY OF THE FIFTEENTH WEEK IN ORDINARY TIME

FIRST READING Year II

Isaiah 38:1-6, 21-22, 7-8   I have heard your prayer and seen your tears.

A reading from the Book of the Prophet Isaiah

When Hezekiah was mortally ill,
> the prophet Isaiah, son of Amoz, came and said to him:
> "Thus says the Lord: Put your house in order,
> for you are about to die; you shall not recover."
Then Hezekiah turned his face to the wall and prayed to the Lord:

> "O Lord, remember how faithfully and wholeheartedly
> I conducted myself in your presence,
> doing what was pleasing to you!"
And Hezekiah wept bitterly.

Then the word of the Lord came to Isaiah: "Go, tell Hezekiah:
> Thus says the Lord, the God of your father David:
> I have heard your prayer and seen your tears.
I will heal you: in three days you shall go up to the Lord's temple;
> I will add fifteen years to your life.
I will rescue you and this city from the hand of the king of Assyria;
> I will be a shield to this city."

Isaiah then ordered a poultice of figs to be taken
> and applied to the boil, that he might recover.
Then Hezekiah asked,
> "What is the sign that I shall go up to the temple of the Lord?"

Isaiah answered:
> "This will be the sign for you from the Lord
> that he will do what he has promised:
> See, I will make the shadow cast by the sun
> on the stairway to the terrace of Ahaz
> go back the ten steps it has advanced."
So the sun came back the ten steps it had advanced.

The word of the Lord.

RESPONSORIAL PSALM

Isaiah 38:10, 11, 12abcd, 16

℟. (see 17b) **You saved my life, O Lord; I shall not die.**

Once I said,
   "In the noontime of life I must depart!
To the gates of the nether world I shall be consigned
   for the rest of my years."

℟. You saved my life, O Lord; I shall not die.

I said, "I shall see the Lord no more
   in the land of the living.
No longer shall I behold my fellow men
   among those who dwell in the world."

℟. You saved my life, O Lord; I shall not die.

My dwelling, like a shepherd's tent,
   is struck down and borne away from me;
You have folded up my life, like a weaver
   who severs the last thread.

℟. You saved my life, O Lord; I shall not die.

Those live whom the Lord protects;
   yours is the life of my spirit.
You have given me health and life.

℟. You saved my life, O Lord; I shall not die.

ALLELUIA

John 10:27

℟. **Alleluia, alleluia.**

My sheep hear my voice, says the Lord;
I know them, and they follow me.

℟. Alleluia, alleluia.

GOSPEL Years I and II

Matthew 12:1-8   The Son of Man is Lord of the sabbath.

✢ A reading from the holy Gospel according to Matthew

**Jesus was going through a field of grain on the sabbath.
His disciples were hungry
   and began to pick the heads of grain and eat them.
When the Pharisees saw this, they said to him,
   "See, your disciples are doing what is unlawful to do on the sabbath."
He said to the them, "Have you not read what David did
   when he and his companions were hungry,
   how he went into the house of God and ate the bread of offering,
   which neither he nor his companions
   but only the priests could lawfully eat?
Or have you not read in the law that on the sabbath
   the priests serving in the temple violate the sabbath
   and are innocent?
I say to you, something greater than the temple is here.
If you knew what this meant, *I desire mercy, not sacrifice*,
   you would not have condemned these innocent men.
For the Son of Man is Lord of the sabbath."**

The Gospel of the Lord.

394 SATURDAY OF THE FIFTEENTH WEEK IN ORDINARY TIME

FIRST READING   Year II

Micah 2:1-5   They covet fields, and seize them; houses, and they take them.

A reading from the Book of the Prophet Micah

**Woe to those who plan iniquity,
  and work out evil on their couches;
In the morning light they accomplish it
  when it lies within their power.
They covet fields, and seize them;
  houses, and they take them;
They cheat an owner of his house,
  a man of his inheritance.
    Therefore thus says the Lord:
Behold, I am planning against this race an evil
  from which you shall not withdraw your necks;
Nor shall you walk with head high,
  for it will be a time of evil.**

**On that day a satire shall be sung over you,
  and there shall be a plaintive chant:
"Our ruin is complete,
  our fields are portioned out among our captors,
The fields of my people are measured out,
  and no one can get them back!"
Thus you shall have no one
  to mark out boundaries by lot
  in the assembly of the Lord.**

The word of the Lord.

RESPONSORIAL PSALM

Psalm 10:1-2, 3-4, 7-8, 14

℟. (12b) **Do not forget the poor, O Lord!**

**Why, O Lord, do you stand aloof?
   Why hide in times of distress?
Proudly the wicked harass the afflicted,
   who are caught in the devices the wicked have contrived.**

℟. **Do not forget the poor, O Lord!**

**For the wicked man glories in his greed,
   and the covetous blasphemes, sets the Lord at nought.
The wicked man boasts, "He will not avenge it";
   "There is no God," sums up his thoughts.**

℟. **Do not forget the poor, O Lord!**

**His mouth is full of cursing, guile and deceit;
   under his tongue are mischief and iniquity.
He lurks in ambush near the villages;
   in hiding he murders the innocent;
   his eyes spy upon the unfortunate.**

℟. **Do not forget the poor, O Lord!**

**You do see, for you behold misery and sorrow,
   taking them in your hands.
On you the unfortunate man depends;
   of the fatherless you are the helper.**

℟. **Do not forget the poor, O Lord!**

ALLELUIA

2 Corinthians 5:19

℟. Alleluia, alleluia.

**God was reconciling the world to himself in Christ,
and entrusting to us the message of reconciliation.**

℟. Alleluia, alleluia.

GOSPEL   Years I and II

Matthew 12:14-21   *He warned them not to make him known to fulfill what had been spoken.*

✢ **A reading from the holy Gospel according to Matthew**

**The Pharisees went out and took counsel against Jesus
   to put him to death.**

**When Jesus realized this, he withdrew from that place.
Many people followed him, and he cured them all,
   but he warned them not to make him known.
This was to fulfill what had been spoken through Isaiah the prophet:**

*Behold, my servant whom I have chosen,
   my beloved in whom I delight;
I shall place my Spirit upon him,
   and he will proclaim justice to the Gentiles.
He will not contend or cry out,
   nor will anyone hear his voice in the streets.
A bruised reed he will not break,
   a smoldering wick he will not quench,
until he brings justice to victory.
   And in his name the Gentiles will hope.*

The Gospel of the Lord.

395 MONDAY OF THE SIXTEENTH WEEK IN ORDINARY TIME

FIRST READING   Year II

Micah 6:1-4, 6-8   *You have been told, O man, what the Lord requires of you.*

A reading from the Book of the Prophet Micah

>   Hear what the Lord says:
> Arise, present your plea before the mountains,
>   and let the hills hear your voice!
> Hear, O mountains, the plea of the Lord,
>   pay attention, O foundations of the earth!
> For the Lord has a plea against his people,
>   and he enters into trial with Israel.
>
> O my people, what have I done to you,
>   or how have I wearied you? Answer me!
> For I brought you up from the land of Egypt,
>   from the place of slavery I released you;
> and I sent before you Moses,
>   Aaron, and Miriam.
>
> With what shall I come before the Lord,
>   and bow before God most high?
> Shall I come before him with burnt offerings,
>   with calves a year old?
> Will the Lord be pleased with thousands of rams,
>   with myriad streams of oil?
> Shall I give my first-born for my crime,
>   the fruit of my body for the sin of my soul?
> You have been told, O man, what is good,
>   and what the Lord requires of you:
> Only to do the right and to love goodness,
>   and to walk humbly with your God.

The word of the Lord.

RESPONSIAL PSALM

Psalm 50:5-6, 8-9, 16bc-17, 21 and 23

℟. (23b) **To the upright I will show the saving power of God.**

"Gather my faithful ones before me,
 those who have made a covenant with me by sacrifice."
And the heavens proclaim his justice;
 for God himself is the judge.

℟. **To the upright I will show the saving power of God.**

"Not for your sacrifices do I rebuke you,
 for your burnt offerings are before me always.
I take from your house no bullock,
 no goats out of your fold."

℟. **To the upright I will show the saving power of God.**

"Why do you recite my statutes,
 and profess my covenant with your mouth,
Though you hate discipline
 and cast my words behind you?"

℟. **To the upright I will show the saving power of God.**

"When you do these things, shall I be deaf to it?
 Or do you think that I am like yourself?
 I will correct you by drawing them up before your eyes.
He that offers praise as a sacrifice glorifies me;
 and to him that goes the right way I will show the salvation of God."

℟. **To the upright I will show the saving power of God.**

ALLELUIA

Psalm 95:8

℟. Alleluia, alleluia.

If today you hear his voice,
harden not your hearts.

℟. Alleluia, alleluia.

GOSPEL   Years I and II

Matthew 12:38-42   At the judgment the queen of the south will arise with this generation and condemn it.

✢ A reading from the holy Gospel according to Matthew

Some of the scribes and Pharisees said to Jesus,
  "Teacher, we wish to see a sign from you."
He said to them in reply,
  "An evil and unfaithful generation seeks a sign,
  but no sign will be given it
  except the sign of Jonah the prophet.
Just as Jonah was in the belly of the whale three days and three nights,
  so will the Son of Man be in the heart of the earth
  three days and three nights.
At the judgment, the men of Nineveh will arise with this generation
  and condemn it, because they repented at the preaching of Jonah;
  and there is something greater than Jonah here.
At the judgment the queen of the south will arise with this generation
  and condemn it, because she came from the ends of the earth
  to hear the wisdom of Solomon;
  and there is something greater than Solomon here."

The Gospel of the Lord.

396 TUESDAY OF THE SIXTEENTH WEEK IN ORDINARY TIME

FIRST READING   Year II

Micah 7:14-15, 18-20   He will cast into the depths of the sea all our sins.

A reading from the Book of the Prophet Micah

Shepherd your people with your staff,
  the flock of your inheritance,
That dwells apart in a woodland,
  in the midst of Carmel.
Let them feed in Bashan and Gilead,
  as in the days of old;
As in the days when you came from the land of Egypt,
  show us wonderful signs.

Who is there like you, the God who removes guilt
  and pardons sin for the remnant of his inheritance;
Who does not persist in anger forever,
  but delights rather in clemency,
And will again have compassion on us,
  treading underfoot our guilt?
You will cast into the depths of the sea
  all our sins;
You will show faithfulness to Jacob,
  and grace to Abraham,
As you have sworn to our fathers
  from days of old.

The word of the Lord.

RESPONSORIAL PSALM

Psalm 85:2-4, 5-6, 7-8

℟. (8a) **Lord, show us your mercy and love.**

**You have favored, O Lord, your land;
 you have brought back the captives of Jacob.
You have forgiven the guilt of your people;
 you have covered all their sins.
You have withdrawn all your wrath;
 you have revoked your burning anger.**

℟. **Lord, show us your mercy and love.**

**Restore us, O God our savior,
 and abandon your displeasure against us.
Will you be ever angry with us,
 prolonging your anger to all generations?**

℟. **Lord, show us your mercy and love.**

**Will you not instead give us life;
 and shall not your people rejoice in you?
Show us, O Lord, your kindness,
 and grant us your salvation.**

℟. **Lord, show us your mercy and love.**

ALLELUIA

John 14:23

℟. Alleluia, alleluia.

Whoever loves me will keep my word,
and my Father will love him
and we will come to him.

℟. Alleluia, alleluia.

GOSPEL   Years I and II

Matthew 12:46-50   Stretching out his hands toward his disciples, he said, "Here are my mother and my brothers."

✠ A reading from the holy Gospel according to Matthew

While Jesus was speaking to the crowds,
   his mother and his brothers appeared outside,
   wishing to speak with him.
Someone told him, "Your mother and your brothers are standing outside,
   asking to speak with you."
But he said in reply to the one who told him,
   "Who is my mother? Who are my brothers?"
And stretching out his hand toward his disciples, he said,
   "Here are my mother and my brothers.
For whoever does the will of my heavenly Father
   is my brother, and sister, and mother."

The Gospel of the Lord.

397 WEDNESDAY OF THE SIXTEENTH WEEK IN ORDINARY TIME

FIRST READING   Year II

Jeremiah 1:1, 4-10   A prophet to the nations I appointed you.

A reading from the beginning of the Book of the Prophet Jeremiah

**The words of Jeremiah, son of Hilkiah,
of a priestly family in Anathoth, in the land of Benjamin.**

The word of the LORD came to me thus:

**Before I formed you in the womb I knew you,
before you were born I dedicated you,
a prophet to the nations I appointed you.
"Ah, Lord GOD!" I said,
"I know not how to speak; I am too young."**

**But the LORD answered me,
Say not, "I am too young."
To whomever I send you, you shall go;
whatever I command you, you shall speak.
Have no fear before them,
because I am with you to deliver you, says the LORD.**

Then the LORD extended his hand and touched my mouth, saying,

**See, I place my words in your mouth!
This day I set you
over nations and over kingdoms,
To root up and to tear down,
to destroy and to demolish,
to build and to plant.**

The word of the Lord.

RESPONSORIAL PSALM

Psalm 71:1-2, 3-4a, 5-6ab, 15 and 17

℟. (see 15ab) **I will sing of your salvation.**

In you, O L֥ord, I take refuge;
  let me never be put to shame.
In your justice rescue me, and deliver me;
  incline your ear to me, and save me.

℟. **I will sing of your salvation.**

Be my rock of refuge,
  a stronghold to give me safety,
    for you are my rock and my fortress.
O my God, rescue me from the hand of the wicked.

℟. **I will sing of your salvation.**

For you are my hope, O Lord;
  my trust, O God, from my youth.
On you I depend from birth;
  from my mother's womb you are my strength.

℟. **I will sing of your salvation.**

My mouth shall declare your justice,
  day by day your salvation.
O God, you have taught me from my youth,
  and till the present I proclaim your wondrous deeds.

℟. **I will sing of your salvation.**

ALLELUIA

℟. Alleluia, alleluia.

The seed is the word of God, Christ is the sower;
all who come to him will live for ever.

℟. Alleluia, alleluia.

GOSPEL   Years I and II

Matthew 13:1-9   The seed produced grain a hundredfold.

✝ A reading from the holy Gospel according to Matthew

On that day, Jesus went out of the house and sat down by the sea.
Such large crowds gathered around him
   that he got into a boat and sat down,
   and the whole crowd stood along the shore.
And he spoke to them at length in parables, saying:
   "A sower went out to sow.
And as he sowed, some seed fell on the path,
   and birds came and ate it up.
Some fell on rocky ground, where it had little soil.
It sprang up at once because the soil was not deep,
   and when the sun rose it was scorched,
   and it withered for lack of roots.
Some seed fell among thorns, and the thorns grew up and choked it.
But some seed fell on rich soil, and produced fruit,
   a hundred or sixty or thirtyfold.
Whoever has ears ought to hear."

The Gospel of the Lord.

398 THURSDAY OF THE SIXTEENTH WEEK IN ORDINARY TIME

FIRST READING   Year II

Jeremiah 2:1-3, 7-8, 12-13   They have forsaken me, the source of living waters; they have dug themselves broken cisterns.

A reading from the Book of the Prophet Jeremiah

This word of the Lord came to me:
  Go, cry out this message for Jerusalem to hear!

I remember the devotion of your youth,
  how you loved me as a bride,
Following me in the desert,
  in a land unsown.
Sacred to the Lord was Israel,
  the first fruits of his harvest;
Should any presume to partake of them,
  evil would befall them, says the Lord.

When I brought you into the garden land
  to eat its goodly fruits,
You entered and defiled my land,
  you made my heritage loathsome.
The priests asked not,
  "Where is the Lord?"
Those who dealt with the law knew me not:
  the shepherds rebelled against me.
The prophets prophesied by Baal,
  and went after useless idols.

Be amazed at this, O heavens,
  and shudder with sheer horror, says the Lord.
Two evils have my people done:
  they have forsaken me, the source of living waters;
They have dug themselves cisterns,
  broken cisterns, that hold no water.

The word of the Lord.

RESPONSORIAL PSALM

Psalm 36:6-7ab, 8-9, 10-11

℟. (10a) **With you is the fountain of life, O Lord.**

O L ORD, your mercy reaches to heaven;
  your faithfulness, to the clouds.
Your justice is like the mountains of God;
  your judgments, like the mighty deep.

℟. **With you is the fountain of life, O Lord.**

How precious is your mercy, O God!
  The children of men take refuge in the shadow of your wings.
They have their fill of the prime gifts of your house;
  from your delightful stream you give them to drink.

℟. **With you is the fountain of life, O Lord.**

For with you is the fountain of life,
  and in your light we see light.
Keep up your mercy toward your friends,
  your just defense of the upright of heart.

℟. **With you is the fountain of life, O Lord.**

ALLELUIA

See Matthew 11:25

℟. **Alleluia, alleluia.**

Blessed are you, Father, Lord of heaven and earth;
you have revealed to little ones the mysteries of the Kingdom.

℟. **Alleluia, alleluia.**

GOSPEL   Years I and II

Matthew 13:10-17   Because knowledge of the mysteries of the Kingdom of heaven has been granted to you, but to them it has not been granted.

☩ A reading from the holy Gospel according to Matthew

The disciples approached Jesus and said,
  "Why do you speak to the crowd in parables?"
He said to them in reply,
  "Because knowledge of the mysteries of the Kingdom of heaven
  has been granted to you, but to them it has not been granted.
To anyone who has, more will be given and he will grow rich;
  from anyone who has not, even what he has will be taken away.
This is why I speak to them in parables, because
  they look but do not see and hear but do not listen or understand.
Isaiah's prophecy is fulfilled in them, which says:

  You shall indeed hear but not understand,
    you shall indeed look but never see.
  Gross is the heart of this people,
    they will hardly hear with their ears,
      they have closed their eyes,
      lest they see with their eyes
    and hear with their ears
  and understand with their hearts and be converted
    and I heal them.

"But blessed are your eyes, because they see,
  and your ears, because they hear.
Amen, I say to you, many prophets and righteous people
  longed to see what you see but did not see it,
  and to hear what you hear but did not hear it."

The Gospel of the Lord.

399 FRIDAY OF THE SIXTEENTH WEEK IN ORDINARY TIME

FIRST READING Year II

Jeremiah 3:14-17   I will appoint over you shepherds after my own heart; all nations will be gathered together at Jerusalem.

A reading from the Book of the Prophet Jeremiah

Return, rebellious children, says the LORD,
   for I am your Master;
I will take you, one from a city, two from a clan,
   and bring you to Zion.
I will appoint over you shepherds after my own heart,
   who will shepherd you wisely and prudently.
When you multiply and become fruitful in the land,
   says the LORD,
They will in those days no longer say,
   "The ark of the covenant of the LORD!"
They will no longer think of it, or remember it,
   or miss it, or make another.

At that time they will call Jerusalem the LORD's throne;
   there all nations will be gathered together
   to honor the name of the LORD at Jerusalem,
   and they will walk no longer in their hardhearted wickedness.

The word of the Lord.

RESPONSORIAL PSALM

Jeremiah 31:10, 11-12abcd, 13

℟. (see 10d) **The Lord will guard us as a shepherd guards his flock.**

Hear the word of the Lord, O nations,
   proclaim it on distant isles, and say:
He who scattered Israel, now gathers them together,
   he guards them as a shepherd his flock.

℟. The Lord will guard us as a shepherd guards his flock.

The Lord shall ransom Jacob,
   he shall redeem him from the hand of his conqueror.
Shouting, they shall mount the heights of Zion,
   they shall come streaming to the Lord's blessings:
The grain, the wine, and the oil,
   the sheep and the oxen.

℟. The Lord will guard us as a shepherd guards his flock.

Then the virgins shall make merry and dance,
   and young men and old as well.
I will turn their mourning into joy,
   I will console and gladden them after their sorrows.

℟. The Lord will guard us as a shepherd guards his flock.

ALLELUIA

See Luke 8:15

℟. **Alleluia, alleluia.**

Blessed are they who have kept the word with a generous heart and yield a harvest through perseverance.

℟. **Alleluia, alleluia.**

GOSPEL   Years I and II

Matthew 13:18-23   *The one who hears the word and understands it will bear much fruit.*

✙ **A reading from the holy Gospel according to Matthew**

Jesus said to his disciples:
"Hear the parable of the sower.
The seed sown on the path is the one who hears the word of the Kingdom
   without understanding it,
   and the Evil One comes and steals away
   what was sown in his heart.
The seed sown on rocky ground
   is the one who hears the word and receives it at once with joy.
But he has no root and lasts only for a time.
When some tribulation or persecution comes because of the word,
   he immediately falls away.
The seed sown among thorns is the one who hears the word,
   but then worldly anxiety and the lure of riches choke the word
   and it bears no fruit.
But the seed sown on rich soil
   is the one who hears the word and understands it,
   who indeed bears fruit and yields a hundred or sixty or thirtyfold."

The Gospel of the Lord.

400 SATURDAY OF THE SIXTEENTH WEEK IN ORDINARY TIME

FIRST READING   Year II

Jeremiah 7:1-11   Has this house which bears my name become in your eyes a den of thieves?

A reading from the Book of the Prophet Jeremiah

The following message came to Jeremiah from the Lord:
   Stand at the gate of the house of the Lord,
   and there proclaim this message:
   Hear the word of the Lord, all you of Judah
   who enter these gates to worship the Lord!
Thus says the Lord of hosts, the God of Israel:
   Reform your ways and your deeds,
   so that I may remain with you in this place.
Put not your trust in the deceitful words:
   "This is the temple of the Lord!
The temple of the Lord! The temple of the Lord!"
Only if you thoroughly reform your ways and your deeds;
   if each of you deals justly with his neighbor;
   if you no longer oppress the resident alien,
   the orphan, and the widow;
   if you no longer shed innocent blood in this place,
   or follow strange gods to your own harm,
   will I remain with you in this place,
   in the land I gave your fathers long ago and forever.

But here you are, putting your trust in deceitful words to your own loss!
Are you to steal and murder, commit adultery and perjury,
   burn incense to Baal,
   go after strange gods that you know not,
   and yet come to stand before me
   in this house which bears my name, and say:
   "We are safe; we can commit all these abominations again"?
Has this house which bears my name
   become in your eyes a den of thieves?
I too see what is being done, says the Lord.

The word of the Lord.

RESPONSORIAL PSALM

Psalm 84:3, 4, 5-6a and 8a, 11

℟. (2) **How lovely is your dwelling place, Lord, mighty God!**

**My soul yearns and pines
   for the courts of the L**ORD**.
My heart and my flesh
   cry out for the living God.**

℟. **How lovely is your dwelling place, Lord, mighty God!**

**Even the sparrow finds a home,
   and the swallow a nest
      in which she puts her young—
Your altars, O L**ORD **of hosts,
   my king and my God!**

℟. **How lovely is your dwelling place, Lord, mighty God!**

**Blessed they who dwell in your house!
   continually they praise you.
Blessed the men whose strength you are!
They go from strength to strength.**

℟. **How lovely is your dwelling place, Lord, mighty God!**

**I had rather one day in your courts
   than a thousand elsewhere;
I had rather lie at the threshold of the house of my God
   than dwell in the tents of the wicked.**

℟. **How lovely is your dwelling place, Lord, mighty God!**

ALLELUIA

James 1:21bc

℟. Alleluia, alleluia.

Humbly welcome the word that has been planted in you and is able to save your souls.

℟. Alleluia, alleluia.

GOSPEL   Years I and II

Matthew 13:24-30   Let them grow together until harvest.

✠ A reading from the holy Gospel according to Matthew

**Jesus proposed a parable to the crowds.
"The Kingdom of heaven may be likened to a man
   who sowed good seed in his field.
While everyone was asleep his enemy came
   and sowed weeds all through the wheat, and then went off.
When the crop grew and bore fruit, the weeds appeared as well.
The slaves of the householder came to him and said,
   'Master, did you not sow good seed in your field?
Where have the weeds come from?'
He answered, 'An enemy has done this.'
His slaves said to him, 'Do you want us to go and pull them up?'
He replied, 'No, if you pull up the weeds
   you might uproot the wheat along with them.
Let them grow together until harvest;
   then at harvest time I will say to the harvesters,
      "First collect the weeds and tie them in bundles for burning;
      but gather the wheat into my barn."'"**

The Gospel of the Lord.

401 MONDAY OF THE SEVENTEENTH WEEK IN ORDINARY TIME

FIRST READING   Year II

Jeremiah 13:1-11   *This people shall be like a loincloth which is good for nothing.*

A reading from the Book of the Prophet Jeremiah

The Lord said to me: Go buy yourself a linen loincloth;
  wear it on your loins, but do not put it in water.
I bought the loincloth, as the Lord commanded, and put it on.
A second time the word of the Lord came to me thus:
  Take the loincloth which you bought and are wearing,
  and go now to the Parath;
  there hide it in a cleft of the rock.
Obedient to the Lord's command, I went to the Parath
  and buried the loincloth.
After a long interval, the Lord said to me:
  Go now to the Parath and fetch the loincloth
  which I told you to hide there.
Again I went to the Parath, sought out and took the loincloth
  from the place where I had hid it.
But it was rotted, good for nothing!
Then the message came to me from the Lord:
Thus says the Lord:
  So also I will allow the pride of Judah to rot,
  the great pride of Jerusalem.
This wicked people who refuse to obey my words,
  who walk in the stubbornness of their hearts,
  and follow strange gods to serve and adore them,
  shall be like this loincloth which is good for nothing.
For, as close as the loincloth clings to a man's loins,
  so had I made the whole house of Israel
  and the whole house of Judah cling to me, says the Lord;
  to be my people, my renown, my praise, my beauty.
But they did not listen.

The word of the Lord.

RESPONSORIAL PSALM

Deuteronomy 32:18-19, 20, 21

℟. (see 18a) **You have forgotten God who gave you birth.**

**You were unmindful of the Rock that begot you,
   You forgot the God who gave you birth.
When the** L<small>ORD</small> **saw this, he was filled with loathing
   and anger toward his sons and daughters.**

℟. **You have forgotten God who gave you birth.**

**"I will hide my face from them," he said,
   "and see what will then become of them.
What a fickle race they are,
   sons with no loyalty in them!"**

℟. **You have forgotten God who gave you birth.**

**"Since they have provoked me with their 'no-god'
   and angered me with their vain idols,
I will provoke them with a 'no-people';
   with a foolish nation I will anger them."**

℟. **You have forgotten God who gave you birth.**

ALLELUIA

James 1:18

℟. **Alleluia, alleluia.**

**The Father willed to give us birth by the word of truth
that we may be a kind of firstfruits of his creatures.**

℟. **Alleluia, alleluia.**

GOSPEL — Years I and II

Matthew 13:31-35   *The mustard seed becomes a large bush and the birds of the sky come and dwell in its branches.*

✠ **A reading from the holy Gospel according to Matthew**

**Jesus proposed a parable to the crowds.
"The Kingdom of heaven is like a mustard seed
   that a person took and sowed in a field.
It is the smallest of all the seeds,
   yet when full-grown it is the largest of plants.
It becomes a large bush,
   and the 'birds of the sky come and dwell in its branches.'"**

**He spoke to them another parable.
"The Kingdom of heaven is like yeast
   that a woman took and mixed with three measures of wheat flour
   until the whole batch was leavened."**

**All these things Jesus spoke to the crowds in parables.
He spoke to them only in parables,
   to fulfill what had been said through the prophet:**

   *I will open my mouth in parables,
      I will announce what has lain hidden from the foundation
      of the world.*

The Gospel of the Lord.

402 TUESDAY OF THE SEVENTEENTH WEEK IN ORDINARY TIME

FIRST READING   Year II

Jeremiah 14:17-22   Remember, Lord, your covenant with us and break it not.

A reading from the Book of the Prophet Jeremiah

Let my eyes stream with tears
  day and night, without rest,
Over the great destruction which overwhelms
  the virgin daughter of my people,
  over her incurable wound.
If I walk out into the field,
  look! those slain by the sword;
If I enter the city,
  look! those consumed by hunger.
Even the prophet and the priest
  forage in a land they know not.

Have you cast Judah off completely?
  Is Zion loathsome to you?
Why have you struck us a blow
  that cannot be healed?
We wait for peace, to no avail;
  for a time of healing, but terror comes instead.
We recognize, O Lord, our wickedness,
  the guilt of our fathers;
  that we have sinned against you.
For your name's sake spurn us not,
  disgrace not the throne of your glory;
  remember your covenant with us, and break it not.
Among the nations' idols is there any that gives rain?
  Or can the mere heavens send showers?
Is it not you alone, O Lord,
  our God, to whom we look?
  You alone have done all these things.

The word of the Lord.

RESPONSORIAL PSALM

Psalm 79:8, 9, 11 and 13

℟. (9) **For the glory of your name, O Lord, deliver us.**

**Remember not against us the iniquities of the past;
may your compassion quickly come to us,
for we are brought very low.**

℟. **For the glory of your name, O Lord, deliver us.**

**Help us, O God our savior,
because of the glory of your name;
Deliver us and pardon our sins
for your name's sake.**

℟. **For the glory of your name, O Lord, deliver us.**

**Let the prisoners' sighing come before you;
with your great power free those doomed to death.
Then we, your people and the sheep of your pasture,
will give thanks to you forever;
through all generations we will declare your praise.**

℟. **For the glory of your name, O Lord, deliver us.**

ALLELUIA

℟. Alleluia, alleluia.

The seed is the word of God, Christ is the sower;
all who come to him will live for ever.

℟. Alleluia, alleluia.

GOSPEL   Years I and II

Matthew 13:36-43   *Just as the weeds are collected now and burned up with fire, so will it be at the end of the age.*

✚   A reading from the holy Gospel according to Matthew

Jesus dismissed the crowds and went into the house.
His disciples approached him and said,
   "Explain to us the parable of the weeds in the field."
He said in reply, "He who sows good seed is the Son of Man,
   the field is the world, the good seed the children of the Kingdom.
The weeds are the children of the Evil One,
   and the enemy who sows them is the Devil.
The harvest is the end of the age, and the harvesters are angels.
Just as weeds are collected and burned up with fire,
   so will it be at the end of the age.
The Son of Man will send his angels,
   and they will collect out of his Kingdom
   all who cause others to sin and all evildoers.
They will throw them into the fiery furnace,
   where there will be wailing and grinding of teeth.
Then the righteous will shine like the sun
   in the Kingdom of their Father.
Whoever has ears ought to hear."

The Gospel of the Lord.

403 WEDNESDAY OF THE SEVENTEENTH WEEK IN ORDINARY TIME

FIRST READING   Year II

Jeremiah 15:10, 16-21   Why is my pain continuous?—If you repent, you shall stand in my presence.

A reading from the Book of the Prophet Jeremiah

Woe to me, mother, that you gave me birth!
 a man of strife and contention to all the land!
I neither borrow nor lend,
 yet all curse me.
When I found your words, I devoured them;
 they became my joy and the happiness of my heart,
Because I bore your name,
  O Lord, God of hosts.
I did not sit celebrating
 in the circle of merrymakers;
Under the weight of your hand I sat alone
 because you filled me with indignation.
Why is my pain continuous,
 my wound incurable, refusing to be healed?
You have indeed become for me a treacherous brook,
 whose waters do not abide!
  Thus the Lord answered me:
If you repent, so that I restore you,
 in my presence you shall stand;
If you bring forth the precious without the vile,
 you shall be my mouthpiece.
Then it shall be they who turn to you,
 and you shall not turn to them;
And I will make you toward this people
 a solid wall of brass.
Though they fight against you,
 they shall not prevail,
For I am with you,
 to deliver and rescue you, says the Lord.
I will free you from the hand of the wicked,
 and rescue you from the grasp of the violent.

The word of the Lord.

RESPONSORIAL PSALM

Psalm 59:2-3, 4, 10-11, 17, 18

℟. (17d) **God is my refuge on the day of distress.**

**Rescue me from my enemies, O my God;
  from my adversaries defend me.
Rescue me from evildoers;
  from bloodthirsty men save me.**

℟. **God is my refuge on the day of distress.**

**For behold, they lie in wait for my life;
  mighty men come together against me,
Not for any offense or sin of mine, O L**ORD.

℟. **God is my refuge on the day of distress.**

**O my strength! for you I watch;
  for you, O God, are my stronghold,
As for my God, may his mercy go before me;
  may he show me the fall of my foes.**

℟. **God is my refuge on the day of distress.**

**But I will sing of your strength
  and revel at dawn in your mercy;
You have been my stronghold,
  my refuge in the day of distress.**

℟. **God is my refuge on the day of distress.**

**O my strength! your praise will I sing;
  for you, O God, are my stronghold,
  my merciful God!**

℟. **God is my refuge on the day of distress.**

ALLELUIA

John 15:15b

℟. Alleluia, alleluia.

I call you my friends, says the Lord,
for I have made known to you all that the Father has told me.

℟. Alleluia, alleluia.

GOSPEL Years I and II

Matthew 13:44-46   He sells all he has and buys that field.

✢ A reading from the holy Gospel according to Matthew

Jesus said to his disciples:
"The Kingdom of heaven is like a treasure buried in a field,
 which a person finds and hides again,
 and out of joy goes and sells all that he has and buys that field.
Again, the Kingdom of heaven is like a merchant
 searching for fine pearls.
When he finds a pearl of great price,
 he goes and sells all that he has and buys it."

The Gospel of the Lord.

404 THURSDAY OF THE SEVENTEENTH WEEK IN ORDINARY TIME

FIRST READING   Year II

Jeremiah 18:1-6   Like the clay in the hand of the potter, so are you in my hand, house of Israel.

A reading from the Book of the Prophet Jeremiah

This word came to Jeremiah from the Lord:
Rise up, be off to the potter's house;
   there I will give you my message.
I went down to the potter's house and there he was,
   working at the wheel.
Whenever the object of clay which he was making
   turned out badly in his hand,
   he tried again,
   making of the clay another object of whatever sort he pleased.
Then the word of the Lord came to me:
   Can I not do to you, house of Israel,
   as this potter has done? says the Lord.
Indeed, like clay in the hand of the potter,
   so are you in my hand, house of Israel.

The word of the Lord.

RESPONSORIAL PSALM

Psalm 146:1b-2, 3-4, 5-6ab

℟. (5a) **Blessed is he whose help is the God of Jacob.**
   or:
℟. **Alleluia.**

Praise the Lord, O my soul;
   I will praise the Lord all my life;
   I will sing praise to my God while I live.

℟. **Blessed is he whose help is the God of Jacob.**
   or:
℟. **Alleluia.**

Put not your trust in princes,
   in the sons of men, in whom there is no salvation.
When his spirit departs he returns to his earth;
   on that day his plans perish.

℟. **Blessed is he whose help is the God of Jacob.**
   or:
℟. **Alleluia.**

Blessed he whose help is the God of Jacob,
   whose hope is in the Lord, his God.
Who made heaven and earth,
   the sea and all that is in them.

℟. **Blessed is he whose help is the God of Jacob.**
   or:
℟. **Alleluia.**

ALLELUIA

See Acts 16:14b

℟. Alleluia, alleluia.

**Open our hearts, O Lord,
to listen to the words of your Son.**

℟. Alleluia, alleluia.

GOSPEL — Years I and II

Matthew 13:47-53   They put what is good into buckets, what is bad they throw away.

✠ A reading from the holy Gospel according to Matthew

**Jesus said to the disciples:
"The Kingdom of heaven is like a net thrown into the sea,
   which collects fish of every kind.
When it is full they haul it ashore
   and sit down to put what is good into buckets.
What is bad they throw away.
Thus it will be at the end of the age.
The angels will go out and separate the wicked from the righteous
   and throw them into the fiery furnace,
      where there will be wailing and grinding of teeth."**

**"Do you understand all these things?"
They answered, "Yes."
And he replied,
   "Then every scribe who has been instructed in the Kingdom of heaven
   is like the head of a household who brings from his storeroom
   both the new and the old."
When Jesus finished these parables, he went away from there.**

The Gospel of the Lord.

405 FRIDAY OF THE SEVENTEENTH WEEK IN ORDINARY TIME

FIRST READING   Year II

Jeremiah 26:1-9   All the people gathered about Jeremiah in the house of the Lord.

A reading from the Book of the Prophet Jeremiah

In the beginning of the reign of Jehoiakim,
  son of Josiah, king of Judah,
  this message came from the Lord:
    Thus says the Lord:
  Stand in the court of the house of the Lord
  and speak to the people of all the cities of Judah
  who come to worship in the house of the Lord;
  whatever I command you, tell them, and omit nothing.
Perhaps they will listen and turn back,
  each from his evil way,
  so that I may repent of the evil I have planned to inflict upon them
  for their evil deeds.
Say to them: Thus says the Lord:
  If you disobey me,
  not living according to the law I placed before you
  and not listening to the words of my servants the prophets,
  whom I send you constantly though you do not obey them,
  I will treat this house like Shiloh,
  and make this the city to which all the nations of the earth
  shall refer when cursing another.

Now the priests, the prophets, and all the people
  heard Jeremiah speak these words in the house of the Lord.
When Jeremiah finished speaking
  all that the Lord bade him speak to all the people,
  the priests and prophets laid hold of him, crying,
  "You must be put to death!
Why do you prophesy in the name of the Lord:
  'This house shall be like Shiloh,' and
  'This city shall be desolate and deserted'?"
And all the people gathered about Jeremiah in the house of the Lord.

The word of the Lord.

RESPONSORIAL PSALM

Psalm 69:5, 8-10, 14

℟. (14c) **Lord, in your great love, answer me.**

**Those outnumber the hairs of my head
    who hate me without cause.
Too many for my strength
    are they who wrongfully are my enemies.
    Must I restore what I did not steal?**

℟. **Lord, in your great love, answer me.**

**Since for your sake I bear insult,
    and shame covers my face.
I have become an outcast to my brothers,
    a stranger to my mother's sons,
Because zeal for your house consumes me,
    and the insults of those who blaspheme you fall upon me.**

℟. **Lord, in your great love, answer me.**

**But I pray to you, O LORD,
    for the time of your favor, O God!
In your great kindness answer me
    with your constant help.**

℟. **Lord, in your great love, answer me.**

ALLELUIA

1 Peter 1:25

℟. **Alleluia, alleluia.**

**The word of the Lord remains forever;
this is the word that has been proclaimed to you.**

℟. **Alleluia, alleluia.**

GOSPEL Years I and II

Matthew 13:54-58   Is he not the carpenter's son? Where did this man get such wisdom and mighty deeds?

☩ A reading from the holy Gospel according to Matthew

Jesus came to his native place and taught the people in their synagogue.
They were astonished and said,
  "Where did this man get such wisdom and mighty deeds?
Is he not the carpenter's son?
Is not his mother named Mary
  and his brothers James, Joseph, Simon, and Judas?
Are not his sisters all with us?
Where did this man get all this?"
And they took offense at him.
But Jesus said to them,
  "A prophet is not without honor except in his native place
  and in his own house."
And he did not work many mighty deeds there
  because of their lack of faith.

The Gospel of the Lord.

406 SATURDAY OF THE SEVENTEENTH WEEK IN ORDINARY TIME

FIRST READING   Year II

Jeremiah 26:11-16, 24   For in truth it was the Lord who sent me to you, to speak all these things for you to hear.

A reading from the Book of the Prophet Jeremiah

The priests and prophets said to the princes and to all the people,
"This man deserves death;
he has prophesied against this city,
as you have heard with your own ears."
Jeremiah gave this answer to the princes and all the people:
"It was the Lord who sent me to prophesy against this house and city
all that you have heard.
Now, therefore, reform your ways and your deeds;
listen to the voice of the Lord your God,
so that the Lord will repent of the evil with which he threatens you.
As for me, I am in your hands;
do with me what you think good and right.
But mark well: if you put me to death,
it is innocent blood you bring on yourselves,
on this city and its citizens.
For in truth it was the Lord who sent me to you,
to speak all these things for you to hear."

Thereupon the princes and all the people
said to the priests and the prophets,
"This man does not deserve death;
it is in the name of the Lord, our God, that he speaks to us."

So Ahikam, son of Shaphan, protected Jeremiah,
so that he was not handed over to the people to be put to death.

The word of the Lord.

RESPONSORIAL PSALM

Psalm 69:15-16, 30-31, 33-34

℟. (14c) **Lord, in your great love, answer me.**

**Rescue me out of the mire; may I not sink!
  may I be rescued from my foes,
  and from the watery depths.
Let not the flood-waters overwhelm me,
  nor the abyss swallow me up,
  nor the pit close its mouth over me.**

℟. **Lord, in your great love, answer me.**

**But I am afflicted and in pain;
  let your saving help, O God, protect me.
I will praise the name of God in song,
  and I will glorify him with thanksgiving.**

℟. **Lord, in your great love, answer me.**

**"See, you lowly ones, and be glad;
  you who seek God, may your hearts revive!
For the L**ORD** hears the poor,
  and his own who are in bonds he spurns not."**

℟. **Lord, in your great love, answer me.**

ALLELUIA

Matthew 5:10

℟. Alleluia, alleluia.

Blessed are they who are persecuted for the sake of righteousness for theirs is the Kingdom of heaven.

℟. Alleluia, alleluia.

GOSPEL Years I and II

Matthew 14:1-12 Herod had John beheaded; John's disciples came and told Jesus.

✠ A reading from the holy Gospel according to Matthew

Herod the tetrarch heard of the reputation of Jesus
   and said to his servants, "This man is John the Baptist.
He has been raised from the dead;
   that is why mighty powers are at work in him."

Now Herod had arrested John, bound him, and put him in prison
   on account of Herodias, the wife of his brother Philip,
   for John had said to him,
   "It is not lawful for you to have her."
Although he wanted to kill him, he feared the people,
   for they regarded him as a prophet.
But at a birthday celebration for Herod,
   the daughter of Herodias performed a dance before the guests
   and delighted Herod so much
   that he swore to give her whatever she might ask for.
Prompted by her mother, she said,
   "Give me here on a platter the head of John the Baptist."
The king was distressed,
   but because of his oaths and the guests who were present,
   he ordered that it be given, and he had John beheaded in the prison.
His head was brought in on a platter and given to the girl,
   who took it to her mother.
His disciples came and took away the corpse
   and buried him; and they went and told Jesus.

The Gospel of the Lord.

407 MONDAY OF THE EIGHTEENTH WEEK IN ORDINARY TIME

FIRST READING Year II

Jeremiah 28:1-17 The Lord has not sent you, and you have raised false confidence in this people.

A reading from the Book of the Prophet Jeremiah

In the beginning of the reign of Zedekiah, king of Judah,
   in the fifth month of the fourth year,
   the prophet Hananiah, son of Azzur, from Gibeon,
   said to me in the house of the Lord
   in the presence of the priests and all the people:
   "Thus says the Lord of hosts, the God of Israel:
   'I will break the yoke of the king of Babylon.
Within two years I will restore to this place
   all the vessels of the temple of the Lord which Nebuchadnezzar,
   king of Babylon, took away from this place to Babylon.
And I will bring back to this place Jeconiah,
   son of Jehoiakim, king of Judah,
   and all the exiles of Judah who went to Babylon,' says the Lord,
   'for I will break the yoke of the king of Babylon.'"

The prophet Jeremiah answered the prophet Hananiah
   in the presence of the priests and all the people assembled
   in the house of the Lord, and said:
   Amen! thus may the Lord do!
May he fulfill the things you have prophesied
   by bringing the vessels of the house of the Lord
   and all the exiles back from Babylon to this place!
But now, listen to what I am about to state in your hearing
   and the hearing of all the people.
From of old, the prophets who were before you and me prophesied
   war, woe, and pestilence against many lands and mighty kingdoms.
But the prophet who prophesies peace
   is recognized as truly sent by the Lord
   only when his prophetic prediction is fulfilled.

Thereupon the prophet Hananiah took the yoke
   from the neck of the prophet Jeremiah and broke it,
   and said in the presence of all the people:
   "Thus says the Lord: 'Even so, within two years
   I will break the yoke of Nebuchadnezzar, king of Babylon,
   from off the neck of all the nations.'"
At that, the prophet Jeremiah went away.

Some time after the prophet Hananiah had broken the yoke
   from off the neck of the prophet Jeremiah,
The word of the Lord came to Jeremiah:
   Go tell Hananiah this:
   Thus says the Lord:
   By breaking a wooden yoke, you forge an iron yoke!
For thus says the Lord of hosts, the God of Israel:
   A yoke of iron I will place on the necks
   of all these nations serving Nebuchadnezzar, king of Babylon,
   and they shall serve him; even the beasts of the field I give him.

To the prophet Hananiah the prophet Jeremiah said:
   Hear this, Hananiah!
The Lord has not sent you,
   and you have raised false confidence in this people.
For this, says the Lord, I will dispatch you from the face of the earth;
   this very year you shall die,
   because you have preached rebellion against the Lord.
That same year, in the seventh month, Hananiah the prophet died.

The word of the Lord.

RESPONSORIAL PSALM

Psalm 119:29, 43, 79, 80, 95, 102

℟. (68b) **Lord, teach me your statutes.**

**Remove from me the way of falsehood,
 and favor me with your law.**

℟. **Lord, teach me your statutes.**

**Take not the word of truth from my mouth,
 for in your ordinances is my hope.**

℟. **Lord, teach me your statutes.**

**Let those turn to me who fear you
 and acknowledge your decrees.**

℟. **Lord, teach me your statutes.**

**Let my heart be perfect in your statutes,
 that I be not put to shame.**

℟. **Lord, teach me your statutes.**

**Sinners wait to destroy me,
 but I pay heed to your decrees.**

℟. **Lord, teach me your statutes.**

**From your ordinances I turn not away,
 for you have instructed me.**

℟. **Lord, teach me your statutes.**

ALLELUIA

Matthew 4:4

℟. **Alleluia, alleluia.**

**One does not live on bread alone,
but on every word that comes forth from the mouth of God.**

℟. **Alleluia, alleluia.**

GOSPEL   Years I and II

In Year A, when the Gospel below is read on the preceding Sunday, Matthew 14:22-36 is read on Monday as below, no. 408.

Matthew 14:13-21   Looking up to heaven, he said the blessing and gave the loaves to the disciples, who in turn gave them to the crowds.

✢ **A reading from the holy Gospel according to Matthew**

When Jesus heard of the death of John the Baptist,
  he withdrew in a boat to a deserted place by himself.
The crowds heard of this and followed him on foot from their towns.
When he disembarked and saw the vast crowd,
  his heart was moved with pity for them, and he cured their sick.
When it was evening, the disciples approached him and said,
   "This is a deserted place and it is already late;
   dismiss the crowds so that they can go to the villages
   and buy food for themselves."
He said to them, "There is no need for them to go away;
  give them some food yourselves."
But they said to him,
  "Five loaves and two fish are all we have here."
Then he said, "Bring them here to me,"
  and he ordered the crowds to sit down on the grass.
Taking the five loaves and the two fish, and looking up to heaven,
  he said the blessing, broke the loaves,
  and gave them to the disciples,
  who in turn gave them to the crowds.
They all ate and were satisfied,
   and they picked up the fragments left over—
  twelve wicker baskets full.
Those who ate were about five thousand men,
  not counting women and children.

The Gospel of the Lord.

408 TUESDAY OF THE EIGHTEENTH WEEK IN ORDINARY TIME

FIRST READING Year II

Jeremiah 30:1-2, 12-15, 18-22 Because of your numerous sins, I have done this to you. See! I will restore the tents of Jacob.

A reading from the Book of the Prophet Jeremiah

**The following message came to Jeremiah from the LORD:
 For thus says the LORD, the God of Israel:
 Write all the words I have spoken to you in a book.**

> **For thus says the LORD:
 Incurable is your wound,
  grievous your bruise;
 There is none to plead your cause,
  no remedy for your running sore,
  no healing for you.
 All your lovers have forgotten you,
  they do not seek you.
 I struck you as an enemy would strike,
  punished you cruelly;
 Why cry out over your wound?
  your pain is without relief.
 Because of your great guilt,
  your numerous sins,
  I have done this to you.**

> **Thus says the LORD:
 See! I will restore the tents of Jacob,
  his dwellings I will pity;
 City shall be rebuilt upon hill,
  and palace restored as it was.
 From them will resound songs of praise,
  the laughter of happy men.
 I will make them not few, but many;
  they will not be tiny, for I will glorify them.
 His sons shall be as of old,
  his assembly before me shall stand firm;
 I will punish all his oppressors.**

His leader shall be one of his own,
> and his rulers shall come from his kin.
When I summon him, he shall approach me;
> how else should one take the deadly risk
> of approaching me? says the Lord.
You shall be my people,
> and I will be your God.

The word of the Lord.

RESPONSORIAL PSALM

Psalm 102:16-18, 19-21, 29 and 22-23

℟. (17) The Lord will build up Zion again, and appear in all his glory.

The nations shall revere your name, O Lord,
> and all the kings of the earth your glory,
When the Lord has rebuilt Zion
> and appeared in his glory;
When he has regarded the prayer of the destitute,
> and not despised their prayer.

℟. The Lord will build up Zion again, and appear in all his glory.

Let this be written for the generation to come,
> and let his future creatures praise the Lord:
"The Lord looked down from his holy height,
> from heaven he beheld the earth,
To hear the groaning of the prisoners,
> to release those doomed to die."

℟. The Lord will build up Zion again, and appear in all his glory.

The children of your servants shall abide,
> and their posterity shall continue in your presence,
That the name of the Lord may be declared on Zion;
> and his praise, in Jerusalem,
When the peoples gather together
> and the kingdoms, to serve the Lord.

℟. The Lord will build up Zion again, and appear in all his glory.

ALLELUIA

John 1:49b

℟. Alleluia, alleluia.

Rabbi, you are the Son of God;
you are the King of Israel.

℟. Alleluia, alleluia.

GOSPEL Years I and II

Matthew 14:22-36   Command me to come to you on the water.

✠ A reading from the holy Gospel according to Matthew

Jesus made the disciples get into a boat
  and precede him to the other side of the sea,
  while he dismissed the crowds.
After doing so, he went up on the mountain by himself to pray.
When it was evening he was there alone.
Meanwhile the boat, already a few miles offshore,
  was being tossed about by the waves, for the wind was against it.
During the fourth watch of the night,
  he came toward them, walking on the sea.
When the disciples saw him walking on the sea they were terrified.
"It is a ghost," they said, and they cried out in fear.
At once Jesus spoke to them, "Take courage, it is I; do not be afraid."
Peter said to him in reply,
  "Lord, if it is you, command me to come to you on the water."
He said, "Come."
Peter got out of the boat and began to walk on the water toward Jesus.
But when he saw how strong the wind was he became frightened;
  and, beginning to sink, he cried out, "Lord, save me!"
Immediately Jesus stretched out his hand and caught him,
  and said to him, "O you of little faith, why did you doubt?"
After they got into the boat, the wind died down.
Those who were in the boat did him homage, saying,
  "Truly, you are the Son of God."

Tuesday of the Eighteenth Week in Ordinary Time II

**After making the crossing, they came to land at Gennesaret.
When the men of that place recognized him,
   they sent word to all the surrounding country.
People brought to him all those who were sick
   and begged him that they might touch only the tassel on his cloak,
   and as many as touched it were healed.**

The Gospel of the Lord.

OR

The following text may be substituted, especially in Year A when the above Gospel is read on Monday.

Matthew 15:1-2, 10-14   Every plant that my heavenly Father has not planted will be uprooted.

✠   **A reading from the holy Gospel according to Matthew**

**Some Pharisees and scribes came to Jesus from Jerusalem and said,
   "Why do your disciples break the tradition of the elders?
They do not wash their hands when they eat a meal."
He summoned the crowd and said to them, "Hear and understand.
It is not what enters one's mouth that defiles the man;
   but what comes out of the mouth is what defiles one."
Then his disciples approached and said to him,
   "Do you know that the Pharisees took offense
   when they heard what you said?"
He said in reply, "Every plant that my heavenly Father has not planted
   will be uprooted.
Let them alone; they are blind guides of the blind.
If a blind man leads a blind man,
   both will fall into a pit."**

The Gospel of the Lord.

409 WEDNESDAY OF THE EIGHTEENTH WEEK IN ORDINARY TIME

FIRST READING   Year II

Jeremiah 31:1-7   With age-old love I have loved you.

A reading from the Book of the Prophet Jeremiah

At that time, says the Lord,
   I will be the God of all the tribes of Israel,
   and they shall be my people.
      Thus says the Lord:
The people that escaped the sword
   have found favor in the desert.
As Israel comes forward to be given his rest,
   the Lord appears to him from afar:
With age-old love I have loved you;
   so I have kept my mercy toward you.
Again I will restore you, and you shall be rebuilt,
   O virgin Israel;
Carrying your festive tambourines,
   you shall go forth dancing with the merrymakers.
Again you shall plant vineyards
   on the mountains of Samaria;
   those who plant them shall enjoy the fruits.
Yes, a day will come when the watchmen
   will call out on Mount Ephraim:
"Rise up, let us go to Zion,
   to the Lord, our God."

   For thus says the Lord:
Shout with joy for Jacob,
   exult at the head of the nations;
   proclaim your praise and say:
The Lord has delivered his people,
   the remnant of Israel.

The word of the Lord.

RESPONSORIAL PSALM

Jeremiah 31:10, 11-12ab, 13

℟. (see 10d) **The Lord will guard us as a shepherd guards his flock.**

Hear the word of the Lord, O nations,
    proclaim it on distant isles, and say:
He who scattered Israel, now gathers them together,
    he guards them as a shepherd his flock.

℟. **The Lord will guard us as a shepherd guards his flock.**

The Lord shall ransom Jacob,
    he shall redeem him from the hand of his conqueror.
Shouting, they shall mount the heights of Zion,
    they shall come streaming to the Lord's blessings.

℟. **The Lord will guard us as a shepherd guards his flock.**

Then the virgins shall make merry and dance,
    and young men and old as well.
I will turn their mourning into joy.
    I will console and gladden them after their sorrows.

℟. **The Lord will guard us as a shepherd guards his flock.**

ALLELUIA

Luke 7:16

℟. **Alleluia, alleluia.**

A great prophet has arisen in our midst
and God has visited his people.

℟. **Alleluia, alleluia.**

GOSPEL — Years I and II

Matthew 15:21-28   O woman, great is your faith!

✠ **A reading from the holy Gospel according to Matthew**

At that time Jesus withdrew to the region of Tyre and Sidon.
And behold, a Canaanite woman of that district came and called out,
   "Have pity on me, Lord, Son of David!
My daughter is tormented by a demon."
But he did not say a word in answer to her.
His disciples came and asked him,
   "Send her away, for she keeps calling out after us."
He said in reply,
   "I was sent only to the lost sheep of the house of Israel."
But the woman came and did him homage, saying, "Lord, help me."
He said in reply,
   "It is not right to take the food of the children
   and throw it to the dogs."
She said, "Please, Lord, for even the dogs eat the scraps
   that fall from the table of their masters."
Then Jesus said to her in reply,
   "O woman, great is your faith!
Let it be done for you as you wish."
And her daughter was healed from that hour.

The Gospel of the Lord.

410 THURSDAY OF THE EIGHTEENTH WEEK IN ORDINARY TIME

FIRST READING   Year II

Jeremiah 31:31-34   The days are coming when I will make a new covenant with the house of Israel and I will remember their sin no more.

A reading from the Book of the Prophet Jeremiah

The days are coming, says the Lord,
  when I will make a new covenant with the house of Israel
  and the house of Judah.
It will not be like the covenant I made with their fathers:
  the day I took them by the hand
  to lead them forth from the land of Egypt;
  for they broke my covenant,
  and I had to show myself their master, says the Lord.
But this is the covenant that I will make
  with the house of Israel after those days, says the Lord.
I will place my law within them, and write it upon their hearts;
  I will be their God, and they shall be my people.
No longer will they have need to teach their friends and relatives
  how to know the Lord.
All, from least to greatest, shall know me, says the Lord,
  for I will forgive their evildoing and remember their sin no more.

The word of the Lord.

RESPONSORIAL PSALM

Psalm 51:12-13, 14-15, 18-19

℟. (12a) **Create a clean heart in me, O God.**

**A clean heart create for me, O God,
 and a steadfast spirit renew within me.
Cast me not out from your presence,
 and your Holy Spirit take not from me.**

℟. **Create a clean heart in me, O God.**

**Give me back the joy of your salvation,
 and a willing spirit sustain in me.
I will teach transgressors your ways,
 and sinners shall return to you.**

℟. **Create a clean heart in me, O God.**

**For you are not pleased with sacrifices;
 should I offer a burnt offering, you would not accept it.
My sacrifice, O God, is a contrite spirit;
 a heart contrite and humbled, O God, you will not spurn.**

℟. **Create a clean heart in me, O God.**

ALLELUIA

Matthew 16:18

℟. **Alleluia, alleluia.**

**You are Peter, and upon this rock I will build my Church,
and the gates of the nether world shall not prevail against it.**

℟. **Alleluia, alleluia.**

GOSPEL Years I and II

Matthew 16:13-23   You are Peter, I will give you the keys to the Kingdom of heaven.

☩ A reading from the holy Gospel according to Matthew

**Jesus went into the region of Caesarea Philippi
and he asked his disciples,
"Who do people say that the Son of Man is?"
They replied, "Some say John the Baptist, others Elijah,
still others Jeremiah or one of the prophets."
He said to them, "But who do you say that I am?"
Simon Peter said in reply,
"You are the Christ, the Son of the living God."
Jesus said to him in reply, "Blessed are you, Simon son of Jonah.
For flesh and blood has not revealed this to you, but my heavenly Father.
And so I say to you, you are Peter,
and upon this rock I will build my Church,
and the gates of the netherworld shall not prevail against it.
I will give you the keys to the Kingdom of heaven.
Whatever you bind on earth shall be bound in heaven;
and whatever you loose on earth shall be loosed in heaven."
Then he strictly ordered his disciples
to tell no one that he was the Christ.**

**From that time on, Jesus began to show his disciples
that he must go to Jerusalem and suffer greatly
from the elders, the chief priests, and the scribes,
and be killed and on the third day be raised.
Then Peter took Jesus aside and began to rebuke him,
"God forbid, Lord! No such thing shall ever happen to you."
He turned and said to Peter,
"Get behind me, Satan! You are an obstacle to me.
You are thinking not as God does, but as human beings do."**

The Gospel of the Lord.

411 FRIDAY OF THE EIGHTEENTH WEEK IN ORDINARY TIME

FIRST READING   Year II

Nahum 2:1, 3; 3:1-3, 6-7   Woe to the city of blood!

A reading from the Book of the Prophet Nahum

See, upon the mountains there advances
   the bearer of good news,
   announcing peace!
Celebrate your feasts, O Judah,
   fulfill your vows!
For nevermore shall you be invaded
   by the scoundrel; he is completely destroyed.
The Lord will restore the vine of Jacob,
   the pride of Israel,
Though ravagers have ravaged them
   and ruined the tendrils.

Woe to the bloody city, all lies,
   full of plunder, whose looting never stops!
The crack of the whip, the rumbling sounds of wheels;
   horses a-gallop, chariots bounding,
Cavalry charging, the flame of the sword, the flash of the spear,
   the many slain, the heaping corpses,
   the endless bodies to stumble upon!
I will cast filth upon you,
   disgrace you and put you to shame;
Till everyone who sees you runs from you, saying,
   "Nineveh is destroyed; who can pity her?
   Where can one find any to console her?"

The word of the Lord.

RESPONSORIAL PSALM

Deuteronomy 32:35cd-36ab, 39abcd, 41

℟. (39c) **It is I who deal death and give life.**

**Close at hand is the day of their disaster,
 and their doom is rushing upon them!
Surely, the L**ORD **shall do justice for his people;
 on his servants he shall have pity.**

℟. **It is I who deal death and give life.**

**"Learn then that I, I alone, am God,
 and there is no god besides me.
It is I who bring both death and life,
 I who inflict wounds and heal them."**

℟. **It is I who deal death and give life.**

**I will sharpen my flashing sword,
 and my hand shall lay hold of my quiver,
"With vengeance I will repay my foes
 and requite those who hate me."**

℟. **It is I who deal death and give life.**

ALLELUIA

Matthew 5:10

℟. Alleluia, alleluia.

Blessed are they who are persecuted for the sake of righteousness; for theirs is the Kingdom of heaven.

℟. Alleluia, alleluia.

GOSPEL Years I and II

Matthew 16:24-28   What can one give in exchange for one's life?

☩ **A reading from the holy Gospel according to Matthew**

**Jesus said to his disciples,
"Whoever wishes to come after me must deny himself,
 take up his cross, and follow me.
For whoever wishes to save his life will lose it,
 but whoever loses his life for my sake will find it.
What profit would there be for one to gain the whole world
 and forfeit his life?
Or what can one give in exchange for his life?
For the Son of Man will come with his angels in his Father's glory,
 and then he will repay each according to his conduct.
Amen, I say to you, there are some standing here
 who will not taste death
 until they see the Son of Man coming in his Kingdom."**

The Gospel of the Lord.

412 SATURDAY OF THE EIGHTEENTH WEEK IN ORDINARY TIME

FIRST READING   Year II

Habakkuk 1:12–2:4   The just, because of their faith, shall live.

A reading from the Book of the Prophet Habakkuk

Are you not from eternity, O Lord,
  my holy God, immortal?
O Lord, you have marked him for judgment,
  O Rock, you have readied him punishment!
Too pure are your eyes to look upon evil,
  and the sight of misery you cannot endure.
Why, then, do you gaze on the faithless in silence
  while the wicked man devours
  one more just than himself?
You have made man like the fish of the sea,
  like creeping things without a ruler.
He brings them all up with his hook,
  he hauls them away with his net,
He gathers them in his seine;
  and so he rejoices and exults.
Therefore he sacrifices to his net,
  and burns incense to his seine;
for thanks to them his portion is generous,
  and his repast sumptuous.
Shall he, then, keep on brandishing his sword
  to slay peoples without mercy?

I will stand at my guard post,
  and station myself upon the rampart,
And keep watch to see what he will say to me,
  and what answer he will give to my complaint.

Then the Lord answered me and said:
   Write down the vision
Clearly upon the tablets,
   so that one can read it readily.
For the vision still has its time,
   presses on to fulfillment, and will not disappoint;
If it delays, wait for it,
   it will surely come, it will not be late.
The rash man has no integrity;
   but the just man, because of his faith, shall live.

The word of the Lord.

RESPONSORIAL PSALM

Psalm 9:8-9, 10-11, 12-13

℟. (11b) You forsake not those who seek you, O Lord.

The Lord sits enthroned forever;
   he has set up his throne for judgment.
He judges the world with justice;
   he governs the peoples with equity.

℟. You forsake not those who seek you, O Lord.

The Lord is a stronghold for the oppressed,
   a stronghold in times of distress.
They trust in you who cherish your name,
   for you forsake not those who seek you, O Lord.

℟. You forsake not those who seek you, O Lord.

Sing praise to the Lord enthroned in Zion;
   proclaim among the nations his deeds;
For the avenger of blood has remembered;
   he has not forgotten the cry of the poor.

℟. You forsake not those who seek you, O Lord.

ALLELUIA

See 2 Timothy 1:10

℟. Alleluia, alleluia.

**Our Savior Jesus Christ has destroyed death
and brought life to light through the Gospel.**

℟. Alleluia, alleluia.

GOSPEL Years I and II

Matthew 17:14-20   If you have faith, nothing will be impossible for you.

☩ A reading from the holy Gospel according to Matthew

**A man came up to Jesus, knelt down before him, and said,
   "Lord, have pity on my son, who is a lunatic and suffers severely;
   often he falls into fire, and often into water.
I brought him to your disciples, but they could not cure him."
Jesus said in reply,
   "O faithless and perverse generation, how long will I be with you?
How long will I endure you?
Bring the boy here to me."
Jesus rebuked him and the demon came out of him,
   and from that hour the boy was cured.
Then the disciples approached Jesus in private and said,
   "Why could we not drive it out?"
He said to them, "Because of your little faith.
Amen, I say to you, if you have faith the size of a mustard seed,
   you will say to this mountain,
   'Move from here to there,' and it will move.
Nothing will be impossible for you."**

The Gospel of the Lord.

413 MONDAY OF THE NINETEENTH WEEK IN ORDINARY TIME

FIRST READING   Year II

Ezekiel 1:2-5, 24-28c   Such was the vision of the likeness of the glory of the LORD.

A reading from the Book of the Prophet Ezekiel

**On the fifth day of the fourth month of the fifth year,
    that is, of King Jehoiachin's exile,
The word of the LORD came to the priest Ezekiel,
    the son of Buzi,
    in the land of the Chaldeans by the river Chebar.—
There the hand of the LORD came upon me.**

**As I looked, a stormwind came from the North,
    a huge cloud with flashing fire enveloped in brightness,
    from the midst of which (the midst of the fire)
    something gleamed like electrum.
Within it were figures resembling four living creatures
    that looked like this: their form was human.**

**Then I heard the sound of their wings,
    like the roaring of mighty waters,
    like the voice of the Almighty.
When they moved, the sound of the tumult was like the din of an army.
And when they stood still, they lowered their wings.**

**Above the firmament over their heads
    something like a throne could be seen,
    looking like sapphire.
Upon it was seated, up above, one who had the appearance of a man.
Upward from what resembled his waist I saw what gleamed like electrum;
    downward from what resembled his waist I saw what looked like fire;
    he was surrounded with splendor.
Like the bow which appears in the clouds on a rainy day
    was the splendor that surrounded him.
Such was the vision of the likeness of the glory of the LORD.**

The word of the Lord.

RESPONSORIAL PSALM

Psalm 148:1-2, 11-12, 13, 14

℟. Heaven and earth are filled with your glory.
   or:
℟. Alleluia.

Praise the Lord from the heavens;
   praise him in the heights;
Praise him, all you his angels;
   praise him, all you his hosts.

℟. Heaven and earth are filled with your glory.
   or:
℟. Alleluia.

Let the kings of the earth and all peoples,
   the princes and all the judges of the earth,
Young men too, and maidens,
   old men and boys,

℟. Heaven and earth are filled with your glory.
   or:
℟. Alleluia.

Praise the name of the Lord,
   for his name alone is exalted;
His majesty is above earth and heaven.

℟. Heaven and earth are filled with your glory.
   or:
℟. Alleluia.

And he has lifted up the horn of his people.
Be this his praise from all his faithful ones,
   from the children of Israel, the people close to him.
   Alleluia.

℟. Heaven and earth are filled with your glory.
   or:
℟. Alleluia.

ALLELUIA

See 2 Thessalonians 2:14

℟. Alleluia, alleluia.

**God has called you through the Gospel
to possess the glory of our Lord Jesus Christ.**

℟. Alleluia, alleluia.

GOSPEL   Years I and II

Matthew 17:22-27   They will kill him and he will be raised. The subjects are exempt from the tax.

✠ **A reading from the holy Gospel according to Matthew**

**As Jesus and his disciples were gathering in Galilee,
  Jesus said to them,
    "The Son of Man is to be handed over to men,
    and they will kill him, and he will be raised on the third day."
And they were overwhelmed with grief.**

**When they came to Capernaum,
    the collectors of the temple tax approached Peter and said,
    "Does not your teacher pay the temple tax?"
"Yes," he said.
When he came into the house, before he had time to speak,
    Jesus asked him, "What is your opinion, Simon?
From whom do the kings of the earth take tolls or census tax?
From their subjects or from foreigners?"
When he said, "From foreigners," Jesus said to him,
    "Then the subjects are exempt.
But that we may not offend them, go to the sea, drop in a hook,
    and take the first fish that comes up.
Open its mouth and you will find a coin worth twice the temple tax.
Give that to them for me and for you."**

The Gospel of the Lord.

414 TUESDAY OF THE NINETEENTH WEEK IN ORDINARY TIME

FIRST READING   Year II

Ezekiel 2:8–3:4   He fed me with this scroll, and it was as sweet as honey in my mouth.

A reading from the Book of the Prophet Ezekiel

The Lord God said to me:
   As for you, son of man, obey me when I speak to you:
   be not rebellious like this house of rebellion,
   but open your mouth and eat what I shall give you.

It was then I saw a hand stretched out to me,
   in which was a written scroll which he unrolled before me.
It was covered with writing front and back,
   and written on it was:
   Lamentation and wailing and woe!

He said to me: Son of man, eat what is before you;
   eat this scroll, then go, speak to the house of Israel.
So I opened my mouth and he gave me the scroll to eat.
Son of man, he then said to me,
   feed your belly and fill your stomach
   with this scroll I am giving you.
I ate it, and it was as sweet as honey in my mouth.
He said: Son of man, go now to the house of Israel,
   and speak my words to them.

The word of the Lord.

RESPONSORIAL PSALM

Psalm 119:14, 24, 72, 103, 111, 131

℟. (103a) **How sweet to my taste is your promise!**

**In the way of your decrees I rejoice,
 as much as in all riches.**

℟. **How sweet to my taste is your promise!**

**Yes, your decrees are my delight;
 they are my counselors.**

℟. **How sweet to my taste is your promise!**

**The law of your mouth is to me more precious
 than thousands of gold and silver pieces.**

℟. **How sweet to my taste is your promise!**

**How sweet to my palate are your promises,
 sweeter than honey to my mouth!**

℟. **How sweet to my taste is your promise!**

**Your decrees are my inheritance forever;
 the joy of my heart they are.**

℟. **How sweet to my taste is your promise!**

**I gasp with open mouth,
 in my yearning for your commands.**

℟. **How sweet to my taste is your promise!**

ALLELUIA

Matthew 11:29ab

℟. Alleluia, alleluia.

Take my yoke upon you and learn from me,
for I am meek and humble of heart.

℟. Alleluia, alleluia.

GOSPEL   Years I and II

Matthew 18:1-5, 10, 12-14   See that you do not despise one of these little ones.

✠ A reading from the holy Gospel according to Matthew

The disciples approached Jesus and said,
 "Who is the greatest in the Kingdom of heaven?"
He called a child over, placed it in their midst, and said,
 "Amen, I say to you, unless you turn and become like children,
  you will not enter the Kingdom of heaven.
Whoever becomes humble like this child
 is the greatest in the Kingdom of heaven.
And whoever receives one child such as this in my name receives me.

"See that you do not despise one of these little ones,
 for I say to you that their angels in heaven
 always look upon the face of my heavenly Father.
What is your opinion?
If a man has a hundred sheep and one of them goes astray,
 will he not leave the ninety-nine in the hills
 and go in search of the stray?
And if he finds it, amen, I say to you, he rejoices more over it
 than over the ninety-nine that did not stray.
In just the same way, it is not the will of your heavenly Father
 that one of these little ones be lost."

The Gospel of the Lord.

415 WEDNESDAY OF THE NINETEENTH WEEK IN ORDINARY TIME

FIRST READING   Year II

Ezekiel 9:1-7; 10:18-22   Mark a "Thau" on the foreheads of those who moan and groan over all the abominations in Jerusalem.

A reading from the Book of the Prophet Ezekiel

The Lord cried loud for me to hear: Come, you scourges of the city!
With that I saw six men coming from the direction
    of the upper gate which faces the north,
    each with a destroying weapon in his hand.
In their midst was a man dressed in linen,
    with a writer's case at his waist.
They entered and stood beside the bronze altar.
Then he called to the man dressed in linen
    with the writer's case at his waist, saying to him:
    Pass through the city, through Jerusalem,
    and mark a "Thau" on the foreheads of those who moan and groan
    over all the abominations that are practiced within it.
To the others I heard the Lord say:
    Pass through the city after him and strike!
Do not look on them with pity nor show any mercy!
Old men, youths and maidens, women and children—wipe them out!
But do not touch any marked with the "Thau"; begin at my sanctuary.
So they began with the men, the elders, who were in front of the temple.
Defile the temple, he said to them, and fill the courts with the slain;
    then go out and strike in the city.

Then the glory of the Lord left the threshold of the temple
    and rested upon the cherubim.
These lifted their wings, and I saw them rise from the earth,
    the wheels rising along with them.
They stood at the entrance of the eastern gate of the Lord's house,
    and the glory of the God of Israel was up above them.
Then the cherubim lifted their wings, and the wheels went along with them,
    while up above them was the glory of the God of Israel.

The word of the Lord.

RESPONSORIAL PSALM

Psalm 113:1-2, 3-4, 5-6

℟. (4b) **The glory of the Lord is higher than the skies.**
   or:
℟. **Alleluia.**

Praise, you servants of the LORD,
   praise the name of the LORD.
Blessed be the name of the LORD
   both now and forever.

℟. The glory of the Lord is higher than the skies.
   or:
℟. Alleluia.

From the rising to the setting of the sun
   is the name of the LORD to be praised.
High above all nations is the LORD;
   above the heavens is his glory.

℟. The glory of the Lord is higher than the skies.
   or:
℟. Alleluia.

Who is like the LORD, our God, who is enthroned on high,
   and looks upon the heavens and the earth below?

℟. The glory of the Lord is higher than the skies.
   or:
℟. Alleluia.

ALLELUIA

2 Corinthians 5:19

℟. Alleluia, alleluia.

**God was reconciling the world to himself in Christ,
and entrusting to us the message of reconciliation.**

℟. Alleluia, alleluia.

GOSPEL Years I and II

Matthew 18:15-20   If your brother listens to you, you have won him over.

☩ **A reading from the holy Gospel according to Matthew**

**Jesus said to his disciples:
"If your brother sins against you,
  go and tell him his fault between you and him alone.
If he listens to you, you have won over your brother.
If he does not listen,
  take one or two others along with you,
  so that every fact may be established
  on the testimony of two or three witnesses.
If he refuses to listen to them, tell the Church.
If he refuses to listen even to the Church,
  then treat him as you would a Gentile or a tax collector.
Amen, I say to you,
  whatever you bind on earth shall be bound in heaven,
  and whatever you loose on earth shall be loosed in heaven.
Again, amen, I say to you, if two of you agree on earth
  about anything for which they are to pray,
  it shall be granted to them by my heavenly Father.
For where two or three are gathered together in my name,
  there am I in the midst of them."**

The Gospel of the Lord.

416 THURSDAY OF THE NINETEENTH WEEK IN ORDINARY TIME

FIRST READING   Year II

Ezekiel 12:1-12   You shall bring out your baggage like an exile in the daytime while they are looking on.

A reading from the Book of the Prophet Ezekiel

The word of the Lord came to me:
Son of man, you live in the midst of a rebellious house;
>   they have eyes to see but do not see,
>   and ears to hear but do not hear,
>   for they are a rebellious house.

Now, son of man, during the day while they are looking on,
>   prepare your baggage as though for exile,
>   and again while they are looking on,
>   migrate from where you live to another place;
>   perhaps they will see that they are a rebellious house.

You shall bring out your baggage like an exile in the daytime
>   while they are looking on;
>   in the evening, again while they are looking on,
>   you shall go out like one of those driven into exile;
>   while they look on, dig a hole in the wall and pass through it;
>   while they look on, shoulder the burden and set out in the darkness;
>   cover your face that you may not see the land,
>   for I have made you a sign for the house of Israel.

I did as I was told.
During the day I brought out my baggage
>   as though it were that of an exile,
>   and at evening I dug a hole through the wall with my hand
>   and, while they looked on, set out in the darkness,
>   shouldering my burden.

Then, in the morning, the word of the Lord came to me:
>   Son of man, did not the house of Israel, that rebellious house,
>   ask you what you were doing?

Tell them: Thus says the Lord God:
>   This oracle concerns Jerusalem
>   and the whole house of Israel within it.

I am a sign for you:
> as I have done, so shall it be done to them;
> as captives they shall go into exile.

The prince who is among them shall shoulder his burden
> and set out in darkness,
>> going through a hole he has dug out in the wall,
>> and covering his face lest he be seen by anyone.

The word of the Lord.

RESPONSORIAL PSALM

Psalm 78:56-57, 58-59, 61-62

℟. (see 7b) **Do not forget the works of the Lord!**

They tempted and rebelled against God the Most High,
> and kept not his decrees.
They turned back and were faithless like their fathers;
> they recoiled like a treacherous bow.

℟. **Do not forget the works of the Lord!**

They angered him with their high places
> and with their idols roused his jealousy.
God heard and was enraged
> and utterly rejected Israel.

℟. **Do not forget the works of the Lord!**

And he surrendered his strength into captivity,
> his glory in the hands of the foe.
He abandoned his people to the sword
> and was enraged against his inheritance.

℟. **Do not forget the works of the Lord!**

ALLELUIA

Psalm 119:135

℟. Alleluia, alleluia.

Let your countenance shine upon your servant
and teach me your statutes.

℟. Alleluia, alleluia.

GOSPEL   Years I and II

Matthew 18:21–19:1   I say to you, not seven times but seventy-seven times.

✠ A reading from the holy Gospel according to Matthew

Peter approached Jesus and asked him,
  "Lord, if my brother sins against me,
  how often must I forgive him?
As many as seven times?"
Jesus answered, "I say to you, not seven times but seventy-seven times.
That is why the Kingdom of heaven may be likened to a king
  who decided to settle accounts with his servants.
When he began the accounting,
  a debtor was brought before him who owed him a huge amount.
Since he had no way of paying it back,
  his master ordered him to be sold,
  along with his wife, his children, and all his property,
  in payment of the debt.
At that, the servant fell down, did him homage, and said,
  'Be patient with me, and I will pay you back in full.'
Moved with compassion the master of that servant
  let him go and forgave him the loan.
When that servant had left, he found one of his fellow servants
  who owed him a much smaller amount.
He seized him and started to choke him, demanding,
  'Pay back what you owe.'
Falling to his knees, his fellow servant begged him,
  'Be patient with me, and I will pay you back.'
But he refused.
Instead, he had the fellow servant put in prison
  until he paid back the debt.

Now when his fellow servants saw what had happened,
  they were deeply disturbed,
    and went to their master and reported the whole affair.
His master summoned him and said to him, 'You wicked servant!
I forgave you your entire debt because you begged me to.
Should you not have had pity on your fellow servant,
  as I had pity on you?'
Then in anger his master handed him over to the torturers
  until he should pay back the whole debt.
So will my heavenly Father do to you,
  unless each of you forgives his brother from his heart."

When Jesus finished these words, he left Galilee
  and went to the district of Judea across the Jordan.

The Gospel of the Lord.

417 FRIDAY OF THE NINETEENTH WEEK IN ORDINARY TIME

FIRST READING   Year II

Long Form

Ezekiel 16:1-15, 60, 63   *You are perfect because of my splendor which I bestowed on you; you became a harlot.*

A reading from the Book of the Prophet Ezekiel

The word of the Lord came to me:
Son of man, make known to Jerusalem her abominations.
Thus says the Lord God to Jerusalem:
  By origin and birth you are of the land of Canaan;
    your father was an Amorite and your mother a Hittite.
As for your birth, the day you were born your navel cord was not cut;
    you were neither washed with water nor anointed,
    nor were you rubbed with salt, nor swathed in swaddling clothes.
No one looked on you with pity or compassion
    to do any of these things for you.
Rather, you were thrown out on the ground as something loathsome,
    the day you were born.

Then I passed by and saw you weltering in your blood.
I said to you: Live in your blood and grow like a plant in the field.
You grew and developed, you came to the age of puberty;
    your breasts were formed, your hair had grown,
    but you were still stark naked.
Again I passed by you and saw that you were now old enough for love.
So I spread the corner of my cloak over you to cover your nakedness;
    I swore an oath to you and entered into a covenant with you;
    you became mine, says the Lord God.
Then I bathed you with water, washed away your blood,
    and anointed you with oil.
I clothed you with an embroidered gown,
    put sandals of fine leather on your feet;
    I gave you a fine linen sash and silk robes to wear.
I adorned you with jewelry: I put bracelets on your arms,
    a necklace about your neck, a ring in your nose,
    pendants in your ears, and a glorious diadem upon your head.

Thus you were adorned with gold and silver;
> your garments were of fine linen, silk, and embroidered cloth.

Fine flour, honey, and oil were your food.

You were exceedingly beautiful, with the dignity of a queen.

You were renowned among the nations for your beauty, perfect as it was,
> because of my splendor which I had bestowed on you,
> says the Lord God.

But you were captivated by your own beauty,
> you used your renown to make yourself a harlot,
> and you lavished your harlotry on every passer-by,
> whose own you became.

Yet I will remember the covenant I made with you when you were a girl,
> and I will set up an everlasting covenant with you,
> that you may remember and be covered with confusion,
> and that you may be utterly silenced for shame
> when I pardon you for all you have done, says the Lord God.

The word of the Lord.

OR

Short Form

Ezekiel 16:59-63   I will remember the covenant I made with you and you will be ashamed.

A reading from the Book of the Prophet Ezekiel

Thus says the Lord:
I will deal with you according to what you have done,
> you who despised your oath, breaking a covenant.

Yet I will remember the covenant I made with you when you were a girl,
> and I will set up an everlasting covenant with you.

Then you shall remember your conduct and be ashamed
> when I take your sisters, those older and younger than you,
> and give them to you as daughters,
> even though I am not bound by my covenant with you.

For I will re-establish my covenant with you,
> that you may know that I am the Lord,
> that you may remember and be covered with confusion,
> and that you may be utterly silenced for shame
> when I pardon you for all you have done, says the Lord God.

The word of the Lord.

RESPONSORIAL PSALM

Isaiah 12:2-3, 4bcd, 5-6

R︎. (1c) **You have turned from your anger.**

**God indeed is my savior;
 I am confident and unafraid.
My strength and my courage is the L**ORD**,
 and he has been my savior.
With joy you will draw water
 at the fountain of salvation.**

R︎. **You have turned from your anger.**

Give thanks to the LORD**, acclaim his name;
 among the nations make known his deeds,
 proclaim how exalted is his name.**

R︎. **You have turned from your anger.**

Sing praise to the LORD **for his glorious achievement;
 let this be known throughout all the earth.
Shout with exultation, O city of Zion,
 for great in your midst
 is the Holy One of Israel!**

R︎. **You have turned from your anger.**

ALLELUIA

See 1 Thessalonians 2:13

R︎. **Alleluia, alleluia.**

**Receive the word of God, not as the word of men,
but, as it truly is, the word of God.**

R︎. **Alleluia, alleluia.**

GOSPEL   Years I and II

Matthew 19:3-12   Because of the hardness of your hearts Moses allowed you to divorce your wives, but from the beginning it was not so.

✠ A reading from the holy Gospel according to Matthew

Some Pharisees approached Jesus, and tested him, saying,
  "Is it lawful for a man to divorce his wife for any cause whatever?"
He said in reply, "Have you not read that from the beginning
  the Creator *made them male and female* and said,
  For this reason a man shall leave his father and mother
  and be joined to his wife, and the two shall become one flesh?
So they are no longer two, but one flesh.
Therefore, what God has joined together, man must not separate."
They said to him, "Then why did Moses command
  that the man give the woman a bill of divorce and dismiss her?"
He said to them, "Because of the hardness of your hearts
  Moses allowed you to divorce your wives,
  but from the beginning it was not so.
I say to you, whoever divorces his wife
  (unless the marriage is unlawful)
  and marries another commits adultery."
His disciples said to him,
  "If that is the case of a man with his wife,
  it is better not to marry."
He answered, "Not all can accept this word,
  but only those to whom that is granted.
Some are incapable of marriage because they were born so;
  some, because they were made so by others;
  some, because they have renounced marriage
  for the sake of the Kingdom of heaven.
Whoever can accept this ought to accept it."

The Gospel of the Lord.

418 SATURDAY OF THE NINETEENTH WEEK IN ORDINARY TIME

FIRST READING   Year II

Ezekiel 18:1-10, 13b, 30-32   I will judge you according to your ways.

A reading from the Book of the Prophet Ezekiel

The word of the Lord came to me:
Son of man, what is the meaning of this proverb
that you recite in the land of Israel:

"Fathers have eaten green grapes,
thus their children's teeth are on edge"?

As I live, says the Lord God:
I swear that there shall no longer be anyone among you
who will repeat this proverb in Israel.
For all lives are mine;
the life of the father is like the life of the son, both are mine;
only the one who sins shall die.

If a man is virtuous—if he does what is right and just,
if he does not eat on the mountains,
nor raise his eyes to the idols of the house of Israel;
if he does not defile his neighbor's wife,
nor have relations with a woman in her menstrual period;
if he oppresses no one,
gives back the pledge received for a debt,
commits no robbery;
if he gives food to the hungry and clothes the naked;
if he does not lend at interest nor exact usury;
if he holds off from evildoing,
judges fairly between a man and his opponent;
if he lives by my statutes and is careful to observe my ordinances,
that man is virtuous—he shall surely live, says the Lord God.

But if he begets a son who is a thief, a murderer,
or lends at interest and exacts usury—
this son certainly shall not live.
Because he practiced all these abominations, he shall surely die;
his death shall be his own fault.

Therefore I will judge you, house of Israel,
  each one according to his ways, says the Lord God.
Turn and be converted from all your crimes,
  that they may be no cause of guilt for you.
Cast away from you all the crimes you have committed,
  and make for yourselves a new heart and a new spirit.
Why should you die, O house of Israel?
For I have no pleasure in the death of anyone who dies,
  says the Lord God. Return and live!

The word of the Lord.

RESPONSORIAL PSALM

Psalm 51:12-13, 14-15, 18-19

℟. (12a) **Create a clean heart in me, O God.**

A clean heart create for me, O God;
  and a steadfast spirit renew within me.
Cast me not out from your presence,
  and your Holy Spirit take not from me.

℟. **Create a clean heart in me, O God.**

Give me back the joy of your salvation,
  and a willing spirit sustain in me.
I will teach transgressors your ways,
  and sinners shall return to you.

℟. **Create a clean heart in me, O God.**

For you are not pleased with sacrifices;
  should I offer a burnt offering, you would not accept it.
My sacrifice, O God, is a contrite spirit;
  a heart contrite and humbled, O God, you will not spurn.

℟. **Create a clean heart in me, O God.**

ALLELUIA

See Matthew 11:25

℟. **Alleluia, alleluia.**

**Blessed are you, Father, Lord of heaven and earth;
you have revealed to little ones the mysteries of the Kingdom.**

℟. **Alleluia, alleluia.**

GOSPEL   Years I and II

Matthew 19:13-15   Let the children come to me, and do not prevent them; for the Kingdom of heaven belongs to such as these.

✢ **A reading from the holy Gospel according to Matthew**

**Children were brought to Jesus
   that he might lay his hands on them and pray.
The disciples rebuked them, but Jesus said,
   "Let the children come to me, and do not prevent them;
   for the Kingdom of heaven belongs to such as these."
After he placed his hands on them, he went away.**

The Gospel of the Lord.

419 MONDAY OF THE TWENTIETH WEEK IN ORDINARY TIME

FIRST READING   Year II

Ezekiel 24:15-23   *Ezekiel shall be a sign for you: all that he did you shall do when it happens.*

A reading from the Book of the Prophet Ezekiel

The word of the Lord came to me:
   Son of man, by a sudden blow
   I am taking away from you the delight of your eyes,
   but do not mourn or weep or shed any tears.
Groan in silence, make no lament for the dead,
   bind on your turban, put your sandals on your feet,
   do not cover your beard, and do not eat the customary bread.
That evening my wife died,
   and the next morning I did as I had been commanded.
Then the people asked me, "Will you not tell us what all these things
   that you are doing mean for us?"
I therefore spoke to the people that morning, saying to them:
   Thus the word of the Lord came to me:
   Say to the house of Israel:
   Thus says the Lord God:
   I will now desecrate my sanctuary, the stronghold of your pride,
   the delight of your eyes, the desire of your soul.
The sons and daughters you left behind shall fall by the sword.
Ezekiel shall be a sign for you:
   all that he did you shall do when it happens.
Thus you shall know that I am the Lord.
You shall do as I have done,
   not covering your beards nor eating the customary bread.
Your turbans shall remain on your heads, your sandals on your feet.
You shall not mourn or weep,
   but you shall rot away because of your sins and groan one to another.

The word of the Lord.

RESPONSORIAL PSALM

Deuteronomy 32:18-19, 20, 21

℟. (see 18a) **You have forgotten God who gave you birth.**

**You were unmindful of the Rock that begot you.
 You forgot the God who gave you birth.
When the Lord saw this, he was filled with loathing
 and anger toward his sons and daughters.**

℟. **You have forgotten God who gave you birth.**

**"I will hide my face from them," he said,
 "and see what will then become of them.
What a fickle race they are,
 sons with no loyalty in them!"**

℟. **You have forgotten God who gave you birth.**

**"Since they have provoked me with their 'no-god'
 and angered me with their vain idols,
I will provoke them with a 'no-people';
 with a foolish nation I will anger them."**

℟. **You have forgotten God who gave you birth.**

ALLELUIA

Matthew 5:3

℟. **Alleluia, alleluia.**

**Blessed are the poor in spirit;
for theirs is the Kingdom of heaven.**

℟. **Alleluia, alleluia.**

GOSPEL   Years I and II

Matthew 19:16-22   If you wish to be perfect, go, sell what you have and you will have treasure in heaven.

✛ A reading from the holy Gospel according to Matthew

A young man approached Jesus and said,
   "Teacher, what good must I do to gain eternal life?"
He answered him, "Why do you ask me about the good?
There is only One who is good.
If you wish to enter into life, keep the commandments."
He asked him, "Which ones?"
And Jesus replied, *"You shall not kill;*
   you shall not commit adultery;
   you shall not steal;
   you shall not bear false witness;
   honor your father and your mother;
   and *you shall love your neighbor as yourself."*
The young man said to him,
   "All of these I have observed. What do I still lack?"
Jesus said to him, "If you wish to be perfect, go,
   sell what you have and give to the poor,
   and you will have treasure in heaven.
Then come, follow me."
When the young man heard this statement, he went away sad,
   for he had many possessions.

The Gospel of the Lord.

420 TUESDAY OF THE TWENTIETH WEEK IN ORDINARY TIME

FIRST READING   Year II

Ezekiel 28:1-10   You are a mortal and not God, however you may think yourself like a god.

A reading from the Book of the Prophet Ezekiel

The word of the LORD came to me: Son of man,
  say to the prince of Tyre:
Thus says the Lord GOD:

> Because you are haughty of heart,
>   you say, "A god am I!
> I occupy a godly throne
>   in the heart of the sea!"—
> And yet you are a man, and not a god,
>   however you may think yourself like a god.
> Oh yes, you are wiser than Daniel,
>   there is no secret that is beyond you.
> By your wisdom and your intelligence
>   you have made riches for yourself;
> You have put gold and silver
>   into your treasuries.
> By your great wisdom applied to your trading
>   you have heaped up your riches;
>   your heart has grown haughty from your riches—
>   therefore thus says the Lord GOD:
> Because you have thought yourself
>   to have the mind of a god,
> Therefore I will bring against you
>   foreigners, the most barbarous of nations.
> They shall draw their swords
>   against your beauteous wisdom,
>   they shall run them through your splendid apparel.
> They shall thrust you down to the pit, there to die
>   a bloodied corpse, in the heart of the sea.
> Will you then say, "I am a god!"
>   when you face your murderers?

**No, you are man, not a god,
     handed over to those who will slay you.
You shall die the death of the uncircumcised
     at the hands of foreigners,
     for I have spoken, says the Lord God.**

The word of the Lord.

RESPONSORIAL PSALM

Deuteronomy 32:26-27ab, 27cd-28, 30, 35cd-36ab

℟. (39c) **It is I who deal death and give life.**

"I would have said, 'I will make an end of them
  and blot out their name from men's memories,'
Had I not feared the insolence of their enemies,
  feared that these foes would mistakenly boast."

℟. **It is I who deal death and give life.**

"'Our own hand won the victory;
  the Lord had nothing to do with it.'"
For they are a people devoid of reason,
  having no understanding.

℟. **It is I who deal death and give life.**

"How could one man rout a thousand,
  or two men put ten thousand to flight,
Unless it was because their Rock sold them
  and the Lord delivered them up?"

℟. **It is I who deal death and give life.**

Close at hand is the day of their disaster,
  and their doom is rushing upon them!
Surely, the Lord shall do justice for his people;
  on his servants he shall have pity.

℟. **It is I who deal death and give life.**

ALLELUIA

2 Corinthians 8:9

℟. Alleluia, alleluia.

**Jesus Christ became poor although he was rich
so that by his poverty you might become rich.**

℟. Alleluia, alleluia.

GOSPEL   Years I and II

Matthew 19:23-30   It is easier for a camel to pass through the eye of a needle than for one who is rich to enter the Kingdom of God.

✟ A reading from the holy Gospel according to Matthew

**Jesus said to his disciples:
"Amen, I say to you, it will be hard for one who is rich
  to enter the Kingdom of heaven.
Again I say to you,
  it is easier for a camel to pass through the eye of a needle
  than for one who is rich to enter the Kingdom of God."
When the disciples heard this, they were greatly astonished and said,
  "Who then can be saved?"
Jesus looked at them and said,
  "For men this is impossible,
  but for God all things are possible."
Then Peter said to him in reply,
  "We have given up everything and followed you.
What will there be for us?"
Jesus said to them, "Amen, I say to you
  that you who have followed me, in the new age,
  when the Son of Man is seated on his throne of glory,
  will yourselves sit on twelve thrones,
  judging the twelve tribes of Israel.
And everyone who has given up houses or brothers or sisters
  or father or mother or children or lands
  for the sake of my name will receive a hundred times more,
  and will inherit eternal life.
But many who are first will be last, and the last will be first."**

The Gospel of the Lord.

421 WEDNESDAY OF THE TWENTIETH WEEK IN ORDINARY TIME

FIRST READING   Year II

Ezekiel 34:1-11   I will save my sheep, that they may no longer be food for their mouths.

A reading from the Book of the Prophet Ezekiel

The word of the Lord came to me:
> Son of man, prophesy against the shepherds of Israel,
> in these words prophesy to them to the shepherds:
> Thus says the Lord God: Woe to the shepherds of Israel
> who have been pasturing themselves!

Should not shepherds, rather, pasture sheep?
You have fed off their milk, worn their wool,
> and slaughtered the fatlings,
> but the sheep you have not pastured.

You did not strengthen the weak nor heal the sick
> nor bind up the injured.

You did not bring back the strayed nor seek the lost,
> but you lorded it over them harshly and brutally.

So they were scattered for the lack of a shepherd,
> and became food for all the wild beasts.

My sheep were scattered
> and wandered over all the mountains and high hills;
> my sheep were scattered over the whole earth,
> with no one to look after them or to search for them.

Therefore, shepherds, hear the word of the Lord:
> As I live, says the Lord God,
> because my sheep have been given over to pillage,
> and because my sheep have become food for every wild beast,
> for lack of a shepherd;
> because my shepherds did not look after my sheep,
> but pastured themselves and did not pasture my sheep;
> because of this, shepherds, hear the word of the Lord:
> Thus says the Lord God:
> I swear I am coming against these shepherds.

I will claim my sheep from them
   and put a stop to their shepherding my sheep
   so that they may no longer pasture themselves.
I will save my sheep,
   that they may no longer be food for their mouths.

For thus says the Lord God:
   I myself will look after and tend my sheep.

The word of the Lord.

RESPONSORIAL PSALM

Psalm 23:1-3a, 3b-4, 5, 6

℟. (1) The Lord is my shepherd; there is nothing I shall want.

The Lord is my shepherd; I shall not want.
   In verdant pastures he gives me repose;
Beside restful waters he leads me;
   he refreshes my soul.

℟. The Lord is my shepherd; there is nothing I shall want.

He guides me in right paths
   for his name's sake.
Even though I walk in the dark valley
   I fear no evil; for you are at my side
With your rod and your staff
   that give me courage.

℟. The Lord is my shepherd; there is nothing I shall want.

You spread the table before me
   in the sight of my foes;
You anoint my head with oil;
   my cup overflows.

℟. The Lord is my shepherd; there is nothing I shall want.

Only goodness and kindness will follow me
   all the days of my life;
And I shall dwell in the house of the Lord
   for years to come.

℟. The Lord is my shepherd; there is nothing I shall want.

ALLELUIA

Hebrews 4:12

℟. Alleluia, alleluia.

The word of God is living and effective,
able to discern reflections and thoughts of the heart.

℟. Alleluia, alleluia.

GOSPEL   Years I and II

Matthew 20:1-16   Are you envious because I am generous?

✠ A reading from the holy Gospel according to Matthew

Jesus told his disciples this parable:
   "The Kingdom of heaven is like a landowner
   who went out at dawn to hire laborers for his vineyard.
After agreeing with them for the usual daily wage,
   he sent them into his vineyard.
Going out about nine o'clock,
   he saw others standing idle in the marketplace,
   and he said to them, 'You too go into my vineyard,
   and I will give you what is just.'
So they went off.
And he went out again around noon,
   and around three o'clock, and did likewise.
Going out about five o'clock,
   he found others standing around, and said to them,
   'Why do you stand here idle all day?'
They answered, 'Because no one has hired us.'
He said to them, 'You too go into my vineyard.'
When it was evening the owner of the vineyard said to his foreman,
   'Summon the laborers and give them their pay,
   beginning with the last and ending with the first.'
When those who had started about five o'clock came,
   each received the usual daily wage.
So when the first came, they thought that they would receive more,
   but each of them also got the usual wage.

And on receiving it they grumbled against the landowner, saying,
   'These last ones worked only one hour,
   and you have made them equal to us,
   who bore the day's burden and the heat.'
He said to one of them in reply,
   'My friend, I am not cheating you.
Did you not agree with me for the usual daily wage?
Take what is yours and go.
What if I wish to give this last one the same as you?
Or am I not free to do as I wish with my own money?
Are you envious because I am generous?'
Thus, the last will be first, and the first will be last."

The Gospel of the Lord.

422 THURSDAY OF THE TWENTIETH WEEK IN ORDINARY TIME

FIRST READING   Year II

Ezekiel 36:23-28   *I will give you a new heart and place a new spirit within you.*

A reading from the Book of the Prophet Ezekiel

Thus says the Lord:
I will prove the holiness of my great name,
profaned among the nations,
in whose midst you have profaned it.
Thus the nations shall know that I am the Lord, says the Lord God,
when in their sight I prove my holiness through you.
For I will take you away from among the nations,
gather you from all the foreign lands,
and bring you back to your own land.
I will sprinkle clean water upon you
to cleanse you from all your impurities,
and from all your idols I will cleanse you.
I will give you a new heart and place a new spirit within you,
taking from your bodies your stony hearts
and giving you natural hearts.
I will put my spirit within you and make you live by my statutes,
careful to observe my decrees.
You shall live in the land I gave your ancestors;
you shall be my people, and I will be your God.

The word of the Lord.

RESPONSORIAL PSALM

Psalm 51:12-13, 14-15, 18-19

℟. (Ezekiel 36:25) **I will pour clean water on you and wash away all your sins.**

A clean heart create for me, O God,
   and a steadfast spirit renew within me.
Cast me not out from your presence,
   and your Holy Spirit take not from me.

℟. **I will pour clean water on you and wash away all your sins.**

Give me back the joy of your salvation,
   and a willing spirit sustain in me.
I will teach transgressors your ways,
   and sinners shall return to you.

℟. **I will pour clean water on you and wash away all your sins.**

For you are not pleased with sacrifices;
   should I offer a burnt offering, you would not accept it.
My sacrifice, O God, is a contrite spirit;
   a heart contrite and humbled, O God, you will not spurn.

℟. **I will pour clean water on you and wash away all your sins.**

ALLELUIA

Psalm 95:8

℟. Alleluia, alleluia.

**If today you hear his voice,
harden not your hearts.**

℟. Alleluia, alleluia.

GOSPEL   Years I and II

Matthew 22:1-14   Invite to the wedding feast whomever you find.

✣ A reading from the holy Gospel according to Matthew

**Jesus again in reply spoke to the chief priests and the elders of the people
  in parables saying,
    "The Kingdom of heaven may be likened to a king
    who gave a wedding feast for his son.
He dispatched his servants to summon the invited guests to the feast,
    but they refused to come.
A second time he sent other servants, saying,
    'Tell those invited: "Behold, I have prepared my banquet,
    my calves and fattened cattle are killed,
    and everything is ready; come to the feast."'
Some ignored the invitation and went away,
    one to his farm, another to his business.
The rest laid hold of his servants,
    mistreated them, and killed them.
The king was enraged and sent his troops,
    destroyed those murderers, and burned their city.
Then the king said to his servants, 'The feast is ready,
    but those who were invited were not worthy to come.
Go out, therefore, into the main roads
    and invite to the feast whomever you find.'
The servants went out into the streets
    and gathered all they found, bad and good alike,
    and the hall was filled with guests.
But when the king came in to meet the guests
    he saw a man there not dressed in a wedding garment.
He said to him, 'My friend, how is it
    that you came in here without a wedding garment?'
But he was reduced to silence.
Then the king said to his attendants, 'Bind his hands and feet,
    and cast him into the darkness outside,
    where there will be wailing and grinding of teeth.'
Many are invited, but few are chosen."**

The Gospel of the Lord.

423 FRIDAY OF THE TWENTIETH WEEK IN ORDINARY TIME

FIRST READING   Year II

Ezekiel 37:1-14   Dry bones, hear the word of the Lord. I will bring you back from your graves, O my people Israel.

A reading from the Book of the Prophet Ezekiel

The hand of the Lord came upon me,
  and led me out in the Spirit of the Lord
  and set me in the center of the plain,
  which was now filled with bones.
He made me walk among the bones in every direction
  so that I saw how many they were on the surface of the plain.
How dry they were!
He asked me:
  Son of man, can these bones come to life?
I answered, "Lord God, you alone know that."
Then he said to me:
  Prophesy over these bones, and say to them:
  Dry bones, hear thc word of the Lord!
Thus says the Lord God to these bones:
  See! I will bring spirit into you, that you may come to life.
I will put sinews upon you, make flesh grow over you,
  cover you with skin, and put spirit in you
  so that you may come to life and know that I am the Lord.
I prophesied as I had been told,
  and even as I was prophesying I heard a noise;
  it was a rattling as the bones came together, bone joining bone.
I saw the sinews and the flesh come upon them,
  and the skin cover them, but there was no spirit in them.
Then the Lord said to me:
  Prophesy to the spirit, prophesy, son of man,
  and say to the spirit: Thus says the Lord God:
  From the four winds come, O spirit,
  and breathe into these slain that they may come to life.
I prophesied as he told me, and the spirit came into them;
  they came alive and stood upright, a vast army.
Then he said to me:
  Son of man, these bones are the whole house of Israel.

They have been saying,
  "Our bones are dried up,
    our hope is lost, and we are cut off."
Therefore, prophesy and say to them: Thus says the Lord God:
  O my people, I will open your graves
    and have you rise from them,
    and bring you back to the land of Israel.
Then you shall know that I am the Lord,
  when I open your graves and have you rise from them,
    O my people!
I will put my spirit in you that you may live,
  and I will settle you upon your land;
    thus you shall know that I am the Lord.
I have promised, and I will do it, says the Lord.

The word of the Lord.

RESPONSORIAL PSALM

Psalm 107:2-3, 4-5, 6-7, 8-9

℟. (1) **Give thanks to the Lord; his love is everlasting.**

Let the redeemed of the Lord say,
  those whom he has redeemed from the hand of the foe
And gathered from the lands,
  from the east and the west, from the north and the south.

℟. **Give thanks to the Lord; his love is everlasting.**

They went astray in the desert wilderness;
  the way to an inhabited city they did not find.
Hungry and thirsty,
  their life was wasting away within them.

℟. **Give thanks to the Lord; his love is everlasting.**

They cried to the Lord in their distress;
  from their straits he rescued them.
And he led them by a direct way
  to reach an inhabited city.

℟. **Give thanks to the Lord; his love is everlasting.**

Let them give thanks to the Lord for his mercy
** and his wondrous deeds to the children of men,**
Because he satisfied the longing soul
** and filled the hungry soul with good things.**

R/. **Give thanks to the Lord; his love is everlasting.**

ALLELUIA

Psalm 25:4b, 5a

R/. **Alleluia, alleluia.**

Teach me your paths, my God,
guide me in your truth.

R/. **Alleluia, alleluia.**

GOSPEL   Years I and II

Matthew 22:34-40   You shall love the Lord, your God, with all your heart and your neighbor as yourself.

☩ **A reading from the holy Gospel according to Matthew**

When the Pharisees heard that Jesus had silenced the Sadducees,
** they gathered together, and one of them,**
** a scholar of the law, tested him by asking,**
** "Teacher, which commandment in the law is the greatest?"**
He said to him,
** "You shall love the Lord, your God, with all your heart,**
** with all your soul, and with all your mind.**
This is the greatest and the first commandment.
The second is like it:
** You shall love your neighbor as yourself.**
The whole law and the prophets depend on these two commandments."

The Gospel of the Lord.

424 SATURDAY OF THE TWENTIETH WEEK IN ORDINARY TIME

FIRST READING   Year II

Ezekiel 43:1-7ab   The glory of God entered the temple.

A reading from the Book of the Prophet Ezekiel

**The angel led me to the gate which faces the east,
    and there I saw the glory of the God of Israel
    coming from the east.
I heard a sound like the roaring of many waters,
    and the earth shone with his glory.
The vision was like that which I had seen
    when he came to destroy the city,
    and like that which I had seen by the river Chebar.
I fell prone as the glory of the Lord entered the temple
    by way of the gate which faces the east,
    but spirit lifted me up and brought me to the inner court.
And I saw that the temple was filled with the glory of the Lord.
Then I heard someone speaking to me from the temple,
    while the man stood beside me.
The voice said to me:
    Son of man, this is where my throne shall be,
    this is where I will set the soles of my feet;
    here I will dwell among the children of Israel forever.**

The word of the Lord.

RESPONSORIAL PSALM

Psalm 85:9ab and 10, 11-12, 13-14

℟. (see 10b) **The glory of the Lord will dwell in our land.**

I will hear what God proclaims;
    the Lord**—for he proclaims peace.**
Near indeed is his salvation to those who fear him,
    glory dwelling in our land.

℟. **The glory of the Lord will dwell in our land.**

Kindness and truth shall meet;
    justice and peace shall kiss.
Truth shall spring out of the earth,
    and justice shall look down from heaven.

℟. **The glory of the Lord will dwell in our land.**

The Lord **himself will give his benefits;**
    our land shall yield its increase.
Justice shall walk before him,
    and salvation, along the way of his steps.

℟. **The glory of the Lord will dwell in our land.**

ALLELUIA

Matthew 23:9b, 10b

℟. **Alleluia, alleluia.**

You have but one Father in heaven;
you have but one master, the Christ.

℟. **Alleluia, alleluia.**

GOSPEL Years I and II

Matthew 23:1-12   They preach but they do not practice.

✚ A reading from the holy Gospel according to Matthew

Jesus spoke to the crowds and to his disciples, saying,
  "The scribes and the Pharisees
  have taken their seat on the chair of Moses.
Therefore, do and observe all things whatsoever they tell you,
  but do not follow their example.
For they preach but they do not practice.
They tie up heavy burdens hard to carry
  and lay them on people's shoulders,
  but they will not lift a finger to move them.
All their works are performed to be seen.
They widen their phylacteries and lengthen their tassels.
They love places of honor at banquets, seats of honor in synagogues,
  greetings in marketplaces, and the salutation 'Rabbi.'
As for you, do not be called 'Rabbi.'
You have but one teacher, and you are all brothers.
Call no one on earth your father;
  you have but one Father in heaven.
Do not be called 'Master';
  you have but one master, the Christ.
The greatest among you must be your servant.
Whoever exalts himself will be humbled;
  but whoever humbles himself will be exalted."

The Gospel of the Lord.

425 MONDAY OF THE TWENTY-FIRST WEEK IN ORDINARY TIME

FIRST READING   Year II

2 Thessalonians 1:1-5, 11-12   May the name of our Lord Jesus be glorified in you and you in him.

A reading from the beginning of the second Letter of Saint Paul to the Thessalonians

Paul, Silvanus, and Timothy to the Church of the Thessalonians
   in God our Father and the Lord Jesus Christ:
   grace to you and peace from God our Father
   and the Lord Jesus Christ.

We ought to thank God always for you, brothers and sisters,
   as is fitting, because your faith flourishes ever more,
   and the love of every one of you for one another grows ever greater.
Accordingly, we ourselves boast of you in the churches of God
   regarding your endurance and faith in all your persecutions
   and the afflictions you endure.

This is evidence of the just judgment of God,
   so that you may be considered worthy of the Kingdom of God
   for which you are suffering.

We always pray for you,
   that our God may make you worthy of his calling
   and powerfully bring to fulfillment every good purpose
   and every effort of faith,
   that the name of our Lord Jesus may be glorified in you,
   and you in him,
   in accord with the grace of our God and Lord Jesus Christ.

The word of the Lord.

RESPONSORIAL PSALM

Psalm 96:1-2a, 2b-3, 4-5

℟. (3) **Proclaim God's marvelous deeds to all the nations.**

Sing to the LORD **a new song;**
    sing to the LORD**, all you lands.**
Sing to the LORD**; bless his name.**

℟. **Proclaim God's marvelous deeds to all the nations.**

Announce his salvation, day after day.
Tell his glory among the nations;
    among all peoples, his wondrous deeds.

℟. **Proclaim God's marvelous deeds to all the nations.**

For great is the LORD **and highly to be praised;**
    awesome is he, beyond all gods.
For all the gods of the nations are things of nought,
    but the LORD **made the heavens.**

℟. **Proclaim God's marvelous deeds to all the nations.**

ALLELUIA

John 10:27

℟. **Alleluia, alleluia.**

My sheep hear my voice, says the Lord;
I know them, and they follow me.

℟. **Alleluia, alleluia.**

GOSPEL   Years I and II

Matthew 23:13-22   Woe to you, blind guides.

☩ A reading from the holy Gospel according to Matthew

Jesus said to the crowds and to his disciples:
"Woe to you, scribes and Pharisees, you hypocrites.
You lock the Kingdom of heaven before men.
You do not enter yourselves,
   nor do you allow entrance to those trying to enter.

"Woe to you, scribes and Pharisees, you hypocrites.
You traverse sea and land to make one convert,
   and when that happens you make him a child of Gehenna
   twice as much as yourselves.

"Woe to you, blind guides, who say,
   'If one swears by the temple, it means nothing,
   but if one swears by the gold of the temple, one is obligated.'
Blind fools, which is greater, the gold,
   or the temple that made the gold sacred?
And you say, 'If one swears by the altar, it means nothing,
   but if one swears by the gift on the altar, one is obligated.'
You blind ones, which is greater, the gift,
   or the altar that makes the gift sacred?
One who swears by the altar swears by it and all that is upon it;
   one who swears by the temple swears by it
   and by him who dwells in it;
   one who swears by heaven swears by the throne of God
   and by him who is seated on it."

The Gospel of the Lord.

426 TUESDAY OF THE TWENTY-FIRST WEEK IN ORDINARY TIME

FIRST READING   Year II

2 Thessalonians 2:1-3a, 14-17   Hold fast to the traditions that you were taught.

A reading from the second Letter of Saint Paul to the Thessalonians

We ask you, brothers and sisters,
 with regard to the coming of our Lord Jesus Christ
 and our assembling with him,
 not to be shaken out of your minds suddenly,
 or to be alarmed either by a "spirit," or by an oral statement,
 or by a letter allegedly from us
 to the effect that the day of the Lord is at hand.
Let no one deceive you in any way.

To this end he has also called you through our Gospel
 to possess the glory of our Lord Jesus Christ.
Therefore, brothers and sisters, stand firm
 and hold fast to the traditions that you were taught,
 either by an oral statement or by a letter of ours.

May our Lord Jesus Christ himself and God our Father,
 who has loved us and given us everlasting encouragement
 and good hope through his grace,
 encourage your hearts and strengthen them
 in every good deed and word.

The word of the Lord.

RESPONSORIAL PSALM

Psalm 96:10, 11-12, 13

℟. (13b) **The Lord comes to judge the earth.**

Say among the nations: The LORD is king.
He has made the world firm, not to be moved;
 he governs the peoples with equity.

℟. **The Lord comes to judge the earth.**

Let the heavens be glad and the earth rejoice;
　let the sea and what fills it resound;
　let the plains be joyful and all that is in them!
Then shall all the trees of the forest exult.

℟. The Lord comes to judge the earth.

Before the LORD, for he comes;
　for he comes to rule the earth.
He shall rule the world with justice
　and the peoples with his constancy.

℟. The Lord comes to judge the earth.

ALLELUIA

Hebrews 4:12

℟. Alleluia, alleluia.

The word of God is living and effective,
able to discern reflections and thoughts of the heart.

℟. Alleluia, alleluia.

GOSPEL   Years I and II

Matthew 23:23-26   But these you should have done, without neglecting the others.

✠ A reading from the holy Gospel according to Matthew

Jesus said:
"Woe to you, scribes and Pharisees, you hypocrites.
You pay tithes of mint and dill and cummin,
　and have neglected the weightier things of the law:
　judgment and mercy and fidelity.
But these you should have done, without neglecting the others.
Blind guides, who strain out the gnat and swallow the camel!

"Woe to you, scribes and Pharisees, you hypocrites.
You cleanse the outside of cup and dish,
　but inside they are full of plunder and self-indulgence.
Blind Pharisee, cleanse first the inside of the cup,
　so that the outside also may be clean."

The Gospel of the Lord.

427 WEDNESDAY OF THE TWENTY-FIRST WEEK IN ORDINARY TIME

FIRST READING   Year II

2 Thessalonians 3:6-10, 16-18   If anyone is unwilling to work, neither should that one eat.

A reading from the second Letter of Saint Paul to the Thessalonians

We instruct you, brothers and sisters,
   in the name of our Lord Jesus Christ,
   to shun any brother
   who walks in a disorderly way
   and not according to the tradition they received from us.
For you know how one must imitate us.
For we did not act in a disorderly way among you,
   nor did we eat food received free from anyone.
On the contrary, in toil and drudgery, night and day we worked,
   so as not to burden any of you.
Not that we do not have the right.
Rather, we wanted to present ourselves as a model for you,
   so that you might imitate us.
In fact, when we were with you, we instructed you that
   if anyone was unwilling to work, neither should that one eat.

May the Lord of peace himself
   give you peace at all times and in every way.
The Lord be with all of you.

This greeting is in my own hand, Paul's.
This is the sign in every letter; this is how I write.
The grace of our Lord Jesus Christ be with all of you.

The word of the Lord.

RESPONSORIAL PSALM

Psalm 128:1-2, 4-5

℟. (1) **Blessed are those who fear the Lord.**

**Blessed are you who fear the LORD,
 who walk in his ways!
For you shall eat the fruit of your handiwork;
 blessed shall you be, and favored.**

℟. **Blessed are those who fear the Lord.**

**Behold, thus is the man blessed
 who fears the LORD.
The LORD bless you from Zion:
 may you see the prosperity of Jerusalem
 all the days of your life.**

℟. **Blessed are those who fear the Lord.**

ALLELUIA

1 John 2:5

℟. **Alleluia, alleluia.**

**Whoever keeps the word of Christ,
the love of God is truly perfected in him.**

℟. **Alleluia, alleluia.**

GOSPEL Years I and II

Matthew 23:27-32   You are the children of those who murdered the prophets.

☩ A reading from the holy Gospel according to Matthew

Jesus said,
  "Woe to you, scribes and Pharisees, you hypocrites.
You are like whitewashed tombs, which appear beautiful on the outside,
  but inside are full of dead men's bones and every kind of filth.
Even so, on the outside you appear righteous,
  but inside you are filled with hypocrisy and evildoing.

"Woe to you, scribes and Pharisees, you hypocrites.
You build the tombs of the prophets
  and adorn the memorials of the righteous,
  and you say, 'If we had lived in the days of our ancestors,
  we would not have joined them in shedding the prophets' blood.'
Thus you bear witness against yourselves
  that you are the children of those who murdered the prophets;
  now fill up what your ancestors measured out!"

The Gospel of the Lord.

428 THURSDAY OF THE TWENTY-FIRST WEEK IN ORDINARY TIME

FIRST READING   Year II

1 Corinthians 1:1-9   In him you were enriched in every way.

A reading from the beginning of the first Letter of Saint Paul to the Corinthians

Paul, called to be an Apostle of Christ Jesus by the will of God,
  and Sosthenes our brother,
  to the Church of God that is in Corinth,
  to you who have been sanctified in Christ Jesus, called to be holy,
  with all those everywhere who call upon the name of our Lord Jesus
    Christ, their Lord and ours.
Grace to you and peace from God our Father
  and the Lord Jesus Christ.

I give thanks to my God always on your account
  for the grace of God bestowed on you in Christ Jesus,
  that in him you were enriched in every way,
  with all discourse and all knowledge,
  as the testimony to Christ was confirmed among you,
  so that you are not lacking in any spiritual gift
  as you wait for the revelation of our Lord Jesus Christ.
He will keep you firm to the end,
  irreproachable on the day of our Lord Jesus Christ.
God is faithful,
  and by him you were called to fellowship with his Son, Jesus Christ our
    Lord.

The word of the Lord.

RESPONSORIAL PSALM

Psalm 145:2-3, 4-5, 6-7

℟. (1) **I will praise your name for ever, Lord.**

**Every day will I bless you,
    and I will praise your name forever and ever.
Great is the** Lord **and highly to be praised;
    his greatness is unsearchable.**

℟. **I will praise your name for ever, Lord.**

**Generation after generation praises your works
    and proclaims your might.
They speak of the splendor of your glorious majesty
    and tell of your wondrous works.**

℟. **I will praise your name for ever, Lord.**

**They discourse of the power of your terrible deeds
    and declare your greatness.
They publish the fame of your abundant goodness
    and joyfully sing of your justice.**

℟. **I will praise your name for ever, Lord.**

ALLELUIA

Matthew 24:42a, 44

℟. **Alleluia, alleluia.**

**Stay awake!
For you do not know when the Son of Man will come.**

℟. **Alleluia, alleluia.**

GOSPEL　Years I and II

Matthew 24:42-51　Stay awake!

✠ A reading from the holy Gospel according to Matthew

Jesus said to his disciples:
"Stay awake!
For you do not know on which day your Lord will come.
Be sure of this:
　if the master of the house
　had known the hour of night when the thief was coming,
　he would have stayed awake
　and not let his house be broken into.
So too, you also must be prepared,
　for at an hour you do not expect, the Son of Man will come.

"Who, then, is the faithful and prudent servant,
　whom the master has put in charge of his household
　to distribute to them their food at the proper time?
Blessed is that servant whom his master on his arrival finds doing so.
Amen, I say to you, he will put him in charge of all his property.
But if that wicked servant says to himself, 'My master is long delayed,'
　and begins to beat his fellow servants,
　and eat and drink with drunkards,
　the servant's master will come on an unexpected day
　and at an unknown hour and will punish him severely
　and assign him a place with the hypocrites,
　where there will be wailing and grinding of teeth."

The Gospel of the Lord.

429 FRIDAY OF THE TWENTY-FIRST WEEK IN ORDINARY TIME

FIRST READING   Year II

1 Corinthians 1:17-25   We proclaim Christ crucified, foolishness to Gentiles, but to those who are called, the wisdom of God.

A reading from the first Letter of Saint Paul to the Corinthians

Brothers and sisters:
Christ did not send me to baptize but to preach the Gospel,
   and not with the wisdom of human eloquence,
   so that the cross of Christ might not be emptied of its meaning.

The message of the cross is foolishness to those who are perishing,
   but to us who are being saved it is the power of God.
For it is written:

   I will destroy the wisdom of the wise,
      and the learning of the learned I will set aside.

Where is the wise one?
Where is the scribe?
Where is the debater of this age?
Has not God made the wisdom of the world foolish?
For since in the wisdom of God
   the world did not come to know God through wisdom,
   it was the will of God through the foolishness of the proclamation
   to save those who have faith.
For Jews demand signs and Greeks look for wisdom,
   but we proclaim Christ crucified,
   a stumbling block to Jews and foolishness to Gentiles,
   but to those who are called, Jews and Greeks alike,
   Christ the power of God and the wisdom of God.
For the foolishness of God is wiser than human wisdom,
   and the weakness of God is stronger than human strength.

The word of the Lord.

RESPONSORIAL PSALM

Psalm 33:1-2, 4-5, 10-11

℟. (5) **The earth is full of the goodness of the Lord.**

Exult, you just, in the LORD**;**
  praise from the upright is fitting.
Give thanks to the LORD **on the harp;**
  with the ten-stringed lyre chant his praises.

℟. **The earth is full of the goodness of the Lord.**

For upright is the word of the LORD**,**
  and all his works are trustworthy.
He loves justice and right;
  of the kindness of the LORD **the earth is full.**

℟. **The earth is full of the goodness of the Lord.**

The LORD **brings to nought the plans of nations;**
  he foils the designs of peoples.
But the plan of the LORD **stands forever;**
  the design of his heart, through all generations.

℟. **The earth is full of the goodness of the Lord.**

ALLELUIA

Luke 21:36

℟. **Alleluia, alleluia.**

Be vigilant at all times and pray,
that you may have the strength to stand before the Son of Man.

℟. **Alleluia, alleluia.**

GOSPEL   Years I and II

Matthew 25:1-13   Behold, the bridegroom! Come out to meet him!

✠ A reading from the holy Gospel according to Matthew

Jesus told his disciples this parable:
"The Kingdom of heaven will be like ten virgins
  who took their lamps and went out to meet the **bridegroom.**
Five of them were foolish and five were wise.
The foolish ones, when taking their lamps,
  brought no oil with them,
  but the wise brought flasks of oil with their lamps.
Since the bridegroom was long delayed,
  they all became drowsy and fell asleep.
At midnight, there was a cry,
  'Behold, the bridegroom! Come out to meet him!'
Then all those virgins got up and trimmed their lamps.
The foolish ones said to the wise,
  'Give us some of your oil,
  for our lamps are going out.'
But the wise ones replied,
  'No, for there may not be enough for us and you.
Go instead to the merchants and buy some for yourselves.'
While they went off to buy it,
  the bridegroom came
  and those who were ready went into the wedding **feast with him.**
Then the door was locked.
Afterwards the other virgins came and said,
  'Lord, Lord, open the door for us!'
But he said in reply,
  'Amen, I say to you, I do not know you.'
Therefore, stay awake,
  for you know neither the day nor the hour."

The Gospel of the Lord.

430 SATURDAY OF THE TWENTY-FIRST WEEK IN ORDINARY TIME

FIRST READING   Year II

1 Corinthians 1:26-31   God chose the weak of the world.

A reading from the first Letter of Saint Paul to the Corinthians

Consider your own calling, brothers and sisters.
Not many of you were wise by human standards,
   not many were powerful,
   not many were of noble birth.
Rather, God chose the foolish of the world to shame the wise,
   and God chose the weak of the world to shame the strong,
   and God chose the lowly and despised of the world,
   those who count for nothing,
   to reduce to nothing those who are something,
   so that no human being might boast before God.
It is due to him that you are in Christ Jesus,
   who became for us wisdom from God,
   as well as righteousness, sanctification, and redemption,
   so that, as it is written,
   Whoever boasts, should boast in the Lord.

The word of the Lord.

RESPONSORIAL PSALM

Psalm 33:12-13, 18-19, 20-21

℟. (12) **Blessed the people the Lord has chosen to be his own.**

**Blessed the nation whose God is the Lord,
 the people he has chosen for his own inheritance.
From heaven the Lord looks down;
 he sees all mankind.**

℟. **Blessed the people the Lord has chosen to be his own.**

**But see, the eyes of the Lord are upon those who fear him,
 upon those who hope for his kindness,
To deliver them from death
 and preserve them in spite of famine.**

℟. **Blessed the people the Lord has chosen to be his own.**

**Our soul waits for the Lord,
 who is our help and our shield,
For in him our hearts rejoice;
 in his holy name we trust.**

℟. **Blessed the people the Lord has chosen to be his own.**

ALLELUIA

John 13:34

℟. **Alleluia, alleluia.**

**I give you a new commandment:
love one another as I have loved you.**

℟. **Alleluia, alleluia.**

GOSPEL   Years I and II

Matthew 25:14-30   Since you have been faithful in small matters, come, share your master's joy.

☩ A reading from the holy Gospel according to Matthew

**Jesus told his disciples this parable:
"A man going on a journey
  called in his servants and entrusted his possessions to them.
To one he gave five talents; to another, two; to a third, one—
  to each according to his ability.
Then he went away.
Immediately the one who received five talents went and traded with them,
  and made another five.
Likewise, the one who received two made another two.
But the man who received one went off and dug a hole in the ground
  and buried his master's money.
After a long time
  the master of those servants came back and settled accounts with them.
The one who had received five talents
  came forward bringing the additional five.
He said, 'Master, you gave me five talents.
See, I have made five more.'
His master said to him, 'Well done, my good and faithful servant.
Since you were faithful in small matters,
  I will give you great responsibilities.
Come, share your master's joy.'
Then the one who had received two talents also came forward and said,
  'Master, you gave me two talents.
See, I have made two more.'
His master said to him, 'Well done, my good and faithful servant.
Since you were faithful in small matters,
  I will give you great responsibilities.
Come, share your master's joy.'
Then the one who had received the one talent came forward and said,
  'Master, I knew you were a demanding person,
  harvesting where you did not plant
  and gathering where you did not scatter;
  so out of fear I went off and buried your talent in the ground.
Here it is back.'
His master said to him in reply, 'You wicked, lazy servant!**

So you knew that I harvest where I did not plant
   and gather where I did not scatter?
Should you not then have put my money in the bank
   so that I could have got it back with interest on my return?
Now then! Take the talent from him and give it to the one with ten.
For to everyone who has,
   more will be given and he will grow rich;
   but from the one who has not,
   even what he has will be taken away.
And throw this useless servant into the darkness outside,
   where there will be wailing and grinding of teeth.'"

The Gospel of the Lord.

431 MONDAY OF THE TWENTY-SECOND WEEK IN ORDINARY TIME

FIRST READING   Year II

1 Corinthians 2:1-5   *I came to you proclaiming Jesus Christ, and him crucified.*

A reading from the first Letter of Saint Paul to the Corinthians

When I came to you, brothers and sisters,
  proclaiming the mystery of God,
  I did not come with sublimity of words or of wisdom.
For I resolved to know nothing while I was with you
  except Jesus Christ, and him crucified.
I came to you in weakness and fear and much trembling,
  and my message and my proclamation
  were not with persuasive words of wisdom,
  but with a demonstration of spirit and power,
  so that your faith might rest not on human wisdom
  but on the power of God.

The word of the Lord.

RESPONSORIAL PSALM

Psalm 119:97, 98, 99, 100, 101, 102

℟. (97) **Lord, I love your commands.**

How I love your law, O LORD**!
It is my meditation all the day.**

℟. **Lord, I love your commands.**

**Your command has made me wiser than my enemies,
for it is ever with me.**

℟. **Lord, I love your commands.**

**I have more understanding than all my teachers
when your decrees are my meditation.**

℟. **Lord, I love your commands.**

**I have more discernment than the elders,
because I observe your precepts.**

℟. **Lord, I love your commands.**

**From every evil way I withhold my feet,
that I may keep your words.**

℟. **Lord, I love your commands.**

**From your ordinances I turn not away,
for you have instructed me.**

℟. **Lord, I love your commands.**

ALLELUIA

See Luke 4:18

℟. **Alleluia, alleluia.**

**The Spirit of the Lord is upon me;
he has sent me to bring glad tidings to the poor.**

℟. **Alleluia, alleluia.**

GOSPEL   Years I and II

Luke 4:16-30   He has sent me to bring glad tidings to the poor. No prophet is accepted in his own native place.

✝ A reading from the holy Gospel according to Luke

Jesus came to Nazareth, where he had grown up,
 and went according to his custom
 into the synagogue on the sabbath day.
He stood up to read and was handed a scroll of the prophet Isaiah.
He unrolled the scroll and found the passage where it was written:

The Spirit of the Lord is upon me,
because he has anointed me
 to bring glad tidings to the poor.
He has sent me to proclaim liberty to captives
 and recovery of sight to the blind,
  to let the oppressed go free,
and to proclaim a year acceptable to the Lord.

Rolling up the scroll,
 he handed it back to the attendant and sat down,
 and the eyes of all in the synagogue looked intently at him.
He said to them,
 "Today this Scripture passage is fulfilled in your hearing."
And all spoke highly of him
 and were amazed at the gracious words that came from his mouth.
They also asked, "Is this not the son of Joseph?"
He said to them, "Surely you will quote me this proverb,
 'Physician, cure yourself,' and say, 'Do here in your native place
 the things that we heard were done in Capernaum.'"
And he said,
 "Amen, I say to you, no prophet is accepted in his own native place.
Indeed, I tell you,
 there were many widows in Israel in the days of Elijah
 when the sky was closed for three and a half years
 and a severe famine spread over the entire land.
It was to none of these that Elijah was sent,
 but only to a widow in Zarephath in the land of Sidon.
Again, there were many lepers in Israel
 during the time of Elisha the prophet;
 yet not one of them was cleansed, but only Naaman the Syrian."

When the people in the synagogue heard this,
   they were all filled with fury.
They rose up, drove him out of the town,
   and led him to the brow of the hill
   on which their town had been built, to hurl him down headlong.
But he passed through the midst of them and went away.

The Gospel of the Lord.

432 TUESDAY OF THE TWENTY-SECOND WEEK IN ORDINARY TIME

FIRST READING   Year II

1 Corinthians 2:10b-16   *Natural persons do not accept what pertains to the Spirit of God: spiritual persons, however, can judge everything.*

A reading from the first Letter of Saint Paul to the Corinthians

Brothers and sisters:
The Spirit scrutinizes everything, even the depths of God.
Among men, who knows what pertains to the man
  except his spirit that is within?
Similarly, no one knows what pertains to God except the Spirit of God.
We have not received the spirit of the world
  but the Spirit who is from God,
  so that we may understand the things freely given us by God.
And we speak about them not with words taught by human wisdom,
  but with words taught by the Spirit,
  describing spiritual realities in spiritual terms.

Now the natural man does not accept what pertains to the Spirit of God,
  for to him it is foolishness, and he cannot understand it,
  because it is judged spiritually.
The one who is spiritual, however, can judge everything
  but is not subject to judgment by anyone.

For "who has known the mind of the Lord, so as to counsel him?"
But we have the mind of Christ.

The word of the Lord.

RESPONSORIAL PSALM

Psalm 145:8-9, 10-11, 12-13ab, 13cd-14

℟. (17) **The Lord is just in all his ways.**

**The LORD is gracious and merciful,
    slow to anger and of great kindness.
The LORD is good to all
    and compassionate toward all his works.**

℟. **The Lord is just in all his ways.**

**Let all your works give you thanks, O LORD,
    and let your faithful ones bless you.
Let them discourse of the glory of your Kingdom
    and speak of your might.**

℟. **The Lord is just in all his ways.**

**Making known to men your might
    and the glorious splendor of your Kingdom.
Your Kingdom is a Kingdom for all ages,
    and your dominion endures through all generations.**

℟. **The Lord is just in all his ways.**

**The LORD is faithful in all his words
    and holy in all his works.
The LORD lifts up all who are falling
    and raises up all who are bowed down.**

℟. **The Lord is just in all his ways.**

ALLELUIA

Luke 7:16

℟. Alleluia, alleluia.

A great prophet has arisen in our midst
and God has visited his people.

℟. Alleluia, alleluia.

GOSPEL   Years I and II

Luke 4:31-37   I know who you are—the Holy One of God!

✚ A reading from the holy Gospel according to Luke

Jesus went down to Capernaum, a town of Galilee.
He taught them on the sabbath,
   and they were astonished at his teaching
   because he spoke with authority.
In the synagogue there was a man with the spirit of an unclean demon,
   and he cried out in a loud voice,
   "What have you to do with us, Jesus of Nazareth?
Have you come to destroy us?
I know who you are—the Holy One of God!"
Jesus rebuked him and said, "Be quiet! Come out of him!"
Then the demon threw the man down in front of them
   and came out of him without doing him any harm.
They were all amazed and said to one another,
   "What is there about his word?
For with authority and power he commands the unclean spirits,
   and they come out."
And news of him spread everywhere in the surrounding region.

The Gospel of the Lord.

433 WEDNESDAY OF THE TWENTY-SECOND WEEK IN ORDINARY TIME

FIRST READING   Year II

1 Corinthians 3:1-9   We are God's co-workers; you are God's field, God's building.

A reading from the first Letter of Saint Paul to the Corinthians

**Brothers and sisters,
 I could not talk to you as spiritual people,
 but as fleshly people, as infants in Christ.
I fed you milk, not solid food,
 because you were unable to take it.
Indeed, you are still not able, even now,
 for you are still of the flesh.
While there is jealousy and rivalry among you,
 are you not of the flesh, and walking
 according to the manner of man?
Whenever someone says, "I belong to Paul," and another,
 "I belong to Apollos," are you not merely men?**

**What is Apollos, after all, and what is Paul?
Ministers through whom you became believers,
 just as the Lord assigned each one.
I planted, Apollos watered, but God caused the growth.
Therefore, neither the one who plants nor the one who waters is anything,
 but only God, who causes the growth.
He who plants and he who waters are one,
 and each will receive wages in proportion to his labor.
For we are God's co-workers;
 you are God's field, God's building.**

The word of the Lord.

RESPONSORIAL PSALM

Psalm 33:12-13, 14-15, 20-21

℟. (12) **Blessed the people the Lord has chosen to be his own.**

**Blessed the nation whose God is the Lord,
 the people he has chosen for his own inheritance.
From heaven the Lord looks down;
 he sees all mankind.**

℟. **Blessed the people the Lord has chosen to be his own.**

**From his fixed throne he beholds
 all who dwell on the earth,
He who fashioned the heart of each,
 he who knows all their works.**

℟. **Blessed the people the Lord has chosen to be his own.**

**Our soul waits for the Lord,
 who is our help and our shield,
For in him our hearts rejoice;
 in his holy name we trust.**

℟. **Blessed the people the Lord has chosen to be his own.**

ALLELUIA

Luke 4:18

℟. **Alleluia, alleluia.**

**The Lord sent me to bring glad tidings to the poor
and to proclaim liberty to captives.**

℟. **Alleluia, alleluia.**

GOSPEL   Years I and II

Luke 4:38-44   To the other towns also I must proclaim the Good News of the Kingdom of God, because for this purpose I have been sent.

✛   A reading from the holy Gospel according to Luke

After Jesus left the synagogue, he entered the house of Simon.
Simon's mother-in-law was afflicted with a severe fever,
　and they interceded with him about her.
He stood over her, rebuked the fever, and it left her.
She got up immediately and waited on them.

At sunset, all who had people sick with various diseases
　brought them to him.
He laid his hands on each of them and cured them.
And demons also came out from many, shouting, "You are the Son of God."
But he rebuked them and did not allow them to speak
　because they knew that he was the Christ.

At daybreak, Jesus left and went to a deserted place.
The crowds went looking for him, and when they came to him,
　they tried to prevent him from leaving them.
But he said to them, "To the other towns also
　I must proclaim the good news of the Kingdom of God,
　because for this purpose I have been sent."
And he was preaching in the synagogues of Judea.

The Gospel of the Lord.

434 THURSDAY OF THE TWENTY-SECOND WEEK IN ORDINARY TIME

FIRST READING   Year II

1 Corinthians 3:18-23   All belong to you, and you to Christ, and Christ to God.

A reading from the first Letter of Saint Paul to the Corinthians

Brothers and sisters:
Let no one deceive himself.
If anyone among you considers himself wise in this age,
   let him become a fool, so as to become wise.
For the wisdom of this world is foolishness in the eyes of God,
   for it is written:

   God catches the wise in their own ruses,

and again:

   The Lord knows the thoughts of the wise, that they are vain.

So let no one boast about human beings, for everything belongs to you,
   Paul or Apollos or Cephas,
   or the world or life or death,
   or the present or the future:
   all belong to you, and you to Christ, and Christ to God.

The word of the Lord.

RESPONSORIAL PSALM

Psalm 24:1bc-2, 3-4ab, 5-6

℟. (1) **To the Lord belongs the earth and all that fills it.**

**The Lord's are the earth and its fullness;
   the world and those who dwell in it.
For he founded it upon the seas
   and established it upon the rivers.**

℟. **To the Lord belongs the earth and all that fills it.**

**Who can ascend the mountain of the Lord?
   or who may stand in his holy place?
He whose hands are sinless, whose heart is clean,
   who desires not what is vain.**

℟. **To the Lord belongs the earth and all that fills it.**

**He shall receive a blessing from the Lord,
   a reward from God his savior.
Such is the race that seeks for him,
   that seeks the face of the God of Jacob.**

℟. **To the Lord belongs the earth and all that fills it.**

ALLELUIA

Matthew 4:19

℟. **Alleluia, alleluia.**

**Come after me, says the Lord,
and I will make you fishers of men.**

℟. **Alleluia, alleluia.**

GOSPEL Years I and II

Luke 5:1-11   They left everything and followed Jesus.

✠ A reading from the holy Gospel according to Luke

While the crowd was pressing in on Jesus and listening to the word of God,
  he was standing by the Lake of Gennesaret.
He saw two boats there alongside the lake;
  the fishermen had disembarked and were washing their nets.
Getting into one of the boats, the one belonging to Simon,
  he asked him to put out a short distance from the shore.
Then he sat down and taught the crowds from the boat.
After he had finished speaking, he said to Simon,
  "Put out into deep water and lower your nets for a catch."
Simon said in reply,
  "Master, we have worked hard all night and have caught nothing,
  but at your command I will lower the nets."
When they had done this, they caught a great number of fish
  and their nets were tearing.
They signaled to their partners in the other boat
  to come to help them.
They came and filled both boats
  so that the boats were in danger of sinking.
When Simon Peter saw this, he fell at the knees of Jesus and said,
  "Depart from me, Lord, for I am a sinful man."
For astonishment at the catch of fish they had made seized him
  and all those with him,
    and likewise James and John, the sons of Zebedee,
  who were partners of Simon.
Jesus said to Simon, "Do not be afraid;
  from now on you will be catching men."
When they brought their boats to the shore,
  they left everything and followed him.

The Gospel of the Lord.

435 FRIDAY OF THE TWENTY-SECOND WEEK IN ORDINARY TIME

FIRST READING   Year II

1 Corinthians 4:1-5   The Lord will manifest the motives of our hearts.

A reading from the first Letter of Saint Paul to the Corinthians

Brothers and sisters:
Thus should one regard us: as servants of Christ
 and stewards of the mysteries of God.
Now it is of course required of stewards
 that they be found trustworthy.
It does not concern me in the least
 that I be judged by you or any human tribunal;
 I do not even pass judgment on myself;
 I am not conscious of anything against me,
 but I do not thereby stand acquitted;
 the one who judges me is the Lord.
Therefore, do not make any judgment before the appointed time,
 until the Lord comes,
 for he will bring to light what is hidden in darkness
 and will manifest the motives of our hearts,
 and then everyone will receive praise from God.

The word of the Lord.

RESPONSORIAL PSALM

Psalm 37:3-4, 5-6, 27-28, 39-40

℟. (39a) **The salvation of the just comes from the Lord.**

Trust in the LORD and do good,
   that you may dwell in the land and be fed in security.
Take delight in the LORD,
   and he will grant you your heart's requests.

℟. **The salvation of the just comes from the Lord.**

Commit to the LORD your way;
   trust in him, and he will act.
He will make justice dawn for you like the light;
   bright as the noonday shall be your vindication.

℟. **The salvation of the just comes from the Lord.**

Turn from evil and do good,
   that you may abide forever;
For the LORD loves what is right,
   and forsakes not his faithful ones.
Criminals are destroyed
   and the posterity of the wicked is cut off.

℟. **The salvation of the just comes from the Lord.**

The salvation of the just is from the LORD;
   he is their refuge in time of distress.
And the LORD helps them and delivers them;
   he delivers them from the wicked and saves them,
   because they take refuge in him.

℟. **The salvation of the just comes from the Lord.**

ALLELUIA

John 8:12

℟. Alleluia, alleluia.

I am the light of the world, says the Lord;
whoever follows me will have the light of life.

℟. Alleluia, alleluia.

GOSPEL   Years I and II

Luke 5:33-39   When the bridegroom is taken away from them, then they will fast.

✠ A reading from the holy Gospel according to Luke

The scribes and Pharisees said to Jesus,
  "The disciples of John the Baptist fast often and offer prayers,
  and the disciples of the Pharisees do the same;
  but yours eat and drink."
Jesus answered them, "Can you make the wedding guests fast
  while the bridegroom is with them?
But the days will come, and when the bridegroom is taken away from them,
  then they will fast in those days."
And he also told them a parable.
"No one tears a piece from a new cloak to patch an old one.
Otherwise, he will tear the new
  and the piece from it will not match the old cloak.
Likewise, no one pours new wine into old wineskins.
Otherwise, the new wine will burst the skins,
  and it will be spilled, and the skins will be ruined.
Rather, new wine must be poured into fresh wineskins.
And no one who has been drinking old wine desires new,
  for he says, 'The old is good.'"

The Gospel of the Lord.

436 SATURDAY OF THE TWENTY-SECOND WEEK IN ORDINARY TIME

FIRST READING   Year II

1 Corinthians 4:6b-15   We go hungry and thirsty and we are poorly clad.

A reading from the first Letter of Saint Paul to the Corinthians

Brothers and sisters:
Learn from myself and Apollos not to go beyond what is written,
   so that none of you will be inflated with pride
   in favor of one person over against another.
Who confers distinction upon you?
What do you possess that you have not received?
But if you have received it,
   why are you boasting as if you did not receive it?
You are already satisfied; you have already grown rich;
   you have become kings without us!
Indeed, I wish that you had become kings,
   so that we also might become kings with you.

For as I see it, God has exhibited us Apostles as the last of all,
   like people sentenced to death,
   since we have become a spectacle to the world,
   to angels and men alike.
We are fools on Christ's account, but you are wise in Christ;
   we are weak, but you are strong;
   you are held in honor, but we in disrepute.
To this very hour we go hungry and thirsty,
   we are poorly clad and roughly treated,
   we wander about homeless and we toil, working with our own hands.
When ridiculed, we bless; when persecuted, we endure;
   when slandered, we respond gently.
We have become like the world's rubbish, the scum of all,
   to this very moment.

I am writing you this not to shame you,
   but to admonish you as my beloved children.
Even if you should have countless guides to Christ,
   yet you do not have many fathers,
   for I became your father in Christ Jesus through the Gospel.

The word of the Lord.

RESPONSORIAL PSALM

Psalm 145:17-18, 19-20, 21

℟. (18) **The Lord is near to all who call upon him.**

**The LORD is just in all his ways
  and holy in all his works.
The LORD is near to all who call upon him,
  to all who call upon him in truth.**

℟. **The Lord is near to all who call upon him.**

**He fulfills the desire of those who fear him,
  he hears their cry and saves them.
The LORD keeps all who love him,
  but all the wicked he will destroy.**

℟. **The Lord is near to all who call upon him.**

**May my mouth speak the praise of the LORD,
  and may all flesh bless his holy name forever and ever.**

℟. **The Lord is near to all who call upon him.**

ALLELUIA

John 14:6

℟. Alleluia, alleluia.

I am the way and the truth and the life, says the Lord;
no one comes to the Father except through me.

℟. Alleluia, alleluia.

GOSPEL   Years I and II

Luke 6:1-5   Why are you doing what is unlawful on the sabbath?

✛ A reading from the holy Gospel according to Luke

While Jesus was going through a field of grain on a sabbath,
   his disciples were picking the heads of grain,
   rubbing them in their hands, and eating them.
Some Pharisees said,
   "Why are you doing what is unlawful on the sabbath?"
Jesus said to them in reply,
   "Have you not read what David did
      when he and those who were with him were hungry?
How he went into the house of God, took the bread of offering,
   which only the priests could lawfully eat,
   ate of it, and shared it with his companions?"
Then he said to them, "The Son of Man is lord of the sabbath."

The Gospel of the Lord.

437 MONDAY OF THE TWENTY-THIRD WEEK IN ORDINARY TIME

FIRST READING Year II

1 Corinthians 5:1-8 Clean out the old yeast; for our Paschal Lamb, Christ, has been sacrificed.

A reading from the first Letter of Saint Paul to the Corinthians

Brothers and sisters:
It is widely reported that there is immorality among you,
    and immorality of a kind not found even among pagans—
    a man living with his father's wife.
And you are inflated with pride.
Should you not rather have been sorrowful?
The one who did this deed should be expelled from your midst.
I, for my part, although absent in body but present in spirit,
    have already, as if present,
    pronounced judgment on the one who has committed this deed,
    in the name of our Lord Jesus:
    when you have gathered together and I am with you in spirit
    with the power of the Lord Jesus,
    you are to deliver this man to Satan
    for the destruction of his flesh,
    so that his spirit may be saved on the day of the Lord.

Your boasting is not appropriate.
Do you not know that a little yeast leavens all the dough?
Clear out the old yeast, so that you may become a fresh batch of dough,
    inasmuch as you are unleavened.
For our Paschal Lamb, Christ, has been sacrificed.
Therefore, let us celebrate the feast,
    not with the old yeast, the yeast of malice and wickedness,
    but with the unleavened bread of sincerity and truth.

The word of the Lord.

RESPONSORIAL PSALM

Psalm 5:5-6, 7, 12

℟. (9) **Lead me in your justice, Lord.**

**For you, O God, delight not in wickedness;
no evil man remains with you;
the arrogant may not stand in your sight.
You hate all evildoers.**

℟. **Lead me in your justice, Lord.**

**You destroy all who speak falsehood;
The bloodthirsty and the deceitful
the Lord abhors.**

℟. **Lead me in your justice, Lord.**

**But let all who take refuge in you
be glad and exult forever.
Protect them, that you may be the joy
of those who love your name.**

℟. **Lead me in your justice, Lord.**

ALLELUIA

John 10:27

℟. **Alleluia, alleluia.**

**My sheep hear my voice, says the Lord;
I know them, and they follow me.**

℟. **Alleluia, alleluia.**

GOSPEL Years I and II

Luke 6:6-11 The scribes and the Pharisees watched him closely to see if he would cure on the sabbath.

✛ A reading from the holy Gospel according to Luke

On a certain sabbath Jesus went into the synagogue and taught,
   and there was a man there whose right hand was withered.
The scribes and the Pharisees watched him closely
   to see if he would cure on the sabbath
   so that they might discover a reason to accuse him.
But he realized their intentions
   and said to the man with the withered hand,
   "Come up and stand before us."
And he rose and stood there.
Then Jesus said to them,
   "I ask you, is it lawful to do good on the sabbath
   rather than to do evil,
   to save life rather than to destroy it?"
Looking around at them all, he then said to him,
   "Stretch out your hand."
He did so and his hand was restored.
But they became enraged
   and discussed together what they might do to Jesus.

The Gospel of the Lord.

438 TUESDAY OF THE TWENTY-THIRD WEEK IN ORDINARY TIME

FIRST READING   Year II

1 Corinthians 6:1-11   A believer goes to court against a believer and that before unbelievers.

A reading from the first Letter of Saint Paul to the Corinthians

**Brothers and sisters:
How can any one of you with a case against another
 dare to bring it to the unjust for judgment
 instead of to the holy ones?
Do you not know that the holy ones will judge the world?
If the world is to be judged by you,
 are you unqualified for the lowest law courts?
Do you not know that we will judge angels?
Then why not everyday matters?
If, therefore, you have courts for everyday matters,
 do you seat as judges people of no standing in the Church?
I say this to shame you.
Can it be that there is not one among you wise enough
 to be able to settle a case between brothers?
But rather brother goes to court against brother,
 and that before unbelievers?**

**Now indeed then it is, in any case,
 a failure on your part that you have lawsuits against one another.
Why not rather put up with injustice?
Why not rather let yourselves be cheated?
Instead, you inflict injustice and cheat, and this to brothers.
Do you not know that the unjust will not inherit the Kingdom of God?
Do not be deceived;
 neither fornicators nor idolaters nor adulterers
 nor boy prostitutes nor sodomites nor thieves
 nor the greedy nor drunkards nor slanderers nor robbers
 will inherit the Kingdom of God.**

That is what some of you used to be;
   but now you have had yourselves washed, you were sanctified,
   you were justified in the name of the Lord Jesus Christ
   and in the Spirit of our God.

The word of the Lord.

RESPONSORIAL PSALM

Psalm 149:1b-2, 3-4, 5-6a and 9b

℟. (see 4) **The Lord takes delight in his people.**

Sing to the LORD **a new song**
   of praise in the assembly of the faithful.
Let Israel be glad in their maker,
   let the children of Zion rejoice in their king.

℟. **The Lord takes delight in his people.**

Let them praise his name in the festive dance,
   let them sing praise to him with timbrel and harp.
For the LORD **loves his people,**
   and he adorns the lowly with victory.

℟. **The Lord takes delight in his people.**

Let the faithful exult in glory;
   let them sing for joy upon their couches;
Let the high praises of God be in their throats.
   This is the glory of all his faithful. Alleluia.

℟. **The Lord takes delight in his people.**

ALLELUIA

See John 15:16

℟. Alleluia, alleluia.

I chose you from the world,
that you may go and bear fruit that will last, says the Lord.

℟. Alleluia, alleluia.

GOSPEL   Years I and II

Luke 6:12-19   He spent the night in prayer. He chose Twelve, whom he also named Apostles.

✠ A reading from the holy Gospel according to Luke

Jesus departed to the mountain to pray,
   and he spent the night in prayer to God.
When day came, he called his disciples to himself,
   and from them he chose Twelve, whom he also named Apostles:
   Simon, whom he named Peter, and his brother Andrew,
   James, John, Philip, Bartholomew,
   Matthew, Thomas, James the son of Alphaeus,
   Simon who was called a Zealot,
   and Judas the son of James,
   and Judas Iscariot, who became a traitor.

And he came down with them and stood on a stretch of level ground.
A great crowd of his disciples and a large number of the people
   from all Judea and Jerusalem
   and the coastal region of Tyre and Sidon
   came to hear him and to be healed of their diseases;
   and even those who were tormented by unclean spirits were cured.
Everyone in the crowd sought to touch him
   because power came forth from him and healed them all.

The Gospel of the Lord.

439 WEDNESDAY OF THE TWENTY-THIRD WEEK IN ORDINARY TIME

FIRST READING   Year II

1 Corinthians 7:25-31   Are you bound to a wife? Do not seek a separation. Are you free of a wife? Then, do not look for a wife.

A reading from the first Letter of Saint Paul to the Corinthians

**Brothers and sisters:
In regard to virgins, I have no commandment from the Lord,
 but I give my opinion as one who by the Lord's mercy is trustworthy.
So this is what I think best because of the present distress:
 that it is a good thing for a person to remain as he is.
Are you bound to a wife? Do not seek a separation.
Are you free of a wife? Then do not look for a wife.
If you marry, however, you do not sin,
 nor does an unmarried woman sin if she marries;
 but such people will experience affliction in their earthly life,
 and I would like to spare you that.**

**I tell you, brothers, the time is running out.
From now on, let those having wives act as not having them,
 those weeping as not weeping,
 those rejoicing as not rejoicing,
 those buying as not owning,
 those using the world as not using it fully.
For the world in its present form is passing away.**

The word of the Lord.

RESPONSORIAL PSALM

Psalm 45:11-12, 14-15, 16-17

℟. (11) **Listen to me, daughter; see and bend your ear.**

**Hear, O daughter, and see; turn your ear,
 forget your people and your father's house.
So shall the king desire your beauty;
 for he is your lord, and you must worship him.**

℟. **Listen to me, daughter; see and bend your ear.**

**All glorious is the king's daughter as she enters;
 her raiment is threaded with spun gold.
In embroidered apparel she is borne in to the king;
 behind her the virgins of her train are brought to you.**

℟. **Listen to me, daughter; see and bend your ear.**

**They are borne in with gladness and joy;
 they enter the palace of the king.
The place of your fathers your sons shall have;
 you shall make them princes through all the land.**

℟. **Listen to me, daughter; see and bend your ear.**

ALLELUIA

Luke 6:23ab

℟. **Alleluia, alleluia.**

**Rejoice and leap for joy!
Your reward will be great in heaven.**

℟. **Alleluia, alleluia.**

GOSPEL — Years I and II

Luke 6:20-26   Blessed are you who are poor. Woe to you who are rich.

☩ **A reading from the holy Gospel according to Luke**

Raising his eyes toward his disciples Jesus said:
    "Blessed are you who are poor,
      for the Kingdom of God is yours.
    Blessed are you who are now hungry,
      for you will be satisfied.
    Blessed are you who are now weeping,
      for you will laugh.
    Blessed are you when people hate you,
      and when they exclude and insult you,
      and denounce your name as evil
      on account of the Son of Man.
Rejoice and leap for joy on that day!
    Behold, your reward
   will be great in heaven. For their
   ancestors treated the prophets
   in the same way.
   But woe to you who are rich,
     for you have received your consolation.
   But woe to you who are filled now,
     for you will be hungry.
   Woe to you who laugh now,
     for you will grieve and weep.
   Woe to you when all speak well of you,
     for their ancestors treated the false
     prophets in this way."

The Gospel of the Lord.

440 THURSDAY OF THE TWENTY-THIRD WEEK IN ORDINARY TIME

FIRST READING Year II

1 Corinthians 8:1b-7, 11-13   When you sin against your brothers, weak as they are, you are sinning against Christ.

A reading from the first Letter of Saint Paul to the Corinthians

Brothers and sisters:
Knowledge inflates with pride, but love builds up.
If anyone supposes he knows something,
  he does not yet know as he ought to know.
But if one loves God, one is known by him.

So about the eating of meat sacrificed to idols:
  we know that *there is no idol in the world*,
  and that *there is no God but one*.
Indeed, even though there are so-called gods in heaven and on earth
  (there are, to be sure, many "gods" and many "lords"),
  yet for us there is

    one God, the Father,
      from whom all things are and for whom we exist,
    and one Lord, Jesus Christ,
      through whom all things are and through whom we exist.

But not all have this knowledge.
There are some who have been so used to idolatry up until now
  that, when they eat meat sacrificed to idols,
  their conscience, which is weak, is defiled.

Thus, through your knowledge, the weak person is brought to destruction,
  the brother for whom Christ died.
When you sin in this way against your brothers
  and wound their consciences, weak as they are,
  you are sinning against Christ.
Therefore, if food causes my brother to sin,
  I will never eat meat again,
  so that I may not cause my brother to sin.

The word of the Lord.

RESPONSORIAL PSALM

Psalm 139:1b-3, 13-14ab, 23-24

℟. (24b) **Guide me, Lord, along the everlasting way.**

O LORD, you have probed me and you know me;
 you know when I sit and when I stand;
 you understand my thoughts from afar.
My journeys and my rest you scrutinize,
 with all my ways you are familiar.

℟. **Guide me, Lord, along the everlasting way.**

Truly you have formed my inmost being;
 you knit me in my mother's womb.
I give you thanks that I am fearfully, wonderfully made;
 wonderful are your works.

℟. **Guide me, Lord, along the everlasting way.**

Probe me, O God, and know my heart;
 try me, and know my thoughts;
See if my way is crooked,
 and lead me in the way of old.

℟. **Guide me, Lord, along the everlasting way.**

ALLELUIA

1 John 4:12

℟. **Alleluia, alleluia.**

If we love one another,
God remains in us,
and his love is brought to perfection in us.

℟. **Alleluia, alleluia.**

GOSPEL   Years I and II

Luke 6:27-38   Be merciful, just as your Father is merciful.

✠ A reading from the holy Gospel according to Luke

Jesus said to his disciples:
"To you who hear I say, love your enemies,
  do good to those who hate you, bless those who curse you,
  pray for those who mistreat you.
To the person who strikes you on one cheek,
  offer the other one as well,
  and from the person who takes your cloak,
  do not withhold even your tunic.
Give to everyone who asks of you,
  and from the one who takes what is yours do not demand it back.
Do to others as you would have them do to you.
For if you love those who love you,
  what credit is that to you?
Even sinners love those who love them.
And if you do good to those who do good to you,
  what credit is that to you?
Even sinners do the same.
If you lend money to those from whom you expect repayment,
  what credit is that to you?
Even sinners lend to sinners,
  and get back the same amount.
But rather, love your enemies and do good to them,
  and lend expecting nothing back;
  then your reward will be great
  and you will be children of the Most High,
  for he himself is kind to the ungrateful and the wicked.
Be merciful, just as also your Father is merciful.

"Stop judging and you will not be judged.
Stop condemning and you will not be condemned.
Forgive and you will be forgiven.
Give and gifts will be given to you;
  a good measure, packed together, shaken down, and overflowing,
  will be poured into your lap.
For the measure with which you measure
  will in return be measured out to you."

The Gospel of the Lord.

441 FRIDAY OF THE TWENTY-THIRD WEEK IN ORDINARY TIME

FIRST READING   Year II

1 Corinthians 9:16-19, 22b-27   *I have become all things to all, to save at least some.*

A reading from the first Letter of Saint Paul to the Corinthians

Brothers and sisters:
If I preach the Gospel, this is no reason for me to boast,
 for an obligation has been imposed on me,
 and woe to me if I do not preach it!
If I do so willingly, I have a recompense,
 but if unwillingly, then I have been entrusted with a stewardship.
What then is my recompense?
That, when I preach, I offer the Gospel free of charge
 so as not to make full use of my right in the Gospel.

Although I am free in regard to all,
 I have made myself a slave to all
 so as to win over as many as possible.
I have become all things to all, to save at least some.
All this I do for the sake of the Gospel,
 so that I too may have a share in it.

Do you not know that the runners in the stadium all run in the race,
 but only one wins the prize?
Run so as to win.
Every athlete exercises discipline in every way.
They do it to win a perishable crown,
 but we an imperishable one.
Thus I do not run aimlessly;
 I do not fight as if I were shadowboxing.
No, I drive my body and train it,
 for fear that, after having preached to others,
 I myself should be disqualified.

The word of the Lord.

RESPONSORIAL PSALM

Psalm 84:3, 4, 5-6, 12

℟. (2) **How lovely is your dwelling place, Lord, mighty God!**

**My soul yearns and pines
   for the courts of the Lord.
My heart and my flesh
   cry out for the living God.**

℟. **How lovely is your dwelling place, Lord, mighty God!**

**Even the sparrow finds a home,
   and the swallow a nest
   in which she puts her young—
Your altars, O Lord of hosts,
   my king and my God!**

℟. **How lovely is your dwelling place, Lord, mighty God!**

**Blessed they who dwell in your house!
   continually they praise you.
Blessed the men whose strength you are!
   their hearts are set upon the pilgrimage.**

℟. **How lovely is your dwelling place, Lord, mighty God!**

**For a sun and a shield is the Lord God;
   grace and glory he bestows;
The Lord withholds no good thing
   from those who walk in sincerity.**

℟. **How lovely is your dwelling place, Lord, mighty God!**

ALLELUIA

See John 17:17b, 17a

℟. Alleluia, alleluia.

Your word, O Lord, is truth;
consecrate us in the truth.

℟. Alleluia, alleluia.

GOSPEL   Years I and II

Luke 6:39-42   Can a blind person guide a blind person?

✛ A reading from the holy Gospel according to Luke

**Jesus told his disciples a parable:
"Can a blind person guide a blind person?
Will not both fall into a pit?
No disciple is superior to the teacher;
   but when fully trained,
   every disciple will be like his teacher.
Why do you notice the splinter in your brother's eye,
   but do not perceive the wooden beam in your own?
How can you say to your brother,
   'Brother, let me remove that splinter in your eye,'
   when you do not even notice the wooden beam in your own eye?
You hypocrite! Remove the wooden beam from your eye first;
   then you will see clearly
   to remove the splinter in your brother's eye."**

The Gospel of the Lord.

442 SATURDAY OF THE TWENTY-THIRD WEEK IN ORDINARY TIME

FIRST READING   Year II

1 Corinthians 10:14-22   We, though many, are one Body, for we all partake of the one bread.

A reading from the first Letter of Saint Paul to the Corinthians

My beloved ones, avoid idolatry.
I am speaking as to sensible people;
  judge for yourselves what I am saying.
The cup of blessing that we bless,
  is it not a participation in the Blood of Christ?
The bread that we break,
  is it not a participation in the Body of Christ?
Because the loaf of bread is one,
  we, though many, are one Body,
  for we all partake of the one loaf.

Look at Israel according to the flesh;
  are not those who eat the sacrifices participants in the altar?
So what am I saying?
That meat sacrificed to idols is anything?
Or that an idol is anything?
No, I mean that what they sacrifice,
  they sacrifice to demons, not to God,
  and I do not want you to become participants with demons.
You cannot drink the cup of the Lord and also the cup of demons.
You cannot partake of the table of the Lord and of the table of demons.
Or are we provoking the Lord to jealous anger?
Are we stronger than him?

The word of the Lord.

RESPONSORIAL PSALM

Psalm 116:12-13, 17-18

℟. (17) **To you, Lord, I will offer a sacrifice of praise.**

How shall I make a return to the LORD
   for all the good he has done for me?
The cup of salvation I will take up,
   and I will call upon the name of the LORD.

℟. **To you, Lord, I will offer a sacrifice of praise.**

To you will I offer sacrifice of thanksgiving,
   and I will call upon the name of the LORD.
My vows to the LORD **I will pay**
   in the presence of all his people.

℟. **To you, Lord, I will offer a sacrifice of praise.**

ALLELUIA

John 14:23

℟. **Alleluia, alleluia.**

Whoever loves me will keep my word,
and my Father will love him,
and we will come to him.

℟. **Alleluia, alleluia.**

GOSPEL   Years I and II

Luke 6:43-49   Why do you call me, "Lord, Lord," but do not do what I command?

✝ A reading from the holy Gospel according to Luke

Jesus said to his disciples:
"A good tree does not bear rotten fruit,
  nor does a rotten tree bear good fruit.
For every tree is known by its own fruit.
For people do not pick figs from thornbushes,
  nor do they gather grapes from brambles.
A good person out of the store of goodness in his heart produces good,
  but an evil person out of a store of evil produces evil;
  for from the fullness of the heart the mouth speaks.

"Why do you call me, 'Lord, Lord,' but not do what I command?
I will show you what someone is like who comes to me,
  listens to my words, and acts on them.
That one is like a man building a house,
  who dug deeply and laid the foundation on rock;
  when the flood came, the river burst against that house
  but could not shake it because it had been well built.
But the one who listens and does not act
  is like a person who built a house on the ground
  without a foundation.
When the river burst against it,
  it collapsed at once and was completely destroyed."

The Gospel of the Lord.

443 MONDAY OF THE TWENTY-FOURTH WEEK IN ORDINARY TIME

FIRST READING   Year II

1 Corinthians 11:17-26, 33   *If there are divisions among you, then you do not eat the Lord's supper.*

A reading from the first Letter of Saint Paul to the Corinthians

Brothers and sisters:
In giving this instruction, I do not praise the fact
 that your meetings are doing more harm than good.
First of all, I hear that when you meet as a Church
 there are divisions among you,
 and to a degree I believe it;
 there have to be factions among you
 in order that also those who are approved among you
 may become known.
When you meet in one place, then,
 it is not to eat the Lord's supper,
 for in eating, each one goes ahead with his own supper,
 and one goes hungry while another gets drunk.
Do you not have houses in which you can eat and drink?
Or do you show contempt for the Church of God
 and make those who have nothing feel ashamed?
What can I say to you? Shall I praise you?
In this matter I do not praise you.

For I received from the Lord what I also handed on to you,
 that the Lord Jesus, on the night he was handed over,
 took bread and, after he had given thanks,
 broke it and said, "This is my Body that is for you.
Do this in remembrance of me."
In the same way also the cup, after supper, saying,
 "This cup is the new covenant in my Blood.
Do this, as often as you drink it, in remembrance of me."
For as often as you eat this bread and drink the cup,
 you proclaim the death of the Lord until he comes.

Therefore, my brothers and sisters,
 when you come together to eat, wait for one another.

The word of the Lord.

RESPONSORIAL PSALM

Psalm 40:7-8a, 8b-9, 10, 17

℟. (1 Corinthians 11:26b) **Proclaim the death of the Lord until he comes again.**

**Sacrifice or oblation you wished not,
   but ears open to obedience you gave me.
Burnt offerings or sin-offerings you sought not;
   then said I, "Behold I come."**

℟. **Proclaim the death of the Lord until he comes again.**

**"In the written scroll it is prescribed for me,
To do your will, O my God, is my delight,
   and your law is within my heart!"**

℟. **Proclaim the death of the Lord until he comes again.**

**I announced your justice in the vast assembly;
   I did not restrain my lips, as you, O LORD, know.**

℟. **Proclaim the death of the Lord until he comes again.**

**May all who seek you
   exult and be glad in you
And may those who love your salvation
   say ever, "The LORD be glorified."**

℟. **Proclaim the death of the Lord until he comes again.**

ALLELUIA

John 3:16

℟. **Alleluia, alleluia.**

**God so loved the world that he gave his only-begotten Son,
so that everyone who believes in him might have eternal life.**

℟. **Alleluia, alleluia.**

GOSPEL   Years I and II

Luke 7:1-10   Not even in Israel have I found such faith.

✠ A reading from the holy Gospel according to Luke

When Jesus had finished all his words to the people,
 he entered Capernaum.
A centurion there had a slave who was ill and about to die,
 and he was valuable to him.
When he heard about Jesus, he sent elders of the Jews to him,
 asking him to come and save the life of his slave.
They approached Jesus and strongly urged him to come, saying,
 "He deserves to have you do this for him,
 for he loves our nation and he built the synagogue for us."
And Jesus went with them,
 but when he was only a short distance from the house,
 the centurion sent friends to tell him,
 "Lord, do not trouble yourself,
 for I am not worthy to have you enter under my roof.
Therefore, I did not consider myself worthy to come to you;
 but say the word and let my servant be healed.
For I too am a person subject to authority,
 with soldiers subject to me.
And I say to one, 'Go,' and he goes;
 and to another, 'Come here,' and he comes;
 and to my slave, 'Do this,' and he does it."
When Jesus heard this he was amazed at him
 and, turning, said to the crowd following him,
 "I tell you, not even in Israel have I found such faith."
When the messengers returned to the house,
 they found the slave in good health.

The Gospel of the Lord.

444 TUESDAY OF THE TWENTY-FOURTH WEEK IN ORDINARY TIME

FIRST READING   Year II

1 Corinthians 12:12-14, 27-31a   *Now you are Christ's Body, and individually parts of it.*

A reading from the first Letter of Saint Paul to the Corinthians

Brothers and sisters:
As a body is one though it has many parts,
   and all the parts of the body, though many, are one body,
   so also Christ.
For in one Spirit we were all baptized into one Body,
   whether Jews or Greeks, slaves or free persons,
   and we were all given to drink of one Spirit.

Now the body is not a single part, but many.

Now you are Christ's Body, and individually parts of it.
Some people God has designated in the Church
   to be, first, Apostles; second, prophets; third, teachers;
   then, mighty deeds;
   then gifts of healing, assistance, administration,
   and varieties of tongues.
Are all Apostles? Are all prophets? Are all teachers?
Do all work mighty deeds? Do all have gifts of healing?
Do all speak in tongues? Do all interpret?
Strive eagerly for the greatest spiritual gifts.

The word of the Lord.

RESPONSORIAL PSALM

Psalm 100:1b-2, 3, 4, 5

℟. (3) **We are his people: the sheep of his flock.**

**Sing joyfully to the Lord, all you lands;
serve the Lord with gladness;
come before him with joyful song.**

℟. **We are his people: the sheep of his flock.**

Know that the Lord is God;
he made us, his we are;
his people, the flock he tends.

℟. **We are his people: the sheep of his flock.**

Enter his gates with thanksgiving,
his courts with praise;
Give thanks to him; bless his name.

℟. **We are his people: the sheep of his flock.**

For he is good, the Lord,
whose kindness endures forever,
and his faithfulness, to all generations.

℟. **We are his people: the sheep of his flock.**

ALLELUIA

Luke 7:16

℟. Alleluia, alleluia.

**A great prophet has arisen in our midst
and God has visited his people.**

℟. Alleluia, alleluia.

GOSPEL Years I and II

Luke 7:11-17   Young man, I tell you, arise!

✝ A reading from the holy Gospel according to Luke

**Jesus journeyed to a city called Nain,
 and his disciples and a large crowd accompanied him.
As he drew near to the gate of the city,
 a man who had died was being carried out,
 the only son of his mother, and she was a widow.
A large crowd from the city was with her.
When the Lord saw her,
 he was moved with pity for her and said to her,
 "Do not weep."
He stepped forward and touched the coffin;
 at this the bearers halted,
 and he said, "Young man, I tell you, arise!"
The dead man sat up and began to speak,
 and Jesus gave him to his mother.
Fear seized them all, and they glorified God, exclaiming,
 "A great prophet has arisen in our midst,"
 and "God has visited his people."
This report about him spread through the whole of Judea
 and in all the surrounding region.**

The Gospel of the Lord.

445 WEDNESDAY OF THE TWENTY-FOURTH WEEK IN ORDINARY TIME

FIRST READING Year II

1 Corinthians 12:31–13:13   So faith, hope, love remain, these three; but the greatest of these is love.

A reading from the first Letter of Saint Paul to the Corinthians

Brothers and sisters:
Strive eagerly for the greatest spiritual gifts.

But I shall show you a still more excellent way.

If I speak in human and angelic tongues
   but do not have love,
   I am a resounding gong or a clashing cymbal.
And if I have the gift of prophecy
   and comprehend all mysteries and all knowledge;
   if I have all faith so as to move mountains,
   but do not have love, I am nothing.
If I give away everything I own,
   and if I hand my body over so that I may boast
   but do not have love, I gain nothing.

Love is patient, love is kind.
It is not jealous, love is not pompous,
   it is not inflated, it is not rude,
   it does not seek its own interests,
   it is not quick-tempered, it does not brood over injury,
   it does not rejoice over wrongdoing
   but rejoices with the truth.
It bears all things, believes all things,
   hopes all things, endures all things.

Love never fails.
If there are prophecies, they will be brought to nothing;
   if tongues, they will cease;
   if knowledge, it will be brought to nothing.
For we know partially and we prophesy partially,
   but when the perfect comes, the partial will pass away.

When I was a child, I used to talk as a child,
>think as a child, reason as a child;
>when I became a man, I put aside childish things.

At present we see indistinctly, as in a mirror,
>but then face to face.

At present I know partially;
>then I shall know fully, as I am fully known.

So faith, hope, love remain, these three;
>but the greatest of these is love.

The word of the Lord.

RESPONSIAL PSALM

Psalm 33:2-3, 4-5, 12 and 22

℟. (12) **Blessed the people the Lord has chosen to be his own.**

Give thanks to the LORD on the harp;
>with the ten-stringed lyre chant his praises.
Sing to him a new song;
>pluck the strings skillfully, with shouts of gladness.

℟. **Blessed the people the Lord has chosen to be his own.**

For upright is the word of the LORD,
>and all his works are trustworthy.
He loves justice and right;
>of the kindness of the LORD the earth is full.

℟. **Blessed the people the Lord has chosen to be his own.**

Blessed the nation whose God is the LORD,
>the people he has chosen for his own inheritance.
May your kindness, O LORD, be upon us
>who have put our hope in you.

℟. **Blessed the people the Lord has chosen to be his own.**

ALLELUIA

See John 6:63c, 68c

℟. Alleluia, alleluia.

Your words, Lord, are Spirit and life,
you have the words of everlasting life.

℟. Alleluia, alleluia.

GOSPEL   Years I and II

Luke 7:31-35   We played the flute for you, but you did not dance. We sang a dirge, but you did not weep.

✛ A reading from the holy Gospel according to Luke

Jesus said to the crowds:
"To what shall I compare the people of this generation?
What are they like?
They are like children who sit in the marketplace and call to one another,

> 'We played the flute for you, but you did not dance.
>   We sang a dirge, but you did not weep.'

For John the Baptist came neither eating food nor drinking wine,
   and you said, 'He is possessed by a demon.'
The Son of Man came eating and drinking and you said,
   'Look, he is a glutton and a drunkard,
   a friend of tax collectors and sinners.'
But wisdom is vindicated by all her children."

The Gospel of the Lord.

446 THURSDAY OF THE TWENTY-FOURTH WEEK IN ORDINARY TIME

FIRST READING   Year II

1 Corinthians 15:1-11   So we preach and so you believed.

A reading from the first Letter of Saint Paul to the Corinthians

I am reminding you, brothers and sisters,
   of the Gospel I preached to you,
   which you indeed received and in which you also stand.
Through it you are also being saved,
   if you hold fast to the word I preached to you,
   unless you believed in vain.
For I handed on to you as of first importance what I also received:
   that Christ died for our sins in accordance with the Scriptures;
   that he was buried;
   that he was raised on the third day in accordance with the Scriptures;
   that he appeared to Cephas, then to the Twelve.
After that, he appeared to more than five hundred brothers at once,
   most of whom are still living, though some have fallen asleep.
After that he appeared to James,
   then to all the Apostles.
Last of all, as to one born abnormally,
   he appeared to me.
For I am the least of the Apostles,
   not fit to be called an Apostle,
   because I persecuted the Church of God.
But by the grace of God I am what I am,
   and his grace to me has not been ineffective.
Indeed, I have toiled harder than all of them;
   not I, however, but the grace of God that is with me.
Therefore, whether it be I or they,
   so we preach and so you believed.

The word of the Lord.

RESPONSORIAL PSALM

Psalm 118:1b-2, 16ab-17, 28

℟. (1) **Give thanks to the Lord, for he is good.**

Give thanks to the LORD**, for he is good,
 for his mercy endures forever.
Let the house of Israel say,
 "His mercy endures forever."**

℟. **Give thanks to the Lord, for he is good.**

"The right hand of the LORD **is exalted;
 the right hand of the L**ORD **has struck with power."
I shall not die, but live,
 and declare the works of the L**ORD**.**

℟. **Give thanks to the Lord, for he is good.**

**You are my God, and I give thanks to you;
 O my God, I extol you.**

℟. **Give thanks to the Lord, for he is good.**

ALLELUIA

Matthew 11:28

℟. **Alleluia, alleluia.**

**Come to me, all you who labor and are burdened,
and I will give you rest, says the Lord.**

℟. **Alleluia, alleluia.**

GOSPEL   Years I and II

Luke 7:36-50   Her many sins have been forgiven; hence, she has shown great love.

✛   **A reading from the holy Gospel according to Luke**

**A certain Pharisee invited Jesus to dine with him,
 and he entered the Pharisee's house and reclined at table.
Now there was a sinful woman in the city
 who learned that he was at table in the house of the Pharisee.**

Bringing an alabaster flask of ointment,
> she stood behind him at his feet weeping
> and began to bathe his feet with her tears.

Then she wiped them with her hair,
> kissed them, and anointed them with the ointment.

When the Pharisee who had invited him saw this he said to himself,
> "If this man were a prophet,
> he would know who and what sort of woman this is who is touching him,
> that she is a sinner."

Jesus said to him in reply,
> "Simon, I have something to say to you."

"Tell me, teacher," he said.

"Two people were in debt to a certain creditor;
> one owed five hundred days' wages and the other owed fifty.

Since they were unable to repay the debt, he forgave it for both.
Which of them will love him more?"

Simon said in reply,
> "The one, I suppose, whose larger debt was forgiven."

He said to him, "You have judged rightly."

Then he turned to the woman and said to Simon,
> "Do you see this woman?

When I entered your house, you did not give me water for my feet,
> but she has bathed them with her tears
> and wiped them with her hair.

You did not give me a kiss,
> but she has not ceased kissing my feet since the time I entered.

You did not anoint my head with oil,
> but she anointed my feet with ointment.

So I tell you, her many sins have been forgiven;
> hence, she has shown great love.

But the one to whom little is forgiven, loves little."

He said to her, "Your sins are forgiven."

The others at table said to themselves,
> "Who is this who even forgives sins?"

But he said to the woman,
> "Your faith has saved you; go in peace."

The Gospel of the Lord.

447 FRIDAY OF THE TWENTY-FOURTH WEEK IN ORDINARY TIME

FIRST READING   Year II

1 Corinthians 15:12-20   If Christ has not been raised, your faith is vain.

A reading from the first Letter of Saint Paul to the Corinthians

Brothers and sisters:
If Christ is preached as raised from the dead,
   how can some among you say there is no resurrection of the dead?
If there is no resurrection of the dead,
   then neither has Christ been raised.
And if Christ has not been raised, then empty too is our preaching;
   empty, too, your faith.
Then we are also false witnesses to God,
   because we testified against God that he raised Christ,
   whom he did not raise if in fact the dead are not raised.
For if the dead are not raised, neither has Christ been raised,
   and if Christ has not been raised, your faith is vain;
   you are still in your sins.
Then those who have fallen asleep in Christ have perished.
If for this life only we have hoped in Christ,
   we are the most pitiable people of all.

But now Christ has been raised from the dead,
   the firstfruits of those who have fallen asleep.

The word of the Lord.

RESPONSORIAL PSALM

Psalm 17:1bcd, 6-7, 8b and 15

℟. (15b) Lord, when your glory appears, my joy will be full.

Hear, O LORD, a just suit;
   attend to my outcry;
   hearken to my prayer from lips without deceit.

℟. Lord, when your glory appears, my joy will be full.

I call upon you, for you will answer me, O God;
> incline your ear to me; hear my word.

Show your wondrous mercies,
> O savior of those who flee
> from their foes to refuge at your right hand.

℟. Lord, when your glory appears, my joy will be full.

Hide me in the shadow of your wings,
But I in justice shall behold your face;
> on waking, I shall be content in your presence.

℟. Lord, when your glory appears, my joy will be full.

ALLELUIA

See Matthew 11:25

℟. Alleluia, alleluia.

**Blessed are you, Father, Lord of heaven and earth;
you have revealed to little ones the mysteries of the Kingdom.**

℟. Alleluia, alleluia.

GOSPEL   Years I and II

Luke 8:1-3   Accompanying them were some women, who provided for them out of their resources.

✢ A reading from the holy Gospel according to Luke

**Jesus journeyed from one town and village to another,
> preaching and proclaiming the good news of the Kingdom of God.
Accompanying him were the Twelve
> and some women who had been cured of evil spirits and infirmities,
> Mary, called Magdalene, from whom seven demons had gone out,
> Joanna, the wife of Herod's steward Chuza,
> Susanna, and many others
> who provided for them out of their resources.**

The Gospel of the Lord.

448 SATURDAY OF THE TWENTY-FOURTH WEEK IN ORDINARY TIME

FIRST READING   Year II

1 Corinthians 15:35-37, 42-49   It is sown corruptible; it is raised incorruptible.

A reading from the first Letter of Saint Paul to the Corinthians

Brothers and sisters:
Someone may say, "How are the dead raised?
With what kind of body will they come back?"

You fool!
What you sow is not brought to life unless it dies.
And what you sow is not the body that is to be
  but a bare kernel of wheat, perhaps, or of some other kind.

So also is the resurrection of the dead.
It is sown corruptible; it is raised incorruptible.
It is sown dishonorable; it is raised glorious.
It is sown weak; it is raised powerful.
It is sown a natural body; it is raised a spiritual body.
If there is a natural body, there is also a spiritual one.

So, too, it is written,
  "The first man, Adam, became a living being,"
  the last Adam a life-giving spirit.
But the spiritual was not first;
  rather the natural and then the spiritual.
The first man was from the earth, earthly;
  the second man, from heaven.
As was the earthly one, so also are the earthly,
  and as is the heavenly one, so also are the heavenly.
Just as we have borne the image of the earthly one,
  we shall also bear the image of the heavenly one.

The word of the Lord.

RESPONSORIAL PSALM

Psalm 56:10c-12, 13-14

℟. (14) **I will walk in the presence of God, in the light of the living.**

Now I know that God is with me.
In God, in whose promise I glory,
in God I trust without fear;
what can flesh do against me?

℟. **I will walk in the presence of God, in the light of the living.**

I am bound, O God, by vows to you;
your thank offerings I will fulfill.
For you have rescued me from death,
my feet, too, from stumbling;
that I may walk before God in the light of the living.

℟. **I will walk in the presence of God, in the light of the living.**

ALLELUIA

See Luke 8:15

℟. **Alleluia, alleluia.**

Blessed are they who have kept the word with a generous heart
and yield a harvest through perseverance.

℟. **Alleluia, alleluia.**

GOSPEL Years I and II

Luke 8:4-15 As for the seed that fell on rich soil, they are the ones who embrace the word and bear much fruit through perseverance.

✠ A reading from the holy Gospel according to Luke

When a large crowd gathered, with people from one town after another
   journeying to Jesus, he spoke in a parable.
"A sower went out to sow his seed.
And as he sowed, some seed fell on the path and was trampled,
   and the birds of the sky ate it up.
Some seed fell on rocky ground, and when it grew,
   it withered for lack of moisture.
Some seed fell among thorns,
   and the thorns grew with it and choked it.
And some seed fell on good soil, and when it grew,
   it produced fruit a hundredfold."
After saying this, he called out,
   "Whoever has ears to hear ought to hear."

Then his disciples asked him
   what the meaning of this parable might be.
He answered,
   "Knowledge of the mysteries of the Kingdom of God
   has been granted to you;
   but to the rest, they are made known through parables
   so that *they may look but not see, and hear but not understand.*

"This is the meaning of the parable.
The seed is the word of God.
Those on the path are the ones who have heard,
   but the Devil comes and takes away the word from their hearts
   that they may not believe and be saved.
Those on rocky ground are the ones who, when they hear,
   receive the word with joy, but they have no root;
   they believe only for a time and fall away in time of temptation.
As for the seed that fell among thorns,
   they are the ones who have heard, but as they go along,
   they are choked by the anxieties and riches and pleasures of life,
   and they fail to produce mature fruit.

But as for the seed that fell on rich soil,
   they are the ones who, when they have heard the word,
   embrace it with a generous and good heart,
   and bear fruit through perseverance."

The Gospel of the Lord.

449 MONDAY OF THE TWENTY-FIFTH WEEK IN ORDINARY TIME

FIRST READING   Year II

Proverbs 3:27-34   The curse of the Lord is on the house of the wicked.

A reading from the Book of Proverbs

**Refuse no one the good on which he has a claim
    when it is in your power to do it for him.
Say not to your neighbor, "Go, and come again,
    tomorrow I will give," when you can give at once.**

**Plot no evil against your neighbor,
    against one who lives at peace with you.
Quarrel not with a man without cause,
    with one who has done you no harm.**

**Envy not the lawless man
    and choose none of his ways:
To the Lord the perverse one is an abomination,
    but with the upright is his friendship.**

**The curse of the Lord is on the house of the wicked,
    but the dwelling of the just he blesses;
When dealing with the arrogant, he is stern,
    but to the humble he shows kindness.**

The word of the Lord.

RESPONSORIAL PSALM

Psalm 15:2-3a, 3bc-4ab, 5

℟. (1) **The just one shall live on your holy mountain, O Lord.**

He who walks blamelessly and does justice;
  who thinks the truth in his heart
  and slanders not with his tongue.

℟. **The just one shall live on your holy mountain, O Lord.**

Who harms not his fellow man,
  nor takes up a reproach against his neighbor;
By whom the reprobate is despised,
  while he honors those who fear the LORD.

℟. **The just one shall live on your holy mountain, O Lord.**

Who lends not his money at usury
  and accepts no bribe against the innocent.
He who does these things
  shall never be disturbed.

℟. **The just one shall live on your holy mountain, O Lord.**

ALLELUIA

Matthew 5:16

℟. **Alleluia, alleluia.**

Let your light shine before others,
that they may see your good deeds and glorify your heavenly Father.

℟. **Alleluia, alleluia.**

GOSPEL — Years I and II

Luke 8:16-18   A lamp is placed on a lampstand so that those who enter may see the light.

✛ A reading from the holy Gospel according to Luke

Jesus said to the crowd:
"No one who lights a lamp conceals it with a vessel
   or sets it under a bed;
   rather, he places it on a lampstand
   so that those who enter may see the light.
For there is nothing hidden that will not become visible,
   and nothing secret that will not be known and come to light.
Take care, then, how you hear.
To anyone who has, more will be given,
   and from the one who has not,
   even what he seems to have will be taken away."

The Gospel of the Lord.

450 TUESDAY OF THE TWENTY-FIFTH WEEK IN ORDINARY TIME

FIRST READING   Year II

Proverbs 21:1-6, 10-13   Various proverbs.

A reading from the Book of Proverbs

Like a stream is the king's heart in the hand of the Lord;
  wherever it pleases him, he directs it.

All the ways of a man may be right in his own eyes,
  but it is the Lord who proves hearts.

To do what is right and just
  is more acceptable to the Lord than sacrifice.

Haughty eyes and a proud heart—
  the tillage of the wicked is sin.

The plans of the diligent are sure of profit,
  but all rash haste leads certainly to poverty.

Whoever makes a fortune by a lying tongue
  is chasing a bubble over deadly snares.

The soul of the wicked man desires evil;
  his neighbor finds no pity in his eyes.

When the arrogant man is punished, the simple are the wiser;
  when the wise man is instructed, he gains knowledge.

The just man appraises the house of the wicked:
  there is one who brings down the wicked to ruin.

He who shuts his ear to the cry of the poor
  will himself also call and not be heard.

The word of the Lord.

RESPONSORIAL PSALM

Psalm 119:1, 27, 30, 34, 35, 44

℟. (35) **Guide me, Lord, in the way of your commands.**

**Blessed are they whose way is blameless,
 who walk in the law of the LORD.**

℟. **Guide me, Lord, in the way of your commands.**

**Make me understand the way of your precepts,
 and I will meditate on your wondrous deeds.**

℟. **Guide me, Lord, in the way of your commands.**

**The way of truth I have chosen;
 I have set your ordinances before me.**

℟. **Guide me, Lord, in the way of your commands.**

**Give me discernment, that I may observe your law
 and keep it with all my heart.**

℟. **Guide me, Lord, in the way of your commands.**

**Lead me in the path of your commands,
 for in it I delight.**

℟. **Guide me, Lord, in the way of your commands.**

**And I will keep your law continually,
 forever and ever.**

℟. **Guide me, Lord, in the way of your commands.**

ALLELUIA

Luke 11:28

℟. Alleluia, alleluia.

**Blessed are those who hear the word of God
and observe it.**

℟. Alleluia, alleluia.

GOSPEL   Years I and II

Luke 8:19-21   My mother and my brothers are those who hear the word of God and act on it.

✠ **A reading from the holy Gospel according to Luke**

**The mother of Jesus and his brothers came to him
 but were unable to join him because of the crowd.
He was told, "Your mother and your brothers are standing outside
 and they wish to see you."
He said to them in reply, "My mother and my brothers
 are those who hear the word of God and act on it."**

The Gospel of the Lord.

451 WEDNESDAY OF THE TWENTY-FIFTH WEEK IN ORDINARY TIME

FIRST READING   Year II

Proverbs 30:5-9   Give me neither poverty nor riches; provide me only with the food I need.

A reading from the Book of Proverbs

Every word of God is tested;
  he is a shield to those who take refuge in him.
Add nothing to his words,
  lest he reprove you, and you will be exposed as a deceiver.

Two things I ask of you,
  deny them not to me before I die:
Put falsehood and lying far from me,
  give me neither poverty nor riches;
  provide me only with the food I need;
Lest, being full, I deny you,
  saying, "Who is the Lord?"
Or, being in want, I steal,
  and profane the name of my God.

The word of the Lord.

RESPONSORIAL PSALM

Psalm 119:29, 72, 89, 101, 104, 163

℟. (105) **Your word, O Lord, is a lamp for my feet.**

Remove from me the way of falsehood,
  and favor me with your law.

℟. Your word, O Lord, is a lamp for my feet.

The law of your mouth is to me more precious
  than thousands of gold and silver pieces.

℟. Your word, O Lord, is a lamp for my feet.

Your word, O Lord, endures forever;
  it is firm as the heavens.

℟. Your word, O Lord, is a lamp for my feet.

From every evil way I withhold my feet,
  that I may keep your words.

℟. **Your word, O Lord, is a lamp for my feet.**

Through your precepts I gain discernment;
  therefore I hate every false way.

℟. **Your word, O Lord, is a lamp for my feet.**

Falsehood I hate and abhor;
  your law I love.

℟. **Your word, O Lord, is a lamp for my feet.**

ALLELUIA

Mark 1:15

℟. **Alleluia, alleluia.**

The Kingdom of God is at hand;
repent and believe in the Gospel.

℟. **Alleluia, alleluia.**

GOSPEL   Years I and II

Luke 9:1-6   He sent them to proclaim the Kingdom of God and to heal the sick.

✠ **A reading from the holy Gospel according to Luke**

Jesus summoned the Twelve and gave them power and authority
  over all demons and to cure diseases,
  and he sent them to proclaim the Kingdom of God
  and to heal the sick.
He said to them, "Take nothing for the journey,
  neither walking stick, nor sack, nor food, nor money,
  and let no one take a second tunic.
Whatever house you enter, stay there and leave from there.
And as for those who do not welcome you,
  when you leave that town,
  shake the dust from your feet in testimony against them."
Then they set out and went from village to village
  proclaiming the Good News and curing diseases everywhere.

The Gospel of the Lord.

452 THURSDAY OF THE TWENTY-FIFTH WEEK IN ORDINARY TIME

FIRST READING   Year II

Ecclesiastes 1:2-11   Nothing is new under the sun.

A reading from the Book of Ecclesiastes

Vanity of vanities, says Qoheleth,
  vanity of vanities! All things are vanity!
What profit has man from all the labor
  which he toils at under the sun?
One generation passes and another comes,
  but the world forever stays.
The sun rises and the sun goes down;
  then it presses on to the place where it rises.
Blowing now toward the south, then toward the north,
  the wind turns again and again, resuming its rounds.
All rivers go to the sea,
  yet never does the sea become full.
To the place where they go,
  the rivers keep on going.
All speech is labored;
  there is nothing one can say.
The eye is not satisfied with seeing
  nor is the ear satisfied with hearing.

What has been, that will be;
  what has been done, that will be done.
Nothing is new under the sun.
Even the thing of which we say, "See, this is new!"
  has already existed in the ages that preceded us.
There is no remembrance of the men of old;
  nor of those to come will there be any remembrance
  among those who come after them.

The word of the Lord.

RESPONSORIAL PSALM

Psalm 90:3-4, 5-6, 12-13, 14 and 17bc

℟. (1) **In every age, O Lord, you have been our refuge.**

**You turn man back to dust,
   saying, "Return, O children of men."
For a thousand years in your sight
   are as yesterday, now that it is past,
   or as a watch of the night.**

℟. **In every age, O Lord, you have been our refuge.**

**You make an end of them in their sleep;
   the next morning they are like the changing grass,
Which at dawn springs up anew,
   but by evening wilts and fades.**

℟. **In every age, O Lord, you have been our refuge.**

**Teach us to number our days aright,
   that we may gain wisdom of heart.
Return, O LORD! How long?
   Have pity on your servants!**

℟. **In every age, O Lord, you have been our refuge.**

**Fill us at daybreak with your kindness,
   that we may shout for joy and gladness all our days.
   Prosper the work of our hands for us!
   Prosper the work of our hands!**

℟. **In every age, O Lord, you have been our refuge.**

ALLELUIA

John 14:6

℟. Alleluia, alleluia.

I am the way and the truth and the life, says the Lord;
no one comes to the Father except through me.

℟. Alleluia, alleluia.

GOSPEL   Years I and II

Luke 9:7-9   John I beheaded. Who then is this about whom I hear such things?

✝ A reading from the holy Gospel according to Luke

Herod the tetrarch heard about all that was happening,
   and he was greatly perplexed because some were saying,
   "John has been raised from the dead";
   others were saying, "Elijah has appeared";
   still others, "One of the ancient prophets has arisen."
But Herod said, "John I beheaded.
Who then is this about whom I hear such things?"
And he kept trying to see him.

The Gospel of the Lord.

453 FRIDAY OF THE TWENTY-FIFTH WEEK IN ORDINARY TIME

FIRST READING   Year II

Ecclesiastes 3:1-11   There is a time for everything under the heavens.

A reading from the Book of Ecclesiastes

**There is an appointed time for everything,
 and a time for every thing under the heavens.
A time to be born, and a time to die;
 a time to plant, and a time to uproot the plant.
A time to kill, and a time to heal;
 a time to tear down, and a time to build.
A time to weep, and a time to laugh;
 a time to mourn, and a time to dance.
A time to scatter stones, and a time to gather them;
 a time to embrace, and a time to be far from embraces.
A time to seek, and a time to lose;
 a time to keep, and a time to cast away.
A time to rend, and a time to sew;
 a time to be silent, and a time to speak.
A time to love, and a time to hate;
 a time of war, and a time of peace.**

**What advantage has the worker from his toil?
I have considered the task that God has appointed
 for the sons of men to be busied about.
He has made everything appropriate to its time,
 and has put the timeless into their hearts,
 without man's ever discovering,
 from beginning to end, the work which God has done.**

The word of the Lord.

RESPONSORIAL PSALM

Psalm 144:1b and 2abc, 3-4

℟. (1) **Blessed be the Lord, my Rock!**

Blessed be the LORD**, my rock,
my mercy and my fortress,
my stronghold, my deliverer,
My shield, in whom I trust.**

℟. Blessed be the Lord, my Rock!

LORD**, what is man, that you notice him;
the son of man, that you take thought of him?
Man is like a breath;
his days, like a passing shadow.**

℟. Blessed be the Lord, my Rock!

ALLELUIA

Mark 10:45

℟. Alleluia, alleluia.

The Son of Man came to serve
and to give his life as a ransom for many.

℟. Alleluia, alleluia.

GOSPEL   Years I and II

Luke 9:18-22   You are the Christ of God. The Son of Man must suffer greatly.

✢ A reading from the holy Gospel according to Luke

Once when Jesus was praying in solitude,
   and the disciples were with him,
   he asked them, "Who do the crowds say that I am?"
They said in reply, "John the Baptist; others, Elijah;
   still others, 'One of the ancient prophets has arisen.'"
Then he said to them, "But who do you say that I am?"
Peter said in reply, "The Christ of God."
He rebuked them and directed them not to tell this to anyone.

He said, "The Son of Man must suffer greatly
   and be rejected by the elders, the chief priests, and the scribes,
   and be killed and on the third day be raised."

The Gospel of the Lord.

454 SATURDAY OF THE TWENTY-FIFTH WEEK IN ORDINARY TIME

FIRST READING   Year II

Ecclesiastes 11:9–12:8   Remember your Creator in the days of your youth, before the dust returns to the earth, and the life breath returns to God.

A reading from the Book of Ecclesiastes

Rejoice, O young man, while you are young
  and let your heart be glad in the days of your youth.
Follow the ways of your heart,
  the vision of your eyes;
Yet understand that as regards all this
  God will bring you to judgment.
Ward off grief from your heart
  and put away trouble from your presence,
  though the dawn of youth is fleeting.

Remember your Creator in the days of your youth,
  before the evil days come
And the years approach of which you will say,
  I have no pleasure in them;
Before the sun is darkened,
  and the light, and the moon, and the stars,
  while the clouds return after the rain;
When the guardians of the house tremble,
  and the strong men are bent,
And the grinders are idle because they are few,
  and they who look through the windows grow blind;
When the doors to the street are shut,
  and the sound of the mill is low;
When one waits for the chirp of a bird,
  but all the daughters of song are suppressed;
And one fears heights,
  and perils in the street;
When the almond tree blooms,
  and the locust grows sluggish
  and the caper berry is without effect,

Because man goes to his lasting home,
 and mourners go about the streets;
Before the silver cord is snapped
 and the golden bowl is broken,
And the pitcher is shattered at the spring,
 and the broken pulley falls into the well,
And the dust returns to the earth as it once was,
 and the life breath returns to God who gave it.

Vanity of vanities, says Qoheleth,
 all things are vanity!

The word of the Lord.

RESPONSORIAL PSALM

Psalm 90:3-4, 5-6, 12-13, 14 and 17

℟. (1) **In every age, O Lord, you have been our refuge.**

**You turn man back to dust,
  saying, "Return, O children of men."
For a thousand years in your sight
  are as yesterday, now that it is past,
  or as a watch of the night.**

℟. **In every age, O Lord, you have been our refuge.**

**You make an end of them in their sleep;
  the next morning they are like the changing grass,
Which at dawn springs up anew,
  but by evening wilts and fades.**

℟. **In every age, O Lord, you have been our refuge.**

**Teach us to number our days aright,
  that we may gain wisdom of heart.
Return, O Lord! How long?
  Have pity on your servants!**

℟. **In every age, O Lord, you have been our refuge.**

**Fill us at daybreak with your kindness,
  that we may shout for joy and gladness all our days.
And may the gracious care of the Lord our God be ours;
  prosper the work of our hands for us!
  Prosper the work of our hands!**

℟. **In every age, O Lord, you have been our refuge.**

ALLELUIA

See 2 Timothy 1:10

℟. Alleluia, alleluia.

**Our Savior Christ Jesus destroyed death
and brought life to light through the Gospel.**

℟. Alleluia, alleluia.

GOSPEL   Years I and II

Luke 9:43b-45   The Son of Man is to be handed over to men. They were afraid to ask him about this saying.

✠ **A reading from the holy Gospel according to Luke**

**While they were all amazed at his every deed,
   Jesus said to his disciples,
   "Pay attention to what I am telling you.
The Son of Man is to be handed over to men."
But they did not understand this saying;
   its meaning was hidden from them
   so that they should not understand it,
   and they were afraid to ask him about this saying.**

The Gospel of the Lord.

455 MONDAY OF THE TWENTY-SIXTH WEEK IN ORDINARY TIME

FIRST READING   Year II

Job 1:6-22   The Lord gave and the Lord has taken away; blessed be the name of the Lord!

A reading from the Book of Job

One day, when the angels of God came to present themselves before the Lord,
   Satan also came among them.
And the Lord said to Satan, "Whence do you come?"
Then Satan answered the Lord and said,
   "From roaming the earth and patrolling it."
And the Lord said to Satan, "Have you noticed my servant Job,
   and that there is no one on earth like him,
   blameless and upright, fearing God and avoiding evil?"
But Satan answered the Lord and said,
   "Is it for nothing that Job is God-fearing?
Have you not surrounded him and his family
   and all that he has with your protection?
You have blessed the work of his hands,
   and his livestock are spread over the land.
But now put forth your hand and touch anything that he has,
   and surely he will blaspheme you to your face."
And the Lord said to Satan,
   "Behold, all that he has is in your power;
   only do not lay a hand upon his person."
So Satan went forth from the presence of the Lord.

And so one day, while his sons and his daughters
   were eating and drinking wine
   in the house of their eldest brother,
   a messenger came to Job and said,
   "The oxen were ploughing and the asses grazing beside them,
   and the Sabeans carried them off in a raid.
They put the herdsmen to the sword,
   and I alone have escaped to tell you."

While he was yet speaking, another came and said,
  "Lightning has fallen from heaven
  and struck the sheep and their shepherds and consumed them;
  and I alone have escaped to tell you."
While he was yet speaking, another messenger came and said,
  "The Chaldeans formed three columns,
  seized the camels, carried them off,
  and put those tending them to the sword,
  and I alone have escaped to tell you."
While he was yet speaking, another came and said,
  "Your sons and daughters were eating and drinking wine
  in the house of their eldest brother,
  when suddenly a great wind came across the desert
  and smote the four corners of the house.
It fell upon the young people and they are dead;
  and I alone have escaped to tell you."
Then Job began to tear his cloak and cut off his hair.
He cast himself prostrate upon the ground, and said,

  "Naked I came forth from my mother's womb,
    and naked shall I go back again.
  The Lord gave and the Lord has taken away;
    blessed be the name of the Lord!"

In all this Job did not sin,
  nor did he say anything disrespectful of God.

The word of the Lord.

RESPONSORIAL PSALM

Psalm 17:1bcd, 2-3, 6-7

℟. (6) **Incline your ear to me and hear my word.**

**Hear, O Lord, a just suit;
    attend to my outcry;
    hearken to my prayer from lips without deceit.**

℟. **Incline your ear to me and hear my word.**

**From you let my judgment come;
    your eyes behold what is right.
Though you test my heart, searching it in the night,
    though you try me with fire, you shall find no malice in me.**

℟. **Incline your ear to me and hear my word.**

**I call upon you, for you will answer me, O God;
    incline your ear to me; hear my word.
Show your wondrous mercies,
    O savior of those who flee
    from their foes to refuge at your right hand.**

℟. **Incline your ear to me and hear my word.**

ALLELUIA

Mark 10:45

℟. **Alleluia, alleluia.**

**The Son of Man came to serve
and to give his life as a ransom for many.**

℟. **Alleluia, alleluia.**

GOSPEL Years I and II

Luke 9:46-50   The one who is least among all of you is the one who is the greatest.

✟ **A reading from the holy Gospel according to Luke**

**An argument arose among the disciples
   about which of them was the greatest.
Jesus realized the intention of their hearts and took a child
   and placed it by his side and said to them,
"Whoever receives this child in my name receives me,
   and whoever receives me receives the one who sent me.
For the one who is least among all of you
   is the one who is the greatest."**

**Then John said in reply,
"Master, we saw someone casting out demons in your name
   and we tried to prevent him
   because he does not follow in our company."
Jesus said to him,
   "Do not prevent him, for whoever is not against you is for you."**

The Gospel of the Lord.

456 TUESDAY OF THE TWENTY-SIXTH WEEK IN ORDINARY TIME

FIRST READING   Year II

Job 3:1-3, 11-17, 20-23   Why is light given to the toilers?

A reading from the Book of Job

Job opened his mouth and cursed his day.
Job spoke out and said:

   Perish the day on which I was born,
      the night when they said, "The child is a boy!"

   Why did I not perish at birth,
      come forth from the womb and expire?
   Or why was I not buried away like an untimely birth,
      like babes that have never seen the light?
   Wherefore did the knees receive me?
      or why did I suck at the breasts?

   For then I should have lain down and been tranquil;
      had I slept, I should then have been at rest
   With kings and counselors of the earth
      who built where now there are ruins
   Or with princes who had gold
      and filled their houses with silver.

   There the wicked cease from troubling,
      there the weary are at rest.

   Why is light given to the toilers,
      and life to the bitter in spirit?
   They wait for death and it comes not;
      they search for it rather than for hidden treasures,
   Rejoice in it exultingly,
      and are glad when they reach the grave:
   Those whose path is hidden from them,
      and whom God has hemmed in!

The word of the Lord.

RESPONSORIAL PSALM

Psalm 88:2-3, 4-5, 6, 7-8

℟. (3) **Let my prayer come before you, Lord.**

O LORD, my God, by day I cry out;
  at night I clamor in your presence.
Let my prayer come before you;
  incline your ear to my call for help.

℟. **Let my prayer come before you, Lord.**

For my soul is surfeited with troubles
  and my life draws near to the nether world.
I am numbered with those who go down into the pit;
  I am a man without strength.

℟. **Let my prayer come before you, Lord.**

My couch is among the dead,
  like the slain who lie in the grave,
Whom you remember no longer
  and who are cut off from your care.

℟. **Let my prayer come before you, Lord.**

You have plunged me into the bottom of the pit,
  into the dark abyss.
Upon me your wrath lies heavy,
  and with all your billows you overwhelm me.

℟. **Let my prayer come before you, Lord.**

ALLELUIA

Mark 10:45

℟. Alleluia, alleluia.

The Son of Man came to serve
and to give his life as a ransom for many.

℟. Alleluia, alleluia.

GOSPEL Years I and II

Luke 9:51-56   He resolutely determined to journey to Jerusalem.

✟ A reading from the holy Gospel according to Luke

When the days for Jesus to be taken up were fulfilled,
 he resolutely determined to journey to Jerusalem,
 and he sent messengers ahead of him.
On the way they entered a Samaritan village
 to prepare for his reception there,
 but they would not welcome him
 because the destination of his journey was Jerusalem.
When the disciples James and John saw this they asked,
 "Lord, do you want us to call down fire from heaven
 to consume them?"
Jesus turned and rebuked them,
 and they journeyed to another village.

The Gospel of the Lord.

457 WEDNESDAY OF THE TWENTY-SIXTH WEEK IN ORDINARY TIME

FIRST READING   Year II

Job 9:1-12, 14-16   How can one be justified before God?

A reading from the Book of Job

Job answered his friends and said:

I know well that it is so;
 but how can a man be justified before God?
Should one wish to contend with him,
 he could not answer him once in a thousand times.
God is wise in heart and mighty in strength;
 who has withstood him and remained unscathed?

He removes the mountains before they know it;
 he overturns them in his anger.
He shakes the earth out of its place,
 and the pillars beneath it tremble.
He commands the sun, and it rises not;
 he seals up the stars.

He alone stretches out the heavens
 and treads upon the crests of the sea.
He made the Bear and Orion,
 the Pleiades and the constellations of the south;
He does great things past finding out,
 marvelous things beyond reckoning.

Should he come near me, I see him not;
 should he pass by, I am not aware of him;
Should he seize me forcibly, who can say him nay?
 Who can say to him, "What are you doing?"

How much less shall I give him any answer,
 or choose out arguments against him!
Even though I were right, I could not answer him,
 but should rather beg for what was due me.
If I appealed to him and he answered my call,
 I could not believe that he would hearken to my words.

The word of the Lord.

RESPONSORIAL PSALM

Psalm 88:10bc-11, 12-13, 14-15

℟. (3) **Let my prayer come before you, Lord.**

**Daily I call upon you, O LORD;
   to you I stretch out my hands.
Will you work wonders for the dead?
   Will the shades arise to give you thanks?**

℟. **Let my prayer come before you, Lord.**

**Do they declare your mercy in the grave,
   your faithfulness among those who have perished?
Are your wonders made known in the darkness,
   or your justice in the land of oblivion?**

℟. **Let my prayer come before you, Lord.**

**But I, O LORD, cry out to you;
   with my morning prayer I wait upon you.
Why, O LORD, do you reject me;
   why hide from me your face?**

℟. **Let my prayer come before you, Lord.**

ALLELUIA

Philippians 3:8-9

℟. Alleluia, alleluia.

**I consider all things so much rubbish
that I may gain Christ and be found in him.**

℟. Alleluia, alleluia.

GOSPEL — Years I and II

Luke 9:57-62 — I will follow you wherever you go.

✠ A reading from the holy Gospel according to Luke

**As Jesus and his disciples were proceeding
on their journey, someone said to him,
"I will follow you wherever you go."
Jesus answered him,
"Foxes have dens and birds of the sky have nests,
but the Son of Man has nowhere to rest his head."
And to another he said, "Follow me."
But he replied, "Lord, let me go first and bury my father."
But he answered him, "Let the dead bury their dead.
But you, go and proclaim the Kingdom of God."
And another said, "I will follow you, Lord,
but first let me say farewell to my family at home."
Jesus answered him, "No one who sets a hand to the plow
and looks to what was left behind is fit for the Kingdom of God."**

The Gospel of the Lord.

458 THURSDAY OF THE TWENTY-SIXTH WEEK IN ORDINARY TIME

FIRST READING Year II

Job 19:21-27   I know that my Vindicator lives.

A reading from the Book of Job

Job said:

Pity me, pity me, O you my friends,
   for the hand of God has struck me!
Why do you hound me as though you were divine,
   and insatiably prey upon me?

Oh, would that my words were written down!
   Would that they were inscribed in a record:
That with an iron chisel and with lead
   they were cut in the rock forever!
But as for me, I know that my Vindicator lives,
   and that he will at last stand forth upon the dust;
Whom I myself shall see:
   my own eyes, not another's, shall behold him,
And from my flesh I shall see God;
   my inmost being is consumed with longing.

The word of the Lord.

RESPONSORIAL PSALM

Psalm 27:7-8a, 8b-9abc, 13-14

℟. (13) **I believe that I shall see the good things of the Lord in the land of the living.**

**Hear, O Lord, the sound of my call;
   have pity on me, and answer me.
Of you my heart speaks; you my glance seeks.**

℟. **I believe that I shall see the good things of the Lord in the land of the living.**

**Your presence, O Lord, I seek.
Hide not your face from me;
   do not in anger repel your servant.
You are my helper: cast me not off.**

℟. **I believe that I shall see the good things of the Lord in the land of the living.**

**I believe that I shall see the bounty of the Lord
   in the land of the living.
Wait for the Lord with courage;
   be stouthearted, and wait for the Lord.**

℟. **I believe that I shall see the good things of the Lord in the land of the living.**

ALLELUIA

Mark 1:15

℟. **Alleluia, alleluia.**

**The Kingdom of God is at hand;
repent and believe in the Gospel.**

℟. **Alleluia, alleluia.**

GOSPEL Years I and II

Luke 10:1-12   Your peace will rest on him.

✢ A reading from the holy Gospel according to Luke

Jesus appointed seventy-two other disciples
   whom he sent ahead of him in pairs
   to every town and place he intended to visit.
He said to them,
   "The harvest is abundant but the laborers are few;
   so ask the master of the harvest
   to send out laborers for his harvest.
Go on your way;
   behold, I am sending you like lambs among wolves.
Carry no money bag, no sack, no sandals;
   and greet no one along the way.
Into whatever house you enter, first say,
   'Peace to this household.'
If a peaceful person lives there,
   your peace will rest on him;
   but if not, it will return to you.
Stay in the same house and eat and drink what is offered to you,
   for the laborer deserves his payment.
Do not move about from one house to another.
Whatever town you enter and they welcome you,
   eat what is set before you,
   cure the sick in it and say to them,
   'The Kingdom of God is at hand for you.'
Whatever town you enter and they do not receive you,
   go out into the streets and say,
   'The dust of your town that clings to our feet,
   even that we shake off against you.'
Yet know this: the Kingdom of God is at hand.
I tell you,
   it will be more tolerable for Sodom on that day
   than for that town."

The Gospel of the Lord.

459 FRIDAY OF THE TWENTY-SIXTH WEEK IN ORDINARY TIME

FIRST READING   Year II

Job 38:1, 12-21; 40:3-5   Have you ever in your lifetime commanded the morning and entered into the sources of the sea?

A reading from the Book of Job

The Lord addressed Job out of the storm and said:

> Have you ever in your lifetime commanded the morning
>   and shown the dawn its place
> For taking hold of the ends of the earth,
>   till the wicked are shaken from its surface?
> The earth is changed as is clay by the seal,
>   and dyed as though it were a garment;
> But from the wicked the light is withheld,
>   and the arm of pride is shattered.
>
> Have you entered into the sources of the sea,
>   or walked about in the depths of the abyss?
> Have the gates of death been shown to you,
>   or have you seen the gates of darkness?
> Have you comprehended the breadth of the earth?
>   Tell me, if you know all:
> Which is the way to the dwelling place of light,
>   and where is the abode of darkness,
> That you may take them to their boundaries
>   and set them on their homeward paths?
> You know, because you were born before them,
>   and the number of your years is great!

Then Job answered the Lord and said:

> Behold, I am of little account; what can I answer you?
>   I put my hand over my mouth.
> Though I have spoken once, I will not do so again;
>   though twice, I will do so no more.

The word of the Lord.

RESPONSORIAL PSALM

Psalm 139:1-3, 7-8, 9-10, 13-14ab

℟. (24b) **Guide me, Lord, along the everlasting way.**

O LORD, you have probed me and you know me;
 you know when I sit and when I stand;
 you understand my thoughts from afar.
My journeys and my rest you scrutinize,
 with all my ways you are familiar.

℟. Guide me, Lord, along the everlasting way.

Where can I go from your spirit?
 From your presence where can I flee?
If I go up to the heavens, you are there;
 if I sink to the nether world, you are present there.

℟. Guide me, Lord, along the everlasting way.

If I take the wings of the dawn,
 if I settle at the farthest limits of the sea,
Even there your hand shall guide me,
 and your right hand hold me fast.

℟. Guide me, Lord, along the everlasting way.

Truly you have formed my inmost being;
 you knit me in my mother's womb.
I give you thanks that I am fearfully, wonderfully made;
 wonderful are your works.

℟. Guide me, Lord, along the everlasting way.

ALLELUIA

Psalm 95:8

℟. Alleluia, alleluia.

If today you hear his voice,
harden not your hearts.

℟. Alleluia, alleluia.

GOSPEL   Years I and II

Luke 10:13-16   Whoever rejects me rejects the one who sent me.

✠ A reading from the holy Gospel according to Luke

Jesus said to them,
   "Woe to you, Chorazin! Woe to you, Bethsaida!
For if the mighty deeds done in your midst
   had been done in Tyre and Sidon,
   they would long ago have repented,
   sitting in sackcloth and ashes.
But it will be more tolerable for Tyre and Sidon
   at the judgment than for you.
And as for you, Capernaum, 'Will you be exalted to heaven?
You will go down to the netherworld.'
Whoever listens to you listens to me.
Whoever rejects you rejects me.
And whoever rejects me rejects the one who sent me."

The Gospel of the Lord.

460 SATURDAY OF THE TWENTY-SIXTH WEEK IN ORDINARY TIME

FIRST READING   Year II

Job 42:1-3, 5-6, 12-17   But now my eye has seen you and I disown what I have said.

A reading from the Book of Job

Job answered the Lord and said:

I know that you can do all things,
   and that no purpose of yours can be hindered.
I have dealt with great things that I do not understand;
   things too wonderful for me, which I cannot know.
I had heard of you by word of mouth,
   but now my eye has seen you.
Therefore I disown what I have said,
   and repent in dust and ashes.

Thus the Lord blessed the latter days of Job
   more than his earlier ones.
For he had fourteen thousand sheep, six thousand camels,
   a thousand yoke of oxen, and a thousand she-asses.
And he had seven sons and three daughters,
   of whom he called the first Jemimah,
   the second Keziah, and the third Kerenhappuch.
In all the land no other women were as beautiful
   as the daughters of Job;
   and their father gave them an inheritance
   along with their brothers.
After this, Job lived a hundred and forty years;
   and he saw his children, his grandchildren,
   and even his great-grandchildren.
Then Job died, old and full of years.

The word of the Lord.

RESPONSORIAL PSALM

Psalm 119:66, 71, 75, 91, 125, 130

℟. (135) **Lord, let your face shine on me.**

**Teach me wisdom and knowledge,
 for in your commands I trust.**

℟. **Lord, let your face shine on me.**

**It is good for me that I have been afflicted,
 that I may learn your statutes.**

℟. **Lord, let your face shine on me.**

**I know, O Lord, that your ordinances are just,
 and in your faithfulness you have afflicted me.**

℟. **Lord, let your face shine on me.**

**According to your ordinances they still stand firm:
 all things serve you.**

℟. **Lord, let your face shine on me.**

**I am your servant; give me discernment
 that I may know your decrees.**

℟. **Lord, let your face shine on me.**

**The revelation of your words sheds light,
 giving understanding to the simple.**

℟. **Lord, let your face shine on me.**

ALLELUIA

See Matthew 11:25

℟. **Alleluia, alleluia.**

**Blessed are you, Father, Lord of heaven and earth;
you have revealed to little ones the mysteries of the Kingdom.**

℟. **Alleluia, alleluia.**

GOSPEL Years I and II

Luke 10:17-24   Rejoice because your names are written in heaven.

✝ A reading from the holy Gospel according to Luke

The seventy-two disciples returned rejoicing and said to Jesus,
"Lord, even the demons are subject to us because of your name."
Jesus said, "I have observed Satan fall like lightning from the sky.
Behold, I have given you the power
'to tread upon serpents' and scorpions
and upon the full force of the enemy
and nothing will harm you.
Nevertheless, do not rejoice because the spirits are subject to you,
but rejoice because your names are written in heaven."

At that very moment he rejoiced in the Holy Spirit and said,
"I give you praise, Father, Lord of heaven and earth,
for although you have hidden these things
from the wise and the learned
you have revealed them to the childlike.
Yes, Father, such has been your gracious will.
All things have been handed over to me by my Father.
No one knows who the Son is except the Father,
and who the Father is except the Son
and anyone to whom the Son wishes to reveal him."

Turning to the disciples in private he said,
"Blessed are the eyes that see what you see.
For I say to you,
many prophets and kings desired to see what you see,
but did not see it,
and to hear what you hear, but did not hear it."

The Gospel of the Lord.

461 MONDAY OF THE TWENTY-SEVENTH WEEK IN ORDINARY TIME

FIRST READING   Year II

Galatians 1:6-12   The Gospel preached by me is not of human origin but through a revelation of Jesus Christ.

A reading from the Letter of Saint Paul to the Galatians

Brothers and sisters:
I am amazed that you are so quickly forsaking
   the one who called you by the grace of Christ
   for a different gospel (not that there is another).
But there are some who are disturbing you
   and wish to pervert the Gospel of Christ.
But even if we or an angel from heaven
   should preach to you a gospel
   other than the one that we preached to you,
   let that one be accursed!
As we have said before, and now I say again,
   if anyone preaches to you a gospel
   other than the one that you received,
   let that one be accursed!

Am I now currying favor with human beings or God?
Or am I seeking to please people?
If I were still trying to please people,
   I would not be a slave of Christ.

Now I want you to know, brothers and sisters,
   that the Gospel preached by me is not of human origin.
For I did not receive it from a human being, nor was I taught it,
   but it came through a revelation of Jesus Christ.

The word of the Lord.

RESPONSORIAL PSALM

Psalm 111:1b-2, 7-8, 9 and 10c

℟. (5) **The Lord will remember his covenant for ever.**
or:
℟. **Alleluia.**

**I will give thanks to the Lord with all my heart
 in the company and assembly of the just.
Great are the works of the Lord,
 exquisite in all their delights.**

℟. **The Lord will remember his covenant for ever.**
or:
℟. **Alleluia.**

**The works of his hands are faithful and just;
 sure are all his precepts,
Reliable forever and ever,
 wrought in truth and equity.**

℟. **The Lord will remember his covenant for ever.**
or:
℟. **Alleluia.**

**He has sent deliverance to his people;
 he has ratified his covenant forever;
 holy and awesome is his name.
 His praise endures forever.**

℟. **The Lord will remember his covenant for ever.**
or:
℟. **Alleluia.**

ALLELUIA

John 13:34

℟. **Alleluia, alleluia.**

**I give you a new commandment:
love one another as I have loved you.**

℟. **Alleluia, alleluia.**

GOSPEL   Years I and II

Luke 10:25-37   Who is my neighbor?

✠   A reading from the holy Gospel according to Luke

There was a scholar of the law who stood up to test Jesus and said,
   "Teacher, what must I do to inherit eternal life?"
Jesus said to him, "What is written in the law?
How do you read it?"
He said in reply,
   "You shall love the Lord, your God,
   with all your heart,
   with all your being,
   with all your strength,
   and with all your mind,
   and your neighbor as yourself."
He replied to him, "You have answered correctly;
   do this and you will live."

But because he wished to justify himself, he said to Jesus,
   "And who is my neighbor?"
Jesus replied,
   "A man fell victim to robbers
   as he went down from Jerusalem to Jericho.
They stripped and beat him and went off leaving him half-dead.
A priest happened to be going down that road,
   but when he saw him, he passed by on the opposite side.
Likewise a Levite came to the place,
   and when he saw him, he passed by on the opposite side.
But a Samaritan traveler who came upon him
   was moved with compassion at the sight.
He approached the victim,
   poured oil and wine over his wounds and bandaged them.
Then he lifted him up on his own animal,
   took him to an inn, and cared for him.
The next day he took out two silver coins
   and gave them to the innkeeper with the instruction,
   'Take care of him.
If you spend more than what I have given you,
   I shall repay you on my way back.'

**Which of these three, in your opinion,
   was neighbor to the robbers' victim?"
He answered, "The one who treated him with mercy."
Jesus said to him, "Go and do likewise."**

The Gospel of the Lord.

462 TUESDAY OF THE TWENTY-SEVENTH WEEK IN ORDINARY TIME

FIRST READING   Year II

Galatians 1:13-24   God was pleased to reveal his Son to me, so that I might proclaim him to the Gentiles.

A reading from the Letter of Saint Paul to the Galatians

Brothers and sisters:
You heard of my former way of life in Judaism,
> how I persecuted the Church of God beyond measure
> and tried to destroy it,
> and progressed in Judaism
> beyond many of my contemporaries among my race,
> since I was even more a zealot for my ancestral traditions.

But when he, who from my mother's womb had set me apart
> and called me through his grace,
> was pleased to reveal his Son to me,
> so that I might proclaim him to the Gentiles,
> I did not immediately consult flesh and blood,
> nor did I go up to Jerusalem
> to those who were Apostles before me;
> rather, I went into Arabia and then returned to Damascus.

Then after three years I went up to Jerusalem to confer with Cephas
> and remained with him for fifteen days.
But I did not see any other of the Apostles,
> only James the brother of the Lord.
(As to what I am writing to you, behold,
> before God, I am not lying.)
Then I went into the regions of Syria and Cilicia.
And I was unknown personally to the churches of Judea
> that are in Christ;
> they only kept hearing that "the one who once was persecuting us
> is now preaching the faith he once tried to destroy."
So they glorified God because of me.

The word of the Lord.

RESPONSORIAL PSALM

Psalm 139:1b-3, 13-14ab, 14c-15

℟. (24b) **Guide me, Lord, along the everlasting way.**

O LORD, you have probed me and you know me;
   you know when I sit and when I stand;
   you understand my thoughts from afar.
My journeys and my rest you scrutinize,
   with all my ways you are familiar.

℟. Guide me, Lord, along the everlasting way.

Truly you have formed my inmost being;
   you knit me in my mother's womb.
I give you thanks that I am fearfully, wonderfully made;
   wonderful are your works.

℟. Guide me, Lord, along the everlasting way.

My soul also you knew full well;
   nor was my frame unknown to you
When I was made in secret,
   when I was fashioned in the depths of the earth.

℟. Guide me, Lord, along the everlasting way.

ALLELUIA

Luke 11:28

℟. Alleluia, alleluia.

Blessed are those who hear the word of God and observe it.

℟. Alleluia, alleluia.

GOSPEL Years I and II

Luke 10:38-42   Martha welcomed him into her house. Mary has chosen the better part.

✢ A reading from the holy Gospel according to Luke

**Jesus entered a village
  where a woman whose name was Martha welcomed him.
She had a sister named Mary
  who sat beside the Lord at his feet listening to him speak.
Martha, burdened with much serving, came to him and said,
    "Lord, do you not care
    that my sister has left me by myself to do the serving?
Tell her to help me."
The Lord said to her in reply,
    "Martha, Martha, you are anxious and worried about many things.
There is need of only one thing.
Mary has chosen the better part
  and it will not be taken from her."**

The Gospel of the Lord.

463 WEDNESDAY OF THE TWENTY-SEVENTH WEEK IN ORDINARY TIME

FIRST READING   Year II

Galatians 2:1-2, 7-14   *They recognized the grace bestowed upon me.*

A reading from the Letter of Saint Paul to the Galatians

Brothers and sisters:
After fourteen years I again went up to Jerusalem with Barnabas,
   taking Titus along also.
I went up in accord with a revelation,
   and I presented to them the Gospel that I preach to the Gentiles—
   but privately to those of repute—
   so that I might not be running, or have run, in vain.
On the contrary,
   when they saw that I had been entrusted with the Gospel to the
      uncircumcised,
   just as Peter to the circumcised,
   for the one who worked in Peter for an apostolate to the circumcised
   worked also in me for the Gentiles,
   and when they recognized the grace bestowed upon me,
   James and Cephas and John,
   who were reputed to be pillars,
   gave me and Barnabas their right hands in partnership,
   that we should go to the Gentiles
   and they to the circumcised.
Only, we were to be mindful of the poor,
   which is the very thing I was eager to do.

And when Cephas came to Antioch,
   I opposed him to his face because he clearly was wrong.
For, until some people came from James,
   he used to eat with the Gentiles;
   but when they came, he began to draw back and separated himself,
   because he was afraid of the circumcised.
And the rest of the Jews acted hypocritically along with him,
   with the result that even Barnabas
   was carried away by their hypocrisy.

But when I saw that they were not on the right road
>   in line with the truth of the Gospel,
>   I said to Cephas in front of all,
"If you, though a Jew,
>   are living like a Gentile and not like a Jew,
>   how can you compel the Gentiles to live like Jews?"

The word of the Lord.

RESPONSORIAL PSALM

Psalm 117:1bc, 2

℟. **Go out to all the world, and tell the Good News.**

**Praise the LORD, all you nations,
glorify him, all you peoples!**

℟. **Go out to all the world, and tell the Good News.**

**For steadfast is his kindness toward us,
and the fidelity of the LORD endures forever.**

℟. **Go out to all the world, and tell the Good News.**

ALLELUIA

Romans 8:15bc

℟. Alleluia, alleluia.

**You have received a spirit of adoption as sons
through which we cry: Abba! Father!**

℟. Alleluia, alleluia.

GOSPEL Years I and II

Luke 11:1-4   Lord, teach us to pray.

✠ **A reading from the holy Gospel according to Luke**

**Jesus was praying in a certain place, and when he had finished,
one of his disciples said to him,
"Lord, teach us to pray just as John taught his disciples."
He said to them, "When you pray, say:**

> **Father, hallowed be your name,
> your Kingdom come.
> Give us each day our daily bread
> and forgive us our sins
> for we ourselves forgive everyone in debt to us,
> and do not subject us to the final test."**

The Gospel of the Lord.

464 THURSDAY OF THE TWENTY-SEVENTH WEEK IN ORDINARY TIME

FIRST READING   Year II

Galatians 3:1-5   Did you receive the Spirit from works of the law, or from faith in what you heard?

A reading from the Letter of Saint Paul to the Galatians

O stupid Galatians!
Who has bewitched you,
   before whose eyes Jesus Christ was publicly portrayed as crucified?
I want to learn only this from you:
   did you receive the Spirit from works of the law,
   or from faith in what you heard?
Are you so stupid?
After beginning with the Spirit,
   are you now ending with the flesh?
Did you experience so many things in vain?—
   if indeed it was in vain.
Does, then, the one who supplies the Spirit to you
   and works mighty deeds among you
   do so from works of the law
   or from faith in what you heard?

The word of the Lord.

RESPONSORIAL PSALM

Luke 1:69-70, 71-72, 73-75

℟. (68) **Blessed be the Lord, the God of Israel; he has come to his people.**

**He has raised up for us a mighty savior,
born of the house of his servant David.**

℟. **Blessed be the Lord, the God of Israel; he has come to his people.**

**Through his holy prophets he promised of old
that he would save us from our enemies,
from the hands of all who hate us.**

℟. **Blessed be the Lord, the God of Israel; he has come to his people.**

**He promised to show mercy to our fathers
and to remember his holy covenant.**

℟. **Blessed be the Lord, the God of Israel; he has come to his people.**

**This was the oath he swore to our father Abraham:
to set us free from the hands of our enemies,
free to worship him without fear,
holy and righteous in his sight
all the days of our life.**

℟. **Blessed be the Lord, the God of Israel; He has come to his people.**

ALLELUIA

See Acts 16:14b

℟. **Alleluia, alleluia.**

**Open our hearts, O Lord,
to listen to the words of your Son.**

℟. **Alleluia, alleluia.**

GOSPEL Years I and II

Luke 11:5-13   Ask and you will receive.

☩ A reading from the holy Gospel according to Luke

Jesus said to his disciples:
"Suppose one of you has a friend
   to whom he goes at midnight and says,
   'Friend, lend me three loaves of bread,
   for a friend of mine has arrived at my house from a journey
   and I have nothing to offer him,'
   and he says in reply from within,
   'Do not bother me; the door has already been locked
   and my children and I are already in bed.
   I cannot get up to give you anything.'
I tell you, if he does not get up to give him the loaves
   because of their friendship,
   he will get up to give him whatever he needs
   because of his persistence.

"And I tell you, ask and you will receive;
   seek and you will find;
   knock and the door will be opened to you.
For everyone who asks, receives;
   and the one who seeks, finds;
   and to the one who knocks, the door will be opened.
What father among you would hand his son a snake
   when he asks for a fish?
Or hand him a scorpion when he asks for an egg?
If you then, who are wicked,
   know how to give good gifts to your children,
   how much more will the Father in heaven give the Holy Spirit
   to those who ask him?"

The Gospel of the Lord.

465 FRIDAY OF THE TWENTY-SEVENTH WEEK IN ORDINARY TIME

FIRST READING   Year II

Galatians 3:7-14   *Those who have faith are blessed along with Abraham who had faith.*

A reading from the Letter of Saint Paul to the Galatians

Brothers and sisters:
Realize that it is those who have faith
   who are children of Abraham.
Scripture, which saw in advance that God
   would justify the Gentiles by faith,
   foretold the good news to Abraham, saying,
   Through you shall all the nations be blessed.
Consequently, those who have faith are blessed
   along with Abraham who had faith.
For all who depend on works of the law are under a curse;
   for it is written, *Cursed be everyone*
   who does not persevere in doing all the things
   written in the book of the law.
And that no one is justified before God by the law is clear,
   for *the one who is righteous by faith will live.*
But the law does not depend on faith;
   rather, *the one who does these things will live by them.*
Christ ransomed us from the curse of the law by becoming a curse for us,
   for it is written, *Cursed be everyone who hangs on a tree,*
   that the blessing of Abraham might be extended
   to the Gentiles through Christ Jesus,
   so that we might receive the promise of the Spirit through faith.

The word of the Lord.

RESPONSORIAL PSALM

Psalm 111:1b-2, 3-4, 5-6

℟. (5) **The Lord will remember his covenant for ever.**

**I will give thanks to the Lord with all my heart
  in the company and assembly of the just.
Great are the works of the Lord,
  exquisite in all their delights.**

℟. **The Lord will remember his covenant for ever.**

**Majesty and glory are his work,
  and his justice endures forever.
He has won renown for his wondrous deeds;
  gracious and merciful is the Lord.**

℟. **The Lord will remember his covenant for ever.**

**He has given food to those who fear him;
  he will forever be mindful of his covenant.
He has made known to his people the power of his works,
  giving them the inheritance of the nations.**

℟. **The Lord will remember his covenant for ever.**

ALLELUIA

John 12:31b-32

℟. **Alleluia, alleluia.**

**The prince of this world will now be cast out,
and when I am lifted up from the earth
I will draw all to myself, says the Lord.**

℟. **Alleluia, alleluia.**

GOSPEL Years I and II

Luke 11:15-26   If it is by the finger of God that I drive out demons, then the Kingdom of God has come upon you.

✠ **A reading from the holy Gospel according to Luke**

**When Jesus had driven out a demon, some of the crowd said:
"By the power of Beelzebul, the prince of demons,
he drives out demons."
Others, to test him, asked him for a sign from heaven.
But he knew their thoughts and said to them,
"Every kingdom divided against itself will be laid waste
and house will fall against house.
And if Satan is divided against himself, how will his kingdom stand?
For you say that it is by Beelzebul that I drive out demons.
If I, then, drive out demons by Beelzebul,
by whom do your own people drive them out?
Therefore they will be your judges.
But if it is by the finger of God that I drive out demons,
then the Kingdom of God has come upon you.
When a strong man fully armed guards his palace,
his possessions are safe.
But when one stronger than he attacks and overcomes him,
he takes away the armor on which he relied
and distributes the spoils.
Whoever is not with me is against me,
and whoever does not gather with me scatters.**

**"When an unclean spirit goes out of someone,
it roams through arid regions searching for rest
but, finding none, it says,
'I shall return to my home from which I came.'
But upon returning, it finds it swept clean and put in order.
Then it goes and brings back seven other spirits
more wicked than itself who move in and dwell there,
and the last condition of that man is worse than the first."**

The Gospel of the Lord.

466 SATURDAY OF THE TWENTY-SEVENTH WEEK IN ORDINARY TIME

FIRST READING   Year II

Galatians 3:22-29   Through faith you are all children of God.

A reading from the Letter of Saint Paul to the Galatians

**Brothers and sisters:
Scripture confined all things under the power of sin,
   that through faith in Jesus Christ
   the promise might be given to those who believe.**

**Before faith came, we were held in custody under law,
   confined for the faith that was to be revealed.
Consequently, the law was our disciplinarian for Christ,
   that we might be justified by faith.
But now that faith has come, we are no longer under a disciplinarian.
For through faith you are all children of God in Christ Jesus.
For all of you who were baptized into Christ
   have clothed yourselves with Christ.
There is neither Jew nor Greek,
   there is neither slave nor free person,
   there is not male and female;
   for you are all one in Christ Jesus.
And if you belong to Christ, then you are Abraham's descendants,
   heirs according to the promise.**

The word of the Lord.

RESPONSORIAL PSALM

Psalm 105:2-3, 4-5, 6-7

℟. (8a) **The Lord remembers his covenant for ever.**
    or:
℟. **Alleluia.**

**Sing to him, sing his praise,
    proclaim all his wondrous deeds.
Glory in his holy name;
    rejoice, O hearts that seek the Lord!**

℟. **The Lord remembers his covenant for ever.**
    or:
℟. **Alleluia.**

**Look to the Lord in his strength;
    seek to serve him constantly.
Recall the wondrous deeds that he has wrought,
    his portents, and the judgments he has uttered.**

℟. **The Lord remembers his covenant for ever.**
    or:
℟. **Alleluia.**

**You descendants of Abraham, his servants,
    sons of Jacob, his chosen ones!
He, the Lord, is our God;
    throughout the earth his judgments prevail.**

℟. **The Lord remembers his covenant for ever.**
    or:
℟. **Alleluia.**

ALLELUIA

Luke 11:28

℟. Alleluia, alleluia.

**Blessed are those who hear the word of God
and observe it.**

℟. Alleluia, alleluia.

GOSPEL   Years I and II

Luke 11:27-28   Blessed is the womb that carried you. Rather, blessed are those who hear the word of God and observe it.

✠ **A reading from the holy Gospel according to Luke**

**While Jesus was speaking,
a woman from the crowd called out and said to him,
"Blessed is the womb that carried you
and the breasts at which you nursed."
He replied, "Rather, blessed are those
who hear the word of God and observe it."**

The Gospel of the Lord.

467 MONDAY OF THE TWENTY-EIGHTH WEEK IN ORDINARY TIME

FIRST READING   Year II

Galatians 4:22-24, 26-27, 31—5:1   We are children not of the slave woman but of the freeborn woman.

A reading from the Letter of Saint Paul to the Galatians

Brothers and sisters:
It is written that Abraham had two sons,
   one by the slave woman and the other by the freeborn woman.
The son of the slave woman was born naturally,
   the son of the freeborn through a promise.
Now this is an allegory.
These women represent two covenants.
One was from Mount Sinai, bearing children for slavery;
   this is Hagar.
But the Jerusalem above is freeborn, and she is our mother.
For it is written:

> *Rejoice, you barren one who bore no children;*
> *break forth and shout, you who were not in labor;*
> *for more numerous are the children of the deserted one*
>   *than of her who has a husband.*

Therefore, brothers and sisters,
   we are children not of the slave woman
   but of the freeborn woman.

For freedom Christ set us free; so stand firm
   and do not submit again to the yoke of slavery.

The word of the Lord.

RESPONSORIAL PSALM

Psalm 113:1b-2, 3-4, 5a and 6-7

℟. (see 2) **Blessed be the name of the Lord forever.**
   or:
℟. **Alleluia, alleluia.**

Praise, you servants of the Lord,
   praise the name of the Lord.
Blessed be the name of the Lord
   both now and forever.

℟. **Blessed be the name of the Lord forever.**
   or:
℟. **Alleluia, alleluia.**

From the rising to the setting of the sun
   is the name of the Lord to be praised.
High above all nations is the Lord;
   above the heavens is his glory.

℟. **Blessed be the name of the Lord forever.**
   or:
℟. **Alleluia, alleluia.**

Who is like the Lord, our God,
   who looks upon the heavens and the earth below?
He raises up the lowly from the dust;
   from the dunghill he lifts up the poor.

℟. **Blessed be the name of the Lord forever.**
   or:
℟. **Alleluia, alleluia.**

ALLELUIA

Psalm 95:8

℟. Alleluia, alleluia.

If today you hear his voice,
harden not your hearts.

℟. Alleluia, alleluia.

GOSPEL   Years I and II

Luke 11:29-32   This generation seeks a sign, but no sign will be given it, except the sign of Jonah.

✠ A reading from the holy Gospel according to Luke

While still more people gathered in the crowd, Jesus said to them,
    "This generation is an evil generation;
    it seeks a sign, but no sign will be given it,
    except the sign of Jonah.
Just as Jonah became a sign to the Ninevites,
    so will the Son of Man be to this generation.
At the judgment
    the queen of the south will rise with the men of this generation
    and she will condemn them,
    because she came from the ends of the earth
    to hear the wisdom of Solomon,
    and there is something greater than Solomon here.
At the judgment the men of Nineveh will arise with this generation
    and condemn it,
    because at the preaching of Jonah they repented,
    and there is something greater than Jonah here."

The Gospel of the Lord.

468 TUESDAY OF THE TWENTY-EIGHTH WEEK IN ORDINARY TIME

FIRST READING   Year II

Galatians 5:1-6   Neither circumcision nor uncircumcision counts for anything, but only faith working through love.

A reading from the Letter of Saint Paul to the Galatians

Brothers and sisters:
For freedom Christ set us free;
   so stand firm and do not submit again to the yoke of slavery.

It is I, Paul, who am telling you
   that if you have yourselves circumcised,
   Christ will be of no benefit to you.
Once again I declare to every man who has himself circumcised
   that he is bound to observe the entire law.
You are separated from Christ,
   you who are trying to be justified by law;
   you have fallen from grace.
For through the Spirit, by faith, we await the hope of righteousness.
For in Christ Jesus,
   neither circumcision nor uncircumcision counts for anything,
   but only faith working through love.

The word of the Lord.

RESPONSORIAL PSALM

Psalm 119:41, 43, 44, 45, 47, 48

℟. (41a) **Let your mercy come to me, O Lord.**

**Let your mercy come to me, O Lord,
your salvation according to your promise.**

℟. **Let your mercy come to me, O Lord.**

**Take not the word of truth from my mouth,
for in your ordinances is my hope.**

℟. **Let your mercy come to me, O Lord.**

**And I will keep your law continually,
forever and ever.**

℟. **Let your mercy come to me, O Lord.**

**And I will walk at liberty,
because I seek your precepts.**

℟. **Let your mercy come to me, O Lord.**

**And I will delight in your commands,
which I love.**

℟. **Let your mercy come to me, O Lord.**

**And I will lift up my hands to your commands
and meditate on your statutes.**

℟. **Let your mercy come to me, O Lord.**

ALLELUIA

Hebrews 4:12

℟. Alleluia, alleluia.

The word of God is living and effective,
able to discern reflections and thoughts of the heart.

℟. Alleluia, alleluia.

GOSPEL Years I and II

Luke 11:37-41   Give alms and behold, everything will be clean for you.

✠ A reading from the holy Gospel according to Luke

After Jesus had spoken,
   a Pharisee invited him to dine at his home.
He entered and reclined at table to eat.
The Pharisee was amazed to see
   that he did not observe the prescribed washing before the meal.
The Lord said to him, "Oh you Pharisees!
Although you cleanse the outside of the cup and the dish,
   inside you are filled with plunder and evil.
You fools!
Did not the maker of the outside also make the inside?
But as to what is within, give alms,
   and behold, everything will be clean for you."

The Gospel of the Lord.

469 WEDNESDAY OF THE TWENTY-EIGHTH WEEK IN ORDINARY TIME

FIRST READING   Year II

Galatians 5:18-25   Those who belong to Christ Jesus have crucified their flesh with its passions and desires.

A reading from the Letter of Saint Paul to the Galatians

**Brothers and sisters:
If you are guided by the Spirit, you are not under the law.
Now the works of the flesh are obvious:
   immorality, impurity, licentiousness, idolatry,
   sorcery, hatreds, rivalry, jealousy,
   outbursts of fury, acts of selfishness,
   dissensions, factions, occasions of envy,
   drinking bouts, orgies, and the like.
I warn you, as I warned you before,
   that those who do such things will not inherit the Kingdom of God.
In contrast, the fruit of the Spirit is love, joy, peace,
   patience, kindness, generosity,
   faithfulness, gentleness, self-control.
Against such there is no law.
Now those who belong to Christ Jesus have crucified their flesh
   with its passions and desires.
If we live in the Spirit, let us also follow the Spirit.**

The word of the Lord.

RESPONSORIAL PSALM

Psalm 1:1-2, 3, 4 and 6

℟. (see John 8:12) **Those who follow you, Lord, will have the light of life.**

**Blessed the man who follows not
   the counsel of the wicked
Nor walks in the way of sinners,
   nor sits in the company of the insolent,
But delights in the law of the Lord
   and meditates on his law day and night.**

℟. **Those who follow you, Lord, will have the light of life.**

**He is like a tree
   planted near running water,
That yields its fruit in due season,
   and whose leaves never fade.
   Whatever he does, prospers.**

℟. **Those who follow you, Lord, will have the light of life.**

**Not so the wicked, not so;
   they are like chaff which the wind drives away.
For the Lord watches over the way of the just,
   but the way of the wicked vanishes.**

℟. **Those who follow you, Lord, will have the light of life.**

ALLELUIA

John 10:27

℟. Alleluia, alleluia.

My sheep hear my voice, says the Lord;
I know them, and they follow me.

℟. Alleluia, alleluia.

GOSPEL   Years I and II

Luke 11:42-46   Woe to Pharisees! Woe also to you scholars of the law!

✠ A reading from the holy Gospel according to Luke

The Lord said:
"Woe to you Pharisees!
You pay tithes of mint and of rue and of every garden herb,
   but you pay no attention to judgment and to love for God.
These you should have done, without overlooking the others.
Woe to you Pharisees!
You love the seat of honor in synagogues
   and greetings in marketplaces.
Woe to you!
You are like unseen graves over which people unknowingly walk."

Then one of the scholars of the law said to him in reply,
   "Teacher, by saying this you are insulting us too."
And he said, "Woe also to you scholars of the law!
You impose on people burdens hard to carry,
   but you yourselves do not lift one finger to touch them."

The Gospel of the Lord.

470 THURSDAY OF THE TWENTY-EIGHTH WEEK IN ORDINARY TIME

FIRST READING   Year II

Ephesians 1:1-10   God chose us in Christ, before the foundation of the world.

A reading from the beginning of the Letter of Saint Paul to the Ephesians

Paul, an Apostle of Christ Jesus by the will of God,
   to the holy ones who are in Ephesus
   and faithful in Christ Jesus:
   grace to you and peace from God our Father and the Lord Jesus Christ.

Blessed be the God and Father of our Lord Jesus Christ,
   who has blessed us in Christ
   with every spiritual blessing in the heavens,
   as he chose us in him, before the foundation of the world,
   to be holy and without blemish before him.
In love he destined us for adoption to himself through Jesus Christ,
   in accord with the favor of his will,
   for the praise of the glory of his grace
   that he granted us in the beloved.

In Christ we have redemption by his Blood,
   the forgiveness of transgressions,
   in accord with the riches of his grace that he lavished upon us.
In all wisdom and insight, he has made known to us
   the mystery of his will in accord with his favor
   that he set forth in him as a plan for the fullness of times,
   to sum up all things in Christ, in heaven and on earth.

The word of the Lord.

RESPONSORIAL PSALM

Psalm 98:1, 2-3ab, 3cd-4, 5-6

℟. (2a) **The Lord has made known his salvation.**

Sing to the L*ord* **a new song,
for he has done wondrous deeds;
His right hand has won victory for him,
his holy arm.**

℟. **The Lord has made known his salvation.**

The L*ord* **has made his salvation known:
in the sight of the nations he has revealed his justice.
He has remembered his kindness and his faithfulness
toward the house of Israel.**

℟. **The Lord has made known his salvation.**

**All the ends of the earth have seen
the salvation by our God.
Sing joyfully to the L***ord***, all you lands;
break into song; sing praise.**

℟. **The Lord has made known his salvation.**

Sing praise to the L*ord* **with the harp,
with the harp and melodious song.
With trumpets and the sound of the horn
sing joyfully before the King, the L***ord***.**

℟. **The Lord has made known his salvation.**

ALLELUIA

John 14:6

℟. Alleluia, alleluia.

I am the way and the truth and the life, says the Lord;
no one comes to the Father except through me.

℟. Alleluia, alleluia.

GOSPEL   Years I and II

Luke 11:47-54   The blood of the prophets is required, from the blood of Abel to the blood of Zechariah.

✠ A reading from the holy Gospel according to Luke

The Lord said:
"Woe to you who build the memorials of the prophets
   whom your fathers killed.
Consequently, you bear witness and give consent
   to the deeds of your ancestors,
   for they killed them and you do the building.
Therefore, the wisdom of God said,
   'I will send to them prophets and Apostles;
   some of them they will kill and persecute'
   in order that this generation might be charged
   with the blood of all the prophets
   shed since the foundation of the world,
   from the blood of Abel to the blood of Zechariah
   who died between the altar and the temple building.
Yes, I tell you, this generation will be charged with their blood!
Woe to you, scholars of the law!
You have taken away the key of knowledge.
You yourselves did not enter and you stopped those trying to enter."
When Jesus left, the scribes and Pharisees
   began to act with hostility toward him
   and to interrogate him about many things,
   for they were plotting to catch him at something he might say.

The Gospel of the Lord.

471 FRIDAY OF THE TWENTY-EIGHTH WEEK IN ORDINARY TIME

FIRST READING   Year II

Ephesians 1:11-14   We first hoped in Christ, and you were sealed with the Holy Spirit.

A reading from the Letter of Saint Paul to the Ephesians

Brothers and sisters:
In Christ we were also chosen,
   destined in accord with the purpose of the One
     who accomplishes all things according to the intention of his will,
     so that we might exist for the praise of his glory,
     we who first hoped in Christ.
In him you also, who have heard the word of truth,
   the Gospel of your salvation, and have believed in him,
   were sealed with the promised Holy Spirit,
   which is the first installment of our inheritance
   toward redemption as God's possession, to the praise of his glory.

The word of the Lord.

RESPONSORIAL PSALM

Psalm 33:1-2, 4-5, 12-13

℟. (12) **Blessed the people the Lord has chosen to be his own.**

Exult, you just, in the LORD**;**
   praise from the upright is fitting.
Give thanks to the LORD **on the harp;**
   with the ten-stringed lyre chant his praises.

℟. **Blessed the people the Lord has chosen to be his own.**

For upright is the word of the LORD**,**
   and all his works are trustworthy.
He loves justice and right;
   of the kindness of the LORD **the earth is full.**

℟. **Blessed the people the Lord has chosen to be his own.**

Blessed the nation whose God is the LORD**,**
   the people he has chosen for his own inheritance.
From heaven the LORD **looks down;**
   he sees all mankind.

℟. **Blessed the people the Lord has chosen to be his own.**

ALLELUIA

Psalm 33:22

℟. Alleluia, alleluia.

May your kindness, Lord, be upon us;
who have put our hope in you.

℟. Alleluia, alleluia.

GOSPEL   Years I and II

Luke 12:1-7   Even the hairs of your head have all been counted.

✠ A reading from the holy Gospel according to Luke

At that time:
So many people were crowding together
   that they were trampling one another underfoot.
Jesus began to speak, first to his disciples,
   "Beware of the leaven—that is, the hypocrisy—of the Pharisees.

"There is nothing concealed that will not be revealed,
   nor secret that will not be known.
Therefore whatever you have said in the darkness
   will be heard in the light,
   and what you have whispered behind closed doors
   will be proclaimed on the housetops.
I tell you, my friends,
   do not be afraid of those who kill the body
   but after that can do no more.
I shall show you whom to fear.
Be afraid of the one who after killing
   has the power to cast into Gehenna;
   yes, I tell you, be afraid of that one.
Are not five sparrows sold for two small coins?
Yet not one of them has escaped the notice of God.
Even the hairs of your head have all been counted.
Do not be afraid.
You are worth more than many sparrows."

The Gospel of the Lord.

472 SATURDAY OF THE TWENTY-EIGHTH WEEK IN ORDINARY TIME

FIRST READING   Year II

Ephesians 1:15-23   He gave Christ as head over all things to the Church, which is his Body.

A reading from the Letter of Saint Paul to the Ephesians

Brothers and sisters:
Hearing of your faith in the Lord Jesus
   and of your love for all the holy ones,
   I do not cease giving thanks for you,
   remembering you in my prayers,
   that the God of our Lord Jesus Christ, the Father of glory,
   may give you a spirit of wisdom and revelation
   resulting in knowledge of him.
May the eyes of your hearts be enlightened,
   that you may know what is the hope that belongs to his call,
   what are the riches of glory
   in his inheritance among the holy ones,
   and what is the surpassing greatness of his power
   for us who believe,
   in accord with the exercise of his great might,
   which he worked in Christ,
   raising him from the dead
   and seating him at his right hand in the heavens,
   far above every principality, authority, power, and dominion,
   and every name that is named
   not only in this age but also in the one to come.
And he put all things beneath his feet
   and gave him as head over all things to the Church,
   which is his Body,
   the fullness of the one who fills all things in every way.

The word of the Lord.

RESPONSORIAL PSALM

Psalm 8:2-3ab, 4-5, 6-7

℟. (7) **You have given your Son rule over the works of your hands.**

O Lord, our Lord,
   how glorious is your name over all the earth!
   You have exalted your majesty above the heavens.
Out of the mouths of babes and sucklings
   you have fashioned praise because of your foes.

℟. **You have given your Son rule over the works of your hands.**

When I behold your heavens, the work of your fingers,
   the moon and the stars which you set in place—
What is man that you should be mindful of him,
   or the son of man that you should care for him?

℟. **You have given your Son rule over the works of your hands.**

You have made him little less than the angels,
   and crowned him with glory and honor.
You have given him rule over the works of your hands,
   putting all things under his feet.

℟. **You have given your Son rule over the works of your hands.**

ALLELUIA

John 15:26b, 27a

℟. **Alleluia, alleluia.**

The Spirit of truth will testify to me, says the Lord,
and you also will testify.

℟. **Alleluia, alleluia.**

GOSPEL Years I and II

Luke 12:8-12   The Holy Spirit will teach you at that moment what you should say.

✢ **A reading from the holy Gospel according to Luke**

Jesus said to his disciples:
"I tell you,
   everyone who acknowledges me before others
   the Son of Man will acknowledge before the angels of God.
But whoever denies me before others
   will be denied before the angels of God.

"Everyone who speaks a word against the Son of Man will be forgiven,
   but the one who blasphemes against the Holy Spirit
   will not be forgiven.
When they take you before synagogues and before rulers and authorities,
   do not worry about how or what your defense will be
   or about what you are to say.
For the Holy Spirit will teach you at that moment what you should say."

The Gospel of the Lord.

473 MONDAY OF THE TWENTY-NINTH WEEK IN ORDINARY TIME

FIRST READING   Year II

Ephesians 2:1-10   God brought us to life with Christ and seated us with him in the heavens.

A reading from the Letter of Saint Paul to the Ephesians

**Brothers and sisters:
You were dead in your transgressions and sins
   in which you once lived following the age of this world,
   following the ruler of the power of the air,
   the spirit that is now at work in the disobedient.
All of us once lived among them in the desires of our flesh,
   following the wishes of the flesh and the impulses,
   and we were by nature children of wrath, like the rest.
But God, who is rich in mercy,
   because of the great love he had for us,
   even when we were dead in our transgressions,
   brought us to life with Christ (by grace you have been saved),
   raised us up with him,
   and seated us with him in the heavens in Christ Jesus,
   that in the ages to come
   he might show the immeasurable riches of his grace
   in his kindness to us in Christ Jesus.
For by grace you have been saved through faith,
   and this is not from you; it is the gift of God;
   it is not from works, so no one may boast.
For we are his handiwork, created in Christ Jesus for good works
   that God has prepared in advance,
   that we should live in them.**

The word of the Lord.

RESPONSORIAL PSALM

Psalm 100:1b-2, 3, 4ab, 4c-5

℟. (3b) **The Lord made us, we belong to him.**

Sing joyfully to the LORD **all you lands;**
   serve the LORD **with gladness;**
   come before him with joyful song.

℟. **The Lord made us, we belong to him.**

Know that the LORD **is God;**
   he made us, his we are;
   his people, the flock he tends.

℟. **The Lord made us, we belong to him.**

Enter his gates with thanksgiving,
   his courts with praise.

℟. **The Lord made us, we belong to him.**

Give thanks to him; bless his name, for he is good:
   the LORD**, whose kindness endures forever,**
   and his faithfulness, to all generations.

℟. **The Lord made us, we belong to him.**

ALLELUIA

Matthew 5:3

℟. Alleluia, alleluia.

Blessed are the poor in spirit;
for theirs is the Kingdom of heaven.

℟. Alleluia, alleluia.

GOSPEL   Years I and II

Luke 12:13-21   And the things you have prepared, to whom will they belong?

✢ A reading from the holy Gospel according to Luke

Someone in the crowd said to Jesus,
   "Teacher, tell my brother to share the inheritance with me."
He replied to him,
   "Friend, who appointed me as your judge and arbitrator?"
Then he said to the crowd,
   "Take care to guard against all greed,
   for though one may be rich,
   one's life does not consist of possessions."

Then he told them a parable.
"There was a rich man whose land produced a bountiful harvest.
He asked himself, 'What shall I do,
   for I do not have space to store my harvest?'
And he said, 'This is what I shall do:
   I shall tear down my barns and build larger ones.
There I shall store all my grain and other goods
   and I shall say to myself, "Now as for you,
   you have so many good things stored up for many years,
   rest, eat, drink, be merry!"'
But God said to him,
   'You fool, this night your life will be demanded of you;
   and the things you have prepared, to whom will they belong?'
Thus will it be for the one who stores up treasure for himself
   but is not rich in what matters to God."

The Gospel of the Lord.

474 TUESDAY OF THE TWENTY-NINTH WEEK IN ORDINARY TIME

FIRST READING Year II

Ephesians 2:12-22   He is our peace; he made both one.

A reading from the Letter of Saint Paul to the Ephesians

Brothers and sisters:
You were at that time without Christ,
   alienated from the community of Israel
   and strangers to the covenants of promise,
   without hope and without God in the world.
But now in Christ Jesus you who once were far off
   have become near by the Blood of Christ.

For he is our peace, he made both one
   and broke down the dividing wall of enmity, through his Flesh,
   abolishing the law with its commandments and legal claims,
   that he might create in himself one new person in place of the two,
   thus establishing peace,
   and might reconcile both with God,
   in one Body, through the cross,
   putting that enmity to death by it.
He came and preached peace to you who were far off
   and peace to those who were near,
   for through him we both have access in one Spirit to the Father.

So then you are no longer strangers and sojourners,
   but you are fellow citizens with the holy ones
   and members of the household of God,
   built upon the foundation of the Apostles and prophets,
   with Christ Jesus himself as the capstone.
Through him the whole structure is held together
   and grows into a temple sacred in the Lord;
   in him you also are being built together
   into a dwelling place of God in the Spirit.

The word of the Lord.

RESPONSORIAL PSALM

Psalm 85:9ab-10, 11-12, 13-14

R/. (see 9) **The Lord speaks of peace to his people.**

**I will hear what God proclaims;
   the LORD—for he proclaims peace.
Near indeed is his salvation to those who fear him,
   glory dwelling in our land.**

R/. **The Lord speaks of peace to his people.**

**Kindness and truth shall meet;
   justice and peace shall kiss.
Truth shall spring out of the earth,
   and justice shall look down from heaven.**

R/. **The Lord speaks of peace to his people.**

**The LORD himself will give his benefits;
   our land shall yield its increase.
Justice shall walk before him,
   and salvation, along the way of his steps.**

R/. **The Lord speaks of peace to his people.**

ALLELUIA

Luke 21:36

℟. Alleluia, alleluia.

**Be vigilant at all times and pray
that you may have the strength to stand before the Son of Man.**

℟. Alleluia, alleluia.

GOSPEL   Years I and II

Luke 12:35-38   Blessed are those servants whom the master finds vigilant on his arrival.

✠ **A reading from the holy Gospel according to Luke**

**Jesus said to his disciples:
"Gird your loins and light your lamps
   and be like servants who await their master's return from a wedding,
   ready to open immediately when he comes and knocks.
Blessed are those servants
   whom the master finds vigilant on his arrival.
Amen, I say to you, he will gird himself,
   have them recline at table, and proceed to wait on them.
And should he come in the second or third watch
   and find them prepared in this way,
   blessed are those servants."**

The Gospel of the Lord.

475 WEDNESDAY OF THE TWENTY-NINTH WEEK IN ORDINARY TIME

FIRST READING   Year II

Ephesians 3:2-12   The mystery of Christ has now been revealed and the Gentiles are coheirs in the promise.

A reading from the Letter of Saint Paul to the Ephesians

Brothers and sisters:
You have heard of the stewardship of God's grace
   that was given to me for your benefit,
   namely, that the mystery was made known to me by revelation,
   as I have written briefly earlier.
When you read this
   you can understand my insight into the mystery of Christ,
   which was not made known to human beings in other generations
   as it has now been revealed
   to his holy Apostles and prophets by the Spirit,
   that the Gentiles are coheirs, members of the same Body,
   and copartners in the promise in Christ Jesus through the Gospel.

Of this I became a minister by the gift of God's grace
   that was granted me in accord with the exercise of his power.
To me, the very least of all the holy ones, this grace was given,
   to preach to the Gentiles the inscrutable riches of Christ,
   and to bring to light for all what is the plan of the mystery
   hidden from ages past in God who created all things,
   so that the manifold wisdom of God
   might now be made known through the Church
   to the principalities and authorities in the heavens.
This was according to the eternal purpose
   that he accomplished in Christ Jesus our Lord,
   in whom we have boldness of speech
   and confidence of access through faith in him.

The word of the Lord.

RESPONSORIAL PSALM

Isaiah 12:2-3, 4bcd, 5-6

℟. (see 3) **You will draw water joyfully from the springs of salvation.**

**God indeed is my savior;
   I am confident and unafraid.
My strength and my courage is the Lord,
   and he has been my savior.
With joy you will draw water
   at the fountain of salvation.**

℟. **You will draw water joyfully from the springs of salvation.**

**Give thanks to the Lord, acclaim his name;
   among the nations make known his deeds,
   proclaim how exalted is his name.**

℟. **You will draw water joyfully from the springs of salvation.**

**Sing praise to the Lord for his glorious achievement;
   let this be known throughout all the earth.
Shout with exultation, O city of Zion,
   for great in your midst
   is the Holy One of Israel!**

℟. **You will draw water joyfully from the springs of salvation.**

ALLELUIA

Matthew 24:42a, 44

℟. **Alleluia, alleluia.**

**Stay awake!
For you do not know on which day your Lord will come.**

℟. **Alleluia, alleluia.**

GOSPEL Years I and II

Luke 12:39-48   Much will be required of the person entrusted with much.

✠ A reading from the holy Gospel according to Luke

Jesus said to his disciples:
"Be sure of this:
  if the master of the house had known the hour
  when the thief was coming,
  he would not have let his house be broken into.
You also must be prepared,
  for at an hour you do not expect, the Son of Man will come."

Then Peter said,
  "Lord, is this parable meant for us or for everyone?"
And the Lord replied,
  "Who, then, is the faithful and prudent steward
  whom the master will put in charge of his servants
  to distribute the food allowance at the proper time?
Blessed is that servant whom his master on arrival finds doing so.
Truly, I say to you, he will put him
  in charge of all his property.
But if that servant says to himself,
  'My master is delayed in coming,'
  and begins to beat the menservants and the maidservants,
  to eat and drink and get drunk,
  then that servant's master will come
  on an unexpected day and at an unknown hour
  and will punish the servant severely
  and assign him a place with the unfaithful.
That servant who knew his master's will
  but did not make preparations nor act in accord with his will
  shall be beaten severely;
  and the servant who was ignorant of his master's will
  but acted in a way deserving of a severe beating
  shall be beaten only lightly.
Much will be required of the person entrusted with much,
  and still more will be demanded of the person entrusted with more."

The Gospel of the Lord.

476 THURSDAY OF THE TWENTY-NINTH WEEK IN ORDINARY TIME

FIRST READING   Year II

Ephesians 3:14-21   Rooted and grounded in love, you may be filled with the fullness of God.

A reading from the Letter of Saint Paul to the Ephesians

Brothers and sisters:
I kneel before the Father,
    from whom every family in heaven and on earth is named,
    that he may grant you in accord with the riches of his glory
    to be strengthened with power through his Spirit in the inner self,
    and that Christ may dwell in your hearts through faith;
    that you, rooted and grounded in love,
    may have strength to comprehend with all the holy ones
    what is the breadth and length and height and depth,
    and to know the love of Christ that surpasses knowledge,
    so that you may be filled with all the fullness of God.

Now to him who is able to accomplish far more than all we ask or imagine,
    by the power at work within us,
    to him be glory in the Church and in Christ Jesus
    to all generations, forever and ever. Amen.

The word of the Lord.

RESPONSORIAL PSALM

Psalm 33:1-2, 4-5, 11-12, 18-19

℟. (5b) The earth is full of the goodness of the Lord.

Exult, you just, in the Lord;
   praise from the upright is fitting.
Give thanks to the Lord on the harp;
   with the ten-stringed lyre chant his praises.

℟. The earth is full of the goodness of the Lord.

For upright is the word of the Lord,
   and all his works are trustworthy.
He loves justice and right;
   of the kindness of the Lord the earth is full.

℟. The earth is full of the goodness of the Lord.

But the plan of the Lord stands forever;
   the design of his heart, through all generations.
Blessed the nation whose God is the Lord,
   the people he has chosen for his own inheritance.

℟. The earth is full of the goodness of the Lord.

But see, the eyes of the Lord are upon those who fear him,
   upon those who hope for his kindness,
To deliver them from death
   and preserve them in spite of famine.

℟. The earth is full of the goodness of the Lord.

ALLELUIA

Philippians 3:8-9

℟. Alleluia, alleluia.

**I consider all things so much rubbish
that I may gain Christ and be found in him.**

℟. Alleluia, alleluia.

GOSPEL   Years I and II

Luke 12:49-53   *I have not come to establish peace but division.*

☩ **A reading from the holy Gospel according to Luke**

**Jesus said to his disciples:
"I have come to set the earth on fire,
  and how I wish it were already blazing!
There is a baptism with which I must be baptized,
  and how great is my anguish until it is accomplished!
Do you think that I have come to establish peace on the earth?
No, I tell you, but rather division.
From now on a household of five will be divided,
  three against two and two against three;
  a father will be divided against his son
  and a son against his father,
  a mother against her daughter
  and a daughter against her mother,
  a mother-in-law against her daughter-in-law
  and a daughter-in-law against her mother-in-law."**

The Gospel of the Lord.

477 FRIDAY OF THE TWENTY-NINTH WEEK IN ORDINARY TIME

FIRST READING   Year II

Ephesians 4:1-6   There is one Body, one Lord, one faith, one baptism.

A reading from the Letter of Saint Paul to the Ephesians

Brothers and sisters:
I, a prisoner for the Lord,
  urge you to live in a manner worthy of the call you have received,
  with all humility and gentleness, with patience,
  bearing with one another through love,
  striving to preserve the unity of the spirit
  through the bond of peace;
  one Body and one Spirit,
  as you were also called to the one hope of your call;
  one Lord, one faith, one baptism;
  one God and Father of all,
  who is over all and through all and in all.

The word of the Lord.

RESPONSORIAL PSALM

Psalm 24:1-2, 3-4ab, 5-6

℟. (see 6) **Lord, this is the people that longs to see your face.**

The Lord's are the earth and its fullness;
  the world and those who dwell in it.
For he founded it upon the seas
  and established it upon the rivers.

℟. **Lord, this is the people that longs to see your face.**

Who can ascend the mountain of the Lord?
  or who may stand in his holy place?
He whose hands are sinless, whose heart is clean,
  who desires not what is vain.

℟. **Lord, this is the people that longs to see your face.**

He shall receive a blessing from the LORD**,**
   a reward from God his savior.
Such is the race that seeks for him,
   that seeks the face of the God of Jacob.

℞. Lord, this is the people that longs to see your face.

ALLELUIA

See Matthew 11:25

℞. Alleluia, alleluia.

Blessed are you, Father, Lord of heaven and earth;
you have revealed to little ones the mysteries of the Kingdom.

℞. Alleluia, alleluia.

GOSPEL   Years I and II

Luke 12:54-59   You know how to interpret the appearance of the earth and sky; why do you not know how to interpret the present time?

✠ A reading from the holy Gospel according to Luke

Jesus said to the crowds,
   "When you see a cloud rising in the west
   you say immediately that it is going to rain—and so it does;
   and when you notice that the wind is blowing from the south
   you say that it is going to be hot—and so it is.
You hypocrites!
You know how to interpret the appearance of the earth and the sky;
   why do you not know how to interpret the present time?

"Why do you not judge for yourselves what is right?
If you are to go with your opponent before a magistrate,
   make an effort to settle the matter on the way;
   otherwise your opponent will turn you over to the judge,
   and the judge hand you over to the constable,
   and the constable throw you into prison.
I say to you, you will not be released
   until you have paid the last penny."

The Gospel of the Lord.

478 SATURDAY OF THE TWENTY-NINTH WEEK IN ORDINARY TIME

FIRST READING Year II

Ephesians 4:7-16   Christ is the head from whom the whole Body grows and builds itself up in love.

A reading from the Letter of Saint Paul to the Ephesians

Brothers and sisters:
Grace was given to each of us
   according to the measure of Christ's gift.
Therefore, it says:

> *He ascended on high and took prisoners captive;*
>   *he gave gifts to men.*

What does "he ascended" mean except that he also descended
   into the lower regions of the earth?
The one who descended is also the one who ascended
   far above all the heavens,
   that he might fill all things.

And he gave some as Apostles, others as prophets,
   others as evangelists, others as pastors and teachers,
   to equip the holy ones for the work of ministry,
   for building up the Body of Christ,
   until we all attain to the unity of faith
   and knowledge of the Son of God, to mature manhood
   to the extent of the full stature of Christ,
   so that we may no longer be infants,
   tossed by waves and swept along by every wind of teaching
   arising from human trickery,
   from their cunning in the interests of deceitful scheming.
Rather, living the truth in love,
   we should grow in every way into him who is the head, Christ,
   from whom the whole Body,
   joined and held together by every supporting ligament,
   with the proper functioning of each part,
   brings about the Body's growth and builds itself up in love.

The word of the Lord.

RESPONSORIAL PSALM

Psalm 122:1-2, 3-4ab, 4cd-5

℟. (1) **Let us go rejoicing to the house of the Lord.**

**I rejoiced because they said to me,
   "We will go up to the house of the L**ORD**."
And now we have set foot
   within your gates, O Jerusalem.**

℟. **Let us go rejoicing to the house of the Lord.**

**Jerusalem, built as a city
   with compact unity.
To it the tribes go up,
   the tribes of the L**ORD**.**

℟. **Let us go rejoicing to the house of the Lord.**

**According to the decree for Israel,
   to give thanks to the name of the L**ORD**.
In it are set up judgment seats,
   seats for the house of David.**

℟. **Let us go rejoicing to the house of the Lord.**

ALLELUIA

Ezekiel 33:11

℟. **Alleluia, alleluia.**

**I take no pleasure in the death of the wicked man, says the Lord,
but rather in his conversion that he may live.**

℟. **Alleluia, alleluia.**

GOSPEL   Years I and II

Luke 13:1-9   *If you do not repent, you will all perish as they did!*

✟ A reading from the holy Gospel according to Luke

Some people told Jesus about the Galileans
  whose blood Pilate had mingled with the blood of their sacrifices.
He said to them in reply,
  "Do you think that because these Galileans suffered in this way
  they were greater sinners than all other Galileans?
By no means!
But I tell you, if you do not repent,
  you will all perish as they did!
Or those eighteen people who were killed
  when the tower at Siloam fell on them—
  do you think they were more guilty
  than everyone else who lived in Jerusalem?
By no means!
But I tell you, if you do not repent,
  you will all perish as they did!"

And he told them this parable:
  "There once was a person who had a fig tree planted in his orchard,
  and when he came in search of fruit on it but found none,
  he said to the gardener,
  'For three years now I have come in search of fruit on this fig tree
  but have found none.
So cut it down.
Why should it exhaust the soil?'
He said to him in reply,
  'Sir, leave it for this year also,
  and I shall cultivate the ground around it and fertilize it;
  it may bear fruit in the future.
If not you can cut it down.'"

The Gospel of the Lord.

479 MONDAY OF THE THIRTIETH WEEK IN ORDINARY TIME

FIRST READING — Year II

Ephesians 4:32–5:8   Walk in love, just as Christ.

A reading from the Letter of Saint Paul to the Ephesians

Brothers and sisters:
Be kind to one another, compassionate,
    forgiving one another as God has forgiven you in Christ.

Be imitators of God, as beloved children, and live in love,
    as Christ loved us and handed himself over for us
    as a sacrificial offering to God for a fragrant aroma.
Immorality or any impurity or greed must not even be mentioned among you,
    as is fitting among holy ones,
      no obscenity or silly or suggestive talk, which is out of place,
      but instead, thanksgiving.
Be sure of this, that no immoral or impure or greedy person,
    that is, an idolater,
      has any inheritance in the Kingdom of Christ and of God.

Let no one deceive you with empty arguments,
    for because of these things
    the wrath of God is coming upon the disobedient.
So do not be associated with them.
For you were once darkness,
    but now you are light in the Lord.
    Live as children of light.

The word of the Lord.

RESPONSORIAL PSALM

Psalm 1:1-2, 3, 4 and 6

℟. (see Ephesians 5:1) **Behave like God as his very dear children.**

**Blessed the man who follows not
  the counsel of the wicked
Nor walks in the way of sinners,
  nor sits in the company of the insolent,
But delights in the law of the Lord
  and meditates on his law day and night.**

℟. **Behave like God as his very dear children.**

**He is like a tree
  planted near running water,
That yields its fruit in due season,
  and whose leaves never fade.
  Whatever he does, prospers.**

℟. **Behave like God as his very dear children.**

**Not so the wicked, not so;
  they are like chaff which the wind drives away.
For the Lord watches over the way of the just,
  but the way of the wicked vanishes.**

℟. **Behave like God as his very dear children.**

ALLELUIA

John 17:17b, 17a

℟. Alleluia, alleluia.

Your word, O Lord, is truth;
consecrate us in the truth.

℟. Alleluia, alleluia.

GOSPEL   Years I and II

Luke 13:10-17   *This daughter of Abraham, ought she not to have been set free on the sabbath day?*

✠ A reading from the holy Gospel according to Luke

Jesus was teaching in a synagogue on the sabbath.
And a woman was there who for eighteen years
   had been crippled by a spirit;
   she was bent over, completely incapable of standing erect.
When Jesus saw her, he called to her and said,
   "Woman, you are set free of your infirmity."
He laid his hands on her,
   and she at once stood up straight and glorified God.
But the leader of the synagogue,
   indignant that Jesus had cured on the sabbath,
   said to the crowd in reply,
   "There are six days when work should be done.
Come on those days to be cured, not on the sabbath day."
The Lord said to him in reply, "Hypocrites!
Does not each one of you on the sabbath
   untie his ox or his ass from the manger
   and lead it out for watering?
This daughter of Abraham,
   whom Satan has bound for eighteen years now,
   ought she not to have been set free on the sabbath day
   from this bondage?"
When he said this, all his adversaries were humiliated;
   and the whole crowd rejoiced at all the splendid deeds done by him.

The Gospel of the Lord.

480 TUESDAY OF THE THIRTIETH WEEK IN ORDINARY TIME

FIRST READING   Year II

Ephesians 5:21-33   This is a great mystery, but I speak in reference to Christ and the Church.

A reading from the Letter of Saint Paul to the Ephesians

Brothers and sisters:
Be subordinate to one another out of reverence for Christ.
Wives should be subordinate to their husbands as to the Lord.
For the husband is head of his wife
   just as Christ is head of the Church,
   he himself the savior of the Body.
As the Church is subordinate to Christ,
   so wives should be subordinate to their husbands in everything.
Husbands, love your wives,
   even as Christ loved the Church
   and handed himself over for her to sanctify her,
   cleansing her by the bath of water with the word,
   that he might present to himself the Church in splendor,
   without spot or wrinkle or any such thing,
   that she might be holy and without blemish.
So also husbands should love their wives as their own bodies.
He who loves his wife loves himself.
For no one hates his own flesh
   but rather nourishes and cherishes it,
   even as Christ does the Church,
   because we are members of his Body.

> *For this reason a man shall leave his father and his mother*
>   *and be joined to his wife,*
> *and the two shall become one flesh.*

This is a great mystery,
   but I speak in reference to Christ and the Church.
In any case, each one of you should love his wife as himself,
   and the wife should respect her husband.

The word of the Lord.

RESPONSORIAL PSALM

Psalm 128:1-2, 3, 4-5

℟. (1a) **Blessed are those who fear the Lord.**

Blessed are you who fear the LORD**,
   who walk in his ways!
For you shall eat the fruit of your handiwork;
   blessed shall you be, and favored.**

℟. **Blessed are those who fear the Lord.**

**Your wife shall be like a fruitful vine
   in the recesses of your home;
Your children like olive plants
   around your table.**

℟. **Blessed are those who fear the Lord.**

**Behold, thus is the man blessed
   who fears the L**ORD**.
The L**ORD **bless you from Zion:
   may you see the prosperity of Jerusalem
   all the days of your life.**

℟. **Blessed are those who fear the Lord.**

ALLELUIA

See Matthew 11:25

℟. **Alleluia, alleluia.**

**Blessed are you, Father, Lord of heaven and earth;
you have revealed to little ones the mysteries of the Kingdom.**

℟. **Alleluia, alleluia.**

GOSPEL Years I and II

Luke 13:18-21   When it was fully grown, it became a large bush.

✠ **A reading from the holy Gospel according to Luke**

**Jesus said, "What is the Kingdom of God like?
To what can I compare it?
It is like a mustard seed that a man took and planted in the garden.
When it was fully grown, it became a large bush
and *the birds of the sky dwelt in its branches.*"**

**Again he said, "To what shall I compare the Kingdom of God?
It is like yeast that a woman took
and mixed in with three measures of wheat flour
until the whole batch of dough was leavened."**

The Gospel of the Lord.

481 WEDNESDAY OF THE THIRTIETH WEEK IN ORDINARY TIME

FIRST READING   Year II

Ephesians 6:1-9   Willingly serving the Lord and not human beings.

A reading from the Letter of Saint Paul to the Ephesians

Children, obey your parents in the Lord, for this is right.
Honor your father and mother.
This is the first commandment with a promise,
   that it may go well with you
   and that you may have a long life on earth.
Fathers, do not provoke your children to anger,
   but bring them up with the training and instruction of the Lord.

Slaves, be obedient to your human masters with fear and trembling,
   in sincerity of heart, as to Christ,
   not only when being watched, as currying favor,
   but as slaves of Christ, doing the will of God from the heart,
   willingly serving the Lord and not men,
   knowing that each will be requited from the Lord
   for whatever good he does, whether he is slave or free.
Masters, act in the same way towards them, and stop bullying,
   knowing that both they and you have a Master in heaven
   and that with him there is no partiality.

The word of the Lord.

RESPONSORIAL PSALM

Psalm 145:10-11, 12-13ab, 13cd-14

℟. (13c) **The Lord is faithful in all his words.**

**Let all your works give you thanks, O LORD,
and let your faithful ones bless you.
Let them discourse of the glory of your Kingdom
and speak of your might.**

℟. **The Lord is faithful in all his words.**

**Making known to men your might
and the glorious splendor of your Kingdom.
Your Kingdom is a Kingdom for all ages,
and your dominion endures through all generations.**

℟. **The Lord is faithful in all his words.**

**The LORD is faithful in all his words
and holy in all his works.
The LORD lifts up all who are falling
and raises up all who are bowed down.**

℟. **The Lord is faithful in all his words.**

ALLELUIA

See 2 Thessalonians 2:14

℟. **Alleluia, alleluia.**

**God has called us through the Gospel
to possess the glory of our Lord Jesus Christ.**

℟. **Alleluia, alleluia.**

GOSPEL Years I and II

Luke 13:22-30   And people will come from the east and the west and will recline at the table in the Kingdom of God.

✢   A reading from the holy Gospel according to Luke

Jesus passed through towns and villages,
   teaching as he went and making his way to Jerusalem.
Someone asked him,
   "Lord, will only a few people be saved?"
He answered them,
   "Strive to enter through the narrow gate,
   for many, I tell you, will attempt to enter
   but will not be strong enough.
After the master of the house has arisen and locked the door,
   then will you stand outside knocking and saying,
   'Lord, open the door for us.'
He will say to you in reply,
   'I do not know where you are from.'
And you will say,
   'We ate and drank in your company and you taught in our streets.'
Then he will say to you,
   'I do not know where you are from.
Depart from me, all you evildoers!'
And there will be wailing and grinding of teeth
   when you see Abraham, Isaac, and Jacob
   and all the prophets in the Kingdom of God
   and you yourselves cast out.
And people will come from the east and the west
   and from the north and the south
   and will recline at table in the Kingdom of God.
For behold, some are last who will be first,
   and some are first who will be last."

The Gospel of the Lord.

482 THURSDAY OF THE THIRTIETH WEEK IN ORDINARY TIME

FIRST READING   Year II

Ephesians 6:10-20   Put on the armor of God, that you may be able, having done everything, to hold your ground.

A reading from the Letter of Saint Paul to the Ephesians

Brothers and sisters:
Draw your strength from the Lord and from his mighty power.
Put on the armor of God so that you may be able to stand firm
   against the tactics of the Devil.
For our struggle is not with flesh and blood
   but with the principalities, with the powers,
   with the world rulers of this present darkness,
   with the evil spirits in the heavens.
Therefore, put on the armor of God,
   that you may be able to resist on the evil day
   and, having done everything, to hold your ground.
So stand fast with your loins girded in truth,
   clothed with righteousness as a breastplate,
   and your feet shod in readiness for the Gospel of peace.
In all circumstances, hold faith as a shield,
   to quench all the flaming arrows of the Evil One.
And take the helmet of salvation and the sword of the Spirit,
   which is the word of God.

With all prayer and supplication,
   pray at every opportunity in the Spirit.
To that end, be watchful with all perseverance and supplication
   for all the holy ones and also for me,
   that speech may be given me to open my mouth,
   to make known with boldness the mystery of the Gospel
   for which I am an ambassador in chains,
   so that I may have the courage to speak as I must.

The word of the Lord.

RESPONSORIAL PSALM

Psalm 144:1b, 2, 9-10

℟. (1b) **Blessed be the Lord, my Rock!**

Blessed be the L<small>ORD</small>, my rock,
   who trains my hands for battle, my fingers for war.

℟. **Blessed be the Lord, my Rock!**

My mercy and my fortress,
   my stronghold, my deliverer,
My shield, in whom I trust,
   who subdues my people under me.

℟. **Blessed be the Lord, my Rock!**

O God, I will sing a new song to you;
   with a ten-stringed lyre I will chant your praise,
You who give victory to kings,
   and deliver David, your servant from the evil sword.

℟. **Blessed be the Lord, my Rock!**

ALLELUIA

See Luke 19:38; 2:14

℟. Alleluia, alleluia.

Blessed is the king who comes in the name of the Lord.
Glory to God in the highest and on earth peace to those on whom his favor rests.

℟. Alleluia, alleluia.

GOSPEL   Years I and II

Luke 13:31-35   It is impossible that a prophet should die outside of Jerusalem.

✠ A reading from the holy Gospel according to Luke

Some Pharisees came to Jesus and said,
  "Go away, leave this area because Herod wants to kill you."
He replied, "Go and tell that fox,
  'Behold, I cast out demons and I perform healings today and tomorrow,
  and on the third day I accomplish my purpose.
Yet I must continue on my way today, tomorrow, and the following day,
  for it is impossible that a prophet should die
  outside of Jerusalem.'

"Jerusalem, Jerusalem,
  you who kill the prophets and stone those sent to you,
  how many times I yearned to gather your children together
  as a hen gathers her brood under her wings,
  but you were unwilling!
Behold, your house will be abandoned.
But I tell you, you will not see me until the time comes when you say,
  Blessed is he who comes in the name of the Lord."

The Gospel of the Lord.

483 FRIDAY OF THE THIRTIETH WEEK IN ORDINARY TIME

FIRST READING   Year II

Philippians 1:1-11   The one who began a good work in you will continue to complete it until the day of Christ Jesus.

A reading from the beginning of the Letter of Saint Paul to the Philippians

Paul and Timothy, slaves of Christ Jesus,
   to all the holy ones in Christ Jesus who are in Philippi,
   with the bishops and deacons:
   grace to you and peace from God our Father and the Lord Jesus Christ.

I give thanks to my God at every remembrance of you,
   praying always with joy in my every prayer for all of you,
   because of your partnership for the Gospel
   from the first day until now.
I am confident of this,
   that the one who began a good work in you
   will continue to complete it
   until the day of Christ Jesus.
It is right that I should think this way about all of you,
   because I hold you in my heart,
   you who are all partners with me in grace,
   both in my imprisonment
   and in the defense and confirmation of the Gospel.
For God is my witness,
   how I long for all of you with the affection of Christ Jesus.
And this is my prayer:
   that your love may increase ever more and more
   in knowledge and every kind of perception,
   to discern what is of value,
   so that you may be pure and blameless for the day of Christ,
   filled with the fruit of righteousness
   that comes through Jesus Christ
   for the glory and praise of God.

The word of the Lord.

RESPONSORIAL PSALM

Psalm 111:1-2, 3-4, 5-6

℟. (2) **How great are the works of the Lord!**
  or:
℟. **Alleluia.**

**I will give thanks to the Lord with all my heart
  in the company and assembly of the just.
Great are the works of the Lord,
  exquisite in all their delights.**

℟. **How great are the works of the Lord!**
  or:
℟. **Alleluia.**

**Majesty and glory are his work,
  and his justice endures forever.
He has won renown for his wondrous deeds;
  gracious and merciful is the Lord.**

℟. **How great are the works of the Lord!**
  or:
℟. **Alleluia.**

**He has given food to those who fear him;
  he will forever be mindful of his covenant.
He has made known to his people the power of his works,
  giving them the inheritance of the nations.**

℟. **How great are the works of the Lord!**
  or:
℟. **Alleluia.**

ALLELUIA

John 10:27

℟. Alleluia, alleluia.

My sheep hear my voice, says the Lord;
I know them, and they follow me.

℟. Alleluia, alleluia.

GOSPEL   Years I and II

Luke 14:1-6   Who among you, if your son or ox falls into a cistern, would not immediately pull him out on the sabbath day?

☩ A reading from the holy Gospel according to Luke

On a sabbath Jesus went to dine
   at the home of one of the leading Pharisees,
   and the people there were observing him carefully.
In front of him there was a man suffering from dropsy.
Jesus spoke to the scholars of the law and Pharisees in reply, asking,
   "Is it lawful to cure on the sabbath or not?"
But they kept silent; so he took the man and,
   after he had healed him, dismissed him.
Then he said to them,
   "Who among you, if your son or ox falls into a cistern,
   would not immediately pull him out on the sabbath day?"
But they were unable to answer his question.

The Gospel of the Lord.

484 SATURDAY OF THE THIRTIETH WEEK IN ORDINARY TIME

FIRST READING   Year II

Philippians 1:18b-26   For to me life is Christ, and death is gain.

A reading from the Letter of Saint Paul to the Philippians

Brothers and sisters:
As long as in every way, whether in pretense or in truth,
    Christ is being proclaimed, and in that I rejoice.

Indeed I shall continue to rejoice,
    for I know that this will result in deliverance for me
    through your prayers and support from the Spirit of Jesus Christ.
My eager expectation and hope
    is that I shall not be put to shame in any way,
    but that with all boldness, now as always,
    Christ will be magnified in my body,
    whether by life or by death.
For to me life is Christ, and death is gain.
If I go on living in the flesh, that means fruitful labor for me.
And I do not know which I shall choose.
I am caught between the two.
I long to depart this life and be with Christ,
    for that is far better.
Yet that I remain in the flesh is more necessary for your benefit.
And this I know with confidence,
    that I shall remain and continue in the service of all of you
    for your progress and joy in the faith,
    so that your boasting in Christ Jesus may abound on account of me
    when I come to you again.

The word of the Lord.

RESPONSORIAL PSALM

Psalm 42:2, 3, 5cdef

℟. **My soul is thirsting for the living God.**

**As the hind longs for the running waters,
 so my soul longs for you, O God.**

℟. **My soul is thirsting for the living God.**

**Athirst is my soul for God, the living God.
 When shall I go and behold the face of God?**

℟. **My soul is thirsting for the living God.**

**I went with the throng
 and led them in procession to the house of God.
Amid loud cries of joy and thanksgiving,
 with the multitude keeping festival.**

℟. **My soul is thirsting for the living God.**

ALLELUIA

Matthew 11:29ab

℟. **Alleluia, alleluia.**

**Take my yoke upon you and learn from me,
for I am meek and humble of heart.**

℟. **Alleluia, alleluia.**

GOSPEL Years I and II

Luke 14:1, 7-11   Everyone who exalts himself will be humbled, but the one who humbles himself will be exalted.

✢ **A reading from the holy Gospel according to Luke**

On a sabbath Jesus went to dine
 at the home of one of the leading Pharisees,
 and the people there were observing him carefully.

He told a parable to those who had been invited,
 noticing how they were choosing the places of honor at the table.
"When you are invited by someone to a wedding banquet,
 do not recline at table in the place of honor.
A more distinguished guest than you may have been invited by him,
 and the host who invited both of you may approach you and say,
 'Give your place to this man,'
 and then you would proceed with embarrassment
 to take the lowest place.
Rather, when you are invited,
 go and take the lowest place
 so that when the host comes to you he may say,
 'My friend, move up to a higher position.'
Then you will enjoy the esteem of your companions at the table.
For everyone who exalts himself will be humbled,
 but the one who humbles himself will be exalted."

The Gospel of the Lord.

485 MONDAY OF THE THIRTY-FIRST WEEK IN ORDINARY TIME

FIRST READING   Year II

Philippians 2:1-4   Complete my joy by being of the same mind.

A reading from the Letter of Saint Paul to the Philippians

Brothers and sisters:
If there is any encouragement in Christ,
  any solace in love,
  any participation in the Spirit,
  any compassion and mercy,
  complete my joy by being of the same mind, with the same love,
  united in heart, thinking one thing.
Do nothing out of selfishness or out of vainglory;
  rather, humbly regard others as more important than yourselves,
  each looking out not for his own interests,
  but also everyone for those of others.

The word of the Lord.

RESPONSORIAL PSALM

Psalm 131:1bcde, 2, 3

R/. In you, O Lord, I have found my peace.

O LORD, my heart is not proud,
  nor are my eyes haughty;
I busy not myself with great things,
  nor with things too sublime for me.

R/. In you, O Lord, I have found my peace.

Nay rather, I have stilled and quieted
  my soul like a weaned child.
Like a weaned child on its mother's lap,
  so is my soul within me.

R/. In you, O Lord, I have found my peace.

O Israel, hope in the LORD,
  both now and forever.

R/. In you, O Lord, I have found my peace.

ALLELUIA

John 8:31b-32

℟. Alleluia, alleluia.

**If you remain in my word, you will truly be my disciples,
and you will know the truth, says the Lord.**

℟. Alleluia, alleluia.

GOSPEL   Years I and II

Luke 14:12-14   Do not invite your friends, but those who are poor and crippled.

✠ A reading from the holy Gospel according to Luke

**On a sabbath Jesus went to dine
   at the home of one of the leading Pharisees.
He said to the host who invited him,
   "When you hold a lunch or a dinner,
   do not invite your friends or your brothers or sisters
   or your relatives or your wealthy neighbors,
   in case they may invite you back and you have repayment.
Rather, when you hold a banquet,
   invite the poor, the crippled, the lame, the blind;
   blessed indeed will you be because of their inability to repay you.
For you will be repaid at the resurrection of the righteous."**

The Gospel of the Lord.

486 TUESDAY OF THE THIRTY-FIRST WEEK IN ORDINARY TIME

FIRST READING — Year II

Philippians 2:5-11   He emptied himself and because of this, God exalted him.

A reading from the Letter of Saint Paul to the Philippians

Brothers and sisters:
Have among yourselves the same attitude
    that is also yours in Christ Jesus,

Who, though he was in the form of God,
    did not regard equality with God
        something to be grasped.
    Rather, he emptied himself,
    taking the form of a slave,
    coming in human likeness;
    and, found human in appearance,
    he humbled himself,
    becoming obedient to death,
        even death on a cross.
Because of this, God greatly exalted him
    and bestowed on him the name
    that is above every name,
    that at the name of Jesus
    every knee should bend,
    of those in heaven and on earth and under the earth,
    and every tongue confess that
    Jesus Christ is Lord,
    to the glory of God the Father.

The word of the Lord.

RESPONSORIAL PSALM

Psalm 22:26b-27, 28-30ab, 30e, 31-32

℟. (26a) **I will praise you, Lord, in the assembly of your people.**

**I will fulfill my vows before those who fear him.
The lowly shall eat their fill;
 they who seek the Lord shall praise him:
 "May your hearts be ever merry!"**

℟. **I will praise you, Lord, in the assembly of your people.**

**All the ends of the earth
 shall remember and turn to the Lord;
All the families of the nations
 shall bow down before him.**

℟. **I will praise you, Lord, in the assembly of your people.**

**For dominion is the Lord's,
 and he rules the nations.
To him alone shall bow down
 all who sleep in the earth.**

℟. **I will praise you, Lord, in the assembly of your people.**

**To him my soul shall live;
 my descendants shall serve him.
Let the coming generation be told of the Lord
 that they may proclaim to a people yet to be born
 the justice he has shown.**

℟. **I will praise you, Lord, in the assembly of your people.**

ALLELUIA

Matthew 11:28

℟. **Alleluia, alleluia.**

**Come to me, all you who labor and are burdened,
and I will give you rest, says the Lord.**

℟. **Alleluia, alleluia.**

GOSPEL   Years I and II

Luke 14:15-24   Go out quickly into highways and hedgerows and make people come in that my home may be filled.

☩ A reading from the holy Gospel according to Luke

One of those at table with Jesus said to him,
 "Blessed is the one who will dine in the Kingdom of God."
He replied to him,
 "A man gave a great dinner to which he invited many.
When the time for the dinner came,
 he dispatched his servant to say to those invited,
 'Come, everything is now ready.'
But one by one, they all began to excuse themselves.
The first said to him,
 'I have purchased a field and must go to examine it;
 I ask you, consider me excused.'
And another said, 'I have purchased five yoke of oxen
 and am on my way to evaluate them;
 I ask you, consider me excused.'
And another said, 'I have just married a woman,
 and therefore I cannot come.'
The servant went and reported this to his master.
Then the master of the house in a rage commanded his servant,
 'Go out quickly into the streets and alleys of the town
 and bring in here the poor and the crippled, the blind and the lame.'
The servant reported, 'Sir, your orders have been carried out
 and still there is room.'
The master then ordered the servant,
 'Go out to the highways and hedgerows
 and make people come in that my home may be filled.
For, I tell you, none of those men who were invited will taste my dinner.'"

The Gospel of the Lord.

487 WEDNESDAY OF THE THIRTY-FIRST WEEK IN ORDINARY TIME

FIRST READING   Year II

Philippians 2:12-18   Work out your salvation. For God is the one who works in you both to desire and to work.

A reading from the Letter of Saint Paul to the Philippians

My beloved, obedient as you have always been,
   not only when I am present but all the more now when I am absent,
   work out your salvation with fear and trembling.
For God is the one who, for his good purpose,
   works in you both to desire and to work.
Do everything without grumbling or questioning,
   that you may be blameless and innocent,
   children of God without blemish
   in the midst of a crooked and perverse generation,
   among whom you shine like lights in the world,
   as you hold on to the word of life,
   so that my boast for the day of Christ may be
   that I did not run in vain or labor in vain.
But, even if I am poured out as a libation
   upon the sacrificial service of your faith,
   I rejoice and share my joy with all of you.
In the same way you also should rejoice and share your joy with me.

The word of the Lord.

RESPONSORIAL PSALM

Psalm 27:1, 4, 13-14

℟. (1a) **The Lord is my light and my salvation.**

**The LORD is my light and my salvation;
 whom should I fear?
The LORD is my life's refuge;
 of whom should I be afraid?**

℟. **The Lord is my light and my salvation.**

**One thing I ask of the LORD;
 this I seek:
To dwell in the house of the LORD
 all the days of my life,
That I may gaze on the loveliness of the LORD
 and contemplate his temple.**

℟. **The Lord is my light and my salvation.**

**I believe that I shall see the bounty of the LORD
 in the land of the living.
Wait for the LORD with courage;
 be stouthearted, and wait for the LORD.**

℟. **The Lord is my light and my salvation.**

ALLELUIA

1 Peter 4:14

℟. **Alleluia, alleluia.**

If you are insulted for the name of Christ, blessed are you, for the Spirit of God rests upon you.

℟. **Alleluia, alleluia.**

GOSPEL Years I and II

Luke 14:25-33 Everyone of you who does not renounce all his possessions cannot be my disciple.

✢ A reading from the holy Gospel according to Luke

Great crowds were traveling with Jesus,
 and he turned and addressed them,
  "If anyone comes to me without hating his father and mother,
  wife and children, brothers and sisters,
  and even his own life,
  he cannot be my disciple.
Whoever does not carry his own cross and come after me
  cannot be my disciple.
Which of you wishing to construct a tower
  does not first sit down and calculate the cost
  to see if there is enough for its completion?
Otherwise, after laying the foundation
  and finding himself unable to finish the work
  the onlookers should laugh at him and say,
  'This one began to build but did not have the resources to finish.'
Or what king marching into battle would not first sit down
  and decide whether with ten thousand troops
  he can successfully oppose another king
  advancing upon him with twenty thousand troops?
But if not, while he is still far away,
  he will send a delegation to ask for peace terms.
In the same way,
  everyone of you who does not renounce all his possessions
  cannot be my disciple."

The Gospel of the Lord.

488 THURSDAY OF THE THIRTY-FIRST WEEK IN ORDINARY TIME

FIRST READING   Year II

Philippians 3:3-8a   But whatever gains I had, I even consider as a loss, because of Christ.

A reading from the Letter of Saint Paul to the Philippians

Brothers and sisters:
We are the circumcision,
    we who worship through the Spirit of God,
    who boast in Christ Jesus and do not put our confidence in flesh,
    although I myself have grounds for confidence even in the flesh.

If anyone else thinks he can be confident in flesh, all the more can I.
Circumcised on the eighth day,
    of the race of Israel, of the tribe of Benjamin,
    a Hebrew of Hebrew parentage,
    in observance of the law a Pharisee,
    in zeal I persecuted the Church,
    in righteousness based on the law I was blameless.

But whatever gains I had,
    these I have come to consider a loss because of Christ.
More than that, I even consider everything as a loss
    because of the supreme good of knowing Christ Jesus my Lord.

The word of the Lord.

RESPONSORIAL PSALM

Psalm 105:2-3, 4-5, 6-7

℟. (3b) **Let hearts rejoice who search for the Lord.**
  or:
℟. **Alleluia.**

**Sing to him, sing his praise,
  proclaim all his wondrous deeds.
Glory in his holy name;
  rejoice, O hearts that seek the Lord!**

℟. **Let hearts rejoice who search for the Lord.**
  or:
℟. **Alleluia.**

**Look to the Lord in his strength;
  seek to serve him constantly.
Recall the wondrous deeds that he has wrought,
  his portents, and the judgments he has uttered.**

℟. **Let hearts rejoice who search for the Lord.**
  or:
℟. **Alleluia.**

**You descendants of Abraham, his servants,
  sons of Jacob, his chosen ones!
He, the Lord, is our God;
  throughout the earth his judgments prevail.**

℟. **Let hearts rejoice who search for the Lord.**
  or:
℟. **Alleluia.**

ALLELUIA

Matthew 11:28

℟. **Alleluia, alleluia.**

**Come to me, all you who labor and are burdened,
and I will give you rest, says the Lord.**

℟. **Alleluia, alleluia.**

GOSPEL Years I and II

Luke 15:1-10   There will be more joy in heaven over one sinner who repents.

✠ A reading from the holy Gospel according to Luke

**The tax collectors and sinners were all drawing near to listen to Jesus,
  but the Pharisees and scribes began to complain, saying,
    "This man welcomes sinners and eats with them."
So Jesus addressed this parable to them.
"What man among you having a hundred sheep and losing one of them
    would not leave the ninety-nine in the desert
    and go after the lost one until he finds it?
And when he does find it,
    he sets it on his shoulders with great joy
    and, upon his arrival home,
    he calls together his friends and neighbors and says to them,
    'Rejoice with me because I have found my lost sheep.'
I tell you, in just the same way
    there will be more joy in heaven over one sinner who repents
    than over ninety-nine righteous people
    who have no need of repentance.**

**"Or what woman having ten coins and losing one
    would not light a lamp and sweep the house,
    searching carefully until she finds it?
And when she does find it,
    she calls together her friends and neighbors
    and says to them,
    'Rejoice with me because I have found the coin that I lost.'
In just the same way, I tell you,
    there will be rejoicing among the angels of God
    over one sinner who repents."**

The Gospel of the Lord.

489 FRIDAY OF THE THIRTY-FIRST WEEK IN ORDINARY TIME

FIRST READING   Year II

Philippians 3:17—4:1   *We await a savior who will change our lowly body to conform with his glorified Body.*

A reading from the Letter of Saint Paul to the Philippians

**Join with others in being imitators of me, brothers and sisters,
    and observe those who thus conduct themselves
    according to the model you have in us.
For many, as I have often told you
    and now tell you even in tears,
    conduct themselves as enemies of the cross of Christ.
Their end is destruction.
Their God is their stomach;
    their glory is in their "shame."
Their minds are occupied with earthly things.
But our citizenship is in heaven,
    and from it we also await a savior, the Lord Jesus Christ.
He will change our lowly body
    to conform with his glorified Body
    by the power that enables him also
    to bring all things into subjection to himself.**

**Therefore, my brothers and sisters,
    whom I love and long for, my joy and crown,
    in this way stand firm in the Lord, beloved.**

The word of the Lord.

RESPONSORIAL PSALM

Psalm 122:1-2, 3-4ab, 4cd-5

℟. (1) **Let us go rejoicing to the house of the Lord.**

**I rejoiced because they said to me,
   "We will go up to the house of the L**ORD**."
And now we have set foot
   within your gates, O Jerusalem.**

℟. **Let us go rejoicing to the house of the Lord.**

**Jerusalem, built as a city
   with compact unity.
To it the tribes go up,
   the tribes of the L**ORD**.**

℟. **Let us go rejoicing to the house of the Lord.**

**According to the decree for Israel,
   to give thanks to the name of the L**ORD**.
In it are set up judgment seats,
   seats for the house of David.**

℟. **Let us go rejoicing to the house of the Lord.**

ALLELUIA

1 John 2:5

℟. **Alleluia, alleluia.**

**Whoever keeps the word of Christ,
the love of God is truly perfected in him.**

℟. **Alleluia, alleluia.**

GOSPEL   Years I and II

Luke 16:1-8   For the children of this world are more prudent in dealing with their own generation than are the children of light.

✠   A reading from the holy Gospel according to Luke

**Jesus said to his disciples, "A rich man had a steward
   who was reported to him for squandering his property.
He summoned him and said,
   'What is this I hear about you?
Prepare a full account of your stewardship,
   because you can no longer be my steward.'
The steward said to himself, 'What shall I do,
   now that my master is taking the position of steward away from me?
I am not strong enough to dig and I am ashamed to beg.
I know what I shall do so that,
   when I am removed from the stewardship,
   they may welcome me into their homes.'
He called in his master's debtors one by one.
To the first he said, 'How much do you owe my master?'
He replied, 'One hundred measures of olive oil.'
He said to him, 'Here is your promissory note.
Sit down and quickly write one for fifty.'
Then to another he said, 'And you, how much do you owe?'
He replied, 'One hundred measures of wheat.'
He said to him, 'Here is your promissory note;
   write one for eighty.'
And the master commended that dishonest steward for acting prudently.
For the children of this world
   are more prudent in dealing with their own generation
   than the children of light."**

The Gospel of the Lord.

490 SATURDAY OF THE THIRTY-FIRST WEEK IN ORDINARY TIME

FIRST READING   Year II

Philippians 4:10-19   I have the strength for everything through him who empowers me.

A reading from the Letter of Saint Paul to the Philippians

Brothers and sisters:
I rejoice greatly in the Lord
   that now at last you revived your concern for me.
You were, of course, concerned about me but lacked an opportunity.
Not that I say this because of need,
   for I have learned, in whatever situation I find myself,
   to be self-sufficient.
I know indeed how to live in humble circumstances;
   I know also how to live with abundance.
In every circumstance and in all things
   I have learned the secret of being well fed and of going hungry,
   of living in abundance and of being in need.
I have the strength for everything through him who empowers me.
Still, it was kind of you to share in my distress.

You Philippians indeed know that at the beginning of the Gospel,
   when I left Macedonia,
   not a single church shared with me
   in an account of giving and receiving, except you alone.
For even when I was at Thessalonica
   you sent me something for my needs,
   not only once but more than once.
It is not that I am eager for the gift;
   rather, I am eager for the profit that accrues to your account.
I have received full payment and I abound.
I am very well supplied because of what I received from you
   through Epaphroditus,
   "a fragrant aroma," an acceptable sacrifice, pleasing to God.
My God will fully supply whatever you need,
   in accord with his glorious riches in Christ Jesus.

The word of the Lord.

RESPONSORIAL PSALM

Psalm 112:1b-2, 5-6, 8a and 9

℟. Blessed the man who fears the Lord.
   or:
℟. Alleluia.

Blessed the man who fears the LORD,
   who greatly delights in his commands.
His posterity shall be mighty upon the earth;
   the upright generation shall be blessed.

℟. Blessed the man who fears the Lord.
   or:
℟. Alleluia.

Well for the man who is gracious and lends,
   who conducts his affairs with justice;
He shall never be moved;
   the just one shall be in everlasting remembrance.

℟. Blessed the man who fears the Lord.
   or:
℟. Alleluia.

His heart is steadfast; he shall not fear.
Lavishly he gives to the poor;
   his generosity shall endure forever;
   his horn shall be exalted in glory.

℟. Blessed the man who fears the Lord.
   or:
℟. Alleluia.

ALLELUIA

2 Corinthians 8:9

℟. Alleluia, alleluia.

**Jesus Christ became poor although he was rich,
so that by his poverty you might become rich.**

℟. Alleluia, alleluia.

GOSPEL   Years I and II

Luke 16:9-15   If, therefore, you are not trustworthy with dishonest wealth, who will trust you with true wealth?

✠ **A reading from the holy Gospel according to Luke**

**Jesus said to his disciples:
"I tell you, make friends for yourselves with dishonest wealth,
  so that when it fails, you will be welcomed into eternal dwellings.
The person who is trustworthy in very small matters
  is also trustworthy in great ones;
  and the person who is dishonest in very small matters
  is also dishonest in great ones.
If, therefore, you are not trustworthy with dishonest wealth,
  who will trust you with true wealth?
If you are not trustworthy with what belongs to another,
  who will give you what is yours?
No servant can serve two masters.
He will either hate one and love the other,
  or be devoted to one and despise the other.
You cannot serve God and mammon."**

**The Pharisees, who loved money,
  heard all these things and sneered at him.
And he said to them,
  "You justify yourselves in the sight of others,
  but God knows your hearts;
  for what is of human esteem is an abomination in the sight of God."**

The Gospel of the Lord.

491 MONDAY OF THE THIRTY-SECOND WEEK IN ORDINARY TIME

FIRST READING   Year II

Titus 1:1-9   Appoint presbyters in every town, as I directed you.

A reading from the beginning of the Letter of Saint Paul to Titus

Paul, a slave of God and Apostle of Jesus Christ
  for the sake of the faith of God's chosen ones
  and the recognition of religious truth,
  in the hope of eternal life
  that God, who does not lie, promised before time began,
  who indeed at the proper time revealed his word
  in the proclamation with which I was entrusted
  by the command of God our savior,
  to Titus, my true child in our common faith:
  grace and peace from God the Father and Christ Jesus our savior.

For this reason I left you in Crete
  so that you might set right what remains to be done
  and appoint presbyters in every town, as I directed you,
  on condition that a man be blameless,
  married only once, with believing children
  who are not accused of licentiousness or rebellious.
For a bishop as God's steward must be blameless, not arrogant,
  not irritable, not a drunkard, not aggressive,
  not greedy for sordid gain, but hospitable, a lover of goodness,
  temperate, just, holy, and self-controlled,
  holding fast to the true message as taught
  so that he will be able both to exhort with sound doctrine
  and to refute opponents.

The word of the Lord.

RESPONSORIAL PSALM

Psalm 24:1b-2, 3-4ab, 5-6

℟. (see 6) **Lord, this is the people that longs to see your face.**

**The LORD's are the earth and its fullness;
 the world and those who dwell in it.
For he founded it upon the seas
 and established it upon the rivers.**

℟. **Lord, this is the people that longs to see your face.**

**Who can ascend the mountain of the LORD?
 or who may stand in his holy place?
He whose hands are sinless, whose heart is clean,
 who desires not what is vain.**

℟. **Lord, this is the people that longs to see your face.**

**He shall receive a blessing from the LORD,
 a reward from God his savior.
Such is the race that seeks for him,
 that seeks the face of the God of Jacob.**

℟. **Lord, this is the people that longs to see your face.**

ALLELUIA

Philippians 2:15d, 16a

℟. Alleluia, alleluia.

**Shine like lights in the world,
as you hold on to the word of life.**

℟. Alleluia, alleluia.

GOSPEL   Years I and II

Luke 17:1-6   If your brother wrongs you seven times in one day, and returns to you seven times saying, "I am sorry," you should forgive him.

✠   A reading from the holy Gospel according to Luke

**Jesus said to his disciples,
   "Things that cause sin will inevitably occur,
   but woe to the one through whom they occur.
It would be better for him if a millstone were put around his neck
   and he be thrown into the sea
   than for him to cause one of these little ones to sin.
Be on your guard!
If your brother sins, rebuke him;
   and if he repents, forgive him.
And if he wrongs you seven times in one day
   and returns to you seven times saying, 'I am sorry,'
   you should forgive him."**

**And the Apostles said to the Lord, "Increase our faith."
The Lord replied, "If you have faith the size of a mustard seed,
   you would say to this mulberry tree,
   'Be uprooted and planted in the sea,' and it would obey you."**

The Gospel of the Lord.

492 TUESDAY OF THE THIRTY-SECOND WEEK IN ORDINARY TIME

FIRST READING   Year II

Titus 2:1-8, 11-14   We live devoutly in this age, as we await the blessed hope, the appearance of our savior Jesus Christ.

A reading from the Letter of Saint Paul to Titus

Beloved:
You must say what is consistent with sound doctrine,
   namely, that older men should be temperate, dignified,
   self-controlled, sound in faith, love, and endurance.
Similarly, older women should be reverent in their behavior,
   not slanderers, not addicted to drink,
   teaching what is good, so that they may train younger women
   to love their husbands and children,
   to be self-controlled, chaste, good homemakers,
   under the control of their husbands,
   so that the word of God may not be discredited.

Urge the younger men, similarly, to control themselves,
   showing yourself as a model of good deeds in every respect,
   with integrity in your teaching, dignity, and sound speech
   that cannot be criticized,
   so that the opponent will be put to shame
   without anything bad to say about us.

For the grace of God has appeared, saving all
   and training us to reject godless ways and worldly desires
   and to live temperately, justly, and devoutly in this age,
   as we await the blessed hope,
   the appearance of the glory of the great God
   and of our savior Jesus Christ,
   who gave himself for us to deliver us from all lawlessness
   and to cleanse for himself a people as his own,
   eager to do what is good.

The word of the Lord.

RESPONSORIAL PSALM

Psalm 37:3-4, 18 and 23, 27 and 29

℟. (39a) **The salvation of the just comes from the Lord.**

**Trust in the Lord and do good,
  that you may dwell in the land and be fed in security.
Take delight in the Lord,
  and he will grant you your heart's requests.**

℟. The salvation of the just comes from the Lord.

**The Lord watches over the lives of the wholehearted;
  their inheritance lasts forever.
By the Lord are the steps of a man made firm,
  and he approves his way.**

℟. The salvation of the just comes from the Lord.

**Turn from evil and do good,
  that you may abide forever;
The just shall possess the land
  and dwell in it forever.**

℟. The salvation of the just comes from the Lord.

ALLELUIA

John 14:23

℟. Alleluia, alleluia.

Whoever loves me will keep my word,
and my Father will love him,
and we will come to him.

℟. Alleluia, alleluia.

GOSPEL   Years I and II

Luke 17:7-10   We are unprofitable servants; we have done what we were obliged to do.

✠ A reading from the holy Gospel according to Luke

Jesus said to the Apostles:
"Who among you would say to your servant
   who has just come in from plowing or tending sheep in the field,
   'Come here immediately and take your place at table'?
Would he not rather say to him,
   'Prepare something for me to eat.
Put on your apron and wait on me while I eat and drink.
You may eat and drink when I am finished'?
Is he grateful to that servant because he did what was commanded?
So should it be with you.
When you have done all you have been commanded, say,
   'We are unprofitable servants;
   we have done what we were obliged to do.'"

The Gospel of the Lord.

493 WEDNESDAY OF THE THIRTY-SECOND WEEK IN ORDINARY TIME

FIRST READING   Year II

Titus 3:1-7   For we ourselves were deluded, but because of his mercy, he saved us.

A reading from the Letter of Saint Paul to Titus

Beloved:
Remind them to be under the control of magistrates and authorities,
 to be obedient, to be open to every good enterprise.
They are to slander no one, to be peaceable, considerate,
 exercising all graciousness toward everyone.
For we ourselves were once foolish, disobedient, deluded,
 slaves to various desires and pleasures,
 living in malice and envy,
 hateful ourselves and hating one another.

But when the kindness and generous love
 of God our savior appeared,
not because of any righteous deeds we had done
 but because of his mercy,
he saved us through the bath of rebirth
 and renewal by the Holy Spirit,
whom he richly poured out on us
 through Jesus Christ our savior,
so that we might be justified by his grace
 and become heirs in hope of eternal life.

The word of the Lord.

RESPONSORIAL PSALM

Psalm 23:1b-3a, 3bc-4, 5, 6

℟. (1) The Lord is my shepherd; there is nothing I shall want.

The Lord is my shepherd; I shall not want.
   In verdant pastures he gives me repose;
Beside restful waters he leads me;
   he refreshes my soul.

℟. The Lord is my shepherd; there is nothing I shall want.

He guides me in right paths
   for his name's sake.
Even though I walk in the dark valley
   I fear no evil; for you are at my side
With your rod and your staff
   that give me courage.

℟. The Lord is my shepherd; there is nothing I shall want.

You spread the table before me
   in the sight of my foes;
You anoint my head with oil;
   my cup overflows.

℟. The Lord is my shepherd; there is nothing I shall want.

Only goodness and kindness follow me
   all the days of my life;
And I shall dwell in the house of the Lord
   for years to come.

℟. The Lord is my shepherd; there is nothing I shall want.

ALLELUIA

1 Thessalonians 5:18

℟. Alleluia, alleluia.

In all circumstances, give thanks,
for this is the will of God for you in Christ Jesus.

℟. Alleluia, alleluia.

GOSPEL Years I and II

Luke 17:11-19   Has none but this foreigner returned to give thanks to God?

✝ A reading from the holy Gospel according to Luke

As Jesus continued his journey to Jerusalem,
   he traveled through Samaria and Galilee.
As he was entering a village, ten lepers met him.
They stood at a distance from him and raised their voice, saying,
   "Jesus, Master! Have pity on us!"
And when he saw them, he said,
   "Go show yourselves to the priests."
As they were going they were cleansed.
And one of them, realizing he had been healed,
   returned, glorifying God in a loud voice;
   and he fell at the feet of Jesus and thanked him.
He was a Samaritan.
Jesus said in reply,
   "Ten were cleansed, were they not?
Where are the other nine?
Has none but this foreigner returned to give thanks to God?"
Then he said to him, "Stand up and go;
   your faith has saved you."

The Gospel of the Lord.

494 THURSDAY OF THE THIRTY-SECOND WEEK IN ORDINARY TIME

FIRST READING   Year II

Philemon 7-20   Have him back, no longer as a slave but more than a slave, a brother, beloved especially to me.

A reading from the Letter of Saint Paul to Philemon

Beloved:
I have experienced much joy and encouragement from your love,
   because the hearts of the holy ones
   have been refreshed by you, brother.
Therefore, although I have the full right in Christ
   to order you to do what is proper,
   I rather urge you out of love,
   being as I am, Paul, an old man,
   and now also a prisoner for Christ Jesus.
I urge you on behalf of my child Onesimus,
   whose father I have become in my imprisonment,
   who was once useless to you but is now useful to both you and me.
I am sending him, that is, my own heart, back to you.
I should have liked to retain him for myself,
   so that he might serve me on your behalf
   in my imprisonment for the Gospel,
   but I did not want to do anything without your consent,
   so that the good you do might not be forced but voluntary.
Perhaps this is why he was away from you for a while,
   that you might have him back forever,
   no longer as a slave but more than a slave, a brother,
   beloved especially to me, but even more so to you,
   as a man and in the Lord.
So if you regard me as a partner, welcome him as you would me.
And if he has done you any injustice
   or owes you anything, charge it to me.
I, Paul, write this in my own hand: I will pay.
May I not tell you that you owe me your very self.
Yes, brother, may I profit from you in the Lord.
Refresh my heart in Christ.

The word of the Lord.

RESPONSORIAL PSALM

Psalm 146:7, 8-9a, 9bc-10

℟. (5a) **Blessed is he whose help is the God of Jacob.**
  or:
℟. **Alleluia.**

The LORD **secures justice for the oppressed,**
  gives food to the hungry.
The LORD **sets captives free.**

℟. **Blessed is he whose help is the God of Jacob.**
  or:
℟. **Alleluia.**

The LORD **gives sight to the blind.**
The LORD **raises up those who were bowed down;**
  the LORD **loves the just.**
The LORD **protects strangers.**

℟. **Blessed is he whose help is the God of Jacob.**
  or:
℟. **Alleluia.**

The fatherless and the widow he **sustains,**
  but the way of the wicked he **thwarts.**
The LORD **shall reign forever;**
  your God, O Zion, through all generations. Alleluia.

℟. **Blessed is he whose help is the God of Jacob.**
  or:
℟. **Alleluia.**

ALLELUIA

John 15:5

℟. Alleluia, alleluia.

I am the vine, you are the branches, says the Lord:
whoever remains in me and I in him will bear much fruit.

℟. Alleluia, alleluia.

GOSPEL Years I and II

Luke 17:20-25   The Kingdom of God is among you.

✠ A reading from the holy Gospel according to Luke

Asked by the Pharisees when the Kingdom of God would come,
   Jesus said in reply,
    "The coming of the Kingdom of God cannot be observed,
    and no one will announce, 'Look, here it is,' or, 'There it is.'
For behold, the Kingdom of God is among you."

Then he said to his disciples,
    "The days will come when you will long to see
    one of the days of the Son of Man, but you will not see it.
There will be those who will say to you,
    'Look, there he is,' or 'Look, here he is.'
Do not go off, do not run in pursuit.
For just as lightning flashes
    and lights up the sky from one side to the other,
    so will the Son of Man be in his day.
But first he must suffer greatly and be rejected by this generation."

The Gospel of the Lord.

495 FRIDAY OF THE THIRTY-SECOND WEEK IN ORDINARY TIME

FIRST READING   Year II

2 John 4-9   Whoever remains in the teaching has the Father and the Son.

A reading from the second Letter of Saint John

[Chosen Lady:]
I rejoiced greatly to find some of your children walking in the truth
   just as we were commanded by the Father.
But now, Lady, I ask you,
   not as though I were writing a new commandment
   but the one we have had from the beginning:
   let us love one another.
For this is love, that we walk according to his commandments;
   this is the commandment, as you heard from the beginning,
   in which you should walk.

Many deceivers have gone out into the world,
   those who do not acknowledge Jesus Christ as coming in the flesh;
   such is the deceitful one and the antichrist.
Look to yourselves that you do not lose what we worked for
   but may receive a full recompense.
Anyone who is so "progressive"
   as not to remain in the teaching of the Christ does not have God;
   whoever remains in the teaching has the Father and the Son.

The word of the Lord.

RESPONSORIAL PSALM

Psalm 119:1, 2, 10, 11, 17, 18

℟. (1b) **Blessed are they who follow the law of the Lord!**

**Blessed are they whose way is blameless,
  who walk in the law of the LORD.**

℟. **Blessed are they who follow the law of the Lord!**

**Blessed are they who observe his decrees,
  who seek him with all their heart.**

℟. **Blessed are they who follow the law of the Lord!**

**With all my heart I seek you;
  let me not stray from your commands.**

℟. **Blessed are they who follow the law of the Lord!**

**Within my heart I treasure your promise,
  that I may not sin against you.**

℟. **Blessed are they who follow the law of the Lord!**

**Be good to your servant, that I may live
  and keep your words.**

℟. **Blessed are they who follow the law of the Lord!**

**Open my eyes, that I may consider
  the wonders of your law.**

℟. **Blessed are they who follow the law of the Lord!**

ALLELUIA

Luke 21:28

℟. **Alleluia, alleluia.**

**Stand erect and raise your heads
because your redemption is at hand.**

℟. **Alleluia, alleluia.**

GOSPEL   Years I and II

Luke 17:26-37   So it will be on the day the Son of Man is revealed.

✠ A reading from the holy Gospel according to Luke

Jesus said to his disciples:
"As it was in the days of Noah,
   so it will be in the days of the Son of Man;
   they were eating and drinking,
   marrying and giving in marriage up to the day
   that Noah entered the ark,
   and the flood came and destroyed them all.
Similarly, as it was in the days of Lot:
   they were eating, drinking, buying,
   selling, planting, building;
   on the day when Lot left Sodom,
   fire and brimstone rained from the sky to destroy them all.
So it will be on the day the Son of Man is revealed.
On that day, someone who is on the housetop
   and whose belongings are in the house
   must not go down to get them,
   and likewise one in the field
   must not return to what was left behind.
Remember the wife of Lot.
Whoever seeks to preserve his life will lose it,
   but whoever loses it will save it.
I tell you, on that night there will be two people in one bed;
   one will be taken, the other left.
And there will be two women grinding meal together;
   one will be taken, the other left."
They said to him in reply, "Where, Lord?"
He said to them, "Where the body is,
   there also the vultures will gather."

The Gospel of the Lord.

496 SATURDAY OF THE THIRTY-SECOND WEEK IN ORDINARY TIME

FIRST READING   Year II

3 John 5-8   We ought to support such persons, so that we may be co-workers in the truth.

A reading from the third Letter of Saint John

**Beloved, you are faithful in all you do for the brothers and sisters,
   especially for strangers;
   they have testified to your love before the Church.
Please help them in a way worthy of God to continue their journey.
For they have set out for the sake of the Name
   and are accepting nothing from the pagans.
Therefore, we ought to support such persons,
   so that we may be co-workers in the truth.**

The word of the Lord.

RESPONSORIAL PSALM

Psalm 112:1-2, 3-4, 5-6

℟. **Blessed the man who fears the Lord.**
   or:
℟. **Alleluia.**

**Blessed the man who fears the LORD,
   who greatly delights in his commands.
His posterity shall be mighty upon the earth;
   the upright generation shall be blessed.**

℟. **Blessed the man who fears the Lord.**
   or:
℟. **Alleluia.**

**Wealth and riches shall be in his house;
   his generosity shall endure forever.
Light shines through the darkness for the upright;
   he is gracious and merciful and just.**

℟. **Blessed the man who fears the Lord.**
   or:
℟. **Alleluia.**

Well for the man who is gracious and lends,
    who conducts his affairs with justice;
He shall never be moved;
    the just one shall be in everlasting remembrance.

℟. **Blessed the man who fears the Lord.**
    or:
℟. **Alleluia.**

ALLELUIA

See 2 Thessalonians 2:14

℟. **Alleluia, alleluia.**

**God has called us through the Gospel,
to possess the glory of our Lord Jesus Christ.**

℟. **Alleluia, alleluia.**

GOSPEL   Years I and II

Luke 18:1-8   Will not God then secure the rights of his chosen ones who call out to him day and night?

✢ **A reading from the holy Gospel according to Luke**

**Jesus told his disciples a parable
    about the necessity for them to pray always without becoming weary.
He said, "There was a judge in a certain town
    who neither feared God nor respected any human being.
And a widow in that town used to come to him and say,
    'Render a just decision for me against my adversary.'
For a long time the judge was unwilling, but eventually he thought,
    'While it is true that I neither fear God nor respect any human being,
    because this widow keeps bothering me
    I shall deliver a just decision for her
    lest she finally come and strike me.'"
The Lord said, "Pay attention to what the dishonest judge says.
Will not God then secure the rights of his chosen ones
    who call out to him day and night?
Will he be slow to answer them?
I tell you, he will see to it that justice is done for them speedily.
But when the Son of Man comes, will he find faith on earth?"**

The Gospel of the Lord.

497 MONDAY OF THE THIRTY-THIRD WEEK IN ORDINARY TIME

FIRST READING   Year II

Revelation 1:1-4; 2:1-5   Realize how far you have fallen and repent.

A reading from the beginning of the Book of Revelation

The revelation of Jesus Christ, which God gave to him,
  to show his servants what must happen soon.
He made it known by sending his angel to his servant John,
    who gives witness to the word of God
    and to the testimony of Jesus Christ by reporting what he saw.
Blessed is the one who reads aloud
    and blessed are those who listen to this prophetic message
    and heed what is written in it, for the appointed time is near.

John, to the seven churches in Asia: grace to you and peace
    from him who is and who was and who is to come,
    and from the seven spirits before his throne.

I heard the Lord saying to me:
"To the angel of the Church in Ephesus, write this:

"'The one who holds the seven stars in his right hand
    and walks in the midst of the seven gold lampstands says this:
    "I know your works, your labor, and your endurance,
  and that you cannot tolerate the wicked;
you have tested those who call themselves Apostles but are not,
    and discovered that they are impostors.
Moreover, you have endurance and have suffered for my name,
    and you have not grown weary.
Yet I hold this against you:
    you have lost the love you had at first.
Realize how far you have fallen.
Repent, and do the works you did at first.
Otherwise, I will come to you
    and remove your lampstand from its place, unless you repent."'"

The word of the Lord.

RESPONSORIAL PSALM

Psalm 1:1-2, 3, 4 and 6

℟. (Revelation 2:17) **Those who are victorious I will feed from the tree of life.**

**Blessed the man who follows not
   the counsel of the wicked
Nor walks in the way of sinners,
   nor sits in the company of the insolent,
But delights in the law of the Lord
   and meditates on his law day and night.**

℟. **Those who are victorious I will feed from the tree of life.**

**He is like a tree
   planted near running water,
That yields its fruit in due season,
   and whose leaves never fade.
   Whatever he does, prospers.**

℟. **Those who are victorious I will feed from the tree of life.**

**Not so the wicked, not so;
   they are like chaff which the wind drives away.
For the Lord watches over the way of the just,
   but the way of the wicked vanishes.**

℟. **Those who are victorious I will feed from the tree of life.**

ALLELUIA

John 8:12

℟. Alleluia, alleluia.

I am the light of the world, says the Lord;
whoever follows me will have the light of life.

℟. Alleluia, alleluia.

GOSPEL   Years I and II

Luke 18:35-43   What do you want me to do for you? Lord, please let me see.

✢ A reading from the holy Gospel according to Luke

**As Jesus approached Jericho
a blind man was sitting by the roadside begging,
and hearing a crowd going by, he inquired what was happening.
They told him,
"Jesus of Nazareth is passing by."
He shouted, "Jesus, Son of David, have pity on me!"
The people walking in front rebuked him,
telling him to be silent,
but he kept calling out all the more,
"Son of David, have pity on me!"
Then Jesus stopped and ordered that he be brought to him;
and when he came near, Jesus asked him,
"What do you want me to do for you?"
He replied, "Lord, please let me see."
Jesus told him, "Have sight; your faith has saved you."
He immediately received his sight
and followed him, giving glory to God.
When they saw this, all the people gave praise to God.**

The Gospel of the Lord.

498 TUESDAY OF THE THIRTY-THIRD WEEK IN ORDINARY TIME

FIRST READING   Year II

Revelation 3:1-6, 14-22   If anyone hears my voice and opens the door, I will enter his house and dine with him.

A reading from the Book of Revelation

I, John, heard the Lord saying to me:
"To the angel of the Church in Sardis, write this:

"'The one who has the seven spirits of God
   and the seven stars says this: "I know your works,
   that you have the reputation of being alive, but you are dead.
Be watchful and strengthen what is left, which is going to die,
   for I have not found your works complete in the sight of my God.
Remember then how you accepted and heard; keep it, and repent.
If you are not watchful, I will come like a thief,
   and you will never know at what hour I will come upon you.
However, you have a few people in Sardis
   who have not soiled their garments;
   they will walk with me dressed in white,
   because they are worthy.

"'The victor will thus be dressed in white,
   and I will never erase his name from the book of life
   but will acknowledge his name in the presence of my Father
   and of his angels.

"'Whoever has ears ought to hear what the Spirit says to the churches.'"

"To the angel of the Church in Laodicea, write this:

"'The Amen, the faithful and true witness,
   the source of God's creation, says this:
   "I know your works;
   I know that you are neither cold nor hot.
I wish you were either cold or hot.
So, because you are lukewarm, neither hot nor cold,
   I will spit you out of my mouth.

For you say, 'I am rich and affluent and have no need of anything,'
   and yet do not realize that you are wretched,
     pitiable, poor, blind, and naked.
I advise you to buy from me gold refined by fire so that you may be rich,
   and white garments to put on
     so that your shameful nakedness may not be exposed,
   and buy ointment to smear on your eyes so that you may see.
Those whom I love, I reprove and chastise.
Be earnest, therefore, and repent.

"'Behold, I stand at the door and knock.
If anyone hears my voice and opens the door,
   then I will enter his house and dine with him,
   and he with me.
I will give the victor the right to sit with me on my throne,
   as I myself first won the victory
   and sit with my Father on his throne.

"'Whoever has ears ought to hear
   what the Spirit says to the churches.'"

The word of the Lord.

RESPONSORIAL PSALM

Psalm 15:2-3a, 3bc-4ab, 5

℟. (Revelation 3:21) **I will seat the victor beside me on my throne.**

**He who walks blamelessly and does justice;
 who thinks the truth in his heart
 and slanders not with his tongue.**

℟. **I will seat the victor beside me on my throne.**

**Who harms not his fellow man,
 nor takes up a reproach against his neighbor;
By whom the reprobate is despised,
 while he honors those who fear the LORD.**

℟. **I will seat the victor beside me on my throne.**

**Who lends not his money at usury
 and accepts no bribe against the innocent.
He who does these things
 shall never be disturbed.**

℟. **I will seat the victor beside me on my throne.**

ALLELUIA

1 John 4:10b

℟. **Alleluia, alleluia.**

**God loved us, and sent his Son
as expiation for our sins.**

℟. **Alleluia, alleluia.**

GOSPEL Years I and II

Luke 19:1-10   *The Son of Man has come to seek and to save what was lost.*

☩ **A reading from the holy Gospel according to Luke**

**At that time Jesus came to Jericho and intended to pass through the town.
Now a man there named Zacchaeus,**
   who was a chief tax collector and also a wealthy man,
   was seeking to see who Jesus was;
   but he could not see him because of the crowd,
   for he was short in stature.
So he ran ahead and climbed a sycamore tree in order to see Jesus,
   who was about to pass that way.
When he reached the place, Jesus looked up and said,
   "Zacchaeus, come down quickly,
   for today I must stay at your house."
**And he came down quickly and received him with joy.
When they saw this, they began to grumble, saying,**
   "He has gone to stay at the house of a sinner."
But Zacchaeus stood there and said to the Lord,
   "Behold, half of my possessions, Lord, I shall give to the poor,
   and if I have extorted anything from anyone
   I shall repay it four times over."
And Jesus said to him,
   "Today salvation has come to this house
   because this man too is a descendant of Abraham.
For the Son of Man has come to seek
   and to save what was lost."

The Gospel of the Lord.

499 WEDNESDAY OF THE THIRTY-THIRD WEEK IN ORDINARY TIME

FIRST READING   Year I

Revelation 4:1-11   Holy is the Lord God almighty, who was, and who is, and who is to come.

A reading from the Book of Revelation

I, John, had a vision of an open door to heaven,
  and I heard the trumpetlike voice
  that had spoken to me before, saying,
  "Come up here and I will show you what must happen afterwards."
At once I was caught up in spirit.
A throne was there in heaven, and on the throne sat one
  whose appearance sparkled like jasper and carnelian.
Around the throne was a halo as brilliant as an emerald.
Surrounding the throne I saw twenty-four other thrones
  on which twenty-four elders sat,
  dressed in white garments and with gold crowns on their heads.
From the throne came flashes of lightning,
  rumblings, and peals of thunder.
Seven flaming torches burned in front of the throne,
  which are the seven spirits of God.
In front of the throne was something that resembled
  a sea of glass like crystal.

In the center and around the throne,
  there were four living creatures
  covered with eyes in front and in back.
The first creature resembled a lion, the second was like a calf,
  the third had a face like that of a man,
  and the fourth looked like an eagle in flight.
The four living creatures, each of them with six wings,
  were covered with eyes inside and out.
Day and night they do not stop exclaiming:
    "Holy, holy, holy is the Lord God almighty,
      who was, and who is, and who is to come."

Whenever the living creatures give glory and honor and thanks
　to the one who sits on the throne, who lives forever and ever,
　the twenty-four elders fall down
　before the one who sits on the throne
　and worship him, who lives forever and ever.
They throw down their crowns before the throne, exclaiming:

　"Worthy are you, Lord our God,
　　to receive glory and honor and power,
　for you created all things;
　　because of your will they came to be and were created."

The word of the Lord.

RESPONSORIAL PSALM

Psalm 150:1b-2, 3-4, 5-6

℟. (1b) Holy, holy, holy Lord, mighty God!

Praise the LḴḴ in his sanctuary,
　praise him in the firmament of his strength.
Praise him for his mighty deeds,
　praise him for his sovereign majesty.

℟. Holy, holy, holy Lord, mighty God!

Praise him with the blast of the trumpet,
　praise him with lyre and harp,
Praise him with timbrel and dance,
　praise him with strings and pipe.

℟. Holy, holy, holy Lord, mighty God!

Praise him with sounding cymbals,
　praise him with clanging cymbals.
Let everything that has breath
　praise the Lord! Alleluia.

℟. Holy, holy, holy Lord, mighty God!

ALLELUIA

See John 15:16

℟. Alleluia, alleluia.

I chose you from the world,
to go and bear fruit that will last, says the Lord.

℟. Alleluia, alleluia.

GOSPEL   Years I and II

Luke 19:11-28   Why did you not put my money in a bank?

✢ A reading from the holy Gospel according to Luke

While a people were listening to Jesus speak,
  he proceeded to tell a parable because he was near Jerusalem
  and they thought that the Kingdom of God
  would appear there immediately.
So he said,
  "A nobleman went off to a distant country
  to obtain the kingship for himself and then to return.
He called ten of his servants and gave them ten gold coins
  and told them, 'Engage in trade with these until I return.'
His fellow citizens, however, despised him
  and sent a delegation after him to announce,
  'We do not want this man to be our king.'
But when he returned after obtaining the kingship,
  he had the servants called, to whom he had given the money,
  to learn what they had gained by trading.
The first came forward and said,
  'Sir, your gold coin has earned ten additional ones.'
He replied, 'Well done, good servant!
You have been faithful in this very small matter;
  take charge of ten cities.'
Then the second came and reported,
  'Your gold coin, sir, has earned five more.'
And to this servant too he said,
  'You, take charge of five cities.'

Then the other servant came and said,
> 'Sir, here is your gold coin;
> I kept it stored away in a handkerchief,
> for I was afraid of you, because you are a demanding man;
> you take up what you did not lay down
> and you harvest what you did not plant.'

He said to him,
> 'With your own words I shall condemn you,
> you wicked servant.

You knew I was a demanding man,
> taking up what I did not lay down
> and harvesting what I did not plant;
> why did you not put my money in a bank?

Then on my return I would have collected it with interest.'
And to those standing by he said,
> 'Take the gold coin from him
> and give it to the servant who has ten.'

But they said to him,
> 'Sir, he has ten gold coins.'

He replied, 'I tell you,
> to everyone who has, more will be given,
> but from the one who has not,
> even what he has will be taken away.

Now as for those enemies of mine who did not want me as their king,
> bring them here and slay them before me.'"

After he had said this,
> he proceeded on his journey up to Jerusalem.

The Gospel of the Lord.

500 THURSDAY OF THE THIRTY-THIRD WEEK IN ORDINARY TIME

FIRST READING   Year I

Revelation 5:1-10   The Lamb that was slain purchased us with his Blood from every nation.

A reading from the Book of Revelation

I, John, saw a scroll in the right hand of the one who sat on the throne.
It had writing on both sides and was sealed with seven seals.
Then I saw a mighty angel who proclaimed in a loud voice,
    "Who is worthy to open the scroll and break its seals?"
But no one in heaven or on earth or under the earth
    was able to open the scroll or to examine it.
I shed many tears because no one was found worthy
    to open the scroll or to examine it.
One of the elders said to me, "Do not weep.
The lion of the tribe of Judah, the root of David, has triumphed,
    enabling him to open the scroll with its seven seals."

Then I saw standing in the midst of the throne
    and the four living creatures and the elders
    a Lamb that seemed to have been slain.
He had seven horns and seven eyes;
    these are the seven spirits of God sent out into the whole world.
He came and received the scroll from the right hand
    of the one who sat on the throne.
When he took it,
    the four living creatures and the twenty-four elders
    fell down before the Lamb.
Each of the elders held a harp and gold bowls filled with incense,
    which are the prayers of the holy ones.
They sang a new hymn:

    "Worthy are you to receive the scroll
        and break open its seals,
            for you were slain and with your Blood you purchased for God
            those from every tribe and tongue, people and nation.
        You made them a kingdom and priests for our God,
            and they will reign on earth."

The word of the Lord.

RESPONSORIAL PSALM

Psalm 149:1b-2, 3-4, 5-6a and 9b

℟. (Revelation 5:10) **The Lamb has made us a kingdom of priests to serve our God.**
   or:
℟. **Alleluia.**

Sing to the LORD **a new song**
   of praise in the assembly of the faithful.
Let Israel be glad in their maker,
   let the children of Zion rejoice in their king.

℟. **The Lamb has made us a kingdom of priests to serve our God.**
   or:
℟. **Alleluia.**

Let them praise his name in the festive dance,
   let them sing praise to him with timbrel and harp.
For the LORD **loves his people,**
   and he adorns the lowly with victory.

℟. **The Lamb has made us a kingdom of priests to serve our God.**
   or:
℟. **Alleluia.**

Let the faithful exult in glory;
   let them sing for joy upon their couches;
Let the high praises of God be in their throats.
   This is the glory of all his faithful. Alleluia.

℟. **The Lamb has made us a kingdom of priests to serve our God.**
   or:
℟. **Alleluia.**

ALLELUIA

Psalm 95:8

℟. Alleluia, alleluia.

If today you hear his voice,
harden not your hearts.

℟. Alleluia, alleluia.

GOSPEL   Years I and II

Luke 19:41-44   If you only knew what makes for peace.

☩ A reading from the holy Gospel according to Luke

**As Jesus drew near Jerusalem,
   he saw the city and wept over it, saying,
   "If this day you only knew what makes for peace—
   but now it is hidden from your eyes.
For the days are coming upon you
   when your enemies will raise a palisade against you;
   they will encircle you and hem you in on all sides.
They will smash you to the ground and your children within you,
   and they will not leave one stone upon another within you
   because you did not recognize the time of your visitation."**

The Gospel of the Lord.

501 FRIDAY OF THE THIRTY-THIRD WEEK IN ORDINARY TIME

FIRST READING   Year II

Revelation 10:8-11   I took the small scroll and swallowed it.

A reading from the Book of Revelation

I, John, heard a voice from heaven speak to me.
Then the voice spoke to me and said:
　"Go, take the scroll that lies open in the hand of the angel
　who is standing on the sea and on the land."
So I went up to the angel and told him to give me the small scroll.
He said to me, "Take and swallow it.
It will turn your stomach sour,
　but in your mouth it will taste as sweet as honey."
I took the small scroll from the angel's hand and swallowed it.
In my mouth it was like sweet honey,
　but when I had eaten it, my stomach turned sour.
Then someone said to me, "You must prophesy again
　about many peoples, nations, tongues, and kings."

The word of the Lord.

RESPONSORIAL PSALM

Psalm 119:14, 24, 72, 103, 111, 131

℟. (103a) How sweet to my taste is your promise!

In the way of your decrees I rejoice,
　as much as in all riches.

℟. How sweet to my taste is your promise!

Yes, your decrees are my delight;
　they are my counselors.

℟. How sweet to my taste is your promise!

The law of your mouth is to me more precious
　than thousands of gold and silver pieces.

℟. How sweet to my taste is your promise!

How sweet to my palate are your promises,
   sweeter than honey to my mouth!

℟. **How sweet to my taste is your promise!**

Your decrees are my inheritance forever;
   the joy of my heart they are.

℟. **How sweet to my taste is your promise!**

I gasp with open mouth
   in my yearning for your commands.

℟. **How sweet to my taste is your promise!**

ALLELUIA

John 10:27

℟. **Alleluia, alleluia.**

My sheep hear my voice, says the Lord;
I know them, and they follow me.

℟. **Alleluia, alleluia.**

GOSPEL   Years I and II

Luke 19:45-48   You have made it a den of thieves.

✠ **A reading from the holy Gospel according to Luke**

Jesus entered the temple area and proceeded to drive out
   those who were selling things, saying to them,
   "It is written, *My house shall be a house of prayer,*
   *but you have made it a den of thieves.***"**
And every day he was teaching in the temple area.
The chief priests, the scribes, and the leaders of the people, meanwhile,
   were seeking to put him to death,
      but they could find no way to accomplish their purpose
      because all the people were hanging on his words.

The Gospel of the Lord.

502 SATURDAY OF THE THIRTY-THIRD WEEK IN ORDINARY TIME

FIRST READING   Year II

Revelation 11:4-12   These two prophets tormented the inhabitants of the earth.

A reading from the Book of Revelation

I, John, heard a voice from heaven speak to me:
Here are my two witnesses:
> These are the two olive trees and the two lampstands
> that stand before the Lord of the earth.

If anyone wants to harm them, fire comes out of their mouths
> and devours their enemies.

In this way, anyone wanting to harm them is sure to be slain.
They have the power to close up the sky
> so that no rain can fall during the time of their prophesying.

They also have power to turn water into blood
> and to afflict the earth with any plague as often as they wish.

When they have finished their testimony,
> the beast that comes up from the abyss
> will wage war against them and conquer them and kill them.

Their corpses will lie in the main street of the great city,
> which has the symbolic names "Sodom" and "Egypt,"
> where indeed their Lord was crucified.

Those from every people, tribe, tongue, and nation
> will gaze on their corpses for three and a half days,
> and they will not allow their corpses to be buried.

The inhabitants of the earth will gloat over them
> and be glad and exchange gifts
> because these two prophets tormented the inhabitants of the earth.

But after the three and a half days,
> a breath of life from God entered them.

When they stood on their feet, great fear fell on those who saw them.
Then they heard a loud voice from heaven say to them, "Come up here."
So they went up to heaven in a cloud as their enemies looked on.

The word of the Lord.

RESPONSORIAL PSALM

Psalm 144:1, 2, 9-10

℟. (1b) **Blessed be the Lord, my Rock!**

Blessed be the LORD**, my rock,
    who trains my hands for battle, my fingers for war.**

℟. **Blessed be the Lord, my Rock!**

**My mercy and my fortress,
    my stronghold, my deliverer,
My shield, in whom I trust,
    who subdues my people under me.**

℟. **Blessed be the Lord, my Rock!**

**O God, I will sing a new song to you;
    with a ten-stringed lyre I will chant your praise,
You who give victory to kings,
    and deliver David, your servant from the evil sword.**

℟. **Blessed be the Lord, my Rock!**

ALLELUIA

See 2 Timothy 1:10

℟. **Alleluia, alleluia.**

**Our Savior Jesus Christ has destroyed death
and brought life to light through the Gospel.**

℟. **Alleluia, alleluia.**

GOSPEL Years I and II

Luke 20:27-40   He is not God of the dead, but of the living.

✠ A reading from the holy Gospel according to Luke

Some Sadducees, those who deny that there is a resurrection,
   came forward and put this question to Jesus, saying,
   "Teacher, Moses wrote for us,
   If someone's brother dies leaving a wife but no child,
   his brother must take the wife
   and raise up descendants for his brother.
Now there were seven brothers;
   the first married a woman but died childless.
Then the second and the third married her,
   and likewise all the seven died childless.
Finally the woman also died.
Now at the resurrection whose wife will that woman be?
For all seven had been married to her."
Jesus said to them,
   "The children of this age marry and remarry;
   but those who are deemed worthy to attain to the coming age
   and to the resurrection of the dead
   neither marry nor are given in marriage.
They can no longer die,
   for they are like angels;
   and they are the children of God
   because they are the ones who will rise.
That the dead will rise
   even Moses made known in the passage about the bush,
   when he called 'Lord'
   the God of Abraham, the God of Isaac, and the God of Jacob;
   and he is not God of the dead, but of the living,
   for to him all are alive."
Some of the scribes said in reply,
   "Teacher, you have answered well."
And they no longer dared to ask him anything.

The Gospel of the Lord.

503 MONDAY OF THE THIRTY-FOURTH OR LAST WEEK IN ORDINARY TIME

FIRST READING   Year II

Revelation 14:1-3, 4b-5   His name and his Father's name are written on their foreheads.

A reading from the Book of Revelation

I, John, looked and there was the Lamb standing on Mount Zion,
  and with him a hundred and forty-four thousand
    who had his name and his Father's name written on their foreheads.
I heard a sound from heaven
  like the sound of rushing water or a loud peal of thunder.
The sound I heard was like that of harpists playing their harps.
They were singing what seemed to be a new hymn before the throne,
  before the four living creatures and the elders.
No one could learn this hymn except the hundred and forty-four thousand
  who had been ransomed from the earth.
These are the ones who follow the Lamb wherever he goes.
They have been ransomed as the first fruits
  of the human race for God and the Lamb.
On their lips no deceit has been found; they are unblemished.

The word of the Lord.

RESPONSORIAL PSALM

Psalm 24:1bc-2, 3-4ab, 5-6

℟. (see 6) **Lord, this is the people that longs to see your face.**

The Lord's are the earth and its fullness;
  the world and those who dwell in it.
For he founded it upon the seas
  and established it upon the rivers.

℟. **Lord, this is the people that longs to see your face.**

Who can ascend the mountain of the LORD?
   or who may stand in his holy place?
He whose hands are sinless, whose heart is clean,
   who desires not what is vain.

℟. **Lord, this is the people that longs to see your face.**

He shall receive a blessing from the LORD,
   a reward from God his savior.
Such is the race that seeks for him,
   that seeks the face of the God of Jacob.

℟. **Lord, this is the people that longs to see your face.**

ALLELUIA

Matthew 24:42a, 44

℟. **Alleluia, alleluia.**

Stay awake!
For you do not know when the Son of Man will come.

℟. **Alleluia, alleluia.**

GOSPEL   Years I and II

Luke 21:1-4   He noticed a poor widow putting in two small coins.

☩ **A reading from the holy Gospel according to Luke**

When Jesus looked up he saw some wealthy people
   putting their offerings into the treasury
   and he noticed a poor widow putting in two small coins.
He said, "I tell you truly,
   this poor widow put in more than all the rest;
   for those others have all made offerings from their surplus wealth,
   but she, from her poverty, has offered her whole livelihood."

The Gospel of the Lord.

504 TUESDAY OF THE THIRTY-FOURTH OR LAST WEEK IN ORDINARY TIME

FIRST READING   Year II

Revelation 14:14-19   The time to reap has come, because the earth's harvest is fully ripe.

A reading from the Book of Revelation

I, John, looked and there was a white cloud,
   and sitting on the cloud one who looked like a son of man,
   with a gold crown on his head and a sharp sickle in his hand.
Another angel came out of the temple,
   crying out in a loud voice to the one sitting on the cloud,
   "Use your sickle and reap the harvest,
   for the time to reap has come,
   because the earth's harvest is fully ripe."
So the one who was sitting on the cloud swung his sickle over the earth,
   and the earth was harvested.

Then another angel came out of the temple in heaven
   who also had a sharp sickle.
Then another angel came from the altar, who was in charge of the fire,
   and cried out in a loud voice
   to the one who had the sharp sickle,
   "Use your sharp sickle and cut the clusters from the earth's vines,
   for its grapes are ripe."
So the angel swung his sickle over the earth and cut the earth's vintage.
He threw it into the great wine press of God's fury.

The word of the Lord.

RESPONSORIAL PSALM

Psalm 96:10, 11-12, 13

℟. (13b) **The Lord comes to judge the earth.**

**Say among the nations: The Lord is king.
He has made the world firm, not to be moved;
 he governs the peoples with equity.**

℟. **The Lord comes to judge the earth.**

**Let the heavens be glad and the earth rejoice;
 let the sea and what fills it resound;
 let the plains be joyful and all that is in them!
Then shall all the trees of the forest exult.**

℟. **The Lord comes to judge the earth.**

**Before the Lord, for he comes;
 for he comes to rule the earth.
He shall rule the world with justice
 and the peoples with his constancy.**

℟. **The Lord comes to judge the earth.**

ALLELUIA

Revelation 2:10c

℟. **Alleluia, alleluia.**

**Remain faithful until death,
and I will give you the crown of life.**

℟. **Alleluia, alleluia.**

GOSPEL Years I and II

Luke 21:5-11   There will not be left a stone upon another stone.

☩ A reading from the holy Gospel according to Luke

While some people were speaking about
how the temple was adorned with costly stones and votive offerings,
Jesus said, "All that you see here—
the days will come when there will not be left
a stone upon another stone that will not be thrown down."

Then they asked him,
"Teacher, when will this happen?
And what sign will there be when all these things are about to happen?"
He answered,
"See that you not be deceived,
for many will come in my name, saying,
'I am he,' and 'The time has come.'
Do not follow them!
When you hear of wars and insurrections,
do not be terrified; for such things must happen first,
but it will not immediately be the end."
Then he said to them,
"Nation will rise against nation, and kingdom against kingdom.
There will be powerful earthquakes, famines, and plagues
from place to place;
and awesome sights and mighty signs will come from the sky."

The Gospel of the Lord.

505 WEDNESDAY OF THE THIRTY-FOURTH OR LAST WEEK IN ORDINARY TIME

FIRST READING   Year II

Revelation 15:1-4   They sang the song of Moses and the song of the Lamb.

A reading from the Book of Revelation

I, John, saw in heaven another sign, great and awe-inspiring:
 seven angels with the seven last plagues,
 for through them God's fury is accomplished.

Then I saw something like a sea of glass mingled with fire.
On the sea of glass were standing those
 who had won the victory over the beast
 and its image and the number that signified its name.
They were holding God's harps,
 and they sang the song of Moses, the servant of God,
 and the song of the Lamb:

> "Great and wonderful are your works,
> Lord God almighty.
> Just and true are your ways,
> O king of the nations.
> Who will not fear you, Lord,
> or glorify your name?
> For you alone are holy.
> All the nations will come
> and worship before you,
> for your righteous acts have been revealed."

The word of the Lord.

RESPONSORIAL PSALM

Psalm 98:1, 2-3ab, 7-8, 9

℟. (Revelation 15:3b) **Great and wonderful are all your works, Lord, mighty God!**

Sing to the LORD **a new song,**
  for he has done wondrous deeds;
His right hand has won victory for him,
  his holy arm.

℟. **Great and wonderful are all your works, Lord, mighty God!**

The LORD **has made his salvation known:**
  in the sight of the nations he has revealed his justice.
He has remembered his kindness and his faithfulness
  toward the house of Israel.

℟. **Great and wonderful are all your works, Lord, mighty God!**

Let the sea and what fills it resound,
  the world and those who dwell in it;
Let the rivers clap their hands,
  the mountains shout with them for joy.

℟. **Great and wonderful are all your works, Lord, mighty God!**

Before the LORD**, for he comes,**
  for he comes to rule the earth;
He will rule the world with justice
  and the peoples with equity.

℟. **Great and wonderful are all your works, Lord, mighty God!**

ALLELUIA

Revelation 2:10c

℟. Alleluia, alleluia.

**Remain faithful until death,
and I will give you the crown of life.**

℟. Alleluia, alleluia.

GOSPEL Years I and II

Luke 21:12-19   You will be hated by all because of my name, but not a hair on your head will be destroyed.

✠ **A reading from the holy Gospel according to Luke**

**Jesus said to the crowd:
"They will seize and persecute you,
  they will hand you over to the synagogues and to prisons,
  and they will have you led before kings and governors
  because of my name.
It will lead to your giving testimony.
Remember, you are not to prepare your defense beforehand,
  for I myself shall give you a wisdom in speaking
  that all your adversaries will be powerless to resist or refute.
You will even be handed over by parents,
  brothers, relatives, and friends,
  and they will put some of you to death.
You will be hated by all because of my name,
  but not a hair on your head will be destroyed.
By your perseverance you will secure your lives."**

The Gospel of the Lord.

506 THURSDAY OF THE THIRTY-FOURTH OR LAST WEEK IN ORDINARY TIME

FIRST READING   Year II

Revelation 18:1-2, 21-23; 19:1-3, 9a   Fallen is Babylon the great.

A reading from the Book of Revelation

**I, John, saw another angel coming down from heaven,
  having great authority,
  and the earth became illumined by his splendor.
He cried out in a mighty voice:**

  **"Fallen, fallen is Babylon the great.
    She has become a haunt for demons.
  She is a cage for every unclean spirit,
    a cage for every unclean bird,
    a cage for every unclean and disgusting beast."**

**A mighty angel picked up a stone like a huge millstone
  and threw it into the sea and said:**

  **"With such force will Babylon the great city be thrown down,
    and will never be found again.
  No melodies of harpists and musicians,
    flutists and trumpeters,
    will ever be heard in you again.
  No craftsmen in any trade
    will ever be found in you again.
  No sound of the millstone
    will ever be heard in you again.
  No light from a lamp
    will ever be seen in you again.
  No voices of bride and groom
    will ever be heard in you again.
  Because your merchants were the great ones of the world,
    all nations were led astray by your magic potion."**

**After this I heard what sounded like
the loud voice of a great multitude in heaven, saying:**

"Alleluia!
**Salvation, glory, and might belong to our God,
for true and just are his judgments.
He has condemned the great harlot
who corrupted the earth with her harlotry.
He has avenged on her the blood of his servants."**

They said a second time:

"Alleluia! Smoke will rise from her forever and ever."

**Then the angel said to me, "Write this:
Blessed are those who have been called
to the wedding feast of the Lamb."**

The word of the Lord.

RESPONSORIAL PSALM

Psalm 100:1b-2, 3, 4, 5

℟. (Revelation 19:9a) **Blessed are they who are called to the wedding feast of the Lamb.**

Sing joyfully to the Lord, all you lands;
serve the Lord with gladness;
come before him with joyful song.

℟. **Blessed are they who are called to the wedding feast of the Lamb.**

Know that the Lord is God;
he made us, his we are;
his people, the flock he tends.

℟. **Blessed are they who are called to the wedding feast of the Lamb.**

Enter his gates with thanksgiving,
his courts with praise;
Give thanks to him; bless his name.

℟. **Blessed are they who are called to the wedding feast of the Lamb.**

For he is good:
the Lord, whose kindness endures forever,
and his faithfulness, to all generations.

℟. **Blessed are they who are called to the wedding feast of the Lamb.**

ALLELUIA

Luke 21:28

℟. **Alleluia, alleluia.**

Stand erect and raise your heads
because your redemption is at hand.

℟. **Alleluia, alleluia.**

GOSPEL Years I and II

Luke 21:20-28   Jerusalem will be trampled underfoot by the Gentiles until the times of the Gentiles are fulfilled.

✠ **A reading from the holy Gospel according to Luke**

**Jesus said to his disciples:
"When you see Jerusalem surrounded by armies,
   know that its desolation is at hand.
Then those in Judea must flee to the mountains.
Let those within the city escape from it,
   and let those in the countryside not enter the city,
   for these days are the time of punishment
   when all the Scriptures are fulfilled.
Woe to pregnant women and nursing mothers in those days,
   for a terrible calamity will come upon the earth
   and a wrathful judgment upon this people.
They will fall by the edge of the sword
   and be taken as captives to all the Gentiles;
   and Jerusalem will be trampled underfoot by the Gentiles
   until the times of the Gentiles are fulfilled.**

"There will be signs in the sun, the moon, and the stars,
   and on earth nations will be in dismay,
   perplexed by the roaring of the sea and the waves.
People will die of fright
   in anticipation of what is coming upon the world,
   for the powers of the heavens will be shaken.
And then they will see the Son of Man
   coming in a cloud with power and great glory.
But when these signs begin to happen,
   stand erect and raise your heads
   because your redemption is at hand."

The Gospel of the Lord.

507 FRIDAY OF THE THIRTY-FOURTH OR LAST WEEK IN ORDINARY TIME

FIRST READING   Year II

Revelation 20:1-4, 11–21:2   The dead were judged according to their deeds. I saw a new Jerusalem, coming down out of heaven from God.

A reading from the Book of Revelation

I, John, saw an angel come down from heaven,
>holding in his hand the key to the abyss and a heavy chain.

He seized the dragon, the ancient serpent,
>which is the Devil or Satan,
>and tied it up for a thousand years and threw it into the abyss,
>which he locked over it and sealed,
>so that it could no longer lead the nations astray
>until the thousand years are completed.

After this, it is to be released for a short time.

Then I saw thrones; those who sat on them were entrusted with judgment.
I also saw the souls of those who had been beheaded
>for their witness to Jesus and for the word of God,
>and who had not worshiped the beast or its image
>nor had accepted its mark on their foreheads or hands.

They came to life and they reigned with Christ for a thousand years.

Next I saw a large white throne and the one who was sitting on it.
The earth and the sky fled from his presence
>and there was no place for them.

I saw the dead, the great and the lowly, standing before the throne,
>and scrolls were opened.

Then another scroll was opened, the book of life.
The dead were judged according to their deeds,
>by what was written in the scrolls.

The sea gave up its dead;
>then Death and Hades gave up their dead.

All the dead were judged according to their deeds.
Then Death and Hades were thrown into the pool of fire.
(This pool of fire is the second death.)
Anyone whose name was not found written in the book of life
>was thrown into the pool of fire.

Then I saw a new heaven and a new earth.
The former heaven and the former earth had passed away,
   and the sea was no more.
I also saw the holy city, a new Jerusalem,
   coming down out of heaven from God,
     prepared as a bride adorned for her husband.

The word of the Lord.

RESPONSORIAL PSALM

Psalm 84:3, 4, 5-6a and 8a

℟. (Revelation 21:3b) **Here God lives among his people.**

My soul yearns and pines
   for the courts of the Lord.
My heart and my flesh
   cry out for the living God.

℟. **Here God lives among his people.**

Even the sparrow finds a home,
   and the swallow a nest
   in which she puts her young—
Your altars, O Lord of hosts,
   my king and my God!

℟. **Here God lives among his people.**

Blessed they who dwell in your house!
   continually they praise you.
Blessed the men whose strength you are!
   They go from strength to strength.

℟. **Here God lives among his people.**

ALLELUIA

Luke 21:28

℟. Alleluia, alleluia.

Stand erect and raise your heads
because your redemption is at hand.

℟. Alleluia, alleluia.

GOSPEL   Years I and II

Luke 21:29-33   When you see these things happening, know that the Kingdom of God is near.

✠ A reading from the holy Gospel according to Luke

Jesus told his disciples a parable.
"Consider the fig tree and all the other trees.
When their buds burst open,
　you see for yourselves and know that summer is now near;
　in the same way, when you see these things happening,
　know that the Kingdom of God is near.
Amen, I say to you, this generation will not pass away
　until all these things have taken place.
Heaven and earth will pass away,
　but my words will not pass away."

The Gospel of the Lord.

508 SATURDAY OF THE THIRTY-FOURTH OR LAST WEEK IN ORDINARY TIME

FIRST READING   Year II

Revelation 22:1-7   Night will be no more, for the Lord God shall give them light.

A reading from the Book of Revelation

John said:
An angel showed me the river of life-giving water,
   sparkling like crystal, flowing from the throne of God
   and of the Lamb down the middle of the street,
On either side of the river grew the tree of life
   that produces fruit twelve times a year, once each month;
   the leaves of the trees serve as medicine for the nations.
Nothing accursed will be found anymore.
The throne of God and of the Lamb will be in it,
   and his servants will worship him.
They will look upon his face, and his name will be on their foreheads.
Night will be no more, nor will they need light from lamp or sun,
   for the Lord God shall give them light,
   and they shall reign forever and ever.

And he said to me, "These words are trustworthy and true,
   and the Lord, the God of prophetic spirits,
   sent his angel to show his servants what must happen soon."
"Behold, I am coming soon."
Blessed is the one who keeps the prophetic message of this book.

The word of the Lord.

RESPONSORIAL PSALM

Psalm 95:1-2, 3-5, 6-7ab

℟. (1 Corinthians 16:22b; see Revelation 22:20c) **Marana tha! Come, Lord Jesus!**

Come, let us sing joyfully to the LORD;
  let us acclaim the Rock of our salvation.
Let us come into his presence with thanksgiving;
  let us joyfully sing psalms to him.

℟. Marana tha! Come, Lord Jesus!

For the LORD is a great God,
  and a great king above all gods;
In his hands are the depths of the earth,
  and the tops of the mountains are his.
His is the sea, for he has made it,
  and the dry land, which his hands have formed.

℟. Marana tha! Come, Lord Jesus!

Come, let us bow down in worship;
  let us kneel before the LORD who made us.
For he is our God,
  and we are the people he shepherds, the flock he guides.

℟. Marana tha! Come, Lord Jesus!

ALLELUIA

Luke 21:36

℟. Alleluia, alleluia.

**Be vigilant at all times and pray
that you may have the strength to stand before the Son of Man.**

℟. Alleluia, alleluia.

GOSPEL   Years I and II

Luke 21:34-36   Be vigilant that you may have the strength to escape the tribulations that are imminent.

✠ **A reading from the holy Gospel according to Luke**

**Jesus said to his disciples:
"Beware that your hearts do not become drowsy
   from carousing and drunkenness
   and the anxieties of daily life,
   and that day catch you by surprise like a trap.
For that day will assault everyone
   who lives on the face of the earth.
Be vigilant at all times
   and pray that you have the strength
   to escape the tribulations that are imminent
   and to stand before the Son of Man."**

The Gospel of the Lord.

ALLELUIA VERSES
FOR WEEKDAYS IN ORDINARY TIME

509 ALLELUIA VERSES FOR WEEKDAYS IN ORDINARY TIME

These texts may be used in place of the texts proposed for each day.

1.

1 Samuel 3:9; John 6:68c

**Speak, O Lord, your servant is listening;
you have the words of everlasting life.**

2.

See Psalm 19:9

**Your words, O Lord, give joy to my heart,
your teaching is light to my eyes.**

3.

Psalm 25:4b, 5a

**Teach me your paths, my God,
and guide me in your truth.**

4.

See Psalm 27:11

**Teach me your way, O Lord,
and lead me on a straight road.**

5.

Psalm 95:8

**If today you hear his voice,
harden not your hearts.**

6.

Psalm 111:7b-8a

**Your laws are all made firm, O Lord,
established for evermore.**

7.

Psalm 119:18

**Unveil my eyes, O Lord,
and I will see the marvels of your law.**

8.

Psalm 119:27

**Instruct me in the way of your rules,
and I will reflect on all your wonders.**

9.

Psalm 119:34

**Teach me the meaning of your law, O Lord,
and I will guard it with all my heart.**

10.

Psalm 119:36a, 29b

**Incline my heart, O God, to your decrees;
and favor me with your law.**

11.

Psalm 119:88

**In your mercy, give me life, O Lord,
and I will do your commands.**

12.

Psalm 119:105

**A lamp for my feet is your word,
and a light to my path.**

13.

Psalm 119:135

**Let your countenance shine upon your servant,
and teach me your statutes.**

14.

See Psalm 130:5

**I hope in the Lord,
my soul trusts in his word.**

15.

Psalm 145:13cd

**The Lord is faithful in all his words
and holy in all his deeds.**

16.

Psalm 147:12a, 15a

Praise the LORD, Jerusalem;
God's word speeds forth to the earth.

17.

Matthew 4:4b

One does not live on bread alone,
but on every word that comes forth from the mouth of God.

18.

See Matthew 11:25

Blessed are you, Father, Lord of heaven and earth;
you have revealed to little ones the mysteries of the Kingdom.

19.

See Luke 8:15

Blessed are they who have kept the word with a generous heart
and yield a harvest through perseverance.

20.

See John 6:63c, 68c

Your words, Lord, are Spirit and life;
you have the words of everlasting life.

21.

John 8:12

I am the light of the world, says the Lord;
whoever follows me will have the light of life.

22.

John 10:27

My sheep hear my voice, says the Lord;
I know them, and they follow me.

23.

John 14:6

I am the way and the truth and the life, says the Lord;
no one comes to the Father except through me.

24.

John 14:23

**Whoever loves me will keep my word,
and my Father will love him,
and we will come to him.**

25.

John 15:15b

**I call you my friends, says the Lord,
for I have made known to you all that the Father has told me.**

26.

See John 17:17b, 17a

**Your word, O Lord, is truth;
consecrate us in the truth.**

27.

See Acts 16:14b

**Open our hearts, O Lord,
to listen to the words of your Son.**

28.

2 Corinthians 5:19

**God was reconciling the world to himself in Christ
and entrusting to us the message of reconciliation.**

29.

See Ephesians 1:17-18

**May the Father of our Lord Jesus Christ
enlighten the eyes of our hearts,
that we may know what is the hope
that belongs to our call.**

30.

Philippians 2:15d, 16a

**Shine like lights in the world,
as you hold on to the word of life.**

31.

See Colossians 3:16a, 17c

**Let the word of Christ dwell in you richly;
giving thanks to God the Father through him.**

32.

See 1 Thessalonians 2:13

**Receive the word of God, not as the word of men,
but as it truly is, the word of God.**

33.

See 2 Thessalonians 2:14

**God has called us through the Gospel,
to share in the glory of our Lord Jesus Christ.**

34.

See 2 Timothy 1:10

**Our Savior Jesus Christ has destroyed death
and brought life to light through the Gospel.**

35.

Hebrews 4:12

**The word of God is living and effective,
able to discern reflections and thoughts of the heart.**

36.

James 1:18

**The Father willed to give us birth by the word of truth,
that we may be a kind of firstfruits of his creatures.**

37.

James 1:21bc

**Humbly welcome the word that has been planted in you
and is able to save your souls.**

38.

1 Peter 1:25

**The word of the Lord remains forever;
this is the word that has been proclaimed to you.**

39.

1 John 2:5

**Whoever keeps the word of Christ
the love of God is truly perfected in him.**

Last Week in Ordinary Time:

1.

Matthew 24:42a, 44

**Stay awake!
For you do not know when the Son of Man will come.**

2.

Luke 21:28

**Stand erect and raise your heads
because your redemption is at hand.**

3.

Luke 21:36

**Be vigilant at all times and pray
that you have may have the strength to stand before the Son of Man.**

4.

Revelation 2:10c

**Remain faithful until death,
and I will give you the crown of life.**

[163]

The following texts for Sundays in Ordinary Time may also be used in place of the texts proposed for each weekday.

1.

1 Samuel 3:9; John 6:68c

**Speak, O Lord, your servant is listening;
you have the words of everlasting life.**

2.

See Matthew 11:25

**Blessed are you, Father, Lord of heaven and earth;
you have revealed to little ones the mysteries of the Kingdom.**

3.

See Luke 19:38; 2:14

**Blessed is the king who comes in the name of the Lord.
Glory to God in the highest and on earth peace to those on whom his favor rests.**

4.

John 1:14a, 12

**The Word of God became flesh and dwelt among us.
To those who accepted him
he gave power to become children of God.**

5.

See John 6:63c, 68c

**Your words, Lord, are Spirit and life;
you have the words of everlasting life.**

6.

John 8:12

**I am the light of the world, says the Lord;
whoever follows me will have the light of life.**

7.

John 10:27

**My sheep hear my voice, says the Lord;
I know them, and they follow me.**

8.

John 14:6

**I am the way and the truth and the life, says the Lord;
no one comes to the Father, except through me.**

9.

John 14:23

**Whoever loves me will keep my word,
and my Father will love him,
and we will come to him.**

10.

John 15:15b

**I call you my friends, says the Lord,
for I have made known to you all that the Father has told me.**

11.

See John 17:17b, 17a

**Your word, O Lord, is truth;
consecrate us in the truth.**

12.

See Acts 16:14b

**Open our hearts, O Lord,
to listen to the words of your Son.**

13.

See Ephesians 1:17-18

**May the Father of our Lord Jesus Christ
enlighten the eyes of our hearts,
that we may know what is the hope
that belongs to our call.**

Last Week in Ordinary Time:

14.

Matthew 24:42a, 44

**Stay awake!
For you do not know when the Son of Man will come.**

15.

Luke 21:36

**Be vigilant at all times and pray
that you may have the strength to stand before the Son of Man.**

16.

Revelation 2:10c

**Remain faithful until death,
and I will give you the crown of life.**

COMMON TEXTS
FOR SUNG RESPONSORIAL PSALMS

COMMON TEXTS FOR SUNG RESPONSORIAL PSALMS

The psalm as a rule is drawn from the Lectionary because the individual psalm texts are directly connected with the individual readings: the choice of psalm depends therefore on the readings.

Nevertheless, in order that the people may be able to join in the responsorial psalm more readily, some texts of responses and psalms have been chosen, according to the different seasons of the year and classes of saints, for optional use, whenever the psalm is sung, in place of the text corresponding to the reading (General Instruction of the Roman Missal, no. 36).

[173] RESPONSES

Season of Advent:
>   **Come, O Lord, and set us free.**

Season of Christmas:
>   **Lord, today we have seen your glory.**

Season of Lent:
>   **Remember, O Lord, your faithfulness and love.**

Season of Easter:
>   **Alleluia** (two or three times)

Ordinary Time:

a) Psalm of praise:
>   **Praise the Lord for he is good.**
>   or:
>   **We praise you, O Lord, for all your works are wonderful.**
>   or:
>   **Sing to the Lord a new song.**

b) Psalm of petition:
>   **The Lord is near to all who call on him.**
>   or:
>   **Hear us, Lord, and save us.**
>   or:
>   **The Lord is kind and merciful.**

[174] PSALMS

Season of Advent:

1.

Psalm 25:4-5ab, 8-9, 10 and 14

℟. (1) **To you, O Lord, I lift my soul.**

**Your ways, O Lord, make known to me;
  teach me your paths,
Guide me in your truth and teach me,
  for you are God my savior.**

℟. **To you, O Lord, I lift my soul.**

**Good and upright is the Lord;
  thus he shows sinners the way.
He guides the humble to justice,
  he teaches the humble his way.**

℟. **To you, O Lord, I lift my soul.**

**All the paths of the Lord are kindness and constancy
  toward those who keep his covenant and his decrees.
The friendship of the Lord is with those who fear him,
  and his covenant, for their instruction.**

℟. **To you, O Lord, I lift my soul.**

2.

Psalm 85:9ab and 10, 11-12, 13-14

℟. (8a) **Lord, show us your mercy and love.**

**I will hear what God proclaims;
  the Lord—for he proclaims peace.
Near indeed is his salvation to those who fear him,
  glory dwelling in our land.**

℟. **Lord, show us your mercy and love.**

**Kindness and truth shall meet;
  justice and peace shall kiss.
Truth shall spring out of the earth,
  and justice shall look down from heaven.**

℟. **Lord, show us your mercy and love.**

The LORD himself will give his benefits;
   our land shall yield its increase.
Justice shall walk before him,
   and salvation, along the way of his steps.

℟. **Lord, show us your mercy and love.**

Season of Christmas:

3.

Psalm 98:1, 2-3ab, 3cd-4, 5-6

℟. (3cd) **All the ends of the earth have seen the saving power of God.**

Sing to the LORD a new song,
   for he has done wondrous deeds;
His right hand has won victory for him,
   his holy arm.

℟. **All the ends of the earth have seen the saving power of God.**

The LORD has made his salvation known:
   in the sight of the nations he has revealed his justice.
He has remembered his kindness and his faithfulness
   toward the house of Israel.

℟. **All the ends of the earth have seen the saving power of God.**

All the ends of the earth have seen
   the salvation by our God.
Sing joyfully to the LORD, all you lands;
   break into song; sing praise.

℟. **All the ends of the earth have seen the saving power of God.**

Sing praise to the LORD with the harp,
   with the harp and melodious song.
With trumpets and the sound of the horn
   sing joyfully before the King, the LORD.

℟. **All the ends of the earth have seen the saving power of God.**

1114   *Common Texts for Sung Responsorial Psalms II*

Epiphany:

4.

Psalm 72:2, 7-8, 10-11, 12-13

℟. (see 11) **Lord, every nation on earth will adore you.**

**O God, with your judgment endow the king,
   and with your justice the king's son;
He shall govern your people with justice
   and your afflicted ones with judgment.**

℟. **Lord, every nation on earth will adore you.**

**Justice shall flower in his days,
   and profound peace, till the moon be no more.
May he rule from sea to sea,
   and from the River to the ends of the earth.**

℟. **Lord, every nation on earth will adore you.**

**The kings of Tarshish and the Isles shall offer gifts;
   the kings of Arabia and Seba shall bring tribute.
All kings shall pay him homage,
   all nations shall serve him.**

℟. **Lord, every nation on earth will adore you.**

**For he shall rescue the poor when he cries out,
   and the afflicted when he has no one to help him.
He shall have pity for the lowly and the poor;
   the lives of the poor he shall save.**

℟. **Lord, every nation on earth will adore you.**

Season of Lent:

5.

Psalm 51:3-4, 5-6ab, 12-13, 14 and 17

℟. (see 3a) **Be merciful, O Lord, for we have sinned.**

**Have mercy on me, O God, in your goodness;
   in the greatness of your compassion wipe out my offense.
Thoroughly wash me from my guilt
   and of my sin cleanse me.**

℟. **Be merciful, O Lord, for we have sinned.**

For I acknowledge my offense,
   and my sin is before me always:
"Against you only have I sinned,
   and done what is evil in your sight."

℟. Be merciful, O Lord, for we have sinned.

A clean heart create for me, O God,
   and a steadfast spirit renew within me.
Cast me not out from your presence,
   and your Holy Spirit take not from me.

℟. Be merciful, O Lord, for we have sinned.

Give me back the joy of your salvation,
   and a willing spirit sustain in me.
O Lord, open my lips,
   and my mouth shall proclaim your praise.

℟. Be merciful, O Lord, for we have sinned.

6.

Psalm 91:1-2, 10-11, 12-13, 14-15

℟. (see 15b) Be with me, Lord, when I am in trouble.

You who dwell in the shelter of the Most High,
   who abide in the shadow of the Almighty,
Say to the Lord, "My refuge and my fortress,
   my God, in whom I trust."

℟. Be with me, Lord, when I am in trouble.

No evil shall befall you,
   nor affliction come near your tent,
For God commands the angels
   to guard you in all your ways.

℟. Be with me, Lord, when I am in trouble.

Upon their hands they shall bear you up,
   lest you dash your foot against the stone.
You shall tread upon the asp and the viper;
   you shall trample down the lion and dragon.

℟. Be with me, Lord, when I am in trouble.

Because he clings to me, I will deliver him;
> I will set him on high because he acknowledges my name.

He shall call upon me, and I will answer him;
> I will be with him in distress;

I will deliver him and glorify him.

℟. Be with me, Lord, when I am in trouble.

7.

Psalm 130:1-2, 3-4, 5-6, 7-8

℟. (7bc) With the Lord there is mercy, and fullness of redemption.

Out of the depths I cry to you, O LORD;
> LORD, hear my voice!

Let your ears be attentive
> to my voice in supplication.

℟. With the Lord there is mercy, and fullness of redemption.

If you, O LORD, mark our iniquities,
> LORD, who can stand?

But with you is forgiveness,
> and so you may be revered.

℟. With the Lord there is mercy, and fullness of redemption.

I trust in the LORD;
> my soul trusts in his word.

My soul waits for the LORD,
> more than sentinels wait for the dawn,

Let Israel wait for the LORD.

℟. With the Lord there is mercy, and fullness of redemption.

For with the LORD is kindness,
> and with him there is plenteous redemption;

And he will redeem Israel
> from all their iniquities.

℟. With the Lord there is mercy, and fullness of redemption.

Holy Week:

8.

Psalm 22:8-9, 17-18a, 19-20, 23-24

℟. (2a) **My God, my God, why have you abandoned me?**

All who see me scoff at me;
   they mock me with parted lips, they wag their heads:
"He relied on the LORD**; let him deliver him,**
   let him rescue him, if he loves him."

℟. **My God, my God, why have you abandoned me?**

Many dogs surround me,
   a pack of evildoers closes in upon me;
They have pierced my hands and my feet;
   I can count all of my bones.

℟. **My God, my God, why have you abandoned me?**

They divide my garments among them;
   and for my vesture they cast lots.
But you, O LORD**, be not far from me;**
   O my help, hasten to aid me.

℟. **My God, my God, why have you abandoned me?**

I will proclaim your name to my brothers and sisters;
   in the midst of the assembly I will praise you:
"You who fear the LORD**, praise him;**
   all you descendants of Jacob, give glory to him;
   revere him, all you descendants of Israel."

℟. **My God, my God, why have you abandoned me?**

Easter Vigil:

9a.

Psalm 136:1-3, 4-6, 7-9, 24-26

℟. **God's love is everlasting.**

Give thanks to the L{ORD}**, for he is good,**
   his mercy endures forever;
Give thanks to the God of gods,
   his mercy endures forever;
Give thanks to the Lord of lords,
   his mercy endures forever.

℟. **God's love is everlasting.**

Who alone does great wonders,
   his mercy endures forever;
Who made the heavens in wisdom,
   his mercy endures forever;
Who spread out the earth upon the waters,
   his mercy endures forever.

℟. **God's love is everlasting.**

Who made the great lights,
   his mercy endures forever;
The sun to rule over the day,
   his mercy endures forever;
The moon and the stars to rule over the night,
   his mercy endures forever.

℟. **God's love is everlasting.**

Who freed us from our foes,
   his mercy endures forever;
Who gives food to all flesh,
   his mercy endures forever;
Give thanks to the God of heaven,
   his mercy endures forever.

℟. **God's love is everlasting.**

9b.

Psalm 136:1 and 3 and 16, 21-23, 24-26

℟. **God's love is everlasting.**

**Give thanks to the Lord, for he is good,
    his mercy endures forever;
Give thanks to the Lord of lords,
    his mercy endures forever;
Who led his people through the wilderness,
    his mercy endures forever.**

℟. **God's love is everlasting.**

**Who made their land a heritage,
    his mercy endures forever;
The heritage of Israel, his servant,
    his mercy endures forever;
Who remembered us in our abjection,
    his mercy endures forever.**

℟. **God's love is everlasting.**

**Who freed us from our foes,
    his mercy endures forever;
Who gives food to all flesh,
    his mercy endures forever;
Give thanks to the God of heaven,
    his mercy endures forever.**

℟. **God's love is everlasting.**

Season of Easter:

10.

Psalm 118:1bc-2 and 4, 16-17, 22-23

℟. (24) **This is the day the Lord has made; let us rejoice and be glad!**

Give thanks to the Lord, for he is good,
   for his mercy endures forever.
Let the house of Israel say,
   "His mercy endures forever."
Let those who fear the Lord say,
   "His mercy endures forever."

℟. **This is the day the Lord has made; let us rejoice and be glad!**

"The right hand of the Lord is exalted;
   the right hand of the Lord has struck with power."
I shall not die, but live
   and declare the works of the Lord.

℟. **This is the day the Lord has made; let us rejoice and be glad!**

The stone which the builders rejected
   has become the cornerstone.
By the Lord has this been done;
   it is wonderful in our eyes.

℟. **This is the day the Lord has made; let us rejoice and be glad!**

11.

Psalm 66:1b-3, 4-5, 6-7a, 16 and 20

℟. (1) **Let all the earth cry out to God with joy, alleluia.**

Shout joyfully to God, all you on earth,
   sing praise to the glory of his name;
   proclaim his glorious praise.
Say to God, "How tremendous are your deeds!"

℟. **Let all the earth cry out to God with joy, alleluia.**

"Let all on earth worship and sing praise to you,
   sing praise to your name!"
Come and see the works of God,
   his tremendous deeds among the children of Adam.

℟. **Let all the earth cry out to God with joy, alleluia.**

He has changed the sea into dry land;
> through the river they passed on foot;
> therefore let us rejoice in him.
He rules by his might forever.

℟. Let all the earth cry out to God with joy, alleluia.

Hear now, all you who fear God, while I declare,
> what he has done for me.
Blessed be God who refused me not
> my prayer or his kindness.

℟. Let all the earth cry out to God with joy, alleluia.

Ascension:

12.

Psalm 47:2-3, 6-7, 8-9

℟. (6a) **God mounts the throne to shouts of joy.**

All you peoples, clap your hands,
> shout to God with cries of gladness,
For the Lord, the Most High, the awesome,
> is the great king over all the earth.

℟. God mounts the throne to shouts of joy.

God mounts his throne amid shouts of joy;
> the Lord, amid trumpet blasts.
Sing praise to God, sing praise;
> sing praise to our king, sing praise.

℟. God mounts the throne to shouts of joy.

For the king of all the earth is God;
> sing hymns of praise.
God reigns over the nations,
> God sits upon his holy throne.

℟. God mounts the throne to shouts of joy.

Pentecost:

13.

Psalm 104:1ab and 24ac, 29bc-30, 31 and 34

℟. (see 30) **Lord, send out your Spirit, and renew the face of the earth.**

Bless the Lord, O my soul!
  O Lord, my God, you are great indeed!
How manifold are your works, O Lord!
  The earth is full of your creatures.

℟. **Lord, send out your Spirit, and renew the face of the earth.**

If you take away their breath, they perish
  and return to their dust.
When you send forth your spirit, they are created,
  and you renew the face of the earth.

℟. **Lord, send out your Spirit, and renew the face of the earth.**

May the glory of the Lord endure forever;
  may the Lord be glad in his works!
Pleasing to him be my theme;
  I will be glad in the Lord.

℟. **Lord, send out your Spirit, and renew the face of the earth.**

Ordinary Time:

14.

Psalm 19:8, 9, 10, 11

℟. (John 6:68c) **Lord, you have the words of everlasting life.**
  or:
℟. (see John 6:63c) **Your words, Lord, are Spirit and life.**

The law of the Lord is perfect,
  refreshing the soul;
The decree of the Lord is trustworthy,
  giving wisdom to the simple.

℟. **Lord, you have the words of everlasting life.**
  or:
℟. **Your words, Lord, are Spirit and life.**

The precepts of the LORD **are right,**
   rejoicing the heart;
The command of the LORD **is clear,**
   enlightening the eye.

℟. **Lord, you have the words of everlasting life.**
   or:
℟. **Your words, Lord, are Spirit and life.**

The fear of the LORD **is pure,**
   enduring forever;
The ordinances of the LORD **are true,**
   all of them just.

℟. **Lord, you have the words of everlasting life.**
   or:
℟. **Your words, Lord, are Spirit and life.**

They are more precious than gold,
   than a heap of purest gold;
Sweeter also than syrup
   or honey from the comb.

℟. **Lord, you have the words of everlasting life.**
   or:
℟. **Your words, Lord, are Spirit and life.**

15.

Psalm 27:1bcde, 4, 13-14

℟. (1a) **The Lord is my light and my salvation.**

The LORD **is my light and my salvation;**
   whom should I fear?
The LORD **is my life's refuge;**
   of whom should I be afraid?

℟. **The Lord is my light and my salvation.**

One thing I ask of the LORD**;**
   this I seek:
To dwell in the house of the LORD
   all the days of my life,
That I may gaze on the loveliness of the LORD
   and contemplate his temple.

℟. **The Lord is my light and my salvation.**

I believe that I shall see the bounty of the LORD
    in the land of the living.
Wait for the LORD **with courage;**
    be stouthearted, and wait for the LORD**.**

℟. **The Lord is my light and my salvation.**

   16.

Psalm 34:2-3, 4-5, 6-7, 8-9

℟. (2) **I will bless the Lord at all times.**
    or:

℟. (9a) **Taste and see the goodness of the Lord.**

I will bless the LORD **at all times;**
    his praise shall be ever in my mouth.
Let my soul glory in the LORD**;**
    the lowly will hear me and be glad.

℟. **I will bless the Lord at all times.**
    or:
℟. **Taste and see the goodness of the Lord.**

Glorify the LORD **with me,**
    let us together extol his name.
I sought the LORD**, and he answered me**
    and delivered me from all my fears.

℟. **I will bless the Lord at all times.**
    or:
℟. **Taste and see the goodness of the Lord.**

Look to him that you may be radiant with joy,
    and your faces may not blush with shame.
When the poor one called out, the LORD **heard,**
    and from all his distress he saved him.

℟. **I will bless the Lord at all times.**
    or:
℟. **Taste and see the goodness of the Lord.**

The angel of the LORD **encamps**
    around those who fear him, and delivers them.
Taste and see how good the LORD **is;**
    blessed the man who takes refuge in him.

℟. **I will bless the Lord at all times.**
    or:
℟. **Taste and see the goodness of the Lord.**

Common Texts for Sung Responsorial Psalms II

17.

Psalm 63:2, 3-4, 5-6, 8-9

℟. (2b) **My soul is thirsting for you, O Lord my God.**

O God, you are my God whom I seek;
  for you my flesh pines and my soul thirsts
    like the earth, parched, lifeless and without water.

℟. **My soul is thirsting for you, O Lord my God.**

Thus have I gazed toward you in the sanctuary
  to see your power and your glory,
For your kindness is a greater good than life;
  my lips shall glorify you.

℟. **My soul is thirsting for you, O Lord my God.**

Thus will I bless you while I live;
  lifting up my hands, I will call upon your name.
As with the riches of a banquet shall my soul be satisfied,
  and with exultant lips my mouth shall praise you.

℟. **My soul is thirsting for you, O Lord my God.**

You are my help,
  and in the shadow of your wings I shout for joy.
My soul clings fast for you;
  your right hand upholds me.

℟. **My soul is thirsting for you, O Lord my God.**

18.

Psalm 95:1-2, 6-7, 8-9

℟. (8) **If today you hear his voice, harden not your hearts.**

Come, let us sing joyfully to the Lord;
  let us acclaim the Rock of our salvation.
Let us come into his presence with thanksgiving;
  let us joyfully sing psalms to him.

℟. **If today you hear his voice, harden not your hearts.**

Come, let us bow down in worship;
  let us kneel before the Lord who made us.
For he is our God,
  and we are the people he shepherds, the flock he guides.

℟. **If today you hear his voice, harden not your hearts.**

Oh, that today you would hear his voice:
   "Harden not your hearts as at Meribah,
   as in the day of Massah in the desert,
Where your fathers tempted me;
   they tested me though they had seen my works."

℟. **If today you hear his voice, harden not your hearts.**

19.

Psalm 100:1b-2, 3, 5

℟. (3c) **We are his people: the sheep of his flock.**

Sing joyfully to the LORD**, all you lands;**
   serve the LORD **with gladness;**
   come before him with joyful song.

℟. **We are his people: the sheep of his flock.**

Know that the LORD **is God;**
   he made us, his we are;
   his people, the flock he tends.

℟. **We are his people: the sheep of his flock.**

The LORD **is good:**
   the LORD**, whose kindness endures forever,**
   and his faithfulness, to all generations.

℟. **We are his people: the sheep of his flock.**

20.

Psalm 103:1bc-2, 3-4, 8 and 10, 12-13

℟. (8a) **The Lord is kind and merciful.**

Bless the LORD**, O my soul;**
   and all my being, bless his holy name.
Bless the LORD**, O my soul,**
   and forget not all his benefits.

℟. **The Lord is kind and merciful.**

He pardons all your iniquities,
   he heals all your ills.
He redeems your life from destruction,
   he crowns you with kindness and compassion.

℟. **The Lord is kind and merciful.**

Merciful and gracious is the L<small>ORD</small>,
   slow to anger and abounding in kindness.
Not according to our sins does he deal with us,
   nor does he requite us according to our crimes.

℟. The Lord is kind and merciful.

As far as the east is from the west,
   so far has he put our transgressions from us.
As a father has compassion on his children,
   so the L<small>ORD</small> has compassion on those who fear him.

℟. The Lord is kind and merciful.

21.

Psalm 145:1b-2, 8-9, 10-11, 13cd-14

℟. (see 1) I will praise your name for ever, my king and my God.

I will extol you, O my God and King,
   and I will bless your name forever and ever.
Every day will I bless you,
   and I will praise your name forever and ever.

℟. I will praise your name for ever, my king and my God.

The L<small>ORD</small> is gracious and merciful,
   slow to anger and of great kindness.
The L<small>ORD</small> is good to all
   and compassionate toward all his works.

℟. I will praise your name for ever, my king and my God.

Let all your works give you thanks, O L<small>ORD</small>,
   and let your faithful ones bless you.
Let them discourse of the glory of your Kingdom
   and speak of your might.

℟. I will praise your name for ever, my king and my God.

The L<small>ORD</small> is faithful in all his words,
   and holy in all his works.
The L<small>ORD</small> lifts up all who are falling
   and raises up all who are bowed down.

℟. I will praise your name for ever, my king and my God.

Last Weeks in Ordinary Time:

22.

Psalm 122:1-2, 3-4ab, 4cd-5, 6-7, 8-9

℟. (see 1) **Let us go rejoicing to the house of the Lord.**

I rejoiced because they said to me,
   "We will go up to the house of the LORD**."**
And now we have set foot
   within your gates, O Jerusalem.

℟. **Let us go rejoicing to the house of the Lord.**

Jerusalem, built as a city
   with compact unity.
To it the tribes go up,
   the tribes of the LORD**.**

℟. **Let us go rejoicing to the house of the Lord.**

According to the decree for Israel,
   to give thanks to the name of the LORD**.**
In it are set up judgment seats,
   seats for the house of David.

℟. **Let us go rejoicing to the house of the Lord.**

Pray for the peace of Jerusalem!
   May those who love you prosper!
May peace be within your walls,
   prosperity in your buildings.

℟. **Let us go rejoicing to the house of the Lord.**

Because of my relatives and friends
   I will say, "Peace be within you!"
Because of the house of the LORD**, our God,**
   I will pray for your good.

℟. **Let us go rejoicing to the house of the Lord.**

PROPER OF SAINTS

JANUARY 1

OCTAVE OF CHRISTMAS

SOLEMNITY OF THE BLESSED VIRGIN MARY, MOTHER OF GOD

See Proper of Seasons, no. 18.

JANUARY 2

510 SAINTS BASIL THE GREAT AND GREGORY NAZIANZEN, BISHOPS AND DOCTORS OF THE CHURCH
MEMORIAL

From the Common of Pastors, p. 1805, or the Common of Doctors of the Church, p. 1838,

OR

FIRST READING

Ephesians 4:1-7, 11-13   For the work of the ministry, for building up the Body of Christ.

A reading from the Letter of Saint Paul to the Ephesians

I, a prisoner for the Lord,
   urge you to live in a manner worthy of the call you have received,
   with all humility and gentleness, with patience,
   bearing with one another through love,
   striving to preserve the unity of the Spirit
   through the bond of peace:
   one Body and one Spirit,
   as you were also called to the one hope of your call;
   one Lord, one faith, one baptism;
   one God and Father of all,
   who is over all and through all and in all.

But grace was given to each of us
   according to the measure of Christ's gift.

And he gave some as Apostles, others as prophets,
   others as evangelists, others as pastors and teachers,
   to equip the holy ones for the work of ministry,
   for building up the Body of Christ,
   until we all attain to the unity of faith
   and knowledge of the Son of God, to mature manhood,
   to the extent of the full stature of Christ.

The word of the Lord.

RESPONSORIAL PSALM

Psalm 23:1b-3a, 4, 5, 6

℟. (1) **The Lord is my shepherd; there is nothing I shall want.**

The LORD **is my shepherd; I shall not want.
    In verdant pastures he gives me repose;
Beside restful waters he leads me;
    he refreshes my soul.**

℟. **The Lord is my shepherd; there is nothing I shall want.**

**Even though I walk in the dark valley
    I fear no evil; for you are at my side
With your rod and your staff
    that give me courage.**

℟. **The Lord is my shepherd; there is nothing I shall want.**

**You spread the table before me
    in the sight of my foes;
You anoint my head with oil;
    my cup overflows.**

℟. **The Lord is my shepherd; there is nothing I shall want.**

**Only goodness and kindness follow me
    all the days of my life;
And I shall dwell in the house of the L**ORD
    for years to come.

℟. **The Lord is my shepherd; there is nothing I shall want.**

ALLELUIA

Matthew 23:9b, 10b

℟. **Alleluia, alleluia.**

**You have but one Father in heaven;
you have but one master, the Christ.**

℟. **Alleluia, alleluia.**

GOSPEL

Matthew 23:8-12   The greatest among you must be your servant.

✝ A reading from the holy Gospel according to Matthew

**Jesus spoke to the crowds and to his disciples:
"Do not be called 'Rabbi.'
You have but one teacher, and you are all brothers.
Call no one on earth your father;
   you have but one Father in heaven.
Do not be called 'Master';
   you have but one master, the Christ.
The greatest among you must be your servant.
Whoever exalts himself will be humbled;
   but whoever humbles himself will be exalted."**

The Gospel of the Lord.

JANUARY 4

[In the Dioceses of the United States]

510A SAINT ELIZABETH ANN SETON, RELIGIOUS MEMORIAL

From the Common of Holy Men and Women: For Religious, p. 1868.

JANUARY 5

[In the Dioceses of the United States]

510B SAINT JOHN NEUMANN, BISHOP MEMORIAL

From the Common of Pastors, p. 1805.

JANUARY 6

[In the Dioceses of the United States]

510C BLESSED ANDRÉ BESSETTE, RELIGIOUS

From the Common of Holy Men and Women: For Religious, p. 1868.

JANUARY 7

511 SAINT RAYMOND OF PEÑAFORT, PRIEST

From the Common of Pastors, p. 1805,

OR

FIRST READING

2 Corinthians 5:14-20   He has given us the ministry of reconciliation.

A reading from the second Letter of Saint Paul to the Corinthians

Brothers and sisters:
The love of Christ impels us,
   once we have come to the conviction that one died for all;
   therefore, all have died.
He indeed died for all,
   so that those who live might no longer live for themselves
   but for him who for their sake died and was raised.

Consequently, from now on we regard no one according to the flesh;
   even if we once knew Christ according to the flesh,
   yet now we know him so no longer.
So whoever is in Christ is a new creation:
   the old things have passed away;
   behold, new things have come.
And all this is from God,
   who has reconciled us to himself through Christ
   and given us the ministry of reconciliation,
   namely, God was reconciling the world to himself in Christ,
   not counting their trespasses against them
   and entrusting to us the message of reconciliation.
So we are ambassadors for Christ,
   as if God were appealing through us.
We implore you on behalf of Christ,
   be reconciled to God.

The word of the Lord.

RESPONSORIAL PSALM

Psalm 103:1bc-2, 3-4, 8-9, 13-14, 17-18

℟. (1) O, bless the Lord, my soul!

Bless the L󰀀ʀᴅ, O my soul;
  and all my being, bless his holy name!
Bless the Lᴏʀᴅ, O my soul;
  and forget not all his benefits.

℟. O, bless the Lord, my soul!

He pardons all your iniquities,
  he heals all your ills.
He redeems your life from destruction,
  he crowns you with kindness and compassion.

℟. O, bless the Lord, my soul!

Merciful and gracious is the Lᴏʀᴅ,
  slow to anger and abounding in kindness.
He will not always chide,
  nor does he keep his wrath forever.

℟. O, bless the Lord, my soul!

As a father has compassion on his children,
  so the Lᴏʀᴅ has compassion on those who fear him,
For he knows how we are formed;
  he remembers that we are dust.

℟. O, bless the Lord, my soul!

But the kindness of the Lᴏʀᴅ is from eternity
  to eternity toward those who fear him,
And his justice toward their children's children
  among those who keep his covenant.

℟. O, bless the Lord, my soul!

ALLELUIA

Luke 21:36

℟. Alleluia, alleluia.

**Be vigilant at all times and pray
that you may have the strength to stand before the Son of Man.**

℟. Alleluia, alleluia.

GOSPEL

Luke 12:35-40   You must also be prepared.

✠ **A reading from the holy Gospel according to Luke**

**Jesus said to his disciples:
"Gird your loins and light your lamps
   and be like servants who await their master's return from a wedding,
   ready to open immediately when he comes and knocks.
Blessed are those servants
   whom the master finds vigilant on his arrival.
Amen, I say to you, he will gird himself,
   have them recline at table, and proceed to wait on them.
And should he come in the second or third watch
   and find them prepared in this way,
   blessed are those servants.
Be sure of this:
   if the master of the house had known the hour
   when the thief was coming,
   he would not have let his house be broken into.
You also must be prepared, for at an hour you do not expect,
   the Son of Man will come."**

The Gospel of the Lord.

JANUARY 13

512 SAINT HILARY, BISHOP AND DOCTOR OF THE CHURCH

From the Common of Pastors, p. 1805, or the Common of Doctors of the Church, p. 1838,

OR

FIRST READING

1 John 2:18-25   Whoever confesses the Son has the Father as well.

A reading from the first Letter of Saint John

Children, it is the last hour;
 and just as you heard that the antichrist was coming,
 so now many antichrists have appeared.
Thus we know this is the last hour.
They went out from us, but they were not really of our number;
 if they had been, they would have remained with us.
Their desertion shows that none of them was of our number.
But you have the anointing that comes from the Holy One,
 and you all have knowledge.
I write to you not because you do not know the truth
 but because you do, and because every lie is alien to the truth.
Who is the liar?
Whoever denies that Jesus is the Christ.
Whoever denies the Father and the Son, this is the antichrist.
Anyone who denies the Son does not have the Father,
 but whoever confesses the Son has the Father as well.

Let what you heard from the beginning remain in you.
If what you heard from the beginning remains in you,
 then you will remain in the Son and in the Father.
And this is the promise that he made us: eternal life.

The word of the Lord.

RESPONSORIAL PSALM

Psalm 110:1, 2, 3, 4

℟. (4b) **You are a priest for ever, in the line of Melchizedek.**

**The Lord said to my Lord: "Sit at my right hand
   till I make your enemies your footstool."**

℟. **You are a priest for ever, in the line of Melchizedek.**

**The scepter of your power the Lord will stretch forth from Zion:
   "Rule in the midst of your enemies."**

℟. **You are a priest for ever, in the line of Melchizedek.**

**"Yours is princely power in the day of your birth, in holy splendor;
   before the daystar, like the dew, I have begotten you."**

℟. **You are a priest for ever, in the line of Melchizedek.**

**The Lord has sworn, and he will not repent:
   "You are a priest forever, according to the order of Melchizedek."**

℟. **You are a priest for ever, in the line of Melchizedek.**

ALLELUIA

Matthew 5:16

℟. **Alleluia, alleluia.**

**Let your light shine before others,
that they may see your good deeds and glorify your heavenly Father.**

℟. **Alleluia, alleluia.**

January 13—Saint Hilary

GOSPEL

Matthew 5:13-19   You are the light of the world.

✠ **A reading from the holy Gospel according to Matthew**

Jesus said to his disciples:
"You are the salt of the earth.
But if salt loses its taste, with what can it be seasoned?
It is no longer good for anything
   but to be thrown out and trampled underfoot.
You are the light of the world.
A city set on a mountain cannot be hidden.
Nor do they light a lamp and then put it under a bushel basket;
   it is set on a lampstand,
   where it gives light to all in the house.
Just so, your light must shine before others,
   that they may see your good deeds
   and glorify your heavenly Father.

"Do not think that I have come to abolish the law or the prophets.
I have come not to abolish but to fulfill.
Amen, I say to you, until heaven and earth pass away,
   not the smallest letter or the smallest part of a letter
   will pass from the law,
   until all things have taken place.
Therefore, whoever breaks one of the least of these commandments
   and teaches others to do so
   will be called least in the Kingdom of heaven.
But whoever obeys and teaches these commandments
   will be called greatest in the Kingdom of heaven."

The Gospel of the Lord.

JANUARY 17

513 SAINT ANTHONY, ABBOT MEMORIAL

From the Common of Holy Men and Women: For Religious, p. 1868,

OR

FIRST READING

Ephesians 6:10-13, 18   Put on the armor of God.

A reading from the Letter of Saint Paul to the Ephesians

Brothers and sisters:
Draw your strength from the Lord and from his mighty power.
Put on the armor of God so that you may be able to stand firm
   against the tactics of the Devil.
For our struggle is not with flesh and blood
   but with the principalities, with the powers,
   with the world rulers of this present darkness,
   with the evil spirits in the heavens.
Therefore, put on the armor of God,
   that you may be able to resist on the evil day
   and, having done everything, to hold your ground.

With all prayer and supplication,
   pray at every opportunity in the Spirit.
To that end, be watchful with all perseverance and supplication
   for all the holy ones.

The word of the Lord.

RESPONSORIAL PSALM

Psalm 16:1-2a and 5, 7-8, 11

℟. (5) **You are my inheritance, O Lord.**

**Keep me, O God, for in you I take refuge;
  I say to the L**ORD**, "My Lord are you."
O L**ORD**, my allotted portion and my cup,
  you it is who hold fast my lot.**

℟. **You are my inheritance, O Lord.**

I bless the LORD **who counsels me;
  even at night my heart exhorts me.
I set the L**ORD **ever before me;
  with him at my right hand I shall not be disturbed.**

℟. **You are my inheritance, O Lord.**

**You will show me the path to life,
  fullness of joys in your presence,
  the delights at your right hand forever.**

℟. **You are my inheritance, O Lord.**

ALLELUIA

John 8:31b-32

℟. **Alleluia, alleluia.**

**If you remain in my word, you will truly be my disciples,
and you will know the truth, says the Lord.**

℟. **Alleluia, alleluia.**

January 17—Saint Anthony

GOSPEL

Matthew 19:16-26   If you wish to be perfect, go, sell what you have.

✠ **A reading from the holy Gospel according to Matthew**

Someone approached Jesus and said,
   "Teacher, what good must I do to gain eternal life?"
Jesus answered him, "Why do you ask me about the good?
There is only One who is good.
If you wish to enter into life, keep the commandments."
He asked him, "Which ones?"
And Jesus replied, *"You shall not kill;*
   you shall not commit adultery;
   you shall not steal;
   you shall not bear false witness;
   honor your father and your mother;
   and *you shall love your neighbor as yourself."*
The young man said to him,
   "All of these I have observed. What do I still lack?"
Jesus said to him, "If you wish to be perfect, go,
   sell what you have and give to the poor,
   and you will have treasure in heaven.
Then come, follow me."
When the young man heard this statement, he went away sad,
   for he had many possessions.
Then Jesus said to his disciples,
   "Amen, I say to you, it will be hard for one who is rich
   to enter the Kingdom of heaven.
Again I say to you,
   it is easier for a camel to pass through the eye of a needle
   than for one who is rich to enter the Kingdom of God."
When the disciples heard this, they were greatly astonished and said,
   "Who then can be saved?"
Jesus looked at them and said,
   "For men this is impossible,
   but for God all things are possible."

The Gospel of the Lord.

JANUARY 20

514 SAINT FABIAN, POPE AND MARTYR

From the Common of Martyrs, p. 1782, or the Common of Pastors: For a Pope, p. 1805,

OR

FIRST READING

1 Peter 5:1-4   Tend the flock of God in your midst.

A reading from the first letter of Saint Peter

Beloved:
I exhort the presbyters among you,
   as a fellow presbyter and witness to the sufferings of Christ
   and one who has a share in the glory to be revealed.
Tend the flock of God in your midst,
   overseeing it not by constraint but willingly,
   as God would have it, not for shameful profit but eagerly.
Do not lord it over those assigned to you,
   but be examples to the flock.
And when the chief Shepherd is revealed,
   you will receive the unfading crown of glory.

The word of the Lord.

RESPONSORIAL PSALM

Psalm 40:2 and 4ab, 7-8a, 8b-9, 10

℟. (8a and 9a) **Here I am, Lord; I come to do your will.**

I have waited, waited for the Lord,
   and he stooped toward me and heard my cry.
And he put a new song into my mouth,
   a hymn to our God.

℟. **Here I am, Lord; I come to do your will.**

Sacrifice or oblation you wished not,
   but ears open to obedience you gave me.
Burnt offerings or sin-offerings you sought not;
   then said I, "Behold I come."

℟. **Here I am, Lord; I come to do your will.**

"In the written scroll it is prescribed for me,
To do your will, O my God, is my delight,
  and your law is within my heart!"

℟. Here I am, Lord; I come to do your will.

I announced your justice in the vast assembly;
  I did not restrain my lips, as you, O LORD, know.

℟. Here I am, Lord; I come to do your will.

ALLELUIA

John 10:14

℟. Alleluia, alleluia.

I am the good shepherd, says the Lord;
I know my sheep, and mine know me.

℟. Alleluia, alleluia.

GOSPEL

John 21:15-17   Feed my lambs, feed my sheep.

✠ A reading from the holy Gospel according to John

After Jesus had revealed himself to his disciples and
  eaten breakfast with them, he said to Simon Peter,
  "Simon, son of John, do you love me more than these?"
Simon Peter answered him, "Yes, Lord, you know that I love you."
Jesus said to him, "Feed my lambs."
He then said to Simon Peter a second time,
  "Simon, son of John, do you love me?"
Simon Peter answered him, "Yes, Lord, you know that I love you."
Jesus said to him, "Tend my sheep."
He said to him the third time,
  "Simon, son of John, do you love me?"
Peter was distressed that he had said to him a third time,
  "Do you love me?" and he said to him,
  "Lord, you know everything; you know that I love you."
Jesus said to him, "Feed my sheep."

The Gospel of the Lord.

JANUARY 20

515 SAINT SEBASTIAN, MARTYR

From the Common of Martyrs, p. 1782,

OR

FIRST READING

1 Peter 3:14-17   Do not be afraid or terrified with fear of them.

A reading from the first Letter of Saint Peter

Beloved:
Even if you should suffer because of righteousness, blessed are you.
Do not be afraid or terrified with fear of them,
   but sanctify Christ as Lord in your hearts.
Always be ready to give an explanation
   to anyone who asks you for a reason for your hope,
   but do it with gentleness and reverence,
   keeping your conscience clear,
   so that, when you are maligned,
   those who defame your good conduct in Christ
   may themselves be put to shame.
For it is better to suffer for doing good,
   if that be the will of God, than for doing evil.

The word of the Lord.

RESPONSORIAL PSALM

Psalm 34:2-3, 4-5, 6-7, 8-9

℟. (5) **The Lord delivered me from all my fears.**

I will bless the Lord at all times;
   his praise shall be ever in my mouth.
Let my soul glory in the Lord;
   the lowly will hear and be glad.

℟. **The Lord delivered me from all my fears.**

Glorify the Lord with me,
   let us together extol his name.
I sought the Lord, and he answered me
   and delivered me from all my fears.

℟. **The Lord delivered me from all my fears.**

Look to him that you may be radiant with joy,
   and your faces may not blush with shame.
When the poor one called out, the LORD heard,
   and from all his distress he saved him.

℟. The Lord delivered me from all my fears.

The angel of the LORD encamps
   around those who fear him, and delivers them.
Taste and see how good the LORD is;
   blessed the man who takes refuge in him.

℟. The Lord delivered me from all my fears.

ALLELUIA

James 1:12

℟. Alleluia, alleluia.

Blessed is the man who perseveres in temptation,
for when he has been proved he will receive the crown of life.

℟. Alleluia, alleluia.

GOSPEL

Matthew 10:28-33   Do not be afraid of those who kill the body.

✠ A reading from the holy Gospel according to Matthew

Jesus said to the Twelve:
"Do not be afraid of those who kill the body
   but cannot kill the soul;
   rather, be afraid of the one who can destroy
   both soul and body in Gehenna.
Are not two sparrows sold for a small coin?
Yet not one of them falls to the ground without your Father's knowledge.
Even all the hairs of your head are counted.
So do not be afraid; you are worth more than many sparrows.
Everyone who acknowledges me before others
   I will acknowledge before my heavenly Father.
But whoever denies me before others,
   I will deny before my heavenly Father."

The Gospel of the Lord.

JANUARY 21

516 SAINT AGNES, VIRGIN AND MARTYR MEMORIAL

From the Common of Martyrs, p. 1782, or the Common of Virgins, p. 1857,

OR

FIRST READING

1 Corinthians 1:26-31   God chose the weak of the world.

A reading from the first Letter of Saint Paul to the Corinthians

Consider your own calling, brothers and sisters.
Not many of you were wise by human standards,
　not many were powerful,
　not many were of noble birth.
Rather, God chose the foolish of the world to shame the wise,
　and God chose the weak of the world to shame the strong,
　and God chose the lowly and despised of the world,
　those who count for nothing,
　to reduce to nothing those who are something,
　so that no human being might boast before God.
It is due to him that you are in Christ Jesus,
　who became for us wisdom from God,
　as well as righteousness, sanctification, and redemption,
　so that, as it is written,
　Whoever boasts, should boast in the Lord.

The word of the Lord.

RESPONSORIAL PSALM

Psalm 23:1b-3a, 4, 5, 6

℟. (1) The Lord is my shepherd; there is nothing I shall want.

The LORD is my shepherd; I shall not want.
　In verdant pastures he gives me repose;
Beside restful waters he leads me;
　he refreshes my soul.

℟. The Lord is my shepherd; there is nothing I shall want.

Even though I walk in the dark valley
  I fear no evil; for you are at my side
With your rod and your staff
  that give me courage.

℟. The Lord is my shepherd; there is nothing I shall want.

You spread the table before me
  in the sight of my foes;
You anoint my head with oil;
  my cup overflows.

℟. The Lord is my shepherd; there is nothing I shall want.

Only goodness and kindness follow me
  all the days of my life;
And I shall dwell in the house of the LORD
  for years to come.

℟. The Lord is my shepherd; there is nothing I shall want.

ALLELUIA

John 15:9b, 5b

℟. Alleluia, alleluia.

Remain in my love, says the Lord;
whoever remains in me and I in him will bear much fruit.

℟. Alleluia, alleluia.

GOSPEL

Matthew 13:44-46   He sells all that he has and buys that field.

✝ A reading from the holy Gospel according to Matthew

Jesus said to his disciples:
"The Kingdom of heaven is like a treasure buried in a field,
  which a person finds and hides again,
    and out of joy goes and sells all that he has and buys that field.
Again, the Kingdom of heaven is like a merchant
  searching for fine pearls.
When he finds a pearl of great price,
  he goes and sells all that he has and buys it."

The Gospel of the Lord.

JANUARY 22

517 SAINT VINCENT, DEACON AND MARTYR

From the Common of Martyrs, p. 1782,

OR

FIRST READING

2 Corinthians 4:7-15   Always carrying about in the body the dying of Jesus.

A reading from the second Letter of Saint Paul to the Corinthians

Brothers and sisters:
We hold this treasure in earthen vessels,
 that the surpassing power may be of God and not from us.
We are afflicted in every way, but not constrained;
 perplexed, but not driven to despair;
 persecuted, but not abandoned;
 struck down, but not destroyed;
 always carrying about in the body the dying of Jesus,
 so that the life of Jesus may also be manifested in our body.
For we who live are constantly being given up to death
 for the sake of Jesus,
 so that the life of Jesus may be manifested in our mortal flesh.

So death is at work in us, but life in you.
Since, then, we have the same spirit of faith,
 according to what is written, *I believed, therefore I spoke*,
 we too believe and therefore speak,
 knowing that the one who raised the Lord Jesus
 will raise us also with Jesus
 and place us with you in his presence.
Everything indeed is for you,
 so that the grace bestowed in abundance on more and more people
 may cause the thanksgiving to overflow for the glory of God.

The word of the Lord.

RESPONSORIAL PSALM

Psalm 34:2-3, 4-5, 6-7, 8-9

℟. (5) **The Lord delivered me from all my fears.**

**I will bless the Lord at all times;
  his praise shall be ever in my mouth.
Let my soul glory in the Lord;
  the lowly will hear and be glad.**

℟. **The Lord delivered me from all my fears.**

**Glorify the Lord with me,
  let us together extol his name.
I sought the Lord, and he answered me
  and delivered me from all my fears.**

℟. **The Lord delivered me from all my fears.**

**Look to him that you may be radiant with joy,
  and your faces may not blush with shame.
When the poor one called out, the Lord heard,
  and from all his distress he saved him.**

℟. **The Lord delivered me from all my fears.**

**The angel of the Lord encamps
  around those who fear him, and delivers them.
Taste and see how good the Lord is;
  blessed the man who takes refuge in him.**

℟. **The Lord delivered me from all my fears.**

ALLELUIA

Matthew 5:10

℟. **Alleluia, alleluia.**

**Blessed are they who are persecuted for the sake of righteousness,
for theirs is the Kingdom of heaven.**

℟. **Alleluia, alleluia.**

January 22—Saint Vincent

GOSPEL

Matthew 10:17-22   You will be led before governors and kings for my sake as a witness before them and the pagans.

✝ **A reading from the holy Gospel according to Matthew**

**Jesus said to the Twelve:
"Beware of men, for they will hand you over to courts
   and scourge you in their synagogues,
   and you will be led before governors and kings for my sake
   as a witness before them and the pagans.
When they hand you over,
   do not worry about how you are to speak
   or what you are to say.
You will be given at that moment what you are to say.
For it will not be you who speak
   but the Spirit of your Father speaking through you.
Brother will hand over brother to death,
   and the father his child;
   children will rise up against parents and have them put to death.
You will be hated by all because of my name,
   but whoever endures to the end will be saved."**

The Gospel of the Lord.

JANUARY 24

518 SAINT FRANCIS DE SALES, BISHOP AND DOCTOR OF THE CHURCH MEMORIAL

From the Common of Pastors, p. 1805, or the Common of Doctors of the Church, p. 1838,

OR

FIRST READING

Ephesians 3:8-12   To preach to the Gentiles the inscrutable riches of Christ.

A reading from the Letter of Saint Paul to the Ephesians

Brothers and sisters:
To me, the very least of all the holy ones, this grace was given,
　to preach to the Gentiles the inscrutable riches of Christ,
　and to bring to light for all what is the plan of the mystery
　hidden from ages past in God who created all things,
　so that the manifold wisdom of God
　　might now be made known through the Church
　to the principalities and authorities in the heavens.
This was according to the eternal purpose
　that he accomplished in Christ Jesus our Lord,
　in whom we have boldness of speech
　and confidence of access through faith in him.

The word of the Lord.

RESPONSORIAL PSALM

Psalm 37:3-4, 5-6, 30-31

℟. (30a) **The mouth of the just murmurs wisdom.**

Trust in the LORD **and do good**
   that you may dwell in the land and be fed in security.
Take delight in the LORD**,**
   and he will grant you your heart's requests.

℟. **The mouth of the just murmurs wisdom.**

Commit to the LORD **your way;**
   trust in him, and he will act.
He will make justice dawn for you like the light;
   bright as the noonday shall be your vindication.

℟. **The mouth of the just murmurs wisdom.**

The mouth of the just tells of wisdom
   and his tongue utters what is right.
The law of his God is in his heart,
   and his steps do not falter.

℟. **The mouth of the just murmurs wisdom.**

ALLELUIA

John 13:34

℟. **Alleluia, alleluia.**

I give you a new commandment:
love one another as I have loved you.

℟. **Alleluia, alleluia.**

GOSPEL

John 15:9-17   You are my friends if you do what I command you.

✝ **A reading from the holy Gospel according to John**

Jesus said to his disciples:
"As the Father loves me, so I also love you.
Remain in my love.
If you keep my commandments, you will remain in my love,
   just as I have kept my Father's commandments
   and remain in his love.

"I have told you this so that my joy be in you
   and your joy be complete.
This is my commandment: love one another as I love you.
No one has greater love than this,
   to lay down one's life for one's friends.
You are my friends if you do what I command you.
I no longer call you slaves,
   because a slave does not know what his master is doing.
I have called you friends,
   because I have told you everything I have heard from my Father.
It was not you who chose me, but I who chose you
   and appointed you to go and bear fruit that will remain,
   so that whatever you ask the Father in my name he may give you.
This I command you: love one another."

The Gospel of the Lord.

JANUARY 25

519 THE CONVERSION OF SAINT PAUL, APOSTLE
FEAST

The following readings may also be used for a votive Mass of Saint Paul.

FIRST READING

First Option

Acts 22:3-16   Get up and have yourself baptized and your sins washed away, calling upon the name of Jesus.

A reading from the Acts of the Apostles

Paul addressed the people in these words:
"I am a Jew, born in Tarsus in Cilicia,
  but brought up in this city.
At the feet of Gamaliel I was educated strictly in our ancestral law
  and was zealous for God, just as all of you are today.
I persecuted this Way to death,
  binding both men and women and delivering them to prison.
Even the high priest and the whole council of elders
  can testify on my behalf.
For from them I even received letters to the brothers
  and set out for Damascus to bring back to Jerusalem
  in chains for punishment those there as well.

"On that journey as I drew near to Damascus,
  about noon a great light from the sky suddenly shone around me.
I fell to the ground and heard a voice saying to me,
  'Saul, Saul, why are you persecuting me?'
I replied, 'Who are you, sir?'
And he said to me,
  'I am Jesus the Nazorean whom you are persecuting.'
My companions saw the light
  but did not hear the voice of the one who spoke to me.
I asked, 'What shall I do, sir?'
The Lord answered me, 'Get up and go into Damascus,
  and there you will be told about everything
  appointed for you to do.'
Since I could see nothing because of the brightness of that light,
  I was led by hand by my companions and entered Damascus.

January 25—The Conversion of Saint Paul 1157

"A certain Ananias, a devout observer of the law,
   and highly spoken of by all the Jews who lived there,
   came to me and stood there and said,
   'Saul, my brother, regain your sight.'
And at that very moment I regained my sight and saw him.
Then he said,
   'The God of our ancestors designated you to know his will,
   to see the Righteous One, and to hear the sound of his voice;
   for you will be his witness before all
   to what you have seen and heard.
Now, why delay?
Get up and have yourself baptized and your sins washed away,
   calling upon his name.'"

The word of the Lord.

OR

1158　*January 25—The Conversion of Saint Paul*

Second Option

Acts 9:1-22　You will be told what you must do.

A reading from the Acts of the Apostles

**Saul, still breathing murderous threats against the disciples of the Lord,
　went to the high priest and asked him
　for letters to the synagogues in Damascus, that,
　if he should find any men or women who belonged to the Way,
　he might bring them back to Jerusalem in chains.
On his journey, as he was nearing Damascus,
　a light from the sky suddenly flashed around him.
He fell to the ground and heard a voice saying to him,
　"Saul, Saul, why are you persecuting me?"
He said, "Who are you, sir?"
The reply came, "I am Jesus, whom you are persecuting.
Now get up and go into the city and you will be told what you must do."
The men who were traveling with him stood speechless,
　for they heard the voice but could see no one.
Saul got up from the ground,
　but when he opened his eyes he could see nothing;
　so they led him by the hand and brought him to Damascus.
For three days he was unable to see, and he neither ate nor drank.**

**There was a disciple in Damascus named Ananias,
　and the Lord said to him in a vision, "Ananias."
He answered, "Here I am, Lord."
The Lord said to him, "Get up and go to the street called Straight
　and ask at the house of Judas for a man from Tarsus named Saul.
He is there praying,
　and in a vision he has seen a man named Ananias
　come in and lay his hands on him,
　that he may regain his sight."
But Ananias replied,
　"Lord, I have heard from many sources about this man,
　what evil things he has done to your holy ones in Jerusalem.
And here he has authority from the chief priests
　to imprison all who call upon your name."
But the Lord said to him,
　"Go, for this man is a chosen instrument of mine
　to carry my name before Gentiles, kings, and children of Israel,
　and I will show him what he will have to suffer for my name."**

So Ananias went and entered the house;
   laying his hands on him, he said,
    "Saul, my brother, the Lord has sent me,
    Jesus who appeared to you on the way by which you came,
   that you may regain your sight and be filled with the Holy Spirit."
Immediately things like scales fell from his eyes
   and he regained his sight.
He got up and was baptized,
   and when he had eaten, he recovered his strength.

He stayed some days with the disciples in Damascus,
   and he began at once to proclaim Jesus in the synagogues,
   that he is the Son of God.
All who heard him were astounded and said,
   "Is not this the man who in Jerusalem
   ravaged those who call upon this name,
   and came here expressly to take them back in chains
   to the chief priests?"
But Saul grew all the stronger
   and confounded the Jews who lived in Damascus,
   proving that this is the Christ.

The word of the Lord.

RESPONSORIAL PSALM

Psalm 117:1bc, 2

℟. (Mark 16:15) **Go out to all the world and tell the Good News.**
   or:
℟. **Alleluia, alleluia.**

Praise the LORD, all you nations;
   glorify him, all you peoples!

℟. **Go out to all the world, and tell the Good News.**
   or:
℟. **Alleluia, alleluia.**

For steadfast is his kindness toward us,
   and the fidelity of the LORD endures forever.

℟. **Go out to all the world, and tell the Good News.**
   or:
℟. **Alleluia, alleluia.**

ALLELUIA

See John 15:16

℟. Alleluia, alleluia.

I chose you from the world,
to go and bear fruit that will last, says the Lord.

℟. Alleluia, alleluia.

GOSPEL

Mark 16:15-18   Go out to all the world and tell the Good News.

✠ A reading from the holy Gospel according to Mark

Jesus appeared to the Eleven and said to them:
"Go into the whole world
    and proclaim the Gospel to every creature.
Whoever believes and is baptized will be saved;
    whoever does not believe will be condemned.
These signs will accompany those who believe:
    in my name they will drive out demons,
    they will speak new languages.
They will pick up serpents with their hands,
    and if they drink any deadly thing, it will not harm them.
They will lay hands on the sick, and they will recover."

The Gospel of the Lord.

JANUARY 26

520 SAINTS TIMOTHY AND TITUS, BISHOPS
MEMORIAL

The first reading for this memorial is proper. From the Common of Pastors, p. 1805,

OR

FIRST READING

First Option

2 Timothy 1:1-8   I recall your sincere faith.

A reading from the beginning of the second Letter of Saint Paul to Timothy

Paul, an Apostle of Christ Jesus by the will of God
   for the promise of life in Christ Jesus,
   to Timothy, my dear child:
   grace, mercy, and peace from God the Father
   and Christ Jesus our Lord.

I am grateful to God,
   whom I worship with a clear conscience as my ancestors did,
   as I remember you constantly in my prayers, night and day.
I yearn to see you again, recalling your tears,
   so that I may be filled with joy,
   as I recall your sincere faith
   that first lived in your grandmother Lois
   and in your mother Eunice
   and that I am confident lives also in you.

For this reason, I remind you to stir into flame
   the gift of God that you have through the imposition of my hands.
For God did not give us a spirit of cowardice
   but rather of power and love and self-control.
So do not be ashamed of your testimony to our Lord,
   nor of me, a prisoner for his sake;
   but bear your share of hardship for the Gospel
   with the strength that comes from God.

The word of the Lord.

OR

Second Option

Titus 1:1-5   To Titus, my beloved son in a common faith.

A reading from the beginning of the Letter of Saint Paul to Titus

**Paul, a slave of God and Apostle of Jesus Christ
for the sake of the faith of God's chosen ones
and the recognition of religious truth,
in the hope of eternal life
that God, who does not lie, promised before time began,
who indeed at the proper time revealed his word
in the proclamation with which I was entrusted
by the command of God our savior,
to Titus, my true child in our common faith:
grace and peace from God the Father and Christ Jesus our savior.**

**For this reason I left you in Crete
so that you might set right what remains to be done
and appoint presbyters in every town, as I directed you.**

The word of the Lord.

RESPONSORIAL PSALM

Psalm 96:1-2a, 2b-3, 7-8a, 10

℟. (3) **Proclaim God's marvelous deeds to all the nations.**

**Sing to the Lord a new song;
sing to the Lord, all you lands.
Sing to the Lord; bless his name.**

℟. **Proclaim God's marvelous deeds to all the nations.**

**Announce his salvation, day after day.
Tell his glory among the nations;
among all peoples, his wondrous deeds.**

℟. **Proclaim God's marvelous deeds to all the nations.**

**Give to the Lord, you families of nations,
give to the Lord glory and praise;
give to the Lord the glory due his name!**

℟. **Proclaim God's marvelous deeds to all the nations.**

Say among the nations: The LORD is king.
He has made the world firm, not to be moved;
> he governs the peoples with equity.

℟. Proclaim God's marvelous deeds to all the nations.

ALLELUIA

Luke 4:18

℟. Alleluia, alleluia.

The Lord sent me to bring glad tidings to the poor
and to proclaim liberty to captives.

℟. Alleluia, alleluia.

GOSPEL

Luke 10:1-9   The harvest is abundant but the laborers are few.

✠ A reading from the holy Gospel according to Luke

The Lord Jesus appointed seventy-two other disciples
> whom he sent ahead of him in pairs
> to every town and place he intended to visit.
He said to them,
> "The harvest is abundant but the laborers are few;
> so ask the master of the harvest
> to send out laborers for his harvest.
Go on your way;
> behold, I am sending you like lambs among wolves.
Carry no money bag, no sack, no sandals;
> and greet no one along the way.
Into whatever house you enter, first say,
> 'Peace to this household.'
If a peaceful person lives there,
> your peace will rest on him;
> but if not, it will return to you.
Stay in the same house and eat and drink what is offered to you,
> for the laborer deserves his pay.
Do not move about from one house to another.
Whatever town you enter and they welcome you,
> eat what is set before you,
> cure the sick in it and say to them,
> 'The Kingdom of God is at hand for you.'"

The Gospel of the Lord.

JANUARY 27

521 SAINT ANGELA MERICI, VIRGIN

From the Common of Virgins, p. 1857, or the Common of Holy Men and Women: For Teachers, p. 1868,

OR

FIRST READING

1 Peter 4:7b-11   Each one has received a special gift; use it to serve one another.

A reading from the first Letter of Saint Peter

Beloved:
Be serious and sober-minded
 so that you will be able to pray.
Above all, let your love for one another be intense,
 because love covers a multitude of sins.
Be hospitable to one another without complaining.
As each one has received a gift, use it to serve one another
 as good stewards of God's varied grace.
Whoever preaches, let it be with the words of God;
 whoever serves, let it be with the strength that God supplies,
 so that in all things God may be glorified through Jesus Christ,
 to whom belong glory and dominion forever and ever. Amen.

The word of the Lord.

RESPONSORIAL PSALM

Psalm 148:1bc-2, 11-13a, 13c-14

℟. (see 12a and 13a) **Young men and women, praise the name of the Lord.**
 or:
℟. **Alleluia.**

Praise the Lord from the heavens;
 praise him in the heights;
Praise him, all you his angels,
 praise him, all you his hosts.

℟. **Young men and women, praise the name of the Lord.**
 or:
℟. **Alleluia.**

Let the kings of the earth and all peoples,
> the princes and all the judges of the earth,
Young men, too, and maidens,
> old men and boys,
Praise the name of the LORD,
> for his name alone is exalted.

℟. Young men and women, praise the name of the Lord.
> or:
℟. Alleluia.

His majesty is above earth and heaven.
He has lifted up the horn of his people.
Be this his praise from all his faithful ones;
> from the children of Israel, the people close to him. Alleluia.

℟. Young men and women, praise the name of the Lord.
> or:
℟. Alleluia.

ALLELUIA

See Matthew 11:25

℟. Alleluia, alleluia.

Blessed are you, Father, Lord of heaven and earth,
you have revealed to little ones the mysteries of the Kingdom.

℟. Alleluia, alleluia.

GOSPEL

Mark 9:34b-37   Whoever receives one child such as this, receives me.

✠ A reading from the holy Gospel according to Mark

The disciples of Jesus had been discussing on the way
> who was the greatest.
Jesus sat down, called the Twelve, and said to them,
> "If anyone wishes to be first,
> he shall be the last of all and the servant of all."
Taking a child, he placed it in their midst,
> and putting his arms around him, he said to them,
> "Whoever receives one child such as this in my name, receives me;
> and whoever receives me,
> receives not me but the One who sent me."

The Gospel of the Lord.

JANUARY 28

522 SAINT THOMAS AQUINAS, PRIEST AND DOCTOR OF THE CHURCH MEMORIAL

From the Common of Doctors of the Church, p. 1838, or the Common of Pastors, p. 1805,

OR

FIRST READING

Wisdom 7:7-10, 15-16   Beyond health and comeliness I loved her.

A reading from the Book of Wisdom

**I prayed, and prudence was given me;
   I pleaded, and the spirit of Wisdom came to me.
I preferred her to scepter and throne,
And deemed riches nothing in comparison with her,
   nor did I liken any priceless gem to her;
Because all gold, in view of her, is a little sand,
   and before her, silver is to be accounted mire.
Beyond health and comeliness I loved her,
And I chose to have her rather than the light,
   because the splendor of her never yields to sleep.**

**Now God grant I speak suitably
   and value these endowments at their worth:
For he is the guide of Wisdom
   and the director of the wise.
For both we and our words are in his hand,
   as well as all prudence and knowledge of crafts.**

The word of the Lord.

RESPONSORIAL PSALM

Psalm 119:9, 10, 11, 12, 13, 14

℟. (12) **Lord, teach me your statutes.**

**How shall a young man be faultless in his way?
   By keeping to your words.**

℟. **Lord, teach me your statutes.**

**With all my heart I seek you;
   let me not stray from your commands.**

℟. **Lord, teach me your statutes.**

January 28—Saint Thomas Aquinas 1167

Within my heart I treasure your promise,
   that I may not sin against you.

℟. **Lord, teach me your statutes.**

Blessed are you, O LORD;
   teach me your statutes.

℟. **Lord, teach me your statutes.**

With my lips I declare
   all the ordinances of your mouth.

℟. **Lord, teach me your statutes.**

In the way of your decrees I rejoice,
   as much as in all riches.

℟. **Lord, teach me your statutes.**

ALLELUIA

Matthew 23:9b, 10b

℟. **Alleluia, alleluia.**

You have but one Father in heaven;
you have but one master, the Christ.

℟. **Alleluia, alleluia.**

GOSPEL

Matthew 23:8-12   Do not be called "Rabbi," you have but one teacher who is Christ.

✢ **A reading from the holy Gospel according to Matthew**

Jesus spoke to the crowds and to his disciples:
"Do not be called 'Rabbi.'
You have but one teacher, and you are all brothers.
Call no one on earth your father;
   you have but one Father in heaven.
Do not be called 'Master';
   you have but one master, the Christ.
The greatest among you must be your servant.
Whoever exalts himself will be humbled;
   but whoever humbles himself will be exalted."

The Gospel of the Lord.

JANUARY 31

523 SAINT JOHN BOSCO, PRIEST MEMORIAL

From the Common of Pastors, p. 1805, or the Common of Holy Men and Women: For Teachers, p. 1868,

OR

FIRST READING

Philippians 4:4-9   Think about whatever is worthy of praise.

A reading from the Letter of Saint Paul to the Philippians

Brothers and sisters:
Rejoice in the Lord always.
I shall say it again: rejoice!
Your kindness should be known to all.
The Lord is near.
Have no anxiety at all, but in everything,
   by prayer and petition, with thanksgiving,
   make your requests known to God.
Then the peace of God that surpasses all understanding
   will guard your hearts and minds in Christ Jesus.

Finally, brothers and sisters,
   whatever is true, whatever is honorable,
   whatever is just, whatever is pure,
   whatever is lovely, whatever is gracious,
   if there is any excellence
   and if there is anything worthy of praise,
   think about these things.
Keep on doing what you have learned and received
   and heard and seen in me.
Then the God of peace will be with you.

The word of the Lord.

RESPONSORIAL PSALM

Psalm 103:1bc-2, 3-4, 8-9, 13-14, 17-18

℟. (1) **O bless the Lord, my soul!**

Bless the LORD**, O my soul;**
  and all my being, bless his holy name.
Bless the LORD**, O my soul,**
  and forget not all his benefits.

℟. **O bless the Lord, my soul!**

He pardons all your iniquities,
  heals all your ills,
He redeems your life from destruction,
  crowns you with kindness and compassion.

℟. **O bless the Lord, my soul!**

Merciful and gracious is the LORD**,**
  slow to anger and abounding in kindness.
He will not always chide,
  nor does he keep his wrath forever.

℟. **O bless the Lord, my soul!**

As a father has compassion on his children,
  so the LORD **has compassion on those who fear him,**
For he knows how we are formed;
  he remembers that we are dust.

℟. **O bless the Lord, my soul!**

But the kindness of the LORD **is from eternity**
  to eternity toward those who fear him,
And his justice toward his children's children
  among those who keep his covenant.

℟. **O bless the Lord, my soul!**

ALLELUIA

Matthew 23:11, 12b

℟. Alleluia, alleluia.

**The greatest among you must be your servant.
Whoever humbles himself will be exalted.**

℟. Alleluia, alleluia.

GOSPEL

Matthew 18:1-5   Unless you turn and become like children, you will not enter the Kingdom of heaven.

✚ **A reading from the holy Gospel according to Matthew**

**The disciples approached Jesus and said,
   "Who is the greatest in the Kingdom of heaven?"
He called a child over, placed it in their midst, and said,
   "Amen, I say to you, unless you turn and become like children,
   you will not enter the Kingdom of heaven.
Whoever humbles himself like this child
   is the greatest in the Kingdom of heaven.
And whoever receives one child such as this in my name receives me."**

The Gospel of the Lord.

FEBRUARY 2

524 THE PRESENTATION OF THE LORD FEAST

FIRST READING

Malachi 3:1-4   There will come to the temple the Lord whom you seek.

A reading from the Book of the Prophet Malachi

Thus says the Lord God:
Lo, I am sending my messenger
  to prepare the way before me;
And suddenly there will come to the temple
  the Lord whom you seek,
And the messenger of the covenant whom you desire.
  Yes, he is coming, says the Lord of hosts.
But who will endure the day of his coming?
  And who can stand when he appears?
For he is like the refiner's fire,
  or like the fuller's lye.
He will sit refining and purifying silver,
  and he will purify the sons of Levi,
Refining them like gold or like silver
  that they may offer due sacrifice to the Lord.
Then the sacrifice of Judah and Jerusalem
  will please the Lord,
  as in the days of old, as in years gone by.

The word of the Lord.

RESPONSORIAL PSALM

Psalm 24:7, 8, 9, 10

℟. (8) **Who is this king of glory? It is the Lord!**

**Lift up, O gates, your lintels;
  reach up, you ancient portals,
    that the king of glory may come in!**

℟. Who is this king of glory? It is the Lord!

**Who is this king of glory?
  The Lord, strong and mighty,
    the Lord, mighty in battle.**

℟. Who is this king of glory? It is the Lord!

**Lift up, O gates, your lintels;
  reach up, you ancient portals,
    that the king of glory may come in!**

℟. Who is this king of glory? It is the Lord!

**Who is this king of glory?
  The Lord of hosts; he is the king of glory.**

℟. Who is this king of glory? It is the Lord!

SECOND READING

Hebrews 2:14-18   He had to become like his brothers and sisters in every way.

A reading from the Letter to the Hebrews

**Since the children share in blood and flesh,
 Jesus likewise shared in them,
 that through death he might destroy the one
 who has the power of death, that is, the Devil,
 and free those who through fear of death
 had been subject to slavery all their life.
Surely he did not help angels
 but rather the descendants of Abraham;
 therefore, he had to become like his brothers and sisters
 in every way,
 that he might be a merciful and faithful high priest before God
 to expiate the sins of the people.
Because he himself was tested through what he suffered,
 he is able to help those who are being tested.**

The word of the Lord.

ALLELUIA

Luke 2:32

℟. **Alleluia, alleluia.**

**A light of revelation to the Gentiles,
and glory for your people Israel.**

℟. **Alleluia, alleluia.**

1174   February 2—The Presentation of the Lord

GOSPEL

Long Form

Luke 2:22-40   My eyes have seen your salvation.

☩ **A reading from the holy Gospel according to Luke**

**When the days were completed for their purification
    according to the law of Moses,
    Mary and Joseph took Jesus up to Jerusalem
    to present him to the Lord,
    just as it is written in the law of the Lord,
    Every male that opens the womb shall be consecrated to the Lord,
    and to offer the sacrifice of
    a pair of turtledoves or two young pigeons,
    in accordance with the dictate in the law of the Lord.**

**Now there was a man in Jerusalem whose name was Simeon.
This man was righteous and devout,
    awaiting the consolation of Israel,
    and the Holy Spirit was upon him.
It had been revealed to him by the Holy Spirit
    that he should not see death
    before he had seen the Christ of the Lord.
He came in the Spirit into the temple;
    and when the parents brought in the child Jesus
    to perform the custom of the law in regard to him,
    he took him into his arms and blessed God, saying:**

   **"Now, Master, you may let your servant go
        in peace, according to your word,
    for my eyes have seen your salvation,
        which you prepared in the sight of all the peoples:
    a light for revelation to the Gentiles,
        and glory for your people Israel."**

**The child's father and mother were amazed at what was said about him;
    and Simeon blessed them and said to Mary his mother,
    "Behold, this child is destined
    for the fall and rise of many in Israel,
    and to be a sign that will be contradicted
    —and you yourself a sword will pierce—
    so that the thoughts of many hearts may be revealed."
There was also a prophetess, Anna,
    the daughter of Phanuel, of the tribe of Asher.**

She was advanced in years,
   having lived seven years with her husband after her marriage,
   and then as a widow until she was eighty-four.
She never left the temple,
   but worshiped night and day with fasting and prayer.
And coming forward at that very time,
   she gave thanks to God and spoke about the child
   to all who were awaiting the redemption of Jerusalem.

When they had fulfilled all the prescriptions
   of the law of the Lord,
   they returned to Galilee, to their own town of Nazareth.
The child grew and became strong, filled with wisdom;
   and the favor of God was upon him.

The Gospel of the Lord.

   OR

February 2—The Presentation of the Lord

Short Form

Luke 2:22-32   My eyes have seen your salvation.

✢ **A reading from the holy Gospel according to Luke**

**When the days were completed for their purification
according to the law of Moses,
Mary and Joseph took Jesus up to Jerusalem
to present him to the Lord,
just as it is written in the law of the Lord,
Every male that opens the womb shall be consecrated to the Lord,
and to offer the sacrifice of
a pair of turtledoves or two young pigeons,
in accordance with the dictate in the law of the Lord.**

**Now there was a man in Jerusalem whose name was Simeon.
This man was righteous and devout,
awaiting the consolation of Israel,
and the Holy Spirit was upon him.
It had been revealed to him by the Holy Spirit
that he should not see death
before he had seen the Christ of the Lord.
He came in the Spirit into the temple;
and when the parents brought in the child Jesus
to perform the custom of the law in regard to him,
he took him into his arms and blessed God, saying:**

> "Now, Master, you may let your servant go
>   in peace, according to your word,
> for my eyes have seen your salvation,
>   which you prepared in the sight of all the peoples:
> a light for revelation to the Gentiles,
>   and glory for your people Israel."

The Gospel of the Lord.

FEBRUARY 3

525 SAINT BLASE, BISHOP AND MARTYR

From the Common of Martyrs, p. 1782, or the Common of Pastors, p. 1805,

OR

FIRST READING

Romans 5:1-5   We boast of our afflictions.

A reading from the Letter of Saint Paul to the Romans

Brothers and sisters:
Since we have been justified by faith,
  we have peace with God through our Lord Jesus Christ,
  through whom we have gained access by faith
  to this grace in which we stand,
  and we boast in hope of the glory of God.
Not only that, but we even boast of our afflictions,
  knowing that affliction produces endurance,
  and endurance, proven character,
  and proven character, hope,
  and hope does not disappoint,
  because the love of God has been poured out into our hearts
  through the Holy Spirit that has been given to us.

The word of the Lord.

RESPONSORIAL PSALM

Psalm 117:1bc, 2

℟. (Mark 16:15) **Go out to all the world and tell the Good News.**
  or:
℟. **Alleluia.**

Praise the LORD, all you nations;
  glorify him, all you peoples!

℟. **Go out to all the world and tell the Good News.**
  or:
℟. **Alleluia.**

February 3—Saint Blase

For steadfast is his kindness toward us,
   and the fidelity of the LORD endures forever.

℟. Go out to all the world and tell the Good News.
   or:
℟. Alleluia.

ALLELUIA

Matthew 28:19a, 20b

℟. Alleluia, alleluia.

Go and teach all nations, says the Lord;
I am with you always, until the end of the world.

℟. Alleluia, alleluia.

GOSPEL

Mark 16:15-20   Go out to all the world and tell the Good News.

✠ A reading from the holy Gospel according to Mark

Jesus appeared to the Eleven and said to them:
"Go into the whole world
   and proclaim the Gospel to every creature.
Whoever believes and is baptized will be saved;
   whoever does not believe will be condemned.
These signs will accompany those who believe:
   in my name they will drive out demons,
   they will speak new languages.
They will pick up serpents with their hands,
   and if they drink any deadly thing, it will not harm them.
They will lay hands on the sick, and they will recover."

So then the Lord Jesus, after he spoke to them,
   was taken up into heaven
   and took his seat at the right hand of God.
But they went forth and preached everywhere,
   while the Lord worked with them
   and confirmed the word through accompanying signs.

The Gospel of the Lord.

FEBRUARY 3

526 SAINT ANSGAR, BISHOP

From the Common of Pastors: For Missionaries, p. 1805,

OR

FIRST READING

Isaiah 52:7-10   All the ends of the earth will behold the salvation of our God.

A reading from the Book of the Prophet Isaiah

> How beautiful upon the mountains
>   are the feet of him who brings glad tidings,
> Announcing peace, bearing good news,
>   announcing salvation, and saying to Zion,
>   "Your God is King!"
>
> Hark! Your sentinels raise a cry,
>   together they shout for joy,
> For they see directly, before their eyes,
>   the LORD restoring Zion.
> Break out together in song,
>   O ruins of Jerusalem!
> For the LORD comforts his people,
>   he redeems Jerusalem.
> The LORD has bared his holy arm
>   in the sight of all the nations;
> All the ends of the earth will behold
>   the salvation of our God.

The word of the Lord.

RESPONSORIAL PSALM

Psalm 96:1-2a, 2b-3, 7-8, 10

℟. (3) **Proclaim God's marvelous deeds to all the nations.**

Sing to the Lord a new song;
   sing to the Lord, all you lands.
Sing to the Lord; bless his name.

℟. **Proclaim God's marvelous deeds to all the nations.**

Announce his salvation, day after day.
Tell his glory among the nations;
   among all peoples, his wondrous deeds.

℟. **Proclaim God's marvelous deeds to all the nations.**

Give to the Lord, you families of nations,
   give to the Lord glory and praise;
   give to the Lord the glory due his name!

℟. **Proclaim God's marvelous deeds to all the nations.**

Say among the nations: The Lord is king.
He has made the world firm, not to be moved;
   he governs the peoples with equity.

℟. **Proclaim God's marvelous deeds to all the nations.**

ALLELUIA

Mark 1:17

℟. Alleluia, alleluia.

Come after me, says the Lord,
and I will make you fishers of men.

℟. Alleluia, alleluia.

GOSPEL

Mark 1:14-20   I will make you fishers of men.

☩ A reading from the holy Gospel according to Mark

After John had been arrested,
> Jesus came to Galilee proclaiming the Gospel of God:
> "This is the time of fulfillment.

The Kingdom of God is at hand.
Repent, and believe in the Gospel."

As he passed by the Sea of Galilee,
> he saw Simon and his brother Andrew casting their nets into the sea;
> they were fishermen.

Jesus said to them,
> "Come after me, and I will make you fishers of men."

Then they left their nets and followed him.
He walked along a little farther
> and saw James, the son of Zebedee, and his brother John.

They too were in a boat mending their nets.
Then he called them.
So they left their father Zebedee in the boat
> along with the hired men and followed him.

The Gospel of the Lord.

FEBRUARY 5

527 SAINT AGATHA, VIRGIN AND MARTYR MEMORIAL

From the Common of Martyrs, p. 1782, or the Common of Virgins, p. 1857,

OR

FIRST READING

1 Corinthians 1:26-31   God chose the weak of the world.

A reading from the first Letter of Saint Paul to the Corinthians

**Consider your own calling, brothers and sisters.
Not many of you were wise by human standards,
not many were powerful,
not many were of noble birth.
Rather, God chose the foolish of the world to shame the wise,
and God chose the weak of the world to shame the strong,
and God chose the lowly and despised of the world,
those who count for nothing,
to reduce to nothing those who are something,
so that no human being might boast before God.
It is due to him that you are in Christ Jesus,
who became for us wisdom from God,
as well as righteousness, sanctification, and redemption,
so that, as it is written,
*Whoever boasts, should boast in the Lord.***

The word of the Lord.

RESPONSORIAL PSALM

Psalm 31:3cd-4, 6 and 8ab, 16bc and 17

℟. (6) **Into your hands, O Lord, I commend my spirit.**

**Be my rock of refuge,
a stronghold to give me safety.
You are my rock and my fortress;
for your name's sake you will lead and guide me.**

℟. **Into your hands, O Lord, I commend my spirit.**

Into your hands I commend my spirit;
 you will redeem me, O Lord, O faithful God.
I will rejoice and be glad because of your mercy.

℟. Into your hands, O Lord, I commend my spirit.

Rescue me from the clutches of my enemies and my persecutors,
Let your face shine upon your servant;
 save me in your kindness.

℟. Into your hands, O Lord, I commend my spirit.

ALLELUIA

1 Peter 4:14

℟. Alleluia, alleluia.

If you are insulted for the name of Christ, blessed are you,
for the Spirit of God rests upon you.

℟. Alleluia, alleluia.

GOSPEL

Luke 9:23-26   Whoever loses his life for my sake will find it.

✛ A reading from the holy Gospel according to Luke

Jesus said to all,
 "If anyone wishes to come after me, he must deny himself
 and take up his cross daily and follow me.
For whoever wishes to save his life will lose it,
 but whoever loses his life for my sake will save it.
What profit is there for one to gain the whole world
 yet lose or forfeit himself?
Whoever is ashamed of me and of my words,
 the Son of Man will be ashamed of when he comes in his glory
 and in the glory of the Father and of the holy angels."

The Gospel of the Lord.

FEBRUARY 6

528 SAINT PAUL MIKI, PRIEST AND MARTYR, AND HIS COMPANIONS, MARTYRS MEMORIAL

From the Common of Martyrs, p. 1782,

OR

FIRST READING

Galatians 2:19-20   I live, no longer I, but Christ lives in me.

A reading from the Letter of Saint Paul to the Galatians

Brothers and sisters:
Through the law I died to the law,
    that I might live for God.
I have been crucified with Christ;
    yet I live, no longer I, but Christ lives in me;
    insofar as I now live in the flesh,
    I live by faith in the Son of God
    who has loved me and given himself up for me.

The word of the Lord.

RESPONSORIAL PSALM

Psalm 126:1bc-2ab, 2cd-3, 4-5, 6

℟. (5) **Those who sow in tears, shall reap rejoicing.**

When the LORD brought back the captives of Zion,
    we were like men dreaming.
Then our mouth was filled with laughter,
    and our tongue with rejoicing.

℟. **Those who sow in tears, shall reap rejoicing.**

Then they said among the nations,
    "The LORD has done great things for them."
The LORD has done great things for us;
    we are glad indeed.

℟. **Those who sow in tears, shall reap rejoicing.**

Restore our fortunes, O Lord,
   like the torrents in the southern desert.
Those who sow in tears
   shall reap rejoicing.

℟. **Those who sow in tears, shall reap rejoicing.**

Although they go forth weeping,
   carrying the seed to be sown,
They shall come back rejoicing,
   carrying their sheaves.

℟. **Those who sow in tears, shall reap rejoicing.**

ALLELUIA

Matthew 28:19a, 20b

℟. **Alleluia, alleluia.**

Go and teach all nations, says the Lord;
I am with you always, until the end of the world.

℟. **Alleluia, alleluia.**

GOSPEL

Matthew 28:16-20   Go and teach all nations.

✠ **A reading from the holy Gospel according to Matthew**

The Eleven disciples went to Galilee,
   to the mountain to which Jesus had ordered them.
When they saw him, they worshiped, but they doubted.
Then Jesus approached and said to them,
   "All power in heaven and on earth has been given to me.
Go, therefore, and make disciples of all nations,
   baptizing them in the name of the Father,
   and of the Son, and of the Holy Spirit,
   teaching them to observe all that I have commanded you.
And behold, I am with you always, until the end of the age."

The Gospel of the Lord.

FEBRUARY 8

529 SAINT JEROME EMILIANI, PRIEST

From the Common of Holy Men and Women: For Teachers, p. 1868,

OR

FIRST READING

Tobit 12:6-13 Prayer and fasting are good: but better than either is almsgiving accompanied by righteousness.

A reading from the Book of Tobit

The angel Raphael said to Tobit and his son:
 "Thank God! Give him the praise and the glory.
Before all the living,
 acknowledge the many good things he has done for you,
 by blessing and extolling his name in song.
Honor and proclaim God's deeds,
 and do not be slack in praising him.
A king's secret it is prudent to keep,
 but the works of God are to be declared and made known.
Praise them with due honor.
Do good, and evil will not find its way to you.
Prayer and fasting are good,
 but better than either is almsgiving accompanied by righteousness.
A little with righteousness is better than abundance with wickedness.
It is better to give alms than to store up gold;
 for almsgiving saves one from death and expiates every sin.
Those who regularly give alms shall enjoy a full life;
 but those habitually guilty of sin are their own worst enemies.

"I will now tell you the whole truth;
 I will conceal nothing at all from you.
I have already said to you,
 'A king's secret it is prudent to keep,
 but the works of God are to be made known with due honor.'
I can now tell you that when you, Tobit, and Sarah prayed,
 it was I who presented and read the record of your prayer
 before the Glory of the Lord;
 and I did the same thing when you used to bury the dead.
When you did not hesitate to get up
 and leave your dinner in order to go and bury the dead,
 I was sent to put you to the test."

The word of the Lord.

RESPONSORIAL PSALM

Psalm 34:2-3, 4-5, 6-7, 8-9, 10-11

℟. (2) **I will bless the Lord at all times.**
　or:
℟. (9) **Taste and see the goodness of the Lord.**

I will bless the LORD **at all times;**
　his praise shall be ever in my mouth.
Let my soul glory in the LORD**;**
　the lowly will hear and be glad.

℟. **I will bless the Lord at all times.**
　or:
℟. **Taste and see the goodness of the Lord.**

Glorify the LORD **with me,**
　let us together extol his name.
I sought the LORD**, and he answered me**
　and delivered me from all my fears.

℟. **I will bless the Lord at all times.**
　or:
℟. **Taste and see the goodness of the Lord.**

Look to him that you may be radiant with joy,
　and your faces may not blush with shame.
When the poor one called out, the LORD **heard,**
　and from all his distress he saved him.

℟. **I will bless the Lord at all times.**
　or:
℟. **Taste and see the goodness of the Lord.**

The angel of the LORD **encamps**
　around those who fear him, and delivers them.
Taste and see how good the LORD **is;**
　blessed the man who takes refuge in him.

℟. **I will bless the Lord at all times.**
　or:
℟. **Taste and see the goodness of the Lord.**

Fear the Lord, you his holy ones,
   for nought is lacking to those who fear him.
The great grow poor and hungry;
   but those who seek the Lord want for no good thing.

℟. I will bless the Lord at all times.
   or:
℟. Taste and see the goodness of the Lord.

ALLELUIA

Matthew 5:3

℟. Alleluia, alleluia.

Blessed are the poor in spirit;
for theirs is the Kingdom of heaven.

℟. Alleluia, alleluia.

GOSPEL

Long Form

Mark 10:17-30   Go, sell what you have and give to the poor; then come, follow me.

✠ A reading from the holy Gospel according to Mark

As Jesus was setting out on a journey, a man ran up,
   knelt down before him, and asked him,
   "Good teacher, what must I do to inherit eternal life?"
Jesus answered him, "Why do you call me good?
No one is good but God alone.
You know the commandments: *You shall not kill;*
   you shall not commit adultery;
   you shall not steal;
   you shall not bear false witness;
   you shall not defraud;
   honor your father and your mother."
He replied and said to him,
   "Teacher, all of these I have observed from my youth."
Jesus, looking at him, loved him and said to him,
   "You are lacking in one thing.
Go, sell what you have, and give to the poor
   and you will have treasure in heaven; then come, follow me."
At that statement his face fell,
   and he went away sad, for he had many possessions.

Jesus looked around and said to his disciples,
   "How hard it is for those who have wealth
   to enter the Kingdom of God!"
The disciples were amazed at his words.
So Jesus again said to them in reply,
   "Children, how hard it is to enter the Kingdom of God!
It is easier for a camel to pass through the eye of a needle
   than for one who is rich to enter the Kingdom of God."
They were exceedingly astonished and said among themselves,
   "Then who can be saved?"
Jesus looked at them and said,
   "For men it is impossible, but not for God.
All things are possible for God."
Peter began to say to him,
   "We have given up everything and followed you."
Jesus said, "Amen, I say to you,
   there is no one who has given up house or brothers or sisters
   or mother or father or children or lands
   for my sake and for the sake of the Gospel
   who will not receive a hundred times more now in this present age:
   houses and brothers and sisters
   and mothers and children and lands,
   with persecutions, and eternal life in the age to come."

The Gospel of the Lord.

OR

February 8—Saint Jerome Emiliani

Short Form

Mark 10:17-27   Go, sell what you have and give to the poor; then come, follow me.

☩ A reading from the holy Gospel according to Mark

As Jesus was setting out on a journey, a man ran up,
   knelt down before him, and asked him,
   "Good teacher, what must I do to inherit eternal life?"
Jesus answered him, "Why do you call me good?
No one is good but God alone.
You know the commandments: *You shall not kill;*
   you shall not commit adultery;
   you shall not steal;
   you shall not bear false witness;
   you shall not defraud;
   honor your father and your mother."
He replied and said to him,
   "Teacher, all of these I have observed from my youth."
Jesus, looking at him, loved him and said to him,
   "You are lacking in one thing.
Go, sell what you have, and give to the poor
   and you will have treasure in heaven; then come, follow me."
At that statement his face fell,
   and he went away sad, for he had many possessions.

Jesus looked around and said to his disciples,
   "How hard it is for those who have wealth
   to enter the Kingdom of God!"
The disciples were amazed at his words.
So Jesus again said to them in reply,
   "Children, how hard it is to enter the Kingdom of God!
It is easier for a camel to pass through the eye of a needle
   than for one who is rich to enter the Kingdom of God."
They were exceedingly astonished and said among themselves,
   "Then who can be saved?"
Jesus looked at them and said,
   "For men it is impossible, but not for God.
All things are possible for God."

The Gospel of the Lord.

FEBRUARY 10

530 SAINT SCHOLASTICA, VIRGIN MEMORIAL

From the Common of Virgins, p. 1857, or the Common of Holy Men and Women: For Religious, p. 1868,

OR

FIRST READING

Song of Songs 8:6-7   Stern as death is love.

A reading from the Song of Songs

Set me as a seal on your heart,
   as a seal on your arm;
For stern as death is love,
   relentless as the nether world is devotion;
   its flames are a blazing fire.
Deep waters cannot quench love,
   nor floods sweep it away.
Were one to offer all he owns to purchase love,
   he would be roundly mocked.

The word of the Lord.

RESPONSORIAL PSALM

Psalm 148:1bc-2, 11-13a, 13c-14

℟. (see 12a and 13a) **Young men and women, praise the name of the Lord.**
   or:
℟. **Alleluia.**

Praise the LORD from the heavens;
   praise him in the heights;
Praise him, all you his angels,
   praise him, all you his hosts.

℟. Young men and women, praise the name of the Lord.
   or:
℟. Alleluia.

Let the kings of the earth and all peoples,
   the princes and all the judges of the earth,
Young men, too, and maidens,
   old men and boys,
Praise the name of the LORD,
   for his name alone is exalted.

℟. Young men and women, praise the name of the Lord.
   or:
℟. Alleluia.

His majesty is above earth and heaven.
He has lifted up the horn of his people.
Be this his praise from all his faithful ones;
   from the children of Israel, the people close to him. Alleluia.

℟. Young men and women, praise the name of the Lord.
   or:
℟. Alleluia.

ALLELUIA

John 14:23

℟. Alleluia, alleluia.

**Whoever loves me will keep my word,
and my Father will love him
and we will come to him.**

℟. Alleluia, alleluia.

GOSPEL

Luke 10:38-42   Martha welcomed him. Mary has chosen the better part.

✠ **A reading from the holy Gospel according to Luke**

**Jesus entered a village
  where a woman whose name was Martha welcomed him.
She had a sister named Mary
  who sat beside the Lord at his feet listening to him speak.
Martha, burdened with much serving, came to him and said,
    "Lord, do you not care
    that my sister has left me by myself to do the serving?
Tell her to help me."
The Lord said to her in reply,
    "Martha, Martha, you are anxious and worried about many things.
There is need of only one thing.
Mary has chosen the better part
    and it will not be taken from her."**

The Gospel of the Lord.

FEBRUARY 11

531 OUR LADY OF LOURDES

From the Common of the Blessed Virgin Mary, p. 1751,

OR

FIRST READING

Isaiah 66:10-14c   I will send peace to her like a river.

A reading from the Book of the Prophet Isaiah

**Rejoice with Jerusalem and be glad because of her,
   all you who love her;
Exult, exult with her,
   all you who were mourning over her!
Oh, that you may suck fully
   of the milk of her comfort,
That you may nurse with delight
   at her abundant breasts!
   For thus says the Lord:
Lo, I will spread prosperity over her like a river,
   and the wealth of the nations like
   an overflowing torrent.
As nurslings, you shall be carried in her arms,
   and fondled in her lap;
As a mother comforts her child,
   so will I comfort you;
   in Jerusalem you shall find your comfort.**

**When you see this, your heart shall rejoice,
   and your bodies flourish like the grass;
The Lord's power shall be known to his servants.**

The word of the Lord.

RESPONSORIAL PSALM

Judith 13:18bcde, 19

℟. (15:9) **You are the highest honor of our race.**

**Blessed are you, daughter, by the Most High God,
 above all the women on earth;
 and blessed be the L**ORD** God,
 the creator of heaven and earth.**

℟. **You are the highest honor of our race.**

**Your deed of hope will never be forgotten
 by those who tell of the might of God.**

℟. **You are the highest honor of our race.**

ALLELUIA

See Luke 1:45

℟. **Alleluia, alleluia.**

**Blessed are you, O Virgin Mary, who believed
that what was spoken to you by the Lord would be fulfilled.**

℟. **Alleluia, alleluia.**

GOSPEL

John 2:1-11   And the mother of Jesus was there.

✠ A reading from the holy Gospel according to John

There was a wedding at Cana in Galilee,
  and the mother of Jesus was there.
Jesus and his disciples were also invited to the wedding.
When the wine ran short,
  the mother of Jesus said to him,
  "They have no wine."
And Jesus said to her,
  "Woman, how does your concern affect me?
My hour has not yet come."
His mother said to the servants,
  "Do whatever he tells you."
Now there were six stone water jars there for Jewish ceremonial washings,
  each holding twenty to thirty gallons.
Jesus told them,
  "Fill the jars with water."
So they filled them to the brim.
Then he told them,
  "Draw some out now and take it to the headwaiter."
So they took it.
And when the headwaiter tasted the water that had become wine,
  without knowing where it came from
  (although they who had drawn the water knew),
  the headwaiter called the bridegroom and said to him,
  "Everyone serves good wine first,
  and then when people have drunk freely, an inferior one;
  but you have kept the good wine until now."
Jesus did this as the beginning of his signs at Cana in Galilee
  and so revealed his glory,
  and his disciples began to believe in him.

The Gospel of the Lord.

FEBRUARY 14

532 SAINTS CYRIL AND METHODIUS, BISHOPS
MEMORIAL

From the Common of Pastors: For Missionaries, p. 1805, or the Common of Holy Men and Women, p. 1868,

OR

FIRST READING

Acts 13:46-49   We now turn to the Gentiles.

A reading from the Acts of the Apostles

Paul and Barnabas spoke out boldly and said,
"It was necessary that the word of God be spoken to you first,
but since you reject it
and condemn yourselves as unworthy of eternal life,
we now turn to the Gentiles.
For so the Lord has commanded us,
I have made you a light to the Gentiles,
that you may be an instrument of salvation
to the ends of the earth."
The Gentiles were delighted when they heard this
and glorified the word of the Lord.
All who were destined for eternal life came to believe,
and the word of the Lord continued to spread
through the whole region.

The word of the Lord.

RESPONSORIAL PSALM

Psalm 117:1bc, 2

℟. (Mark 16:15) **Go out to all the world and tell the Good News.**
   or:
℟. **Alleluia.**

Praise the LORD, all you nations;
   glorify him, all you peoples!

℟. **Go out to all the world and tell the Good News.**
   or:
℟. **Alleluia.**

**For steadfast is his kindness toward us,
and the fidelity of the Lord endures forever.**

℟. **Go out to all the world and tell the Good News.**
   or:
℟. **Alleluia.**

ALLELUIA

Luke 4:18

℟. **Alleluia, alleluia.**

**The Lord sent me to bring glad tidings to the poor
and to proclaim liberty to captives.**

℟. **Alleluia, alleluia.**

GOSPEL

Luke 10:1-9   The harvest is abundant but the laborers are few.

✠ **A reading from the holy Gospel according to Luke**

**The Lord Jesus appointed seventy-two other disciples
whom he sent ahead of him in pairs
to every town and place he intended to visit.
He said to them,
"The harvest is abundant but the laborers are few;
so ask the master of the harvest
to send out laborers for his harvest.
Go on your way;
behold, I am sending you like lambs among wolves.
Carry no money bag, no sack, no sandals;
and greet no one along the way.
Into whatever house you enter, first say,
'Peace to this household.'
If a peaceful person lives there,
your peace will rest on him;
but if not, it will return to you.
Stay in the same house and eat and drink what is offered to you,
for the laborer deserves his payment.
Do not move about from one house to another.
Whatever town you enter and they welcome you,
eat what is set before you,
cure the sick in it and say to them,
'The Kingdom of God is at hand for you.'"**

The Gospel of the Lord.

FEBRUARY 17

533 SEVEN FOUNDERS OF THE ORDER OF SERVITES, RELIGIOUS

From the Common of Holy Men and Women: For Religious, p. 1868,

OR

FIRST READING

Romans 8:26-30   Those God justified he also glorified.

A reading from the Letter of Saint Paul to the Romans

Brothers and sisters:
The Spirit comes to the aid of our weakness;
   for we do not know how to pray as we ought,
   but the Spirit himself intercedes with inexpressible groanings.
And the one who searches hearts
   knows what is the intention of the Spirit,
   because he intercedes for the holy ones
   according to God's will.

We know that all things work for good for those who love God,
   who are called according to his purpose.
For those he foreknew he also predestined
   to be conformed to the image of his Son,
   so that he might be the firstborn
   among many brothers.
And those he predestined he also called;
   and those he called he also justified;
   and those he justified he also glorified.

The word of the Lord.

RESPONSORIAL PSALM

Psalm 34:2-3, 4-5, 6-7, 8-9, 10-11

℟. (2) **I will bless the Lord at all times.**
   or:
℟. (9) **Taste and see the goodness of the Lord.**

I will bless the LORD** at all times;**
   his praise shall be ever in my mouth.
Let my soul glory in the LORD**;**
   the lowly will hear and be glad.

℟. **I will bless the Lord at all times.**
   or:
℟. **Taste and see the goodness of the Lord.**

Glorify the LORD** with me,**
   let us together extol his name.
I sought the LORD**, and he answered me**
   and delivered me from all my fears.

℟. **I will bless the Lord at all times.**
   or:
℟. **Taste and see the goodness of the Lord.**

Look to him that you may be radiant with joy,
   and your faces may not blush with shame.
When the poor one called out, the LORD** heard,**
   and from all his distress he saved him.

℟. **I will bless the Lord at all times.**
   or:
℟. **Taste and see the goodness of the Lord.**

The angel of the LORD** encamps**
   around those who fear him, and delivers them.
Taste and see how good the LORD** is;**
   blessed the man who takes refuge in him.

℟. **I will bless the Lord at all times.**
   or:
℟. **Taste and see the goodness of the Lord.**

Fear the LORD**, you his holy ones,**
   for nought is lacking to those who fear him.
The great grow poor and hungry;
   but those who seek the LORD **want for no good thing.**

℟. **I will bless the Lord at all times.**
   or:
℟. **Taste and see the goodness of the Lord.**

ALLELUIA

Matthew 5:3

℟. **Alleluia, alleluia.**

Blessed are the poor in spirit;
for theirs is the Kingdom of heaven.

℟. **Alleluia, alleluia.**

GOSPEL

Matthew 19:27-29   You who have followed me will receive a hundred times more.

☩ **A reading from the holy Gospel according to Matthew**

Peter said to Jesus,
   "We have given up everything and followed you.
What will there be for us?"
Jesus said to them "Amen, I say to you
   that you who have followed me, in the new age,
   when the Son of Man is seated on his throne of glory,
   will yourselves sit on twelve thrones,
   judging the twelve tribes of Israel.
And everyone who has given up houses or brothers or sisters
   or father or mother or children or lands
   for the sake of my name will receive a hundred times more,
   and will inherit eternal life."

The Gospel of the Lord.

FEBRUARY 21

534 SAINT PETER DAMIAN, BISHOP AND DOCTOR OF THE CHURCH

From the Common of Doctors of the Church, p. 1838, or the Common of Pastors, p. 1805, or the Common of Holy Men and Women: For Religious, p. 1868,

OR

FIRST READING

2 Timothy 4:1-5   Perform the work of an evangelist; fulfill your ministry.

A reading from the second Letter of Saint Paul to Timothy

Beloved:
I charge you in the presence of God and of Christ Jesus,
  who will judge the living and the dead,
  and by his appearing and his kingly power:
  proclaim the word;
  be persistent whether it is convenient or inconvenient;
  convince, reprimand, encourage through all patience and teaching.
For the time will come when people will not tolerate sound doctrine
  but, following their own desires and insatiable curiosity,
  will accumulate teachers and will stop listening to the truth
  and will be diverted to myths.
But you, be self-possessed in all circumstances;
  put up with hardship;
  perform the work of an evangelist;
  fulfill your ministry.

The word of the Lord.

RESPONSORIAL PSALM

Psalm 16:1-2, 5, 7-8, 11

℟. (see 5a) **You are my inheritance, O Lord.**

Keep me, O God, for in you I take refuge.
  I say to the LORD**, "My Lord are you."**
O LORD**, my allotted portion and my cup,**
  you it is who hold fast my lot.

℟. **You are my inheritance, O Lord.**

I bless the LORD **who counsels me;**
  even in the night my heart exhorts me.
I set the LORD **ever before me;**
  with him at my right hand I shall not be disturbed.

℟. **You are my inheritance, O Lord.**

You will show me the path to life,
  fullness of joys in your presence,
    the delights at your right hand forever.

℟. **You are my inheritance, O Lord.**

ALLELUIA

John 15:9b, 5b

℟. **Alleluia, alleluia.**

Remain in my love, says the Lord;
whoever remains in me and I in him will bear much fruit.

℟. **Alleluia, alleluia.**

February 21—Saint Peter Damian

GOSPEL

John 15:1-8 Whoever remains in me, and I in them, will bear much fruit.

☩ **A reading from the holy Gospel according to John**

Jesus said to his disciples:
"I am the true vine, and my Father is the vine grower.
He takes away every branch in me that does not bear fruit,
   and every one that does he prunes so that it bears more fruit.
You are already pruned because of the word that I spoke to you.
Remain in me, as I remain in you.
Just as a branch cannot bear fruit on its own
   unless it remains on the vine,
   so neither can you unless you remain in me.
I am the vine, you are the branches.
Whoever remains in me and I in him will bear much fruit,
   because without me you can do nothing.
Anyone who does not remain in me
   will be thrown out like a branch and wither;
   people will gather them and throw them into a fire
   and they will be burned.
If you remain in me and my words remain in you,
   ask for whatever you want and it will be done for you.
By this is my Father glorified,
   that you bear much fruit and become my disciples."

The Gospel of the Lord.

FEBRUARY 22

535 THE CHAIR OF SAINT PETER, APOSTLE   FEAST

For a votive Mass of Saint Peter the readings are also as follows.

FIRST READING

1 Peter 5:1-4   As a fellow presbyter and witness to the sufferings of Christ.

A reading from the first Letter of Saint Peter

Beloved:
I exhort the presbyters among you,
   as a fellow presbyter and witness to the sufferings of Christ
   and one who has a share in the glory to be revealed.
Tend the flock of God in your midst,
   overseeing not by constraint but willingly,
   as God would have it, not for shameful profit but eagerly.
Do not lord it over those assigned to you,
   but be examples to the flock.
And when the chief Shepherd is revealed,
   you will receive the unfading crown of glory.

The word of the Lord.

RESPONSORIAL PSALM

Psalm 23:1-3a, 4, 5, 6

℟. (1) **The Lord is my shepherd; there is nothing I shall want.**

The LORD is my shepherd; I shall not want.
   In verdant pastures he gives me repose;
Beside restful waters he leads me;
   he refreshes my soul.

℟. **The Lord is my shepherd; there is nothing I shall want.**

Even though I walk in the dark valley
   I fear no evil; for you are at my side
With your rod and your staff
   that give me courage.

℟. **The Lord is my shepherd; there is nothing I shall want.**

You spread the table before me
   in the sight of my foes;
You anoint my head with oil;
   my cup overflows.

R̷. The Lord is my shepherd; there is nothing I shall want.

Only goodness and kindness follow me
   all the days of my life;
And I shall dwell in the house of the LORD
   for years to come.

R̷. The Lord is my shepherd; there is nothing I shall want.

ALLELUIA

Matthew 16:18

R̷. Alleluia, alleluia.

You are Peter, and upon this rock I will build my Church;
the gates of the netherworld shall not prevail against it.

R̷. Alleluia, alleluia.

GOSPEL

Matthew 16:13-19   You are Peter. I will give you the keys to the Kingdom of heaven.

✛ A reading from the holy Gospel according to Matthew

When Jesus went into the region of Caesarea Philippi
   he asked his disciples,
      "Who do people say that the Son of Man is?"
They replied, "Some say John the Baptist, others Elijah,
   still others Jeremiah or one of the prophets."
He said to them, "But who do you say that I am?"
Simon Peter said in reply,
   "You are the Christ, the Son of the living God."
Jesus said to him in reply, "Blessed are you, Simon son of Jonah.
For flesh and blood has not revealed this to you, but my heavenly Father.
And so I say to you, you are Peter,
   and upon this rock I will build my Church,
   and the gates of the netherworld shall not prevail against it.
I will give you the keys to the Kingdom of heaven.
Whatever you bind on earth shall be bound in heaven;
   and whatever you loose on earth shall be loosed in heaven."

The Gospel of the Lord.

FEBRUARY 23

536 SAINT POLYCARP, BISHOP AND MARTYR
MEMORIAL

From the Common of Martyrs, p. 1782, or the Common of Pastors, p. 1805,

OR

FIRST READING

Revelation 2:8-11   I know your tribulation and poverty.

A reading from the Book of Revelation

"To the angel of the Church in Smyrna, write this:

"'The first and the last, who once died but came to life, says this:
 "I know your tribulation and poverty, but you are rich.
I know the slander of those who claim to be Jews and are not,
 but rather are members of the assembly of Satan.
Do not be afraid of anything that you are going to suffer.
Indeed, the Devil will throw some of you into prison,
 that you may be tested,
 and you will face an ordeal for ten days.
Remain faithful until death, and I will give you the crown of life.

"'"Whoever has ears ought to hear what the Spirit says to the churches.
The victor shall not be harmed by the second death."'"

The word of the Lord.

RESPONSORIAL PSALM

Psalm 31:3cd-4, 6 and 8ab, 16bc and 17

℟. (6) **Into your hands, O Lord, I commend my spirit.**

Be my rock of refuge,
 a stronghold to give me safety.
You are my rock and my fortress;
 for your name's sake you will lead and guide me.

℟. **Into your hands, O Lord, I commend my spirit.**

Into your hands I commend my spirit;
 you will redeem me, O Lord, O faithful God.
I will rejoice and be glad because of your mercy.

℟. **Into your hands, O Lord, I commend my spirit.**

Rescue me from the clutches of my enemies and my persecutors,
Let your face shine upon your servant;
   save me in your kindness.

℞. Into your hands, O Lord, I commend my spirit.

ALLELUIA

See *Te Deum*

℞. Alleluia, alleluia.

We praise you, O God,
we acclaim you as Lord;
the white-robed army of martyrs praise you.

℞. Alleluia, alleluia.

GOSPEL

John 15:18-21   If they persecuted me, they will also persecute you.

✠ A reading from the holy Gospel according to John

Jesus said to his disciples:
"If the world hates you, realize that it hated me first.
If you belonged to the world, the world would love its own;
   but because you do not belong to the world,
   and I have chosen you out of the world,
   the world hates you.
Remember the word I spoke to you,
   'No slave is greater than his master.'
If they persecuted me, they will also persecute you.
If they kept my word, they will also keep yours.
And they will do all these things to you on account of my name,
   because they do not know the one who sent me."

The Gospel of the Lord.

MARCH 3

[In the Dioceses of the United States]

536A SAINT KATHARINE DREXEL, VIRGIN

From the Common of Virgins, p. 1857, or the Common of Holy Men and Women: For Religious, p. 1868.

MARCH 4

537 SAINT CASIMIR

From the Common of Holy Men and Women, p. 1868,

OR

FIRST READING

Philippians 3:8-14   I continue my pursuit toward the goal, the prize of God's heavenly call, in Christ Jesus.

A reading from the Letter of Saint Paul to the Philippians

Brothers and sisters:
I consider everything as a loss
  because of the supreme good of knowing Christ Jesus my Lord.
For his sake I have accepted the loss of all things
  and I consider them so much rubbish,
  that I may gain Christ and be found in him,
  not having any righteousness of my own based on the law
  but that which comes through faith in Christ,
  the righteousness from God,
  depending on faith to know him and the power of his resurrection
  and the sharing of his sufferings by being conformed to his death,
  if somehow I may attain the resurrection from the dead.

It is not that I have already taken hold of it
  or have already attained perfect maturity,
  but I continue my pursuit in hope that I may possess it,
  since I have indeed been taken possession of by Christ Jesus.
Brothers and sisters, I for my part
  do not consider myself to have taken possession.
Just one thing: forgetting what lies behind
  but straining forward to what lies ahead,
  I continue my pursuit toward the goal,
  the prize of God's upward calling, in Christ Jesus.

The word of the Lord.

RESPONSORIAL PSALM

Psalm 15:2-3ab, 3cd-4ab, 5

℟. (1) **The just one shall live on your holy mountain, O Lord.**

**He who walks blamelessly and does justice;
    who thinks the truth in his heart
    and slanders not with his tongue.**

℟. **The just one shall live on your holy mountain, O Lord.**

**Who harms not his fellow man,
    nor takes up a reproach against his neighbor;
By whom the reprobate is despised,
    while he honors those who fear the L**ORD**.**

℟. **The just one shall live on your holy mountain, O Lord.**

**Who lends not his money at usury
    and accepts no bribe against the innocent.
He who does these things
    shall never be disturbed.**

℟. **The just one shall live on your holy mountain, O Lord.**

ALLELUIA

John 13:34

℟. **Alleluia, alleluia.**

**I give you a new commandment:
love one another as I have loved you.**

℟. **Alleluia, alleluia.**

GOSPEL

John 15:9-17   You are my friends if you do what I command you.

☩ **A reading from the holy Gospel according to John**

Jesus said to his disciples:
"As the Father loves me, so I also love you.
Remain in my love.
If you keep my commandments, you will remain in my love,
 just as I have kept my Father's commandments
 and remain in his love.

"I have told you this so that my joy might be in you
 and your joy might be complete.
This is my commandment: love one another as I love you.
No one has greater love than this,
 to lay down one's life for one's friends.
You are my friends if you do what I command you.
I no longer call you slaves,
 because a slave does not know what his master is doing.
I have called you friends,
 because I have told you everything I have heard from my Father.
It was not you who chose me, but I who chose you
 and appointed you to go and bear fruit that will remain,
 so that whatever you ask the Father in my name he may give you.
This I command you: love one another."

The Gospel of the Lord.

MARCH 7

538 SAINTS PERPETUA AND FELICITY, MARTYRS
MEMORIAL

From the Common of Martyrs, p. 1782,

> OR

FIRST READING

Romans 8:31b-39   Neither death nor life will be able to separate us from the love of God.

A reading from the Letter of Saint Paul to the Romans

Brothers and sisters:
If God is for us, who can be against us?
He who did not spare his own Son
  but handed him over for us all,
  how will he not also give us everything else along with him?
Who will bring a charge against God's chosen ones?
It is God who acquits us.
Who will condemn?
It is Christ Jesus who died, rather, was raised,
  who also is at the right hand of God,
  who indeed intercedes for us.
What will separate us from the love of Christ?
Will anguish, or distress, or persecution, or famine,
  or nakedness, or peril, or the sword?
As it is written:

> *For your sake we are being slain all the day;*
>   *we are looked upon as sheep to be slaughtered.*

No, in all these things we conquer overwhelmingly
  through him who loved us.
For I am convinced that neither death, nor life,
  nor angels, nor principalities,
  nor present things, nor future things,
  nor powers, nor height, nor depth,
  nor any other creature will be able to separate us
  from the love of God in Christ Jesus our Lord.

The word of the Lord.

RESPONSORIAL PSALM

Psalm 124:2-3, 4-5, 7-8

℟. (7) **Our soul has escaped like a bird from the fowler's snare.**

Had not the Lord been with us—
　when men rose up against us,
Then would they have swallowed us alive,
　when their fury was inflamed against us.

℟. **Our soul has escaped like a bird from the fowler's snare.**

Then would the waters have overwhelmed us;
The torrent would have swept over us;
　over us then would have swept
　the raging waters.

℟. **Our soul has escaped like a bird from the fowler's snare.**

Broken was the snare,
　and we were freed.
Our help is in the name of the Lord,
　who made heaven and earth.

℟. **Our soul has escaped like a bird from the fowler's snare.**

ALLELUIA

Matthew 5:10

℟. **Alleluia, alleluia.**

**Blessed are they who are persecuted for the sake of righteousness,
for theirs is the Kingdom of heaven.**

℟. **Alleluia, alleluia.**

GOSPEL

Matthew 10:34-39 I have come to bring not peace but the sword.

✢ A reading from the holy Gospel according to Matthew

**Jesus said to his Apostles:
"Do not think that I have come to bring peace upon the earth.
I have come to bring not peace but the sword.
For I have come to set**

   **a man 'against his father,
      a daughter against her mother,
   and a daughter-in-law against her mother-in-law;
      and one's enemies will be those of his household.'**

**"Whoever loves father or mother more than me is not worthy of me,
   and whoever loves son or daughter more than me is not worthy of me;
   and whoever does not take up his cross
   and follow after me is not worthy of me.
Whoever finds his life will lose it,
   and whoever loses his life for my sake will find it."**

The Gospel of the Lord.

MARCH 8

539 SAINT JOHN OF GOD, RELIGIOUS

From the Common of Holy Men and Women: For Religious, p. 1868, or For Those Who Work for the Underprivileged, p. 1868,

OR

FIRST READING

1 John 3:14-18   We ought to lay down our lives for our brothers.

A reading from the first Letter of Saint John

Beloved:
We know that we have passed from death to life
   because we love our brothers.
Whoever does not love remains in death.
Everyone who hates his brother is a murderer,
   and you know that anyone who is a murderer
      does not have eternal life remaining in him.
The way we came to know love
   was that he laid down his life for us;
   so we ought to lay down our lives for our brothers.
If someone who has worldly means
   sees a brother in need and refuses him compassion,
   how can the love of God remain in him?
Children, let us love not in word or speech
   but in deed and truth.

The word of the Lord.

RESPONSORIAL PSALM

Psalm 112:1bc-2, 3-4, 5-7a, 7b-8, 9

℟. (1) **Blessed the man who fears the Lord.**
   or:
℟. **Alleluia.**

Blessed the man who fears the LORD,
   who greatly delights in his commands.
His posterity shall be mighty upon the earth;
   the upright generation shall be blessed.

℟. **Blessed the man who fears the Lord.**
   or:
℟. **Alleluia.**

Wealth and riches shall be in his house;
   his generosity shall endure forever.
Light shines through the darkness for the upright;
   he is gracious and merciful and just.

℟. **Blessed the man who fears the Lord.**
   or:
℟. **Alleluia.**

Well for the man who is gracious and lends,
   who conducts his affairs with justice;
He shall never be moved;
   the just man shall be in everlasting remembrance.

℟. **Blessed the man who fears the Lord.**
   or:
℟. **Alleluia.**

An evil report he shall not fear.
   His heart is firm, trusting in the LORD.
His heart is steadfast; he shall not fear
   till he looks down upon his foes.

℟. **Blessed the man who fears the Lord.**
   or:
℟. **Alleluia.**

Lavishly he gives to the poor,
   his generosity shall endure forever;
   his horn shall be exalted in glory.

℟. **Blessed the man who fears the Lord.**
   or:
℟. **Alleluia.**

ALLELUIA

John 13:34

℟. Alleluia, alleluia.

I give you a new commandment:
love one another as I have loved you.

℟. Alleluia, alleluia.

GOSPEL

Matthew 25:31-40   Whatever you did for one of these least brothers of mine, you did for me.

✠ A reading from the holy Gospel according to Matthew

Jesus said to his disciples:
"When the Son of Man comes in his glory,
   and all the angels with him,
   he will sit upon his glorious throne,
   and all the nations will be assembled before him.
And he will separate them one from another,
   as a shepherd separates the sheep from the goats.
He will place the sheep on his right and the goats on his left.
Then the king will say to those on his right,
   'Come, you who are blessed by my Father.
Inherit the kingdom prepared for you from the foundation of the world.
For I was hungry and you gave me food,
   I was thirsty and you gave me drink,
   a stranger and you welcomed me,
   naked and you clothed me,
   ill and you cared for me,
   in prison and you visited me.'
Then the righteous will answer him and say,
   'Lord, when did we see you hungry and feed you,
   or thirsty and give you drink?
When did we see you a stranger and welcome you,
   or naked and clothe you?
When did we see you ill or in prison, and visit you?'
And the king will say to them in reply,
   'Amen, I say to you, whatever you did
   for one of the least brothers of mine, you did for me.'"

The Gospel of the Lord.

MARCH 9

540 SAINT FRANCES OF ROME, RELIGIOUS

From the Common of Holy Men and Women, p. 1868,

OR

FIRST READING

Proverbs 31:10-13, 19-20, 30-31   *The woman who fears the Lord is to be praised.*

A reading from the Book of Proverbs

**When one finds a worthy wife,
    her value is far beyond pearls.
Her husband, entrusting his heart to her,
    has an unfailing prize.
She brings him good, and not evil,
    all the days of her life.
She obtains wool and flax
    and makes cloth with skillful hands.
She puts her hands to the distaff,
    and her fingers ply the spindle.
She reaches out her hands to the poor,
    and extends her arms to the needy.
Charm is deceptive and beauty fleeting;
    the woman who fears the Lord is to be praised.
Give her a reward of her labors,
    and let her works praise her at the city gates.**

The word of the Lord.

RESPONSORIAL PSALM

Psalm 34:2-3, 4-5, 6-7, 8-9, 10-11

℟. (2) **I will bless the Lord at all times.**
    or:
℟. (9) **Taste and see the goodness of the Lord.**

I will bless the Lord at all times;
    his praise shall be ever in my mouth.
Let my soul glory in the Lord;
    the lowly will hear and be glad.

℟. **I will bless the Lord at all times.**
    or:
℟. **Taste and see the goodness of the Lord.**

Glorify the LORD **with me,**
   let us together extol his name.
I sought the LORD**, and he answered me**
   and delivered me from all my fears.

℟. I will bless the Lord at all times.
   or:
℟. Taste and see the goodness of the Lord.

Look to him that you may be radiant with joy,
   and your faces may not blush with shame.
When the poor one called out, the LORD **heard,**
   and from all his distress he saved him.

℟. I will bless the Lord at all times.
   or:
℟. Taste and see the goodness of the Lord.

The angel of the LORD **encamps**
   around those who fear him, and delivers them.
Taste and see how good the LORD **is;**
   blessed the man who takes refuge in him.

℟. I will bless the Lord at all times.
   or:
℟. Taste and see the goodness of the Lord.

Fear the LORD**, you his holy ones,**
   for nought is lacking to those who fear him.
The great grow poor and hungry;
   but those who seek the LORD want for no good thing.

℟. I will bless the Lord at all times.
   or:
℟. Taste and see the goodness of the Lord.

ALLELUIA

John 13:34

℟. Alleluia, alleluia.

I give you a new commandment:
love one another as I have loved you.

℟. Alleluia, alleluia.

GOSPEL

Matthew 22:34-40 You shall love the Lord your God, and your neighbor as yourself.

✛ A reading from the holy Gospel according to Matthew

When the Pharisees heard that Jesus had silenced the Sadducees,
   they gathered together, and one of them,
   a scholar of the law, tested him by asking,
   "Teacher, which commandment in the law is the greatest?"
He said to him,
   "You shall love the Lord, your God,
   with all your heart,
   with all your soul,
   and with all your mind.
This is the greatest and the first commandment.
The second is like it:
   You shall love your neighbor as yourself.
The whole law and the prophets depend on these two commandments."

The Gospel of the Lord.

MARCH 17

541 SAINT PATRICK, BISHOP

From the Common of Pastors: For Missionaries, p. 1805,

OR

FIRST READING

1 Peter 4:7b-11   Each one has received a gift; use it to serve one another.

A reading from the first Letter of Saint Peter

Beloved:
Be serious and sober-minded
  so that you will be able to pray.
Above all, let your love for one another be intense,
  because love covers a multitude of sins.
Be hospitable to one another without complaining.
As each one has received a gift, use it to serve one another
  as good stewards of God's varied grace.
Whoever preaches, let it be with the words of God;
  whoever serves, let it be with the strength that God supplies,
  so that in all things God may be glorified through Jesus Christ,
  to whom belong glory and dominion forever and ever. Amen.

The word of the Lord.

RESPONSORIAL PSALM

Psalm 96:1-2a, 2b-3, 7-8b, 10

℟. (3) **Proclaim God's marvelous deeds to all the nations.**

**Sing to the Lord a new song;
  sing to the Lord, all you lands.
Sing to the Lord; bless his name.**

℟. **Proclaim God's marvelous deeds to all the nations.**

**Announce his salvation, day after day.
Tell his glory among the nations;
  among all peoples, his wondrous deeds.**

℟. **Proclaim God's marvelous deeds to all the nations.**

**Give to the Lord, you families of nations,
  give to the Lord glory and praise;
  give to the Lord the glory due his name!**

℟. **Proclaim God's marvelous deeds to all the nations.**

**Say among the nations: The Lord is king.
He has made the world firm, not to be moved;
  he governs the peoples with equity.**

℟. **Proclaim God's marvelous deeds to all the nations.**

ALLELUIA

Mark 1:17

℟. **Alleluia, alleluia.**

**Come after me, says the Lord,
and I will make you fishers of men.**

℟. **Alleluia, alleluia.**

GOSPEL

Luke 5:1-11   At your command I will lower the nets.

✠ **A reading from the holy Gospel according to Luke**

While the crowd was pressing in on Jesus and listening to the word of God,
  he was standing by the Lake of Gennesaret.
He saw two boats there alongside the lake;
  the fishermen had disembarked and were washing their nets.
Getting into one of the boats, the one belonging to Simon,
  he asked him to put out a short distance from the shore.
Then he sat down and taught the crowds from the boat.
After he had finished speaking, he said to Simon,
  "Put out into deep water and lower your nets for a catch."
Simon said in reply,
  "Master, we have worked hard all night and have caught nothing,
  but at your command I will lower the nets."
When they had done this, they caught a great number of fish
  and their nets were tearing.
They signaled to their partners in the other boat
  to come to help them.
They came and filled both boats
  so that they were in danger of sinking.
When Simon Peter saw this, he fell at the knees of Jesus and said,
  "Depart from me, Lord, for I am a sinful man."
For astonishment at the catch of fish they had made seized him
  and all those with him,
  and likewise James and John, the sons of Zebedee,
  who were partners of Simon.
Jesus said to Simon, "Do not be afraid;
  from now on you will be catching men."
When they brought their boats to the shore,
  they left everything and followed him.

The Gospel of the Lord.

MARCH 18

542 SAINT CYRIL OF JERUSALEM, BISHOP AND DOCTOR OF THE CHURCH

From the Common of Pastors, p. 1805, or the Common of Doctors of the Church, p. 1838,

OR

FIRST READING

John 5:1-5   The victory that conquers the world is our faith.

A reading from the first Letter of Saint John

Beloved:
Everyone who believes that Jesus is the Christ is begotten by God,
   and everyone who loves the Father
   loves also the one begotten by him.
In this way we know that we love the children of God
   when we love God and obey his commandments.
For the love of God is this,
   that we keep his commandments.
And his commandments are not burdensome,
   for whoever is begotten by God conquers the world.
And the victory that conquers the world is our faith.
Who indeed is the victor over the world
   but the one who believes that Jesus is the Son of God?

The word of the Lord.

RESPONSORIAL PSALM

Psalm 19:8, 9, 10, 11

℟. (10) **The judgments of the Lord are true, and all of them are just.**
or:
℟. (John 6:63) **Your words, Lord, are Spirit and life.**

**The law of the Lord is perfect,
refreshing the soul.
The decree of the Lord is trustworthy,
giving wisdom to the simple.**

℟. **The judgments of the Lord are true, and all of them are just.**
or:
℟. **Your words, Lord, are Spirit and life.**

**The precepts of the Lord are right,
rejoicing the heart.
The command of the Lord is clear,
enlightening the eye.**

℟. **The judgments of the Lord are true, and all of them are just.**
or:
℟. **Your words, Lord, are Spirit and life.**

**The fear of the Lord is pure,
enduring forever.
The ordinances of the Lord are true,
all of them just.**

℟. **The judgments of the Lord are true, and all of them are just.**
or:
℟. **Your words, Lord, are Spirit and life.**

**They are more precious than gold,
than a heap of purest gold;
Sweeter also than syrup
or honey from the comb.**

℟. **The judgments of the Lord are true, and all of them are just.**
or:
℟. **Your words, Lord, are Spirit and life.**

ALLELUIA

John 15:9b, 5b

℟. Alleluia, alleluia.

**Remain in my love, says the Lord;
whoever remains in me and I in him will bear much fruit.**

℟. Alleluia, alleluia.

GOSPEL

John 15:1-8   Whoever remains in me and I in him will bear much fruit.

✠ A reading from the holy Gospel according to John

**Jesus said to his disciples:
"I am the true vine, and my Father is the vine grower.
He takes away every branch in me that does not bear fruit,
   and everyone that does he prunes so that it bears more fruit.
You are already pruned because of the word that I spoke to you.
Remain in me, as I remain in you.
Just as a branch cannot bear fruit on its own
   unless it remains on the vine,
   so neither can you unless you remain in me.
I am the vine, you are the branches.
Whoever remains in me and I in him will bear much fruit,
   because without me you can do nothing.
Anyone who does not remain in me
   will be thrown out like a branch and wither;
   people will gather them and throw them into a fire
   and they will be burned.
If you remain in me and my words remain in you,
   ask for whatever you want and it will be done for you.
By this is my Father glorified,
   that you bear much fruit and become my disciples."**

The Gospel of the Lord.

MARCH 19

543 SAINT JOSEPH, HUSBAND OF THE BLESSED VIRGIN MARY SOLEMNITY

FIRST READING

2 Samuel 7:4-5a, 12-14a, 16   The Lord God will give him the throne of David, his father (Luke 1:32).

A reading from the second Book of Samuel

The Lord spoke to Nathan and said:
"Go, tell my servant David,
  'When your time comes and you rest with your ancestors,
  I will raise up your heir after you, sprung from your loins,
  and I will make his kingdom firm.
It is he who shall build a house for my name.
And I will make his royal throne firm forever.
I will be a father to him,
  and he shall be a son to me.
Your house and your kingdom shall endure forever before me;
  your throne shall stand firm forever.'"

The word of the Lord.

RESPONSORIAL PSALM

Psalm 89:2-3, 4-5, 27 and 29

℟. (37) **The son of David will live for ever.**

The promises of the Lord I will sing forever;
  through all generations my mouth shall proclaim your faithfulness,
For you have said, "My kindness is established forever";
  in heaven you have confirmed your faithfulness.

℟. **The son of David will live for ever.**

"I have made a covenant with my chosen one,
  I have sworn to David my servant:
Forever will I confirm your posterity
  and establish your throne for all generations."

℟. **The son of David will live for ever.**

"He shall say of me, 'You are my father,
  my God, the Rock, my savior.'
Forever I will maintain my kindness toward him,
  and my covenant with him stands firm."

℟. The son of David will live for ever.

SECOND READING

Romans 4:13, 16-18, 22   Abraham believed, hoping against hope.

A reading from the Letter of Saint Paul to the Romans

Brothers and sisters:
It was not through the law
  that the promise was made to Abraham and his descendants
  that he would inherit the world,
  but through the righteousness that comes from faith.
For this reason, it depends on faith,
  so that it may be a gift,
  and the promise may be guaranteed to all his descendants,
  not to those who only adhere to the law
  but to those who follow the faith of Abraham,
  who is the father of all of us, as it is written,
  I have made you father of many nations.
He is our father in the sight of God,
  in whom he believed, who gives life to the dead
  and calls into being what does not exist.
He believed, hoping against hope,
  that he would become *the father of many nations,*
  according to what was said, *Thus shall your descendants be.*
That is why *it was credited to him as righteousness.*

The word of the Lord.

VERSE BEFORE THE GOSPEL OR ALLELUIA

Psalm 84:5

℟. [Alleluia, alleluia.]

Blessed are those who dwell in your house, O Lord;
they never cease to praise you.

℟. [Alleluia, alleluia.]

GOSPEL

First Option

Matthew 1:16, 18-21, 24a   Joseph did as the angel of the Lord had commanded him.

✠ **A reading from the holy Gospel according to Matthew**

**Jacob was the father of Joseph, the husband of Mary.
Of her was born Jesus who is called the Christ.**

**Now this is how the birth of Jesus Christ came about.
When his mother Mary was betrothed to Joseph,
  but before they lived together,
  she was found with child through the Holy Spirit.
Joseph her husband, since he was a righteous man,
  yet unwilling to expose her to shame,
  decided to divorce her quietly.
Such was his intention when, behold,
  the angel of the Lord appeared to him in a dream and said,
  "Joseph, son of David,
  do not be afraid to take Mary your wife into your home.
For it is through the Holy Spirit
  that this child has been conceived in her.
She will bear a son and you are to name him Jesus,
  because he will save his people from their sins."
When Joseph awoke,
  he did as the angel of the Lord had commanded him
  and took his wife into his home.**

The Gospel of the Lord.

OR

March 19—Saint Joseph, Husband of the Blessed Virgin Mary

Second Option

Luke 2:41-51a   Your father and I have been looking for you with great anxiety.

✠ A reading from the holy Gospel according to Luke

Each year Jesus' parents went to Jerusalem for the feast of Passover,
    and when he was twelve years old,
    they went up according to festival custom.
After they had completed its days, as they were returning,
    the boy Jesus remained behind in Jerusalem,
    but his parents did not know it.
Thinking that he was in the caravan,
    they journeyed for a day
    and looked for him among their relatives and acquaintances,
    but not finding him,
    they returned to Jerusalem to look for him.
After three days they found him in the temple,
    sitting in the midst of the teachers,
    listening to them and asking them questions,
    and all who heard him were astounded
    at his understanding and his answers.
When his parents saw him,
    they were astonished,
    and his mother said to him,
    "Son, why have you done this to us?
Your father and I have been looking for you with great anxiety."
And he said to them,
    "Why were you looking for me?
Did you not know that I must be in my Father's house?"
But they did not understand what he said to them.
He went down with them and came to Nazareth,
    and was obedient to them.

The Gospel of the Lord.

MARCH 23

544 SAINT TORIBIO DE MOGROVEJO, BISHOP

From the Common of Pastors, p. 1805,

OR

FIRST READING

2 Timothy 1:13-14; 2:1-3 Guard this rich trust with the help of the Holy Spirit.

A reading from the second Letter of Saint Paul to Timothy

Beloved:
Take as your norm the sound words that you heard from me,
   in the faith and love that are in Christ Jesus.
Guard this rich trust with the help of the Holy Spirit
   who dwells within us.

My child, be strong in the grace that is in Christ Jesus.
And what you heard from me through many witnesses
   entrust to faithful people
   who will have the ability to teach others as well.
Bear your share of hardship along with me
   like a good soldier of Christ Jesus.

The word of the Lord.

RESPONSORIAL PSALM

Psalm 96:1-2a, 2b-3, 7-8c, 10

℟. (3) **Proclaim God's marvelous deeds to all the nations.**

Sing to the Lord a new song;
   sing to the Lord, all you lands.
Sing to the Lord; bless his name.

℟. **Proclaim God's marvelous deeds to all the nations.**

Announce his salvation, day after day.
Tell his glory among the nations;
   among all peoples, his wondrous deeds.

℟. **Proclaim God's marvelous deeds to all the nations.**

Give to the LORD, **you families of nations,**
   give to the LORD **glory and praise;**
   give to the LORD **the glory due his name!**

℟. Proclaim God's marvelous deeds to all the nations.

Say among the nations: The LORD **is king.**
He has made the world firm, not to be moved;
   he governs the peoples with equity.

℟. Proclaim God's marvelous deeds to all the nations.

ALLELUIA

John 10:14

℟. Alleluia, alleluia.

I am the good shepherd, says the Lord;
I know my sheep, and mine know me.

℟. Alleluia, alleluia.

GOSPEL

Matthew 9:35-38   The harvest is abundant but the laborers are few.

✝ A reading from the holy Gospel according to Matthew

Jesus went around to all the towns and villages,
   teaching in their synagogues,
   proclaiming the Gospel of the Kingdom,
   and curing every disease and illness.
At the sight of the crowds, his heart was moved with pity for them
   because they were troubled and abandoned,
   like sheep without a shepherd.
Then he said to his disciples,
   "The harvest is abundant but the laborers are few;
   so ask the master of the harvest
   to send out laborers for his harvest."

The Gospel of the Lord.

MARCH 25

545 THE ANNUNCIATION OF THE LORD SOLEMNITY

FIRST READING

Isaiah 7:10-14; 8:10   Behold, the virgin shall conceive.

A reading from the Book of the Prophet Isaiah

**The LORD spoke to Ahaz, saying:
Ask for a sign from the LORD, your God;
   let it be deep as the nether world, or high as the sky!
But Ahaz answered,
   "I will not ask! I will not tempt the LORD!"
Then Isaiah said:
   Listen, O house of David!
Is it not enough for you to weary people,
   must you also weary my God?
Therefore the Lord himself will give you this sign:
   the virgin shall be with child, and bear a son,
   and shall name him Emmanuel,
   which means "God is with us!"**

The word of the Lord.

RESPONSORIAL PSALM

Psalm 40:7-8a, 8b-9, 10, 11

℟. (8a and 9a) **Here I am, Lord; I come to do your will.**

**Sacrifice or oblation you wished not,
   but ears open to obedience you gave me.
Holocausts or sin-offerings you sought not;
   then said I, "Behold I come."**

℟. **Here I am, Lord; I come to do your will.**

**"In the written scroll it is prescribed for me,
To do your will, O my God, is my delight,
   and your law is within my heart!"**

℟. **Here I am, Lord; I come to do your will.**

**I announced your justice in the vast assembly;
   I did not restrain my lips, as you, O LORD, know.**

℟. **Here I am, Lord; I come to do your will.**

1234 March 25—The Annunciation of the Lord

Your justice I kept not hid within my heart;
 your faithfulness and your salvation I have spoken of;
I have made no secret of your kindness and your truth
 in the vast assembly.

℟. Here I am, Lord; I come to do your will.

SECOND READING

Hebrews 10:4-10   As is written of me in the scroll, behold, I come to do your will, O God.

A reading from the Letter to the Hebrews

Brothers and sisters:
It is impossible that the blood of bulls and goats
 takes away sins.
For this reason, when Christ came into the world, he said:

 "Sacrifice and offering you did not desire,
  but a body you prepared for me;
 in holocausts and sin offerings you took no delight.
 Then I said, 'As is written of me in the scroll,
 behold, I come to do your will, O God.'"

First he says, "Sacrifices and offerings,
 holocausts and sin offerings,
 you neither desired nor delighted in."
These are offered according to the law.
Then he says, "Behold, I come to do your will."
He takes away the first to establish the second.
By this "will," we have been consecrated
 through the offering of the Body of Jesus Christ once for all.

The word of the Lord.

VERSE BEFORE THE GOSPEL OR ALLELUIA

John 1:14ab

℟. [Alleluia, alleluia.]

The Word of God became flesh and made his dwelling among us;
and we saw his glory.

℟. [Alleluia, alleluia.]

GOSPEL

Luke 1:26-38   Behold, you will conceive in your womb and bear a son.

✠ A reading from the holy Gospel according to Luke

The angel Gabriel was sent from God
   to a town of Galilee called Nazareth,
   to a virgin betrothed to a man named Joseph,
   of the house of David,
   and the virgin's name was Mary.
And coming to her, he said,
   "Hail, full of grace! The Lord is with you."
But she was greatly troubled at what was said
   and pondered what sort of greeting this might be.
Then the angel said to her,
   "Do not be afraid, Mary,
   for you have found favor with God.
Behold, you will conceive in your womb and bear a son,
   and you shall name him Jesus.
He will be great and will be called Son of the Most High,
   and the Lord God will give him the throne of David his father,
   and he will rule over the house of Jacob forever,
   and of his Kingdom there will be no end."
But Mary said to the angel,
   "How can this be,
   since I have no relations with a man?"
And the angel said to her in reply,
   "The Holy Spirit will come upon you,
   and the power of the Most High will overshadow you.
Therefore the child to be born
   will be called holy, the Son of God.
And behold, Elizabeth, your relative,
   has also conceived a son in her old age,
   and this is the sixth month for her who was called barren;
   for nothing will be impossible for God."
Mary said, "Behold, I am the handmaid of the Lord.
May it be done to me according to your word."
Then the angel departed from her.

The Gospel of the Lord.

APRIL 2

546 SAINT FRANCIS OF PAOLA, HERMIT

From the Common of Holy Men and Women: For Religious, p. 1868,

OR

FIRST READING

Philippians 3:8-14   I continue my pursuit toward the goal, the prize of God's upward calling, in Christ Jesus.

A reading from the Letter of Saint Paul to the Philippians

Brothers and sisters:
I consider everything as a loss
   because of the supreme good of knowing Christ Jesus my Lord.
For his sake I have accepted the loss of all things
   and I consider them so much rubbish,
   that I may gain Christ and be found in him,
   not having any righteousness of my own based on the law
   but that which comes through faith in Christ,
   the righteousness from God,
     depending on faith to know him and the power of his resurrection
     and the sharing of his sufferings by being conformed to his death,
     if somehow I may attain the resurrection from the dead.

It is not that I have already taken hold of it
   or have already attained perfect maturity,
     but I continue my pursuit in hope that I may possess it,
     since I have indeed been taken possession of by Christ Jesus.
Brothers and sisters, I for my part
   do not consider myself to have taken possession.
Just one thing: forgetting what lies behind
   but straining forward to what lies ahead,
   I continue my pursuit toward the goal,
   the prize of God's upward calling, in Christ Jesus.

The word of the Lord.

RESPONSORIAL PSALM

Psalm 16:1-2a and 5, 7-8, 11

℟. (see 5a) **You are my inheritance, O Lord.**

**Keep me, O God, for in you I take refuge.
   I say to the L**ORD**, "My Lord are you."
O L**ORD**, my allotted portion and my cup,
   you it is who hold fast my lot.**

℟. **You are my inheritance, O Lord.**

I bless the LORD **who counsels me;
   even in the night my heart exhorts me.
I set the L**ORD **always before me;
   with him at my right hand I shall not be disturbed.**

℟. **You are my inheritance, O Lord.**

**You will show me the path to life,
   fullness of joys in your presence,
      the delights at your right hand forever.**

℟. **You are my inheritance, O Lord.**

ALLELUIA

Matthew 5:3

℟. **Alleluia, alleluia.**

**Blessed are the poor in spirit;
for theirs is the Kingdom of God.**

℟. **Alleluia, alleluia.**

GOSPEL

Luke 12:32-34   Your Father is pleased to give you the Kingdom.

✠ **A reading from the holy Gospel according to Luke**

**Jesus said to his disciples:
"Do not be afraid any longer, little flock,
   for your Father is pleased to give you the Kingdom.
Sell your belongings and give alms.
Provide money bags for yourselves that do not wear out,
   an inexhaustible treasure in heaven
   that no thief can reach nor moth destroy.
For where your treasure is, there also will your heart be."**

The Gospel of the Lord.

APRIL 4

547 SAINT ISIDORE, BISHOP AND DOCTOR OF THE CHURCH

From the Common of Pastors, p. 1805, or the Common of Doctors of the Church, p. 1838,

OR

FIRST READING

2 Corinthians 4:1-2, 5-7   We preach Jesus Christ as Lord, and ourselves as your slaves for the sake of Jesus.

A reading from the second Letter of Saint Paul to the Corinthians

Brothers and sisters:
Since we have this ministry through the mercy shown us,
   we are not discouraged.
Rather, we have renounced shameful, hidden things;
   not acting deceitfully or falsifying the word of God,
   but by the open declaration of the truth
   we commend ourselves to everyone's conscience in the sight of God.
For we do not preach ourselves but Jesus Christ as Lord,
   and ourselves as your slaves for the sake of Jesus.
For God who said, "Let light shine out of darkness,"
   has shone in our hearts to bring to light
   the knowledge of the glory of God on the face of Jesus Christ.

But we hold this treasure in earthen vessels,
   that the surpassing power may be of God and not from us.

The word of the Lord.

RESPONSORIAL PSALM

Psalm 37:3-4, 5-6, 30-31

℟. (30a) **The mouth of the just murmurs wisdom.**

Trust in the Lord and do good,
   that you may dwell in the land and be fed in security.
Take delight in the Lord,
   and he will grant you your heart's requests.

℟. **The mouth of the just murmurs wisdom.**

Commit to the LORD **your way;**
    trust in him, and he will act.
He will make justice dawn for you like the light;
    bright as the noonday shall be your vindication.

℟. **The mouth of the just murmurs wisdom.**

The mouth of the just tells of wisdom
    and his tongue utters what is right.
The law of his God is in his heart,
    and his steps do not falter.

℟. **The mouth of the just murmurs wisdom.**

ALLELUIA

John 15:5

℟. **Alleluia, alleluia.**

I am the vine, you are the branches, says the Lord;
whoever remains in me and I in him will bear much fruit.

℟. **Alleluia, alleluia.**

GOSPEL

Luke 6:43-45   From the fullness of the heart the mouth speaks.

✚ **A reading from the holy Gospel according to Luke**

Jesus said to his disciples:
"**A good tree does not bear rotten fruit,**
    nor does a rotten tree bear good fruit.
For every tree is known by its own fruit.
For people do not pick figs from thornbushes,
    nor do they gather grapes from brambles.
A good person out of the store of goodness in his heart produces good,
    but an evil person out of a store of evil produces evil;
    for from the fullness of the heart the mouth speaks."

The Gospel of the Lord.

APRIL 5

548 SAINT VINCENT FERRER, PRIEST

From the Common of Pastors: For Missionaries, p. 1805,

OR

FIRST READING

2 Timothy 4:1-5   Perform the work of an evangelist; fulfill your ministry.

A reading from the second Letter of Saint Paul to Timothy

Beloved:
I charge you in the presence of God and of Christ Jesus,
   who will judge the living and the dead,
   and by his appearing and his kingly power:
   proclaim the word;
   be persistent whether it is convenient or inconvenient;
   convince, reprimand, encourage through all patience and teaching.
For the time will come when people will not tolerate sound doctrine
   but, following their own desires and insatiable curiosity,
   will accumulate teachers and will stop listening to the truth
   and will be diverted to myths.
But you, be self-possessed in all circumstances;
   put up with hardship;
   perform the work of an evangelist;
   fulfill your ministry.

The word of the Lord.

RESPONSORIAL PSALM

Psalm 40:2, 4, 7-8, 8-9, 10, 11

℟. (8a and 9a) **Here I am, Lord; I come to do your will.**

I have waited, waited for the LORD**,
 and he stooped toward me and heard my cry.
And he put a new song into my mouth,
 a hymn to our God.**

℟. **Here I am, Lord; I come to do your will.**

**Sacrifice or oblation you wished not,
 but ears open to obedience you gave me.
Burnt offerings or sin-offerings you sought not;
 then said I, "Behold I come."**

℟. **Here I am, Lord; I come to do your will.**

**"In the written scroll it is prescribed for me,
To do your will, O my God, is my delight,
 and your law is within my heart!"**

℟. **Here I am, Lord; I come to do your will.**

**I announced your justice in the vast assembly;
 I did not restrain my lips, as you, O L**ORD**, know.**

℟. **Here I am, Lord; I come to do your will.**

**Your justice I kept not hid within my heart;
 your faithfulness and your salvation I have spoken of;
I have made no secret of your kindness and your truth
 in the vast assembly.**

℟. **Here I am, Lord; I come to do your will.**

ALLELUIA

Luke 21:36

℟. Alleluia, alleluia.

**Be vigilant at all times
and pray that you may have the strength to stand before the Son of Man.**

℟. Alleluia, alleluia.

GOSPEL

Luke 12:35-40   You also must be prepared.

☩ **A reading from the holy Gospel according to Luke**

**Jesus said to his disciples:
"Gird your loins and light your lamps
   and be like servants who await their master's return from a wedding,
   ready to open immediately when he comes and knocks.
Blessed are those servants
   whom the master finds vigilant on his arrival.
Amen, I say to you, he will gird himself,
   have them recline at table, and proceed to wait on them.
And should he come in the second or third watch
   and find them prepared in this way,
   blessed are those servants.
Be sure of this:
   if the master of the house had known the hour
   when the thief was coming,
   he would not have let his house be broken into.
You also must be prepared, for at an hour you do not expect,
   the Son of Man will come."**

The Gospel of the Lord.

APRIL 7

549 SAINT JOHN BAPTIST DE LA SALLE, PRIEST
MEMORIAL

From the Common of Pastors, p. 1805, or the Common of Holy Men and Women: For Teachers, p. 1868,

OR

FIRST READING

2 Timothy 1:13-14; 2:1-3   Guard this rich trust with the help of the Holy Spirit.

A reading from the second Letter of Saint Paul to Timothy

Beloved:
Take as your norm the sound words that you heard from me,
   in the faith and love that are in Christ Jesus.
Guard this rich trust with the help of the Holy Spirit
   that dwells within us.

My child, be strong in the grace that is in Christ Jesus.
And what you heard from me through many witnesses
   entrust to faithful people
   who will have the ability to teach others as well.
Bear your share of hardship along with me
   like a good soldier of Christ Jesus.

The word of the Lord.

RESPONSORIAL PSALM

Psalm 1:1-2, 3, 4 and 6

℟. (40:5a) **Blessed are they who hope in the Lord.**
   or:
℟. (2a) **Blessed are they who delight in the law of the Lord.**
   or:
℟. (92:13-14) **The just will flourish like the palm tree in the garden of the Lord.**

**Blessed the man who follows not
   the counsel of the wicked
Nor walks in the way of sinners,
   nor sits in the company of the insolent,
But delights in the law of the L**ORD
   and meditates on his law day and night.

℟. **Blessed are they who hope in the Lord.**
   or:
℟. **Blessed are they who delight in the law of the Lord.**
   or:
℟. **The just will flourish like the palm tree in the garden of the Lord.**

**He is like a tree
   planted near running water,
That yields its fruit in due season,
   and whose leaves never fade.
   Whatever he does, prospers.**

℟. **Blessed are they who hope in the Lord.**
   or:
℟. **Blessed are they who delight in the law of the Lord.**
   or:
℟. **The just will flourish like the palm tree in the garden of the Lord.**

**Not so, the wicked, not so;
   they are like chaff which the wind drives away.
For the L**ORD **watches over the way of the just,
   but the way of the wicked vanishes.**

℟. **Blessed are they who hope in the Lord.**
   or:
℟. **Blessed are they who delight in the law of the Lord.**
   or:
℟. **The just will flourish like the palm tree in the garden of the Lord.**

ALLELUIA

Matthew 23:11, 12b

℟. **Alleluia, alleluia.**

**The greatest among you must be your servant.
Whoever humbles himself will be exalted.**

℟. **Alleluia, alleluia.**

GOSPEL

Matthew 18:1-5   Unless you turn and become like children, you will not enter the Kingdom of heaven.

✠   **A reading from the holy Gospel according to Matthew**

**The disciples approached Jesus and said,
   "Who is the greatest in the Kingdom of heaven?"
He called a child over, placed it in their midst, and said,
   "Amen, I say to you, unless you turn and become like children,
   you will not enter the Kingdom of heaven.
Whoever humbles himself like this child
   is the greatest in the Kingdom of heaven.
And whoever receives one child such as this in my name receives me."**

The Gospel of the Lord.

APRIL 11

550 SAINT STANISLAUS, BISHOP, MARTYR MEMORIAL

From the Common of Martyrs, p. 1782, or the Common of Pastors, p. 1805,

OR

FIRST READING

Revelation 12:10-12a   Love for life did not deter them from death.

A reading from the Book of Revelation

I, John, heard a loud voice in heaven say:
  "Now have salvation and power come,
    and the Kingdom of our God
    and the authority of his Anointed.
  For the accuser of our brothers is cast out,
    who accuses them before our God day and night.
  They conquered him by the Blood of the Lamb
    and by the word of their testimony;
    love for life did not deter them from death.
  Therefore, rejoice, you heavens,
    and you who dwell in them."

The word of the Lord.

RESPONSORIAL PSALM

Psalm 34:2-3, 4-5, 6-7, 8-9

℟. (5) **The Lord delivered me from all my fears.**

I will bless the Lord at all times;
  his praise shall be ever in my mouth.
Let my soul glory in the Lord;
  the lowly will hear and be glad.

℟. **The Lord delivered me from all my fears.**

Glorify the Lord with me,
  let us together extol his name.
I sought the Lord, and he answered me
  and delivered me from all my fears.

℟. **The Lord delivered me from all my fears.**

Look to him that you may be radiant with joy,
   and your faces may not blush with shame.
When the poor one called out, the Lord heard,
   and from all his distress he saved him.

℟. **The Lord delivered me from all my fears.**

The angel of the Lord encamps
   around those who fear him, and delivers them.
Taste and see how good the Lord is;
   blessed the man who takes refuge in him.

℟. **The Lord delivered me from all my fears.**

Fear the Lord, you his holy ones,
   for nought is lacking to those who fear him.
The great grow poor and hungry;
   but those who seek the Lord want for no good thing.

℟. **The Lord delivered me from all my fears.**

ALLELUIA

2 Corinthians 1:3b-4a

℟. **Alleluia, alleluia.**

Blessed be the Father of compassion and God of all encouragement, who encourages us in our every affliction.

℟. **Alleluia, alleluia.**

GOSPEL

John 17:11b-19   The world hated them.

✠ A reading from the holy Gospel according to John

Jesus raised his eyes to heaven and prayed, saying:
"Holy Father, keep them in your name that you have given me,
   so that they may be one just as we are one.
When I was with them I protected them in your name that you gave me,
   and I guarded them, and none of them was lost
   except the son of destruction,
   in order that the Scripture might be fulfilled.
But now I am coming to you.
I speak this in the world
   so that they may share my joy completely.
I gave them your word, and the world hated them,
   because they do not belong to the world
   any more than I belong to the world.
I do not ask that you take them out of the world
   but that you keep them from the Evil One.
They do not belong to the world
   any more than I belong to the world.
Consecrate them in the truth.
Your word is truth.
As you sent me into the world,
   so I sent them into the world.
And I consecrate myself for them,
   so that they also may be consecrated in truth."

The Gospel of the Lord.

APRIL 13

551 SAINT MARTIN I, POPE AND MARTYR

From the Common of Martyrs, p. 1782, or the Common of Pastors: For a Pope, p. 1805,

OR

FIRST READING

2 Timothy 2:8-13; 3:10-12   All who want to live religiously in Christ Jesus will be persecuted.

A reading from the second Letter of Saint Paul to Timothy

Beloved:
Remember Jesus Christ, raised from the dead, a descendant of David:
    such is my Gospel, for which I am suffering,
    even to the point of chains, like a criminal.
But the word of God is not chained.
Therefore, I bear with everything for the sake of those who are chosen,
    so that they too may obtain the salvation that is in Christ Jesus,
    together with eternal glory.
This saying is trustworthy:

    If we have died with him
        we shall also live with him;
    if we persevere
        we shall also reign with him.
    But if we deny him
        he will deny us.
    If we are unfaithful
        he remains faithful,
            for he cannot deny himself.

You have followed my teaching, way of life,
    purpose, faith, patience, love,
    endurance, persecutions, and sufferings,
    such as happened to me in Antioch, Iconium, and Lystra,
    persecutions that I endured.
Yet from all these things the Lord delivered me.
In fact, all who want to live religiously in Christ Jesus
    will be persecuted.

The word of the Lord.

RESPONSORIAL PSALM

Psalm 126:1bc-2, 2-3, 4-5, 6

℟. (5) Those who sow in tears, shall reap rejoicing.

When the LORD brought back the captives of Zion,
    we were like men dreaming.
Then our mouth was filled with laughter,
    and our tongue with rejoicing.

℟. Those who sow in tears, shall reap rejoicing.

Then they said among the nations,
    "The LORD has done great things for them."
The LORD has done great things for us;
    we are glad indeed.

℟. Those who sow in tears, shall reap rejoicing.

Restore our fortunes, O LORD,
    like the torrents in the southern desert.
Those that sow in tears
    shall reap rejoicing.

℟. Those who sow in tears, shall reap rejoicing.

Although they go forth weeping,
    carrying the seed to be sown,
They shall come back rejoicing,
    carrying their sheaves.

℟. Those who sow in tears, shall reap rejoicing.

ALLELUIA

See *Te Deum*

℟. Alleluia, alleluia.

We praise you, O God,
we acclaim you as Lord;
the white-robed army of martyrs praise you.

℟. Alleluia, alleluia.

GOSPEL

John 15:18-21   If they persecuted me, they will also persecute you.

✠ A reading from the holy Gospel according to John

Jesus said to his disciples:
"If the world hates you, realize that it hated me first.
If you belonged to the world, the world would love its own;
  but because you do not belong to the world,
  and I have chosen you out of the world,
  the world hates you.
Remember the word I spoke to you,
  'No slave is greater than his master.'
If they persecuted me, they will also persecute you.
If they kept my word, they will also keep yours.
And they will do all these things to you on account of my name,
  because they do not know the One who sent me."

The Gospel of the Lord.

APRIL 21

552 SAINT ANSELM, BISHOP AND DOCTOR OF THE CHURCH

From the Common of Pastors, p. 1805, or the Common of Doctors of the Church, p. 1838,

OR

FIRST READING

Ephesians 3:14-19 To know the love of Christ, that surpasses knowledge.

A reading from the Letter of Saint Paul to the Ephesians

Brothers and sisters:
I kneel before the Father,
   from whom every family in heaven and on earth is named,
   that he may grant you in accord with the riches of his glory
   to be strengthened with power through his Spirit in the inner self,
   and that Christ may dwell in your hearts through faith;
   that you, rooted and grounded in love,
   may have strength to comprehend with all the holy ones
   what is the breadth and length and height and depth,
   and to know the love of Christ that surpasses knowledge,
   so that you may be filled with all the fullness of God.

The word of the Lord.

RESPONSORIAL PSALM

Psalm 34:2-3, 4-5, 6-7, 8-9, 10-11

℟. (2) **I will bless the Lord at all times.**
   or:
℟. (9) **Taste and see the goodness of the Lord.**

I will bless the LORD **at all times;**
   his praise shall be ever in my mouth.
Let my soul glory in the LORD;
   the lowly will hear and be glad.

℟. **I will bless the Lord at all times.**
   or:
℟. **Taste and see the goodness of the Lord.**

Glorify the L͟o͟r͟d͟ with me,
   let us together extol his name.
I sought the L͟o͟r͟d͟, and he answered me
   and delivered me from all my fears.

℟. I will bless the Lord at all times.
   or:
℟. Taste and see the goodness of the Lord.

Look to him that you may be radiant with joy,
   and your faces may not blush with shame.
When the poor one called out, the L͟o͟r͟d͟ heard,
   and from all his distress he saved him.

℟. I will bless the Lord at all times.
   or:
℟. Taste and see the goodness of the Lord.

The angel of the L͟o͟r͟d͟ encamps
   around those who fear him, and delivers them.
Taste and see how good the L͟o͟r͟d͟ is;
   blessed the man who takes refuge in him.

℟. I will bless the Lord at all times.
   or:
℟. Taste and see the goodness of the Lord.

Fear the L͟o͟r͟d͟, you his holy ones,
   for nought is lacking to those who fear him.
The great grow poor and hungry;
   but those who seek the L͟o͟r͟d͟ want for no good thing.

℟. I will bless the Lord at all times.
   or:
℟. Taste and see the goodness of the Lord.

ALLELUIA

John 6:63, 68c

℟. Alleluia, alleluia.

Your words, Lord, are spirit and life;
you have the words of eternal life.

℟. Alleluia, alleluia.

GOSPEL

Matthew 7:21-29   He taught them as one having authority.

✙ A reading from the holy Gospel according to Matthew

Jesus said to his disciples:
"Not everyone who says to me, 'Lord, Lord,'
  will enter the Kingdom of heaven,
  but only the one who does the will of my Father in heaven.
Many will say to me on that day,
  'Lord, Lord, did we not prophesy in your name?
Did we not drive out demons in your name?
Did we not do mighty deeds in your name?'
Then I will declare to them solemnly,
  'I never knew you. Depart from me, you evildoers.'

"Everyone who listens to these words of mine and acts on them
  will be like a wise man who built his house on rock.
The rain fell, the floods came,
  and the winds blew and buffeted the house.
But it did not collapse; it had been set solidly on rock.
And everyone who listens to these words of mine
  but does not act on them
  will be like a fool who built his house on sand.
The rain fell, the floods came,
  and the winds blew and buffeted the house.
And it collapsed and was completely ruined."

When Jesus finished these words,
  the crowds were astonished at his teaching,
  for he taught them as one having authority,
  and not as their scribes.

The Gospel of the Lord.

APRIL 23

553 SAINT GEORGE, MARTYR

From the Common of Martyrs, p. 1782,

OR

FIRST READING

Revelation 21:5-7   The victor will inherit these gifts.

A reading from the Book of Revelation

The One who was seated on the throne said:
"Behold, I make all things new."
Then he said, "Write these words down,
    for they are trustworthy and true."
He said to me, "They are accomplished.
I am the Alpha and the Omega, the beginning and the end.
To the thirsty I will give a gift
    from the spring of life-giving water.
The victor will inherit these gifts,
    and I shall be his God,
    and he will be my son."

The word of the Lord.

RESPONSORIAL PSALM

Psalm 126:1bc-2, 2-3, 4-5, 6

℟. (5) **Those who sow in tears, shall reap rejoicing.**

When the Lord brought back the captives of Zion,
    we were like men dreaming.
Then our mouth was filled with laughter,
    and our tongue with rejoicing.

℟. **Those who sow in tears, shall reap rejoicing.**

Then they said among the nations,
    "The Lord has done great things for them."
The Lord has done great things for us;
    we are glad indeed.

℟. **Those who sow in tears, shall reap rejoicing.**

Restore our fortunes, O Lord,
   like the torrents in the southern desert.
Those that sow in tears
   shall reap rejoicing.

℟. **Those who sow in tears, shall reap rejoicing.**

Although they go forth weeping,
   carrying the seed to be sown,
They shall come back rejoicing,
   carrying their sheaves.

℟. **Those who sow in tears, shall reap rejoicing.**

ALLELUIA

1 Peter 4:14

℟. **Alleluia, alleluia.**

If you are insulted for the name of Christ, blessed are you,
for the Spirit of God rests upon you.

℟. **Alleluia, alleluia.**

GOSPEL

Luke 9:23-26   Whoever loses his life for my sake will save it.

✠ **A reading from the holy Gospel according to Luke**

Jesus said to all,
   "If anyone wishes to come after me, he must deny himself
   and take up his cross daily and follow me.
For whoever wishes to save his life will lose it,
   but whoever loses his life for my sake will save it.
What profit is there for one to gain the whole world
   yet lose or forfeit himself?
Whoever is ashamed of me and of my words,
   the Son of Man will be ashamed of when he comes in his glory
   and in the glory of the Father and of the holy angels."

The Gospel of the Lord.

APRIL 23

553A SAINT ADALBERT, BISHOP AND MARTYR

From the Common of Martyrs, p. 1782, or the Common of Pastors, p. 1805,

OR

FIRST READING

2 Corinthians 6:4-10   We are treated as dying and behold we live.

A reading from the second Letter of Saint Paul to the Corinthians

Brothers and sisters:
In everything we commend ourselves as ministers of God,
   through much endurance, in afflictions, hardships, constraints,
   beatings, imprisonments, riots, labors, vigils, fasts;
   by purity, knowledge, patience, kindness,
   in the Holy Spirit, in unfeigned love, in truthful speech,
   in the power of God;
   with weapons of righteousness at the right and at the left;
   through glory and dishonor, insult and praise.
We are treated as deceivers and yet are truthful;
   as unrecognized and yet acknowledged;
   as dying and behold we live;
   as chastised and yet not put to death;
   as sorrowful yet always rejoicing;
   as poor yet enriching many;
   as having nothing and yet possessing all things.

The word of the Lord.

RESPONSORIAL PSALM

Psalm 31:3cd-4, 6 and 8ab, 16bc and 17

℟. (6) **Into your hands, O Lord, I commend my spirit.**

Be my rock of refuge,
   a stronghold to give me safety.
You are my rock and my fortress;
   for your name's sake you will lead and guide me.

℟. **Into your hands, O Lord, I commend my spirit.**

1258   April 23—Saint Adalbert

Into your hands I commend my spirit;
   you will redeem me, O LORD**, O faithful God.**
I will rejoice and be glad because of your mercy.

℟. **Into your hands, O Lord, I commend my spirit.**

Rescue me from the clutches of my enemies and my persecutors,
Let your face shine upon your servant;
   save me in your kindness.

℟. **Into your hands, O Lord, I commend my spirit.**

ALLELUIA

John 17:19

℟. **Alleluia, alleluia.**

I consecrate myself for them,
so that they also may be consecrated in the truth.

℟. **Alleluia, alleluia.**

GOSPEL

John 10:11-16   A good shepherd lays down his life for the sheep.

✠ **A reading from the holy Gospel according to John**

Jesus said:
"I am the good shepherd.
A good shepherd lays down his life for the sheep.
A hired man, who is not a shepherd
   and whose sheep are not his own,
      sees a wolf coming and leaves the sheep and runs away,
      and the wolf catches and scatters them.
This is because he works for pay and has no concern for the sheep.
I am the good shepherd,
   and I know mine and mine know me,
      just as the Father knows me and I know the Father;
      and I will lay down my life for the sheep.
I have other sheep that do not belong to this fold.
These also I must lead, and they will hear my voice,
   and there will be one flock, one shepherd."

The Gospel of the Lord.

APRIL 24

554 SAINT FIDELIS OF SIGMARINGEN, PRIEST AND MARTYR

From the Common of Martyrs, p. 1782, or the Common of Pastors, p. 1805,

OR

FIRST READING

Colossians 1:24-29 I am a minister of the Church in accordance with God's stewardship.

A reading from the Letter of Saint Paul to the Colossians

Brothers and sisters:
I rejoice in my sufferings for your sake,
   and in my flesh I am filling up
   what is lacking in the afflictions of Christ
   on behalf of his Body, which is the Church,
   of which I am a minister
   in accordance with God's stewardship given to me
   to bring to completion for you the word of God,
   the mystery hidden from ages and from generations past.
But now it has been manifested to his holy ones,
   to whom God chose to make known the riches of the glory
   of this mystery among the Gentiles;
   it is Christ in you, the hope for glory.
It is him whom we proclaim,
   admonishing everyone and teaching everyone with all wisdom,
   that we may present everyone perfect in Christ.
For this I labor and struggle,
   in accord with the exercise of his power working within me.

The word of the Lord.

RESPONSORIAL PSALM

Psalm 34:2-3, 4-5, 6-7, 8-9

℟. (5) **The Lord delivered me from all my fears.**

I will bless the LORD **at all times;**
 his praise shall be ever in my mouth.
Let my soul glory in the LORD**;**
 the lowly will hear and be glad.

℟. **The Lord delivered me from all my fears.**

Glorify the LORD **with me,**
 let us together extol his name.
I sought the LORD**, and he answered me**
 and delivered me from all my fears.

℟. **The Lord delivered me from all my fears.**

Look to him that you may be radiant with joy,
 and your faces may not blush with shame.
When the poor one called out, the LORD **heard,**
 and from all his distress he saved him.

℟. **The Lord delivered me from all my fears.**

The angel of the LORD **encamps**
 around those who fear him, and delivers them.
Taste and see how good the LORD **is;**
 blessed the man who takes refuge in him.

℟. **The Lord delivered me from all my fears.**

ALLELUIA

John 13:34

℟. Alleluia, alleluia.

I give you a new commandment:
love one another as I have loved you.

℟. Alleluia, alleluia.

GOSPEL

John 17:20-26   I wish that where I am they also may be with me.

✠ A reading from the holy Gospel according to John

Jesus raised his eyes to heaven and said:
"Holy Father, I pray not only for these,
  but also for those who will believe in me through their word,
  so that they may all be one,
  as you, Father, are in me and I in you,
  that they also may be in us,
  that the world may believe that you sent me.
And I have given them the glory you gave me,
  so that they may be one, as we are one,
  I in them and you in me,
  that they may be brought to perfection as one,
  that the world may know that you sent me,
  and that you loved them even as you loved me.
Father, they are your gift to me.
I wish that where I am they also may be with me,
  that they may see my glory that you gave me,
  because you loved me before the foundation of the world.
Righteous Father, the world also does not know you,
  but I know you, and they know that you sent me.
I made known to them your name and I will make it known,
  that the love with which you loved me
  may be in them and I in them."

The Gospel of the Lord.

APRIL 25

555 SAINT MARK, EVANGELIST FEAST

FIRST READING

1 Peter 5:5b-14   Mark, my son, sends you greetings.

A reading from the First Letter of Saint Peter

Beloved:
Clothe yourselves with humility
   in your dealings with one another, for:

   *God opposes the proud
      but bestows favor on the humble.*

So humble yourselves under the mighty hand of God,
   that he may exalt you in due time.
Cast all your worries upon him because he cares for you.

Be sober and vigilant.
Your opponent the Devil is prowling around like a roaring lion
   looking for someone to devour.
Resist him, steadfast in faith,
   knowing that your brothers and sisters throughout the world
   undergo the same sufferings.
The God of all grace
   who called you to his eternal glory through Christ Jesus
   will himself restore, confirm, strengthen, and establish you
   after you have suffered a little.
To him be dominion forever. Amen.

I write you this briefly through Silvanus,
   whom I consider a faithful brother,
   exhorting you and testifying that this is the true grace of God.
Remain firm in it.
The chosen one at Babylon sends you greeting, as does Mark, my son.
Greet one another with a loving kiss.
Peace to all of you who are in Christ.

The word of the Lord.

RESPONSORIAL PSALM

Psalm 89:2-3, 6-7, 16-17

℟. (2) **For ever I will sing the goodness of the Lord.**
   or:
℟. **Alleluia.**

The favors of the Lord I will sing forever;
   through all generations my mouth shall proclaim your faithfulness.
For you have said, "My kindness is established forever";
   in heaven you have confirmed your faithfulness.

℟. **For ever I will sing the goodness of the Lord.**
   or:
℟. **Alleluia.**

The heavens proclaim your wonders, O Lord,
   and your faithfulness, in the assembly of the holy ones.
For who in the skies can rank with the Lord?
   Who is like the Lord among the sons of God?

℟. **For ever I will sing the goodness of the Lord.**
   or:
℟. **Alleluia.**

Blessed the people who know the joyful shout;
   in the light of your countenance, O Lord, they walk.
At your name they rejoice all the day,
   and through your justice they are exalted.

℟. **For ever I will sing the goodness of the Lord.**
   or:
℟. **Alleluia.**

ALLELUIA

1 Corinthians 1:23a-24b

℟. **Alleluia, alleluia.**

**We proclaim Christ crucified;
he is the power of God and the wisdom of God.**

℟. **Alleluia, alleluia.**

GOSPEL

Mark 16:15-20   Proclaim the Gospel to every creature.

✛ **A reading from the holy Gospel according to Mark**

**Jesus appeared to the Eleven and said to them:
"Go into the whole world
   and proclaim the Gospel to every creature.
Whoever believes and is baptized will be saved;
   whoever does not believe will be condemned.
These signs will accompany those who believe:
   in my name they will drive out demons,
   they will speak new languages.
They will pick up serpents with their hands,
   and if they drink any deadly thing, it will not harm them.
They will lay hands on the sick, and they will recover."**

**Then the Lord Jesus, after he spoke to them,
   was taken up into heaven
   and took his seat at the right hand of God.
But they went forth and preached everywhere,
   while the Lord worked with them
   and confirmed the word through accompanying signs.**

The Gospel of the Lord.

APRIL 28

556 SAINT PETER CHANEL, PRIEST AND MARTYR

From the Common of Martyrs, p. 1782, or the Common of Pastors: For Missionaries, p. 1805,

OR

FIRST READING

1 Corinthians 1:18-25   It was the will of God through the foolishness of the proclamation to save those who have faith.

A reading from the first Letter of Saint Paul to the Corinthians

Brothers and sisters:
The message of the cross is foolishness to those who are perishing,
   but to us who are being saved it is the power of God.
For it is written:

> *I will destroy the wisdom of the wise,*
>   *and the learning of the learned I will set aside.*

Where is the wise one?
Where is the scribe?
Where is the debater of this age?
Has not God made the wisdom of the world foolish?
For since in the wisdom of God
   the world did not come to know God through wisdom,
   it was the will of God through the foolishness of the proclamation
   to save those who have faith.
For Jews demand signs and Greeks look for wisdom,
   but we proclaim Christ crucified,
   a stumbling block to Jews and foolishness to Gentiles,
   but to those who are called, Jews and Greeks alike,
   Christ the power of God and the wisdom of God.
For the foolishness of God is wiser than human wisdom,
   and the weakness of God is stronger than human strength.

The word of the Lord.

RESPONSORIAL PSALM

Psalm 117:1bc, 2

℟. (Mark 16:15) **Go out to all the world and tell the Good News.**
   or:
℟. **Alleluia.**

Praise the Lord, all you nations;
   glorify him, all you peoples!

℟. **Go out to all the world and tell the Good News.**
   or:
℟. **Alleluia.**

For steadfast is his kindness toward us,
   and the fidelity of the Lord endures forever.

℟. **Go out to all the world and tell the Good News.**
   or:
℟. **Alleluia.**

ALLELUIA

Mark 1:17

℟. **Alleluia, alleluia.**

Come after me, says the Lord,
and I will make you fishers of men.

℟. **Alleluia, alleluia.**

GOSPEL

Mark 1:14-20   I will make you fishers of men.

✠ A reading from the holy Gospel according to Mark

After John the Baptist had been arrested,
>   Jesus came to Galilee proclaiming the Gospel of God:
>   "This is the time of fulfillment.

The Kingdom of God is at hand.
Repent, and believe in the Gospel."

As he passed by the Sea of Galilee,
>   he saw Simon and his brother Andrew casting their nets into the sea;
>   they were fishermen.

Jesus said to them,
>   "Come after me, and I will make you fishers of men."

Then they left their nets and followed him.
He walked along a little farther
>   and saw James, the son of Zebedee, and his brother John.

They too were in a boat mending their nets.
Then he called them.
So they left their father Zebedee in the boat
>   along with the hired men and followed him.

The Gospel of the Lord.

APRIL 28

556A SAINT LOUIS MARY DE MONTFORT, PRIEST

From the Common of Pastors: For Missionaries, p. 1805,

OR

FIRST READING

1 Corinthians 1:18-25   It was the will of God through the foolishness of the proclamation to save those who have faith.

A reading from the first Letter of Saint Paul to the Corinthians

Brothers and sisters:
The message of the cross is foolishness to those who are perishing,
  but to us who are being saved it is the power of God.
For it is written:
  I will destroy the wisdom of the wise,
    and the learning of the learned I will set aside.

Where is the wise one?
Where is the scribe?
Where is the debater of this age?
Has not God made the wisdom of the world foolish?
For since in the wisdom of God
  the world did not come to know God through wisdom,
  it was the will of God through the foolishness of the proclamation
  to save those who have faith.
For Jews demand signs and Greeks look for wisdom,
  but we proclaim Christ crucified,
  a stumbling block to Jews and foolishness to Gentiles,
  but to those who are called, Jews and Greeks alike,
  Christ the power of God and the wisdom of God.
For the foolishness of God is wiser than human wisdom,
  and the weakness of God is stronger than human strength.

The word of the Lord.

RESPONSORIAL PSALM

Psalm 40:2 and 4, 7-8a, 8b-9, 10

℟. (8a and 9a) **Here I am, Lord; I come to do your will.**

I have waited, waited for the LORD**,**
  and he stooped toward me and heard my cry.
And he put a new song into my mouth,
  a hymn to our God.

℟. **Here I am, Lord; I come to do your will.**

Sacrifice or offering you wished not,
  but ears open to obedience you gave me.
Burnt offerings or sin-offerings you sought not;
  then said I, "Behold I come."

℟. Here I am, Lord; I come to do your will.

In the written scroll it is prescribed for me,
To do your will, O my God, is my delight,
  and your law is within my heart!"

℟. Here I am, Lord; I come to do your will.

I announced your justice in the vast assembly;
  I did not restrain my lips, as you, O Lord, know.

℟. Here I am, Lord; I come to do your will.

ALLELUIA

Luke 4:18

℟. Alleluia, alleluia.

The Lord sent me to bring glad tidings to the poor
and to proclaim liberty to captives.

℟. Alleluia, alleluia.

GOSPEL

Matthew 28:16-20   Go, therefore, and make disciples of all nations.

✚ A reading from the holy Gospel according to Matthew

The Eleven disciples went to Galilee,
  to the mountain to which Jesus had ordered them.
When they saw him, they worshiped, but they doubted.
Then Jesus approached and said to them,
  "All power in heaven and on earth has been given to me.
Go, therefore, and make disciples of all nations,
  baptizing them in the name of the Father,
  and of the Son, and of the Holy Spirit,
  teaching them to observe all that I have commanded you.
And behold, I am with you always, until the end of the age."

The Gospel of the Lord.

APRIL 29

557 SAINT CATHERINE OF SIENA, VIRGIN AND DOCTOR OF THE CHURCH MEMORIAL

From the Common of Virgins, p. 1857,

OR

FIRST READING

1 John 1:5–2:2   The Blood of his Son Jesus cleanses us from all sin.

A reading from the first Letter of Saint John

Beloved:
This is the message that we have heard from Jesus Christ
and proclaim to you: God is light,
and in him there is no darkness at all.
If we say, "We have fellowship with him,"
while we continue to walk in darkness,
we lie and do not act in truth.
But if we walk in the light as he is in the light,
then we have fellowship with one another,
and the Blood of his Son Jesus cleanses us from all sin.
If we say, "We are without sin," we deceive ourselves,
and the truth is not in us.
If we acknowledge our sins, he is faithful and just
and will forgive our sins and cleanse us from every wrongdoing.
If we say, "We have not sinned," we make him a liar,
and his word is not in us.

My children, I am writing this to you so that you may not commit sin.
But if anyone does sin, we have an Advocate with the Father,
Jesus Christ the righteous one.
He is expiation for our sins,
and not for our sins only but for those of the whole world.

The word of the Lord.

RESPONSORIAL PSALM

Psalm 103:1-2, 3-4, 8-9, 13-14, 17-18

℟. (1) **O bless the Lord, my soul!**

Bless the Lord, O my soul;
  and all my being, bless his holy name!
Bless the Lord, O my soul;
  and forget not all his benefits.

℟. **O bless the Lord, my soul!**

He pardons all your iniquities,
  he heals all your ills.
He redeems your life from destruction,
  he crowns you with kindness and compassion.

℟. **O bless the Lord, my soul!**

Merciful and gracious is the Lord,
  slow to anger and abounding in kindness.
He will not always chide,
  nor does he keep his wrath forever.

℟. **O bless the Lord, my soul!**

As a father has compassion on his children,
  so the Lord has compassion on those who fear him,
For he knows how we are formed;
  he remembers that we are dust.

℟. **O bless the Lord, my soul!**

But the kindness of the Lord is from eternity
  to eternity toward those who fear him,
And his justice toward his children's children
  among those who keep his covenant.

℟. **O bless the Lord, my soul!**

ALLELUIA

See Matthew 11:25

℟. Alleluia, alleluia.

**Blessed are you, Father, Lord of heaven and earth;
you have revealed to little ones the mysteries of the Kingdom.**

℟. Alleluia, alleluia.

GOSPEL

Matthew 11:25-30   You have hidden these things from the wise and the learned and have revealed them to the childlike.

✠ A reading from the holy Gospel according to Matthew

**At that time Jesus responded:
"I give praise to you, Father, Lord of heaven and earth,
   for although you have hidden these things
   from the wise and the learned
   you have revealed them to the childlike.
Yes, Father, such has been your gracious will.
All things have been handed over to me by my Father.
No one knows the Son except the Father,
   and no one knows the Father except the Son
   and anyone to whom the Son wishes to reveal him."**

**"Come to me, all you who labor and are burdened,
   and I will give you rest.
Take my yoke upon you and learn from me,
   for I am meek and humble of heart;
   and you will find rest for yourselves.
For my yoke is easy, and my burden light."**

The Gospel of the Lord.

APRIL 30

558 SAINT PIUS V, POPE, RELIGIOUS

From the Common of Pastors: For a Pope, p. 1805,

OR

FIRST READING

1 Corinthians 4:1-5   As servants of Christ and stewards of the mysteries of God.

A reading from the first Letter of Saint Paul to the Corinthians

Brothers and sisters:
Thus should one regard us: as servants of Christ
   and stewards of the mysteries of God.
Now it is of course required of stewards
   that they be found trustworthy.
It does not concern me in the least
   that I be judged by you or any human tribunal;
   I do not even pass judgment on myself;
   I am not conscious of anything against me,
   but I do not thereby stand acquitted;
   the one who judges me is the Lord.
Therefore do not make any judgment before the appointed time,
   until the Lord comes,
   for he will bring to light what is hidden in darkness
   and will manifest the motives of our hearts,
   and then everyone will receive praise from God.

The word of the Lord.

RESPONSORIAL PSALM

Psalm 110:1, 2, 3, 4

℟. (4b) **You are a priest for ever, in the line of Melchizedek.**

The Lord said to my Lord: "Sit at my right hand
   till I make your enemies your footstool."

℟. **You are a priest for ever, in the line of Melchizedek.**

The scepter of your power the Lord will stretch forth from Zion:
   "Rule in the midst of your enemies."

℟. **You are a priest for ever, in the line of Melchizedek.**

"Yours is princely power in the day of your birth, in holy splendor;
  before the daystar, like the dew, I have begotten you."

℟. You are a priest for ever, in the line of Melchizedek.

The Lord has sworn, and he will not repent:
  "You are a priest forever, according to the order of Melchizedek."

℟. You are a priest for ever, in the line of Melchizedek.

ALLELUIA

John 10:14

℟. Alleluia, alleluia.

I am the good shepherd, says the Lord;
I know my sheep, and mine know me.

℟. Alleluia, alleluia.

GOSPEL

John 21:15-17   Feed my lambs, feed my sheep.

✠ A reading from the holy Gospel according to John

After Jesus had revealed himself to his disciples
    and eaten breakfast with them, he said to Simon Peter,
   "Simon, son of John, do you love me more than these?"
Simon Peter answered him, "Yes, Lord, you know that I love you."
Jesus said to him, "Feed my lambs."
He then said to Simon Peter a second time,
   "Simon, son of John, do you love me?"
Simon Peter answered him, "Yes, Lord, you know that I love you."
Jesus said to him, "Tend my sheep."
He said to him the third time,
   "Simon, son of John, do you love me?"
Peter was distressed that Jesus had said to him a third time,
   "Do you love me?" and he said to him,
   "Lord, you know everything; you know that I love you."
Jesus said to him, "Feed my sheep."

The Gospel of the Lord.

MAY 1

559 SAINT JOSEPH THE WORKER

The Gospel for this memorial is proper.

FIRST READING

First Option

Genesis 1:26—2:3   Fill the earth and subdue it.

A reading from the Book of Genesis

**God said:
"Let us make man in our image, after our likeness.
Let them have dominion over the fish of the sea,
   the birds of the air, and the cattle,
   and over all the wild animals
   and all the creatures that crawl on the ground."**

**God created man in his image;
   in the divine image he created him;
   male and female he created them.**

**God blessed them, saying:
   "Be fertile and multiply;
   fill the earth and subdue it.
Have dominion over the fish of the sea, the birds of the air,
   and all the living things that move on the earth."
God also said:
   "See, I give you every seed-bearing plant all over the earth
   and every tree that has seed-bearing fruit on it to be your food;
   and to all the animals of the land, all the birds of the air,
   and all the living creatures that crawl on the ground,
   I give all the green plants for food."
And so it happened.
God looked at everything he had made, and he found it very good.
Evening came, and morning followed—the sixth day.**

**Thus the heavens and the earth and all their array were completed.
Since on the seventh day God was finished with the work he had been doing,
   God rested on the seventh day from all the work he had undertaken.
So God blessed the seventh day and made it holy,
   because on it he rested from all the work he had done in creation.**

The word of the Lord.

Second Option

Colossians 3:14-15, 17, 23-24   Whatever you do, do from the heart, as for the Lord and not for men.

A reading from the Letter of Saint Paul to the Colossians

Brothers and sisters:
Over all these things put on love, that is, the bond of perfection.
And let the peace of Christ control your hearts,
   the peace into which you were also called in one Body.
And be thankful.
And whatever you do, in word or in deed,
   do everything in the name of the Lord Jesus,
   giving thanks to God the Father through him.
Whatever you do, do from the heart,
   as for the Lord and not for men,
   knowing that you will receive from the Lord
   the due payment of the inheritance;
   be slaves of the Lord Christ.

The word of the Lord.

RESPONSORIAL PSALM

Psalm 90:2, 3-4, 12-13, 14 and 16

℟. (see 17b) **Lord, give success to the work of our hands.**
or:
℟. **Alleluia.**

**Before the mountains were begotten
and the earth and the world were brought forth,
from everlasting to everlasting you are God.**

℟. **Lord, give success to the work of our hands.**
or:
℟. **Alleluia.**

**You turn men back to dust,
saying, "Return, O children of men."
For a thousand years in your sight
are as yesterday, now that it is past,
or as a watch of the night.**

℟. **Lord, give success to the work of our hands.**
or:
℟. **Alleluia.**

**Teach us to number our days aright,
that we may gain wisdom of heart.
Return, O Lord! How long?
Have pity on your servants!**

℟. **Lord, give success to the work of our hands.**
or:
℟. **Alleluia.**

**Fill us at daybreak with your kindness,
that we may shout for joy and gladness all our days.
Let your work be seen by your servants
and your glory by their children.**

℟. **Lord, give success to the work of our hands.**
or:
℟. **Alleluia.**

ALLELUIA

Psalm 68:20

℟. Alleluia, alleluia.

Blessed be the Lord day by day,
God, our salvation, who bears our burdens.

℟. Alleluia, alleluia.

GOSPEL

Matthew 13:54-58   Is he not the carpenter's son?

✢ A reading from the holy Gospel according to Matthew

Jesus came to his native place and taught the people in their synagogue.
They were astonished and said,
    "Where did this man get such wisdom and mighty deeds?
Is he not the carpenter's son?
Is not his mother named Mary
    and his brothers James, Joseph, Simon, and Judas?
Are not his sisters all with us?
Where did this man get all this?"
And they took offense at him.
But Jesus said to them,
    "A prophet is not without honor except in his native place
    and in his own house."
And he did not work many mighty deeds there
    because of their lack of faith.

The Gospel of the Lord.

MAY 2

560 SAINT ATHANASIUS, BISHOP AND DOCTOR OF THE CHURCH MEMORIAL

From the Common of Pastors, p. 1805, or the Common of Doctors of the Church, p. 1838,

OR

FIRST READING

1 John 5:1-5   The victory that conquers the world is our faith.

A reading from the first Letter of Saint John

Beloved:
Everyone who believes that Jesus is the Christ is begotten by God,
   and everyone who loves the Father
   loves also the one begotten by him.
In this way we know that we love the children of God
   when we love God and obey his commandments.
For the love of God is this,
   that we keep his commandments.
And his commandments are not burdensome,
   for whoever is begotten by God conquers the world.
And the victory that conquers the world is our faith.
Who indeed is the victor over the world
   but the one who believes that Jesus is the Son of God?

The word of the Lord.

RESPONSORIAL PSALM

Psalm 37:3-4, 5-6, 30-31

R. (30a) **The mouth of the just murmurs wisdom.**

Trust in the Lord and do good
   that you may dwell in the land and be fed in security.
Take delight in the Lord,
   and he will grant you your heart's requests.

R. **The mouth of the just murmurs wisdom.**

Commit to the LORD **your way;**
    trust in him, and he will act.
He will make justice dawn for you like the light;
    bright as the noonday shall be your vindication.

℞. **The mouth of the just murmurs wisdom.**

The mouth of the just tells of wisdom
    and his tongue utters what is right.
The law of his God is in his heart,
    and his steps do not falter.

℞. **The mouth of the just murmurs wisdom.**

ALLELUIA

Matthew 5:10

℞. **Alleluia, alleluia.**

Blessed are they who are persecuted for the sake of righteousness,
for theirs is the Kingdom of heaven.

℞. **Alleluia, alleluia.**

GOSPEL

Matthew 10:22-25   When they persecute you in one town, flee to another.

✚ **A reading from the holy Gospel according to Matthew**

Jesus said to the Twelve:
"You will be hated by all because of my name,
    but whoever endures to the end will be saved.
When they persecute you in one town, flee to another.
Amen, I say to you, you will not finish the towns of Israel
    before the Son of Man comes.
No disciple is above his teacher,
    no slave above his master.
It is enough for the disciple that he become like the teacher,
    and the slave that he become like the master.
If they have called the master of the house Beelzebub,
    how much more those of his household!"

The Gospel of the Lord.

MAY 3

561 SAINTS PHILIP AND JAMES, APOSTLES FEAST

FIRST READING

1 Corinthians 15:1-8   After that he appeared to James, then to all the Apostles.

A reading from the first Letter of Saint Paul to the Corinthians

I am reminding you, brothers and sisters,
   of the Gospel I preached to you,
   which you indeed received and in which you also stand.
Through it you are also being saved,
   if you hold fast to the word I preached to you,
   unless you believed in vain.
For I handed on to you as of first importance what I also received:
   that Christ died for our sins
      in accordance with the Scriptures;
   that he was buried;
   that he was raised on the third day
      in accordance with the Scriptures;
   that he appeared to Cephas, then to the Twelve.
After that, he appeared to more
   than five hundred brothers and sisters at once,
   most of whom are still living,
   though some have fallen asleep.
After that he appeared to James,
   then to all the Apostles.
Last of all, as to one born abnormally,
   he appeared to me.

The word of the Lord.

RESPONSORIAL PSALM

Psalm 19:2-3, 4-5

℟. (5) **Their message goes out through all the earth.**
or:
℟. **Alleluia.**

**The heavens declare the glory of God;
and the firmament proclaims his handiwork.
Day pours out the word to day;
and night to night imparts knowledge.**

℟. **Their message goes out through all the earth.**
or:
℟. **Alleluia.**

**Not a word nor a discourse
whose voice is not heard;
Through all the earth their voice resounds,
and to the ends of the world, their message.**

℟. **Their message goes out through all the earth.**
or:
℟. **Alleluia.**

ALLELUIA

John 14:6b, 9c

℟. **Alleluia, alleluia.**

**I am the way, the truth, and the life, says the Lord;
Philip, whoever has seen me has seen the Father.**

℟. **Alleluia, alleluia.**

GOSPEL

John 14:6-14   Have I been with you so long and you still do not know me?

✢   A reading from the holy Gospel according to John

**Jesus said to Thomas, "I am the way and the truth and the life.
No one comes to the Father except through me.
If you know me, then you will also know my Father.
From now on you do know him and have seen him."
Philip said to him,
  "Master, show us the Father, and that will be enough for us."
Jesus said to him, "Have I been with you for so long a time
  and you still do not know me, Philip?
Whoever has seen me has seen the Father.
How can you say, 'Show us the Father'?
Do you not believe that I am in the Father and the Father is in me?
The words that I speak to you I do not speak on my own.
The Father who dwells in me is doing his works.
Believe me that I am in the Father and the Father is in me,
  or else, believe because of the works themselves.
Amen, amen, I say to you,
  whoever believes in me will do the works that I do,
  and will do greater ones than these,
  because I am going to the Father.
And whatever you ask in my name, I will do,
  so that the Father may be glorified in the Son.
If you ask anything of me in my name, I will do it."**

The Gospel of the Lord.

MAY 10

[In the Dioceses of the United States]

561A   BLESSED DAMIEN JOSEPH DE VEUSTER OF MOLOKA'I, PRIEST

From the Common of Pastors, p. 1805, or the Common of Holy Men and Women, p. 1868.

MAY 12

562 SAINTS NEREUS AND ACHILLEUS, MARTYRS

From the Common of Martyrs, p. 1782,

OR

FIRST READING

Revelation 7:9-17   These are the ones who have survived the time of great distress.

A reading from the Book of Revelation

I, John, had a vision of a great multitude,
   which no one could count,
   from every nation, race, people, and tongue.
They stood before the throne and before the Lamb,
   wearing white robes and holding palm branches in their hands.
They cried out in a loud voice:

   "Salvation comes from our God, who is seated on the throne,
     and from the Lamb."

All the angels stood around the throne
   and around the elders and the four living creatures.
They prostrated themselves before the throne,
   worshiped God, and exclaimed:

   "Amen. Blessing and glory, wisdom and thanksgiving,
     honor, power, and might
     be to our God forever and ever. Amen."

Then one of the elders spoke up and said to me,
   "Who are these wearing white robes, and where did they come from?"
I said to him, "My lord, you are the one who knows."
He said to me,
   "These are the ones who have survived the time of great distress;
   they have washed their robes
   and made them white in the Blood of the Lamb.

   "For this reason they stand before God's throne
     and worship him day and night in his temple.
     The One who sits on the throne will shelter them.
   They will not hunger or thirst anymore,
     nor will the sun or any heat strike them.

**For the Lamb who is in the center of the throne
   will shepherd them
   and lead them to springs of life-giving water,
   and God will wipe away every tear from their eyes."**

The word of the Lord.

RESPONSORIAL PSALM

Psalm 124:2-3, 4-5, 7-8

℟. (7) **Our soul has been rescued like a bird from the fowler's snare.**

Had not the LORD **been with us—
   when men rose up against us,
   then would they have swallowed us alive,
When their fury was inflamed against us.**

℟. **Our soul has been rescued like a bird from the fowler's snare.**

**Then would the waters have overwhelmed us;
The torrent would have swept over us;
   over us then would have swept the raging waters.**

℟. **Our soul has been rescued like a bird from the fowler's snare.**

**Broken was the snare,
   and we were freed.
Our help is in the name of the L**ORD**,
   who made heaven and earth.**

℟. **Our soul has been rescued like a bird from the fowler's snare.**

ALLELUIA

Matthew 5:10

℟. Alleluia, alleluia.

**Blessed are they who are persecuted for the sake of righteousness,
for theirs is the Kingdom of heaven.**

℟. Alleluia, alleluia.

GOSPEL

Matthew 10:17-22   You will be led before governors and kings for my sake as a witness before them and the pagans.

☩ **A reading from the holy Gospel according to Matthew**

**Jesus said to the Twelve:
"Beware of men, for they will hand you over to courts
    and scourge you in their synagogues,
    and you will be led before governors and kings for my sake
    as a witness before them and the pagans.
When they hand you over,
    do not worry about how you are to speak
    or what you are to say.
You will be given at that moment what you are to say.
For it will not be you who speak
    but the Spirit of your Father speaking through you.
Brother will hand over brother to death,
    and the father his child;
    children will rise up against parents and have them put to death.
You will be hated by all because of my name,
    but whoever endures to the end will be saved."**

The Gospel of the Lord.

MAY 12

563 SAINT PANCRAS, MARTYR

From the Common of Martyrs, p. 1782,

OR

FIRST READING

Revelation 19:1, 5-9a   Blessed are those who have been called to the wedding feast of the Lamb.

A reading from the Book of Revelation

**I, John, heard what sounded like the loud voice
  of a great multitude in heaven, saying:**

> "Alleluia!
> Salvation, glory, and might belong to our God."

Then a voice coming from a heavenly throne said:

> "Praise our God, all you his servants,
>   and you who revere him, small and great."

**Then I heard something like the sound of a great multitude
  or the sound of rushing water or mighty peals of thunder,
  as they said:**

> "Alleluia!
> The Lord has established his reign,
>   our God, the almighty.
> Let us rejoice and be glad
>   and give him glory.
> For the wedding day of the Lamb has come,
>   his bride has made herself ready.
> She was allowed to wear
>   a bright, clean linen garment."

(The linen represents the righteous deeds of the holy ones.)

**Then an angel said to me, "Write this:
  Blessed are those who have been called
  to the wedding feast of the Lamb."**

The word of the Lord.

RESPONSORIAL PSALM

Psalm 103:1-2, 3-4, 8-9, 13-14, 17-18

℟. (1) O bless the Lord, my soul!

Bless the Lord, O my soul;
  and all my being, bless his holy name!
Bless the Lord, O my soul;
  and forget not all his benefits.

℟. O bless the Lord, my soul!

He pardons all your iniquities,
  he heals all your ills.
He redeems your life from destruction,
  he crowns you with kindness and compassion.

℟. O bless the Lord, my soul!

Merciful and gracious is the Lord,
  slow to anger and abounding in kindness.
He will not always chide,
  nor does he keep his wrath forever.

℟. O bless the Lord, my soul!

As a father has compassion on his children,
  so the Lord has compassion on those who fear him,
For he knows how we are formed;
  he remembers that we are dust.

℟. O bless the Lord, my soul!

But the kindness of the Lord is from eternity
  to eternity toward those who fear him,
And his justice toward his children's children
  among those who keep his covenant.

℟. O bless the Lord, my soul!

ALLELUIA

See Matthew 11:25

℟. **Alleluia, alleluia.**

**Blessed are you, Father, Lord of heaven and earth,
you have revealed to little ones the mysteries of the Kingdom.**

℟. **Alleluia, alleluia.**

GOSPEL

Matthew 11:25-30   Although you have hidden these things from the wise and learned you have revealed them to the childlike.

✠ **A reading from the holy Gospel according to Matthew**

**At that time Jesus responded:
"I give praise to you, Father, Lord of heaven and earth,
    for although you have hidden these things
    from the wise and the learned
    you have revealed them to the childlike.
Yes, Father, such has been your gracious will.
All things have been handed over to me by my Father.
No one knows the Son except the Father,
    and no one knows the Father except the Son
    and anyone to whom the Son wishes to reveal him."**

**"Come to me, all you who labor and are burdened,
    and I will give you rest.
Take my yoke upon you and learn from me,
    for I am meek and humble of heart;
    and you will find rest for yourselves.
For my yoke is easy, and my burden light."**

The Gospel of the Lord.

MAY 14

564 SAINT MATTHIAS, APOSTLE FEAST

FIRST READING

Acts 1:15-17, 20-26   The lot fell upon Matthias, and he was counted with the Eleven Apostles.

A reading from the Acts of the Apostles

Peter stood up in the midst of the brothers and sisters
 (there was a group of about one hundred and twenty persons
 in the one place).
He said, "My brothers and sisters,
 the Scripture had to be fulfilled
 which the Holy Spirit spoke beforehand
 through the mouth of David, concerning Judas,
 who was the guide for those who arrested Jesus.
Judas was numbered among us
 and was allotted a share in this ministry.
For it is written in the Book of Psalms:

*Let his encampment become desolate,
 and may no one dwell in it.*

and:

May another take his office.

Therefore, it is necessary that one of the men
 who accompanied us the whole time
 the Lord Jesus came and went among us,
 beginning from the baptism of John
 until the day on which he was taken up from us,
 become with us a witness to his resurrection."
So they proposed two, Joseph called Barsabbas,
 who was also known as Justus, and Matthias.
Then they prayed,
 "You, Lord, who know the hearts of all,
 show which one of these two you have chosen
 to take the place in this apostolic ministry
 from which Judas turned away to go to his own place."
Then they gave lots to them, and the lot fell upon Matthias,
 and he was counted with the Eleven Apostles.

The word of the Lord.

RESPONSORIAL PSALM

Psalm 113:1-2, 3-4, 5-6, 7-8

℟. (8) **The Lord will give him a seat with the leaders of his people.**
or:
℟. **Alleluia.**

Praise, you servants of the LORD,
 praise the name of the LORD.
Blessed be the name of the LORD
 both now and forever.

℟. **The Lord will give him a seat with the leaders of his people.**
or:
℟. **Alleluia.**

From the rising to the setting of the sun
 is the name of the LORD to be praised.
High above all nations is the LORD;
 above the heavens is his glory.

℟. **The Lord will give him a seat with the leaders of his people.**
or:
℟. **Alleluia.**

Who is like the LORD, our God, who is enthroned on high
 and looks upon the heavens and the earth below?

℟. **The Lord will give him a seat with the leaders of his people.**
or:
℟. **Alleluia.**

He raises up the lowly from the dust;
 from the dunghill he lifts up the poor
To seat them with princes,
 with the princes of his own people.

℟. **The Lord will give him a seat with the leaders of his people.**
or:
℟. **Alleluia.**

ALLELUIA

See John 15:16

℟. Alleluia, alleluia.

I chose you from the world,
to go and bear fruit that will last, says the Lord.

℟. Alleluia, alleluia.

GOSPEL

John 15:9-17   It was not you who chose me, but I who chose you.

✢ A reading from the holy Gospel according to John

Jesus said to his disciples:
"As the Father loves me, so I also love you.
Remain in my love.
If you keep my commandments, you will remain in my love,
    just as I have kept my Father's commandments
    and remain in his love.

"I have told you this so that my joy might be in you
    and your joy might be complete.
This is my commandment: love one another as I love you.
No one has greater love than this,
    to lay down one's life for one's friends.
You are my friends if you do what I command you.
I no longer call you slaves,
    because a slave does not know what his master is doing.
I have called you friends,
    because I have told you everything I have heard from my Father.
It was not you who chose me, but I who chose you
    and appointed you to go and bear fruit that will remain,
    so that whatever you ask the Father in my name he may give you.
This I command you: love one another."

The Gospel of the Lord.

MAY 15

[In the Dioceses of the United States]

564A SAINT ISIDORE

From the Common of Holy Men and Women, p. 1868.

MAY 18

565 SAINT JOHN I, POPE, MARTYR

From the Common of Martyrs, p. 1782, or the Common of Pastors: For a Pope, p. 1805,

OR

FIRST READING

Revelation 3:14b, 20-22   I will dine with him and he with me.

A reading from the Book of Revelation

**"'The Amen, the faithful and true witness,
the source of God's creation, says this:**

**"'Behold, I stand at the door and knock.
If anyone hears my voice and opens the door,
then I will enter his house and dine with him
and he with me.
I will give the victor the right to sit with me on my throne,
as I myself first won the victory
and sit with my Father on his throne.**

**"'Whoever has ears ought to hear
what the Spirit says to the churches.'"**

The word of the Lord.

RESPONSORIAL PSALM

Psalm 23:1-3a, 4, 5, 6

℟. (1) The Lord is my shepherd; there is nothing I shall want.

The LORD is my shepherd; I shall not want.
  In verdant pastures he gives me repose;
Beside restful waters he leads me;
  he refreshes my soul.

℟. The Lord is my shepherd; there is nothing I shall want.

Even though I walk in the dark valley
  I fear no evil; for you are at my side
With your rod and your staff
  that give me courage.

℟. The Lord is my shepherd; there is nothing I shall want.

You spread the table before me
  in the sight of my foes;
You anoint my head with oil;
  my cup overflows.

℟. The Lord is my shepherd; there is nothing I shall want.

Only goodness and kindness follow me
  all the days of my life;
And I shall dwell in the house of the LORD
  for years to come.

℟. The Lord is my shepherd; there is nothing I shall want.

ALLELUIA

John 15:15

℟. Alleluia, alleluia.

I call you my friends, says the Lord,
For I have made known to you all that the Father has told me.

℟. Alleluia, alleluia.

GOSPEL

Luke 22:24-30   I confer a kingdom on you, just as my Father has conferred one on me.

✠ A reading from the holy Gospel according to Luke

An argument broke out among the Apostles
 about which of them should be regarded as the greatest.
Jesus said to them,
 "The kings of the Gentiles lord it over them
 and those in authority over them are addressed as 'Benefactors';
 but among you it shall not be so.
Rather, let the greatest among you be as the youngest,
 and the leader as the servant.
For who is greater:
 the one seated at table or the one who serves?
Is it not the one seated at table?
I am among you as the one who serves.
It is you who have stood by me in my trials;
 and I confer a kingdom on you,
 just as my Father has conferred one on me,
 that you may eat and drink at my table in my Kingdom;
 and you will sit on thrones
 judging the twelve tribes of Israel."

The Gospel of the Lord.

MAY 20

566 SAINT BERNARDINE OF SIENA, PRIEST

From the Common of Pastors: For Missionaries, p. 1805,

OR

FIRST READING

Acts 4:8-12   There is no salvation through anyone else.

A reading from the Acts of the Apostles

Peter, filled with the Holy Spirit, answered them:
"Leaders of the people and elders:
  If we are being examined today
  about a good deed done to a cripple,
  namely, by what means he was saved,
  then all of you and all the people of Israel should know
  that it was in the name of Jesus Christ the Nazorean
  whom you crucified, whom God raised from the dead;
  in his name this man stands before you healed.
He is the stone rejected by you, the builders,
  which has become the cornerstone.
There is no salvation through anyone else,
  nor is there any other name under heaven
  given to the human race by which we are to be saved."

The word of the Lord.

RESPONSORIAL PSALM

Psalm 40:2, 4, 7-8, 8-9, 10, 11

℟. (8a and 9a) Here am I, Lord; I come to do your will.

I have waited, waited for the LORD,
   and he stooped toward me and heard my cry.
And he put a new song into my mouth,
   a hymn to our God.

℟. Here am I, Lord; I come to do your will.

Sacrifice or oblation you wished not,
   but ears open to obedience you gave me.
Burnt offerings or sin-offerings you sought not;
   then said I, "Behold I come."

℟. Here am I, Lord; I come to do your will.

"In the written scroll it is prescribed for me,
To do your will, O my God, is my delight,
   and your law is within my heart!"

℟. Here am I, Lord; I come to do your will.

I announced your justice in the vast assembly;
   I did not restrain my lips, as you, O LORD, know.

℟. Here am I, Lord; I come to do your will.

Your justice I kept not hid within my heart;
   your faithfulness and your salvation I have spoken of;
I have made no secret of your kindness and your truth
   in the vast assembly.

℟. Here am I, Lord; I come to do your will.

ALLELUIA

John 8:12

℟. Alleluia, alleluia.

I am the light of the world, says the Lord;
whoever follows me will have the light of life.

℟. Alleluia, alleluia.

GOSPEL

Luke 9:57-62   I will follow you wherever you go.

✛ A reading from the holy Gospel according to Luke

As Jesus and his disciples were proceeding
  on their journey to Jerusalem,
  someone said to him,
  "I will follow you wherever you go."
Jesus answered him,
  "Foxes have dens and birds of the sky have nests,
  but the Son of Man has nowhere to rest his head."
And to another he said, "Follow me."
But he replied, "Lord, let me go first and bury my father."
But he answered him, "Let the dead bury their dead.
But you, go and proclaim the Kingdom of God."
And another said, "I will follow you, Lord,
  but first let me say farewell to my family at home."
Jesus said, "No one who sets a hand to the plow
  and looks to what was left behind is fit for the Kingdom of God."

The Gospel of the Lord.

MAY 25

567 SAINT BEDE THE VENERABLE, PRIEST AND DOCTOR OF THE CHURCH

From the Common of Pastors, p. 1805, or the Common of Doctors of the Church, p. 1838,

OR

FIRST READING

1 Corinthians 2:10b-16   We have the mind of Christ.

A reading from the first Letter of Saint Paul to the Corinthians

Brothers and sisters:
The Spirit scrutinizes everything, even the depths of God.
Among men, who knows what pertains to the man
   except his spirit that is within?
Similarly, no one knows what pertains to God except the Spirit of God.
We have not received the spirit of the world
   but the Spirit who is from God,
   so that we may understand the things freely given us by God.
And we speak about them not with words taught by human wisdom,
   but with words taught by the Spirit,
   describing spiritual realities in spiritual terms.

Now the natural man does not accept what pertains to the Spirit of God,
   for to him it is foolishness, and he cannot understand it,
   because it is judged spiritually.
The one who is spiritual, however, can judge everything
   but is not subject to judgment by anyone.

For *who has known the mind of the Lord, so as to counsel him?*
But we have the mind of Christ.

The word of the Lord.

RESPONSORIAL PSALM

Psalm 119:9, 10, 11, 12, 13, 14

℟. (12) **Lord, teach me your statutes.**

**How shall a young man be faultless in his way?
   By keeping to your words.**

℟. **Lord, teach me your statutes.**

**With all my heart I seek you;
   let me not stray from your commands.**

℟. **Lord, teach me your statutes.**

**Within my heart I treasure your promise,
   that I may not sin against you.**

℟. **Lord, teach me your statutes.**

**Blessed are you, O LORD;
   teach me your statutes.**

℟. **Lord, teach me your statutes.**

**With my lips I declare
   all the ordinances of your mouth.**

℟. **Lord, teach me your statutes.**

**In the way of your decrees I rejoice,
   as much as in all riches.**

℟. **Lord, teach me your statutes.**

ALLELUIA

See John 6:63, 68c

℟. **Alleluia, alleluia.**

**Your words, Lord, are Spirit and life;
you have the words of everlasting life.**

℟. **Alleluia, alleluia.**

GOSPEL

Matthew 7:21-29   He taught them as one having authority.

✠ A reading from the holy Gospel according to **Matthew**

Jesus said to his disciples:
"Not everyone who says to me, 'Lord, Lord,'
   will enter the Kingdom of heaven,
   but only the one who does the will of my Father in heaven.
Many will say to me on that day,
   'Lord, Lord, did we not prophesy in your name?
Did we not drive out demons in your name?
Did we not do mighty deeds in your name?'
Then I will declare to them solemnly,
   'I never knew you. Depart from me, you evildoers.'

"Everyone who listens to these words of mine and acts on them
   will be like a wise man who built his house on rock.
The rain fell, the floods came,
   and the winds blew and buffeted the house.
But it did not collapse; it had been set solidly on rock.
And everyone who listens to these words of mine
   but does not act on them
   will be like a fool who built his house on sand.
The rain fell, the floods came,
   and the winds blew and buffeted the house.
And it collapsed and was completely ruined."

When Jesus finished these words,
   the crowds were astonished at his teaching,
   for he taught them as one having authority,
   and not as their scribes.

The Gospel of the Lord.

MAY 25

568 SAINT GREGORY VII, POPE, RELIGIOUS

From the Common of Pastors: For a Pope, p. 1805,

OR

FIRST READING

Acts 20:17-18a, 28-32, 36 Keep watch over yourselves and over the whole flock of which the Holy Spirit has appointed you overseers in which you tend the Church of God.

A reading from the Acts of the Apostles

From Miletus Paul had the presbyters
   of the Church at Ephesus summoned.
When they came to him, he addressed them,
   "Keep watch over yourselves and over the whole flock
   of which the Holy Spirit has appointed you overseers,
   in which you tend the Church of God
   that he acquired with his own Blood.
I know that after my departure savage wolves will come among you,
   and they will not spare the flock.
And from your own group,
   some will come forward perverting the truth
   to draw the disciples away after them.
So be vigilant and remember that for three years, night and day,
   I unceasingly admonished each of you with tears.
And now I commend you to God
   and to that gracious word of his that can build you up
   and give you the inheritance among all who are consecrated."

When he had finished speaking
   he knelt down and prayed with them all.

The word of the Lord.

RESPONSORIAL PSALM

Psalm 110:1, 2, 3, 4

℟. (4b) **You are a priest for ever, in the line of Melchizedek.**

The LORD said to my Lord: "Sit at my right hand
   till I make your enemies your footstool."

℟. **You are a priest for ever, in the line of Melchizedek.**

The scepter of your power the L ORD will stretch forth from Zion:
   "Rule in the midst of your enemies."

℟. You are a priest for ever, in the line of Melchizedek.

"Yours is princely power in the day of your birth, in holy splendor;
   before the daystar, like the dew, I have begotten you."

℟. You are a priest for ever, in the line of Melchizedek.

The L ORD has sworn, and he will not repent:
   "You are a priest forever, according to the order of Melchizedek."

℟. You are a priest for ever, in the line of Melchizedek.

ALLELUIA

Mark 1:17

℟. Alleluia, alleluia.

Come after me, says the Lord,
and I will make you fishers of men.

℟. Alleluia, alleluia.

GOSPEL

Matthew 16:13-19   You are Peter and upon this rock I will build my Church.

✠ A reading from the holy Gospel according to Matthew

When Jesus went into the region of Caesarea Philippi
   he asked his disciples,
   "Who do people say that the Son of Man is?"
They replied, "Some say John the Baptist, others Elijah,
   still others Jeremiah or one of the prophets."
He said to them, "But who do you say that I am?"
Simon Peter said in reply,
   "You are the Christ, the Son of the living God."
Jesus said to him in reply, "Blessed are you, Simon son of Jonah.
For flesh and blood has not revealed this to you, but my heavenly Father.
And so I say to you, you are Peter,
   and upon this rock I will build my Church,
   and the gates of the netherworld shall not prevail against it.
I will give you the keys to the Kingdom of heaven.
Whatever you bind on earth shall be bound in heaven;
   and whatever you loose on earth shall be loosed in heaven."

The Gospel of the Lord.

MAY 25

569 SAINT MARY MAGDALENE DE' PAZZI, VIRGIN

From the Common of Virgins, p. 1857, or the Common of Holy Men and Women: For Religious, p. 1868,

OR

FIRST READING

1 Corinthians 7:25-35   *A virgin is anxious about the things of the Lord.*

A reading from the first Letter of Saint Paul to the Corinthians

In regard to virgins, I have no commandment from the Lord,
> but I give my opinion as one who by the Lord's mercy is trustworthy.

So this is what I think best because of the present distress:
> that it is a good thing for a person to remain as he is.

Are you bound to a wife? Do not seek a separation.
Are you free of a wife? Then do not look for a wife.
If you marry, however, you do not sin,
> nor does an unmarried woman sin if she marries;
> but such people will experience affliction in their earthly life,
> and I would like to spare you that.

I tell you, brothers and sisters, the time is running out.
From now on, let those having wives act as not having them,
> those weeping as not weeping,
> those rejoicing as not rejoicing,
> those buying as not owning,
> those using the world as not using it fully.

For the world in its present form is passing away.

I should like you to be free of anxieties.
An unmarried man is anxious about the things of the Lord,
> how he may please the Lord.

But a married man is anxious about the things of the world,
> how he may please his wife, and he is divided.

An unmarried woman or a virgin is anxious about the things of the Lord,
> so that she may be holy in both body and spirit.

A married woman, on the other hand,
> is anxious about the things of the world,
> how she may please her husband.

I am telling you this for your own benefit,
> not to impose a restraint upon you,
> but for the sake of propriety
> and adherence to the Lord without distraction.

The word of the Lord.

RESPONSORIAL PSALM

Psalm 148:1-2, 11-13, 13-14

℟. (see 12a and 13a) **Young men and women, praise the name of the Lord.**
   or:
℟. **Alleluia.**

Praise the LORD from the heavens;
   praise him in the heights;
Praise him, all you his angels,
   praise him, all you his hosts.

℟. Young men and women, praise the name of the Lord.
   or:
℟. Alleluia.

Let the kings of the earth and all peoples,
   the princes and all the judges of the earth,
Young men, too, and maidens,
   old men and boys,
Praise the name of the LORD,
   for his name alone is exalted.

℟. Young men and women, praise the name of the Lord.
   or:
℟. Alleluia.

His majesty is above earth and heaven.
He has lifted up the horn of his people.
Be this his praise from all his faithful ones;
   from the children of Israel, the people close to him. Alleluia.

℟. Young men and women, praise the name of the Lord.
   or:
℟. Alleluia.

ALLELUIA

John 8:31b-32

℟. Alleluia, alleluia.

**If you remain in my word, you will truly be my disciples,
and you will know the truth, says the Lord.**

℟. Alleluia, alleluia.

GOSPEL

Mark 3:31-35   Whoever does the will of God is my brother and sister and mother.

☩   A reading from the holy Gospel according to Mark

**The mother of Jesus and his brothers arrived at the house.
Standing outside, they sent word to him and called him.
A crowd seated around him told him,
    "Your mother and your brothers and your sisters
    are outside asking for you."
But he said to them in reply,
    "Who are my mother and my brothers?"
And looking around at those seated in the circle he said,
    "Here are my mother and my brothers.
For whoever does the will of God
    is my brother and sister and mother."**

The Gospel of the Lord.

MAY 26

570 SAINT PHILIP NERI, PRIEST MEMORIAL

From the Common of Pastors, p. 1805, or the Common of Holy Men and Women: For Religious, p. 1868,

OR

FIRST READING

Philippians 4:4-9   Think about whatever is worthy of praise.

A reading from the Letter of Saint Paul to the Philippians

Brothers and sisters:
Rejoice in the Lord always.
I shall say it again: rejoice!
Your kindness should be known to all.
The Lord is near.
Have no anxiety at all, but in everything,
   by prayer and petition, with thanksgiving,
   make your requests known to God.
Then the peace of God that surpasses all understanding
   will guard your hearts and minds in Christ Jesus.

Finally, brothers and sisters,
   whatever is true, whatever is honorable,
   whatever is just, whatever is pure,
   whatever is lovely, whatever is gracious,
   if there is any excellence
   and if there is anything worthy of praise,
   think about these things.
Keep on doing what you have learned and received
   and heard and seen in me.
Then the God of peace will be with you.

The word of the Lord.

RESPONSORIAL PSALM

Psalm 34:2-3, 4-5, 6-7, 8-9, 10-11

℟. (2) **I will bless the Lord at all times.**
   or:
℟. (9) **Taste and see the goodness of the Lord.**

I will bless the LORD **at all times;**
   his praise shall be ever in my mouth.
Let my soul glory in the LORD**;**
   the lowly will hear and be glad.

℟. **I will bless the Lord at all times.**
   or:
℟. **Taste and see the goodness of the Lord.**

Glorify the LORD **with me,**
   let us together extol his name.
I sought the LORD**, and he answered me**
   and delivered me from all my fears.

℟. **I will bless the Lord at all times.**
   or:
℟. **Taste and see the goodness of the Lord.**

Look to him that you may be radiant with joy,
   and your faces may not blush with shame.
When the poor one called out, the LORD **heard,**
   and from all his distress he saved him.

℟. **I will bless the Lord at all times.**
   or:
℟. **Taste and see the goodness of the Lord.**

The angel of the LORD **encamps**
   around those who fear him, and delivers them.
Taste and see how good the LORD **is;**
   blessed the man who takes refuge in him.

℟. **I will bless the Lord at all times.**
   or:
℟. **Taste and see the goodness of the Lord.**

Fear the Lord, you his holy ones,
  for nought is lacking to those who fear him.
The great grow poor and hungry;
  but those who seek the Lord want for no good thing.

℟. I will bless the Lord at all times.

or:

℟. Taste and see the goodness of the Lord.

ALLELUIA

John 15:9b, 5b

℟. Alleluia, alleluia.

Remain in my love, says the Lord;
whoever remains in me and I in him will bear much fruit.

℟. Alleluia, alleluia.

GOSPEL

John 17:20-26   I wish that where I am they also may be with me.

✠ A reading from the holy Gospel according to John

Jesus raised his eyes to heaven and said:
"Holy Father, I pray not only for these,
  but also for those who will believe in me through their word,
  so that they may all be one,
  as you, Father, are in me and I in you,
  that they also may be in us,
  that the world may believe that you sent me.
And I have given them the glory you gave me,
  so that they may be one, as we are one,
  I in them and you in me,
  that they may be brought to perfection as one,
  that the world may know that you sent me,
  and that you loved them even as you loved me.
Father, they are your gift to me.
I wish that where I am they also may be with me,
  that they may see my glory that you gave me,
  because you loved me before the foundation of the world.
Righteous Father, the world also does not know you,
  but I know you, and they know that you sent me.
I made known to them your name and I will make it known,
  that the love with which you loved me
  may be in them and I in them."

The Gospel of the Lord.

MAY 27

571 SAINT AUGUSTINE OF CANTERBURY, BISHOP

From the Common of Pastors: For Missionaries, p. 1805,

OR

FIRST READING

1 Thessalonians 2:2b-8   We were determined to share with you not only the Gospel of God, but our very selves as well.

A reading from the first Letter of Saint Paul to the Thessalonians

Brothers and sisters:
We drew courage through our God
    to speak to you the Gospel of God with much struggle.
Our exhortation was not from delusion or impure motives,
    nor did it work through deception.
But as we were judged worthy by God to be entrusted with the Gospel,
    that is how we speak,
    not as trying to please men,
    but rather God, who judges our hearts.
Nor, indeed, did we ever appear with flattering speech, as you know,
    or with a pretext for greed—God is witness—
    nor did we seek praise from men,
    either from you or from others,
    although we were able to impose our weight as Apostles of Christ.
Rather, we were gentle among you,
    as a nursing mother cares for her children.
With such affection for you, we were determined to share with you
    not only the Gospel of God, but our very selves as well,
    so dearly beloved had you become to us.

The word of the Lord.

RESPONSORIAL PSALM

Psalm 96:1-2a, 2b-3, 7-8a, 10

℟. (3) **Proclaim God's marvelous deeds to all the nations.**

Sing to the LORD a new song;
    sing to the LORD, all you lands.
Sing to the LORD; bless his name.

℟. **Proclaim God's marvelous deeds to all the nations.**

Announce his salvation, day after day.
Tell his glory among the nations;
   among all peoples, his wondrous deeds.

℟. Proclaim God's marvelous deeds to all the nations.

Give to the LORD, you families of nations,
   give to the LORD glory and praise;
   give to the LORD the glory due his name!

℟. Proclaim God's marvelous deeds to all the nations.

Say among the nations: The LORD is king.
He has made the world firm, not to be moved;
   he governs the peoples with equity.

℟. Proclaim God's marvelous deeds to all the nations.

ALLELUIA

John 10:14

℟. Alleluia, alleluia.

I am the good shepherd, says the Lord;
I know my sheep, and mine know me.

℟. Alleluia, alleluia.

GOSPEL

Matthew 9:35-38   The harvest is abundant but the laborers are few.

✠ A reading from the holy Gospel according to Matthew

Jesus went around to all the towns and villages,
   teaching in their synagogues,
   proclaiming the Gospel of the Kingdom,
   and curing every disease and illness.
At the sight of the crowds, his heart was moved with pity for them
   because they were troubled and abandoned,
   like sheep without a shepherd.
Then he said to his disciples,
   "The harvest is abundant but the laborers are few;
   so ask the master of the harvest
   to send out laborers for his harvest."

The Gospel of the Lord.

MAY 31

572 VISITATION OF THE BLESSED VIRGIN MARY
FEAST

FIRST READING

First Option

Zephaniah 3:14-18a   The King of Israel, the Lord, is in your midst.

A reading from the Book of the Prophet Zephaniah

> Shout for joy, O daughter Zion!
>   Sing joyfully, O Israel!
> Be glad and exult with all your heart,
>   O daughter Jerusalem!
> The LORD has removed the judgment against you,
>   he has turned away your enemies;
> The King of Israel, the LORD, is in your midst,
>   you have no further misfortune to fear.
> On that day, it shall be said to Jerusalem:
>   Fear not, O Zion, be not discouraged!
> The LORD, your God, is in your midst,
>   a mighty savior;
> He will rejoice over you with gladness,
>   and renew you in his love,
> He will sing joyfully because of you,
>   as one sings at festivals.

The word of the Lord.

OR

Second Option

Romans 12:9-16   Contribute to the needs of the holy ones, exercise hospitality.

A reading from the Letter of Saint Paul to the Romans

Brothers and sisters:
Let love be sincere;
  hate what is evil,
  hold on to what is good;
  love one another with mutual affection;
  anticipate one another in showing honor.
Do not grow slack in zeal,
  be fervent in spirit,
  serve the Lord.

Rejoice in hope,
  endure in affliction,
  persevere in prayer.
Contribute to the needs of the holy ones,
  exercise hospitality.
Bless those who persecute you,
  bless and do not curse them.
Rejoice with those who rejoice,
  weep with those who weep.
Have the same regard for one another;
  do not be haughty but associate with the lowly;
  do not be wise in your own estimation.

The word of the Lord.

RESPONSORIAL PSALM

Isaiah 12:2-3, 4bcd, 5-6

℟. (6) **Among you is the great and Holy One of Israel.**

God indeed is my savior;
  I am confident and unafraid.
My strength and my courage is the LORD**,**
  and he has been my savior.
With joy you will draw water
  at the fountain of salvation.

℟. **Among you is the great and Holy One of Israel.**

Give thanks to the LORD**, acclaim his name;**
  among the nations make known his deeds,
  proclaim how exalted is his name.

℟. **Among you is the great and Holy One of Israel.**

Sing praise to the LORD **for his glorious achievement;**
  let this be known throughout all the earth.
Shout with exultation, O city of Zion,
  for great in your midst
  is the Holy One of Israel!

℟. **Among you is the great and Holy One of Israel.**

ALLELUIA

See Luke 1:45

℟. Alleluia, alleluia.

**Blessed are you, O Virgin Mary, who believed
that what was spoken to you by the Lord would be fulfilled.**

℟. Alleluia, alleluia.

GOSPEL

Luke 1:39-56   And how does this happen to me, that the mother of my Lord should come to me?

✠ A reading from the holy Gospel according to Luke

**Mary set out
and traveled to the hill country in haste
to a town of Judah,
where she entered the house of Zechariah
and greeted Elizabeth.
When Elizabeth heard Mary's greeting,
the infant leaped in her womb,
and Elizabeth, filled with the Holy Spirit,
cried out in a loud voice and said,
"Most blessed are you among women,
and blessed is the fruit of your womb.
And how does this happen to me,
that the mother of my Lord should come to me?
For at the moment the sound of your greeting reached my ears,
the infant in my womb leaped for joy.
Blessed are you who believed
that what was spoken to you by the Lord
would be fulfilled."**

**And Mary said:
"My soul proclaims the greatness of the Lord;
my spirit rejoices in God my Savior,
for he has looked with favor on his lowly servant.
From this day all generations will call me blessed:
the Almighty has done great things for me,
and holy is his Name.**

He has mercy on those who fear him
>in every generation.
He has shown the strength of his arm,
>he has scattered the proud in their conceit.
He has cast down the mighty from their thrones,
>and has lifted up the lowly.
He has filled the hungry with good things,
>and the rich he has sent away empty.
He has come to the help of his servant Israel
>for he has remembered his promise of mercy,
>the promise he made to our fathers,
>to Abraham and his children for ever."

Mary remained with her about three months
>and then returned to her home.

The Gospel of the Lord.

1316 *The Immaculate Heart of the Blessed Virgin Mary*

SATURDAY FOLLOWING THE SECOND SUNDAY AFTER PENTECOST

573 THE IMMACULATE HEART OF THE BLESSED VIRGIN MARY MEMORIAL

The Gospel for this memorial is proper. From the Common of the Blessed Virgin Mary, p. 1751,

OR

FIRST READING

Isaiah 61:9-11   I rejoice heartily in the LORD.

A reading from the Book of the Prophet Isaiah

> Thus says the LORD:
> The descendants of my people shall be renowned among the nations,
>   and their offspring among the peoples;
> All who see them shall acknowledge them
>   as a race the LORD has blessed.
>
> I rejoice heartily in the LORD,
>   in my God is the joy of my soul;
> For he has clothed me with a robe of salvation,
>   and wrapped me in a mantle of justice,
> Like a bridegroom adorned with a diadem,
>   like a bride bedecked with her jewels.
> As the earth brings forth its plants,
>   and a garden makes its growth spring up,
> So will the Lord GOD make justice and praise
>   spring up before all the nations.

The word of the Lord.

RESPONSORIAL PSALM

1 Samuel 2:1, 4-5, 6-7, 8abcd

℟. (see 1) **My heart exults in the Lord, my Savior.**

"My heart exults in the LORD,
  my horn is exalted in my God.
I have swallowed up my enemies;
  I rejoice in my victory."

℟. **My heart exults in the Lord, my Savior.**

"The bows of the mighty are broken,
  while the tottering gird on strength.
The well-fed hire themselves out for bread,
  while the hungry batten on spoil.
The barren wife bears seven sons,
  while the mother of many languishes."

℟. **My heart exults in the Lord, my Savior.**

"The LORD puts to death and gives life;
  he casts down to the nether world;
  he raises up again.
The LORD makes poor and makes rich,
  he humbles, and also exalts."

℟. **My heart exults in the Lord, my Savior.**

"He raises the needy from the dust;
  from the dung heap he lifts up the poor,
To seat them with nobles
  and make a glorious throne their heritage."

℟. **My heart exults in the Lord, my Savior.**

ALLELUIA

See Luke 2:19

℟. Alleluia, alleluia.

**Blessed is the Virgin Mary who kept the word of God
and pondered it in her heart.**

℟. Alleluia, alleluia.

GOSPEL

Luke 2:41-51   His mother kept all these things in her heart.

✠ **A reading from the holy Gospel according to Luke**

**Each year Jesus' parents went to Jerusalem for the feast of Passover,
    and when he was twelve years old,
    they went up according to festival custom.
After they had completed its days, as they were returning,
    the boy Jesus remained behind in Jerusalem,
    but his parents did not know it.
Thinking that he was in the caravan,
    they journeyed for a day
    and looked for him among their relatives and acquaintances,
    but not finding him,
    they returned to Jerusalem to look for him.
After three days they found him in the temple,
    sitting in the midst of the teachers,
    listening to them and asking them questions,
    and all who heard him were astounded
    at his understanding and his answers.
When his parents saw him,
    they were astonished,
    and his mother said to him,
    "Son, why have you done this to us?
Your father and I have been looking for you with great anxiety."
And he said to them,
    "Why were you looking for me?
Did you not know that I must be in my Father's house?"
But they did not understand what he said to them.
He went down with them and came to Nazareth,
    and was obedient to them;
    and his mother kept all these things in her heart.**

The Gospel of the Lord.

JUNE 1

574 SAINT JUSTIN, MARTYR MEMORIAL

From the Common of Martyrs, p. 1782,

> OR

FIRST READING

1 Corinthians 1:18-25   It was the will of God through the foolishness of the proclamation to save those who have faith.

A reading from the first Letter of Saint Paul to the Corinthians

Brothers and sisters:
The message of the cross is foolishness to those who are perishing,
    but to us who are being saved it is the power of God.
For it is written:

> *I will destroy the wisdom of the wise,*
>   *and the learning of the learned I will set aside.*

Where is the wise one?
Where is the scribe?
Where is the debater of this age?
Has not God made the wisdom of the world foolish?
For since in the wisdom of God
    the world did not come to know God through wisdom,
    it was the will of God through the foolishness of the proclamation
    to save those who have faith.
For Jews demand signs and Greeks look for wisdom,
    but we proclaim Christ crucified,
    a stumbling block to Jews and foolishness to Gentiles,
    but to those who are called, Jews and Greeks alike,
    Christ the power of God and the wisdom of God.
For the foolishness of God is wiser than human wisdom,
    and the weakness of God is stronger than human strength.

The word of the Lord.

RESPONSORIAL PSALM

Psalm 34:2-3, 4-5, 6-7, 8-9

℟. (5) **The Lord delivered me from all my fears.**

**I will bless the Lord at all times;
　his praise shall be ever in my mouth.
Let my soul glory in the Lord;
　the lowly will hear and be glad.**

℟. **The Lord delivered me from all my fears.**

**Glorify the Lord with me,
　let us together extol his name.
I sought the Lord, and he answered me
　and delivered me from all my fears.**

℟. **The Lord delivered me from all my fears.**

**Look to him that you may be radiant with joy,
　and your faces may not blush with shame.
When the poor one called out, the Lord heard,
　and from all his distress he saved him.**

℟. **The Lord delivered me from all my fears.**

**The angel of the Lord encamps
　around those who fear him, and delivers them.
Taste and see how good the Lord is;
　blessed the man who takes refuge in him.**

℟. **The Lord delivered me from all my fears.**

ALLELUIA

Matthew 5:16

℟. **Alleluia, alleluia.**

**Let your light shine before others,
that they may see your good deeds and glorify your heavenly Father.**

℟. **Alleluia, alleluia.**

GOSPEL

Matthew 5:13-19   You are the light of the world.

☩ **A reading from the holy Gospel according to Matthew**

**Jesus said to his disciples:
"You are the salt of the earth.
But if salt loses its taste, with what can it be seasoned?
It is no longer good for anything
   but to be thrown out and trampled underfoot.
You are the light of the world.
A city set on a mountain cannot be hidden.
Nor do they light a lamp and then put it under a bushel basket;
   it is set on a lampstand,
   where it gives light to all in the house.
Just so, your light must shine before others,
   that they may see your good deeds
   and glorify your heavenly Father.**

**"Do not think that I have come to abolish the law or the prophets.
I have come not to abolish but to fulfill.
Amen, I say to you, until heaven and earth pass away,
   not the smallest letter or the smallest part of a letter
   will pass from the law,
   until all things have taken place.
Therefore, whoever breaks one of the least of these commandments
   and teaches others to do so
   will be called least in the Kingdom of heaven.
But whoever obeys and teaches these commandments
   will be called greatest in the Kingdom of heaven."**

The Gospel of the Lord.

JUNE 2

575 SAINTS MARCELLINUS AND PETER, MARTYRS

From the Common of Martyrs, p. 1782,

OR

FIRST READING

2 Corinthians 6:4-10   We are treated as dying and behold we live.

A reading from the second Letter of Saint Paul to the Corinthians

Brothers and sisters:
In everything we commend ourselves as ministers of God,
  through much endurance, in afflictions, hardships,
  constraints, beatings, imprisonments, riots,
  labors, vigils, fasts;
  by purity, knowledge, patience, kindness,
  in the Holy Spirit, in unfeigned love, in truthful speech,
  in the power of God;
  with weapons of righteousness at the right and at the left;
  through glory and dishonor, insult and praise.
We are treated as deceivers and yet are truthful;
  as unrecognized and yet acknowledged;
  as dying and behold we live;
  as chastised and yet not put to death;
  as sorrowful yet always rejoicing;
  as poor yet enriching many;
  as having nothing and yet possessing all things.

The word of the Lord.

RESPONSORIAL PSALM

Psalm 124:2-3, 4-5, 7b-8

℟. (7) **Our soul has been rescued like a bird from the fowler's snare.**

**Had not the Lord been with us—
When men rose up against us,
 then would they have swallowed us alive
When their fury was inflamed against us.**

℟. **Our soul has been rescued like a bird from the fowler's snare.**

**Then would the waters have overwhelmed us;
The torrent would have swept over us;
 over us then would have swept
 the raging waters.**

℟. **Our soul has been rescued like a bird from the fowler's snare.**

**Broken was the snare,
 and we were freed.
Our help is in the name of the Lord,
 who made heaven and earth.**

℟. **Our soul has been rescued like a bird from the fowler's snare.**

ALLELUIA

2 Corinthians 1:3b-4a

℟. **Alleluia, alleluia.**

Blessed be the Father of compassion and the God of all encouragement, who encourages us in every affliction.

℟. **Alleluia, alleluia.**

GOSPEL

John 17:11b-19   The world hated them.

✞   A reading from the holy Gospel according to John

Jesus raised his eyes to heaven and prayed, saying:
 "Holy Father, keep them in your name that you have given me,
  so that they may be one just as we are one.
When I was with them I protected them in your name that you gave me,
  and I guarded them, and none of them was lost
  except the son of destruction,
  in order that the Scripture might be fulfilled.
But now I am coming to you.
I speak this in the world
  so that they may share my joy completely.
I gave them your word, and the world hated them,
  because they do not belong to the world
  any more than I belong to the world.
I do not ask that you take them out of the world
  but that you keep them from the Evil One.
They do not belong to the world
  any more than I belong to the world.
Consecrate them in the truth. Your word is truth.
As you sent me into the world,
  so I sent them into the world.
And I consecrate myself for them,
  so that they also may be consecrated in truth."

The Gospel of the Lord.

JUNE 3

576 SAINT CHARLES LWANGA AND COMPANIONS, MARTYRS MEMORIAL

From the Common of Martyrs, p. 1782,

OR

FIRST READING

2 Maccabees 7:1-2, 9-14   We are ready to die rather than transgress the laws of our ancestors.

A reading from the second Book of Maccabees

It happened that seven brothers with their mother were arrested
  and tortured with whips and scourges by the king,
  to force them to eat pork in violation of God's law.
One of the brothers, speaking for the others, said:
  "What do you expect to achieve by questioning us?
We are ready to die rather than transgress the laws of our ancestors."

At the point of death he said:
  "You accursed fiend, you are depriving us of this present life,
  but the King of the world will raise us up to live again forever.
It is for his laws that we are dying."

After him, the third suffered their cruel sport.
He put out his tongue at once when told to do so,
  and bravely held out his hands, as he spoke these noble words:
  "It was from Heaven that I received these;
  for the sake of God's laws I disdain them;
  from him I hope to receive them again."
Even the king and his attendants marveled at the young man's courage,
  because he regarded his sufferings as nothing.

After he had died,
  they tortured and maltreated the fourth brother in the same way.
When he was near death, he said,
  "It is my choice to die at the hands of men
  with the God-given hope of being restored to life by him;
  but for you, there will be no resurrection to life."

The word of the Lord.

RESPONSORIAL PSALM

Psalm 124:2-3, 4-5, 7b-8

℟. (7) **Our soul has been rescued like a bird from the fowler's snare.**

**Had not the Lord been with us—
When men rose up against us,
  then would they have swallowed us alive
When their fury was inflamed against us.**

℟. **Our soul has been rescued like a bird from the fowler's snare.**

**Then would the waters have overwhelmed us;
The torrent would have swept over us;
  over us then would have swept
  the raging waters.**

℟. **Our soul has been rescued like a bird from the fowler's snare.**

**Broken was the snare,
  and we were freed.
Our help is in the name of the Lord,
  who made heaven and earth.**

℟. **Our soul has been rescued like a bird from the fowler's snare.**

ALLELUIA

Matthew 5:3

℟. **Alleluia, alleluia.**

**Blessed are the poor in spirit;
theirs is the Kingdom of heaven.**

℟. **Alleluia, alleluia.**

GOSPEL

Matthew 5:1-12a   Rejoice and be glad, for your reward will be great in heaven.

✢ **A reading from the holy Gospel according to Matthew**

**When Jesus saw the crowds, he went up the mountain,
and after he had sat down, his disciples came to him.
He began to teach them, saying:
"Blessed are the poor in spirit,
for theirs is the Kingdom of heaven.
Blessed are they who mourn,
for they will be comforted.
Blessed are the meek,
for they will inherit the land.
Blessed are they who hunger and thirst for righteousness,
for they will be satisfied.
Blessed are the merciful,
for they will be shown mercy.
Blessed are the clean of heart,
for they will see God.
Blessed are the peacemakers,
for they will be called children of God.
Blessed are they who are persecuted for the sake of righteousness,
for theirs is the Kingdom of heaven.
Blessed are you when they insult you and persecute you
and utter every kind of evil against you falsely because of me.
Rejoice and be glad,
for your reward will be great in heaven."**

The Gospel of the Lord.

JUNE 5

577 SAINT BONIFACE, BISHOP AND MARTYR
MEMORIAL

From the Common of Martyrs, p. 1782, or the Common of Pastors: For Missionaries, p. 1805,

OR

FIRST READING

Acts 26:19-23   Christ proclaims light to both the Jews and the Gentiles.

A reading from the Acts of the Apostles

Paul said:
"King Agrippa, I was not disobedient to the heavenly vision.
On the contrary, first to those in Damascus and in Jerusalem
 and throughout the whole country of Judea,
 and then to the Gentiles,
 I preached the need to repent and turn to God,
 and to do works giving evidence of repentance.
That is why the Jews seized me when I was in the temple
 and tried to kill me.
But I have enjoyed God's help to this very day,
 and so I stand here testifying to small and great alike,
 saying nothing different from what the prophets and Moses foretold,
 that the Messiah must suffer and that,
 as the first to rise from the dead,
 he would proclaim light both to our people and to the Gentiles."

The word of the Lord.

RESPONSORIAL PSALM

Psalm 117:1bc, 2

℟. (Mark 16:15) **Go out to all the world and tell the Good News.**
  or:
℟. **Alleluia.**

Praise the LORD, all you nations;
 glorify him, all you peoples!

℟. **Go out to all the world and tell the Good News.**
  or:
℟. **Alleluia.**

For steadfast is his kindness toward us,
  and the fidelity of the Lord endures forever.

℟. **Go out to all the world and tell the Good News.**
  or:
℟. **Alleluia.**

ALLELUIA

John 10:14

℟. **Alleluia, alleluia.**

I am the good shepherd, says the Lord,
I know my sheep, and mine know me.

℟. **Alleluia, alleluia.**

GOSPEL

John 10:11-16   A good shepherd lays down his life for his sheep.

✠ **A reading from the holy Gospel according to John**

Jesus said:
"I am the good shepherd.
A good shepherd lays down his life for the sheep.
A hired man, who is not a shepherd
  and whose sheep are not his own,
    sees a wolf coming and leaves the sheep and runs away,
    and the wolf catches and scatters them.
This is because he works for pay and has no concern for the sheep.
I am the good shepherd,
  and I know mine and mine know me,
    just as the Father knows me and I know the Father;
    and I will lay down my life for the sheep.
I have other sheep that do not belong to this fold.
These also I must lead, and they will hear my voice,
  and there will be one flock, one shepherd."

The Gospel of the Lord.

JUNE 6

578 SAINT NORBERT, BISHOP

From the Common of Pastors, p. 1805, or the Common of Holy Men and Women: For Religious, p. 1868,

OR

FIRST READING

Ezekiel 34:11-16   As a shepherd tends his flock so will I tend my sheep.

A reading from the Book of the Prophet Ezekiel

Thus says the Lord God:
   I myself will look after and tend my sheep.
As a shepherd tends his flock
   when he finds himself among his scattered sheep,
   so will I tend my sheep.
I will rescue them from every place where they were scattered
   when it was cloudy and dark.
I will lead them out from among the peoples
   and gather them from the foreign lands;
   I will bring them back to their own country
   and pasture them upon the mountains of Israel
   in the land's ravines and all its inhabited places.
In good pastures will I pasture them,
   and on the mountain heights of Israel
   shall be their grazing ground.
There they shall lie down on good grazing ground,
   and in rich pastures shall they be pastured
   on the mountains of Israel.
I myself will pasture my sheep;
   I myself will give them rest, says the Lord God.
The lost I will seek out,
   the strayed I will bring back,
   the injured I will bind up,
   the sick I will heal,
   but the sleek and the strong I will destroy,
   shepherding them rightly.

The word of the Lord.

RESPONSORIAL PSALM

Psalm 23:1-3a, 4, 5, 6

℟. (1) **The Lord is my shepherd; there is nothing I shall want.**

The Lord is my shepherd; I shall not want.
   In verdant pastures he gives me repose;
Beside restful waters he leads me;
   he refreshes my soul.

℟. **The Lord is my shepherd; there is nothing I shall want.**

Even though I walk in the dark valley
   I fear no evil; for you are at my side
With your rod and your staff
   that give me courage.

℟. **The Lord is my shepherd; there is nothing I shall want.**

You spread the table before me
   in the sight of my foes;
You anoint my head with oil;
   my cup overflows.

℟. **The Lord is my shepherd; there is nothing I shall want.**

Only goodness and kindness follow me
   all the days of my life;
And I shall dwell in the house of the Lord
   for years to come.

℟. **The Lord is my shepherd; there is nothing I shall want.**

ALLELUIA

Matthew 5:3

℟. Alleluia, alleluia.

**Blessed are the poor in spirit;
for theirs is the Kingdom of heaven.**

℟. Alleluia, alleluia.

GOSPEL

Luke 14:25-33   Everyone of you who does not renounce all his possessions cannot be my disciple.

✠ A reading from the holy Gospel according to Luke

**Great crowds were traveling with Jesus,
   and he turned and addressed them,
   "If anyone comes to me without hating his father and mother,
   wife and children, brothers and sisters,
   and even his own life,
   he cannot be my disciple.
Whoever does not carry his own cross and come after me
   cannot be my disciple.
Which of you wishing to construct a tower
   does not first sit down and calculate the cost
   to see if there is enough for its completion?
Otherwise, after laying the foundation
   and finding himself unable to finish the work
   the onlookers should laugh at him and say,
   'This one began to build but did not have the resources to finish.'
Or what king marching into battle would not first sit down
   and decide whether with ten thousand troops
   he can successfully oppose another king
   advancing upon him with twenty thousand troops?
But if not, while he is still far away,
   he will send a delegation to ask for peace terms.
In the same way,
   everyone of you who does not renounce all his possessions
   cannot be my disciple."**

The Gospel of the Lord.

JUNE 9

579 SAINT EPHREM, DEACON AND DOCTOR OF THE CHURCH

From the Common of Doctors of the Church, p. 1838,

> OR

FIRST READING

Colossians 3:12-17   And over all these put on love, that is, the bond of perfection.

A reading from the Letter of Saint Paul to the Colossians

Brothers and sisters:
Put on, as God's chosen ones, holy and beloved,
   heartfelt compassion, kindness, humility, gentleness, and patience,
   bearing with one another and forgiving one another,
   if one has a grievance against another;
   as the Lord has forgiven you, so must you also do.
And over all these put on love,
   that is, the bond of perfection.
And let the peace of Christ control your hearts,
   the peace into which you were also called in one Body.
And be thankful.
Let the word of Christ dwell in you richly,
   as in all wisdom you teach and admonish one another,
   singing psalms, hymns, and spiritual songs
   with gratitude in your hearts to God.
And whatever you do, in word or in deed,
   do everything in the name of the Lord Jesus,
   giving thanks to God the Father through him.

The word of the Lord.

RESPONSORIAL PSALM

Psalm 37:3-4, 5-6, 30-31

℟. (30a) **The mouth of the just murmurs wisdom.**

Trust in the Lord and do good,
   that you may dwell in the land and be fed in security.
Take delight in the Lord,
   and he will grant you your heart's requests.

℟. **The mouth of the just murmurs wisdom.**

June 9—Saint Ephrem

Commit to the LORD **your way;**
   trust in him, and he will act.
He will make justice dawn for you like the light;
   bright as the noonday shall be your vindication.

℟. **The mouth of the just murmurs wisdom.**

The mouth of the just tells of wisdom
   and his tongue utters what is right.
The law of his God is in his heart,
   and his steps do not falter.

℟. **The mouth of the just murmurs wisdom.**

ALLELUIA

John 15:5

℟. **Alleluia, alleluia.**

I am the vine, you are the branches, says the Lord:
whoever remains in me and I in him will bear much fruit.

℟. **Alleluia, alleluia.**

GOSPEL

Luke 6:43-45   What a person says comes from what is in his heart.

✠ **A reading from the holy Gospel according to Luke**

Jesus said to his disciples:
"A good tree does not bear rotten fruit,
   nor does a rotten tree bear good fruit.
For every tree is known by its own fruit.
For people do not pick figs from thornbushes,
   nor do they gather grapes from brambles.
A good person, out of the store of goodness in his heart produces good,
   but an evil person out of a store of evil produces evil,
   for from the fullness of the heart the mouth speaks."

The Gospel of the Lord.

JUNE 11

580 SAINT BARNABAS, APOSTLE MEMORIAL

FIRST READING

Acts 11:21b-26; 13:1-3   Barnabas was a good man, filled with the Holy Spirit and with faith.

A reading from the Acts of the Apostles

In those days a great number who believed turned to the Lord.
The news about them reached the ears of the Church in Jerusalem,
    and they sent Barnabas to go to Antioch.
When he arrived and saw the grace of God,
    he rejoiced and encouraged them all
    to remain faithful to the Lord in firmness of heart,
    for he was a good man, filled with the Holy Spirit and faith.
And a large number of people was added to the Lord.
Then he went to Tarsus to look for Saul,
    and when he had found him he brought him to Antioch.
For a whole year they met with the Church
    and taught a large number of people,
    and it was in Antioch that the disciples
    were first called Christians.

Now there were in the Church at Antioch prophets and teachers:
    Barnabas, Symeon who was called Niger,
    Lucius of Cyrene,
    Manaen who was a close friend of Herod the tetrarch, and Saul.
While they were worshiping the Lord and fasting, the Holy Spirit said,
    "Set apart for me Barnabas and Saul
    for the work to which I have called them."
Then, completing their fasting and prayer,
    they laid hands on them and sent them off.

The word of the Lord.

RESPONSORIAL PSALM

Psalm 98:1, 2-3ab, 3cd-4, 5-6

℟. (see 2b) **The Lord has revealed to the nations his saving power.**

Sing to the LORD **a new song,**
for he has done wondrous deeds;
His right hand has won victory for him,
his holy arm.

℟. **The Lord has revealed to the nations his saving power.**

The LORD **has made his salvation known:**
in the sight of the nations he has revealed his justice.
He has remembered his kindness and his faithfulness
toward the house of Israel.

℟. **The Lord has revealed to the nations his saving power.**

All the ends of the earth have seen
the salvation by our God.
Sing joyfully to the LORD**, all you lands;**
break into song; sing praise.

℟. **The Lord has revealed to the nations his saving power.**

Sing praise to the LORD **with the harp,**
with the harp and melodious song.
With trumpets and the sound of the horn
sing joyfully before the King, the LORD**.**

℟. **The Lord has revealed to the nations his saving power.**

ALLELUIA

Matthew 28:19a, 20b

℟. Alleluia, alleluia.

Go and teach all nations, says the Lord;
I am with you always, until the end of the world.

℟. Alleluia, alleluia.

GOSPEL

Matthew 10:7-13   Without cost you have received; without cost you are to give.

✠ **A reading from the holy Gospel according to Matthew**

**Jesus said to the Twelve:
"As you go, make this proclamation:
   'The Kingdom of heaven is at hand.'
Cure the sick, raise the dead, cleanse the lepers, drive out demons.
Without cost you have received; without cost you are to give.
Do not take gold or silver or copper for your belts;
   no sack for the journey, or a second tunic,
   or sandals, or walking stick.
The laborer deserves his keep.
Whatever town or village you enter,
   look for a worthy person in it,
   and stay there until you leave.
As you enter a house, wish it peace.
If the house is worthy, let your peace come upon it;
   if not, let your peace return to you."

The Gospel of the Lord.**

JUNE 13

581 SAINT ANTHONY OF PADUA, PRIEST AND DOCTOR OF THE CHURCH MEMORIAL

From the Common of Pastors, p. 1805, or the Common of Doctors of the Church, p. 1838, or the Common of Holy Men and Women: For Religious, p. 1868,

OR

FIRST READING

Isaiah 61:1-3d   The Lord God anointed me and sent me to bring good news to the poor.

A reading from the Book of the Prophet Isaiah

> The spirit of the Lord God is upon me,
>   because the Lord has anointed me;
> He has sent me to bring glad tidings to the lowly,
>   to heal the brokenhearted,
> To proclaim liberty to the captives
>   and release to the prisoners,
> To announce a year of favor from the Lord
>   and a day of vindication by our God,
>   to comfort all who mourn;
> To place on those who mourn in Zion
>   a diadem instead of ashes,
> To give them oil of gladness in place of mourning,
>   a glorious mantle instead of a listless spirit.

The word of the Lord.

RESPONSORIAL PSALM

Psalm 89:2-3, 4-5, 21-22, 25 and 27

℟. (2) **For ever I will sing the goodness of the Lord.**

The favors of the LORD **I will sing forever;**
　through all generations my mouth shall proclaim your faithfulness.
For you have said, "My kindness is established forever";
　in heaven you have confirmed your faithfulness.

℟. **For ever I will sing the goodness of the Lord.**

"I have made a covenant with my chosen one,
　I have sworn to David my servant:
Forever will I confirm your posterity
　and establish your throne for all generations."

℟. **For ever I will sing the goodness of the Lord.**

"I have found David, my servant;
　with my holy oil I have anointed him,
That my hand may be always with him,
　and that my arm may make him strong."

℟. **For ever I will sing the goodness of the Lord.**

"My faithfulness and my mercy shall be with him,
　and through my name shall his horn be exalted.
He shall say of me, 'You are my father,
　my God, the Rock, my savior.'"

℟. **For ever I will sing the goodness of the Lord.**

ALLELUIA

Luke 4:18

℟. Alleluia, alleluia.

The Lord sent me to bring glad tidings to the poor
and to proclaim liberty to captives.

℟. Alleluia, alleluia.

GOSPEL

Luke 10:1-9   The harvest is abundant but the laborers are few.

✠ A reading from the holy Gospel according to Luke

The Lord Jesus appointed seventy-two other disciples
   whom he sent ahead of him in pairs
   to every town and place he intended to visit.
He said to them,
   "The harvest is abundant but the laborers are few;
   so ask the master of the harvest
   to send out laborers for his harvest.
Go on your way;
   behold, I am sending you like lambs among wolves.
Carry no money bag, no sack, no sandals;
   and greet no one along the way.
Into whatever house you enter, first say,
   'Peace to this household.'
If a peaceful person lives there,
   your peace will rest on him;
   but if not, it will return to you.
Stay in the same house and eat and drink what is offered to you,
   for the laborer deserves his payment.
Do not move about from one house to another.
Whatever town you enter and they welcome you,
   eat what is set before you,
   cure the sick in it and say to them,
   'The Kingdom of God is at hand for you.'"

The Gospel of the Lord.

JUNE 19

582 SAINT ROMUALD, ABBOT

From the Common of Holy Men and Women: For Religious, p. 1868,

OR

FIRST READING

Philippians 3:8-14   I continue my pursuit toward the goal, the prize of God's heavenly calling, in Christ Jesus.

A reading from the Letter of Saint Paul to the Philippians

Brothers and sisters:
I consider everything as a loss
   because of the supreme good of knowing Christ Jesus my Lord.
For his sake I have accepted the loss of all things
   and I consider them so much rubbish,
   that I may gain Christ and be found in him,
   not having any righteousness of my own based on the law
   but that which comes through faith in Christ,
   the righteousness from God,
   depending on faith to know him and the power of his resurrection
   and the sharing of his sufferings by being conformed to his death,
   if somehow I may attain the resurrection from the dead.

It is not that I have already taken hold of it
   or have already attained perfect maturity,
   but I continue my pursuit in hope that I may possess it,
   since I have indeed been taken possession of by Christ Jesus.
Brothers and sisters, I for my part
   do not consider myself to have taken possession.
Just one thing: forgetting what lies behind
   but straining forward to what lies ahead,
   I continue my pursuit toward the goal,
   the prize of God's upward calling, in Christ Jesus.

The word of the Lord.

June 19—Saint Romuald

RESPONSORIAL PSALM

Psalm 131:1bcde, 2, 3

℟. In you, Lord, I have found my peace.

O Lord, my heart is not proud,
 nor are my eyes haughty;
I busy not myself with great things,
 nor with things too sublime for me.

℟. In you, Lord, I have found my peace.

Nay rather, I have stilled and quieted
 my soul like a weaned child.
Like a weaned child on its mother's lap,
 so is my soul within me.

℟. In you, Lord, I have found my peace.

O Israel, hope in the Lord,
 both now and forever.

℟. In you, Lord, I have found my peace.

ALLELUIA

Matthew 5:3

℟. Alleluia, alleluia.

Blessed are the poor in spirit,
the Kingdom of heaven is theirs!

℟. Alleluia, alleluia.

GOSPEL

Luke 14:25-33   Any one of you who does not renounce all his possessions cannot be my disciple.

✠ A reading from the holy Gospel according to Luke

Great crowds were traveling with Jesus,
  and he turned and addressed them,
  "If anyone comes to me without hating his father and mother,
  wife and children, brothers and sisters,
  and even his own life,
  he cannot be my disciple.
Whoever does not carry his own cross and come after me
  cannot be my disciple.
Which of you wishing to construct a tower
  does not first sit down and calculate the cost
  to see if there is enough for its completion?
Otherwise, after laying the foundation
  and finding himself unable to finish the work
  the onlookers should laugh at him and say,
  'This one began to build but did not have the resources to finish.'
Or what king marching into battle would not first sit down
  and decide whether with ten thousand troops
  he can successfully oppose another king
  advancing upon him with twenty thousand troops?
But if not, while he is still far away,
  he will send a delegation to ask for peace terms.
In the same way,
  everyone of you who does not renounce all his possessions
  cannot be my disciple."

The Gospel of the Lord.

JUNE 21

583 SAINT ALOYSIUS GONZAGA, RELIGIOUS
MEMORIAL

From the Common of Holy Men and Women: For Religious, p. 1868,

OR

FIRST READING

1 John 5:1-5   The victory that conquers the world is our faith.

A reading from the first Letter of Saint John

Beloved:
Everyone who believes that Jesus is the Christ is begotten by God,
  and everyone who loves the Father
  loves also the one begotten by him.
In this way we know that we love the children of God
  when we love God and obey his commandments.
For the love of God is this,
  that we keep his commandments.
And his commandments are not burdensome,
  for whoever is begotten by God conquers the world.
And the victory that conquers the world is our faith.
Who indeed is the victor over the world
  but the one who believes that Jesus is the Son of God?

The word of the Lord.

RESPONSORIAL PSALM

Psalm 16:1-2a and 5, 7-8, 11

℟. (see 5a) **You are my inheritance, O Lord.**

Keep me, O God, for in you I take refuge.
  I say to the Lord, "My Lord are you."
O Lord, my allotted portion and my cup,
  you it is who hold fast my lot.

℟. **You are my inheritance, O Lord.**

I bless the Lord who counsels me;
  even in the night my heart exhorts me.
I set the Lord always before me;
  with him at my right hand I shall not be disturbed.

℟. **You are my inheritance, O Lord.**

You will show me the path to life,
- fullness of joys in your presence,
- the delights at your right hand forever.

℟. You are my inheritance, O Lord.

ALLELUIA

John 13:34

℟. Alleluia, alleluia.

I give you a new commandment:
love one another as I have loved you.

℟. Alleluia, alleluia.

GOSPEL

Matthew 22:34-40   You shall love the Lord your God, and your neighbor as yourself.

✠ A reading from the holy Gospel according to Matthew

When the Pharisees heard that Jesus had silenced the Sadducees,
- they gathered together, and one of them
- a scholar of the law, tested him by asking,
- "Teacher, which commandment in the law is the greatest?"

Jesus said to him, "You shall love the Lord, your God,
- with all your heart,
- with all your soul,
- and with all your mind.

This is the greatest and the first commandment.
The second is like it:
- You shall love your neighbor as yourself.

The whole law and the prophets depend on these two commandments."

The Gospel of the Lord.

JUNE 22

584 SAINT PAULINUS OF NOLA, BISHOP

From the Common of Pastors, p. 1805,

OR

FIRST READING

2 Corinthians 8:9-15   Christ was rich but he became poor for your sake: to make you rich out of his poverty.

A reading from the second Letter of Saint Paul to the Corinthians

Brothers and sisters:
You know the gracious act of our Lord Jesus Christ,
 that for your sake he became poor although he was rich,
 so that by his poverty you might become rich.
And I am giving counsel in this matter,
 for it is appropriate for you who began not only to act
 but to act willingly last year:
 complete it now, so that your eager willingness may be matched
 by your completion of it out of what you have.
For if the eagerness is there,
 it is acceptable according to what one has,
 not according to what one does not have;
 not that others should have relief while you are burdened,
 but that as a matter of equality
 your surplus at the present time should supply their needs,
 so that their surplus may also supply your needs,
 that there may be equality.
As it is written:

Whoever had much did not have more,
 and whoever had little did not have less.

The word of the Lord.

RESPONSORIAL PSALM

Psalm 40:2 and 4ab, 7-8a, 8b-9, 10

℟. (8a and 9a) **Here I am, Lord; I come to do your will.**

I have waited, waited for the LORD,
   and he stooped toward me and heard my cry.
And he put a new song into my mouth,
   a hymn to our God.

℟. **Here I am, Lord; I come to do your will.**

Sacrifice or oblation you wished not,
   but ears open to obedience you gave me.
Burnt offerings or sin-offerings you sought not;
   then said I, "Behold I come."

℟. **Here I am, Lord; I come to do your will.**

"In the written scroll it is prescribed for me,
To do your will, O my God, is my delight,
   and your law is within my heart!"

℟. **Here I am, Lord; I come to do your will.**

I announced your justice in the vast assembly;
   I did not restrain my lips, as you, O LORD, know.

℟. **Here I am, Lord; I come to do your will.**

Your justice I kept not hid within my heart;
   your faithfulness and your salvation I have spoken of;
I have made no secret of your kindness and your truth
   in the vast assembly.

℟. **Here I am, Lord; I come to do your will.**

ALLELUIA

Matthew 5:3

℟. Alleluia, alleluia.

**Blessed are the poor in spirit;
the Kingdom of heaven is theirs!**

℟. Alleluia, alleluia.

GOSPEL

Luke 12:32-34   It has pleased the Father to give you the Kingdom.

✠ **A reading from the holy Gospel according to Luke**

**Jesus said to his disciples:
"Do not be afraid any longer, little flock,
   for your Father is pleased to give you the Kingdom.
Sell your belongings and give alms.
Provide money bags for yourselves that do not wear out,
   an inexhaustible treasure in heaven
   that no thief can reach nor moth destroy.
For where your treasure is, there also will your heart be."**

The Gospel of the Lord.

JUNE 22

585 SAINT JOHN FISHER, BISHOP AND MARTYR AND SAINT THOMAS MORE, MARTYR

From the Common of Martyrs, p. 1782,

> OR

FIRST READING

1 Peter 4:12-19   Rejoice to the extent that you share in the sufferings of Christ.

A reading from the first Letter of Saint Peter

**Beloved, do not be surprised that a trial by fire is occurring among you,
    as if something strange were happening to you.
But rejoice to the extent that you share in the sufferings of Christ,
    so that when his glory is revealed
    you may also rejoice exultantly.
If you are insulted for the name of Christ, blessed are you,
    for the Spirit of glory and of God rests upon you.
But let no one among you be made to suffer
    as a murderer, a thief, an evildoer, or as an intriguer.
But whoever is made to suffer as a Christian should not be ashamed
    but glorify God because of the name.
For it is time for the judgment to begin with the household of God;
    if it begins with us, how will it end
    for those who fail to obey the Gospel of God?**

*And if the righteous one is barely saved,
    where will the godless and the sinner appear?*

**As a result, those who suffer in accord with God's will
    hand their souls over to a faithful creator as they do good.**

The word of the Lord.

RESPONSORIAL PSALM

Psalm 126:1bc-2ab, 2cd-3, 4-5, 6

℟. (5) **Those who sow in tears shall reap rejoicing.**

**When the Lord brought back the captives of Zion,
   we were like men dreaming.
Then our mouth was filled with laughter,
   and our tongue with rejoicing.**

℟. **Those who sow in tears shall reap rejoicing.**

**Then they said among the nations,
   "The Lord has done great things for them."
The Lord has done great things for us;
   we are glad indeed.**

℟. **Those who sow in tears shall reap rejoicing.**

**Restore our fortunes, O Lord,
   like the torrents in the southern desert.
Those who sow in tears
   shall reap rejoicing.**

℟. **Those who sow in tears shall reap rejoicing.**

**Although they go forth weeping,
   carrying the seed to be sown,
They shall come back rejoicing,
   carrying their sheaves.**

℟. **Those who sow in tears shall reap rejoicing.**

ALLELUIA

Matthew 5:10

℟. Alleluia, alleluia.

Blessed are they who are persecuted for the sake of righteousness, for theirs is the Kingdom of heaven.

℟. Alleluia, alleluia.

GOSPEL

Matthew 10:34-39   I have come to bring not peace but the sword.

✛ **A reading from the holy Gospel according to Matthew**

**Jesus said to the Twelve:
"Do not think that I have come to bring peace upon the earth.
I have come to bring not peace but the sword.
For I have come to set**

> **a man 'against his father,
> a daughter against her mother,
> and a daughter-in-law against her mother-in-law;
> and one's enemies will be those of his household.'**

**"Whoever loves father or mother more than me is not worthy of me,
and whoever loves son or daughter more than me is not worthy of me;
and whoever does not take up his cross
and follow after me is not worthy of me.
Whoever finds his life will lose it,
and whoever loses his life for my sake will find it."**

The Gospel of the Lord.

JUNE 24

THE NATIVITY OF SAINT JOHN THE BAPTIST
SOLEMNITY

586 VIGIL

FIRST READING

Jeremiah 1:4-10   Before I formed you in the womb I knew you.

A reading from the Book of the Prophet Jeremiah

In the days of King Josiah, the word of the Lord came to me, saying:

> Before I formed you in the womb I knew you,
>   before you were born I dedicated you,
>   a prophet to the nations I appointed you.
>
> "Ah, Lord God!" I said,
>   "I know not how to speak; I am too young."
> But the Lord answered me,
> Say not, "I am too young."
>   To whomever I send you, you shall go;
>   whatever I command you, you shall speak.
> Have no fear before them,
>   because I am with you to deliver you, says the Lord.

Then the Lord extended his hand and touched my mouth, saying,

> See, I place my words in your mouth!
>   This day I set you
>   over nations and over kingdoms,
> to root up and to tear down,
>   to destroy and to demolish,
>   to build and to plant.

The word of the Lord.

RESPONSORIAL PSALM

Psalm 71:1-2, 3-4a, 5-6ab, 15ab and 17

℟. (6) **Since my mother's womb, you have been my strength.**

In you, O Lord, I take refuge;
 let me never be put to shame.
In your justice rescue me, and deliver me;
 incline your ear to me, and save me.

℟. **Since my mother's womb, you have been my strength.**

Be my rock of refuge,
 a stronghold to give me safety,
 for you are my rock and my fortress.
O my God, rescue me from the hand of the wicked.

℟. **Since my mother's womb, you have been my strength.**

For you are my hope, O Lord;
 my trust, O Lord, from my youth.
On you I depend from birth;
 from my mother's womb you are my strength.

℟. **Since my mother's womb, you have been my strength.**

My mouth shall declare your justice,
 day by day your salvation.
O God, you have taught me from my youth,
 and till the present I proclaim your wondrous deeds.

℟. **Since my mother's womb, you have been my strength.**

June 24—The Nativity of Saint John the Baptist—Vigil

SECOND READING

1 Peter 1:8-12 *The prophets who prophesied about the grace that was to be yours searched and investigated it.*

A reading from the first Letter of Saint Peter

Beloved:
Although you have not seen Jesus Christ you love him;
   even though you do not see him now yet believe in him,
   you rejoice with an indescribable and glorious joy,
   as you attain the goal of your faith, the salvation of your souls.

Concerning this salvation,
   prophets who prophesied about the grace that was to be yours
   searched and investigated it,
   investigating the time and circumstances
   that the Spirit of Christ within them indicated
   when he testified in advance
   to the sufferings destined for Christ
   and the glories to follow them.
It was revealed to them that they were serving not themselves but you
   with regard to the things that have now been announced to you
   by those who preached the Good News to you
   through the Holy Spirit sent from heaven,
   things into which angels longed to look.

The word of the Lord.

ALLELUIA

See John 1:7; Luke 1:17

℟. **Alleluia, alleluia.**

**He came to testify to the light,
to prepare a people fit for the Lord.**

℟. **Alleluia, alleluia.**

GOSPEL

Luke 1:5-17   Your wife Elizabeth will bear you a son and you shall name him John.

✠ A reading from the holy Gospel according to Luke

In the days of Herod, King of Judea,
   there was a priest named Zechariah
   of the priestly division of Abijah;
   his wife was from the daughters of Aaron,
   and her name was Elizabeth.
Both were righteous in the eyes of God,
   observing all the commandments
   and ordinances of the Lord blamelessly.
But they had no child, because Elizabeth was barren
   and both were advanced in years.
Once when he was serving
   as priest in his division's turn before God,
   according to the practice of the priestly service,
   he was chosen by lot
   to enter the sanctuary of the Lord to burn incense.
Then, when the whole assembly of the people was praying outside
   at the hour of the incense offering,
   the angel of the Lord appeared to him,
   standing at the right of the altar of incense.
Zechariah was troubled by what he saw, and fear came upon him.
But the angel said to him, "Do not be afraid, Zechariah,
   because your prayer has been heard.
Your wife Elizabeth will bear you a son,
   and you shall name him John.
And you will have joy and gladness,
   and many will rejoice at his birth,
   for he will be great in the sight of the Lord.
John will drink neither wine nor strong drink.
He will be filled with the Holy Spirit even from his mother's womb,
   and he will turn many of the children of Israel
   to the Lord their God.
He will go before him in the spirit and power of Elijah
   to turn their hearts toward their children
   and the disobedient to the understanding of the righteous,
   to prepare a people fit for the Lord."

The Gospel of the Lord.

587 MASS DURING THE DAY

FIRST READING

Isaiah 49:1-6   I will make you a light to the nations.

A reading from the Book of the Prophet Isaiah

**Hear me, O coastlands,
   listen, O distant peoples.
The L**ord** called me from birth,
   from my mother's womb he gave me my name.
He made of me a sharp-edged sword
   and concealed me in the shadow of his arm.
He made me a polished arrow,
   in his quiver he hid me.
You are my servant, he said to me,
   Israel, through whom I show my glory.**

**Though I thought I had toiled in vain,
   and for nothing, uselessly, spent my strength,
yet my reward is with the L**ord**,
   my recompense is with my God.
For now the L**ord** has spoken
   who formed me as his servant from the womb,
that Jacob may be brought back to him
   and Israel gathered to him;
and I am made glorious in the sight of the L**ord**,
   and my God is now my strength!
It is too little, he says, for you to be my servant,
   to raise up the tribes of Jacob,
   and restore the survivors of Israel;
I will make you a light to the nations,
   that my salvation may reach to the ends of the earth.**

The word of the Lord.

RESPONSORIAL PSALM

Psalm 139:1b-3, 13-14ab, 14c-15

℟. (14) **I praise you, for I am wonderfully made.**

O LORD, you have probed me, you know me:
 you know when I sit and when I stand;
 you understand my thoughts from afar.
My journeys and my rest you scrutinize,
 with all my ways you are familiar.

℟. **I praise you for I am wonderfully made.**

Truly you have formed my inmost being;
 you knit me in my mother's womb.
I give you thanks that I am fearfully, wonderfully made;
 wonderful are your works.

℟. **I praise you, for I am wonderfully made.**

My soul also you knew full well;
 nor was my frame unknown to you
When I was made in secret,
 when I was fashioned in the depths of the earth.

℟. **I praise you, for I am wonderfully made.**

SECOND READING

Acts 13:22-26   John heralded his coming by proclaiming a baptism of repentance.

A reading from the Acts of the Apostles

**In those days, Paul said:
"God raised up David as king;
of him God testified,
*I have found David, son of Jesse, a man after my own heart;
he will carry out my every wish.*
From this man's descendants God, according to his promise,
has brought to Israel a savior, Jesus.
John heralded his coming by proclaiming a baptism of repentance
to all the people of Israel;
and as John was completing his course, he would say,
'What do you suppose that I am? I am not he.
Behold, one is coming after me;
I am not worthy to unfasten the sandals of his feet.'**

**"My brothers, sons of the family of Abraham,
and those others among you who are God-fearing,
to us this word of salvation has been sent."**

The word of the Lord.

ALLELUIA

See Luke 1:76

℟. **Alleluia, alleluia.**

**You, child, will be called prophet of the Most High,
for you will go before the Lord to prepare his way.**

℟. **Alleluia, alleluia.**

GOSPEL

Luke 1:57-66, 80   John is his name.

✠ **A reading from the holy Gospel according to Luke**

**When the time arrived for Elizabeth to have her child
she gave birth to a son.
Her neighbors and relatives heard
that the Lord had shown his great mercy toward her,
and they rejoiced with her.
When they came on the eighth day to circumcise the child,
they were going to call him Zechariah after his father,
but his mother said in reply,
"No. He will be called John."
But they answered her,
"There is no one among your relatives who has this name."
So they made signs, asking his father what he wished him to be called.
He asked for a tablet and wrote, "John is his name,"
and all were amazed.
Immediately his mouth was opened, his tongue freed,
and he spoke blessing God.
Then fear came upon all their neighbors,
and all these matters were discussed
throughout the hill country of Judea.
All who heard these things took them to heart, saying,
"What, then, will this child be?"
For surely the hand of the Lord was with him.
The child grew and became strong in spirit,
and he was in the desert until the day
of his manifestation to Israel.**

The Gospel of the Lord.

JUNE 27

588 SAINT CYRIL OF ALEXANDRIA, BISHOP AND DOCTOR OF THE CHURCH

From the Common of Pastors, p. 1805, or the Common of Doctors of the Church, p. 1838,

OR

FIRST READING

2 Timothy 4:1-5   Perform the work of an evangelist; fulfill your ministry.

A reading from the second Letter of Saint Paul to Timothy

Beloved:
I charge you in the presence of God and of Christ Jesus,
    who will judge the living and the dead,
    and by his appearing and his kingly power:
    proclaim the word;
    be persistent whether it is convenient or inconvenient;
    convince, reprimand, encourage through all patience and teaching.
For the time will come when people will not tolerate sound doctrine
    but, following their own desires and insatiable curiosity,
    will accumulate teachers and will stop listening to the truth
    and will be diverted to myths.
But you, be self-possessed in all circumstances;
    put up with hardship;
    perform the work of an evangelist;
    fulfill your ministry.

The word of the Lord.

RESPONSORIAL PSALM

Psalm 89:2-3, 4-5, 21-22, 25 and 27

℟. (2) **For ever I will sing the goodness of the Lord.**

The favors of the L<small>ORD</small> **I will sing forever;**
  through all generations my mouth shall proclaim your faithfulness.
For you have said, "My kindness is established forever";
  in heaven you have confirmed your faithfulness.

℟. **For ever I will sing the goodness of the Lord.**

"I have made a covenant with my chosen one,
  I have sworn to David my servant:
Forever will I confirm your posterity
  and establish your throne for all generations."

℟. **For ever I will sing the goodness of the Lord.**

"I have found David, my servant;
  with my holy oil I have anointed him,
That my hand may be always with him,
  and that my arm may make him strong."

℟. **For ever I will sing the goodness of the Lord.**

"My faithfulness and my mercy shall be with him,
  and through my name shall his horn be exalted.
He shall say of me, 'You are my father,
  my God, the Rock, my savior.'"

℟. **For ever I will sing the goodness of the Lord.**

ALLELUIA

Matthew 5:16

℟. Alleluia, alleluia.

**Let your light shine before others
that they may see your good deeds and glorify your heavenly Father.**

℟. Alleluia, alleluia.

GOSPEL

Matthew 5:13-19   You are the light of the world.

☩ **A reading from the holy Gospel according to Matthew**

**Jesus said to his disciples:
"You are the salt of the earth.
But if salt loses its taste, with what can it be seasoned?
It is no longer good for anything
   but to be thrown out and trampled underfoot.
You are the light of the world.
A city set on a mountain cannot be hidden.
Nor do they light a lamp and then put it under a bushel basket;
   it is set on a lampstand,
   where it gives light to all in the house.
Just so, your light must shine before others,
   that they may see your good deeds
   and glorify your heavenly Father.**

**"Do not think that I have come to abolish the law or the prophets.
I have come not to abolish but to fulfill.
Amen, I say to you, until heaven and earth pass away,
   not the smallest letter or the smallest part of a letter
   will pass from the law,
   until all things have taken place.
Therefore, whoever breaks one of the least of these commandments
   and teaches others to do so
   will be called least in the Kingdom of heaven.
But whoever obeys and teaches these commandments
   will be called greatest in the Kingdom of heaven."**

The Gospel of the Lord.

JUNE 28

589 SAINT IRENAEUS, BISHOP AND MARTYR
MEMORIAL

From the Common of Martyrs, p. 1782, or the Common of Doctors of the Church, p. 1838,

OR

FIRST READING

2 Timothy 2:22b-26   A slave of the Lord should be gentle with everyone, correcting with kindness.

A reading from the second Letter of Saint Paul to Timothy

Beloved:
Pursue righteousness, faith, love, and peace,
   along with those who call on the Lord with purity of heart.
Avoid foolish and ignorant debates,
   for you know that they breed quarrels.
A slave of the Lord should not quarrel,
   but should be gentle with everyone,
   able to teach, tolerant, correcting opponents with kindness.
It may be that God will grant them repentance
   that leads to knowledge of the truth,
   and that they may return to their senses out of the Devil's snare,
   where they are entrapped by him, for his will.

The word of the Lord.

RESPONSORIAL PSALM

Psalm 37:3-4, 5-6, 30-31

℟. (30a) **The mouth of the just murmurs wisdom.**

Trust in the Lord and do good
   that you may dwell in the land and be fed in security.
Take delight in the Lord,
   and he will grant you your heart's requests.

℟. **The mouth of the just murmurs wisdom.**

Commit to the Lord your way;
   trust in him, and he will act.
He will make justice dawn for you like the light;
   bright as the noonday shall be your vindication.

℟. **The mouth of the just murmurs wisdom.**

1364 *June 28—Saint Irenaeus*

The mouth of the just tells of wisdom
   and his tongue utters what is right.
The law of his God is in his heart,
   and his steps do not falter.

℟. **The mouth of the just murmurs wisdom.**

ALLELUIA

John 15:9b, 5b

℟. **Alleluia, alleluia.**

Remain in my love, says the Lord;
whoever remains in me and I in him will bear much fruit.

℟. **Alleluia, alleluia.**

GOSPEL

John 17:20-26   *I wish that those you have given me may be with me.*

✠ **A reading from the holy Gospel according to John**

Jesus raised his eyes to heaven and said:
"Holy Father, I pray not only for these,
   but also for those who will believe in me through their word,
   so that they may all be one,
   as you, Father, are in me and I in you,
   that they also may be in us,
   that the world may believe that you sent me.
And I have given them the glory you gave me,
   so that they may be one, as we are one,
   I in them and you in me,
   that they may be brought to perfection as one,
   that the world may know that you sent me,
   and that you loved them even as you loved me.
Father, they are your gift to me.
I wish that where I am they also may be with me,
   that they may see my glory that you gave me,
   because you loved me before the foundation of the world.
Righteous Father, the world also does not know you,
   but I know you, and they know that you sent me.
I made known to them your name and I will make it known,
   that the love with which you loved me
   may be in them and I in them."

The Gospel of the Lord.

JUNE 29

SAINTS PETER AND PAUL, APOSTLES SOLEMNITY

590 VIGIL

For a votive Mass of Saint Peter the readings are taken from the feast of the Chair of Saint Peter, Apostle, February 22, no. 535. For a votive Mass of Saint Paul the readings are taken from the feast of the Conversion of Saint Paul, Apostle, no. 519.

FIRST READING

Acts 3:1-10   What I do have I give you: in the name of Jesus, rise and walk.

A reading from the Acts of the Apostles

Peter and John were going up to the temple area
　for the three o'clock hour of prayer.
And a man crippled from birth was carried
　and placed at the gate of the temple called "the Beautiful Gate"
　every day to beg for alms from the people who entered the temple.
When he saw Peter and John about to go into the temple,
　he asked for alms.
But Peter looked intently at him, as did John,
　and said, "Look at us."
He paid attention to them, expecting to receive something from them.
Peter said, "I have neither silver nor gold,
　but what I do have I give you:
　in the name of Jesus Christ the Nazorean, rise and walk."
Then Peter took him by the right hand and raised him up,
　and immediately his feet and ankles grew strong.
He leaped up, stood, and walked around,
　and went into the temple with them,
　walking and jumping and praising God.
When all the people saw the man walking and praising God,
　they recognized him as the one who used to sit begging
　at the Beautiful Gate of the temple,
　and they were filled with amazement and astonishment
　at what had happened to him.

The word of the Lord.

RESPONSORIAL PSALM

Psalm 19:2-3, 4-5

℟. (5) **Their message goes out through all the earth.**

**The heavens declare the glory of God;
   and the firmament proclaims his handiwork.
Day pours out the word to day;
   and night to night imparts knowledge.**

℟. **Their message goes out through all the earth.**

**Not a word nor a discourse
   whose voice is not heard;
through all the earth their voice resounds,
   and to the ends of the world, their message.**

℟. **Their message goes out through all the earth.**

SECOND READING

Galatians 1:11-20   From my mother's womb, God set me apart.

A reading from the Letter of Saint Paul to the Galatians

**I want you to know, brothers and sisters,
that the Gospel preached by me is not of human origin.
For I did not receive it from a human being, nor was I taught it,
   but it came through a revelation of Jesus Christ.**

**For you heard of my former way of life in Judaism,
   how I persecuted the Church of God beyond measure
   and tried to destroy it, and progressed in Judaism
   beyond many of my contemporaries among my race,
   since I was even more a zealot for my ancestral traditions.
But when God, who from my mother's womb had set me apart
   and called me through his grace,
   was pleased to reveal his Son to me,
   so that I might proclaim him to the Gentiles,
   I did not immediately consult flesh and blood,
   nor did I go up to Jerusalem
   to those who were Apostles before me;
   rather, I went into Arabia and then returned to Damascus.**

**Then after three years I went up to Jerusalem
   to confer with Cephas and remained with him for fifteen days.
But I did not see any other of the Apostles,
   only James the brother of the Lord.**

—As to what I am writing to you, behold,
  before God, I am not lying.

The word of the Lord.

ALLELUIA

John 21:17

℟. **Alleluia, alleluia.**

**Lord, you know everything:
you know that I love you.**

℟. **Alleluia, alleluia.**

GOSPEL

John 21:15-19   Feed my lambs, feed my sheep.

✠ **A reading from the holy Gospel according to John**

**Jesus had revealed himself to his disciples
   and, when they had finished breakfast, said to Simon Peter,
   "Simon, son of John, do you love me more than these?"
Simon Peter answered him, "Yes, Lord, you know that I love you."
Jesus said to him, "Feed my lambs."
He then said to Simon Peter a second time,
   "Simon, son of John, do you love me?"
Simon Peter answered him, "Yes, Lord, you know that I love you."
He said to him, "Tend my sheep."
He said to him the third time,
   "Simon, son of John, do you love me?"
Peter was distressed that he had said to him a third time,
   "Do you love me?" and he said to him,
   "Lord, you know everything; you know that I love you."
Jesus said to him, "Feed my sheep.
Amen, amen, I say to you, when you were younger,
   you used to dress yourself and go where you wanted;
   but when you grow old, you will stretch out your hands,
   and someone else will dress you
   and lead you where you do not want to go."
He said this signifying by what kind of death he would glorify God.
And when he had said this, he said to him, "Follow me."**

The Gospel of the Lord.

591 MASS DURING THE DAY

FIRST READING

Acts 12:1-11 Now I know for certain that the Lord rescued me from the hand of Herod.

A reading from the Acts of the Apostles

In those days, King Herod laid hands upon some members of the Church to harm them.
He had James, the brother of John, killed by the sword,
and when he saw that this was pleasing to the Jews
he proceeded to arrest Peter also.
—It was the feast of Unleavened Bread.—
He had him taken into custody and put in prison
under the guard of four squads of four soldiers each.
He intended to bring him before the people after Passover.
Peter thus was being kept in prison,
but prayer by the Church was fervently being made
to God on his behalf.

On the very night before Herod was to bring him to trial,
Peter, secured by double chains,
was sleeping between two soldiers,
while outside the door guards kept watch on the prison.
Suddenly the angel of the Lord stood by him,
and a light shone in the cell.
He tapped Peter on the side and awakened him, saying,
"Get up quickly."
The chains fell from his wrists.
The angel said to him, "Put on your belt and your sandals."
He did so.
Then he said to him, "Put on your cloak and follow me."
So he followed him out,
not realizing that what was happening through the angel was real;
he thought he was seeing a vision.
They passed the first guard, then the second,
and came to the iron gate leading out to the city,
which opened for them by itself.
They emerged and made their way down an alley,
and suddenly the angel left him.

The word of the Lord.

RESPONSORIAL PSALM

Psalm 34:2-3, 4-5, 6-7, 8-9

℟. (5) **The angel of the Lord will rescue those who fear him.**

I will bless the LORD **at all times;**
  his praise shall be ever in my mouth.
Let my soul glory in the LORD**;**
  the lowly will hear me and be glad.

℟. **The angel of the Lord will rescue those who fear him.**

Glorify the LORD **with me,**
  let us together extol his name.
I sought the LORD**, and he answered me**
  and delivered me from all my fears.

℟. **The angel of the Lord will rescue those who fear him.**

Look to him that you may be radiant with joy,
  and your faces may not blush with shame.
When the poor one called out, the LORD **heard,**
  and from all his distress he saved him.

℟. **The angel of the Lord will rescue those who fear him.**

The angel of the LORD **encamps**
  around those who fear him, and delivers them.
Taste and see how good the LORD **is;**
  blessed the man who takes refuge in him.

℟. **The angel of the Lord will rescue those who fear him.**

1370   June 29—Saints Peter and Paul—Mass During the Day

SECOND READING

2 Timothy 4:6-8, 17-18   From now on the crown of righteousness awaits me.

A reading from the second Letter of Saint Paul to Timothy

**I, Paul, am already being poured out like a libation,
   and the time of my departure is at hand.
I have competed well; I have finished the race;
   I have kept the faith.
From now on the crown of righteousness awaits me,
      which the Lord, the just judge,
      will award to me on that day, and not only to me,
      but to all who have longed for his appearance.**

**The Lord stood by me and gave me strength,
   so that through me the proclamation might be completed
   and all the Gentiles might hear it.
And I was rescued from the lion's mouth.
The Lord will rescue me from every evil threat
   and will bring me safe to his heavenly Kingdom.
To him be glory forever and ever. Amen.**

The word of the Lord.

ALLELUIA

Matthew 16:18

℟. Alleluia, alleluia.

**You are Peter and upon this rock I will build my Church,
and the gates of the netherworld shall not prevail against it.**

℟. Alleluia, alleluia.

GOSPEL

Matthew 16:13-19   You are Peter, and I will give you the keys to the Kingdom of heaven.

✠ **A reading from the holy Gospel according to Matthew**

**When Jesus went into the region of Caesarea Philippi
he asked his disciples,
"Who do people say that the Son of Man is?"
They replied, "Some say John the Baptist, others Elijah,
still others Jeremiah or one of the prophets."
He said to them, "But who do you say that I am?"
Simon Peter said in reply,
"You are the Christ, the Son of the living God."
Jesus said to him in reply, "Blessed are you, Simon son of Jonah.
For flesh and blood has not revealed this to you, but my heavenly Father.
And so I say to you, you are Peter,
and upon this rock I will build my Church,
and the gates of the netherworld shall not prevail against it.
I will give you the keys to the Kingdom of heaven.
Whatever you bind on earth shall be bound in heaven;
and whatever you loose on earth shall be loosed in heaven."**

The Gospel of the Lord.

JUNE 30

592 THE FIRST HOLY MARTYRS OF THE HOLY ROMAN CHURCH

From the Common of Martyrs, p. 1782,

OR

FIRST READING

Romans 8:31b-39   Neither death nor life will be able to separate us from the love of Christ.

A reading from the Letter of Saint Paul to the Romans

Brothers and sisters:
If God is for us, who can be against us?
He did not spare his own Son
    but handed him over for us all,
    how will he not also give us everything else along with him?
Who will bring a charge against God's chosen ones?
It is God who acquits us.
Who will condemn?
It is Christ Jesus who died, rather, was raised,
    who also is at the right hand of God,
    who indeed intercedes for us.
What will separate us from the love of Christ?
Will anguish, or distress, or persecution, or famine,
    or nakedness, or peril, or the sword?
As it is written:

> *For your sake we are being slain all the day;*
>   *we are looked upon as sheep to be slaughtered.*

No, in all these things we conquer overwhelmingly
    through him who loved us.
For I am convinced that neither death, nor life,
    nor angels, nor principalities,
    nor present things, nor future things,
    nor powers, nor height, nor depth,
    nor any other creature will be able to separate us
    from the love of God in Christ Jesus our Lord.

The word of the Lord.

RESPONSORIAL PSALM

Psalm 124:2-3, 4-5, 7b-8

℟. (7) **Our soul has been rescued like a bird from the fowler's snare.**

**Had not the Lord been with us—
   when men rose up against us,
      then would they have swallowed us alive
When their fury was inflamed against us.**

℟. **Our soul has been rescued like a bird from the fowler's snare.**

**Then would the waters have overwhelmed us;
The torrent would have swept over us;
   over us then would have swept
      the raging waters.**

℟. **Our soul has been rescued like a bird from the fowler's snare.**

**Broken was the snare,
   and we were freed.
Our help is in the name of the Lord,
   who made heaven and earth.**

℟. **Our soul has been rescued like a bird from the fowler's snare.**

ALLELUIA

Matthew 5:10

℟. **Alleluia, alleluia.**

**Blessed are they who are persecuted for the sake of righteousness,
for theirs is the Kingdom of heaven.**

℟. **Alleluia, alleluia.**

June 30—The First Holy Martyrs of the Holy Roman Church

GOSPEL

Matthew 24:4-13   You will be hated by all nations because of my name.

✟ **A reading from the holy Gospel according to Matthew**

**Jesus said to his disciples:
"See that no one deceives you.
For many will come in my name, saying,
  'I am the Christ,' and they will deceive many.
You will hear of wars and reports of wars;
   see that you are not alarmed,
   for these things must happen, but it will not yet be the end.
Nation will rise against nation, and kingdom against kingdom;
   there will be famines and earthquakes from place to place.
All these are the beginning of the labor pains.
Then they will hand you over to persecution,
   and they will kill you.
You will be hated by all nations because of my name.
And then many will be led into sin;
   they will betray and hate one another.
Many false prophets will arise and deceive many;
   and because of the increase of evildoing,
   the love of many will grow cold.
But the one who perseveres to the end will be saved."**

The Gospel of the Lord.

JULY 1

[In the Dioceses of the United States]

592A BLESSED JUNIPERO SERRA, PRIEST

From the Common of Pastors: For Missionaries, p. 1805, or the Common of Holy Men and Women: For Religious, p. 1868.

JULY 3

593 SAINT THOMAS, APOSTLE FEAST

FIRST READING

Ephesians 2:19-22   Built upon the foundation of the Apostles.

A reading from the Letter of Saint Paul to the Ephesians

Brothers and sisters:
You are no longer strangers and sojourners,
   but you are fellow citizens with the holy ones
   and members of the household of God,
   built upon the foundation of the Apostles and prophets,
   with Christ Jesus himself as the capstone.
Through him the whole structure is held together
   and grows into a temple sacred in the Lord;
   in him you also are being built together
   into a dwelling place of God in the Spirit.

The word of the Lord.

RESPONSORIAL PSALM

Psalm 117:1bc, 2

℟. (Mark 16:15) **Go out to all the world and tell the Good News.**

Praise the LORD, all you nations;
   glorify him, all you peoples!

℟. Go out to all the world and tell the Good News.

For steadfast is his kindness for us,
   and the fidelity of the LORD endures forever.

℟. Go out to all the world and tell the Good News.

ALLELUIA

John 20:29

℟. **Alleluia, alleluia.**

You believe in me, Thomas, because you have seen me, says the Lord; blessed are those who have not seen, but still believe!

℟. **Alleluia, alleluia.**

GOSPEL

John 20:24-29   My Lord and my God!

✢ **A reading from the holy Gospel according to John**

Thomas, called Didymus, one of the Twelve,
  was not with them when Jesus came.
So the other disciples said to him, "We have seen the Lord."
But Thomas said to them,
  "Unless I see the mark of the nails in his hands
  and put my finger into the nailmarks
  and put my hand into his side, I will not believe."
Now a week later his disciples were again inside
  and Thomas was with them.
Jesus came, although the doors were locked,
  and stood in their midst and said, "Peace be with you."
Then he said to Thomas, "Put your finger here and see my hands,
  and bring your hand and put it into my side,
  and do not be unbelieving, but believe."
Thomas answered and said to him, "My Lord and my God!"
Jesus said to him, "Have you come to believe because you have seen me?
Blessed are those who have not seen and have believed."

The Gospel of the Lord.

JULY 4

594 SAINT ELIZABETH OF PORTUGAL

From the Common of Holy Men and Women: For Those Who Work for the Underprivileged, p. 1868,

OR

FIRST READING

1 John 3:14-18   We ought to lay down our lives for our brothers.

A reading from the first Letter of Saint John

Beloved:
We know that we have passed from death to life
   because we love our brothers.
Whoever does not love remains in death.
Everyone who hates his brother is a murderer,
   and you know that anyone who is a murderer
   does not have eternal life remaining in him.
The way we came to know love
   was that he laid down his life for us;
   so we ought to lay down our lives for our brothers.
If someone who has worldly means
   sees a brother in need and refuses him compassion,
   how can the love of God remain in him?
Children, let us love not in word or speech
   but in deed and truth.

The word of the Lord.

RESPONSORIAL PSALM

Psalm 112:1-2, 3-4, 5-6, 7-8, 9

℟. (1) **Blessed the man who fears the Lord.**
   or:
℟. **Alleluia.**

Blessed the man who fears the Lord,
   who greatly delights in his commands.
His posterity shall be might upon the earth;
   the upright generation shall be blessed.

℟. **Blessed the man who fears the Lord.**
   or:
℟. **Alleluia.**

Wealth and riches shall be in his house;
   his generosity shall endure forever.
Light shines through the darkness for the upright;
   he is gracious and merciful and just.

℟. Blessed the man who fears the Lord.
   or:
℟. Alleluia.

Well for the man who is gracious and lends,
   who conducts his affairs with justice;
He shall never be moved;
   the just one shall be in everlasting remembrance.

℟. Blessed the man who fears the Lord.
   or:
℟. Alleluia.

An evil report he shall not fear.
   His heart is firm, trusting in the LORD.
His heart is steadfast; he shall not fear
   till he looks down upon his foes.

℟. Blessed the man who fears the Lord.
   or:
℟. Alleluia.

Lavishly he gives to the poor,
   his generosity shall endure forever;
   his horn shall be exalted in glory.

℟. Blessed the man who fears the Lord.
   or:
℟. Alleluia.

ALLELUIA

John 13:34

℟. Alleluia, alleluia.

I give you a new commandment:
love one another as I have loved you.

℟. Alleluia, alleluia.

1380 July 4—Saint Elizabeth of Portugal

GOSPEL

Long Form

Matthew 25:31-46 Whatever you did for the least of my brothers, you did for me.

✝ **A reading from the holy Gospel according to Matthew**

**Jesus said to his disciples:
"When the Son of Man comes in his glory,
   and all the angels with him,
   he will sit upon his glorious throne,
   and all the nations will be assembled before him.
And he will separate them one from another,
   as a shepherd separates the sheep from the goats.
He will place the sheep on his right and the goats on his left.
Then the king will say to those on his right,
   'Come, you who are blessed by my Father.
Inherit the kingdom prepared for you from the foundation of the world.
For I was hungry and you gave me food,
   I was thirsty and you gave me drink,
   a stranger and you welcomed me,
   naked and you clothed me,
   ill and you cared for me,
   in prison and you visited me.'
Then the righteous will answer him and say,
   'Lord, when did we see you hungry and feed you,
   or thirsty and give you drink?
When did we see you a stranger and welcome you,
   or naked and clothe you?
When did we see you ill or in prison, and visit you?'
And the king will say to them in reply,
   'Amen, I say to you, whatever you did
   for these least brothers of mine, you did for me.'
Then he will say to those on his left,
   'Depart from me, you accursed,
   into the eternal fire prepared for the Devil and his angels.
For I was hungry and you gave me no food,
   I was thirsty and you gave me no drink,
   a stranger and you gave me no welcome,
   naked and you gave me no clothing,
   ill and in prison, and you did not care for me.'
Then they will answer and say,
   'Lord, when did we see you hungry or thirsty
   or a stranger or naked or ill or in prison,
   and not minister to your needs?'**

He will answer them, 'Amen, I say to you,
   what you did not do for one of these least ones,
   you did not do for me.'
And these will go off to eternal punishment,
   but the righteous to eternal life."

The Gospel of the Lord.

OR

Short Form

Matthew 25:31-40   Whatever you did for the least of my brothers, you did for me.

✠ **A reading from the holy Gospel according to Matthew**

Jesus said to his disciples:
"When the Son of Man comes in his glory,
   and all the angels with him,
   he will sit upon his glorious throne,
   and all the nations will be assembled before him.
And he will separate them one from another,
   as a shepherd separates the sheep from the goats.
He will place the sheep on his right and the goats on his left.
Then the king will say to those on his right,
   'Come, you who are blessed by my Father.
Inherit the kingdom prepared for you from the foundation of the world.
For I was hungry and you gave me food,
   I was thirsty and you gave me drink,
   a stranger and you welcomed me,
   naked and you clothed me,
   ill and you cared for me,
   in prison and you visited me.'
Then the righteous will answer him and say,
   'Lord, when did we see you hungry and feed you,
   or thirsty and give you drink?
When did we see you a stranger and welcome you,
   or naked and clothe you?
When did we see you ill or in prison, and visit you?'
And the king will say to them in reply,
   'Amen, I say to you, whatever you did
   for one of the least brothers of mine, you did for me.'"

The Gospel of the Lord.

[In the Dioceses of the United States]

594A INDEPENDENCE DAY

From the Masses for Various Needs and Occasions, II. For Civil Needs: 13. For the Nation, nos. 882–886, p. 786, volume IV, or 14. For Peace and Justice, nos. 887–891, p. 821, volume IV.

JULY 5

595 SAINT ANTHONY MARY ZACCARIA, PRIEST

From the Common of Pastors, p. 1805, or the Common of Holy Men and Women: For Teachers, p. 1868, or For Religious, p. 1868,

OR

FIRST READING

2 Timothy 1:13-14; 2:1-3   Guard this rich trust with the help of the Holy Spirit.

A reading from the second Letter of Saint Paul to Timothy

Beloved:
Take as your norm the sound words that you heard from me,
   in the faith and love that are in Christ Jesus.
Guard this rich trust with the help of the Holy Spirit
   who dwells within us.

My child, be strong in the grace that is in Christ Jesus.
And what you heard from me through many witnesses
   entrust to faithful people
   who will have the ability to teach others as well.
Bear your share of hardship along with me
   like a good soldier of Christ Jesus.

The word of the Lord.

RESPONSORIAL PSALM

Psalm 1:1-2, 3, 4 and 6

℟. (40:5a) **Blessed are they who hope in the Lord.**
or:
℟. (2a) **Blessed are they who delight in the law of the Lord.**
or:
℟. (92:13-14) **The just will flourish like the palm tree in the garden of the Lord.**

Blessed the man who follows not
the counsel of the wicked
Nor walks in the way of sinners,
nor sits in the company of the insolent,
But delights in the law of the LORD
and meditates on his law day and night.

℟. **Blessed are they who hope in the Lord.**
or:
℟. **Blessed are they who delight in the law of the Lord.**
or:
℟. **The just will flourish like the palm tree in the garden of the Lord.**

He is like a tree
planted near running water,
That yields its fruit in due season,
and whose leaves never fade.
Whatever he does, prospers.

℟. **Blessed are they who hope in the Lord.**
or:
℟. **Blessed are they who delight in the law of the Lord.**
or:
℟. **The just will flourish like the palm tree in the garden of the Lord.**

Not so, the wicked, not so;
they are like chaff which the wind drives away.
For the LORD watches over the way of the just,
but the way of the wicked vanishes.

℟. **Blessed are they who hope in the Lord.**
or:
℟. **Blessed are they who delight in the law of the Lord.**
or:
℟. **The just will flourish like the palm tree in the garden of the Lord.**

ALLELUIA

See Matthew 11:25

℟. Alleluia, alleluia.

Blessed are you, Father, Lord of heaven and earth;
you have revealed to little ones the mysteries of the Kingdom.

℟. Alleluia, alleluia.

GOSPEL

Mark 10:13-16   Let the children come to me.

✝ A reading from the holy Gospel according to Mark

People were bringing children to Jesus that he might touch them,
   but the disciples rebuked them.
When Jesus saw this he became indignant and said to them,
   "Let the children come to me; do not prevent them,
   for the Kingdom of God belongs to such as these.
Amen, I say to you,
   whoever does not accept the Kingdom of God like a child
   will not enter it."
Then he embraced them and blessed them,
   placing his hands on them.

The Gospel of the Lord.

JULY 6

596 SAINT MARIA GORETTI, VIRGIN AND MARTYR

From the Common of Martyrs, p. 1782, or the Common of Virgins, p. 1857,

OR

FIRST READING

1 Corinthians 6:13c-15a, 17-20   Your bodies are members of the Body of Christ.

A reading from the first Letter of Saint Paul to the Corinthians

Brothers and sisters:
The body is not for immorality, but for the Lord,
   and the Lord is for the body;
   God raised the Lord and will also raise us by his power.

Do you not know that your bodies are members of Christ?
Whoever is joined to the Lord becomes one spirit with him.
Avoid immorality.
Every other sin a person commits is outside the body,
   but the immoral person sins against his own body.
Do you not know that your body
   is a temple of the Holy Spirit within you,
   whom you have from God, and that you are not your own?
For you have been purchased at a price.
Therefore glorify God in your body.

The word of the Lord.

RESPONSORIAL PSALM

Psalm 31:3cd-4, 6 and 8ab, 16bc and 17

R. (6) **Into your hands, O Lord, I commend my spirit.**

Be my rock of refuge,
   a stronghold to give me safety.
You are my rock and my fortress;
   for your name's sake you will lead and guide me.

R. **Into your hands, O Lord, I commend my spirit.**

Into your hands I commend my spirit;
   you will redeem me, O Lord, O faithful God.
I will rejoice and be glad because of your mercy.

R. **Into your hands, O Lord, I commend my spirit.**

Rescue me from the clutches of my enemies and my persecutors,
Let your face shine upon your servant;
   save me in your kindness.

℟. Into your hands, O Lord, I commend my spirit.

ALLELUIA

James 1:12

℟. Alleluia, alleluia.

Blessed is the man who perseveres in temptation,
for when he has been proved he will receive the crown of life.

℟. Alleluia, alleluia.

GOSPEL

John 12:24-26   If it dies, it produces much fruit.

✣ A reading from the holy Gospel according to John

Jesus said to his disciples:
"Amen, amen, I say to you,
   unless a grain of wheat falls to the ground and dies,
   it remains just a grain of wheat;
   but if it dies, it produces much fruit.
Whoever loves his life loses it,
   and whoever hates his life in this world
   will preserve it for eternal life.
Whoever serves me must follow me,
   and where I am, there also will my servant be.
The Father will honor whoever serves me."

The Gospel of the Lord.

JULY 11

597 SAINT BENEDICT, ABBOT MEMORIAL

From the Common of Holy Men and Women: For Religious, p. 1868,

OR

FIRST READING

Proverbs 2:1-9   Inclining your heart to understanding.

A reading from the Book of Proverbs

My son, if you receive my words
  and treasure my commands,
Turning your ear to wisdom,
  inclining your heart to understanding;
Yes, if you call to intelligence,
  and to understanding raise your voice;
If you seek her like silver,
  and like hidden treasures search her out:

Then will you understand the fear of the Lord;
  the knowledge of God you will find;
For the Lord gives wisdom,
  from his mouth come knowledge and understanding;
He has counsel in store for the upright,
  he is the shield of those who walk honestly,
Guarding the paths of justice,
  protecting the way of his pious ones.

Then you will understand rectitude and justice,
  honesty, every good path.

The word of the Lord.

RESPONSORIAL PSALM

Psalm 34:2-3, 4-5, 6-7, 8-9, 10-11

℟. (2) **I will bless the Lord at all times.**
  or:
℟. (9) **Taste and see the goodness of the Lord.**

I will bless the Lord at all times;
  his praise shall be ever in my mouth.
Let my soul glory in the Lord;
  the lowly will hear and be glad.

℟. I will bless the Lord at all times.
   or:
℟. Taste and see the goodness of the Lord.

Glorify the LORD **with me,**
   let us together extol his name.
I sought the LORD**, and he answered me**
   and delivered me from all my fears.

℟. I will bless the Lord at all times.
   or:
℟. Taste and see the goodness of the Lord.

Look to him that you may be radiant with joy,
   and your faces may not blush with shame.
When the poor one called out, the LORD **heard,**
   and from all his distress he saved him.

℟. I will bless the Lord at all times.
   or:
℟. Taste and see the goodness of the Lord.

The angel of the LORD **encamps**
   around those who fear him, and delivers them.
Taste and see how good the LORD **is;**
   blessed the man who takes refuge in him.

℟. I will bless the Lord at all times.
   or:
℟. Taste and see the goodness of the Lord.

Fear the LORD**, you his holy ones,**
   for nought is lacking to those who fear him.
The great grow poor and hungry;
   but those who seek the LORD **want for no good thing.**

℟. I will bless the Lord at all times.
   or:
℟. Taste and see the goodness of the Lord.

ALLELUIA

Matthew 5:3

℟. Alleluia, alleluia.

**Blessed are the poor in spirit;
the Kingdom of heaven is theirs!**

℟. Alleluia, alleluia.

GOSPEL

Matthew 19:27-29   You who have followed me will receive a hundred times more.

✠ **A reading from the holy Gospel according to Matthew**

**Peter said to Jesus,
   "We have given up everything and followed you.
What will there be for us?"
Jesus said to them, "Amen, I say to you
   that you who have followed me, in the new age,
   when the Son of Man is seated on his throne of glory,
   will yourselves sit on twelve thrones,
   judging the twelve tribes of Israel.
And everyone who has given up houses or brothers or sisters
   or father or mother or children or lands
   for the sake of my name will receive a hundred times more,
   and will inherit eternal life."**

The Gospel of the Lord.

JULY 13

598 SAINT HENRY

From the Common of Holy Men and Women, p. 1868,

OR

FIRST READING

Micah 6:6-8   You have been told, O man, what is good.

A reading from the Book of the Prophet Micah

With what shall I come before the LORD**,
  and bow before God most high?
Shall I come before him with burnt offerings,
  with calves a year old?
Will the L**ORD **be pleased with thousands of rams,
  with myriad streams of oil?
Shall I give my first-born for my crime,
  the fruit of my body for the sin of my soul?
You have been told, O man, what is good,
  and what the L**ORD **requires of you:
Only to do the right and to love goodness,
  and to walk humbly with your God.**

The word of the Lord.

RESPONSORIAL PSALM

Psalm 1:1-2, 3, 4 and 6

℟. (40:5a) **Blessed are they who hope in the Lord.**
or:
℟. (2a) **Blessed are they who delight in the law of the Lord.**
or:
℟. (92:13-14) **The just will flourish like the palm tree in the garden of the Lord.**

**Blessed the man who follows not
  the counsel of the wicked
Nor walks in the way of sinners,
  nor sits in the company of the insolent,
But delights in the law of the Lord
  and meditates on his law day and night.**

℟. **Blessed are they who hope in the Lord.**
or:
℟. **Blessed are they who delight in the law of the Lord.**
or:
℟. **The just will flourish like the palm tree in the garden of the Lord.**

**He is like a tree
  planted near running water,
That yields its fruit in due season,
  and whose leaves never fade.
  Whatever he does, prospers.**

℟. **Blessed are they who hope in the Lord.**
or:
℟. **Blessed are they who delight in the law of the Lord.**
or:
℟. **The just will flourish like the palm tree in the garden of the Lord.**

**Not so, the wicked, not so;
  they are like chaff which the wind drives away.
For the Lord watches over the way of the just,
  but the way of the wicked vanishes.**

℟. **Blessed are they who hope in the Lord.**
or:
℟. **Blessed are they who delight in the law of the Lord.**
or:
℟. **The just will flourish like the palm tree in the garden of the Lord.**

ALLELUIA

John 14:23

℟. Alleluia, alleluia.

Whoever loves me will keep my word
and my Father will love him
and we will come to him.

℟. Alleluia, alleluia.

GOSPEL

Matthew 7:21-27   The house built on rock and the house built on sand.

✠ A reading from the holy Gospel according to Matthew

**Jesus said to his disciples:
"Not everyone who says to me, 'Lord, Lord,'
    will enter the Kingdom of heaven,
    but only the one who does the will of my Father in heaven.
Many will say to me on that day,
    'Lord, Lord, did we not prophesy in your name?
Did we not drive out demons in your name?
Did we not do mighty deeds in your name?'
Then I will declare to them solemnly,
    'I never knew you. Depart from me, you evildoers.'

"Everyone who listens to these words of mine and acts on them
    will be like a wise man who built his house on rock.
The rain fell, the floods came,
    and the winds blew and buffeted the house.
But it did not collapse; it had been set solidly on rock.
And everyone who listens to these words of mine
    but does not act on them
    will be like a fool who built his house on sand.
The rain fell, the floods came,
    and the winds blew and buffeted the house.
And it collapsed and was completely ruined."

The Gospel of the Lord.**

JULY 14

599 SAINT CAMILLUS DE LELLIS, PRIEST

In the United States this memorial is transferred to July 18, p. 1400.

JULY 14

[In the Dioceses of the United States]

599A BLESSED KATERI TEKAKWITHA, VIRGIN
MEMORIAL

From the Common of Virgins, p. 1857.

JULY 15

600 SAINT BONAVENTURE, BISHOP AND DOCTOR OF THE CHURCH MEMORIAL

From the Common of Pastors, p. 1805, or the Common of Doctors of the Church, p. 1838,

OR

FIRST READING

Ephesians 3:14-19   To know the love of Christ that surpasses knowledge.

A reading from the Letter of Saint Paul to the Ephesians

Brothers and sisters:
I kneel before the Father,
> from whom every family in heaven and on earth is named,
> that he may grant you in accord with the riches of his glory
> to be strengthened with power through his Spirit in the inner self,
> and that Christ may dwell in your hearts through faith;
> that you, rooted and grounded in love,
> may have strength to comprehend with all the holy ones
> what is the breadth and length and height and depth,
> and to know the love of Christ that surpasses knowledge,
> so that you may be filled with all the fullness of God.

The word of the Lord.

RESPONSORIAL PSALM

Psalm 119:9, 10, 11, 12, 13, 14

℟. (12) **Lord, teach me your statutes.**

How shall a young man be faultless in his way?
> **By keeping to your words.**

℟. **Lord, teach me your statutes.**

With all my heart I seek you;
> **let me not stray from your commands.**

℟. **Lord, teach me your statutes.**

Within my heart I treasure your promise,
> **that I may not sin against you.**

℟. **Lord, teach me your statutes.**

Blessed are you, O Lord;
　　teach me your statutes.

℟. **Lord, teach me your statutes.**

With my lips I declare
　　all the ordinances of your mouth.

℟. **Lord, teach me your statutes.**

In the way of your decrees I rejoice,
　　as much as in all riches.

℟. **Lord, teach me your statutes.**

ALLELUIA

Matthew 23:9b, 10b

℟. **Alleluia, alleluia.**

You have but one Father in heaven;
you have one master, the Christ.

℟. **Alleluia, alleluia.**

GOSPEL

Matthew 23:8-12   The greatest among you must be your servant.

✢ **A reading from the holy Gospel according to Matthew**

Jesus spoke to the crowds and to his disciples:
"Do not be called 'Rabbi.'
You have but one teacher, and you are all brothers.
Call no one on earth your father;
　　you have but one Father in heaven.
Do not be called 'Master';
　　you have but one master, the Christ.
The greatest among you must be your servant.
Whoever exalts himself will be humbled;
　　but whoever humbles himself will be exalted."

The Gospel of the Lord.

JULY 16

601 OUR LADY OF MOUNT CARMEL

From the Common of the Blessed Virgin Mary, p. 1751,

OR

FIRST READING

Zechariah 2:14-17   Rejoice, O daughter of Zion! See, I am coming.

A reading from the Book of the Prophet Zechariah

Sing and rejoice, O daughter Zion!
See, I am coming to dwell among you, says the Lord.
Many nations shall join themselves to the Lord on that day,
   and they shall be his people,
   and he will dwell among you,
   and you shall know that the Lord of hosts has sent me to you.
The Lord will possess Judah as his portion in the holy land,
   and he will again choose Jerusalem.
Silence, all, in the presence of the Lord!
   for he stirs forth from his holy dwelling.

The word of the Lord.

RESPONSORIAL PSALM

Luke 1:46-47, 48-49, 50-51, 52-53, 54-55

℟. (49) **The Almighty has done great things for me, and holy is his Name.**
  or:
℟. **O Blessed Virgin Mary, you carried the Son of the eternal Father.**

"My soul proclaims the greatness of the Lord,
  my spirit rejoices in God my savior."

℟. **The Almighty has done great things for me, and holy is his Name.**
  or:
℟. **O Blessed Virgin Mary, you carried the Son of the eternal Father.**

"For he has looked with favor on his lowly servant.
From this day all generations will call me blessed:
  the Almighty has done great things for me,
  and holy is his Name."

℟. **The Almighty has done great things for me, and holy is his Name.**
  or:
℟. **O Blessed Virgin Mary, you carried the Son of the eternal Father.**

"He has mercy on those who fear him
  in every generation.
He has shown the strength of his arm,
  he has scattered the proud in their conceit."

℟. **The Almighty has done great things for me, and holy is his Name.**
  or:
℟. **O Blessed Virgin Mary, you carried the Son of the eternal Father.**

"He has cast down the mighty from their thrones,
  and has lifted up the lowly.
He has filled the hungry with good things,
  and the rich he has sent away empty."

℟. **The Almighty has done great things for me, and holy is his Name.**
  or:
℟. **O Blessed Virgin Mary, you carried the Son of the eternal Father.**

"He has come to the help of his servant Israel
  for he has remembered his promise of mercy,
  the promise he made to our fathers,
  to Abraham and his children for ever."

℟. **The Almighty has done great things for me, and holy is his Name.**
  or:
℟. **O Blessed Virgin Mary, you carried the Son of the eternal Father.**

ALLELUIA

Luke 11:28

℟. Alleluia, alleluia.

**Blessed are those who hear the word of God
and observe it.**

℟. Alleluia, alleluia.

GOSPEL

Matthew 12:46-50   Stretching out his hands toward his disciples, he said, "Here are my mother and my brothers."

✢ **A reading from the holy Gospel according to Matthew**

**While Jesus was speaking to the crowds,
   his mother and his brothers appeared outside,
   wishing to speak with him.
Someone told him, "Your mother and your brothers are standing outside,
   asking to speak with you."
But he said in reply to the one who told him,
   "Who is my mother? Who are my brothers?"
And stretching out his hand toward his disciples, he said,
   "Here are my mother and my brothers.
For whoever does the will of my heavenly Father
   is my brother, and sister, and mother."**

The Gospel of the Lord.

JULY 18

601A SAINT CAMILLUS DE LELLIS, PRIEST

In the United States this memorial is transferred to this date from July 14. From the Common of Holy Men and Women: For Those Who Work for the Underprivileged, p. 1868,

OR

FIRST READING

1 John 3:14-18   We ought to lay down our lives for our brothers.

A reading from the first Letter of Saint John

Beloved:
We know that we have passed from death to life
    because we love our brothers.
Whoever does not love remains in death.
Everyone who hates his brother is a murderer,
    and you know that anyone who is a murderer
    does not have eternal life remaining in him.
The way we came to know love
    was that he laid down his life for us;
    so we ought to lay down our lives for our brothers.
If someone who has worldly means
    sees a brother in need and refuses him compassion,
    how can the love of God remain in him?
Children, let us love not in word or speech
    but in deed and truth.

The word of the Lord.

RESPONSORIAL PSALM

Psalm 112:1-2, 3-4, 5-7a, 7b-8, 9

℟. (1) **Blessed the man who fears the Lord.**
  or:
℟. **Alleluia.**

Blessed the man who fears the LORD,
  who greatly delights in his commands.
His posterity shall be might upon the earth;
  the upright generation shall be blessed.

℟. **Blessed the man who fears the Lord.**
  or:
℟. **Alleluia.**

Wealth and riches shall be in his house;
  his generosity shall endure forever.
Light shines through the darkness for the upright;
  he is gracious and merciful and just.

℟. **Blessed the man who fears the Lord.**
  or:
℟. **Alleluia.**

Well for the man who is gracious and lends,
  who conducts his affairs with justice;
He shall never be moved;
  the just one shall be in everlasting remembrance.

℟. **Blessed the man who fears the Lord.**
  or:
℟. **Alleluia.**

An evil report he shall not fear.
  His heart is firm, trusting in the LORD.
His heart is steadfast; he shall not fear
  till he looks down upon his foes.

℟. **Blessed the man who fears the Lord.**
  or:
℟. **Alleluia.**

Lavishly he gives to the poor,
  his generosity shall endure forever;
  his horn shall be exalted in glory.

℟. **Blessed the man who fears the Lord.**
  or:
℟. **Alleluia.**

ALLELUIA

John 13:34

℟. **Alleluia, alleluia.**

**I give you a new commandment:
love one another as I have loved you.**

℟. **Alleluia, alleluia.**

GOSPEL

John 15:9-17   You are my friends if you do what I command you.

✠   **A reading from the holy Gospel according to John**

Jesus said to his disciples:
"As the Father loves me, so I also love you.
Remain in my love.
If you keep my commandments, you will remain in my love,
   just as I have kept my Father's commandments
   and remain in his love.

"I have told you this so that my joy might be in you
   and your joy might be complete.
This is my commandment: love one another as I love you.
No one has greater love than this,
   to lay down one's life for one's friends.
You are my friends if you do what I command you.
I no longer call you slaves,
   because a slave does not know what his master is doing.
I have called you friends,
   because I have told you everything I have heard from my Father.
It was not you who chose me, but I who chose you
   and appointed you to go and bear fruit that will remain,
   so that whatever you ask the Father in my name he may give you.
This I command you: love one another."

The Gospel of the Lord.

JULY 21

602 SAINT LAWRENCE OF BRINDISI, PRIEST AND DOCTOR OF THE CHURCH

From the Common of Pastors, p. 1805, or the Common of Doctors of the Church, p. 1838,

OR

FIRST READING

2 Corinthians 4:1-2, 5-7   We preach Jesus Christ as Lord, with ourselves as your servants for Jesus' sake.

A reading from the second Letter of Saint Paul to the Corinthians

Brothers and sisters:
Since we have this ministry through the mercy shown us,
  we are not discouraged.
Rather, we have renounced shameful, hidden things;
  not acting deceitfully or falsifying the word of God,
  but by the open declaration of the truth
  we commend ourselves to everyone's conscience in the sight of God.
For we do not preach ourselves but Jesus Christ as Lord,
  and ourselves as your slaves for the sake of Jesus.
For God who said, *Let light shine out of darkness,*
  has shone in our hearts to bring to light
  the knowledge of the glory of God on the face of Jesus Christ.

But we hold this treasure in earthen vessels,
  that the surpassing power may be of God and not from us.

The word of the Lord.

RESPONSORIAL PSALM

Psalm 40:2 and 4ab, 7-8a, 8b-9, 10, 11

℟. (8a and 9a) **Here I am, Lord; I come to do your will.**

I have waited, waited for the L֚ord,
  and he stooped toward me and heard my cry.
And he put a new song into my mouth,
  a hymn to our God.

℟. **Here I am, Lord; I come to do your will.**

July 21—Saint Lawrence of Brindisi

Sacrifice or oblation you wished not,
  but ears open to obedience you gave me.
Burnt offerings or sin-offerings you sought not;
  then said I, "Behold I come."

℟. Here I am, Lord; I come to do your will.

"In the written scroll it is prescribed for me,
To do your will, O my God, is my delight,
  and your law is within my heart!"

℟. Here I am, Lord; I come to do your will.

"I announced your justice in the vast assembly;
  I did not restrain my lips, as you, O Lord, know."

℟. Here I am, Lord; I come to do your will.

"Your justice I kept not hid within my heart;
  your faithfulness and your salvation I have spoken of;
I have made no secret of your kindness and your truth
  in the vast assembly."

℟. Here I am, Lord; I come to do your will.

ALLELUIA

℟. Alleluia, alleluia.

The seed is the word of God, Christ the sower;
all who come to him will live for ever.

℟. Alleluia, alleluia.

GOSPEL

Long Form

Mark 4:1-10, 13-20   The sower went out to sow.

✠ A reading from the holy Gospel according to Mark

On another occasion, Jesus began to teach by the sea.
A very large crowd gathered around him
  so that he got into a boat on the sea and sat down.
And the whole crowd was beside the sea on land.
And he taught them at length in parables,
  and in the course of his instruction he said to them,
  "Hear this! A sower went out to sow.

And as he sowed, some seed fell on the path,
   and the birds came and ate it up.
Other seed fell on rocky ground where it had little soil.
It sprang up at once because the soil was not deep.
And when the sun rose, it was scorched and it withered for lack of roots.
Some seed fell among thorns, and the thorns grew up and choked it
   and it produced no grain.
And some seed fell on rich soil and produced fruit.
It came up and grew and yielded thirty, sixty, and a hundredfold."
He added, "Whoever has ears to hear ought to hear."

And when he was alone,
   those present along with the Twelve
   questioned him about the parables.
Jesus said to them, "Do you not understand this parable?
Then how will you understand any of the parables?
The sower sows the word.
These are the ones on the path where the word is sown.
As soon as they hear, Satan comes at once
   and takes away the word sown in them.
And these are the ones sown on rocky ground who,
   when they hear the word, receive it at once with joy.
But they have no roots; they last only for a time.
Then when tribulation or persecution comes because of the word,
   they quickly fall away.
Those sown among thorns are another sort.
They are the people who hear the word,
   but worldly anxiety, the lure of riches,
   and the craving for other things intrude and choke the word,
   and it bears no fruit.
But those sown on rich soil are the ones who hear the word and accept it
   and bear fruit thirty and sixty and a hundredfold."

The Gospel of the Lord.

OR

July 21—Saint Lawrence of Brindisi

Short Form

Mark 4:1-9   The sower went out to sow.

☩ **A reading from the holy Gospel according to Mark**

**On another occasion, Jesus began to teach by the sea.
A very large crowd gathered around him
   so that he got into a boat on the sea and sat down.
And the whole crowd was beside the sea on land.
And he taught them at length in parables,
   and in the course of his instruction he said to them,
   "Hear this! A sower went out to sow.
And as he sowed, some seed fell on the path,
   and the birds came and ate it up.
Other seed fell on rocky ground where it had little soil.
It sprang up at once because the soil was not deep.
And when the sun rose, it was scorched and it withered for lack of roots.
Some seed fell among thorns, and the thorns grew up and choked it
   and it produced no grain.
And some seed fell on rich soil and produced fruit.
It came up and grew and yielded thirty, sixty, and a hundredfold."**

The Gospel of the Lord.

JULY 22

603 SAINT MARY MAGDALENE MEMORIAL

The Gospel for this memorial is proper.

FIRST READING

First Option

Song of Songs 3:1-4b   I have found him whom my heart loves.

A reading from the Song of Songs

The Bride says:
On my bed at night I sought him
  whom my heart loves—
  I sought him but I did not find him.
I will rise then and go about the city;
  in the streets and crossings I will seek
Him whom my heart loves.
  I sought him but I did not find him.
The watchmen came upon me,
  as they made their rounds of the city:
  Have you seen him whom my heart loves?
I had hardly left them
  when I found him whom my heart loves.

The word of the Lord.

OR

July 22—Saint Mary Magdalene

Second Option

2 Corinthians 5:14-17 Even if we once knew Christ according to the flesh, yet now we know him so no longer.

A reading from the second Letter of Saint Paul to the Corinthians

Brothers and sisters:
The love of Christ impels us,
  once we have come to the conviction that one died for all;
  therefore, all have died.
He indeed died for all,
  so that those who live might no longer live for themselves
  but for him who for their sake died and was raised.

Consequently, from now on we regard no one according to the flesh;
  even if we once knew Christ according to the flesh,
  yet now we know him so no longer.
So whoever is in Christ is a new creation:
  the old things have passed away;
  behold, new things have come.

The word of the Lord.

RESPONSORIAL PSALM

Psalm 63:2, 3-4, 5-6, 8-9

℟. (2) **My soul is thirsting for you, O Lord my God.**

O God, you are my God whom I seek;
    for you my flesh pines and my soul thirsts
    like the earth, parched, lifeless and without water.

℟. **My soul is thirsting for you, O Lord my God.**

Thus have I gazed toward you in the sanctuary
    to see your power and your glory,
For your kindness is a greater good than life;
    my lips shall glorify you.

℟. **My soul is thirsting for you, O Lord my God.**

Thus will I bless you while I live;
    lifting up my hands, I will call upon your name.
As with the riches of a banquet shall my soul be satisfied,
    and with exultant lips my mouth shall praise you.

℟. **My soul is thirsting for you, O Lord my God.**

You are my help,
    and in the shadow of your wings I shout for joy.
My soul clings fast to you;
    your right hand upholds me.

℟. **My soul is thirsting for you, O Lord my God.**

ALLELUIA

℟. **Alleluia, alleluia.**

Tell us Mary, what did you see on the way?
I saw the glory of the risen Christ, I saw his empty tomb.

℟. **Alleluia, alleluia.**

July 22—Saint Mary Magdalene

GOSPEL

John 20:1-2, 11-18   Woman, why are you weeping? Whom are you looking for?

✣   A reading from the holy Gospel according to John

On the first day of the week,
   Mary Magdalene came to the tomb early in the morning,
   while it was still dark,
   and saw the stone removed from the tomb.
So she ran and went to Simon Peter
   and to the other disciple whom Jesus loved, and told them,
   "They have taken the Lord from the tomb,
   and we don't know where they put him."

Mary stayed outside the tomb weeping.
And as she wept, she bent over into the tomb
   and saw two angels in white sitting there,
   one at the head and one at the feet
   where the Body of Jesus had been.
And they said to her, "Woman, why are you weeping?"
She said to them, "They have taken my Lord,
   and I don't know where they laid him."
When she had said this, she turned around and saw Jesus there,
   but did not know it was Jesus.
Jesus said to her, "Woman, why are you weeping?
Whom are you looking for?"
She thought it was the gardener and said to him,
   "Sir, if you carried him away,
   tell me where you laid him,
   and I will take him."
Jesus said to her, "Mary!"
She turned and said to him in Hebrew,
   "Rabbouni," which means Teacher.
Jesus said to her,
   "Stop holding on to me, for I have not yet ascended to the Father.
But go to my brothers and tell them,
   'I am going to my Father and your Father,
   to my God and your God.'"
Mary Magdalene went and announced to the disciples,
   "I have seen the Lord,"
   and then reported what he told her.

The Gospel of the Lord.

JULY 23

604 SAINT BRIDGET OF SWEDEN, RELIGIOUS

From the Common of Holy Men and Women: For Religious, p. 1868,

OR

FIRST READING

Galatians 2:19-20   Yet I live, no longer I, but Christ lives in me.

A reading from the Letter of Saint Paul to the Galatians

Brothers and sisters:
Through the law I died to the law,
   that I might live for God.
I have been crucified with Christ;
   yet I live, no longer I, but Christ lives in me;
   insofar as I now live in the flesh,
   I live by faith in the Son of God
   who has loved me and given himself up for me.

The word of the Lord.

RESPONSORIAL PSALM

Psalm 34:2-3, 4-5, 6-7, 8-9, 10-11

℟. (2) **I will bless the Lord at all times.**
  or:
℟. (9) **Taste and see the goodness of the Lord.**

I will bless the Lord at all times;
   his praise shall be ever in my mouth.
Let my soul glory in the Lord;
   the lowly will hear me and be glad.

℟. **I will bless the Lord at all times.**
  or:
℟. **Taste and see the goodness of the Lord.**

Glorify the Lord with me,
   let us together extol his name.
I sought the Lord, and he answered me
   and delivered me from all my fears.

℟. **I will bless the Lord at all times.**
  or:
℟. **Taste and see the goodness of the Lord.**

Look to him that you may be radiant with joy,
 and your faces may not blush with shame.
When the poor one called out, the L ORD heard,
 and from all his distress he saved him.

℟. I will bless the Lord at all times.
 or:
℟. Taste and see the goodness of the Lord.

The angel of the L ORD encamps
 around those who fear him, and delivers them.
Taste and see how good the L ORD is;
 blessed the man who takes refuge in him.

℟. I will bless the Lord at all times.
 or:
℟. Taste and see the goodness of the Lord.

Fear the L ORD, you his holy ones,
 for nought is lacking to those who fear him.
The great grow poor and hungry;
 but those who seek the L ORD want for no good thing.

℟. I will bless the Lord at all times.
 or:
℟. Taste and see the goodness of the Lord.

ALLELUIA

John 15:9b, 5b

℟. Alleluia, alleluia.

Remain in my love, says the Lord;
whoever remains in me and I in him will bear much fruit.

℟. Alleluia, alleluia.

GOSPEL

John 15:1-8 Whoever remains in me, and I in him will bear much fruit.

☩ **A reading from the holy Gospel according to John**

Jesus said to his disciples:
"I am the true vine, and my Father is the vine grower.
He takes away every branch in me that does not bear fruit,
   and every one that does he prunes so that it bears more fruit.
You are already pruned because of the word that I spoke to you.
Remain in me, as I remain in you.
Just as a branch cannot bear fruit on its own
   unless it remains on the vine,
   so neither can you unless you remain in me.
I am the vine, you are the branches.
Whoever remains in me and I in him will bear much fruit,
   because without me you can do nothing.
Anyone who does not remain in me
   will be thrown out like a branch and wither;
   people will gather them and throw them into a fire
   and they will be burned.
If you remain in me and my words remain in you,
   ask for whatever you want and it will be done for you.
By this is my Father glorified,
   that you bear much fruit and become my disciples."

The Gospel of the Lord.

JULY 25

605 SAINT JAMES, APOSTLE FEAST

FIRST READING

2 Corinthians 4:7-15   Always carrying about in the body the dying of Jesus.

A reading from the second Letter of Saint Paul to the Corinthians

Brothers and sisters:
We hold this treasure in earthen vessels,
  that the surpassing power may be of God and not from us.
We are afflicted in every way, but not constrained;
   perplexed, but not driven to despair;
   persecuted, but not abandoned;
   struck down, but not destroyed;
   always carrying about in the body the dying of Jesus,
   so that the life of Jesus may also be manifested in our body.
For we who live are constantly being given up to death
   for the sake of Jesus,
   so that the life of Jesus may be manifested in our mortal flesh.

So death is at work in us, but life in you.
Since, then, we have the same spirit of faith,
   according to what is written, *I believed, therefore I spoke*,
   we too believe and therefore speak,
   knowing that the one who raised the Lord Jesus
   will raise us also with Jesus
   and place us with you in his presence.
Everything indeed is for you,
   so that the grace bestowed in abundance on more and more people
   may cause the thanksgiving to overflow for the glory of God.

The word of the Lord.

RESPONSORIAL PSALM

Psalm 126:1bc-2ab, 2cd-3, 4-5, 6

℟. (5) **Those who sow in tears shall reap rejoicing.**

**When the Lord brought back the captives of Zion,
   we were like men dreaming.
Then our mouth was filled with laughter,
   and our tongue with rejoicing.**

℟. **Those who sow in tears shall reap rejoicing.**

**Then they said among the nations,
   "The Lord has done great things for them."
The Lord has done great things for us;
   we are glad indeed.**

℟. **Those who sow in tears shall reap rejoicing.**

**Restore our fortunes, O Lord,
   like the torrents in the southern desert.
Those that sow in tears
   shall reap rejoicing.**

℟. **Those who sow in tears shall reap rejoicing.**

**Although they go forth weeping,
   carrying the seed to be sown,
They shall come back rejoicing,
   carrying their sheaves.**

℟. **Those who sow in tears shall reap rejoicing.**

ALLELUIA

See John 15:16

℟. Alleluia, alleluia.

I chose you from the world,
to go and bear fruit that will last, says the Lord.

℟. Alleluia, alleluia.

GOSPEL

Matthew 20:20-28   You will drink my chalice.

✠ A reading from the holy Gospel according to Matthew

The mother of the sons of Zebedee approached Jesus with her sons
   and did him homage, wishing to ask him for something.
He said to her,
   "What do you wish?"
She answered him,
   "Command that these two sons of mine sit,
   one at your right and the other at your left, in your Kingdom."
Jesus said in reply,
   "You do not know what you are asking.
Can you drink the chalice that I am going to drink?"
They said to him, "We can."
He replied,
   "My chalice you will indeed drink,
   but to sit at my right and at my left, this is not mine to give
   but is for those for whom it has been prepared by my Father."
When the ten heard this,
   they became indignant at the two brothers.
But Jesus summoned them and said,
   "You know that the rulers of the Gentiles lord it over them,
   and the great ones make their authority over them felt.
But it shall not be so among you.
Rather, whoever wishes to be great among you shall be your servant;
   whoever wishes to be first among you shall be your slave.
Just so, the Son of Man did not come to be served
   but to serve and to give his life as a ransom for many."

The Gospel of the Lord.

JULY 26

606 SAINTS JOACHIM AND ANNE, PARENTS OF THE BLESSED VIRGIN MARY MEMORIAL

FIRST READING

Sirach 44:1, 10-15   Their name lives on and on.

A reading from the Book of Sirach

**Now will I praise those godly men,
  our ancestors, each in his own time:
These were godly men
  whose virtues have not been forgotten;
Their wealth remains in their families,
  their heritage with their descendants;
Through God's covenant with them their family endures,
  their posterity for their sake.**

**And for all time their progeny will endure,
  their glory will never be blotted out;
Their bodies are peacefully laid away,
  but their name lives on and on.
At gatherings their wisdom is retold,
  and the assembly proclaims their praise.**

The word of the Lord.

RESPONSORIAL PSALM

Psalm 132:11, 13-14, 17-18

℟. (Luke 1:32) **God will give him the throne of David, his father.**

**The Lord swore to David
  a firm promise from which he will not withdraw:
"Your own offspring
  I will set upon your throne."**

℟. **God will give him the throne of David, his father.**

**For the Lord has chosen Zion;
  he prefers her for his dwelling.
"Zion is my resting place forever;
  in her will I dwell, for I prefer her."**

℟. **God will give him the throne of David, his father.**

"In her will I make a horn to sprout forth for David;
   I will place a lamp for my anointed.
His enemies I will clothe with shame,
   but upon him my crown shall shine."

℟. God will give him the throne of David, his father.

ALLELUIA

See Luke 2:25c

℟. Alleluia, alleluia.

They yearned for the comforting of Israel,
and the Holy Spirit rested upon them.

℟. Alleluia, alleluia.

GOSPEL

Matthew 13:16-17   Many prophets and righteous people longed to see what you see.

✠ A reading from the holy Gospel according to Matthew

Jesus said to his disciples:
"Blessed are your eyes, because they see,
   and your ears, because they hear.
Amen, I say to you, many prophets and righteous people
   longed to see what you see but did not see it,
   and to hear what you hear but did not hear it."

The Gospel of the Lord.

JULY 29

607 SAINT MARTHA MEMORIAL

The Gospel for this memorial is proper. From the Common of Holy Men and Women, p. 1868,

OR

FIRST READING

1 John 4:7-16   If we love one another, God remains in us.

A reading from the first Letter of Saint John

**Beloved, let us love one another,
because love is of God;
everyone who loves is begotten by God and knows God.
Whoever is without love does not know God, for God is love.
In this way the love of God was revealed to us:
God sent his only-begotten Son into the world
so that we might have life through him.
In this is love:
not that we have loved God, but that he loved us
and sent his Son as expiation for our sins.
Beloved, if God so loved us,
we also must love one another.
No one has ever seen God.
Yet, if we love one another, God remains in us,
and his love is brought to perfection in us.**

**This is how we know that we remain in him and he in us,
that he has given us of his Spirit.
Moreover, we have seen and testify
that the Father sent his Son as savior of the world.
Whoever acknowledges that Jesus is the Son of God,
God remains in him and he in God.
We have come to know and to believe in the love God has for us.**

**God is love, and whoever remains in love
remains in God and God in him.**

The word of the Lord.

July 29—Saint Martha

RESPONSORIAL PSALM

Psalm 34:2-3, 4-5, 6-7, 8-9, 10-11

℟. (2) **I will bless the Lord at all times.**
   or:
℟. (9) **Taste and see the goodness of the Lord.**

I will bless the LORD **at all times;**
   his praise shall be ever in my mouth.
Let my soul glory in the LORD**;**
   the lowly will hear me and be glad.

℟. **I will bless the Lord at all times.**
   or:
℟. **Taste and see the goodness of the Lord.**

Glorify the LORD **with me,**
   let us together extol his name.
I sought the LORD**, and he answered me**
   and delivered me from all my fears.

℟. **I will bless the Lord at all times.**
   or:
℟. **Taste and see the goodness of the Lord.**

Look to him that you may be radiant with joy,
   and your faces may not blush with shame.
When the poor one called out, the LORD **heard,**
   and from all his distress he saved him.

℟. **I will bless the Lord at all times.**
   or:
℟. **Taste and see the goodness of the Lord.**

The angel of the LORD **encamps**
   around those who fear him, and delivers them.
Taste and see how good the LORD **is;**
   blessed the man who takes refuge in him.

℟. **I will bless the Lord at all times.**
   or:
℟. **Taste and see the goodness of the Lord.**

Fear the Lord, you his holy ones,
    for nought is lacking to those who fear him.
The great grow poor and hungry;
    but those who seek the Lord want for no good thing.

℟. I will bless the Lord at all times.
  or:
℟. Taste and see the goodness of the Lord.

ALLELUIA

John 8:12

℟. Alleluia, alleluia.

I am the light of the world, says the Lord;
whoever follows me will have the light of life.

℟. Alleluia, alleluia.

1422   July 29—Saint Martha

GOSPEL

First Option

John 11:19-27   I have come to believe that you are the Christ, the Son of God.

✢ **A reading from the holy Gospel according to John**

**Many of the Jews had come to Martha and Mary
   to comfort them about their brother [Lazarus, who had died].
When Martha heard that Jesus was coming,
   she went to meet him;
   but Mary sat at home.
Martha said to Jesus,
   "Lord, if you had been here,
   my brother would not have died.
But even now I know that whatever you ask of God,
   God will give you."
Jesus said to her,
   "Your brother will rise."
Martha said to him,
   "I know he will rise,
   in the resurrection on the last day."
Jesus told her,
   "I am the resurrection and the life;
   whoever believes in me, even if he dies, will live,
   and anyone who lives and believes in me will never die.
Do you believe this?"
She said to him, "Yes, Lord.
I have come to believe that you are the Christ, the Son of God,
   the one who is coming into the world."**

The Gospel of the Lord.

   OR

Second Option

Luke 10:38-42   Martha, Martha, you are anxious and worried about many things.

✠ **A reading from the holy Gospel according to Luke**

**Jesus entered a village
 where a woman whose name was Martha welcomed him.
She had a sister named Mary
 who sat beside the Lord at his feet listening to him speak.
Martha, burdened with much serving, came to him and said,
 "Lord, do you not care
 that my sister has left me by myself to do the serving?
Tell her to help me."
The Lord said to her in reply,
 "Martha, Martha, you are anxious and worried about many things.
There is need of only one thing.
Mary has chosen the better part
 and it will not be taken from her."**

The Gospel of the Lord.

JULY 30

608 SAINT PETER CHRYSOLOGUS, BISHOP AND DOCTOR OF THE CHURCH

From the Common of Pastors, p. 1805, the Common of Doctors of the Church, p. 1838,

OR

FIRST READING

Ephesians 3:8-12   To preach to the Gentiles the inscrutable riches of Christ.

A reading from the Letter of Saint Paul to the Ephesians

Brothers and sisters:
To me, the very least of all the holy ones, this grace was given,
 to preach to the Gentiles the inscrutable riches of Christ,
 and to bring to light for all what is the plan of the mystery
 hidden from ages past in God who created all things,
 so that the manifold wisdom of God
 might now be made known through the Church
 to the principalities and authorities in the heavens.
This was according to the eternal purpose
 that he accomplished in Christ Jesus our Lord,
 in whom we have boldness of speech
 and confidence of access through faith in him.

The word of the Lord.

RESPONSORIAL PSALM

Psalm 119:9, 10, 11, 12, 13, 14

℟. (12) **Lord, teach me your statutes.**

How shall a young man be faultless in his way?
 By keeping to your words.

℟. **Lord, teach me your statutes.**

With all my heart I seek you;
 let me not stray from your commands.

℟. **Lord, teach me your statutes.**

Within my heart I treasure your promise,
 that I may not sin against you.

℟. **Lord, teach me your statutes.**

Blessed are you, O LORD;
   teach me your statutes.

℟. **Lord, teach me your statutes.**

With my lips I declare
   all the ordinances of your mouth.

℟. **Lord, teach me your statutes.**

In the way of your decrees I rejoice,
   as much as in all riches.

℟. **Lord, teach me your statutes.**

ALLELUIA

John 15:5

℟. **Alleluia, alleluia.**

I am the vine, you are the branches, says the Lord:
whoever remains in me, and I in him, will bear much fruit.

℟. **Alleluia, alleluia.**

GOSPEL

Luke 6:43-45   From the fullness of the heart the mouth speaks.

✠ **A reading from the holy Gospel according to Luke**

Jesus said to his disciples:
"A good tree does not bear rotten fruit,
   nor does a rotten tree bear good fruit.
For every tree is known by its own fruit.
For people do not pick figs from thornbushes,
   nor do they gather grapes from brambles.
A good person out of the store of goodness in his heart produces good,
   but an evil person out of a store of evil produces evil;
   for from the fullness of the heart the mouth speaks."

The Gospel of the Lord.

JULY 31

609 SAINT IGNATIUS OF LOYOLA, PRIEST — MEMORIAL

From the Common of Pastors, p. 1805, or the Common of Holy Men and Women: For Religious, p. 1868,

OR

FIRST READING

1 Corinthians 10:31—11:1   Do everything for the glory of God.

A reading from the first Letter of Saint Paul to the Corinthians

Brothers and sisters:
Whether you eat or drink, or whatever you do,
   do everything for the glory of God.
Avoid giving offense, whether to Jews or Greeks
   or the Church of God,
   just as I try to please everyone in every way,
   not seeking my own benefit but that of the many,
   that they may be saved.
Be imitators of me, as I am of Christ.

The word of the Lord.

RESPONSORIAL PSALM

Psalm 34:2-3, 4-5, 6-7, 8-9, 10-11

℟. (2) **I will bless the Lord at all times.**
   or:
℟. (9) **Taste and see the goodness of the Lord.**

I will bless the LORD at all times;
   his praise shall be ever in my mouth.
Let my soul glory in the LORD;
   the lowly will hear me and be glad.

℟. **I will bless the Lord at all times.**
   or:
℟. **Taste and see the goodness of the Lord.**

Glorify the Lꜜꜜ with me,
   let us together extol his name.
I sought the Lꜜꜜ, and he answered me
   and delivered me from all my fears.

℟. I will bless the Lord at all times.
   or:
℟. Taste and see the goodness of the Lord.

Look to him that you may be radiant with joy,
   and your faces may not blush with shame.
When the poor one called out, the Lꜜꜜ heard,
   and from all his distress he saved him.

℟. I will bless the Lord at all times.
   or:
℟. Taste and see the goodness of the Lord.

The angel of the Lꜜꜜ encamps
   around those who fear him, and delivers them.
Taste and see how good the Lꜜꜜ is;
   blessed the man who takes refuge in him.

℟. I will bless the Lord at all times.
   or:
℟. Taste and see the goodness of the Lord.

Fear the Lꜜꜜ, you his holy ones,
   for nought is lacking to those who fear him.
The great grow poor and hungry;
   but those who seek the Lꜜꜜ want for no good thing.

℟. I will bless the Lord at all times.
   or:
℟. Taste and see the goodness of the Lord.

ALLELUIA

Matthew 5:3

℟. Alleluia, alleluia.

Blessed are the poor in spirit,
for theirs is the Kingdom of heaven.

℟. Alleluia, alleluia.

GOSPEL

Luke 14:25-33   Everyone of you who does not renounce all his possessions cannot be my disciple.

✜ A reading from the holy Gospel according to Luke

Great crowds were traveling with Jesus,
   and he turned and addressed them,
   "If anyone comes to me without hating his father and mother,
   wife and children, brothers and sisters,
   and even his own life,
   he cannot be my disciple.
Whoever does not carry his own cross and come after me
   cannot be my disciple.
Which of you wishing to construct a tower
   does not first sit down and calculate the cost
   to see if there is enough for its completion?
Otherwise, after laying the foundation
   and finding himself unable to finish the work
   the onlookers should laugh at him and say,
   'This one began to build but did not have the resources to finish.'
Or what king marching into battle would not first sit down
   and decide whether with ten thousand troops
   he can successfully oppose another king
   advancing upon him with twenty thousand troops?
But if not, while he is still far away,
   he will send a delegation to ask for peace terms.
In the same way,
   everyone of you who does not renounce all his possessions
   cannot be my disciple."

The Gospel of the Lord.

AUGUST 1

610 SAINT ALPHONSUS LIGUORI, BISHOP AND DOCTOR OF THE CHURCH MEMORIAL

From the Common of Pastors, p. 1805, or the Common of Doctors of the Church, p. 1838,

OR

FIRST READING

Romans 8:1-4   The law of the spirit of life in Christ Jesus has set you free from the law of sin and death.

A reading from the Letter of Saint Paul to the Romans

Brothers and sisters:
Now there is no condemnation for those who are in Christ Jesus.
For the law of the spirit of life in Christ Jesus
   has freed you from the law of sin and death.
For what the law, weakened by the flesh, was powerless to do,
   this God has done:
      by sending his own Son in the likeness of sinful flesh
      and for the sake of sin, he condemned sin in the flesh,
      so that the righteous decree of the law might be fulfilled in us,
      who live not according to the flesh but according to the spirit.

The word of the Lord.

RESPONSORIAL PSALM

Psalm 119:9, 10, 11, 12, 13, 14

℟. (12) **Lord, teach me your statutes.**

How shall a young man be faultless in his way?
  By keeping to your words.

℟. **Lord, teach me your statutes.**

With all my heart I seek you;
  let me not stray from your commands.

℟. **Lord, teach me your statutes.**

Within my heart I treasure your promise,
  that I may not sin against you.

℟. **Lord, teach me your statutes.**

Blessed are you, O Lord;
  teach me your statutes.

℟. **Lord, teach me your statutes.**

With my lips I declare
  all the ordinances of your mouth.

℟. **Lord, teach me your statutes.**

In the way of your decrees I rejoice,
  as much as in all riches.

℟. **Lord, teach me your statutes.**

ALLELUIA

Matthew 5:16

℟. **Alleluia, alleluia.**

Let your light shine before others,
that they may see your good deeds and glorify your heavenly Father.

℟. **Alleluia, alleluia.**

GOSPEL

Matthew 5:13-19   You are the light of the world.

✢ A reading from the holy Gospel according to Matthew

Jesus said to his disciples:
"You are the salt of the earth.
But if salt loses its taste, with what can it be seasoned?
It is no longer good for anything
   but to be thrown out and trampled underfoot.
You are the light of the world.
A city set on a mountain cannot be hidden.
Nor do they light a lamp and then put it under a bushel basket;
   it is set on a lampstand,
   where it gives light to all in the house.
Just so, your light must shine before others,
   that they may see your good deeds
   and glorify your heavenly Father.

"Do not think that I have come to abolish the law or the prophets.
I have come not to abolish but to fulfill.
Amen, I say to you, until heaven and earth pass away,
   not the smallest letter or the smallest part of a letter
   will pass from the law,
   until all things have taken place.
Therefore, whoever breaks one of the least of these commandments
   and teaches others to do so
   will be called least in the Kingdom of heaven.
But whoever obeys and teaches these commandments
   will be called greatest in the Kingdom of heaven."

The Gospel of the Lord.

AUGUST 2

611 SAINT EUSEBIUS OF VERCELLI, BISHOP

From the Common of Pastors, p. 1805,

OR

FIRST READING

1 John 5:1-5   The victory that conquers the world is our faith.

A reading from the first Letter of Saint John

Beloved:
Everyone who believes that Jesus is the Christ is begotten by God,
　and everyone who loves the Father
　loves also the one begotten by him.
In this way we know that we love the children of God
　when we love God and obey his commandments.
For the love of God is this,
　that we keep his commandments.
And his commandments are not burdensome,
　for whoever is begotten by God conquers the world.
And the victory that conquers the world is our faith.
Who indeed is the victor over the world
　but the one who believes that Jesus is the Son of God?

The word of the Lord.

RESPONSORIAL PSALM

Psalm 89:2-3, 4-5, 21-22, 25 and 27

℟. (2) **For ever I will sing the goodness of the Lord.**

The favors of the L<small>ORD</small> **I will sing forever;**
   through all generations my mouth shall proclaim your faithfulness.
For you have said, "My kindness is established forever";
   in heaven you have confirmed your faithfulness.

℟. **For ever I will sing the goodness of the Lord.**

"I have made a covenant with my chosen one,
   I have sworn to David my servant:
Forever will I confirm your posterity
   and establish your throne for all generations."

℟. **For ever I will sing the goodness of the Lord.**

"I have found David, my servant;
   with my holy oil I have anointed him,
That my hand may be always with him,
   and that my arm may make him strong."

℟. **For ever I will sing the goodness of the Lord.**

"My faithfulness and my mercy shall be with him,
   and through my name shall his horn be exalted.
He shall say of me, 'You are my father,
   my God, the Rock, my savior.'"

℟. **For ever I will sing the goodness of the Lord.**

ALLELUIA

Matthew 5:3

℟. Alleluia, alleluia.

**Blessed are the poor in spirit,
for theirs is the Kingdom of heaven.**

℟. Alleluia, alleluia.

GOSPEL

Matthew 5:1-12a   Rejoice and be glad, for your reward will be great in heaven.

✠ **A reading from the holy Gospel according to Matthew**

When Jesus saw the crowds, he went up the mountain,
  and after he had sat down, his disciples came to him.
He began to teach them, saying:

> "Blessed are the poor in spirit,
>   for theirs is the Kingdom of heaven.
> Blessed are they who mourn,
>   for they will be comforted.
> Blessed are the meek,
>   for they will inherit the land.
> Blessed are they who hunger and thirst for righteousness,
>   for they will be satisfied.
> Blessed are the merciful,
>   for they will be shown mercy.
> Blessed are the clean of heart,
>   for they will see God.
> Blessed are the peacemakers,
>   for they will be called children of God.
> Blessed are they who are persecuted for the sake of righteousness,
>   for theirs is the Kingdom of heaven.
> Blessed are you when they insult you and persecute you
>   and utter every kind of evil against you falsely because of me.
> Rejoice and be glad,
>   for your reward will be great in heaven."

The Gospel of the Lord.

AUGUST 2

611A PETER JULIAN EYMARD, PRIEST

From the Common of Pastors, p. 1805, or the Common of Holy Men and Women: For Religious, p. 1868,

OR

FIRST READING

Acts 4:32-35 The community of believers was of one heart and mind.

A reading from the Acts of the Apostles

The community of believers was of one heart and mind,
  and no one claimed that any of his possessions was his own,
  but they had everything in common.
With great power the Apostles bore witness
  to the resurrection of the Lord Jesus,
  and great favor was accorded them all.
There was no needy person among them,
  for those who owned property or houses would sell them,
  bring the proceeds of the sale,
  and put them at the feet of the Apostles,
  and they were distributed to each according to need.

The word of the Lord.

August 2—Peter Julian Eymard

RESPONSORIAL PSALM

Psalm 34:2-3, 4-5, 6-7, 8-9, 10-11

℟. (9) **Taste and see the goodness of the Lord.**

I will bless the Lord at all times;
   his praise shall be ever in my mouth.
Let my soul glory in the Lord;
   the lowly will hear and be glad.

℟. **Taste and see the goodness of the Lord.**

Glorify the Lord with me,
   let us together extol his name.
I sought the Lord, and he answered me
   and delivered me from all my fears.

℟. **Taste and see the goodness of the Lord.**

Look to him that you may be radiant with joy,
   and your faces may not blush with shame.
When the poor one called out, the Lord heard,
   and from all his distress he saved him.

℟. **Taste and see the goodness of the Lord.**

The angel of the Lord encamps
   around those who fear him, and delivers them.
Taste and see how good the Lord is;
   blessed the man who takes refuge in him.

℟. **Taste and see the goodness of the Lord.**

Fear the Lord, you his holy ones,
   for nought is lacking to those who fear him.
The great grow poor and hungry;
   but those who seek the Lord want for no good thing.

℟. **Taste and see the goodness of the Lord.**

ALLELUIA

John 15:4a, 5b

℟. Alleluia, alleluia.

**Remain in me, as I remain in you, says the Lord;
whoever remains in me will bear much fruit.**

℟. Alleluia, alleluia.

GOSPEL

John 15:1-8   Whoever remains in me, and I in him, will bear much fruit.

☩ A reading from the holy Gospel according to John

Jesus said to his disciples:
"I am the true vine, and my Father is the vine grower.
**He takes away every branch in me that does not bear fruit,
   and everyone that does he prunes so that it bears more fruit.**
You are already pruned because of the word that I spoke to you.
Remain in me, as I remain in you.
Just as a branch cannot bear fruit on its own
   unless it remains on the vine,
   so neither can you unless you remain in me.
I am the vine, you are the branches.
**Whoever remains in me and I in him will bear much fruit,
   because without me you can do nothing.**
Anyone who does not remain in me
   will be thrown out like a branch and wither;
   people will gather them and throw them into a fire
   and they will be burned.
If you remain in me and my words remain in you,
   ask for whatever you want and it will be done for you.
By this is my Father glorified,
   that you bear much fruit and become my disciples."

The Gospel of the Lord.

AUGUST 4

612 SAINT JOHN MARY VIANNEY, PRIEST MEMORIAL

From the Common of Pastors, p. 1805,

OR

FIRST READING

Ezekiel 3:17-21   I have appointed you a watchman for the house of Israel.

A reading from the Book of the Prophet Ezekiel

The word of the Lord came to me:
Son of man, I have appointed you a watchman
   for the house of Israel.
When you hear a word from my mouth,
   you shall warn them for me.

If I say to the wicked man,
   You shall surely die;
   and you do not warn him or speak out
   to dissuade him from his wicked conduct so that he may live:
   the wicked man shall die for his sins,
   but I will hold you responsible for his death.
If, on the other hand, you have warned the wicked man,
   yet he has not turned away from his evil
   nor from his wicked conduct,
   then he shall die for his sin,
   but you shall save your life.

If a virtuous man turns away from virtue and does wrong
   when I place a stumbling block before him, he shall die.
He shall die for his sin,
   and his virtuous deeds shall not be remembered;
   but I will hold you responsible for his death
   if you did not warn him.
When, on the other hand, you have warned a virtuous man not to sin,
   and he has in fact not sinned,
   he shall surely live because of the warning,
   and you shall save your own life.

The word of the Lord.

RESPONSORIAL PSALM

Psalm 117:1bc, 2

℟. (Mark 16:15) **Go out to all the world and tell the Good News.**

**Praise the Lord, all you nations;
  glorify him, all you peoples!**

℟. **Go out to all the world and tell the Good News.**

**For steadfast is his kindness toward us,
  and the fidelity of the Lord endures forever.**

℟. **Go out to all the world and tell the Good News.**

ALLELUIA

Luke 4:18

℟. **Alleluia, alleluia.**

**The Lord sent me to bring glad tidings to the poor
and to proclaim liberty to captives.**

℟. **Alleluia, alleluia.**

GOSPEL

Matthew 9:35—10:1 At the sight of the crowds, his heart was moved with pity for them.

✠ **A reading from the holy Gospel according to Matthew**

**Jesus went around to all the towns and villages,
  teaching in their synagogues, proclaiming the Gospel of the Kingdom,
  and curing every disease and illness.
At the sight of the crowds,
  his heart was moved with pity for them
  because they were troubled and abandoned,
  like sheep without a shepherd.
Then he said to his disciples,
  "The harvest is abundant but the laborers are few;
  so ask the master of the harvest
  to send out laborers for his harvest."**

**Then he summoned his twelve disciples
  and gave them authority over unclean spirits
  to drive them out and to cure every disease and every illness.**

The Gospel of the Lord.

AUGUST 5

613 DEDICATION OF THE BASILICA OF SAINT MARY MAJOR IN ROME

From the Common of the Blessed Virgin Mary, p. 1751,

OR

FIRST READING

Revelation 21:1-5a   I saw a new Jerusalem, prepared as a bride adorned for her husband.

A reading from the Book of Revelation

I, John, saw a new heaven and a new earth.
The former heaven and the former earth had passed away,
   and the sea was no more.
I also saw the holy city, a new Jerusalem,
   coming down out of heaven from God,
   prepared as a bride adorned for her husband.
I heard a loud voice from the throne saying,
   "Behold, God's dwelling is with the human race.
He will dwell with them and they will be his people
   and God himself will always be with them as their God.
He will wipe every tear from their eyes,
   and there shall be no more death or mourning, wailing or pain,
   for the old order has passed away."

The One who sat on the throne said,
   "Behold, I make all things new."

The word of the Lord.

RESPONSORIAL PSALM

Judith 13:18, 19, 20

℟. (15:9) **You are the highest honor of our race.**

**Blessed are you, daughter, by the Most High God,
 above all the women on earth;
 and blessed be the Lord God,
 the creator of heaven and earth.**

℟. **You are the highest honor of our race.**

**Your deed of hope will never be forgotten
 by those who tell of the might of God.**

℟. **You are the highest honor of our race.**

ALLELUIA

Luke 11:28

℟. **Alleluia, alleluia.**

**Blessed are those who hear the word of God
and observe it.**

℟. **Alleluia, alleluia.**

GOSPEL

Luke 11:27-28   Blessed is the womb that carried you.

☩ **A reading from the holy Gospel according to Luke**

**While Jesus was speaking,
 a woman from the crowd called out and said to him,
 "Blessed is the womb that carried you
 and the breasts at which you nursed."
He replied, "Rather, blessed are those
 who hear the word of God and observe it."**

The Gospel of the Lord.

AUGUST 6

614 THE TRANSFIGURATION OF THE LORD FEAST

FIRST READING

Daniel 7:9-10, 13-14   His clothing was snow bright.

A reading from the Book of the Prophet Daniel

As I watched:

> Thrones were set up
>   and the Ancient One took his throne.
> His clothing was bright as snow,
>   and the hair on his head as white as wool;
> his throne was flames of fire,
>   with wheels of burning fire.
> A surging stream of fire
>   flowed out from where he sat;
> thousands upon thousands were ministering to him,
>   and myriads upon myriads attended him.

The court was convened and the books were opened.

As the visions during the night continued, I saw:

> One like a Son of man coming,
>   on the clouds of heaven;
> when he reached the Ancient One
>   and was presented before him,
> the one like a Son of man received dominion, glory, and kingship;
>   all peoples, nations, and languages serve him.
> His dominion is an everlasting dominion
>   that shall not be taken away,
>   his kingship shall not be destroyed.

The word of the Lord.

RESPONSORIAL PSALM

Psalm 97:1-2, 5-6, 9

R/. (1a and 9a) The Lord is king, the Most High over all the earth.

The LORD is king; let the earth rejoice;
  let the many islands be glad.
Clouds and darkness are round about him,
  justice and judgment are the foundation of his throne.

R/. The Lord is king, the Most High over all the earth.

The mountains melt like wax before the Lord,
   before the Lord of all the earth.
The heavens proclaim his justice,
   and all peoples see his glory.

℟. The Lord is king, the Most High over all the earth.

Because you, O Lord, are the Most High over all the earth,
   exalted far above all gods.

℟. The Lord is king, the Most High over all the earth.

SECOND READING

2 Peter 1:16-19   We ourselves heard this voice come from heaven.

A reading from the second Letter of Saint Peter

Beloved:
We did not follow cleverly devised myths
   when we made known to you
      the power and coming of our Lord Jesus Christ,
      but we had been eyewitnesses of his majesty.
For he received honor and glory from God the Father
   when that unique declaration came to him from the majestic glory,
   "This is my Son, my beloved, with whom I am well pleased."
We ourselves heard this voice come from heaven
   while we were with him on the holy mountain.
Moreover, we possess the prophetic message that is altogether reliable.
You will do well to be attentive to it,
   as to a lamp shining in a dark place,
   until day dawns and the morning star rises in your hearts.

The word of the Lord.

ALLELUIA

Matthew 17:5c

℟. Alleluia, alleluia.

This is my beloved Son, with whom I am well pleased;
listen to him.

℟. Alleluia, alleluia.

GOSPEL

A

Matthew 17:1-9   His face shone like the sun.

✢ A reading from the holy Gospel according to Matthew

Jesus took Peter, James, and his brother, John,
   and led them up a high mountain by themselves.
And he was transfigured before them;
   his face shone like the sun
   and his clothes became white as light.
And behold, Moses and Elijah appeared to them,
   conversing with him.
Then Peter said to Jesus in reply,
   "Lord, it is good that we are here.
If you wish, I will make three tents here,
   one for you, one for Moses, and one for Elijah."
While he was still speaking, behold,
   a bright cloud cast a shadow over them,
   then from the cloud came a voice that said,
   "This is my beloved Son, with whom I am well pleased;
   listen to him."
When the disciples heard this, they fell prostrate
   and were very much afraid.
But Jesus came and touched them, saying,
   "Rise, and do not be afraid."
And when the disciples raised their eyes,
   they saw no one else but Jesus alone.

As they were coming down from the mountain,
   Jesus charged them,
      "Do not tell the vision to anyone
      until the Son of Man has been raised from the dead."

The Gospel of the Lord.

GOSPEL

B

Mark 9:2-10   This is my beloved Son.

✠ **A reading from the holy Gospel according to Mark**

Jesus took Peter, James, and his brother John,
   and led them up a high mountain apart by themselves.
And he was transfigured before them,
   and his clothes became dazzling white,
   such as no fuller on earth could bleach them.
Then Elijah appeared to them along with Moses,
   and they were conversing with Jesus.
Then Peter said to Jesus in reply,
   "Rabbi, it is good that we are here!
Let us make three tents:
   one for you, one for Moses, and one for Elijah."
He hardly knew what to say, they were so terrified.
Then a cloud came, casting a shadow over them;
   from the cloud came a voice,
   "This is my beloved Son. Listen to him."
Suddenly, looking around, they no longer saw anyone
   but Jesus alone with them.

As they were coming down from the mountain,
   he charged them not to relate what they had seen to anyone,
   except when the Son of Man had risen from the dead.
So they kept the matter to themselves,
   questioning what rising from the dead meant.

The Gospel of the Lord.

GOSPEL

C

Luke 9:28b-36   While Jesus was praying his face changed in appearance.

✠ **A reading from the holy Gospel according to Luke**

Jesus took Peter, John, and James
  and went up a mountain to pray.
While he was praying his face changed in appearance
  and his clothing became dazzling white.
And behold, two men were conversing with him, Moses and Elijah,
  who appeared in glory and spoke of his exodus
  that he was going to accomplish in Jerusalem.
Peter and his companions had been overcome by sleep,
  but becoming fully awake,
  they saw his glory and the two men standing with him.
As they were about to part from him, Peter said to Jesus,
  "Master, it is good that we are here;
  let us make three tents,
  one for you, one for Moses, and one for Elijah."
But he did not know what he was saying.
While he was still speaking,
  a cloud came and cast a shadow over them,
  and they became frightened when they entered the cloud.
Then from the cloud came a voice that said,
  "This is my chosen Son; listen to him."
After the voice had spoken, Jesus was found alone.
They fell silent and did not at that time
  tell anyone what they had seen.

The Gospel of the Lord.

AUGUST 7

615 SAINT SIXTUS II, POPE AND MARTYR, AND HIS COMPANIONS, MARTYRS

From the Common of Martyrs, p. 1782,

OR

FIRST READING

Wisdom 3:1-9   As sacrificial offerings he took them to himself.

A reading from the Book of Wisdom

The souls of the just are in the hand of God,
   and no torment shall touch them.
They seemed, in the view of the foolish, to be dead;
   and their passing away was thought an affliction
   and their going forth from us, utter destruction.
But they are in peace.
For if before men, indeed they be punished,
   yet is their hope full of immortality;
Chastised a little, they shall be greatly blessed,
   because God tried them
   and found them worthy of himself.
As gold in the furnace, he proved them,
   and as sacrificial offerings he took them to himself.
In the time of their visitation they shall shine,
   and shall dart about as sparks through stubble;
They shall judge nations and rule over peoples,
   and the Lord shall be their King forever.
Those who trust in him shall understand truth,
   and the faithful shall abide with him in love:
Because grace and mercy are with his holy ones,
   and his care is with his elect.

The word of the Lord.

RESPONSORIAL PSALM

Psalm 126:1bc-2ab, 2cd-3, 4-5, 6

℟. (5) **Those who sow in tears shall reap rejoicing.**

When the L**ORD** **brought back the captives of Zion,**
   we were like men dreaming.
Then our mouth was filled with laughter,
   and our tongue with rejoicing.

℟. **Those who sow in tears shall reap rejoicing.**

Then they said among the nations,
   "The L**ORD** **has done great things for them."**
The L**ORD** **has done great things for us;**
   we are glad indeed.

℟. **Those who sow in tears shall reap rejoicing.**

Restore our fortunes, O L**ORD,**
   like the torrents in the southern desert.
Those who sow in tears
   shall reap rejoicing.

℟. **Those who sow in tears shall reap rejoicing.**

Although they go forth weeping,
   carrying the seed to be sown,
They shall come back rejoicing,
   carrying their sheaves.

℟. **Those who sow in tears shall reap rejoicing.**

ALLELUIA

James 1:12

℟. **Alleluia, alleluia.**

**Blessed is the man who perseveres in temptation,
for when he has been proved he will receive the crown of life.**

℟. **Alleluia, alleluia.**

GOSPEL

Matthew 10:28-33   Do not be afraid of those who kill the body.

✠ **A reading from the holy Gospel according to Matthew**

**Jesus said to his Apostles:
"Do not be afraid of those who kill the body
   but cannot kill the soul;
   rather, be afraid of the one who can destroy
   both soul and body in Gehenna.
Are not two sparrows sold for a small coin?
Yet not one of them falls to the ground without your Father's knowledge.
Even all the hairs of your head are counted.
So do not be afraid; you are worth more than many sparrows.
Everyone who acknowledges me before others
   I will acknowledge before my heavenly Father.
But whoever denies me before others,
   I will deny before my heavenly Father."**

The Gospel of the Lord.

AUGUST 7

616 SAINT CAJETAN, PRIEST

From the Common of Pastors, p. 1805, or the Common of Holy Men and Women: For Religious, p. 1868,

OR

FIRST READING

Sirach 2:7-11   You who fear the Lord, believe in him, hope in him, love him.

A reading from the Book of Sirach

**You who fear the Lord, wait for his mercy,
  turn not away lest you fall.
You who fear the Lord, trust him,
  and your reward will not be lost.
You who fear the Lord, hope for good things,
  for lasting joy and mercy.
You who fear the Lord, love him
  and your hearts will be enlightened.
Study the generations long past and understand;
  has anyone hoped in the Lord and been disappointed?
Has anyone persevered in his commandments and been forsaken?
  Has anyone called upon him and been rebuffed?
Compassionate and merciful is the Lord;
  he forgives sins, he saves in time of trouble
  and he is a protector to all who seek him in truth.**

The word of the Lord.

RESPONSORIAL PSALM

Psalm 112:1-2, 3-4, 5-6, 7-8, 9

℟. (1) **Blessed the man who fears the Lord.**
  or:
℟. **Alleluia.**

Blessed the man who fears the LORD,
  who greatly delights in his commands.
His posterity shall be mighty upon the earth;
  the upright generation shall be blessed.

℟. **Blessed the man who fears the Lord.**
  or:
℟. **Alleluia.**

Wealth and riches shall be in his house;
  his generosity shall endure forever.
Light shines through the darkness for the upright;
  he is gracious and merciful and just.

℟. **Blessed the man who fears the Lord.**
  or:
℟. **Alleluia.**

Well for the man who is gracious and lends,
  who conducts his affairs with justice;
He shall never be moved;
  the just one shall be in everlasting remembrance.

℟. **Blessed the man who fears the Lord.**
  or:
℟. **Alleluia.**

An evil report he shall not fear.
  His heart is firm, trusting in the LORD.
His heart is steadfast; he shall not fear
  till he looks down upon his foes.

℟. **Blessed the man who fears the Lord.**
  or:
℟. **Alleluia.**

Lavishly he gives to the poor,
  his generosity shall endure forever;
  his horn shall be exalted in glory.

℟. **Blessed the man who fears the Lord.**
  or:
℟. **Alleluia.**

ALLELUIA

Matthew 5:3

℟. Alleluia, alleluia.

**Blessed are the poor in spirit;
for theirs is the Kingdom of heaven.**

℟. Alleluia, alleluia.

GOSPEL

Luke 12:32-34   Your Father is pleased to give you the Kingdom.

✠ **A reading from the holy Gospel according to Luke**

**Jesus said to his disciples:
"Do not be afraid any longer, little flock,
   for your Father is pleased to give you the Kingdom.
Sell your belongings and give alms.
Provide money bags for yourselves that do not wear out,
   an inexhaustible treasure in heaven
   that no thief can reach nor moth destroy.
For where your treasure is, there also will your heart be."**

The Gospel of the Lord.

AUGUST 8

617 SAINT DOMINIC, PRIEST MEMORIAL

From the Common of Pastors: For Missionaries, p. 1805, or the Common of Holy Men and Women: For Religious, p. 1868,

OR

FIRST READING

1 Corinthians 2:1-10a   We speak God's wisdom, mysterious, hidden.

A reading from the first Letter of Saint Paul to the Corinthians

**When I came to you, brothers and sisters,
proclaiming the mystery of God,
I did not come with sublimity of words or of wisdom.
For I resolved to know nothing while I was with you
except Jesus Christ, and him crucified.
I came to you in weakness and fear and much trembling,
and my message and my proclamation
were not with persuasive words of wisdom,
but with a demonstration of spirit and power,
so that your faith might rest not on human wisdom
but on the power of God.**

**Yet we do speak a wisdom to those who are mature,
but not a wisdom of this age,
nor of the rulers of this age who are passing away.
Rather, we speak God's wisdom, mysterious, hidden,
which God predetermined before the ages for our glory,
and which none of the rulers of this age knew;
for, if they had known it,
they would not have crucified the Lord of glory.
But as it is written:**

*What eye has not seen, and ear has not heard,
and what has not entered the human heart,
what God has prepared for those who love him,*

this God has revealed to us through the Spirit.

The word of the Lord.

RESPONSORIAL PSALM

Psalm 96:1-2a, 2b-3, 7-8a, 10

℟. (3) **Proclaim God's marvelous deeds to all the nations.**

Sing to the Lord a new song;
  sing to the Lord, all you lands.
Sing to the Lord; bless his name.

℟. **Proclaim God's marvelous deeds to all the nations.**

Announce his salvation, day after day.
Tell his glory among the nations;
  among all peoples, his wondrous deeds.

℟. **Proclaim his marvelous deeds to all the nations.**

Give to the Lord, you families of nations,
  give to the Lord glory and praise;
  give to the Lord the glory due his name!

℟. **Proclaim God's marvelous deeds to all the nations.**

Say among the nations: The Lord is king.
He has made the world firm, not to be moved;
  he governs the peoples with equity.

℟. **Proclaim God's marvelous deeds to all the nations.**

ALLELUIA

John 8:12

℟. Alleluia, alleluia.

I am the light of the world, says the Lord;
whoever follows me will have the light of life.

℟. Alleluia, alleluia.

GOSPEL

Luke 9:57-62   I will follow you wherever you go.

☩ A reading from the holy Gospel according to Luke

As Jesus and his disciples were proceeding on their journey
   someone said to him, "I will follow you wherever you go."
Jesus answered him,
   "Foxes have dens and birds of the sky have nests,
   but the Son of Man has nowhere to rest his head."
And to another he said, "Follow me."
But he replied, "Lord, let me go first and bury my father."
But he answered him, "Let the dead bury their dead.
But you, go and proclaim the Kingdom of God."
And another said, "I will follow you, Lord,
   but first let me say farewell to my family at home."
He said, "No one who sets a hand to the plow
   and looks to what was left behind is fit for the Kingdom of God."

The Gospel of the Lord.

AUGUST 10

618 SAINT LAWRENCE, DEACON AND MARTYR FEAST

FIRST READING

2 Corinthians 9:6-10   God loves a cheerful giver.

A reading from the second Letter of Saint Paul to the Corinthians

Brothers and sisters:
Whoever sows sparingly will also reap sparingly,
 and whoever sows bountifully will also reap bountifully.
Each must do as already determined, without sadness or compulsion,
 for God loves a cheerful giver.
Moreover, God is able to make every grace abundant for you,
 so that in all things, always having all you need,
 you may have an abundance for every good work.
As it is written:

*He scatters abroad, he gives to the poor;
 his righteousness endures forever.*

The one who supplies seed to the sower and bread for food
 will supply and multiply your seed
 and increase the harvest of your righteousness.

The word of the Lord.

RESPONSORIAL PSALM

Psalm 112:1-2, 5-6, 7-8, 9

℟. (5) **Blessed the man who is gracious and lends to those in need.**

Blessed the man who fears the L ord,
 who greatly delights in his commands.
His posterity shall be mighty upon the earth;
 the upright generation shall be blessed.

℟. **Blessed the man who is gracious and lends to those in need.**

Well for the man who is gracious and lends,
 who conducts his affairs with justice;
He shall never be moved;
 the just one shall be in everlasting remembrance.

℟. **Blessed the man who is gracious and lends to those in need.**

An evil report he shall not fear;
   his heart is firm, trusting in the Lord.
His heart is steadfast; he shall not fear
   till he looks down upon his foes.

℟. Blessed the man who is gracious and lends to those in need.

Lavishly he gives to the poor,
   his generosity shall endure forever;
   his horn shall be exalted in glory.

℟. Blessed the man who is gracious and lends to those in need.

ALLELUIA

John 8:12bc

℟. Alleluia, alleluia.

Whoever follows me will not walk in darkness
but will have the light of life, says the Lord.

℟. Alleluia, alleluia.

GOSPEL

John 12:24-26   The Father will honor whoever serves me.

✠ A reading from the holy Gospel according to John

Jesus said to his disciples:
"Amen, amen, I say to you,
   unless a grain of wheat falls to the ground and dies,
   it remains just a grain of wheat;
   but if it dies, it produces much fruit.
Whoever loves his life loses it,
   and whoever hates his life in this world
   will preserve it for eternal life.
Whoever serves me must follow me,
   and where I am, there also will my servant be.
The Father will honor whoever serves me."

The Gospel of the Lord.

AUGUST 11

619 SAINT CLARE, VIRGIN MEMORIAL

From the Common of Virgins, p. 1857, or the Common of Holy Men and Women: For Religious, p. 1868,

OR

FIRST READING

Philippians 3:8-14   I continue my pursuit toward the goal, the prize of God's upward calling, in Christ Jesus.

A reading from the Letter of Saint Paul to the Philippians

Brothers and sisters:
I consider everything as a loss
   because of the supreme good of knowing Christ Jesus my Lord.
For his sake I have accepted the loss of all things
   and I consider them so much rubbish,
   that I may gain Christ and be found in him,
   not having any righteousness of my own based on the law
   but that which comes through faith in Christ,
   the righteousness from God,
   depending on faith to know him and the power of his resurrection
   and the sharing of his sufferings by being conformed to his death,
   if somehow I may attain the resurrection from the dead.

It is not that I have already taken hold of it
   or have already attained perfect maturity,
   but I continue my pursuit in hope that I may possess it,
   since I have indeed been taken possession of by Christ Jesus.
Brothers and sisters, I for my part
   do not consider myself to have taken possession.
Just one thing: forgetting what lies behind
   but straining forward to what lies ahead,
   I continue my pursuit toward the goal,
   the prize of God's upward calling, in Christ Jesus.

The word of the Lord.

RESPONSORIAL PSALM

Psalm 16:1b-2a, 5, 7-8, 11

℟. (see 5a) **You are my inheritance, O Lord.**

Keep me, O God, for in you I take refuge.
 I say to the LORD**, "My Lord are you."**
O LORD**, my allotted portion and my cup,**
 you it is who hold fast my lot.

℟. **You are my inheritance, O Lord.**

I bless the LORD **who counsels me;**
 even in the night my heart exhorts me.
I set the LORD **ever before me;**
 with him at my right hand I shall not be disturbed.

℟. **You are my inheritance, O Lord.**

You will show me the path to life,
 fullness of joys in your presence,
 the delights at your right hand forever.

℟. **You are my inheritance, O Lord.**

ALLELUIA

Matthew 5:3

℟. **Alleluia, alleluia.**

Blessed are the poor in spirit;
the Kingdom of heaven is theirs!

℟. **Alleluia, alleluia.**

August 11—Saint Clare

GOSPEL

Matthew 19:27-29   You who have followed me will receive a hundred times more.

✟ **A reading from the holy Gospel according to Matthew**

**Peter said to Jesus,
    "We have given up everything and followed you.
What will there be for us?"
Jesus said to them, "Amen, I say to you
    that you who have followed me, in the new age,
    when the Son of Man is seated on his throne of glory,
    will yourselves sit on twelve thrones,
    judging the twelve tribes of Israel.
And everyone who has given up houses or brothers or sisters
    or father or mother or children or lands
    for the sake of my name will receive a hundred times more,
    and will inherit eternal life."**

The Gospel of the Lord.

AUGUST 13

620 SAINT PONTIAN, POPE AND MARTYR AND SAINT HIPPOLYTUS, PRIEST AND MARTYR

From the Common of Martyrs, p. 1782, or the Common of Pastors, p. 1805,

OR

FIRST READING

1 Peter 4:12-19   Rejoice to the extent you share in the sufferings of Christ.

A reading from the first Letter of Saint Peter

Beloved, do not be surprised that a trial by fire is occurring among you,
    as if something strange were happening to you.
But rejoice to the extent that you share in the sufferings of Christ,
    so that when his glory is revealed
    you may also rejoice exultantly.
If you are insulted for the name of Christ, blessed are you,
    for the Spirit of glory and of God rests upon you.
But let no one among you be made to suffer
    as a murderer, a thief, an evildoer, or as an intriguer.
But whoever is made to suffer as a Christian should not be ashamed
    but glorify God because of the name.
For it is time for the judgment to begin with the household of God;
    if it begins with us, how will it end
    for those who fail to obey the Gospel of God?

And if the righteous one is barely saved,
    where will the godless and the sinner appear?

As a result, those who suffer in accord with God's will
    hand their souls over to a faithful creator as they do good.

The word of the Lord.

RESPONSORIAL PSALM

Psalm 124:2-3, 4-5, 7-8

℟. (7) **Our soul has been rescued like a bird from the fowler's snare.**

Had not the Lord been with us—
    when men rose up against us,
Then would they have swallowed us alive
    when their fury was inflamed against us.

℟. **Our soul has been rescued like a bird from the fowler's snare.**

Then would the waters have overwhelmed us;
The torrent would have swept over us;
   over us then would have swept
   the raging waters.

℟. Our soul has been rescued like a bird from the fowler's snare.

Broken was the snare,
   and we were freed.
Our help is in the name of the Lord,
   who made heaven and earth.

℟. Our soul has been rescued like a bird from the fowler's snare.

ALLELUIA

See *Te Deum*

℟. Alleluia, alleluia.

We praise you, O God,
we acclaim you as Lord;
the white-robed army of martyrs praise you.

℟. Alleluia, alleluia.

GOSPEL

John 15:18-21   If they persecuted me, they will also persecute you.

✠ A reading from the holy Gospel according to John

Jesus said to his disciples:
"If the world hates you, realize that it hated me first.
If you belonged to the world, the world would love its own;
   but because you do not belong to the world,
   and I have chosen you out of the world,
   the world hates you.
Remember the word I spoke to you,
   'No slave is greater than his master.'
If they persecuted me, they will also persecute you.
If they kept my word, they will also keep yours.
And they will do all these things to you on account of my name,
   because they do not know the one who sent me."

The Gospel of the Lord.

AUGUST 14

620A SAINT MAXIMILIAN MARY KOLBE, PRIEST AND MARTYR MEMORIAL

From the Common of Martyrs, p. 1782, or the Common of Pastors, p. 1805,

OR

FIRST READING

First Option

Wisdom 3:1-9   As sacrificial offerings he took them to himself.

A reading from the Book of Wisdom

**The souls of the just are in the hand of God,
   and no torment shall touch them.
They seemed, in the view of the foolish, to be dead;
   and their passing away was thought an affliction
   and their going forth from us, utter destruction.
But they are in peace.
For if before men, indeed they be punished,
   yet is their hope full of immortality;
Chastised a little, they shall be greatly blessed,
   because God tried them
   and found them worthy of himself.
As gold in the furnace, he proved them,
   and as sacrificial offerings he took them to himself.
In the time of their visitation they shall shine,
   and shall dart about as sparks through stubble;
They shall judge nations and rule over peoples,
   and the Lord shall be their King forever.
Those who trust in him shall understand truth,
   and the faithful shall abide with him in love:
Because grace and mercy are with his holy ones,
   and his care is with his elect.**

The word of the Lord.

OR

1464   August 14—Saint Maximilian Mary Kolbe

Second Option

1 John 3:14-18   We should lay down our lives for our brothers.

A reading from the first Letter of Saint John

**Beloved:
We know that we have passed from death to life
   because we love our brothers.
Whoever does not love remains in death.
Everyone who hates his brother is a murderer,
   and you know that no murderer has eternal life remaining in him.
The way we came to know love
   was that he laid down his life for us;
   so we ought to lay down our lives for our brothers.
If someone who has worldly means
sees a brother in need and refuses him compassion,
   how can the love of God remain in him?
Children, let us love not in word or speech
   but in deed and truth.**

The word of the Lord.

RESPONSORIAL PSALM

Psalm 116:10-11, 12-13, 16ac-17

℟. (15) **Precious in the eyes of the Lord is the death of his faithful ones.**

**I believed, even when I said,
   "I am greatly afflicted";
I said in my alarm,
   "No man is dependable."**

℟. **Precious in the eyes of the Lord is the death of his faithful ones.**

How shall I make a return to the LORD
   **for all the good he has done for me?
The cup of salvation I will take up,
   and I will call upon the name of the L**ORD.

℟. **Precious in the eyes of the Lord is the death of his faithful ones.**

O LORD, **I am your servant;
   you have loosed my bonds.
To you will I offer sacrifice of thanksgiving,
   and I will call upon the name of the L**ORD.

℟. **Precious in the eyes of the Lord is the death of his faithful ones.**

ALLELUIA

John 12:25

℟. Alleluia, alleluia.

**If you hate your life in this world,
you will preserve it to life eternal.**

℟. Alleluia, alleluia.

GOSPEL

John 15:12-16   This is my commandment: love one another.

✠ **A reading from the holy Gospel according to John**

**Jesus said to his disciples:
"This is my commandment: love one another as I love you.
No one has greater love than this,
   to lay down one's life for one's friends.
You are my friends if you do what I command you.
I no longer call you slaves,
   because a slave does not know what his master is doing.
I have called you friends,
   because I have told you everything I have heard from my Father.
I was not you who chose me, but I who chose you
   and appointed you to go and bear fruit that will remain,
   so that whatever you ask the Father in my name he may give you."**

The Gospel of the Lord.

AUGUST 15

621 THE ASSUMPTION OF THE BLESSED VIRGIN MARY SOLEMNITY

VIGIL

FIRST READING

1 Chronicles 15:3-4, 15-16; 16:1-2   They brought in the ark of God and set it within the tent which David had pitched for it.

A reading from the first Book of Chronicles

David assembled all Israel in Jerusalem to bring the ark of the LORD
    to the place which he had prepared for it.
David also called together the sons of Aaron and the Levites.

The Levites bore the ark of God on their shoulders with poles,
    as Moses had ordained according to the word of the LORD**.**

David commanded the chiefs of the Levites
    to appoint their kinsmen as chanters,
    to play on musical instruments, harps, lyres, and cymbals,
    to make a loud sound of rejoicing.

They brought in the ark of God and set it within the tent
    which David had pitched for it.
Then they offered up burnt offerings and peace offerings to God.
When David had finished offering up the burnt offerings and peace offerings,
    he blessed the people in the name of the LORD**.**

The word of the Lord.

RESPONSORIAL PSALM

Psalm 132:6-7, 9-10, 13-14

℟. (8) **Lord, go up to the place of your rest, you and the ark of your holiness.**

Behold, we heard of it in Ephrathah;
    we found it in the fields of Jaar.
Let us enter his dwelling,
    let us worship at his footstool.

℟. **Lord, go up to the place of your rest, you and the ark of your holiness.**

May your priests be clothed with justice;
 let your faithful ones shout merrily for joy.
For the sake of David your servant,
 reject not the plea of your anointed.

℟. **Lord, go up to the place of your rest, you and the ark of your holiness.**

For the LORD **has chosen Zion;**
 he prefers her for her dwelling.
"Zion is my resting place forever;
 in her will I dwell, for I prefer her."

℟. **Lord, go up to the place of your rest, you and the ark of your holiness.**

SECOND READING

1 Corinthians 15:54b-57   God gave us victory through Jesus Christ.

A reading from the first Letter of Saint Paul to the Corinthians

Brothers and sisters:
When that which is mortal clothes itself with immortality,
 then the word that is written shall come about:

 Death is swallowed up in victory.
 Where, O death, is your victory?
 Where, O death, is your sting?

The sting of death is sin,
 and the power of sin is the law.
But thanks be to God who gives us the victory
 through our Lord Jesus Christ.

The word of the Lord.

ALLELUIA

Luke 11:28

℟. Alleluia, alleluia.

**Blessed are they who hear the word of God
and observe it.**

℟. Alleluia, alleluia.

GOSPEL

Luke 11:27-28   Blessed is the womb that carried you!

✛ **A reading from the holy Gospel according to Luke**

**While Jesus was speaking,
a woman from the crowd called out and said to him,
"Blessed is the womb that carried you
and the breasts at which you nursed."
He replied,
"Rather, blessed are those
who hear the word of God and observe it."**

The Gospel of the Lord.

622 MASS DURING THE DAY

FIRST READING

Revelation 11:19a; 12:1-6a, 10ab   A woman clothed with the sun, with the moon beneath her feet.

A reading from the Book of Revelation

**God's temple in heaven was opened,
 and the ark of his covenant could be seen in the temple.**

**A great sign appeared in the sky, a woman clothed with the sun,
 with the moon under her feet,
 and on her head a crown of twelve stars.
She was with child and wailed aloud in pain as she labored to give birth.
Then another sign appeared in the sky;
 it was a huge red dragon, with seven heads and ten horns,
 and on its heads were seven diadems.
Its tail swept away a third of the stars in the sky
 and hurled them down to the earth.
Then the dragon stood before the woman about to give birth,
 to devour her child when she gave birth.
She gave birth to a son, a male child,
 destined to rule all the nations with an iron rod.
Her child was caught up to God and his throne.
The woman herself fled into the desert
 where she had a place prepared by God.**

**Then I heard a loud voice in heaven say:
 "Now have salvation and power come,
  and the Kingdom of our God
  and the authority of his Anointed One."**

The word of the Lord.

August 15—Assumption of the Blessed Virgin Mary—Mass During the Day

RESPONSORIAL PSALM

Psalm 45:10, 11, 12, 16

℟. (10bc) **The queen stands at your right hand, arrayed in gold.**

The queen takes her place at your right hand in gold of Ophir.

℟. **The queen stands at your right hand, arrayed in gold.**

**Hear, O daughter, and see; turn your ear,
  forget your people and your father's house.**

℟. **The queen stands at your right hand, arrayed in gold.**

**So shall the king desire your beauty;
  for he is your lord.**

℟. **The queen stands at your right hand, arrayed in gold.**

**They are borne in with gladness and joy;
  they enter the palace of the king.**

℟. **The queen stands at your right hand, arrayed in gold.**

August 15—Assumption of the Blessed Virgin Mary—Mass During the Day

SECOND READING

1 Corinthians 15:20-27   Christ, the firstfruits; then those who belong to him.

A reading from the first Letter of Saint Paul to the Corinthians

**Brothers and sisters:
Christ has been raised from the dead,
   the firstfruits of those who have fallen asleep.
For since death came through man,
   the resurrection of the dead came also through man.
For just as in Adam all die,
   so too in Christ shall all be brought to life,
   but each one in proper order:
   Christ the firstfruits;
   then, at his coming, those who belong to Christ;
   then comes the end,
   when he hands over the Kingdom to his God and Father,
   when he has destroyed every sovereignty
   and every authority and power.
For he must reign until he has put all his enemies under his feet.
The last enemy to be destroyed is death,
   for "he subjected everything under his feet."**

The word of the Lord.

ALLELUIA

℟. **Alleluia, alleluia.**

**Mary is taken up to heaven;
a chorus of angels exults.**

℟. **Alleluia, alleluia.**

GOSPEL

Luke 1:39-56   The Almighty has done great things for me; he has raised up the lowly.

✠ A reading from the holy Gospel according to Luke

Mary set out
   and traveled to the hill country in haste
   to a town of Judah,
   where she entered the house of Zechariah
   and greeted Elizabeth.
When Elizabeth heard Mary's greeting,
   the infant leaped in her womb,
   and Elizabeth, filled with the Holy Spirit,
   cried out in a loud voice and said,
   "Blessed are you among women,
   and blessed is the fruit of your womb.
And how does this happen to me,
   that the mother of my Lord should come to me?
For at the moment the sound of your greeting reached my ears,
   the infant in my womb leaped for joy.
Blessed are you who believed
   that what was spoken to you by the Lord
   would be fulfilled."

And Mary said:

   "My soul proclaims the greatness of the Lord;
      my spirit rejoices in God my Savior
      for he has looked with favor on his lowly servant.
   From this day all generations will call me blessed:
      the Almighty has done great things for me
      and holy is his Name.
      He has mercy on those who fear him
      in every generation.
   He has shown the strength of his arm,
      and has scattered the proud in their conceit.
   He has cast down the mighty from their thrones,
      and has lifted up the lowly.
   He has filled the hungry with good things,
      and the rich he has sent away empty.

**He has come to the help of his servant Israel
for he has remembered his promise of mercy,
the promise he made to our fathers,
to Abraham and his children forever."**

**Mary remained with her about three months
and then returned to her home.**

The Gospel of the Lord.

AUGUST 16

623 SAINT STEPHEN OF HUNGARY

From the Common of Holy Men and Women, p. 1868,

>OR

FIRST READING

Deuteronomy 6:3-9   Love the Lord, your God, with all your heart.

A reading from the Book of Deuteronomy

**Moses said to the people:
"Hear, Israel, and be careful to observe these commandments,
    that you may grow and prosper the more,
    in keeping with the promise of the Lord, the God of your fathers,
    to give you a land flowing with milk and honey.**

**"Hear, O Israel! The Lord is our God, the Lord alone!
Therefore, you shall love the Lord, your God,
    with all your heart,
    and with all your soul,
    and with all your strength.
Take to heart these words which I enjoin on you today.
Drill them into your children.
Speak of them at home and abroad, whether you are busy or at rest.
Bind them at your wrist as a sign
    and let them be as a pendant on your forehead.
Write them on the doorposts of your houses and on your gates."**

The word of the Lord.

RESPONSORIAL PSALM

Psalm 112:1bc-2, 3-4, 5-6, 7-8, 9

℟. (1) **Blessed the man who fears the Lord.**

**Blessed the man who fears the Lord,
 who greatly delights in his commands.
His posterity shall be mighty upon the earth;
 the upright generation shall be blessed.**

℟. **Blessed the man who fears the Lord.**

**Wealth and riches shall be in his house;
 his generosity shall endure forever.
Light shines through the darkness for the upright;
 he is gracious and merciful and just.**

℟. **Blessed the man who fears the Lord.**

**Well for the man who is gracious and lends,
 who conducts his affairs with justice;
He shall never be moved;
 the just one shall be in everlasting remembrance.**

℟. **Blessed the man who fears the Lord.**

**An evil report he shall not fear;
 his heart is firm, trusting in the Lord.
His heart is steadfast; he shall not fear
 till he looks down upon his foes.**

℟. **Blessed the man who fears the Lord.**

**Lavishly he gives to the poor,
 his generosity shall endure forever;
 his horn shall be exalted in glory.**

℟. **Blessed the man who fears the Lord.**

ALLELUIA

John 14:23

℟. Alleluia, alleluia.

Whoever loves me will keep my word,
and my Father will love him,
and we will come to him.

℟. Alleluia, alleluia.

GOSPEL

Long Form

Matthew 25:14-30 Since you were faithful in small matters, come, share your master's joy.

✠ A reading from the holy Gospel according to Matthew

**Jesus told his disciples this parable:
"A man who was going on a journey
   called in his servants and entrusted his possessions to them.
To one he gave five talents; to another, two; to a third, one—
   to each according to his ability.
Then he went away.
Immediately the one who received five talents went and traded with them,
   and made another five.
Likewise, the one who received two made another two.
But the one who received one went off and dug a hole in the ground
   and buried his master's money.
After a long time
   the master of those servants came back
   and settled accounts with them.
The one who had received five talents
   came forward bringing the additional five.
He said, 'Master, you gave me five talents.
See, I have made five more.'
His master said to him,
   'Well done, my good and faithful servant.
Since you were faithful in small matters,
   I will give you great responsibilities.
Come, share your master's joy.'
Then the one who had received two talents also came forward and said,
   'Master, you gave me two talents.**

See, I have made two more.'
His master said to him,
   'Well done, my good and faithful servant.
Since you were faithful in small matters,
   I will give you great responsibilities.
Come, share your master's joy.'
Then the one who had received the one talent came forward and said,
   'Master, I knew you were a demanding person,
   harvesting where you did not plant
   and gathering where you did not scatter;
   so out of fear I went off and buried your talent in the ground.
Here it is back.'
His master said to him in reply, 'You wicked, lazy servant!
So you knew that I harvest where I did not plant
   and gather where I did not scatter?
Should you not then have put my money in the bank
   so that I could have got it back with interest on my return?
Now then! Take the talent from him and give it to the one with ten.
For to everyone who has, more will be given and he will grow rich;
   but from the one who has not, even what he has will be taken away.
And throw this useless servant into the darkness outside,
   where there will be wailing and grinding of teeth!'"

The Gospel of the Lord.

OR

Short Form

Matthew 25:14-23 Since you were faithful in small matters, come, share your master's joy.

✝ **A reading from the holy Gospel according to Matthew**

**Jesus told his disciples this parable:
"A man who was going on a journey called in his servants
 and entrusted his possessions to them.
To one he gave five talents; to another, two; to a third, one—
 to each according to his ability.
Then he went away.
Immediately the one who received five talents went and traded with them,
 and made another five.
Likewise, the one who received two made another two.
But the man who received one went off and dug a hole in the ground
 and buried his master's money.
After a long time
 the master of those servants came back
 and settled accounts with them.
The one who had received five talents came forward
 bringing the additional five.
He said, 'Master, you gave me five talents.
See, I have made five more.'
His master said to him,
 'Well done, my good and faithful servant.
Since you were faithful in small matters,
 I will give you great responsibilities.
Come, share your master's joy.'
Then the one who had received two talents also came forward and said,
 'Master, you gave me two talents.
See, I have made two more.'
His master said to him,
 'Well done, my good and faithful servant.
Since you were faithful in small matters,
 I will give you great responsibilities.
Come, share your master's joy!'"**

The Gospel of the Lord.

AUGUST 18

[In the Dioceses of the United States]

623A SAINT JANE FRANCES DE CHANTAL, RELIGIOUS

In the United States this memorial is transferred to this date from December 12. From the Common of Holy Men and Women: For Religious, p. 1868,

OR

FIRST READING

Proverbs 31:10-13, 19-20, 30-31   The woman who fears the Lord will be praised.

A reading from the Book of Proverbs

**When one finds a worthy wife,
  her value is far beyond pearls.
Her husband, entrusting his heart to her,
  has an unfailing prize.
She brings him good, and not evil,
  all the days of her life.
She obtains wool and flax
  and makes cloth with skillful hands.
She puts her hands to the distaff,
  and her fingers ply the spindle.
She reaches out her hands to the poor,
  and extends her arms to the needy.
Charm is deceptive and beauty fleeting;
  the woman who fears the Lord is to be praised.
Give her a reward of her labors,
  and let her works praise her at the city gates.**

The word of the Lord.

RESPONSORIAL PSALM

Psalm 131:1bcde, 2, 3

℟. **In you, Lord, I have found my peace.**

**O Lord, my heart is not proud,
  nor are my eyes haughty;
I busy not myself with great things,
  nor with things too sublime for me.**

℟. **In you, Lord, I have found my peace.**

Nay rather, I have stilled and quieted
  my soul like a weaned child.
Like a weaned child on its mother's lap,
  so is my soul within me.

℟. In you, Lord, I have found my peace.

O Israel, hope in the LORD,
  both now and forever.

℟. In you, Lord, I have found my peace.

ALLELUIA

John 8:31b-32

℟. Alleluia, alleluia.

If you remain in my word, you will truly be my disciples,
and you will know the truth, says the Lord.

℟. Alleluia, alleluia.

GOSPEL

Mark 3:31-35   Whoever does the will of God is my brother and sister and mother.

✠ A reading from the holy Gospel according to Mark

The mother of Jesus and his brothers arrived.
Standing outside they sent word to him and called him.
A crowd seated around him told him,
  "Your mother and your brothers and your sisters
  are outside asking for you."
But he said to them in reply,
  "Who are my mother and my brothers?"
And looking around at those seated in the circle he said,
  "Here are my mother and my brothers.
For whoever does the will of God
  is my brother and sister and mother."

The Gospel of the Lord.

AUGUST 19

624 SAINT JOHN EUDES, PRIEST

From the Common of Pastors, p. 1805, or the Common of Holy Men and Women, p. 1868,

OR

FIRST READING

Ephesians 3:14-19   To know the love of Christ that surpasses all knowledge.

A reading from the Letter of Saint Paul to the Ephesians

Brothers and sisters:
I kneel before the Father,
   from whom every family in heaven and on earth is named,
   that he may grant you, in accord with the riches of his glory,
   to be strengthened with power through his Spirit in the inner self,
   and that Christ may dwell in your hearts through faith;
   that you, rooted and grounded in love,
   may have strength to comprehend with all the holy ones
   what is the breadth and length and height and depth,
   and to know the love of Christ that surpasses knowledge,
   so that you may be filled with all the fullness of God.

The word of the Lord.

RESPONSORIAL PSALM

Psalm 131:1bcde, 2, 3

℟. In you, Lord, I have found my peace.

O Lord, my heart is not proud,
   nor are my eyes haughty;
I busy not myself with great things,
   nor with things too sublime for me.

℟. In you, Lord, I have found my peace.

Nay rather, I have stilled and quieted
   my soul like a weaned child.
Like a weaned child on its mother's lap,
   so is my soul within me.

℟. In you, Lord, I have found my peace.

O Israel, hope in the LORD,
> both now and forever.

℟. In you, Lord, I have found my peace.

ALLELUIA

See Matthew 11:25

℟. Alleluia, alleluia.

**Blessed are you, Father, Lord of heaven and earth;
you have revealed to little ones the mysteries of the Kingdom.**

℟. Alleluia, alleluia.

GOSPEL

Matthew 11:25-30   You have hidden these things from the wise and revealed them to the childlike.

☩ **A reading from the holy Gospel according to Matthew**

**At that time Jesus answered:
"I give praise to you, Father, Lord of heaven and earth,
> for although you have hidden these things
> from the wise and the learned
> you have revealed them to the childlike.
Yes, Father, such has been your gracious will.
All things have been handed over to me by my Father.
No one knows the Son except the Father,
> and no one knows the Father except the Son
> and anyone to whom the Son wishes to reveal him.**

**"Come to me, all you who labor and are burdened,
> and I will give you rest.
Take my yoke upon you and learn from me,
> for I am meek and humble of heart;
> and you will find rest for yourselves.
For my yoke is easy, and my burden light."**

The Gospel of the Lord.

AUGUST 20

625 SAINT BERNARD, ABBOT AND DOCTOR OF THE CHURCH MEMORIAL

From the Common of Doctors of the Church, p. 1838, or the Common of Holy Men and Women: For Religious, p. 1868,

OR

FIRST READING

Sirach 15:1-6   He will be filled with the spirit of wisdom and understanding.

A reading from the Book of Sirach

He who fears the Lord will do this;
  he who is practiced in the law will come to wisdom.
Motherlike she will meet him,
  like a young bride she will embrace him,
Nourish him with the bread of understanding,
  and give him the water of learning to drink.
He will lean upon her and not fall,
  he will trust in her and not be put to shame.
She will exalt him above his fellows;
  and in the midst of the assembly she will open his mouth
  and fill him with the spirit of wisdom and understanding,
  and clothe him with the robe of glory.
Joy and gladness he will find,
  an everlasting name he will inherit.

The word of the Lord.

RESPONSORIAL PSALM

Psalm 119:9, 10, 11, 12, 13, 14

℟. (12) **Lord, teach me your statutes.**

**How shall a young man be faultless in his way?
By keeping to your words.**

℟. **Lord, teach me your statutes.**

**With all my heart I seek you;
let me not stray from your commands.**

℟. **Lord, teach me your statutes.**

**Within my heart I treasure your promise,
that I may not sin against you.**

℟. **Lord, teach me your statutes.**

**Blessed are you, O LORD;
teach me your statutes.**

℟. **Lord, teach me your statutes.**

**With my lips I declare
all the ordinances of your mouth.**

℟. **Lord, teach me your statutes.**

**In the way of your decrees I rejoice,
as much as in all riches.**

℟. **Lord, teach me your statutes.**

ALLELUIA

John 15:9b, 5b

℟. Alleluia, alleluia.

**Remain in my love, says the Lord;
whoever lives in me and I in him will bear much fruit.**

℟. Alleluia, alleluia.

GOSPEL

John 17:20-26   I wish that where I am they also may be with me.

✠ A reading from the holy Gospel according to John

**Jesus raised his eyes to heaven and said:
"Holy Father,
I pray not only for these,
but also for those who will believe in me through their word,
so that they may all be one,
as you, Father, are in me and I in you,
that they also may be in us,
that the world may believe that you sent me.
And I have given them the glory you gave me,
so that they may be one, as we are one,
I in them and you in me,
that they may be brought to perfection as one,
that the world may know that you sent me,
and that you loved them even as you loved me.
Father, they are your gift to me.
I wish that where I am they also may be with me,
that they may see my glory that you gave me,
because you loved me before the foundation of the world.
Righteous Father, the world also does not know you,
but I know you, and they know that you sent me.
I made known to them your name and I will make it known,
that the love with which you loved me
may be in them and I in them."**

The Gospel of the Lord.

AUGUST 21

626 SAINT PIUS X, POPE MEMORIAL

From the Common of Pastors: For a Pope, p. 1805,

OR

FIRST READING

1 Thessalonians 2:2b-8   We were determined to share with you not only the Gospel of God, but our very selves as well.

A reading from the first Letter of Saint Paul to the Thessalonians

Brothers and sisters:
We drew courage through our God
   to speak to you the Gospel of God with much struggle.
Our exhortation was not from delusion or impure motives,
   nor did it work through deception.
But as we were judged worthy by God to be entrusted with the Gospel,
   that is how we speak,
   not as trying to please men,
   but rather God, who judges our hearts.
Nor, indeed, did we ever appear with flattering speech, as you know,
   or with a pretext for greed—God is witness—nor did we seek praise
   from men, either from you or from others,
   although we were able to impose our weight as Apostles of Christ.
Rather, we were gentle among you,
   as a nursing mother cares for her children.
With such affection for you,
   we were determined to share with you not only the Gospel of God,
   but our very selves as well, so dearly beloved had you become to us.

The word of the Lord.

RESPONSORIAL PSALM

Psalm 89:2-3, 4-5, 21-22, 25 and 27

℟. (2) **For ever I will sing the goodness of the Lord.**

The favors of the Lord I will sing forever;
   through all generations my mouth shall proclaim your faithfulness.
For you have said, "My kindness is established forever";
   in heaven you have confirmed your faithfulness.

℟. **For ever I will sing the goodness of the Lord.**

"I have made a covenant with my chosen one,
   I have sworn to David my servant:
Forever will I confirm your posterity
   and establish your throne for all generations."

℟. **For ever I will sing the goodness of the Lord.**

"I have found David, my servant;
   with my holy oil I have anointed him,
That my hand may be always with him,
   and that my arm may make him strong."

℟. **For ever I will sing the goodness of the Lord.**

"My faithfulness and my mercy shall be with him,
   and through my name shall his horn be exalted.
He shall say of me, 'You are my father,
   my God, the rock, my savior.'"

℟. **For ever I will sing the goodness of the Lord.**

ALLELUIA

John 10:14

℟. Alleluia, alleluia.

I am the good shepherd, says the Lord;
I know my sheep, and mine know me.

℟. Alleluia, alleluia.

GOSPEL

John 21:15-17   Feed my lambs, feed my sheep.

✠ A reading from the holy Gospel according to John

After Jesus had revealed himself to his disciples and
    eaten breakfast with them,
    he said to Simon Peter,
    "Simon, son of John, do you love me more than these?"
Simon Peter answered him, "Yes, Lord, you know that I love you."
Jesus said to him, "Feed my lambs."
He then said to Simon Peter a second time,
    "Simon, son of John, do you love me?"
Simon Peter answered him, "Yes, Lord, you know that I love you."
He said to him, "Tend my sheep."
He said to him the third time,
    "Simon, son of John, do you love me?"
Peter was distressed that he had said to him a third time,
    "Do you love me?" and he said to him,
    "Lord, you know everything; you know that I love you."
[Jesus] said to him, "Feed my sheep."

The Gospel of the Lord.

AUGUST 22

627 THE QUEENSHIP OF THE BLESSED VIRGIN MARY
MEMORIAL

From the Common of the Blessed Virgin Mary, p. 1751,

OR

FIRST READING

Isaiah 9:1-6   A son is given us.

A reading from the Book of the Prophet Isaiah

> The people who walked in darkness
>   have seen a great light;
> Upon those who dwelt in the land of gloom
>   a light has shone.
> You have brought them abundant joy
>   and great rejoicing,
> As they rejoice before you as at the harvest,
>   as men make merry when dividing spoils.
> For the yoke that burdened them,
>   the pole on their shoulder,
> And the rod of their taskmaster
>   you have smashed, as on the day of Midian.
> For every boot that tramped in battle,
>   every cloak rolled in blood,
>   will be burned as fuel for flames.
>
> For a child is born to us, a son is given us;
>   upon his shoulder dominion rests.
> They name him Wonder-Counselor, God-Hero,
>   Father-Forever, Prince of Peace.
> His dominion is vast
>   and forever peaceful,
> From David's throne, and over his kingdom,
>   which he confirms and sustains
> By judgment and justice,
>   both now and forever.
> The zeal of the Lord of hosts will do this!

The word of the Lord.

RESPONSORIAL PSALM

Psalm 113:1-2, 3-4, 5-6, 7-8

℟. (2) **Blessed be the name of the Lord for ever.**
or:
℟. **Alleluia.**

**Praise, you servants of the Lord,
  praise the name of the Lord.
Blessed be the name of the Lord
  both now and forever.**

℟. **Blessed be the name of the Lord for ever.**
or:
℟. **Alleluia.**

**From the rising to the setting of the sun
  is the name of the Lord to be praised.
High above all nations is the Lord;
  above the heavens is his glory.**

℟. **Blessed be the name of the Lord for ever.**
or:
℟. **Alleluia.**

**Who is like the Lord, our God, who is enthroned on high
  and looks upon the heavens and the earth below?**

℟. **Blessed be the name of the Lord for ever.**
or:
℟. **Alleluia.**

**He raises up the lowly from the dust;
  from the dunghill he lifts up the poor
To seat them with princes,
  with the princes of his own people.**

℟. **Blessed be the name of the Lord for ever.**
or:
℟. **Alleluia.**

ALLELUIA

See Luke 1:28

℟. **Alleluia, alleluia.**

**Hail, Mary, full of grace, the Lord is with you;
blessed are you among women.**

℟. **Alleluia, alleluia.**

GOSPEL

Luke 1:26-38   You will conceive in your womb and bear a son.

✠ **A reading from the holy Gospel according to Luke**

The angel Gabriel was sent from God
   to a town of Galilee called Nazareth,
   to a virgin betrothed to a man named Joseph,
   of the house of David,
   and the virgin's name was Mary.
And coming to her, he said,
   "Hail, full of grace! The Lord is with you."
But she was greatly troubled at what was said
   and pondered what sort of greeting this might be.
Then the angel said to her,
   "Do not be afraid, Mary,
   for you have found favor with God.
Behold, you will conceive in your womb and bear a son,
   and you shall name him Jesus.
He will be great and will be called Son of the Most High,
   and the Lord God will give him the throne of David his father,
   and he will rule over the house of Jacob forever,
   and of his Kingdom there will be no end."
But Mary said to the angel,
   "How can this be,
   since I have no relations with a man?"
And the angel said to her in reply,
   "The Holy Spirit will come upon you,
   and the power of the Most High will overshadow you.
Therefore the child to be born
   will be called holy, the Son of God.
And behold, Elizabeth, your relative,
   has also conceived a son in her old age,
   and this is the sixth month for her who was called barren;
   for nothing will be impossible for God."
Mary said, "Behold, I am the handmaid of the Lord.
May it be done to me according to your word."
Then the angel departed from her.

The Gospel of the Lord.

AUGUST 23

628 SAINT ROSE OF LIMA, VIRGIN

From the Common of Virgins, p. 1857, or the Common of Holy Men and Women: For Religious, p. 1868,

OR

FIRST READING

2 Corinthians 10:17–11:2   I betrothed you to one husband to present you as a chaste virgin to Christ.

A reading from the second Letter of Saint Paul to the Corinthians

Brothers and sisters:
"Whoever boasts, should boast in the Lord."
For it is not the one who recommends himself who is approved,
　but he whom the Lord recommends.

If only you would put up with a little foolishness from me!
Please put up with me.
For I am jealous of you with the jealousy of God,
　since I betrothed you to one husband
　to present you as a chaste virgin to Christ.

The word of the Lord.

RESPONSORIAL PSALM

Psalm 148:1bc-2, 11-13a, 13c-14

℟. (see 12a and 13a) **Young men and women, praise the name of the Lord.**
　or:
℟. **Alleluia.**

Praise the Lord from the heavens;
　praise him in the heights;
Praise him, all you his angels,
　praise him, all you his hosts.

℟. **Young men and women, praise the name of the Lord.**
　or:
℟. **Alleluia.**

Let the kings of the earth and all peoples,
   the princes and all the judges of the earth,
Young men, too, and maidens,
   old men and boys,
Praise the name of the LORD,
   for his name alone is exalted.

℟. Young men and women, praise the name of the Lord.
   or:
℟. Alleluia.

His majesty is above earth and heaven.
He has lifted up the horn of his people.
Be this his praise from all his faithful ones;
   from the children of Israel, the people close to him. Alleluia.

℟. Young men and women, praise the name of the Lord.
   or:
℟. Alleluia.

ALLELUIA

John 15:9b, 5b

℟. Alleluia, alleluia.

Remain in my love, says the Lord;
whoever lives in me and I in him will bear much fruit.

℟. Alleluia, alleluia.

GOSPEL

Matthew 13:44-46   He sells all that he has and buys that field.

✠ A reading from the holy Gospel according to Matthew

Jesus said to his disciples:
"The Kingdom of heaven is like a treasure buried in a field,
   which a person finds and hides again,
   and out of joy goes and sells all that he has and buys that field.
Again, the Kingdom of heaven is like a merchant
   searching for fine pearls.
When he finds a pearl of great price,
   he goes and sells all that he has and buys it."

The Gospel of the Lord.

AUGUST 24

629 SAINT BARTHOLOMEW, APOSTLE FEAST

FIRST READING

Revelation 21:9b-14   On the foundation of the city were inscribed the names of the twelve Apostles of the Lamb.

A reading from the Book of Revelation

The angel spoke to me, saying,
  "Come here.
I will show you the bride, the wife of the Lamb."
He took me in spirit to a great, high mountain
  and showed me the holy city Jerusalem
  coming down out of heaven from God.
It gleamed with the splendor of God.
Its radiance was like that of a precious stone,
  like jasper, clear as crystal.
It had a massive, high wall,
  with twelve gates where twelve angels were stationed
  and on which names were inscribed,
  the names of the twelve tribes of the children of Israel.
There were three gates facing east,
  three north, three south, and three west.
The wall of the city had twelve courses of stones as its foundation,
  on which were inscribed the twelve names
  of the twelve Apostles of the Lamb.

The word of the Lord.

RESPONSORIAL PSALM

Psalm 145:10-11, 12-13, 17-18

℟. (12) **Your friends make known, O Lord, the glorious splendor of your Kingdom.**

Let all your works give you thanks, O LORD,
 and let your faithful ones bless you.
Let them discourse of the glory of your Kingdom
 and speak of your might.

℟. **Your friends make known, O Lord, the glorious splendor of your Kingdom.**

Making known to men your might
 and the glorious splendor of your Kingdom.
Your Kingdom is a Kingdom for all ages,
 and your dominion endures through all generations.

℟. **Your friends make known, O Lord, the glorious splendor of your Kingdom.**

The LORD is just in all his ways
 and holy in all his works.
The LORD is near to all who call upon him,
 to all who call upon him in truth.

℟. **Your friends make known, O Lord, the glorious splendor of your Kingdom.**

ALLELUIA

John 1:49b

℟. **Alleluia, alleluia.**

Rabbi, you are the Son of God;
you are the King of Israel.

℟. **Alleluia, alleluia.**

GOSPEL

John 1:45-51   Here is a true child of Israel. There is no duplicity in him.

✛ A reading from the holy Gospel according to John

Philip found Nathanael and told him,
  "We have found the one about whom Moses wrote in the law,
  and also the prophets, Jesus son of Joseph, from Nazareth."
But Nathanael said to him,
  "Can anything good come from Nazareth?"
Philip said to him, "Come and see."
Jesus saw Nathanael coming toward him and said of him,
  "Here is a true child of Israel.
There is no duplicity in him."
Nathanael said to him, "How do you know me?"
Jesus answered and said to him,
  "Before Philip called you, I saw you under the fig tree."
Nathanael answered him,
  "Rabbi, you are the Son of God; you are the King of Israel."
Jesus answered and said to him,
  "Do you believe
  because I told you that I saw you under the fig tree?
You will see greater things than this."
And he said to him, "Amen, amen, I say to you,
  you will see heaven opened and the angels of God
  ascending and descending on the Son of Man."

The Gospel of the Lord.

AUGUST 25

630 SAINT LOUIS OF FRANCE

From the Common of Holy Men and Women, p. 1868,

OR

FIRST READING

Isaiah 58:6-11   Share your bread with the hungry.

A reading from the Book of the Prophet Isaiah

Thus says the Lord:
  This is the fasting that I wish:
    releasing those bound unjustly,
    untying the thongs of the yoke;
  Setting free the oppressed,
    breaking every yoke;
  Sharing your bread with the hungry,
    sheltering the oppressed and the homeless;
  Clothing the naked when you see them,
    and not turning your back on your own.

  Then your light shall break forth like the dawn,
    and your wound shall quickly be healed;
  Your vindication shall go before you,
    and the glory of the Lord shall be your rear guard.
  Then you shall call, and the Lord will answer,
    you shall cry for help, and he will say: Here I am!
  If you remove from your midst oppression,
    false accusation and malicious speech;
  If you bestow your bread on the hungry
    and satisfy the afflicted;
  Then light shall rise for you in the darkness,
    and the gloom shall become for you like midday;
  Then the Lord will guide you always
    and give you plenty even on the parched land.
  He will renew your strength,
    and you shall be like a watered garden,
    like a spring whose water never fails.

The word of the Lord.

August 25—Saint Louis of France

RESPONSORIAL PSALM

Psalm 112:1-2, 3-4, 5-7, 7-8, 9

℟. (1) **Blessed the man who fears the Lord.**
or:
℟. **Alleluia.**

Blessed the man who fears the LORD**,
 who greatly delights in his commands.
His posterity shall be mighty upon the earth;
 the upright generation shall be blessed.**

℟. **Blessed the man who fears the Lord.**
or:
℟. **Alleluia.**

**Wealth and riches shall be in his house;
 his generosity shall endure forever.
Light shines through the darkness for the upright;
 he is gracious and merciful and just.**

℟. **Blessed the man who fears the Lord.**
or:
℟. **Alleluia.**

**Well for the man who is gracious and lends,
 who conducts his affairs with justice;
He shall never be moved;
 the just one shall be in everlasting remembrance.**

℟. **Blessed the man who fears the Lord.**
or:
℟. **Alleluia.**

**An evil report he shall not fear;
 his heart is firm, trusting in the L**ORD**.
His heart is steadfast; he shall not fear
 till he looks down upon his foes.**

℟. **Blessed the man who fears the Lord.**
or:
℟. **Alleluia.**

**Lavishly he gives to the poor,
 his generosity shall endure forever;
 his horn shall be exalted in glory.**

℟. **Blessed the man who fears the Lord.**
or:
℟. **Alleluia.**

ALLELUIA

John 13:34

℟. Alleluia, alleluia.

I give you a new commandment:
love one another, as I have loved you.

℟. Alleluia, alleluia.

GOSPEL

Matthew 22:34-40   You shall love the Lord, your God, and your neighbor as yourself.

✠ A reading from the holy Gospel according to Matthew

When the Pharisees heard that Jesus had silenced the Sadducees,
   they gathered together, and one of them,
   a scholar of the law, tested him by asking,
   "Teacher, which commandment in the law is the greatest?"
He said to him,
   "You shall love the Lord, your God, with all your heart,
   with all your soul, and with all your mind.
This is the greatest and the first commandment.
The second is like it:
   You shall love your neighbor as yourself.
The whole law and the prophets depend on these two commandments."

The Gospel of the Lord.

AUGUST 25

631 SAINT JOSEPH CALASANZ, PRIEST

From the Common of Pastors, p. 1805, or the Common of Holy Men and Women: For Teachers, p. 1868,

OR

FIRST READING

Long Form

1 Corinthians 12:31–13:13   Love never fails.

A reading from the first Letter of Saint Paul to the Corinthians

Brothers and sisters:
Strive eagerly for the greatest spiritual gifts.

But I shall show you a still more excellent way.

If I speak in human and angelic tongues
   but do not have love,
   I am a resounding gong or a clashing cymbal.
And if I have the gift of prophecy
   and comprehend all mysteries and all knowledge;
   if I have all faith so as to move mountains,
   but do not have love, I am nothing.
If I give away everything I own,
   and if I hand my body over so that I may boast
   but do not have love, I gain nothing.

Love is patient, love is kind.
It is not jealous, love is not pompous,
   it is not inflated, it is not rude,
   it does not seek its own interests,
   it is not quick-tempered, it does not brood over injury, it does not rejoice
      over wrongdoing
   but rejoices with the truth.
It bears all things, believes all things,
   hopes all things, endures all things.

Love never fails.
If there are prophecies, they will be brought to nothing;
   if tongues, they will cease;
   if knowledge, it will be brought to nothing.
For we know partially and we prophesy partially,
   but when the perfect comes, the partial will pass away.

When I was a child, I used to talk as a child,
  think as a child, reason as a child;
    when I became a man, I put aside childish things.
At present we see indistinctly, as in a mirror,
  but then face to face.
At present I know partially;
  then I shall know fully, as I am fully known.
So faith, hope, love remain, these three;
  but the greatest of these is love.

The word of the Lord.

OR

Short Form

1 Corinthians 13:4-13   Love never fails.

A reading from the first Letter of Saint Paul to the Corinthians

Brothers and sisters:
Love is patient, love is kind.
It is not jealous, it is not pompous,
  it is not inflated, it is not rude,
  it does not seek its own interests,
    it is not quick-tempered, it does not brood over injury, it does not rejoice over wrongdoing
  but rejoices with the truth.
It bears all things, believes all things,
  hopes all things, endures all things.

Love never fails.
If there are prophecies, they will be brought to nothing;
  if tongues, they will cease;
  if knowledge, it will be brought to nothing.
For we know partially and we prophesy partially,
  but when the perfect comes, the partial will pass away.
When I was a child, I used to talk as a child,
  think as a child, reason as a child;
    when I became a man, I put aside childish things.
At present we see indistinctly, as in a mirror,
  but then face to face.
At present I know partially;
  then I shall know fully, as I am fully known.
So faith, hope, love remain, these three;
  but the greatest of these is love.

The word of the Lord.

RESPONSORIAL PSALM

Psalm 34:2-3, 4-5, 6-7, 8-9, 10-11

℟. (2) I will bless the Lord at all times.
  or:
℟. (9) Taste and see the goodness of the Lord.

I will bless the Lord at all times;
  his praise shall be ever in my mouth.
Let my soul glory in the Lord;
  the lowly will hear me and be glad.

℟. I will bless the Lord at all times.
  or:
℟. Taste and see the goodness of the Lord.

Glorify the Lord with me,
  let us together extol his name.
I sought the Lord, and he answered me
  and delivered me from all my fears.

℟. I will bless the Lord at all times.
  or:
℟. Taste and see the goodness of the Lord.

Look to him that you may be radiant with joy,
  and your faces may not blush with shame.
When the poor one called out, the Lord heard,
  and from all his distress he saved him.

℟. I will bless the Lord at all times.
  or:
℟. Taste and see the goodness of the Lord.

The angel of the Lord encamps
  around those who fear him, and delivers them.
Taste and see how good the Lord is;
  blessed the man who takes refuge in him.

℟. I will bless the Lord at all times.
  or:
℟. Taste and see the goodness of the Lord.

Fear the Lord, you his holy ones,
> for nought is lacking to those who fear him.
The great grow poor and hungry;
> but those who seek the Lord want for no good thing.

℟. I will bless the Lord at all times.

or:

℟. Taste and see the goodness of the Lord.

ALLELUIA

John 15:9b, 5b

℟. Alleluia, alleluia.

**Remain in my love, says the Lord;
whoever remains in me and I in him will bear much fruit.**

℟. Alleluia, alleluia.

GOSPEL

Matthew 18:1-5   Unless you become like children, you will not enter the Kingdom of heaven.

✠ A reading from the holy Gospel according to Matthew

The disciples approached Jesus and said,
> "Who is the greatest in the Kingdom of heaven?"
He called a child over, placed it in their midst, and said,
> "Amen, I say to you, unless you turn and become like children,
> you will not enter the Kingdom of heaven.
Whoever humbles himself like this child
> is the greatest in the Kingdom of heaven.
And whoever receives one child such as this in my name receives me."

The Gospel of the Lord.

AUGUST 27

632 SAINT MONICA MEMORIAL

From the Common of Holy Men and Women, p. 1868,

OR

FIRST READING

Sirach 26:1-4, 13-16 Like the sun rising in the Lord's heavens, the beauty of a virtuous wife is the radiance of her home.

A reading from the Book of Sirach

**Blessed the husband of a good wife,
    twice-lengthened are his days;
A worthy wife brings joy to her husband,
    peaceful and full is his life.
A good wife is a generous gift
    bestowed upon him who fears the Lord;
Be he rich or poor, his heart is content,
    and a smile is ever on his face.**

**A gracious wife delights her husband,
    her thoughtfulness puts flesh on his bones;
A gift from the Lord is her governed speech,
    and her firm virtue is of surpassing worth.
Choicest of blessings is a modest wife,
    priceless her chaste soul.
A holy and decent woman adds grace upon grace;
    indeed, no price is worthy of her temperate soul.
Like the sun rising in the Lord's heavens,
    the beauty of a virtuous wife is the radiance of her home.**

The word of the Lord.

RESPONSORIAL PSALM

Psalm 131:1bcde, 2, 3

℟. In you, Lord, I have found my peace.

O Lord, my heart is not proud,
   nor are my eyes haughty;
I busy not myself with great things,
   nor with things too sublime for me.

℟. In you, Lord, I have found my peace.

Nay rather, I have stilled and quieted
   my soul like a weaned child.
Like a weaned child on its mother's lap,
   so is my soul within me.

℟. In you, Lord, I have found my peace.

O Israel, hope in the Lord,
   both now and forever.

℟. In you, Lord, I have found my peace.

ALLELUIA

John 8:12

℟. Alleluia, alleluia.

I am the light of the world, says the Lord;
whoever follows me will have the light of life.

℟. Alleluia, alleluia.

GOSPEL

Luke 7:11-17   She bore me in the arms of her prayer, that you might say to the son of the widow: Young man, I say to you, arise (Saint Augustine, Confessions, book 6, no. 2).

☩   A reading from the holy Gospel according to Luke

Jesus journeyed to a city called Nain,
   and his disciples and a large crowd accompanied him.
As he drew near to the gate of the city,
   a man who had died was being carried out,
   the only son of his mother, and she was a widow.
A large crowd from the city was with her.
When the Lord saw her,
   he was moved with pity for her and said to her,
   "Do not weep."
He stepped forward and touched the coffin;
   at this the bearers halted,
   and he said, "Young man, I tell you, arise!"
The dead man sat up and began to speak,
   and Jesus gave him to his mother.
Fear seized them all, and they glorified God, exclaiming,
   "A great prophet has arisen in our midst,"
   and "God has visited his people."
This report about him spread through the whole of Judea
   and in all the surrounding region.

The Gospel of the Lord.

AUGUST 28

633 SAINT AUGUSTINE, BISHOP AND DOCTOR OF THE CHURCH MEMORIAL

From the Common of Pastors, p. 1805, or the Common of Doctors of the Church, p. 1838,

OR

FIRST READING

1 John 4:7-16   If we love one another, God will live in us.

A reading from the first Letter of Saint John

Beloved, let us love one another,
  because love is of God;
  everyone who loves is begotten by God and knows God.
Whoever is without love does not know God, for God is love.
In this way the love of God was revealed to us:
  God sent his only-begotten Son into the world
  so that we might have life through him.
In this is love:
  not that we have loved God, but that he loved us
  and sent his Son as expiation for our sins.
Beloved, if God so loved us,
  we also must love one another.
No one has ever seen God.
Yet, if we love one another, God remains in us,
  and his love is brought to perfection in us.

This is how we know that we remain in him and he in us,
  that he has given us of his Spirit.
Moreover, we have seen and testify
  that the Father sent his Son as savior of the world.
Whoever acknowledges that Jesus is the Son of God,
  God remains in him and he in God.
We have come to know and to believe in the love God has for us.

God is love, and whoever remains in love
  remains in God and God in him.

The word of the Lord.

RESPONSORIAL PSALM

Psalm 119:9, 10, 11, 12, 13, 14

℟. (12) **Lord, teach me your statutes.**

**How shall a young man be faultless in his way?
By keeping to your words.**

℟. **Lord, teach me your statutes.**

**With all my heart I seek you;
let me not stray from your commands.**

℟. **Lord, teach me your statutes.**

**Within my heart I treasure your promise,
that I may not sin against you.**

℟. **Lord, teach me your statutes.**

**Blessed are you, O Lord;
teach me your statutes.**

℟. **Lord, teach me your statutes.**

**With my lips I declare
all the ordinances of your mouth.**

℟. **Lord, teach me your statutes.**

**In the way of your decrees I rejoice,
as much as in all riches.**

℟. **Lord, teach me your statutes.**

ALLELUIA

Matthew 23:9b, 10b

℟. Alleluia, alleluia.

You have but one Father, in heaven;
you have but one master, the Christ.

℟. Alleluia, alleluia.

GOSPEL

Matthew 23:8-12   Do not be called 'Master'; you have one master, the Christ.

✠ A reading from the holy Gospel according to Matthew

Jesus spoke to his disciples:
"Do not be called 'Rabbi.'
You have but one teacher, and you are all brothers.
Call no one on earth your father;
   you have but one Father in heaven.
Do not be called 'Master';
   you have but one master, the Christ.
The greatest among you must be your servant.
Whoever exalts himself will be humbled;
   but whoever humbles himself will be exalted."

The Gospel of the Lord.

AUGUST 29

634 THE MARTYRDOM OF SAINT JOHN THE BAPTIST
MEMORIAL

The Gospel for this memorial is proper.

FIRST READING

Jeremiah 1:17-19   Stand up and tell them all that I command you.

A reading from the Book of the Prophet Jeremiah

**The word of the Lord came to me thus:
   Gird your loins;
      stand up and tell them
      all that I command you.
   Be not crushed on their account,
      as though I would leave you crushed before them;
   For it is I this day
      who have made you a fortified city,
   A pillar of iron, a wall of brass,
      against the whole land:
   Against Judah's kings and princes,
      against its priests and people.
   They will fight against you, but not prevail over you,
      for I am with you to deliver you, says the Lord.**

The word of the Lord.

RESPONSORIAL PSALM

Psalm 71:1-2, 3-4a, 5-6ab, 15ab and 17

℟. (see 15ab) **I will sing your salvation.**

**In you, O Lord, I take refuge;
    let me never be put to shame.
In your justice rescue me, and deliver me;
    incline your ear to me, and save me.**

℟. **I will sing your salvation.**

**Be my rock of refuge,
    a stronghold to give me safety,
    for you are my rock and my fortress.
O my God, rescue me from the hand of the wicked.**

℟. **I will sing your salvation.**

**For you are my hope, O Lord;
    my trust, O God, from my youth.
On you I depend from birth;
    from my mother's womb you are my strength.**

℟. **I will sing your salvation.**

**My mouth shall declare your justice,
    day by day your salvation.
O God, you have taught me from my youth,
    and till the present I proclaim your wondrous deeds.**

℟. **I will sing your salvation.**

ALLELUIA

Matthew 5:10

℟. **Alleluia, alleluia.**

**Blessed are those who are persecuted for the sake of righteousness,
for theirs is the Kingdom of heaven.**

℟. **Alleluia, alleluia.**

August 29—The Martyrdom of Saint John the Baptist

GOSPEL

Mark 6:17-29   I want you to give me at once on a platter the head of John the Baptist.

✠ **A reading from the holy Gospel according to Mark**

Herod was the one who had John the Baptist arrested and bound in prison
  on account of Herodias,
  the wife of his brother Philip, whom he had married.
John had said to Herod,
  "It is not lawful for you to have your brother's wife."
Herodias harbored a grudge against him
  and wanted to kill him but was unable to do so.
Herod feared John, knowing him to be a righteous and holy man,
  and kept him in custody.
When he heard him speak he was very much perplexed,
  yet he liked to listen to him.
She had an opportunity one day when Herod, on his birthday,
  gave a banquet for his courtiers,
  his military officers, and the leading men of Galilee.
Herodias' own daughter came in
  and performed a dance that delighted Herod and his guests.
The king said to the girl,
  "Ask of me whatever you wish and I will grant it to you."
He even swore many things to her,
  "I will grant you whatever you ask of me,
  even to half of my kingdom."
She went out and said to her mother,
  "What shall I ask for?"
She replied, "The head of John the Baptist."
The girl hurried back to the king's presence and made her request,
  "I want you to give me at once
  on a platter the head of John the Baptist."
The king was deeply distressed,
  but because of his oaths and the guests
  he did not wish to break his word to her.
So he promptly dispatched an executioner with orders
  to bring back his head.
He went off and beheaded him in the prison.
He brought in the head on a platter and gave it to the girl.
The girl in turn gave it to her mother.
When his disciples heard about it,
  they came and took his body and laid it in a tomb.

The Gospel of the Lord.

SEPTEMBER 3

635 SAINT GREGORY THE GREAT, POPE AND DOCTOR OF THE CHURCH MEMORIAL

From the Common of Pastors: For a Pope, p. 1805, or the Common of Doctors of the Church, p. 1838,

OR

FIRST READING

2 Corinthians 4:1-2, 5-7   We preach Jesus Christ as Lord and ourselves as your slaves for the sake of Jesus.

A reading from the second Letter of Saint Paul to the Corinthians

Brothers and sisters:
Since we have this ministry through the mercy shown us,
 we are not discouraged.
Rather, we have renounced shameful, hidden things;
 not acting deceitfully or falsifying the word of God,
 but by the open declaration of the truth
 we commend ourselves to everyone's conscience in the sight of God.
For we do not preach ourselves but Jesus Christ as Lord,
 and ourselves as your slaves for the sake of Jesus.
For God who said, "Let light shine out of darkness,"
 has shone in our hearts to bring to light
 the knowledge of the glory of God on the face of Jesus Christ.

But we hold this treasure in earthen vessels,
 that the surpassing power may be of God and not from us.

The word of the Lord.

September 3—Saint Gregory the Great

RESPONSORIAL PSALM

Psalm 96:1-2a, 2b-3, 7-8, 10

℟. (3) **Proclaim God's marvelous deeds to all the nations.**

Sing to the LORD **a new song;**
   sing to the LORD**, all you lands.**
Sing to the LORD**; bless his name.**

℟. **Proclaim God's marvelous deeds to all the nations.**

Announce his salvation, day after day.
Tell his glory among the nations;
   among all peoples, his wondrous deeds.

℟. **Proclaim God's marvelous deeds to all the nations.**

Give to the LORD**, you families of nations,**
   give to the LORD **glory and praise;**
   give to the LORD **the glory due his name!**

℟. **Proclaim God's marvelous deeds to all the nations.**

Say among the nations: The LORD **is king.**
He has made the world firm, not to be moved;
   he governs the peoples with equity.

℟. **Proclaim God's marvelous deeds to all the nations.**

ALLELUIA

John 15:15b

℟. **Alleluia, alleluia.**

I call you my friends, says the Lord,
for I have made known to you all that the Father has told me.

℟. **Alleluia, alleluia.**

GOSPEL

Luke 22:24-30   I confer a kingdom on you, just as my Father has conferred one on me.

✝ **A reading from the holy Gospel according to Luke**

An argument broke out among the Apostles
  about which of them should be regarded as the greatest.
Jesus said to them,
    "The kings of the Gentiles lord it over them
    and those in authority over them are addressed as 'Benefactors';
    but among you it shall not be so.
Rather, let the greatest among you be as the youngest,
    and the leader as the servant.
For who is greater:
    the one seated at table or the one who serves?
Is it not the one seated at table?
I am among you as the one who serves.
It is you who have stood by me in my trials;
    and I confer a kingdom on you,
    just as my Father has conferred one on me,
    that you may eat and drink at my table in my Kingdom;
    and you will sit on thrones
    judging the twelve tribes of Israel."

The Gospel of the Lord.

SEPTEMBER 8

636 THE NATIVITY OF THE BLESSED VIRGIN MARY
FEAST

FIRST READING

First Option

Micah 5:1-4a   The time when she who is to give birth has borne.

A reading from the Book of the Prophet Micah

The LORD says:
>You, Bethlehem-Ephrathah,
>>too small to be among the clans of Judah,
>
>From you shall come forth for me
>>one who is to be ruler in Israel;
>
>Whose origin is from of old,
>>from ancient times.
>
>(Therefore the Lord will give them up, until the time
>>when she who is to give birth has borne,
>
>And the rest of his brethren shall return
>>to the children of Israel.)
>
>He shall stand firm and shepherd his flock
>>by the strength of the LORD,
>>in the majestic name of the LORD, his God;
>
>And they shall remain, for now his greatness
>>shall reach to the ends of the earth;
>>he shall be peace.

The word of the Lord.

OR

Second Option

Romans 8:28-30   For those he foreknew he also predestined.

A reading from the Letter of Saint Paul to the Romans

Brothers and sisters:
We know that all things work for good for those who love God,
   who are called according to his purpose.
For those he foreknew he also predestined
   to be conformed to the image of his Son,
   so that he might be the firstborn
   among many brothers.
And those he predestined he also called;
   and those he called he also justified;
   and those he justified he also glorified.

The word of the Lord.

RESPONSORIAL PSALM

Psalm 13:6ab, 6c

℟. (Isaiah 61:10) **With delight I rejoice in the Lord.**

Though I trusted in your mercy,
   let my heart rejoice in your salvation.

℟. **With delight I rejoice in the Lord.**

Let me sing of the LORD**, "He has been good to me."**

℟. **With delight I rejoice in the Lord.**

ALLELUIA

℟. **Alleluia, alleluia.**

Blessed are you, holy Virgin Mary, deserving of all praise;
from you rose the sun of justice, Christ our God.

℟. **Alleluia, alleluia.**

September 8—The Nativity of the Blessed Virgin Mary

GOSPEL

Long Form

Matthew 1:1-16, 18-23   For it is through the Holy Spirit that this child has been conceived in her.

✠ **A reading from the holy Gospel according to Matthew**

**The Book of the genealogy of Jesus Christ,
   the son of David, the son of Abraham.**

**Abraham became the father of Isaac,
   Isaac the father of Jacob,
   Jacob the father of Judah and his brothers.
Judah became the father of Perez and Zerah,
   whose mother was Tamar.
Perez became the father of Hezron,
   Hezron the father of Ram,
   Ram the father of Amminadab.
Amminadab became the father of Nahshon,
   Nahshon the father of Salmon,
   Salmon the father of Boaz,
   whose mother was Rahab.
Boaz became the father of Obed,
   whose mother was Ruth.
Obed became the father of Jesse,
   Jesse the father of David the king.**

**David became the father of Solomon,
   whose mother had been the wife of Uriah.
Solomon became the father of Rehoboam,
   Rehoboam the father of Abijah,
   Abijah the father of Asaph.
Asaph became the father of Jehoshaphat,
   Jehoshaphat the father of Joram,
   Joram the father of Uzziah.
Uzziah became the father of Jotham,
   Jotham the father of Ahaz,
   Ahaz the father of Hezekiah.
Hezekiah became the father of Manasseh,
   Manasseh the father of Amos,
   Amos the father of Josiah.
Josiah became the father of Jechoniah and his brothers
   at the time of the Babylonian exile.**

September 8—The Nativity of the Blessed Virgin Mary   1519

After the Babylonian exile,
>Jechoniah became the father of Shealtiel,
>Shealtiel the father of Zerubbabel,
>Zerubbabel the father of Abiud.

Abiud became the father of Eliakim,
>Eliakim the father of Azor,
>Azor the father of Zadok.

Zadok became the father of Achim,
>Achim the father of Eliud,
>Eliud the father of Eleazar.

Eleazar became the father of Matthan,
>Matthan the father of Jacob,
>Jacob the father of Joseph, the husband of Mary.

Of her was born Jesus who is called the Christ.

Now this is how the birth of Jesus Christ came about.
When his mother Mary was betrothed to Joseph,
>but before they lived together,
>she was found with child through the Holy Spirit.

Joseph her husband, since he was a righteous man,
>yet unwilling to expose her to shame,
>decided to divorce her quietly.

Such was his intention when, behold,
>the angel of the Lord appeared to him in a dream and said,
>"Joseph, son of David,
>do not be afraid to take Mary your wife into your home.

For it is through the Holy Spirit
>that this child has been conceived in her.

She will bear a son and you are to name him Jesus,
>because he will save his people from their sins."

All this took place to fulfill
>what the Lord had said through the prophet:

>>*Behold, the virgin shall be with child and bear a son,*
>>>*and they shall name him Emmanuel,*

>which means "God is with us."

The Gospel of the Lord.

OR

1520 *September 8—The Nativity of the Blessed Virgin Mary*

Short Form

Matthew 1:18-23   For it is through the Holy Spirit that this child has been conceived in her.

✠ A reading from the holy Gospel according to Matthew

This is how the birth of Jesus Christ came about.
When his mother Mary was betrothed to Joseph,
> but before they lived together,
> she was found with child through the Holy Spirit.

Joseph her husband, since he was a righteous man,
> yet unwilling to expose her to shame,
> decided to divorce her quietly.

Such was his intention when, behold,
> the angel of the Lord appeared to him in a dream and said,
> "Joseph, son of David,
> do not be afraid to take Mary your wife into your home.

For it is through the Holy Spirit
> that this child has been conceived in her.

She will bear a son and you are to name him Jesus,
> because he will save his people from their sins."

All this took place to fulfill
> what the Lord had said through the prophet:

> *Behold, the virgin shall be with child and bear a son,*
>> *and they shall name him Emmanuel,*

> which means "God is with us."

The Gospel of the Lord.

SEPTEMBER 9

[In the Dioceses of the United States]

636A SAINT PETER CLAVER, PRIEST AND RELIGIOUS MEMORIAL

From the Common of Pastors: For Missionaries, p. 1805.

SEPTEMBER 13

637 SAINT JOHN CHRYSOSTOM, BISHOP AND DOCTOR OF THE CHURCH MEMORIAL

From the Common of Pastors, p. 1805, or the Common of Doctors of the Church, p. 1838,

OR

FIRST READING

Ephesians 4:1-7, 11-13   For the work of ministry, for the building up of the Body of Christ.

A reading from the Letter of Saint Paul to the Ephesians

Brothers and sisters:
I, a prisoner for the Lord,
　urge you to live in a manner worthy of the call you have received,
　with all humility and gentleness, with patience,
　bearing with one another through love,
　striving to preserve the unity of the Spirit
　through the bond of peace:
　one Body and one Spirit,
　as you were also called to the one hope of your call;
　one Lord, one faith, one baptism;
　one God and Father of all,
　who is over all and through all and in all.

But grace was given to each of us
　according to the measure of Christ's gift.

And he gave some as Apostles, others as prophets,
　others as evangelists, others as pastors and teachers,
　to equip the holy ones for the work of ministry,
　for building up the Body of Christ,
　until we all attain to the unity of faith
　and knowledge of the Son of God, to mature manhood,
　to the extent of the full stature of Christ.

The word of the Lord.

RESPONSORIAL PSALM

Psalm 40:2 and 4, 7-8a, 8b-9, 10, 11

℟. (8a and 9a) Here I am, Lord; I come to do your will.

I have waited, waited for the LORD,
  and he stooped toward me and heard my cry.
And he put a new song into my mouth,
  a hymn to our God.

℟. Here I am, Lord; I come to do your will.

Sacrifice or oblation you wished not,
  but ears open to obedience you gave me.
Burnt offerings or sin-offerings you sought not;
  then said I, "Behold I come."

℟. Here I am, Lord; I come to do your will.

"In the written scroll it is prescribed for me,
To do your will, O my God, is my delight,
  and your law is within my heart!"

℟. Here I am, Lord; I come to do your will.

I announced your justice in the vast assembly;
  I did not restrain my lips, as you, O LORD, know.

℟. Here I am, Lord; I come to do your will.

Your justice I kept not hid within my heart;
  your faithfulness and your salvation I have spoken of;
I have made no secret of your kindness and your truth
  in the vast assembly.

℟. Here I am, Lord; I come to do your will.

ALLELUIA

℟. **Alleluia, alleluia.**

**The seed is the word of God, Christ is the sower;
all who come to him will live for ever.**

℟. **Alleluia, alleluia.**

September 13—Saint John Chrysostom

GOSPEL

Long Form

Mark 4:1-10, 13-20   The sower went out to sow.

✜ A reading from the holy Gospel according to Mark

On another occasion, Jesus began to teach by the sea.
A very large crowd gathered around him
   so that he got into a boat on the sea and sat down.
And the whole crowd was beside the sea on land.
And he taught them at length in parables,
   and in the course of his instruction he said to them,
   "Hear this! A sower went out to sow.
And as he sowed, some seed fell on the path,
   and the birds came and ate it up.
Other seed fell on rocky ground where it had little soil.
It sprang up at once because the soil was not deep.
And when the sun rose, it was scorched and it withered for lack of roots.
Some seed fell among thorns,
   and the thorns grew up and choked it
   and it produced no grain.
And some seed fell on rich soil and produced fruit.
It came up and grew and yielded thirty, sixty, and a hundredfold."
He added, "Whoever has ears to hear ought to hear."

And when he was alone,
   those present along with the Twelve
   questioned him about the parables.
Jesus answered them,
   "Do you not understand this parable?
Then how will you understand any of the parables?
The sower sows the word.
These are the ones on the path where the word is sown.
As soon as they hear, Satan comes at once
   and takes away the word sown in them.
And these are the ones sown on rocky ground who,
   when they hear the word, receive it at once with joy.
But they have no root; they last only for a time.
Then when tribulation or persecution comes because of the word,
   they quickly fall away.
Those sown among thorns are another sort.
They are the people who hear the word,
   but worldly anxiety, the lure of riches,
   and the craving for other things intrude and choke the word,
   and it bears no fruit.

But those sown on rich soil are the ones who hear the word and accept it
 and bear fruit thirty and sixty and a hundredfold."

The Gospel of the Lord.

OR

Short Form

Mark 4:1-9   The sower went out to sow.

☩ A reading from the holy Gospel according to Mark

On another occasion, Jesus began to teach by the sea.
A very large crowd gathered around him
 so that he got into a boat on the sea and sat down.
And the whole crowd was beside the sea on land.
And he taught them at length in parables,
 and in the course of his instruction he said to them,
 "Hear this! A sower went out to sow.
And as he sowed, some seed fell on the path,
 and the birds came and ate it up.
Other seed fell on rocky ground where it had little soil.
It sprang up at once because the soil was not deep.
And when the sun rose, it was scorched and it withered for lack of roots.
Some seed fell among thorns,
 and the thorns grew up and choked it
 and it produced no grain.
And some seed fell on rich soil and produced fruit.
It came up and grew and yielded thirty, sixty, and a hundredfold."
He added, "Whoever has ears to hear ought to hear."

The Gospel of the Lord.

SEPTEMBER 14

638 THE EXALTATION OF THE HOLY CROSS FEAST

FIRST READING

Numbers 21:4b-9   Whenever anyone who had been bitten by a serpent looked at the bronze serpent, he lived.

A reading from the Book of Numbers

**With their patience worn out by the journey,
 the people complained against God and Moses,
 "Why have you brought us up from Egypt to die in this desert,
 where there is no food or water?
We are disgusted with this wretched food!"**

In punishment the LORD **sent among the people saraph serpents,
 which bit the people so that many of them died.
Then the people came to Moses and said,
 "We have sinned in complaining against the L**ORD **and you.
Pray the L**ORD **to take the serpents from us."
So Moses prayed for the people, and the L**ORD **said to Moses,
 "Make a saraph and mount it on a pole,
 and if any who have been bitten look at it, they will live."
Moses accordingly made a bronze serpent and mounted it on a pole,
 and whenever anyone who had been bitten by a serpent
 looked at the bronze serpent, he lived.**

The word of the Lord.

RESPONSORIAL PSALM

Psalm 78:1bc-2, 34-35, 36-37, 38

℟. (see 7b) **Do not forget the works of the Lord!**

**Hearken, my people, to my teaching;
 incline your ears to the words of my mouth.
I will open my mouth in a parable,
 I will utter mysteries from of old.**

℟. **Do not forget the works of the Lord!**

**While he slew them they sought him
 and inquired after God again,
Remembering that God was their rock
 and the Most High God, their redeemer.**

℟. **Do not forget the works of the Lord!**

September 14—The Exaltation of the Holy Cross

But they flattered him with their mouths
   and lied to him with their tongues,
Though their hearts were not steadfast toward him,
   nor were they faithful to his covenant.

℟. **Do not forget the works of the Lord!**

But he, being merciful, forgave their sin
   and destroyed them not;
Often he turned back his anger
   and let none of his wrath be roused.

℟. **Do not forget the works of the Lord!**

SECOND READING

Philippians 2:6-11   He humbled himself; because of this God greatly exalted him.

A reading from the Letter of Saint Paul to the Philippians

Brothers and sisters:
   Christ Jesus, though he was in the form of God,
     did not regard equality with God something to be grasped.
   Rather, he emptied himself,
   taking the form of a slave,
   coming in human likeness;
   and found human in appearance,
   he humbled himself,
   becoming obedient to death,
     even death on a cross.
Because of this, God greatly exalted him
   and bestowed on him the name
   that is above every name,
   that at the name of Jesus
   every knee should bend,
   of those in heaven and on earth and under the earth,
   and every tongue confess that
   Jesus Christ is Lord,
   to the glory of God the Father.

The word of the Lord.

ALLELUIA

℟. Alleluia, alleluia.

We adore you, O Christ, and we bless you,
because by your Cross you have redeemed the world.

℟. Alleluia, alleluia.

GOSPEL

John 3:13-17   So the Son of Man must be lifted up.

✠ A reading from the holy Gospel according to John

Jesus said to Nicodemus:
"No one has gone up to heaven
   except the one who has come down from heaven, the Son of Man.
And just as Moses lifted up the serpent in the desert,
   so must the Son of Man be lifted up,
   so that everyone who believes in him may have eternal life."

For God so loved the world that he gave his only Son,
   so that everyone who believes in him might not perish
   but might have eternal life.
For God did not send his Son into the world to condemn the world,
   but that the world might be saved through him.

The Gospel of the Lord.

SEPTEMBER 15

639 OUR LADY OF SORROWS MEMORIAL

The Gospel for this memorial is proper.

FIRST READING

Hebrews 5:7-9   Christ learned obedience and became the source of eternal salvation.

A reading from the letter to the Hebrews

**In the days when Christ was in the flesh,
   he offered prayers and supplications with loud cries and tears
   to the one who was able to save him from death,
   and he was heard because of his reverence.
Son though he was, he learned obedience from what he suffered;
   and when he was made perfect,
   he became the source of eternal salvation for all who obey him.**

The word of the Lord.

RESPONSORIAL PSALM

Psalm 31:2 and 3b, 3cd-4, 5-6, 15-16, 20

℟. (17) **Save me, O Lord, in your kindness.**

**In you, O Lord, I take refuge;
   let me never be put to shame.
In your justice rescue me,
   make haste to deliver me!**

℟. **Save me, O Lord, in your kindness.**

**Be my rock of refuge,
   a stronghold to give me safety.
You are my rock and my fortress;
   for your name's sake you will lead and guide me.**

℟. **Save me, O Lord, in your kindness.**

**You will free me from the snare they set for me,
   for you are my refuge.
Into your hands I commend my spirit;
   you will redeem me, O Lord, O faithful God.**

℟. **Save me, O Lord, in your kindness.**

1530 *September 15—Our Lady of Sorrows*

But my trust is in you, O Lord,
  I say, "You are my God."
In your hands is my destiny; rescue me
  from the clutches of my enemies and my persecutors.

℟. Save me, O Lord, in your kindness.

How great is your goodness, O Lord,
  which you have in store for those who fear you,
And which, toward those who take refuge in you,
  you show in the sight of the children of men.

℟. Save me, O Lord, in your kindness.

The sequence *Stabat Mater* may follow.

SEQUENCE (OPTIONAL)

Stabat Mater

At the cross her station keeping,
Stood the mournful Mother weeping,
  Close to Jesus to the last.

Through her heart, his sorrow sharing,
All his bitter anguish bearing,
  Now at length the sword had passed.

Oh, how sad and sore distressed
Was that Mother highly blessed
  Of the sole begotten One!

Christ above in torment hangs,
She beneath beholds the pangs
  Of her dying, glorious Son.

Is there one who would not weep,
'Whelmed in miseries so deep,
  Christ's dear Mother to behold?

Can the human heart refrain
From partaking in her pain,
  In that mother's pain untold?

Bruised, derided, cursed, defiled,
She beheld her tender Child,
  All with bloody scourges rent.

For the sins of his own nation
Saw him hang in desolation
  Till his spirit forth he sent.

O sweet Mother! font of love,
Touch my spirit from above,
   Make my heart with yours accord.

Make me feel as you have felt;
Make my soul to glow and melt
   With the love of Christ, my Lord.

Holy Mother, pierce me through,
In my heart each wound renew
   Of my Savior crucified.

Let me share with you his pain,
Who for all our sins was slain,
   Who for me in torments died.

Let me mingle tears with you,
Mourning him who mourned for me,
   All the days that I may live.

By the cross with you to stay,
There with you to weep and pray,
   Is all I ask of you to give.

Virgin of all virgins blest!
Listen to my fond request:
   Let me share your grief divine.

Let me to my latest breath,
In my body bear the death
   Of that dying Son of yours.

Wounded with his every wound,
Steep my soul till it has swooned
   In his very Blood away.

Be to me, O Virgin, nigh,
Lest in flames I burn and die,
   In his awful judgment day.

Christ, when you shall call me hence,
Be your Mother my defense,
   Be your cross my victory.

While my body here decays,
May my soul your goodness praise,
   Safe in heaven eternally.
   Amen. (Alleluia)

ALLELUIA

℟. Alleluia, alleluia.

Blessed are you, O Virgin Mary;
without dying you won the martyr's crown
beneath the Cross of the Lord.

℟. Alleluia, alleluia.

GOSPEL

First Option

John 19:25-27   *How that loving mother was pierced with grief and anguish when she saw the sufferings of her Son (Stabat Mater).*

✠ A reading from the holy Gospel according to John

Standing by the cross of Jesus were his mother
 and his mother's sister, Mary the wife of Clopas,
 and Mary Magdalene.
When Jesus saw his mother and the disciple there whom he loved
 he said to his mother, "Woman, behold, your son."
Then he said to the disciple,
 "Behold, your mother."
And from that hour the disciple took her into his home.

The Gospel of the Lord.

OR

Second Option

Luke 2:33-35   *And you yourself a sword will pierce.*

✠ A reading from the holy Gospel according to Luke

Jesus' father and mother were amazed at what was said about him;
 and Simeon blessed them and said to Mary his mother,
 "Behold, this child is destined
 for the fall and rise of many in Israel,
 and to be a sign that will be contradicted
 and you yourself a sword will pierce
 so that the thoughts of many hearts may be revealed."

The Gospel of the Lord.

SEPTEMBER 16

640 SAINT CORNELIUS, POPE AND MARTYR, AND SAINT CYPRIAN, BISHOP AND MARTYR MEMORIAL

From the Common of Martyrs, p. 1782, or the Common of Pastors, p. 1805,

OR

FIRST READING

2 Corinthians 4:7-15   Always carrying about in the body the dying of Jesus.

A reading from the second Letter of Saint Paul to the Corinthians

Brothers and sisters:
We hold this treasure in earthen vessels,
  that the surpassing power may be of God and not from us.
We are afflicted in every way, but not constrained;
  perplexed, but not driven to despair;
  persecuted, but not abandoned;
  struck down, but not destroyed;
  always carrying about in the body the dying of Jesus,
  so that the life of Jesus may also be manifested in our body.
For we who live are constantly being given up to death
  for the sake of Jesus,
  so that the life of Jesus may be manifested in our mortal flesh.

So death is at work in us, but life in you.
Since, then, we have the same spirit of faith,
  according to what is written, *I believed, therefore I spoke,*
  we too believe and therefore speak,
  knowing that the one who raised the Lord Jesus
  will raise us also with Jesus
  and place us with you in his presence.
Everything indeed is for you,
  so that the grace bestowed in abundance on more and more people
  may cause the thanksgiving to overflow for the glory of God.

The word of the Lord.

RESPONSORIAL PSALM

Psalm 126:1bc-2ab, 2cd-3, 4-5, 6

℟. (5) **Those who sow in tears shall reap rejoicing.**

When the LORD brought back the captives of Zion,
  we were like men dreaming.
Then our mouth was filled with laughter,
  and our tongue with rejoicing.

℟. **Those who sow in tears shall reap rejoicing.**

Then they said among the nations,
  "The LORD has done great things for them."
The LORD has done great things for us;
  we are glad indeed.

℟. **Those who sow in tears shall reap rejoicing.**

Restore our fortunes, O LORD,
  like the torrents in the southern desert.
Those who sow in tears
  shall reap rejoicing.

℟. **Those who sow in tears shall reap rejoicing.**

Although they go forth weeping,
  carrying the seed to be sown,
They shall come back rejoicing,
  carrying their sheaves.

℟. **Those who sow in tears shall reap rejoicing.**

ALLELUIA

2 Corinthians 1:3b-4

℟. **Alleluia, alleluia.**

Blessed be the Father of compassion and God of all encouragement,
who encourages us in our every affliction.

℟. **Alleluia, alleluia.**

GOSPEL

John 17:11b-19   The world hated them.

✢ A reading from the holy Gospel according to John

**Jesus raised his eyes to heaven and prayed, saying:
"Holy Father, keep them in your name that you have given me,
  so that they may be one just as we are one.
When I was with them I protected them in your name that you gave me,
  and I guarded them, and none of them was lost
  except the son of destruction,
  in order that the Scripture might be fulfilled.
But now I am coming to you.
I speak this in the world
  so that they may share my joy completely.
I gave them your word, and the world hated them,
  because they do not belong to the world
  any more than I belong to the world.
I do not ask that you take them out of the world
  but that you keep them from the Evil One.
They do not belong to the world
  any more than I belong to the world.
Consecrate them in the truth.
Your word is truth.
As you sent me into the world,
  so I sent them into the world.
And I consecrate myself for them,
  so that they also may be consecrated in truth."**

The Gospel of the Lord.

SEPTEMBER 17

641 SAINT ROBERT BELLARMINE, BISHOP AND DOCTOR OF THE CHURCH

From the Common of Pastors, p. 1805, or the Common of Doctors of the Church, p. 1838,

OR

FIRST READING

Wisdom 7:7-10, 15-16   Beyond health and comeliness I loved her.

A reading from the Book of Wisdom

I prayed, and prudence was given me;
  I pleaded, and the spirit of Wisdom came to me.
I preferred her to scepter and throne,
And deemed riches nothing in comparison with her,
  nor did I liken any priceless gem to her;
Because all gold, in view of her, is a little sand,
  and before her, silver is to be accounted mire.
Beyond health and comeliness I loved her,
And I chose to have her rather than the light,
  because the splendor of her never yields to sleep.

Now God grant I speak suitably
  and value these endowments at their worth:
For he is the guide of Wisdom
  and the director of the wise.
For both we and our words are in his hand,
  as well as all prudence and knowledge of crafts.

The word of the Lord.

RESPONSORIAL PSALM

Psalm 19:8, 9, 10, 11

℟. (10) **The judgments of the Lord are true, and all of them are just.**
  or:
℟. (John 6:63) **Your words, Lord, are Spirit and life.**

The law of the Lord is perfect,
  refreshing the soul;
The decree of the Lord is trustworthy,
  giving wisdom to the simple.

℟. **The judgments of the Lord are true, and all of them are just.**
  or:
℟. **Your words, Lord, are Spirit and life.**

The precepts of the Lord are right,
  rejoicing the heart.
The command of the Lord is clear,
  enlightening the eye.

℟. **The judgments of the Lord are true, and all of them are just.**
  or:
℟. **Your words, Lord, are Spirit and life.**

The fear of the Lord is pure,
  enduring forever;
The ordinances of the Lord are true,
  all of them just.

℟. **The judgments of the Lord are true, and all of them are just.**
  or:
℟. **Your words, Lord, are Spirit and life.**

They are more precious than gold,
  than a heap of purest gold;
Sweeter also than syrup
  or honey from the comb.

℟. **The judgments of the Lord are true, and all of them are just.**
  or:
℟. **Your words, Lord, are Spirit and life.**

ALLELUIA

See John 6:63c, 68c

℟. Alleluia, alleluia.

Your words, Lord, are Spirit and life;
you have the words of everlasting life.

℟. Alleluia, alleluia.

GOSPEL

Matthew 7:21-29   He taught them as one having authority.

✛ **A reading from the holy Gospel according to Matthew**

Jesus said to his disciples:
"Not everyone who says to me, 'Lord, Lord,'
 will enter the Kingdom of heaven,
 but only the one who does the will of my Father in heaven.
Many will say to me on that day,
 'Lord, Lord, did we not prophesy in your name?
Did we not drive out demons in your name?
Did we not do mighty deeds in your name?'
Then I will declare to them solemnly,
 'I never knew you. Depart from me, you evildoers.'

"Everyone who listens to these words of mine and acts on them
 will be like a wise man who built his house on rock.
The rain fell, the floods came,
 and the winds blew and buffeted the house.
But it did not collapse; it had been set solidly on rock.
And everyone who listens to these words of mine
 but does not act on them
 will be like a fool who built his house on sand.
The rain fell, the floods came,
 and the winds blew and buffeted the house.
And it collapsed and was completely ruined."

When Jesus finished these words,
 the crowds were astonished at his teaching,
 for he taught them as one having authority,
 and not as their scribes.

The Gospel of the Lord.

SEPTEMBER 19

642 SAINT JANUARIUS, BISHOP AND MARTYR

From the Common of Martyrs, p. 1782, or the Common of Pastors, p. 1805,

OR

FIRST READING

Hebrews 10:32-36 You endured a great contest of suffering.

A reading from the Letter to the Hebrews

Brothers and sisters:
Remember the days past when, after you had been enlightened,
   you endured a great contest of suffering.
At times you were publicly exposed to abuse and affliction;
   at other times you associated yourselves with those so treated.
You even joined in the sufferings of those in prison
   and joyfully accepted the confiscation of your property,
   knowing that you had a better and lasting possession.
Therefore, do not throw away your confidence;
   it will have great recompense.
You need endurance to do the will of God and receive what he has promised.

The word of the Lord.

RESPONSORIAL PSALM

Psalm 126:1 bc-2ab, 2cd-3, 4-5, 6

℟. (5) **Those who sow in tears shall reap rejoicing.**

When the LORD brought back the captives of Zion,
   we were like men dreaming.
Then our mouth was filled with laughter,
   and our tongue with rejoicing.

℟. **Those who sow in tears shall reap rejoicing.**

Then they said among the nations,
   "The LORD has done great things for them."
The LORD has done great things for us;
   we are glad indeed.

℟. **Those who sow in tears shall reap rejoicing.**

Restore our fortunes, O Lord,
  like the torrents in the southern desert.
Those who sow in tears
  shall reap rejoicing.

℟. Those who sow in tears shall reap rejoicing.

Although they go forth weeping,
  carrying the seed to be sown,
They shall come back rejoicing,
  carrying their sheaves.

℟. Those who sow in tears shall reap rejoicing.

ALLELUIA

James 1:12

℟. Alleluia, alleluia.

Blessed is the man who perseveres in temptation,
for when he has been proved he will receive the crown of life.

℟. Alleluia, alleluia.

GOSPEL

John 12:24-26   If a grain of wheat falls to the ground and dies, it produces much fruit.

✠ **A reading from the holy Gospel according to John**

Jesus said to his disciples:
"Amen, amen, I say to you,
  unless a grain of wheat falls to the ground and dies,
  it remains just a grain of wheat;
  but if it dies, it produces much fruit.
Whoever loves his life loses it,
  and whoever hates his life in this world
  will preserve it for eternal life.
Whoever serves me must follow me,
  and where I am, there also will my servant be.
The Father will honor whoever serves me."

The Gospel of the Lord.

SEPTEMBER 20

642A SAINT ANDREW KIM TAEGŎN, PRIEST AND MARTYR, AND SAINT PAUL CHŎNG HASANG, CATECHIST AND MARTYR, AND THEIR COMPANIONS, MARTYRS MEMORIAL

From the Common of Martyrs, p. 1782,

OR

FIRST READING

First Option

Wisdom 3:1-9   As sacrificial offerings he took them to himself.

A reading from the Book of Wisdom

**The souls of the just are in the hand of God,
   and no torment shall touch them.
They seemed, in the view of the foolish, to be dead;
   and their passing away was thought an affliction
   and their going forth from us, utter destruction.
But they are in peace.
For if before men, indeed they be punished,
   yet is their hope full of immortality;
Chastised a little, they shall be greatly blessed,
   because God tried them
   and found them worthy of himself.
As gold in the furnace, he proved them,
   and as sacrificial offerings he took them to himself.
In the time of their visitation they shall shine,
   and shall dart about as sparks through stubble;
They shall judge nations and rule over peoples,
   and the Lord shall be their King forever.
Those who trust in him shall understand truth,
   and the faithful shall abide with him in love:
Because grace and mercy are with his holy ones,
   and his care is with his elect.**

The word of the Lord.

OR

1542 September 20—Saints Andrew Kim Taegŏn and Paul Chŏng Hasang

Second Option

Romans 8:31b-39   Neither death nor life will be able to separate us from the love of God.

A reading from the Letter of Saint Paul to the Romans

Brothers and sisters:
If God is for us, who can be against us?
He who did not spare his own Son
   but handed him over for us all,
   how will he not also give us everything else along with him?
Who will bring a charge against God's chosen ones?
It is God who acquits us.
   Who will condemn?
It is Christ Jesus who died, rather, was raised,
   who also is at the right hand of God,
   who indeed intercedes for us.
What will separate us from the love of Christ?
Will anguish, or distress, or persecution, or famine,
   or nakedness, or peril, or the sword?
As it is written:

   For your sake we are being slain all the day;
      we are looked upon as sheep to be slaughtered.

No, in all these things we conquer overwhelmingly
   through him who loved us.
For I am convinced that neither death, nor life,
   nor angels, nor principalities,
   nor present things, nor future things,
   nor powers, nor height, nor depth,
   nor any other creature will be able to separate us
   from the love of God in Christ Jesus our Lord.

The word of the Lord.

RESPONSORIAL PSALM

Psalm 126:1bc-2ab, 2cd-3, 4-5, 6

℟. (5) **Those who sow in tears shall reap rejoicing.**

When the Lord **brought back the captives of Zion,**
   we were like men dreaming.
Then our mouth was filled with laughter,
   and our tongue with rejoicing.

℟. **Those who sow in tears shall reap rejoicing.**

Then they said among the nations,
  "The Lord has done great things for them."
The Lord has done great things for us;
  we are glad indeed.

℟. Those who sow in tears shall reap rejoicing.

Restore our fortunes, O Lord,
  like the torrents in the southern desert.
Those who sow in tears
  shall reap rejoicing.

℟. Those who sow in tears shall reap rejoicing.

Although they go forth weeping,
  carrying the seed to be sown,
They shall come back rejoicing,
  carrying their sheaves.

℟. Those who sow in tears shall reap rejoicing.

ALLELUIA

1 Peter 4:14

℟. Alleluia, alleluia.

If you are insulted for the name of Christ, blessed are you,
for the Spirit of God rests upon you.

℟. Alleluia, alleluia.

GOSPEL

Luke 9:23-26   Whoever loses his life for my sake will save it.

✝ A reading from the holy Gospel according to Luke

Jesus said to all,
  "If anyone wishes to come after me, he must deny himself
  and take up his cross daily and follow me.
For whoever wishes to save his life will lose it,
  but whoever loses his life for my sake will save it.
What profit is there for one to gain the whole world
  yet lose or forfeit himself?
Whoever is ashamed of me and of my words,
  the Son of Man will be ashamed of when he comes in his glory
  and in the glory of the Father and of the holy angels."

The Gospel of the Lord.

SEPTEMBER 21

643 SAINT MATTHEW, APOSTLE AND EVANGELIST
FEAST

FIRST READING

Ephesians 4:1-7, 11-13   He gave some as Apostles, others as evangelists.

A reading from the Letter of Saint Paul to the Ephesians

Brothers and sisters:
I, a prisoner for the Lord,
  urge you to live in a manner worthy of the call you have received,
  with all humility and gentleness, with patience,
  bearing with one another through love,
  striving to preserve the unity of the Spirit
  through the bond of peace:
  one Body and one Spirit,
  as you were also called to the one hope of your call;
  one Lord, one faith, one baptism;
  one God and Father of all,
  who is over all and through all and in all.

But grace was given to each of us
  according to the measure of Christ's gift.

And he gave some as Apostles, others as prophets,
  others as evangelists, others as pastors and teachers,
  to equip the holy ones for the work of ministry,
  for building up the Body of Christ,
  until we all attain to the unity of faith
  and knowledge of the Son of God, to mature manhood,
  to the extent of the full stature of Christ.

The word of the Lord.

RESPONSORIAL PSALM

Psalm 19:2-3, 4-5

℟. (5) Their message goes out through all the earth.

The heavens declare the glory of God;
  and the firmament proclaims his handiwork.
Day pours out the word to day,
  and night to night imparts knowledge.

℟. Their message goes out through all the earth.

Not a word nor a discourse
   whose voice is not heard;
Through all the earth their voice resounds,
   and to the ends of the world, their message.

℟. **Their message goes out through all the earth.**

ALLELUIA

See *Te Deum*

℟. **Alleluia, alleluia.**

We praise you, O God,
we acclaim you as Lord;
the glorious company of Apostles praise you.

℟. **Alleluia, alleluia.**

GOSPEL

Matthew 9:9-13   Follow me. And he got up and followed him.

✠ **A reading from the holy Gospel according to Matthew**

As Jesus passed by,
   he saw a man named Matthew sitting at the customs post.
He said to him, "Follow me."
And he got up and followed him.
While he was at table in his house,
   many tax collectors and sinners came
   and sat with Jesus and his disciples.
The Pharisees saw this and said to his disciples,
   "Why does your teacher eat with tax collectors and sinners?"
He heard this and said,
   "Those who are well do not need a physician, but the sick do.
Go and learn the meaning of the words,
   I desire mercy, not sacrifice.
I did not come to call the righteous but sinners."

The Gospel of the Lord.

SEPTEMBER 26

644 SAINTS COSMAS AND DAMIAN, MARTYRS

From the Common of Martyrs, p. 1782,

OR

FIRST READING

Wisdom 3:1-9   As sacrificial offerings he took them to himself.

A reading from the Book of Wisdom

**The souls of the just are in the hand of God,
   and no torment shall touch them.
They seemed, in the view of the foolish, to be dead;
   and their passing away was thought an affliction
   and their going forth from us, utter destruction.
But they are in peace.
For if before men, indeed, they be punished,
   yet is their hope full of immortality;
Chastised a little, they shall be greatly blessed,
   because God tried them
   and found them worthy of himself.
As gold in the furnace, he proved them,
   and as sacrificial offerings he took them to himself.
In the time of their visitation they shall shine,
   and shall dart about as sparks through stubble;
They shall judge nations and rule over peoples,
   and the Lord shall be their King forever.
Those who trust in him shall understand truth,
   and the faithful shall abide with him in love:
Because grace and mercy are with his holy ones,
   and his care is with his elect.**

The word of the Lord.

September 26—Saints Cosmas and Damian

RESPONSORIAL PSALM

Psalm 126:1bc-2ab, 2cd-3, 4-5, 6

℟. (5) **Those who sow in tears shall reap rejoicing.**

**When the Lord brought back the captives of Zion,
 we were like men dreaming.
Then our mouth was filled with laughter,
 and our tongue with rejoicing.**

℟. **Those who sow in tears shall reap rejoicing.**

**Then they said among the nations,
 "The Lord has done great things for them."
The Lord has done great things for us;
 we are glad indeed.**

℟. **Those who sow in tears shall reap rejoicing.**

**Restore our fortunes, O Lord,
 like the torrents in the southern desert.
Those who sow in tears
 shall reap rejoicing.**

℟. **Those who sow in tears shall reap rejoicing.**

**Although they go forth weeping,
 carrying the seed to be sown,
They shall come back rejoicing,
 carrying their sheaves.**

℟. **Those who sow in tears shall reap rejoicing.**

ALLELUIA

James 1:12

℟. Alleluia, alleluia.

**Blessed is the man who perseveres in temptation,
for when he has been proved he will receive the crown of life.**

℟. Alleluia, alleluia.

GOSPEL

Matthew 10:28-33   Do not be afraid of those who kill the body.

✠ **A reading from the holy Gospel according to Matthew**

**Jesus said to his Apostles:
"Do not be afraid of those who kill the body
   but cannot kill the soul;
   rather, be afraid of the one who can destroy
   both soul and body in Gehenna.
Are not two sparrows sold for a small coin?
Yet not one of them falls to the ground without your Father's knowledge.
Even all the hairs of your head are counted.
So do not be afraid; you are worth more than many sparrows.
Everyone who acknowledges me before others
   I will acknowledge before my heavenly Father.
But whoever denies me before others,
   I will deny before my heavenly Father."**

The Gospel of the Lord.

SEPTEMBER 27

645 SAINT VINCENT DE PAUL, PRIEST MEMORIAL

From the Common of Pastors: For Missionaries, p. 1805, or the Common of Holy Men and Women: For Those Who Work for the Underprivileged, p. 1868,

OR

FIRST READING

1 Corinthians 1:26-31   God chose the weak of the world to shame the strong.

A reading from the first Letter of Saint Paul to the Corinthians

**Consider your own calling, brothers and sisters.
Not many of you were wise by human standards,
not many were powerful,
not many were of noble birth.
Rather, God chose the foolish of the world to shame the wise,
and God chose the weak of the world to shame the strong,
and God chose the lowly and despised of the world,
those who count for nothing,
to reduce to nothing those who are something,
so that no human being might boast before God.
It is due to him that you are in Christ Jesus,
who became for us wisdom from God,
as well as righteousness, sanctification, and redemption,
so that, as it is written,
Whoever boasts, should boast in the Lord.

The word of the Lord.**

RESPONSORIAL PSALM

Psalm 112:1bc-2, 3-4, 5-7, 7-8, 9

℟. (1) **Blessed the man who fears the Lord.**
  or:
℟. **Alleluia.**

Blessed the man who fears the LORD,
  who greatly delights in his commands.
His posterity shall be mighty upon the earth;
  the upright generation shall be blessed.

℟. Blessed the man who fears the Lord.
  or:
℟. Alleluia.

Wealth and riches shall be in his house;
  his generosity shall endure forever.
Light shines through the darkness for the upright;
  he is gracious and merciful and just.

℟. Blessed the man who fears the Lord.
  or:
℟. Alleluia.

Well for the man who is gracious and lends,
  who conducts his affairs with justice;
He shall never be moved;
  the just one shall be in everlasting remembrance.

℟. Blessed the man who fears the Lord.
  or:
℟. Alleluia.

An evil report he shall not fear.
  His heart is firm, trusting in the LORD.
His heart is steadfast; he shall not fear
  till he looks down upon his foes.

℟. Blessed the man who fears the Lord.
  or:
℟. Alleluia.

Lavishly he gives to the poor,
  his generosity shall endure forever;
  his horn shall be exalted in glory.

℟. Blessed the man who fears the Lord.
  or:
℟. Alleluia.

ALLELUIA

John 10:14

℟. Alleluia, alleluia.

I am the good shepherd, says the Lord;
I know my sheep, and mine know me.

℟. Alleluia, alleluia.

GOSPEL

Matthew 9:35-38   The harvest is abundant but the laborers are few.

✣ A reading from the holy Gospel according to Matthew

Jesus went around to all the towns and villages,
   teaching in their synagogues,
   proclaiming the Gospel of the Kingdom,
   and curing every disease and illness.
At the sight of the crowds, his heart was moved with pity for them
   because they were troubled and abandoned,
   like sheep without a shepherd.
Then he said to his disciples,
   "The harvest is abundant but the laborers are few;
   so ask the master of the harvest
   to send out laborers for his harvest."

The Gospel of the Lord.

SEPTEMBER 28

645A SAINT LAWRENCE RUIZ, MARTYR, AND HIS COMPANIONS, MARTYRS

From the Common of Martyrs, p. 1782.

SEPTEMBER 28

646 SAINT WENCESLAUS, MARTYR

From the Common of Martyrs, p. 1782,

OR

FIRST READING

1 Peter 3:14-17   Do not be afraid or terrified with fear of them.

A reading from the first Letter of Saint Peter

**Beloved:
Even if you should suffer because of righteousness, blessed are you.
Do not be afraid or terrified with fear of them,
   but sanctify Christ as Lord in your hearts.
Always be ready to give an explanation
   to anyone who asks you for a reason for your hope,
   but do it with gentleness and reverence,
   keeping your conscience clear,
   so that, when you are maligned,
   those who defame your good conduct in Christ
   may themselves be put to shame.
For it is better to suffer for doing good,
   if that be the will of God, than for doing evil.**

The word of the Lord.

RESPONSORIAL PSALM

Psalm 126:1bc-2ab, 2cd-3, 4-5, 6

℟. (5) **Those who sow in tears shall reap rejoicing.**

**When the LORD brought back the captives of Zion,
   we were like men dreaming.
Then our mouth was filled with laughter,
   and our tongue with rejoicing.**

℟. **Those who sow in tears shall reap rejoicing.**

**Then they said among the nations,
   "The LORD has done great things for them."
The LORD has done great things for us;
   we are glad indeed.**

℟. **Those who sow in tears shall reap rejoicing.**

Restore our fortunes, O Lord,
   like the torrents in the southern desert.
Those who sow in tears
   shall reap rejoicing.

℟. Those who sow in tears shall reap rejoicing.

Although they go forth weeping,
   carrying the seed to be sown,
They shall come back rejoicing,
   carrying their sheaves.

℟. Those who sow in tears shall reap rejoicing.

ALLELUIA

Matthew 5:10

℟. Alleluia, alleluia.

Blessed are they who are persecuted for the sake of righteousness,
for theirs is the Kingdom of heaven.

℟. Alleluia, alleluia.

GOSPEL

Matthew 10:34-39   I have come to bring not peace, but the sword.

✠ **A reading from the holy Gospel according to Matthew**

Jesus said to his Apostles:
"Do not think that I have come to bring peace upon the earth.
I have come to bring not peace but the sword.
For I have come to set

   a man 'against his father,
      a daughter against her mother,
   and a daughter-in-law against her mother-in-law;
      and one's enemies will be those of his household.'

"Whoever loves father or mother more than me is not worthy of me,
   and whoever loves son or daughter more than me is not worthy of me;
   and whoever does not take up his cross
   and follow after me is not worthy of me.
Whoever finds his life will lose it,
   and whoever loses his life for my sake will find it."

The Gospel of the Lord.

SEPTEMBER 29

647 SAINTS MICHAEL, GABRIEL, AND RAPHAEL, ARCHANGELS FEAST

FIRST READING

First Option

Daniel 7:9-10, 13-14   Thousands upon thousands were ministering to him.

A reading from the Book of the Prophet Daniel

As I watched:

> Thrones were set up
>   and the Ancient One took his throne.
> His clothing was bright as snow,
>   and the hair on his head as white as wool;
> His throne was flames of fire,
>   with wheels of burning fire.
> A surging stream of fire
>   flowed out from where he sat;
> Thousands upon thousands were ministering to him,
>   and myriads upon myriads attended him.

The court was convened, and the books were opened.
As the visions during the night continued, I saw

> One like a son of man coming,
>   on the clouds of heaven;
> When he reached the Ancient One
>   and was presented before him,
> He received dominion, glory, and kingship;
>   nations and peoples of every language serve him.
> His dominion is an everlasting dominion
>   that shall not be taken away,
>   his kingship shall not be destroyed.

The word of the Lord.

OR

Second Option

Revelation 12:7-12ab   Michael and his angels battled against the dragon.

A reading from the Book of Revelation

**War broke out in heaven;
   Michael and his angels battled against the dragon.
The dragon and its angels fought back,
   but they did not prevail
   and there was no longer any place for them in heaven.
The huge dragon, the ancient serpent,
   who is called the Devil and Satan,
   who deceived the whole world,
   was thrown down to earth,
   and its angels were thrown down with it.**

**Then I heard a loud voice in heaven say:
   "Now have salvation and power come,
     and the Kingdom of our God
     and the authority of his Anointed.
   For the accuser of our brothers is cast out,
     who accuses them before our God day and night.
   They conquered him by the Blood of the Lamb
     and by the word of their testimony;
     love for life did not deter them from death.
   Therefore, rejoice, you heavens,
     and you who dwell in them."**

The word of the Lord.

RESPONSORIAL PSALM

Psalm 138:1-2ab, 2cde-3, 4-5

℟. (1) **In the sight of the angels I will sing your praises, Lord.**

I will give thanks to you, O LORD**, with all my heart,
   for you have heard the words of my mouth;
   in the presence of the angels I will sing your praise;
I will worship at your holy temple
   and give thanks to your name.**

℟. **In the sight of the angels I will sing your praises, Lord.**

1556 *September 29—Saints Michael, Gabriel, and Raphael*

Because of your kindness and your truth;
 for you have made great above all things
 your name and your promise.
When I called, you answered me;
 you built up strength within me.

℟. **In the sight of the angels I will sing your praises, Lord.**

All the kings of the earth shall give thanks to you, O Lord,
 when they hear the words of your mouth;
And they shall sing of the ways of the Lord:
 "Great is the glory of the Lord."

℟. **In the sight of the angels I will sing your praises, Lord.**

ALLELUIA

Psalm 103:21

℟. **Alleluia, alleluia.**

Bless the Lord, all you angels,
you ministers, who do his will.

℟. **Alleluia, alleluia.**

GOSPEL

John 1:47-51 You will see the sky opened and the angels of God ascending and descending on the Son of Man.

✜ **A reading from the holy Gospel according to John**

Jesus saw Nathanael coming toward him and said of him,
 "Here is a true child of Israel.
There is no duplicity in him."
Nathanael said to him, "How do you know me?"
Jesus answered and said to him,
 "Before Philip called you, I saw you under the fig tree."
Nathanael answered him,
 "Rabbi, you are the Son of God; you are the King of Israel."
Jesus answered and said to him,
 "Do you believe
 because I told you that I saw you under the fig tree?
You will see greater things than this."
And he said to him, "Amen, amen, I say to you,
 you will see heaven opened
  and the angels of God ascending and descending on the Son of Man."

The Gospel of the Lord.

SEPTEMBER 30

648 SAINT JEROME, PRIEST AND DOCTOR OF THE CHURCH MEMORIAL

From the Common of Doctors of the Church, p. 1838, or the Common of Pastors, p. 1805,

OR

FIRST READING

2 Timothy 3:14-17   All Scripture is inspired by God and is useful for teaching.

A reading from the second Letter of Saint Paul to Timothy

Beloved:
Remain faithful to what you have learned and believed,
 because you know from whom you learned it,
 and that from infancy you have known the sacred Scriptures,
 which are capable of giving you wisdom for salvation
 through faith in Christ Jesus.
All Scripture is inspired by God
 and is useful for teaching, for refutation, for correction,
 and for training in righteousness,
 so that one who belongs to God may be competent,
 equipped for every good work.

The word of the Lord.

RESPONSORIAL PSALM

Psalm 119:9, 10, 11, 12, 13, 14

R. (12) **Lord, teach me your statutes.**

How shall a young man be faultless in his way?
 By keeping to your words.

R. Lord, teach me your statutes.

With all my heart I seek you;
 let me not stray from your commands.

R. Lord, teach me your statutes.

Within my heart I treasure your promise,
 that I may not sin against you.

R. Lord, teach me your statutes.

1558 September 30—Saint Jerome

Blessed are you, O Lord;
   teach me your statutes.

℟. **Lord, teach me your statutes.**

With my lips I declare
   all the ordinances of your mouth.

℟. **Lord, teach me your statutes.**

In the way of your decrees I rejoice,
   as much as in all riches.

℟. **Lord, teach me your statutes.**

ALLELUIA

See Acts 16:14b

℟. **Alleluia, alleluia.**

Open our hearts, O Lord,
to listen to the words of your Son.

℟. **Alleluia, alleluia.**

GOSPEL

Matthew 13:47-52   Both the new and the old.

✠ **A reading from the holy Gospel according to Matthew**

Jesus said to the disciples:
"**The Kingdom of heaven is like a net thrown into the sea,**
   which collects fish of every kind.
When it is full they haul it ashore
   and sit down to put what is good into buckets.
What is bad they throw away.
Thus it will be at the end of the age.
The angels will go out and separate the wicked from the righteous
   and throw them into the fiery furnace,
   where there will be wailing and grinding of teeth."
Jesus asked them:
"**Do you understand all these things?**"
They answered, "Yes."
And he replied,
   "**Then every scribe who has been instructed in the Kingdom of heaven**
   is like the head of a household who brings from his storeroom
   both the new and the old."

The Gospel of the Lord.

OCTOBER 1

649 SAINT THÉRÈSE OF THE CHILD JESUS, VIRGIN AND DOCTOR OF THE CHURCH MEMORIAL

From the Common for Virgins, p. 1857, or the Common of Holy Men and Women: For Religious, p. 1868,

OR

FIRST READING

Isaiah 66:10-14c   I will spread prosperity over her like a river.

A reading from the Book of the Prophet Isaiah

**Rejoice with Jerusalem and be glad because of her,
 all you who love her;
Exult, exult with her,
 all you who were mourning over her!
Oh, that you may suck fully
 of the milk of her comfort,
That you may nurse with delight
 at her abundant breasts!
 For thus says the Lord:
Lo, I will spread prosperity over her like a river,
 and the wealth of the nations like
 an overflowing torrent.
As nurslings, you shall be carried in her arms,
 and fondled in her lap;
As a mother comforts her son,
 so will I comfort you;
 in Jerusalem you shall find your comfort.**

**When you see this, your heart shall rejoice,
 and your bodies flourish like the grass;
The Lord's power shall be known to his servants.**

The word of the Lord.

RESPONSORIAL PSALM

Psalm 131:1bcde, 2, 3

℟. In you, Lord, I have found my peace.

O Lord, my heart is not proud,
　　nor are my eyes haughty;
I busy not myself with great things,
　　nor with things too sublime for me.

℟. In you, Lord, I have found my peace.

Nay rather, I have stilled and quieted
　　my soul like a weaned child.
Like a weaned child on its mother's lap,
　　so is my soul within me.

℟. In you, Lord, I have found my peace.

O Israel, hope in the Lord,
　　both now and forever.

℟. In you, Lord, I have found my peace.

ALLELUIA

See Matthew 11:25

℟. Alleluia, alleluia.

**Blessed are you, Father, Lord of heaven and earth;
you have revealed to little ones the mysteries of the Kingdom.**

℟. Alleluia, alleluia.

GOSPEL

Matthew 18:1-4　Unless you become like children, you will not enter the Kingdom of heaven.

✠ A reading from the holy Gospel according to Matthew

The disciples approached Jesus and said,
　　"Who is the greatest in the Kingdom of heaven?"
He called a child over, placed it in their midst, and said,
　　"Amen, I say to you, unless you turn and become like children,
　　you will not enter the Kingdom of heaven.
Whoever humbles himself like this child
　　is the greatest in the Kingdom of heaven."

The Gospel of the Lord.

OCTOBER 2

650 THE GUARDIAN ANGELS MEMORIAL

FIRST READING

Exodus 23:20-23   My angel will go before you.

A reading from the Book of Exodus

Thus says the Lord:
"See, I am sending an angel before you,
  to guard you on the way and bring you to the place I have prepared.
Be attentive to him and heed his voice.
Do not rebel against him, for he will not forgive your sin.
My authority resides in him.
If you heed his voice and carry out all I tell you,
  I will be an enemy to your enemies and a foe to your foes.

"My angel will go before you and bring you to the
  Amorites, Hittites, Perizzites,
  Canaanites, Hivites, and Jebusites;
  and I will wipe them out."

The word of the Lord.

RESPONSORIAL PSALM

Psalm 91:1-2, 3-4ab, 4c-6, 10-11

℟. (11) **The Lord has put angels in charge of you, to guard you in all your ways.**

You who dwell in the shelter of the Most High,
  who abide in the shadow of the Almighty,
Say to the Lord, "My refuge and my fortress,
  my God, in whom I trust."

℟. The Lord has put angels in charge of you, to guard you in all your ways.

For he will rescue you from the snare of the fowler,
  from the destroying pestilence.
With his pinions he will cover you,
  and under his wings you shall take refuge.

℟. The Lord has put angels in charge of you, to guard you in all your ways.

1562 October 2—The Guardian Angels

His faithfulness is a buckler and a shield.
You shall not fear the terror of the night
   nor the arrow that flies by day;
Nor the pestilence that roams in darkness,
   nor the devastating plague at noon.

℟. The Lord has put angels in charge of you, to guard you in all your ways.

No evil shall befall you,
   nor shall affliction come near your tent,
For to his angels he has given command about you,
   that they guard you in all your ways.

℟. The Lord has put angels in charge of you, to guard you in all your ways.

ALLELUIA

Psalm 103:21

℟. Alleluia, alleluia.

Bless the LORD, all you angels,
you ministers, who do his will.

℟. Alleluia, alleluia.

GOSPEL

Matthew 18:1-5, 10 Their angels in heaven always look upon the face of my heavenly Father.

✠ A reading from the holy Gospel according to Matthew

The disciples approached Jesus and said,
   "Who is the greatest in the Kingdom of heaven?"
He called a child over, placed it in their midst, and said,
   "Amen, I say to you, unless you turn and become like children,
   you will not enter the Kingdom of heaven.
Whoever humbles himself like this child
   is the greatest in the Kingdom of heaven.
And whoever receives one child such as this in my name receives me.

"See that you do not despise one of these little ones,
   for I say to you that their angels in heaven
   always look upon the face of my heavenly Father."

The Gospel of the Lord.

OCTOBER 4

651 SAINT FRANCIS OF ASSISI, RELIGIOUS MEMORIAL

From the Common of Holy Men and Women: For Religious, p. 1868,

OR

FIRST READING

Galatians 6:14-18   Through the cross the world has been crucified.

A reading from the Letter of Saint Paul to the Galatians

Brothers and sisters:
May I never boast except in the cross of our Lord Jesus Christ,
   through which the world has been crucified to me,
   and I to the world.
For neither does circumcision mean anything, nor does uncircumcision,
   but only a new creation.
Peace and mercy be to all who follow this rule and to the Israel of God.

From now on, let no one make troubles for me;
   for I bear the marks of Jesus on my body.

The grace of our Lord Jesus Christ be with your spirit,
   brothers and sisters. Amen.

The word of the Lord.

RESPONSORIAL PSALM

Psalm 16:1b-2a and 5, 7-8, 11

℟. (see 5a) **You are my inheritance, O Lord.**

Keep me, O God, for in you I take refuge.
   I say to the LORD, "My Lord are you."
O LORD, my allotted portion and my cup,
   you it is who hold fast my lot.

℟. **You are my inheritance, O Lord.**

I bless the LORD who counsels me;
   even in the night my heart exhorts me.
I set the LORD ever before me;
   with him at my right hand I shall not be disturbed.

℟. **You are my inheritance, O Lord.**

October 4—Saint Francis of Assisi

**You will show me the path to life,
fullness of joys in your presence,
the delights at your right hand forever.**

℞. **You are my inheritance, O Lord.**

ALLELUIA

See Matthew 11:25

℞. **Alleluia, alleluia.**

**Blessed are you, Father, Lord of heaven and earth;
you have revealed to little ones the mysteries of the Kingdom.**

℞. **Alleluia, alleluia.**

GOSPEL

Matthew 11:25-30   You have hidden these things from the learned and you have revealed them to the childlike.

✠ **A reading from the holy Gospel according to Matthew**

**At that time Jesus answered:
"I give praise to you, Father, Lord of heaven and earth,
for although you have hidden these things
from the wise and the learned
you have revealed them to the childlike.
Yes, Father, such has been your gracious will.
All things have been handed over to me by my Father.
No one knows the Son except the Father,
and no one knows the Father except the Son
and anyone to whom the Son wishes to reveal him.**

**"Come to me, all you who labor and are burdened,
and I will give you rest.
Take my yoke upon you and learn from me,
for I am meek and humble of heart;
and you will find rest for yourselves.
For my yoke is easy, and my burden light."**

The Gospel of the Lord.

OCTOBER 6

652 SAINT BRUNO, PRIEST

From the Common of Pastors, p. 1805, or the Common of Holy Men and Women: For Religious, p. 1868,

OR

FIRST READING

Philippians 3:8-14   I continue my pursuit towards the goal, the prize of God's upward calling, in Christ Jesus.

A reading from the Letter of Saint Paul to the Philippians

Brothers and sisters:
I consider everything as a loss
   because of the supreme good of knowing Christ Jesus my Lord.
For his sake I have accepted the loss of all things
   and I consider them so much rubbish,
   that I may gain Christ and be found in him,
   not having any righteousness of my own based on the law
   but that which comes through faith in Christ,
   the righteousness from God,
   depending on faith to know him and the power of his resurrection
   and the sharing of his sufferings by being conformed to his death,
   if somehow I may attain the resurrection from the dead.

It is not that I have already taken hold of it
   or have already attained perfect maturity,
   but I continue my pursuit in hope that I may possess it,
   since I have indeed been taken possession of by Christ Jesus.
Brothers and sisters, I for my part
   do not consider myself to have taken possession.
Just one thing: forgetting what lies behind
   but straining forward to what lies ahead,
   I continue my pursuit toward the goal,
   the prize of God's upward calling, in Christ Jesus.

The word of the Lord.

RESPONSORIAL PSALM

Psalm 1:1-2, 3, 4 and 6

℟. (40:5a) **Blessed are they who hope in the Lord.**
   or:
℟. (2a) **Blessed are they who delight in the law of the Lord.**
   or:
℟. (92:13-14) **The just will flourish like the palm tree in the garden of the Lord.**

Blessed the man who follows not
   the counsel of the wicked
Nor walks in the way of sinners,
   nor sits in the company of the insolent,
But delights in the law of the Lord
   and meditates on his law day and night.

℟. **Blessed are they who hope in the Lord.**
   or:
℟. **Blessed are they who delight in the law of the Lord.**
   or:
℟. **The just will flourish like the palm tree in the garden of the Lord.**

He is like a tree
   planted near running water,
That yields its fruit in due season,
   and whose leaves never fade.
   Whatever he does, prospers.

℟. **Blessed are they who hope in the Lord.**
   or:
℟. **Blessed are they who delight in the law of the Lord.**
   or:
℟. **The just will flourish like the palm tree in the garden of the Lord.**

Not so, the wicked, not so;
   they are like chaff which the wind drives away.
For the Lord watches over the way of the just,
   but the way of the wicked vanishes.

℟. **Blessed are they who hope in the Lord.**
   or:
℟. **Blessed are they who delight in the law of the Lord.**
   or:
℟. **The just will flourish like the palm tree in the garden of the Lord.**

ALLELUIA

John 8:12

℟. Alleluia, alleluia.

**I am the light of the world, says the Lord;
whoever follows me will have the light of life.**

℟. Alleluia, alleluia.

GOSPEL

Luke 9:57-62   I will follow you wherever you go.

✠ **A reading from the holy Gospel according to Luke**

**As Jesus and his disciples were proceeding
    on their journey
    someone said to him, "I will follow you wherever you go."
Jesus answered him,
    "Foxes have dens and birds of the sky have nests,
    but the Son of Man has nowhere to rest his head."
And to another he said, "Follow me."
But he replied, "Lord, let me go first and bury my father."
But he answered him, "Let the dead bury their dead.
But you, go and proclaim the Kingdom of God."
And another said, "I will follow you, Lord,
    but first let me say farewell to my family at home."
He said, "No one who sets a hand to the plow
    and looks to what was left behind is fit for the Kingdom of God."**

The Gospel of the Lord.

OCTOBER 6

[In the Dioceses of the United States]

652A BLESSED MARIE-ROSE DUROCHER, VIRGIN

From the Common of Virgins, p. 1857, or the Common of Holy Men and Women: For Religious, p. 1868.

OCTOBER 7

653 OUR LADY OF THE ROSARY MEMORIAL

From the Common of the Blessed Virgin Mary, p. 1751,

OR

FIRST READING

Acts 1:12-14   All these devoted themselves with one accord to prayer together with Mary, the Mother of Jesus.

A reading from the Acts of the Apostles

After Jesus had been taken up into heaven,
   the Apostles returned to Jerusalem
   from the mount called Olivet, which is near Jerusalem,
   a sabbath day's journey away.

When they entered the city
   they went to the upper room where they were staying,
   Peter and John and James and Andrew,
   Philip and Thomas, Bartholomew and Matthew,
   James son of Alphaeus, Simon the Zealot,
   and Judas son of James.
All these devoted themselves with one accord to prayer,
   together with some women,
   and Mary the mother of Jesus, and his brothers.

The word of the Lord.

RESPONSORIAL PSALM

Luke 1:46-47, 48-49, 50-51, 52-53, 54-55

℞. (49) **The Almighty has done great things for me, and holy is his Name.**
or:
℞. **O Blessed Virgin Mary, you carried the Son of the eternal Father.**

"My soul proclaims the greatness of the Lord,
  my spirit rejoices in God my Savior."

℞. **The Almighty has done great things for me, and holy is his Name.**
or:
℞. **O Blessed Virgin Mary, you carried the Son of the eternal Father.**

"For he has looked upon his lowly servant.
From this day all generations will call me blessed:
  the Almighty has done great things for me,
  and holy is his Name."

℞. **The Almighty has done great things for me, and holy is his Name.**
or:
℞. **O Blessed Virgin Mary, you carried the Son of the eternal Father.**

"He has mercy on those who fear him
  in every generation.
He has shown the strength of his arm,
  he has scattered the proud in their conceit."

℞. **The Almighty has done great things for me, and holy is his Name.**
or:
℞. **O Blessed Virgin Mary, you carried the Son of the eternal Father.**

"He has cast down the mighty from their thrones,
  and has lifted up the lowly.
He has filled the hungry with good things,
  and the rich he has sent away empty."

℞. **The Almighty has done great things for me, and holy is his Name.**
or:
℞. **O Blessed Virgin Mary, you carried the Son of the eternal Father.**

"He has come to the help of his servant Israel
  for he has remembered his promise of mercy,
  the promise he made to our fathers,
  to Abraham and his children forever."

℞. **The Almighty has done great things for me, and holy is his Name.**
or:
℞. **O Blessed Virgin Mary, you carried the Son of the eternal Father.**

ALLELUIA

See Luke 1:28

℟. Alleluia, alleluia.

Hail Mary, full of grace, the Lord is with you; blessed are you among women.

℟. Alleluia, alleluia.

GOSPEL

Luke 1:26-38   You will conceive in your womb and bear a son.

✠ **A reading from the holy Gospel according to Luke**

**The angel Gabriel was sent from God
    to a town of Galilee called Nazareth,
    to a virgin betrothed to a man named Joseph,
    of the house of David,
    and the virgin's name was Mary.
And coming to her, he said,
    "Hail, full of grace! The Lord is with you."
But she was greatly troubled at what was said
    and pondered what sort of greeting this might be.
Then the angel said to her,
    "Do not be afraid, Mary,
    for you have found favor with God.
Behold, you will conceive in your womb and bear a son,
    and you shall name him Jesus.
He will be great and will be called Son of the Most High,
    and the Lord God will give him the throne of David his father,
    and he will rule over the house of Jacob forever,
    and of his Kingdom there will be no end."
But Mary said to the angel,
    "How can this be,
    since I have no relations with a man?"
And the angel said to her in reply,
    "The Holy Spirit will come upon you,
    and the power of the Most High will overshadow you.
Therefore the child to be born
    will be called holy, the Son of God.
And behold, Elizabeth, your relative,
    has also conceived a son in her old age,
    and this is the sixth month for her who was called barren;
    for nothing will be impossible for God."
Mary said, "Behold, I am the handmaid of the Lord.
May it be done to me according to your word."
Then the angel departed from her.**

The Gospel of the Lord.

OCTOBER 9

654 SAINT DENIS, BISHOP AND MARTYR, AND HIS COMPANIONS, MARTYRS

From the Common of Martyrs, p. 1782,

OR

FIRST READING

2 Corinthians 6:4-10   As dying and behold we live.

A reading from the second Letter of Saint Paul to the Corinthians

Brothers and sisters:
In everything we commend ourselves as ministers of God,
   through much endurance, in afflictions, hardships, constraints,
   beatings, imprisonments, riots, labors, vigils, fasts;
   by purity, knowledge, patience, kindness,
   in the Holy Spirit, in unfeigned love, in truthful speech,
   in the power of God;
   with weapons of righteousness at the right and at the left;
   through glory and dishonor, insult and praise.
We are treated as deceivers and yet are truthful;
   as unrecognized and yet acknowledged;
   as dying and behold we live;
   as chastised and yet not put to death;
   as sorrowful yet always rejoicing;
   as poor yet enriching many;
   as having nothing and yet possessing all things.

The word of the Lord.

RESPONSORIAL PSALM

Psalm 126:1bc-2ab, 2cd-3, 4-5, 6

℟. (5) **Those who sow in tears shall reap rejoicing.**

When the LORD **brought back the captives of Zion,**
   we were like men dreaming.
Then our mouth was filled with laughter,
   and our tongue with rejoicing.

℟. **Those who sow in tears shall reap rejoicing.**

Then they said among the nations,
   "The LORD **has done great things for them."**
The LORD **has done great things for us;**
   we are glad indeed.

℟. **Those who sow in tears shall reap rejoicing.**

Restore our fortunes, O LORD**,**
   like the torrents in the southern desert.
Those who sow in tears
   shall reap rejoicing.

℟. **Those who sow in tears shall reap rejoicing.**

Although they go forth weeping,
   carrying the seed to be sown,
They shall come back rejoicing,
   carrying their sheaves.

℟. **Those who sow in tears shall reap rejoicing.**

ALLELUIA

John 8:12

℟. Alleluia, alleluia.

I am the light of the world, says the Lord;
whoever follows me will have the light of life.

℟. Alleluia, alleluia.

GOSPEL

Matthew 5:13-16   You are the light of the world.

✠ A reading from the holy Gospel according to Matthew

Jesus said to his disciples:
"You are the salt of the earth.
But if salt loses its taste, with what can it be seasoned?
It is no longer good for anything
   but to be thrown out and trampled underfoot.
You are the light of the world.
A city set on a mountain cannot be hidden.
Nor do they light a lamp and then put it under a bushel basket;
   it is set on a lampstand,
   where it gives light to all in the house.
Just so, your light must shine before others,
   that they may see your good deeds
   and glorify your heavenly Father."

The Gospel of the Lord.

OCTOBER 9

655 SAINT JOHN LEONARDI, PRIEST

From the Common of Pastors, p. 1805, or the Common of Holy Men and Women: For Those Who Work for the Underprivileged, p. 1868,

OR

FIRST READING

2 Corinthians 4:1-2, 5-7 We preach Jesus Christ as Lord, and ourselves as your slaves for the sake of Jesus.

A reading from the second Letter of Saint Paul to the Corinthians

Brothers and sisters:
Since we have this ministry through the mercy shown us,
   we are not discouraged.
Rather, we have renounced shameful, hidden things;
   not acting deceitfully or falsifying the word of God,
   but by the open declaration of the truth
   we commend ourselves to everyone's conscience in the sight of God.
For we do not preach ourselves but Jesus Christ as Lord,
   and ourselves as your slaves for the sake of Jesus.
For God who said, *Let light shine out of darkness,*
   has shone in our hearts to bring to light
   the knowledge of the glory of God on the face of Jesus Christ.

But we hold this treasure in earthen vessels,
   that the surpassing power may be of God and not from us.

The word of the Lord.

October 9—Saint John Leonardi

RESPONSORIAL PSALM

Psalm 96:1-2, 2-3, 7-8, 10

℟. (3) **Proclaim God's marvelous deeds to all the nations.**

Sing to the Lord a new song;
 sing to the Lord, all you lands.
Sing to the Lord; bless his name.

℟. **Proclaim God's marvelous deeds to all the nations.**

Announce his salvation, day after day.
Tell his glory among the nations;
 among all peoples, his wondrous deeds.

℟. **Proclaim God's marvelous deeds to all the nations.**

Give to the Lord, you families of nations,
 give to the Lord glory and praise;
 give to the Lord the glory due his name!

℟. **Proclaim God's marvelous deeds to all the nations.**

Say among the nations: The Lord is king.
He has made the world firm, not to be moved;
 he governs the peoples with equity.

℟. **Proclaim God's marvelous deeds to all the nations.**

ALLELUIA

Mark 1:17

℟. **Alleluia, alleluia.**

Come after me, says the Lord,
and I will make you fishers of men.

℟. **Alleluia, alleluia.**

GOSPEL

Luke 5:1-11   At your command I will lower the nets.

✚ **A reading from the holy Gospel according to Luke**

While the crowd was pressing in on Jesus and listening to the word of God,
    he was standing by the Lake of Gennesaret.
He saw two boats there alongside the lake;
    the fishermen had disembarked and were washing their nets.
Getting into one of the boats, the one belonging to Simon,
    he asked him to put out a short distance from the shore.
Then he sat down and taught the crowds from the boat.
After he had finished speaking, he said to Simon,
    "Put out into deep water and lower your nets for a catch."
Simon said in reply,
    "Master, we have worked hard all night and have caught nothing,
    but at your command I will lower the nets."
When they had done this, they caught a great number of fish
    and their nets were tearing.
They signaled to their partners in the other boat
    to come to help them.
They came and filled both boats
    so that they were in danger of sinking.
When Simon Peter saw this, he fell at the knees of Jesus and said,
    "Depart from me, Lord, for I am a sinful man."
For astonishment at the catch of fish they had made seized him
    and all those with him,
    and likewise James and John, the sons of Zebedee,
    who were partners of Simon.
Jesus said to Simon, "Do not be afraid;
    from now on you will be catching men."
When they brought their boats to the shore,
    they left everything and followed him.

The Gospel of the Lord.

OCTOBER 14

656 SAINT CALLISTUS I, POPE AND MARTYR

From the Common of Martyrs, p. 1782, or the Common of Pastors: For a Pope, p. 1805,

OR

FIRST READING

1 Peter 5:1-4   Tend the flock of God in your midst.

A reading from the first Letter of Saint Peter

Beloved:
I exhort the presbyters among you,
   as a fellow presbyter and witness to the sufferings of Christ
   and one who has a share in the glory to be revealed.
Tend the flock of God in your midst,
   overseeing it not by constraint but willingly,
   as God would have it, not for shameful profit but eagerly.
Do not lord it over those assigned to you,
   but be examples to the flock.
And when the chief Shepherd is revealed,
   you will receive the unfading crown of glory.

The word of the Lord.

RESPONSORIAL PSALM

Psalm 40:2 and 4ab, 7-8a, 8b-9, 10, 11

℟. (8a and 9a) **Here I am, Lord; I come to do your will.**

I have waited, waited for the LORD**,**
  and he stooped toward me and heard my cry.
And he put a new song into my mouth,
  a hymn to our God.

℟. **Here I am, Lord; I come to do your will.**

Sacrifice or oblation you wished not,
  but ears open to obedience you gave me.
Burnt offerings or sin-offerings you sought not;
  then said I, "Behold I come."

℟. **Here I am, Lord; I come to do your will.**

"In the written scroll it is prescribed for me,
To do your will, O my God, is my delight,
  and your law is within my heart!"

℟. **Here I am, Lord; I come to do your will.**

I announced your justice in the vast assembly;
  I did not restrain my lips, as you, O LORD**, know.**

℟. **Here I am, Lord; I come to do your will.**

Your justice I kept not hid within my heart;
  your faithfulness and your salvation I have spoken of;
I have made no secret of your kindness and your truth
  in the vast assembly.

℟. **Here I am, Lord; I come to do your will.**

ALLELUIA

John 15:15b

℟. Alleluia, alleluia.

I call you my friends, says the Lord,
for I have made known to you all that the Father has told me.

℟. Alleluia, alleluia.

GOSPEL

Luke 22:24-30   I confer a kingdom on you, just as my Father conferred one on me.

✚ A reading from the holy Gospel according to Luke

An argument broke out among the Apostles
  about which of them should be regarded as the greatest.
Jesus said to them,
  "The kings of the Gentiles lord it over them
    and those in authority over them are addressed as 'Benefactors';
  but among you it shall not be so.
Rather, let the greatest among you be as the youngest,
  and the leader as the servant.
For who is greater:
  the one seated at table or the one who serves?
Is it not the one seated at table?
I am among you as the one who serves.
It is you who have stood by me in my trials;
  and I confer a kingdom on you,
  just as my Father has conferred one on me,
  that you may eat and drink at my table in my Kingdom;
  and you will sit on thrones
  judging the twelve tribes of Israel."

The Gospel of the Lord.

OCTOBER 15

657 SAINT TERESA OF JESUS, VIRGIN AND DOCTOR OF THE CHURCH MEMORIAL

From the Common of Virgins, p. 1857, or the Common of Holy Men and Women: For Religious, p. 1868,

OR

FIRST READING

Romans 8:22-27   The Spirit himself intercedes with inexpressible groanings.

A reading from the Letter of Saint Paul to the Romans

Brothers and sisters:
We know that all creation is groaning in labor pains even until now;
  and not only that, but we ourselves,
  who have the firstfruits of the Spirit,
  we also groan within ourselves
  as we wait for adoption, the redemption of our bodies.
For in hope we were saved.
Now hope that sees for itself is not hope.
For who hopes for what one sees?
But if we hope for what we do not see, we wait with endurance.

In the same way, the Spirit too comes to the aid of our weakness;
  for we do not know how to pray as we ought,
  but the Spirit himself intercedes with inexpressible groanings.
And the one who searches hearts
  knows what is the intention of the Spirit,
  because he intercedes for the holy ones
  according to God's will.

The word of the Lord.

1582   October 15—Saint Teresa of Jesus

RESPONSORIAL PSALM

Psalm 19:8, 9, 10, 11

℟. (10) **The judgments of the Lord are true, and all of them are just.**
   or:
℟. (John 6:63) **Your words, Lord, are Spirit and life.**

The law of the LORD **is perfect,
   refreshing the soul.
The decree of the L**ORD **is trustworthy,
   giving wisdom to the simple.**

℟. The judgments of the Lord are true, and all of them are just.
   or:
℟. Your words, Lord, are Spirit and life.

The precepts of the LORD **are right,
   rejoicing the heart;
The command of the L**ORD **is clear,
   enlightening the eye.**

℟. The judgments of the Lord are true, and all of them are just.
   or:
℟. Your words, Lord, are Spirit and life.

The fear of the LORD **is pure,
   enduring forever;
The ordinances of the L**ORD **are true,
   all of them just.**

℟. The judgments of the Lord are true, and all of them are just.
   or:
℟. Your words, Lord, are Spirit and life.

**They are more precious than gold,
   than a heap of purest gold;
Sweeter also than syrup
   or honey from the comb.**

℟. The judgments of the Lord are true, and all of them are just.
   or:
℟. Your words, Lord, are Spirit and life.

ALLELUIA

John 15:9b, 5b

℟. **Alleluia, alleluia.**

**Remain in my love, says the Lord;
whoever remains in me and I in him will bear much fruit.**

℟. **Alleluia, alleluia.**

GOSPEL

John 15:1-8   Whoever remains in me and I in him will bear much fruit.

✠ **A reading from the holy Gospel according to John**

**Jesus said to his disciples:
"I am the true vine, and my Father is the vine grower.
He takes away every branch in me that does not bear fruit,
   and everyone that does he prunes so that it bears more fruit.
You are already pruned because of the word that I spoke to you.
Remain in me, as I remain in you.
Just as a branch cannot bear fruit on its own
   unless it remains on the vine,
   so neither can you unless you remain in me.
I am the vine, you are the branches.
Whoever remains in me and I in him will bear much fruit,
   because without me you can do nothing.
Anyone who does not remain in me
   will be thrown out like a branch and wither;
   people will gather them and throw them into a fire
   and they will be burned.
If you remain in me and my words remain in you,
   ask for whatever you want and it will be done for you.
By this is my Father glorified,
   that you bear much fruit and become my disciples."**

The Gospel of the Lord.

OCTOBER 16

658 SAINT HEDWIG, RELIGIOUS

From the Common of Holy Men and Women: For Religious, p. 1868,

OR

FIRST READING

Sirach 26:1-4, 13-16   Like the sun rising, the beauty of a virtuous wife is the radiance of her home.

A reading from the Book of Sirach

Blessed the husband of a good wife,
  twice-lengthened are his days;
A worthy wife brings joy to her husband,
  peaceful and full is his life.
A good wife is a generous gift
  bestowed upon him who fears the LORD**;**
Be he rich or poor, his heart is content,
  and a smile is ever on his face.

A gracious wife delights her husband,
  her thoughtfulness puts flesh on his bones;
A gift from the LORD **is her governed speech,**
  and her firm virtue is of surpassing worth.
Choicest of blessings is a modest wife,
  priceless her chaste soul.
A holy and decent woman adds grace upon grace;
  indeed, no price is worthy of her temperate soul.
Like the sun rising in the LORD**'s heavens,**
  the beauty of a virtuous wife is the radiance of her home.

The word of the Lord.

RESPONSORIAL PSALM

Psalm 128:1-2, 3, 4-5

℟. (1) **Blessed are those who fear the Lord.**

Blessed are you who fear the LORD**,**
  who walk in his ways!
For you shall eat the fruit of your handiwork;
  blessed shall you be, and favored.

℟. **Blessed are those who fear the Lord.**

Your wife shall be like a fruitful vine
   in the recesses of your home;
Your children like olive plants
   around your table.

℟. Blessed are those who fear the Lord.

Behold, thus is the man blessed
   who fears the Lord.
The Lord bless you from Zion:
   may you see the prosperity of Jerusalem
   all the days of your life.

℟. Blessed are those who fear the Lord.

ALLELUIA

John 8:31b-32

℟. Alleluia, alleluia.

If you remain in my word, you will truly be my disciples,
and you will know the truth, says the Lord.

℟. Alleluia, alleluia.

GOSPEL

Mark 3:31-35   Whoever does the will of God is my brother and sister and mother.

✠ A reading from the holy Gospel according to Mark

Jesus' mother and his brothers arrived.
Standing outside, they sent word to him and called him.
A crowd seated around him told him,
   "Your mother and your brothers and your sisters
   are outside asking for you."
But he said to them in reply,
   "Who are my mother and my brothers?"
And looking around at those seated in the circle he said,
   "Here are my mother and my brothers.
For whoever does the will of God
   is my brother and sister and mother."

The Gospel of the Lord.

OCTOBER 16

659 SAINT MARGARET MARY ALACOQUE, VIRGIN

From the Common of Virgins, p. 1857, or the Common of Holy Men and Women: For Religious, p. 1868,

OR

FIRST READING

Ephesians 3:14-19   To know the love of Christ that surpasses knowledge.

A reading from the Letter of Saint Paul to the Ephesians

Brothers and sisters:
I kneel before the Father,
  from whom every family in heaven and on earth is named,
  that he may grant you in accord with the riches of his glory
  to be strengthened with power through his Spirit in the inner self,
  and that Christ may dwell in your hearts through faith;
  that you, rooted and grounded in love,
  may have strength to comprehend with all the holy ones
  what is the breadth and length and height and depth,
  and to know the love of Christ that surpasses knowledge,
  so that you may be filled with all the fullness of God.

The word of the Lord.

RESPONSORIAL PSALM

Psalm 23:1b-3a, 4, 5, 6

℟. (1) **The Lord is my shepherd; there is nothing I shall want.**

The LORD is my shepherd; I shall not want.
  In verdant pastures he gives me repose;
Beside restful waters he leads me;
  he refreshes my soul.

℟. **The Lord is my shepherd; there is nothing I shall want.**

Even though I walk in the dark valley
  I fear no evil; for you are at my side
With your rod and your staff
  that give me courage.

℟. **The Lord is my shepherd; there is nothing I shall want.**

October 16—Saint Margaret Mary Alacoque 1587

You spread the table before me
  in the sight of my foes;
You anoint my head with oil;
  my cup overflows.

℟. **The Lord is my shepherd; there is nothing I shall want.**

Only goodness and kindness follow me
  all the days of my life;
And I shall dwell in the house of the LORD
  for years to come.

℟. **The Lord is my shepherd; there is nothing I shall want.**

ALLELUIA

See Matthew 11:25

℟. **Alleluia, alleluia.**

Blessed are you, Father, Lord of heaven and earth;
you have revealed to little ones the mysteries of the Kingdom.

℟. **Alleluia, alleluia.**

GOSPEL

Matthew 11:25-30   You have hidden these things from the wise and the learned and have revealed them to the childlike.

✠   **A reading from the holy Gospel according to Matthew**

At that time Jesus answered:
"I give praise to you, Father, Lord of heaven and earth,
  for although you have hidden these things
    from the wise and the learned
    you have revealed them to the childlike.
Yes, Father, such has been your gracious will.
All things have been handed over to me by my Father.
No one knows the Son except the Father,
  and no one knows the Father except the Son
    and anyone to whom the Son wishes to reveal him.

"Come to me, all you who labor and are burdened,
  and I will give you rest.
Take my yoke upon you and learn from me,
  for I am meek and humble of heart;
  and you will find rest for yourselves.
For my yoke is easy, and my burden light."

The Gospel of the Lord.

OCTOBER 17

660 SAINT IGNATIUS OF ANTIOCH, BISHOP AND MARTYR MEMORIAL

From the Common of Martyrs, p. 1782, or the Common of Pastors, p. 1805,

OR

FIRST READING

Philippians 3:17—4:1   Our citizenship is in heaven.

A reading from the Letter of Saint Paul to the Philippians

**Join with others in being imitators of me, brothers and sisters,
and observe those who thus conduct themselves
according to the model you have in us.
For many, as I have often told you
and now tell you even in tears
conduct themselves as enemies of the cross of Christ.
Their end is destruction.
Their God is their stomach;
their glory is in their "shame."
Their minds are occupied with earthly things.
But our citizenship is in heaven,
and from it we also await a savior, the Lord Jesus Christ.
He will change our lowly body
to conform with his glorified Body
by the power that enables him also
to bring all things into subjection to himself.**

**Therefore, my brothers and sisters,
whom I love and long for, my joy and crown,
in this way stand firm in the Lord, beloved.**

The word of the Lord.

RESPONSORIAL PSALM

Psalm 34:2-3, 4-5, 6-7, 8-9

℟. (5) **The Lord delivered me from all my fears.**

I will bless the LORD **at all times;**
   his praise shall be ever in my mouth.
Let my soul glory in the LORD**;**
   the lowly will hear me and be glad.

℟. **The L**ORD **delivered me from all my fears.**

Glorify the LORD **with me,**
   let us together extol his name.
I sought the LORD**, and he answered me**
   and delivered me from all my fears.

℟. **The L**ORD **set me free from all my fears.**

Look to him that you may be radiant with joy,
   and your faces may not blush with shame.
When the poor one called out, the LORD **heard,**
   and from all his distress he saved him.

℟. **The L**ORD **delivered me from all my fears.**

The angel of the LORD **encamps**
   around those who fear him, and delivers them.
Taste and see how good the LORD **is;**
   blessed the man who takes refuge in him.

℟. **The L**ORD **delivered me from all my fears.**

ALLELUIA

James 1:12

℟. Alleluia, alleluia.

**Blessed is the man who perseveres in temptation,
for when he has been proved he will receive the crown of life.**

℟. Alleluia, alleluia.

GOSPEL

John 12:24-26   If a grain of wheat falls to the ground and dies, it produces much fruit.

☩ A reading from the holy Gospel according to John

**Jesus said to his disciples:
"Amen, amen, I say to you,
    unless a grain of wheat falls to the ground and dies,
    it remains just a grain of wheat;
    but if it dies, it produces much fruit.
Whoever loves his life loses it,
    and whoever hates his life in this world
    will preserve it for eternal life.
Whoever serves me must follow me,
    and where I am, there also will my servant be.
The Father will honor whoever serves me."**

The Gospel of the Lord.

OCTOBER 18

661 SAINT LUKE, EVANGELIST FEAST

FIRST READING

2 Timothy 4:10-17b   Luke is the only one with me.

A reading from the second Letter of Saint Paul to Timothy

Beloved:
Demas, enamored of the present world,
 deserted me and went to Thessalonica,
 Crescens to Galatia, and Titus to Dalmatia.
Luke is the only one with me.
Get Mark and bring him with you,
 for he is helpful to me in the ministry.
I have sent Tychicus to Ephesus.
When you come, bring the cloak I left with Carpus in Troas,
 the papyrus rolls, and especially the parchments.

Alexander the coppersmith did me a great deal of harm;
 the Lord will repay him according to his deeds.
You too be on guard against him,
 for he has strongly resisted our preaching.

At my first defense no one appeared on my behalf,
 but everyone deserted me.
May it not be held against them!
But the Lord stood by me and gave me strength,
 so that through me the proclamation might be completed
 and all the Gentiles might hear it.

The word of the Lord.

RESPONSORIAL PSALM

Psalm 145:10-11, 12-13, 17-18

℟. (12) **Your friends make known, O Lord, the glorious splendor of your Kingdom.**

**Let all your works give you thanks, O LORD,
  and let your faithful ones bless you.
Let them discourse of the glory of your Kingdom
  and speak of your might.**

℟. **Your friends make known, O Lord, the glorious splendor of your Kingdom.**

**Making known to men your might
  and the glorious splendor of your Kingdom.
Your Kingdom is a Kingdom for all ages,
  and your dominion endures through all generations.**

℟. **Your friends make known, O Lord, the glorious splendor of your Kingdom.**

**The LORD is just in all his ways
  and holy in all his works.
The LORD is near to all who call upon him,
  to all who call upon him in truth.**

℟. **Your friends make known, O Lord, the glorious splendor of your Kingdom.**

ALLELUIA

See John 15:16

℟. **Alleluia, alleluia.**

**I chose you from the world,
to go and bear fruit that will last, says the Lord.**

℟. **Alleluia, alleluia.**

GOSPEL

Luke 10:1-9   The harvest is abundant but the laborers are few.

☩ **A reading from the holy Gospel according to Luke**

**The Lord Jesus appointed seventy-two disciples
   whom he sent ahead of him in pairs
   to every town and place he intended to visit.
He said to them,
   "The harvest is abundant but the laborers are few;
   so ask the master of the harvest
   to send out laborers for his harvest.
Go on your way;
   behold, I am sending you like lambs among wolves.
Carry no money bag, no sack, no sandals;
   and greet no one along the way.
Into whatever house you enter,
   first say, 'Peace to this household.'
If a peaceful person lives there,
   your peace will rest on him;
   but if not, it will return to you.
Stay in the same house and eat and drink what is offered to you,
   for the laborer deserves payment.
Do not move about from one house to another.
Whatever town you enter and they welcome you,
   eat what is set before you,
   cure the sick in it and say to them,
   'The Kingdom of God is at hand for you.'"**

The Gospel of the Lord.

OCTOBER 19

[In the Dioceses of the United States]

662 SAINTS JOHN DE BRÉBEUF AND ISAAC JOGUES, PRIESTS AND MARTYRS, AND THEIR COMPANIONS, MARTYRS MEMORIAL

From the Common of Martyrs, p. 1782, or the Common of Pastors: For Missionaries, p. 1805,

OR

FIRST READING

2 Corinthians 4:7-15   We carry about in our body the dying of Jesus.

A reading from the second Letter of Saint Paul to the Corinthians

Brothers and sisters:
We hold this treasure in earthen vessels,
   that the surpassing power may be of God and not from us.
We are afflicted in every way, but not constrained;
   perplexed, but not driven to despair;
   persecuted, but not abandoned;
   struck down, but not destroyed;
   always carrying about in the body the dying of Jesus,
   so that the life of Jesus may also be manifested in our body.
For we who live are constantly being given up to death
   for the sake of Jesus,
   so that the life of Jesus may be manifested in our mortal flesh.

So death is at work in us, but life in you.
Since, then, we have the same spirit of faith,
   according to what is written, *I believed, therefore I spoke,*
   we too believe and therefore speak,
   knowing that the one who raised the Lord Jesus
   will raise us also with Jesus
   and place us with you in his presence.
Everything indeed is for you,
   so that the grace bestowed in abundance on more and more people
   may cause the thanksgiving to overflow for the glory of God.

The word of the Lord.

RESPONSORIAL PSALM

Psalm 126:1bc-2ab, 2cd-3, 4-5, 6

℟. (5) **Those who sow in tears shall reap rejoicing.**

**When the Lord brought back the captives of Zion,
 we were like men dreaming.
Then our mouth was filled with laughter,
 and our tongue with rejoicing.**

℟. **Those who sow in tears shall reap rejoicing.**

**Then they said among the nations,
 "The Lord has done great things for them."
The Lord has done great things for us;
 we are glad indeed.**

℟. **Those who sow in tears shall reap rejoicing.**

**Restore our fortunes, O Lord,
 like the torrents in the southern desert.
Those who sow in tears
 shall reap rejoicing.**

℟. **Those who sow in tears shall reap rejoicing.**

**Although they go forth weeping,
 carrying the seed to be sown,
They shall come back rejoicing,
 carrying their sheaves.**

℟. **Those who sow in tears shall reap rejoicing.**

ALLELUIA

Matthew 28:19a, 20b

℟. **Alleluia, alleluia.**

**Go and teach all nations, says the Lord;
I am with you always, until the end of the world.**

℟. **Alleluia, alleluia.**

GOSPEL

Matthew 28:16-20   Go, therefore, and make disciples of all nations.

✟ A reading from the holy Gospel according to Matthew

The Eleven disciples went to Galilee,
   to the mountain to which Jesus had ordered them.
When they saw him, they worshiped, but they doubted.
Then Jesus approached and said to them,
   "All power in heaven and on earth has been given to me.
Go, therefore, and make disciples of all nations,
   baptizing them in the name of the Father,
   and of the Son, and of the Holy Spirit,
   teaching them to observe all that I have commanded you.
And behold, I am with you always, until the end of the age."

The Gospel of the Lord.

OCTOBER 20

[In the Dioceses of the United States]

663 SAINT PAUL OF THE CROSS, PRIEST

From the Common of Pastors, p. 1805, or the Common of Holy Men and Women: For Religious, p. 1868,

OR

FIRST READING

1 Corinthians 1:18-25   It was the will of God through the foolishness of the proclamation to save those who have faith.

A reading from the first Letter of Saint Paul to the Corinthians

Brothers and sisters:
The message of the cross is foolishness to those who are perishing,
   but to us who are being saved it is the power of God.
For it is written:

> *I will destroy the wisdom of the wise,*
>   *and the learning of the learned I will set aside.*

Where is the wise one?
Where is the scribe?
Where is the debater of this age?
Has not God made the wisdom of the world foolish?
For since in the wisdom of God
   the world did not come to know God through wisdom,
   it was the will of God through the foolishness of the proclamation
   to save those who have faith.
For Jews demand signs and Greeks look for wisdom,
   but we proclaim Christ crucified,
   a stumbling block to Jews and foolishness to Gentiles,
   but to those who are called, Jews and Greeks alike,
   Christ the power of God and the wisdom of God.
For the foolishness of God is wiser than human wisdom,
   and the weakness of God is stronger than human strength.

The word of the Lord.

RESPONSORIAL PSALM

Psalm 117:1bc, 2

℟. (Mark 16:15) **Go out to all the world and tell the Good News.**

**Praise the Lord, all you nations;
  glorify him, all you peoples!**

℟. **Go out to all the world and tell the Good News.**

**For steadfast is his kindness toward us,
  and the fidelity of the Lord endures forever.**

℟. **Go out to all the world and tell the Good News.**

ALLELUIA

Matthew 5:6

℟. **Alleluia, alleluia.**

**Blessed are those who hunger and thirst for righteousness;
for they will be satisfied.**

℟. **Alleluia, alleluia.**

GOSPEL

Matthew 16:24-27 Whoever loses his life for my sake will save it.

✠ **A reading from the holy Gospel according to Matthew**

**Jesus said to his disciples,
  "Whoever wishes to come after me must deny himself,
  take up his cross, and follow me.
For whoever wishes to save his life will lose it,
  but whoever loses his life for my sake will find it.
What profit would there be for one to gain the whole world
  and forfeit his life?
Or what can one give in exchange for his life?
For the Son of Man will come with his angels in his Father's glory,
  and then he will repay each one according to his conduct."**

The Gospel of the Lord.

OCTOBER 23

664 SAINT JOHN OF CAPISTRANO, PRIEST

From the Common of Pastors: For Missionaries, p. 1805,

> OR

FIRST READING

2 Corinthians 5:14-20   God has given us the ministry of reconciliation.

A reading from the second Letter of Saint Paul to the Corinthians

Brothers and sisters:
The love of Christ impels us,
   once we have come to the conviction that one died for all;
   therefore, all have died.
He indeed died for all,
   so that those who live might no longer live for themselves
   but for him who for their sake died and was raised.

Consequently, from now on we regard no one according to the flesh;
   even if we once knew Christ according to the flesh,
   yet now we know him so no longer.
So whoever is in Christ is a new creation:
   the old things have passed away;
   behold, new things have come.
And all this is from God,
   who has reconciled us to himself through Christ
   and given us the ministry of reconciliation,
   namely, God was reconciling the world to himself in Christ,
   not counting their trespasses against them
   and entrusting to us the message of reconciliation.
So we are ambassadors for Christ,
   as if God were appealing through us.
We implore you on behalf of Christ,
   be reconciled to God.

The word of the Lord.

RESPONSORIAL PSALM

Psalm 16:1b-2a and 5, 7-8, 11

℟. (see 5a) **You are my inheritance, O Lord.**

**Keep me, O God, for in you I take refuge.
 I say to the L**ORD**, "My Lord are you."
O L**ORD**, my allotted portion and my cup,
 you it is who hold fast my lot.**

℟. **You are my inheritance, O Lord.**

I bless the LORD **who counsels me;
 even in the night my heart exhorts me.
I set the L**ORD **ever before me;
 with him at my right hand I shall not be disturbed.**

℟. **You are my inheritance, O Lord.**

**You will show me the path to life,
 fullness of joys in your presence,
 the delights at your right hand forever.**

℟. **You are my inheritance, O Lord.**

ALLELUIA

John 8:12

℟. Alleluia, alleluia.

I am the light of the world, says the Lord;
whoever follows me will have the light of life.

℟. Alleluia, alleluia.

GOSPEL

Luke 9:57-62   I will follow you wherever you go.

☩ A reading from the holy Gospel according to Luke

As Jesus and his disciples were proceeding on their journey
  someone said to him, "I will follow you wherever you go."
Jesus answered him,
  "Foxes have dens and birds of the sky have nests,
  but the Son of Man has nowhere to rest his head."
And to another he said, "Follow me."
But he replied, "Lord, let me go first and bury my father."
But he answered him, "Let the dead bury their dead.
But you, go and proclaim the Kingdom of God."
And another said, "I will follow you, Lord,
  but first let me say farewell to my family at home."
He said, "No one who sets a hand to the plow
  and looks to what was left behind is fit for the Kingdom of God."

The Gospel of the Lord.

OCTOBER 24

665 SAINT ANTHONY MARY CLARET, BISHOP

From the Common of Pastors: For Missionaries, p. 1805,

OR

FIRST READING

Isaiah 52:7-10   All the ends of the earth will behold the salvation of our God.

A reading from the Book of the Prophet Isaiah

> How beautiful upon the mountains
>   are the feet of him who brings glad tidings,
> Announcing peace, bearing good news,
>   announcing salvation, and saying to Zion,
>   "Your God is King!"
> Hark! Your sentinels raise a cry,
>   together they shout for joy,
> For they see directly, before their eyes,
>   the Lord restoring Zion.
> Break out together in song,
>   O ruins of Jerusalem!
> For the Lord comforts his people,
>   he redeems Jerusalem.
> The Lord has bared his holy arm
>   in the sight of all the nations;
> All the ends of the earth will behold
>   the salvation of our God.

The word of the Lord.

RESPONSORIAL PSALM

Psalm 96:1-2a, 2b-3, 7-8, 10

℟. (3) **Proclaim God's marvelous deeds to all the nations.**

Sing to the Lord a new song;
  sing to the Lord, all you lands.
Sing to the Lord; bless his name.

℟. **Proclaim God's marvelous deeds to all the nations.**

Announce his salvation, day after day.
Tell his glory among the nations;
  among all peoples, his wondrous deeds.

℟. **Proclaim God's marvelous deeds to all the nations.**

October 24—Saints Anthony Mary Claret **1603**

Give to the LORD**, you families of nations,**
  give to the LORD **glory and praise;**
  give to the LORD **the glory due his name!**

℟. **Proclaim God's marvelous deeds to all the nations.**

Say among the nations: The LORD **is king.**
He has made the world firm, not to be moved;
  he governs the peoples with equity.

℟. **Proclaim God's marvelous deeds to all the nations.**

ALLELUIA

Mark 1:17

℟. **Alleluia, alleluia.**

Come after me, says the Lord,
and I will make you fishers of men.

℟. **Alleluia, alleluia.**

GOSPEL

Mark 1:14-20   I will make you fishers of men.

✠ **A reading from the holy Gospel according to Mark**

After John the Baptist had been arrested,
  Jesus came to Galilee proclaiming the Gospel of God:
  "This is the time of fulfillment.
The Kingdom of God is at hand.
Repent, and believe in the Gospel."

As he passed by the Sea of Galilee,
  he saw Simon and his brother Andrew casting their nets into the sea;
  they were fishermen.
Jesus said to them,
  "Come after me, and I will make you fishers of men."
Then they abandoned their nets and followed him.
He walked along a little farther
  and saw James, the son of Zebedee, and his brother John.
They too were in a boat mending their nets.
Then he called them.
So they left their father Zebedee in the boat
  along with the hired men and followed him.

The Gospel of the Lord.

OCTOBER 28

666 SAINTS SIMON AND JUDE, APOSTLES FEAST

For a votive Mass of the Apostles, or of a single Apostle, the readings are as follows.

FIRST READING

Ephesians 2:19-22   Built upon the foundation of the Apostles.

A reading from the Letter of Saint Paul to the Ephesians

Brothers and sisters:
You are no longer strangers and sojourners,
　but you are fellow citizens with the holy ones
　and members of the household of God,
　built upon the foundation of the Apostles and prophets,
　with Christ Jesus himself as the capstone.
Through him the whole structure is held together
　and grows into a temple sacred in the Lord;
　in him you also are being built together
　into a dwelling place of God in the Spirit.

The word of the Lord.

RESPONSORIAL PSALM

Psalm 19:2-3, 4-5

℟. (5a) **Their message goes out through all the earth.**

**The heavens declare the glory of God,
　and the firmament proclaims his handiwork.
Day pours out the word to day,
　and night to night imparts knowledge.**

℟. **Their message goes out through all the earth.**

**Not a word nor a discourse
　whose voice is not heard;
Through all the earth their voice resounds,
　and to the ends of the world, their message.**

℟. **Their message goes out through all the earth.**

ALLELUIA

See *Te Deum*

℟. Alleluia, alleluia.

We praise you, O God,
we acclaim you as Lord;
the glorious company of Apostles praise you.

℟. Alleluia, alleluia.

GOSPEL

Luke 6:12-16   From them Jesus chose Twelve, whom he also named Apostles.

☩ A reading from the holy Gospel according to Luke

Jesus went up to the mountain to pray,
   and he spent the night in prayer to God.
When day came, he called his disciples to himself,
   and from them he chose Twelve, whom he also named Apostles:
   Simon, whom he named Peter, and his brother Andrew,
   James, John, Philip, Bartholomew, Matthew,
   Thomas, James the son of Alphaeus,
   Simon who was called a Zealot,
   and Judas the son of James,
   and Judas Iscariot, who became a traitor.

The Gospel of the Lord.

NOVEMBER 1

667 ALL SAINTS SOLEMNITY

FIRST READING

Revelation 7:2-4, 9-14   I had a vision of a great multitude, which no one could count, from every nation, race, people and tongue.

A reading from the Book of Revelation

I, John, saw another angel come up from the East,
  holding the seal of the living God.
He cried out in a loud voice to the four angels
  who were given power to damage the land and the sea,
  "Do not damage the land or the sea or the trees
  until we put the seal on the foreheads of the servants of our God."
I heard the number of those who had been marked with the seal,
  one hundred and forty-four thousand marked
  from every tribe of the children of Israel.

After this I had a vision of a great multitude,
  which no one could count,
  from every nation, race, people, and tongue.
They stood before the throne and before the Lamb,
  wearing white robes and holding palm branches in their hands.
They cried out in a loud voice:

  "Salvation comes from our God, who is seated on the throne,
  and from the Lamb."

All the angels stood around the throne
  and around the elders and the four living creatures.
They prostrated themselves before the throne,
  worshiped God, and exclaimed:

  "Amen. Blessing and glory, wisdom and thanksgiving,
    honor, power, and might
    be to our God forever and ever. Amen."

Then one of the elders spoke up and said to me,
  "Who are these wearing white robes, and where did they come from?"
I said to him, "My lord, you are the one who knows."
He said to me,
  "These are the ones who have survived the time of great distress;
  they have washed their robes
  and made them white in the Blood of the Lamb."

The word of the Lord.

RESPONSORIAL PSALM

Psalm 24:1bc-2, 3-4ab, 5-6

℟. (see 6) **Lord, this is the people that longs to see your face.**

The Lord's are the earth and its fullness;
  the world and those who dwell in it.
For he founded it upon the seas
  and established it upon the rivers.

℟. **Lord, this is the people that longs to see your face.**

Who can ascend the mountain of the Lord?
  or who may stand in his holy place?
One whose hands are sinless, whose heart is clean,
  who desires not what is vain.

℟. **Lord, this is the people that longs to see your face.**

He shall receive a blessing from the Lord,
  a reward from God his savior.
Such is the race that seeks him,
  that seeks the face of the God of Jacob.

℟. **Lord, this is the people that longs to see your face.**

SECOND READING

1 John 3:1-3   We shall see God as he is.

A reading from the first Letter of Saint John

Beloved:
See what love the Father has bestowed on us
  that we may be called the children of God.
Yet so we are.
The reason the world does not know us
  is that it did not know him.
Beloved, we are God's children now;
  what we shall be has not yet been revealed.
We do know that when it is revealed we shall be like him,
  for we shall see him as he is.
Everyone who has this hope based on him makes himself pure,
  as he is pure.

The word of the Lord.

ALLELUIA

Matthew 11:28

℟. Alleluia, alleluia.

Come to me, all you who labor and are burdened,
and I will give you rest, says the Lord.

℟. Alleluia, alleluia.

GOSPEL

Matthew 5:1-12a   Rejoice and be glad, for your reward will be great in heaven.

✠ A reading from the holy Gospel according to Matthew

When Jesus saw the crowds, he went up the mountain,
  and after he had sat down, his disciples came to him.
He began to teach them, saying:

> "Blessed are the poor in spirit,
>   for theirs is the Kingdom of heaven.
> Blessed are they who mourn,
>   for they will be comforted.
> Blessed are the meek,
>   for they will inherit the land.
> Blessed are they who hunger and thirst for righteousness,
>   for they will be satisfied.
> Blessed are the merciful,
>   for they will be shown mercy.
> Blessed are the clean of heart,
>   for they will see God.
> Blessed are the peacemakers,
>   for they will be called children of God.
> Blessed are they who are persecuted for the sake of righteousness,
>   for theirs is the Kingdom of heaven.
> Blessed are you when they insult you and persecute you
>   and utter every kind of evil against you falsely because of me.
> Rejoice and be glad,
>   for your reward will be great in heaven."

The Gospel of the Lord.

NOVEMBER 2

668 THE COMMEMORATION OF ALL THE FAITHFUL DEPARTED (ALL SOULS)

The following readings or those given in the Masses for the Dead, nos. 1011–1015, may be used.

FIRST READING

1.

Wisdom 3:1-9   As sacrificial offerings he took them to himself.

A reading from the Book of Wisdom

The souls of the just are in the hand of God,
  and no torment shall touch them.
They seemed, in the view of the foolish, to be dead;
  and their passing away was thought an affliction
  and their going forth from us, utter destruction.
But they are in peace.
For if before men, indeed they be punished,
  yet is their hope full of immortality;
chastised a little, they shall be greatly blessed,
  because God tried them
  and found them worthy of himself.
As gold in the furnace, he proved them,
  and as sacrificial offerings he took them to himself.
In the time of their visitation they shall shine,
  and shall dart about as sparks through stubble;
they shall judge nations and rule over peoples,
  and the Lord shall be their King forever.
Those who trust in him shall understand truth,
  and the faithful shall abide with him in love:
because grace and mercy are with his holy ones,
  and his care is with his elect.

The word of the Lord.

2.

Wisdom 4:7-14   An unsullied life, the attainment of old age.

A reading from the Book of Wisdom

**The just man, though he die early,
    shall be at rest.
For the age that is honorable comes not
    with the passing of time,
    nor can it be measured in terms of years.
Rather, understanding is the hoary crown for men,
    and an unsullied life, the attainment of old age.
He who pleased God was loved;
    he who lived among sinners was transported—**
snatched away, lest wickedness pervert his mind
    or deceit beguile his soul;
for the witchery of paltry things obscures what is right
    and the whirl of desire transforms the innocent mind.
Having become perfect in a short while,
    he reached the fullness of a long career;
    for his soul was pleasing to the Lord,
    therefore he sped him out of the midst of wickedness.
But the people saw and did not understand,
    nor did they take this into account.

The word of the Lord.

3.

Isaiah 25:6, 7-9   The Lord will destroy death forever.

A reading from the Book of the Prophet Isaiah

On this mountain the Lord of hosts
    will provide for all peoples.
On this mountain he will destroy
    the veil that veils all peoples,
the web that is woven over all nations;
    he will destroy death forever.
The Lord God will wipe away
    the tears from all faces;
the reproach of his people he will remove
    from the whole earth; for the Lord has spoken.
    On that day it will be said:
"Behold our God, to whom we looked to save us!
    This is the Lord for whom we looked;
    let us rejoice and be glad that he has saved us!"

The word of the Lord.

RESPONSORIAL PSALM

1.

Psalm 23:1-3a, 3b-4, 5, 6

℟. (1) **The Lord is my shepherd; there is nothing I shall want.**
   or:
℟. **Though I walk in the valley of darkness, I fear no evil, for you are with me.**

The LORD **is my shepherd; I shall not want.**
   In verdant pastures he gives me repose;
beside restful waters he leads me;
   he refreshes my soul.

℟. **The Lord is my shepherd; there is nothing I shall want.**
   or:
℟. **Though I walk in the valley of darkness, I fear no evil, for you are with me.**

He guides me in right paths
   for his name's sake.
Even though I walk in the dark valley
   I fear no evil; for you are at my side
with your rod and your staff
   that give me courage.

℟. **The Lord is my shepherd; there is nothing I shall want.**
   or:
℟. **Though I walk in the valley of darkness, I fear no evil, for you are with me.**

You spread the table before me
   in the sight of my foes;
You anoint my head with oil;
   my cup overflows.

℟. **The Lord is my shepherd; there is nothing I shall want.**
   or:
℟. **Though I walk in the valley of darkness, I fear no evil, for you are with me.**

Only goodness and kindness follow me
   all the days of my life;
and I shall dwell in the house of the LORD
   for years to come.

℟. **The Lord is my shepherd; there is nothing I shall want.**
   or:
℟. **Though I walk in the valley of darkness, I fear no evil, for you are with me.**

2.

Psalm 25:6 and 7b, 17-18, 20-21

℟. (1) **To you, O Lord, I lift my soul.**
or:
℟. (3a) **No one who waits for you, O Lord, will ever be put to shame.**

Remember that your compassion, O Lord,
  and your kindness are from of old.
In your kindness remember me,
  because of your goodness, O Lord.

℟. **To you, O Lord, I lift my soul.**
or:
℟. **No one who waits for you, O Lord, will ever be put to shame.**

Relieve the troubles of my heart,
  and bring me out of my distress.
Put an end to my affliction and my suffering;
  and take away all my sins.

℟. **To you, O Lord, I lift my soul.**
or:
℟. **No one who waits for you, O Lord, will ever be put to shame.**

Preserve my life, and rescue me;
  let me not be put to shame, for I take refuge in you.
Let integrity and uprightness preserve me,
  because I wait for you, O Lord.

℟. **To you, O Lord, I lift my soul.**
or:
℟. **No one who waits for you, O Lord, will ever be put to shame.**

3.

Psalm 27:1, 4, 7 and 8b and 9a, 13-14

℟. (1) **The Lord is my light and my salvation.**
or:
℟. (13) **I believe that I shall see the good things of the Lord in the land of the living.**

The Lord is my light and my salvation;
  whom should I fear?
The Lord is my life's refuge;
  of whom should I be afraid?

℟. The Lord is my light and my salvation.
or:
℟. I believe that I shall see the good things of the Lord in the land of the living.

One thing I ask of the Lord;
  this I seek:
To dwell in the house of the Lord
  all the days of my life,
That I may gaze on the loveliness of the Lord
  and contemplate his temple.

℟. The Lord is my light and my salvation.
or:
℟. I believe that I shall see the good things of the Lord in the land of the living.

Hear, O Lord, the sound of my call;
  have pity on me and answer me.
Your presence, O Lord, I seek.
  Hide not your face from me.

℟. The Lord is my light and my salvation.
or:
℟. I believe that I shall see the good things of the Lord in the land of the living.

I believe that I shall see the bounty of the Lord
  in the land of the living.
Wait for the Lord with courage;
  be stouthearted, and wait for the Lord!

℟. The Lord is my light and my salvation.
or:
℟. I believe that I shall see the good things of the Lord in the land of the living.

1614   November 2—The Commemoration of All the Faithful Departed

SECOND READING

1.

Romans 5:5-11   Justified by his Blood, we will be saved through Christ from the wrath.

A reading from the Letter of Saint Paul to the Romans

Brothers and sisters:
Hope does not disappoint,
   because the love of God has been poured out into our hearts
   through the Holy Spirit that has been given to us.
For Christ, while we were still helpless,
   died at the appointed time for the ungodly.
Indeed, only with difficulty does one die for a just person,
   though perhaps for a good person
   one might even find courage to die.
But God proves his love for us
   in that while we were still sinners Christ died for us.
How much more then, since we are now justified by his Blood,
   will we be saved through him from the wrath.
Indeed, if, while we were enemies,
   we were reconciled to God through the death of his Son,
   how much more, once reconciled,
   will we be saved by his life.
Not only that,
   but we also boast of God through our Lord Jesus Christ,
   through whom we have now received reconciliation.

The word of the Lord.

2.

Romans 5:17-21   Where sin increased, grace overflowed all the more.

A reading from the Letter of Saint Paul to the Romans

Brothers and sisters:
If, by the transgression of the one,
   death came to reign through that one,
   how much more will those who receive the abundance of grace
   and of the gift of justification
   come to reign in life through the one Jesus Christ.
In conclusion, just as through one transgression
   condemnation came upon all,
   so, through one righteous act,
   acquittal and life came to all.

For just as through the disobedience of the one man
　the many were made sinners,
　so through the obedience of one
　the many will be made righteous.
The law entered in so that transgression might increase
　but, where sin increased, grace overflowed all the more, so that,
　as sin reigned in death,
　grace also might reign through justification for eternal life
　through Jesus Christ our Lord.

The word of the Lord.

3.

Romans 6:3-9　Let us walk in newness of life.

A reading from the Letter of Saint Paul to the Romans

Brothers and sisters:
Are you unaware that we who were baptized into Christ Jesus
　were baptized into his death?
We were indeed buried with him through baptism into death,
　so that, just as Christ was raised from the dead
　by the glory of the Father,
　we too might live in newness of life.

For if we have grown into union with him through a death like his,
　we shall also be united with him in the resurrection.
We know that our old self was crucified with him,
　so that our sinful body might be done away with,
　that we might no longer be in slavery to sin.
For a dead person has been absolved from sin.
If, then, we have died with Christ,
　we believe that we shall also live with him.
We know that Christ, raised from the dead, dies no more;
　death no longer has power over him.

The word of the Lord.

1616   November 2—The Commemoration of All the Faithful Departed

4.

Romans 8:14-23   We wait for the redemption of our bodies.

A reading from the Letter of Saint Paul to the Romans

Brothers and sisters:
Those who are led by the Spirit of God are sons of God.
For you did not receive a spirit of slavery to fall back into fear,
  but you received a spirit of adoption,
  through which we cry, "*Abba*, Father!"
The Spirit itself bears witness with our spirit
  that we are children of God,
  and if children, then heirs,
  heirs of God and joint heirs with Christ,
  if only we suffer with him
  so that we may also be glorified with him.
I consider that the sufferings of this present time are as nothing
  compared with the glory to be revealed for us.
For creation awaits with eager expectation
  the revelation of the children of God;
  for creation was made subject to futility,
  not of its own accord but because of the one who subjected it,
  in hope that creation itself
  would be set free from slavery to corruption
  and share in the glorious freedom of the children of God.
We know that all creation is groaning in labor pains even until now;
  and not only that, but we ourselves,
  who have the firstfruits of the Spirit,
  we also groan within ourselves
  as we wait for adoption, the redemption of our bodies.

The word of the Lord.

5.

Romans 8:31b-35, 37-39   What will separate us from the love of God?

A reading from the Letter of Saint Paul to the Romans

Brothers and sisters:
If God is for us, who can be against us?
He who did not spare his own Son
  but handed him over for us all,
  will he not also give us everything else along with him?
Who will bring a charge against God's chosen ones?
It is God who acquits us.
Who will condemn?

It is Christ Jesus who died, rather, was raised,
  who also is at the right hand of God,
  who indeed intercedes for us.
What will separate us from the love of Christ?
Will anguish, or distress or persecution, or famine,
  or nakedness, or peril, or the sword?

No, in all these things, we conquer overwhelmingly
  through him who loved us.
For I am convinced that neither death, nor life,
  nor angels, nor principalities,
  nor present things, nor future things,
  nor powers, nor height, nor depth,
  nor any other creature will be able to separate us
  from the love of God in Christ Jesus our Lord.

The word of the Lord.

6.

Romans 14:7-9, 10c-12   Whether we live or die, we are the Lord's.

A reading from the Letter of Saint Paul to the Romans

Brothers and sisters:
None of us lives for oneself, and no one dies for oneself.
For if we live, we live for the Lord,
  and if we die, we die for the Lord;
  so then, whether we live or die, we are the Lord's.
For this is why Christ died and came to life,
  that he might be Lord of both the dead and the living.
Why then do you judge your brother?
Or you, why do you look down on your brother?
For we shall all stand before the judgment seat of God;
  for it is written:

As I live, says the Lord, every knee shall bend before me,
  and every tongue shall give praise to God.

So then each of us shall give an account of himself to God.

The word of the Lord.

7.

1 Corinthians 15:20-28   In Christ all shall be brought to life.

A reading from the first Letter of Saint Paul to the Corinthians

Brothers and sisters:
Christ has been raised from the dead,
   the firstfruits of those who have fallen asleep.
For since death came through a human being,
   the resurrection of the dead came also through a human being.
For just as in Adam all die,
   so too in Christ shall all be brought to life,
   but each one in proper order:
   Christ the firstfruits;
   then, at his coming, those who belong to Christ;
   then comes the end,
   when he hands over the Kingdom to his God and Father.

For he must reign until he has put all his enemies under his feet.
The last enemy to be destroyed is death,
   for "he subjected everything under his feet."
But when it says that everything has been subjected,
   it is clear that it excludes the one who subjected everything to him.
When everything is subjected to him,
   then the Son himself will also be subjected
   to the one who subjected everything to him,
   so that God may be all in all.

The word of the Lord.

8.

1 Corinthians 15:51-57   Death is swallowed up in victory.

A reading from the first Letter of Saint Paul to the Corinthians

Brothers and sisters:
Behold, I tell you a mystery.
We shall not all fall asleep, but we will all be changed,
   in an instant, in the blink of an eye, at the last trumpet.
For the trumpet will sound,
   the dead will be raised incorruptible,
   and we shall be changed.
For that which is corruptible must clothe itself with incorruptibility,
   and that which is mortal must clothe itself with immortality.

And when this which is corruptible clothes itself with incorruptibility
  and this which is mortal clothes itself with immortality,
    then the word that is written shall come about:

Death is swallowed up in victory.
Where, O death, is your victory?
Where, O death, is your sting?

The sting of death is sin,
  and the power of sin is the law.
But thanks be to God who gives us the victory
  through our Lord Jesus Christ.

The word of the Lord.

9.

2 Corinthians 4:14—5:1   What is seen is transitory; what is unseen is eternal.

A reading from the second Letter of Saint Paul to the Corinthians

Brothers and sisters:
We know that the One who raised the Lord Jesus
  will raise us also with Jesus
  and place us with you in his presence.
Everything indeed is for you,
  so that the grace bestowed in abundance on more and more people
  may cause the thanksgiving to overflow for the glory of God.
Therefore, we are not discouraged;
  rather, although our outer self is wasting away,
  our inner self is being renewed day by day.
For this momentary light affliction
  is producing for us an eternal weight of glory beyond all comparison,
  as we look not to what is seen but to what is unseen;
    for what is seen is transitory, but what is unseen is eternal.
For we know that if our earthly dwelling, a tent,
  should be destroyed,
  we have a building from God,
  a dwelling not made with hands, eternal in heaven.

The word of the Lord.

10.

2 Corinthians 5:1, 6-10   We have an eternal dwelling in heaven.

A reading from the second Letter of Saint Paul to the Corinthians

Brothers and sisters:
We know that if our earthly dwelling, a tent,
   should be destroyed,
   we have a building from God,
   a dwelling not made with hands,
   eternal in heaven.

We are always courageous,
   although we know that while we are at home in the body
   we are away from the Lord,
   for we walk by faith, not by sight.
Yet we are courageous,
   and we would rather leave the body and go home to the Lord.
Therefore, we aspire to please him,
   whether we are at home or away.
For we must all appear before the judgment seat of Christ,
   so that each one may receive recompense,
   according to what he did in the body, whether good or evil.

The word of the Lord.

11.

Philippians 3:20-21   The Lord Jesus will change our lowly body to conform with his glorified Body.

A reading from the Letter of Saint Paul to the Philippians

Brothers and sisters:
Our citizenship is in heaven,
   and from it we also await a savior, the Lord Jesus Christ.
He will change our lowly body
   to conform with his glorified Body
   by the power that enables him also
   to bring all things into subjection to himself.

The word of the Lord.

12.

1 Thessalonians 4:13-18   We shall always be with the Lord.

A reading from the first Letter of Saint Paul to the Thessalonians

**We do not want you to be unaware, brothers and sisters,
   about those who have fallen asleep,
   so that you may not grieve like the rest, who have no hope.
For if we believe that Jesus died and rose,
   so too will God, through Jesus,
   bring with him those who have fallen asleep.
Indeed, we tell you this, on the word of the Lord,
   that we who are alive,
   who are left until the coming of the Lord,
   will surely not precede those who have fallen asleep.
For the Lord himself, with a word of command,
   with the voice of an archangel and with the trumpet of God,
   will come down from heaven,
   and the dead in Christ will rise first.
Then we who are alive, who are left,
   will be caught up together with them in the clouds
   to meet the Lord in the air.
Thus we shall always be with the Lord.
Therefore, console one another with these words.**

The word of the Lord.

13.

2 Timothy 2:8-13   If we have died with Christ, we shall also live with him.

A reading from the second Letter of Saint Paul to Timothy

Beloved:
Remember Jesus Christ, raised from the dead, a descendant of David:
  such is my Gospel, for which I am suffering,
    even to the point of chains, like a criminal.
But the word of God is not chained.
Therefore, I bear with everything for the sake of those who are chosen,
  so that they too may obtain the salvation that is in Christ Jesus,
    together with eternal glory.
This saying is trustworthy:

  If we have died with him
    we shall also live with him;
  if we persevere
    we shall also reign with him.
  But if we deny him
    he will deny us.
  If we are unfaithful
    he remains faithful,
      for he cannot deny himself.

The word of the Lord.

ALLELUIA VERSE AND VERSE BEFORE THE GOSPEL

1.

Matthew 25:34

Come, you who are blessed by my Father;
inherit the kingdom prepared for you from the foundation of the world.

2.

See John 3:16

God so loved the world that he gave us his only Son,
that everyone who sees the Son and believes in him
may have eternal life.

3.

See John 6:40

This is the will of my Father, says the Lord,
that everyone who sees the Son and believes in him
may have eternal life.

4.

John 6:51

**I am the living bread that came down from heaven, says the Lord;
whoever eats this bread will live forever.**

5.

John 11:25a, 26

**I am the resurrection and the life, says the Lord;
whoever believes in me will never die.**

GOSPEL

1.

Matthew 5:1-12a   Rejoice and be glad, for your reward will be great in heaven.

✠ A reading from the holy Gospel according to Matthew

**When Jesus saw the crowds, he went up the mountain,
   and after he had sat down, his disciples came to him.
He began to teach them, saying:**

**"Blessed are the poor in spirit,
   for theirs is the Kingdom of heaven.
Blessed are they who mourn,
   for they will be comforted.
Blessed are the meek,
   for they will inherit the land.
Blessed are they who hunger and thirst for righteousness,
   for they will be satisfied.
Blessed are the merciful,
   for they will be shown mercy.
Blessed are the clean of heart,
   for they will see God.
Blessed are the peacemakers,
   for they will be called children of God.
Blessed are they who are persecuted for the sake of righteousness,
   for theirs is the Kingdom of heaven.
Blessed are you when they insult you and persecute you
   and utter every kind of evil against you falsely because of me.
Rejoice and be glad,
   for your reward will be great in heaven."**

The Gospel of the Lord.

2.

Matthew 11:25-30   Come to me . . . and I will give you rest.

✟ **A reading from the holy Gospel according to Matthew**

**At that time Jesus exclaimed:
"I give praise to you, Father, Lord of heaven and earth,
for although you have hidden these things
from the wise and the learned
you have revealed them to little ones.
Yes, Father, such has been your gracious will.
All things have been handed over to me by my Father.
No one knows the Son except the Father,
and no one knows the Father except the Son
and anyone to whom the Son wishes to reveal him."**

**"Come to me, all you who labor and are burdened,
and I will give you rest.
Take my yoke upon you and learn from me,
for I am meek and humble of heart;
and you will find rest for yourselves.
For my yoke is easy, and my burden light."**

The Gospel of the Lord.

3.

Matthew 25:31-46   Come, you who are blessed by my Father.

✟ **A reading from the holy Gospel according to Matthew**

**Jesus said to his disciples:
"When the Son of Man comes in his glory,
and all the angels with him,
he will sit upon his glorious throne,
and all the nations will be assembled before him.
And he will separate them one from another,
as a shepherd separates the sheep from the goats.
He will place the sheep on his right and the goats on his left.
Then the king will say to those on his right,
'Come, you who are blessed by my Father.
Inherit the kingdom prepared for you from the foundation of the world.
For I was hungry and you gave me food,
I was thirsty and you gave me drink,
a stranger and you welcomed me,
naked and you clothed me,
ill and you cared for me,
in prison and you visited me.'**

Then the righteous will answer him and say,
	'Lord, when did we see you hungry and feed you,
		or thirsty and give you drink?
When did we see you a stranger and welcome you,
		or naked and clothe you?
When did we see you ill or in prison, and visit you?'
And the king will say to them in reply,
	'Amen, I say to you, whatever you did
		for one of these least brothers of mine, you did for me.'

"Then he will say to those on his left,
	'Depart from me, you accursed,
		into the eternal fire prepared for the Devil and his angels.
For I was hungry and you gave me no food,
	I was thirsty and you gave me no drink,
	a stranger and you gave me no welcome,
	naked and you gave me no clothing,
	ill and in prison, and you did not care for me.'
Then they will answer and say,
	'Lord, when did we see you hungry or thirsty
		or a stranger or naked or ill or in prison,
		and not minister to your needs?'
He will answer them, 'Amen, I say to you,
	what you did not do for one of the least of these,
	you did not do for me.'
And these will go off to eternal punishment,
	but the righteous to eternal life."

The Gospel of the Lord.

4.

Luke 7:11-17   Young man, I tell you, arise!

✠ A reading from the holy Gospel according to Luke

Jesus journeyed to a city called Nain,
  and his disciples and a large crowd accompanied him.
As he drew near to the gate of the city,
  a man who had died was being carried out,
  the only son of his mother, and she was a widow.
A large crowd from the city was with her.
When the Lord saw her,
  he was moved with pity for her and said to her,
  "Do not weep."
He stepped forward and touched the coffin;
  at this the bearers halted,
  and he said, "Young man, I tell you, arise!"
The dead man sat up and began to speak,
  and Jesus gave him to his mother.
Fear seized them all, and they glorified God, exclaiming,
  "A great prophet has arisen in our midst,"
  and "God has visited his people."
This report about him spread through the whole of Judea
  and in all the surrounding region.

The Gospel of the Lord.

5.

Luke 23:44-46, 50, 52-53; 24:1-6a   Father, into your hands, I commend my spirit.

✢ A reading from the holy Gospel according to Luke

It was about noon and darkness came over the whole land
   until three in the afternoon
   because of an eclipse of the sun.
Then the veil of the temple was torn down the middle.
Jesus cried out in a loud voice,
   "Father, into your hands I commend my spirit";
   and when he had said this he breathed his last.

Now there was a virtuous and righteous man named Joseph who,
   though he was a member of the council,
   went to Pilate and asked for the Body of Jesus.
After he had taken the Body down,
   he wrapped it in a linen cloth
   and laid him in a rock-hewn tomb
   in which no one had yet been buried.

At daybreak on the first day of the week
   they took the spices they had prepared
   and went to the tomb.
They found the stone rolled away from the tomb;
   but when they entered,
   they did not find the Body of the Lord Jesus.
While they were puzzling over this, behold,
   two men in dazzling garments appeared to them.
They were terrified and bowed their faces to the ground.
They said to them,
   "Why do you seek the living one among the dead?
He is not here, but he has been raised."

The Gospel of the Lord.

6.

Luke 24:13-16, 28-35   Was it not necessary that the Christ should suffer these things and enter into his glory?

✠ A reading from the holy Gospel according to Luke

That very day, the first day of the week,
  two of Jesus' disciples were going
  to a village seven miles from Jerusalem called Emmaus,
   and they were conversing about all the things that had occurred.
And it happened that while they were conversing and debating,
  Jesus himself drew near and walked with them,
   but their eyes were prevented from recognizing him.
As they approached the village to which they were going,
  he gave the impression that he was going on farther.
But they urged him, "Stay with us,
  for it is nearly evening and the day is almost over."
So he went in to stay with them.
And it happened that, while he was with them at table,
  he took bread, said the blessing,
   broke it, and gave it to them.
With that their eyes were opened and they recognized him,
  but he vanished from their sight.
Then they said to each other,
  "Were not our hearts burning within us
   while he spoke to us on the way and opened the Scriptures to us?"
So they set out at once and returned to Jerusalem
  where they found gathered together
   the Eleven and those with them who were saying,
   "The Lord has truly been raised and has appeared to Simon!"
Then the two recounted to them
  what had taken place on the way
   and how he was made known to them in the breaking of bread.

The Gospel of the Lord.

7.

John 5:24-29   Whoever hears my word and believes has passed from death to life.

✠ A reading from the holy Gospel according to John

Jesus answered the Jews and said to them:
  "Amen, amen, I say to you, whoever hears my word
   and believes in the one who sent me
   has eternal life and will not come to condemnation,
   but has passed from death to life.

Amen, amen, I say to you, the hour is coming and is now here
  when the dead will hear the voice of the Son of God,
  and those who hear will live.
For just as the Father has life in himself,
  so also he gave to his Son the possession of life in himself.
And he gave him power to exercise judgment,
  because he is the Son of Man.
Do not be amazed at this,
  because the hour is coming in which all who are in the tombs
  will hear his voice and will come out,
  those who have done good deeds
  to the resurrection of life,
  but those who have done wicked deeds
  to the resurrection of condemnation."

The Gospel of the Lord.

8.

John 6:37-40   Everyone who believes in the Son will have eternal life and I shall raise him up on the last day.

✠ **A reading from the holy Gospel according to John**

Jesus said to the crowds:
  "Everything that the Father gives me will come to me,
  and I will not reject anyone who comes to me,
  because I came down from heaven not to do my own will
  but the will of the one who sent me.
And this is the will of the one who sent me,
  that I should not lose anything of what he gave me,
  but that I should raise it on the last day.
For this is the will of my Father,
  that everyone who sees the Son and believes in him
  may have eternal life,
  and I shall raise him on the last day."

The Gospel of the Lord.

9.

John 6:51-58   Whoever eats this bread will live forever. I will raise him on the last day.

✚ A reading from the holy Gospel according to John

Jesus said to the crowds:
"I am the living bread that came down from heaven;
 whoever eats this bread will live forever;
 and the bread that I will give is my Flesh
 for the life of the world."

The Jews quarreled among themselves, saying,
 "How can this man give us his Flesh to eat?"
Jesus said to them,
 "Amen, amen, I say to you,
 unless you eat the Flesh of the Son of Man and drink his Blood,
 you do not have life within you.
He who eats my Flesh and drinks my Blood
 has eternal life,
 and I will raise him on the last day.
For my Flesh is true food,
 and my Blood is true drink.
Whoever eats my Flesh and drinks my Blood
 remains in me and I in him.
Just as the living Father sent me
 and I have life because of the Father,
 so also whoever feeds on me
 will have life because of me.
This is the bread that came down from heaven.
Unlike your ancestors who ate and still died,
 whoever eats this bread will live forever."

The Gospel of the Lord.

10.

John 11:17-27   I am the resurrection and the life.

✢ A reading from the holy Gospel according to John

When Jesus arrived in Bethany,
   he found that Lazarus had already been in the tomb for four days.
Now Bethany was near Jerusalem, only about two miles away.
And many of the Jews had come to Martha and Mary
   to comfort them about their brother.
When Martha heard that Jesus was coming,
   she went to meet him;
   but Mary sat at home.
Martha said to Jesus,
   "Lord, if you had been here,
   my brother would not have died.
But even now I know that whatever you ask of God,
   God will give you."
Jesus said to her,
   "Your brother will rise."
Martha said to him,
   "I know he will rise,
   in the resurrection on the last day."
Jesus told her,
   "I am the resurrection and the life;
   he who believes in me, even if he dies, will live,
   and everyone who lives and believes in me will never die.
Do you believe this?"
She said to him, "Yes, Lord.
I have come to believe that you are the Christ, the Son of God,
   the one who is coming into the world."

The Gospel of the Lord.

11.

John 11:32-45   Lazarus, come out!

✞ A reading from the holy Gospel according to John

When Mary, the sister of Lazarus, came to where Jesus was and saw him,
   she fell at his feet and said to him,
   "Lord, if you had been here,
   my brother would not have died."
When Jesus saw her weeping and the Jews who had come with her weeping,
   he became perturbed and deeply troubled, and said,
   "Where have you laid him?"
They said to him, "Sir, come and see."
And Jesus wept.
So the Jews said, "See how he loved him."
But some of them said,
   "Could not the one who opened the eyes of the blind man
   have done something so that this man would not have died?"

So Jesus, perturbed again, came to the tomb.
It was a cave, and a stone lay across it.
Jesus said, "Take away the stone."
Martha, the dead man's sister, said to him,
   "Lord, by now there will be a stench;
   he has been dead for four days."
Jesus said to her,
   "Did I not tell you that if you believe
   you will see the glory of God?"
So they took away the stone.
And Jesus raised his eyes and said,
   "Father, I thank you for hearing me.
I know that you always hear me;
   but because of the crowd here I have said this,
   that they may believe that you sent me."
And when he had said this,
   he cried out in a loud voice,
   "Lazarus, come out!"
The dead man came out,
   tied hand and foot with burial bands,
   and his face was wrapped in a cloth.
So Jesus said to them,
   "Untie him and let him go."

Now many of the Jews who had come to Mary
   and seen what he had done began to believe in him.

The Gospel of the Lord.

12.

John 14:1-6   In my Father's house there are many dwelling places.

✠ A reading from the holy Gospel according to John

Jesus said to his disciples:
"Do not let your hearts be troubled.
You have faith in God; have faith also in me.
In my Father's house there are many dwelling places.
If there were not,
    would I have told you that I am going to prepare a place for you?
And if I go and prepare a place for you,
    I will come back again and take you to myself,
    so that where I am you also may be.
Where I am going you know the way."
Thomas said to him,
    "Master, we do not know where you are going;
    how can we know the way?"
Jesus said to him, "I am the way and the truth and the life.
No one comes to the Father except through me."

The Gospel of the Lord.

NOVEMBER 3

669 SAINT MARTIN DE PORRES, RELIGIOUS

From the Common of Holy Men and Women: For Religious, p. 1868,

> OR

FIRST READING

Philippians 4:4-9   Think about whatever is worthy of praise.

A reading from the Letter of Saint Paul to the Philippians

Brothers and sisters:
Rejoice in the Lord always.
I shall say it again: rejoice!
Your kindness should be known to all.
The Lord is near.
Have no anxiety at all, but in everything,
   by prayer and petition, with thanksgiving,
   make your requests known to God.
Then the peace of God that surpasses all understanding
   will guard your hearts and minds in Christ Jesus.

Finally, brothers and sisters,
   whatever is true, whatever is honorable,
   whatever is just, whatever is pure,
   whatever is lovely, whatever is gracious,
   if there is any excellence
   and if there is anything worthy of praise,
   think about these things.
Keep on doing what you have learned and received
   and heard and seen in me.
Then the God of peace will be with you.

The word of the Lord.

RESPONSORIAL PSALM

Psalm 131:1bcde, 2, 3

℟. In you, Lord, I have found my peace.

O LORD, my heart is not proud,
   nor are my eyes haughty;
I busy not myself with great things,
   nor with things too sublime for me.

℟. In you, Lord, I have found my peace.

November 3—Saint Martin de Porres   1635

Nay rather, I have stilled and quieted
>my soul like a weaned child.

Like a weaned child on its mother's lap,
>so is my soul within me.

℟. In you, Lord, I have found my peace.

O Israel, hope in the Lord,
>both now and forever.

℟. In you, Lord, I have found my peace.

ALLELUIA

John 13:34

℟. Alleluia, alleluia.

I give you a new commandment:
love one another as I have loved you.

℟. Alleluia, alleluia.

GOSPEL

Matthew 22:34-40   Love the Lord your God, and your neighbor as yourself.

✢ A reading from the holy Gospel according to Matthew

When the Pharisees heard that Jesus had silenced the Sadducees,
>they gathered together, and one of them
>a scholar of the law, tested him by asking,
>"Teacher, which commandment in the law is the greatest?"

He said to him,
>"You shall love the Lord, your God, with all your heart,
>with all your soul, and with all your mind.

This is the greatest and the first commandment.
The second is like it:
>You shall love your neighbor as yourself.

The whole Law and the Prophets depend on these two commandments."

The Gospel of the Lord.

NOVEMBER 4

670 SAINT CHARLES BORROMEO, BISHOP MEMORIAL

From the Common of Pastors, p. 1805,

OR

FIRST READING

Romans 12:3-13   We have gifts that differ according to the grace given to us.

A reading from the Letter of Saint Paul to the Romans

Brothers and sisters:
By the grace given to me I tell everyone among you
not to think of himself more highly than one ought to think,
 but to think soberly,
 each according to the measure of faith that God has apportioned.
For as in one body we have many parts,
 and all the parts do not have the same function,
 so we, though many, are one Body in Christ
 and individually parts of one another.
Since we have gifts that differ according to the grace given to us,
 let us exercise them:
 if prophecy, in proportion to the faith;
 if ministry, in ministering;
 if one is a teacher, in teaching;
 if one exhorts, in exhortation;
 if one contributes, in generosity;
 if one is over others, with diligence;
 if one does acts of mercy, with cheerfulness.

Let love be sincere;
 hate what is evil,
 hold on to what is good;
 love one another with mutual affection;
 anticipate one another in showing honor.
Do not grow slack in zeal,
 be fervent in spirit,
 serve the Lord.
Rejoice in hope,
 endure in affliction,
 persevere in prayer.
Contribute to the needs of the holy ones,
 exercise hospitality.

The word of the Lord.

RESPONSORIAL PSALM

Psalm 89:2-3, 4-5, 21-22, 25 and 27

℟. (see 2a) **For ever I will sing the goodness of the Lord.**

The favors of the Lord **I will sing forever;**
  through all generations my mouth shall proclaim your faithfulness.
For you have said, "My kindness is established forever";
  in heaven you have confirmed your faithfulness.

℟. **For ever I will sing the goodness of the Lord.**

"I have made a covenant with my chosen one,
  I have sworn to David my servant:
Forever will I confirm your posterity
  and establish your throne for all generations."

℟. **For ever I will sing the goodness of the Lord.**

"I have found David, my servant;
  with my holy oil I have anointed him,
That my hand may be always with him,
  and that my arm may make him strong."

℟. **For ever I will sing the goodness of the Lord.**

"My faithfulness and my mercy shall be with him,
  and through my name shall his horn be exalted.
He shall say of me, 'You are my father,
  my God, the rock, my savior.'"

℟. **For ever I will sing the goodness of the Lord.**

ALLELUIA

John 10:14

℟. **Alleluia, alleluia.**

I am the good shepherd, says the Lord;
I know my sheep, and mine know me.

℟. **Alleluia, alleluia.**

GOSPEL

John 10:11-16   A good shepherd lays down his life for his sheep.

✝ A reading from the holy Gospel according to John

Jesus said:
"I am the good shepherd.
A good shepherd lays down his life for the sheep.
A hired man, who is not a shepherd
   and whose sheep are not his own,
   sees a wolf coming and leaves the sheep and runs away,
   and the wolf catches and scatters them.
This is because he works for pay and has no concern for the sheep.
I am the good shepherd,
   and I know mine and mine know me,
   just as the Father knows me and I know the Father;
   and I will lay down my life for the sheep.
I have other sheep that do not belong to this fold.
These also I must lead, and they will hear my voice,
   and there will be one flock, one shepherd."

The Gospel of the Lord.

NOVEMBER 9

671 THE DEDICATION OF THE LATERAN BASILICA IN ROME FEAST

FIRST READING

Ezekiel 47:1-2, 8-9, 12   I saw water flowing from the temple, and all who were touched by it were saved (see Roman Missal, antiphon for the blessing and sprinkling of water during the season of Easter).

A reading from the Book of the Prophet Ezekiel

The angel brought me
 back to the entrance of the temple,
 and I saw water flowing out
 from beneath the threshold of the temple toward the east,
 for the façade of the temple was toward the east;
 the water flowed down from the southern side of the temple,
 south of the altar.
He led me outside by the north gate,
 and around to the outer gate facing the east,
 where I saw water trickling from the southern side.
He said to me,
 "This water flows into the eastern district down upon the Arabah,
 and empties into the sea, the salt waters, which it makes fresh.
Wherever the river flows,
 every sort of living creature that can multiply shall live,
 and there shall be abundant fish,
 for wherever this water comes the sea shall be made fresh.
Along both banks of the river, fruit trees of every kind shall grow;
 their leaves shall not fade, nor their fruit fail.
Every month they shall bear fresh fruit,
 for they shall be watered by the flow from the sanctuary.
Their fruit shall serve for food, and their leaves for medicine."

The word of the Lord.

RESPONSORIAL PSALM

Psalm 46:2-3, 5-6, 8-9

℟. (5) **The waters of the river gladden the city of God, the holy dwelling of the Most High!**

**God is our refuge and our strength,
an ever-present help in distress.
Therefore, we fear not, though the earth be shaken
and mountains plunge into the depths of the sea.**

℟. **The waters of the river gladden the city of God, the holy dwelling of the Most High!**

**There is a stream whose runlets gladden the city of God,
the holy dwelling of the Most High.
God is in its midst; it shall not be disturbed;
God will help it at the break of dawn.**

℟. **The waters of the river gladden the city of God, the holy dwelling of the Most High!**

**The Lord of hosts is with us;
our stronghold is the God of Jacob.
Come! behold the deeds of the Lord,
the astounding things he has wrought on earth.**

℟. **The waters of the river gladden the city of God, the holy dwelling of the Most High!**

November 9—The Dedication of the Lateran Basilica in Rome   1641

SECOND READING

1 Corinthians 3:9c-11, 16-17   You are God's temple.

A reading from the first Letter of Saint Paul to the Corinthians

Brothers and sisters:
You are God's building.
According to the grace of God given to me,
  like a wise master builder I laid a foundation,
  and another is building upon it.
But each one must be careful how he builds upon it,
  for no one can lay a foundation other than the one that is there,
  namely, Jesus Christ.

Do you not know that you are the temple of God,
  and that the Spirit of God dwells in you?
If anyone destroys God's temple,
  God will destroy that person;
  for the temple of God, which you are, is holy.

The word of the Lord.

ALLELUIA

2 Chronicles 7:16

  ℟. **Alleluia, alleluia.**

I have chosen and consecrated this house, says the Lord,
that my name may be there forever.

  ℟. **Alleluia, alleluia.**

GOSPEL

John 2:13-22   Jesus was speaking about the temple of his Body.

☩ A reading from the holy Gospel according to John

Since the Passover of the Jews was near,
   Jesus went up to Jerusalem.
He found in the temple area those who sold oxen, sheep, and doves,
   as well as the money-changers seated there.
He made a whip out of cords
   and drove them all out of the temple area, with the sheep and oxen,
   and spilled the coins of the money-changers
   and overturned their tables,
   and to those who sold doves he said,
   "Take these out of here,
   and stop making my Father's house a marketplace."
His disciples recalled the words of Scripture,
   Zeal for your house will consume me.
At this the Jews answered and said to him,
   "What sign can you show us for doing this?"
Jesus answered and said to them,
   "Destroy this temple and in three days I will raise it up."
The Jews said,
   "This temple has been under construction for forty-six years,
   and you will raise it up in three days?"
But he was speaking about the temple of his Body.
Therefore, when he was raised from the dead,
   his disciples remembered that he had said this,
   and they came to believe the Scripture
   and the word Jesus had spoken.

The Gospel of the Lord.

NOVEMBER 10

672 SAINT LEO THE GREAT, POPE AND DOCTOR OF THE CHURCH MEMORIAL

From the Common of Pastors: For a Pope, p. 1805, or the Common of Doctors of the Church, p. 1838,

OR

FIRST READING

Sirach 39:6-11   He who studies the law of the Most High will be filled with the spirit of understanding.

A reading from the Book of Sirach

If it pleases the Lord Almighty,
   he who studies the law of the Most High
   will be filled with the spirit of understanding;
He will pour forth his words of wisdom
   and in prayer give thanks to the Lord,
Who will direct his knowledge and his counsel,
   as he meditates upon his mysteries.
He will show the wisdom of what he has learned
   and glory in the law of the Lord's covenant.
Many will praise his understanding;
   his fame can never be effaced;
Unfading will be his memory,
   through all generations his name will live;
Peoples will speak of his wisdom,
   and in assembly sing his praises.

The word of the Lord.

RESPONSORIAL PSALM

Psalm 37:3-4, 5-6, 30-31

R. (30a) **The mouth of the just murmurs wisdom.**

Trust in the Lord and do good
   that you may dwell in the land and be fed in security.
Take delight in the Lord,
   and he will grant you your heart's requests.

R. **The mouth of the just murmurs wisdom.**

Commit to the Lord your way;
   trust in him, and he will act.
He will make justice dawn for you like the light;
   bright as the noonday shall be your vindication.

℟. **The mouth of the just murmurs wisdom.**

The mouth of the just tells of wisdom
   and his tongue utters what is right.
The law of his God is in his heart,
   and his steps do not falter.

℟. **The mouth of the just murmurs wisdom.**

ALLELUIA

Mark 1:17

℟. **Alleluia, alleluia.**

Come after me, says the Lord,
and I will make you fishers of men.

℟. **Alleluia, alleluia.**

GOSPEL

Matthew 16:13-19   You are Peter, and upon this rock I will build my Church.

✠ **A reading from the holy Gospel according to Matthew**

When Jesus went into the region of Caesarea Philippi
   he asked his disciples,
      "Who do people say that the Son of Man is?"
They replied, "Some say John the Baptist, others Elijah,
   still others Jeremiah or one of the prophets."
He said to them, "But who do you say that I am?"
Simon Peter said in reply,
   "You are the Christ, the Son of the living God."
Jesus said to him in reply, "Blessed are you, Simon son of Jonah.
For flesh and blood has not revealed this to you, but my heavenly Father.
And so I say to you, you are Peter,
   and upon this rock I will build my Church,
   and the gates of the netherworld shall not prevail against it.
I will give you the keys to the Kingdom of heaven.
Whatever you bind on earth shall be bound in heaven;
   and whatever you loose on earth shall be loosed in heaven."

The Gospel of the Lord.

NOVEMBER 11

673 SAINT MARTIN OF TOURS, BISHOP MEMORIAL

From the Common of Pastors, p. 1805, or the Common of Holy Men and Women: For Religious, p. 1868,

OR

FIRST READING

Isaiah 61:1-3abcd   The Lord anointed me and sent me to bring glad tidings to the lowly.

A reading from the Book of the Prophet Isaiah

> The Spirit of the Lord God is upon me,
>   because the Lord has anointed me;
> He has sent me to bring glad tidings to the lowly,
>   to heal the brokenhearted,
> To proclaim liberty to the captives
>   and release to the prisoners,
> To announce a year of favor from the Lord
>   and a day of vindication by our God,
>   to comfort all who mourn;
> To place on those who mourn in Zion
>   a diadem instead of ashes,
> To give them oil of gladness in place of mourning,
>   a glorious mantle instead of a listless spirit.

The word of the Lord.

1646   November 11—Saint Martin of Tours

RESPONSORIAL PSALM

Psalm 89:2-3, 4-5, 21-22, 25 and 27

℟. (see 2a) **For ever I will sing the goodness of the Lord.**

The favors of the Lord **I will sing forever;**
   through all generations my mouth shall proclaim your faithfulness.
For you have said, "My kindness is established forever";
   in heaven you have confirmed your faithfulness.

℟. **For ever I will sing the goodness of the Lord.**

"I have made a covenant with my chosen one,
   I have sworn to David my servant:
Forever will I confirm your posterity
   and establish your throne for all generations."

℟. **For ever I will sing the goodness of the Lord.**

"I have found David, my servant;
   with my holy oil I have anointed him,
That my hand may be always with him,
   and that my arm may make him strong."

℟. **For ever I will sing the goodness of the Lord.**

"My faithfulness and my mercy shall be with him,
   and through my name shall his horn be exalted.
He shall say of me, 'You are my father,
   my God, the rock, my savior.'"

℟. **For ever I will sing the goodness of the Lord.**

ALLELUIA

John 13:34

℟. **Alleluia, alleluia.**

I give you a new commandment:
love one another as I have loved you.

℟. **Alleluia, alleluia.**

GOSPEL

Matthew 25:31-40   Whatever you did for one of these least brothers of mine, you did for me.

✠ **A reading from the holy Gospel according to Matthew**

Jesus said to his disciples:
"When the Son of Man comes in his glory,
   and all the angels with him,
   he will sit upon his glorious throne,
   and all the nations will be assembled before him.
And he will separate them one from another,
   as a shepherd separates the sheep from the goats.
He will place the sheep on his right and the goats on his left.
Then the king will say to those on his right,
   'Come, you who are blessed by my Father.
Inherit the kingdom prepared for you from the foundation of the world.
For I was hungry and you gave me food,
   I was thirsty and you gave me drink,
   a stranger and you welcomed me,
   naked and you clothed me,
   ill and you cared for me,
   in prison and you visited me.'
Then the righteous will answer him and say,
   'Lord, when did we see you hungry and feed you,
   or thirsty and give you drink?
When did we see you a stranger and welcome you,
   or naked and clothe you?
When did we see you ill or in prison, and visit you?'
And the king will say to them in reply,
   'Amen, I say to you, whatever you did
   for one of the least brothers of mine, you did for me.'"

The Gospel of the Lord.

NOVEMBER 12

674 SAINT JOSAPHAT, BISHOP AND MARTYR
MEMORIAL

From the Common of Martyrs, p. 1782, or the Common of Pastors, p. 1805,

OR

FIRST READING

Ephesians 4:1-7, 11-13   For the work of ministry, for building up the Body of Christ.

A reading from the Letter of Saint Paul to the Ephesians

Brothers and sisters:
I, a prisoner for the Lord,
  urge you to live in a manner worthy of the call you have received,
  with all humility and gentleness, with patience,
  bearing with one another through love,
  striving to preserve the unity of the Spirit
  through the bond of peace:
  one Body and one Spirit,
  as you were also called to the one hope of your call;
  one Lord, one faith, one baptism;
  one God and Father of all,
  who is over all and through all and in all.

But grace was given to each of us
  according to the measure of Christ's gift.

And he gave some as Apostles, others as prophets,
  others as evangelists, others as pastors and teachers,
  to equip the holy ones for the work of ministry,
  for building up the Body of Christ,
  until we all attain to the unity of faith
  and knowledge of the Son of God, to mature manhood,
  to the extent of the full stature of Christ.

The word of the Lord.

RESPONSORIAL PSALM

Psalm 1:1-2, 3, 4 and 6

℟. (40:5a) **Blessed are they who hope in the Lord.**
   or:
℟. (2a) **Blessed are they who delight in the law of the Lord.**
   or:
℟. (92:13-14) **The just will flourish like the palm tree in the garden of the Lord.**

Blessed the man who follows not
   the counsel of the wicked
Nor walks in the way of sinners,
   nor sits in the company of the insolent,
But delights in the law of the Lord
   and meditates on his law day and night.

℟. **Blessed are they who hope in the Lord.**
   or:
℟. **Blessed are they who delight in the law of the Lord.**
   or:
℟. **The just will flourish like the palm tree in the garden of the Lord.**

He is like a tree
   planted near running water,
That yields its fruit in due season,
   and whose leaves never fade.
   Whatever he does, prospers.

℟. **Blessed are they who hope in the Lord.**
   or:
℟. **Blessed are they who delight in the law of the Lord.**
   or:
℟. **The just will flourish like the palm tree in the garden of the Lord.**

Not so, the wicked, not so;
   they are like chaff which the wind drives away.
For the Lord watches over the way of the just,
   but the way of the wicked vanishes.

℟. **Blessed are they who hope in the Lord.**
   or:
℟. **Blessed are they who delight in the law of the Lord.**
   or:
℟. **The just will flourish like the palm tree in the garden of the Lord.**

1650 *November 12—Saint Josaphat*

ALLELUIA

John 15:9b, 5b

℟. Alleluia, alleluia.

**Remain in my love, says the Lord;
whoever lives in me and I in him will bear much fruit.**

℟. Alleluia, alleluia.

GOSPEL

John 17:20-26   *I wish that where I am they also may be with me.*

✠ A reading from the holy Gospel according to John

**Jesus raised his eyes to heaven and said:
"Holy Father,
   I pray not only for these,
   but also for those who will believe in me through their word,
   so that they may all be one,
   as you, Father, are in me and I in you,
   that they also may be in us,
   that the world may believe that you sent me.
And I have given them the glory you gave me,
   so that they may be one, as we are one,
   I in them and you in me,
   that they may be brought to perfection as one,
   that the world may know that you sent me,
   and that you loved them even as you loved me.
Father, they are your gift to me.
I wish that where I am they also may be with me,
   that they may see my glory that you gave me,
   because you loved me before the foundation of the world.
Righteous Father, the world also does not know you,
   but I know you, and they know that you sent me.
I made known to them your name and I will make it known,
   that the love with which you loved me
   may be in them and I in them."**

The Gospel of the Lord.

NOVEMBER 13

[In the Dioceses of the United States]

674A SAINT FRANCES XAVIER CABRINI, VIRGIN
MEMORIAL

From the Common of Virgins, p. 1857, or the Common of Holy Men and Women: For Religious, p. 1868.

NOVEMBER 15

675 SAINT ALBERT THE GREAT, BISHOP AND DOCTOR OF THE CHURCH

From the Common of Pastors, p. 1805, or the Common of Doctors of the Church, p. 1838,

OR

FIRST READING

Sirach 15:1-6   She will fill him with the spirit of wisdom and understanding.

A reading from the Book of Sirach

He who fears the Lord will do this;
  he who is practiced in the law will come to wisdom.
Motherlike she will meet him,
  like a young bride she will embrace him,
Nourish him with the bread of understanding,
  and give him the water of learning to drink.
He will lean upon her and not fall,
  he will trust in her and not be put to shame.
She will exalt him above his fellows;
  and in the midst of the assembly she will open his mouth
  and fill him with the spirit of wisdom and understanding,
  and clothe him with the robe of glory.
Joy and gladness he will find,
  an everlasting name he will inherit.

The word of the Lord.

RESPONSORIAL PSALM

Psalm 119:9, 10, 11, 12, 13, 14

℟. (12) **Lord, teach me your statutes.**

How shall a young man be faultless in his way?
  By keeping to your words.

℟. **Lord, teach me your statutes.**

With all my heart I seek you;
  let me not stray from your commands.

℟. **Lord, teach me your statutes.**

Within my heart I treasure your promise,
  that I may not sin against you.

℟. **Lord, teach me your statutes.**

Blessed are you, O LORD**;**
  teach me your statutes.

℟. **Lord, teach me your statutes.**

With my lips I declare
  all the ordinances of your mouth.

℟. **Lord, teach me your statutes.**

In the way of your decrees I rejoice,
  as much as in all riches.

℟. **Lord, teach me your statutes.**

1654　*November 15—Saint Albert the Great*

ALLELUIA

See Acts 16:14b

℟. **Alleluia, alleluia.**

**Open our hearts, O Lord,
to listen to the words of your Son.**

℟. **Alleluia, alleluia.**

GOSPEL

Matthew 13:47-52　Both the new and the old.

✠ **A reading from the holy Gospel according to Matthew**

**Jesus said to the crowds:
"The Kingdom of heaven is like a net thrown into the sea,
　which collects fish of every kind.
When it is full they haul it ashore
　and sit down to put what is good into buckets.
What is bad they throw away.
Thus it will be at the end of the age.
The angels will go out and separate the wicked from the righteous
　and throw them into the fiery furnace,
　　where there will be wailing and grinding of teeth.
Do you understand all these things?"
They answered, "Yes."
And he replied,
　"Then every scribe who has been instructed in the Kingdom of heaven
　is like the head of a household who brings from his storeroom
　both the new and the old."**

The Gospel of the Lord.

NOVEMBER 16

676 SAINT MARGARET OF SCOTLAND

From the Common of Holy Men and Women: For Those Who Work for the Underprivileged, p. 1868,

OR

FIRST READING

Isaiah 58:6-11   Sharing your bread with the hungry.

A reading from the Book of the Prophet Isaiah

Thus says the Lord:
   This is the fasting that I wish:
      releasing those bound unjustly,
      untying the thongs of the yoke;
   Setting free the oppressed,
      breaking every yoke;
   Sharing your bread with the hungry,
      sheltering the oppressed and the homeless;
   Clothing the naked when you see them,
      and not turning your back on your own.
   Then your light shall break forth like the dawn,
      and your wound shall quickly be healed;
   Your vindication shall go before you,
      and the glory of the Lord shall be your rear guard.
   Then you shall call, and the Lord will answer,
      you shall cry for help, and he will say: Here I am!
   If you remove from your midst oppression,
      false accusation and malicious speech;
   If you bestow your bread on the hungry
      and satisfy the afflicted;
   Then light shall rise for you in darkness,
      and the gloom shall become for you like midday;
   Then the Lord will guide you always
      and give you plenty even on the parched land.
   He will renew your strength,
      and you shall be like a watered garden,
      like a spring whose water never fails.

The word of the Lord.

RESPONSORIAL PSALM

Psalm 112:1-2, 3-4, 5-6, 7-8, 9

℟. (1) **Blessed the man who fears the Lord.**
   or:
℟. **Alleluia.**

Blessed the man who fears the LORD**,**
   who greatly delights in his commands.
His posterity shall be might upon the earth;
   the upright generation shall be blessed.

℟. **Blessed the man who fears the Lord.**
   or:
℟. **Alleluia.**

Wealth and riches shall be in his house;
   his generosity shall endure forever.
Light shines through the darkness for the upright;
   he is gracious and merciful and just.

℟. **Blessed the man who fears the Lord.**
   or:
℟. **Alleluia.**

Well for the man who is gracious and lends,
   who conducts his affairs with justice;
He shall never be moved;
   the just one shall be in everlasting remembrance.

℟. **Blessed the man who fears the Lord.**
   or:
℟. **Alleluia.**

An evil report he shall not fear.
   His heart is firm, trusting in the LORD**.**
His heart is steadfast; he shall not fear
   till he looks down upon his foes.

℟. **Blessed the man who fears the Lord.**
   or:
℟. **Alleluia.**

Lavishly he gives to the poor,
   his generosity shall endure forever;
   his horn shall be exalted in glory.

℟. **Blessed the man who fears the Lord.**
   or:
℟. **Alleluia.**

ALLELUIA

John 13:34

℟. Alleluia, alleluia.

I give you a new commandment:
love one another as I have loved you.

℟. Alleluia, alleluia.

GOSPEL

John 15:9-17   You are my friends if you do what I command you.

☩ A reading from the holy Gospel according to John

Jesus said to his disciples:
"As the Father loves me, so I also love you.
Remain in my love.
If you keep my commandments, you will remain in my love,
   just as I have kept my Father's commandments
   and remain in his love.

"I have told you this so that my joy might be in you
   and your joy might be complete.
This is my commandment: love one another as I love you.
No one has greater love than this,
   to lay down one's life for one's friends.
You are my friends if you do what I command you.
I no longer call you slaves,
   because a slave does not know what his master is doing.
I have called you friends,
   because I have told you everything I have heard from my Father.
It was not you who chose me, but I who chose you
   and appointed you to go and bear fruit that will remain,
   so that whatever you ask the Father in my name he may give you.
This I command you: love one another."

The Gospel of the Lord.

NOVEMBER 16

677 SAINT GERTRUDE, VIRGIN

From the Common of Virgins, p. 1857, or the Common of Holy Men and Women: For Religious, p. 1868,

OR

FIRST READING

Ephesians 3:14-19 To know the love of Christ that surpasses knowledge.

A reading from the Letter of Saint Paul to the Ephesians

Brothers and sisters:
I kneel before the Father,
> from whom every family in heaven and on earth is named,
> that he may grant you in accord with the riches of his glory
> to be strengthened with power through his Spirit in the inner self,
> and that Christ may dwell in your hearts through faith;
> that you, rooted and grounded in love,
> may have strength to comprehend with all the holy ones
> what is the breadth and length and height and depth,
> and to know the love of Christ that surpasses knowledge,
> so that you may be filled with all the fullness of God.

The word of the Lord.

RESPONSORIAL PSALM

Psalm 23:1b-3a, 4, 5, 6

℟. (1) **The Lord is my shepherd; there is nothing I shall want.**

The LORD **is my shepherd; I shall not want.
In verdant pastures he gives me repose;
Beside restful waters he leads me;
he refreshes my soul.**

℟. **The Lord is my shepherd; there is nothing I shall want.**

**Even though I walk in the dark valley
I fear no evil; for you are at my side
With your rod and your staff
that give me courage.**

℟. **The Lord is my shepherd; there is nothing I shall want.**

**You spread the table before me
in the sight of my foes;
You anoint my head with oil;
my cup overflows.**

℟. **The Lord is my shepherd; there is nothing I shall want.**

**Only goodness and kindness follow me
all the days of my life;
And I shall dwell in the house of the L**ORD
for years to come.

℟. **The Lord is my shepherd; there is nothing I shall want.**

ALLELUIA

John 15:9b, 5b

℟. **Alleluia, alleluia.**

**Remain in my love, says the Lord;
whoever remains in me and I in him will bear much fruit.**

℟. **Alleluia, alleluia.**

GOSPEL

John 15:1-8 He who remains in me and I in him will bear much fruit.

☩ A reading from the holy Gospel according to John

Jesus said to his disciples:
"I am the true vine, and my Father is the vine grower.
He takes away every branch in me that does not bear fruit,
   and every one that does he prunes so that it bears more fruit.
You are already pruned because of the word that I spoke to you.
Remain in me, as I remain in you.
Just as a branch cannot bear fruit on its own
   unless it remains on the vine,
   so neither can you unless you remain in me.
I am the vine, you are the branches.
Whoever remains in me and I in him will bear much fruit,
   because without me you can do nothing.
Anyone who does not remain in me
   will be thrown out like a branch and wither;
   people will gather them and throw them into a fire
   and they will be burned.
If you remain in me and my words remain in you,
   ask for whatever you want and it will be done for you.
By this is my Father glorified,
   that you bear much fruit and become my disciples."

The Gospel of the Lord.

NOVEMBER 17

678 SAINT ELIZABETH OF HUNGARY, RELIGIOUS MEMORIAL

From the Common of Holy Men and Women: For Those Who Work for the Underprivileged, p. 1868, or For Religious, p. 1868,

OR

FIRST READING

1 John 3:14-18   We should lay down our lives for our brothers.

A reading from the first Letter of Saint John

Beloved:
We know that we have passed from death to life
  because we love our brothers.
Whoever does not love remains in death.
Everyone who hates his brother is a murderer,
  and you know that anyone who is a murderer
  does not have eternal life remaining in him.
The way we came to know love
  was that he laid down his life for us;
  so we ought to lay down our lives for our brothers.
If someone who has worldly means
  sees a brother in need and refuses him compassion,
  how can the love of God remain in him?
Children, let us love not in word or speech
  but in deed and truth.

The word of the Lord.

RESPONSORIAL PSALM

Psalm 34:2-3, 4-5, 6-7, 8-9, 10-11

℟. (2) **I will bless the Lord at all times.**
  or:
℟. (9) **Taste and see the goodness of the Lord.**

I will bless the LORD at all times;
  his praise shall be ever in my mouth.
Let my soul glory in the LORD;
  the lowly will hear and be glad.

℟. **I will bless the Lord at all times.**
  or:
℟. **Taste and see the goodness of the Lord.**

Glorify the LORD **with me,**
   let us together extol his name.
I sought the LORD**, and he answered me**
   and delivered me from all my fears.

℟. I will bless the Lord at all times.
   or:
℟. Taste and see the goodness of the Lord.

Look to him that you may be radiant with joy,
   and your faces may not blush with shame.
When the poor one called out, the LORD **heard,**
   and from all his distress he saved him.

℟. I will bless the Lord at all times.
   or:
℟. Taste and see the goodness of the Lord.

The angel of the LORD **encamps**
   around those who fear him, and delivers them.
Taste and see how good the LORD **is;**
   blessed the man who takes refuge in him.

℟. I will bless the Lord at all times.
   or:
℟. Taste and see the goodness of the Lord.

Fear the LORD**, you his holy ones,**
   for nought is lacking to those who fear him.
The great grow poor and hungry;
   but those who seek the L**ORD** want for no good thing.

℟. I will bless the Lord at all times.
   or:
℟. Taste and see the goodness of the Lord.

ALLELUIA

John 13:34

℟. Alleluia, alleluia.

I give you a new commandment:
love one another as I have loved you.

℟. Alleluia, alleluia.

GOSPEL

Luke 6:27-38   Be merciful, just as your Father is merciful.

✠ A reading from the holy Gospel according to Luke

Jesus said to his disciples:
"To you who hear I say,
   love your enemies, do good to those who hate you,
   bless those who curse you, pray for those who mistreat you.
To the person who strikes you on one cheek,
   offer the other one as well,
   and from the person who takes your cloak,
   do not withhold even your tunic.
Give to everyone who asks of you,
   and from the one who takes what is yours do not demand it back.
Do to others as you would have them do to you.
For if you love those who love you,
   what credit is that to you?
Even sinners love those who love them.
And if you do good to those who do good to you,
   what credit is that to you?
Even sinners do the same.
If you lend money to those from whom you expect repayment,
   what credit is that to you?
Even sinners lend to sinners,
   and get back the same amount.
But rather, love your enemies and do good to them,
   and lend expecting nothing back;
   then your reward will be great
   and you will be children of the Most High,
   for he himself is kind to the ungrateful and the wicked.
Be merciful, just as also your Father is merciful.
"Stop judging and you will not be judged.
Stop condemning and you will not be condemned.
Forgive and you will be forgiven.
Give and gifts will be given to you;
   a good measure, packed together, shaken down, and overflowing,
   will be poured into your lap.
For the measure with which you measure
   will in return be measured out to you."

The Gospel of the Lord.

NOVEMBER 18

679 DEDICATION OF THE BASILICA OF SAINTS PETER AND PAUL, APOSTLES

The readings for this memorial are proper.

FIRST READING

Acts 28:11-16, 30-31   And thus we came to Rome.

A reading from the Acts of the Apostles

After three months
 we set sail on a ship that had wintered at the island [of Malta].
It was an Alexandrian ship with the Dioscuri
 as its figurehead.
We put in at Syracuse and stayed there three days,
 and from there we sailed round the coast and arrived at Rhegium.
After a day, a south wind came up and in two days we reached Puteoli.
There we found some brothers
 and were urged to stay with them for seven days.
And thus we came to Rome.
The brothers from there heard about us
 and came as far as the Forum of Appius and Three Taverns to meet us.
On seeing them, Paul gave thanks to God and took courage.
When he entered Rome,
 Paul was allowed to live by himself,
 with the soldier who was guarding him.

He remained for two full years in his lodgings.
He received all who came to him,
 and with complete assurance and without hindrance
  he proclaimed the Kingdom of God
  and taught about the Lord Jesus Christ.

The word of the Lord.

RESPONSORIAL PSALM

Psalm 98:1, 2-3ab, 3cd-4, 5-6

℟. (see 2b) **The Lord has revealed to the nations his saving power.**

**Sing to the Lord a new song,
   for he has done wondrous deeds;
His right hand has won victory for him,
   his holy arm.**

℟. **The Lord has revealed to the nations his saving power.**

**The Lord has made his salvation known:
   in the sight of the nations he has revealed his justice.
He has remembered his kindness and his faithfulness
   toward the house of Israel.**

℟. **The Lord has revealed to the nations his saving power.**

**All the ends of the earth have seen
   the salvation by our God.
Sing joyfully to the Lord, all you lands;
   break into song; sing praise.**

℟. **The Lord has revealed to the nations his saving power.**

**Sing praise to the Lord with the harp,
   with the harp and melodious song.
With trumpets and the sound of the horn
   sing joyfully before the King, the Lord.**

℟. **The Lord has revealed to the nations his saving power.**

ALLELUIA

See *Te Deum*

℟. **Alleluia, alleluia.**

**We praise you, O God,
we acclaim you as Lord;
the glorious company of Apostles praise you.**

℟. **Alleluia, alleluia.**

1666   November 18—Dedication of the Basilica of Saints Peter and Paul

GOSPEL

Matthew 14:22-33   Command me to come to you on the water.

✝ A reading from the holy Gospel according to Matthew

After the crowd had eaten their fill,
Jesus made the disciples get into the boat
    and precede him to the other side,
    while he dismissed the crowds.
After doing so, he went up on the mountain by himself to pray.
When it was evening he was there alone.
Meanwhile the boat, already a few miles offshore,
    was being tossed about by the waves, for the wind was against it.
During the fourth watch of the night,
    he came toward them, walking on the sea.
When the disciples saw him walking on the sea they were terrified.
"It is a ghost," they said, and they cried out in fear.
At once Jesus spoke to them, "Take courage, it is I; do not be afraid."
Peter said to him in reply,
    "Lord, if it is you, command me to come to you on the water."
He said, "Come."
Peter got out of the boat and began to walk on the water toward Jesus.
But when he saw how strong the wind was he became frightened;
    and, beginning to sink, he cried out, "Lord, save me!"
Immediately Jesus stretched out his hand and caught him,
    and said to him, "O you of little faith, why did you doubt?"
After they got into the boat, the wind died down.
Those who were in the boat did him homage, saying,
    "Truly, you are the Son of God."

The Gospel of the Lord.

NOVEMBER 18

[In the Dioceses of the United States]

679A SAINT ROSE PHILIPPINE DUCHESNE, VIRGIN

From the Common of Virgins, p. 1857, or the Common of Holy Men and Women: For Religious, p. 1868.

NOVEMBER 21

680 THE PRESENTATION OF THE VIRGIN MARY
MEMORIAL

From the Common of the Blessed Virgin Mary, p. 1751,

OR

FIRST READING

Zechariah 2:14-17   Rejoice, O daughter of Zion! See, I am coming.

A reading from the Book of the Prophet Zechariah

Sing and rejoice, O daughter Zion!
See, I am coming to dwell among you, says the Lord.
Many nations shall join themselves to the Lord on that day,
   and they shall be his people,
   and he will dwell among you,
   and you shall know that the Lord of hosts has sent me to you.
The Lord will possess Judah as his portion in the holy land,
   and he will again choose Jerusalem.
Silence, all mankind, in the presence of the Lord!
   He stirs forth from his holy dwelling.

The word of the Lord.

November 21—The Presentation of the Virgin Mary

RESPONSORIAL PSALM

Luke 1:46-47, 48-49, 50-51, 52-53, 54-55

℟. (49) **The Almighty has done great things for me, and holy is his Name.**
   or:
℟. **O Blessed Virgin Mary, you carried the Son of the eternal Father.**

"My soul proclaims the greatness of the Lord,
   my spirit rejoices in God my Savior."

℟. **The Almighty has done great things for me, and holy is his Name.**
   or:
℟. **O Blessed Virgin Mary, you carried the Son of the eternal Father.**

"For he has looked upon his lowly servant.
From this day all generations will call me blessed:
   the Almighty has done great things for me,
   and holy is his Name."

℟. **The Almighty has done great things for me, and holy is his Name.**
   or:
℟. **O Blessed Virgin Mary, you carried the Son of the eternal Father.**

"He has mercy on those who fear him
   in every generation.
He has shown the strength of his arm,
   he has scattered the proud in their conceit."

℟. **The Almighty has done great things for me, and holy is his Name.**
   or:
℟. **O Blessed Virgin Mary, you carried the Son of the eternal Father.**

"He has cast down the mighty from their thrones,
   and has lifted up the lowly.
He has filled the hungry with good things,
   and the rich he has sent away empty."

℟. **The Almighty has done great things for me, and holy is his Name.**
   or:
℟. **O Blessed Virgin Mary, you carried the Son of the eternal Father.**

"He has come to the help of his servant Israel
   for he has remembered his promise of mercy,
   the promise he made to our fathers,
   to Abraham and his children forever."

℟. **The Almighty has done great things for me, and holy is his Name.**
   or:
℟. **O Blessed Virgin Mary, you carried the Son of the eternal Father.**

ALLELUIA

Luke 11:28

℟. Alleluia, alleluia.

**Blessed are those who hear the word of God
and observe it.**

℟. Alleluia, alleluia.

GOSPEL

Matthew 12:46-50   Stretching out his hands toward his disciples, he said, Here are my mother and my brothers.

✠ A reading from the holy Gospel according to Matthew

**While Jesus was speaking to the crowds,
   his mother and his brothers appeared outside,
      wishing to speak with him.
Someone told him, "Your mother and your brothers are standing outside,
   asking to speak with you."
But he said in reply to the one who told him,
   "Who is my mother?
Who are my brothers?"
And stretching out his hand toward his disciples, he said,
   "Here are my mother and my brothers.
For whoever does the will of my heavenly Father
   is my brother, and sister, and mother."**

The Gospel of the Lord.

NOVEMBER 22

681 SAINT CECILIA, VIRGIN AND MARTYR — MEMORIAL

From the Common of Martyrs, p. 1782, or the Common of Virgins, p. 1857,

OR

FIRST READING

Hosea 2:16bc, 17cd, 21-22   I will espouse you to me forever.

A reading from the Book of the Prophet Hosea

**Thus says the Lord:
I will lead her into the desert
    and speak to her heart.
She shall respond there as in the days of her youth,
    when she came up from the land of Egypt.**

**I will espouse you to me forever:
    I will espouse you in right and in justice,
    in love and in mercy;
I will espouse you in fidelity,
    and you shall know the Lord.**

The word of the Lord.

RESPONSORIAL PSALM

Psalm 45:11-12, 14-15, 16-17

℟. (11) **Listen to me, daughter; see and bend your ear.**
    or:
℟. **The bridegroom is here; let us go out to meet Christ the Lord.**

**Hear, O daughter, and see; turn your ear,
    forget your people and your father's house.
So shall the king desire your beauty;
    for he is your lord, and you must worship him.**

℟. **Listen to me, daughter; see and bend your ear.**
    or:
℟. **The bridegroom is here; let us go out to meet Christ the Lord.**

**All glorious is the king's daughter as she enters;
    her raiment is threaded with spun gold.
In embroidered apparel she is borne in to the king;
    behind her the virgins of her train are brought to you.**

℟. **Listen to me, daughter; see and bend your ear.**
    or:
℟. **The bridegroom is here; let us go out to meet Christ the Lord.**

**They are borne in with gladness and joy;
    they enter the palace of the king.
The place of your fathers your sons shall have;
    you shall make them princes through all the land.**

℟. **Listen to me, daughter; see and bend your ear.**
    or:
℟. **The bridegroom is here; let us go out to meet Christ the Lord.**

ALLELUIA

℟. Alleluia, alleluia.

This is the wise bridesmaid, whom the Lord found waiting;
at his coming, she went in with him to the wedding feast.

℟. Alleluia, alleluia.

GOSPEL

Matthew 25:1-13   Behold, the bridegroom! Come out to meet him!

☩ A reading from the holy Gospel according to Matthew

Jesus told his disciples this parable:
"The Kingdom of heaven will be like ten virgins
   who took their lamps and went out to meet the bridegroom.
Five of them were foolish and five were wise.
The foolish ones, when taking their lamps,
   brought no oil with them,
   but the wise brought flasks of oil with their lamps.
Since the bridegroom was long delayed,
   they all became drowsy and fell asleep.
At midnight, there was a cry,
   'Behold, the bridegroom! Come out to meet him!'
Then all those virgins got up and trimmed their lamps.
The foolish ones said to the wise,
   'Give us some of your oil,
   for our lamps are going out.'
But the wise ones replied,
   'No, for there may not be enough for us and you.
Go instead to the merchants and buy some for yourselves.'
While they went off to buy it,
   the bridegroom came
   and those who were ready went into the wedding feast with him.
Then the door was locked.
Afterwards the other virgins came and said,
   'Lord, Lord, open the door for us!'
But he said in reply,
   'Amen, I say to you, I do not know you.'
Therefore, stay awake,
   for you know neither the day nor the hour."

The Gospel of the Lord.

NOVEMBER 23

682 SAINT CLEMENT I, POPE AND MARTYR

From the Common of Martyrs, p. 1782, or the Common of Pastors: For a Pope, p. 1805,

OR

FIRST READING

1 Peter 5:1-4   Tend the flock of God in your midst!

A reading from the first Letter of Saint Peter

Beloved:
I exhort the presbyters among you,
   as a fellow presbyter and witness to the sufferings of Christ
   and one who has a share in the glory to be revealed.
Tend the flock of God in your midst,
   overseeing it not by constraint but willingly,
   as God would have it, not for shameful profit but eagerly.
Do not lord it over those assigned to you,
   but be examples to the flock.
And when the chief Shepherd is revealed,
   you will receive the unfading crown of glory.

The word of the Lord.

RESPONSORIAL PSALM

Psalm 89:2-3, 4-5, 21-22, 25 and 27

R?. For ever I will sing the goodness of the Lord.

The favors of the Lord I will sing forever;
   through all generations my mouth shall proclaim your faithfulness.
For you have said, "My kindness is established forever";
   in heaven you have confirmed your faithfulness.

R?. For ever I will sing the goodness of the Lord.

"I have made a covenant with my chosen one,
   I have sworn to David my servant:
Forever will I confirm your posterity
   and establish your throne for all generations."

R?. For ever I will sing the goodness of the Lord.

"I have found David, my servant;
   with my holy oil I have anointed him,
That my hand may be always with him,
   and that my arm may make him strong."

℟. For ever I will sing the goodness of the Lord.

"My faithfulness and my mercy shall be with him,
   and through my name shall his horn be exalted.
He shall say of me, 'You are my father,
   my God, the rock, my savior.'"

℟. For ever I will sing the goodness of the Lord.

ALLELUIA

Mark 1:17

℟. Alleluia, alleluia.

Come after me, says the Lord,
and I will make you fishers of men.

℟. Alleluia, alleluia.

GOSPEL

Matthew 16:13-19   You are Peter, and upon this rock I will build my Church.

✠ A reading from the holy Gospel according to Matthew

When Jesus went into the region of Caesarea Philippi
   he asked his disciples,
      "Who do people say that the Son of Man is?"
They replied, "Some say John the Baptist, others Elijah,
   still others Jeremiah or one of the prophets."
He said to them, "But who do you say that I am?"
Simon Peter said in reply,
   "You are the Christ, the Son of the living God."
Jesus said to him in reply, "Blessed are you, Simon son of Jonah.
For flesh and blood has not revealed this to you, but my heavenly Father.
And so I say to you, you are Peter,
   and upon this rock I will build my Church,
   and the gates of the netherworld shall not prevail against it.
I will give you the keys to the Kingdom of heaven.
Whatever you bind on earth shall be bound in heaven;
   and whatever you loose on earth shall be loosed in heaven."

The Gospel of the Lord.

NOVEMBER 23

683 SAINT COLUMBAN, ABBOT

From the Common of Pastors: For Missionaries, p. 1805, or the Common of Holy Men and Women: For Religious, p. 1868,

OR

FIRST READING

Isaiah 52:7-10   All the ends of the earth will behold the salvation.

A reading from the Book of the Prophet Isaiah

> How beautiful upon the mountains
>   are the feet of him who brings glad tidings,
> Announcing peace, bearing good news,
>   announcing salvation, and saying to Zion,
>   "Your God is King!"
>
> Hark! Your sentinels raise a cry,
>   together they shout for joy,
> For they see directly, before their eyes,
>   the Lord restoring Zion.
> Break out together in song,
>   O ruins of Jerusalem!
> For the Lord comforts his people,
>   he redeems Jerusalem.
> The Lord has bared his holy arm
>   in the sight of all the nations;
> All the ends of the earth will behold
>   the salvation of our God.

The word of the Lord.

RESPONSORIAL PSALM

Psalm 96:1-2a, 2b-3, 7-8a, 10

℟. (3) **Proclaim God's marvelous deeds to all the nations.**

Sing to the Lord a new song;
  sing to the Lord, all you lands.
Sing to the Lord; bless him name.

℟. **Proclaim God's marvelous deeds to all the nations.**

Announce his salvation, day after day.
Tell his glory among the nations;
  among all peoples, his wondrous deeds.

℟. **Proclaim God's marvelous deeds to all the nations.**

Give to the Lord, you families of nations,
   give to the Lord glory and praise;
   give to the Lord the glory due his name!

℟. **Proclaim God's marvelous deeds to all the nations.**

Say among the nations: The Lord is king.
He has made the world firm, not to be moved;
   he governs the peoples with equity.

℟. **Proclaim God's marvelous deeds to all the nations.**

ALLELUIA

John 8:12

℟. Alleluia, alleluia.

I am the light of the world, says the Lord;
whoever follows me will have the light of life.

℟. Alleluia, alleluia.

GOSPEL

Luke 9:57-62   I will follow you wherever you go.

☩ A reading from the holy Gospel according to Luke

As Jesus and his disciples were proceeding on their journey,
   someone said to him, "I will follow you wherever you go."
Jesus answered him,
   "Foxes have dens and birds of the sky have nests,
   but the Son of Man has nowhere to rest his head."
And to another he said, "Follow me."
But he replied, "Lord, let me go first and bury my father."
But he answered him, "Let the dead bury their dead.
But you, go and proclaim the Kingdom of God."
And another said, "I will follow you, Lord,
   but first let me say farewell to my family at home."
He said, "No one who sets a hand to the plow
   and looks to what was left behind is fit for the Kingdom of God."

The Gospel of the Lord.

NOVEMBER 23

[In the Dioceses of the United States]

683A BLESSED MIGUEL AGUSTÍN PRO, PRIEST AND MARTYR

From the Common of Martyrs, p. 1782, or the Common of Pastors, p. 1805.

NOVEMBER 24

683B SAINT ANDREW DUNG-LAC, PRIEST AND MARTYR, AND HIS COMPANIONS, MARTYRS

From the Common of Martyrs, p. 1782.

NOVEMBER 30

684 SAINT ANDREW, APOSTLE FEAST

FIRST READING

Romans 10:9-18   Thus faith comes from what is heard, and what is heard comes through the word of Christ.

A reading from the Letter of Saint Paul to the Romans

Brothers and sisters:
If you confess with your mouth that Jesus is Lord
   and believe in your heart that God raised him from the dead,
   you will be saved.
For one believes with the heart and so is justified,
   and one confesses with the mouth and so is saved.
The Scripture says,
   No one who believes in him will be put to shame.
There is no distinction between Jew and Greek;
   the same Lord is Lord of all,
   enriching all who call upon him.
For everyone who calls on the name of the Lord will be saved.

But how can they call on him in whom they have not believed?
And how can they believe in him of whom they have not heard?
And how can they hear without someone to preach?
And how can people preach unless they are sent?
As it is written,
   How beautiful are the feet of those who bring the good news!
But not everyone has heeded the good news;
   for Isaiah says, *Lord, who has believed what was heard from us?*
Thus faith comes from what is heard,
   and what is heard comes through the word of Christ.
But I ask, did they not hear?
Certainly they did; for

   *Their voice has gone forth to all the earth,
     and their words to the ends of the world.*

The word of the Lord.

RESPONSORIAL PSALM

Psalm 19:8, 9, 10, 11

℟. (10) **The judgments of the Lord are true, and all of them are just.**
   or:
℟. (John 6:63) **Your words, Lord, are Spirit and life.**

The law of the Lord is perfect,
   refreshing the soul;
The decree of the Lord is trustworthy,
   giving wisdom to the simple.

℟. **The judgments of the Lord are true, and all of them are just.**
   or:
℟. **Your words, Lord, are Spirit and life.**

The precepts of the Lord are right,
   rejoicing the heart;
The command of the Lord is clear,
   enlightening the eye.

℟. **The judgments of the Lord are true, and all of them are just.**
   or:
℟. **Your words, Lord, are Spirit and life.**

The fear of the Lord is pure,
   enduring forever;
The ordinances of the Lord are true,
   all of them just.

℟. **The judgments of the Lord are true, and all of them are just.**
   or:
℟. **Your words, Lord, are Spirit and life.**

They are more precious than gold,
   than a heap of purest gold;
Sweeter also than syrup
   or honey from the comb.

℟. **The judgments of the Lord are true, and all of them are just.**
   or:
℟. **Your words, Lord, are Spirit and life.**

ALLELUIA

Matthew 4:19

℟. Alleluia, alleluia.

Come after me, says the Lord,
and I will make you fishers of men.

℟. Alleluia, alleluia.

GOSPEL

Matthew 4:18-22   Immediately they left their nets and followed him.

✢ A reading from the holy Gospel according to Matthew

As Jesus was walking by the Sea of Galilee, he saw two brothers,
   Simon who is called Peter, and his brother Andrew,
   casting a net into the sea; they were fishermen.
He said to them,
   "Come after me, and I will make you fishers of men."
At once they left their nets and followed him.
He walked along from there and saw two other brothers,
   James, the son of Zebedee, and his brother John.
They were in a boat, with their father Zebedee, mending their nets.
He called them, and immediately they left their boat and their father
   and followed him.

The Gospel of the Lord.

FOURTH THURSDAY IN NOVEMBER

[In the Dioceses of the United States]

684A THANKSGIVING DAY

From Masses for Various Needs and Occasions: III. For Various Public Needs, 26. In Thanksgiving, nos. 943–947.

DECEMBER 3

685 SAINT FRANCIS XAVIER, PRIEST MEMORIAL

From the Common of Pastors: For Missionaries, p. 1805,

OR

FIRST READING

1 Corinthians 9:16-19, 22-23   Woe to me if I do not preach the Gospel!

A reading from the first Letter of Saint Paul to the Corinthians

Brothers and sisters:
If I preach the Gospel, this is no reason for me to boast,
   for an obligation has been imposed on me,
   and woe to me if I do not preach it!
If I do so willingly, I have a recompense,
   but if unwillingly, then I have been entrusted with a stewardship.
What then is my recompense?
That, when I preach,
   I offer the Gospel free of charge
   so as not to make full use of my right in the Gospel.
Although I am free in regard to all,
   I have made myself a slave to all
   so as to win over as many as possible.
To the weak I became weak, to win over the weak.
I have become all things to all, to save at least some.
All this I do for the sake of the Gospel,
   so that I too may have a share in it.

The word of the Lord.

RESPONSORIAL PSALM

Psalm 117:1bc, 2

℟. (Mark 16:15) **Go out to all the world and tell the Good News.**

Praise the Lord, all you nations;
   glorify him, all you peoples!

℟. **Go out to all the world and tell the Good News.**

For steadfast is his kindness toward us,
   and the fidelity of the Lord endures forever.

℟. **Go out to all the world and tell the Good News.**

ALLELUIA

Matthew 28:19a, 20b

℟. Alleluia, alleluia.

Go and teach all nations, says the Lord;
I am with you always, until the end of the world.

℟. Alleluia, alleluia.

GOSPEL

Mark 16:15-20   Go into the whole world and proclaim the Gospel to every creature.

✜ A reading from the holy Gospel according to Mark

Jesus appeared to the Eleven and said to them:
"Go into the whole world
   and proclaim the Gospel to every creature.
Whoever believes and is baptized will be saved;
   whoever does not believe will be condemned.
These signs will accompany those who believe:
   in my name they will drive out demons,
   they will speak new languages.
They will pick up serpents with their hands,
   and if they drink any deadly thing, it will not harm them.
They will lay hands on the sick, and they will recover."

So the Lord Jesus, after he spoke to them,
   was taken up into heaven
   and took his seat at the right hand of God.
But they went forth and preached everywhere,
   while the Lord worked with them
   and confirmed the word through accompanying signs.

The Gospel of the Lord.

DECEMBER 4

686 JOHN OF DAMASCUS, PRESBYTER, RELIGIOUS, DOCTOR OF THE CHURCH

From the Common of Pastors, p. 1805, or the Common of Doctors of the Church, p. 1838,

OR

FIRST READING

2 Timothy 1:13-14; 2:1-3   Guard this rich trust with the help of the Holy Spirit.

A reading from the second Letter of Saint Paul to Timothy

Beloved:
Take as your norm the sound words that you heard from me,
   in the faith and love that are in Christ Jesus.
Guard this rich trust with the help of the Holy Spirit
   that dwells within us.

My child, be strong in the grace that is in Christ Jesus.
And what you heard from me through many witnesses
   entrust to faithful people
   who will have the ability to teach others as well.
Bear your share of hardship along with me
   like a good soldier of Christ Jesus.

The word of the Lord.

December 4—John of Damascus 1685

RESPONSORIAL PSALM

Psalm 19:8, 9, 10, 11

℟. (10) **The judgments of the Lord are true, and all of them are just.**
   or:
℟. (John 6:63) **Your words, Lord, are Spirit and life.**

**The law of the Lord is perfect,
   refreshing the soul;
The decree of the Lord is trustworthy,
   giving wisdom to the simple.**

℟. **The judgments of the Lord are true, and all of them are just.**
   or:
℟. **Your words, Lord, are Spirit and life.**

**The precepts of the Lord are right,
   rejoicing the heart;
The command of the Lord is clear,
   enlightening the eye.**

℟. **The judgments of the Lord are true, and all of them are just.**
   or:
℟. **Your words, Lord, are Spirit and life.**

**The fear of the Lord is pure,
   enduring forever;
The ordinances of the Lord are true,
   all of them just.**

℟. **The judgments of the Lord are true, and all of them are just.**
   or:
℟. **Your words, Lord, are Spirit and life.**

**They are more precious than gold,
   than a heap of purest gold;
Sweeter also than syrup
   or honey from the comb.**

℟. **The judgments of the Lord are true, and all of them are just.**
   or:
℟. **Your words, Lord, are Spirit and life.**

ALLELUIA

John 14:23

℟. Alleluia, alleluia.

**All who love me will keep my words,
and my Father will love them,
and we will come to them.**

℟. Alleluia, alleluia.

GOSPEL

Long Form

Matthew 25:14-30   Since you were faithful in small matters, I will give you great responsibilities.

✠ A reading from the holy Gospel according to Matthew

**Jesus told his disciples this parable:
"A man going on a journey
 called in his servants and entrusted his possessions to them.
To one he gave five talents; to another, two; to a third, one—
 to each according to his ability.
Then he went away.
Immediately the one who received five talents went and traded with them,
 and made another five.
Likewise, the one who received two made another two.
But the man who received one went off and dug a hole in the ground
 and buried his master's money.
After a long time
 the master of those servants came back
 and settled accounts with them.
The one who had received five talents
 came forward bringing the additional five.
He said, 'Master, you gave me five talents.
See, I have made five more.'
His master said to him, 'Well done, my good and faithful servant.
Since you were faithful in small matters,
 I will give you great responsibilities.
Come, share your master's joy.'
Then the one who had received two talents also came forward and said,
 'Master, you gave me two talents.
See, I have made two more.'
His master said to him, 'Well done, my good and faithful servant.**

Since you were faithful in small matters,
   I will give you great responsibilities.
Come, share your master's joy.'
Then the one who had received the one talent came forward and said,
   'Master, I knew you were a demanding person,
   harvesting where you did not plant
   and gathering where you did not scatter;
   so out of fear I went off and buried your talent in the ground.
Here it is back.'
His master said to him in reply, 'You wicked, lazy servant!
So you knew that I harvest where I did not plant
   and gather where I did not scatter?
Should you not then have put my money in the bank
   so that I could have got it back with interest on my return?
Now then! Take the talent from him and give it to the one with ten.
For to everyone who has, more will be given and he will grow rich;
   but from the one who has not, even what he has will be taken away.
And throw this useless servant into the darkness outside,
   where there will be wailing and grinding of teeth.'"

The Gospel of the Lord.

   OR

December 4—John of Damascus

Short Form

Matthew 25:14-23   Since you were faithful in small matters, I will give you great responsibilities.

✠ **A reading from the holy Gospel according to Matthew**

Jesus told his disciples this parable:
"A man going on a journey
  called in his servants and entrusted his possessions to them.
To one he gave five talents; to another, two; to a third, one—
  to each according to his ability.
Then he went away.
Immediately the one who received five talents went and traded with them,
  and made another five.
Likewise, the one who received two made another two.
But the man who received one went off and dug a hole in the ground
  and buried his master's money.
After a long time
  the master of those servants came back
  and settled accounts with them.
The one who had received five talents
  came forward bringing the additional five.
He said, 'Master, you gave me five talents.
See, I have made five more.'
His master said to him, 'Well done, my good and faithful servant.
Since you were faithful in small matters,
  I will give you great responsibilities.
Come, share your master's joy.'
Then the one who had received two talents also came forward and said,
  'Master, you gave me two talents.
See, I have made two more.'
His master said to him, 'Well done, my good and faithful servant.
Since you were faithful in small matters,
  I will give you great responsibilities.
Come, share your master's joy.'"

The Gospel of the Lord.

DECEMBER 6

687 SAINT NICHOLAS, BISHOP

From the Common of Pastors, p. 1805,

OR

FIRST READING

Isaiah 6:1-8   Whom shall I send? Who will go for us?

A reading from the Book of the Prophet Isaiah

In the year King Uzziah died,
   I saw the Lord seated on a high and lofty throne,
   with the train of his garment filling the temple.
Seraphim were stationed above; each of them had six wings:
   with two they veiled their faces,
   with two they veiled their feet,
   and with two they hovered aloft.

"Holy, holy, holy is the Lord of hosts!"
   they cried, one to the other.
"All the earth is filled with his glory!"
At the sound of that cry, the frame of the door shook
   and the house was filled with smoke.

Then I said, "Woe is me, I am doomed!
For I am a man of unclean lips,
   living among a people of unclean lips;
   yet my eyes have seen the King, the Lord of hosts!"
Then one of the seraphim flew to me,
   holding an ember which he had taken with tongs from the altar.

He touched my mouth with it and said,
"See, now that this has touched your lips,
   your wickedness is removed, your sin purged."

Then I heard the voice of the Lord saying,
   "Whom shall I send? Who will go for us?"
"Here I am," I said, "send me!"

The word of the Lord.

RESPONSORIAL PSALM

Psalm 40:2 and 4, 7-8a, 8b-9, 10, 11

℟. (8a and 9a) **Here I am, Lord; I come to do your will.**

**I have waited, waited for the LORD,
 and he stooped toward me and heard my cry.
And he put a new song into my mouth,
 a hymn to our God.**

℟. **Here I am, Lord; I come to do your will.**

**Sacrifice or oblation you wished not,
 but ears open to obedience you gave me.
Burnt offerings or sin-offerings you sought not;
 then said I, "Behold I come."**

℟. **Here I am, Lord; I come to do your will.**

**"In the written scroll it is prescribed for me,
To do your will, O my God, is my delight,
 and your law is within my heart!"**

℟. **Here I am, Lord; I come to do your will.**

**I announced your justice in the vast assembly;
 I did not restrain my lips, as you, O LORD, know.**

℟. **Here I am, Lord; I come to do your will.**

**Your justice I kept not hid within my heart;
 your faithfulness and your salvation I have spoken of;
I have made no secret of your kindness and your truth
 in the vast assembly.**

℟. **Here I am, Lord; I come to do your will.**

ALLELUIA

Luke 4:18

℟. **Alleluia, alleluia.**

**The Lord sent me to bring glad tidings to the poor
and to proclaim liberty to captives.**

℟. **Alleluia, alleluia.**

GOSPEL

Luke 10:1-9   The harvest is abundant but the laborers are few.

✠ A reading from the holy Gospel according to Luke

The Lord Jesus appointed seventy-two disciples
   whom he sent ahead of him in pairs
   to every town and place he intended to visit.
He said to them,
   "The harvest is abundant but the laborers are few;
   so ask the master of the harvest
   to send out laborers for his harvest.
Go on your way;
   behold, I am sending you like lambs among wolves.
Carry no money bag, no sack, no sandals;
   and greet no one along the way.
Into whatever house you enter,
   first say, 'Peace to this household.'
If a peaceful person lives there,
   your peace will rest on him;
   but if not, it will return to you.
Stay in the same house and eat and drink what is offered to you,
   for the laborer deserves his payment.
Do not move about from one house to another.
Whatever town you enter and they welcome you,
   eat what is set before you,
   cure the sick in it and say to them,
   'The Kingdom of God is at hand for you.'"

The Gospel of the Lord.

DECEMBER 7

688 SAINT AMBROSE, BISHOP AND DOCTOR OF THE CHURCH MEMORIAL

From the Common of Pastors, p. 1805, or the Common of Doctors of the Church, p. 1838,

OR

FIRST READING

Ephesians 3:8-12   To preach to the Gentiles the inscrutable riches of Christ.

A reading from the Letter of Saint Paul to the Ephesians

Brothers and sisters:
To me, the very least of all the holy ones, this grace was given,
   to preach to the Gentiles the inscrutable riches of Christ,
   and to bring to light for all what is the plan of the mystery
   hidden from ages past in God who created all things,
   so that the manifold wisdom of God
   might now be made known through the Church
   to the principalities and authorities in the heavens.
This was according to the eternal purpose
   that he accomplished in Christ Jesus our Lord,
   in whom we have boldness of speech
   and confidence of access through faith in him.

The word of the Lord.

RESPONSORIAL PSALM

Psalm 89:2-3, 4-5, 21-22, 25 and 27

℟. For ever I will sing the goodness of the Lord.

The favors of the Lord I will sing forever;
   through all generations my mouth shall proclaim your faithfulness.
For you have said, "My kindness is established forever";
   in heaven you have confirmed your faithfulness.

℟. For ever I will sing the goodness of the Lord.

"I have made a covenant with my chosen one,
   I have sworn to David my servant:
Forever will I confirm your posterity
   and establish your throne for all generations."

℟. For ever I will sing the goodness of the Lord.

"I have found David, my servant;
   with my holy oil I have anointed him,
That my hand may be always with him,
   and that my arm may make him strong."

℟. For ever I will sing the goodness of the Lord.

"My faithfulness and my mercy shall be with him,
   and through my name shall his horn be exalted.
He shall say of me, 'You are my father,
   my God, the rock, my savior.'"

℟. For ever I will sing the goodness of the Lord.

ALLELUIA

John 10:14

℟. Alleluia, alleluia.

I am the good shepherd, says the Lord;
I know my sheep, and mine know me.

℟. Alleluia, alleluia.

GOSPEL

John 10:11-16   The good shepherd lays down his life for his sheep.

✠ A reading from the holy Gospel according to John

Jesus said:
"I am the good shepherd.
A good shepherd lays down his life for the sheep.
A hired man, who is not a shepherd
   and whose sheep are not his own,
      sees a wolf coming and leaves the sheep and runs away,
      and the wolf catches and scatters them.
This is because he works for pay and has no concern for the sheep.
I am the good shepherd,
   and I know mine and mine know me,
      just as the Father knows me and I know the Father;
      and I will lay down my life for the sheep.
I have other sheep that do not belong to this fold.
These also I must lead, and they will hear my voice,
   and there will be one flock, one shepherd."

The Gospel of the Lord.

DECEMBER 8

689 THE IMMACULATE CONCEPTION OF THE BLESSED VIRGIN MARY SOLEMNITY

FIRST READING

Genesis 3:9-15, 20   I will put enmity between your offspring and hers.

A reading from the Book of Genesis

After the man, Adam, had eaten of the tree,
   the Lord God called to the man and asked him, "Where are you?"
He answered, "I heard you in the garden;
   but I was afraid, because I was naked,
   so I hid myself."
Then he asked, "Who told you that you were naked?
You have eaten, then,
   from the tree of which I had forbidden you to eat!"
The man replied, "The woman whom you put here with me—
   she gave me fruit from the tree, and so I ate it."
The Lord God then asked the woman,
   "Why did you do such a thing?"
The woman answered, "The serpent tricked me into it, so I ate it."

Then the Lord God said to the serpent:
   "Because you have done this, you shall be banned
     from all the animals
     and from all the wild creatures;
   on your belly shall you crawl,
     and dirt shall you eat
     all the days of your life.
   I will put enmity between you and the woman,
     and between your offspring and hers;
   he will strike at your head,
     while you strike at his heel."

The man called his wife Eve,
   because she became the mother of all the living.

The word of the Lord.

RESPONSORIAL PSALM

Psalm 98:1, 2-3ab, 3cd-4

℟. (1) **Sing to the Lord a new song, for he has done marvelous deeds.**

Sing to the LORD **a new song,
 for he has done wondrous deeds;
His right hand has won victory for him,
 his holy arm.**

℟. **Sing to the Lord a new song, for he has done marvelous deeds.**

The LORD **has made his salvation known:
 in the sight of the nations he has revealed his justice.
He has remembered his kindness and his faithfulness
 toward the house of Israel.**

℟. **Sing to the Lord a new song, for he has done marvelous deeds.**

**All the ends of the earth have seen
 the salvation by our God.
Sing joyfully to the L**ORD**, all you lands;
 break into song; sing praise.**

℟. **Sing to the Lord a new song, for he has done marvelous deeds.**

SECOND READING

Ephesians 1:3-6, 11-12   He chose us in Christ before the foundation of the world.

A reading from the Letter of Saint Paul to the Ephesians

Brothers and sisters:
Blessed be the God and Father of our Lord Jesus Christ,
   who has blessed us in Christ
   with every spiritual blessing in the heavens,
   as he chose us in him, before the foundation of the world,
   to be holy and without blemish before him.
In love he destined us for adoption to himself through Jesus Christ,
   in accord with the favor of his will,
   for the praise of the glory of his grace
   that he granted us in the beloved.

In him we were also chosen,
   destined in accord with the purpose of the One
   who accomplishes all things according to the intention of his will,
   so that we might exist for the praise of his glory,
   we who first hoped in Christ.

The word of the Lord.

ALLELUIA

See Luke 1:28

℟. Alleluia, alleluia.

Hail, Mary, full of grace, the Lord is with you;
blessed are you among women.

℟. Alleluia, alleluia.

GOSPEL

Luke 1:26-38   Hail, full of grace! The Lord is with you.

✠ A reading from the holy Gospel according to Luke

The angel Gabriel was sent from God
   to a town of Galilee called Nazareth,
   to a virgin betrothed to a man named Joseph,
   of the house of David,
   and the virgin's name was Mary.
And coming to her, he said,
   "Hail, full of grace! The Lord is with you."
But she was greatly troubled at what was said
   and pondered what sort of greeting this might be.
Then the angel said to her,
   "Do not be afraid, Mary,
   for you have found favor with God.
Behold, you will conceive in your womb and bear a son,
   and you shall name him Jesus.
He will be great and will be called Son of the Most High,
   and the Lord God will give him the throne of David his father,
   and he will rule over the house of Jacob forever,
   and of his Kingdom there will be no end."
But Mary said to the angel,
   "How can this be,
   since I have no relations with a man?"
And the angel said to her in reply,
   "The Holy Spirit will come upon you,
   and the power of the Most High will overshadow you.
Therefore the child to be born
   will be called holy, the Son of God.
And behold, Elizabeth, your relative,
   has also conceived a son in her old age,
   and this is the sixth month for her who was called barren;
   for nothing will be impossible for God."
Mary said, "Behold, I am the handmaid of the Lord.
May it be done to me according to your word."
Then the angel departed from her.

The Gospel of the Lord.

DECEMBER 9

[In the Dioceses of the United States]

689A BLESSED JUAN DIEGO, HERMIT

From the Common of Holy Men and Women, p. 1868.

DECEMBER 11

690 SAINT DAMASUS I, POPE

From the Common of Pastors: For a Pope, p. 1805,

OR

FIRST READING

Acts 20:17-18a, 28-32, 36   Keep watch over yourselves and over the whole flock for which the Holy Spirit has appointed overseers to tend the Church of God.

A reading from the Acts of the Apostles

**From Miletus Paul had the presbyters
  of the Church at Ephesus summoned.
When they came to him, he addressed them,
  "Keep watch over yourselves and over the whole flock
  of which the Holy Spirit has appointed you overseers,
  in which you tend the Church of God
  that he acquired with his own Blood.
I know that after my departure savage wolves will come among you,
  and they will not spare the flock.
And from your own group,
  men will come forward perverting the truth
  to draw the disciples away after them.
So be vigilant and remember that for three years, night and day,
  I unceasingly admonished each of you with tears.
And now I commend you to God
  and to that gracious word of his that can build you up
  and give you the inheritance among all who are consecrated."**

**When he had finished speaking
  he knelt down and prayed with them all.**

The word of the Lord.

RESPONSORIAL PSALM

Psalm 110:1, 2, 3, 4

℟. (4b) **You are a priest for ever, in the line of Melchizedek.**

The Lord said to my Lord: "Sit at my right hand
till I make your enemies your footstool."

℟. **You are a priest for ever, in the line of Melchizedek.**

The scepter of your power the Lord will stretch forth from Zion:
"Rule in the midst of your enemies."

℟. **You are a priest for ever, in the line of Melchizedek.**

"Yours is princely power in the day of your birth, in holy splendor;
before the daystar, like the dew, I have begotten you."

℟. **You are a priest for ever, in the line of Melchizedek.**

The Lord has sworn, and he will not repent:
"You are a priest forever, according to the order of Melchizedek."

℟. **You are a priest for ever, in the line of Melchizedek.**

ALLELUIA

John 15:15b

℟. **Alleluia, alleluia.**

I call you my friends, says the Lord,
for I have made known to you all that the Father has told me.

℟. **Alleluia, alleluia.**

GOSPEL

John 15:9-17   I no longer call you slaves. I have called you friends.

✠ **A reading from the holy Gospel according to John**

Jesus said to his disciples:
"As the Father loves me, so I also love you.
Remain in my love.
If you keep my commandments, you will remain in my love,
just as I have kept my Father's commandments
and remain in his love.

"I have told you this so that my joy might be in you
and your joy might be complete.
This is my commandment: love one another as I love you.
No one has greater love than this,
to lay down one's life for one's friends.
You are my friends if you do what I command you.
I no longer call you slaves,
because a slave does not know what his master is doing.
I have called you friends,
because I have told you everything I have heard from my Father.
It was not you who chose me, but I who chose you
and appointed you to go and bear fruit that will remain,
so that whatever you ask the Father in my name he may give you.
This I command you: love one another."

The Gospel of the Lord.

DECEMBER 12

[In the Dioceses of the United States]

690A OUR LADY OF GUADALUPE FEAST

From the Common of the Blessed Virgin Mary, p. 1751.

OR

FIRST READING

First Option

Zechariah 2:14-17   Rejoice, O daughter Zion! See, I am coming.

A reading from the Book of the Prophet Zechariah

**Sing and rejoice, O daughter Zion!
See, I am coming to dwell among you, says the Lord.
Many nations shall join themselves to the Lord on that day,
   and they shall be his people,
   and he will dwell among you,
   and you shall know that the Lord of hosts has sent me to you.
The Lord will possess Judah as his portion in the holy land,
   and he will again choose Jerusalem.
Silence, all mankind, in the presence of the Lord!
   For he stirs forth from his holy dwelling.**

The word of the Lord.

OR

Second Option

Revelation 11:19a; 12:1-6a, 10ab   A great sign appeared in the sky.

A reading from the Book of Revelation

**God's temple in heaven was opened,
   and the ark of his covenant could be seen in the temple.**

**A great sign appeared in the sky, a woman clothed with the sun,
   with the moon under her feet,
   and on her head a crown of twelve stars.
She was with child and wailed aloud in pain as she labored to give birth.
Then another sign appeared in the sky;
   it was a huge red dragon, with seven heads and ten horns,
   and on its heads were seven diadems.
Its tail swept away a third of the stars in the sky
   and hurled them down to the earth.**

Then the dragon stood before the woman about to give birth,
   to devour her child when she gave birth.
She gave birth to a son, a male child,
   destined to rule all the nations with an iron rod.
Her child was caught up to God and his throne.
The woman herself fled into the desert
   where she had a place prepared by God.
Then I heard a loud voice in heaven say:
   "Now have salvation and power come,
      and the Kingdom of our God
      and the authority of his Anointed."

The word of the Lord.

RESPONSORIAL PSALM

Judith 13:18bcde, 19

℟. (15:9d) **You are the highest honor of our race.**

**Blessed are you, daughter, by the Most High God,
   above all the women on earth;
   and blessed be the L**ORD **God,
   the creator of heaven and earth.**

℟. **You are the highest honor of our race.**

**Your deed of hope will never be forgotten
   by those who tell of the might of God.**

℟. **You are the highest honor of our race.**

ALLELUIA

℟. **Alleluia, alleluia.**

**Blessed are you, holy Virgin Mary, deserving of all praise;
from you rose the sun of justice, Christ our God.**

℟. **Alleluia, alleluia.**

GOSPEL

First Option

Luke 1:26-38   Behold, you will conceive in your womb and bear a son.

✠ A reading from the holy Gospel according to Luke

The angel Gabriel was sent from God
   to a town of Galilee called Nazareth,
   to a virgin betrothed to a man named Joseph,
   of the house of David,
   and the virgin's name was Mary.
And coming to her, he said,
   "Hail, full of grace! The Lord is with you."
But she was greatly troubled at what was said
   and pondered what sort of greeting this might be.
Then the angel said to her,
   "Do not be afraid, Mary,
   for you have found favor with God.
Behold, you will conceive in your womb and bear a son,
   and you shall name him Jesus.
He will be great and will be called Son of the Most High,
   and the Lord God will give him the throne of David his father,
   and he will rule over the house of Jacob forever,
   and of his Kingdom there will be no end."
But Mary said to the angel,
   "How can this be,
   since I have no relations with a man?"
And the angel said to her in reply,
   "The Holy Spirit will come upon you,
   and the power of the Most High will overshadow you.
Therefore the child to be born
   will be called holy, the Son of God.
And behold, Elizabeth, your relative,
   has also conceived a son in her old age,
   and this is the sixth month for her who was called barren;
   for nothing will be impossible for God."
Mary said, "Behold, I am the handmaid of the Lord.
May it be done to me according to your word."
Then the angel departed from her.

The Gospel of the Lord.

OR

Second Option

Luke 1:39-47   Blessed is she who believed.

✠ **A reading from the holy Gospel according to Luke**

**Mary set out
   and traveled to the hill country in haste
   to a town of Judah,
   where she entered the house of Zechariah
   and greeted Elizabeth.
When Elizabeth heard Mary's greeting,
   the infant leaped in her womb,
   and Elizabeth, filled with the Holy Spirit,
   cried out in a loud voice and said,
   "Most blessed are you among women,
   and blessed is the fruit of your womb.
And how does this happen to me,
   that the mother of my Lord should come to me?
For at the moment the sound of your greeting reached my ears,
   the infant in my womb leaped for joy.
Blessed are you who believed
   that what was spoken to you by the Lord
   would be fulfilled."

And Mary said:

   "My soul proclaims the greatness of the Lord;
      my spirit rejoices in God my savior."

The Gospel of the Lord.**

DECEMBER 12

691 SAINT JANE FRANCES DE CHANTAL, RELIGIOUS

In the United States this memorial is transferred to August 18, p. 1479.

DECEMBER 13

692 SAINT LUCY, VIRGIN AND MARTYR MEMORIAL

From the Common of Martyrs, p. 1782, or the Common of Virgins, p. 1857,

OR

FIRST READING

2 Corinthians 10:17–11:2   I betrothed you to one husband to present you as a chaste virgin to Christ.

A reading from the second Letter of Saint Paul to the Corinthians

Brothers and sisters:
"Whoever boasts, should boast in the Lord."
For it is not the one who recommends himself who is approved,
 but the one whom the Lord recommends.

If only you would put up with a little foolishness from me!
Please put up with me.
For I am jealous of you with the jealousy of God,
 since I betrothed you to one husband
 to present you as a chaste virgin to Christ.

The word of the Lord.

RESPONSORIAL PSALM

Psalm 31:3cd-4, 6 and 8ab, 16bc and 17

℟. (6) **Into your hands, O Lord, I commend my spirit.**

Be my rock of refuge,
 a stronghold to give me safety.
You are my rock and my fortress;
 for your name's sake you will lead and guide me.

℟. **Into your hands, O Lord, I commend my spirit.**

Into your hands I commend my spirit;
 you will redeem me, O Lord, O faithful God.
I will rejoice and be glad because of your mercy.

℟. **Into your hands, O Lord, I commend my spirit.**

Rescue me from the clutches of my enemies and my persecutors,
Let your face shine upon your servant;
 save me in your kindness.

℟. **Into your hands, O Lord, I commend my spirit.**

ALLELUIA

℟. Alleluia, alleluia.

This is the wise virgin, whom the Lord found waiting;
at his coming, she went in with him to the wedding feast.

℟. Alleluia, alleluia.

GOSPEL

Matthew 25:1-13   Behold, the bridegroom! Come out to meet him!

✠ A reading from the holy Gospel according to Matthew

Jesus told his disciples this parable:
"The Kingdom of heaven will be like ten virgins
 who took their lamps and went out to meet the bridegroom.
Five of them were foolish and five were wise.
The foolish ones, when taking their lamps,
 brought no oil with them,
 but the wise brought flasks of oil with their lamps.
Since the bridegroom was long delayed,
 they all became drowsy and fell asleep.
At midnight, there was a cry,
 'Behold, the bridegroom! Come out to meet him!'
Then all those virgins got up and trimmed their lamps.
The foolish ones said to the wise,
 'Give us some of your oil,
 for our lamps are going out.'
But the wise ones replied,
 'No, for there may not be enough for us and you.
Go instead to the merchants and buy some for yourselves.'
While they went off to buy it,
 the bridegroom came
 and those who were ready went into the wedding feast with him.
Then the door was locked.
Afterwards the other virgins came and said,
 'Lord, Lord, open the door for us!'
But he said in reply,
 'Amen, I say to you, I do not know you.'
Therefore, stay awake,
 for you know neither the day nor the hour."

The Gospel of the Lord.

DECEMBER 14

693 SAINT JOHN OF THE CROSS, PRIEST AND DOCTOR OF THE CHURCH MEMORIAL

From the Common of Pastors, p. 1805, or the Common of Doctors of the Church, p. 1838,

OR

FIRST READING

1 Corinthians 2:1-10a   We speak God's wisdom, mysteriously hidden.

A reading from the first Letter of Saint Paul to the Corinthians

When I came to you, brothers and sisters,
   proclaiming the mystery of God,
   I did not come with sublimity of words or of wisdom.
For I resolved to know nothing while I was with you
   except Jesus Christ, and him crucified.
I came to you in weakness and fear and much trembling,
   and my message and my proclamation
   were not with persuasive words of wisdom,
   but with a demonstration of spirit and power,
   so that your faith might rest not on human wisdom
   but on the power of God.

Yet we do speak a wisdom to those who are mature,
   but not a wisdom of this age,
   nor of the rulers of this age who are passing away.
Rather, we speak God's wisdom, mysterious, hidden,
   which God predetermined before the ages for our glory,
   and which none of the rulers of this age knew
   for, if they had known it,
   they would not have crucified the Lord of glory.
But as it is written:

   *What eye has not seen, and ear has not heard,
      and what has not entered the human heart,
      what God has prepared for those who love him,*

this God has revealed to us through the Spirit.

The word of the Lord.

RESPONSORIAL PSALM

Psalm 37:3-4, 5-6, 30-31

℟. (30a) **The mouth of the just murmurs wisdom.**

Trust in the LORD and do good,
 that you may dwell in the land and be fed in security.
Take delight in the LORD,
 and he will grant you your heart's request.

℟. **The mouth of the just murmurs wisdom.**

Commit to the LORD your way;
 trust in him, and he will act.
He will make justice dawn for you like the light;
 bright as the noonday shall be your vindication.

℟. **The mouth of the just murmurs wisdom.**

The mouth of the just tells of wisdom
 and his tongue utters what is right.
The law of his God is in his heart,
 and his steps do not falter.

℟. **The mouth of the just murmurs wisdom.**

ALLELUIA

Matthew 5:3

℟. **Alleluia, alleluia.**

Blessed are the poor in spirit;
the Kingdom of heaven is theirs.

℟. **Alleluia, alleluia.**

GOSPEL

Luke 14:25-33 Every one of you who does not renounce all his possessions cannot be my disciple.

✠ **A reading from the holy Gospel according to Luke**

**Great crowds were traveling with Jesus,
and he turned and addressed them,
"If anyone comes to me without hating his father and mother,
wife and children, brothers and sisters,
and even his own life,
he cannot be my disciple.
Whoever does not carry his own cross and come after me
cannot be my disciple.
Which of you wishing to construct a tower
does not first sit down and calculate the cost
to see if there is enough for its completion?
Otherwise, after laying the foundation
and finding himself unable to finish the work
the onlookers should laugh at him and say,
'This one began to build but did not have the resources to finish.'
Or what king marching into battle would not first sit down
and decide whether with ten thousand troops
he can successfully oppose another king
advancing upon him with twenty thousand troops?
But if not, while he is still far away,
he will send a delegation to ask for peace terms.
In the same way,
every one of you who does not renounce all his possessions
cannot be my disciple."**

The Gospel of the Lord.

DECEMBER 21

694 SAINT PETER CANISIUS, PRIEST AND DOCTOR OF THE CHURCH

From the Common of Pastors, p. 1805, or the Common of Doctors of the Church, p. 1838,

OR

FIRST READING

2 Timothy 4:1-5   Perform the work of an evangelist; fulfill your ministry.

A reading from the second Letter of Saint Paul to Timothy

Beloved:
I charge you in the presence of God and of Christ Jesus,
  who will judge the living and the dead,
  and by his appearing and his kingly power:
  proclaim the word;
  be persistent whether it is convenient or inconvenient;
  convince, reprimand, encourage through all patience and teaching.
For the time will come when people will not tolerate sound doctrine but,
  following their own desires and insatiable curiosity,
  will accumulate teachers and will stop listening to the truth
  and will be diverted to myths.
But you, be self-possessed in all circumstances;
  put up with hardship;
  perform the work of an evangelist;
  fulfill your ministry.

The word of the Lord.

RESPONSORIAL PSALM

Psalm 40:2 and 4, 7-8a, 8b-9, 10, 11

℟. (8a and 9a) **Here I am, Lord; I come to do your will.**

I have waited, waited for the LORD**,**
 and he stooped toward me and heard my cry.
And he put a new song into my mouth,
 a hymn to our God.

℟. Here I am, Lord; I come to do your will.

Sacrifice or oblation you wished not,
 but ears open to obedience you gave me.
Burnt offerings or sin-offerings you sought not;
 then said I, "Behold I come."

℟. Here I am, Lord; I come to do your will.

"In the written scroll it is prescribed for me,
To do your will, O my God, is my delight,
 and your law is within my heart!"

℟. Here I am, Lord; I come to do your will.

I announced your justice in the vast assembly;
 I did not restrain my lips, as you, O LORD**, know.**

℟. Here I am, Lord; I come to do your will.

Your justice I kept not hid within my heart;
 your faithfulness and your salvation I have spoken of;
I have made no secret of your kindness and your truth
 in the vast assembly.

℟. Here I am, Lord; I come to do your will.

ALLELUIA

Matthew 5:16

℟. Alleluia, alleluia.

Let your light shine before others,
that they may see your good deeds and glorify your heavenly Father.

℟. Alleluia, alleluia.

GOSPEL

Matthew 5:13-19   You are the light of the world.

✚ A reading from the holy Gospel according to Matthew

Jesus said to his disciples:
"You are the salt of the earth.
But if salt loses its taste, with what can it be seasoned?
It is no longer good for anything
　but to be thrown out and trampled underfoot.
You are the light of the world.
A city set on a mountain cannot be hidden.
Nor do they light a lamp and then put it under a bushel basket;
　it is set on a lampstand,
　where it gives light to all in the house.
Just so, your light must shine before others,
　that they may see your good deeds
　and glorify your heavenly Father.

"Do not think that I have come to abolish the law or the prophets.
I have come not to abolish but to fulfill.
Amen, I say to you, until heaven and earth pass away,
　not the smallest letter or the smallest part of a letter
　will pass from the law,
　until all things have taken place.
Therefore, whoever breaks one of the least of these commandments
　and teaches others to do so
　will be called least in the Kingdom of heaven.
But whoever obeys and teaches these commandments
　will be called greatest in the Kingdom of heaven."

The Gospel of the Lord.

DECEMBER 23

695 SAINT JOHN OF KANTY, PRIEST

From the Common of Pastors: For Those Who Work for the Underprivileged, p. 1805,

OR

FIRST READING

James 2:14-17   Faith of itself, if it does not have works, is dead.

A reading from the Letter of Saint James

What good is it, my brothers and sisters,
 if someone says he has faith but does not have works?
Can that faith save him?
If a brother or sister has nothing to wear
 and has no food for the day,
 and one of you says to them,
 "Go in peace, keep warm, and eat well,"
 but you do not give them the necessities of the body,
 what good is it?
So also faith of itself,
 if it does not have works, is dead.

The word of the Lord.

RESPONSORIAL PSALM

Psalm 112:1bc-2, 3-4, 5-7, 6-8, 9

℟. (1) **Blessed the man who fears the Lord.**
  or:
℟. **Alleluia.**

Blessed the man who fears the Lord,
 who greatly delights in his commands.
His posterity shall be might upon the earth;
 the upright generation shall be blessed.

℟. **Blessed the man who fears the Lord.**
  or:
℟. **Alleluia.**

Wealth and riches shall be in his house;
    his generosity shall endure forever.
Light shines through the darkness for the upright;
    he is gracious and merciful and just.

℟. Blessed the man who fears the Lord.
    or:
℟. Alleluia.

Well for the man who is gracious and lends,
    who conducts his affairs with justice;
He shall never be moved;
    the just one shall be in everlasting remembrance.

℟. Blessed the man who fears the Lord.
    or:
℟. Alleluia.

An evil report he shall not fear;
    his heart is firm, trusting in the Lord.
His heart is steadfast; he shall not fear
    till he looks down upon his foes.

℟. Blessed the man who fears the Lord.
    or:
℟. Alleluia.

Lavishly he gives to the poor,
    his generosity shall endure forever;
    his horn shall be exalted in glory.

℟. Blessed the man who fears the Lord.
    or:
℟. Alleluia.

ALLELUIA

John 13:34

℟. Alleluia, alleluia.

I give you a new commandment:
love one another as I have loved you.

℟. Alleluia, alleluia.

GOSPEL

Luke 6:27-38   Be merciful, just as your Father is merciful.

✠ A reading from the holy Gospel according to Luke

Jesus said to his disciples:
"To you who hear I say,
  love your enemies, do good to those who hate you,
  bless those who curse you, pray for those who mistreat you.
To the person who strikes you on one cheek,
  offer the other one as well,
  and from the person who takes your cloak,
  do not withhold even your tunic.
Give to everyone who asks of you,
  and from the one who takes what is yours do not demand it back.
Do to others as you would have them do to you.
For if you love those who love you,
  what credit is that to you?
Even sinners love those who love them.
And if you do good to those who do good to you,
  what credit is that to you?
Even sinners do the same.
If you lend money to those from whom you expect repayment,
  what credit is that to you?
Even sinners lend to sinners,
  and get back the same amount.
But rather, love your enemies and do good to them,
  and lend expecting nothing back;
  then your reward will be great
  and you will be children of the Most High,
  for he himself is kind to the ungrateful and the wicked.
Be merciful, just as your Father is merciful.

"Stop judging and you will not be judged.
Stop condemning and you will not be condemned.
Forgive and you will be forgiven.
Give and gifts will be given to you;
  a good measure, packed together, shaken down, and overflowing,
  will be poured into your lap.
For the measure with which you measure
  will in return be measured out to you."

The Gospel of the Lord.

DECEMBER 26

696 SAINT STEPHEN, FIRST MARTYR FEAST

FIRST READING

Acts 6:8-10; 7:54-59   I see the heavens opened.

A reading from the Acts of the Apostles

Stephen, filled with grace and power,
   was working great wonders and signs among the people.
Certain members of the so-called Synagogue of Freedmen,
   Cyrenians, and Alexandrians,
   and people from Cilicia and Asia,
   came forward and debated with Stephen,
   but they could not withstand the wisdom and the spirit with which he spoke.

When they heard this, they were infuriated,
   and they ground their teeth at him.
But he, filled with the Holy Spirit,
   looked up intently to heaven
   and saw the glory of God and Jesus standing at the right hand of God,
   and he said,
   "Behold, I see the heavens opened and the Son of Man
   standing at the right hand of God."
But they cried out in a loud voice, covered their ears,
   and rushed upon him together.
They threw him out of the city, and began to stone him.
The witnesses laid down their cloaks
   at the feet of a young man named Saul.
As they were stoning Stephen, he called out
   "Lord Jesus, receive my spirit."

The word of the Lord.

RESPONSORIAL PSALM

Psalm 31:3cd-4, 6 and 8ab, 16bc and 17

R. (6) **Into your hands, O Lord, I commend my spirit.**

Be my rock of refuge,
   a stronghold to give me safety.
You are my rock and my fortress;
   for your name's sake you will lead and guide me.

R. **Into your hands, O Lord, I commend my spirit.**

Into your hands I commend my spirit;
   you will redeem me, O Lord, O faithful God.
I will rejoice and be glad because of your mercy.

℟. **Into your hands, O Lord, I commend my spirit.**

Rescue me from the clutches of my enemies and my persecutors,
Let your face shine upon your servant;
   save me in your kindness.

℟. **Into your hands, O Lord, I commend my spirit.**

ALLELUIA

Psalm 118:26a, 27a

℟. **Alleluia, alleluia.**

Blessed is he who comes in the name of the Lord:
the Lord is God and has given us light.

℟. **Alleluia, alleluia.**

GOSPEL

Matthew 10:17-22   For it will not be you who speak but the Spirit of your Father.

✢ **A reading from the holy Gospel according to Matthew**

Jesus said to his disciples:
"Beware of men, for they will hand you over to courts
   and scourge you in their synagogues,
   and you will be led before governors and kings for my sake
   as a witness before them and the pagans.
When they hand you over,
   do not worry about how you are to speak
   or what you are to say.
You will be given at that moment what you are to say.
For it will not be you who speak
   but the Spirit of your Father speaking through you.
Brother will hand over brother to death,
   and the father his child;
   children will rise up against parents and have them put to death.
You will be hated by all because of my name,
   but whoever endures to the end will be saved."

The Gospel of the Lord.

DECEMBER 27

697 SAINT JOHN, APOSTLE AND EVANGELIST FEAST

FIRST READING

1 John 1:1-4   What we have seen and heard we proclaim now to you.

A reading from the beginning of the first Letter of Saint John

Beloved:
   What was from the beginning,
   what we have heard,
   what we have seen with our eyes,
   what we looked upon
   and touched with our hands
   concerns the Word of life—
   for the life was made visible;
   we have seen it and testify to it
   and proclaim to you the eternal life
   that was with the Father and was made visible to us—
   what we have seen and heard
   we proclaim now to you,
   so that you too may have fellowship with us;
   for our fellowship is with the Father
   and with his Son, Jesus Christ.
We are writing this so that our joy may be complete.

The word of the Lord.

RESPONSORIAL PSALM

Psalm 97:1-2, 5-6, 11-12

℟. (12) **Rejoice in the Lord, you just!**

The LORD is king; let the earth rejoice;
   let the many isles be glad.
Clouds and darkness are around him,
   justice and judgment are the foundation of his throne.

℟. **Rejoice in the Lord, you just!**

The mountains melt like wax before the LORD,
   before the LORD of all the earth.
The heavens proclaim his justice,
   and all peoples see his glory.

℟. **Rejoice in the Lord, you just!**

Light dawns for the just;
  and gladness, for the upright of heart.
Be glad in the LORD**, you just,**
  and give thanks to his holy name.

℟. **Rejoice in the Lord, you just!**

ALLELUIA

See *Te Deum*

℟. **Alleluia, alleluia.**

We praise you, O God,
we acclaim you as Lord;
the glorious company of Apostles praise you.

℟. **Alleluia, alleluia.**

GOSPEL

John 20:1a and 2-8   The other disciple ran faster than Peter and arrived at the tomb first.

✠ **A reading from the holy Gospel according to John**

On the first day of the week,
  Mary Magdalene ran and went to Simon Peter
  and to the other disciple whom Jesus loved, and told them,
  "They have taken the Lord from the tomb,
  and we do not know where they put him."
So Peter and the other disciple went out and came to the tomb.
They both ran, but the other disciple ran faster than Peter
  and arrived at the tomb first;
  he bent down and saw the burial cloths there, but did not go in.
When Simon Peter arrived after him,
  he went into the tomb and saw the burial cloths there,
  and the cloth that had covered his head,
  not with the burial cloths but rolled up in a separate place.
Then the other disciple also went in,
  the one who had arrived at the tomb first,
  and he saw and believed.

The Gospel of the Lord.

DECEMBER 28

698 THE HOLY INNOCENTS, MARTYRS FEAST

FIRST READING

1 John 1:5–2:2   The Blood of his Son Jesus Christ cleanses us from all sin.

A reading from the first Letter of Saint John

Beloved:
This is the message that we have heard from Jesus Christ
   and proclaim to you:
   God is light, and in him there is no darkness at all.
If we say, "We have fellowship with him,"
   while we continue to walk in darkness,
   we lie and do not act in truth.
But if we walk in the light as he is in the light,
   then we have fellowship with one another,
   and the Blood of his Son Jesus cleanses us from all sin.
If we say, "We are without sin,"
   we deceive ourselves, and the truth is not in us.
If we acknowledge our sins, he is faithful and just
   and will forgive our sins and cleanse us from every wrongdoing.
If we say, "We have not sinned," we make him a liar,
   and his word is not in us.

My children, I am writing this to you
   so that you may not commit sin.
But if anyone does sin, we have an Advocate with the Father,
   Jesus Christ the righteous one.
He is expiation for our sins,
   and not for our sins only but for those of the whole world.

The word of the Lord.

RESPONSORIAL PSALM

Psalm 124:2-3, 4-5, 7cd-8

℟. (7) **Our soul has been rescued like a bird from the fowler's snare.**

Had not the LORD **been with us—
When men rose up against us,
   then would they have swallowed us alive,
When their fury was inflamed against us.**

℟. **Our soul has been rescued like a bird from the fowler's snare.**

**Then would the waters have overwhelmed us;
The torrent would have swept over us;
   over us then would have swept the raging waters.**

℟. **Our soul has been rescued like a bird from the fowler's snare.**

**Broken was the snare,
   and we were freed.
Our help is in the name of the L**ORD**,
   who made heaven and earth.**

℟. **Our soul has been rescued like a bird from the fowler's snare.**

ALLELUIA

See *Te Deum*

℟. **Alleluia, alleluia.**

**We praise you, O God,
we acclaim you as Lord;
the white-robed army of martyrs praise you.**

℟. **Alleluia, alleluia.**

GOSPEL

Matthew 2:13-18   He ordered the massacre of all boys in Bethlehem.

✠ A reading from the holy Gospel according to Matthew

When the magi had departed, behold,
    the angel of the Lord appeared to Joseph in a dream and said,
    "Rise, take the child and his mother, flee to Egypt,
    and stay there until I tell you.
Herod is going to search for the child to destroy him."
Joseph rose and took the child and his mother by night
    and departed for Egypt.
He stayed there until the death of Herod,
    that what the Lord had said through the prophet might be fulfilled,
    Out of Egypt I called my son.

When Herod realized that he had been deceived by the magi,
    he became furious.
He ordered the massacre of all the boys in Bethlehem and its vicinity
    two years old and under,
    in accordance with the time he had ascertained from the magi.
Then was fulfilled what had been said through Jeremiah the prophet:

   *A voice was heard in Ramah,
      sobbing and loud lamentation;
   Rachel weeping for her children,
      and she would not be consoled,
      since they were no more.*

The Gospel of the Lord.

DECEMBER 29

699 SAINT THOMAS BECKET, BISHOP AND MARTYR

From the Common of Martyrs, p. 1782, or the Common of Pastors, p. 1805,

OR

FIRST READING

2 Timothy 2:8-13; 3:10-12   All who want to live religiously in Christ Jesus will be persecuted.

A reading from the second Letter of Saint Paul to Timothy

Beloved:
Remember Jesus Christ, raised from the dead, a descendant of David:
   such is my Gospel, for which I am suffering,
   even to the point of chains, like a criminal.
But the word of God is not chained.
Therefore, I bear with everything for the sake of those who are chosen,
   so that they too may obtain the salvation that is in Christ Jesus,
   together with eternal glory.
This saying is trustworthy:

  If we have died with him
    we shall also live with him;
  if we persevere
    we shall also reign with him.
  But if we deny him
    he will deny us.
  If we are unfaithful
    he remains faithful,
    for he cannot deny himself.

You have followed my teaching, way of life,
   purpose, faith, patience, love,
   endurance, persecutions, and sufferings,
   such as happened to me in Antioch, Iconium, and Lystra,
   persecutions that I endured.
Yet from all these things the Lord delivered me.
In fact, all who want to live religiously in Christ Jesus
   will be persecuted.

The word of the Lord.

RESPONSORIAL PSALM

Psalm 34:2-3, 4-5, 6-7, 8-9

℟. (5) **The Lord delivered me from all my fears.**

I will bless the LORD **at all times;**
 his praise shall be ever in my mouth.
Let my soul glory in the LORD**;**
 the lowly will hear and be glad.

℟. **The Lord delivered me from all my fears.**

Glorify the LORD **with me,**
 let us together extol his name.
I sought the LORD**, and he answered me**
 and delivered me from all my fears.

℟. **The Lord delivered me from all my fears.**

Look to him that you may be radiant with joy,
 and your faces may not blush with shame.
When the poor one called out, the LORD **heard,**
 and from all his distress he saved him.

℟. **The Lord delivered me from all my fears.**

The angel of the LORD **encamps**
 around those who fear him, and delivers them.
Taste and see how good the LORD **is;**
 blessed the man who takes refuge in him.

℟. **The Lord delivered me from all my fears.**

ALLELUIA

Matthew 5:6

℟. Alleluia, alleluia.

**Blessed are those who hunger and thirst for righteousness;
for they will be satisfied.**

℟. Alleluia, alleluia.

GOSPEL

Matthew 16:24-27   Whoever loses his life for my sake will save it.

✠ **A reading from the holy Gospel according to Matthew**

**Jesus said to all,
   "Whoever wishes to come after me, must deny himself,
      take up his cross, and follow me.
For whoever wishes to save his life will lose it,
   but whoever loses his life for my sake will save it.
What profit would there be for one to gain the whole world
   and forfeit his life? Or what can one give
   in exchange for his life?
For the Son of Man will come with his angels in his Father's glory,
   and then he will repay each one according to his conduct."**

The Gospel of the Lord.

DECEMBER 31

700 SAINT SYLVESTER I, POPE

From the Common of Pastors: For a Pope, p. 1805,

OR

FIRST READING

Ezekiel 34:11-16 As a shepherd tends his flock, so will I tend my sheep.

A reading from the Book of the Prophet Ezekiel

Thus says the Lord GOD:
  I myself will look after and tend my sheep.
As a shepherd tends his flock
  when he finds himself among his scattered sheep,
  so will I tend my sheep.
I will rescue them from every place where they were scattered
  when it was cloudy and dark.
I will lead them out from among the peoples
  and gather them from the foreign lands;
  I will bring them back to their own country
  and pasture them upon the mountains of Israel
  in the land's ravines and all its inhabited places.
In good pastures will I pasture them,
  and on the mountain heights of Israel
  shall be their grazing ground.
There they shall lie down on good grazing ground,
  and in rich pastures shall they be pastured
  on the mountains of Israel.
I myself will pasture my sheep;
  I myself will give them rest, says the Lord GOD.
The lost I will seek out,
  the strayed I will bring back,
  the injured I will bind up,
  the sick I will heal,
  but the sleek and the strong I will destroy,
  shepherding them rightly.

The word of the Lord.

RESPONSORIAL PSALM

Psalm 23:1-3a, 4, 5, 6

℟. (1) The Lord is my shepherd; there is nothing I shall want.

The Lord is my shepherd; I shall not want.
   In verdant pastures he gives me repose;
Beside restful waters he leads me;
   he refreshes my soul.

℟. The Lord is my shepherd; there is nothing I shall want.

Even though I walk in the dark valley
   I fear no evil; for you are at my side
With your rod and your staff
   that give me courage.

℟. The Lord is my shepherd; there is nothing I shall want.

You spread the table before me
   in the sight of my foes;
You anoint my head with oil;
   my cup overflows.

℟. The Lord is my shepherd; there is nothing I shall want.

Only goodness and kindness follow me
   all the days of my life;
And I shall dwell in the house of the Lord
   for years to come.

℟. The Lord is my shepherd; there is nothing I shall want.

ALLELUIA

Mark 1:17

℟. Alleluia, alleluia.

Come after me, says the Lord,
and I will make you fishers of men.

℟. Alleluia, alleluia.

December 31—Saint Sylvester I

GOSPEL

Matthew 16:13-19   You are Peter and upon this rock I will build my Church.

☩ **A reading from the holy Gospel according to Matthew**

**When Jesus went into the region of Caesarea Philippi
he asked his disciples,
"Who do people say that the Son of Man is?"
They replied, "Some say John the Baptist, others Elijah,
still others Jeremiah or one of the prophets."
He said to them, "But who do you say that I am?"
Simon Peter said in reply,
"You are the Christ, the Son of the living God."
Jesus said to him in reply, "Blessed are you, Simon son of Jonah.
For flesh and blood has not revealed this to you, but my heavenly Father.
And so I say to you, you are Peter,
and upon this rock I will build my Church,
and the gates of the netherworld shall not prevail against it.
I will give you the keys to the Kingdom of heaven.
Whatever you bind on earth shall be bound in heaven;
and whatever you loose on earth shall be loosed in heaven."**

The Gospel of the Lord.

COMMONS

THE COMMON OF THE ANNIVERSARY OF THE DEDICATION OF A CHURCH

701 READING I FROM THE OLD TESTAMENT

1.

1 Kings 8:22-23, 27-30   May your eyes watch night and day over this temple.

A reading from the first Book of Kings

In those days:
Solomon stood before the altar of the Lord
   in the presence of the whole community of Israel,
   and stretching forth his hands toward heaven, he said,
   "Lord, God of Israel, there is no God like you
   in heaven above or on earth below;
   you keep your covenant of mercy with your servants
   who are faithful to you with their whole heart.

"Can it indeed be that God dwells on earth?
If the heavens and the highest heavens cannot contain you,
   how much less this temple which I have built!
Look kindly on the prayer and petition of your servant,
   O Lord, my God,
   and listen to the cry of supplication I, your servant,
   utter before you this day.
May your eyes watch night and day over this temple,
   the place where you have decreed you shall be honored;
   may you heed the prayer which I, your servant, offer in this place.
Listen to the petitions of your servant
   and of your people Israel
   which they offer in this place.
Listen from your heavenly dwelling and grant pardon."

The word of the Lord.

2.

2 Chronicles 5:6-10, 13–6:2   I have truly built a princely house and dwelling, where you may abide forever.

A reading from the second Book of Chronicles

King Solomon and the entire community of Israel
   gathered about him before the ark
   were sacrificing sheep and oxen so numerous
   that they could not be counted or numbered.
The priests brought the ark of the covenant of the Lord
   to its place beneath the wings of the cherubim in the sanctuary,
   the holy of holies of the temple.
The cherubim had their wings spread out over the place of the ark,
   sheltering the ark and its poles from above.
The poles were long enough so that their ends could be seen
   from that part of the holy place nearest the sanctuary;
   however, they could not be seen beyond.
The ark has remained there to this day.
There was nothing in it but the two tablets
   which Moses put there on Horeb,
   the tablets of the covenant which the Lord made
   with the children of Israel at their departure from Egypt.

When the trumpeters and singers were heard as a single voice
   praising and giving thanks to the Lord,
   and when they raised the sound
   of the trumpets, cymbals and other musical instruments
   to "give thanks to the Lord, for he is good,
   for his mercy endures forever,"
   the building of the Lord's temple was filled with a cloud.
The priests could not continue to minister because of the cloud,
   since the Lord's glory filled the house of God.

Then Solomon said:
   "The Lord intends to dwell in the dark cloud.
I have truly built you a princely house and dwelling,
   where you may abide forever."

The word of the Lord.

3.

Isaiah 56:1, 6-7   My house shall be called a house of prayer for all peoples.

A reading from the Book of the Prophet Isaiah

> Thus says the Lord:
>
> **Observe what is right, do what is just;**
> **for my salvation is about to come,**
> **my justice, about to be revealed.**
>
> **The foreigners who join themselves to the Lord,**
> **ministering to him,**
> **Loving the name of the Lord,**
> **and becoming his servants—**
> **All who keep the sabbath free from profanation**
> **and hold to my covenant,**
> **Them I will bring to my holy mountain**
> **and make joyful in my house of prayer;**
> **Their burnt offerings and sacrifices**
> **will be acceptable on my altar,**
> **For my house shall be called**
> **a house of prayer for all peoples.**

The word of the Lord.

4.

Ezekiel 43:1-2, 3c-7a   The temple was filled with the glory of the Lord.

A reading from the Book of the Prophet Ezekiel

The angel led me to the gate which faces the east,
and there I saw the glory of the God of Israel
coming from the east.
I heard a sound like the roaring of many waters,
and the earth shone with his glory.
I fell prone as the glory of the Lord entered the temple
by way of the gate which faces the east,
but spirit lifted me up and brought me to the inner court.
And I saw that the temple was filled with the glory of the Lord.
Then I heard someone speaking to me from the temple,
while the man stood beside me.
The voice said to me:
Son of man, this is where my throne shall be,
this is where I will set the soles of my feet;
here I will dwell among the children of Israel forever.

The word of the Lord.

5.

Ezekiel 47:1-2, 8-9, 12   I saw water flowing from the temple, and all who were touched by it were saved (see Roman Missal, antiphon for the blessing and sprinkling of water during the season of Easter).

A reading from the Book of the Prophet Ezekiel

The angel brought me back to the entrance of the temple,
   and I saw water flowing out
   from beneath the threshold of the temple toward the east,
   for the façade of the temple was toward the east;
   the water flowed down from the right side of the temple,
   south of the altar.
He led me outside by the north gate,
   and around to the outer gate facing the east,
   where I saw water trickling from the right side.
He said to me,
   "This water flows into the eastern district down upon the Arabah,
   and empties into the sea, the salt waters, which it makes fresh.
Wherever the river flows,
   every sort of living creature that can multiply shall live,
   and there shall be abundant fish,
   for wherever this water comes the sea shall be made fresh.
Along both banks of the river, fruit trees of every kind shall grow;
   their leaves shall not fade, nor their fruit fail.
Every month they shall bear fresh fruit,
   for they shall be watered by the flow from the sanctuary.
Their fruit shall serve for food, and their leaves for medicine."

The word of the Lord.

702 READING I FROM THE NEW TESTAMENT DURING THE SEASON OF EASTER

First Option

Acts 7:44-50   The Most High does not dwell in houses made by human hands.

A reading from the Acts of the Apostles

Stephen said to the people, the elders and the scribes:
"Our ancestors had the tent of testimony in the desert
  just as the One who spoke to Moses directed him
  to make it according to the pattern he had seen.
Our ancestors who inherited it
  brought it with Joshua when they dispossessed the nations
  that God drove out from before our ancestors,
  up to the time of David,
  who found favor in the sight of God
  and asked that he might find a dwelling place
  for the house of Jacob.
But Solomon built a house for him.
Yet the Most High does not dwell in houses made by human hands.
As the prophet says:

  The heavens are my throne,
    the earth is my footstool.
  What kind of house can you build for me?
      says the Lord,
    or what is to be my resting place?
  Did not my hand make all these things?"

The word of the Lord.

Second Option

Revelation 21:1-5a   Behold, God's dwelling is with the human race.

A reading from the Book of Revelation

**I, John, saw a new heaven and a new earth.
The former heaven and the former earth had passed away,
    and the sea was no more.
I also saw the holy city, a new Jerusalem,
    coming down out of heaven from God,
    prepared as a bride adorned for her husband.
I heard a loud voice from the throne saying,
    "Behold, God's dwelling is with the human race.
He will dwell with them and they will be his people
    and God himself will always be with them as their God.
He will wipe every tear from their eyes,
    and there shall be no more death or mourning, wailing or pain,
    for the old order has passed away."**

**The One who sat on the throne said,
    "Behold, I make all things new."**

The word of the Lord.

Third Option

Revelation 21:9-14   I will show you the bride, the wife of the Lamb.

A reading from the Book of Revelation

**The angel spoke to me, saying:
"Come here. I will show you the bride, the wife of the Lamb."
He took me in spirit to a great, high mountain
    and showed me the holy city Jerusalem
    coming down out of heaven from God.
It gleamed with the splendor of God.
Its radiance was like that of a precious stone,
    like jasper, clear as crystal.
It had a massive, high wall,
    with twelve gates where twelve angels were stationed
    and on which names were inscribed,
    the names of the twelve tribes of the children of Israel.
There were three gates facing east,
    three north, three south, and three west.
The wall of the city had twelve courses of stones as its foundation,
    on which were inscribed the twelve names
    of the twelve Apostles of the Lamb.**

The word of the Lord.

703 RESPONSORIAL PSALM

1.

1 Chronicles 29:10, 11, 12

℟. (13b) **We praise your glorious name, O mighty God.**

"Blessed may you be, O Lord,
 God of Israel our father,
 from eternity to eternity."

℟. **We praise your glorious name, O mighty God.**

"Yours, O Lord, are grandeur and power,
 majesty, splendor, and glory.
For all in heaven and on earth is yours."

℟. **We praise your glorious name, O mighty God.**

"Yours, O Lord, is the sovereignty;
 you are exalted as head over all.
Riches and honor are from you."

℟. **We praise your glorious name, O mighty God.**

"You have dominion over all.
In your hands are power and might;
 it is yours to give grandeur and strength to all."

℟. **We praise your glorious name, O mighty God.**

2.

Psalm 46:2-3, 5-6, 8-9

℟. (5) **There is a stream whose runlets gladden the city of God, the holy dwelling of the Most High!**

God is our refuge and our strength,
   an ever-present help in distress.
Therefore we fear not, though the earth be shaken
   and mountains plunge into the depths of the sea.

℟. **There is a stream whose runlets gladden the city of God, the holy dwelling of the Most High!**

There is a stream whose runlets gladden the city of God,
   the holy dwelling of the Most High.
God is in its midst; it shall not be disturbed;
   God will help it at the break of dawn.

℟. **There is a stream whose runlets gladden the city of God, the holy dwelling of the Most High!**

The Lord of hosts is with us;
   our stronghold is the God of Jacob.
Come! behold the deeds of the Lord,
   the astounding things he has wrought on earth.

℟. **There is a stream whose runlets gladden the city of God, the holy dwelling of the Most High!**

3.

Psalm 84:3, 4, 5 and 10, 11

℟. How lovely is your dwelling-place, Lord, mighty God!
   or:
℟. Here God lives among his people.

My soul yearns and pines
   for the courts of the LORD.
My heart and my flesh
   cry out for the living God.

℟. How lovely is your dwelling-place, Lord, mighty God!
   or:
℟. Here God lives among his people.

Even the sparrow finds a home,
   and the swallow a nest
   in which she puts her young—
Your altars, O LORD **of hosts,**
   my king and my God!

℟. How lovely is your dwelling-place, Lord, mighty God!
   or:
℟. Here God lives among his people.

Blessed they who dwell in your house!
   continually they praise you.
O God, behold our shield,
   and look upon the face of your anointed.

℟. How lovely is your dwelling-place, Lord, mighty God!
   or:
℟. Here God lives among his people.

I had rather one day in your courts
   than a thousand elsewhere;
I had rather lie at the threshold of the house of my God
   than dwell in the tents of the wicked.

℟. How lovely is your dwelling-place, Lord, mighty God!
   or:
℟. Here God lives among his people.

4.

Psalm 95:1-2, 3-5, 6-7

℟. (2) **Let us come before the Lord and praise him.**

Come, let us sing joyfully to the LORD**;**
  let us acclaim the Rock of our salvation.
Let us come into his presence with thanksgiving;
  let us joyfully sing psalms to him.

℟. **Let us come before the Lord and praise him.**

For the LORD **is a great God,**
  and a great king above all gods;
In his hands are the depths of the earth,
  and the tops of the mountains are his.
His is the sea, for he has made it,
  and the dry land, which his hands have formed.

℟. **Let us come before the Lord and praise him.**

Come, let us bow down in worship;
  let us kneel before the LORD **who made us.**
For he is our God,
  and we are the people he shepherds, the flock he guides.

℟. **Let us come before the Lord and praise him.**

5.

Psalm 122:1-2, 3-4ab, 8-9

℟. (1) **Let us go rejoicing to the house of the Lord!**

I rejoiced because they said to me,
  "We will go up to the house of the LORD**."**
And now we have set foot
  within your gates, O Jerusalem.

℟. **Let us go rejoicing to the house of the Lord!**

Jerusalem, built as a city
  with compact unity.
To it the tribes go up,
  the tribes of the LORD**.**

℟. **Let us go rejoicing to the house of the Lord!**

Because of my relatives and friends
  I will say, "Peace be within you!"
Because of the house of the LORD**, our God,**
  I will pray for your good.

℟. **Let us go rejoicing to the house of the Lord!**

704 READING II FROM THE NEW TESTAMENT

First Option

1 Corinthians 3:9c-11, 16-17   You are God's temple.

A reading from the first Letter of Saint Paul to the Corinthians

Brothers and sisters:
You are God's building.

According to the grace of God given to me,
  like a wise master builder I laid a foundation,
  and another is building upon it.
But each one must be careful how he builds upon it,
  for no one can lay a foundation other than the one that is there,
  namely, Jesus Christ.
Do you not know that you are the temple of God,
  and that the Spirit of God dwells in you?
If anyone destroys God's temple,
  God will destroy that person;
  for the temple of God, which you are, is holy.

The word of the Lord.

Second Option

Ephesians 2:19-22   Through him the whole structure is held together and grows into a temple sacred in the Lord.

A reading from the Letter of Saint Paul to the Ephesians

Brothers and sisters:
You are no longer strangers and sojourners,
  but you are fellow citizens with the holy ones
  and members of the household of God,
  built upon the foundation of the Apostles and prophets,
  with Christ Jesus himself as the capstone.
Through him the whole structure is held together
  and grows into a temple sacred in the Lord;
  in him you also are being built together
  into a dwelling place of God in the Spirit.

The word of the Lord.

Third Option

Hebrews 12:18-19, 22-24 You have approached Mount Zion and the city of the living God.

A reading from the Letter to the Hebrews

Brothers and sisters:
You have not approached that which could be touched
   and a blazing fire and gloomy darkness
   and storm and a trumpet blast
   and a voice speaking words such that those who heard
   begged that no message be further addressed to them.
No, you have approached Mount Zion
   and the city of the living God, the heavenly Jerusalem,
   and countless angels in festal gathering,
   and the assembly of the firstborn enrolled in heaven,
   and God the judge of all,
   and the spirits of the just made perfect,
   and Jesus, the mediator of a new covenant,
   and the sprinkled Blood that speaks more eloquently
   than that of Abel.

The word of the Lord.

Fourth Option

1 Peter 2:4-9   Like living stones, let yourselves be built into a spiritual house.

A reading from the first Letter of Saint Peter

Beloved:
Come to the Lord, a living stone, rejected by human beings
  but chosen and precious in the sight of God,
  and, like living stones,
  let yourselves be built into a spiritual house
  to be a holy priesthood to offer spiritual sacrifices
  acceptable to God through Jesus Christ.
For it says in Scripture:

Behold, I am laying a stone in Zion,
  a cornerstone, chosen and precious,
and whoever believes in it shall not be put to shame.

Therefore, its value is for you who have faith,
  but for those without faith:

The stone which the builders rejected
  has become the cornerstone,

and

A stone which will make people stumble,
  and a rock that will make them fall.

They stumble by disobeying the word, as is their destiny.

You are "a chosen race, a royal priesthood,
  a holy nation, a people of his own,
  so that you may announce the praises" of him
  who called you out of darkness into his wonderful light.

The word of the Lord.

705 ALLELUIA VERSE AND VERSE BEFORE THE GOSPEL

1.

2 Chronicles 7:16

**I have chosen and consecrated this house, says the Lord,
that my name may be there forever.**

2.

Isaiah 66:1

**"The heavens are my throne, the earth is my footstool," says the Lord;
What kind of house can you build for me?**

3.

Ezekiel 37:27

**My dwelling shall be with them, says the Lord;
I will be their God and they shall be my people.**

4.

See Matthew 7:8

**In my house, says the Lord, everyone who asks will receive;
The one who seeks, finds; and to the one who knocks, the door will be opened.**

5.

Matthew 16:18

**You are Peter, and upon this rock I will build my Church,
and the gates of the netherworld shall not prevail against it.**

706 GOSPEL

First Option

Matthew 16:13-19   You are Peter: I will give you the keys to the Kingdom of heaven.

✠ A reading from the holy Gospel according to Matthew

**When Jesus went into the region of Caesarea Philippi
he asked his disciples,
"Who do people say that the Son of Man is?"
They replied, "Some say John the Baptist, others Elijah,
still others Jeremiah or one of the prophets."
He said to them, "But who do you say that I am?"
Simon Peter said in reply,
"You are the Christ, the Son of the living God."
Jesus said to him in reply, "Blessed are you, Simon son of Jonah.
For flesh and blood has not revealed this to you, but my heavenly Father.
And so I say to you, you are Peter,
and upon this rock I will build my Church,
and the gates of the netherworld shall not prevail against it.
I will give you the keys to the Kingdom of heaven.
Whatever you bind on earth shall be bound in heaven;
and whatever you loose on earth shall be loosed in heaven."**

The Gospel of the Lord.

Second Option

Luke 19:1-10 Today salvation has come to this house.

✠ **A reading from the holy Gospel according to Luke**

At that time, Jesus came to Jericho and intended to pass through the town.
Now a man there named Zacchaeus,
   who was a chief tax collector and also a wealthy man,
   was seeking to see who Jesus was;
   but he could not see him because of the crowd,
   for he was short in stature.
So he ran ahead and climbed a sycamore tree in order to see Jesus,
   who was about to pass that way.
When he reached the place, Jesus looked up and said,
   "Zacchaeus, come down quickly,
   for today I must stay at your house."
And he came down quickly and received him with joy.
When they saw this, they began to grumble, saying,
   "He has gone to stay at the house of a sinner."
But Zacchaeus stood there and said to the Lord,
   "Behold, half of my possessions, Lord, I shall give to the poor,
   and if I have extorted anything from anyone
   I shall repay it four times over."
And Jesus said to him,
   "Today salvation has come to this house
   because this man too is a descendant of Abraham.
For the Son of Man has come to seek
   and to save what was lost."

The Gospel of the Lord.

Third Option

John 2:13-22   Jesus was speaking about the temple of his Body.

✠ **A reading from the holy Gospel according to John**

Since the Passover of the Jews was near,
   Jesus went up to Jerusalem.
He found in the temple area those who sold oxen, sheep, and doves,
   as well as the money-changers seated there.
He made a whip out of cords
   and drove them all out of the temple area, with the sheep and oxen,
   and spilled the coins of the money-changers
   and overturned their tables,
   and to those who sold doves he said,
   "Take these out of here,
   and stop making my Father's house a marketplace."
His disciples recalled the words of Scripture,
   Zeal for your house will consume me.
At this the Jews answered and said to him,
   "What sign can you show us for doing this?"
Jesus answered and said to them,
   "Destroy this temple and in three days I will raise it up."
The Jews said,
   "This temple has been under construction for forty-six years,
   and you will raise it up in three days?"
But he was speaking about the temple of his Body.
Therefore, when he was raised from the dead,
   his disciples remembered that he had said this,
   and they came to believe the Scripture
   and the word Jesus had spoken.

The Gospel of the Lord.

Fourth Option

John 4:19-24   True worshipers will worship the Father in Spirit and truth.

✠ **A reading from the holy Gospel according to John**

The Samaritan woman said to Jesus,
  "Sir, I can see that you are a prophet.
Our ancestors worshiped on this mountain;
  but you people say that the place to worship is in Jerusalem."
Jesus said to her,
  "Believe me, woman, the hour is coming
  when you will worship the Father
  neither on this mountain nor in Jerusalem.
You people worship what you do not understand;
  we worship what we understand,
  because salvation is from the Jews.
But the hour is coming, and is now here,
  when true worshipers will worship the Father in Spirit and truth;
  and indeed the Father seeks such people to worship him.
God is Spirit, and those who worship him
  must worship in Spirit and truth."

The Gospel of the Lord.

THE COMMON OF THE BLESSED VIRGIN MARY

707 READING I FROM THE OLD TESTAMENT

1.

Genesis 3:9-15, 20   I will put enmity between your offspring and the offspring of the woman.

A reading from the Book of Genesis

After the man, Adam, had eaten of the tree,
 the Lord God called to the man and asked him, "Where are you?"
He answered, "I heard you in the garden;
 but I was afraid, because I was naked,
 so I hid myself."
Then he asked, "Who told you that you were naked?
You have eaten, then,
 from the tree of which I had forbidden you to eat!"
The man replied, "The woman whom you put here with me—
 she gave me fruit from the tree, and so I ate it."
The Lord God then asked the woman,
 "Why did you do such a thing?"
The woman answered, "The serpent tricked me into it, so I ate it."

Then the Lord God said to the serpent:

 "Because you have done this, you shall be banned
  from all the animals
  and from all the wild creatures;
 On your belly shall you crawl,
  and dirt shall you eat
  all the days of your life.
 I will put enmity between you and the woman,
  and between your offspring and hers;
 He will strike at your head,
  while you strike at his heel."

The man called his wife Eve,
 because she became the mother of all the living.

The word of the Lord.

The Common of the Blessed Virgin Mary

2.

Genesis 12:1-7   The Lord spoke to our ancestors, to Abraham and to his descendants for ever (Luke 1:55).

A reading from the Book of Genesis

The Lord said to Abram:
"Go forth from the land of your kinsfolk
 and from your father's house to a land that I will show you.

 "I will make of you a great nation,
  and I will bless you;
 I will make your name great,
  so that you will be a blessing.
 I will bless those who bless you
  and curse those who curse you.
 All the communities of the earth
  shall find blessing in you."

Abram went as the Lord directed him, and Lot went with him.
Abram was seventy-five years old when he left Haran.
Abram took his wife Sarai, his brother's son Lot,
 all the possessions that they had accumulated,
 and the persons they had acquired in Haran,
 and they set out for the land of Canaan.
When they came to the land of Canaan, Abram passed through the land
 as far as the sacred place at Shechem,
 by the terebinth of Moreh.
(The Canaanites were then in the land.)

The Lord appeared to Abram and said,
 "To your descendants I will give this land."
So Abram built an altar there to the Lord who had appeared to him.

The word of the Lord.

3.

2 Samuel 7:1-5, 8b-11, 16   The Lord God will give him the throne of David his father (Luke 1:32).

A reading from the second Book of Samuel

When King David was settled in his palace,
 and the Lord had given him rest from his enemies on every side,
 he said to Nathan the prophet,
 "Here I am living in a house of cedar,
 while the ark of God dwells in a tent!"
Nathan answered the king,

The Common of the Blessed Virgin Mary 1753

"Go, do whatever you have in mind,
   for the Lord is with you."
But that night the Lord spoke to Nathan and said:
   "Go tell my servant David, 'Thus says the Lord:
   Should you build me a house to dwell in?'

"'It was I who took you from the pasture
   and from the care of the flock
   to be commander of my people Israel.
I have been with you wherever you went,
   and I have destroyed all your enemies before you.
And I will make you famous like the great ones of the earth.
I will fix a place for my people Israel;
   I will plant them so that they may dwell in their place
   without further disturbance.
Neither shall the wicked continue to afflict them as they did of old,
   since the time I first appointed judges over my people Israel.
I will give you rest from all your enemies.
The Lord also reveals to you
   that he will establish a house for you.
Your house and your kingdom shall endure forever before me;
   your throne shall stand firm forever.'"

The word of the Lord.

4.

1 Chronicles 15:3-4, 15-16; 16:1-2   They brought in the ark of God and set it within the tent which David had pitched for it.

A reading from the first Book of Chronicles

David assembled all Israel in Jerusalem to bring the ark of the Lord
   to the place which he had prepared for it.
David also called together the sons of Aaron and the Levites.

The Levites bore the ark of God on their shoulders with poles,
   as Moses had ordained according to the word of the Lord.

David commanded the chiefs of the Levites
   to appoint their brethren as chanters,
   to play on musical instruments, harps, lyres, and cymbals
   to make a loud sound of rejoicing.

They brought in the ark of God and set it within the tent
   which David had pitched for it.
Then they offered up burnt offerings and peace offerings to God.
When David had finished offering up the burnt offerings and peace offerings,
   he blessed the people in the name of the Lord.

The word of the Lord.

5.

Proverbs 8:22-31   Mary, seat of Wisdom.

A reading from the Book of Proverbs

The Wisdom of God says:
"The Lord begot me, the first-born of his ways,
   the forerunner of his prodigies of long ago;
From of old I was poured forth,
   at the first, before the earth.
When there were no depths I was brought forth,
   when there were no fountains or springs of water;
Before the mountains were settled into place,
   before the hills, I was brought forth;
While as yet the earth and fields were not made,
   nor the first clods of the world.

"When he established the heavens I was there,
   when he marked out the vault over the face of the deep;
When he made firm the skies above,
   when he fixed fast the foundations of the earth;
When he set for the sea its limit,
   so that the waters should not transgress his command;
Then was I beside him as his craftsman,
   and I was his delight day by day,
Playing before him all the while,
   playing on the surface of his earth;
   and I found delight in the sons of men."

The word of the Lord.

6.

Sirach 24:1-2, 3-4, 8-12, 18-21   Mary, seat of Wisdom.

A reading from the Book of Sirach

Wisdom sings her own praises and is honored in God,
   before her own people she proclaims her glory;
In the assembly of the Most High she opens her mouth,
   in the presence of his power she declares her worth.

"From the mouth of the Most High I came forth
   the first-born before all creatures.
I made that in the heavens there should arise
   light that never fades
   and mistlike covered the earth.
In the highest heavens did I dwell,
   my throne on a pillar of cloud.

"Then the Creator of all gave me his command,
   and he who formed me chose the spot for my tent,
Saying, 'In Jacob make your dwelling,
   in Israel your inheritance
   and among my chosen put down your roots.'
Before all ages, in the beginning, he created me,
   and through all ages I shall not cease to be.
In the holy tent I ministered before him,
   and in Zion I fixed my abode.
Thus in the chosen city he has given me rest,
   in Jerusalem is my domain.
I have struck root among the glorious people,
   in the portion of the Lord**, his heritage**
   and in the company of the holy ones do I linger.

"Come to me, all you that yearn for me,
   and be filled with my fruits;
You will remember me as sweeter than honey,
   better to have than the honeycomb
   my memory is unto everlasting generations.
Whoever eats of me will hunger still,
   whoever drinks of me will thirst for more;
Whoever obeys me will not be put to shame,
   whoever serves me will never fail."

The word of the Lord.

7.

Isaiah 7:10-14; 8:10   The virgin shall conceive and bear a son.

A reading from the Book of the Prophet Isaiah

**The LORD spoke to Ahaz:
Ask for a sign from the LORD, your God;
   let it be deep as the nether world, or high as the sky!
But Ahaz answered,
   "I will not ask! I will not tempt the LORD!"
Then Isaiah said:
   Listen, O house of David!
Is it not enough for you to weary people,
   must you also weary my God?
Therefore the Lord himself will give you this sign:
   the virgin shall conceive, and bear a son,
   and shall name him Emmanuel
   which means "God is with us."**

The word of the Lord.

8.

Isaiah 9:1-6 A son is given us.

A reading from the Book of the Prophet Isaiah

**The people who walked in darkness
   have seen a great light;
Upon those who dwelt in the land of gloom
   a light has shone.
You have brought them abundant joy
   and great rejoicing,
As they rejoice before you as at the harvest,
   as people make merry when dividing spoils.
For the yoke that burdened them,
   the pole on their shoulder,
And the rod of their taskmaster
   you have smashed, as on the day of Midian.
For every boot that tramped in battle,
   every cloak rolled in blood,
   will be burned as fuel for flames.**

**For a child is born to us, a son is given us;
   upon his shoulder dominion rests.
They name him Wonder-Counselor, God-Hero,
   Father-Forever, Prince of Peace.
His dominion is vast
   and forever peaceful,
From David's throne, and over his kingdom,
   which he confirms and sustains
By judgment and justice,
   both now and forever.
The zeal of the Lord of hosts will do this!**

The word of the Lord.

9.

Isaiah 61:9-11   I rejoice heartily in the LORD.

A reading from the Book of the Prophet Isaiah

**Thus says the LORD:
Their descendants shall be renowned among the nations,
   and their offspring among the peoples;
All who see them shall acknowledge them
   as a race the LORD has blessed.**

**I rejoice heartily in the LORD,
   in my God is the joy of my soul;
For he has clothed me with a robe of salvation,
   and wrapped me in a mantle of justice,
Like a bridegroom adorned with a diadem,
   like a bride bedecked with her jewels.
As the earth brings forth its plants,
   and a garden makes its growth spring up,
So will the Lord GOD make justice and praise
   spring up before all the nations.**

The word of the Lord.

The Common of the Blessed Virgin Mary 1759

10.

Micah 5:1-4a   Until the time when she who is to give birth has borne.

A reading from the Book of the Prophet Micah

The LORD **says:**
You, Bethlehem-Ephrathah,
   too small to be among the clans of Judah,
From you shall come forth for me
   one who is to be ruler in Israel;
Whose origin is from of old,
   from ancient times.
(Therefore the Lord will give them up, until the time
   when she who is to give birth has borne,
And the rest of his brethren shall return
   to the children of Israel.)
He shall stand firm and shepherd his flock
   by the strength of the LORD**,**
   in the majestic name of the LORD**, his God;**
And they shall remain, for now his greatness
   shall reach to the ends of the earth;
   he shall be peace.

The word of the Lord.

11.

Zechariah 2:14-17   Rejoice, O daughter Zion! See, I am coming.

A reading from the Book of the Prophet Zechariah

Sing and rejoice, O daughter Zion!
See, I am coming to dwell among you, says the LORD**.**
Many nations shall join themselves to the LORD **on that day,**
   and they shall be his people,
   and he will dwell among you,
   and you shall know that the LORD **of hosts has sent me to you.**
The LORD **will possess Judah as his portion in the holy land,**
   and he will again choose Jerusalem.
Silence, all mankind, in the presence of the LORD**!**
   for he stirs forth from his holy dwelling.

The word of the Lord.

The Common of the Blessed Virgin Mary

708 READING I FROM THE NEW TESTAMENT DURING THE SEASON OF EASTER

1.

Acts 1:12-14   All these devoted themselves with one accord to prayer with Mary, the mother of Jesus.

A reading from the Acts of the Apostles

**After Jesus had been taken up to heaven,
the Apostles returned to Jerusalem
from the mount called Olivet, which is near Jerusalem,
a sabbath day's journey away.**

**When they entered the city
they went to the upper room where they were staying,
Peter and John and James and Andrew,
Philip and Thomas, Bartholomew and Matthew,
James son of Alphaeus, Simon the Zealot,
and Judas son of James.
All these devoted themselves with one accord to prayer,
together with some women,
and Mary the mother of Jesus, and his brothers.**

The word of the Lord.

2.

Revelation 11:19a; 12:1-6a, 10ab   A great sign appeared in the sky.

A reading from the Book of Revelation

God's temple in heaven was opened,
   and the ark of his covenant could be seen in the temple.

A great sign appeared in the sky, a woman clothed with the sun,
   with the moon under her feet,
   and on her head a crown of twelve stars.
She was with child and wailed aloud in pain
   as she labored to give birth.
Then another sign appeared in the sky;
   it was a huge red dragon, with seven heads and ten horns,
   and on its heads were seven diadems.
Its tail swept away a third of the stars in the sky
   and hurled them down to the earth.
Then the dragon stood before the woman about to give birth,
   to devour her child when she gave birth.
She gave birth to a son, a male child,
   destined to rule all the nations with an iron rod.
Her child was caught up to God and his throne.
The woman herself fled into the desert
   where she had a place prepared by God.

Then I heard a loud voice in heaven say:
   "Now have salvation and power come,
      and the Kingdom of our God
      and the authority of his Anointed."

The word of the Lord.

3.

Revelation 21:1-5a   I also saw a new Jerusalem, prepared as a bride adorned for her husband.

A reading from the Book of Revelation

I, John, saw a new heaven and a new earth.
The former heaven and the former earth had passed away,
  and the sea was no more.
I also saw the holy city, a new Jerusalem,
  coming down out of heaven from God,
  prepared as a bride adorned for her husband.
I heard a loud voice from the throne saying,
  "Behold, God's dwelling is with the human race.
He will dwell with them and they will be his people
  and God himself will always be with them as their God.
He will wipe every tear from their eyes,
  and there shall be no more death or mourning, wailing or pain,
  for the old order has passed away."

The One who sat on the throne said,
  "Behold, I make all things new."

The word of the Lord.

709 RESPONSORIAL PSALM

1.

1 Samuel 2:1, 4-5, 6-7, 8abcd

℟. (see 1b) **My heart exults in the Lord, my Savior.**

"My heart exults in the LORD,
 my horn is exalted in my God.
I have swallowed up my enemies;
 I rejoice in my victory."

℟. My heart exults in the Lord, my Savior.

"The bows of the mighty are broken,
 while the tottering gird on strength.
The well-fed hire themselves out for bread,
 while the hungry batten on spoil.
The barren wife bears seven sons,
 while the mother of many languishes."

℟. My heart exults in the Lord, my Savior.

"The LORD puts to death and gives life;
 he casts down to the nether world;
 he raises up again.
The LORD makes poor and makes rich,
 he humbles, he also exalts."

℟. My heart exults in the Lord, my Savior.

"He raises the needy from the dust;
 from the dung heap he lifts up the poor,
To seat them with nobles
 and make a glorious throne their heritage."

℟. My heart exults in the Lord, my Savior.

2.

Judith 13:18bcde, 19

℟. (15:9d) **You are the highest honor of our race.**

"Blessed are you, daughter, by the Most High God,
 above all the women on earth;
 and blessed be the L<small>ORD</small> God,
 the creator of heaven and earth."

℟. **You are the highest honor of our race.**

"Your deed of hope will never be forgotten
 by those who tell of the might of God."

℟. **You are the highest honor of our race.**

3.

Psalm 45:11-12, 14-15, 16-17

℟. (11) **Listen to me, daughter; see and bend your ear.**

Hear, O daughter, and see; turn your ear,
 forget your people and your father's house.
So shall the king desire your beauty;
 for he is your lord, and you must worship him.

℟. **Listen to me, daughter; see and bend your ear.**

All glorious is the king's daughter as she enters;
 her raiment is threaded with spun gold.
In embroidered apparel she is borne in to the king;
 behind her the virgins of her train are brought to you.

℟. **Listen to me, daughter; see and bend your ear.**

They are borne in with gladness and joy;
 they enter the palace of the king.
The place of your fathers your sons shall have;
 you shall make them princes through all the land.

℟. **Listen to me, daughter; see and bend your ear.**

4.

Psalm 113:1b-2, 3-4, 5-6, 7

℟. **Blessed be the name of the Lord for ever.**
   or:
℟. **Alleluia.**

Praise, you servants of the LORD**,
   praise the name of the L**ORD**.
Blessed be the name of the L**ORD
   both now and forever.

℟. **Blessed be the name of the Lord for ever.**
   or:
℟. **Alleluia.**

**From the rising to the setting of the sun
   is the name of the L**ORD **to be praised.
High above all nations is the L**ORD**;
   above the heavens is his glory.**

℟. **Blessed be the name of the Lord for ever.**
   or:
℟. **Alleluia.**

Who is like the LORD**, our God, who is enthroned on high
   and looks upon the heavens and the earth below?**

℟. **Blessed be the name of the Lord for ever.**
   or:
℟. **Alleluia.**

**He raises up the lowly from the dust;
   from the dunghill he lifts up the poor
To seat them with princes,
   with the princes of his own people.**

℟. **Blessed be the name of the Lord for ever.**
   or:
℟. **Alleluia.**

5.

Luke 1:46-47, 48-49, 50-51, 52-53, 54-55

℟. (49) **The Almighty has done great things for me, and holy is his Name.**
or:
℟. **O Blessed Virgin Mary, you carried the Son of the eternal Father.**

"My soul proclaims the greatness of the Lord,
  my spirit rejoices in God my Savior."

℟. The Almighty has done great things for me, and holy is his Name.
or:
℟. O Blessed Virgin Mary, you carried the Son of the eternal Father.

"For he has looked with favor on his lowly servant.
From this day all generations will call me blessed:
  the Almighty has done great things for me
  and holy is his Name."

℟. The Almighty has done great things for me, and holy is his Name.
or:
℟. O Blessed Virgin Mary, you carried the Son of the eternal Father.

"He has mercy on those who fear him
  in every generation.
He has shown the strength of his arm,
  he has scattered the proud in their conceit."

℟. The Almighty has done great things for me, and holy is his Name.
or:
℟. O Blessed Virgin Mary, you carried the Son of the eternal Father.

"He has cast down the mighty from their thrones,
  and has lifted up the lowly.
He has filled the hungry with good things,
  and the rich he has sent away empty."

℟. The Almighty has done great things for me, and holy is his Name.
or:
℟. O Blessed Virgin Mary, you carried the Son of the eternal Father.

"He has come to the help of his servant Israel
  for he has remembered his promise of mercy,
the promise he made to our fathers,
  to Abraham and his children for ever."

℟. The Almighty has done great things for me, and holy is his name.
or:
℟. O Blessed Virgin Mary, you carried the Son of the eternal Father.

The Common of the Blessed Virgin Mary 1767

710 READING II FROM THE NEW TESTAMENT

First Option

Romans 5:12, 17-19   Where sin increased, grace overflowed all the more.

A reading from the Letter of Saint Paul to the Romans

Brothers and sisters:
Through one man sin entered the world,
   and through sin, death,
   and thus death came to all men, inasmuch as all sinned.

For if, by the transgression of the one,
   death came to reign through that one,
   how much more will those who receive the abundance of grace
   and of the gift of justification
   come to reign in life through the one Jesus Christ.
In conclusion, just as through one transgression
   condemnation came upon all,
   so, through one righteous act,
   acquittal and life came to all.
For just as through the disobedience of the one man
   the many were made sinners,
   so, through the obedience of the one,
   the many will be made righteous.

The word of the Lord.

Second Option

Romans 8:28-30   Those he foreknew he also predestined.

A reading from the Letter of Saint Paul to the Romans

Brothers and sisters:
We know that all things work for good for those who love God,
   who are called according to his purpose.
For those he foreknew he also predestined
   to be conformed to the image of his Son,
   so that he might be the firstborn
   among many brothers.
And those he predestined he also called;
   and those he called he also justified;
   and those he justified he also glorified.

The word of the Lord.

1768   *The Common of the Blessed Virgin Mary*

Third Option

Galatians 4:4-7   God sent his Son, born of a woman.

A reading from the Letter of Saint Paul to the Galatians

**Brothers and sisters:
When the fullness of time had come, God sent his Son,
    born of a woman, born under the law,
    to ransom those under the law,
    so that we might receive adoption as sons.
As proof that you are sons,
    God sent the spirit of his Son into our hearts,
    crying out, "Abba, Father!"
So you are no longer a slave but a son,
    and if a son then also an heir, through God.**

The word of the Lord.

Fourth Option

Ephesians 1:3-6, 11-12   God chose us in Christ, before the world began.

A reading from the Letter of Saint Paul to the Ephesians

**Blessed be the God and Father of our Lord Jesus Christ,
    who has blessed us in Christ
    with every spiritual blessing in the heavens,
    as he chose us in him, before the foundation of the world,
    to be holy and without blemish before him.
In love he destined us for adoption to himself through Jesus Christ,
    in accord with the favor of his will,
    for the praise of the glory of his grace
    that he granted us in the beloved.**

**In him we were also chosen,
    destined in accord with the purpose of the One
    who accomplishes all things according to the intention of his will,
    so that we might exist for the praise of his glory,
    we who first hoped in Christ.**

The word of the Lord.

711 ALLELUIA VERSE AND VERSE BEFORE THE GOSPEL

1.

See Luke 1:28

**Hail, Mary, full of grace, the Lord is with you;
blessed are you among women.**

2.

See Luke 1:45

**Blessed are you, O Virgin Mary, who believed
that what was spoken to you by the Lord would be fulfilled.**

3.

See Luke 2:19

**Blessed is the Virgin Mary who kept the word of God
and pondered it in her heart.**

4.

Luke 11:28

**Blessed are those who hear the word of God
and observe it.**

5.

**Blessed are you, holy Virgin Mary, deserving of all praise;
from you rose the sun of justice, Christ our God.**

6.

**Blessed are you, O Virgin Mary;
without dying you won the martyr's crown
beneath the Cross of the Lord.**

712 GOSPEL

1. Long Form

Matthew 1:1-16, 18-23   For it is through the Holy Spirit that this child has been conceived in her.

☩ A reading from the holy Gospel according to Matthew

The book of the genealogy of Jesus Christ,
  the son of David, the son of Abraham.

Abraham became the father of Isaac,
  Isaac the father of Jacob,
  Jacob the father of Judah and his brothers.
Judah became the father of Perez and Zerah,
  whose mother was Tamar.
Perez became the father of Hezron,
  Hezron the father of Ram,
  Ram the father of Amminadab.
Amminadab became the father of Nahshon,
  Nahshon the father of Salmon,
  Salmon the father of Boaz,
  whose mother was Rahab.
Boaz became the father of Obed,
  whose mother was Ruth.
Obed became the father of Jesse,
  Jesse the father of David the king.

David became the father of Solomon,
  whose mother had been the wife of Uriah.
Solomon became the father of Rehoboam,
  Rehoboam the father of Abijah,
  Abijah the father of Asaph.
Asaph became the father of Jehoshaphat,
  Jehoshaphat the father of Joram,
  Joram the father of Uzziah.
Uzziah became the father of Jotham,
  Jotham the father of Ahaz,
  Ahaz the father of Hezekiah.
Hezekiah became the father of Manasseh,
  Manasseh the father of Amos,
  Amos the father of Josiah.
Josiah became the father of Jechoniah and his brothers
  at the time of the Babylonian exile.

After the Babylonian exile,
> Jechoniah became the father of Shealtiel,
> Shealtiel the father of Zerubbabel,
> Zerubbabel the father of Abiud.

Abiud became the father of Eliakim,
> Eliakim the father of Azor,
> Azor the father of Zadok.

Zadok became the father of Achim,
> Achim the father of Eliud,
> Eliud the father of Eleazar.

Eleazar became the father of Matthan,
> Matthan the father of Jacob,
> Jacob the father of Joseph, the husband of Mary.

Of her was born Jesus who is called the Christ.

Now this is how the birth of Jesus Christ came about.
When his mother Mary was betrothed to Joseph,
> but before they lived together,
> she was found with child through the Holy Spirit.

Joseph her husband, since he was a righteous man,
> yet unwilling to expose her to shame,
> decided to divorce her quietly.

Such was his intention when, behold,
> the angel of the Lord appeared to him in a dream and said,
> "Joseph, son of David,
> do not be afraid to take Mary your wife into your home.

For it is through the Holy Spirit
> that this child has been conceived in her.

She will bear a son and you are to name him Jesus,
> because he will save his people from their sins."

All this took place to fulfill
> what the Lord had said through the prophet:

> *Behold, the virgin shall be with child and bear a son,*
> > *and they shall name him Emmanuel,*

> which means "God is with us."

The Gospel of the Lord.

1772　*The Common of the Blessed Virgin Mary*

OR Short Form

Matthew 1:18-23　For it is through the Holy Spirit that this child has been conceived in her.

✠ A reading from the holy Gospel according to Matthew

This is how the birth of Jesus Christ came about.
When his mother Mary was betrothed to Joseph,
   but before they lived together,
   she was found with child through the Holy Spirit.
Joseph her husband, since he was a righteous man,
   yet unwilling to expose her to shame,
   decided to divorce her quietly.
Such was his intention when, behold,
   the angel of the Lord appeared to him in a dream and said,
   "Joseph, son of David,
   do not be afraid to take Mary your wife into your home.
For it is through the Holy Spirit
   that this child has been conceived in her.
She will bear a son and you are to name him Jesus,
   because he will save his people from their sins."
All this took place to fulfill
   what the Lord had said through the prophet:

   Behold, the virgin shall be with child and bear a son,
     and they shall name him Emmanuel,

   which means "God is with us."

The Gospel of the Lord.

The Common of the Blessed Virgin Mary 1773

2.

Matthew 2:13-15, 19-23   Take the child and his mother and flee to Egypt.

✠ A reading from the holy Gospel according to Matthew

When the magi had departed, behold,
   the angel of the Lord appeared to Joseph in a dream and said,
   "Rise, take the child and his mother, flee to Egypt,
   and stay there until I tell you.
Herod is going to search for the child to destroy him."
Joseph rose and took the child and his mother by night
   and departed for Egypt.
He stayed there until the death of Herod,
   that what the Lord had said through the prophet might be fulfilled,
   Out of Egypt I called my son.

When Herod had died, behold,
   the angel of the Lord appeared in a dream
   to Joseph in Egypt and said,
   "Rise, take the child and his mother and go to the land of Israel,
   for those who sought the child's life are dead."
He rose, took the child and his mother,
   and went to the land of Israel.
But when he heard that Archelaus was ruling over Judea
   in place of his father Herod,
   he was afraid to go back there.
And because he had been warned in a dream,
   he departed for the region of Galilee.
He went and dwelt in a town called Nazareth,
   so that what had been spoken through the prophets might be fulfilled,
   He shall be called a Nazorean.

The Gospel of the Lord.

3.

Matthew 12:46-50   Stretching out his hand toward his disciples, he said, here are my mother and my brothers.

✠ A reading from the holy Gospel according to Matthew

While Jesus was speaking to the crowds,
   his mother and his brothers appeared outside,
     wishing to speak with him.
Someone told him, "Your mother and your brothers are standing outside,
   asking to speak with you."
But he said in reply to the one who told him,
   "Who is my mother? Who are my brothers?"
And stretching out his hand toward his disciples, he said,
   "Here are my mother and my brothers.
For whoever does the will of my heavenly Father
   is my brother, and sister, and mother."

The Gospel of the Lord.

4.

Luke 1:26-38   Behold, you will conceive in your womb and bear a son.

✠ A reading from the holy Gospel according to Luke

The angel Gabriel was sent from God
   to a town of Galilee called Nazareth,
   to a virgin betrothed to a man named Joseph,
   of the house of David,
   and the virgin's name was Mary.
And coming to her, he said,
   "Hail, full of grace! The Lord is with you."
But she was greatly troubled at what was said
   and pondered what sort of greeting this might be.
Then the angel said to her,
   "Do not be afraid, Mary,
   for you have found favor with God.
Behold, you will conceive in your womb and bear a son,
   and you shall name him Jesus.
He will be great and will be called Son of the Most High,
   and the Lord God will give him the throne of David his father,
   and he will rule over the house of Jacob forever,
   and of his Kingdom there will be no end."
But Mary said to the angel,
   "How can this be,
   since I have no relations with a man?"

And the angel said to her in reply,
   "The Holy Spirit will come upon you,
      and the power of the Most High will overshadow you.
Therefore the child to be born
   will be called holy, the Son of God.
And behold, Elizabeth, your relative,
   has also conceived a son in her old age,
   and this is the sixth month for her who was called barren;
   for nothing will be impossible for God."
Mary said, "Behold, I am the handmaid of the Lord.
May it be done to me according to your word."
Then the angel departed from her.

The Gospel of the Lord.

5.

Luke 1:39-47   Blessed is she who believed.

✣   A reading from the holy Gospel according to Luke

Mary set out
   and traveled to the hill country in haste
   to a town of Judah,
   where she entered the house of Zechariah
   and greeted Elizabeth.
When Elizabeth heard Mary's greeting,
   the infant leaped in her womb,
   and Elizabeth, filled with the Holy Spirit,
   cried out in a loud voice and said,
   "Most blessed are you among women,
   and blessed is the fruit of your womb.
And how does this happen to me,
   that the mother of my Lord should come to me?
For at the moment the sound of your greeting reached my ears,
   the infant in my womb leaped for joy.
Blessed are you who believed
   that what was spoken to you by the Lord
   would be fulfilled."

And Mary said:

   "My soul proclaims the greatness of the Lord;
      my spirit rejoices in God my savior."

The Gospel of the Lord.

6.

Luke 2:1-14   She gave birth to her firstborn son.

✠ A reading from the holy Gospel according to Luke

In those days a decree went out from Caesar Augustus
   that the whole world should be enrolled.
This was the first enrollment,
   when Quirinius was governor of Syria.
So all went to be enrolled, each to his own town.
And Joseph too went up from Galilee from the town of Nazareth
   to Judea, to the city of David that is called Bethlehem,
   because he was of the house and family of David,
   to be enrolled with Mary, his betrothed, who was with child.
While they were there,
   the time came for her to have her child,
   and she gave birth to her firstborn son.
She wrapped him in swaddling clothes and laid him in a manger,
   because there was no room for them in the inn.

Now there were shepherds in that region living in the fields
   and keeping the night watch over their flock.
The angel of the Lord appeared to them
   and the glory of the Lord shone around them,
   and they were struck with great fear.
The angel said to them,
   "Do not be afraid;
   for behold, I proclaim to you good news of great joy
   that will be for all the people.
For today in the city of David
   a savior has been born for you who is Christ and Lord.
And this will be a sign for you:
   you will find an infant wrapped in swaddling clothes
   and lying in a manger."
And suddenly there was a multitude of the heavenly host with the angel,
   praising God and saying:

     "Glory to God in the highest
     and on earth peace to those on whom his favor rests."

The Gospel of the Lord.

7.

Luke 2:15b-19   Mary kept all these things, reflecting on them in her heart.

✠ A reading from the holy Gospel according to Luke

The shepherds said to one another,
  "Let us go, then, to Bethlehem
  to see this thing that has taken place,
  which the Lord has made known to us."
So they went in haste and found Mary and Joseph
  and the infant lying in the manger.
When they saw this,
  they made known the message
  that had been told them about this child.
All who heard it were amazed
  by what had been told them by the shepherds.
And Mary kept all these things,
  reflecting on them in her heart.

The Gospel of the Lord.

8.

Luke 2:27-35   You yourself a sword will pierce.

✠ A reading from the holy Gospel according to Luke

Simeon came in the Spirit into the temple;
  and when the parents brought in the child Jesus
  to perform the custom of the law in regard to him,
  he took him into his arms and blessed God, saying:

"Lord, now let your servant go in peace;
  your word has been fulfilled;
my own eyes have seen the salvation
  which you prepared in the sight of every people:
a light to reveal you to the nations
  and the glory of your people Israel."

The child's father and mother were amazed at what was said about him;
  and Simeon blessed them and said to Mary his mother,
  "Behold, this child is destined
  for the fall and rise of many in Israel,
  and to be a sign that will be contradicted
  and you yourself a sword will pierce
  so that the thoughts of many hearts may be revealed."

The Gospel of the Lord.

9.

Luke 2:41-52   Your father and I have been looking for you.

✠ A reading from the holy Gospel according to Luke

Each year Jesus' parents went to Jerusalem for the feast of Passover,
   and when he was twelve years old,
   they went up according to festival custom.
After they had completed its days, as they were returning,
   the boy Jesus remained behind in Jerusalem,
   but his parents did not know it.
Thinking that he was in the caravan,
   they journeyed for a day
   and looked for him among their relatives and acquaintances,
   but not finding him,
   they returned to Jerusalem to look for him.
After three days they found him in the temple,
   sitting in the midst of the teachers,
   listening to them and asking them questions,
   and all who heard him were astounded
   at his understanding and his answers.
When his parents saw him,
   they were astonished,
   and his mother said to him,
   "Son, why have you done this to us?
Your father and I have been looking for you with great anxiety."
And he said to them,
   "Why were you looking for me?
Did you not know that I must be in my Father's house?"
But they did not understand what he said to them.
He went down with them and came to Nazareth,
   and was obedient to them;
   and his mother kept all these things in her heart.
And Jesus advanced in wisdom and age and favor
   before God and man.

The Gospel of the Lord.

10.

Luke 11:27-28   Blessed is the womb that carried you.

✛ **A reading from the holy Gospel according to Luke**

**While Jesus was speaking,
 a woman from the crowd called out and said to him,
 "Blessed is the womb that carried you
 and the breasts at which you nursed."
He replied, "Rather, blessed are those
 who hear the word of God and observe it."**

The Gospel of the Lord.

11.

John 2:1-11   The mother of Jesus was there.

✠ A reading from the holy Gospel according to John

There was a wedding in Cana at Galilee,
   and the mother of Jesus was there.
Jesus and his disciples were also invited to the wedding.
When the wine ran short,
   the mother of Jesus said to him,
   "They have no wine."
And Jesus said to her,
   "Woman, how does your concern affect me?
My hour has not yet come."
His mother said to the servers,
   "Do whatever he tells you."
Now there were six stone water jars there for Jewish ceremonial washings,
   each holding twenty to thirty gallons.
Jesus told them,
   "Fill the jars with water."
So they filled them to the brim.
Then he told them,
   "Draw some out now and take it to the headwaiter."
So they took it.
And when the headwaiter tasted the water that had become wine,
   without knowing where it came from
   although the servers who had drawn the water knew,
   the headwaiter called the bridegroom and said to him,
   "Everyone serves good wine first,
   and then when people have drunk freely, an inferior one;
   but you have kept the good wine until now."
Jesus did this as the beginning of his signs in Cana in Galilee
   and so revealed his glory,
   and his disciples began to believe in him.

The Gospel of the Lord.

12.

John 19:25-27   Behold, your son. Behold, your mother.

✠ A reading from the holy Gospel according to John

Standing by the cross of Jesus were his mother
  and his mother's sister, Mary the wife of Clopas,
  and Mary Magdalene.
When Jesus saw his mother and the disciple there whom he loved,
  he said to his mother, "Woman, behold, your son."
Then he said to the disciple,
  "Behold, your mother."
And from that hour the disciple took her into his home.

The Gospel of the Lord.

THE COMMON OF MARTYRS

713 READING I FROM THE OLD TESTAMENT

1.

2 Chronicles 24:18-22   Zechariah was stoned to death in the court of the LORD's temple.

A reading from the second Book of Chronicles

The princes of Judah forsook the temple of the LORD,
   the God of their fathers,
   and began to serve the sacred poles and the idols;
   and because of this crime of theirs,
   wrath came upon Judah and Jerusalem.
Although prophets were sent to them to convert them to the LORD,
   the people would not listen to their warnings.
Then the spirit of God possessed Zechariah,
   son of Jehoiada the priest.
He took his stand above the people and said to them:
   "God says, 'Why are you transgressing the LORD's commands,
   so that you cannot prosper?
Because you have abandoned the LORD, he has abandoned you.'"
But the people conspired against him,
   and at the king's order they stoned him to death
   in the court of the LORD's temple.
Thus King Joash was unmindful of the devotion shown him
   by Jehoiada, Zechariah's father, and slew his son.
And as he was dying, he said, "May the LORD see and avenge."

The word of the Lord.

2.

2 Maccabees 6:18, 21, 24-31   I am suffering it with joy in my soul because of my devotion to him.

A reading from the second Book of Maccabees

Eleazar, one of the foremost scribes,
   a man of advanced age and noble appearance,
   was being forced to open his mouth to eat pork.
Those in charge of that unlawful ritual meal took the man **aside privately**,
   because of their long acquaintance with him,
   and urged him to bring meat of his own providing,
   such as he could legitimately eat,
   and to pretend to be eating some of the meat of the **sacrifice**
   prescribed by the king.

He told them:
>   "At our age it would be unbecoming to make such a pretense;
>   many young men would think the ninety-year-old Eleazar
>   had gone over to an alien religion.
> Should I thus pretend for the sake of a brief moment of life,
>   they would be led astray by me,
>   while I would bring shame and dishonor on my old age.
> Even if, for the time being, I avoid the punishment of men,
>   I shall never, whether alive or dead,
>   escape the hands of the Almighty.
> Therefore, by manfully giving up my life now,
>   I will prove myself worthy of my old age,
>   and I will leave to the young a noble example
>   of how to die willingly and generously for the revered and holy laws."

He spoke thus,
>   and went immediately to the instrument of torture.
Those who shortly before had been kindly disposed
>   now became hostile toward him because what he had said
>   seemed to them utter madness.
When he was about to die under the blows,
>   he groaned and said:
>   "The LORD in his holy knowledge knows full well that,
>   although I could have escaped death,
>   I am not only enduring terrible pain in my body from this scourging,
>   but also suffering it with joy in my soul
>   because of my devotion to him."
This is how he died,
>   leaving in his death a model of courage
>   and an unforgettable example of virtue
>   not only for the young but for the whole nation.

The word of the Lord.

3.

2 Maccabees 7:1-2, 9-14   We are ready to die rather than transgress the laws of our ancestors.

A reading from the second Book of Maccabees

**It happened that seven brothers with their mother were arrested
    and tortured with whips and scourges by the king,
    to force them to eat pork in violation of God's law.
One of the brothers, speaking for the others, said:
    "What do you expect to achieve by questioning us?
We are ready to die rather than transgress the laws of our ancestors."**

**At the point of death, the second brother said:
    "You accursed fiend, you are depriving us of this present life,
    but the King of the world will raise us up to live again forever.
It is for his laws that we are dying."**

**After him the third suffered their cruel sport.
He put out his tongue at once when told to do so,
    and bravely held out his hands, as he spoke these noble words:
    "It was from Heaven that I received these;
    for the sake of his laws I disdain them;
    from him I hope to receive them again."
Even the king and his attendants marveled at the young man's courage,
    because he regarded his sufferings as nothing.**

**After he had died,
    they tortured and maltreated the fourth brother in the same way.
When he was near death, he said,
    "It is my choice to die at the hands of men
    with the hope God gives of being raised up by him;
    but for you, there will be no resurrection to life."**

The word of the Lord.

4.

2 Maccabees 7:1, 20-23, 27b-29   This most admirable mother bore it courageously because of her hope in the Lord.

A reading from the second Book of Maccabees

**It happened that seven brothers with their mother were arrested
  and tortured with whips and scourges by the king,
  to force them to eat pork in violation of God's law.**

**Most admirable and worthy of everlasting remembrance was the mother,
  who saw her seven sons perish in a single day,
  yet bore it courageously because of her hope in the Lord.
Filled with a noble spirit that stirred her womanly heart with manly courage
  she exhorted each of them
  in the language of their forefathers with these words:
  "I do not know how you came into existence in my womb;
  it was not I who gave you the breath of life,
  nor was it I who set in order
  the elements of which each of you is composed.
Therefore, since it is the Creator of the universe
  who shapes each man's beginning,
  as he brings about the origin of everything,
  he, in his mercy,
  will give you back both breath and life,
  because you now disregard yourselves for the sake of his law."**

**"Son, have pity on me, who carried you in my womb for nine months,
  nursed you for three years, brought you up,
  educated and supported you to your present age.
I beg you, child, to look at the heavens and the earth
  and see all that is in them;
  then you will know that God did not make them out of existing things;
  and in the same way the human race came into existence.
Do not be afraid of this executioner,
  but be worthy of your brothers and accept death,
  so that in the time of mercy I may receive you again with them."**

The word of the Lord.

5.

Wisdom 3:1-9 As sacrificial offerings he took them to himself.

A reading from the Book of Wisdom

The souls of the just are in the hand of God,
 and no torment shall touch them.
They seemed, in the view of the foolish, to be dead;
 and their passing away was thought an affliction
 and their going forth from us, utter destruction.
But they are in peace.
For if before men, indeed, they be punished,
 yet is their hope full of immortality;
Chastised a little, they shall be greatly blessed,
 because God tried them
 and found them worthy of himself.
As gold in the furnace, he proved them,
 and as sacrificial offerings he took them to himself.
In the time of their visitation they shall shine,
 and shall dart about as sparks through stubble;
They shall judge nations and rule over peoples,
 and the LORD shall be their King forever.
Those who trust in him shall understand truth,
 and the faithful shall abide with him in love:
Because grace and mercy are with his holy ones,
 and his care is with his elect.

The word of the Lord.

6.

Sirach 51:1-8 You redeemed me, true to the greatness of your mercy and of your name.

A reading from the Book of Sirach

I give you thanks, O Lord and King;
  I praise you, O God my savior!
I will make known your name,
  for you have been a helper and a protector to me.
You have kept back my body from the pit,
  and from the scourge of a slanderous tongue,
  from lips that went over to falsehood.
And in the sight of those who stood by,
  you have delivered me,
According to the multitude of the mercy of your name,
  and from them that did roar, prepared to devour me,
And from the power of those who sought my life;
  from many a danger you have saved me,
  from flames that hemmed me in on every side;
From the midst of unremitting fire when I was not burnt
  from the deep belly of the nether world;
From deceiving lips and painters of lies,
  from the arrows of dishonest tongues.
My soul was at the point of death,
  my life was nearing the depths of the nether world;
They encompassed me on every side, but there was no one to help me,
  I looked for one to sustain me, but could find no one.
But then I remembered the mercies of the Lord,
  his kindness through ages past;
For he saves those who take refuge in him,
  and rescues them from every evil.

The word of the Lord.

The Common of Martyrs

714 READING I FROM THE NEW TESTAMENT DURING THE SEASON OF EASTER

First Option

Acts 7:55-60   Lord Jesus, receive my spirit.

A reading from the Acts of the Apostles

**Stephen, filled with the Holy Spirit,
  looked up intently to heaven and saw the glory of God
  and Jesus standing at the right hand of God,
  and he said, "Behold, I see the heavens opened
  and the Son of Man standing at the right hand of God."
But they cried out in a loud voice,
  covered their ears, and rushed upon him together.
They threw him out of the city, and began to stone him.
The witnesses laid down their cloaks
  at the feet of a young man named Saul.
As they were stoning Stephen, he called out,
  "Lord Jesus, receive my spirit."
Then he fell to his knees and cried out in a loud voice,
  "Lord, do not hold this sin against them";
  and when he said this, he fell asleep.**

The word of the Lord.

Second Option

Revelation 7:9-17   These are the ones who have survived the time of great distress.

A reading from the Book of Revelation

**I, John, had a vision of a great multitude,
  which no one could count,
  from every nation, race, people, and tongue.
They stood before the throne and before the Lamb,
  wearing white robes and holding palm branches in their hands.
They cried out in a loud voice:**

  **"Salvation comes from our God, who is seated on the throne,
    and from the Lamb."**

**All the angels stood around the throne
  and around the elders and the four living creatures.
They prostrated themselves before the throne,
  worshiped God, and exclaimed:**

"Amen. Blessing and glory, wisdom and thanksgiving,
  honor, power, and might
    be to our God forever and ever. Amen."

Then one of the elders spoke up and said to me,
  "Who are these wearing white robes, and where did they come from?"
I said to him, "My lord, you are the one who knows."
He said to me,
  "These are the ones who have survived the time of great distress;
  they have washed their robes
  and made them white in the Blood of the Lamb.

"For this reason they stand before God's throne
  and worship him day and night in his temple.
  The One who sits on the throne will shelter them.
They will not hunger or thirst anymore,
  nor will the sun or any heat strike them.
For the Lamb who is in the center of the throne will shepherd them
  and lead them to springs of life-giving water,
  and God will wipe away every tear from their eyes."

The word of the Lord.

Third Option

Revelation 12:10-12b *Love for life did not deter them from death.*

A reading from the Book of Revelation

I, John, heard a loud voice in heaven say:
  "Now have salvation and power come,
    and the Kingdom of our God
    and the authority of his Anointed.
  For the accuser of our brothers is cast out,
    who accuses them before our God day and night.
  They conquered him by the Blood of the Lamb
    and by the word of their testimony;
    love for life did not deter them from death.
  Therefore, rejoice, you heavens,
    and you who dwell in them."

The word of the Lord.

1790 *The Common of Martyrs*

Fourth Option

Revelation 21:5-7   The victor will inherit these gifts.

A reading from the Book of Revelation

**The One who was seated on the throne said:
"Behold, I make all things new."
Then he said, "Write these words down,
   for they are trustworthy and true."
He said to me, "They are accomplished.
I am the Alpha and the Omega, the beginning and the end.
To the thirsty I will give a gift
   from the spring of life-giving water.
The victor will inherit these gifts,
   and I shall be his God,
   and he will be my son."**

The word of the Lord.

715 RESPONSORIAL PSALM

First Option

Psalm 31:3cd-4, 6 and 8ab, 16bc and 17

℟. (6) **Into your hands, O Lord, I commend my spirit.**

**Be my rock of refuge,
 a stronghold to give me safety.
You are my rock and my fortress;
 for your name's sake you will lead and guide me.**

℟. **Into your hands, O Lord, I commend my spirit.**

**Into your hands I commend my spirit;
 you will redeem me, O LORD, O faithful God.
I will rejoice and be glad because of your mercy.**

℟. **Into your hands, O Lord, I commend my spirit.**

**Rescue me from the clutches of my enemies and my persecutors,
Let your face shine upon your servant;
 save me in your kindness.**

℟. **Into your hands, O Lord, I commend my spirit.**

Second Option

Psalm 34:2-3, 4-5, 6-7, 8-9

℟. (5) **The Lord delivered me from all my fears.**

**I will bless the LORD at all times;
 his praise shall be ever in my mouth.
Let my soul glory in the LORD;
 the lowly will hear me and be glad.**

℟. **The Lord delivered me from all my fears.**

**Glorify the LORD with me,
 let us together extol his name.
I sought the LORD, and he answered me
 and delivered me from all my fears.**

℟. **The Lord delivered me from all my fears.**

1792 *The Common of Martyrs*

Look to him that you may be radiant with joy,
   and your faces may not blush with shame.
When the afflicted man called out, the LORD **heard,**
   and from all his distress he saved him.

℟. The Lord delivered me from all my fears.

The angel of the LORD **encamps**
   around those who fear him, and delivers them.
Taste and see how good the LORD **is;**
   blessed the man who takes refuge in him.

℟. The Lord delivered me from all my fears.

Third Option

Psalm 124:2-3, 4-5, 7cd-8

℟. (7) Our soul has been rescued like a bird from the fowler's snare.

Had not the LORD **been with us—**
When men rose up against us,
   then would they have swallowed us alive
When their fury was inflamed against us.

℟. Our soul has been rescued like a bird from the fowler's snare.

Then would the waters have overwhelmed us;
The torrent would have swept over us;
   over us then would have swept
      the raging waters.

℟. Our soul has been rescued like a bird from the fowler's snare.

Broken was the snare,
   and we were freed.
Our help is in the name of the LORD**,**
   who made heaven and earth.

℟. Our soul has been rescued like a bird from the fowler's snare.

Fourth Option

Psalm 126:1bc-2ab, 2cd-3, 4-5, 6

℟. (5) **Those who sow in tears shall reap rejoicing.**

**When the Lord brought back the captives of Zion,
we were like men dreaming.
Then our mouth was filled with laughter,
and our tongue with rejoicing.**

℟. **Those who sow in tears shall reap rejoicing.**

**Then they said among the nations,
"The Lord has done great things for them."
The Lord has done great things for us;
we are glad indeed.**

℟. **Those who sow in tears shall reap rejoicing.**

**Restore our fortunes, O Lord,
like the torrents in the southern desert.
Those who sow in tears
shall reap rejoicing.**

℟. **Those who sow in tears shall reap rejoicing.**

**Although they go forth weeping,
carrying the seed to be sown,
They shall come back rejoicing,
carrying their sheaves.**

℟. **Those who sow in tears shall reap rejoicing.**

1794   *The Common of Martyrs*

716 READING II FROM THE NEW TESTAMENT

1.

Romans 5:1-5   We even boast of our afflictions.

A reading from the Letter of Saint Paul to the Romans

Brothers and sisters:
Since we have been justified by faith,
    we have peace with God through our Lord Jesus Christ,
    through whom we have gained access by faith
    to this grace in which we stand,
    and we boast in hope of the glory of God.
Not only that, but we even boast of our afflictions,
    knowing that affliction produces endurance,
    and endurance, proven character,
    and proven character, hope,
    and hope does not disappoint,
    because the love of God has been poured out into our hearts
    through the Holy Spirit that has been given to us.

The word of the Lord.

2.

Romans 8:31b-39   Neither death nor life will be able to separate us from the love of God.

A reading from the Letter of Saint Paul to the Romans

Brothers and sisters:
If God is for us, who can be against us?
He who did not spare his own Son
    but handed him over for us all,
    how will he not also give us everything else along with him?
Who will bring a charge against God's chosen ones?
It is God who acquits us.
Who will condemn?
Christ Jesus it is who died—or, rather, was raised—
    who also is at the right hand of God,
    who indeed intercedes for us.
What will separate us from the love of Christ?
Will anguish, or distress, or persecution, or famine,
    or nakedness, or peril, or the sword?

As it is written:

> *For your sake we are being slain all the day;*
> *we are looked upon as sheep to be slaughtered.*

No, in all these things we conquer overwhelmingly
   through him who loved us.
For I am convinced that neither death, nor life,
   nor angels, nor principalities,
   nor present things, nor future things,
   nor powers, nor height, nor depth,
   nor any other creature will be able to separate us
   from the love of God in Christ Jesus our Lord.

The word of the Lord.

3.

2 Corinthians 4:7-15   Always carrying about in the body the dying of Jesus.

A reading from the second Letter of Saint Paul to the Corinthians

Brothers and sisters:
We hold this treasure in earthen vessels,
   that the surpassing power may be of God and not from us.
We are afflicted in every way, but not constrained;
   perplexed, but not driven to despair;
   persecuted, but not abandoned;
   struck down, but not destroyed;
   always carrying about in the body the dying of Jesus,
   so that the life of Jesus may also be manifested in our body.
For we who live are constantly being given up to death
   for the sake of Jesus,
   so that the life of Jesus may be manifested in our mortal flesh.

So death is at work in us, but life in you.
Since, then, we have the same spirit of faith,
   according to what is written, *I believed, therefore I spoke*,
   we too believe and therefore speak,
   knowing that the one who raised the Lord Jesus
   will raise us also with Jesus
   and place us with you in his presence.
Everything indeed is for you,
   so that the grace bestowed in abundance on more and more people
   may cause the thanksgiving to overflow for the glory of God.

The word of the Lord.

4.

2 Corinthians 6:4-10   We are treated as dying and behold we live.

A reading from the second Letter of Saint Paul to the Corinthians

**Brothers and sisters:
In everything we commend ourselves as ministers of God,
   through much endurance, in afflictions, hardships, constraints,
   beatings, imprisonments, riots, labors, vigils, fasts;
   by purity, knowledge, patience, kindness,
   in the Holy Spirit, in unfeigned love, in truthful speech,
   in the power of God;
   with weapons of righteousness at the right and at the left;
   through glory and dishonor, insult and praise.
We are treated as deceivers and yet are truthful;
   as unrecognized and yet acknowledged;
   as dying and behold we live;
   as chastised and yet not put to death;
   as sorrowful yet always rejoicing;
   as poor yet enriching many;
   as having nothing and yet possessing all things.**

The word of the Lord.

5.

2 Timothy 2:8-13; 3:10-12   All who want to live religiously in Christ Jesus will be persecuted.

A reading from the second Letter of Saint Paul to Timothy

**Beloved:
Remember Jesus Christ, raised from the dead, a descendant of David:
   such is my Gospel, for which I am suffering,
   even to the point of chains, like a criminal.
But the word of God is not chained.
Therefore, I bear with everything for the sake of those who are chosen,
   so that they too may obtain the salvation that is in Christ Jesus,
   together with eternal glory.
This saying is trustworthy:

   If we have died with him
      we shall also live with him;
   if we persevere
      we shall also reign with him.
   But if we deny him
      he will deny us.**

If we are unfaithful
  he remains faithful,
    for he cannot deny himself.

You have followed my teaching, way of life,
  purpose, faith, patience, love,
  endurance, persecutions, and sufferings,
  such as happened to me in Antioch, Iconium, and Lystra,
  persecutions that I endured.
Yet from all these things the Lord delivered me.
In fact, all who want to live religiously in Christ Jesus
  will be persecuted.

The word of the Lord.

6.

Hebrews 10:32-36   You endured a great contest of suffering.

A reading from the Letter to the Hebrews

Brothers and sisters:
Remember the days past when, after you had been enlightened,
  you endured a great contest of suffering.
At times you were publicly exposed to abuse and affliction;
  at other times you associated yourselves with those so treated.
You even joined in the sufferings of those in prison
  and joyfully accepted the confiscation of your property,
    knowing that you had a better and lasting possession.
Therefore, do not throw away your confidence;
  it will have great recompense.
You need endurance to do the will of God and receive what he has promised.

The word of the Lord.

1798   The Common of Martyrs

7.

James 1:2-4, 12   Blessed is the man who perseveres in the face of temptation.

A reading from the Letter of Saint James

Consider it all joy, my brothers and sisters,
   when you encounter various trials,
      for you know that the testing of your faith produces perseverance.
And let perseverance be perfect,
   so that you may be perfect and complete, lacking in nothing.

Blessed is the man who perseveres in temptation,
   for when he has been proved he will receive the crown of life
      that he promised to those who love him.

The word of the Lord.

8.

1 Peter 3:14-17   Do not be afraid or terrified with fear of them.

A reading from the first Letter of Saint Peter

Beloved:
Even if you should suffer because of righteousness, blessed are you.
Do not be afraid or terrified with fear of them,
   but sanctify Christ as Lord in your hearts.
Always be ready to give an explanation
   to anyone who asks you for a reason for your hope,
   but do it with gentleness and reverence,
   keeping your conscience clear,
   so that, when you are maligned,
      those who defame your good conduct in Christ
         may themselves be put to shame.
For it is better to suffer for doing good,
   if that be the will of God, than for doing evil.

The word of the Lord.

9.

1 Peter 4:12-19   Rejoice to the extent that you share in the sufferings of Christ.

A reading from the first Letter of Saint Peter

Beloved, do not be surprised that a trial by fire is occurring among you,
   as if something strange were happening to you.
But rejoice to the extent that you share in the sufferings of Christ,
   so that when his glory is revealed
   you may also rejoice exultantly.

If you are insulted for the name of Christ, blessed are you,
> for the Spirit of glory and of God rests upon you.

But let no one among you be made to suffer
> as a murderer, a thief, an evildoer, or as an intriguer.

But whoever is made to suffer as a Christian should not be ashamed
> but glorify God because of the name.

For it is time for the judgment to begin with the household of God;
> if it begins with us, how will it end
> for those who fail to obey the Gospel of God?

And if the righteous one is barely saved,
> *where will the godless and the sinner appear?*

As a result, those who suffer in accord with God's will
> hand their souls over to a faithful creator as they do good.

The word of the Lord.

10.

1 John 5:1-5   The victory that conquers the world is our faith.

A reading from the first Letter of Saint John

Beloved:
Everyone who believes that Jesus is the Christ is begotten by God,
> and everyone who loves the Father
> loves also the one begotten by him.

In this way we know that we love the children of God
> when we love God and obey his commandments.

For the love of God is this,
> that we keep his commandments.

And his commandments are not burdensome,
> for whoever is begotten by God conquers the world.

And the victory that conquers the world is our faith.
Who indeed is the victor over the world
> but the one who believes that Jesus is the Son of God?

The word of the Lord.

1800   *The Common of Martyrs*

717 ALLELUIA VERSE AND VERSE BEFORE THE GOSPEL

1.

Matthew 5:10

Blessed are they who are persecuted for the sake of righteousness, for theirs is the Kingdom of heaven.

2.

John 17:19

I consecrate myself for them, so that they also may be consecrated in the truth.

3.

2 Corinthians 1:3b-4a

Blessed be the Father of compassion and God of all encouragement, who encourages us in our every affliction.

4.

James 1:12

Blessed is the man who perseveres in temptation, for when he has been proved he will receive the crown of life.

5.

1 Peter 4:14

If you are insulted for the name of Christ, blessed are you, for the Spirit of God rests upon you.

6.

See *Te Deum*

We praise you, O God, we acclaim you as Lord; the white-robed army of martyrs praise you.

718 GOSPEL

1.

Matthew 10:17-22   You will be led before governors and kings for my sake, as a witness before them and the pagans.

✠ **A reading from the holy Gospel according to Matthew**

**Jesus said to his Apostles:
"Beware of men, for they will hand you over to courts
   and scourge you in their synagogues,
   and you will be led before governors and kings for my sake
   as a witness before them and the pagans.
When they hand you over,
   do not worry about how you are to speak
   or what you are to say.
You will be given at that moment what you are to say.
For it will not be you who speak
   but the Spirit of your Father speaking through you.
Brother will hand over brother to death,
   and the father his child;
   children will rise up against parents and have them put to death.
You will be hated by all because of my name,
   but whoever endures to the end will be saved."**

The Gospel of the Lord.

2.

Matthew 10:28-33   Do not be afraid of those who kill the body.

✠ **A reading from the holy Gospel according to Matthew**

**Jesus said to his Apostles:
"Do not be afraid of those who kill the body
   but cannot kill the soul;
   rather, be afraid of the one who can destroy
   both soul and body in Gehenna.
Are not two sparrows sold for a small coin?
Yet not one of them falls to the ground without your Father's knowledge.
Even all the hairs of your head are counted.
So do not be afraid; you are worth more than many sparrows.
Everyone who acknowledges me before others
   I will acknowledge before my heavenly Father.
But whoever denies me before others,
   I will deny before my heavenly Father."**

The Gospel of the Lord.

3.

Matthew 10:34-39   I have come to bring not peace but the sword.

✠ A reading from the holy Gospel according to Matthew

Jesus said to his Apostles:
"Do not think that I have come to bring peace upon the earth.
I have come to bring not peace but the sword.
For I have come to set
    a man 'against his father,
        a daughter against her mother,
    and a daughter-in-law against her mother-in-law;
        and one's enemies will be those of one's household.'

"Whoever loves father or mother more than me is not worthy of me,
    and whoever loves son or daughter more than me is not worthy of me;
    and whoever does not take up his cross
    and follow after me is not worthy of me.
Whoever finds his life will lose it,
    and whoever loses his life for my sake will find it."

The Gospel of the Lord.

4.

Luke 9:23-26   Whoever loses his life for my sake will save it.

✠ A reading from the holy Gospel according to Luke

Jesus said to all,
    "If anyone wishes to come after me, he must deny himself
    and take up his cross daily and follow me.
For whoever wishes to save his life will lose it,
    but whoever loses his life for my sake will save it.
What profit is there for one to gain the whole world
    yet lose or forfeit himself?
Whoever is ashamed of me and of my words,
    the Son of Man will be ashamed of when he comes in his glory
    and in the glory of the Father and of the holy angels."

The Gospel of the Lord.

5.

John 12:24-26 If a grain of wheat falls to the ground and dies, it produces much fruit.

✠ **A reading from the holy Gospel according to John**

Jesus said to his disciples:
"Amen, amen, I say to you,
   unless a grain of wheat falls to the ground and dies,
   it remains just a grain of wheat;
   but if it dies, it produces much fruit.
Whoever loves his life loses it,
   and whoever hates his life in this world
   will preserve it for eternal life.
Whoever serves me must follow me,
   and where I am, there also will my servant be.
The Father will honor whoever serves me."

The Gospel of the Lord.

6.

John 15:18-21 If they persecuted me, they will also persecute you.

✠ **A reading from the holy Gospel according to John**

Jesus said to his disciples:
"If the world hates you, realize that it hated me first.
If you belonged to the world, the world would love its own;
   but because you do not belong to the world,
   and I have chosen you out of the world,
   the world hates you.
Remember the word I spoke to you,
   'No slave is greater than his master.'
If they persecuted me, they will also persecute you.
If they kept my word, they will also keep yours.
And they will do all these things to you on account of my name,
   because they do not know the one who sent me."

The Gospel of the Lord.

7.

John 17:11b-19   The world hated them.

✟ A reading from the holy Gospel according to John

Lifting his eyes to heaven, Jesus prayed, saying:
"Holy Father, keep them in your name that you have given me,
   so that they may be one just as we are one.
When I was with them I protected them in your name that you gave me,
   and I guarded them, and none of them was lost
   except the son of destruction,
   in order that the Scripture might be fulfilled.
But now I am coming to you.
I speak this in the world
   so that they may share my joy completely.
I gave them your word, and the world hated them,
   because they do not belong to the world
   any more than I belong to the world.
I do not ask that you take them out of the world
   but that you keep them from the Evil One.
They do not belong to the world
   any more than I belong to the world.
Consecrate them in the truth.
Your word is truth.
As you sent me into the world,
   so I sent them into the world.
And I consecrate myself for them,
   so that they also may be consecrated in truth."

The Gospel of the Lord.

THE COMMON OF PASTORS

719 READING I FROM THE OLD TESTAMENT OUTSIDE THE EASTER SEASON

1.

Exodus 32:7-14   Then he spoke of exterminating them, but Moses, his chosen one, withstood him in the breach to turn back his destructive wrath (Psalm 106:23).

A reading from the Book of Exodus

The Lord said to Moses,
    "Go down at once to your people,
    whom you brought out of the land of Egypt,
    for they have become depraved.
They have soon turned aside from the way I pointed out to them,
    making for themselves a molten calf and worshiping it,
    sacrificing to it and crying out,
    'This is your God, O Israel,
    who brought you out of the land of Egypt!'
I see how stiff necked this people is," continued the Lord to Moses.
"Let me alone, then,
    that my wrath may blaze up against them to consume them.
Then I will make of you a great nation."

But Moses implored the Lord, his God, saying,
    "Why, O Lord, should your wrath blaze up against your own people,
    whom you brought out of the land of Egypt
    with such great power and with so strong a hand?
Why should the Egyptians say,
    'With evil intent he brought them out,
    that he might kill them in the mountains
    and exterminate them from the face of the earth'?
Let your blazing wrath die down;
    relent in punishing your people.
Remember your servants Abraham, Isaac, and Israel,
    and how you swore to them by your own self, saying,
    'I will make your descendants as numerous as the stars in the sky;
    and all this land that I promised,
    I will give your descendants as their perpetual heritage.'"
So the Lord relented in the punishment
    he had threatened to inflict on his people.

The word of the Lord.

1806   *The Common of Pastors*

2.

Deuteronomy 10:8-9   The Lord himself is his heritage.

A reading from the Book of Deuteronomy

**Moses summoned all of Israel and said to them:
"At that time the Lord set apart the tribe of Levi
  to carry the ark of the covenant of the Lord,
  to be in attendance before the Lord and minister to him,
  and to give blessings in his name,
  as they have done to this day.
For this reason,
  Levi has no share in the heritage with his brothers;
  the Lord himself is his heritage,
  as the Lord, your God, has told him."**

The word of the Lord.

3.

1 Samuel 16:1b, 6-13a   There—anoint him, for this is he!

A reading from the first Book of Samuel

**The Lord said to Samuel:
"Fill your horn with oil, and be on your way.
I am sending you to Jesse of Bethlehem,
  for I have chosen my king from among his sons."

As Jesse and his sons came to the sacrifice,
  Samuel looked at Eliab and thought,
  "Surely the Lord's anointed is here before him."
But the Lord said to Samuel:
  "Do not judge from his appearance or from his lofty stature,
  because I have rejected him.
Not as man sees does God see,
  because he sees the appearance
  but the Lord looks into the heart."
Then Jesse called Abinadab and presented him before Samuel,
  who said, "The Lord has not chosen him."
Next Jesse presented Shammah, but Samuel said,
  "The Lord has not chosen this one either."
In the same way Jesse presented seven sons before Samuel,
  but Samuel said to Jesse,
  "The Lord has not chosen any one of these."
Then Samuel asked Jesse,
  "Are these all the sons you have?"
Jesse replied,
  "There is still the youngest, who is tending the sheep."**

Samuel said to Jesse,
> "Send for him;
> we will not begin the sacrificial banquet until he arrives here."

Jesse sent and had the young man brought to them.
He was ruddy, a youth handsome to behold
> and making a splendid appearance.

The Lord said,
> "There—anoint him, for this is he!"

Then Samuel, with the horn of oil in hand,
> anointed him in the midst of his brothers;
> and from that day on, the spirit of the Lord rushed upon David.

The word of the Lord.

4.

Isaiah 6:1-8   Whom shall I send? Who will go for us?

A reading from the Book of the Prophet Isaiah

In the year King Uzziah died,
> I saw the Lord seated on a high and lofty throne,
> with the train of his garment filling the temple.

Seraphim were stationed above; each of them had six wings:
> with two they veiled their faces,
> with two they veiled their feet,
> and with two they hovered aloft.

"Holy, holy, holy is the Lord of hosts!"
> they cried, one to the other.

"All the earth is filled with his glory!"
At the sound of that cry, the frame of the door shook
> and the house was filled with smoke.

Then I said, "Woe is me, I am doomed!
For I am a man of unclean lips,
> living among a people of unclean lips;
> yet my eyes have seen the King, the Lord of hosts!"

Then one of the seraphim flew to me,
> holding an ember which he had taken with tongs from the altar.

He touched my mouth with it and said,
> "See, now that this has touched your lips,
> your wickedness is removed, your sin purged."

Then I heard the voice of the Lord saying,
> "Whom shall I send? Who will go for us?"

"Here I am," I said; "send me!"

The word of the Lord.

1808 The Common of Pastors

5. For Missionaries

Isaiah 52:7-10   All the ends of the earth will behold the salvation of our God.

A reading from the Book of the Prophet Isaiah

> How beautiful upon the mountains
>   are the feet of him who brings glad tidings,
> Announcing peace, bearing good news,
>   announcing salvation, and saying to Zion,
>   "Your God is King!"
> Hark! Your sentinels raise a cry,
>   together they shout for joy,
> For they see directly, before their eyes,
>   the Lord restoring Zion.
> Break out together in song,
>   O ruins of Jerusalem!
> For the Lord comforts his people,
>   he redeems Jerusalem.
> The Lord has bared his holy arm
>   in the sight of all the nations;
> All the ends of the earth will behold
>   the salvation of our God.

The word of the Lord.

6.

Isaiah 61:1-3a   The Lord has anointed me; he has sent me to bring glad tidings to the lowly.

A reading from the Book of the Prophet Isaiah

> The spirit of the Lord God is upon me,
>   because the Lord has anointed me;
> He has sent me to bring glad tidings to the lowly,
>   to heal the brokenhearted,
> To proclaim liberty to the captives
>   and release to the prisoners,
> To announce a year of favor from the Lord
>   and a day of vindication by our God,
>   to comfort all who mourn;
> To place on those who mourn in Zion
>   a diadem instead of ashes,
> To give them oil of gladness in place of mourning,
>   a glorious mantle instead of a listless spirit.

The word of the Lord.

7.

Jeremiah 1:4-9   To whomever I send you, you shall go.

A reading from the Book of the Prophet Jeremiah

The word of the Lord **came to me thus:**

> Before I formed you in the womb I knew you,
>   before you were born I dedicated you,
>   a prophet to the nations I appointed you.
>
> "Ah, Lord, God!" I said,
>   "I know not how to speak; I am too young."

But the Lord **answered me,**

> Say not, "I am too young."
> To whomever I send you, you shall go;
>   whatever I command you, you shall speak.
> Have no fear before them,
>   because I am with you to deliver you, says the Lord.

Then the Lord **extended his hand and touched my mouth, saying,**

> See, I place my words in your mouth!

The word of the Lord.

8.

Ezekiel 3:17-21   I have appointed you a watchman for the house of Israel.

A reading from the Book of the Prophet Ezekiel

The word of the Lord came to me:
    Son of man, I have appointed you a watchman
    for the house of Israel.
When you hear a word from my mouth,
    you shall warn them for me.

If I say to the wicked man,
    You shall surely die;
    and you do not warn him or speak out
    to dissuade him from his wicked conduct so that he may live:
    the wicked man shall die for his sin,
    but I will hold you responsible for his death.
If, on the other hand, you have warned the wicked man,
    yet he has not turned away from his evil
    nor from his wicked conduct,
    then he shall die for his sin,
    but you shall save your life.

If a virtuous man turns away from virtue and does wrong
    when I place a stumbling block before him, he shall die.
He shall die for his sin,
    and his virtuous deeds shall not be remembered;
    but I will hold you responsible for his death
    if you did not warn him.
When, on the other hand, you have warned a virtuous man not to sin,
    and he has in fact not sinned,
    he shall surely live because of the warning,
    and you shall save your own life.

The word of the Lord.

9.

Ezekiel 34:11-16   As a shepherd tends his flock, so will I tend my sheep.

A reading from the Book of the Prophet Ezekiel

Thus says the Lord God:
   I myself will look after and tend my sheep.
As a shepherd tends his flock
   when he finds himself among his scattered sheep,
   so will I tend my sheep.
I will rescue them from every place where they were scattered
   when it was cloudy and dark.
I will lead them out from among the peoples
   and gather them from the foreign lands;
   I will bring them back to their own country
   and pasture them upon the mountains of Israel
   in the land's ravines and all its inhabited places.
In good pastures will I pasture them,
   and on the mountain heights of Israel
   shall be their grazing ground.
There they shall lie down on good grazing ground,
   and in rich pastures shall they be pastured
   on the mountains of Israel.
I myself will pasture my sheep;
   I myself will give them rest, says the Lord God.
The lost I will seek out,
   the strayed I will bring back,
   the injured I will bind up,
   the sick I will heal,
   but the sleek and the strong I will destroy,
   shepherding them rightly.

The word of the Lord.

1812   *The Common of Pastors*

720 READING I FROM THE NEW TESTAMENT DURING THE SEASON OF EASTER

1. For Missionaries

Acts 13:46-49   We now turn to the Gentiles.

A reading from the Acts of the Apostles

Paul and Barnabas spoke out boldly and said,
"It was necessary that the word of God be spoken to you first,
but since you reject it
and condemn yourselves as unworthy of eternal life,
we now turn to the Gentiles.
For so the Lord has commanded us,
*I have made you a light to the Gentiles,
that you may be an instrument of salvation
to the ends of the earth."*

The Gentiles were delighted when they heard this
and glorified the word of the Lord.
All who were destined for eternal life came to believe,
and the word of the Lord continued to spread
through the whole region.

The word of the Lord.

2.

Acts 20:17-18a, 28-32, 36   Keep watch over yourselves and over the whole flock of which the Holy Spirit has appointed you overseers, in which you tend the Church of God.

A reading from the Acts of the Apostles

From Miletus Paul had the presbyters
of the Church at Ephesus summoned.
When they came to him, he addressed them,
"Keep watch over yourselves and over the whole flock
of which the Holy Spirit has appointed you overseers,
in which you tend the Church of God
that he acquired with his own Blood.
I know that after my departure savage wolves will come among you,
and they will not spare the flock.
And from your own group,
men will come forward perverting the truth
to draw the disciples away after them.

So be vigilant and remember that for three years, night and day,
   I unceasingly admonished each of you with tears.
And now I commend you to God
   and to that gracious word of his that can build you up
   and give you the inheritance among all who are consecrated."

When he had finished speaking
   he knelt down and prayed with them all.

The word of the Lord.

3. For Missionaries

Acts 26:19-23   He would proclaim light both to our people and to the Gentiles.

A reading from the Acts of the Apostles

Paul said:
"King Agrippa, I was not disobedient to the heavenly vision.
On the contrary, first to those in Damascus and in Jerusalem
   and throughout the whole country of Judea,
   and then to the Gentiles,
   I preached the need to repent and turn to God,
   and to do works giving evidence of repentance.
That is why the Jews seized me when I was in the temple
   and tried to kill me.
But I have enjoyed God's help to this very day,
   and so I stand here testifying to small and great alike,
saying nothing different from what the prophets and Moses foretold,
   that the Christ must suffer and that,
   as the first to rise from the dead,
   he would proclaim light both to our people and to the Gentiles."

The word of the Lord.

721 RESPONSORIAL PSALM

1.

Psalm 16:1-2a and 5, 7-8, 11

℟. (see 5a) **You are my inheritance, O Lord.**

Keep me, O God, for in you I take refuge;
  I say to the Lord, "My Lord are you."
O Lord, my allotted portion and my cup,
  you it is who hold fast my lot.

℟. **You are my inheritance, O Lord.**

I bless the Lord who counsels me;
  even in the night my heart exhorts me.
I set the Lord ever before me;
  with him at my right hand I shall not be disturbed.

℟. **You are my inheritance, O Lord.**

You will show me the path to life,
  fullness of joys in your presence,
  the delights at your right hand forever.

℟. **You are my inheritance, O Lord.**

2.

Psalm 23:1-3a, 4, 5, 6

℟. (1) **The Lord is my shepherd; there is nothing I shall want.**

The Lord is my shepherd; I shall not want.
  In verdant pastures he gives me repose;
Beside restful waters he leads me;
  he refreshes my soul.

℟. **The Lord is my shepherd; there is nothing I shall want.**

Even though I walk in the dark valley
  I fear no evil; for you are at my side
With your rod and your staff
  that give me courage.

℟. **The Lord is my shepherd; there is nothing I shall want.**

You spread the table before me
   in the sight of my foes;
You anoint my head with oil;
   my cup overflows.

℟. The Lord is my shepherd; there is nothing I shall want.

Only goodness and kindness follow me
   all the days of my life;
And I shall dwell in the house of the LORD
   for years to come.

℟. The Lord is my shepherd; there is nothing I shall want.

3.

Psalm 40:2 and 4, 7-8a, 8b-9, 10

℟. (8a and 9a) Here I am, Lord; I come to do your will.

I have waited, waited for the LORD**,**
   and he stooped toward me and heard my cry.
And he put a new song into my mouth,
   a hymn to our God.

℟. Here I am, Lord; I come to do your will.

Sacrifice or offering you wished not,
   but ears open to obedience you gave me.
Burnt offerings or sin-offerings you sought not;
   then said I, "Behold I come."

℟. Here I am, Lord; I come to do your will.

"In the written scroll it is prescribed for me,
To do your will, O my God, is my delight,
   and your law is within my heart!"

℟. Here I am, Lord; I come to do your will.

I announced your justice in the vast assembly;
   I did not restrain my lips, as you, O LORD**, know.**

℟. Here I am, Lord; I come to do your will.

1816   *The Common of Pastors*

4.

Psalm 89:2-3, 4-5, 21-22, 25 and 27

℟. (2) For ever I will sing the goodness of the Lord.

The favors of the LORD **I will sing forever;**
  through all generations my mouth shall proclaim your faithfulness.
For you have said, "My kindness is established forever";
  in heaven you have confirmed your faithfulness.

℟. **For ever I will sing the goodness of the Lord.**

"I have made a covenant with my chosen one,
  I have sworn to David my servant:
Forever will I confirm your posterity
  and establish your throne for all generations."

℟. **For ever I will sing the goodness of the Lord.**

"I have found David, my servant;
  with my holy oil I have anointed him,
That my hand may be always with him,
  and that my arm may make him strong."

℟. **For ever I will sing the goodness of the Lord.**

"My faithfulness and my mercy shall be with him,
  and through my name shall his horn be exalted.
He shall say of me, 'You are my father,
  my God, the Rock, my savior.'"

℟. **For ever I will sing the goodness of the Lord.**

5.

Psalm 96:1-2a, 2b-3, 7-8a, 10

℟. **(3) Proclaim God's marvelous deeds to all the nations.**

Sing to the LORD **a new song;**
  sing to the LORD**, all you lands.**
Sing to the LORD**; bless his name.**

℟. **Proclaim God's marvelous deeds to all the nations.**

Announce his salvation, day after day.
Tell his glory among the nations;
  among all peoples, his wondrous deeds.

℟. **Proclaim God's marvelous deeds to all the nations.**

Give to the LORD, you families of nations,
　　give to the LORD glory and praise;
　　give to the LORD the glory due his name!

℟. **Proclaim God's marvelous deeds to all the nations.**

Say among the nations: The LORD is king.
He has made the world firm, not to be moved;
　　he governs the peoples with equity.

℟. **Proclaim God's marvelous deeds to all the nations.**

6.

Psalm 106:19-20, 21-22, 23

℟. (4a) **Remember us, O Lord, as you favor your people.**

Our fathers made a calf in Horeb
　　and adored a molten image;
They exchanged their glory
　　for the image of a grass-eating bullock.

℟. **Remember us, O Lord, as you favor your people.**

They forgot the God who had saved them,
　　who had done great deeds in Egypt,
Wondrous deeds in the land of Ham,
　　terrible things at the Red Sea.

℟. **Remember us, O Lord, as you favor your people.**

Then he spoke of exterminating them,
　　but Moses, his chosen one,
Withstood him in the breach
　　to turn back his destructive wrath.

℟. **Remember us, O Lord, as you favor your people.**

7.

Psalm 110:1, 2, 3, 4

℟. (4b) **You are a priest for ever, in the line of Melchizedek.**

The L**ord**** said to my Lord: "Sit at my right hand
till I make your enemies your footstool."**

℟. **You are a priest for ever, in the line of Melchizedek.**

The scepter of your power the L**ord**** will stretch forth from Zion:
"Rule in the midst of your enemies."**

℟. **You are a priest for ever, in the line of Melchizedek.**

**"Yours is princely power in the day of your birth, in holy splendor;
before the daystar, like the dew, I have begotten you."**

℟. **You are a priest for ever, in the line of Melchizedek.**

The L**ord**** has sworn, and he will not repent:
"You are a priest forever, according to the order of Melchizedek."**

℟. **You are a priest for ever, in the line of Melchizedek.**

8.

Psalm 117:1bc, 2

℟. (Mark 16:15) **Go out to all the world and tell the Good News.**
   or:
℟. **Alleluia.**

Praise the L**ord****, all you nations;
glorify him, all you peoples!**

℟. **Go out to all the world, and tell the Good News.**
   or:
℟. **Alleluia.**

**For steadfast is his kindness toward us,
and the fidelity of the L****ord**** endures forever.**

℟. **Go out to all the world, and tell the Good News.**
   or:
℟. **Alleluia.**

722 READING II FROM THE NEW TESTAMENT

1.

Romans 12:3-13   Since we have gifts that differ according to the grace given to us.

A reading from the Letter of Saint Paul to the Romans

Brothers and sisters:
By the grace given to me I tell everyone among you
   not to think of himself more highly than one ought to think,
   but to think soberly,
   each according to the measure of faith that God has apportioned.
For as in one body we have many parts,
   and all the parts do not have the same function,
   so we, though many, are one Body in Christ
   and individually parts of one another.
Since we have gifts that differ according to the grace given to us,
   let us exercise them:
   if prophecy, in proportion to the faith;
   if ministry, in ministering;
   if one is a teacher, in teaching;
   if one exhorts, in exhortation;
   if one contributes, in generosity;
   if one is over others, with diligence;
   if one does acts of mercy, with cheerfulness.

Let love be sincere;
   hate what is evil,
   hold on to what is good;
   love one another with mutual affection;
   anticipate one another in showing honor.
Do not grow slack in zeal,
   be fervent in spirit,
   serve the Lord.
Rejoice in hope,
   endure in affliction,
   persevere in prayer.
Contribute to the needs of the holy ones,
   exercise hospitality.

The word of the Lord.

1820 The Common of Pastors

2. For Missionaries

1 Corinthians 1:18-25 It was the will of God through the foolishness of the proclamation to save those who have faith.

A reading from the first Letter of Saint Paul to the Corinthians

Brothers and sisters:
The message of the cross is foolishness to those who are perishing,
  but to us who are being saved it is the power of God.
For it is written:
  I will destroy the wisdom of the wise,
    and the learning of the learned I will set aside.

Where is the wise one?
Where is the scribe?
Where is the debater of this age?
Has not God made the wisdom of the world foolish?
For since in the wisdom of God
  the world did not come to know God through wisdom,
  it was the will of God through the foolishness of the proclamation
  to save those who have faith.
For Jews demand signs and Greeks look for wisdom,
  but we proclaim Christ crucified,
  a stumbling block to Jews and foolishness to Gentiles,
  but to those who are called, Jews and Greeks alike,
  Christ the power of God and the wisdom of God.
For the foolishness of God is wiser than human wisdom,
  and the weakness of God is stronger than human strength.

The word of the Lord.

3.

1 Corinthians 4:1-5 Thus should one regard us: as servants of Christ and stewards of the mysteries of God.

A reading from the first Letter of Saint Paul to the Corinthians

Brothers and sisters:
Thus should one regard us: as servants of Christ
  and stewards of the mysteries of God.
Now it is of course required of stewards that they be found trustworthy.
It does not concern me in the least
  that I be judged by you or any human tribunal;
  I do not even pass judgment on myself;
  I am not conscious of anything against me,
  but I do not thereby stand acquitted;
  the one who judges me is the Lord.

Therefore do not make any judgment
   before the appointed time,
   until the Lord comes,
   for he will bring to light what is hidden in darkness
   and will manifest the motives of our hearts,
   and then everyone will receive praise from God.

The word of the Lord.

4.

1 Corinthians 9:16-19, 22-23   Woe to me if I do not preach it!

A reading from the first Letter of Saint Paul to the Corinthians

Brothers and sisters:
If I preach the Gospel, this is no reason for me to boast,
   for an obligation has been imposed on me,
   and woe to me if I do not preach it!
If I do so willingly, I have a recompense,
   but if unwillingly, then I have been entrusted with a stewardship.
What then is my recompense?
That, when I preach,
   I offer the Gospel free of charge
   so as not to make full use of my right in the Gospel.

Although I am free in regard to all,
   I have made myself a slave to all
   so as to win over as many as possible.
To the weak I became weak, to win over the weak.
I have become all things to all, to save at least some.
All this I do for the sake of the Gospel,
   so that I too may have a share in it.

The word of the Lord.

5.

2 Corinthians 3:1-6a He has indeed qualified us as ministers of a new covenant.

A reading from the second Letter of Saint Paul to the Corinthians

Brothers and sisters:
Are we beginning to commend ourselves again?
Do we need, as some do,
  letters of recommendation to you or from you?
You are our letter, written on our hearts,
  known and read by all,
  shown to be a letter of Christ administered by us,
  written not in ink but by the Spirit of the living God,
  not on tablets of stone but on tablets that are hearts of flesh.

Such confidence we have through Christ toward God.
Not that of ourselves we are qualified
  to take credit for anything as coming from us;
  rather, our qualification comes from God,
  who has indeed qualified us as ministers of a new covenant,
  not of letter but of spirit.

The word of the Lord.

6.

2 Corinthians 4:1-2, 5-7 We preach Jesus Christ as Lord, and ourselves as your slaves for the sake of Jesus.

A reading from the second Letter of Saint Paul to the Corinthians

Brothers and sisters:
Since we have this ministry through the mercy shown us,
  we are not discouraged.
Rather, we have renounced shameful, hidden things;
  not acting deceitfully or falsifying the word of God,
  but by the open declaration of the truth
  we commend ourselves to everyone's conscience in the sight of God.
For we do not preach ourselves but Jesus Christ as Lord,
  and ourselves as your slaves for the sake of Jesus.
For God who said, *Let light shine out of darkness*,
  has shone in our hearts to bring to light
  the knowledge of the glory of God on the face of Jesus Christ.

But we hold this treasure in earthen vessels,
  that the surpassing power may be of God and not from us.

The word of the Lord.

7.

2 Corinthians 5:14-20   He gave us the ministry of reconciliation.

A reading from the Second Letter of Saint Paul to the Corinthians

Brothers and sisters:
The love of Christ impels us,
  once we have come to the conviction that one died for all;
  therefore, all have died.
He indeed died for all,
  so that those who live might no longer live for themselves
  but for him who for their sake died and was raised.

Consequently, from now on we regard no one according to the flesh;
  even if we once knew Christ according to the flesh,
  yet now we know him so no longer.
So whoever is in Christ is a new creation:
  the old things have passed away;
  behold, new things have come.
And all this is from God,
  who has reconciled us to himself through Christ
  and given us the ministry of reconciliation,
  namely, God was reconciling the world to himself in Christ,
  not counting their trespasses against them
  and entrusting to us the message of reconciliation.
So we are ambassadors for Christ,
  as if God were appealing through us.
We implore you on behalf of Christ,
  be reconciled to God.

The word of the Lord.

8.

Ephesians 4:1-7, 11-13   In the work of ministry, in building up the Body of Christ.

A reading from the Letter of Saint Paul to the Ephesians

Brothers and sisters,
I, a prisoner for the Lord,
   urge you to live in a manner worthy of the call you have received,
   with all humility and gentleness, with patience,
   bearing with one another through love,
   striving to preserve the unity of the spirit
   through the bond of peace:
   one Body and one Spirit,
   as you were also called to the one hope of your call;
   one Lord, one faith, one baptism;
   one God and Father of all,
   who is over all and through all and in all.

But grace was given to each of us
   according to the measure of Christ's gift.

And he gave some as Apostles, others as prophets,
   others as evangelists, others as pastors and teachers,
   to equip the holy ones for the work of ministry,
   for building up the Body of Christ,
   until we all attain to the unity of faith
   and knowledge of the Son of God, to mature to manhood,
   to the extent of the full stature of Christ.

The word of the Lord.

9.

Colossians 1:24-29   On behalf of his Body, which is the Church, of which I am a minister in accordance with God's stewardship given to me to bring to completion for you the word of God.

A reading from the Letter of Saint Paul to the Colossians

Brothers and sisters:
I rejoice in my sufferings for your sake,
   and in my flesh I am filling up
   what is lacking in the afflictions of Christ
   on behalf of his Body, which is the Church,
   of which I am a minister
   in accordance with God's stewardship given to me
   to bring to completion for you the word of God,
   the mystery hidden from ages and from generations past.

But now it has been manifested to his holy ones,
> to whom God chose to make known the riches of the glory
> of this mystery among the Gentiles;
> it is Christ in you, the hope for glory.

It is he whom we proclaim,
> admonishing everyone and teaching everyone with all wisdom,
> that we may present everyone perfect in Christ.

For this I labor and struggle,
> in accord with the exercise of his power working within me.

The word of the Lord.

10.

1 Thessalonians 2:2b-8   We were determined to share with you not only the Gospel of God but our very selves as well.

A reading from the first Letter of Saint Paul to the Thessalonians

Brothers and sisters:
We drew courage through our God
> to speak to you the Gospel of God with much struggle.

Our exhortation was not from delusion or impure motives,
> nor did it work through deception.

But as we were judged worthy by God to be entrusted with the Gospel,
> that is how we speak,
> not as trying to please men,
> but rather God, who judges our hearts.

Nor, indeed, did we ever appear with flattering speech, as you know,
> or with a pretext for greed—God is witness—nor did we seek praise
> from men, either from you or from others,
> although we were able to impose our weight as Apostles of Christ.

Rather, we were gentle among you,
> as a nursing mother cares for her children.

With such affection for you,
> we were determined to share with you not only the Gospel of God,
> but our very selves as well, so dearly beloved had you become to us.

The word of the Lord.

1826 The Common of Pastors

11.

2 Timothy 1:13-14; 2:1-3   Guard this rich trust with the help of the Holy Spirit who dwells within us.

A reading from the second Letter of Saint Paul to Timothy

Beloved:
Take as your norm the sound words that you heard from me,
   in the faith and love that are in Christ Jesus.
Guard this rich trust with the help of the Holy Spirit
   who dwells within us.
So you, my child, be strong in the grace that is in Christ Jesus.
And what you heard from me through many witnesses
   entrust to faithful people
   who will have the ability to teach others as well.
Bear your share of hardship along with me
   like a good soldier of Christ Jesus.

The word of the Lord.

12.

2 Timothy 4:1-5   Perform the work of an evangelist, fulfill your ministry.

A reading from the second Letter of Saint Paul to Timothy

Beloved:
I charge you in the presence of God and of Christ Jesus,
   who will judge the living and the dead,
   and by his appearing and his kingly power:
   proclaim the word;
   be persistent whether it is convenient or inconvenient;
   convince, reprimand, encourage through all patience and teaching.
For the time will come when people will not tolerate sound doctrine but,
   following their own desires and insatiable curiosity,
   will accumulate teachers and will stop listening to the truth
   and will be diverted to myths.
But you, be self-possessed in all circumstances;
   put up with hardship;
   perform the work of an evangelist;
   fulfill your ministry.

The word of the Lord.

13.

1 Peter 5:1-4   Tend the flock of God in your midst.

A reading from the first Letter of Saint Peter

**Beloved:
I exhort the presbyters among you,
   as a fellow presbyter and witness to the sufferings of Christ
   and one who has a share in the glory to be revealed.
Tend the flock of God in your midst,
   overseeing it not by constraint but willingly,
   as God would have it, not for shameful profit but eagerly.
Do not lord it over those assigned to you,
   but be examples to the flock.
And when the chief Shepherd is revealed,
   you will receive the unfading crown of glory.**

The word of the Lord.

1828   *The Common of Pastors*

723 ALLELUIA VERSE AND VERSE BEFORE THE GOSPEL

1.

Matthew 23:9b, 10b

**You have but one Father in heaven;
you have but one master, the Christ!**

2.

Matthew 28:19a, 20bc

**Go, and teach all nations, says the Lord;
I am with you always, until the end of the world.**

3.

Mark 1:17

**Come after me, says the Lord,
and I will make you fishers of men.**

4.

Luke 4:18

**The Lord sent me to bring glad tidings to the poor
and to proclaim liberty to captives.**

5.

John 10:14

**I am the good shepherd, says the Lord;
I know my sheep, and mine know me.**

6.

John 15:5

**I am the vine, you are the branches, says the Lord:
whoever remains in me and I in him will bear much fruit.**

7.

John 15:15b

**I call you my friends, says the Lord,
for I have made known to you all that the Father has told me.**

8.

2 Corinthians 5:19

**God was reconciling the world to himself in Christ,
and entrusting to us the message of reconciliation.**

1830   *The Common of Pastors*

724   GOSPEL

1.

Matthew 9:35-38   The harvest is abundant but the laborers are few.

✠   A reading from the holy Gospel according to Matthew

Jesus went around to all the towns and villages,
  teaching in their synagogues,
  proclaiming the Gospel of the Kingdom,
  and curing every disease and illness.
At the sight of the crowds, his heart was moved with pity for them
  because they were troubled and abandoned,
  like sheep without a shepherd.
Then he said to his disciples,
  "The harvest is abundant but the laborers are few;
  so ask the master of the harvest
  to send out laborers for his harvest."

The Gospel of the Lord.

2. For a Pope

Matthew 16:13-19   You are Peter, and upon this rock I will build my Church.

✠   A reading from the holy Gospel according to Matthew

Jesus went into the region of Caesarea Philippi
  and he asked his disciples,
  "Who do people say that the Son of Man is?"
They replied, "Some say John the Baptist, others Elijah,
  still others Jeremiah or one of the prophets."
He said to them, "But who do you say that I am?"
Simon Peter said in reply,
  "You are the Christ, the Son of the living God."
Jesus said to him in reply, "Blessed are you, Simon son of Jonah.
For flesh and blood has not revealed this to you, but my heavenly Father.
And so I say to you, you are Peter,
  and upon this rock I will build my Church,
  and the gates of the netherworld shall not prevail against it.
I will give you the keys to the Kingdom of heaven.
Whatever you bind on earth shall be bound in heaven;
  and whatever you loose on earth shall be loosed in heaven."

The Gospel of the Lord.

3.

Matthew 23:8-12   The greatest among you must be your servant.

☩ A reading from the holy Gospel according to Matthew

Jesus spoke to his disciples:
"Do not be called 'Rabbi.'
You have but one teacher, and you are all brothers.
Call no one on earth your father;
   you have but one Father in heaven.
Do not be called 'Master';
   you have but one master, the Christ.
The greatest among you must be your servant.
Whoever exalts himself will be humbled;
   but whoever humbles himself will be exalted."

The Gospel of the Lord.

4. For Missionaries

Matthew 28:16-20   Go, therefore, and make disciples of all nations.

☩ A reading from the holy Gospel according to Matthew

The Eleven disciples went to Galilee,
   to the mountain to which Jesus had ordered them.
When they saw him, they worshiped, but they doubted.
Then Jesus approached and said to them,
   "All power in heaven and on earth has been given to me.
Go, therefore, and make disciples of all nations,
   baptizing them in the name of the Father,
   and of the Son, and of the Holy Spirit,
   teaching them to observe all that I have commanded you.
And behold, I am with you always, until the end of the age."

The Gospel of the Lord.

1832 *The Common of Pastors*

5.

Mark 1:14-20   I will make you fishers of men.

☩   A reading from the holy Gospel according to Mark

After John had been arrested,
   Jesus came to Galilee proclaiming the Gospel of God:
   "This is the time of fulfillment.
The Kingdom of God is at hand.
Repent, and believe in the Gospel."

As he passed by the Sea of Galilee,
   he saw Simon and his brother Andrew casting their nets into the sea;
   they were fishermen.
Jesus said to them,
   "Come after me, and I will make you fishers of men."
Then they abandoned their nets and followed him.
He walked along a little farther
   and saw James, the son of Zebedee, and his brother John.
They too were in a boat mending their nets.
Then he called them.
So they left their father Zebedee in the boat
   along with the hired men and followed him.

The Gospel of the Lord.

6. For Missionaries

Mark 16:15-20   Go into the whole world and proclaim the Gospel to every creature.

☩   A reading from the holy Gospel according to Mark

Jesus appeared to the Eleven and said to them:
"Go into the whole world
   and proclaim the Gospel to every creature.
Whoever believes and is baptized will be saved;
   whoever does not believe will be condemned.
These signs will accompany those who believe:
   in my name they will drive out demons,
   they will speak new languages.
They will pick up serpents with their hands,
   and if they drink any deadly thing, it will not harm them.
They will lay hands on the sick, and they will recover."

So then the Lord Jesus, after he spoke to them,
   was taken up into heaven
   and took his seat at the right hand of God.
But they went forth and preached everywhere,
   while the Lord worked with them
   and confirmed the word through accompanying signs.

The Gospel of the Lord.

7. For Missionaries

Luke 5:1-11   At your command I will lower the nets.

✠ **A reading from the holy Gospel according to Luke**

While the crowd was pressing in on Jesus and listening to the word of God,
   he was standing by the Lake of Gennesaret.
He saw two boats there alongside the lake;
   the fishermen had disembarked and were washing their nets.
Getting into one of them, the one belonging to Simon,
   he asked him to put out a short distance from the shore.
Then he sat down and taught the crowds from the boat.
After he had finished speaking, he said to Simon,
   "Put out into deep water and lower your nets for a catch."
Simon said in reply,
   "Master, we have worked hard all night and have caught nothing,
   but at your command I will lower the nets."
When they had done this, they caught a great number of fish
   and their nets were tearing.
They signaled to their partners in the other boat
   to come to help them.
They came and filled both boats
   so that the boats were in danger of sinking.
When Simon Peter saw this, he fell at the knees of Jesus and said,
   "Depart from me, Lord, for I am a sinful man."
For astonishment at the catch of fish they had made seized him
   and all those with him,
   and likewise James and John, the sons of Zebedee,
   who were partners of Simon.
Jesus said to Simon, "Do not be afraid;
   from now on you will be catching men."
When they brought their boats to the shore,
   they left everything and followed him.

The Gospel of the Lord.

1834 *The Common of Pastors*

8.

Luke 10:1-9   The harvest is abundant but the laborers are few.

✠   A reading from the holy Gospel according to Luke

The Lord Jesus appointed seventy-two disciples
   whom he sent ahead of him in pairs
   to every town and place he intended to visit.
He said to them,
   "The harvest is abundant but the laborers are few;
   so ask the master of the harvest
   to send out laborers for his harvest.
Go on your way;
   behold, I am sending you like lambs among wolves.
Carry no money bag, no sack, no sandals;
   and greet no one along the way.
Into whatever house you enter,
   first say, 'Peace to this household.'
If a peaceful person lives there,
   your peace will rest on him;
   but if not, it will return to you.
Stay in the same house and eat and drink what is offered to you,
   for the laborer deserves his payment.
Do not move about from one house to another.
Whatever town you enter and they welcome you,
   eat what is set before you,
   cure the sick in it and say to them,
   'The Kingdom of God is at hand for you.'"

The Gospel of the Lord.

9.

Luke 22:24-30   I confer a kingdom on you, just as my Father has conferred one on me.

✠   A reading from the holy Gospel according to Luke

An argument broke out among the Apostles
   about which of them should be regarded as the greatest.
Jesus said to them,
   "The kings of the Gentiles lord it over them
   and those in authority over them are addressed as 'Benefactors;'
   but among you it shall not be so.
Rather, let the greatest among you be as the youngest,
   and the leader as the servant.

For who is greater:
> the one seated at table or the one who serves?

Is it not the one seated at table?
I am among you as the one who serves.
It is you who have stood by me in my trials;
> and I confer a kingdom on you,
>> just as my Father has conferred one on me,
>
> that you may eat and drink at my table in my Kingdom;
> and you will sit on thrones
> judging the twelve tribes of Israel."

The Gospel of the Lord.

10.

John 10:11-16   A good shepherd lays down his life for the sheep.

✝ A reading from the holy Gospel according to John

Jesus said:
"I am the good shepherd.
A good shepherd lays down his life for the sheep.
A hired man, who is not a shepherd
> and whose sheep are not his own,
> sees a wolf coming and leaves the sheep and runs away,
> and the wolf catches and scatters them.

This is because he works for pay and has no concern for the sheep.
I am the good shepherd,
> and I know mine and mine know me,
> just as the Father knows me and I know the Father;
> and I will lay down my life for the sheep.

I have other sheep that do not belong to this fold.
These also I must lead, and they will hear my voice,
> and there will be one flock, one shepherd."

The Gospel of the Lord.

11.

John 15:9-17   I no longer call you slaves; I have called you friends.

☩ A reading from the holy Gospel according to John

Jesus said to his disciples:
"As the Father loves me, so I also love you.
Remain in my love.
If you keep my commandments, you will remain in my love,
    just as I have kept my Father's commandments
    and remain in his love.

"I have told you this so that my joy might be in you
    and your joy might be complete.
This is my commandment: love one another as I love you.
No one has greater love than this,
    to lay down one's life for one's friends.
You are my friends if you do what I command you.
I no longer call you slaves,
    because a slave does not know what his master is doing.
I have called you friends,
    because I have told you everything I have heard from my Father.
It was not you who chose me, but I who chose you
    and appointed you to go and bear fruit that will remain,
    so that whatever you ask the Father in my name he may give you.
This I command you: love one another."

The Gospel of the Lord.

12. For a Pope

John 21:15-17   Feed my lambs, feed my sheep.

✛ A reading from the holy Gospel according to John

After Jesus had revealed himself to his disciples and
   eaten breakfast with them, he said to Simon Peter,
    "Simon, son of John, do you love me more than these?"
Simon Peter answered him, "Yes, Lord, you know that I love you."
Jesus said to him, "Feed my lambs."
He then said to Simon Peter a second time,
    "Simon, son of John, do you love me?"
Simon Peter answered him, "Yes, Lord, you know that I love you."
He said to him, "Tend my sheep."
He said to him the third time,
    "Simon, son of John, do you love me?"
Peter was distressed that he had said to him a third time,
   "Do you love me?" and he said to him,
   "Lord, you know everything; you know that I love you."
Jesus said to him, "Feed my sheep."

The Gospel of the Lord.

THE COMMON OF DOCTORS OF THE CHURCH

725 READING I FROM THE OLD TESTAMENT

First Option

1 Kings 3:11-14   I give you a wise and understanding heart.

A reading from the first Book of Kings

The LORD said to Solomon:
"Because you have asked for this—not for a long life for yourself,
   nor for riches, nor for the life of your enemies,
   but for understanding so that you may know what is right—
   I do as you requested.
I give you a heart so wise and understanding
   that there has never been anyone like you up to now,
   and after you there will come no one to equal you.
In addition, I give you what you have not asked for,
   such riches and glory that among kings there is not your like.
And if you follow me by keeping my statutes and commandments,
   as your father David did,
   I will give you a long life."

The word of the Lord.

Second Option

Wisdom 7:7-10, 15-16   Beyond health and comeliness I loved her.

A reading from the Book of Wisdom

I prayed, and prudence was given me;
   I pleaded, and the spirit of wisdom came to me.
I preferred her to scepter and throne,
And deemed riches nothing in comparison with her,
   nor did I liken any priceless gem to her;
Because all gold, in view of her, is a little sand,
   and before her, silver is to be accounted mire.
Beyond health and comeliness I loved her,
And I chose to have her rather than the light,
   because the splendor of her never yields to sleep.

Now God grant I speak suitably
   and value these endowments at their worth:
For he is the guide of Wisdom
   and the director of the wise.
For both we and our words are in his hand,
   as well as all prudence and knowledge of crafts.

The word of the Lord.

Third Option

Sirach 15:1-6 *She will fill him with the spirit of wisdom and understanding.*

A reading from the Book of Sirach

He who fears the Lord will do this;
   he who is practiced in the law will come to wisdom.
Motherlike she will meet him,
   like a young bride she will embrace him,
Nourish him with the bread of understanding,
   and give him the water of learning to drink.
He will lean upon her and not fall,
   he will trust in her and not be put to shame.
She will exalt him above his fellows;
   and in the midst of the assembly she will open his mouth
   and fill him with the spirit of wisdom and understanding,
   and clothe him with the robe of glory.
Joy and gladness he will find,
   an everlasting name he will inherit.

The word of the Lord.

Fourth Option

Sirach 39:6e-10 *He who studies the law of the Most High will be filled with the spirit of understanding.*

A reading from the Book of Sirach

If it pleases the Lord Almighty,
   he who studies the law of the Most High
   will be filled with the spirit of understanding;
He will pour forth his words of wisdom
   and in prayer give thanks to the Lord,
Who will direct his knowledge and his counsel,
   as he meditates upon his mysteries.
He will show the wisdom of what he has learned
   and glory in the law of the Lord's covenant.
Many will praise his understanding;
   his fame can never be effaced;
Unfading will be his memory,
   through all generations his name will live;
Peoples will speak of his wisdom,
   and in assembly sing his praises.

The word of the Lord.

1840   *The Common of Doctors of the Church*

726 READING I FROM THE NEW TESTAMENT DURING THE SEASON OF EASTER

First Option

Acts 2:14a, 22-24, 32-36   God has made him both Lord and Christ.

A reading from the Acts of the Apostles

**On the day of the Pentecost, Peter stood up with the Eleven,
  raised his voice, and proclaimed to them:**

**"You who are children of Israel, hear these words.
Jesus the Nazorean was a man commended to you by God
  with mighty deeds, wonders, and signs,
    which God worked through him in your midst, as you yourselves know.
This man, delivered up by the set plan and foreknowledge of God,
  you killed, using lawless men to crucify him.
But God raised him up, releasing him from the throes of death,
  because it was impossible for him to be held by it.**

**"God raised this Jesus; of this we are all witnesses.
Exalted at the right hand of God,
  he received the promise of the Holy Spirit from the Father
  and poured it forth, as you both see and hear.
For David did not go up into heaven, but he himself said:**

> *The Lord said to my Lord,*
> *'Sit at my right hand*
>   *until I make your enemies your footstool.'*

**Therefore let the whole house of Israel know for certain
  that God has made him both Lord and Christ,
    this Jesus whom you crucified."**

The word of the Lord.

Second Option

Acts 13:26-33   What God promised to our fathers he has brought to fulfillment by raising up Jesus.

A reading from the Acts of the Apostles

When Paul came to Antioch in Pisidia, he said in the synagogue:
"My brothers, sons of the family of Abraham,
and those others among you who are God-fearing,
to us this word of salvation has been sent.
The inhabitants of Jerusalem and their leaders failed to recognize him,
and by condemning him they fulfilled the oracles of the prophets
that are read sabbath after sabbath.
For even though they found no grounds for a death sentence,
they asked Pilate to have him put to death,
and when they had accomplished all that was written about him,
they took him down from the tree and placed him in a tomb.
But God raised him from the dead,
and for many days he appeared to those
who had come up with him from Galilee to Jerusalem.
These are now his witnesses before the people.
We ourselves are proclaiming this good news to you
that what God promised our fathers
he has brought to fulfillment for us, their children, by raising up Jesus,
as it is written in the second psalm,
You are my Son; this day I have begotten you."

The word of the Lord.

1842   *The Common of Doctors of the Church*

727 RESPONSORIAL PSALM

First Option

Psalm 19:8, 9, 10, 11

℟. (10) **The judgments of the Lord are true, and all of them are just.**
   or:
℟. (John 6:63) **Your words, Lord, are Spirit and life.**

**The law of the Lord is perfect,
   refreshing the soul;
The decree of the Lord is trustworthy,
   giving wisdom to the simple.**

℟. **The judgments of the Lord are true, and all of them are just.**
   or:
℟. **Your words, Lord, are Spirit and life.**

**The precepts of the Lord are right,
   rejoicing the heart;
The command of the Lord is clear,
   enlightening the eye.**

℟. **The judgments of the Lord are true, and all of them are just.**
   or:
℟. **Your words, Lord, are Spirit and life.**

**The fear of the Lord is pure,
   enduring forever;
The ordinances of the Lord are true,
   all of them just.**

℟. **The judgments of the Lord are true, and all of them are just.**
   or:
℟. **Your words, Lord, are Spirit and life.**

**They are more precious than gold,
   than a heap of purest gold;
Sweeter also than syrup
   or honey from the comb.**

℟. **The judgments of the Lord are true, and all of them are just.**
   or:
℟. **Your words, Lord, are Spirit and life.**

Second Option

Psalm 37:3-4, 5-6, 30-31

℟. (30a) **The mouth of the just murmurs wisdom.**

Trust in the L<small>ORD</small> and do good,
 that you may dwell in the land and be fed in security.
Take delight in the L<small>ORD</small>,
 and he will grant you your heart's requests.

℟. **The mouth of the just murmurs wisdom.**

Commit to the L<small>ORD</small> your way;
 trust in him, and he will act.
He will make justice dawn for you like the light;
 bright as the noonday shall be your vindication.

℟. **The mouth of the just murmurs wisdom.**

The mouth of the just tells of wisdom
 and his tongue utters what is right.
The law of his God is in his heart,
 and his steps do not falter.

℟. **The mouth of the just murmurs wisdom.**

The Common of Doctors of the Church

Third Option

Psalm 119:9, 10, 11, 12, 13, 14

℟. (12b) **Lord, teach me your statutes.**

**How can a young man be faultless in his way?
By keeping to your words.**

℟. **Lord, teach me your statutes.**

**With all my heart I seek you;
let me not stray from your commands.**

℟. **Lord, teach me your statutes.**

**Within my heart I treasure your promise,
that I may not sin against you.**

℟. **Lord, teach me your statutes.**

**Blessed are you, O Lord;
teach me your statutes.**

℟. **Lord, teach me your statutes.**

**With my lips I declare
all the ordinances of your mouth.**

℟. **Lord, teach me your statutes.**

**In the way of your decrees
I rejoice as much as in all riches.**

℟. **Lord, teach me your statutes.**

And we speak about them not with words taught by human wisdom,
>	but with words taught by the Spirit,
>		describing spiritual realities in spiritual terms.

Now the natural man does not accept what pertains to the Spirit of God,
>	for to him it is foolishness, and he cannot understand it,
>		because it is judged spiritually.
The one who is spiritual, however, can judge everything
>	but is not subject to judgment by anyone.

For *who has known the mind of the Lord, so as to counsel him?*
But we have the mind of Christ.

The word of the Lord.

4.

Ephesians 3:8-12   This grace was given, to preach to the Gentiles the inscrutable riches of Christ.

A reading from the Letter of Saint Paul to the Ephesians

Brothers and sisters:
To me, the very least of all the holy ones, this grace was given,
>	to preach to the Gentiles the inscrutable riches of Christ,
>	and to bring to light for all what is the plan of the mystery
>	hidden from ages past in God who created all things,
>	so that the manifold wisdom of God
>		might now be made known through the Church
>	to the principalities and authorities in the heavens.
This was according to the eternal purpose
>	that he accomplished in Christ Jesus our Lord,
>	in whom we have boldness of speech
>		and confidence of access through faith in him.

The word of the Lord.

5.

Ephesians 4:1-7, 11-13   In the work of ministry, in building up the Body of Christ.

A reading from the Letter of Saint Paul to the Ephesians

Brothers and sisters:
I, a prisoner for the Lord,
   urge you to live in a manner worthy of the call you have received,
   with all humility and gentleness, with patience,
   bearing with one another through love,
   striving to preserve the unity of the Spirit
   through the bond of peace:
   one Body and one Spirit,
   as you were also called to the one hope of your call;
   one Lord, one faith, one baptism;
   one God and Father of all,
   who is over all and through all and in all.

But grace was given to each of us
   according to the measure of Christ's gift.

And he gave some as Apostles, others as prophets,
   others as evangelists, others as pastors and teachers,
   to equip the holy ones for the work of ministry,
   for building up the Body of Christ,
   until we all attain to the unity of faith
   and knowledge of the Son of God, to mature manhood,
   to the extent of the full stature of Christ.

The word of the Lord.

The Common of Doctors of the Church 1849

6.

2 Timothy 1:13-14; 2:1-3   Guard this rich trust with the help of the Holy Spirit who dwells within us.

A reading from the second Letter of Saint Paul to Timothy

Beloved:
Take as your norm the sound words that you heard from me,
   in the faith and love that are in Christ Jesus.
Guard this rich trust with the help of the Holy Spirit
   that dwells within us.

My child, be strong in the grace that is in Christ Jesus.
And what you heard from me through many witnesses
   entrust to faithful people
   who will have the ability to teach others as well.
Bear your share of hardship along with me
   like a good soldier of Christ Jesus.

The word of the Lord.

7.

2 Timothy 4:1-5   Perform the work of an evangelist; fulfill your ministry.

A reading from the second Letter of Saint Paul to Timothy

Beloved:
I charge you in the presence of God and of Christ Jesus,
   who will judge the living and the dead,
   and by his appearing and his kingly power:
   proclaim the word;
   be persistent whether it is convenient or inconvenient;
   convince, reprimand, encourage through all patience and teaching.
For the time will come
   when people will not tolerate sound doctrine but,
   following their own desires and insatiable curiosity,
   will accumulate teachers and will stop listening to the truth
   and will be diverted to myths.
But you, be self-possessed in all circumstances;
   put up with hardship;
   perform the work of an evangelist;
   fulfill your ministry.

The word of the Lord.

1850   *The Common of Doctors of the Church*

729 ALLELUIA VERSE AND VERSE BEFORE THE GOSPEL

1.

Matthew 5:16

**Let your light shine before others,
that they may see your good deeds and glorify your heavenly Father.**

2.

Matthew 23:9b, 10b

**You have but one Father in heaven.
You have but one master, the Christ.**

3.

See John 6:63c, 68c

**Your words, Lord, are Spirit and life;
you have the words of everlasting life.**

4.

John 15:5

**I am the vine, you are the branches, says the Lord:
whoever remains in me and I in him will bear much fruit.**

5.

See Acts 16:14b

**Open our hearts, O Lord,
to listen to the words of your Son.**

6.

1 Corinthians 1:18

**The message about the cross is foolishness to those who are perishing,
but to us who are being saved it is the power of God.**

7.

1 Corinthians 2:7

**We speak God's wisdom, mysterious, hidden,
which God predetermined before the ages for our glory.**

8.

**The seed is the word of God, Christ is the sower;
all who come to him will live for ever.**

730 GOSPEL

1.

Matthew 5:13-19   You are the light of the world.

✝ A reading from the holy Gospel according to Matthew

Jesus said to his disciples:
"You are the salt of the earth.
But if salt loses its taste, with what can it be seasoned?
It is no longer good for anything
   but to be thrown out and trampled underfoot.
You are the light of the world.
A city set on a mountain cannot be hidden.
Nor do they light a lamp and then put it under a bushel basket;
   it is set on a lampstand,
   where it gives light to all in the house.
Just so, your light must shine before others,
   that they may see your good deeds
   and glorify your heavenly Father.

"Do not think that I have come to abolish the law or the prophets.
I have come not to abolish but to fulfill.
Amen, I say to you, until heaven and earth pass away,
   not the smallest letter or the smallest part of a letter
   will pass from the law,
   until all things have taken place.
Therefore, whoever breaks one of the least of these commandments
   and teaches others to do so
   will be called least in the Kingdom of heaven.
But whoever obeys and teaches these commandments
   will be called greatest in the Kingdom of heaven."

The Gospel of the Lord.

2.

Matthew 7:21-29   He taught them as one having authority.

✠ **A reading from the holy Gospel according to Matthew**

Jesus said to his disciples:
"Not everyone who says to me, 'Lord, Lord,'
  will enter the Kingdom of heaven,
  but only the one who does the will of my Father in heaven.
Many will say to me on that day,
  'Lord, Lord, did we not prophesy in your name?
Did we not drive out demons in your name?
Did we not do mighty deeds in your name?'
Then I will declare to them solemnly,
  'I never knew you. Depart from me, you evildoers.'

"Everyone who listens to these words of mine and acts on them
  will be like a wise man who built his house on rock.
The rain fell, the floods came,
  and the winds blew and buffeted the house.
But it did not collapse; it had been set solidly on rock.
And everyone who listens to these words of mine
  but does not act on them
  will be like a fool who built his house on sand.
The rain fell, the floods came,
  and the winds blew and buffeted the house.
And it collapsed and was completely ruined."

When Jesus finished these words,
  the crowds were astonished at his teaching,
  for he taught them as one having authority,
  and not as their scribes.

The Gospel of the Lord.

1854 The Common of Doctors of the Church

3.

Matthew 13:47-52   The new and the old.

✠ **A reading from the holy Gospel according to Matthew**

**Jesus said to the crowds:
"The Kingdom of heaven is like a net thrown into the sea,
  which collects fish of every kind.
When it is full they haul it ashore
  and sit down to put what is good into buckets.
What is bad they throw away.
Thus it will be at the end of the age.
The angels will go out and separate the wicked from the righteous
  and throw them into the fiery furnace,
  where there will be wailing and grinding of teeth.**

**"Do you understand all these things?"
They answered, "Yes."
And he replied,
  "Then every scribe who has been instructed in the Kingdom of heaven
  is like the head of a household who brings from his storeroom
  both the new and the old."**

The Gospel of the Lord.

4.

Matthew 23:8-12   Do not be called "Rabbi." You have but one teacher, who is Christ.

✠ **A reading from the holy Gospel according to Matthew**

**Jesus said to his disciples:
"Do not be called 'Rabbi.'
You have but one teacher, and you are all brothers.
Call no one on earth your father;
  you have but one Father in heaven.
Do not be called 'Master';
  you have but one master, the Christ.
The greatest among you must be your servant.
Whoever exalts himself will be humbled;
  whoever humbles himself will be exalted."**

The Gospel of the Lord.

5. Long Form

Mark 4:1-10, 13-20   The sower went out to sow.

✠   A reading from the holy Gospel according to Mark

On another occasion, Jesus began to teach by the sea.
A very large crowd gathered around him
   so that he got into a boat on the sea and sat down.
And the whole crowd was beside the sea on land.
And he taught them at length in parables,
   and in the course of his instruction he said to them,
   "Hear this! A sower went out to sow.
And as he sowed, some seed fell on the path,
   and the birds came and ate it up.
Other seed fell on rocky ground where it had little soil.
It sprang up at once because the soil was not deep.
And when the sun rose, it was scorched and it withered for lack of roots.
Some seed fell among thorns,
   and the thorns grew up and choked it
   and it produced no grain.
And some seed fell on rich soil and produced fruit.
It came up and grew and yielded thirty, sixty, and a hundredfold."
He added, "Whoever has ears to hear ought to hear."

And when he was alone,
   those present along with the Twelve
   questioned him about the parables.
He said to them,
   "Do you not understand this parable?
Then how will you understand any of the parables?
The sower sows the word.
These are the ones on the path where the word is sown.
As soon as they hear, Satan comes at once
   and takes away the word sown in them.
And these are the ones sown on rocky ground who,
   when they hear the word, receive it at once with joy.
But they have no roots; they last only for a time.
Then when tribulation or persecution comes because of the word,
   they quickly fall away.
Those sown among thorns are another sort.
They are the people who hear the word,
   but worldly anxiety, the lure of riches,
   and the craving for other things intrude and choke the word,
   and it bears no fruit.
But those sown on rich soil are the ones who hear the word and accept it
   and bear fruit thirty and sixty and a hundredfold."

The Gospel of the Lord.

OR Short Form

Mark 4:1-9   A sower went out to sow.

✠ A reading from the holy Gospel according to Mark

On another occasion, Jesus began to teach by the sea.
A very large crowd gathered around him
   so that he got into a boat on the sea and sat down.
And the whole crowd was beside the sea on land.
And he taught them at length in parables,
   and in the course of his instruction he said to them,
   "Hear this! A sower went out to sow.
And as he sowed, some seed fell on the path,
   and the birds came and ate it up.
Other seed fell on rocky ground where it had little soil.
It sprang up at once because the soil was not deep.
And when the sun rose, it was scorched and it withered for lack of roots.
Some seed fell among thorns,
   and the thorns grew up and choked it
   and it produced no grain.
And some seed fell on rich soil and produced fruit.
It came up and grew and yielded thirty, sixty, and a hundredfold."
He added, "Whoever has ears to hear ought to hear."

The Gospel of the Lord.

6.

Luke 6:43-45   From the fullness of the heart the mouth speaks.

✠ A reading from the holy Gospel according to Luke

Jesus said to his disciples:
"A good tree does not bear rotten fruit,
   nor does a rotten tree bear good fruit.
For every tree is known by its own fruit.
For people do not pick figs from thorn bushes,
   nor do they gather grapes from brambles.
A good person out of the store of goodness in his heart produces good,
   but an evil person out of a store of evil produces evil;
   for from the fullness of the heart the mouth speaks."

The Gospel of the Lord.

THE COMMON OF VIRGINS

731 READING I FROM THE OLD TESTAMENT

First Option

Song of Songs 8:6-7   Stern as death is love.

A reading from the Song of Songs

**Set me as a seal on your heart,
    as a seal on your arm;
For stern as death is love,
    relentless as the nether world is devotion;
    its flames are a blazing fire.
Deep waters cannot quench love,
    nor floods sweep it away.
Were one to offer all he owns to purchase love,
    he would be roundly mocked.**

The word of the Lord.

Second Option

Hosea 2:16bc, 17cd, 21-22   I will espouse you to me forever.

A reading from the Book of the Prophet Hosea

**Thus says the Lord:
I will lead her into the desert
    and speak to her heart.
She shall respond there as in the days of her youth,
    when she came up from the land of Egypt.
I will espouse you to me forever:
    I will espouse you in right and in justice,
    in love and in mercy;
I will espouse you in fidelity,
    and you shall know the Lord.**

The word of the Lord.

The Common of Virgins

732 READING I FROM THE NEW TESTAMENT DURING THE SEASON OF EASTER

First Option

Revelation 19:1, 5-9a   Blessed are those who have been called to the wedding feast of the Lamb.

A reading from the Book of Revelation

I, John, heard what sounded like the loud voice
  of a great multitude in heaven, saying:

  "Alleluia!
  Salvation, glory, and might belong to our God."

A voice coming from the throne said:

  "Praise our God, all you his servants,
    and you who revere him, small and great."

Then I heard something like the sound of a great multitude
  or the sound of rushing water or mighty peals of thunder,
  as they said:

  "Alleluia!
  The Lord has established his reign,
    our God, the almighty.
  Let us rejoice and be glad
    and give him glory.
  For the wedding day of the Lamb has come,
    his bride has made herself ready.
  She was allowed to wear
    a bright, clean linen garment."
The linen represents the righteous deeds of the holy ones.

Then the angel said to me,
  "Write this:
  Blessed are those who have been called
  to the wedding feast of the Lamb."

The word of the Lord.

Second Option

Revelation 21:1-5a I saw the new Jerusalem, prepared as a bride adorned for her husband.

A reading from the Book of Revelation

I, John, saw a new heaven and a new earth.
The former heaven and the former earth had passed away,
   and the sea was no more.
I also saw the holy city, a new Jerusalem,
   coming down out of heaven from God,
   prepared as a bride adorned for her husband.
I heard a loud voice from the throne saying,
   "Behold, God's dwelling is with the human race.
He will dwell with them and they will be his people
   and God himself will always be with them as their God.
He will wipe every tear from their eyes,
   and there shall be no more death or mourning, wailing or pain,
   for the old order has passed away."

The One who sat on the throne said,
   "Behold, I make all things new."

The word of the Lord.

1860 *The Common of Virgins*

733 RESPONSORIAL PSALM

First Option

Psalm 45:11-12, 14-15, 16-17

℞. (11) **Listen to me, daughter; see and bend your ear.**
   or:
℞. **The bridegroom is here; let us go out to meet Christ the Lord.**

Hear, O daughter, and see; turn your ear,
   forget your people and your father's house.
So shall the king desire your beauty;
   for he is your lord, and you must worship him.

℞. Listen to me, daughter; see and bend your ear.
   or:
℞. The bridegroom is here; let us go out to meet Christ the Lord.

All glorious is the king's daughter as she enters;
   her raiment is threaded with spun gold.
In embroidered apparel she is borne in to the king;
   behind her the virgins of her train are brought to you.

℞. Listen to me, daughter; see and bend your ear.
   or:
℞. The bridegroom is here; let us go out to meet Christ the Lord.

They are borne in with gladness and joy;
   they enter the palace of the king.
The place of your fathers your sons shall have;
   you shall make them princes through all the land.

℞. Listen to me, daughter; see and bend your ear.
   or:
℞. The bridegroom is here; let us go out to meet Christ the Lord.

Second Option

Psalm 148:1bc-2, 11-12, 13, 14

℟. (see 12a and 13a) **Young men and women, praise the name of the Lord.**
  or:
℟. **Alleluia.**

Praise the LORD **from the heavens;**
  praise him in the heights;
Praise him, all you his angels,
  praise him, all you his hosts.

℟. **Young men and women, praise the name of the Lord.**
  or:
℟. **Alleluia.**

Let the kings of the earth and all peoples,
  the princes and all the judges of the earth,
Young men, too, and maidens,
  old men and boys,
Praise the name of the LORD**,**
  for his name alone is exalted.

℟. **Young men and women, praise the name of the Lord.**
  or:
℟. **Alleluia.**

His majesty is above earth and heaven.
He has lifted up the horn of his people.
Be this his praise from all his faithful ones;
  from the children of Israel, the people close to him. Alleluia.

℟. **Young men and women, praise the name of the Lord.**
  or:
℟. **Alleluia.**

The Common of Virgins

734 READING II FROM THE NEW TESTAMENT

First Option

1 Corinthians 7:25-35   A virgin is anxious about the things of the Lord.

A reading from the first Letter of Saint Paul to the Corinthians

Brothers and sisters:
In regard to virgins, I have no commandment from the Lord,
 but I give my opinion as one who by the Lord's mercy is trustworthy.
So this is what I think best because of the present distress:
 that it is a good thing for a person to remain as he is.
Are you bound to a wife? Do not seek a separation.
Are you free of a wife? Then do not look for a wife.
If you marry, however, you do not sin,
 nor does an unmarried woman sin if she marries;
 but such people will experience affliction in their earthly life,
 and I would like to spare you that.

I tell you, brothers, the time is running out.
From now on, let those having wives act as not having them,
 those weeping as not weeping,
 those rejoicing as not rejoicing,
 those buying as not owning,
 those using the world as not using it fully.
For the world in its present form is passing away.

I should like you to be free of anxieties.
An unmarried man is anxious about the things of the Lord,
 how he may please the Lord.
But a married man is anxious about the things of the world,
 how he may please his wife, and he is divided.
An unmarried woman or a virgin is anxious about the things of the Lord,
 so that she may be holy in both body and spirit.
A married woman, on the other hand,
 is anxious about the things of the world,
 how she may please her husband.
I am telling you this for your own benefit,
 not to impose a restraint upon you,
 but for the sake of propriety
 and adherence to the Lord without distraction.

The word of the Lord.

Second Option

2 Corinthians 10:17–11:2   I betrothed you to one husband, to present you as a chaste virgin to Christ.

A reading from the second Letter of Saint Paul to the Corinthians

Brothers and sisters:
"Whoever boasts, should boast in the Lord."
For it is not the one who recommends himself who is approved,
but the one whom the Lord recommends.

If only you would put up with a little foolishness from me!
Please put up with me.
For I am jealous of you with the jealousy of God,
since I betrothed you to one husband
to present you as a chaste virgin to Christ.

The word of the Lord.

1864　*The Common of Virgins*

735 ALLELUIA VERSE AND VERSE BEFORE THE GOSPEL

1.

John 14:23

Whoever loves me will keep my word
and my Father will love him,
and we will come to him.

2.

This is the wise virgin, whom the Lord found waiting;
at his coming, she went in with him to the wedding feast.

3.

Come, bride of Christ, and receive the crown,
which the Lord has prepared for you for ever.

736 GOSPEL

First Option

Matthew 19:3-12   For the sake of the Kingdom of heaven.

☩ **A reading from the holy Gospel according to Matthew**

Some Pharisees approached Jesus, and tested him, saying,
  "Is it lawful for a man to divorce his wife for any cause whatever?"
He said in reply,
  "Have you not read that from the beginning
  the Creator *made them male and female* and said,
  For this reason a man shall leave his father and mother
  and be joined to his wife, and the two shall become one flesh?
So they are no longer two, but one flesh.
Therefore, what God has joined together, man must not separate."
They said to him,
  "Then why did Moses command that the man give the woman
  a bill of divorce and dismiss her?"
He said to them,
  "Because of the hardness of your hearts
  Moses allowed you to divorce your wives,
  but from the beginning it was not so.
I say to you, whoever divorces his wife
  (unless the marriage is unlawful)
  and marries another commits adultery."
His disciples said to him,
  "If that is the case of a man with his wife,
  it is better not to marry."
He answered, "Not all can accept this word,
  but only those to whom that is granted.
Some are incapable of marriage because they were born so;
  some, because they were made so by others;
  some, because they have renounced marriage
  for the sake of the Kingdom of heaven.
Whoever can accept this ought to accept it."

The Gospel of the Lord.

1866   *The Common of Virgins*

Second Option

Matthew 25:1-13   Behold, the bridegroom! Come out to meet him!

☩ **A reading from the holy Gospel according to Matthew**

**Jesus told his disciples this parable:
"The Kingdom of heaven will be like ten virgins
   who took their lamps and went out to meet the bridegroom.
Five of them were foolish and five were wise.
The foolish ones, when taking their lamps,
   brought no oil with them,
   but the wise brought flasks of oil with their lamps.
Since the bridegroom was long delayed,
   they all became drowsy and fell asleep.
At midnight, there was a cry,
   'Behold, the bridegroom! Come out to meet him!'
Then all those virgins got up and trimmed their lamps.
The foolish ones said to the wise,
   'Give us some of your oil,
   for our lamps are going out.'
But the wise ones replied,
   'No, for there may not be enough for us and you.
Go instead to the merchants and buy some for yourselves.'
While they went off to buy it,
   the bridegroom came
   and those who were ready went into the wedding feast with him.
Then the door was locked.
Afterwards the other virgins came and said,
   'Lord, Lord, open the door for us!'
But he said in reply,
   'Amen, I say to you, I do not know you.'
Therefore, stay awake,
   for you know neither the day nor the hour."**

The Gospel of the Lord.

Third Option

Luke 10:38-42 — Martha welcomed him. Mary has chosen the better part.

✠ **A reading from the holy Gospel according to Luke**

Jesus entered a village
   where a woman whose name was Martha welcomed him.
She had a sister named Mary
   who sat beside the Lord at his feet listening to him speak.
Martha, burdened with much serving, came to him and said,
    "Lord, do you not care
   that my sister has left me by myself to do the serving?
Tell her to help me."
The Lord said to her in reply,
    "Martha, Martha, you are anxious and worried about many things.
There is need of only one thing.
Mary has chosen the better part
   and it will not be taken from her."

The Gospel of the Lord.

THE COMMON OF HOLY MEN AND WOMEN

737 READING I FROM THE OLD TESTAMENT

1.

Genesis 12:1-4a   Go forth from the land of your kinsfolk and from your father's house.

A reading from the Book of Genesis

The LORD said to Abram:
"Go forth from the land of your kinsfolk
  and from your father's house to a land that I will show you.

  "I will make of you a great nation,
    and I will bless you;
  I will make your name great,
    so that you will be a blessing.
  I will bless those who bless you
    and curse those who curse you.
  All the communities of the earth
    shall find blessing in you."

Abram went as the LORD directed him.

The word of the Lord.

2.

Leviticus 19:1-2, 17-18   You shall love your neighbor as yourself.

A reading from the Book of Leviticus

The LORD said to Moses,
  "Speak to the whole assembly of the children of Israel and tell them:
  Be holy, for I, the LORD, your God, am holy.

"You shall not bear hatred for your brother in your heart.
Though you may have to reprove your fellow citizen
  do not incur sin because of him.
Take no revenge and cherish no grudge against any of your people.
You shall love your neighbor as yourself.
I am the LORD."

The word of the Lord.

3.

Deuteronomy 6:3-9   Love the Lord your God with all your heart.

A reading from the Book of Deuteronomy

Moses said to the people:
"Hear, Israel, and be careful to observe these commandments,
    that you may grow and prosper the more,
        in keeping with the promise of the Lord, the God of your fathers,
        to give you a land flowing with milk and honey.

"Hear, O Israel! The Lord is our God, the Lord alone!
Therefore, you shall love the Lord, your God,
    with all your heart,
    and with all your soul,
    and with all your strength.
Take to heart these words which I enjoin on you today.
Drill them into your children.
Speak of them at home and abroad, whether you are busy or at rest.
Bind them at your wrist as a sign
    and let them be as a pendant on your forehead.
Write them on the doorposts of your houses and on your gates."

The word of the Lord.

4. For Religious

Deuteronomy 10:8-9   The Lord himself is our heritage.

A reading from the Book of Deuteronomy

Moses summoned all of Israel and said to them:
"At that time the Lord set apart the tribe of Levi
    to carry the ark of the covenant of the Lord,
    to be in attendance before the Lord and minister to him,
    and to give blessings in his name,
    as they have done to this day.
For this reason,
    Levi has no share in the heritage with his brothers;
    the Lord himself is his heritage,
    as the Lord, your God, has told him."

The word of the Lord.

The Common of Holy Men and Women

5. For Religious

1 Kings 19:4-9a, 11-15a   Go outside and stand on the mountain before the Lord.

A reading from the first Book of Kings

Elijah went a day's journey into the desert,
   until he came to a broom tree and sat beneath it.
He prayed for death saying:
   "This is enough, O Lord!
Take my life, for I am no better than my fathers."
He lay down and fell asleep under the broom tree,
   but then an angel touched him and ordered him to get up and eat.
He looked and there at his head was a hearth cake
   and a jug of water.
After he ate and drank, he lay down again,
   but the angel of the Lord came back a second time,
   touched him, and ordered,
   "Get up and eat, else the journey will be too long for you!"
He got up, ate, and drank;
   then strengthened by that food,
   he walked forty days and forty nights to the mountain of God, Horeb.

There he came to a cave, where he took shelter.
Then the Lord said to him,
   "Go outside and stand on the mountain before the Lord;
   the Lord will be passing by."
A strong and heavy wind was rending the mountains
   and crushing rocks before the Lord—
   but the Lord was not in the wind.
After the wind there was an earthquake—
   but the Lord was not in the earthquake.
After the earthquake there was fire—
   but the Lord was not in the fire.
After the fire there was a tiny whispering sound.
When he heard this,
   Elijah hid his face in his cloak
   and went and stood at the entrance of the cave.
A voice said to him, "Elijah, why are you here?"
He replied, "I have been most zealous for the Lord, the God of hosts.
But the children of Israel have forsaken your covenant,
   torn down your altars, and put your prophets to the sword.
I alone am left, and they seek to take my life."
The Lord said to him,
   "Go, take the road back to the desert near Damascus."

The word of the Lord.

6. For Religious

1 Kings 19:16b, 19-21   Elisha left and followed Elijah.

A reading from the first Book of Kings

The Lord said to Elijah:
"You shall anoint Elisha, son of Shaphat of Abel-meholah,
  as prophet to succeed you."

Elijah set out and came upon Elisha, son of Shaphat,
  as he was plowing with twelve yoke of oxen;
  he was following the twelfth.
Elijah went over to him and threw his cloak over him.
Elisha left the oxen, ran after Elijah, and said,
  "Please, let me kiss my father and mother goodbye,
  and I will follow you."
Elijah answered, "Go back!
Have I done anything to you?"
Elisha left him, and taking the yoke of oxen, slaughtered them;
  he used the plowing equipment for fuel to boil their flesh,
  and gave it to his people to eat.
Then he left and followed Elijah as his attendant.

The word of the Lord.

7.

Tobit 8:4b-8   Allow us to live together to a happy old age.

A reading from the Book of Tobit

On their wedding night Tobiah arose from bed and said to his wife,
   "My love, get up. Let us pray and beg our Lord
   to have mercy on us and to grant us deliverance."
She got up, and they started to pray
   and beg that deliverance might be theirs.
He began with these words:

   "Blessed are you, O God of our fathers;
      praised be your name forever and ever.
   Let the heavens and all your creation
      praise you forever.
   You made Adam and you gave him his wife Eve
      to be his help and support;
      and from these two the human race descended.
   You said, 'It is not good for the man to be alone;
      let us make him a partner like himself.'
   Now, Lord, you know that I take this wife of mine
      not because of lust,
      but for a noble purpose.
   Call down your mercy on me and on her,
      and allow us to live together to a happy old age."

They said together, "Amen, amen."

The word of the Lord.

8. For Those Who Work for the Underprivileged

Tobit 12:6-14a   *Prayer and fasting are good, but better than either is almsgiving accompanied by righteousness.*

A reading from the Book of Tobit

**The angel Raphael said to Tobit and his son:
"Thank God!
Give him the praise and the glory.
Before all the living,**
  acknowledge the many good things he has done for you,
  by blessing and extolling his name in song.
Before all people, honor and proclaim God's deeds,
  and do not be slack in praising him.
A king's secret it is prudent to keep,
  but the works of God are to be declared and made known.
Praise them with due honor.
Do good, and evil will not find its way to you.
Prayer and fasting are good,
  but better than either is almsgiving accompanied by righteousness.
A little with righteousness is better than abundance with wickedness.
It is better to give alms than to store up gold;
  for almsgiving saves one from death and expiates every sin.
Those who regularly give alms shall enjoy a full life;
  but those habitually guilty of sin are their own worst enemies.

"I will now tell you the whole truth;
  I will conceal nothing at all from you.
I have already said to you,
  'A king's secret it is prudent to keep,
  but the works of God are to be made known with due honor.'
I can now tell you that when you, Tobit, and Sarah prayed,
  it was I who presented and read the record of your prayer
  before the Glory of the Lord;
  and I did the same thing when you used to bury the dead.
When you did not hesitate to get up
  and leave your dinner in order to go and bury the dead,
  I was sent to put you to the test."

The word of the Lord.

1874 *The Common of Holy Men and Women*

9. For Widows

Judith 8:2-8   She was a very God-fearing woman.

A reading from the Book of Judith

**Judith's husband, Manasseh, of her own tribe and clan,
   had died at the time of the barley harvest.
While he was in the field supervising those who bound the sheaves,
   he suffered sunstroke;
   and he died of this illness in Bethulia, his native city.
Manasseh was buried with his fathers
   in the field between Dothan and Balamon.
The widowed Judith remained three years and four months at home,
   where she set up a tent for herself on the roof of her house.
She put sackcloth about her loins and wore widow's weeds.
She fasted all the days of her widowhood,
   except sabbath eves and sabbaths, new moon eves and new moons,
   feastdays and holidays of the house of Israel.
She was beautifully formed and lovely to behold.**

**Her husband, Manasseh, the son of Joseph,
   the son of Ahitub, the son of Melchis,
   the son of Eliab, the son of Nathanael,
   the son of Sarasadai, the son of Simeon,
   had left her gold and silver,
   servants and maids, livestock and fields,
   which she was maintaining.
No one had a bad word to say about her,
   for she was a very God-fearing woman.**

The word of the Lord.

10.

Esther C:1-7, 10   I acted as I did so as not to place the honor of man above that of God.

A reading from the Book of Esther

**Mordecai prayed:
"O God of Abraham, God of Isaac, God of Jacob, blessed are you;
   O Lord God, almighty King, all things are in your power,
   and there is no one to oppose you in your will to save Israel.
You made heaven and earth
   and every wonderful thing under the heavens.
You are L**ORD** of all,
   and there is no one who can resist you, L**ORD**.
You know all things.**

You know, O L<small>ORD</small>, that
   gladly would I have kissed the soles of Haman's feet
   for the salvation of Israel.
But I acted as I did so as not to place the honor of man
   above that of God.
I will not bow down to anyone but you, my L<small>ORD</small> and God.
Hear my prayer; have pity on your inheritance
   and turn our sorrow into joy:
   thus we shall live to sing praise to your name, O L<small>ORD</small>.
Do not silence those who praise you."

The word of the Lord.

11.

Proverbs 31:10-13, 19-20, 30-31   The woman who fears the L<small>ORD</small> is to be praised.

A reading from the Book of Proverbs

When one finds a worthy wife,
   her value is far beyond pearls.
Her husband, entrusting his heart to her,
   has an unfailing prize.
She brings him good, and not evil,
   all the days of her life.
She obtains wool and flax
   and cloth with skillful hands.
She puts her hands to the distaff,
   and her fingers ply the spindle.
She reaches out her hands to the poor,
   and extends her arms to the needy.
Charm is deceptive and beauty fleeting;
   the woman who fears the L<small>ORD</small> is to be praised.
Give her a reward of her labors,
   and let her works praise her at the city gates.

The word of the Lord.

The Common of Holy Men and Women

12.

Sirach 2:7-13 You who fear the LORD, believe him, hope in him, love him.

A reading from the Book of Sirach

**You who fear the LORD, wait for his mercy,
  turn not away lest you fall.
You who fear the LORD, trust him,
  and your reward will not be lost.
You who fear the LORD, hope for good things,
  for lasting joy and mercy.
You who fear the Lord, love him
  and your hearts will be enlightened.
Study the generations long past and understand;
  has anyone hoped in the LORD and been disappointed?
Has anyone persevered in his commandments and been forsaken?
  Has anyone called upon him and been rebuffed?
Compassionate and merciful is the LORD;
  he forgives sins, he saves in time of trouble
  and he is a protector to all who seek him in truth.**

The word of the Lord.

13.

Sirach 3:17-24 Humble yourself and you will find favor with God.

A reading from the Book of Sirach

**My child, conduct your affairs with humility,
  and you will be loved more than a giver of gifts.
Humble yourself the more, the greater you are,
  and you will find favor with God.
The greater you are,
  the more you must humble yourself in all things,
  and you will find grace before God.
For great is the power of God;
  by the humble he is glorified.
What is too sublime for you, seek not,
  into things beyond your strength search not.
What is committed to you, attend to;
  for it is not necessary for you to see with your eyes
  those things which are hidden.
With what is too much for you meddle not,
  when shown things beyond human understanding.**

Their own opinion has misled many,
   and false reasoning unbalanced their judgment.
Where the pupil of the eye is missing, there is no light,
   and where there is no knowledge, there is no wisdom.

The word of the Lord.

14.

Sirach 26:1-4, 13-16   Like the sun rising in the Lord's heavens, the beauty of a virtuous wife is the radiance of her home.

A reading from the Book of Sirach

Blessed the husband of a good wife,
   twice-lengthened are his days;
A worthy wife brings joy to her husband,
   peaceful and full is his life.
A good wife is a generous gift
   bestowed upon him who fears the Lord;
Be he rich or poor, his heart is content,
   and a smile is ever on his face.

A gracious wife delights her husband,
   her thoughtfulness puts flesh on his bones;
A gift from the Lord is her governed speech,
   and her firm virtue is of surpassing worth.
Choicest of blessings is a modest wife,
   priceless her chaste soul.
A holy and decent woman adds grace upon grace;
   indeed, no price is worthy of her temperate soul.
Like the sun rising in the Lord's heavens,
   the beauty of a virtuous wife is the radiance of her home.

The word of the Lord.

15. For Those Who Work for the Underprivileged

Isaiah 58:6-11   Share your bread with the hungry.

A reading from the Book of the Prophet Isaiah

Thus says the Lord:
This is the fasting that I wish:
　releasing those bound unjustly,
　untying the thongs of the yoke;
Setting free the oppressed,
　breaking every yoke;
Sharing your bread with the hungry,
　sheltering the oppressed and the homeless;
Clothing the naked when you see them,
　and not turning your back on your own.
Then your light shall break forth like the dawn,
　and your wound shall quickly be healed;
Your vindication shall go before you,
　and the glory of the Lord shall be your rear guard.
Then you shall call, and the Lord will answer,
　you shall cry for help, and he will say: Here I am!
If you remove from your midst oppression,
　false accusation and malicious speech;
If you bestow your bread on the hungry
　and satisfy the afflicted;
Then light shall rise for you in darkness,
　and the gloom shall become for you like midday;
Then the Lord will guide you always
　and give you plenty even on the parched land.
He will renew your strength,
　and you shall be like a watered garden,
　like a spring whose water never fails.

The word of the Lord.

16.

Jeremiah 20:7-9   It becomes like fire burning in my heart.

A reading from the Book of the Prophet Jeremiah

You duped me, O Lord, and I let myself be duped;
  you were too strong for me, and you triumphed.
All the day I am an object for laughter;
  everyone mocks me.
Whenever I speak, I must cry out,
  violence and outrage is my message;
The word of the Lord has brought me
  derision and reproach all the day.
I say to myself, I will not mention him,
  I will speak in his name no more.
But then it becomes like fire burning in my heart,
  imprisoned in my bones;
I grow weary holding it in,
  I cannot endure it.

The word of the Lord.

17.

Micah 6:6-8   You have been told, O man, what the Lord requires of you.

A reading from the Book of the Prophet Micah

With what shall I come before the Lord,
  and bow before God most high?
Shall I come before him with burnt offerings,
  with calves a year old?
Will the Lord be pleased with thousands of rams,
  with myriad streams of oil?
Shall I give my first-born for my crime,
  the fruit of my body for the sin of my soul?
You have been told, O man, what is good,
  and what the Lord requires of you:
Only to do the right and to love goodness,
  and to walk humbly with your God.

The word of the Lord.

18.

Zephaniah 2:3; 3:12-13   But I will leave as a remnant in your midst a people humble and lowly.

A reading from the Book of the Prophet Zephaniah

Seek the Lord, all you humble of the earth,
  who have observed his law;
Seek justice, seek humility;
  perhaps you may be sheltered
  on the day of the Lord's anger.

But I will leave as a remnant in your midst
  a people humble and lowly,
Who shall take refuge in the name of the Lord:
  the remnant of Israel.
They shall do no wrong
  and speak no lies;
Nor shall there be found in their mouths
  a deceitful tongue;
They shall pasture and couch their flocks
  with none to disturb them.

The word of the Lord.

738 READING I FROM THE NEW TESTAMENT DURING THE SEASON OF EASTER

First Option   For Religious

Acts 4:32-35   The community of believers was of one heart and mind.

A reading from the Acts of the Apostles

**The community of believers was of one heart and mind,
 and no one claimed that any of his possessions was his own,
 but they had everything in common.
With great power the Apostles bore witness
 to the resurrection of the Lord Jesus,
 and great favor was accorded them all.
There was no needy person among them,
 for those who owned property or houses would sell them,
 bring the proceeds of the sale,
 and put them at the feet of the Apostles,
 and they were distributed to each according to need.**

The word of the Lord.

Second Option

Revelation 3:14b, 20-22   I will dine with him and he with me.

A reading from the Book of Revelation

**"'The Amen, the faithful and true witness,
 the source of God's creation, says this:**

**"'"Behold, I stand at the door and knock.
If anyone hears my voice and opens the door,
 then I will enter his house and dine with him,
 and he with me.
I will give the victor the right to sit with me on my throne,
 as I myself first won the victory
 and sit with my Father on his throne.**

**"'"Whoever has ears ought to hear
 what the Spirit says to the churches."'"**

The word of the Lord.

1882 *The Common of Holy Men and Women*

Third Option

Revelation 19:1, 5-9a   Blessed are those who have been called to the wedding feast of the Lamb.

A reading from the Book of Revelation

I, John, heard what sounded like the loud voice
  of a great multitude in heaven, saying:
    "Alleluia!
  Salvation, glory, and might belong to our God."

A voice coming from the throne said:

  "Praise our God, all you his servants,
    and you who revere him, small and great."

Then I heard something like the sound of a great multitude
  or the sound of rushing water or mighty peals of thunder,
  as they said:

    "Alleluia!
  The Lord has established his reign,
    our God, the almighty.
  Let us rejoice and be glad
    and give him glory.
  For the wedding day of the Lamb has come,
    his bride has made herself ready.
  She was allowed to wear
    a bright, clean linen garment."
(The linen represents the righteous deeds of the holy ones.)

Then the angel said to me,
  "Write this:
  Blessed are those who have been called
  to the wedding feast of the Lamb."

The word of the Lord.

Fourth Option

Revelation 21:5-7   To the thirsty I will give a gift from the spring of life-giving water.

A reading from the Book of Revelation

**The One who was seated on the throne said:
"Behold, I make all things new."
Then he said, "Write these words down,
   for they are trustworthy and true."
He said to me, "They are accomplished.
I am the Alpha and the Omega,
   the beginning and the end.
To the thirsty I will give a gift
   from the spring of life-giving water.
The victor will inherit these gifts,
   and I shall be his God,
   and he will be my son."**

The word of the Lord.

739 RESPONSORIAL PSALM

1.

Psalm 1:1-2, 3, 4 and 6

℟. (40:5a) **Blessed are they who hope in the Lord.**
or:
℟. (2a) **Blessed are they who delight in the law of the Lord.**
or:
℟. (92:13-14) **The just will flourish like the palm tree in the garden of the Lord.**

**Blessed the man who follows not
  the counsel of the wicked
Nor walks in the way of sinners,
  nor sits in the company of the insolent,
But delights in the law of the Lord
  and meditates on his law day and night.**

℟. **Blessed are they who hope in the Lord.**
or:
℟. **Blessed are they who delight in the law of the Lord.**
or:
℟. **The just will flourish like the palm tree in the garden of the Lord.**

**He is like a tree
  planted near running water,
That yields its fruit in due season,
  and whose leaves never fade.
  Whatever he does, prospers.**

℟. **Blessed are they who hope in the Lord.**
or:
℟. **Blessed are they who delight in the law of the Lord.**
or:
℟. **The just will flourish like the palm tree in the garden of the Lord.**

**Not so, the wicked, not so;
  they are like chaff which the wind drives away.
For the Lord watches over the way of the just,
  but the way of the wicked vanishes.**

℟. **Blessed are they who hope in the Lord.**
or:
℟. **Blessed are they who delight in the law of the Lord.**
or:
℟. **The just will flourish like the palm tree in the garden of the Lord.**

2.

Psalm 15:2-3a, 3bc-4ab, 5

℟. (1) **The just one shall live on your holy mountain, O Lord.**

He who walks blamelessly and does justice;
   who thinks the truth in his heart
   and slanders not with his tongue.

℟. **The just one shall live on your holy mountain, O Lord.**

Who harms not his fellow man,
   nor takes up a reproach against his neighbor;
By whom the reprobate is despised,
   while he honors those who fear the Lord.

℟. **The just one shall live on your holy mountain, O Lord.**

Who lends not his money at usury
   and accepts no bribe against the innocent.
He who does these things
   shall never be disturbed.

℟. **The just one shall live on your holy mountain, O Lord.**

3.

Psalm 16:1-2ab and 5, 7-8, 11

℟. (see 5a) **You are my inheritance, O Lord.**

Keep me, O God, for in you I take refuge;
   I say to the Lord, "My Lord are you."
O Lord, my allotted portion and my cup,
   you it is who hold fast my lot.

℟. **You are my inheritance, O Lord.**

I bless the Lord who counsels me;
   even in the night my heart exhorts me.
I set the Lord ever before me;
   with him at my right hand I shall not be disturbed.

℟. **You are my inheritance, O Lord.**

You will show me the path to life,
   fullness of joys in your presence,
   the delights at your right hand forever.

℟. **You are my inheritance, O Lord.**

The Common of Holy Men and Women

4.

Psalm 23:1-3, 4, 5, 6

℟. (1) The Lord is my shepherd; there is nothing I shall want.

The Lord is my shepherd; I shall not want.
   In verdant pastures he gives me repose;
Beside restful waters he leads me;
   he refreshes my soul.
He guides me on right paths
   for his name's sake.

℟. The Lord is my shepherd; there is nothing I shall want.

Even though I walk in the dark valley
   I fear no evil; for you are at my side
With your rod and your staff
   that give me courage.

℟. The Lord is my shepherd; there is nothing I shall want.

You spread the table before me
   in the sight of my foes;
You anoint my head with oil;
   my cup overflows.

℟. The Lord is my shepherd; there is nothing I shall want.

Only goodness and kindness follow me
   all the days of my life;
And I shall dwell in the house of the Lord
   for years to come.

℟. The Lord is my shepherd; there is nothing I shall want.

5.

Psalm 34:2-3, 4-5, 6-7, 8-9, 10-11

℟. (2) I will bless the Lord at all times.
   or:
℟. (9) Taste and see the goodness of the Lord.

I will bless the Lord at all times;
   his praise shall be ever in my mouth.
Let my soul glory in the Lord;
   the lowly will hear and be glad.

℟. I will bless the Lord at all times.
   or:
℟. Taste and see the goodness of the Lord.

Glorify the LORD **with me,**
　　let us together extol his name.
I sought the LORD**, and he answered me**
　　and delivered me from all my fears.

℟. **I will bless the Lord at all times.**
　　or:
℟. **Taste and see the goodness of the Lord.**

Look to him that you may be radiant with joy,
　　and your faces may not blush with shame.
When the poor one called out, the LORD **heard,**
　　and from all his distress he saved him.

℟. **I will bless the Lord at all times.**
　　or:
℟. **Taste and see the goodness of the Lord.**

The angel of the LORD **encamps**
　　around those who fear him, and delivers them.
Taste and see how good the LORD **is;**
　　blessed the man who takes refuge in him.

℟. **I will bless the Lord at all times.**
　　or:
℟. **Taste and see the goodness of the Lord.**

Fear the LORD**, you his holy ones,**
　　for nought is lacking to those who fear him.
The great grow poor and hungry;
　　but those who seek the LORD **want for no good thing.**

℟. **I will bless the Lord at all times.**
　　or:
℟. **Taste and see the goodness of the Lord.**

6.

Psalm 103:1bc-2, 3-4, 8-9, 13-14, 17-18a

℟. (1) **O bless the Lord, my soul!**

Bless the LORD**, O my soul;
   and all my being, bless his holy name.
Bless the L**ORD**, O my soul,
   and forget not all his benefits.**

℟. **O bless the Lord, my soul!**

**He pardons all your iniquities,
   he heals all your ills,
He redeems your life from destruction,
   crowns you with kindness and compassion.**

℟. **O bless the Lord, my soul!**

Merciful and gracious is the LORD**,
   slow to anger and abounding in kindness.
He will not always chide,
   nor does he keep his wrath forever.**

℟. **O bless the Lord, my soul!**

**As a father has compassion on his children,
   so the L**ORD **has compassion on those who fear him,
For he knows how we are formed;
   he remembers that we are dust.**

℟. **O bless the Lord, my soul!**

But the kindness of the LORD **is from eternity
   to eternity toward those who fear him,
And his justice toward his children's children
   among those who keep his covenant.**

℟. **O bless the Lord, my soul!**

7.

Psalm 112:1-2, 3-4, 5-7a, 7b-8, 9

℟. (1) **Blessed the man who fears the Lord.**
   or:
℟. **Alleluia.**

Blessed the man who fears the LORD**,**
   who greatly delights in his commands.
His posterity shall be mighty upon the earth;
   the upright generation shall be blessed.

℟. **Blessed the man who fears the Lord.**
   or:
℟. **Alleluia.**

Wealth and riches shall be in his house;
   his generosity shall endure forever.
Light shines through the darkness for the upright;
   he is gracious and merciful and just.

℟. **Blessed the man who fears the Lord.**
   or:
℟. **Alleluia.**

Well for the man who is gracious and lends,
   who conducts his affairs with justice;
He shall never be moved;
   the just one shall be in everlasting remembrance.

℟. **Blessed the man who fears the Lord.**
   or:
℟. **Alleluia.**

An evil report he shall not fear;
   his heart is firm, trusting in the LORD**.**
His heart is steadfast; he shall not fear
   till he looks down upon his foes.

℟. **Blessed the man who fears the Lord.**
   or:
℟. **Alleluia.**

Lavishly he gives to the poor,
    his generosity shall endure forever;
his horn shall be exalted in glory.

℟. **Blessed the man who fears the Lord.**
    or:
℟. **Alleluia.**

8.

Psalm 128:1-2, 3, 4-5

℟. **Blessed are those who fear the Lord.**

Blessed are you who fear the LORD**,**
    who walk in his ways!
For you shall eat the fruit of your handiwork;
    blessed shall you be, and favored.

℟. **Blessed are those who fear the Lord.**

Your wife shall be like a fruitful vine
    in the recesses of your home;
Your children like olive plants
    around your table.

℟. **Blessed are those who fear the Lord.**

Behold, thus is the man blessed
    who fears the LORD**.**
The LORD **bless you from Zion:**
    may you see the prosperity of Jerusalem
    all the days of your life.

℟. **Blessed are those who fear the Lord.**

9.

Psalm 131:1bcde, 2, 3

℟. In you, Lord, I have found my peace.

O Lord, my heart is not proud,
   nor are my eyes haughty;
I busy not myself with great things,
   nor with things too sublime for me.

℟. In you, Lord, I have found my peace.

Nay rather, I have stilled and quieted
   my soul like a weaned child.
Like a weaned child on its mother's lap,
   so is my soul within me.

℟. In you, Lord, I have found my peace.

O Israel, hope in the Lord,
   both now and forever.

℟. In you, Lord, I have found my peace.

740 READING II FROM THE NEW TESTAMENT

1.

Romans 8:26-30   Those he justified he also glorified.

A reading from the Letter of Saint Paul to the Romans

Brothers and sisters:
The Spirit comes to the aid of our weakness;
  for we do not know how to pray as we ought,
  but the Spirit himself intercedes with inexpressible groanings.
And the one who searches hearts
  knows what is the intention of the Spirit,
  because he intercedes for the holy ones
  according to God's will.

We know that all things work for good for those who love God,
  who are called according to his purpose.
For those he foreknew he also predestined
  to be conformed to the image of his Son,
  so that he might be the firstborn
  among many brothers.
And those he predestined he also called;
  and those he called he also justified;
  and those he justified he also glorified.

The word of the Lord.

2.

1 Corinthians 1:26-31   God chose the weak of the world.

A reading from the first Letter of Saint Paul to the Corinthians

**Consider your own calling, brothers and sisters.
Not many of you were wise by human standards,
not many were powerful,
not many were of noble birth.
Rather, God chose the foolish of the world to shame the wise,
and God chose the weak of the world to shame the strong,
and God chose the lowly and despised of the world,
those who count for nothing,
to reduce to nothing those who are something,
so that no human being might boast before God.
It is due to him that you are in Christ Jesus,
who became for us wisdom from God,
as well as righteousness, sanctification, and redemption,
so that, as it is written,
*Whoever boasts, should boast in the Lord.***

The word of the Lord.

1894 *The Common of Holy Men and Women*

3. Long Form

1 Corinthians 12:31—13:13   Love never fails.

A reading from the first Letter of Saint Paul to the Corinthians

Brothers and sisters:
Strive eagerly for the greatest spiritual gifts.
But I shall show you a still more excellent way.

If I speak in human and angelic tongues
   but do not have love,
   I am a resounding gong or a clashing cymbal.
And if I have the gift of prophecy
   and comprehend all mysteries and all knowledge;
   if I have all faith so as to move mountains,
   but do not have love, I am nothing.
If I give away everything I own,
   and if I hand my body over so that I may boast
   but do not have love, I gain nothing.

Love is patient, love is kind.
It is not jealous, love is not pompous,
   it is not inflated, it is not rude,
   it does not seek its own interests,
   it is not quick-tempered, it does not brood over injury,
      it does not rejoice over wrongdoing
   but rejoices with the truth.
It bears all things, believes all things,
   hopes all things, endures all things.

Love never fails.
If there are prophecies, they will be brought to nothing;
   if tongues, they will cease;
   if knowledge, it will be brought to nothing.
For we know partially and we prophesy partially,
   but when the perfect comes, the partial will pass away.
When I was a child, I used to talk as a child,
   think as a child, reason as a child;
   when I became a man, I put aside childish things.
At present we see indistinctly, as in a mirror,
   but then face to face.
At present I know partially;
   then I shall know fully, as I am fully known.
So faith, hope, love remain, these three;
   but the greatest of these is love.

The word of the Lord.

OR Short Form

1 Corinthians 13:4-13   Love never fails.

A reading from the first Letter of Saint Paul to the Corinthians

Brothers and sisters:
Love is patient, love is kind.
It is not jealous, love is not pompous,
   it is not inflated, it is not rude,
   it does not seek its own interests,
   it is not quick-tempered, it does not brood over injury,
   it does not rejoice over wrongdoing but rejoices with the truth.
It bears all things, believes all things,
   hopes all things, endures all things.

Love never fails.
If there are prophecies, they will be brought to nothing;
   if tongues, they will cease;
   if knowledge, it will be brought to nothing.
For we know partially and we prophesy partially,
   but when the perfect comes, the partial will pass away.
When I was a child, I used to talk as a child,
   think as a child, reason as a child;
   when I became a man, I put aside childish things.
At present we see indistinctly, as in a mirror,
   but then face to face.
At present I know partially;
   then I shall know fully, as I am fully known.
So faith, hope, love remain, these three;
   but the greatest of these is love.

The word of the Lord.

1896   *The Common of Holy Men and Women*

4.

2 Corinthians 10:17–11:2   I betrothed you to one husband, to present you as a chaste virgin to Christ.

A reading from the second Letter of Saint Paul to the Corinthians

Brothers and sisters:
Whoever boasts, should boast in the Lord.
For it is not the one who recommends himself who is approved,
but the one whom the Lord recommends.

If only you would put up with a little foolishness from me!
Please put up with me.
For I am jealous of you with the jealousy of God,
since I betrothed you to one husband
to present you as a chaste virgin to Christ.

The word of the Lord.

5.

Galatians 2:19-20   I live, no longer I, but Christ lives in me.

A reading from the Letter of Saint Paul to the Galatians

Brothers and sisters:
Through the law I died to the law,
that I might live for God.
I have been crucified with Christ;
yet I live, no longer I, but Christ lives in me;
insofar as I now live in the flesh,
I live by faith in the Son of God
who has loved me and given himself up for me.

The word of the Lord.

6.

Galatians 6:14-16   Through which the world has been crucified to me and I to the world.

A reading from the Letter of Saint Paul to the Galatians

Brothers and sisters:
May I never boast except in the cross of our Lord Jesus Christ,
    through which the world has been crucified to me,
    and I to the world.
For neither does circumcision mean anything, nor does uncircumcision,
    but only a new creation.
Peace and mercy be to all who follow this rule
    and to the Israel of God.

The word of the Lord.

7.

Ephesians 3:14-19   To know the love of Christ which surpasses knowledge.

A reading from the Letter of Saint Paul to the Ephesians

Brothers and sisters:
I kneel before the Father,
    from whom every family in heaven and on earth is named,
    that he may grant you in accord with the riches of his glory
    to be strengthened with power through his Spirit in the inner self,
    and that Christ may dwell in your hearts through faith;
    that you, rooted and grounded in love,
    may have strength to comprehend with all the holy ones
    what is the breadth and length and height and depth,
    and to know the love of Christ that surpasses knowledge,
    so that you may be filled with all the fullness of God.

The word of the Lord.

1898　*The Common of Holy Men and Women*

8.

Ephesians 6:10-13, 18　Put on the armor of God.

A reading from the Letter of Saint Paul to the Ephesians

Brothers and sisters:
Draw your strength from the Lord and from his mighty power.
Put on the armor of God so that you may be able to stand firm
　against the tactics of the Devil.
For our struggle is not with flesh and blood
　but with the principalities, with the powers,
　with the world rulers of this present darkness,
　with the evil spirits in the heavens.
Therefore, put on the armor of God,
　that you may be able to resist on the evil day
　and, having done everything, to hold your ground.

With all prayer and supplication,
　pray at every opportunity in the Spirit.
To that end, be watchful with all perseverance and supplication
　for all the holy ones.

The word of the Lord.

9.

Philippians 3:8-14   I continue my pursuit toward the goal, the prize of God's upward calling, in Christ Jesus.

A reading from the Letter of Saint Paul to the Philippians

Brothers and sisters:
I consider everything as a loss
    because of the supreme good of knowing Christ Jesus my Lord.
For his sake I have accepted the loss of all things
    and I consider them so much rubbish,
    that I may gain Christ and be found in him,
    not having any righteousness of my own based on the law
    but that which comes through faith in Christ,
    the righteousness from God,
    depending on faith to know him and the power of his resurrection
    and the sharing of his sufferings by being conformed to his death,
    if somehow I may attain the resurrection from the dead.

It is not that I have already taken hold of it
    or have already attained perfect maturity,
    but I continue my pursuit in hope that I may possess it,
    since I have indeed been taken possession of by Christ Jesus.
Brothers and sisters, I for my part
    do not consider myself to have taken possession.
Just one thing: forgetting what lies behind
    but straining forward to what lies ahead,
    I continue my pursuit toward the goal,
    the prize of God's upward calling, in Christ Jesus.

The word of the Lord.

1900 *The Common of Holy Men and Women*

10.

Philippians 4:4-9   Think about whatever is worthy of praise.

A reading from the Letter of Saint Paul to the Philippians

Brothers and sisters:
Rejoice in the Lord always.
I shall say it again: rejoice!
Your kindness should be known to all.
The Lord is near.
Have no anxiety at all, but in everything,
   by prayer and petition, with thanksgiving,
   make your requests known to God.
Then the peace of God that surpasses all understanding
   will guard your hearts and minds in Christ Jesus.

Finally, brothers and sisters,
   whatever is true, whatever is honorable,
   whatever is just, whatever is pure,
   whatever is lovely, whatever is gracious,
   if there is any excellence
   and if there is anything worthy of praise,
   think about these things.
Keep on doing what you have learned and received
   and heard and seen in me.
Then the God of peace will be with you.

The word of the Lord.

11.

Colossians 3:12-17   Over all these put on love, that is, the bond of perfection.

A reading from the Letter of Saint Paul to the Colossians

Brothers and sisters:
Put on, as God's chosen ones, holy and beloved,
   heartfelt compassion, kindness, humility, gentleness, and patience,
   bearing with one another and forgiving one another,
   if one has a grievance against another;
   as the Lord has forgiven you, so must you also do.
And over all these put on love,
   that is, the bond of perfection.
And let the peace of Christ control your hearts,
   the peace into which you were also called in one Body.
And be thankful.

Let the word of Christ dwell in you richly,
    as in all wisdom you teach and admonish one another,
    singing psalms, hymns, and spiritual songs
    with gratitude in your hearts to God.
And whatever you do, in word or in deed,
    do everything in the name of the Lord Jesus,
    giving thanks to God the Father through him.

The word of the Lord.

12. For Widows

1 Timothy 5:3-10   The real widow, who is all alone, has set her hope on God.

A reading from the first Letter of Saint Paul to Timothy

Beloved:
Honor widows who are truly widows.
But if a widow has children or grandchildren,
    let these first learn to perform their religious duty
    to their own family and to make recompense to their parents,
    for this is pleasing to God.
The real widow, who is all alone,
    has set her hope on God
    and continues in supplications and prayers night and day.
But the one who is self-indulgent is dead while she lives.
Command this, so that they may be irreproachable.
And whoever does not provide for relatives and especially family members
    has denied the faith and is worse than an unbeliever.

Let a widow be enrolled if she is not less than sixty years old,
    married only once, with a reputation for good works,
    namely, that she has raised children, practiced hospitality,
    washed the feet of the holy ones, helped those in distress,
    involved herself in every good work.

The word of the Lord.

13.

James 2:14-17   Faith of itself, if it does not have works, is dead.

A reading from the Letter of Saint James

What good is it, my brothers and sisters,
**   if someone says he has faith but does not have works?**
Can that faith save him?
If a brother or sister has nothing to wear
**   and has no food for the day,**
**   and one of you says to them,**
**   "Go in peace, keep warm, and eat well,"**
**   but you do not give them the necessities of the body,**
**   what good is it?**
So also faith of itself,
**   if it does not have works, is dead.**

The word of the Lord.

14.

1 Peter 3:1-9   Holy women hoped in God.

A reading from the first Letter of Saint Peter

You wives should be subordinate to your husbands so that,
   even if some disobey the word,
   they may be won over without a word by their wives' conduct
   when they observe your reverent and chaste behavior.
Your adornment should not be an external one:
   braiding the hair, wearing gold jewelry, or dressing in fine clothes,
   but rather the hidden character of the heart,
   expressed in the imperishable beauty
   of a gentle and calm disposition,
   which is precious in the sight of God.
For this is also how the holy women who hoped in God
   once used to adorn themselves
   and were subordinate to their husbands;
   thus Sarah obeyed Abraham, calling him "lord."
You are her children when you do what is good and fear no intimidation.

Likewise, you husbands should live with your wives in understanding,
   showing honor to the weaker female sex,
   since we are joint heirs of the gift of life,
   so that your prayers may not be hindered.

Finally, all of you, be of one mind, sympathetic,
   loving toward one another, compassionate, humble.
Do not return evil for evil, or insult for insult;
   but, on the contrary, a blessing, because to this you were called,
   that you might inherit a blessing.

The word of the Lord.

1904 *The Common of Holy Men and Women*

15.

1 Peter 4:7b-11   As each one has received a gift, use it to serve one another.

A reading from the first Letter of Saint Peter

Beloved:
Be serious and sober-minded
   so that you will be able to pray.
Above all, let your love for one another be intense,
   because love covers a multitude of sins.
Be hospitable to one another without complaining.
As each one has received a gift, use it to serve one another
   as good stewards of God's varied grace.
Whoever preaches, let it be with the words of God;
   whoever serves, let it be with the strength that God supplies,
   so that in all things God may be glorified through Jesus Christ,
   to whom belong glory and dominion forever and ever. Amen.

The word of the Lord.

16. For Those Who Work for the Underprivileged

1 John 3:14-18   We ought to lay down our lives for our brothers.

A reading from the first Letter of Saint John

Beloved:
We know that we have passed from death to life
   because we love our brothers.
Whoever does not love remains in death.
Everyone who hates his brother is a murderer,
   and you know that anyone who is a murderer
   does not have eternal life remaining in him.
The way we came to know love
   was that he laid down his life for us;
   so we ought to lay down our lives for our brothers.
If someone who has worldly means
   sees a brother in need and refuses him compassion,
   how can the love of God remain in him?
Children, let us love not in word or speech
   but in deed and truth.

The word of the Lord.

17.

1 John 4:7-16   If we love one another, God remains in us.

A reading from the first Letter of Saint John

Beloved, let us love one another,
   because love is of God;
   everyone who loves is begotten by God and knows God.
Whoever is without love does not know God, for God is love.
In this way the love of God was revealed to us:
   God sent his only-begotten Son into the world
   so that we might have life through him.
In this is love:
   not that we have loved God, but that he loved us
   and sent his Son as expiation for our sins.
Beloved, if God so loved us,
   we also must love one another.
No one has ever seen God.
Yet, if we love one another, God remains in us,
   and his love is brought to perfection in us.

This is how we know that we remain in him and he in us,
   that he has given us of his Spirit.
Moreover, we have seen and testify
   that the Father sent his Son as savior of the world.
Whoever acknowledges that Jesus is the Son of God,
   God remains in him and he in God.
We have come to know and to believe in the love God has for us.

God is love, and whoever remains in love
   remains in God and God in him.

The word of the Lord.

18.

1 John 5:1-5   The victory that conquers the world is our faith.

A reading from the first Letter of Saint John

Beloved:
Everyone who believes that Jesus is the Christ is begotten by God,
  and everyone who loves the Father
  loves also the one begotten by him.
In this way we know that we love the children of God
  when we love God and obey his commandments.
For the love of God is this,
  that we keep his commandments.
And his commandments are not burdensome,
  for whoever is begotten by God conquers the world.
And the victory that conquers the world is our faith.
Who indeed is the victor over the world
  but the one who believes that Jesus is the Son of God?

The word of the Lord.

741 ALLELUIA VERSE AND VERSE BEFORE THE GOSPEL

1.

Matthew 5:3

**Blessed are the poor in spirit;
for theirs is the Kingdom of heaven.**

2.

Matthew 5:6

**Blessed are those who hunger and thirst for righteousness,
for they will be satisfied.**

3.

Matthew 5:8

**Blessed are the clean of heart,
for they will see God.**

4.

See Matthew 11:25

**Blessed are you, Father, Lord of heaven and earth;
you have revealed to little ones the mysteries of the Kingdom.**

5.

Matthew 11:28

**Come to me, all you who labor and are burdened,
and I will give you rest, says the Lord.**

6.

Matthew 23:11, 12b

**The greatest among you must be your servant.
Whoever humbles himself will be exalted.**

7.

Luke 21:36

**Be vigilant at all times
and pray that you may have the strength to stand before the Son of Man.**

8.

John 8:12

**I am the light of the world, says the Lord;
whoever follows me will have the light of life.**

9.

John 8:31b-32

**If you remain in my word, you will truly be my disciples,
and you will know the truth, says the Lord.**

10.

John 13:34

**I give you a new commandment:
love one another as I have loved you.**

11.

John 14:23

**Whoever loves me will keep my word
and my Father will love him
and we will come to him.**

12.

John 15:4a, 5b

**Remain in me, as I remain in you, says the Lord;
whoever remains in me will bear much fruit.**

13.

John 15:9b, 5b

**Remain in my love, says the Lord;
whoever remains in me and I in him will bear much fruit.**

742 GOSPEL

1.

Matthew 5:1-12a Rejoice and be glad, for your reward will be great in heaven.

✛ A reading from the holy Gospel according to Matthew

When Jesus saw the crowds, he went up the mountain,
   and after he had sat down, his disciples came to him.
He began to teach them, saying:

   "Blessed are the poor in spirit,
      for theirs is the Kingdom of heaven.
   Blessed are they who mourn,
      for they will be comforted.
   Blessed are the meek,
      for they will inherit the land.
   Blessed are they who hunger and thirst for righteousness,
      for they will be satisfied.
   Blessed are the merciful,
      for they will be shown mercy.
   Blessed are the clean of heart,
      for they will see God.
   Blessed are the peacemakers,
      for they will be called children of God.
   Blessed are they who are persecuted for the sake of righteousness,
      for theirs is the Kingdom of heaven.
   Blessed are you when they insult you and persecute you
      and utter every kind of evil against you falsely because of me.
   Rejoice and be glad,
      for your reward will be great in heaven."

The Gospel of the Lord.

2.

Matthew 5:13-16   You are the light of the world.

✠ A reading from the holy Gospel according to Matthew

Jesus said to his disciples:
"You are the salt of the earth.
But if salt loses its taste, with what can it be seasoned?
It is no longer good for anything
　but to be thrown out and trampled underfoot.
You are the light of the world.
A city set on a mountain cannot be hidden.
Nor do they light a lamp and then put it under a bushel basket;
　it is set on a lamp stand,
　where it gives light to all in the house.
Just so, your light must shine before others,
　that they may see your good deeds
　and glorify your heavenly Father."

The Gospel of the Lord.

3.

Matthew 7:21-27   The house built on rock and the house built on sand.

✠ A reading from the holy Gospel according to Matthew

Jesus said to his disciples:
"Not everyone who says to me, 'Lord, Lord,'
　will enter the Kingdom of heaven,
　but only the one who does the will of my Father in heaven.
Many will say to me on that day,
　'Lord, Lord, did we not prophesy in your name?
Did we not drive out demons in your name?
Did we not do mighty deeds in your name?'
Then I will declare to them solemnly,
　'I never knew you. Depart from me, you evildoers.'

"Everyone who listens to these words of mine and acts on them
　will be like a wise man who built his house on rock.
The rain fell, the floods came,
　and the winds blew and buffeted the house.
But it did not collapse; it had been set solidly on rock.
And everyone who listens to these words of mine
　but does not act on them
　will be like a fool who built his house on sand.

The Common of Holy Men and Women   1911

The rain fell, the floods came,
  and the winds blew and buffeted the house.
And it collapsed and was completely ruined."

The Gospel of the Lord.

4.

Matthew 11:25-30   Although you have hidden these things from the wise and the learned, you have revealed them to the childlike.

✢ **A reading from the holy Gospel according to Matthew**

At that time Jesus exclaimed:
"I give praise to you, Father, Lord of heaven and earth,
  for although you have hidden these things
  from the wise and the learned
  you have revealed them to the childlike.
Yes, Father, such has been your gracious will.
All things have been handed over to me by my Father.
No one knows the Son except the Father,
  and no one knows the Father except the Son
  and anyone to whom the Son wishes to reveal him."

"Come to me, all you who labor and are burdened,
  and I will give you rest.
Take my yoke upon you and learn from me,
  for I am meek and humble of heart;
  and you will find rest for yourselves.
For my yoke is easy, and my burden light."

The Gospel of the Lord.

5.

Matthew 13:44-46   He sells all that he has and buys that field.

✢ **A reading from the holy Gospel according to Matthew**

Jesus said to the crowds:
"The Kingdom of heaven is like a treasure buried in a field,
  which a person finds and hides again,
  and out of joy goes and sells all that he has and buys that field.
Again, the Kingdom of heaven is like a merchant
  searching for fine pearls.
When he finds a pearl of great price,
  he goes and sells all that he has and buys it."

The Gospel of the Lord.

6.

Matthew 16:24-27   Whoever loses his life for my sake will find it.

✠ A reading from the holy Gospel according to Matthew

Jesus said to his disciples,
  "Whoever wishes to come after me must deny himself,
    take up his cross, and follow me.
For whoever wishes to save his life will lose it,
  but whoever loses his life for my sake will find it.
What profit would there be for one to gain the whole world
  and forfeit his life?
Or what can one give in exchange for his life?
For the Son of Man will come with his angels in his Father's glory,
  and then he will repay each one according to his conduct."

The Gospel of the Lord.

7.

Matthew 18:1-5   Unless you turn and become like children, you will not enter the Kingdom of heaven.

✠ A reading from the holy Gospel according to Matthew

The disciples approached Jesus and said,
  "Who is the greatest in the Kingdom of heaven?"
He called a child over, placed it in their midst, and said,
  "Amen, I say to you, unless you turn and become like children,
    you will not enter the Kingdom of heaven.
Whoever humbles himself like this child
  is the greatest in the Kingdom of heaven.
And whoever receives one child such as this in my name receives me."

The Gospel of the Lord.

8. For Religious

Matthew 19:3-12   For the sake of the Kingdom of heaven.

☩ **A reading from the holy Gospel according to Matthew**

Some Pharisees approached Jesus and tested him, saying,
  "Is it lawful for a man to divorce his wife for any cause whatever?"
He said in reply,
  "Have you not read that from the beginning
  the Creator *made them male and female* and said,
  For this reason a man shall leave his father and mother
  and be joined to his wife, and the two shall become one flesh?
So they are no longer two, but one flesh.
Therefore, what God has joined together, man must not separate."
They said to him,
  "Then why did Moses command that the man give the woman
  a bill of divorce and dismiss her?"
He said to them, "Because of the hardness of your hearts
  Moses allowed you to divorce your wives,
  but from the beginning it was not so.
I say to you, whoever divorces his wife
  (unless the marriage is unlawful)
  and marries another commits adultery."
His disciples said to him,
  "If that is the case of a man with his wife,
  it is better not to marry."
He answered, "Not all can accept this word,
  but only those to whom that is granted.
Some are incapable of marriage because they were born so;
  some, because they were made so by others;
  some, because they have renounced marriage
  for the sake of the Kingdom of heaven.
Whoever can accept this ought to accept it."

The Gospel of the Lord.

9.

Matthew 19:27-29   You who have followed me will receive a hundred times more.

☩ A reading from the holy Gospel according to Matthew

Peter said to Jesus,
   "We have given up everything and followed you.
What will there be for us?"
Jesus said to them, "Amen, I say to you
   that you who have followed me, in the new age,
   when the Son of Man is seated on his throne of glory,
   will yourselves sit on twelve thrones,
   judging the twelve tribes of Israel.
And everyone who has given up houses or brothers or sisters
   or father or mother or children or lands
   for the sake of my name will receive a hundred times more,
   and will inherit eternal life."

The Gospel of the Lord.

10.

Matthew 22:34-40   Love the Lord your God and your neighbor as yourself.

☩ A reading from the holy Gospel according to Matthew

When the Pharisees heard that Jesus had silenced the Sadducees,
   they gathered together, and one of them
   a scholar of the law, tested him by asking,
   "Teacher, which commandment in the law is the greatest?"
He said to him,
   "You shall love the Lord, your God, with all your heart,
   with all your soul, and with all your mind.
This is the greatest and the first commandment.
The second is like it:
   You shall love your neighbor as yourself.
The whole law and the prophets depend on these two commandments."

The Gospel of the Lord.

11.

Matthew 25:1-13 Behold, the bridegroom! Come out to meet him!

✠ **A reading from the holy Gospel according to Matthew**

Jesus told his disciples this parable:
"The Kingdom of heaven will be like ten virgins
    who took their lamps and went out to meet the bridegroom.
Five of them were foolish and five were wise.
The foolish ones, when taking their lamps,
    brought no oil with them,
    but the wise brought flasks of oil with their lamps.
Since the bridegroom was long delayed,
    they all became drowsy and fell asleep.
At midnight, there was a cry,
    'Behold, the bridegroom!
    Come out to meet him!'
Then all those virgins got up and trimmed their lamps.
The foolish ones said to the wise,
    'Give us some of your oil,
    for our lamps are going out.'
But the wise ones replied,
    'No, for there may not be enough for us and you.
Go instead to the merchants and buy some for yourselves.'
While they went off to buy it,
    the bridegroom came
    and those who were ready went into the wedding feast with him.
Then the door was locked.
Afterwards the other virgins came and said,
    'Lord, Lord, open the door for us!'
But he said in reply,
    'Amen, I say to you, I do not know you.'
Therefore, stay awake,
    for you know neither the day nor the hour."

The Gospel of the Lord.

12. Long Form

Matthew 25:14-30   Since you were faithful in small matters, come, share your master's joy.

✠ A reading from the holy Gospel according to Matthew

Jesus told his disciples this parable:
"A man who was going on a journey called in his servants
   and entrusted his possessions to them.
To one he gave five talents;
   to another, two; to a third, one—
   to each according to his ability.
Then he went away.
Immediately the one who received five talents went and traded with them,
   and made another five.
Likewise, the one who received two made another two.
But the man who received one went off and dug a hole in the ground
   and buried his master's money.
After a long time
   the master of those servants came back
   and settled accounts with them.
The one who had received five talents
   came forward bringing the additional five.
He said, 'Master, you gave me five talents.
See, I have made five more.'
His master said to him, 'Well done, my good and faithful servant.
Since you were faithful in small matters,
   I will give you great responsibilities.
Come, share your master's joy.'
Then the one who had received two talents also came forward and said,
   'Master, you gave me two talents.
See, I have made two more.'
His master said to him, 'Well done, my good and faithful servant.
Since you were faithful in small matters,
   I will give you great responsibilities.
Come, share your master's joy.'
Then the one who had received the one talent came forward and said,
   'Master, I knew you were a demanding person,
   harvesting where you did not plant
   and gathering where you did not scatter;
   so out of fear I went off and buried your talent in the ground.
Here it is back.'
His master said to him in reply, 'You wicked, lazy servant!
So you knew that I harvest where I did not plant
   and gather where I did not scatter?
Should you not then have put my money in the bank
   so that I could have got it back with interest on my return?

The Common of Holy Men and Women 1917

Now then! Take the talent from him and give it to the one with ten.
For to everyone who has
   more will be given and he will grow rich;
   but from the one who has not
   even what he has will be taken away.
And throw this useless servant into the darkness outside,
   where there will be wailing and grinding of teeth.'"

The Gospel of the Lord.

OR Short Form

Matthew 25:14-23   Since you were faithful in small matters, come, share your master's joy.

✛ **A reading from the holy Gospel according to Matthew**

Jesus told his disciples this parable:
"A man who was going on a journey
   called in his servants and entrusted his possessions to them.
To one he gave five talents;
   to another, two; to a third, one—
   to each according to his ability.
Then he went away.
Immediately the one who received five talents went and traded with them,
   and made another five.
Likewise, the one who received two made another two.
But the man who received one went off and dug a hole in the ground
   and buried his master's money.
After a long time
   the master of those servants came back and settled accounts with them.
The one who had received five talents came forward
   bringing the additional five.
He said, 'Master, you gave me five talents.
See, I have made five more.'
His master said to him, 'Well done, my good and faithful servant.
Since you were faithful in small matters,
   I will give you great responsibilities.
Come, share your master's joy.'
Then the one who had received two talents also came forward and said,
   'Master, you gave me two talents.
See, I have made two more.'
His master said to him, 'Well done, my good and faithful servant.
Since you were faithful in small matters,
   I will give you great responsibilities.
Come, share your master's joy.'"

The Gospel of the Lord.

14.

Mark 3:31-35   Whoever does the will of God is my brother and sister and mother.

✠ A reading from the holy Gospel according to Mark

The mother of Jesus and his brothers arrived.
Standing outside they sent word to him and called him.
A crowd seated around him told him,
 "Your mother and your brothers and your sisters
 are outside asking for you."
But he said to them in reply,
 "Who are my mother and my brothers?"
And looking around at those seated in the circle he said,
 "Here are my mother and my brothers.
For whoever does the will of God
 is my brother and sister and mother."

The Gospel of the Lord.

15. For Teachers

Mark 9:34-37   Whoever receives such a child as this, receives me.

✠ A reading from the holy Gospel according to Mark

Jesus' disciples had been discussing among themselves
 who was the greatest.
Then he sat down, called the Twelve, and said to them,
 "If anyone wishes to be first,
 he shall be the last of all and the servant of all."
Taking a child he placed it in their midst,
 and putting his arms around it he said to them,
 "Whoever receives one child such as this in my name, receives me;
 and whoever receives me,
 receives not me but the One who sent me."

The Gospel of the Lord.

16. For Teachers

Mark 10:13-16   Let the children come to me; do not prevent them.

✣ **A reading from the holy Gospel according to Mark**

**People were bringing children to Jesus that he might touch them,
   but the disciples rebuked them.
When Jesus saw this he became indignant and said to them,
   "Let the children come to me; do not prevent them,
   for the Kingdom of God belongs to such as these.
Amen, I say to you,
   whoever does not accept the Kingdom of God like a child
   will not enter it."
Then he embraced them and blessed them,
   placing his hands on them.**

The Gospel of the Lord.

17. For Religious

Long Form

Mark 10:17-30   Go, sell what you have, and give to the poor; then come, follow me.

✠ A reading from the holy Gospel according to Mark

As Jesus was setting out on a journey,
   a man ran up, knelt down before him, and asked him,
   "Good teacher, what must I do to inherit eternal life?"
Jesus answered him, "Why do you call me good?
No one is good but God alone.
You know the commandments:
   You shall not kill;
   you shall not commit adultery;
   you shall not steal;
   you shall not bear false witness;
   you shall not defraud;
   honor your father and your mother."
He replied and said to him,
   "Teacher, all of these I have observed from my youth."
Jesus, looking at him, loved him and said to him,
   "You are lacking in one thing.
Go, sell what you have, and give to the poor
   and you will have treasure in heaven; then come, follow me."
At that statement his face fell,
   and he went away sad, for he had many possessions.

Jesus looked around and said to his disciples,
   "How hard it is for those who have wealth
   to enter the Kingdom of God!"
The disciples were amazed at his words.
So Jesus again said to them in reply,
   "Children, how hard it is to enter the Kingdom of God!
It is easier for a camel to pass through the eye of a needle
   than for one who is rich to enter the Kingdom of God."
They were exceedingly astonished
   and said among themselves, "Then who can be saved?"
Jesus looked at them and said,
   "For men it is impossible, but not for God.
All things are possible for God."
Peter began to say to him,
   "We have given up everything and followed you."

Jesus said, "Amen, I say to you,
   there is no one who has given up house or brothers or sisters
   or mother or father or children or lands for my sake
   and for the sake of the Gospel
   who will not receive a hundred times more now in this present age:
   houses and brothers and sisters and mothers and children and lands,
   with persecutions, and eternal life in the age to come."

The Gospel of the Lord.

OR Short Form

Mark 10:17-27   Go, sell what you have, and give to the poor; then come, follow me.

☩ A reading from the holy Gospel according to Mark

As Jesus was setting out on a journey,
   a man ran up, knelt down before him, and asked him,
   "Good teacher, what must I do to inherit eternal life?"
Jesus answered him, "Why do you call me good?
No one is good but God alone.
You know the commandments:
   You shall not kill;
   you shall not commit adultery;
   you shall not steal;
   you shall not bear false witness;
   you shall not defraud;
   honor your father and your mother."
He replied and said to him,
   "Teacher, all of these I have observed from my youth."
Jesus, looking at him, loved him and said to him,
   "You are lacking in one thing.
Go, sell what you have, and give to the poor
   and you will have treasure in heaven; then come, follow me."
At that statement his face fell,
   and he went away sad, for he had many possessions.

Jesus looked around and said to his disciples,
   "How hard it is for those who have wealth
   to enter the Kingdom of God!"
The disciples were amazed at his words.
So Jesus again said to them in reply,
   "Children, how hard it is to enter the Kingdom of God!
It is easier for a camel to pass through the eye of a needle
   than for one who is rich to enter the Kingdom of God."
They were exceedingly astonished
   and said among themselves, "Then who can be saved?"
Jesus looked at them and said,
   "For men it is impossible, but not for God.
All things are possible for God."

The Gospel of the Lord.

18.

Luke 6:27-38   Be merciful, just as your Father is merciful.

✝ A reading from the holy Gospel according to Luke

**Jesus said to his disciples:
"To you who hear I say,
   love your enemies, do good to those who hate you,
   bless those who curse you, pray for those who mistreat you.
To the person who strikes you on one cheek,
   offer the other one as well,
   and from the person who takes your cloak,
   do not withhold even your tunic.
Give to everyone who asks of you,
   and from the one who takes what is yours do not demand it back.
Do to others as you would have them do to you.
For if you love those who love you,
   what credit is that to you?
Even sinners love those who love them.
And if you do good to those who do good to you,
   what credit is that to you?
Even sinners do the same.
If you lend money to those from whom you expect repayment,
   what credit is that to you?
Even sinners lend to sinners,
   and get back the same amount.
But rather, love your enemies and do good to them,
   and lend expecting nothing back;
   then your reward will be great
   and you will be children of the Most High,
   for he himself is kind to the ungrateful and the wicked.
Be merciful, just as also your Father is merciful.**

**"Stop judging and you will not be judged.
Stop condemning and you will not be condemned.
Forgive and you will be forgiven.
Give and gifts will be given to you;
   a good measure, packed together, shaken down, and overflowing,
   will be poured into your lap.
For the measure with which you measure
   will in return be measured out to you."**

The Gospel of the Lord.

1926 *The Common of Holy Men and Women*

19. For Religious

Luke 9:57-62   I will follow you wherever you go.

✠ **A reading from the holy Gospel according to Luke**

**As Jesus and his disciples were proceeding on their journey,
someone said to him, "I will follow you wherever you go."
Jesus answered him,
"Foxes have dens and birds of the sky have nests,
but the Son of Man has nowhere to rest his head."
And to another he said, "Follow me."
But he replied, "Lord, let me go first and bury my father."
But he answered him, "Let the dead bury their dead.
But you, go and proclaim the Kingdom of God."
And another said, "I will follow you, Lord,
but first let me say farewell to my family at home."
Jesus said to him, "No one who sets a hand to the plow
and looks to what was left behind is fit for the Kingdom of God."**

The Gospel of the Lord.

20.

Luke 10:38-42   Martha welcomed him. Mary has chosen the better part.

✠ **A reading from the holy Gospel according to Luke**

**Jesus entered a village
where a woman whose name was Martha welcomed him.
She had a sister named Mary
who sat beside the Lord at his feet listening to him speak.
Martha, burdened with much serving, came to him and said,
"Lord, do you not care
that my sister has left me by myself to do the serving?
Tell her to help me."
The Lord said to her in reply,
"Martha, Martha, you are anxious and worried about many things.
There is need of only one thing.
Mary has chosen the better part and it will not be taken from her."**

The Gospel of the Lord.

21. For Religious

Luke 12:32-34   Your Father is pleased to give you the Kingdom.

✠ **A reading from the holy Gospel according to Luke**

**Jesus said to his disciples:
"Do not be afraid any longer, little flock,
   for your Father is pleased to give you the Kingdom.
Sell your belongings and give alms.
Provide money bags for yourselves that do not wear out,
   an inexhaustible treasure in heaven
   that no thief can reach nor moth destroy.
For where your treasure is, there also will your heart be."**

The Gospel of the Lord.

22.

Luke 12:35-40   You also must be prepared.

✠ **A reading from the holy Gospel according to Luke**

**Jesus said to his disciples:
"Gird your loins and light your lamps
   and be like servants who await their master's return from a wedding,
   ready to open immediately when he comes and knocks.
Blessed are those servants whom the master finds vigilant on his arrival.
Amen, I say to you, he will gird himself,
   have them recline at table, and proceed to wait on them.
And should he come in the second or third watch
   and find them prepared in this way,
   blessed are those servants.
Be sure of this:
   if the master of the house had known the hour
   when the thief was coming,
   he would not have let his house be broken into.
You also must be prepared, for at an hour you do not expect,
   the Son of Man will come."**

The Gospel of the Lord.

1928   *The Common of Holy Men and Women*

23. For Religious

Luke 14:25-33   Everyone of you who does not renounce all his possessions cannot be my disciple.

✣   **A reading from the holy Gospel according to Luke**

Great crowds were traveling with Jesus,
  and he turned and addressed them,
  "If anyone comes to me without hating his father and mother,
  wife and children, brothers and sisters,
  and even his own life,
  he cannot be my disciple.
Whoever does not carry his own cross and come after me
  cannot be my disciple.
Which of you wishing to construct a tower
  does not first sit down and calculate the cost
  to see if there is enough for its completion?
Otherwise, after laying the foundation
  and finding himself unable to finish the work
  the onlookers should laugh at him and say,
  'This one began to build but did not have the resources to finish.'
Or what king marching into battle would not first sit down
  and decide whether with ten thousand troops
  he can successfully oppose another king
  advancing upon him with twenty thousand troops?
But if not, while he is still far away,
  he will send a delegation to ask for peace terms.
In the same way,
  everyone of you who does not renounce all his possessions
  cannot be my disciple."

The Gospel of the Lord.

24.

John 15:1-8   Whoever remains in me, and I in him, will bear much fruit.

✣   **A reading from the holy Gospel according to John**

Jesus said to his disciples:
"I am the true vine, and my Father is the vine grower.
He takes away every branch in me that does not bear fruit,
  and everyone that does he prunes so that it bears more fruit.
You are already pruned because of the word that I spoke to you.
Remain in me, as I remain in you.

Just as a branch cannot bear fruit on its own
  unless it remains on the vine,
  so neither can you unless you remain in me.
I am the vine, you are the branches.
Whoever remains in me and I in him will bear much fruit,
  because without me you can do nothing.
Anyone who does not remain in me
  will be thrown out like a branch and wither;
  people will gather them and throw them into a fire
  and they will be burned.
If you remain in me and my words remain in you,
  ask for whatever you want and it will be done for you.
By this is my Father glorified,
  that you bear much fruit and become my disciples."

The Gospel of the Lord.

25.

John 15:9-17   You are my friends if you do what I command you.

✠ **A reading from the holy Gospel according to John**

Jesus said to his disciples:
"As the Father loves me, so I also love you.
Remain in my love.
If you keep my commandments, you will remain in my love,
  just as I have kept my Father's commandments
  and remain in his love.

"I have told you this so that my joy might be in you
  and your joy might be complete.
This is my commandment: love one another as I love you.
No one has greater love than this,
  to lay down one's life for one's friends.
You are my friends if you do what I command you.
I no longer call you slaves,
  because a slave does not know what his master is doing.
I have called you friends,
  because I have told you everything I have heard from my Father.
It was not you who chose me, but I who chose you
  and appointed you to go and bear fruit that will remain,
  so that whatever you ask the Father in my name he may give you.
This I command you: love one another."

The Gospel of the Lord.

26.

John 17:20-26   I wish that where I am they also may be with me.

✢ A reading from the holy Gospel according to John

Jesus raised his eyes to heaven and said:
"Holy Father, I pray not only for these,
   but also for those who will believe in me through their word,
   so that they may all be one,
   as you, Father, are in me and I in you,
   that they also may be in us,
   that the world may believe that you sent me.
And I have given them the glory you gave me,
   so that they may be one, as we are one,
   I in them and you in me,
   that they may be brought to perfection as one,
   that the world may know that you sent me,
   and that you loved them even as you loved me.
Father, they are your gift to me.
I wish that where I am they also may be with me,
   that they may see my glory that you gave me,
   because you loved me before the foundation of the world.
Righteous Father, the world also does not know you,
   but I know you, and they know that you sent me.
I made known to them your name and I will make it known,
   that the love with which you loved me
   may be in them and I in them."

The Gospel of the Lord.

APPENDIX I

SEQUENCE

This sequence is for optional use. The Latin text is given here for use in those particular circumstances where it may be pastorally suitable, and especially where it is sung according to the plain chant melody found in the Graduale Romanum.

OUR LADY OF SORROWS

This sequence may be sung in its entirety or in the shorter form beginning with the verse *Sancta Mater.*

Stabat Mater dolorosa
iuxta crucem lacrimosa,
dum pendebat Filius.

Cuius animam gementem,
contristatam et dolentem
pertransivit gladius.

O quam tristis et afflicta
fuit illa benedicta
mater Unigeniti!

Quæ mærebat et dolebat
pia Mater, dum videbat
Nati pœnas incliti.

Quis est homo qui non fleret,
Matrem Christi si videret
in tanto supplicio?

Quis non posset contristari,
piam Matrem contemplari
dolentem cum Filio?

Pro peccatis suæ gentis
vidit Iesum in tormentis,
et flagellis subditum.

Vidit suum dulcem Natum
morientem desolatum,
dum emisit spiritum.

Eia, Mater, fons amoris,
me sentire vim doloris
fac, ut tecum lugeam.

Fac ut ardeat cor meum
in amando Christum Deum,
ut sibi complaceam.

*Sancta Mater, istud agas
Crucifixi fige plagas
cordi meo valide.

Tui Nati vulnerati,
tam dignati pro me pati,
pœnas mecum divide.

Fac me tecum pie flere,
Crucifixo condolere,
donec ego vixero.

Iuxta crucem tecum stare,
ac me tibi sociare
in planctu desidero.

Virgo virginum præclara,
mihi iam non sis amara:
fac me tecum plangere.

Fac ut portem Christi mortem,
passionis fac me sortem,
et plagas recolere.

Fac me plagis vulnerari,
cruce hac inebriari,
et cruore Filii.

Flammis urar ne succensus,
per te, Virgo, sim defensus
in die iudicii.

Fac me cruce custodiri,
morte Christi præmuniri,
confoveri gratia.

Quando corpus morietur,
fac ut animæ donetur
Paradisi gloria.

(*Graduale Romanum* 1974, pp. 602–605)

APPENDIX II

TABLE OF READINGS

Weekdays, Year I, are indicated by WI following the Lectionary number; Year II by WII; Proper of the Saints by PS; Commons by COM; Ritual Masses by RM; Masses for Various Needs by MVN; Votive Masses by VM; and Masses for the Dead by MD.

Genesis 1:1-19 329WI
Genesis 1:11-12 912MVN
Genesis 1:14-18 902MVN
Genesis 1:20–2:4a 330WI
Genesis 1:26–2:3 559PS 882MVN 907MVN
Genesis 1:26-28, 31a 801RM
Genesis 2:4b-9, 15-17 331WI
Genesis 2:4b-9, 15 882MVN 907MVN
Genesis 2:18-25 332WI
Genesis 2:18-24 801RM
Genesis 3:1-8 333WI
Genesis 3:9-24 334WI
Genesis 3:9-15, 20 689PS 707COM 1002VM
Genesis 4:1-15, 25 335WI
Genesis 4:3-10 882MVN 897MVN
Genesis 6:5-8; 7:1-5, 10 336WI
Genesis 8:6-13, 20-22 337WI
Genesis 9:1-13 338WI
Genesis 11:1-9 339WI
Genesis 12:1-9 371WI
Genesis 12:1-7 707COM
Genesis 12:1-4a 737COM 743RM 811RM 857MVN
Genesis 13:2, 5-18 372WI
Genesis 14:18-20 785RM 976VM
Genesis 15:1-12, 17-18 373WI
Genesis 15:1-6, 18a 751RM
Genesis 16:1-12, 15-16 374WI
Genesis 17:1, 9-10, 15-22 375WI
Genesis 17:1-8 751RM
Genesis 17:3-9 254WI 254WII
Genesis 18:1-15 376WI
Genesis 18:16-33 377WI
Genesis 19:15-29 378WI
Genesis 21:5, 8-20 379WI
Genesis 22:1-19 380WI
Genesis 23:1-4, 19; 24:1-8, 62-67 381WI
Genesis 24:48-51, 58-67 801RM

Genesis 27:1-5, 15-29 382WI
Genesis 28:10-22a 383WI
Genesis 28:11-18 817RM
Genesis 32:22-32 384WI
Genesis 35:1-4, 6-7a 751RM
Genesis 37:3-4, 12-13a, 17b-28 234WI 234WII
Genesis 41:55-57; 42:5-7a, 17-24a 385WI
Genesis 44:18-21, 23b-29; 45:1-5 386WI
Genesis 46:1-7, 28-30 387WI
Genesis 49:2, 8-10 193WI 193WII
Genesis 49:29-32; 50:15-26a 388WI

Exodus 1:8-14, 22 389WI
Exodus 2:1-15a 390WI
Exodus 3:1-6, 9-12 391WI 857MVN
Exodus 3:11-15 983VM
Exodus 3:13-20 392WI
Exodus 11:10–12:14 393WI
Exodus 12:1-8, 11-14 969VM
Exodus 12:21-27 976VM 989VM
Exodus 12:37-42 394WI
Exodus 14:5-18 395WI
Exodus 14:21–15:1 396WI
Exodus 16:1-5, 9-15 397WI
Exodus 16:2-4, 12-15 785RM 976VM
Exodus 17:1-7 236WI 236WII
Exodus 17:3-7 756RM
Exodus 19:1-2, 9-11, 16-20b 398WI
Exodus 20:1-17* 399WI
Exodus 23:20-23 650PS
Exodus 24:3-8 400WI 785RM 976VM 989VM
Exodus 32:7-14 247WI 247WII 719COM
Exodus 32:15-24, 30-34 401WI
Exodus 33:7-11; 34:5b-9, 28 402WI
Exodus 34:4b-6, 8-9 995VM
Exodus 34:29-35 403WI
Exodus 40:16-21, 34-38 404WI

* Readings with a longer and shorter option are indicated with an asterisk.
The numbers in the columns are the Lectionary reference numbers, not the page numbers.

Leviticus 19:1-2, 11-18 224WI 224WII
Leviticus 19:1-2, 17-18 737COM
Leviticus 23:1, 4-11, 15-16, 27, 34b-37 405WI
Leviticus 25:1, 8-17 406WI

Numbers 3:5-9 770RM
Numbers 6:22-27 882MVN 902MVN
Numbers 11:4b-15 407WI
Numbers 11:11b-12, 14-17, 24-25a 770RM
Numbers 12:1-13 408WI
Numbers 13:1-2, 25–14:1, 26-29, 34-35 409WI
Numbers 20:1-13 410WI
Numbers 21:4-9 252WI 252WII 638PS
Numbers 24:2-7, 15-17a 187WI 187WII

Deuteronomy 1:9-14 775RM
Deuteronomy 4:1, 5-9 239WI 239WII
Deuteronomy 4:32-40 411WI
Deuteronomy 6:1-7 748RM
Deuteronomy 6:3-9 623PS 737COM 780RM
Deuteronomy 6:4-13 412WI
Deuteronomy 7:6-11 995VM
Deuteronomy 8:2-3, 14b-16a 785RM 976VM
Deuteronomy 8:7-18 917MVN
Deuteronomy 10:8-9 719COM 737COM
Deuteronomy 10:12-22 413WI 995VM
Deuteronomy 10:17-19 927MVN
Deuteronomy 24:17-22 922MVN 927MVN
Deuteronomy 26:16-19 229WI 229WII
Deuteronomy 30:1-4 867MVN
Deuteronomy 30:10-14 780RM 838MVN
Deuteronomy 30:15-20 220WI 220WII 751RM
Deuteronomy 31:1-8 414WI
Deuteronomy 34:1-12 415WI

Joshua 3:7-10a, 11, 13-17 416WI
Joshua 8:30-35 817RM
Joshua 24:1-13 417WI
Joshua 24:1-2a, 15-17, 18b-25a 751RM
Joshua 24:14-29 418WI

Judges 2:11-19 419WI
Judges 6:11-24a 420WI
Judges 9:6-15 421WI
Judges 11:29-39a 422WI
Judges 13:2-7, 24-25a 195WI 195WII

Ruth 1:1, 3-6, 14b-16, 22 423WI
Ruth 2:1-3, 8-11; 4:13-17 424WI

1 Samuel 1:1-8 305WII
1 Samuel 1:9-20 306WII
1 Samuel 1:24-28 198WI 198WII
1 Samuel 3:1-10, 19-20 307WII
1 Samuel 3:1-10 811RM 857MVN
1 Samuel 4:1-11 308WII
1 Samuel 8:4-7, 10-22a 309WII
1 Samuel 9:1-4, 17-19; 10:1a 310WII
1 Samuel 15:16-23 311WII
1 Samuel 16:1-13 312WII
1 Samuel 16:1b, 6-13a 719COM
1 Samuel 17:32-33, 37, 40-51 313WII
1 Samuel 18:6-9; 19:1-7 314WII
1 Samuel 24:3-21 315WII
1 Samuel 26:2, 7-9, 12-13, 22-23 958MVN

2 Samuel 1:1-4, 11-12, 19, 23-27 316WII
2 Samuel 5:1-7, 10 317WII
2 Samuel 6:12b-15, 17-19 318WII
2 Samuel 7:1-5, 8b-12, 14a, 16 200WI 200WII
2 Samuel 7:1-5, 8b-11, 16 707COM
2 Samuel 7:4-17 319WII
2 Samuel 7:4-5a, 12-14a, 16 543PS
2 Samuel 7:18-19, 24, 29 320WII
2 Samuel 11:1-4a, 5-10a, 13-17 321WII
2 Samuel 12:1-7a, 10-17 322WII
2 Samuel 15:13-14, 30; 16:5-13a 323WII
2 Samuel 18:9-10, 14b, 24-25a, 30–19:3 324WII
2 Samuel 24:2, 9-17 325WII

1 Kings 2:1-4, 10-12 326WII
1 Kings 3:4-13 328WII
1 Kings 3:11-14 725COM 882MVN
1 Kings 8:1-7, 9-13 329WII
1 Kings 8:22-23, 27-30 330WII 701COM
1 Kings 8:55-61 943MVN
1 Kings 10:1-10 331WII
1 Kings 11:4-13 332WII
1 Kings 11:29-32; 12:19 333WII
1 Kings 12:26-32; 13:33-34 334WII
1 Kings 17:1-6 359WII
1 Kings 17:7-16 360WII
1 Kings 18:20-39 361WII
1 Kings 18:41-46 362WII
1 Kings 19:1-8 790RM
1 Kings 19:4-9a, 11-15a 737COM 811RM 852MVN
1 Kings 19:4-8 785RM 796RM 976VM

Appendix II—Table of Readings 1939

1 Kings 19:9a, 11-16 363WII
1 Kings 19:16b, 19-21 737COM 811RM
  857MVN
1 Kings 19:19-21 364WII
1 Kings 21:1-16 365WII
1 Kings 21:17-29 366WII

2 Kings 2:1, 6-14 367WII
2 Kings 4:18b-21, 32-37 250WI 250WII
2 Kings 5:1-15a 237WI 237WII
2 Kings 5:9-15a 751RM
2 Kings 11:1-4, 9-18, 20 369WII
2 Kings 17:5-8, 13-15a, 18 371WII
2 Kings 19:9b-11, 14-21, 31-35a, 36 372WII
2 Kings 20:1-6 933MVN
2 Kings 22:8-13; 23:1-3 373WII
2 Kings 24:8-17 374WII
2 Kings 25:1-12 375WII

1 Chronicles 15:3-4, 15-16; 16:1-2 621PS
  707COM

2 Chronicles 5:6-10, 13–6:2 701COM
2 Chronicles 24:17-25 370WII
2 Chronicles 24:18-22 713COM

Ezra 1:1-6 449WI
Ezra 6:7-8, 12b, 14-20 450WI
Ezra 9:5-9 451WI

Nehemiah 2:1-8 457WI
Nehemiah 8:1-4a, 5-6, 7b-12 458WI
Nehemiah 8:2-4a, 5-6, 8-10 780RM 816RM

Tobit 1:3; 2:1a-8 353WI
Tobit 2:9-14 354WI
Tobit 3:1-11a, 16-17a 355WI
Tobit 6:10-11; 7:1, 9-17; 8:4-9a 356WI
Tobit 7:6-14 801RM
Tobit 8:4b-8 737COM 801RM
Tobit 11:5-17 357WI
Tobit 12:1, 5-15, 20 358WI
Tobit 12:6-13 529PS 737COM

Judith 8:2-8 737COM

Esther 4:17, n; p-r; aa-bb, gg-hh 227WI 227WII
Esther 4:17b-17e, 17i-17l 877MVN 882MVN
  938MVN
Esther 4:17b-17g, 17l 737COM

1 Maccabees 1:10-15, 41-43, 54-57, 62-64
  497WI
1 Maccabees 2:15-29 500WI
1 Maccabees 2:49-52, 57-64 877MVN
1 Maccabees 4:36-37, 52-59 501WI
1 Maccabees 4:52-59 817RM
1 Maccabees 6:1-13 502WI

2 Maccabees 6:18-31 498WI
2 Maccabees 6:18, 21, 24-31 713COM
2 Maccabees 7:1, 20-31 499WI
2 Maccabees 7:1, 20-23, 27b-29 713COM
2 Maccabees 7:1-2, 9-14 576PS 713COM
2 Maccabees 12:43-46 1011MD

Job 1:6-22 455WII
Job 3:1-3, 11-17, 20-23 456WII 790RM
Job 7:1-4, 6-11 790RM
Job 7:12-21 790RM
Job 9:1-12, 14-16 457WII
Job 19:1, 23-27a 1011MD
Job 19:21-27 458WII
Job 19:23-27a 790RM 796RM
Job 31:16-20, 24-25, 31-32 882MVN 922MVN
Job 38:1, 12-21; 40:3-5 459WII
Job 42:1-3, 5-6, 12-16 460WII

Proverbs 2:1-9 597PS 806RM
Proverbs 3:27-34 449WII
Proverbs 4:7-13 806RM
Proverbs 8:22-31 707COM
Proverbs 9:1-6 785RM 976VM
Proverbs 21:1-6, 10-13 450WII
Proverbs 30:5-9 451WII
Proverbs 31:10-13, 19-20, 30-31 540PS
  691PS 737COM

Ecclesiastes 1:2-11 452WII
Ecclesiastes 3:1-11 453WII
Ecclesiastes 11:9–12:8 454WII

Song of Songs 2:8-14 197WI 197WII 811RM
Song of Songs 2:8-10, 14, 16a; 8:6-7a 801RM
Song of Songs 3:1-4a 603PS
Song of Songs 8:6-7 530PS 731COM
  811RM 852MVN

Wisdom 1:1-7 491WI
Wisdom 2:1a, 12-22 248WI 248WII 969VM
Wisdom 2:23–3:9 492WI

1940 *Appendix II—Table of Readings*

Wisdom 3:1-9* 615PS 644PS 713COM
   1011MD
Wisdom 4:7-15 1011MD
Wisdom 6:1-11 493WI
Wisdom 7:7-10, 15-16 522PS 641PS
   725COM
Wisdom 7:22–8:1 494WI
Wisdom 9:9-11, 13-18 790RM
Wisdom 13:1-9 495WI
Wisdom 18:14-16; 19:6-9 496WI

Sirach 1:1-10 341WI
Sirach 2:1-13 342WI
Sirach 2:7-13 616PS 737COM
Sirach 3:19-26 737COM
Sirach 4:12-22 343WI
Sirach 5:1-10 344WI
Sirach 6:5-17 345WI
Sirach 15:1-6 625PS 675PS 725COM
Sirach 17:1-13 346WI
Sirach 17:20-28 347WI
Sirach 24:1-2, 5-7, 12-16, 26-30 707COM
Sirach 26:1-4, 16-21 632PS 658PS 737COM
   801RM
Sirach 35:1-15 348WI
Sirach 36:1-2a, 5-6, 13-19 349WI
Sirach 39:1, 5-8 775RM
Sirach 39:8-14 672PS 725COM
Sirach 42:15-26 350WI
Sirach 44:1, 9-13 351WI
Sirach 44:1, 10-15 606PS
Sirach 47:2-13 327WII
Sirach 48:1-15 368WII
Sirach 48:1-4, 9-11 186WI 186WII
Sirach 50:24-26 943MVN
Sirach 51:1-12 713COM
Sirach 51:11-17 983VM
Sirach 51:17-27 352WI

Isaiah 1:10, 16-20 231WI 231WII
Isaiah 1:10-17 389WII
Isaiah 2:1-5 175WI 175WII 872MVN
Isaiah 4:2-6 175WI 175WII
Isaiah 6:1-8 388WII 687PS 719COM
Isaiah 6:1-2a, 3-8 775RM
Isaiah 6:1, 6-8 857MVN
Isaiah 7:1-9 390WII
Isaiah 7:10-14; 8:10 545PS 707COM
Isaiah 7:10-14 196WI 196WII
Isaiah 9:1-6 627PS 707COM 887MVN

Isaiah 10:5-7, 13-16 391WII
Isaiah 11:1-10 176WI 176WII
Isaiah 11:1-4a 764RM
Isaiah 25:6-10a 177WI 177WII 963MVN
Isaiah 25:6a, 7-9 1011MD 1017MD
Isaiah 25:6a, 7-8b 1023MD
Isaiah 26:1-6 178WI 178WII
Isaiah 26:7-9, 12, 16-19 392WII
Isaiah 29:17-24 179WI 179WII
Isaiah 30:19-21, 23-26 180WI 180WII
Isaiah 32:15-18 882MVN 887MVN
Isaiah 35:1-10 181WI 181WII 790RM
Isaiah 38:1-6, 21-22, 7-8 393WII
Isaiah 40:1-11 182WI 182WII
Isaiah 40:25-31 183WI 183WII
Isaiah 41:8-10, 13-14 877MVN
Isaiah 41:13-20 184WI 184WII
Isaiah 42:1-7 257WI 257WII
Isaiah 42:1-3 764RM
Isaiah 44:1-5 811RM
Isaiah 44:1-3 751RM
Isaiah 45:6b-8, 18, 21b-25 189WI 189WII
Isaiah 48:17-19 185WI 185WII
Isaiah 49:1-6 258WI 258WII 587PS
Isaiah 49:8-15 246WI 246WII
Isaiah 49:13-15 995VM
Isaiah 50:4-9a 259WI 259WII 958MVN
   969VM
Isaiah 52:7-10 526PS 665PS 683PS
   719COM
Isaiah 52:13–53:12 790RM 969VM 982VM
Isaiah 53:1-5, 10-11 933MVN
Isaiah 54:1-10 190WI 190WII
Isaiah 55:1-3, 6-9 892MVN
Isaiah 55:6-13 912MVN
Isaiah 55:6-9 948MVN
Isaiah 55:10-11 225WI 225WII 780RM
Isaiah 56:1-3a, 6-8 191WI 191WII
Isaiah 56:1, 6-7 701COM 827MVN
   872MVN
Isaiah 57:15-19 887MVN
Isaiah 58:1-9a 221WI 221WII
Isaiah 58:6-11 630PS 676PS 737COM
   882MVN 922MVN
Isaiah 58:9b-14 222WI 222WII
Isaiah 60:1-6 827MVN 872MVN
Isaiah 61:1-3a, 6a, 8b-9 260WI 260WII
   764RM
Isaiah 61:1-3a 581PS 673PS 719COM
   770RM 790RM 833MVN 843MVN

Isaiah 61:9-11 573PS 707COM 811RM
  852MVN
Isaiah 63:7-9 943MVN
Isaiah 65:17-21 244WI 244WII
Isaiah 66:10-14c 531PS 649PS

Jeremiah 1:1, 4-10 397WII
Jeremiah 1:1, 7-19 634PS
Jeremiah 1:4-10 586PS
Jeremiah 1:4-9 719COM 770RM 775RM
  843MVN 857MVN
Jeremiah 2:1-3, 7-8, 12-13 398WII
Jeremiah 3:14-17 399WII
Jeremiah 7:1-11 400WII
Jeremiah 7:23-28 240WI
Jeremiah 11:18-20 249WI 249WII
Jeremiah 13:1-11 401WII
Jeremiah 14:17-22 402WII
Jeremiah 15:10, 16-21 403WII
Jeremiah 17:5-10 233WI 233WII
Jeremiah 18:1-6 404WII
Jeremiah 18:18-20 232WI 232WII
Jeremiah 20:7-9 737COM 857MVN
Jeremiah 20:10-13 255WI 255WII
Jeremiah 23:5-8 194WI 194WII
Jeremiah 26:1-9 405WII
Jeremiah 26:11-16, 24 406WII
Jeremiah 28:1-17 407WII
Jeremiah 30:1-2, 12-15, 18-22 408WII
Jeremiah 31:1-7 409WII
Jeremiah 31:1-4 995VM
Jeremiah 31:31-37 811RM
Jeremiah 31:31-34 410WII 751RM 892MVN
Jeremiah 31:31-32a, 33-34a 801RM

Lamentations 2:2, 10-14, 18-19 376WII
Lamentations 3:17-26 938MVN 1011MD
Lamentations 3:22-26 1017MD 1023MD

Baruch 1:15-22 459WI
Baruch 4:5-12, 27-29 460WI

Ezekiel 1:2-5, 24-28c 413WII
Ezekiel 2:8–3:4 414WII
Ezekiel 3:16-21 612PS 719COM 882MVN
Ezekiel 9:1-7; 10:18-22 415WII
Ezekiel 12:1-12 416WII
Ezekiel 16:1-15, 60, 63 417WII
Ezekiel 16:59-63 417WII
Ezekiel 18:1-10, 13b, 30-32 418WII

Ezekiel 18:21-28 228WI 228WII
Ezekiel 18:21-23, 30-32 948MVN
Ezekiel 24:15-24 419WII
Ezekiel 28:1-10 420WII
Ezekiel 34:1-11 421WII
Ezekiel 34:11-16 578PS 700PS 719COM
  827MVN 995VM
Ezekiel 36:23-28 422WII
Ezekiel 36:24-28 751RM 756RM 764RM
  862MVN 867MVN
Ezekiel 37:1-14 423WII
Ezekiel 37:15-19, 21b-22, 26-28 867MVN
Ezekiel 37:21-28 256WI 256WII
Ezekiel 43:1-7a 424WII
Ezekiel 43:1-2, 4-7a 701COM
Ezekiel 47:1-9, 12 245WI 245WII 756RM
Ezekiel 47:1-2, 8-9, 12 671PS 701COM

Daniel 1:1-6, 8-20 503WI
Daniel 2:31-45 504WI
Daniel 3:14-20, 91-92, 95 253WI 253WII
Daniel 3:25, 34-43 238WI 238WII 877MVN
  938MVN
Daniel 5:1-6, 13-14, 16-17, 23-28 505WI
Daniel 6:12-28 506WI
Daniel 7:2-14 507WI
Daniel 7:9-10, 13-14 614PS 647PS
Daniel 7:15-27 508WI
Daniel 9:4b-10 230WI 230WII
Daniel 12:1-3 1011MD
Daniel 13:1-9, 15-17, 19-30, 33-62 251WI
  251WII

Hosea 2:16, 17b-18, 21-22 383WII
Hosea 2:16b, 17b, 21-22 681PS 731COM
  827MVN
Hosea 2:16, 21-22 811RM 852MVN
Hosea 6:1-6 242WI 242WII
Hosea 8:4-7, 11-13 384WII
Hosea 10:1-3, 7-8, 12 385WII
Hosea 11:1-4, 8c-9 386WII
Hosea 11:1, 3-4, 8c-9 749RM 995VM
Hosea 14:2-10 241WI 241WII

Joel 1:13-15; 2:1-2 465WI
Joel 2:12-18 219WI 219WII 948MVN
Joel 2:21-24, 26-27 917MVN
Joel 2:23a–3:1-3a 764RM
Joel 3:1a-5 862MVN
Joel 4:12-21 466WI

1942 Appendix II—Table of Readings

Amos 2:6-10, 13-16 377WII
Amos 3:1-8; 4:11-12 378WII
Amos 5:4, 14-15, 21-24 892MVN
Amos 5:14-15, 21-24 379WII
Amos 7:10-17 380WII
Amos 8:4-6, 9-12 381WII
Amos 9:11-15 382WII

Jonah 1:1–2:1, 11 461WI
Jonah 3:1-10 226WI 226WII 462WI
 948MVN
Jonah 3:10–4:11 872MVN
Jonah 4:1-11 463WI

Micah 2:1-5 394WII
Micah 4:1-4 897MVN
Micah 5:1-4a 636PS 707COM
Micah 6:1-4, 6-8 395WII
Micah 6:6-8 598PS 737COM
Micah 7:7-9 243WI 243WII
Micah 7:14-15, 18-20 235WI 235WII 396WII

Nahum 2:1-3; 3:1-3, 6-7 411WII

Habakkuk 1:12–2:4 412WII

Zephaniah 2:3–3:12-13 737COM
Zephaniah 3:1-2, 9-13 188WI 188WII
Zephaniah 3:14-18 572PS
Zephaniah 3:14-18a 197WI 197WII 827MVN
Zephaniah 3:14-15 943MVN
Zephaniah 3:16-20 867MVN

Haggai 1:1-8 452WI
Haggai 1:15b–2:9 453WI

Zechariah 2:5-9, 14-15a 454WI
Zechariah 2:14-17 601PS 680PS 707COM
Zechariah 8:1-8 455WI
Zechariah 8:20-23 456WI 872MVN
Zechariah 9:9-10 897MVN
Zechariah 12:10-11; 13:6-7 969VM

Malachi 3:1-4, 23-24 199WI 199WII
Malachi 3:1-4 524PS
Malachi 3:13-20a 464WI

Matthew 1:1-16, 18-23* 636PS 712COM
Matthew 1:1-17 193WI 193WII
Matthew 1:16, 18-21, 24a 543PS

Matthew 1:18-25 988VM
Matthew 1:18-24 194WI 194WII
Matthew 2:13-15, 19-23 712COM 931MVN
Matthew 2:13-18 698PS
Matthew 4:12-17, 23-25 212WI 212WII
Matthew 4:18-22 684PS
Matthew 5:1-12 359WI 359WII
Matthew 5:1-12a 576PS 611PS 667PS
 742COM 768RM 795RM 805RM
 815RM 866MVN 881MVN 886MVN
 891MVN 896MVN 1016MD
Matthew 5:2-12a 763RM
Matthew 5:13-19 512PS 574PS 588PS
 610PS 694PS 730COM
Matthew 5:13-16 360WI 360WII 654PS
 742COM 763RM 774RM 805RM
Matthew 5:14-19 784RM
Matthew 5:17-19 239WI 239WII 361WI
 361WII
Matthew 5:20-26 228WI 228WII 362WI
 362WII
Matthew 5:20-24 886MVN 901MVN
Matthew 5:23-24 822RM
Matthew 5:27-32 363WI 363WII
Matthew 5:33-37 364WI 364WII
Matthew 5:38-48 886MVN 891MVN
 962MVN
Matthew 5:38-42 365WI 365WII
Matthew 5:43-48 229WI 229WII 366WI
 366WII
Matthew 6:1-6, 16-18 219WI 219WII 367WI
 367WII
Matthew 6:7-15 225WI 225WII 368WI
 368WII
Matthew 6:9-13 749RM
Matthew 6:19-23 369WI 369WII
Matthew 6:24-34 370WI 370WII
Matthew 6:31-34 906MVN 911MVN
Matthew 7:1-5 371WI 371WII
Matthew 7:6, 12-14 372WI 372WII
Matthew 7:7-12 227WI 227WII
Matthew 7:7-11 942MVN 947MVN
Matthew 7:15-20 373WI 373WII
Matthew 7:21-29 374WI 374WII 552PS
 567PS 641PS 730COM
Matthew 7:21, 24-29* 805RM
Matthew 7:21, 24-27 178WI 178WII
Matthew 7:21-27 598PS 742COM
Matthew 8:1-4 375WI 375WII 795RM
Matthew 8:5-17* 376WI 376WII 795RM

Appendix II—Table of Readings 1943

Matthew 8:5-11 175WI 175WII
Matthew 8:14-17 937MVN
Matthew 8:18-22 377WI 377WII
Matthew 8:23-27 378WI 378WII
Matthew 8:28-34 379WI 379WII
Matthew 9:1-8 380WI 380WII 952MVN
Matthew 9:9-13 381WI 381WII 643PS
Matthew 9:14-17 382WI 382WII
Matthew 9:14-15 221WI 221WII
Matthew 9:18-26 383WI 383WII
Matthew 9:27-31 179WI 179WII
Matthew 9:32-38 384WI 384WII
Matthew 9:35–10:1, 6-8 180WI 180WII
Matthew 9:35–10:1 612PS
Matthew 9:35-38 544PS 571PS 645PS
  724COM 774RM 779RM 861MVN
Matthew 10:1-5a 774RM
Matthew 10:1-7 385WI 385WII
Matthew 10:7-15 386WI 386WII
Matthew 10:7-13 580PS
Matthew 10:16-23 387WI 387WII
Matthew 10:17-22 517PS 562PS 696PS
  718COM 881MVN
Matthew 10:22-25a 560PS
Matthew 10:24-33 388WI 388WII
Matthew 10:26-33 881MVN
Matthew 10:28-33 515PS 615PS 644PS
  718COM
Matthew 10:34–11:1 389WI 389WII
Matthew 10:34-39 538PS 585PS 646PS
  718COM
Matthew 11:11-15 184WI 184WII
Matthew 11:16-19 185WI 185WII
Matthew 11:20-24 390WI 390WII
Matthew 11:25-30 557PS 563PS 624PS
  651PS 659PS 742COM 763RM 795RM
  815RM 856MVN 947MVN 1000VM
  1016MD 1022MD 1026MD
Matthew 11:25-27 391WI 391WII
Matthew 11:28-30 183WI 183WII 392WI
  392WII
Matthew 12:1-8 393WI 393WII
Matthew 12:14-21 394WI 394WII
Matthew 12:38-42 395WI 395WII
Matthew 12:46-50 396WI 396WII 601PS
  680PS 712COM
Matthew 13:1-9 397WI 397WII 916MVN
Matthew 13:10-17 398WI 398WII
Matthew 13:16-17 606PS
Matthew 13:18-23 399WI 399WII

Matthew 13:24-30 400WI 400WII
Matthew 13:31-35 401WI 401WII
Matthew 13:36-43 402WI 402WII
Matthew 13:44-46 403WI 403WII 516PS
  628PS 648PS 675PS 742COM
Matthew 13:47-53 404WI 404WII
Matthew 13:47-52 730COM
Matthew 13:54-58 405WI 405WII 559PS
Matthew 14:1-12 406WI 406WII
Matthew 14:12-16, 22-26 789RM
Matthew 14:13-21 407WI 407WII
Matthew 14:22-36 407WI, 408WI 407WII,
  408WII
Matthew 14:22-33 679PS
Matthew 15:1-2, 10-14 408WI 408WII
Matthew 15:21-28 409WI 409WII
Matthew 15:29-37 177WI 177WII
Matthew 15:29-31 795RM
Matthew 16:13-23 410WI 410WII
Matthew 16:13-19 535PS 568PS 591PS
  672PS 682PS 700PS 706COM 724COM
  831MVN
Matthew 16:13-18 748RM
Matthew 16:24-28 411WI 411WII
Matthew 16:24-27 663PS 699PS 742COM
  755RM 768RM 815RM 856MVN
  866MVN
Matthew 17:1-9 614PS
Matthew 17:10-13 186WI 186WII
Matthew 17:14-20 412WI 412WII
Matthew 17:22-27 413WI 413WII
Matthew 18:1-5, 10, 12-14 414WI 414WII
Matthew 18:1-5, 10 650PS
Matthew 18:1-5 523PS 549PS 631PS
  649PS 742COM
Matthew 18:12-14 182WI 182WII
Matthew 18:15-20 415WI 415WII 831MVN
  842MVN 956MVN
Matthew 18:19-22 871MVN
Matthew 18:21–19:1 416WI 416WII
Matthew 18:21-35 238WI 238WII
Matthew 19:3-12 417WI 417WII 736COM
  742COM 815RM 856MVN
Matthew 19:3-6 805RM
Matthew 19:13-15 418WI 418WII
Matthew 19:16-26 513PS
Matthew 19:16-22 419WI 419WII
Matthew 19:23-30 420WI 420WII
Matthew 19:27-29 533PS 597PS 619PS
  742COM

Matthew 20:1-16a 421WI 421WII
Matthew 20:17-28 232WI 232WII
Matthew 20:20-28 605PS 826RM 847MVN
    851MVN
Matthew 20:25-28 774RM
Matthew 21:23-27 187WI 187WII
Matthew 21:28-32 188WI 188WII
Matthew 21:33-43, 45-46 234WI 234WII
Matthew 22:1-14* 422WI 422WII
Matthew 22:15-21 886MVN
Matthew 22:34-40 423WI 423WII 540PS
    583PS 630PS 669PS 742COM
Matthew 22:35-40 760RM 805RM
Matthew 23:1-12 231WI, 424WI 231WII,
    424WII
Matthew 23:8-12 510PS 522PS 600PS
    633PS 724COM 730COM 810RM
Matthew 23:13-22 425WI 425WII
Matthew 23:23-26 426WI 426WII
Matthew 23:27-32 427WI 427WII
Matthew 24:4-13 592PS
Matthew 24:42-51 428WI 428WII
Matthew 25:1-13 429WI 429WII 681PS
    692PS 736COM 742COM 815RM
    967MVN 1016MD
Matthew 25:14-30* 430WI 430WII 623PS
    686PS 742COM 768RM 866MVN
    886MVN 911MVN
Matthew 25:31-46* 224WI 224WII 539PS
    594PS 742COM 886MVN 926MVN
    931MVN 932MVN 1016MD
Matthew 25:31-40 673PS 795RM
Matthew 26:14-25 259WI 259WII
Matthew 26:47-56 975VM
Matthew 27:33-50 975VM
Matthew 28:8-15 261WI 261WII
Matthew 28:16-20 528PS 662PS 724COM
    831MVN 847MVN 876MVN
Matthew 28:18-20 755RM 760RM

Mark 1:1-8, 14-15 952MVN
Mark 1:7-11 209WI 209WII
Mark 1:9-11 755RM 760RM 768RM
Mark 1:14-20 305WI 305WII 526PS 556PS
    665PS 724COM 779RM
Mark 1:21-28 306WI 306WII
Mark 1:29-39 307WI 307WII
Mark 1:35-39 569 784RM
Mark 1:40-45 308WI 308WII
Mark 2:1-12 309WI 309WII 795RM

Mark 2:13-17 310WI 310WII
Mark 2:18-22 311WI 311WII
Mark 2:23-28 312WI 312WII
Mark 3:1-6 313WI 313WII
Mark 3:7-12 314WI 314WII
Mark 3:13-19 315WI 315WII
Mark 3:20-21 316WI 316WII
Mark 3:22-30 317WI 317WII
Mark 3:31-35 318WI 318WII 569PS 658PS
    691PS 742COM 815RM 856MVN
    866MVN
Mark 4:1-20 319WI 319WII
Mark 4:1-10, 13-20* 602PS 637PS 730COM
Mark 4:1-9 866MVN
Mark 4:21-25 320WI 320WII
Mark 4:26-34 321WI 321WII
Mark 4:26-29 916MVN
Mark 4:35-41 322WI 322WII 795RM
    942MVN
Mark 5:1-20 323WI 323WII
Mark 5:18-20 947MVN
Mark 5:21-43* 324WI 324WII
Mark 6:1-6 325WI 325WII
Mark 6:7-13 326WI 326WII
Mark 6:14-29 327WI 327WII
Mark 6:17-29 634PS
Mark 6:30-34 328WI 328WII 842MVN
Mark 6:34-44 213WI 213WII 926MVN
Mark 6:45-52 214WI 214WII
Mark 6:53-56 329WI 329WII
Mark 7:1-13 330WI 330WII
Mark 7:14-23 331WI 331WII
Mark 7:24-30 332WI 332WII
Mark 7:31-37 333WI 333WII
Mark 8:1-10 334WI 334WII
Mark 8:11-13 335WI 335WII
Mark 8:14-21 336WI 336WII
Mark 8:22-26 337WI 337WII
Mark 8:27-33 338WI 338WII
Mark 8:31-34 974VM
Mark 8:34–9:1 339WI 339WII
Mark 9:2-13 340WI 340WII
Mark 9:2-10 614PS
Mark 9:14-29 341WI 341WII
Mark 9:30-37 342WI 342WII
Mark 9:34-37 521PS 742COM
Mark 9:38-40 343WI 343WII
Mark 9:41-50 344WI 344WII
Mark 10:1-12 345WI 345WII
Mark 10:6-9 805RM

Appendix II—Table of Readings 1945

Mark 10:13-16 346WI 346WII 595PS
 742COM 755RM 760RM
Mark 10:17-30* 529PS 742COM
Mark 10:17-27 347WI 347WII 861MVN
Mark 10:24b-30 815RM
Mark 10:28-31 348WI 348WII
Mark 10:28-30 861MVN
Mark 10:32-45 349WI 349WII
Mark 10:46-52 350WI 350WII 795RM
Mark 11:11-26 351WI 351WII
Mark 11:27-33 352WI 352WII
Mark 12:1-12 353WI 353WII 974VM
Mark 12:13-17 354WI 354WII
Mark 12:18-27 355WI 355WII
Mark 12:28b-34* 241WI, 356WI 241WII,
 356WII 760RM
Mark 12:35-37 357WI 357WII
Mark 12:38-44* 358WI 358WII
Mark 14:12-16, 22-26 826RM 981VM 994VM
Mark 14:32-41 975VM
Mark 14:55-65 975VM
Mark 15:1-15 975VM
Mark 15:16-20 975VM 981VM 994VM
Mark 15:33-46 1026MD
Mark 15:33-39; 16:1-6* 975VM 1016MD
Mark 16:9-15 266WI 266WII
Mark 16:15-20 525PS 555PS 685PS
 724COM 795RM 851MVN 876MVN
 937MVN
Mark 16:15-16, 19-20 755RM
Mark 16:15-18 519PS

Luke 1:5-25 195WI 195WII
Luke 1:5-17 586PS
Luke 1:26-38 196WI 196WII 545PS 627PS
 653PS 689PS 712COM 815RM
Luke 1:39-56 572PS 622PS
Luke 1:39-55 947MVN
Luke 1:39-47 712COM 1002VM
Luke 1:39-45 197WI 197WII
Luke 1:46-56 198WI 198WII
Luke 1:57-66, 80 587PS
Luke 1:57-66 199WI 199WII
Luke 1:67-79 200WI 200WII
Luke 2:1-14 712COM
Luke 2:15b-19 712COM
Luke 2:16-21 988VM
Luke 2:22-40* 524PS
Luke 2:22-35 202WI 202WII
Luke 2:27-35 712COM

Luke 2:33-35 639PS
Luke 2:36-40 203WI 203WII
Luke 2:41-52 712COM
Luke 2:41-51 573PS
Luke 2:41-51a 543PS
Luke 3:7-18 896MVN
Luke 3:23-28 210WI 210WII
Luke 4:14-22a 215WI 215WII
Luke 4:16-30 431WI 431WII
Luke 4:16-22a 768RM
Luke 4:16-21 260WI 260WII 784RM
Luke 4:24-30 237WI 237WII
Luke 4:31-37 432WI 432WII
Luke 4:38-44 433WI 433WII
Luke 5:1-11 434WI 434WII 541PS 655PS
 724COM 779RM 861MVN
Luke 5:12-16 216WI 216WII
Luke 5:17-26 181WI 181WII
Luke 5:27-32 222WI 222WII
Luke 5:33-39 435WI 435WII
Luke 6:1-5 436WI 436WII
Luke 6:6-11 437WI 437WII
Luke 6:12-19 438WI 438WII 666PS
Luke 6:20-26 439WI 439WII
Luke 6:27-38 440WI 440WII 678PS 695PS
 742COM 962MVN
Luke 6:36-38 230WI 230WII
Luke 6:39-42 441WI 441WII
Luke 6:43-49 442WI 442WII
Luke 6:43-45 547PS 579PS 608PS 730COM
Luke 7:1-10 443WI 443WII
Luke 7:11-17 444WI 444WII 632PS
 1016MD
Luke 7:19-23 189WI 189WII 795RM
Luke 7:24-30 190WI 190WII
Luke 7:31-35 445WI 445WII
Luke 7:36-50 446WI 446WII 952MVN
Luke 8:1-3 447WI 447WII
Luke 8:4-15 448WI 448WII
Luke 8:4-10a, 11b-15 768RM
Luke 8:16-18 449WI 449WII
Luke 8:19-21 450WI 450WII
Luke 9:1-6 451WI 451WII
Luke 9:7-9 452WI 452WII
Luke 9:11b-17 789RM 981VM
Luke 9:18-22 453WI 453WII
Luke 9:22-25 220WI 220WII
Luke 9:23-26 527PS 553PS 718COM
Luke 9:28b-36 614PS
Luke 9:43b-45 454WI 454WII

1946 Appendix II—Table of Readings

Luke 9:46-50 455WI 455WII
Luke 9:49-56 871MVN
Luke 9:51-56 456WI 456WII
Luke 9:57-62 457WI 457WII 566PS 617PS
    652PS 664PS 683PS 742COM 815RM
    861MVN
Luke 10:1-9 520PS 532PS 581PS 661PS
    687PS 724COM 774RM 847MVN
    851MVN
Luke 10:1-12 458WI 458WII
Luke 10:5-6, 8-9 795RM
Luke 10:13-16 459WI 459WII
Luke 10:17-24 460WI 460WII 947MVN
Luke 10:21-24 176WI 176WII 768RM
Luke 10:25-37 461WI 461WII 795RM
    931MVN
Luke 10:38-42 462WI 462WII 530PS 607PS
    736COM 742COM 815RM 856MVN
Luke 11:1-4 463WI 463WII
Luke 11:5-13 464WI 464WII 795RM
Luke 11:14-23 240WI 240WII
Luke 11:15-26 465WI 465WII
Luke 11:27-28 466WI 466WII 613PS
    621PS 712COM 815RM
Luke 11:29-32 226WI, 467WI 226WII,
    467WII
Luke 11:37-41 468WI 468WII
Luke 11:42-46 469WI 469WII
Luke 11:47-54 470WI 470WII
Luke 12:1-7 471WI 471WII
Luke 12:8-12 472WI 472WII
Luke 12:13-21 473WI 473WII
Luke 12:15-21 886MVN 921MVN
Luke 12:32-34 584PS 616PS 742COM
Luke 12:35-44 774RM 795RM 810RM
Luke 12:35-40 511PS 548PS 742COM
    886MVN 906MVN 967MVN 1016MD
Luke 12:35-38 474WI 474WII
Luke 12:39-48 475WI 475WII
Luke 12:49-53 476WI 476WII
Luke 12:54-59 477WI 477WII
Luke 13:1-9 478WI 478WII
Luke 13:10-17 479WI 479WII
Luke 13:18-21 480WI 480WII
Luke 13:22-30 481WI 481WII
Luke 13:31-35 482WI 482WII
Luke 14:1-6 483WI 483WII
Luke 14:1, 7-11 484WI 484WII
Luke 14:12-14 485WI 485WII 886MVN
    926MVN

Luke 14:15-24 486WI 486WII
Luke 14:25-33 487WI 487WII 578PS
    582PS 609PS 693PS 742COM 861MVN
Luke 15:1-10 488WI 488WII 1000VM
Luke 15:1-3, 11-32 235WI 235WII 896MVN
    952MVN 1000VM
Luke 16:1-8 489WI 489WII
Luke 16:9-15 490WI 490WII
Luke 16:19-31 233WI 233WII 886MVN
    926MVN
Luke 17:1-6 491WI 491WII
Luke 17:7-10 492WI 492WII
Luke 17:11-19 493WI 493WII 921MVN
    947MVN
Luke 17:20-25 494WI 494WII
Luke 17:26-37 495WI 495WII
Luke 18:1-8 496WI 496WII 942MVN
Luke 18:9-14 242WI 242WII 795RM
Luke 18:35-43 497WI 497WII
Luke 19:1-10 498WI 498WII 706COM
Luke 19:11-28 499WI 499WII
Luke 19:41-44 500WI 500WII
Luke 19:45-48 501WI 501WII
Luke 20:27-40 502WI 502WII
Luke 21:1-4 503WI 503WII
Luke 21:5-11 504WI 504WII
Luke 21:12-19 505WI 505WII
Luke 21:20-28 506WI 506WII
Luke 21:29-33 507WI 507WII
Luke 21:34-36 508WI 508WII 967MVN
Luke 22:14-20, 24-30 774RM
Luke 22:14-20 982VM
Luke 22:24-30 565PS 635PS 656PS
    724COM 847MVN 886MVN
Luke 22:24-27 810RM
Luke 22:39-44 981VM 994VM
Luke 22:39-43 937MVN
Luke 23:33-34, 39-46 975VM
Luke 23:33, 39-43 1016MD
Luke 23:39-46 967MVN
Luke 23:44-46, 50, 52-53; 24:1-6a* 1016MD
Luke 24:13-35* 263WI 263WII 789RM
    981VM 1016MD
Luke 24:35-48 264WI 264WII 974VM
Luke 24:44-53 755RM 876MVN
Luke 24:44-48 784RM
Luke 24:46-48 952MVN

John 1:1-18* 204WI 204WII
John 1:1-5, 9-14, 16-18 755RM

Appendix II—Table of Readings 1947

John 1:19-28 205WI 205WII
John 1:29-34 206WI 206WII 755RM
John 1:35-51* 861MVN
John 1:35-42 207WI 207WII 743RM
 779RM
John 1:43-51 208WI 208WII
John 1:45-51 629PS 779RM
John 1:47-51 647PS
John 2:1-11 210WI 210WII 531PS
 712COM 805RM
John 2:13-22 671PS 706COM
John 3:1-8 267WI 267WII
John 3:1-6 755RM 760RM
John 3:7b-15 268WI 268WII
John 3:13-17 638PS
John 3:16-21 269WI 269WII 755RM 763RM
John 3:22-30 217WI 217WII
John 3:31-36 270WI 270WII
John 4:5-42* 236WI 236WII
John 4:5-14 760RM
John 4:19-24 706COM 822RM
John 4:43-54 244WI 244WII
John 5:1-16 245WI 245WII
John 5:17-30 246WI 246WII
John 5:24-29 1016MD
John 5:31-47 247WI 247WII
John 5:33-36 191WI 191WII
John 6:1-15 271WI 271WII 789RM 981VM
John 6:16-21 272WI 272WII
John 6:22-29 273WI 273WII
John 6:24-35 789RM 981VM
John 6:30-35 274WI 274WII
John 6:35-40 275WI 275WII 795RM
John 6:37-40* 1016MD 1022MD
John 6:41-50 789RM 800RM 981VM
John 6:44-51 276WI 276WII
John 6:44-47 760RM
John 6:51-58 789RM 800RM 981VM
 1016MD 1022MD
John 6:52-59 277WI 277WII
John 6:53-58 795RM
John 6:60-69 278WI 278WII
John 7:1-2, 10, 25-30 248WI 248WII
John 7:14-18 784RM
John 7:34b-39a 760RM 768RM
John 7:40-53 249WI 249WII
John 8:1-11 251WI 251WII
John 8:12-20 251WI 251WII
John 8:21-30 252WI 252WII
John 8:31-42 253WI 253WII

John 8:51-59 254WI 254WII
John 9:1-41* 243WI 243WII
John 9:1-7 760RM 795RM
John 10:1-10 279WI 279WII
John 10:11-18 279WI 279WII 795RM
 1000VM
John 10:11-16 577PS 670PS 688PS
 724COM 774RM 847MVN 871MVN
John 10:22-30 280WI 280WII
John 10:31-42 255WI 255WII
John 11:1-45* 250WI 250WII
John 11:17-27* 1016MD
John 11:19-27 607PS
John 11:32-45 1016MD
John 11:32-38, 40 1022MD
John 11:45-56 256WI 256WII
John 11:45-52 871MVN 876MVN
John 12:1-11 257WI 257WII
John 12:23-28* 1016MD
John 12:24-26 596PS 618PS 642PS 660PS
 718COM 774RM 815RM
John 12:31-36a 822RM 974VM
John 12:44-50 281WI 281WII 748RM
 755RM
John 13:1-15 871MVN
John 13:16-20 282WI 282WII
John 13:21-33, 36-38 258WI 258WII
John 14:1-6 283WI 283WII 1016MD
John 14:6-14 561PS 988VM
John 14:7-14 284WI 284WII
John 14:15-23, 26-27 763RM
John 14:15-17 768RM
John 14:21-26 285WI 285WII
John 14:23-29 842MVN 891MVN
John 14:23-26 768RM
John 14:27-31a 286WI 286WII
John 15:1-11 755RM 760RM
John 15:1-8 287WI 287WII 534PS 542PS
 604PS 657PS 677PS 742COM 815RM
 831MVN 856MVN 866MVN 937MVN
 1000VM
John 15:1-6 763RM
John 15:9-17 518PS 537PS 564PS 599PS
 690PS 724COM 742COM 774RM
 815RM 837MVN 847MVN 861MVN
 947MVN 1000VM
John 15:9-12 805RM 886MVN 901MVN
John 15:9-11 288WI 288WII
John 15:12-17 289WI 289WII 956MVN
John 15:12-16 805RM

John 15:18-21, 26–16:4 881MVN
John 15:18-21, 26-27 768RM
John 15:18-21 290WI 290WII 536PS
    551PS 620PS 718COM 866MVN
John 15:26–16:4a 291WI 291WII
John 16:5-11 292WI 292WII
John 16:5b-7, 12-13a 768RM
John 16:12-15 293WI 293WII
John 16:16-20 294WI 294WI
John 16:20-23a 295WI 295WII
John 16:20-22 947MVN
John 16:23b-28 296WI 296WII
John 16:29-33 297WI 297WII
John 17:1-11a 298WI 298WII 871MVN
John 17:6, 14-19 774RM
John 17:11b, 17-23 831MVN 837MVN
    876MVN
John 17:11b-19 299WI 299WII 550PS
    575PS 640PS 718COM 871MVN
    881MVN
John 17:20-26* 300WI 300WII 554PS
    570PS 589PS 625PS 674PS 742COM
    805RM 815RM 871MVN 1000VM
John 17:24-26 1016MD
John 19:17-18, 25-39 1016MD
John 19:25-30 1022MD
John 19:25-27 639PS 712COM 1002VM
John 19:28-37 975VM
John 19:31-37 981VM 994VM 1000VM
John 19:31-35 760RM
John 20:1-2, 11-18 603PS
John 20:2-8 697PS
John 20:11-18 262WI 262WII
John 20:19-23 774RM 891MVN
John 20:24-29 593PS
John 21:1-14 265WI 265WII 789RM 981VM
John 21:15-19 301WI 301WII 590PS
John 21:15-17 514PS 558PS 626PS
    724COM 774RM 831MVN 847MVN
John 21:20-25 302WI 302WII

Acts of the Apostles 1:3-8 765RM 873MVN
Acts of the Apostles 1:12-14 653PS
    708COM 1002VM
Acts of the Apostles 1:15-17, 20-26 564PS
Acts of the Apostles 2:1-6, 14, 22b-23, 32-33
    765RM
Acts of the Apostles 2:1-11 863MVN
Acts of the Apostles 2:14, 22-33 261WI
    261WII
Acts of the Apostles 2:14a, 22-24, 32-36
    726COM
Acts of the Apostles 2:14a, 36-40a, 41-42
    752RM
Acts of the Apostles 2:36-41 262WI 262WII
Acts of the Apostles 2:42-47 786RM 807RM
    812RM 818RM 828MVN 853MVN
    977VM
Acts of the Apostles 3:1-10 263WI 263WII
    590PS 791RM 984VM
Acts of the Apostles 3:11-26 264WI 264WII
Acts of the Apostles 3:11-16 791RM
Acts of the Apostles 3:13-15, 17-19 893MVN
Acts of the Apostles 4:1-5, 18-21 878MVN
Acts of the Apostles 4:1-12 265WI 265WII
Acts of the Apostles 4:8-12 566PS 791RM
    984VM
Acts of the Apostles 4:13-21 266WI 266WII
Acts of the Apostles 4:23-31 267WI 267WII
    878MVN
Acts of the Apostles 4:32-37 268WI 268WII
Acts of the Apostles 4:32-35 738COM
    812RM
Acts of the Apostles 5:17-26 269WI 269WII
Acts of the Apostles 5:27b-32, 40b-42
    878MVN 984VM
Acts of the Apostles 5:27-33 270WI 270WII
Acts of the Apostles 5:34-42 271WI 271WII
Acts of the Apostles 6:1-7 272WI 272WII
Acts of the Apostles 6:1-7b 771RM
Acts of the Apostles 6:8-10; 7:54-59 696PS
Acts of the Apostles 6:8-15 273WI 273WII
Acts of the Apostles 7:44-50 702COM
Acts of the Apostles 7:51–8:1a 274WI 274WII
Acts of the Apostles 7:55-60 714COM
    959MVN
Acts of the Apostles 8:1b-8 275WI 275WII
Acts of the Apostles 8:1, 4, 14-17 765RM
Acts of the Apostles 8:26-40 276WI 276WII
    771RM
Acts of the Apostles 8:26-38 752RM
Acts of the Apostles 9:1-22 519PS
Acts of the Apostles 9:1-20 277WI 277WII
Acts of the Apostles 9:31-42 278WI 278WII
Acts of the Apostles 10:1, 33-34a, 37-44
    765RM
Acts of the Apostles 10:34-43* 970VM
    1012MD
Acts of the Apostles 10:34a, 37-43 786RM
    977VM

Acts of the Apostles 10:37-43 771RM
Acts of the Apostles 11:1-18 279WI 279WII
Acts of the Apostles 11:19-26 280WI
  280WII 873MVN
Acts of the Apostles 11:21b-26, 13:1-3 580PS
Acts of the Apostles 11:27-30 883MVN
  923MVN
Acts of the Apostles 12:1-11 591PS
Acts of the Apostles 12:24–13:5a 281WI
  281WII
Acts of the Apostles 13:13-25 282WI
  282WII
Acts of the Apostles 13:22-26 587PS
Acts of the Apostles 13:26-33 726COM
  970VM
Acts of the Apostles 13:26b-33 283WI
  283WII
Acts of the Apostles 13:32-39 791RM
Acts of the Apostles 13:44-52 284WI 284WII
Acts of the Apostles 13:46-49 532PS
  720COM 873MVN
Acts of the Apostles 14:5-18 285WI 285WII
Acts of the Apostles 14:19-28 286WI 286WII
Acts of the Apostles 14:21-23 776RM
Acts of the Apostles 15:1-6 287WI 287WII
Acts of the Apostles 15:7-21 288WI 288WII
Acts of the Apostles 15:22-31 289WI 289WII
Acts of the Apostles 16:1-10 290WI 290WII
Acts of the Apostles 16:11-15 291WI 291WII
Acts of the Apostles 16:22-34 292WI 292WII
Acts of the Apostles 17:15, 22–18:1 293WI
  293WII
Acts of the Apostles 18:1-8 294WI 294WII
Acts of the Apostles 18:9-18 295WI 295WII
Acts of the Apostles 18:23-28 296WI 296WII
Acts of the Apostles 19:1-8 297WI 297WII
Acts of the Apostles 19:1b-6a 765RM
Acts of the Apostles 20:17-18a, 28-32, 36
  568PS 690PS 720COM 771RM
Acts of the Apostles 20:17-27 298WI 298WII
Acts of the Apostles 20:28-38 299WI 299WII
Acts of the Apostles 22:3-16 519PS
Acts of the Apostles 22:30; 23:6-11 300WI
  300WII
Acts of the Apostles 25:13b-21 301WI
  301WII
Acts of the Apostles 26:19-23 577PS
  720COM
Acts of the Apostles 28:7-10, 11-16, 30-31
  679PS

Acts of the Apostles 28:7-10 934MVN
Acts of the Apostles 28:16-20, 30-31 302WI
  302WII

Romans 1:1-7 467WI
Romans 1:16-25 468WI
Romans 2:1-11 469WI
Romans 3:21-30 470WI
Romans 4:1-8 471WI
Romans 4:13, 16-18, 22 543PS
Romans 4:13, 16-18 472WI
Romans 4:20-25 473WI
Romans 5:1-2, 5-8 765RM
Romans 5:1-5 525PS 716COM
Romans 5:5-11 998VM 1014MD
Romans 5:12, 15b, 17-19, 20b-21 474WI
Romans 5:12, 17-19 710COM
Romans 5:17-21 1014MD
Romans 6:2-14 949MVN
Romans 6:2-4, 12-14 863MVN
Romans 6:3-11* 752RM 812RM
Romans 6:3-9* 1014MD
Romans 6:3-4, 8-9 1020MD
Romans 6:3-5 757RM
Romans 6:12-18 475WI
Romans 6:19-23 476WI
Romans 7:18-25a 477WI
Romans 8:1-11 478WI
Romans 8:1-4 610PS
Romans 8:12-17 479WI
Romans 8:14-17, 26-27 749RM
Romans 8:14-23 1014MD
Romans 8:14-17 765RM 792RM
Romans 8:18-30 883MVN 939MVN
Romans 8:18-27 792RM
Romans 8:18-25 480WI
Romans 8:22-27 657PS
Romans 8:26-30 481WI 533PS 740COM
Romans 8:26-27 765RM
Romans 8:28-39 761RM
Romans 8:28-32, 35, 37-39 752RM
Romans 8:28-32 757RM
Romans 8:28-30 636PS 710COM
Romans 8:31b-39 482WI 538PS 592PS
  716COM 863MVN 939MVN
Romans 8:31b-35, 37-39 792RM 802RM
  1014MD
Romans 9:1-5 483WI
Romans 10:8-13 748RM
Romans 10:9-18 684PS 873MVN

Romans 11:1-2a, 11-12, 25-29 484WI
Romans 11:29-36 485WI
Romans 12:1-2, 9-18* 802RM
Romans 12:1-13 812RM 863MVN
Romans 12:3-13 670PS 722COM 953MVN
Romans 12:4-8 771RM
Romans 12:5-16a 486WI
Romans 12:9-16b 572PS 928MVN
Romans 13:8-10 487WI
Romans 14:7-12 488WI
Romans 14:7-9, 10c-12 964MVN 1014MD
Romans 14:7-9 1020MD
Romans 15:14-21 489WI
Romans 16:3-9, 16, 22-27 490WI

1 Corinthians 1:1-3 986VM
1 Corinthians 1:1-9 428WII
1 Corinthians 1:3-9 944MVN
1 Corinthians 1:10-13 868MVN
1 Corinthians 1:17-25 429WII
1 Corinthians 1:18-25 556PS 574PS 663PS
   722COM 728COM 792RM 972VM
1 Corinthians 1:22-31 812RM 853MVN
1 Corinthians 1:26-31 430WII 516PS
   527PS 645PS 740COM
1 Corinthians 2:1-10a 617PS 693PS
   728COM
1 Corinthians 2:1-5 431WII 781RM
1 Corinthians 2:10b-16 432WII 567PS
   728COM
1 Corinthians 3:1-9 433WII
1 Corinthians 3:18-23 434WII
1 Corinthians 3:6-10 918MVN
1 Corinthians 3:9c-11, 16-17 704COM
   828MVN
1 Corinthians 4:1-5 435WII 558PS
   722COM
1 Corinthians 4:6b-15 436WII
1 Corinthians 5:1-8 437WII
1 Corinthians 6:1-11 438WII
1 Corinthians 6:13c-15a, 17-20 596PS 802RM
1 Corinthians 7:25-35 569PS 734COM
   812RM 853MVN
1 Corinthians 7:25-31 439WII
1 Corinthians 7:29-31 903MVN
1 Corinthians 8:1b-7, 11-13 440WII
1 Corinthians 9:16-19, 22b-27 441WII
1 Corinthians 9:16-19, 22-23 685PS
   722COM 776RM 848MVN
1 Corinthians 10:14-22 442WII

1 Corinthians 10:14-22a 823RM
1 Corinthians 10:16-21 820RM
1 Corinthians 10:16-17 786RM 797RM
   979VM
1 Corinthians 10:31–11:1 609PS
1 Corinthians 11:17-26, 33 443WII
1 Corinthians 11:23-26 786RM 797RM
   823RM 844MVN 979VM
1 Corinthians 12:3b-7, 12-13 828MVN
   848MVN 863MVN
1 Corinthians 12:4-13 765RM
1 Corinthians 12:4-11 776RM
1 Corinthians 12:12-14, 27-31a 444WII
1 Corinthians 12:12-22, 24b-27 792RM
1 Corinthians 12:12-13 752RM, 757RM
1 Corinthians 12:31–13:13* 445WII 631PS
   740COM 761RM 953MVN
1 Corinthians 12:31–13:8a 802RM
1 Corinthians 15:1-11* 446WII
1 Corinthians 15:1-8* 561PS 748RM
1 Corinthians 15:12-20 447WII 792RM
1 Corinthians 15:20-24a, 25-28* 1014MD
1 Corinthians 15:20-27 622PS
1 Corinthians 15:20-23 1020MD
1 Corinthians 15:35-37, 42-49 448WII
1 Corinthians 15:51-57 1014MD
1 Corinthians 15:54b-57 621PS

2 Corinthians 1:1-7 359WI
2 Corinthians 1:18-22 360WI
2 Corinthians 3:1-6a 722COM
2 Corinthians 3:4-11 361WI
2 Corinthians 3:15–4:1, 3-6 362WI
2 Corinthians 4:1-2, 5-7 547PS 602PS 635PS
   655PS 722COM 771RM 844MVN
2 Corinthians 4:7-15 363WI 517PS 605PS
   640PS 662PS 716COM
2 Corinthians 4:10-18 934MVN
2 Corinthians 4:14–5:1 1014MD
2 Corinthians 4:16-18 792RM
2 Corinthians 5:1, 6-10 792RM 1014MD
2 Corinthians 5:14-21 364WI
2 Corinthians 5:14-20 511PS 664PS
   722COM 771RM 844MVN 858MVN
2 Corinthians 5:14-17 603PS
2 Corinthians 5:17–6:2 893MVN
2 Corinthians 5:20–6:2 219WI 219WII
2 Corinthians 6:1-10 365WI
2 Corinthians 6:4-10 575PS 654PS
   716COM

Appendix II—Table of Readings 1951

2 Corinthians 8:1-5, 9-15 883MVN 923MVN
2 Corinthians 8:1-9 366WI
2 Corinthians 8:9-15 584PS
2 Corinthians 9:6-15 883MVN 923MVN
2 Corinthians 9:6-11 367WI
2 Corinthians 9:6-10 618PS
2 Corinthians 9:8-11 913MVN
2 Corinthians 10:17–11:2 628PS 692PS 740COM
2 Corinthians 11:1-11 368WI
2 Corinthians 11:18, 21b-30 369WI
2 Corinthians 12:1-10 370WI
2 Corinthians 12:7b-10 934MVN

Galatians 1:6-12 461WII
Galatians 1:11-20 590PS
Galatians 1:13-24 462WII
Galatians 2:1-2, 7-14 463WII
Galatians 2:19-20 528PS 604PS 740COM
Galatians 3:1-5 464WII
Galatians 3:7-14 465WII
Galatians 3:22-29 466WII
Galatians 3:26-28 752RM 757RM
Galatians 4:4-7 710COM 749RM 1002VM
Galatians 4:12-19 792RM
Galatians 4:22-24, 26-27, 31–5:1 467WII
Galatians 5:1-6 468WII
Galatians 5:16-17, 22-23a, 24-25 765RM
Galatians 5:17-26 883MVN 898MVN
Galatians 5:18-25 469WII
Galatians 6:14-18 651PS
Galatians 6:14-16 740COM

Ephesians 1:1-10 470WII
Ephesians 1:3a, 4a, 13-19a 765RM
Ephesians 1:3-14 761RM 812RM 828MVN 863MVN 944MVN
Ephesians 1:3-10, 13-14 752RM
Ephesians 1:3-10 998VM
Ephesians 1:3-6, 11-12 689PS 710COM 1002VM
Ephesians 1:3-5 1020MD
Ephesians 1:11-14 471WII
Ephesians 1:15-23 472WII
Ephesians 2:1-10 473WII
Ephesians 2:12-22 474WII
Ephesians 2:13-18 972VM
Ephesians 2:19-22 593PS 666PS 704COM 828MVN 868MVN

Ephesians 3:2-12 475WII 873MVN
Ephesians 3:8-12 518PS 608PS 688PS 728COM 998VM
Ephesians 3:14-21 476WII
Ephesians 3:14-19 552PS 600PS 624PS 659PS 677PS 740COM 998VM
Ephesians 4:1-7, 11-13 510PS 637PS 643PS 674PS 722COM 728COM 761RM 771RM 844MVN 848MVN
Ephesians 4:1-6 477WII 752RM 757RM 765RM 807RM 863MVN 868MVN
Ephesians 4:7-16 478WII
Ephesians 4:11-16 834MVN
Ephesians 4:30–5:2 868MVN 883MVN 898MVN
Ephesians 4:32–5:8 479WII
Ephesians 5:2a, 21-33* 802RM
Ephesians 5:21-33 480WII
Ephesians 6:1-9 481WII
Ephesians 6:10-20 482WII
Ephesians 6:10-13, 18 513PS 740COM

Philippians 1:1-11 483WII
Philippians 1:18b-26 484WII
Philippians 1:8-11 998VM
Philippians 1:27-30 878MVN
Philippians 2:1-13 868MVN
Philippians 2:1-4 485WII 812RM 839MVN 853MVN
Philippians 2:5-11 486WII
Philippians 2:6-11 638PS 978VM 986VM
Philippians 2:12-18 487WII
Philippians 2:25-30 792RM
Philippians 3:3-8a 488WII
Philippians 3:8-14 537PS 546PS 582PS 619PS 652PS 740COM 812RM 858MVN 972VM
Philippians 3:17–4:1, 20-21 660PS
Philippians 3:17–4:1* 489WII
Philippians 4:4-9 523PS 570PS 669PS 740COM
Philippians 4:4-8 761RM
Philippians 4:6-9 888MVN
Philippians 4:10-19 490WII

Colossians 1:1-8 433WI
Colossians 1:9-14 434WI
Colossians 1:15-20 435WI
Colossians 1:21-23 436WI
Colossians 1:22-29 792RM

1952 Appendix II—Table of Readings

Colossians 1:24–2:3 437WI
Colossians 1:24-29 554PS 722COM
   844MVN 848MVN
Colossians 2:6-15 438WI
Colossians 3:1-11 439WI
Colossians 3:1-4 812RM
Colossians 3:9b-17 752RM 868MVN
   883MVN
Colossians 3:12-17 440WI 579PS 740COM
   802RM 807RM 812RM 944MVN
   986VM
Colossians 3:12-15 888MVN 959MVN
Colossians 3:14-15, 17, 23-24 559PS

1 Thessalonians 1:1-5, 8b-10 425WI
1 Thessalonians 2:1-8 426WI
1 Thessalonians 2:2b-8 571PS 626PS
   722COM 844MVN
1 Thessalonians 2:9-13 427WI
1 Thessalonians 3:7-13 428WI
1 Thessalonians 4:1-3a, 7-12 812RM
1 Thessalonians 4:1b-2, 9-12 908MVN
1 Thessalonians 4:1-8 429WI
1 Thessalonians 4:9-11 430WI
1 Thessalonians 4:13-18* 431WI 1014MD
1 Thessalonians 4:13-14, 18 1020MD
1 Thessalonians 5:1-6, 9-11 432WI
1 Thessalonians 5:16-24 761RM

2 Thessalonians 1:1-5, 11b-12 425WII
2 Thessalonians 2:1-3a, 14-17 426WII
2 Thessalonians 3:6-10, 16-18 427WII
2 Thessalonians 3:6-12, 16 908MVN

1 Timothy 1:1-2, 12-14 441WI
1 Timothy 1:15-17 442WI
1 Timothy 2:1-8 443WI 873MVN
1 Timothy 2:5-8 868MVN
1 Timothy 3:1-13 444WI
1 Timothy 3:8-10, 12-13 771RM
1 Timothy 3:14-16 445WI
1 Timothy 4:12-16 446WI 771RM
1 Timothy 5:3-10 740COM
1 Timothy 6:2c-12 447WI
1 Timothy 6:6-11, 17-19 883MVN 918MVN
1 Timothy 6:13-16 448WI

2 Timothy 1:1-3, 6-12 355WII
2 Timothy 1:1-8 520PS
2 Timothy 1:6-14 771RM

2 Timothy 1:13-14; 2:1-3 544PS 549PS
   595PS 686PS 722COM 728COM
2 Timothy 2:8-13; 3:10-12 699PS 551PS
   716COM
2 Timothy 2:8-15 356WII
2 Timothy 3:8-13 1014MD
2 Timothy 3:10-17 357WII
2 Timothy 3:10-12, 14-15 776RM
2 Timothy 3:14-17 781RM
2 Timothy 3:22b-26 589PS
2 Timothy 4:1-8 358WII
2 Timothy 4:1-5 534PS 548PS 588PS 694PS
   722COM 728COM 781RM 848MVN
2 Timothy 4:6-8, 17-18 591PS
2 Timothy 4:10-17b 661PS

Titus 1:1-9 491WII
Titus 1:1-5 520PS
Titus 2:1-8, 11-14 492WII
Titus 3:1-7 493WII
Titus 3:4-7 752RM

Philemon 7-20 494WII

Hebrews 1:1-6 305WI
Hebrews 2:5-12 306WI
Hebrews 2:14-18 307WI 524PS
Hebrews 3:7-14 308WI
Hebrews 4:1-5, 11 309WI
Hebrews 4:12-16 310WI
Hebrews 4:12-13 781RM
Hebrews 4:14-16; 5:7-9 792RM
Hebrews 5:1-10 311WI 771RM 834MVN
   858MVN
Hebrews 5:7-9 639PS 972VM
Hebrews 6:10-20 312WI
Hebrews 7:1-3, 15-17 313WI
Hebrews 7:25–8:6 314WI
Hebrews 8:6-13 315WI
Hebrews 9:2-3, 11-14 316WI
Hebrews 9:11-15 786RM 979VM 992VM
Hebrews 9:15, 24-28 317WI
Hebrews 10:1-10 318WI
Hebrews 10:4-10 545PS
Hebrews 10:11-18 319WI
Hebrews 10:12-23 982VM
Hebrews 10:19-25 320WI
Hebrews 10:22-25 752RM
Hebrews 10:32-39 321WI
Hebrews 10:32-36 642PS 716COM

Appendix II—Table of Readings 1953

Hebrews 11:1-7 340WI
Hebrews 11:1-2, 8-19* 322WI
Hebrews 11:13-16 928MVN
Hebrews 11:32-40 323WI
Hebrews 12:1-4 324WI
Hebrews 12:2-13 878MVN
Hebrews 12:4-7, 11-15 325WI
Hebrews 12:18-19, 21-24 326WI
Hebrews 12:18-19, 22-24 704COM 979VM 992VM
Hebrews 13:1-2, 7-8, 17-18 807RM
Hebrews 13:1-3, 14-16 928MVN
Hebrews 13:1-8 327WI
Hebrews 13:8-15 820RM
Hebrews 13:15-17, 20-21 328WI

James 1:1-11 335WII
James 1:2-4, 12 716COM 939MVN
James 1:12-18 336WII
James 1:19-27 337WII
James 2:1-9 338WII
James 2:14-24, 26 339WII
James 2:14-17 695PS 740COM
James 3:1-10 340WII
James 3:13-18 341WII 883MVN 888MVN
James 4:1-10 342WII 883MVN 898MVN
James 4:13-17 343WII
James 4:13-15 903MVN
James 5:1-6 344WII
James 5:7-8, 16c-18 913MVN
James 5:9-12 345WII
James 5:13-20 346WII
James 5:13-16 792RM 934MVN

1 Peter 1:3-9 347WII 792RM 812RM 853MVN 878MVN
1 Peter 1:8-12 586PS
1 Peter 1:10-16 348WII
1 Peter 1:17-21 979VM 992VM
1 Peter 1:18-25 349WII
1 Peter 2:2-5, 9-12 350WII
1 Peter 2:4-10 863MVN
1 Peter 2:4-5, 9-10 752RM 757RM
1 Peter 2:4-9 704COM 828MVN
1 Peter 3:1-9 740COM 802RM
1 Peter 3:14-17 515PS 646PS 716COM
1 Peter 4:7-13 351WII
1 Peter 4:7b-11 521PS 541PS 740COM 771RM
1 Peter 4:12-19 558PS 620PS 716COM

1 Peter 5:1-4 514PS 535PS 656PS 682PS 722COM 771RM 807RM
1 Peter 5:5b-14 555PS

2 Peter 1:2-7 353WII
2 Peter 1:16-19 614PS
2 Peter 3:12-15a, 17-18 354WII

1 John 1:1-4 697PS 781RM
1 John 1:5–2:2 557PS 698PS 949MVN
1 John 2:1-5 893MVN
1 John 2:3-11 202WI 202WII
1 John 2:12-17 203WI 203WII
1 John 2:18-25 512PS
1 John 2:18-21 204WI 204WII
1 John 2:22-28 205WI 205WII
1 John 2:29–3:6 206WI 206WII
1 John 3:1-3 667PS
1 John 3:1-2 792RM 1014MD
1 John 3:7-10 207WI 207WII
1 John 3:11-21 208WI 208WII
1 John 3:14-18 539PS 594PS 599PS 678PS 740COM 953MVN
1 John 3:14-16 1014MD
1 John 3:18-24 802RM
1 John 3:22–4:6 212WI 212WII
1 John 4:7-16 607PS 633PS 740COM 812RM 998VM
1 John 4:7-12 802RM
1 John 4:7-10 213WI 213WII
1 John 4:9-15 868MVN
1 John 4:11-18 214WI 214WII
1 John 4:19–5:4 215WI 215WII
1 John 5:1-5 542PS 560PS 583PS 611PS 716COM 740COM
1 John 5:4-8 979VM 992VM
1 John 5:5-13 209WI 209WII 216WI 216WII
1 John 5:14-21 210WI 210WII

2 John 4-9 495WII

3 John 5-8 496WII

Jude 17, 20b-25 352WII

Revelation 1:1-4; 2:1-5a 497WII
Revelation 1:5-8 260WI 260WII 970VM 977VM 990VM
Revelation 2:8-11 536PS
Revelation 3:1-6, 14-22 498WII

Revelation 3:14b, 20-22 565PS 738COM
  797RM 812RM 853MVN 996VM
Revelation 4:1-11 499WII
Revelation 5:1-10 500WII
Revelation 5:6-12 970VM 996VM
Revelation 7:2-4, 9-14 667PS 828MVN
Revelation 7:9-17 562PS 714COM
Revelation 7:9-10, 14b-17 878MVN
Revelation 7:9-10, 15-17 1018MD
Revelation 7:9-14 977VM 990VM
Revelation 8:3-4 818RM
Revelation 10:8-11 501WII
Revelation 11:4-12 502WII
Revelation 11:19a–12:1-6a, 10ab 622PS
  708COM
Revelation 12:7-12a 647PS
Revelation 12:10-12a 550PS 714COM
Revelation 14:1-3, 4b-5 503WII
Revelation 14:13 1012MD

Revelation 14:14-19 504WII
Revelation 15:1-4 505WII
Revelation 18:1-2, 21-23; 19:1-3, 9a 506WII
Revelation 19:1, 5-9a 563PS 732COM
  738COM 752RM 802RM
Revelation 20:1-4, 11–21:2 507WII
Revelation 20:11; 21:1 1012MD
Revelation 21:1-7 792RM
Revelation 21:1-5a, 6b-7 939MVN 1012MD
Revelation 21:1-5a 613PS 702COM
  708COM 732COM 816RM 828MVN
Revelation 21:1a, 3-5a 1018MD
Revelation 21:5-7 553PS 714COM
  738COM
Revelation 21:9b-14 629PS 702COM
  816RM 828MVN
Revelation 22:1-7 508WII
Revelation 22:12-14, 16-17, 20 812RM
Revelation 22:17, 20-21 792RM 797RM

APPENDIX III

TABLE OF RESPONSORIAL PSALMS AND CANTICLES

I. RESPONSORIAL PSALMS

Psalm 1   185, 220, 233, 344, 464, 469, 476, 479, 497, 549, 595, 598, 652, 674, 739, 808
Psalm 2   212, 267, 283, 879
Psalm 3   323, 498
Psalm 4   360
Psalm 5   365, 378, 437
Psalm 6   793
Psalm 7   249
Psalm 8   264, 306, 330, 472, 753, 884, 904
Psalm 9   412, 465, 502
Psalm 10   394
Psalm 11   302
Psalm 12   340
Psalm 13   481, 636
Psalm 15   337, 372, 449, 498, 537, 739
Psalm 16   261, 300, 361, 364, 418, 441, 513, 534, 546, 583, 619, 651, 664, 721, 739, 777, 824, 845, 859
Psalm 17   250, 384, 447, 455, 499
Psalm 18   255, 327, 412
Psalm 19   224, 310, 341, 352, 380, 399, 458, 468, 495, 542, 561, 590, 641, 643, 657, 666, 684, 686, 727, 748, 782, 829, 840, 845, 849, 854, 874
Psalm 21   310, 421
Psalm 22   324, 486, 766, 924, 971
Psalm 23   177, 251, 328, 421, 493, 510, 516, 535, 565, 578, 659, 668, 677, 700, 721, 739, 749, 753, 758, 766, 772, 787, 798, 824, 869, 978, 997, 1013, 1019
Psalm 24   196, 318, 320, 434, 477, 478, 491, 503, 524, 667, 777, 813
Psalm 25   187, 199, 238, 355, 356, 668, 793, 829, 997, 1013, 1019, 1024
Psalm 26   378
Psalm 27   179, 243, 257, 271, 327, 363, 432, 458, 487, 488, 668, 753, 758, 762, 793, 813, 829, 845, 854, 859, 879, 1013
Psalm 28   443
Psalm 29   336
Psalm 30   190, 244
Psalm 31   232, 274, 323, 367, 527, 536, 553A, 596, 639, 692, 696, 715
Psalm 32   325, 333, 347, 471, 753
Psalm 33   197, 262, 272, 339, 350, 371, 385, 429, 430, 433, 445, 471, 476, 743, 803, 813, 997
Psalm 34   188, 225, 248, 269, 270, 338, 359, 369, 370, 379, 492, 515, 517, 529, 533, 540, 550, 552, 554, 570, 574, 591, 597, 604, 607, 609, 611A, 631, 660, 678, 699, 715, 739, 753, 758, 787, 793, 798, 803, 808, 813, 849, 978, 997
Psalm 36   398
Psalm 37   321, 331, 342, 387, 435, 492, 518, 547, 560, 579, 589, 672, 693, 727
Psalm 40   307, 314, 318, 422, 443, 474, 514, 545, 548, 566, 556A, 584, 602, 637, 656, 687, 694, 721, 813, 859, 978, 982, 991
Psalm 41   965, 971
Psalm 42   237, 279, 484, 753, 762, 793, 798, 1013, 1019
Psalm 43   453
Psalm 44   308
Psalm 45   439, 622, 681, 709, 733, 813, 854
Psalm 46   245, 671, 703
Psalm 47   295, 296, 316
Psalm 48   326, 372, 390
Psalm 49   343, 344, 447, 904
Psalm 50   231, 311, 335, 348, 377, 379, 389, 395, 400, 500
Psalm 51   219, 221, 226, 242, 321, 322, 366, 387, 408, 410, 418, 422, 753, 894, 950
Psalm 52   433
Psalm 54   436
Psalm 55   342, 971
Psalm 56   314, 448
Psalm 57   289, 315
Psalm 59   403
Psalm 60   371
Psalm 61   762
Psalm 62   437, 469

Appendix III—Table of Responsorial Psalms and Canticles

Psalm 63   352, 603, 753, 762, 793, 813, 1013
Psalm 65   362, 762, 914
Psalm 66   275, 276, 415, 753
Psalm 67   191, 281, 406, 829, 874, 919
Psalm 68   297, 298, 299, 479
Psalm 69   259, 390, 405, 406, 460, 485, 971
Psalm 71   195, 258, 358, 397, 586, 634, 793
Psalm 72   176, 193, 194, 213, 214, 215, 889, 899
Psalm 74   376
Psalm 77   411
Psalm 78   309, 397, 416, 638, 787, 978
Psalm 79   230, 349, 374, 402, 459
Psalm 80   186, 316, 386, 884, 940
Psalm 81   241, 333, 405, 407
Psalm 82   493
Psalm 84   330, 400, 404, 441, 507, 703, 772, 813, 819, 845, 859
Psalm 85   181, 189, 315, 362, 382, 396, 420, 424, 474, 864, 884, 889, 899, 940, 954
Psalm 86   222, 324, 463, 793, 960
Psalm 87   280, 456
Psalm 88   456, 457
Psalm 89   200, 260, 282, 309, 312, 317, 319, 370, 543, 555, 581, 588, 611, 626, 670, 673, 682, 688, 721, 753, 772, 835
Psalm 90   334, 354, 428, 452, 454, 559, 793, 904, 909
Psalm 91   353, 383, 650
Psalm 92   808
Psalm 93   268, 341, 388
Psalm 94   336, 391, 484
Psalm 95   236, 240, 308, 410, 508, 703, 819
Psalm 96   182, 202, 203, 204, 288, 351, 425, 426, 431, 504, 520, 526, 541, 544, 571, 617, 635, 655, 665, 683, 721, 766, 772, 829, 849, 874
Psalm 97   305, 368, 429, 466, 614, 697
Psalm 98   205, 206, 207, 284, 294, 317, 348, 365, 430, 434, 467, 470, 489, 505, 580, 679, 689, 777, 829, 874
Psalm 99   361, 403
Psalm 100   208, 290, 350, 435, 444, 448, 473, 506, 772, 813, 864, 869, 884, 954
Psalm 101   444
Psalm 102   252, 338, 392, 408, 455, 793, 935
Psalm 103   183, 235, 301, 325, 345, 346, 364, 377, 391, 402, 511, 523, 557, 563, 739, 749, 793, 803, 864, 950, 960, 997, 1013
Psalm 104   329, 331, 766, 914
Psalm 105   234, 254, 263, 307, 373, 385, 386, 388, 392, 466, 472, 488, 496
Psalm 106   247, 332, 334, 374, 381, 401, 409, 419, 721
Psalm 107   423, 884, 914, 924, 929
Psalm 109   482
Psalm 110   311, 313, 319, 512, 558, 568, 690, 721, 772, 787, 829, 845, 978
Psalm 111   312, 347, 368, 445, 446, 461, 465, 483
Psalm 112   339, 353, 354, 367, 487, 490, 496, 539, 594, 601A, 616, 618, 623, 630, 645, 676, 695, 739, 803, 854, 884, 924
Psalm 113   415, 442, 467, 564, 627, 709, 864, 945, 985
Psalm 114   416
Psalm 115   285, 380, 384, 1013
Psalm 116   278, 305, 337, 363, 393, 442, 620A, 772, 787, 798, 978, 991, 1013
Psalm 117   277, 463, 519. 525, 532, 556, 577, 593, 612, 663, 685, 721, 766, 772, 829, 874
Psalm 118   178, 265, 266, 446, 819, 869, 971
Psalm 119   229, 273, 328, 335, 343, 345, 357, 360, 373, 381, 407, 414, 431, 450, 451, 460, 468, 477, 494, 495, 497, 501, 522, 567, 600, 608, 610, 625, 633, 648, 675, 727, 782, 819
Psalm 121   359, 762, 929
Psalm 122   175, 287, 450, 478, 489, 703, 819, 869, 884, 889, 1013
Psalm 123   355, 793, 829, 854, 879, 884, 940
Psalm 124   389, 475, 538, 562, 575, 576, 592, 620, 698, 715, 879
Psalm 126   449, 480, 528, 551, 553, 585, 605, 615, 640, 642, 642A, 644, 646, 654, 662, 715, 753, 919
Psalm 127   884, 909
Psalm 128   332, 356, 375, 424, 427, 480, 658, 739, 803
Psalm 130   228, 462, 470, 894, 950, 1013
Psalm 131   485, 486, 582, 623A, 624, 632, 649, 669, 739
Psalm 132   320, 329, 369, 606, 621
Psalm 135   382
Psalm 136   394, 417
Psalm 137   375, 457
Psalm 138   227, 292, 647, 945
Psalm 139   426, 427, 440, 459, 462, 491, 587
Psalm 141   346
Psalm 143   793, 1013
Psalm 144   313, 453, 482, 502

Psalm 145   184, 246, 286, 340, 383, **428**, **432**, 436, 438, 439, 481, 490, 629, 661, 766, 787, 798, 803, 945, 978

Psalm 146   357, 366, 404, 423, 494

Psalm 147   180, 209, 216, 239, 349, 413, **483**, 782, 787, 978

Psalm 148   293, 413, 521, 530, 569, 628, 733, 803, 854, 1019

Psalm 149   210, 217, 291, 351, 425, 438, 452, 500

Psalm 150   440, 499

II. OLD TESTAMENT CANTICLES

Exod 15:1-17   395, 396
Deut 32:3-41   401, 411, 414, 419, 420
1 Sam 2:1-8   198, 306, 573, 709
1 Chr 29:10-12   326, 501, 703, 945
Tob 13:2-9   358, 451, 929
Jdt 13:18-20   531, 613, 690A, 709, 1002

Isa 12:2-6   417, 475, 572, 985, 997
Isa 38:10-16   393, 793, 935
Jer 31:10-13   256, 399, 409, 454, 869
Dan 3:52-56   253, 398, 503
Dan 3:57-87   504, 505, 506, 507, 508
Jonah 2:3-8   461

III. NEW TESTAMENT CANTICLES

Luke 1:46-55   376, 601, 653, 680, 709, 1002

Luke 1:69-75   322, 464, 473

Lectionary for Mass, Classic edition,
was designed by Frank Kacmarcik, Obl.S.B.
The text was set at The Liturgical Press
in Cheltenham typeface
designed by Bertam Goodhue.

National Publishing Company, Philadelphia,
Pennsylvania, printed the book on
Domtar Volume Opaque paper,
and the endsheets are Beckett Blazer Blue.
It is bound in red Sturdite,
Morocco embossed, over binderboard.

The book was completed on the feast of
All Saints, 2001.